Latin Sermon Collections from Later Medieval England

Until the Reformation, almost all sermons were written down in Latin. This is the first scholarly study systematically to describe and analyze the collections of Latin sermons from the golden age of medieval preaching in England, the fourteenth and fifteenth centuries. Basing his studies on the extant manuscripts, Siegfried Wenzel analyzes these sermons and the occasions when they were given. Larger issues of preaching in the later Middle Ages, such as the pastoral concern about preaching, originality in sermon making, and the attitudes of orthodox preachers to Lollardy, receive detailed attention. The surviving sermons and their collections are listed for the first time in full inventories, which supplement the critical and contextual material Wenzel presents. This book is an important contribution to the study of medieval preaching, and will be essential for scholars of late medieval literature, history and religious thought.

SIEGFRIED WENZEL is Emeritus Professor of English at the University of Pennsylvania. He is a Fellow of the Medieval Academy of America and has held fellowships from the National Endowment for the Humanities, the American Council of Learned Societies and the Guggenheim Foundation. His many publications on medieval literature and thought include *Preachers, Poets and the Early English Lyric* (1986) and *Macaronic Sermons: Bilingualism and Preaching in Late Medieval England* (1994).

CAMBRIDGE STUDIES IN MEDIEVAL LITERATURE

General editor
Alastair Minnis, *University of York*

Editorial board
Zygmunt G. Barański, *University of Cambridge*
Christopher C. Baswell, *University of California, Los Angeles*
John Burrow, *University of Bristol*
Mary Carruthers, *New York University*
Rita Copeland, *University of Pennsylvania*
Simon Gaunt, *King's College, London*
Steven Kruger, *City University of New York*
Nigel Palmer, *University of Oxford*
Winthrop Wetherbee, *Cornell University*
Jocelyn Wogan-Browne, *Fordham University*

This series of critical books seeks to cover the whole area of literature written in the major medieval languages – the main European vernaculars, and medieval Latin and Greek – during the period c. 1100–1500. Its chief aim is to publish and stimulate fresh scholarship and criticism on medieval literature, special emphasis being placed on understanding major works of poetry, prose, and drama in relation to the contemporary culture and learning which fostered them.

Recent titles in the series
Rita Copeland *Pedagogy, Intellectuals and Dissent in the Later Middle Ages:*
Lollardy and Ideas of Learning
Kantik Ghosh *The Wycliffite Heresy: Authority and the Interpretation of Texts*
Mary C. Erler *Women, Reading, and Piety in Late Medieval England*
D. H. Green *The Beginnings of Medieval Romance: Fact and Fiction, 1150–1220*
J. A. Burrow *Gestures and Looks in Medieval Narrative*
Ardis Butterfield *Poetry and Music in Medieval France: From Jean Renart to*
Guillaume de Machaut
Emily Steiner *Documentary Culture and the Making of Medieval English Literature*
William E. Burgwinkle *Sodomy, Masculinity and Law in Medieval Literature*
Nick Havely *Dante and the Franciscans: Poverty and the Papacy in the Commedia*

A complete list of titles in the series can be found at the end of the volume.

Latin Sermon Collections from Later Medieval England

Orthodox Preaching in the Age of Wyclif

SIEGFRIED WENZEL

CAMBRIDGE
UNIVERSITY PRESS

PUBLISHED BY THE PRESS SYNDICATE OF THE UNIVERSITY OF CAMBRIDGE
The Pitt Building, Trumpington Street, Cambridge, United Kingdom

CAMBRIDGE UNIVERSITY PRESS
The Edinburgh Building, Cambridge, CB2 2RU, UK
40 West 20th Street, New York, NY 10011–4211, USA
477 Williamstown Road, Port Melbourne, VIC 3207, Australia
Ruiz de Alarcón 13, 28014 Madrid, Spain
Dock House, The Waterfront, Cape Town 8001, South Africa

http://www.cambridge.org

First published 2005

Printed in the United Kingdom at the University Press, Cambridge

Typeface Adobe Garamond 11/13 pt.   *System* LATEX 2ε   [TB]

A catalogue record for this book is available from the British Library

Library of Congress Cataloguing in Publication data
Wenzel, Siegfried, 1928–
Latin sermon collections from later Medieval England : orthodox preaching in the age of Wyclif / Siegfried
Wenzel.
p.   cm. – (Cambridge studies in medieval literature ; 53)
Includes bibliographical references and index.
ISBN 0 521 84182 8 (hb)
1. Christian literature, Latin (Medieval and modern) – England – History and criticism.   2. Latin prose
literature, Medieval and modern – England – History and criticism.   3. Preaching – England – History –
Middle Ages, 600-1500.   4. Sermons, Medieval – England – Manuscripts – Catalogs.
5. Sermons, Medieval – England – History and criticism.   6. Wycliffe, John, d. 1384 – Contemporaries.   7.
Sermons, Latin – Manuscripts – Catalogs.   8. Sermons, Latin – History and criticism.   I. Title.   II. Series.
PA8045.E5W45   2004
875'.4093823 – dc22   2004047388

ISBN 0 521 84182 8 hardback

gratefully to Grace and Philology

Contents

Contents

Contents

Part II Occasions of Preaching

Part III Orthodox Preaching

Preface

Our knowledge of the preaching that took place in England during the later Middle Ages has over the past seventy years uniquely relied on the magisterial work of G. R. Owst. In his *Preaching in Medieval England: An Introduction to Sermon Manuscripts of the Period c. 1350–1458* (1926), Owst dealt with the various kinds of clergymen who preached, the occasions on which sermons were given, the various types of sermons and of related sermon books such as *artes praedicandi* and *exempla* collections, the forms that sermons took, and the "theory and practice of sacred eloquence" in general. A few years later, in a second volume entitled *Literature and Pulpit in Medieval England* (1933), he continued to present the material he had gathered, but now argued that medieval preachers shared the same world as contemporary poets and pleaded that the former be read and studied as parallels to, and often even sources for, specific images, stories, and attitudes of social complaint that so delight the modern reader of *The Canterbury Tales*, *Piers Plowman*, and medieval drama. Both volumes were infused with a sometimes breathtaking amount of knowledge and information about late-medieval preaching: they quoted over four hundred manuscripts, brought for the first time the names of outstanding preachers of the period together, and provided a vast number of excerpts and snippets of interest to social historians and literary scholars. Their learning and collected material, which will retain its great value, was also clothed in a lively style. Owst could easily weave together samples from sermon texts, external information, illustrative stories, general reflections on medieval mentalities, and the like, which at least for a more general audience makes his work eminently readable (my favorite short example is his calling Richard Rolle "an English Jacopone, clad in his sister's frock").[1] Owst's work was a great achievement for its time, especially when one considers that the sermon

---

[1] Owst, *Preaching*, p. 110. I hasten to say that I certainly would not endorse Owst's style and approach in general, which, as Helen L. Spencer has aptly said, "with its grand panoramas . . . can distract a reader from the real and enduring value of his work," *English*, pp. 13–14.

editions by Devlin and Ross, Gwynn's work on FitzRalph, or Charland's study of the *artes praedicandi* were then still much in the future.[2]

But its shortcomings were immediately evident. Quite apart from his occasionally condescending tone and his frequent characterization of sermons and preachers as "quaint," substantive failures were felt to be serious enough to diminish his work's scholarly value. Neither volume contains an index of manuscripts cited. More importantly, although Owst subtitled his first book *An Introduction to Sermon Manuscripts*, neither it nor its successor offers a detailed description of even a single manuscript. Hardly ever is any attention given to the affiliation (monastic? mendicant? secular? university?), audience (clerical? lay?), or occasion (Lent? post-Easter? saint's feast?) of quoted sermons. Then there is the constant confusion between sermons and sermon handbooks. To be sure, the latter were written to be used by preachers and thus do reflect preaching in later medieval England; but they cannot *tout court* be taken as evidence of actual preaching. And unfortunately Owst misplaced by half a century a sermon handbook from which he quoted most abundantly, Bromyard's *Summa praedicantium*, which was produced in the 1330s, not at the end of the century as he believed.[3] At an even more important level, Owst completely undervalued monastic preaching in the period his two books covered. He opined that the pulpit "share[d] in the general decline of cloister fame and cloister influence" and ended his discussion by speaking of "the actual dearth of fresh monastic sermon literature for the period under our examination." Yet he was reasonably familiar with the sermons by Brinton, Repingdon, and Rypon from whom he quoted extensively – monastic writers who, as my book will show, made significant contributions to preaching in late-medieval England. Rypon particularly was clearly an important moral theologian, exegete, and orator, an intellect far above the purveyor of quaint stories we meet in Owst's pages. Given these shortcomings, it is no wonder that the call for a more scholarly and fundamental study beginning with a careful account of the surviving collections has been voiced again and again. As the author of a much-read survey of *The English Church in the Fourteenth Century* said in 1955: "What we badly need is a systematic catalogue or repertory of mediaeval English preachers and their sermons."[4] Pantin's call has still not found a response, and it is symptomatic that the recent volume on the medieval sermon in the prestigious series "Typologie des sources du moyen âge occidental" contains discussions of Latin sermons in the twelfth century, and after 1200 for the Continent and especially Italy, as well as of vernacular sermons in Old and Middle English, but lacks

---

[2] Brinton, *Sermons*; *Middle English Sermons*; Gwynn, "Sermon-Diary"; Charland, *Artes praedicandi*.
[3] Owst, *Preaching*, pp. 68–69. [4] Pantin, *English Church*, p. 235.

entirely a corresponding chapter on Latin sermon collections produced in later medieval England.

One result of this gap in our knowledge is that studies of specific aspects of late-medieval preaching, of the Church, or of the religious and devotional life in England during the fourteenth and fifteenth centuries simply lack one if not the major basis that would be found in surviving sermon texts. To give but one example: Miri Rubin's rich study of the Eucharist in late-medieval culture[5] devotes some twenty pages to "Preaching on Corpus Christi" (pp. 213–232) and, after noting "the absence of specific preaching material for the most doctrinal of feasts" (p. 214), analyzes seven texts, of which only three or four are genuine sermons.[6] The collections surveyed in my book, however, include at least two dozen Latin sermons that are explicitly marked "in festo Corporis Christi" or "de Corpore Christi," and this number can be easily increased by unmarked sermons or sermons for Maundy Thursday or Easter that likewise deal with the Eucharist and Holy Communion – a substantial body of material that may or may not significantly alter our understanding of the topic but surely demands to be taken into consideration. Investigations of other topics, such as visitation or Good-Friday devotion, have similarly suffered from scholarly unawareness of source material.[7]

This book sets out to remedy this situation. In contrast to Owst's work it focuses not on *preaching* but more narrowly on the surviving *sermons*. It will provide, if not a formal catalogue or repertory, at least a survey and guide to the subject. My aim is to identify, describe, and analyze surviving collections of Latin sermons that were produced in England between c. 1350 and c. 1450.[8] I concentrate on Latin sermons for two reasons. As is generally known, even if medieval preachers had preached their sermons, or were about to do so, in the vernacular, they wrote them down in Latin, and they continued this practice at least to the end of the fifteenth century. Whatever the relation between a written sermon and its actual delivery may have been, the overwhelming majority of surviving texts are in Latin. My second reason is that in the past two or three generations, English sermons have been much better served than their Latin siblings – or, perhaps one should say, parents. Thus, at least half a dozen

---

[5] Rubin, *Corpus Christi*.

[6] Mirk's *Festial*, the *Speculum sacerdotale*, a sermon from collection A, and a sermon from the Lollard *English Wycliffite Sermons*. Rubin glances at Maundy Thursday sermons by Brinton and others at pp. 215–216.

[7] The rich material on Good-Friday preaching has begun to be opened up in the unpublished dissertation by Johnson, "Preaching the Passion."

[8] Of the collections analyzed in this book Owst does not cite Sheppey (mentioned but not examined) and Dygon, nor collections B, CO, D, E, F, G, H, J, N, P1, P2, R, S, U, X, Y, and Z.

collections in English have been critically edited,[9] as against only one in Latin,[10] and it does not appear that this imbalance is likely to change in the near future. The collected sermons of such major figures as FitzRalph, Waldeby, Rypon, or Nicholas Philip, and at least some of the anonymous collections, still call for modern editions. Meanwhile, an account of what Latin collections exist and what they look like is indeed badly needed. Moreover, sermons in English have recently been receiving much attention from highly qualified students, notably H. Leith Spencer,[11] and by concentrating on Latin sermons my work wishes not to compete but to fill a real gap. It is my great hope that this account of manuscript sermon collections will lead other scholars to undertake more detailed investigations.

A "collection" is a group of similar objects gathered as such for a purpose that concerns the entire group. A stamp collection brings together stamps. These may be from different periods, or from different countries, or may depict a common topic such as flowers or artists, or they could just have been kept as the collector received envelopes with pretty stamps from foreign countries. But they are all stamps, not railroad tickets, and what has caused them to be brought together is the collector's delight in having such a collection, or perhaps his curiosity in what they may reveal about a given time or place, or simply their potential monetary value. Keeping a few current stamps in the drawer of one's desk to put on the monthly bills is not the same as making a collection. The same applies to sermons. It would be otiose to specify a minimum number of sermons a manuscript must hold in order to be considered a collection. The important factor is that a small or large number of sermons were brought together to form a collection of texts intended for use in the pulpit, not as parts of a book that gathers material for such different purposes as meditation on the Passion of Christ or arguing for the Immaculate Conception. In the absence of an author's prologue it is of course often impossible to say what motivated an anonymous scribe to copy a number of sermons, and the defining lines between sermon collection, notebook, and anthology are vague and fluid.[12] But by and large, as the following chapters will show, sermon collections contain substantial numbers of sermons – certainly more than one or two separate items – in close proximity, whether they fill a section of a medieval manuscript, a booklet, or an entire codex. I should add

---

[9] *Middle English Sermons*, ed. Ross; *Mirk's Festial*, ed. Erbe; and *Speculum sacerdotale*, ed. Weatherly; the *English Wycliffite Sermons*, ed. Hudson and Gradon; and another group of *Lollard Sermons*, ed. Cigman. A revised and expanded version of Mirk's *Festial* was edited in an unpublished dissertation by Steckman, "Fifteenth Century Festival Book," and sections of that collection have been edited by Powell in *Advent and Nativity Sermons*.

[10] Brinton, *Sermons*.

[11] Spencer, *English Preaching*.

[12] See Wenzel, "Sermon Collections."

that although I generally disregard manuscripts that contain only a few scattered sermons, I have now and then paid attention to several that have preserved single items that enjoyed some currency elsewhere.

A few words should be said about how one recognizes a handwritten medieval sermon. The question has vexed a number of scholars.[13] Unfortunately, not all sermon texts are in their manuscripts marked as sermons, whether by titles, subscriptions, or rubrics, and the potential difficulty in identifying a sermon is further compounded by the fact that sermons share a number of formal characteristics with religious treatises, especially an initial quotation from the Bible, sometimes followed by a division. The best-known example is Chaucer's Parson's Tale, which opens with a quotation of Jeremiah 6:16 and then divides its main topic, penitence, into six parts.[14] None the less, there are additional formal features that are characteristic of the medieval sermon in the period with which we are concerned, and their combination will usually allow us to count a text as a sermon without much doubt. These are the structural features of what I call the scholastic sermon, to be further described in my "Prolegomena." A text, therefore, that begins with a (usually biblical) thema, leads to a division whose members are then developed, and typically (though not always in concrete cases) ends with a closing formula such as "to which may he lead us who reigns with the Father and the Holy Spirit" can be confidently considered to be a sermon. A further characteristic would be an address ("Beloved"), after the initial thema, or in the body of the sermon, or in both places.

The chronological limits of this survey – c. 1350 and c. 1450 – were set by the fact that, as was already recognized by Owst, this was the golden age of preaching in post-Conquest England before the Renaissance. To be sure, there were preachers in England before 1350, and several collections, generally of the thirteenth century, have been preserved in one or more manuscripts. But this very limited earlier material furnishes nothing like the concentrated, systematic, vigorous, and rhetorically crafted sermon literature of the hundred years under consideration. At the other end, after 1450, preaching of course continued and even became a major concern of English bishops and theologians, but it has left few if any traces in surviving manuscripts. Most of the collections here studied were therefore made during the period in which Wyclif and his followers, whose moral seriousness and attention to the biblical text inspired and infused their own preaching, exerted a major impact on the intellectual and spiritual life of the period. Given that sermon texts from the time of Brinton to about 1450,

---

[13] See for instance the repeated definitions of "sermon" in the collective volume Kienzle, ed., *The Sermon*, pp. 144–159, 203–212, 325–327, 449–450, 562–565, 761–763, 862–864.

[14] See further discussion and examples of religious treatises that similarly begin with a biblical quotation in Wenzel, "Notes," pp. 248–251.

other than those by Wyclif and the Lollards,[15] have been very little studied, the question naturally arose for me how these texts compare with those by Wyclif and the Lollards, and thus the reader will find brief remarks about their orthodoxy in the individual descriptions. One may wonder whether, with respect to the sermon collections of this period, "Latin" and "orthodox" are synonymous. It turns out that they are nearly so, for apart from Wyclif's work, I know of only one Latin collection that takes doctrinal positions characteristic of Lollardy.[16] This relation of the material this book investigates to Wycliffite preaching is indicated in the book's subtitle.

After discussing and defining a number of larger issues concerning late-medieval sermons in the "Prolegomena," the first major part of this study offers detailed accounts of over thirty collections I have identified, and considers such aspects as the nature and composition of the respective manuscript, the sermons in the collection, and what is known or may be deduced about their occasion, authorship, date, important structural features, affiliation, and orthodoxy. The collections fall easily into two major types, unified and miscellaneous, a distinction that will be explained later, and they are in Part One examined in the order of their date of composition as far as this can be established. In Part Two I evaluate this material in terms of the occasions when sermons were preached, and discuss, for each separate occasion, first the official requirements for delivering such sermons, next what evidence we have that sermons for the specified occasion were indeed preached, and finally what actual sermons for this occasion have survived in the collections. In doing so a few words will be said about their specific contents. These two major parts, on collections and occasions, lead in Part Three to a series of chapters that focus on several controversial issues raised by Lollard preachers or by modern historians and cull relevant material from the sermons found in the collections. Thus, "An English theology," after scanning the astonishing breadth and chronological range of sources that have been directly or indirectly utilized by the sermon writers, examines more closely major English authors whose works are frequently cited, particularly Bromyard, Holcot, and – most importantly – Grosseteste, who with FitzRalph had a deep influence on moral concerns voiced from both orthodox and heterodox pulpits. "Preaching and the pastoral office" discusses specifically the concern that orthodox preachers of the period had for the priestly office and particularly for the demand to instruct and guide their flocks. "The word of God and *pastoralia*" addresses the

---

[15] Foremost is the work of Anne Hudson, as it can be found in many publications, especially in *Premature* and her new edition, with Pamela Gradon, of *English Wycliffite Sermons*, and further by several of their students, including H. Leith Spencer.

[16] Oxford, Bodleian Library, MS Laud misc. 200 and related manuscripts; see Von Nolcken, "Unremarked," and below, Part One, section 16.

relation, in the orthodox sermons, between preaching the gospel and furnishing instruction on the basics of Christian faith and morals. "The preacher's voice" asks how much freedom a preacher had in shaping and presenting his message and deals at some length with the putative revival of the ancient homily form, which, in contrast to the scholastic sermon, dealt with the entire text of the lection. The next chapter in this part, "Orthodox and heterodox," examines how Lollard teaching and agitation are reflected in the orthodox sermons. A concluding section, "Final reflections," then draws together some major insights into late-medieval preaching in England for which the Latin sermon collections provide new material. Lastly, in "Inventories," I furnish lists of all the sermons contained in the respective collections, to give a sequential account of the material and to provide other investigators of sermon literature with a database for future identifications.[17]

---

[17] An electronic list of all sermons in alphabetical order may be obtained at nominal cost from <swenzel@email.unc.edu>.

Acknowledgments

As this book is the fruit of prolonged research in many libraries, it is my first and most pleasant task to thank the libraries that hold the manuscripts described here, their librarians and staff, for giving me access to their holdings and for providing me with microfilms of the sermon collections. I am especially grateful to Christine Ferdinand (Magdalen College, Oxford), Julia Walworth (Senate House, London, and now Merton College, Oxford), and Joe Wisdom (St. Paul's Cathedral Library, London) for facilitating the work. I thank A. Ian Doyle, Malcolm Parkes, Anne Hudson, Jeremy Catto, Mary McLoughlin, and Ralph Hanna for sundry pieces of relevant information, and Christina Von Nolcken has kindly shared photographic material with me. Richard W. Pfaff has been a constant source of information on matters related to the medieval Church in England and its liturgy. I am further grateful for permission to draw on material that was previously published in *Macaronic Sermons* (University of Michigan Press) and in *History of Universities* 14 (1995/96; Oxford University Press).

And I gratefully acknowledge permission to quote small excerpts from manuscripts in the possession of: the Trustees of the British Library; the Dean and Chapter of Hereford Cathedral; Lincoln Cathedral Library; the Dean and Chapter of Worcester Cathedral; the Bodleian Library, Oxford; the Master and Fellows of Balliol College, Oxford; the President and Fellows of Corpus Christi College, Oxford; the President and Fellows of Magdalen College, Oxford; the Warden and Fellows of Merton College, Oxford; the President and Fellows of Trinity College, Oxford; the Syndics of Cambridge University Library; the Master and Fellows of Gonville and Caius College, Cambridge; the Master and Fellows of Jesus College, Cambridge; the Master and Fellows of Pembroke College, Cambridge; the John Rylands University Library, Manchester; and the Médiathèque municipale of Arras (France).

This book is dedicated to the two who, at the moment in my life when retirement from teaching and relocation were joined by the untimely death of my beloved wife, gave me much strength and consolation.

Editorial conventions

In transcribed passages I keep the spelling of the manuscripts but add modern punctuation. Cardinal numbers of books and chapters are given as Arabic numbers ("1 Cor 6") regardless of their original form in the transcribed text (e.g., "primo Cor. vi"). Ordinal numbers in the original texts are consistently expanded (e.g., "v" as "quinque"). Biblical references are to the Latin Vulgate, but for the names of the books I follow modern English practice. Translations are my own except where otherwise indicated. I have used the following diacritical marks and abbreviations:

[]	Square brackets enclose material not in the quoted text.
[!]	Used for "*sic*" to indicate that a word or spelling is thus found in the quoted text.
< >	Angle brackets indicate material found in the margin.
\ /	Slashes enclose material that in quoted texts appears written between the lines.
/	The single slash in excerpts indicates change of folio or page.
f., ff.	folio, folios

Notes on the text

In referring to specific Sundays of the Church year, I occasionally use an abbreviated form, such as "3 Lent" for the third Sunday in Lent. The Sundays with their sigla (as used in the inventories) are listed on pp. 403–405. Individual sermons are referred to by the siglum of the respective collection (listed below) and sermon number (for example, "A-50," "RY-6," etc.).

Documentation in the footnotes is given in a simplified form, referring the reader to the "Works cited" on pp. 672–698, where full bibliographical data can be found. There I distinguish between manuscripts and printed material (including dissertations), but do not separate printed sources from secondary literature.

Sigla for the sermon collections

A	Cambridge, University Library, MS Ii.3.8
B	Cambridge, University Library, MS Kk.4.24
BR	Thomas Brinton, Sermons: London, British Library, MS Harley 3760; edited in Brinton, *Sermons*.
C	Cambridge, Gonville and Caius College, MS 356/583
CA	Cambridge, Gonville and Caius College, MS 334/727
CO	Oxford, Magdalen College, MS 96 ("Collectarium")
D	Toulouse, Bibliothèque Municipale, MS 342
DY	Oxford, Magdalen College, MS 79, probably by John Dygon
E	Hereford, Cathedral Library, MS O.iii.5
F	Oxford, Bodleian Library, MS Auct. F. infra 1.2
FE	John Felton, *Sermones dominicales*: Lincoln, Cathedral Chapter Library, MS 204 (B.5.1)
FI	Richard FitzRalph, Sermons: Oxford, Bodleian Library, MS Bodley 144
G	Cambridge, University Library, MS Gg.6.26
H	London, British Library, MS Harley 331
I	London, British Library, MS Harley 2388
J	Cambridge, Jesus College, MS 13
K	Cambridge, Corpus Christi College, MS 392
L	Oxford Bodleian Library, MS Laud misc. 200
M	Manchester, John Rylands Library, MS 367
N	Oxford, Bodleian Library, MS Barlow 24
O	Oxford, Bodleian Library, MS Bodley 649
P1	Cambridge, Pembroke College, MS 199
P2	Cambridge, Pembroke College, MS 257
Q	Oxford, Bodleian Library, MS Lat. th. d. 1
R	Oxford, Bodleian Library, MS Laud misc. 706
RE	Philip Repingdon, *Sermones dominicales*: Oxford, Corpus Christi College, MS 54

Sigla

RY Robert Rypon, Sermons: London, British Library, MS Harley 4894
S   Oxford, Balliol College, MS 149
SH John Sheppey, Sermons: Oxford, New College, MS 92
T   Oxford, Magdalen College, MS 93
U   London, University of London, MS 657
V   Oxford, Trinity College, MS 42
W   Worcester, Cathedral Library, MS F.10
WA John Waldeby, *Novum opus dominicale*: Oxford, Bodleian Library, MS Laud misc. 77
X   Worcester, Cathedral Library, MS F.126
Y   London, St. Paul's Cathedral Library, MS 8
Z   Arras, Bibliothèque de la Ville, MS 254

Abbreviations

BL	London, British Library
BN	Paris, Bibliothèque Nationale
BRUC	Emden, *A Biographical Register of the University of Cambridge to 1500*
BRUO	Emden, *A Biographical Register of the University of Oxford to AD 1500*
CCSL	Corpus Christianorum, Series Latina
Coxe	Coxe, *Catalogus codicum manuscriptorum qui in collegiis aulisque Oxoniensibus hodie adservantur*
CUL	Cambridge, University Library
EETS	Early English Text Society, original series
EETS, es	Early English Text Society, extra series
Friedberg	*Corpus iuris canonici*, ed. Aemilius [Emil] Friedberg
Pantin, *Documents*	*Documents Illustrating the Activities of the General and Provincial Chapters of the English Black Monks, 1215–1540*, ed. William A. Pantin.
PL	J. P. Migne, ed., *Patrologiae cursus completus, Series latina*, 217 vols. (Paris, 1844–1864)
SC	Madan et al., *A Summary Catalogue of Western Manuscripts in the Bodleian Library at Oxford*
Schneyer	Schneyer, *Repertorium der lateinischen Sermones des Mittelalters für die Zeit von 1150–1350*
Wilkins, *Concilia*	*Concilia Magnae Britanniae et Hiberniae, AD 446–1718*, ed. David Wilkins.

Prolegomena

Before turning to the surviving collections it will be helpful to define some basic terms and to introduce several general considerations that will recur in subsequent sections and chapters. A preliminary caveat is in order. In discussing such matters as types of collections, audience, sermon structure, and so forth, one is – quite naturally – tempted to think in binary terms: collections may be systematic or random, the audience clerical or lay, the form of sermons ancient or modern, etc. Such opposites are more than theoretical, they have solid historical foundations and indeed occur in the surviving material. However, one must also be aware that the interval between the two poles often forms a continuum where many cases share characteristics of both. My preliminary discussion in this chapter will call attention to such greater variety, but a fuller consideration will be found only later, in the analyses of individual collections, their occasions, and the subsequent chapters.

I. TYPES OF COLLECTIONS

On the basis of the liturgical occasions of the sermons they contain and their order, one can distinguish between two types of sermon collections, systematic and random. Systematic collections, or sermon cycles, contain one or several sermons for each of the occasions that follow the Church's liturgy in a regular order.[1] Thus, a *de tempore* cycle offers sermons for the Sundays of the year from the first Sunday of Advent to the last (normally the twenty-fifth) Sunday after Trinity. In contrast, a *de sanctis* cycle brings sermons for the feasts of the saints, normally from St. Andrew (Nov. 30) to St. Katherine (Nov. 25).[2] This

---

[1] A brief exposition of the liturgical calendar and *de tempore* and *de sanctis* sermon cycles can be found in Spencer, *English*, pp. 23–33.

[2] Generic sermons for classes of saints (one martyr, several martyrs, one virgin, etc.) could form a separate cycle (*De sanctis in communi*) or be part of a *de sanctis* cycle.

basic distinction leaves it unclear where to place major feasts that were celebrated on a fixed date and hence might occur on any day of the week, not necessarily Sunday, such as Christmas (Dec. 25), Circumcision (Jan. 1), or Epiphany (Jan. 6), and feasts that held a firm position in the liturgical season but did not fall on a Sunday, such as Good Friday (before Easter Sunday) or Corpus Christi (Thursday after Trinity Sunday).[3] Consequently, sermons for such occasions can be found in either *de tempore* or *de sanctis* cycles. Medieval titles will sometimes signal this fact by speaking of *sermones de sanctis et de festis*.[4] Another group of sermons whose position is not always certain are those for special occasions, such as dedication of a church, funerals, visitations, synods, elections, etc., or common sermons for saints, as for instance sermons for any martyr, confessor, virgin, and so on. In regular cycles these tend to appear at the end of either *de tempore*[5] or *de sanctis* cycles,[6] or else they may form separate cycles. Besides the two kinds of cycles for the entire year, one may also find cycles for specific seasons, particularly Lent, with such titles as *(Opus) Quadragesimale* or *Sermones quadragesimales*. Lastly, in some instances a systematic sermon sequence may have been written on a given biblical text, such as successive verses from the first chapter of the Gospel of John or the Psalms, and in such cases it may not always be clear for what occasion these were intended.

The other type, the random sermon collection, gathers sermons haphazardly for a variety of occasions: Sundays, feast days, saints' feasts, and special occasions, without ordering them according to their place in the Church year. One will want to ask whether their collectors merely copied them as they came to hand, or whether they followed some principle of order, however vague this might be. In some cases such sermons clearly follow the chronological order in which they were preached, as is the case – to a large extent, though not entirely – in the sermons by FitzRalph, Brinton, and Nicholas Philip. Other random collections suggest thematic concerns of the collector or scribe, in that four or five sermons for a special occasion (such as Easter or a synod), or else on a particular topic (such as the blood of Christ), are "bunched" together. And of course it is always possible that a group of sermons in a larger, basically random collection stand together because they derive from a common source, as must be the case with collection X.

---

[3] For these categories in the thirteenth century, see d'Avray, *Preaching*, pp. 78–79.

[4] For example: Jacobus de Voragine ("Januensis"), *Sermones de sanctis et de festis*, in Oxford, Lincoln College, MS 88, inventoried in Schneyer 3:246–66.

[5] For example, Oxford, Merton College, MS 216 contains a *de tempore* cycle on the Sunday epistles and gospels, followed by sermons on such special occasions as dedication, celebration of Holy Orders, synod, visitation, election, and for peace.

[6] In MS Bodley 50 (early fourteenth century), a set of sermons for special occasions appears at the end of a *de tempore* cycle, and another, different set at the end of the *sanctis* cycle.

The distinction between regular cycle and random collection concerns much more than the order of arrangement – it amounts to being a genuinely generic distinction. Cycles are quite evidently products of the scholarly study, systematic expositions of the lections for Sundays, feast days, or saints' feasts in homiletic form, made to be consulted with ease. In contrast, in so far as one can generalize, random collections tend to gather "real" sermons, which were actually preached.[7] The dividing line between the two is not always clear and sharp, and each collection will challenge its student in its own way to decide how close to actual preaching its pieces are, what exactly their *Sitz im Leben* might have been. None the less, it can be said categorically that random collections are likely to bring the reader much closer to what was actually said from the pulpit than regular cycles.

I have so far avoided the term "model sermon collections," used extensively by David d'Avray in his important study of mendicant preaching as it was diffused from the university of Paris in the thirteenth century.[8] D'Avray defines this genre as "sermons written for a proximate public of users and an ultimate public of listeners," that is, as sermons produced to serve as models for other preachers to use in their own preaching.[9] In my view, the notion of "model sermon" applies far beyond the material from thirteenth-century mendicant authors studied by d'Avray, not only chronologically but also generically, beyond systematic cycles. If one extends the intention of producing models from the authors to collectors and scribes, it surely becomes reasonable to claim that any sermon that got written down could, and probably was intended to, function as a model to be used by other preachers, whether they were confrères, students, or simple vicars. Proof of this can be found amply in the surviving texts, and it is of various kinds. Many sermons contain, in the midst of their development, commands to "tell the story" or "note the example," commands that could only be directed to a fellow preacher who was using the text as a model for his own practice. Moreover, many sermons in random collections contain cross references to other sermons in the same manuscript. We shall find such features even in the most "personal" collections, those by FitzRalph and Brinton.[10] FitzRalph's collection, usually referred to as a "sermon diary," clearly served other functions beyond recording the bishop's preaching tours or his arguments against the Franciscans for his own

---

[7] I use the term "real sermon" for what d'Avray calls "live sermons," *Preaching*, pp. 144, 179. These may utilize material from model sermon collections, but in contrast to the latter they have such discourse characteristics as address forms, a closing formula, and features of orality.

[8] See above, note 3. Model sermon collections are discussed passim.

[9] D'Avray, *Preaching*, p. 105. He then discusses the implication that the "ultimate public of listeners" was the laity, the *populus*, which he rejects with good evidence, ibid., pp. 111–125.

[10] For these two elements in thirteenth-century model sermons, see d'Avray, *Preaching*, pp. 105–108.

recollection: the number of surviving copies of the entire collection or of parts speaks for its usefulness as a model for other preachers.

The distinction between systematic and random collections I have here drawn focuses on the liturgical occasions of the sermons they contain and their order in the collection. Later, in Part One, I will introduce an additional, different distinction between unified, miscellaneous, and mixed collections. That distinction, as will be explained there, rests on more external features, such as the sources and preservation of the individual sermons collected as well as certain scribal aspects. These two distinctions do not coincide but may overlap in various ways; a random collection, for instance, may be unified or else miscellaneous.

2. VERSIONS, COPIES, AND REDACTIONS

Many of the collections here examined contain a usually small number of sermons that are shared, that is, that have also been preserved in one or more other collections, and on occasion even occur as single items in manuscripts not included in this survey. These separate appearances or *versions* of a sermon may differ textually from each other significantly. When the respective texts agree in substance, I call them *copies* of the same sermon. Copies usually show some differences in spelling, word order, even individual words and phrases; but these are of scribal origin or scribal errors, including eyeskips. In contrast, versions that agree to a large measure in their structure and their verbal substance, but show variations that, rather than being mere scribal errors or preferences, affect the substance of the respective sermon, I call *redactions*. For example, William of Rimington preached a synodal sermon at York in 1373, on *Luceat lux vestra*, "Let your light shine before men" (Matthew 5:16). It develops twelve aspects of light and applies them to the priestly life. A sermon in Cambridge, Corpus Christi College, MS 392 (K), of the later fifteenth century, repeats the complete text and introduces only a few minor changes, most notably reducing the invitation to pray for "the prince", "the duke" (of Lancaster), "my Lord Percy," and benefactors to "etc." This I consider a *copy* of the original Rimington sermon. In contrast, what is basically the same sermon in Hereford Cathedral MS O.iii.5 (E) also omits these specific personalities for whom the congregation is asked to pray, but its changes go further: of Rimington's twelve aspects of light, this sermon selects four and rearranges their order (1, 2, 5, 3 of Rimington's sections). Yet another version of *Luceat lux*, in MS Harley 1615, similarly presents basically the text of Rimington, but omits the complete protheme (including the entire invitation to pray) and in addition also selects from Rimington's aspects of light, but now five of them, with some reordering (1, 4, 3, 7, 12 of Rimington's sections). Further, it adds some material not present in Rimington. These versions of *Luceat lux* in the

Hereford and the Harley manuscripts, I therefore call *redactions* of Rimington's sermon.

In some instances, the substantive differences between two versions are so great that one may, and indeed must, wonder if these texts can still be considered versions of the same sermon. The composition of such texts is more complex than mere subtraction of material from the original version and some addition of new material, such as prooftexts or exemplary narratives. It is clear that now and then two or even three different sermon writers used the same distinction or division for the basic structure of their sermon or part thereof but developed its members with different materials, though here again there may be some overlapping. Their compositional work obviously stands in a tradition of biblical commentary and preaching handbooks that all suggested basic patterns and matters for amplification which thus could be combined in various ways, to produce pieces that may very much look alike but are in effect different sermons.

A good demonstration of all these variations is furnished by a group of sermons on *Surrexit Dominus vere* (E-2, H-8, Z-26, and P2–46). The first three use the same structure:

Protheme:

> Bodily medicine, if taken by a person with the right complexion, is helpful, otherwise it can be fatal. Thus the Eucharist can be healthy only for the right complexion. The latter can be improved by penance.

Prayer.
Introduction: On true "rising," which applies to Christ.
Division: True resurrection has three signs: speaking, eating, and walking.
Part 1: Speaking. The youth of Luke 7. In true confession.
Part 2: Eating. The daughter of Jairus. Six conditions of eating the Body of Christ correctly (Exodus 12):

1. Non crudum
2. Sed assum igne
3. Renes accingetis
4. Calciamenta in pedibus
5. Baculos in manibus
6. Comedetis festinanter

Part 3: Walking. Lazarus. Israelites want to return to Egypt > warning against recidivism.

Manna.

Conclusion.

In their verbal substance, H and Z agree to a very large extent; the only exceptions are small scribal variants and a longer insertion in Z (which is also used in Z-38). The two are, therefore, copies of the same sermon. E, in contrast, while following the same structure and loosely sharing the verbal substance of H and Z, omits material here (part 3), adds some there (e.g., three impediments to true confession in part 1), changes the six conditions in part 2 to make them seven, and has a different prayer and conclusion. E is, therefore, a different redaction. Against these three versions, however, P2–46 has an entirely different structure:

Thema

Part A: Resurrection is shown by three signs, which were in Christ at Easter:

    1. Bodily movement: Lazarus
    2. Eating: the daughter of Jairus
    3. Speaking: the youth of Luke 7

Part B: Christ's resurrection had three qualities, which must also be in our rising from sin:

    1. Timely
    2. True
    3. Lasting

Closing formula

While part A is very similar to the overall structure in the first three sermons, in P2 it forms only the first part in the overall bipartite structure that is characteristic of P2 sermons, and after citing the biblical *figurae* its development is entirely different. For part B there are no similarities. P2–46, therefore, is a quite different sermon from the first three, even if it makes use of what must have been a common *distinctio*, the three signs of true resurrection.

The differences and variations between individual versions of a sermon are matters that can only be fully investigated in a text-critical study, and my remarks on shared sermons, copies, and redactions in the following sections on individual sermon collections cannot do more than trace some general lines of relationship.[11]

---

[11] On departures from the standardized text presumably found in mendicant model sermons see d'Avray, *Preaching*, pp. 101–103. He has since offered a splendid sophisticated study of this matter in d'Avray, *Marriage*.

3. OCCASIONS

The occasions for which sermons were written, a particular Sunday, the feast of a saint, or a special occasion such as the bishop's visitation or the election of a prioress, can be established from various kinds of evidence. Best among them is a rubric, a running title, or a marginal note, either at the head of the sermon or in the top margin, which directly and specifically names the occasion. Such rubrics were often used to compile indexes of sermon themata in the same manuscript, and the latter occasionally also list the occasions. Where we lack such rubrication, which is unfortunately true of very many surviving sermons, one can still infer the intended occasion from several other elements. In regular *de tempore* cycles the sermons follow the liturgical order, and hence their position in the cycle speaks for their intended occasion. Random sermon collections, however, are a different matter, and much of their material remains unassigned. Yet often the text of a sermon contains a reference to a specific Sunday or feast on which it was written or spoken – such remarks as "the gospel of this Sunday mentions" or "the saint whose memory we celebrate today." A similar identification may also appear at the beginning of the sermon, where the sermon's thema is identified with its scriptural source and then followed by a remark that the thema comes from the day's lection, as for instance: "*De celo querebant*, Luce 11, et in euangelio hodierno" (O-7), or "*Ingredere ciuitatem*, Actuum 9, et in epistula hodierna" (J/5-18), or "Dominica 2 quadragesime. *Miserere mei, Domine.* Mathei 15 et in euangelio presentis dominice" (H-2).

A final way to determine a sermon's occasion is by inference from the chosen thema. Since by the end of the Middle Ages the epistle and gospel readings at Mass were fairly well fixed,[12] and since preachers were encouraged to choose their themata from these readings,[13] it is likely that a sermon on "Jesus was casting out a devil," or "And he was mute" (Luke 11:14), or "Every kingdom divided against itself shall be brought to desolation" (Luke 11:17), or "Blessed is the womb that bore you" (Luke 11:27), or "Blessed are those that hear the word of God and keep it" (Luke 11:28) was intended for the third Sunday of Lent. Likely, but by no means certain. The sermons here studied that have clear rubrics show that, apart from evident mistakes made by the scribes, individual preachers many times chose their themata from biblical texts other than those prescribed for the given occasion, or that they used a text from an official lection on another day than that for

---

[12] Clear evidence from the collections shows the normal use of the lection according to the Sarum rite. For some exceptions see the following remarks about Pecham.

[13] Thus Robert Basevorn, *Forma praedicandi*, 15, and Thomas Waleys, *De modo componendi sermones*, 2; both in Charland, *Artes praedicandi*, pp. 249 and 342.

which it was prescribed.[14] Further, the collections also reveal the use of different competing patterns of describing a given Sunday. For example, some collections count the Sundays after Trinity as such while others call and count them as Sundays "after the octave of Pentecost." This of course amounts to the same thing and causes little confusion except where a scribe has contented himself with designating such an occasion simply as "Dominica 3" or another number, without reference to the starting point of his counting. Matters are more complicated and potentially confusing for the Sundays between Christmas and Septuagesima and for those after Easter. Thus, the copyist of Repingdon's Sunday sermons (which follow Sarum use) in Oxford, Corpus Christi College, MS 54 assigned the sermon for the Sunday after the Octave of Epiphany (T11a in my inventories) to "Dominica 1 post oct' Epiphanie," but another scribe who foliated the manuscript and wrote the sermon occasions in the top margin labeled this sermon simply as "Dominica 1 post Epiph'." Similarly, a sermon on *Bonum semen seminasti in agro tuo* (Matthew 13:27, for T15) is correctly rubricated "Dominica 5 post oct[avam] Epiphanie" in Cambridge, Pembroke College, MS 200 but appears as "5 post Epiphaniam" in U-6. Matters become even more complicated when the gospel on the wedding feast at Cana (John 2:1–11), officially read on "Dominica secunda post octabas Epiphanie" (T12, the second Sunday after the octave of Epiphany),[15] is used not only in sermons that are rubricated "Dominica 2" (C-23) but also "Dominica 3 post Nativitatem" (X-77, table). And there is yet a further complication: the coexistence of different uses that on some Sundays employed variant readings. For instance, collection X includes a copy of the Sunday collations on the gospels by Archbishop John Pecham. A sermon on *Medius autem vestrum stetit* ("But one has stood in the midst of you," John 1:26) is designated for the fourth Sunday in Advent in the sermon index at the end of the collection, but the rubric next to the sermon assigns it to the third. Rather than being a simple scribal error, as was the case in the previous examples, here the discrepancy signals that Pecham, a Franciscan, evidently followed the gospel readings according to the Franciscan, not the Sarum use.[16] In my inventories I have used inference from the official readings rather discreetly and distinguished among the various

---

[14] Other possibilities were choosing a thema from the day's office, which could include an antiphon (for instance, DY-47) or part of a canticle (DY-23); and, in some academic sermons, from outside the liturgy altogether (W-55, W-120).

[15] Thus in the Sarum use: *Sarum Missal*, pp. 41–42.

[16] Another instance of Franciscan use is the sermon for 4 Advent in Cambridge, Pembroke College, MS 200. The preacher chooses as his thema Luke 3:3 (instead of John 1:19–28) and adds, "in today's gospel after the use of some churches" ("secundum consuetudinem quarundam ecclesiarum in euangelio hodierno," f. 14v). For the differences between the Franciscan and the Dominican use, see the discussion and table in O'Carroll, "Lectionary."

kinds of evidence for the occasion of a given sermon typographically, as will be explained in the headnote there.

The features of rubrication and internal references apply as well to saints' sermons, where the particular saint may be mentioned by name in the body of the sermon, and to sermons for special occasions. In the latter case, the chosen thema may reflect the occasion; thus, makers of visitation sermons liked such themata as "You shall visit your brethren" (1 Samuel 17:18), "I come seeking fruit" (Luke 13:7), or "I have come down into my garden . . . to look if the vineyard has flourished" (Canticles 6:10), and an otherwise unrubricated sermon with such a thema may at least be suspected to have been intended for visitation, especially if it is addressed to the clergy and discusses duties of the pastoral office or the religious life.

4. AUDIENCE

Again, a rubric will occasionally tell us what audience a given sermon was intended for or given to, by specifying *ad clerum, ad populum, ad studentes,* and the like. Next to rubrics, address forms furnish similar information. Sermons addressed to "Reverendi," "Reverendi mei," or "Reverendi domini" were obviously directed to the clergy. Likewise, such addresses as "Magistri" or, later in the fifteenth century, more exuberant forms like "Honorandi magistri" or "Viri prudentissimi" or "Studiosissimi magistri, patres atque domini," characterize sermons before academic audiences. A simple "Domini" or "Domini mei" may be a touch ambiguous; it probably addresses a clerical audience, but it could of course also be directed to lay nobility. Lastly, "Karissimi fratres" most probably addresses the members of a religious order, monastic or mendicant, whereas a simple "Karissimi" leaves the audience undetermined; it could be either clerical or lay. A third category of evidence are references in the body of the sermon. Obviously, remarks on how to preach, on the dignity of priesthood, or on clerical failings point to a clerical audience, whereas directions on how to make one's confession to one's parish priest, how to act toward one's wife or husband, how to educate one's children, or urgings to tithe well equally clearly reveal a lay audience. The subsequent chapters on individual sermon collections will present much evidence for all these cases.

Determining a sermon's audience runs into two problems, however. One is that a good many sermons simply lack evidence of any kind altogether. The other, more interestingly, is that internal references often suggest that the audience was mixed, composed of both clerics and layfolk. Again, my later analysis will reveal many instances where this is the case, and I believe that the respective sermons were indeed preached before a mixed audience, such as would have been present at a bishop's sermon in his cathedral, including at visitations; or at monks' preaching in a monastic cathedral; or at public university sermons; or at the first sermon at a synod. Other students of sermons who have paid close attention to what their texts reveal about the sermons' audience have come to similar conclusions regarding mixed audiences.[17]

One further kind of evidence about a sermon's audience could be the language in which it was preached. Conventional wisdom has it that, at least in an earlier period, sermons to the layfolk were spoken in the vernacular, and sermons to the clergy in Latin. In the century with which this study is concerned, however, this distinction clearly broke down, as is patently shown for instance in the license to preach given in 1417 to the famous canon lawyer William Lyndwood allowing him, indiscriminately, "to preach the word of God to the clergy and the people in Latin or in the vernacular,"[18] which I take to mean that Lyndwood could preach to any audience in either tongue. Moreover, in whichever language sermons might have been preached, through the fifteenth century, the majority were written down in Latin. Careful study of the linguistic texture of sermon texts, especially those carrying both Latin and English elements, might reveal the language of the "original" sermon as preached. But for determining the audience, this criterion is, at least in a general way, of little use.

5. DATING

Where an individual sermon or an entire collection is connected with a named preacher, the date of its composition or delivery can, at least in a general way, be established from biographical information found elsewhere. In optimum cases, rubrics may furnish very specific dates, as with FitzRalph's sermons. Random collections are more problematic, in fact they are mostly closed to an even approximate dating. Here again, references in the sermons themselves to historical events will help. What information I have been able to detect will be found in the analyses of the collections. For dating the actual manuscripts I follow the evidence of the handwriting. I have included a few manuscripts that were apparently written after 1450 but contain material that originated earlier in the century.

6. ORTHODOXY

As pointed out in the Preface, my analyses of individual collections will usually include some remarks about their authors' orthodoxy. Such evidence is provided

---

[17] For example, Carruthers, "'Know thyself'."

[18] "Verbum Dei clero et populo in lingua Latina seu vulgari licite proponere et praedicare," Wilkins, *Concilia* 3:389.

by clearcut attacks on or criticism of the Lollards, who are often mentioned by name as a group, or else by taking clearly orthodox positions on doctrinal and pastoral matters that were subjects of contemporary controversy, such as the doctrine of the Eucharist (of which there is very little discussion in these texts), the dignity of priesthood without regard to the holder's moral standing, the need for private confession, whether to the penitent's parish priest or another authorized person, and the validity of pilgrimages and image worship.

7. SERMON FORM

Histories of medieval preaching, from both the later Middle Ages and modern times, have customarily distinguished between two fundamentally different forms the medieval preacher's discourse could take.[19] One is the homily or "ancient form," which deals with the entire biblical lection for the liturgical occasion and tends first to repeat it literally and then to give a moral or "mystic" exegesis of the text. The other form is that of the "modern" or "university" or "scholastic" sermon,[20] which is based on a short biblical text that provides the verbal base for an extended treatment by means of a main division and perhaps subsequent subdivisions, the main parts of the sermon being called *membra* or, more often, *principalia*. To these essential elements of the scholastic sermon: thema, division, and developed principals, may be added one or two introductory sections. The first is the protheme or antetheme (often called "antithema" in medieval texts), which briefly introduces the sermon's main topic, in a few instances with a thema of its own, and may lead to the preacher's request of his audience to pray for him and themselves. This can be followed by the *introductio thematis*, where the preacher might explain the nature of the feast day, or the position of the day's lection in the gospel or in the Church year, and then lead up to the repetition of the thema in order to divide it. A full scholastic sermon would, thus, have the following structure and parts:

Thema.
Protheme.
Prayer.
Restatement of thema.
Introduction to the thema.

[19] See especially the longer discussion in Spencer, *English*, pp. 235–247, with samples.
[20] I prefer here, as I have done earlier, the label "scholastic sermon" as a matter of convenience, for the reasons given in Wenzel, *Preachers*, pp. 61–62. Rouse and Rouse, *Preachers*, use the term "school sermon" and trace the development of the form in the thirteenth century, p. 66 and passim.

Restatement of the thema.
Division.
Development of the announced parts.
Closing formula.[21]

In discussing individual collections, I occasionally speak of "full sermons," by which I mean not that all the structural elements just mentioned are present but rather that the texts under discussion record a complete development of the principal parts. This would be in distinction to sermon outlines or skeleton sermons, which may only furnish a thema, main division, and perhaps some biblical or other prooftexts, but do not develop the main parts. They are often written in schematic form. Another kind of sermon that is not full in this sense would be a sermon text that gives a complete, developed protheme or introduction but then breaks off with "etc."

For the division itself, preaching handbooks distinguish between two types. The first is the *divisio ab intus*, when a division is based on the very *words* of the thema. In contrast, the *divisio ab extra* takes a *concept* that is suggested by these words and divides it into parts. For example, in the thema "There shall be one sheepfold and one shepherd" (John 10:16) a preacher may find Christ's prediction or warning that the Church is to be one in faith ("one sheepfold") and that its lord is one God alone ("one shepherd"). But he may also find that the image or notion of "sheepfold" can be applied to the soul, and as a sheepfold has four walls, so the soul should have four cardinal virtues to build it up and protect it.[22] The first would be a *divisio ab intus*, the second *ab extra*. Both types of division can be found everywhere in extant sermons, and very often they occur together in the same sermon. In this case, after the *divisio ab intus*, which characteristically begins with such a formula as "in his/istis verbis," the preacher continues with the formula "pro processu/materia sermonis" and gives a *divisio ab extra*, whose members are then developed in due order. Careful preachers would confirm the members of either division with, normally, biblical passages that express the same thought and contain the respective words of the thema. A good example of the whole process occurs in a sermon by John Waldeby on the thema *Signum de caelo quaerebant ab eo*, "They sought from him a sign from heaven" (Luke 11:16). The entire division runs as follows:

---

[21] Schematic analyses of scholastic sermons from our period can be found in Fletcher, *Preaching*, pp. 52–54 (Q-60); 71–74 (FE-6); and 74–76 (FE-37); in Spencer, *English*, pp. 247–65 and 335–358 (several, with some errors in the Latin); and in Wenzel, *Macaronic*, pp. 212 (S-7), 268–69 (O-7), and 308–9 (W-154).

[22] For the entire text and commentary see Wenzel, *Preachers*, pp. 88–89.

[*divisio ab intus:*]
In which words are two things briefly shown:

> first, God's own kindness and justice, "a sign from heaven"; second, the
> malice and cunning of the Jewish crowd, "they sought from him."

The first is apparent because every sign that God gave to men from heaven is
either to help the desolate, and thus it is a sign of mercy; or it is to punish the
obstinate, and thus it is a sign of justice. Joel 3: "I will show wonders in heaven
above and signs on the earth below" [Joel 2:30]. The second is apparent because
"they were asking for a sign from heaven," etc., but not believing him even as
he was showing him a very great sign. And thus they were like Pharaoh, who
did not believe Moses despite any signs, whereas God said to Moses, in Exodus
7: "I will multiply signs and portents" [Exodus 7:3]. Whence John says: "You
will seek me and not find me and thus die in your sin" [John 7:36, 8:21], just as
Herod was "seeking the child in order to kill him," Luke 3 [Matthew 2:13].

[*divisio ab extra:*]
But for the matter of this sermon we should notice that "heaven" is understood
in three ways:

> as the sky, as in Luke 8: "The birds of heaven eat it," that is in the sky [Luke
> 8:5]; secondly as the starry heaven, Kings 23: "Josias took them," etc., "those
> who were offering incense to Baal and the signs and the heavenly host"
> [2 Kgs 23:5]; and thirdly as the empyreum; the Psalmist says: "The heaven
> of heavens to the Lord" [Psalm 113:16], that is the empyreum, which is the
> first heaven of all heavens and the dwelling place of God and all the saints.

In the manuscript, the two divisions are neatly marked in the margin as *divisio
principalis* and *materia collacionis*.[23] The members of the second division are then

---

[23] "<diuisio principalis> In quibus verbis duo notantur breuiter: primo ipsius Dei benignitas
et iusticia, 'signum de celo'; secundo cetus Iudaici malignitas et versucia, 'querebant ab eo.'
Primum sic patet quia omne signum quod Deus ostendit de celo hominibus aut est ad iuuan-
dum desolatos, et sic est signum misericordie, aut ad puniendum obstinatos, et sic est signum
iusticie. Ioelis 3: 'Dabo prodigia in celo sursum et signa in terra deorsum.' Secundum patet eo
quod 'temptantes signum de celo,' etc. et non credentes sibi cum tamen ostendisset eis signum
maximum, similes Pharaoni, qui non credidit propter aliqua signa Moysi, cum tamen dixit
Deus ad Moysen, Exodi 7: 'Multiplicabo signa atque portenta.' Vnde Johannes: 'Queritis me et
non inuenietis, et in peccato vestro moriemini,' sicut 'Herodes querebat puerum ad perdendum
eum,' Luce 3. <materia collacionis> Sed pro materia collacionis est aduertendum quod celum
tripliciter accipitur: pro celo aereo, / vt Luce 8, 'Volucres celi comederunt illud,' idest aeris;
secundo accipitur pro celo sidereo, Regum 23: 'Tulit Iosias eos,' etc., 'qui adolebant incensum
Baal et signis et omni milicie celi'; tercio accipitur pro celo empireo; Psalmista: 'Celum celi
Domino,' idest celum empireum, quod est celum principale omnium celorum, habitacio Dei
et omnium sanctorum." Oxford, Bodleian Library, MS Laud misc. 77, f. 74r–v (WA-30).

used for the three main parts of the sermon: "First, then, let us seek from the sky a sign from God of reconciliation against sin, which is offensive to his divine majesty," and so forth.[24] As this example shows, making a good division is an art that requires biblical knowledge and ingenuity, on which the structure and logical and rhetorical success of the entire sermon depend.[25]

In teaching the principles of scholastic sermon structure, fourteenth-century writers of *artes praedicandi* recognized and accepted individual variations of this basic structural model. Clearly, individual preachers modified the model and its components according to their preferences, and my discussion will now and then comment on peculiar structural formats that characterize individual collections. But despite such variations, the majority of the sermons here surveyed follow the basic structure of the scholastic sermon, no matter by whom and to whom they were preached.[26] Contemporary *artes praedicandi* were further aware that the other type of sermon structure, the homily, was used in earlier times as well as in contemporary Italy, and we shall see in chapter 49 of Part Three that the ancient homily form was also used by English preachers in the late fourteenth and fifteenth centuries.

In connection with "sermon" and "homily" another term that occurs in a number of the collections calls for some discussion. By the later Middle Ages, the word *collatio* had had a long and diversified history that was anchored in the monastic life. In earlier times it referred to instructional conversations or conferences among monks, eventually signaling a brief address given to a monastic community in the evening before their evening meal, whence the term acquired its meaning of "a lighter meal." In the scholastic age it came to refer to a spiritual address or sermon given to a community of monks or friars in the afternoon, which often continued to develop a thema or topic already treated in the main sermon given earlier in the day. Closer to the Renaissance, the term eventually came to be used for any kind of speech.

In our collections the term appears in about a hundred sermons, and although its usage calls for more detailed investigation, the following observations can be

---

[24] The text quoted in the previous note continues: "Quod igitur fecerunt Iudei per maliciam conuertamus nos ad penitenciam et signum de celo queramus a Deo. Primo de celo aereo queramus a Deo signum reconsiliacionis contra peccatum, quod est offensum diuine magestatis. Secundo de celo sidereo queramus a Deo signum curacionis contra peccatum, quod est consumptiuum humane fragilitatis. Tercio de celo empyreo queramus a Deo signum premiacionis contra peccatum, quod est exclusium eterne felicitatis. De primo signo scribitur Genesis 14; de secundo patet Regum 19 et Ysaie 20; de tercio patet Apocalipsis 16," ibid., f. 74v.

[25] I have discussed this art in Wenzel, *Preachers*, pp. 66–100.

[26] The same seems to have been true of thirteenth-century preaching; see Rouse and Rouse, *Preachers*, pp. 76–77. It is also true of English sermons in our period; see Spencer, *English*, pp. 265–268.

made. First of all, *collatio* is in fact very often employed by monks and friars or in monastic sermons. Rypon especially used it with great regularity, as did Brinton and others. Many of these sermons were directed to a clerical audience, whether at visitations, synods, the university, or unspecified occasions. As we shall see later, in these milieux monastic preachers and friars took a surprisingly large share. Furthermore, in very many instances the word *collatio* is used with the qualifier "short": *brevis*, *brevissima*, or *exilis*. Though this collocation may be no more than a rhetorical *captatio benevolentiae* not unknown to modern professors and after-dinner speakers ("In my brief remarks I shall . . ."), one may wonder whether in a written sermon text it may not indeed indicate that the discourse in question was not a full-blown sermon but a shorter address in sermon form. It would therefore seem that the word continued to have kept its old connotations of brevity, monastic affiliation, and special sermon occasion. However, there are important exceptions. FitzRalph, a secular priest and bishop, speaks of a *collacio* he gave to his *familia* in his chapel. More significantly, about a dozen sermons that refer to themselves as *collaciones* are clearly not monastic or addressed to the clergy. A good example comes in a rhetorically simple but full sermon on the feast of the Circumcision, dealing with the thema "Be circumcised to the Lord" (Jeremiah 4:4). Its anonymous preacher addresses his audience with "Beloved" (*karissimi*) and begins: "Today the Church celebrates the feast of the Lord's circumcision, who was circumcised on the eighth day after his birth." He then refers to the gospel of the day with its back-reference to the Annunciation and the angel's command to name the child "Jesus" (Luke 2:21 and 1:31). In his main division he speaks of three spiritual circumcisions – of our mind, flesh, and soul – which form "the matter of this collation" (*de quibus ad presens erit materia nostre collacionis*). He develops all three at some leisure, and in doing so addresses "you who have children and servants under your care."[27] Here, then, *collatio* is applied to a sermon given to a lay audience on a general feast day of the Church. It is therefore possible but by no means necessary to think that "collacio" in these sermons points to a monastic or mendicant milieu or to a time of preaching different from that of the regular liturgy or Mass. Conversely, one should also keep in mind that, since the term *collatio* is nearly always used in such set phrases as "pro materia collacionis" (as above) or "in principio huius

---

[27] H-14: "Circumcidimini Domino, Jeremie 4 capitulo. Karissimi, hodie celebrat Ecclesia festum de circumcisione Domini, qui circumcisus fuit in octaua die a sua nativitate, et hoc est quia dicitur in euangelio hodierno 'Postquam consummati sunt'. . ." (f. 41); "sed pro vlteriori processu est notandum quod triplex est circumcisio spiritualis, de quibus ad presens erit materia nostre collacionis. Prima circumcisio . . ." (f. 41); "Karissimi, pro omnipotentis Dei amore, vos qui sub uobis habetis pueros et seruientes" (f. 42v). The sermon ends f. 43.

collacionis," the term may, by the fifteenth century, have lost its earlier specific meaning.[28]

8. ACTUAL DELIVERY

All texts examined in this study must be considered to be the result of a literary effort and activity that reflects the form of their actual delivery at best dimly. In the absence of unedited verbatim transcripts of the preacher's words, we can only guess at what was actually said in the pulpit and heard by the congregation. Nor can we ever from the surviving sermon texts know how inspired and inspiring the actual words of a gifted preacher were. Occasional reports by witnesses have left faint echoes here and there, such as Margery Kempe's remarks on the sermons she heard in Lynn and elsewhere. But we lack transcripts or recordings of the actual words that may have lit a spiritual or emotional fire, such as observers of Continental preachers occasionally report[29] or that the novelist Lawrence Durrell, for example, created in Narouz's preaching to the Copts.[30]

All we have, then, are written texts, and their relation to the actual discourse remains a matter of uncertain speculation. It is entirely possible that a preacher carried a written text into the pulpit and used it, verbatim or selectively, for his sermon, and that such a text has been preserved.[31] If, however, he did not preach from a written text – whether that was a complete sermon, an outline, or only notes – his preaching may have been recorded in a process called *reportatio*: someone in his audience would have jotted down essential parts of the sermon, including major proof-texts, in shorthand form and probably on wax tablets, and

---

[28] Proof may come from sermon A-43, which has "Pro induccione istius breuissime [!] sermonis et collacionis," but later says "Pro processu istius sermonis," ff. 138v and 139.

[29] Cf. d'Avray, *Preaching*, p. 61, on Berthold von Regensburg. For charismatic preaching among the early Franciscans and discussions of the relationship between divine inspiration and the recourse to learned techniques, see Roest, *History*, pp. 278–279. As Moorman put it, the histrionics characteristic of some early Franciscans "were not normally adopted by other Franciscan preachers," *History*, p. 522.

[30] Lawrence Durrell, *Mountolive*, pp. 108–110. On the inspired preaching of St. Francis, see Delcorno, "Origini," pp. 147–158.

[31] A special case in this connection is the preacher's reading out a text from a model sermon collection or a "postil," that is, a biblical commentary on the lection of the day, such as were made by Repingdon and the authors of the English Wycliffite sermons (cf. below, Part One, section 7). The century which this book deals with stands halfway between the early Middle Ages, in which preachers were expected to read out homilies from the Fathers, and Martin Luther, who in the 1520s composed postils for the use of the Reformed clergy who lacked the knowledge or skill to write their own sermons; Brecht, *Luther*, 2:250–251, 256, and 278–279. A synodal sermon of 1435 (Q-25) still repeats the canon that among the books a priest should own for his own instruction should be one containing "omelias per circulum anni diebus dominicis et singulis festibus aptas" (f. 88v); cf. *Decretum*, D. 38, c. 5, Friedberg 1:141.

later expanded them at leisure. In expanding his jottings the *reportator* had much freedom to complete the citations and check their sources, to add ornaments, and in general to make the sermon more literary. The text thus edited may or may not have been submitted to the preacher for his approval. This process is well documented for the entire medieval period, from the preaching of St. Augustine[32] on through the similar technique of *reportatio* of scholastic lectures[33] to fifteenth-century preaching in Italy.[34] But in contrast to lecture notes taken by university students and to notes taken of the sermons of Bernardine of Siena, the preaching reflected in the present study has left no significant actual *reportationes*.[35] We come perhaps closest to them in the repertory of Cambridge sermons in Cambridge, Gonville and Caius College, MS 356 (C).[36] But even here the reflective labors of the transcriber show.[37] Similarly, Archbishop FitzRalph left a sermon diary in which he "reports" what he said when and where and to whom, and he often uses such expressions as "here I said" or "it was argued." He thus was his own *reportator*. But here, too, what was actually said has clearly been subjected to selection, and of course even the sermons that he reports that he gave in the vernacular are written down in Latin.[38]

If the Cambridge university sermons and FitzRalph furnish information about their actual delivery, other collections conversely are certainly based on actual preaching but show unmistakable signs of literary redaction. Thus, both Waldeby and Rypon claim that what they present in writing was in fact preached. Yet it is hard to imagine that Rypon's often tediously academic exposition or his frequent cross references were in fact thus spoken from the pulpit; and Waldeby tells us that "the moral mattter that I had formerly preached at York" and which lay scattered "in cedulis et membranis," he gathered into twelve sermons "in due (or

---

[32] See Deferrari, "St. Augustine's Method."   [33] See, for example, Hamesse, "*Reportatio*."

[34] In a number of studies by Delcorno; see for instance his "Diffrazione" and his edition of Bernardino da Siena, *Prediche volgari*. Rusconi, "Reportatio," makes wide-ranging use of secondary literature on *reportatio* of sermons and other genres.

[35] Some recent studies of academic and sermon *reportatio* in England are listed in Wenzel, *Macaronic*, p. 106, n. 1.

[36] Wenzel, "Sermon Repertory."   [37] Ibid., pp. 57–58, 59–60.

[38] A rather unique remark about the relation between the delivery and the writing down of a sermon has been left by an anonymous preacher of the fifteenth century, who jotted down notes after speaking at greater length to the people: "De hiis que in presenti sermone dixi et alias scripsi uel modo scribere volo sed solum sub breuitate tangere verbum breue quod alias non memini me scripsisse sicut plerumque facio de prolixo sermone ad populum dico aliquid breue notans ad memoriam sermone succincto." London, BL, MS Royal 5.C.iii, f. 238ra. The mid-fifteenth century codex, composed of many booklets, is a genuine miscellany, perhaps an anthology or collection of excerpts or works, including a *Forma predicandi*; see Warner and Gilson, *Western Manuscripts*, 1:105–106; and Briggs, *Giles of Rome*, pp. 161–162.

continuous) order"[39] – far from the crowds of York in his retreat at Tickhill. All this implies a significant gap between actual preaching and extant sermon texts, a gap that should prevent us from making quick and easy inferences from extant texts to such matters as their occasion, audience, or language of delivery. For example, we might assume that a sermon full of quotations from canon law was preached, not to a lay but to a clerical audience. This assumption can be proven to be true where other indications as well point to a clerical audience. But the mere presence of canon law quotation is no argument for a clerical audience, because these quotations may in fact have been added by the redactor or the preacher if he edited his own sermons. For instance, Bishop Brinton's sermons brim with such citations. Sermon 54, according to its rubric, was preached on Passion Sunday and contains six quotes from canon law. Its editor speculated that "Bishop Brinton delivered this sermon . . . to a congregation which if we may judge by the number of allusions in the sermon to canon law, consisted largely of clergy."[40] This may well have been the case. But what are we then to make of sermon 56, which was preached on Good Friday in Rochester Cathedral, hence before a congregation that at least included a large portion of layfolk, and contains ten references to canon law? Or what of Brinton's funeral sermon for the Black Prince delivered at Rochester in 1376? Here eulogy of the prince's virtues brings the bishop to consider the current moral decay among knights and the clergy. The latter are criticized for failing to correct their temporal overlords, and the criticism is supported from canon law: "We prelates, who according to God's law have the office of judging the great as well as the small, *Extravagantes De iudiciis, Nouit*."[41] I have no doubt that in delivering this sermon Brinton did remind his audience of the clergy's God-given command to chastize the mighty; but I doubt very much that he would have actually cited the canon. Though the canon speaks at length of the pope's and higher clergy's obligation to chastize temporal lords, Brinton's reference to "God's law" ultimately is to Deuteronomy 1:17 (which is in fact quoted in the canon *Novit*).[42] It looks, therefore, as if the canonistic reference was a footnote added by the sermon's redactor.

Another example in which the preacher's putative words are neatly mixed with remarks that betray the effort to make an actual sermon into a model for

---

[39] ". . . venit in memoriam quedam materia moralis in exposicione symboli quam dudum populo predicaueram in Eborum. Ne vero dicta materia per obliuionem delibaret a posterum memoria nisi esset exaratum in scriptura, me totum vestrum rogastis intime quatinus quicquid de ista materia fuerat in cedulis et membranis sparsim intitulatum colligerem in seriosum tractatum duodecim sermones iuxta numerum articulorum fidei continentem." Cambridge, Gonville and Caius College, MS 334 (CA), f. 150rb. The prologue is addressed to Thomas de la Mare, abbot of St. Albans.

[40] Brinton, *Sermons*, p. 241.   [41] Sermon 78; Brinton, *Sermons*, p. 357.   [42] Friedberg 2:244.

other readers occurs in the Palm Sunday sermon Q-28 on the thema *Ecce*. Its introduction begins with a decidedly "personal" tone:

> Beloved, having been asked to make a short sermon, I have taken a short word, which has only two syllables: "Behold." . . . In order to show why this word "behold" is used today, I say it is my desire that you look especially at the gospel for the blessing of the palms. For in this gospel, so it seems to me, are three necessary lessons . . .

But then first-person statements yield to third-person instructions:

> And let the gospel be recited if it so pleases. After this has been done, or not done, if there is still leave on account of the shortness of time, it should be said . . .[43]

It is evident that here an actual sermon has become a model or instruction for other preachers.

If the gap between a sermon's oral delivery and its written form is thus constant and significant, we must indeed exercise great caution in equating the two: on principle, medieval sermon texts, as they have been preserved, must not be thought to have actually been preached that way.[44] But the modern reader's quest to come close to the actual delivery is not entirely hopeless. It stands to reason that sermons that contain a good number of "popular" elements – such as proverbs, allusions to games, snatches of vernacular songs – that include English material in the Latin text to the point of becoming genuinely macaronic, and that hold such marks of orality as addresses to the audience, imperatives in the singular ("go to your curate!"), rhetorical questions, the use of the inclusive first person plural, and a more leisurely style of telling narrative exempla, may indeed reflect actual preaching quite closely.[45] And there are some cases whose very rambling reminds one of modern preachers *in actu* who no longer bother to write out their sermons

---

[43] "Karissimi, rogatus breuem sermonem facere, ideo breue verbum as[sumpsi], quod est nisi due sillabe, scilicet *ecce* . . . et hoc ad ostendendum quare accepitur hoc verbum *ecce* isto die, dico quod voluntas esset mea vt specialiter intuemini euangelium benediccionis palmarum. Quia in isto euangelio michi videtur quod sunt tres necessarie lecciones, ymmo tria exempla bona conuersacionis in eo includuntur . . . Et recitetur euangelium si placet. Quo facto uel non facto, si forte fuerit dimissio propter breuitatem temporis, dicendum . . . ," Q-28, f. 96v.

[44] An interesting case from an earlier age is Grosseteste's sermon 22, *Legimus hodie in Ecclesia*, in which he says that in writing down his sermon he omitted some light moralizations he had spoken for the instruction of the simple: "Hec ergo breuiter dicta sint de coapcione eorum que fiebant in mundi condicione et in archa Noe ad ea que fiunt in ecclesie materialis dedicacione, omissis in scripcione quibusdam leuibus moralibus ad simplicium instruccionem dictis," MS Royal 6.E., f. 96rb.

[45] Probably the finest example are the macaronic sermons in O.

in advance or who never had a course in composition.[46] Such sermons are more likely to be found in random collections and, in this respect, form a stark contrast to regular sermon cycles. Yet even here one will, on closer inspection, hesitate to think of them as the preacher's *ipsissima verba*, for even sermons that have such marks of orality will occasionally contain an instruction to the preacher to "find the story" or to "tell here the story of . . ."[47]

[46] An example is given in Part One, section 24, p. 143.
[47] "Quere narracionem," O-29, f.153v.

PART I

The Collections

I

Overview

With respect to their contents, the collections to be analyzed in this part can be separated into two or three major types. First are what I will call "unified" collections. These contain sermons that are attributed to a single named author or collector, or else are unified by a specific milieu in which they were preached (e.g., Cambridge University), or by peculiar structural or stylistic features (e.g., macaronic sermons of a distinct style). Such collections usually do not share their material widely with others. In contrast, "miscellaneous" collections do precisely that: they share individual sermons among themselves and thus may be assumed to have drawn their material from several different sources. This material could have been gathered by one or by more collectors, and the texts may be written in one or in several hands.[1] Occasionally, both unified and miscellaneous types occur in the same manuscript and were written by the same scribe. This combination I will call a "mixed" collection, of which Cambridge, University Library, MS Kk.4.24 (B) is a good example: here a unified collection of sermons in regular liturgical order, ascribed to Bromyard, is followed by a random series of sermons, some of which also occur elsewhere, the whole codex being written by the same hand. It should thus be clear that "collection" and "manuscript" are not synonymous. A manuscript may indeed contain nothing but a sermon collection – whether unified, miscellaneous, or mixed – but many manuscripts contain a sermon collection together with other material, such as treatises of various kinds or collections of exempla. Similarly, "booklets" – that is, physically discrete units of one or more gatherings that make up a codex, are written by one or several different scribes, and often have blank leaves at their ends – are not *per se* coterminous with the parts of a mixed collection. Although its parts may differ in many ways, a mixed collection is normally

---

[1] Further discussion of the general characteristics of miscellaneous collections, with specific details, can be found in the sections on S and H.

written by a single scribe, and the resulting book shows clear signs that it was conceived as a unit, such as continuous medieval foliation and an index.

The following sections first examine the unified collections in roughly chronological order:

Sheppey (SH, d. 1360)
FitzRalph (FI, d. 1360)
Oxford, Bodleian Library, Auct. F. infra 1.2 (F, c. 1366?)
Waldeby (WA, d. 1372)
Brinton (BR, d. 1389)
Repingdon (RE, 1382–94)
Felton (FE, 1431)
Mirk (1382–1390?)
Rypon (RY, 1401–1410)
Cambridge, Pembroke 199 (P1, post 1400)
Cambridge, Pembroke 257 (P2, post 1400)
Cambridge, Gonville and Caius 356 (C, 1417 and 1424–5)
Oxford, Bodleian Library, Bodley 649 (O, 1415x1421)
Oxford, Bodleian Library, Laud misc. 706 (R, post 1412)
Oxford, Bodleian Library, Laud misc. 200 (L)
Oxford, Bodleian Library, Lat. th. d. 1 (Q, 1430–1436)
Dygon (DY, d. c. 1449)
Oxford, Magdalen 96 (CO)

I have included here MS Bodley 649, which, properly speaking, forms a mixed collection, and add to its discussion MS Laud misc. 706, which, though by itself of the miscellaneous type, shares four sermons from Bodley 649's unified part. In contrast to Bodley 649, two other collections that are similarly mixed (B and V) will be found in the next group, the miscellaneous collections. I have further included here Oxford, Bodleian Library, MS Auct. F. infra 1.2, because it contains a series of FitzRalph's sermons that are named and dated.

Next I examine the following miscellaneous collections, together with some individual authors:

Oxford, Balliol College 149 (S)
Chambron
Toulouse, Bibliothèque Municipale 342 (D)
Cambridge, University Library, Kk.4.24 (B/2)
Cambridge, Jesus College 13 (J)
Worcester Cathedral F.126 (X)

Worcester Cathedral F.10 (W)
Hereford Cathedral O.iii.5 (E)
Oxford, Trinity College 42 (V)
Alkerton
Wimbledon
Cambridge, University Library Ii.3.8 (A)
London, British Library, Royal 18.B.xxiii
Arras, Bibliothèque de la Ville 184 (254) (Z)
London, St. Paul's Cathedral 8 (Y)
London, British Library, Harley 331 (H)
Manchester, Rylands Library, Latin 367 (M)
Oxford, Bodleian Library, Barlow 24 (N)
Cambridge, Corpus Christi College 392 (K)

The final section, "On the margins," discusses some additional collections that were made before and after the period of 1350–1450, including Cambridge, University Library, Gg.6.26 (G) and London University 657 (U), and looks at the inclusion of sermons in books that are not primarily sermon collections.

I present these collections in the presumed chronological order of their composition, though establishing such an order is somewhat hazardous, since the scripts cannot be precisely dated and many of these manucripts are written in more than one hand ranging throughout the fifteenth century. Furthermore, miscellaneous collections tend to include individual sermons whose original dates of composition range widely, often over a century and more. Several individual preachers, such as Chambron, Rimington, Wimbledon, and Alkerton, are taken up after or within the chapters on the respective major manuscripts where their work is found.

2

John Sheppey (SH)

I begin this survey with a small group of sermons which, although they barely reach the threshold of our period, yet possess a number of unusual advantages for this study. For one thing, we know their author as well as the occasions and dates of his sermons. They reflect English preaching before our period because their author collected and studied the work of English preachers who were active in the two preceding generations. And they also foreshadow some of the major features of later collections.

John Sheppey was a Benedictine monk at Rochester who studied at Oxford in the early 1330s and incepted in theology in 1332.[1] He then served as prior of his monastery (1333–1350) and as bishop of Rochester (1353–1360), where his tomb and effigy can still be seen. At his death, the archdeacon of his diocese, William Reed, who later became bishop of Chichester, bought three "volumes" of sermons that Sheppey had gathered "in his time at the university of Oxford" and bound two of them together (in MS New College, 92). The resulting two manuscripts Reed then gave, respectively, to Merton and to New College. Thus, we know more about the earliest history of Sheppey's collections than about any other discussed in this study.

Merton College, MS 248, a parchment codex of 225 leaves, is made up of several booklets written mostly in two columns.[2] According to the owner's note, this is the "tercium volumen sermonum per dominum Johannem de Schepeya . . . pro suo tempore in vniuersitate Oxon' collectorum." Except for the final section (ff. 194–225v), the volume is written by several fourteenth-century hands. It begins

---

[1] For a succinct and up-to-date survey of Sheppey's life and the sermon manuscripts see Stacpoole, "Jean Sheppey;" see also Greatrex, *Register*, pp. 634–635. G. Mifsud has studied Sheppey's life and sermon work in his unpublished B. Litt. thesis, "John Sheppey."

[2] The contents are listed in Coxe 1:96–97. See also Powicke, *Medieval Books of Merton College*, p. 171 ("Rede's Library"). Powicke's statement that "Sheppey's own sermons, or fables, occupy ff. 30–62" should probably read "ff. 30–42"; but these are not sermons. Mifsud, "John Sheppey," discusses this manuscript in chapter VI.

with a copy of the (here unidentified) *Communiloquium* by the Franciscan John of Wales, which Sheppey says he acquired from the Dominican William of Hotoft, and some other material.[3] This is followed by excerpts from a Latin translation of Aesop's fables (ff. 25v–29v) and *Flores moralium antiquorum* (ff. 30–42), both preceded by topical indices (ff. 20–26, in four columns). The final section (ff. 194–225v) contains three works written in thirteenth-century hands. The middle part of the codex, ff. 43–193v, holds over two hundred sermons of varying lengths and shapes.[4] These appear in several booklets that occasionally bear the names of contemporary preachers[5] and show individual differences in form and style. Some items which I have counted as sermons give only a thema and division, while a series of sermons on themata from the Psalms is said to be excerpted "de quadam postilla super psalterium per magistrum Petrum de Ylkalay" (f. 101ra).

The other volume, Oxford, New College, MS 92, contains an owner's note stating that it is made up of four booklets that William Reed purchased or received as a gift from various sources.[6] Reed must have had these bound together and then, as already mentioned, given the book to New College. The four original booklets are:[7]

(1) Sheppey's collection of *Sermones vasconici*, ff. 1–40, which he may have made on one of his trips to the Continent and reworked for an English audience; with various indices for this booklet.

(2) *Sermones permixti*, ff. 40–138: forty-eight numbered sermons *de tempore* and *de sanctis* of the late thirteenth and early fourteenth century, without apparent connection to Sheppey. A number of these sermons also occur in Worcester Cathedral MS Q.46 and have been studied by Little and

---

[3] "Habui a fratre Willelmo de Hotoft predicatore," f. 1. This copy is highly abbreviated and incomplete. For John of Wales and his *Communiloquium*, see Jenny Swanson, *John of Wales*; Swanson does not mention this manuscript.

[4] As far as I can tell, the last sermon ends on 184v and is followed by excerpts, mostly from Augustine's homilies on the Epistle of John. The sermons listed in Schneyer 3:765–775 seem to have nothing to do with MS Merton 248 or, for that matter, with John Sheppey.

[5] They are, in alphabetical order: M. Lawrence Bretone, OFM; Robert Droyane, OFM; Henricus de Cruce, OFM; William Hotoft; Peter de Ilkalay; Philip Lancham or Laueham, OP; Laȝerne; Mauleuerer; Oliver; John Riddliton, OP; Sawcemere (or Sawremere); Stanchawe; Symon, OP; P. Tanny, OP. See also Little and Pelster, *Oxford Theology*, pp. 176–7, n. 5.

[6] "Liber M. Willelmi Reed, Episcopi Cicestr', cuius partem primam et terciam, quas scripsit venerabilis pater dominus Johannes de Schepeya Episcopus Roffen', emit de executoribus eiusdem. Partem vero secundam emit de venerabili patre domino Thoma Tryllek, episcopo Roffen'. Sed quartam partem habuit ex dono reuerendi domini sui M. Nicholai de Sandwyco quam Oxon' reportari fecit. Oretis igitur [pro] singulis supradictis," front pastedown. The manuscript contents are listed in Coxe, vol. 1, pt. 7, pp. 30–32.

[7] Listed in this order after Reed's note referred to in the preceding footnote, front pastedown.

Pelster.[8] An index on f. 40r–v lists sixty-nine sermons, i.e. all contained in booklets 2–4. A medieval hand has entered the respective numbers in the upper right corner of the versos of all three booklets.

(3) Sheppey's own sermons and some other material, ff. 139–187.

(4) Two Oxford sermons collected by M. Nicholas de Sandwyco, ff. 190–194.

The nineteen pieces in the third booklet, described on the front pastedown as "sermons edited, written, and preached by the venerable father Dom John de Schepeya, bishop,"[9] include a dozen full sermons. Either their rubrics or labels in the table, or else references in the texts, indicate that two are for Ash Wednesday (one dated 1353, see below), four are funeral sermons,[10] two were preached at St. Paul's, London (1336 and 1337), one preached at the election of an abbess, perhaps to the nuns of Malling, and the remaining three were for Holy Thursday 1343, for Corpus Christi, and perhaps for Pentecost. They are in Latin with a fair amount of English mixed in. The last of them, SH-19 without date, also appears in the Merton collection and seemingly represents Sheppey's copy of a sermon he had heard at Oxford.[11]

The second Ash Wednesday sermon in the booklet (SH-12) seems to be chronologically the last of Sheppey's preserved sermons; it is dated "1353" (i.e. February 26, 1354). In it Sheppey, now bishop of Rochester, speaks of various sins among the laity and the clergy of his diocese. The main part of this sermon develops the need to weep for our sins "as a father weeps over his son that is led to the gallows; as a friend weeps over his friend who is about to be thrown into an abyss; as a master weeps over his student who is to be degraded; and as a workman weeps over his work that is about to be shamefully deformed."[12] A marginal note in

---

[8] Little and Pelster, see note 5.

[9] "Sermones editi, scripti, et predicati per venerabilem patrem dominum Joh' de Schepeya episcopum."

[10] They are for "Dominus Nicholas Malameyn," 1349 (f. 148v); "Domina de Cobham," 1344, but not preached because the archbishop of Canterbury gave [his own] sermon (f. 152); "Stephanus" (f. 160); and an unnamed person (f. 164, incomplete).

[11] Oxford, Merton College, MS 248, ff. 176rb–177rb. SH-19 hovers somewhere between a copy and a redaction. It has the same structure and substance as the version in Merton, but some of its variations in details are more than scribal. For example, to Merton's "prouerbialiter dicitur" Sheppey has added "in nostra lingua," f. 177ra. In Merton, the sermon is followed by "Frater J. [blank] predicator," but this may belong to the following sermon.

[12] "Circa primum est breuiter aduertendum quod vos qui per peccatum Dominum offendistis flebitis propter peccata vestra, sicud pater propter filium ductum ad suspendium. Secundo flebitis sicud amicus super amicum cito precipitandum. Tercio sicud magister super discipulum degradandum. Quarto sicud artifex super opus suum turpiter deformandum. Hec materia sermonis," f. 156v, followed by a rhymed English division. Only the first three parts are developed in the extant text.

Sheppey's hand indicates that the division comes from Bromyard's *Distinctions*,[13] from which Sheppey has taken the fourfold division as well as some other verbal material, including a simile involving Welsh thieves that are led to the gallows. Later on, in the text itself, he refers to another of Bromyard's distinctions,[14] and on the same page he points once more to Bromyard, this time to the *Summa praedicantium*.[15] The latter work is also referred to in another sermon by Sheppey, that for Corpus Christi.[16]

These citations alone reveal in a nutshell the interest this learned Benedictine took in preaching. He had been to university even before the important constitutions of Benedict XII were issued (which demanded that monasteries send young monks to the university in order to learn how to preach) and had read the preaching work of one of the most influential English Dominicans carefully. He had also listened to contemporary Dominican and Franciscan friars and collected their sermons as well as an abbreviated version of a major aid for preachers, John of Wales' *Communiloquium*. The monastery to which he returned continued to cultivate a keen interest in sermon-making: one of Sheppey's successors, Thomas Brinton, left a much larger and important collection of sermons (BR, see below), and Rochester priory owned a number of basic aids for preaching, including Bromyard's *Summa praedicantium*, a work from which Brinton, too, was to quote again and again.[17] Sheppey preached in various places and on various occasions including Ash Wednesday, as Brinton was to do later also. And both men have left us the fruit of their study and preaching in written form. In addition, Sheppey's work demonstrates another more general feature of preaching in late-medieval England: the field is no longer dominated by the mendicant orders; instead, learned monks move very much into the foreground. This is shown, first of all, by the proportionately large number of Benedictine collections from the 1370s to 1450.[18] It can, I think, also be shown by examining a sermon feature which the studies of Beryl Smalley linked closely to the friars, the use of classical and pseudo-classical material in their sermons. While the few friars whose work

---

[13] "De istis nota in d[istinccionibus] brom3ard d[istinccione] lv," f. 156v margin.

[14] "Quere de hoc in d[istinccionibus] brom3ard d[instinccione] 97, membro 2, ad hoc signum o-o," f. 158v. It is hard to tell whether the reference is accurate.

[15] In a marginal note: "Si velis plus de compassione vide in brom3ard c. 12," f. 158v. The reference is to *Summa praedicantium*, "Compassio," C.XII; cf. London, British Library, MS Royal 7.E.iv, ff. 101rb–102rb.

[16] "Pro tercio, videlicet quod cum magna reuerencia debet adorari et sumi, nota E.6.13. Et iunge quod Deus non potuit fecisse aliquid magis conueniens saluti nostre, ibidem 21. Et quod iste panis dat vitam eternam, ibidem 17," f. 171 insert. In the Royal MS, the paragraphs alluded to appear on ff. 155vb–156ra, 156va–b, and 155vb.

[17] The book is extant as London, British Library, MS Royal 7.E.iv.

[18] See below the discussions of Brinton, Rypon, MSS O and R, the Worcester collections X and W, and perhaps J.

we know in this period continued to use some of this traditional material, it is Benedictine preachers who came to excel in exploring "the classics" for their sermons. Judging by those texts that have been preserved, it is Benedictine sermons that in our period are rhetorically crafted and innovative.[19]

[19] I have examined the continuing interests of the "classicizing friars" in Wenzel, "Classics" and commented on the elevated rhetoric of fifteenth-century Benedictine preaching, ibid., p. 141, as well as in *Monastic Preaching*, pp. 19–20.

3

Richard FitzRalph (FI)

As did John Sheppey's, so FitzRalph's life straddled the threshold to the century covered in this study, and thus a good deal of his preaching occurred before 1350. But his work, too, should be included here for a number of reasons that echo and yet differ from those given for the inclusion of Sheppey. First and foremost, he has left a unique sermon diary, in which he noted precisely where, when, in what language, and often before what audience he preached. Second, his work gives us a splendid insight into the preaching activities of a fourteenth-century bishop. And lastly, FitzRalph exerted a strong and often acknowledged influence on later fourteenth- and fifteenth-century preachers, both orthodox and Lollard.[1]

Born around the beginning of the century in Dundalk, Ireland, FitzRalph studied at Oxford and advanced to a doctorate in theology (1331) and the chancel-lorship of the university (1332–1334). Throughout his life he spent four extended periods at Avignon (1334–5, 1337–44, 1349–51, and 1357–60) and probably died there in 1360. In 1335 he was appointed dean of Lichfield cathedral, and in 1347 archbishop of Armagh and primate of Ireland.[2]

His sermons have been preserved in three complete and several partial manuscripts, and some of them appear elsewhere as single items in differ-ent sermon collections.[3] They amount to some 90 items in the complete

---

[1] He is quoted in W-68 (=FI-39), W-149 (=FI-26), and DY-66 (citing his sermons on almsgiving). His *Summa de questionibus Armenorum* is cited in A-40 and in Oxford, Magdalen College, MS 156 (see below, section 18 on Dygon). For single sermons copied in other collections see below, note 3.

[2] A full and recent study of FitzRalph's life, thought, and work is Walsh, *Fourteenth-Century Scholar*. FitzRalph's important contribution to the controversy between the secular clergy and the mendicant orders has been analyzed in Szittya, *Antifraternal Tradition*, chap. 3, pp. 123–51.

[3] See Gwynn, "Sermon-Diary." In addition, several articles by Gwynn in *Studies: an Irish Quarterly Review* 22–26 (1933–37) are still valuable for FitzRalph's preaching activity. Walsh, *Fourteenth-Century Scholar*, offers a detailed discussion of the sermons in chronological order in chapter 3, "The Preacher and His Sermon Diary," and chapters 4–5. For single sermons that appear in other

manuscripts,[4] to which should be added an academic *introitus*, a sermon in praise of scripture and Peter Lombard.[5]

Almost all of the sermons are dated by year and feast day, thus furnishing a chronological picture[6] not only of FitzRalph's preaching activity but of changes in his views and of the development of strongly held positions with respect to such favorite topics as the Beatific Vision, the Immaculate Conception, almsgiving, the mendicant orders' claim of following Christ's voluntary poverty, and their privileges in hearing confession and burying the dead.[7] Often the exposition of his thoughts on such topics extends through a series of sermons; for instance, his condemnation of usurers, false judges, people who receive stolen goods and thieves, and Irish parishioners who are remiss in tithing occupies at least nine consecutive sermons (44–52) given at various locations in 1355. During his active years, FitzRalph preached in many places and before the most widely diversified audiences, ranging from the papal curia and the cardinals as well as houses of the mendicant orders at Avignon, through his constituencies at Lichfield and in his diocese, to what must have been humbler audiences in country parishes in England and Ireland. In his final years he engaged in a running controversy with the friars in a series of sermons given at St. Paul's Cross, but he had already preached in London earlier, at public processions.

Given this diversity of occasions, his sermons belong to all types: *de tempore*, *de sanctis*, and for such special occasions as synods and visitations.[8] Among the saints, "nostra Maria" and saints Katherine, Thomas Becket, Dominic, Martin, and Nicholas received special panegyrics. He would preach in Latin or in English,

collections, see Walsh, ibidem, p. 471, last paragraph, and p. 208, n. 70; and Szittya, *Antifraternal Tradition*, p. 127, n. 15. Of the sermon collections here surveyed, B/2, J/5, and F/3 contain pieces of his work: B/2-82 is FI-67 (shortened), one of FitzRalph's antifraternal sermons preached at St. Paul's Cross; J/5-42 is FI-73, an Avignon sermon; and F/3 contains thirteen sermons preached in London and at Avignon, apparently copied *en bloc* from one of the major collections.

4 Walsh speaks of "ninety-two" and "95 items," pp. 182 and 183 n. 2, respectively. Gwynn lists ninety-two items from Oxford MS Bodley 144; these include several *proposiciones* in sermon form and one *responsio* in non-sermon form. In my inventory I follow this manuscript and add FitzRalph's *introitus*. Notice that the modern reader who numbered the sermons in Bodley 144 in pencil assigned the numbers 5 and 6 to the same sermon (FI-5).

5 *Luminis impetus laetificat civitatem Dei*, in Oxford, Oriel College, MS 15, f. 1ra–va. See Walsh, *Fourteenth-Century Scholar*, p. 59 and n. 95; and Wenzel, "Academic Sermons," p. 309.

6 Their appearance in the full manuscripts, however, is not straightforwardly chronological, which has led to speculations about how the diary originated and possible scribal interference. See Walsh, *Fourteenth-Century Scholar*, pp. 182, 184–187, 221–224.

7 In addition, the sermons also reveal a good deal of FitzRalph's personality; see Walsh, ibid., especially pp. 218–221.

8 Two synodal sermons have been edited by Gwynn, "Two Sermons."

as his audiences required; and now and then he records that he began a sermon in Latin, outlining its structure, and then continued in the vernacular.[9] In his processional sermon in London after the victory at Crécy (FI-23) he even began by giving three reasons why he spoke at once in English. As one might expect, in several sermons FitzRalph expounded such catechetical matters as the Creed (8, 31), the Ten Commandments (55, 56), the Lord's Prayer (26), the Hail Mary (4), the seven deadly sins (29), and the sacraments (37, report only). In these instances his tone and style are considerably more learned and demanding than the mere listing of such items that one finds in the work of lesser preachers. If we can judge by the preserved complete sermons, in general FitzRalph used a somewhat academic style of preaching that here and there verged on that of a theological discussion, with *dubia* and objections and responses. The latter is especially noteworthy in his discussion of the ideal of poverty among the friars and in his argumentation in favor of the Immaculate Conception, sermons that read rather like treatises or theological pamphlets and evidently were copied separately for that reason.[10] But the same measured tone can also be found in sermons that criticize and condemn moral and social evils, such as postponing almsgiving until after death, or usury, or confession to friars and being buried among them (67, 20), where FitzRalph relies on reasoned argument rather than impassioned rhetoric.[11]

It must of course be remembered that most of his sermons are not what he actually spoke from the pulpit but, rather, *post factum* reports made by himself and consistently written in Latin. They are full of first-person singular phrases, such as "here I said" or "I argued (*suasi*)," or more usually statements in the passive voice, such as "first the prayer was said," or "her whole history was recited," or "it was shown," or "it was argued" (*suasum fuit*), and so on. A good brief example is

---

[9] In sermon 18, after the main division, FitzRalph reports: "Hucusque in latino; consequenter prosecucio fiebat in anglico isto modo . . ." (f. 30). In Sermon 6 he says: "Vt sub breuibus verbis ac leuibus et latino describam sermonis nostri materiam et postmodum loquar ad populum expressius atque rusticius in vulgari, videtur michi . . ." MS Bodley 144, f. 4. Walsh's account of the language of sermon 6 (*Fourteenth-Century Scholar*, p. 225) is inaccurate; also, both Gwynn and Walsh failed to notice that this sermon is indeed dated in MS Bodley 144 apart from the *tabula*, though in the colophon: "Hic sermo dictus fuit in choro ecclesie Lich' in festo Cene dominice anno Domini 1345" (f. 7v).

[10] Cf. Walsh, *Fourteenth-Century Scholar*, p. 187.

[11] There are exceptions to this rationally controlled style. One is sermon 68, which Szittya calls "the most intemperate outburst of FitzRalph's career" (*Antifraternal Tradition*, p. 129). His sermons in praise of saints frequently are panegyric in tone; for instance, FI-79 for St. Thomas of Canterbury or FI-85 for the Blessed Virgin.

the sermon delivered to the people of Drogheda in mid-Lent of 1355, on "Cast out this bondwoman and her son" (Gen 21:10):

> First I introduced the prayer, referrring to the five barley loaves [of the day's gospel] which are dry and arid, that is, knowledge derived from the five senses without grace to order them . . . For the introduction I explained the epistle reading by interpreting the names of Sarah, Hagar, Ishmael, and Isaac. Then I gave the development by showing that this servant Hagar stands for cupidity, which is a stranger to our nature and converts or rather subverts it. And her son Ishmael stands for the action of this cupidity by which one desires to abound in wordly goods.[12]

FitzRalph then preached against cupidity, which he showed to exist in the acquisition of goods, their preservation for one's family, and reluctance to give them up at death. After that,

> I returned to the words "Cast out" and showed that it is much better to cast out this cupidity and her aforementioned son than to reject or flee them. Where I described two ways of acquiring virtue . . . And afterwards I exhorted to reiterate one's confession and showed how the act of confession, which is part of satisfaction, often merits a reward in heaven that is no smaller than a similar act that is not part of satisfaction . . . And so I made an end to the sermon.[13]

The result is at best a partial picture of what his actual preaching was like, tracing its logical and structural development but unquestionably filtering out much of its substance and color. In keeping such a personal record of his preaching FitzRalph also notes other sermons in which he used the same material or developed the same points. This practice of cross referencing occurs in other sermon collections as well and is a handy device to send *readers* to relevant material elsewhere in a

---

[12] For the sake of readability I have rendered FitzRalph's passive verb forms as first-person singular ones. "*Eice ancilla hanc et filium eius*, Genesis 21, et excepto pronomine in epistula hodierna. Primo fuit oracio introducta per quinque panes ordeacios, scilicet scienciam acceptam ex quinque sensibus sine gracia regulante siccos et aridos . . . Introduccio fiebat exponendo epistulam per interpretacionem nominum Sara, Agar, Ymael, et Ysaac. Et prosecucio fiebat intelligendo per ancillam hanc Agar cupiditatem, que aduena est nostre nature et eam semper conuertens, immo magis subuertens. Et per filium eius Ysmael actum huius cupiditatis quo quis cupit bonis mundanis conformiter cupiditat' affluere," FI-46, f. 65v.

[13] "Deinde ad uerbum 'eice' reuersum, atque ostensum quod magis expedit exercere saltem cum toto mentis conatu extra iacere hanc cupiditatem et filium eius predictum quam pellere aut paulatim fugere. Vbi declarata [!] fuerant duo modi acquirendi virtutem . . . Et consequenter de iteracione confessionis fuit suasum, et ibi fuit ostensum qualiter actus confessionis, que est pars satisfaccionis, non numquam non meretur minus premium in celo quam actus consimilis qui non est satisfactorius . . . Et sic fiebat finis sermonis." Ibid., ff. 65v–66.

collection. But as one reads through FitzRalph's great controversial sermons of St. Paul's Cross, one gets the impression that, from early on, FitzRalph kept this record of what he had said when and where perhaps more as a personal aide-memoire to protect himself in attacks and controversies. Such scholarly accuracy also shows in another feature that one rarely or ever encounters elsewhere: now and then FitzRalph would qualify a quotation and its source by an added "as I recall" or "in so far as it occurs to me."[14]

[14] "Quantum recordor" (FI-80, 85), "quantum michi occurrit" (78, 80).

4

Oxford, Bodleian Library, MS
Auct. F. infra 1.2 (F)

Although formally this manuscript belongs with what I have called miscellaneous collections, I discuss it at this point because of its connection with FitzRalph, and because its sermons, like Sheppey's, point back to the earlier fourteenth and even the late thirteenth centuries, in fact to the academic milieu found in one of Sheppey's booklets. The manuscript itself was made after 1350: it is written by various hands of the second half of the fourteenth century, probably of the third quarter; and it includes several sermons preached by FitzRalph in the 1350s as well as one sermon by Richard Kilvington, who was a master by 1366.[1]

The codex is composed of five booklets (A–E), which are easily distinguishable by their contents as well as their handwriting:[2]

A. *De pauperie Salvatoris* by FitzRalph, written in hand *a*, a clear Anglicana formata (ff. 1–84).

B. Eight sermons, written in a different Anglicana hand (*b*), though hand *a* seems to take over again on f. 97rb (ff. 85–103). They are random *de tempore* sermons and will be referred to as F/1.[3] At least one sermon (F/1-2) is addressed to "Reuerendi domini et magistri" (together with "Karissimi").

C. Works by Augustine, Bede, and others, written in hand *c*, a more formal Anglicana bookhand (ff. 104–229vb). The contents of these eleven quires are listed in a different hand on f. 230v, beginning with "Liber monasterii Radyng" and adding to the titles the respective medieval folio numbers. This original distinctness of this booklet is also shown by its medieval foliation,

---

[1] The sermon, F/4-2, is marked for 2 Advent and was preached the day before the feast of the Immaculate Conception. The Second Sunday in Advent fell on December 7 in 1365, 1371, 1376, 1382, 1393, and 1399 (as well as earlier and later years). On Kilvington see *BRUO* 2:1051.

[2] In using capital letters for the booklets I follow *SC* 1:120–121, which is, however, insufficient and inaccurate in its analysis of booklet D.

[3] F/1-5 bears a rubric "Dominica 4 post epiphaniam"; another copy of this sermon, in X-86, is for the Christmas season. F/1-4, which is also X-28, is there assigned to 2 Advent. F/1-6, also in BL, Add. 38818 (Basevorn?), may be for Sexagesima.

in ink (modern f. 104) and pencil (passim). The medieval foliation is used in the table on f. 230v.

D. A collection of sermon material, written by hand *a* (ff. 231–320). The booklet comprises three different matters:

1. "Hic incipiunt antethemata multa": about sixty-six prothemes, all leading to the normal prayer, without indication of their intended occasion (ff. 231ra–236vb).[4] These will be referred to as F/2.

2. Thirteen sermons by FitzRalph, corresponding to nos. 65–66, 69–75, 83–84, 67–68 in Gwynn's inventory, with the standard headnotes indicating time and place of their delivery (ff. 237ra–287vb). 67–68, which form a quire, apparently occur here out of order by misplacement,[5] which in turn may suggest that the thirteen sermons here (together with *De pauperie Salvatoris* in booklet A) were once part of a larger collection of FitzRalph's works. These sermons will be referred to as F/3.

3. Thirty sermons written by hand *a* (ff. 288ra–337rb; 338–339 blank). The second, on *Erunt signa in sole*, is entitled "Sermo magistri Ricardi kilwyngton' de aduentu Domini" and was preached on December 7. It is followed by the rubric "Incipiunt sermones et materie diuerse de eleccione" (f. 293vb, within the column), which introduces nine items dealing with election (F/4-3 to 11). However, only two of them (3 and 4) are properly speaking sermons, while the remaining seven pieces are copies of lectures 119–125 from Holcot's commentary on the Book of Wisdom, which deal with election. They in turn are followed by some more sermons (F/4-12 to 30) for a dead person and for martyrs and confessors.[6] The booklet ends with a list of the sermons in sections 2–3, written by a small and more current hand (with some omissions; f. 337rb). The pieces in this third section of booklet D will be referred to as F/4.

E. Fifty-eight sermons written in an Anglicana hand *d*, which is much smaller than *a* (ff. 340–401). There may be a change of hand on ff. 397rb. This booklet must have been written after 1360, because it contains a

---

[4] The text is written continuously, but as a rule the items are separated by double slashes, underlining, and a marginal note "prothema." Several items, however, lack the marginal note as well as a biblical thema (see my inventory), but they consistently end with an invitation to pray. Schneyer 7:671–2 lists only ten items, and rather selectively.

[5] Sermons 65–66 are introduced as *Primus sermo* and *Secundus sermo*, respectively; sermon 67 as *Tercius sermo*; the other FitzRalph sermons are not numbered.

[6] The indications of the occasions as marked in the top margins (by the text hand) are not always closely related to the sermon texts. For example, F/4-14 is clearly a sermon in honor of St. Thomas Becket but marked "Sermo de martiribus." Similarly, F/4-17, for St. Augustine, and F/4-18, for St. Augustine of Canterbury, are marked "Sermo de confess'."

freestanding invitation to pray for a number of persons and groups including FitzRalph: "inter mortuos recommendo ita specialiter sicut scio animam illius doctoris eximii Armachani" (395vb). This booklet breaks off incomplete. The sermons here gathered will be referred to as F/5. They include pieces for major feast days, saints, and special occasions in a very random order.

The entire volume received the title *Collectarium* in the fifteenth century and was given to the Benedictine monastery of Reading by its abbot Thomas Erle (abbot 1409–1430).[7] It thus reflects the work of collectors in its overall composition. It does so also in the individual booklets. Especially interesting is booklet E, which shares a number of sermons with two manuscripts – Oxford, New College, MS 92 and Worcester Cathedral MS Q.46 – which are of great importance for our knowledge of university preaching and disputation in the 1290s and have been studied by Little and Pelster.[8] In MS Q.46 the Worcester monk John Dumbleton collected sermons he had heard or read at Oxford from 1290 to 1293. Many of these bear indications of their occasions as well as preachers' names, so that Pelster could reconstruct a calendar of university preaching at Oxford during those years.[9] Of the sermons in Q.46 that can be dated to the academic year of 1292–1293, thirty-four also occur in Oxford, New College, MS 92 (with the same occasions and preachers' names noted), where – in contrast to Q.46 – they stand in the correct chronological sequence. As we saw earlier, New College, MS 92 combines four originally different booklets that were evidently brought together by bishop William Reed. One of these four contains Sheppey's own sermons; another (the second booklet), sixty-nine *Sermones permixti* (ff. 40–138). It is the latter booklet that contains the Oxford sermons of 1292–93.[10] Now, booklet E of MS Auct. F. infra 1.2 shares five sermons with the New College manuscript,[11] and another three with Q.46.[12] Pelster concluded his examination of the two earlier manuscripts with the resigned sigh, "There is practically no hope of discovering other MSS. of this collection." Yet MS Auct. F. infra 1.2 at least shows that those Oxford sermons of the 1290s kept their popularity into the post-1350 period. In addition, it may be worth

---

[7] Interestingly, the sermon by Kilvington, F/4-2, quotes the rare work *De concepcione Virginis gloriose* by Nicholas de Sancto Albano, which seems to have been uniquely preserved in another Reading manuscript, now Oxford, Bodleian Library, MS Auct. D.4.18; see Sharpe, *Handlist*, p. 393.

[8] Little and Pelster, *Oxford Theology*.   [9] Ibid., pp. 154–165.

[10] The *Sermones permixti* of the New College manuscript are listed in Schneyer 6:246–7, but his inventory was apparently culled from Pelster's and is quite untrustworthy. The sermons of Worcester Q.46 are inventoried in Schneyer 6:239–246.

[11] F/5-36, 37, 47, 48, and 50.   [12] F/5-28, 49, and 57.

pointing out that many more of the sermons in booklet E of Auct. F. infra 1.2 show structural practices that are very much like what one finds in the older Oxford sermons and differ from sermons written a century later, especially in their habit of beginning the protheme with a biblical quotation that differs from the thema proper; of indicating the source of the thema only after the protheme; and of devoting the protheme to a brief discussion of the preacher's office. It is, therefore, quite possible that this booklet preserves more witnesses of late thirteenth-century university preaching than has so far been realized. A very minor but potentially telling detail of the scribal work involved in composing booklet E is the erroneous copying, on f. 371va, of thirty-two lines that had appeared earlier on f. 368ra, in exactly the same position. The second copy, which is almost photographic, has been canceled with "va – cat," and the scribe then resumed copying the correct text.

These earlier Oxford sermons are not the only material that Auct. F. infra 1.2 shares with other collections. Booklet E additionally contains one sermon that also appears in collection X[13] and several others that evidently are also found elsewhere.[14] Similarly, booklet B has two sermons likewise copied in X, and another in the collection of sermons that may have been made by Robert Basevorn.[15] Its sermon F/1-7 agrees to a large extent with E-19 in its substance, although with constant differences in wording; but F/1-7 eventually speaks against hypocrisy in acquiring spiritual benefices and honors, whereas E-19 discusses the duties of a visitator of a religious house. Hence, the two sermons probably are different redactions derived from a common source.[16]

---

[13] F/5-55 in X-251 but without protheme.

[14] F/5-23 in Valencia 284 (Schneyer 6:211); F/5-31 in Bodley 4 and elsewhere (Schneyer 6:137, 249; 7:68, 78); perhaps also F/5-9 in Vatican, MS Vat. lat. 11444 (Schneyer 6:215); F/5-12 in Charleville 31 (Schneyer 6:367); and F/5-43 in Vatican, MS Borghese 166 (Schneyer 6:484).

[15] See above, n. 3.

[16] F/1-7 also mentions the example of St. Francis, which is omitted in E-19.

5

John Waldeby (WA)

Judging by the number of extant manuscripts as well as his own words, John Waldeby was one of the most popular preachers surveyed in this book, and he has deservedly drawn some scholarly attention.[1] He entered the convent of the Austin friars in Lincoln in the early 1330s and then studied at Oxford, where he had became a doctor of theology by 1354. In 1354 he was at the convent in York and licensed to hear confessions. Except for a brief journey to the General Chapter of the Austin friars at Perugia in 1354, he stayed in York until his death shortly after 1372. Perhaps he served as prior provincial of the English Austin Friars in 1366.[2] As he tells us himself, his preaching in York drew such large crowds that, in order to get some writing done, he had to withdraw to the quieter convent of Tickhill.[3] He was highly esteemed by Thomas de la Mare, the powerful and well-known abbot of St Albans. The latter, during his nine-year tenure as prior of Tynemouth, in the 1340s, spent three years "studying how to preach the word of God, in both English and Latin," for which he surrounded himself with "clerics and masters, both secular and mendicants" who were to teach him.[4] Waldeby is not mentioned by name as De la Mare's teacher, but the two men became close friends, and in his early years in York Waldeby wrote up a series of sermons on the Creed at the Benedictine abbot's request and dedicated that work to him.

---

[1] Especially in Morrin, *John Waldeby*, with good discussion of his sermon structure and style. See also *BRUO* 3:1958; Gwynn, *English Austin Friars*, pp. 114–123; and Roth, *English Austin Friars*, 1:400–404.

[2] Apart from the dates mentioned, the chronology is not entirely certain; see the works cited in the previous note. Morrin, *John Waldeby*, gives a tentative chronology of Waldeby's academic career on pp. 15–16.

[3] Prologue to his treatise on the Creed, MS Caius 334, f. 150rb–va.

[4] Walsingham, *Gesta abbatum*, vol. 2, p. 380. Since De la Mare became abbot of St. Albans in 1349 (till 1396), he must have been prior of Tynemouth in the preceding nine years.

This is one of three extant treatises on basic catechetical matters[5] from Waldeby's hand: the Pater Noster, the Ave Maria, and the Credo.[6] While all three works are presumably based on Waldeby's preaching in York, in the course of writing up his sermons Waldeby gave them an overall form that approaches that of a treatise. His work on the Creed – "moral matter that I formerly preached to the people in York"[7] – is referred to as a *tractatus* throughout. But its component parts, dealing with the twelve articles of faith, are called *sermones* or *collaciones* and have such sermon features as thema, addresses, the typical closing formula, and, beyond such formal characteristics, a moral concern with the vices, pious stories, memorial verses, and so on. At the same time the treatise contains a good deal of theological learning, including a number of *dubia*. If the treatise stems from Waldeby's actual preaching in York, this work would share the function of his *Novum opus dominicale*, as we shall see. The work on the Pater Noster is similarly called *tractatus* and reads much like an academic commentary on the Lord's Prayer, although again the term *collacio* occurs here and there, and some of its parts end with a closing formula that is typical of sermons. Its seven parts deal with the seven deadly sins as they are opposed by the seven petitions. Finally, the work on the Ave Maria comprises five parts devoted to the major feasts in honor of the Blessed Virgin. They are, by Waldeby himself, called "homilies" (*omelie*).[8]

These formal characteristics and moral concerns reappear in Waldeby's *Novum opus dominicale*, a regular sermon cycle on the Sunday gospels of the church year.[9] This work has been preserved in two known copies. The more important one is Oxford, Bodleian Library, MS Laud misc. 77, of the fifteenth century.[10] In contrast to the second manuscript (Bodley 687), here the sixty sermons run from 14 Trinity to 13 Trinity.[11] This curious order is explained by Waldeby himself in the first item, which serves as, and is actually called, the "prohemium" to the

---

[5] See the further discussion of *pastoralia* in Part Three, chapter 48.

[6] Waldeby's oeuvre was listed in the catalogue of the York Austin friars compiled in 1372; see *Friars' Libraries*, pp. xxiv–xxxv and 11–154. For Waldeby's works in the York library see ibid., index, p. 264.

[7] "Quedam materia moralis in exposicione symboli quam dudum populo predicaueram in Eborum," Cambridge, Gonville and Caius College, MS 334, f. 150rb.

[8] The work has been edited in Morrin, *John Waldeby*, pp. 81–135.

[9] Also called *Opus doctrinale*; see *Friars' Libraries*, p. 141. Waldeby apparently also composed a cycle of saints' sermons, but that work is not known to have survived; see ibidem. In contrast to most other collections Waldeby uses the lections of the Franciscan use for the Sundays after Trinity, and he counts the latter "after Pentecost"; see above, "Prolegomena," p. 9.

[10] Described by Morrin, *John Waldeby*, p. 76.

[11] In Bodley 687 they run more regularly from 1 Advent to 24 Trinity.

entire cycle.[12] After a discourse on "Preach the Gospel to every creature" (Mark 16:15), Waldeby turns to his own work and the activity in which it originated:

> Since the teaching of the Gospel has such power and efficacy that it makes its teachers, readers, and followers spiritually children of God, makes them spiritually practitioners of the divine commandments, and in the end renders them recipients of the eternal rewards, as has been shown in this preface, I therefore desire, with the help of Christ, the author of the gospels, hastily and as it were stealthily in the midst of my other business, to compile short and simple collations for each Sunday gospel through the year, to serve as introduction for the youths who have been designated as my students. Let them derive usefulness and profit from the progress from what is easier to what is more difficult, so that they find plain and common things in this work and later study new and more subtle ones.[13]

Waldeby continues to explain that, since around Michaelmas worldly activity in both fields and markets slows down whereas preachers are busy teaching the people, he will

> start this work with the Sundays that occur at this time, and I shall publish and read these sermons in their order, in the cathedra in place of the ordinary lectures, as time will allow.[14]

He will not always identify his authorities nor write out fully the stories and biblical figures, "so that my hearers may look them up more diligently in their books, and on that occasion know and understand the text of the Bible more

[12] This was not realized by Owst, who apparently did not examine either manuscript (Owst, *Preaching*, p. 64, n. 2), nor by Gwynn, who declared that "there is no preface to this work in the two extant manuscripts" (Gwynn, *English Austin Friars*, p. 117 n. 3).

[13] "Quia igitur euangelica doctrina tante virtutis et efficacie est quod illius doctores et auditores et obseruatores tamquam filios Dei spiritualiter gignit, factores diuinorum mandatorum spiritualiter efficit, possessoresque premiorum eternorum finaliter perficit, sicut deductum est in hoc prohemio. [*marg:* epilogus] Idcirco / raptim et quasi furtiue inter ceteras occupaciones meas volo, fauente Christo euangeliorum auctore, de singulis euangeliis dominicalibus per anni circulum singulas compilare collaciones breues et leues pro introduccione iuuenum qui mihi in studentes annotantur. vt eorum utilitas et profectus sit a facilioribus et ad difficiliora progressus, vt ipsi plana et communia in hoc opusculo videant et postea noua et subtilia studeant." WA-1, f. 2r–v.

[14] "Et quia circa festum sancti Michaelis cessat occupacio mundialis circa colleccionem messium nec diebus dominicis communiter vltra tempus illud exercentur mercata, sed predicatores tam seculares quam regulares ecclesiastica exercent iudicia et plebi spiritualia proponunt dogmata, idcirco de dominicis que illo tempore occurrunt huius operis exordium sumam et in cathedra loco leccionum ordinariarum per ordinem sermones publicabo provt tempus permiserit et legam." Ibid., f.2v.

deeply and better."[15] And he ends by comparing himself to the woman who anointed Christ, who did what she could in anointing his body for the burial, and whose name will remain in memory wherever the Gospel is preached (cf. Mark 14:3–9).[16]

In this manuscript, the *Novum opus dominicale* bears a colophon according to which the work was "compiled" by Friar John of Waldeby, OSA, DTh, in 1365.[17] The colophon is written in a different hand from the text, cursive and evidently much later. If the date given is accurate, Waldeby's changing from lecturing *in cathedra* to reading the sermons for the benefit of "the youths" assigned to him might reflect his teaching in the York convent. If the date is not accurate, this activity could go back – but less plausibly – to his teaching at Oxford. As he had omitted stories in the sermons to save time and space, he now, at the end of the sermons, added a dozen folios of just such material, since "not all who are going to own these sermons have [Gregory's] *Dialogues*, the *Legends of the Saints*, the *Speculum historiale*, and other books available" to which he had referred.[18]

While following the scholastic sermon structure in general – with protheme, often leading to prayer, perhaps an *introductio thematis*, division, and development of the principal parts – in his *Novum opus dominicale* Waldeby yet uses a peculiar variation. In a number of his sermons (though not all) he divides his thema first into two parts and confirms them, and then offers a second division into three parts, which form the principal parts to be developed. These two divisions are referred to – in the text as well as occasionally in the margins – as *divisio principalis*," beginning with the words "In quibus verbis duo notantur," and

---

[15] "Auctoritates vero non semper connotabo nec historias seu figuras [!] per scripturarum ad plenum exarabo, vt audientes ipsas in libris diligencius inquirant et occasione illa profundius et melius textum biblie sciant et cognoscant." Ibidem.

[16] Ibidem. For Waldeby's preaching technique see Morrin, *John Waldeby*, pp. 42–63; Roth, *English Austin Friars*, 1:401–404.

[17] "Explicit tractatus qui dicitur novum opus dominicale continens sermones per omnes dominicas tocius anni cum quibusdam festis principalibus. Quem tractatum compilauit frater Iohannes de Waldeby ordinis sancti Augustini sacre pagine professor sub anno Domini 1365." MS Laud misc. 77, f. 151v. Followed by four hexameters reproduced in Morrin, *John Waldeby*, p. 76.

[18] "Quoniam omnes historias et narraciones in sermonibus prelibatis seriose in ipsis sermonibus inserens tractatum faceret nimis prolixum, nec pro tunc quando sermones compilaui ad historias plene scribendi tempus occurrebat optimum, id circo michi videbatur michi expediens ipsas historias / in vnum colligere et plene ac plane inscribere, eo quod non omnes predictos sermones habituri libros *Dialogorum*, *Legendam sanctorum*, *Speculum historiale*, et libros alios habent ad quos pro eisdem historiis requirendis fit transmissio. Hunc igitur ordinem in historiis scribendis obseruabo: seriose scribam eas et historiis que in primo sermone adducuntur premittam numerum correspondentem, et sic historias aductas in sermone secundo signabo numero correspondente, et sic successiue faciam vsque ad finem compilacionis. Historias vero Biblie famosas et notas et historias plene in sermonibus scriptas in hoc opusculo nullatenus explicabo." Laud misc. 77, f. 140r–v. The *Narraciones* follow ff. 140v–151v.

materia collacionis, beginning "Sed pro materia collacionis est aduertendum."[19] All this is fairly standard procedure in scholastic sermons, and the two divisions are in fact a *divisio ab intus* followed by a *divisio ab extra*. What sets Waldeby slightly apart is his consistently dividing the thema into two and then three parts. One may perhaps detect another hallmark of his preaching in his fondness for anecdotes, especially for somewhat funny ones called *trufae*, in both text and margins.[20] Readers of Middle-English literature will find here such popular old acquaintances as the man in the moon or the owl and the nightingale, both in WA-35.

CAMBRIDGE, GONVILLE AND CAIUS COLLEGE, MS 334/727 (CA)

Waldeby's three "catechetical" sermon cycles have been preserved in several manuscripts, including Cambridge, Gonville and Caius College, 334 (ff. 112–172).[21] In its first part, before Waldeby's genuine works, appears a short run of five sermons (ff. 1–8), for which I know of no parallels, as well as a copy of Wimbledon's *Redde rationem* in Latin (ff. 10v–18). After Waldeby's three treatises, in the second part of the manuscript, appear another fourteen sermons[22] (ff. 172va–198ra). On the basis of an ambiguous note in the manuscript (f. 2v), Owst considered them part of Waldeby's corpus.[23] But at least seven of these occur in other collections, several even in more than one.[24] One of them is by Holcot, another the very popular *Quae utilitas in sanguine meo*, which is often found appended to the sermons by Michael of Hungary, in both manuscript and printed books.

[19] For an example, see "Prolegomena," pp. 13–14.   [20] Cf. Wenzel, "Joyous Art," p. 310.

[21] See Morrin, *John Waldeby*, pp. 36 and 67–68, giving a more detailed analysis than James, *Descriptive Catalogue . . . Gonville and Caius College*, 1:376–377.

[22] There are actually fifteen items, but the two on *Poenitet me fecisse* (ff. 176va–177ra and 193rb–195rb) probably represent the introduction and main part of one and the same sermon.

[23] See Morrin, *John Waldeby*, p. 36.   [24] In H, B (and H), S, W, and Z (and H).

6

Thomas Brinton (BR)

A native of Norfolk, Thomas Brinton became a Benedictine monk at the priory of Norwich, where he found not only a decent library but a learned environment, which he shared with one of the best Benedictine theologians of the later fourteenth century, the future cardinal Adam Easton. Apparently Brinton was sent to study, first at Cambridge – sermon 32 relates a story "tempore quo studui Cantabrigie" – and later to Oxford, where he incepted as doctor of canon law in 1364.[1] By then he evidently enjoyed a reputation as preacher, for he was called home, with Adam Easton, "in order to preach the customary sermons in the cathedral."[2] Before and after his doctorate he spent several years at the papal curia at Avignon and in Rome, where he served as proctor of the general chapter of the English Benedictines and preached before the pope. In Rome he was also involved in the founding of what became the English College. In January of 1373 Pope Gregory XI appointed him bishop of Rochester, against the election of the priory monks, and for the next decade Brinton took part in a number of major political events of Church and state: the parliaments of 1376 and 1377, the peace negotiations with France (1380), the commission that tried the rebels of the Peasants' Revolt (1381), and the Blackfriars Council, which condemned Wyclif's teaching (1382). Much of this active life is reflected in his sermons, whose audiences ranged from the general public to the clergy, from his monastic brethren to the pope and cardinals. For the last seven years of his life he was in ill health and died, apparently in his late sixties, in 1389.

British Library MS Harley 3760, unfortunately defective at its beginning, preserves 105 of a numbered sequence of 108 sermons that a later hand has

---

[1] For Brinton's life see *BRUO* 1:268–9; Devlin in Brinton, *Sermons*, 1:ix–xviii; and Greatrex, *Register*, pp. 487–488. Many of the details and dates of his life find support in his sermons. For Brinton's frequent references to canon law see Prolegomena, pp. 19–20, and note 17.

[2] Knowles, *Religious Orders*, 2:58.

ascribed to "Brunton."[3] They have been edited by Sister Mary Aquinas Devlin.[4] Most of them bear an indication of the liturgical occasion of their delivery, and in some instances the rubrics further mention the place and audience where they were preached. Together with internal references to historical situations, this evidence allows us to think that a large portion of the sermons follow the liturgical calendar selectively through several years.[5] Though the calendar proposed by the editor remains tentative, it is at least clear that Brinton preached in his cathedral in Rochester; at several religious houses; before the clergy in Rochester and London, including convocation at the archbishop's mandate; at various funerals or memorial services, including that of the Black Prince; and possibly at the coronation of Richard II, for which we have an independent summary by Walsingham.[6] There is, further, the strong probability that at least two sermons, which both ask in astonishment why "in this glorious city where a firm faith ought to flourish more vigorously . . . the perfidious Jews are tolerated (*permissi*) with much favor and are not being converted from their errors through the persuasion and teaching of many holy fathers, prelates, and doctors,"[7] were preached at Avignon.[8]

[3] "Sermones domini Thome Brunton' Roffensis episcopi," f. 312. I have adopted the name form used in current handbooks.

[4] See note 1. In my references I give only the (continuous) pagination. Unfortunately the edition is marred by many misprints and editorial errors, among which the constant misreading of *verum* for *vnde, quod* for *quasi, bonum* for *beatum,* and *exempla* for *Extra[vagantes]* are the most glaring. As some of these function as structural markers, the modern reader's task is made considerably more burdensome than need be. There is also some confusion between Sts. Matthew and Matthias (p. 104). Owst devoted several pages to "Brunton" (*Preaching,* pp. 15–20 and 577–588) and quoted from the bishop's sermons throughout his two volumes; see the indexes.

[5] Eleanor H. Kellogg, "Bishop Brunton." In her edition of 1954 Devlin made some additions but also some errors (Brinton, *Sermons,* 1:xxxv–xxxviii, and the headnotes to the individual sermons), and uncertainties remain.

[6] Devlin discusses the parallels between Walsingham's account and sermon 44 on pp. xxvii–xxviii. But it must be said that these parallels are not entirely convincing. Walsingham mentions four points on which Brinton admonished his audience: (1) against dissensions between lords and the people, (2) against oppression by the lords, (3) to help king and realm without murmuring, and (4) to be examples of sexual purity to the young and innocent king (Walsingham, *Historia anglicana,* pp. 338–339). Brinton's sermon 44, in its main part, makes two points: (1) poor and rich belong together and must be for each other, (2) especially so in prayers, and especially in processions, which are being neglected by both parties. For Walsingham's fourth point there is nothing even faintly similar in BR-44. It is also baffling that in his second point Brinton should complain at sparse attendance at processions "pro rege vel pace regni" (199) in a sermon supposedly made at a procession that, as Walsingham says, was attended by "plebis multitudine copiosa" (p. 338).

[7] Brinton, *Sermons,* p. 383. It should be pointed out that elsewhere Brinton praises the Jews for their charity: sermon 35 (p. 148).

[8] See now Margaret Harvey, "Preaching." Apart from the curious reference to crowds of Jews in "this city," one of these sermons is in honor of the Franciscan saint Louis of Anjou (or Toulouse),

Like his contemporaries, Brinton clings to the scholastic sermon form.[9] He also uses a good deal of conventional material. This in itself is not remarkable in late medieval preaching, but Brinton not only draws on conventional material but throughout his collection repeats himself again and again. Thus, one of his favorite similes, "In the sea of Marseilles, of four ships hardly one perishes; in the sea of this life, of four souls hardly one survives," recurs in at least six sermons, whenever he likens the world to the sea.[10] Such repeated use of material goes beyond similes, quotations, and stories and includes paragraph-length arguments, such as his exposé and rebuttal of Wyclif's errors:

> I call "pseudo-prophets" those who teach and affirm false things about the sacraments of the Church, especially about baptism. They say that when a bishop or priest is in deadly sin, he does not in effect consecrate or baptize. About confession they say that if someone is duly contrite, any external confession is superfluous and useless. About the Eucharist they say that the substance of material bread and wine remains after the consecration in the sacrament of the altar. To which I answer . . .[11]

Similarly, an entire protheme is used in two different sermons.[12] However much such repetition may offend against our ideals of a written composition, it surely reflects the reality of the busy life of a bishop who preached earnestly and frequently. His sermons also show that his preaching was powerful, driven by a zeal for reform in personal and social morals, imaginative, and often humanized with an observation from his own life. In his last sermons, for instance, he movingly complains of his failing health (sermon 108) and that he has been preaching all his life to no avail (sermon 107). The perceived lack of success in his pastoral work is echoed in the apparent lack of popularity of his written work. The sermons survive in only one manuscript, and I know of only one sermon that found its way into a later collection.[13]

As is already suggested by their conventional and repetitive features, Brinton's sermons present themselves as typical literary productions of the genre, whether they were written up before or after delivery. They have occasionally been called

who died in 1297, was canonized in 1317, and apparently was not very popular in England, although his name and details from his life occur in a sermon preached at Oxford in the 1380s: S-15.

[9] But notice my remarks on the structure of some his sermons, in Part Three, chapter 49, pp. 366–367.

[10] Pp. 97, 106, 141, 163, 261, 427.

[11] Sermon 101 (466); verbally repeated in sermon 107 (495).

[12] For example, sermons 35 (145) and 89 (403–404).   [13] Brinton's Sermon 36 in A-57.

"sermon notes" (rather than complete sermons),[14] and I can see two stylistic features that might lead – or rather mislead – readers to apply that label. One is the frequent formula *hic predico contra . . .* followed by some moral failing among either clergy or laity. Since the material that immediately follows renders the entire statement complete, the formula does not seem to indicate matter that Brinton preached but did not write out, but instead means something like "I am saying this against . . ."[15] In contrast, the other formula, *dic quomodo*, normally follows a point or quotation without further development[16] and thus is clearly Brinton's shorthand way to signal that the point could or should be expanded. For instance, in the protheme to a sermon on "An armed man keeps his court" (Luke 11:21), Brinton states that nowadays there is manifold fighting, contradiction, and dissent in the city of the Church, who is attacked "not only by Jews, pagans, and heretics, but also by false Christians. Tell how, by concluding with the Psalm verse 'I have seen impiety and contradiction in the city'."[17] But imperatives such as *dic quomodo* or *narra* occur quite regularly in complete sermons of the later Middle Ages[18] and do not make these texts "sermon notes."

Given Brinton's personality as well as his position as bishop of Rochester and his involvement in contemporary political issues, it is no wonder that, in contrast to such collections as Waldeby's, his sermons should address a number of political and ecclesiastical concerns of his time and voice a good deal of social criticism.[19] He frequently reminds all classes of society of their ordained tasks in state and Church and does not hesitate to criticize both high and low in their failings. To quote but one out of many cases: sermon 28, dealing with unity in Church and realm and apparently preached to the clergy in 1373, declares that "we prelates, who ought to uphold the Church like columns, as it were with *one* shoulder," fail to speak up against encroachments of the Church's rights and against public oppression of the poor. In the secular area, "maintainers" are similarly tolerated in their unjust oppression, so that "if one has harmed his neighbor . . . , he rather chooses to give ten pounds to a powerful and rich person that he may maintain him in his evil ways, than to give the neighbor he has harmed ten

---

[14] Cf. Brinton, *Sermons*, pp. xviii and xxvii; Devlin also refers to the manuscript as a "digest" (p. v). In her review of Devlin's edition, Beryl Smalley even calls Brinton's oeuvre "notes or schemes" (*Journal of Theological Studies* 6 (1955), p. 313).

[15] What is preached against includes moral failures of all sorts, among clergy and laity.

[16] Though on occasion he indicates how this may be done, with the help of exempla (pp. 247, 468), a chronicle story (349), learned authorities (297, 305), or the bishop's mandate (466).

[17] BR-81, p. 368.

[18] Such as "nota narracionem," "narra," "dic ut placet," and others. Brinton similarly uses "dic historiam" (268) and "dic ut scis" (500).

[19] For the content of Brinton's preaching see Owst, *Preaching* and *Literature*, passim; Brinton, *Sermons*, pp. xxi–xxxi; and Brandt, "Church and Society."

pounds as justice would require." There should be one law and equal justice for all classes of society, and donations made from ill-gotten gains can never be considered charitable gifts.[20] Hence Brinton's sermons contain a good deal of theological and canonistic reflection on public issues of his day. One example is his determination on how the power to absolve from sins applies to the rebels of 1381, especially their claim that they "had no scruples in this matter."[21] Another is his well-known use of the fable of Belling the Cat in one of his London sermons, which is thought to be reflected in Langland's *Piers Plowman*.[22]

Although Brinton sat on a council that condemned Wyclif's teaching, his sermons are relatively bare of anti-Lollard remarks. In BR-80 he remarks that the lower classes "rather listen to the shouts of those who teach errors than to true preachers. Tell how,"[23] and in BR-101 he refers to pseudo-prophets who teach errors about the sacraments, who have been condemned "by mandate of the bishop of London."[24] He is more forthcoming in condemning those who participated in the Peasants' Revolt and the murder of Archbishop Sudbury.[25]

---

[20] Pp. 113, 115–116.

[21] "Dicunt se non habere conscienciam super isto," BR-99 (457). On the idiom see *Dictionary of Medieval Latin from British Sources, "conscientia"* 3.b (p. 446).

[22] See Owst, "'Angel'," and *Literature*, pp. 577–588; Eleanor Kellogg, "Bishop Brunton"; and Bennett, "Date."

[23] "Immo mediocres et populares cicius audiunt clamores docencium errores quam veros predicatores. Dic quomodo" (362).

[24] P. 466. See further below, Part Three, chapter 50, p. 381.   [25] Sermons 99–100.

7

Philip Repingdon (RE)

With FitzRalph and Brinton, Philip Repingdon is the third bishop who made an important and extant contribution to preaching in our period.[1] In contrast to them, however, he stood considerably closer to the dividing line between orthodoxy and Lollardism — or rather, he found himself at Oxford at the moment when Wyclif's teaching and the serious desire for reform that lay behind it began to cause public concern. As an Augustinian canon from Leicester, Repingdon was sent to the university and incepted in theology in 1382. In that crucial year of his life he was asked by chancellor Rigg, who sympathized strongly with Wyclif's teaching and for a while was unwilling to listen to warnings from Canterbury, to deliver the Corpus Christi sermon at the Augustinian priory of St. Frideswide. In it Repingdon defended Wyclif's doctrine on the Eucharist. This and other positions proved too much for Archbishop Courtenay, who had him suspended from preaching and from all academic acts. During the year, then, Repingdon had several confrontations with Church authority. As he failed to appear at a later meeting with the archbishop, he was excommunicated. By the late fall, however, he abjured his heterodox views and was allowed to return to his academic functions. A distinguished career in the English Church followed. In 1394 Repingdon became abbot of St. Mary-in-the-Meadows, Leicester. He served as chancellor of Oxford University in 1400, and in 1404 he was appointed to the see of Lincoln, which he resigned in 1419. In 1408 he was even created a cardinal by pope Gregory XII, though after the latter's deposition Repingdon's cardinalate was annulled. It would thus appear that his abjuration of Wyclif's doctrines marked a genuine change or perhaps adjustment of views in a man who had moral reform and the good of the Church close to his heart, and who was neither opportunist nor secret

[1] Repingdon and his work have been studied in detail in an unpublished dissertation by Forde, "Writings." See also Archer, "Preaching." Forde's article "New Sermon Evidence" offers salient information about the manuscripts of Repingdon's sermons and "later redactions" (p. 174), as well as their sources, date, and orthodoxy.

Lollard.[2] Repingdon showed great and serious dedication to his episcopal duties. Arundel even said of him that "noo bischop of þis londe pursueþ now scharplier hem þat holden þat wei [i.e. the Lollards] þan he doiþ."[3] His administrative care is witnessed in the full register that he left.[4] And of his personal kindness and concern for individuals there is no better testimony than that of Margery Kempe, who visited him in 1413 or early 1414 and whom he encouraged to write down her visions.[5]

Repingdon left a collection of *Sermones super evangelia dominicalia* that has been preserved in at least eight manuscripts. These are not actual, "real" sermons preached by him, as are those by FitzRalph and Brinton, but rather form a unified lengthy, systematic, and scholarly exposition of the Sunday gospels.[6] The work must date back to Repingdon's Oxford days, i.e. 1382–1394. The fifty-three pieces deal with the Sunday gospels from 1 Advent to 24 Trinity in the regular order of the Church year.[7] Each sermon – or rather "homily," as they are called in some manuscripts – deals with the entire gospel lection of the day. The lection is initially divided into parts,[8] and these are then taken up seriatim. If the lection contains more than one gospel story or event, all the stories are treated in order. Repingdon usually places the lection in its larger biblical or liturgical context. He also pays close attention to narrative variations among the

---

[2] Differing views of Repingdon's later position and character are reviewed in Forde, "Writings," 1:5–54. Forde himself addresses Repingdon's ideological position in discussing the content of his sermons at vol. 1, pp. 280–337, and takes the view that "there is some integrity between his known 1382 views and his episcopal actions but that the views expressed in these sermons are those of a reformer working within the Church, not a radical without" (p. 280). See also vol. 1, pp. 339–341 for a summarizing comparison of Repingdon and Wyclif.

[3] In his interrogation of William Thorpe: *Two Wycliffite Texts*, p. 42.

[4] *Register Philip Repingdon.* For a brief evaluation see Davies, "Episcopate," p. 80.

[5] *The Book of Margery Kempe*, pp. 33–36; for the date, see ibid., p. 273. Notice that at that time the prohibitions issued by Archbishop Arundel against English books were in full force.

[6] Forde shows that "Repyngdon's *Sermones super Evangelia Dominicalia* are compilations written in the so-called 'ancient' form, that they are 'model sermons' and were not intended primarily for oral delivery and that Repyngdon's purpose in writing them was to make available biblical scholarship in a practical way to an educated readership," "Writings," 1:193.

[7] My account follows Oxford, Corpus Christi College, MS 54. There are some variations in the manuscripts regarding the number and numbering of the sermons; see the comparative table in Forde, "Writings," 1:111–112. I refer to the sermons by the consecutive numbers are they appear in the Corpus manuscript. The cycle has a sermon for Easter Monday but none for such non-dominical feasts as Good Friday, Ascension, or Corpus Christi. The manuscript has been described by Forde, "Writings," 2:118–121.

[8] Forde calls such initial divisions "framing devices," probably in order to avoid confusion with the *divisio thematis* of the scholastic sermon ("Writings," 1:203–215). But notice that later, in discussing Repingdon's position in the putative revival of the ancient homily form, Forde speaks of "thematically divided sermons" (p. 270).

evangelists. In expounding the reading, he uses and quotes a variety of earlier and very popular theologians, both Continental and English, such as "Januensis," "Parisiensis," Gorran, John of Abbéville, Grosseteste, Nottingham, several *postillatores*, and many others,[9] making this one of the most learned works of its kind. His exposition often proceeds by questions that are put and then answered.[10] Occasionally Repingdon's exposition even includes a scholastic *quaestio*, and in fact he is one of the few sermon writers who quote such fourteenth-century theologians as Duns Scotus and Bradwardine.[11] All these features are characteristic of what modern scholars have called "model sermon collections" that were produced at universities and mendicant *studia* from the early thirteenth century on. Like them, Repingdon's sermon cycle lacks structural elements and other stylistic features that are characteristic of genuine sermons: they do not develop a thema but expound the entire lection; they do not address an audience; and they frequently do not end with the typical closing formula.[12] Thus they essentially constitute an extended commentary on the Sunday pericopes or gospel lections; in Simon Forde's words, they "were literary *compilationes*, intended to be read as a means of disseminating current biblical scholarship in a liturgical format."[13] In that, they do precisely what their major sources had done before them.

As to their theological teaching, Repingdon's sermons seem to be entirely orthodox. Apart from his touching on the question of whether unworthy priests administer the sacraments validly,[14] another rare echo of his reformist concerns

---

[9] Forde, "Writings," 2:6–9, provides a list of works cited in Repingdon's sermons.

[10] For example, his sermon on the Fourth Sunday after Easter discusses the reason why Christ had to ascend before sending the Holy Spirit with a succession of *videtur . . . , contra hoc . . . ,* and *respondetur,* RE-24, f. 179va.

[11] The sermon for Trinity Sunday (RE-28) quotes Duns Scotus, "Doctor subtilis," repeatedly, ff. 213va–214vb. In a long treatment that is almost a treatise on baptism and other sacraments, Repingdon raises the question whether sacraments given by an unworthy priest are valid; after first stating the standard view that "it is not necessary that a priest be holy, only that he be a priest" (f. 215va), he then adds: "It seems to me patent that being a good priest adds a special merit, just as being a bad one adds a detestable demerit. Hence, in the ministry good priests are to be preferred to bad ones, and openly bad ones are to be refused. With that the *Doctor subtilis* agrees" (f. 216va). Bradwardine is cited in Repingdon's sermon for Passion Sunday: "Doctor profundus *De causa Dei* libro 1, capitulo 1, parte 32" (f. 134vb). Elsewhere, in discussing the first article of faith Repingdon refers to the distinction between *potentia absoluta* and *potentia ordinata* (RE-50, f. 364rb).

[12] But there are occasional statements that envision the work of preaching; for instance: "Pro processu est hic sciendum quod preter sensum litteralem qui breuiter in suis locis exprimetur ad sensum misticum sunt tria declaranda" (RE-42, f. 317rb). And a few sermons do have closing formulas: RE-4, 10, 16, 21, 22, 30, 33, 39, 45, 50, 51. On the latter Forde comments: "it would be difficult to say whether Repyngdon had a 'policy' for concluding his sermons with such prayers or whether these are merely scribal variations or indeed additions," 1:205–206.

[13] Forde, "New Sermon Evidence," p. 169.   [14] Above, note 11.

occurs, perhaps, in his accusing both friars and monks of bending biblical texts that speak against their form of life: "If a mendicant friar interprets the scriptures and they suggest anything against his mendicancy . . . , he will either pass it over entirely in silence or obfuscate it with a gloss that goes against the text." Similarly, monks will not hear of scriptural truths that clearly speak against defects of their order, whereas they eagerly explore the faults of others.[15]

In contrast to other sermon collections, both unified and miscellaneous, Repingdon's sermon cycle enjoyed a good deal of popularity. Beside the eight manuscripts that contain the entire collection,[16] the cycle was subjected to a redaction that is extant in two manuscripts, M and N. Since both also gather other material (thus making them "mixed" collections), they will be treated later.

---

[15] "Si enim frater ordinis mendicancium interpres fuerit scripturarum, si qua forte contra eius mendicacionem sonuerint vel eorum temporale emolumentum in aliquo iuste retrahere poterit, vel ea omnino silebit vel ea cum glosa textui contradicente obscurabit. Sic possessionatus qui [ms que] contra sui et secularis contra sui graduum defectus veritates scripturarum manifeste sonantes nec voluntarie audiet nec reserabit . . . omnes alienorum defectuum sunt exploratores et suorum desides inspectores" (RE-51, f. 366vb).

[16] Forde, "Writings," 1:109–110 lists eight manuscripts that "contain largely the same version of the complete sermon-cycle," plus the two manuscripts that hold what I call a redaction (Forde's Br and R), and two more manuscripts that "merely contain a few short extracts."

8

John Felton (FE)

Though writing at least a generation later than Repingdon, Felton produced a sermon collection that can profitably be compared with Repingdon's: it, too, is a temporal cycle and relies heavily on earlier works of the kind, but in contrast to Repingdon's its individual pieces are built very much like actual sermons.

John Felton was vicar of the church of St. Mary Magdalene in Oxford from 1397 to 1434.[1] He evidently did not finish his university education, yet among his contemporaries and later he enjoyed the reputation of a great preacher and even of sanctity. In the short and conventional prologue to his sermon collection, which was finished in 1431, he tells us that he made a compilation of sermons based on the Sunday gospels through the year, and that he did so "from the morsels I have gathered that fell from the tables of my lords, namely, Januensis, Parisiensis, Lugdunensis, Odo, and others."[2] The result is a cycle of fifty-eight sermons[3] following the regular sequence of the Church year and covering all Sundays as well as the feast of the Holy Innocents.[4] For three Sundays, 4 Advent,

[1] See the basic study by Fletcher, "Magnus Predicator," which discusses what is known about Felton, the manuscripts and their English dialect features, Felton's work as sermon compiler and as reader, the structure of his sermons, and their influence in the later fifteenth century. Fletcher also edits two sermons, 6 and 37, with schematic analyses and translation. Sermon 6 has also been analyzed by Spencer, *English*, pp. 342–346.

[2] The prologue is edited by Fletcher, *Preaching*, p. 59 n. 7. The authorities cited are Jacobus de Voragine, Peraldus, Nicholas of Aquaville, and Odo of Cheriton. The "others" include, *inter alios*, Grosseteste (both genuine and spurious works) and the anonymous *Fasciculus morum*. See also Fletcher, *Preaching*, pp. 67–68.

[3] The sermons are numbered in the rubrics and the alphabetical table of sermon topics. My references and quotations are to Lincoln Cathedral MS 204, which is described in R. M. Thomson, *Catalogue . . . Lincoln Cathedral*, p. 166, with a list of the sermons found in this manuscript. Individual manuscripts have some divergences; for example, University of Pennsylvania MS Lat. 35 contains 59 sermons (two for 12 Trinity, on the thema "Adducunt ei surdum et mutum") but counts two of them twice.

[4] Fletcher claims that one sermon is for Epiphany (*Preaching*, p. 69), but the item in question, sermon 7, is marked "Sexta die a nativitate Domini," which refers to the Sunday after Christmas. It also has the gospel lection for that day according to the Sarum Use; see *Sarum Missal*, p. 34.

Easter, and 5 Trinity, Felton furnished two sermons each. The second sermon for 4 Advent and that for Holy Innocents take their themata from the epistle reading of the day, but the other sermons are all based on the respective gospel lections.

Felton's work of gathering, not just morsels but large chunks from earlier sermon collections, can be neatly seen in his sermon for 3 Lent. After a brief paragraph that leads to the invitation to pray, he copies, with acknowledgment, a paragraph from Januensis' first sermon for this Sunday (the four ways of tempting, with rationale for the three Sundays in Lent), and next Januensis' entire second sermon. This is followed by large sections from sermons 3 and 4 of William Peraldus for the same Sunday. Then Felton turns to a treatise on the sins of the tongue, *De lingua*, which he attributes to "Lincolniensis," and excerpts lengthy paragraphs with precise acknowledgment.[5] Next he adds a series of *exempla*, some fully told, others only referred to; they carry no source identification, but probably come from a collection of such stories. He closes with another paragraph on how the devil particularly tries to hinder people from confessing their sins, which is similar in style to the material from *De lingua* but carries no source identification.

This accumulative or pastiche work does not make for a clearly structured sermon,[6] but in other cases it is evident that, rather than furnishing a running commentary or *postillatio* on the lections, Felton aimed at producing a scholastic sermon.[7] A brief protheme, leading to the invitation to pray, is there followed by a short *introductio thematis*, which in turn leads to the announcement of two, three, or four aspects of the announced thema or, more often, of the entire gospel lection. These are then developed in detail and with further subdivisions. The *introductio thematis* is only occasionally separated from the main division by a second repetition of the thema.[8] But that Felton had such a structure in mind can be clearly seen in sermon 18, on the text "Have pity on me, Lord" (Matthew 15:22). Its protheme is a citation from the *Summa iusticie* by "Lincolniensis," that "God's grace is necessary to the preacher as well as to the hearer of God's word."

[5] Felton's references to part and chapter (2.28 and 3.17, respectively) agree with the version of *De lingua* found in British Library MSS Arundel 200 and Harley 5275, but not with that in Arundel 47.

[6] That Felton's use of the scholastic sermon structure is less than rigorous and transparent is neatly reflected in his sermon 6, *Sequuntur agnum*, which has yielded two different analyses, by Spencer (*English*, pp. 342–347; also in "English Vernacular," 1:267–273) and by Fletcher (*Preaching*, pp. 71–73) respectively. The stumbling block here is that at one point the sermon seems to end with the standard closing formula but then continues with what in effect is the development of the second part announced in the formal division. Fletcher considers this "extra material" (p. 73), whereas Spencer calls this a "continuation" of the "third" and "fourth principal" (presumably on the basis of marginal letters, pp. 345–346).

[7] See also further comments in Part Three, chapter 49, "The Preacher's Voice," p. 362.

[8] A good example is sermon 37, edited by Fletcher, *Preaching*, p. 100, lines 27–37.

This leads to the preacher's request, "Therefore you shall pray in the beginning, etc." The thema is repeated, and the preacher continues: "For the *introductio*, let the gospel be repeated," meaning that at this point, in this sermon, the preacher retells the entire gospel lection as his *introductio thematis*. This is followed by a second repetition of the thema, after which the preacher gives a division: "In these words there are two things: first, something useful and necessary, namely pity, when I say 'Have pity'; and second, something honorable and fearsome, when it is said 'Lord'." These two members of the division are confirmed, from Scripture and etymology respectively. After this division (technically a *divisio ab intus*), a second one follows:

> In this gospel mention is made of Christ, in whom there was great pity; second of the Canaanite woman, in whom there was great humility; third, of her daughter, in whom there was affliction; and fourth, of the disciples, in whom there was great compassion.

These four aspects or parts of the gospel are then developed at some length.[9]

In many instances, the invitation to pray contains a personal element, a statement in the first person singular. For example, sermon 44, on the gospel text "Whoever exalts himself shall be humbled" (Luke 18:14), begins with a simile:

> If someone were to scatter gold and silver or precious stones, every one of you would look and put his hand to it and gather as much as he could.

The preacher continues that he is scattering, not material things like gold but something more precious, the words of God. After proving this point by reason and example (here authoritative quotations), he concludes:

> That I may scatter this treasure for you it is necessary for you to look, that is, to understand; and to gather, that is, to retain; and to put your hand to it, that is, to do good works. And that this may be so, let us pray.[10]

[9] "*Miserere mei, Domine*, Mathei 15. Dicit Lincolniensis in libro *De summa iusticie* quod gracia Dei est necessaria tam predicatori quam verbum Dei audienti. Hoc ostenditur . . . Ideo in principio orabitis, etc. Miserere mei, Domine. Repetatur euangelium pro introduccione. Miserere, etc. In quibus verbis ecce duo: primo res vtilis et necessaria, scilicet misericordia, cum dico 'Miserere'; secundo, res honorabilis et timenda, cum dicitur 'Domine.' Pro primo, Trenorum 3: 'Misericordia Dei est quod non sumus consumpti'. Pro secundo patet per ethimologiam: dicitur enim 'dominus' quasi 'dans munus', et ideo honorabilis, vel 'dans minas', et ideo timendus. In isto euangelio fit mencio de Christo, in quo erat magna miseracio; secundo de muliere Chananea, in qua erat magna humiliaco; tercio de filia, in qua erat vexacio; quarto de discipulis, in quibus erat magna compassio. Primo, in Christo erat . . . ," FE-18, f. 28vb.

[10] "*Omnis qui se exaltat humiliabitur*, etc., Luce 18. Karissimi, Si quis spargeret aurum et argentum vel lapides preciosos, quilibet vestrum respiceret et manum apponeret et colligeret quantum posset. Sed ego non spargo vobis huiusmodi sed preciosiora, scilicet verba Dei, et hoc patet tam

But this is as "personal" as these sermons get. Moreover, concentrating on expounding the gospel lections of the day, they are devoid of specific social and moral criticism, of the complaint at the decadent or evil times, that one finds so often in other preachers' works. Felton never goes beyond such a generality as, "But certainly there are many nowadays who do not want to follow Christ on this way (i.e., of mercy) but rather Gehazi, the leprous servant of Elisha."[11]

Similarly, the *Sermones dominicales* contain little to identify their audience. One would surmise that as Sunday sermons they were intended for a lay congregation. But at least some of them may have been directed to clerical ears, as is suggested by many elements that range from the address form "Reuerendi"[12] to the treatment, in sermon 26 on "I am the good shepherd" (John 10:11), of three questions that, as the development makes clear, are to be asked of priests: "Who has brought you here, for what reason did you want to come; second, how have you lived; and third, how have you ruled?"[13] All these features point to Felton's work being a typical model sermon collection that, in contrast to the sermons by Brinton or later random collections, does not reflect his actual preaching very directly.

The cycle's orthodoxy is established negatively by the absence of Wycliffite elements, and positively by such remarks as "contra lollardos et hereticos."[14] Like Repingdon's sermons on the Sunday gospels, Felton's cycle enjoyed a good deal of popularity. The entire cycle has been preserved in twenty-nine manuscripts.[15] In addition, one or two individual sermons appear separately,[16] and some material seems to have been used in a collection of English sermons.[17]

---

racione quam exemplo . . . Cum ergo spargam vobis hunc thesaurum, necesse est vt respiciatis, idest intelligatis, et colligatis, idest retiniatis [!], et manum apponatis, idest operibus impleatis. Et vt ita fiat, oremus," FE-44, f. 77vb. Similarly Fletcher, *Preaching*, p. 100, line 2.

[11] Sermon 37; see Fletcher, *Preaching*, p. 110, lines 235–237.

[12] FE-50, f. 90va: "non sic vos, reuerendi."

[13] "Sciendum est quod tribus questionibus respondebunt in dignitatibus constituti: prima questio erit quis te huc adduxit, ob quam causam venire voluisti; secunda questio erit qualiter vixisti; tercia, qualiter rexisti" (FE-26, f. 42vb). A longer development follows. The three questions are also utilized in Wimbledon's sermon on "Redde rationem vilicationis tuae" and in many other places.

[14] FE-20, f. 34va.   [15] Listed in Fletcher, *Preaching*, pp. 62–63.

[16] FE-23, which is missing in the Lincoln manuscript, appears also as J/5-36. Similarly, FE-24, which in the Lincoln MS is incomplete, appears in Bodleian Library, MS Bodley 687, ff. 74v–76, after the *Fasciculus morum*.

[17] Fletcher argues that an English version of Felton's sermon 21 appears in Gloucester, Cathedral Library MS 22 (*Preaching*, pp. 80–84).

9

Mirk's *Festial*

Though this work was written in English, it warrants inclusion in this study because it contains several unusual features whose importance for the history of preaching in the later Middle Ages has so far not been sufficiently appreciated. Like Repingdon, John Mirk was an Augustinian canon, living at Lilleshall Abbey, Shropshire. Little else is known about him, but from manuscript attributions it emerges that he composed three important aids for parish priests: the *Manuale sacerdotis* in Latin,[1] a handbook called *Instructions for Parish Priests* in English verse,[2] and the *Festial* or *Liber festivalis* in English prose.[3] It is the last which calls for attention here.

Like Felton's cycle of sermons on the Sunday gospels, Mirk's *Festial* begins with a preface that states his intention to help simple priests who lack books and education in their task of teaching their parishioners:

> On account of my insufficient learning I understand how it goes with others of the same rank who have the cure of souls and are required to teach their parishioners all the main feasts that occur in the year, showing them what the saints suffered and did for God's love, so that the people should have greater devotion to God's saints and come to the church more willingly to serve God and pray to the holy saints for their help. But as many excuse themselves by the lack of books and their simple education, I have, in order to help such simple clerics as I am myself, drawn the following treatise from the *Golden Legend* with some addition, so that whoever wishes to study in it shall find readily for all the principal feasts of the year a short sermon that is necessary for him to teach

---

[1] See Fletcher, "Manuscripts." The work has been edited in an unpublished dissertation by Girsch, "Edition."

[2] Available in two editions, by Peacock and by Kristensson.

[3] *Mirk's Festial*, edited by Erbe. The planned second part, with introduction and notes, did not appear. A more recent and fuller critical edition is Wakelin, "Edition." The sermon on the Conversion of St. Paul has been translated by Jeffrey, *The Law of Love*, pp. 320–324.

and for others to learn. And since this treatise speaks entirely of feasts, I desire and pray that it may be called a *Festial*. It begins on the first Sunday of Advent, in worship of God and of all the saints that are written about in it.[4]

In contrast to Felton, however, he does not produce a *de tempore* cycle but a curious mixture of sermons *de tempore* and *de sanctis*. For the period from Advent through Corpus Christi, Mirk combines sermons for selected Sundays, for non-dominical feasts (Christmas, Circumcision, etc.), and for saints' feasts (nos. 1–41), while after Corpus Christi he gives only pieces for saints' days through the feast of St. Katherine, adding a sermon for the dedication of a church and another that expounds the Pater Noster (nos. 42–69). Thus, although the series follows the order of the calendar, it is neither a *de tempore* nor a *de sanctis* collection, nor really a combination of the two.[5] But it does, structurally, exactly the same as the *Legenda aurea*, which similarly furnishes chapters of liturgical instruction for selected Sundays, non-dominical feasts, and saints' days from Advent through Pentecost (Corpus Christi was added in a later expansion) and then focuses on saints' feasts for the remainder of the Church year.

A second peculiarity is that the sermons in the *Festial* do not begin with the announcement of a thema[6] but instead at once address their audience, normally with "Good men and women."[7] Next, they refer to "this day" and explain its liturgical meaning. This usually leads to some division, whose members are then developed. For example, the sermon on Sexagesima begins by stating that "this day is called, in Holy Church, the Sunday in Sexagesima" and explains that *sexagesima* means "three score." This number, the preacher explains, reminds us of how short our life is in comparison with that of the biblical patriarchs. But even in our short time we can please God and come to heaven. For this we must do three things: suffer tribulation meekly, give alms wisely, and hate sin especially. These points are then developed. For the first point the preacher cites the example of St. Paul, quoting the epistle of the day (2 Cor 11:19 ff.). On the

---

[4] My translation of the preface printed in Horstmann, *Altenglische Legenden*, p. cxiv n. 1. The preface appears in only one manuscript and was not reproduced in Erbe's edition. It has recently been printed again by Powell, "John Mirk's *Festial*," p. 86.

[5] Two items, however, are not properly sermons: 29 (a set of instructions to parish priests on liturgical questions commonly asked by parishioners) and 46 (the story of Nero's death, as an example for priests not to "speak ribaldry"). To the sixty-nine pieces in his base manuscript, the last being an exposition of the Pater Noster, Erbe added five more pieces from a different manuscript. More recent scholarship has shown that a redaction of the *Festial* cycle separates the *de sanctis* from the *de tempore* sermons.

[6] An exception is no. 20.

[7] However, other address forms occur here and there, such as one to "God's servants" (pp. 44, 47). As stated earlier, items 29 and 46 are directed to priests, as are 72 and 73.

second point he returns to the number sixty and now explains it as six times ten, "the six works of charity that come out of the Ten Commandments." That these works must be done wisely, God shows in today's gospel of the sower that went out to sow his seed (Luke 8:4–15), of which verses 5–8 are quoted in English. For the seed that fell beside the way, the preacher tells a story about a rich man whose good works were blown away by the wind of vainglory. The third point, to resist sin, is then developed with the story of Noah and the Flood, which was read in the Office for Sexagesima week and shows God's vengeance on sin. It is followed by another illustrative story, this one about St. Dominic's vision of Christ with three spears and Mary's intercession. The sermon ends with an invitation to pray and the normal closing formula.

The sermon for Sexagesima thus creates a texture that not only explains the day's meaning but weaves together the day's gospel and epistle readings as well as material from the week's Office. The same can be observed in practically all Sunday sermons in this collection. But in contrast to the more usual scholastic sermon structure, Mirk does not expound and unfold a short text taken from the days's lection. Instead his priority seems to be aiming at instructing the audience about the meaning of the specific liturgical occasion. Thus nearly all Sunday sermons begin with the formula "This day is called" or "this is [such and such a day]." Although such liturgical instructions can occasionally also be found in genuine scholastic sermons, especially in those that are closely derived from model cycles such as Repingdon's, they nowhere make their appearance with the same systematic dominance as they do in Mirk's *Festial.*[8]

This peculiarity is even more noticeable in Mirk's saints sermons. These begin normally, after the address, with the formula "such a day ȝe schull haue [saint's name]'s daye"[9] and then simply speak of the respective saint's life and his or her miracles, occasionally using a division to list the saint's major virtues. The narrative material used by Mirk comes from a variety of sources, foremost but not exclusively the *Legenda aurea.* This opening formula of sermons for saints' days calls for further comment. A typical instance is the following:

> Good men and woymen, such a day ȝe schull haue þe Holyrode-day. þe whech day ȝe schull not fast þe euen, but comyth to þe chyrch as cristen pepull, in worschip of hym þat deyd on þe rode for saluacyon of mankynd.[10]

Use of the future tense and the statement that no fast for the vigil is prescribed (on other occasions such fasting is prescribed and announced) indicate that this

---

[8] See for instance the liturgical notes at the beginning of FE-14 and M/3-14 for Septuagesima Sunday.

[9] Mirk, *Mirk's Festial,* p. 6 and passim.   [10] P. 142.

is not a sermon preached on Holyrood day but rather an announcement made in advance,[11] presumably on the preceding Sunday. The formula "such a day," therefore, means "on such and such a day this week" or "on the coming X-day," with X to be filled in with the respective weekday on which the feast was going to fall. This is made quite clear in several sermons of this type where "such a" is followed by "N," the usual abbreviation for *nomen*, the specific name to be supplied by a reader or speaker.[12] Another case that clearly shows the function of such formulas occurs in the sermon for Trinity Sunday. At its end, the preacher says, "On next Thursday you shall have a high feast in Holy Church, the feast of Corpus Christi. On which day you shall come to church . . ." (sermon 40); and the following sermon in the collection (41) is a separate sermon for the holy day.[13]

The practice of announcing a coming saint's feast on its preceding Sunday and explaining it at some length has left its trace also in another work that in many respects is very similar to the *Festial* though apparently not textually related to it. This is the anonymous *Speculum sacerdotale*, surviving in English in a single manuscript of the later fifteenth century.[14] After an introduction in two parts (see below) it offers sixty-nine chapters that deal with liturgical occasions from Advent to the feast of St. Thomas the Apostle, mixing, as does Mirk's *Festial*, feast days and saints' feasts through Corpus Christi and then discussing only saints' feasts. As the title says, it is a handbook for priests, addressing them here and there directly and even furnishing detailed instructions on how to give penance. If the chapters that deal with the feasts have an initial address, it is a simple "Sires." But all the pieces for a liturgical occasion have the formula "yn sych a day ye schull haue the feste . . . ," whether this is a major feast or a saint's day. These pieces then usually end with an exhortation to "come to church and pray," or else to "worship." As in Mirk, the explanations of the saints' feasts normally contain a good deal of narrative material, heavily copied from the *Legenda aurea*.[15]

---

[11] Mirk used the word *prononce* for this; see p. 252.

[12] Thus sermons 53, 56–57, 60, 62–64, 66–68. Sermon 59 speaks of "next week."

[13] Thus, the feast of Corpus Christi has its own sermon, instead of a mere announcement.

[14] Edited by Weatherly, *Speculum sacerdotale*. Extensive quotations from its prologue appear in Owst, *Preaching*, pp. 244–245 and 355–356; and *Literature*, pp. 123–124 and 135. Another collection of sermons that frequently begin with such formulas as "Frendis, on Thursday next come ye shall haue the feste of . . ." and similar ones, and end by asking the congregation to kneel and pray, appears in Oxford, Bodleian Library, MS Greaves 54, which also includes some revised pieces from Mirk's *Festial*. See Spencer, *English*, pp. 183–184 and 315–316.

[15] The notes in Weatherly's edition (pp. 255–289) identify the sources, and there is a good conspectus of the major source for each chapter – predominantly the *Legenda aurea* and John Beleth's *Rationale divinorum officiorum* – on pp. xxvii–xxix.

The sixty-nine chapters of the *Speculum* are preceded by an introductory chapter in two parts.[16] The first is a translation of the prologue to the very popular *Martyrologium* by Usuardus (died c. 875), entitled "De sollempnitatibus sanctorum feriandis."[17] This is followed by another prologue, evidently an English translation of a Latin treatise *Ad sacerdotes quomodo populum instruerent* (beginning "Inter sacratissimas sancte vniuersalis ecclesie consuetudines"), whose authorship is not known to me. Both prologues together also survive in Latin in at least two English manuscripts,[18] where they introduce a number of short sermon-like sections on the Church feasts, exactly as they do in the *Speculum sacerdotale*.[19] These short Latin "sermons" also appear without the prologues in two further manuscripts.[20]

It is the second prologue, "Inter sacratissimas" or, in the English translation, "Among alle other holy customes," that is of particular interest here. In it, the anonymous author explains the use of this material as follows:

> In alle the chirches of the worlde, the prestes of hem whiche are sette to the gouernaunce of the parishenus, aftur the redyng of the gospel and of the offertorie at masse, turne hem vnto the peple and schewe openliche vnto hem alle the solempnitees and festes whiche shall falle and be hadde in the weke folowynge. And afturward that they make hem to pray for pees to be grauntyd and for the clergie, for the people . . . Therfore, ye serteyne prestes which ben dere and famyliare vn-to / me before alle other, vn-to you I redresse my speche . . . I haue here disposyd and writen aftur my sympilnes of the solempnytees of alle seyntes the whiche schulden worshipfully eche Sonneday be schewid vn-to your peple.[21]

This "proclamacion" or "pronunsyng" of the feasts that occur in the following week, made during Mass each Sunday, evidently was part of the medieval liturgy

---

[16] In *Speculum sacerdotale*, respectively pp. 1–2, lines 2–12, and pp. 2–3, lines 13–34.

[17] PL 123:599 f.

[18] London, British Library, MS Harley 2345, ff. 56vb–69ra, probably of the thirteenth century; and Oxford, Bodleian Library, MS Bodley 440, ff. 1 ff., dated to the last quarter of the fourteenth century.

[19] Many of these Latin sermons also begin with such formulas as *hodie* or *(in) illa die habebitis*, as in the *Speculum*. Such formulas do not occur in the sources of the *Speculum* that have been identified by Weatherly.

[20] Oxford, Bodleian Library, MS Bodley 110, ff. 58 ff.; and MS Rawlinson A.362, an imperfect copy, discussed by Spencer, *English*, p. 365 n.8.

[21] P. 2; I have slightly altered the punctuation. The demand of a prayer "afterwards," i.e. at the end of the announcement before Mass continues, is also reflected in many pieces of the *Festial*, as for instance: "Now pray we to Seynt Mathew . . . þat he wyll pray for vs, þat we may be sauet, boþe body and sowle. Amen," *Mirk's Festial*, p. 257.

from much earlier times on, constituting the so-called "prone."[22] The texts assembled in the *Speculum* and the *Festial,* thus, reflect a development from what once was no more than a simple announcement to a full guide for preaching (*Speculum sacerdotale*) or a regular sermon cycle (Mirk's *Festial*), whose ultimate aim is "that God may be glorified in youre chirches be the maters i-writen aftur, and deuocion and wytt of the peple may be the more informyd to worschepyng and glorifyinge of him that is almyghty, here God."[23] The relation of such preaching aids to the *Legenda aurea,* through such thirteenth-century sermon collections as MS Harley 2345, remains to be studied in detail.

In Mirk's *Festial* we, therefore, find not merely a vernacular sermon book[24] but evidence of a peculiar kind of preaching. It shares with medieval preaching in general the preacher's intent to instruct his congregation in the basic matters

---

[22] Cf. Spencer, *English,* p. 31, with reference to Cross, *Oxford Dictionary of the Christian Church,* p. 1131. On the prone see further: Lecoy de la Marche, *Chaire,* pp. 223–224; Gatch, *Preaching,* p. 51–59; Foley, "Song," p. 219 and notes; and Bériou, review article of Roberts, p. 228. Notice that Gratian's *Decretum* includes the demand to announce future feast days: "Tempora feriandi in missa sunt laicis annuncianda," followed by a list of feasts; *De consecratione III.1* (Friedberg 1:1353). A simple announcement of this kind can still be heard or read in some churches today, both Roman Catholic and Anglican.

[23] Ibid., p. 3. The Latin text for the passages quoted is as follows: "Per ecclesias vbique terrarum diffusas sacerdotes Dei qui singulis parochiis suis presunt, lecto euangelio, offertorio cantato, ad populum sibi commissum solempnitates sequenti septimana futuras ille [!] sancte ac religiose seruandas esse publica voce pronunciant. Et deinde pro pace nobis celitus concedenda, pro clero et pro populo et pro benefactoribus suis, et pro infirmis parochie si in ea fuerint, et pro peregrinantibus, et pro hiis quoque qui vltra mare consistunt, pro fructibus terre vt eos omnipotens Deus fidelibus suis misericorditer conferret, pro viuis deinde ac mortuis preces facere precipiunt ac predicant . . . Inde est, fratres karissimi, sacerdotes inter alias [!] mihi non mediocriter familiares. quod crebris vestris precibus pulsatus. immo inoportuna exaccione conpulsus, de solempnitatibus sanctorum dominique eius dominicis diebus venerabiliter populo pronunciandis pro viribus aliqua scribere disposui. vt ex hiis que scribimus / per vos in parochiis vestris Deus glorificetur et nostrum ministerium exaltetur et honoretur, deuotique populi vobis commissi ad cultum diuinum magis ac magis informetur." MS Bodley 440, f. 1r–v.

[24] That the unknown English author's primary intent was to furnish a *vernacular* sermon collection has been inferred from his statement: "Sires myn, taketh here youre werke, occupacion, and besynes that ye mowe haue therby a more profitable forme and better matere; that is to say, of the pronunsyng of solempnitees and festyuall tymes, right as ye haue hadde and saide sermones in the same tymes here afore endytid to youre honde in Latyn or Romayne tonge" (*Speculum sacerdotale,* ed. Weatherly, p. 3). But notice that this linguistic remark also occurs in the corresponding and earlier Latin text: "Accipite hoc opusculum et munusculum nostrum vt, sicut per manum nostram singulis diebus dominicis et quibuslibet festiuitatibus dicendos latina et romana lingua dictos habetis, ita quoque quod ex hoc opere ad pronunciandas solempnitates formam commodiorem materiamque meliorem habeatis" (MS Harley 2345, f. 57ra; MS Bodley 440, f. 1v). What the unknown author of the Latin seems to be saying is that he had earlier produced Latin sermons *de tempore* and *de sanctis* and is now sending along material for the announcement of the coming feast days.

of faith,[25] to explain the meaning of the Church's liturgy, to lead people from vices to virtues, and to stir up their devotion. But it carries out these intentions by emphasizing information about the liturgy, the meaning of a given occasion. As Mirk himself says in the prologue to his *Festial*, he wrote these pieces to instruct simple priests, not how to preach the word of God but to "teach their parishioners all the main feasts that occur in the year." If guided by the *Festial*, for some Sundays and the major Christian feasts the preacher would do so by combining liturgical explanation with moral applications derived from the day's epistle, gospel, and Office readings. For the saints' feasts he would, without regard to the day's lections, present to his audience the saint's life, virtues, and miracles. The latter – preaching the saints – was evidently done on the Sunday preceding the feast, not only during the season between Corpus Christi and Advent but also on the Sundays after Epiphany and after Easter (for which there are no specified sermons in the collection). Whether such preaching was an innovation of the fourteenth century[26] is debatable, since the prescription for such preaching in *Speculum sacerdotale* and its Latin source goes back at least to the thirteenth century.

It is equally debatable whether the sermons in Mirk's *Festial* were actually preached in this form. Its preface presents this work as an aid for other preachers, not as a record of Mirk's own preaching. While it contains some local references, its overabundance of narrative material would speak against actual delivery in this form. But whatever Mirk's *Festial* may reveal about the background and actual practice of preaching in medieval parishes around 1400, its liturgical instruction, moral appeal, and host of stories made the work highly successful, to the point of becoming "central to preaching in English in the fifteenth century,"[27] with

---

[25] The *pastoralia* appear in sermons 15 (seven deadly sins), 16 (works of mercy), 17 (parts of the Creed), 23 (Decalogue), 30 (chief virtues and vices), 38 (gifts of the Holy Spirit and seven deadly sins).

[26] Spencer (*English*, p. 31) thinks this new custom is referred to by Thomas Waleys in his *ars praedicandi*, but she mistranslates Waleys's "*de* dominica immediate praecedente" as "*on* the Sunday . . ." (my emphasis). What Waleys is concerned with (and criticizes) is not that the Sunday sermon deals with a coming saint's feast but some preachers' choice of their thema: "Nowadays, however, some have newly established the habit of taking their thema from the Sunday immediately preceding the feast [of the saint], whatever that Sunday may be, to preach on the feast of the saint within the current week. And they have so much committed themselves to this usage, if it should be called usage, that whether any [thema] that fits the feast of the saint be found in the gospel of that Sunday or not, they still take their thema from it . . . They often take a thema which they try to adapt with labor and violence to the saint . . ." Waleys is therefore not concerned with when saints' sermons were preached. Notice also that the pieces in the *Festial* and the *Speculum sacerdotale* have no themata. My quotation translates the passage in Thomas Waleys, "De modo componendi sermones," in Charland, *Artes praedicandi*, pp. 342–3.

[27] Fletcher, "Unnoticed," p. 514.

its main period of influence being the second half of the fifteenth and the early sixteenth century.[28] The first modern editor of the cycle used six manuscripts for his edition, and between 1483(?) and 1532 the collection was printed more than twenty times.[29] Recent scholarship has shown that throughout the fifteenth century, the original work was abridged, enlarged, rearranged, and utilized in a number of vernacular sermon cycles.[30]

Mirk's original work was written before AD 1415 and has been recently dated to the period of 1382 to 1390.[31] The sermons refer to Mirk's monastery at Lilleshall[32] and to St. Alkmund as "the patron of this church," which would be Shrewsbury, St. Alkmund.[33] The collection's orthodoxy is confirmed by several critical references to Lollards and by traditional views on controversial topics.[34]

---

[28] Spencer, *English*, p. 311.   [29] Lewis et al., *Index of Printed Middle English Prose*, item 734.

[30] Wakelin, "Manuscripts," describes and discusses twenty-seven manuscripts with *Festial* sermons. To these Fletcher, in "Unnoticed," has added another ten. Many of these contain *Festial* sermons in a variety of forms. See further Mirk, *Advent and Nativity Sermons*, pp. 22–25. Basically, the *Festial* exists in two versions, called Group A (where the *de tempore* and *de sanctis* sermons are mixed) and Group B (*de tempore* and *de sanctis* sermons separated, and slightly expanded). Group B was used as the basis for parts of a more learned vernacular sermon cycle extant in two manuscripts (Harley 2247 and Royal 18.B.xxv), for which a date of composition "sometime after 1429" has been suggested. This cycle (called HR) then furnished material for collections in CUL MS Gg.6.16 and in four other manuscripts of the late fifteenth century, the latter evidently written by the same scribe. These relations have been studied by Wakelin, "Manuscripts"; Fletcher, "Unnoticed"; and Fletcher and Powell, "Origins." See also Mirk, *Advent and Nativity Sermons*, pp. 7–8; on pp. 147–50 Powell provides a useful conspectus of *Festial* sermons in the HR group as well as the sources for sermons in HR that were added to *Festial* material. Spencer, *English*, pp. 311–316, summarizes all these findings. See in addition Powell, "Preaching at Syon Abbey." Dr. Powell is currently preparing a critical edition of the *Festial*.

[31] Powell, "New Dating."   [32] *Mirk's Festial*, p. 281.

[33] Ibid., p. 240; see Fletcher, "John Mirk."

[34] The Lollards are mentioned by name in *Mirk's Festial*, pp. 171 and 164 (here as "Lombardes"). Orthodox statements appear: on the power of priesthood, the Eucharist, and image worship, in the sermon for Corpus Christi, pp. 168–175; on pilgrimages, p. 85.

Robert Rypon (RY)

With Robert Rypon we return to the standard and conventional scholastic sermon in Latin. A Benedictine monk from Durham Priory, he was trained at Oxford, where he had become a bachelor in theology by 1392–1393 and incepted as doctor of theology by 1406. At home he served as subprior for about two decades and was prior of Finchley, a dependency of Durham Cathedral priory, at the turn of the century (1397–1405). He evidently was occasionally sent out from the priory to preach in the countryside.[1] Rypon died at some time after 1419. Like his fellow Benedictines Sheppey and Brinton, he left an important collection of sermons.[2]

Orderliness is the first impression one gets of the fifty-nine sermons ascribed to him in the unique manuscript, British Library, MS Harley 4894, which once belonged to Durham Priory. Almost a de luxe book, it is written in a careful Secretary bookhand of the early fifteenth century with some Anglicana features. All sermons bear clear indications of their occasions. Each begins with an enlarged, flourished, and illuminated capital, and the first page as well as the opening of the synodal sermons (f. 193) have a decorated border. The text is surrounded by large margins with annotations that call attention to the major sermon parts and to their subject matter; only rarely do they register a correction. The left margins also contain letters that, in the order of the alphabet, divide the pages for each sermon into two halves. These letters are then utilized in an alphabetical table of topics (Abraham – Zona) with references to the respective sermon and section (ff. 217v–231v). A prologue there (f. 217r–v) explains the method of indexing; it also stipulates that to these sermons others are to be added, for different occasions

---

[1] The Durham Accounts speak of him as preaching "apud Heghinton, Billyngham, et S'cam. Hildam, etc." in 1389–1390; *Extracts from the Account Rolls* 3:596. For Heighington and Billingham see Barlow, *Durham*, passim. There also was a church of St. Hilda's in Durham. In sermon 19 Rypon says to an unspecified audience: "Which you have often received from me and my confrères before these times" ("quod a me et confratribus meis accepistis frequenter ante hec tempora"), f. 70.

[2] *BRUO* 3:1618. Emden's reference to MS Harley 2398 must be an error.

such as visitations, processions, and the publication of miracles, but I do not find any such entries. This, then, is a book to be taken from the shelves and read at leisure.

The sermons are grouped according to the standard classification of *de tempore* sermons, saints sermons, and sermons for special occasions, but they do not form a complete cycle. Conversely, for many of the selected occasions there is more than one sermon; so we get one sermon each on 1 Advent, 4 Advent, and the Sunday after Epiphany; but then twelve sermons for 1 Lent, nine for 2 Lent, four for 3 Lent, three for 4 Lent, one for Passion Sunday, two for Palm Sunday, two for Easter, six for Rogation Days, one for Trinity, and one for 9 Trinity. Next follows a group of saints' sermons: one for John the Baptist, three for Mary Magdalene, and three for Oswald, the seventh-century king of Northumbria, martyr, and one of the patron saints of Durham.[3] These finally lead to a group of eight synodal sermons, which may originally have constituted a separate booklet. They are directed to the clergy of the diocese, the final one being incomplete, and they all deal with the gospel of Christ sending out his apostles (Luke 10:1–7). In the other groups, the themata are taken from either the gospel or the epistle readings. In the body of his sermons, Rypon often refers to and utilizes parts of the lection beyond his thema; in fact, he tends to cover the entire lection, although structurally the sermons – which he consistently calls *collaciones* – follow the scholastic sermon pattern, with a longer protheme leading to prayer and then the division.[4]

It should be noted that not only the synodal sermons but many others as well are addressed to the clergy.[5] One might even think that Rypon's entire preaching activity as it is reflected in these sermons was directed to priests and curates, were it not that a number of sermons are free of any reference to their audience, while one actually first addresses priests ("Vos sacerdotes") and a few words later parents ("et vos infantum parentes et amici"), thus suggesting a mixed audience (RY-12).

This orderliness has one major exception. On grounds of its thema (Luke 7:37) as well as internal references, the sermon marked as the ninth for 2 Lent really is for St. Mary Magdalene (ff. 86v–89v). But the saint's feast day, July 22, is nowhere near 2 Lent. Perhaps the sermon was placed there because the collector inadvertently confused its thema, *Mulier erat in civitate peccatrix*, with that of the preceding sermon for 2 Lent, *Mulier egressa clamavit*, even though

---

[3] Cf. below, p. 72 at note 20, and Part Two, chapter 41, pp. 263–264.

[4] See further Part Three, chapter 49, pp. 364–365.

[5] The clergy is explicitly addressed in sermons 1, 3, 4, and the synodal sermons (52–59). A clerical audience can further be inferred from Rypon's discussion of preachers and their office, in sermons 6, 16, 23, 34, 37, 43, 50, 51.

its opening words make explicit reference to Mary Magdalene. Another possible reason for the misplacement is that the sermon contains a longer discussion of the seven deadly sins, a favorite topic of Lenten sermons including Rypon's. In addition to this misplacement, there are some other, though minor, errors in the rubrication.[6]

The sermons are very carefully worked out and structured in a complex way that suggests texts created for reading rather than oral delivery. This feature is strengthened by cross references to matters in the same sermon ("The authority for this was quoted immediately above," *pro isto est auctoritas supra proximo allegata*, f. 3v) or to other sermons that occur both before (*supra*) and after (*infra*) the reference. Very often the reference is quite specific and notes the respective part of the sermon referred to: *vide supra in primo sermone quadragesime in secunda parte principali* (f. 49), or *nota supra in sermone 2 prime dominice quadragesime, in primo principali prope finem eiusdem* (f. 118). Such careful and explicit attention to what was or will be said at what point is characteristic of Rypon's style throughout his sermons. For instance, he often tells his reader not only what the main members of his sermons are and which principal part he is beginning or ending (as is standard practice in scholastic sermons), but how, after a complex division, he will distribute parts of the members announced, as in this case: "Hence I shall proceed a little in the first principal part, then combine the second principal with the first, and thirdly say a little about the third principal and thus quickly come to the end."[7] Or: "Since the third member of the main division contains in part the second member, for the sake of brevity I combine the third with the second."[8] Such meticulous attention to structure goes beyond the customary divisions, subdivisions, and distinctions of the scholastic sermon; it creates an impression of academic fussiness.

Other features strengthen this academic tenor. For once, the sermons are rather long and labored. Even Owst registered some impatience with Rypon's sermon style,[9] but the cause is perhaps less that Rypon quotes authorities – all sermon writers of the period did that – but that he belabors matters *à fonds*. A fine example occurs in his sermon for 3 Lent. It begins with the remark that in

---

[6] RY-3 and 4, for 3 Lent, are here labeled "Sermo 1" and "Sermo 2 dominice quarte quadragesime" (ff. 96v and 101), but the repeated rubrics at the respective divisions get the occasion right, though they still number the sermons 1 and 2. These mislabelings are copied into the table.

[7] "Vnde est primo paululum procedendum in primo principali, deinde combinabitur pro compendio secundum principale cum primo, et tercio dicetur modicum de tercio principali, et sic statissime fiet finis," RY-57, f. 208v.

[8] "Quia vero tercium membrum principalis diuisionis continet in parte secundum membrum, ideo pro breuitate combino tercium cum secundo," RY-3, f. 7v.

[9] "No mere independent statement is good enough for the writer, but above it and below he must quote from . . ." etc., Owst, *Preaching*, p. 54.

the biblical text the sermon thema, *Erat Iesus eiciens daemonium* (Luke 11:14), is linked to the preceding narrative with the copula *et*. In the preceding biblical text, Rypon explains (i.e. Luke 11:2–13), Jesus had taught his disciples the Our Father and then added two examples that showed the need for insistent prayer and its effectiveness. Luke's gospel then uses the copula *et* to continue with the lection for this Sunday, *et erat Iesus eiciens*, to show that casting out a devil, whether physical or spiritual, requires God's help; hence it must be preceded by prayer. At this point Rypon becomes extremely technical:

> In order to understand this better, we should notice that the copula *et* sometimes links true statements, sometimes totally false ones, and sometimes statements that are both true and false or a true statement and a false one. If a false or a true statement is linked with a false one, then one *et* is enough, or even too much. But if two true statements are linked, then we have to see whether, if the first remains true, the second could be false. If this is the case, then one *et* is enough. For example, these two statements are both together true: "You are standing or sitting here and you are listening to a sermon." The first statement, "You are standing or sitting," can remain true until the end of the sermon; while perhaps the second, "You are listening to a sermon," can right now be false, because maybe you are asleep or are chattering or turn off your hearing. In such linked statements one *et* is enough. But if two true statements are linked with the copula and the second remains true as long as it is known to be true; and as long as it is true, the first also must necessarily be true; then the copula *et*, or something like it, must be placed before both the first and the second statement. This is the case for instance in the common prayer:
>
> > *Actiones nostras, quaesumus, aspirando* \scilicet per graciam/ *praeveni et adiuvando prosequere, ut cuncta nostra operatio et locutio et a te semper incipiat et per te incepta finiatur.* ["Begin, we pray, our actions with your inspiration and foster them with your help, so that all our work and speech may take its beginning from you and come to its end with you."]

In the second part of this prayer, beginning with *ut cuncta nostra operatio*, etc., are put two *et*s, when we say: "*et a te semper incipiat et per te,*" etc. The reason for this is that if the second statement, *et per te incepta finiatur*, is true, then the first, *et a te semper incipiat*, must necessarily be true also. This can refer to our work or speech. For a deed that has its end in God has of necessity begun in God. The opposite is not true, because it does not follow that every work that has been begun in God also ends in God. For many people begin to do good now during Lent, to leave their sins and start a new life, but they do not always finish it because they do not persevere. Whence the adverb *semper* denotes perseverance, and if the beginning of a good work lacks perseverance, the end is not well linked with the beginning, nor the beginning with the end.

Therefore we should not place one *et* before the beginning and another before the end, but only one in the middle as the copula, because one *et* is then placed deceitfully with regard to the truth of the work, whereas when the end of the work is proven to exist, then the beginning is fittingly linked with the end, and vice-versa.

This is *grammatica* and *logica* applied to biblical exegesis with a vengeance, and one may rightly doubt that Rypon was writing a sermon for actual delivery, let alone preaching this way. But notice his illustrating his grammatical point with references to a sermon audience and to Lenten practices. And even better, the quoted excerpt leads precisely to the point of Rypon's disquisition –

Therefore, that the end of the current work, namely our preaching, may be linked with the beginning in reality and effectiveness, let us start with the aforementioned prayer, *Actiones nostras*, etc.[10]

---

[10] "Pro cuius declaracione clariori notandum quod plerumque coniunguntur cum hac nota *et* preposiciones vere, quandoque proposiciones in toto false, et interdum proposiciones vere et false, seu proposicio vera preposicioni false. Si proprosicio falsa aut proposicio vera cum proposicione falsa copulentur, tunc sufficit, immo nimium est, vnum *et*. Si vero due proposiciones vere copulentur, tunc vlterius est videndum an prima illarum manente vera possit secunda esse falsa. Quod si sit, tunc sufficit vnum *et*, vt verbi gracia iste due sunt simul vere: 'Tu stas vel sedes hic et audis sermonem.' Prima istarum potest manere vera vsque finem sermonis, ista videlicet 'Tu stas vel sedes hic,' et forsan secunda statim erit falsa, scilicet 'Tu audis sermonem,' quia forsan dormitabis aut garulabis seu aures tuas auertes. In talibus vtique proposicionibus copulatis sufficit vnum *et*. Sed si sint due proposiciones vere copulatiue coniuncte, et secunda maneat vera pro toto tempore pro quo nota [*MS*: nata] est esse vera, et cum ipsa existente vera, necesse est primam fuisse veram, tunc debet hec copula *et* vel sibi equiualens preponi tam prime quam secunde, vt verbi gracia in ista oracione communi: 'Acciones nostras, quesumus, aspirando \scilicet per graciam/ preueni et adiuuando prosequere, vt cuncta nostra operacio et locucio et a te semper incipiat et per te incepta finiatur.' In secunda parte huius oracionis, que incipit ibi 'vt cuncta nostra o[pe]racio,' etc., ponuntur due *et* – cum dicitur 'et a te semper incipiat et per te,' etc. Cuius causa est quia si ista sit vera 'et per te incepta finiatur,' necesse est quod prima sit vera, scilicet ista 'et a te semper incipiat,' scilicet operacio et locucio. Nam operacio que finit in Deo necessario incepit in Deo, sed non e contrario, nam non sequitur quod scilicet operacio incipit in Deo quod finit in Deo; nam nonnulli iam in quadragesima incipiunt bene facere et dimittere sua peccata nouamque vitam inchoare, sed non semper finiunt [*MS*: incipiunt], quia non perseuerant. Vnde hoc aduerbium temporis *semper* notat perseueranciam, quod si incepcioni [*MS*: incepcio] bone operacionis desit perseuerancia, tunc non vere copulatur finis cum principio, nec principium cum fine. Ideo non debet poni vnum *et* ante principium et aliud ante finem, sed in medio copulatiue. Nam frustratorie quoad operio [*read* operis?] veritatem ponitur vnum *et*, sed fine operacionis verificate [*read* verificato?], tunc congrue copulatur principium cum fine, et econtra. Igitur in signum vere copulacionis realis ponitur vnum *et* ante principium et aliud ante finem. Perinde, vt presentis operis, scilicet nostre predicacionis, finis cum principio realiter et effectualiter copuletur, premittamus oracionem predictam, scilicet Acciones, etc." RY-28, f. 101v. The prayer is from the Saturday in the first week of Lent.

– the invitation to pray which, in the scholastic sermon form, ends the protheme and opens the way to the following division!

Surely this is high rhetorical craftsmanship, which may not have pleased Wyclif or the Lollards but probably delighted and gave much aesthetic pleasure to a learned audience. At the same time, it should be pointed out that Rypon's sermons show a much greater engagement with the biblical text than was the case with Waldeby's or Brinton's, a matter that will receive further attention in a later chapter. Not everything in his sermons, however, is abstraction, and Rypon does insert a pious tale or *exemplum* here and there, including a *narracio licet in parte iocosa* that is the closest known analogue to Chaucer's "Friar's Tale,"[11] and an account from "Maunvyle in tractatu suo *De mirabilibus mundi*," i.e. *Mandeville's Travels*.[12]

Other elements are similarly distinctive of Rypon's oeuvre. One is his great interest in the seven deadly sins. These recur throughout his sermons, in and out of Lent, and here they receive more detailed and practical attention than in other contemporary collections, usually by listing and explaining their species or branches at some length. Another feature is his concern about and emphasis on preaching. Scholastic sermon writers frequently insert a few words on the preacher's office and moral duties, usually in their prothemes, but Rypon goes beyond this and derives such teachings not just from a single word of his thema but from the entire lection. Thus, his sermon for the first Sunday in Advent is on *Ecce rex tuus venit tibi* (Matt 21:5), but in its protheme he uses the complete narrative of Jesus entering Jerusalem to speak of the *officium predicatoris* and the *officium auditoris verbi Dei*. For the former he finds seven features that lie hidden in the day's gospel and can be brought forth by moral exegesis: the preacher must be sent as the two disciples were sent (Matthew 21:1), he must go into the village (*castellum*) and untie the ass he shall find there, that is, the sinner bound with the devil's fetters, and so on. This and similar sermons clearly reveal how important a role preaching had for him in the pastoral office. In dealing with these topics, Rypon of course also criticizes contemporary abuses, and thus provided Owst with much quotable material.[13] It is clear, though, that in spite of his moral seriousness and his emphasis on the office of preaching Rypon was no follower of Wyclif. In at least four sermons (9, 11, 21, 59) he mentions Lollards and condemns them for their false doctrines. Conversely, he devotes a good deal of space to an

---

[11] RY-28, ff. 103v–104. See Owst, *Literature*, pp. 162–3; full transcription and translation by Nicholson, "Rypon Analogue." See also below, note 23.

[12] "Dicit Maunvyle in tractatu suo *De mirabilibus mundi* quod est quedam insula in qua moratur quedam gens que viuit solum ex odore cuiusdam generis pomi," RY-31, f. 118v. The passage occurs in *Travels of Sir John Mandeville*, ch. 22, p. 137.

[13] In his two volumes there are some 120 citations of Rypon.

orthodox exposition of such controversial topics as image worship (9) and oral confession (28).[14]

References to "nowadays" and modern times take a more concrete form in several allusions to specific historical events. A Lenten sermon refers to the Schism as having lasted for some time;[15] more specifically, the appearance of the comet in 1401 is referred to as recent[16] as is the victory at Homildon Hill (1402),[17] and yet another Lenten sermon states that the Great Schism has lasted for 32 years.[18] This would date Rypon's preaching activity to the first decade of the fifteenth century (or at least 1401–1410) and makes it likely that the multiple sermons for the same Sunday or feast day were preached over several years.[19] It is also clear that at least the synodal sermons were preached in Durham Cathedral. In the first, Rypon laments the non-observance of the "ancient custom" whereby the rectors and vicars of the diocese came to "this church" to honor its patron saints Oswald and Cuthbert.[20] Elsewhere he mentions his personal experience:

> In hearing confessions, I myself have encountered many people plagued by demons; and some of you know well how someone recently, in the suburbs of this town, killed himself at the suggestion of the devil. And I have often heard, indeed experienced it myself, that people become renewed and freed from demonic vexations through exorcisms and conditional baptism . . . and also through first blessings and hallowings.[21]

---

[14] Though it should be noted that in the latter case Rypon also speaks sharply against the misapprehension of indulgences that underlies the activities of Chaucer's Pardoner; see the passage quoted in Owst, *Preaching,* p. 358.

[15] "In scismate iam diu prothdolor contingere videtur nonnullis discretis superbiam ambiciorum et inanem gloriam precipue esse causas," RY-8, f. 27.

[16] "Quedam arra subuersionis nuper contigit, et hoc in maioribus regni sicut constat, et indies in signis apparet, vtpote aquarum inundanciis, fructuum paucitate, et in stella comata iam apparente, videlicet anno Domini MCCCC primo in quadragesima," RY-31, f. 116v.

[17] "Perinde mater nostra, scilicet Christus Deus noster, volens sui filii lacrimas mitigare nuper benedicto altissimo pomum, idest victoriam, mirabiliter nobis donauit et graciosissime sine nostro quasi detrimento apud montem vocatum Homildoun de hostibus nostris Scottis," RY-21, f. 78v.

[18] "Quod scisma durauit iam per 32 annos et amplius secundum tempus conuersacionis Christi hic in terris," RY-15, f. 55.

[19] Support for this view comes from RY-42, whose structural scheme is much like that of RY-41.

[20] RY-52, f. 194v, quoted in English translation by Owst, *Preaching,* p. 216.

[21] "Nonnullos demonibus vexatos egomet expertus sum in auditu confessionum, immo et quidam vestrum satis norunt quomodo nuper quidam in suburbiis huius ville seipsum interfecit ex suggestione demonis. Et indubie sepius audiui immo et egomet expertus sum quod per excercismos [!] et per baptismum sub condicione . . . necnon per primas benediciones seu sanctificaciones innouati sunt et fuerunt a vexacionibus liberati," RY-12, f. 42. Rypon was appointed penitentiary for Durham diocese in 1413; *BRUO* 3:1618.

Another personal remark appears in his first sermon for Palm Sunday, where Rypon narrates what "happened in my time at Oxford some time ago": a cleric presented himself for admission to a higher degree and, as is the custom Oxford, swore on the gospels that he proposed to incept within a year. But then he left university and told the chancellor and officials that he had changed his mind. The lighthearted excuse, however, left a mark on his life: "since he was a notary public, he was held most false among all in England."[22] There are further references to Oxford, but not personal ones.[23]

The substance of his sermons establishes Rypon as an important preacher in an important period, and as perhaps the one who, in the years between FitzRalph and Reginald Pecock, combined learning, thought, and originality[24] more than any other. Yet we know his work from only a single manuscript, a collection none the less that calls for closer intellectual and historical study.

[22] "Sicut dudum in meo tempore contigit in Oxonia. Quidam clericus se optulit licenciari et admitti, vt moris est ibidem, vt fieret magister vel doctor in certa facultate. Mos est in Oxonia quod quisquis sic licenciatus iuret super euangelia quod proponit incipere infra annum computandum ab illo die quo licenciatus <fuit>. Iste clericus licenciatus <fuit> scienter periurus, quia habens propositum suum contrarium iuramento quando exiit ad certum locum regraciaturus cancellario et officiariis ac regend' vniuersitatis et aliis valentibus sue licenciacioni astantibus, dixit: 'Meum propositum est mutatum,' credens ex hoc suum excusare iuramentum. Set non dubium quin posterius nunquam viguit quoad Deum nisi forsan prope mortem penituerit, et quia publicus notarius fuit, reputabatur inter omnes Anglie falsissimus," RY-33, f. 127.

[23] A superstitious woman near Oxford lets a monk pass by her left side; when he throws a stone and breaks the pot of milk she is carrying, she says, "I knew I would have a mishap if I met a monk!" But when the monk gives her sixpence on the condition that she would never believe so again, she exclaims, "Blessed be God, now I know that my belief was false!" RY-9, f. 33v. Christ appears to the future St. Edmund in the "Cowmede" near Oxford (a popular sermon *exemplum*; RY-12 and 13, ff. 42v and 47).

[24] See for instance his treatment of the seven deadly sins analyzed in Wenzel, "Preaching the Seven Deadly Sins."

II

Cambridge, Pembroke College, MS 199 (P1)

In its present form this volume contains three items, each apparently written in a different hand:[1]

(1) Jordan of Quedlinburg, OEA, *Meditationes de passione Christi*, here anonymous (ff. 1–36);
(2) a series of forty-three sermons (ff. 41–141);
(3) Wyclif's *Sermones quadraginta*, here anonymous and without title (ff. 142–221).

Item (1) is a separate booklet; items (2) and (3) stand together in a second booklet, though they are written by different hands and the medieval quiring system distinguishes between them; the changeover occurs within a quire. I have discussed the volume, its composition, and Wyclif's sermons elsewhere[2] and am here concerned only with item (2).

The forty-three sermons of this anonymous collection form a partial *de tempore* cycle from Advent to Good Friday, with up to three sermons per Sunday or feast. About two thirds of them are addressed to *Reuerendi*, and the collection in general has a strong academic tone. Of its forty-three sermons, fourteen also occur in Cambridge, Pembroke College, MS 257. As the two collections have other significant features in common, they should be discussed together.

---

[1] Items 1 and 2 are in the same script, a Gothic textura *valde fracta*; some pages in item 2 look much like the script of item 1, and it is possible that both items were written by the same scribe.
[2] Wenzel, "New Version."

Cambridge, Pembroke College, MS 257 (P2)

This paper manuscript was written later in the fifteenth century than Pembroke College 199. It contains seventy-one *de tempore* sermons written in two columns in one hand of mixed Anglicana and Secretary features. These are followed by copies of three more sermons by the French Dominican Guilelmus de Malliaco (died c. 1300), written in single columns in a late fifteenth-century Secretary hand,[1] and a treatise on the Eucharist in the layout and script of the first hand.[2] On the front flyleaf appears a list of the sermons, in scripts that correspond to those of the main text.[3]

Of the seventy-one sermons, the first sixty-eight form a regular *de tempore* cycle from 1 Advent to Corpus Christi, while three added sermons (69–71) deal with the Passion (including Chambron's Good Friday sermon *Quare rubrum* found elsewhere). Many Sundays and major feasts have two or even three sermons, and their themata are taken from either the day's gospel or the epistle. Twenty sermons are addressed to *Reuerendi*, including one to *Reuerendi magistri*, while

---

[1] Cf. Schneyer 2:488.

[2] Description and collation in James, *Descriptive Catalogue . . . Pembroke College*, pp. 232–233. His remark on the final sermons is inaccurate. Also, while the main hand varies a good deal in firmness and care, it is hardly "ugly."

[3] In the text of the sermons, the scribe made a major mistake: Sermon 18 ends with a closing formula (f. 39va), to which three different divisions of the same thema *(Amice, non facio tibi iniuriam)* are added, plus the beginning development of the first part. This much may well be the beginning of the second part that is so characteristic of these sermons (see below). But instead of giving a full development, the scribe then began, without break, a new sermon on a different thema, *Pauci sunt electi* (P2-19), and copied it to its end. A quotation in this new sermon, on f. 40ra, however, begins a new line and with an enlarged capital ("Nemo laudat Deum nisi etc."). Whoever wrote the list on the front flyleaf took this to be a different sermon and entered it, but the entry was later canceled. At the same time, the maker of the list did not recognize *Pauci sunt electi* as a new, separate sermon. That it is so indeed is made clear by its internal structure as well as a marginal "sermo." Furthermore, most of the sermons bear medieval numbers, but these contain errors and in addition do not correspond to the numbers assigned by the maker of the list.

five contain the address form *Karissimi* (one of them has both). In the sermons shared with P1, the scribe of P2 frequently omits the address form *Reuerendi mei*, though conversely, in one case (P2–35) he has added it.

As already mentioned, P2 shares fourteen pieces with sermon cycle (2) of P1. In addition to sharing a number of sermons, both collections have two identical major features. One is their academic tone: they frequently discuss theological questions,[4] and they do so by constantly quoting Aristotle and St. Thomas Aquinas. Aquinas, usually cited as "sanctus Thomas," is quoted in other collections surveyed in this study as well, but here his name appears with great regularity and with accurate identifications and quotations from his *Summa* as well as minor works. Next to Aquinas stand quotations from Albertus Magnus and Fishacre – a triad of Dominican theologians whose presence would point to a Dominican origin of this sermon cycle.[5]

The sermons' development can, on occasion, become almost absurdly abstract. For instance, a Quinquagesima sermon in P1 on *Nichil sum*, "I am nothing" (1 Corinthians 13:2), develops the notion that man is nothing by utilizing the fourfold proof set out in Aristotle's *Topics*, namely, by example, enthymeme, induction, and syllogism, each of which is explained in some detail. In the second part of the sermon, the preacher continues to develop the two words of his thema in terms of deprivation and positing of being, and in doing so quotes Socrates' dictum that "Nothing and the chimera are brothers" and tells a *nichil* joke. In both manuscripts, the sermons do have their quota of similes and stories, though the latter lack the popular quality found elsewhere. As a positive mark, these sermons contain an impressive breadth of authorities cited, in which the name of Lactantius recurs unusually often, and *Pamphilius on Love* (quoted as "Pamphilius ad Galileam") appears on one occasion.[6]

The other major feature concerns their structure. All sermons are built on the model of the scholastic sermon, but most of them use it with a peculiar twist. Only a few begin with a genuine protheme or the invitation to pray. A large number, instead, divide the thema at once into two or three parts, often with a rhyming division in English. The announced parts are then developed and neatly marked off. Then, instead of ending the sermon, the preacher returns to the thema or to another verse from the day's lection, divides it, again frequently with rhyming English lines, and develops its parts as well. In terms of scholastic sermon

---

[4] For example, sermons in P1 discuss why Adam was created from dust (f. 85rb), why the Son was incarnated rather than the Father or the Holy Spirit (f. 65ra), or why Christ was incarnated as a child (f. 68rb).

[5] There is further a citation of "doctor Hilwardby" in P2–57, f. 176rb, presumably Robert Kilwardby, OP (d. 1279).

[6] P1–24, f. 86rb.

structure, one could consider the first section a form of the *introductio thematis*, and the second section the sermon's main part.[7] But here the two sections are of equal length, and in some cases the first is even considerably longer than the second. In addition, rather than gradually working up to the sermon's main part, as a normal *introductio thematis* would do, these sermons enter at once into the main development. They must therefore be more accurately considered as having an overall bipartite structure, something like a double plot.

The two collections, P1 and P2, are thus closely related through their shared items as well as characteristic features. Analysis of the shared material reveals that both collections contain independent variants (markedly eyeskips in P1 and major omissions in P2), which would establish them to be independent copies from a hitherto unidentified source. Moreover, P1, the smaller collection, contains sermons that are not in P2, and conversely, in the liturgical season that is covered by both collections, P2 contains pieces not in P1. It would therefore seem that the two manuscripts represent the results not only of independent copying but also of severally selecting items from a common source. In this process, P2 gives some indication of being copied later than P1 (see below) and perhaps for a wider audience, as it often omits the address form *Reuerendi mei* found in P1. Also, the English material that occurs in the shared sermons has northern forms in P1 but non-northern ones in P2.[8]

The sermons contain some criticism of contemporary society and of the clergy, though usually put in rather general terms. A couple of such passages are relevant to the dating of the cycle. A shared sermon tells us that England has been beset by its enemies since the deaths of King Edward, "the [Black] Prince," and other dukes, and laments that nowadays knights and soldiers engage "in commerce, in legal business, and in false views to destroy God's Church."[9]

---

[7] This view would hold of several sermons which begin their second part with the standard formula *pro processu* (e.g., ff. 75rb, 109vb, 14vb, 129rb). But other sermons simply start a new division, after finishing the first part with a repetition of the thema (e.g., ff. 42va, 44ra with *sequitur*, 45ra, etc.). See also the structural outline of P2–46 above, in "Prolegomena," p. 6.

[8] Characteristic are (in the order of P1: P2): *lastand:lastyng, es:ys; qwas:whos; qwham:wham.*

[9] "Quamdiu vixit rex Edwardus, princeps, seu alii duces nostri, nunquam audebant inimici nostri faciem ponere contra nos. Sed illis mortuis continue molestamur. Quare enim modo non faciunt ut solebant racio potest esse . . . Sed iam illi, scilicet milites et armigeri, qui sunt et debent esse instrumenta bellorum, non solum actibus armorum sed magis intromittunt se cum mercimoniis, cum iure in assisis, cum opinionibus [P2: operacionibus] falsis ad destruendum Ecclesiam Dei quam cum actibus armorum. Igitur quamdiu sic fecerint, nunquam bene terram istam defendent." P1–29, f. 103va; P2–29, f. 77rb. In another sermon, P1–12 (not in P2), the writer speaks of the transience of worldly joy and again refers to Edward III and the Black Prince: "Ad oculum enim possumus istud percipere de predecessoribus huius regni, videlicet de rege, principe, et aliis nobilibus ac proximis nostris. Vix autem est aliqua memoria eorum quelibet in hac vita," f. 62va.

Another sermon, also extant in both collections, refers to what must be the Great Schism:

> These days the Church is in discord. So is also every kingdom in the world and every community. And this for two reasons. One and foremost is the discord of the Church.[10]

In P2 the same passage appears rather garbled, which may be a result of scribal error or else a poor effort to omit a historical reference no longer pertinent.[11] The *termini* of the original cycle, thus, are 1378 and c. 1417. Both versions have several eucharistic sermons, and while one of them, P2–67, mentions heretics in general, they lack the anti-Lollard stance and tone one normally finds in orthodox sermons from c. 1400. One may therefore think that the original cycle originated early in the reign of Richard II.[12] P1 was probably written not much later.

P2 contains two further remarks that may locate the cycle in place and time. An Ascension sermon speaks of God's power to provide and likens it to the provisions that kings and lords make for their knights in their retirement, "just as the lord our king has in fact ordained in Windsor for our doughty knights."[13] The reference must be to Edward III's foundation of Windsor College in 1348, which made provisions for twenty-six poor knights.[14] The preceding sermon, for Rogation Days, speaks of the power of prayer and of the intercession of saints, especially in battle, and that for that reason kings and temporal lords have frequently endowed the Church:

[10] "Istis diebus iam Ecclesia est in dissencione; quodlibet eciam regnum mundi et quelibet communitas. Et huius duplex potest esse causa. Prima et principalis est dissencio Ecclesie," P1–4, f. 46va.

[11] "Nunc Ecclesia est diuisum [!] quodlibet regnum contra aliud et quelibet ciuitas, et omni istorum ut suppono in Ecclesia est causa," P2–2, f. 4vb.

[12] See also Wenzel, "New Version," pp. 160–161.

[13] "Prouidetur per reges et dominos ut honeste et honorifice habeant ad viuendum, sicut dominus noster rex de facto ordinauit in Wendessore pro probis militibus," P2–61, f. 187va.

[14] See A. K. B. Roberts, *St. George's Chapel*. "In including poor knights in the college of St. George, Edward III intended both to provide for some of those who after fighting with him in France had been brought to poverty through adverse fortune, and also to strengthen the connexion of the college with the Order of the Garter by maintaining in the persons of the poor knights deputies in prayer for the Knights-Companion. The poor knights enjoyed an income equal to that of the canons, 40s. a year and a daily allowance of 12d. In return, as bedesmen, they were / required to attend three times a day in choir, at High Mass, the Lady Mass and Vespers and Compline, and to say 150 Aves and fifteen Pater Nosters at these services," ibid., pp. 11–12.

An example of this is blessed Athelstan and other kings of this realm, who in reverence of this saint granted goods to this monastery and this town, because they had been helped . . .[15]

The author's orthodoxy is shown in a eucharistic miracle story. A sinful woman fails to adore the Host carried in procession, but does so when her friends tell her of God's mercy. Then the Host says, "Woman, your sins are forgiven," first in Latin and then, when the woman tells the priest that she does not know Latin, "in lingua illius provincie" (f. 111ra). Regarding the sacrament of Penance, the preacher twice enjoins his audience that confession must be made to one's curate, but then adds the mendicant position that friars admitted by the bishops are likewise authorized to hear confessions, with a slap on the wrist of those who argue otherwise.[16]

Through several shared sermons as well as structural features, one other collection can be associated with P1 and P2: **Oxford, Bodleian Library, MS Bodley 857**.

This fifteenth-century manuscript, written in apparently a single hand by "Castell de Wyroull",[17] is a pastoral manual that, according to two inscriptions, belonged to William Marshall, chaplain of Pesholme (Peaseholm, Yorkshire).[18] It contains a mélange of material of use to a parish priest, including extracts from the *Gesta Romanorum* as well as two runs of sermons. The first is the temporal cycle by Nicholas de Aquavilla (ff. 1–82), to which two more Aquavilla sermons and another for the dedication of a church have been added. The second run, at the end of the volume (ff. 153–172v), is an anonymous run of seventeen sermons.[19] Of these seventeen, nearly half appear also elsewhere:

---

[15] "Exemplum de beato Athelstano et aliis regibus huius regni, qui bona concesserunt ob reuerenciam huius sancti huic monasterio et ville, quia erant adiuti . . . ," P2–60, f. 186vb.

[16] "Puram oris confessionem, que facienda est potestatem habenti et scienciam, videlicet curato ordinario, fratribus eciam ab episcopo admissis, qui equalem auctoritatem absoluendi habent, nec eis confessi tenentur eadem peccata iterato confiteri proprio sacerdoti, quia dicere oppositum est erroneum, nec aliquis dicit oppositum nisi ex ignorancia vel malicia," P1–33, f. 115va–b. "Alii qui per inuidiam obloquuntur aliis, dicentes quod parochiani sui tenentur et debent suis curatis confiteri et nullo modo aliis," P1–38, f. 130vb.

[17] See ff. 82 and 152v.

[18] Ff. iv and 82. See the description of the manuscript, no. 2760, in *SC* 2:530–531.

[19] Of ff. 172–173 only strips are left, and the text on f. 173v seems to end incomplete. Sermon 17 is followed by, apparently, another sermon. On f. 160 a paragraph of five and a half lines is marked "Antethema."

Bod 857	P1	P2	Others
1			J/5-2; Balliol 219;[20] New College 305
2			
3	09		C-21 (see below)
4			
5			
6	34	32	
7			
8			
9		08	
10	11	07	
11	05		
12			
13	13	10	
14	14		
15			
16			
17			

Of the sermons not shared with P1/P2, several have the same structure, quote Thomas Aquinas, and have occasional verbal parallels with P1/P2. Some of these are for saints' feasts, whereas P1/P2 only contain *de tempore* sermons. It is, thus, possible that Bodley 857 is yet another independent derivative of the underlying source, which must have been a major collection. The distinguishing features of P1/P2 also occur in isolated sermons in other collections, such as B/2-81 and 84, and thus may point to further connections.[21]

Finally, collection **Y/3** also shares at least three sermons with P1/P2. It will be discussed in greater detail in the section devoted to St. Paul's Cathedral MS 8.

---

[20] See Mynors, *Catalogue . . . Balliol College*, pp. 213–215.

[21] Notice also the similar but not identical structure in the second run of sermons in Oxford, Merton College, MS 236, noted below, pp. 215–216.

13

Cambridge, Gonville and Caius College, MS 356/583 (C)

This fifteenth-century paper manuscript furnishes a unique and important insight into university preaching in the early decades of the century, specifically at Cambridge.[1] Hard to read, and presenting its text in a highly abbreviated form, the volume contains a repertory of 156 sermons that I believe were preached in the academic years of 1417 and 1424–1425. With but few exceptions the sermons follow strictly the order of the Church year as well as the university calendar, with rubrics indicating the beginnings of terms. As a result, pieces *de tempore* and *de sanctis* and others for special occasions appear mixed together. All items are nothing but very short sermon notes, recording leading ideas, distinctions, authorities, and images "on the fly," apparently as they caught the note-taker's attention and interest. The manuscript, however, is not a set of the preacher's original notes but clearly a copy of what the note-taker had heard from the pulpit. The notes for individual sermons vary in length from less than a line to over 114 lines. All bear an indication of the occasion on which they were preached, and nearly all record the sermon thema. Exceptions to the latter practice occur in five instances where the scribe records that a sermon is or was missing ("vacat sermo"), presumably indicating that the sermon either was not given (as in one case "propter pluuiam," no. 65) or was not available to the scribe. In the sixth instance he tells us that "I was out of town but have heard that the sermon was about hierarchies, how men are taken up at the fall of the angels" (26).

The quoted remark ("I have heard") is one of various indications that the reporter was not the preacher himself. In fact, whoever recorded the pieces mentions a number of different preachers, including the Franciscan friar Meltoun (3), someone named Hyn[wood?] (1), the chancellor (45, 79), the prior of Colchester (155), and an unnamed Dominican *doctor* (152). In addition a number of sermons

---

[1] I have analyzed the manuscript in detail and given an inventory of the sermons in "Sermon Repertory," which contains full documentation for the remarks made in the following paragraphs.

are said to have been preached by "the same man," sometimes on successive days, sometimes over a period of one or more years. As one might expect, the audience of these sermons was primarily clerical, which is substantiated by their address forms and by the presence of at least one synodal sermon (141). At the same time, several sermons address *karissimi*, which could point to the laity or a mixed audience; and one piece is actually marked "ad populum" (13). Rubrics occasionally tell us that the entire sermon was preached in Latin (36, 89, 100, 111, 119, 132) or else in English (13, 58, 140, perhaps 40), and there are cases where part of a sermon was said in Latin (93, 107, 127), with the rest presumably spoken in English.

To this variety of preachers, audiences, and languages should be added the variety of locations where the sermons were given. The church of the Blessed Virgin Mary – presumably the university church of Cambridge – is mentioned twice (36, 120). But other sermons were given at Bury (St. Edmunds: 1, 2, 148), Cotoun (8), and St. Botulph's (13, 88); and one sermon is said to have been preached at St. Paul's Cross, London (151). This would mean that the repertory covers more than strictly university sermons, and several of the recorded items also fall outside the normal university calendar. Yet a number of pieces bear clear references to the university and its students, and some even seem to be marked as *sermones examinatorii*. Moreover, two sermons report an ongoing hostility between friars or religious and secular clergy. It would, thus, appear that the collection was made by a Cambridge student, either for his own future use or that of his religious house, a student who also had access to other repertories, books, quires, and perhaps even single paper sheets in which sermons had been recorded.

Whoever this person was, his notes show a strong interest in sermon structure. Most of the sermons included have the characteristic scholastic form, and the note-taker was eager to include remarks on their structural parts. Thus, he almost always notes where the invitation to pray was said[2] and indicates the division ("pro materia" or similar expressions) and the principal parts ("primo dixi," etc.). He also notes when a preacher omitted one or more principal parts or when, on a different occasion, the same thema had received a different development. But not all preaching recorded here followed the scholastic sermon form. The reporter tells us that some pieces were developed as homilies that dealt with the entire biblical lection and furnished a running commentary. Of no. 11, for example, we read that "Here he [the preacher] spoke the entire sermon by way of

---

[2] In the texts the invitation is indicated with the abbreviation *comm.* for *commendatio*, as I have argued in "Sermon Repertory," p. 54. For another example of such a *commendatio* see below, section 34, p. 196.

a moralization of the entire gospel without divisions."[3] But whether the preachers used the scholastic sermon form or *postillacio*, the texture of the actual sermons clearly included the normal devices of "popular" preaching. Thus, besides learned references to "Ovid's *De vetula*," to Alan of Lille's poems, and of course to a fair number of later medieval theologians including Thomas Aquinas, Bonaventure, Fishacre, and Holcot, the note-taker also recorded several popular *exempla* and a number of English glosses and phrases in his otherwise Latin context, much like what we find in contemporary non-university-related sermons or collections. In fact, as university sermons these pieces may strike the reader as remarkably unacademic.

One sermon contains a tantalizing remark. No. 21 ends by saying: "Note this matter in another repertory, with the same members but the textual matter a little changed," thereby referring to a sermon that has the same structure but some variation in the development of its parts.[4] This fits exactly a sermon on the same thema that has survived in two copies, P1-9 and Bodley 857-3. The two divisions and the parts announced in C-21 and P1-9 are the same (though C-21 introduces the second main part with "pro materia"), but their development, despite a few parallels, differs, not just *paululum* but a good deal. Whether either of these two codices is the "other repertory" referred to, and whether this information can be used to date collection P1, is not clear.

As far as I can see, the collection contains no reference to the Lollards, and the undeveloped nature of the texts gives no indication about the Cambridge preachers' stand on controversial topics. One sermon (76) was preached at a procession for victory in the war in France, a public occasion for which at this time a Lollard preacher would hardly have been invited. The same would be true of three sermons for the dedication of a church (72, 74–75), given by the same preacher.

---

[3] See further Part Three, chapter 49, p. 358.
[4] "Nota istam materiam in alio repertorio et eadem membra, set materia paululum variata," p. 19.

14

Oxford, Bodleian Library, MS Bodley 649 (O)

This remarkable manuscript has received a great deal of attention from historians and literary scholars.[1] According to the typology offered earlier, it is a "mixed" collection, containing a unified collection followed by a miscellaneous one. But the whole is written in a single fifteenth-century hand, which in both parts begins each sermon with a flourished Lombard letter[2] and regularly leaves a blank space of about six or seven lines between sermons. The codex is regularly constructed: eleven quires of twelve leaves each (ff. 1–134) contain the first set (ff. 1–133, 133v and 134 are blank except for a pen trial on 134v); seven more quires contain the second set (ff. 145–228). The volume bears a continuous medieval foliation, possibly entered by the scribe, which jumps from 134 to 145, perhaps leaving space for a quire that was to hold an index. The scribe in all likelihood was one John Swetstock, whose name was once visible and now appears only abbreviated on f. 48.

The first set, O/1 (ff. 1–133), holds twenty-five sermons. The initial thirteen are for the Sundays in Lent and (apparently) Holy Thursday, in correct liturgical order; they are followed by two other Lenten sermons and then further sermons, in no particular order, of which several can, on internal evidence, be assigned to other Sundays, several saints' feasts, and the funeral of the knight John D. The

---

[1] I have discussed it in some detail in Wenzel, *Macaronic*, pp. 49–55, to which the following paragraphs are indebted; the sermons are inventoried ibidem pp. 160–165. See also a similar inventory in Horner, "Benedictines . . . in Fifteenth-Century England." Discussions of the sermons appear in: Haines, "'Wilde Wittes'"; Haines, "Church, Society"; Haines, "'Our Master Mariner'"; Haines, *Ecclesia Anglicana*, ch. 13. The following sermons have been edited: O-7 in Wenzel, *Macaronic*, pp. 268–307; O-25 in Haines, "'Our Master Mariner'"; O-42 (partially) in Palmer, "'Antiquitus depingebatur'," pp. 236–238. Professor Horner is currently preparing an edition and translation of the macaronic sermons from O/1.

[2] Two exceptions are sermons 30 and 33; on the other hand, one *narracio* outside the sermons opens with a Lombard letter, f. 206. The first initial of set 1 is more elaborate than any other in the volume and is set into a simple, partial border; the first initial of set 2 (f. 145) is more decorated than the other Lombard letters.

entire set is distinguished by a keen concern with the state of the nation, voicing dismay at England's moral and military decay and, on the other hand, joy at the victories of King Henry V, "our master mariner, our worthy prince." Equally heartfelt is the sermons' outspoken condemnation of "those poisonmongers," the Lollards. I should add, though, that lament at the state of the realm, exultation over the king, and condemnation of the Lollards are always at best part of moral-devotional exhortation, here to penance – these sermons are concerned with individual salvation, not politics.[3] Another dominant feature of this collection, and one that allows me to call it unified, is its strong macaronic character. Twenty-two of the twenty-five sermons are fully macaronic in the terminology I have adopted elsewhere,[4] and one is very nearly so. The two sermons without English elements (20–21) are addressed to the clergy and deal with the dignity of priesthood and its duties; their Latin style is different from the macaronic sermons, more rhetorical, and very reminiscent of some of the sermons in W. All were evidently written by a single author, who repeats the same verbal material in different sermons,[5] and who was a Benedictine monk and had associations with Oxford; this may have been Paunteley (see the following collection, R). Their date of composition lies between 1415 and 1421. Many use such addresses as "Reuerendi domini," "Venerandi domini," "Domini mei," or plain "Domini," thus pointing to a clerical audience. On the other hand, remarks within the sermons make it clear that at least some were directed to a mixed audience of clergy and layfolk.[6] Four sermons of this set also appear in another Benedictine collection, manuscript R. Though the text in R is generally inferior, R was not copied from O/1, since O/1 contains occasionally blanks that in R are

---

[3] An apparent exception is O-15, which, after summarizing the points of the sermon, adds two exempla moralized with reference to England's king.

[4] Wenzel, *Macaronic*, pp. 13–30, especially 25–30 (type C).

[5] One can gain a good impression of the repetition of topics and verbal material from the notes in Haines, "Church, Society."

[6] A fine example is O-24. In moralizing the story of Moses' ascent to Mount Sinai while all the people were waiting at the bottom, the preacher first addresses the clergy: "It is not enough for you who are an excellent cleric to sit in your study and keep your knowledge locked up for yourself, but you must descend from the mountain and inform the people" and next warns the lay people: "No lay person should climb the mountain . . . The limits you must not pass are the twelve articles of faith . . . Do not pass beyond these limits, for if you touch the mountain, you will die. Keep yourselves within these limits . . ." ("Non sufficit tibi qui es excellens clericus residere in studio et seruare scienciam clausam tibi ipsi, sed oportet te descendere de monte et populum informare . . . Et in figura quod nullus laicus ascenderet montem, intromitteret de altis scripturis nec clerimonia, cunctus populus / expectabat ad radicem montis . . . Limites quas non excedes sunt duodecim articuli fidei, quos sancti apostoli per inspiracionem Spiritus Sancti plantauerunt in tuo Credo. Ne excedas istas limites, quia tetigeris montem, es nisi mortuus. Serua te infra limites et scias qui sunt," f. 126r–v).

completed. Hence, both texts seem to derive independently from a common ancestor.

Though written by the same hand, the twenty sermons of the second set, O/2 (ff. 145–227), differ strikingly from set 1. They lack its nationalistic and anti-Lollard tone and elements; they are mostly in Latin; and they differ from O/1 in their style. As one enters the set, one is immediately reminded of the work of the "classicizing friars" that Beryl Smalley has written about, and in fact, rather than being associated with the Benedictine order as O/1 was, they contain several details that suggest Franciscan authorship. Thus, O-42 speaks of the poverty of the *fratres minores* and quotes "Sanctus Antonius de ordine Minorum in suis sermonibus" (f. 208), to my knowledge a unique citation in English sermons of the period. O-44, a sermon for St. Barnabas, enjoins its audience to have compassion with Christ who, in the poor members of his mystical body, is suffering hunger, thirst, and nakedness. The preacher then adds a quotation that condemns those who are "like dogs that, with a spiteful tooth, gnaw the bones of the poor, that is they hate the robe of Benedict and the sackcloth of Jerome – and with regard to the Fratres Minores, the nakedness of the Apostle, whose life, to tell the truth, is the apostolic life."[7] The same sermon and several others rely in their development heavily on the use of "classical" moralized *picturae*.[8]

Though all sermons of O/2 share this "popular" tone, at least one sermon is addressed to the clergy.[9] In further contrast to set 1, they seem to have been gathered from several different sources, and in copying them, the scribe must have worked from an exemplar or exemplars that he sometimes did not understand or that perhaps were defective. They are, moreover, interspersed with other preaching matter, such as short notes, distinctions, moralized "pictures," and stories. The sermons are for Sundays, saints' feasts, and the souls of the dead, in no liturgical order. It might also be worth emphasizing that, with two possible exceptions, the twenty sermons of O/2 are for different occasions than those of O/1.

O/2 also differs from O/1 with regard to the material it shares with other collections. Whereas O/1 shares sermons only with one other, Benedictine collection (R, see below), O/2 contains material that can also be found in several

---

[7] "Quasi canes dente liuido ossa pauperum fratrum corrodentes, idest odientes tunicam Benedicti, tactum [*read* saccum] Ieronimi, et quantum ad pauperes fratres minores nuditatem Apostoli, quia, vt verius dicam, vita eorum vita est apostolica," f. 220. The sermon gives this as part of a quotation from Augustine, *De duodecim abusivis*. In fact, the quoted text occurs verbatim in Hugh of Folieto, *De claustro animae*, Book 2, prologue (PL 176:1051), except for the words referring to the Franciscans ("et quantum . . . apostolica").

[8] Such *picturae* are used in set 1 also, but not with the same insistence. In O-45, for instance, moralized *picturae* form the primary mode of dilation in all four main parts of the sermon.

[9] O-43, "Reuerendi."

non-Benedictine manuscripts. Moreover, at least two of the five sermons so shared are not simply different copies but redactions. O-30 occurs also as A-27; O-37 in Oxford, Merton College, MS 248, ff. 97vb–99rb, in a quire of sermons evidently ascribed to "Sawcemere" or "Sawremere" in one of the collections made by John Sheppey; and O-39 as A-26, here in a slightly fuller form. In these three cases, the differences among the respective copies are mostly scribal. In contrast, O-32, here incomplete, occurs complete in B/2-71, from which it differs in many details that would make it eligible to being called a separate redaction. A third version of the same sermon, in W-91, is definitely a redaction. Finally, O-31 is a variant of the popular Good-Friday sermon *Amore langueo*, which has been preserved in at least four other manuscripts.[10] Here the sermon has the same overall structure of applying seven signs of lovesickness to Christ's passion, but their development is shorter, omits all the English, and has some other major changes in its arrangement and substance.

It would appear, then, that in this manuscript one scribe has assembled material from different sources to make up a collection (O) that provides models for the Sundays in Lent and for some Sundays later in the Church year, for a number of saints' feasts, and for a few special occasions (e.g., O-21 on the dignity of the priesthood, perhaps given at a synod?). His attention seems to have been particularly engaged by genuinely macaronic sermons. And his orthodoxy is shown by many explicit condemnations of the Lollards as well as remarks about the Eucharist, private confession, image worship, pilgrimages, and even the ordination of women (O-16).

---

[10] B-88, S-7, T-7, and Dublin, Trinity College, MS 277 (ff. 185–198). A semi-critical edition of this sermon appears in Wenzel, *Macaronic*, pp. 212–267.

15

Oxford, Bodleian Library, MS Laud misc. 706 (R)

As indicated, four sermons of the first set in MS Bodley 649 (O/1) also appear in MS Laud misc. 706.[1] Patrick Horner, who has studied the latter manuscript in detail, describes it as "a composite manuscript assembled from sermons made and collected by Benedictine monks at Oxford in the fifteenth century."[2] According to an *ex libris* on its last folio, the book belonged to John Paunteley, Benedictine monk of St. Peter's Abbey, Gloucester, who had been ordained a priest in 1392 and incepted as "professor sacre pagine" at Oxford.[3] On 3 May 1412 he preached the funeral sermon of his abbot, Walter Froucetur, which is preserved as R-3. Some of the sermons, however, may go back to earlier times. The first sermon here, on "How shall the realm stand?" and for the third Sunday of Lent, applies a story from Augustine's *De urbis excidio* to contemporary England and declares:

> In our East a frightful cloud is rising up against us, by which I understand the kingdom of France. Our enemies, the French, are preparing arms with high council and the support and help of all their friends and are lifting their bow to our destruction![4]

Against this danger, the preacher urges going to confession and prayer. Fear of an imminent French invasion disturbed England particularly in the late 1380s, and the sermon could well belong to that time.

[1] That R is not the source of O may be argued from the fact that the sermons in set 1 of O form a structurally, thematically, and linguistically coherent group ("unified collection"), whereas the four O sermons in R are scattered among other pieces with different structures and concerns.

[2] Horner, "Benedictines . . . in Fifteenth-Century England," p. 320, based on his unpublished dissertation, "Edition." The article contains a list of sermons on pp. 329–332. In *Macaronic* I have offered a corrected and slightly expanded list of sermons (pp. 173–177) and discussion of the manuscript (pp. 53–55). Here I use the (modern) foliation as it appears in the manuscript.

[3] See *BRUO* 3:1437.

[4] "In oriente nostro horrenda nubes incipit nobis oriri, per quam intelligo regnum Francie. Nostri aduersarii Gallici cum summo concilio et omnium amicorum fauore et auxilio arma parant et archum erigunt in nostrum exterminium," f. 1. The cloud from the East is part of Augustine's story in *De urbis excidio sermo*, 7 (PL 40:722).

The manuscript, consisting of several booklets, is written by several hands, all of the early fifteenth century.[5] Besides several scientific treatises at the end, it contains some thirty-three sermons forming a random collection of pieces that range, linguistically, from entirely Latin through various degrees of macaronic to entirely English texts.[6] As far as their occasions can be determined, among the *de tempore* sermons pieces for Lent and Easter predominate, though they are not copied in regular liturgical order. The five *de sanctis* sermons include one for St. Birinus (also O-19) and another for St. Alban, the latter in a very florid, classicizing style characteristic of monastic preaching of the early fifteenth century.[7] Of the four sermons for special occasions, one is the funeral sermon for Walter Froucetur,[8] another a memorial sermon for Thomas Beauchamp, earl of Warwick,[9] the third is for the visitation of a Benedictine house,[10] and the fourth for the general chapter of the *Cistercian* order.[11] Besides those sermons whose occasion would have required a clerical audience (chapter, visitation, etc.), several *de tempore* sermons also are addressed to the clergy, one of them in fact bearing the rubric "coram quodam episcopo."[12] Two sermons were clearly preached to a

---

[5] One of the scribes was "frater Ricardus Cotell," whose name appears on f. 134.

[6] Two sermons in Latin contain references to *alia lingua*, which is probably English. R-17, addressed to a clerical audience, declares: "On this matter [i.e., the Church's power of forgiveness] I can adduce many other notable authorities, both from other doctors and from the *Decretals* and the *Decretum*. But [their] prolixness does not allow it. However, I intend to speak of this more diffusely in the/an other tongue" ("De ista materia plures alias auctoritates notabiles tam de aliis doctoribus quam de decretalibus et decretis possum [*ms*: passionem] adducere, set prolixitas non permittit. Tamen in alia lingua de hoc diffusius loqui intendo," f. 86). R-25, a sermon for 3 Lent to an unspecified audience, in discussing the stability of the three orders of society, says, "On these matters very briefly in the/an other tongue" ("De hiis breuissime in alia lingua," f. 138).

[7] R-31 calls St. Alban "noster patronus beatissimus" (f. 154); similarly, the English sermon R-30 speaks of pilgrimages to "owr gloryous patroun synt Albone" (f. 149v). Hence, both sermons were possibly preached at St. Albans monastery. For the florid style see below, n.16.

[8] Edited by Horner, "John Paunteley's Sermon." In the manuscript the abbot's name appears as "Froucetur."

[9] R-14, edited by Horner, "Sermon on the Anniversary." Beauchamp died on April 8, 1401. The sermon bears the marginal rubric "Sermo obiti," f. 72, and speaks of "iste venerabilis dominus, ad cuius exequias nos omnes venimus ad presens," f. 73v.

[10] R-18.

[11] R-6, not Benedictine, as Horner implies ("Benedictines . . . in Fifteenth-Century England," p. 318).

[12] R-4. Also addressed to the clergy are sermons 11, 17, 19, 23, 24, 27, 32, 33. Notice that sermon 10 has a note "per visitacionem" in the top margin of f. 53, but the sermon is not concerned with visitation, whereas the next sermon, R-11, deals with priestly failings, a topic more appropriate to a visitation sermon.

university audience, presumably at Oxford.[13] Finally, besides the four sermons already mentioned, shared with collection O, one more piece in this manuscript occurs also in a different monastic collection (R-5 in W-4).

The praise of Henry V and the strong condemnation of the Lollards that are so characteristic of MS Bodley 649 occur here again in the sermons shared by the two manuscripts. Beyond those, R has further anti-Lollard passages in sermons 17, 20, 28, 30, and 32, which not only condemn the Lollards by name but furnish brief sketches of their heterodox teachings.[14] In contrast to Lollard teaching, R-19 includes a brief discussion of the scriptural basis for auricular confession.

In addition to these topics, it is worth mentioning that Laud misc. 706 also shows a great interest in monastic perfection, praising its virtues and lamenting its decay.[15] I suspect that this interest accounts for the inclusion of the sermon for a Cistercian general chapter (R-6) in what is clearly a Benedictine product and may in fact represent the collecting efforts of Dom John Paunteley. Several of these sermons appear in the florid style associated with monastic preaching of the period,[16] while others, such as R-10, are filled with such elements of popular appeal as the well-known *exemplum* of the peasant who is so overcome by sweet-smelling perfumes that he faints;[17] or the juggler's trick of making fools blow into a box filled with dust and getting their faces dirty;[18] or "the stones of Winefride, which are blood-red from the blood that was shed there in the martyrdom of that virgin, and which can never be washed of the blood by the running water."[19]

---

[13] R-15 alludes to conflict between clerics and lay people and rhetorically addresses different faculties ("Tu qui es acutus sophista, . . . philosophus, . . . iurista," f. 80r–v. R-24 includes "this university" and "the town" in its initial prayer, f. 129.

[14] R-17, dealing with speech in religious and the clergy, and with wrong silence, discusses the Lollards' denial of the sacrament of penance. R-20, in English and delivered at a monastery, accuses Lollards of presuming to be the worthiest to have temporal dominion, of usurping the office of prelacy, and of "destroying the blessed sacrament" of the Eucharist. R-30, also in English, talks about their denial of image worship.

[15] See Wenzel, *Monastic Preaching*, passim.

[16] Sermons 5, 29, 31; for the florid style see Wenzel, *Monastic Preaching*, pp. 19–20 and *Macaronic*, pp. 128–129.

[17] See Tubach, *Index Exemplorum*, no. 3645; here in R-10, f. 56v.

[18] R-10, f. 56.

[19] "De lapidibus Wenefride, qui sanguinolenti ex sanguine ibidem fuso in martirio eiusdem virginis nunquam possunt per aquam currentem a sanguine mundari," R-10, f. 54.

16

Oxford, Bodleian Library, MS Laud misc. 200 (L)

Although anonymous, this is a unified collection of Latin sermons made by a *Wycliffite* author.[1] It combines a regular series of forty-two sermons on the gospels for the Sundays and major non-dominical feasts from 1 Advent to 1 Trinity (with four saints sermons included in the correct liturgical position), the last sermon ending incomplete (L-1 to 42), with an equally regular sequence of thirteen sermons for the saints' feasts from Andrew to John the Baptist, all but one again on the respective gospel lections (L-43 to 55).[2] Parts of the cycle have also been preserved in five other fifteenth-century manuscripts.[3] The entire collection as a whole, both *de tempore* and *de sanctis* sermons, is unified by its use of a peculiar sermon structure and by clear Wycliffite positions of its unknown author. In MS Laud misc. 200 it is written in one hand,[4] and the sermons contain many cross references.

The structure this author has used is somewhat reminiscent of Repingdon or of the Repingdon-derived collection M/3. Essentially the sermons here fall into two parts. In the first, the author gives a moral-psychological interpretation of the entire gospel reading. Sometimes this is done phrase by phrase, similar to the *postillatio* format of Repingdon, but at other times the author recounts the gospel more discursively by giving it a comprehensive moral interpretation and then going through its parts in linear order, thus achieving, as it were, a psychological narrative. A good example of the latter is the sermon for Easter Monday on "On

---

[1] See the fine study by Von Nolcken, "Unremarked." I am grateful to Professor Von Nolcken for lending me a printout of the sermons.

[2] The sermons are listed in Von Nolcken, "Unremarked," pp. 247–249, the first run also in Schneyer 9:42–46. Since Von Nolcken does not give the *initia* of sermons 1–42, and since Schneyer's account has a number of errors, I have included all the sermons in my inventories. As this is a unified collection, I have numbered all sermons consecutively (L).

[3] Discussed by Von Nolcken, "Unremarked," pp. 236–238 and 247–248.

[4] A fifteenth-century textura; see ibidem, p. 235, n. 16.

that day two of Jesus's disciples went to a town called Emmaus . . . And they told what had happened on the way; and how they knew him in the breaking of the bread" (Luke 24:13–35). The author explains:

> These two disciples, Luke and Cleophas, stand for the body and the soul. Luke, whose name means "rising," stands for the soul that rises from sins to the contemplative life. Cleophas, whose name means "the gathering of one who passes by," stands for the body that is troubled about many things and goes along laboriously in the active life. These two disciples walk spiritually toward the town of Emmaus when, one in mind, they desire to know the Lord's counsel intimately, which is the faith of Christians.[5]

The subsequent details of the gospel narrative are interpreted in similar terms, and the author concludes:

> They went to Jerusalem and told the other disciples how they knew him in the breaking of the bread. Thus must soul and body return to the vision of peace, which is the spiritual Jerusalem, and rest firmly in faith and teach others what they themselves had learned by explaining (*per declaracionem*) the word of God, which is indicated by the breaking of the bread.[6]

After such an initial exegetical section, the author normally extracts two or three points from the lection in the form of a division and confirms them, exactly as it was done in scholastic sermons. For example, in the sermon for 1 Advent, on *Cum adpropinquasset Iesus Hierosolymis et venisset Bethfage* ("When Jesus approached Jerusalem and came to Bethphage," Matthew 21:1–9), he says,

> In hoc euangelio possunt tria naturaliter tangi, scilicet:
>> aduentus desiderabilis Redemptoris,
>> solucio notabilis peccatoris,
>> et honor laudabilis Creatoris.
> De primo dicitur ibidem: Ecce rex tuus uenit tibi . . .

---

[5] "Duo ex discipulis Iesu ibant ipsa die in castellum, etc., Luce 24. Isti duo discipuli Lucas et Cleophas significant corpus et animam. Lucas, qui interpretatur consurgens, signat animam surgentem a peccatis ad vitam / contemplatiuam. Cleophas, qui interpretatur congregacio transeuntis, signat corpus turbatum erga plurima et transiens laboriose in vita actiua. Isti duo discipuli ambulant in castellum Emaus quando vnanimes consensu desiderant intime congoscere consilium Domini, quod est fides Christianorum," L-31, f. 115r–v.

[6] "Transierunt Ierusalem et narrauerunt discipulis aliis quomodo cognouerunt eum in fraccione panis. Sic debent anima et corpus redire in visionem pacis, que est spirituale Ierusalem, et quietari firmiter in fide, et docere alios que ipsi didicerunt per declaracionem verbi Dei, que per fraccionem panis signatur," f. 116.

("In this gospel three topics can be naturally touched on, namely: the desirable advent of the Redeemer, the noteworthy deliverance of a sinner, and the praise-worthy honor of the Creator. Of the first topic the gospel says, 'Behold, your king comes to you' . . .")[7]

The three parts, which are called *principalia*, are then developed in the regular fashion of standard scholastic sermons, with subdivisions and prooftexts and leading frequently to the normal closing formula. Although there are no address forms, this structural format represents an interesting combination of the ancient homily and the scholastic sermon, as we shall see in a later chapter.[8]

Though overall these sermons are not abnormally long, they and their peculiar structure evidently lent themselves to partitioning, so that the scribe of MS Laud misc. 200 several times began a principal part with the enlarged initial he usually employs at the opening of a new sermon and at least on one occasion even rubricated such a part as "another sermon for Easter time."[9] But attention to the lection for the respective day as well as to structural characteristics leaves no doubt that the author of this collection intended one sermon for each occasion, with the mentioned complex features.

The author's Wycliffite sympathies pervade the entire collection. Though not strident, they are firm and frequently expressed. Besides criticizing the clergy for their moral failures and speaking of persecution from the official Church, they turn, doctrinally, mostly against the need for auricular confession and the practices of pilgrimages and image worship.[10] Also, the sermons are pervaded with a strong sense that the primary foundation of Christian faith is the Gospel. Hence other quoted authorities are very limited in number and concentrate on the Church Fathers (Augustine, Gregory, Jerome, Ambrose, and Pseudo-Chrysostom) and Grosseteste.[11] In conformity with Wyclif's condemnation of pious stories and fanciful narratives, the author refrains from using such, and when he does occasionally employ similes to illustrate a point, he stays away from *De rerum proprietatibus, De mirabilibus mundi*, or similar sources.[12]

---

[7] L-1, f. 3.

[8] Von Nolcken has analyzed another sermon in "Unremarked," pp. 245–246.

[9] "Materia alterius sermonis pro tempore pasche," after L-31, f. 117. Hence the discrepancies between Schneyer's list (9:42–46) and Von Nolcken's (correct) account.

[10] Further details can be found in Von Nolcken, "Unremarked," pp. 239–245.

[11] There are a few scattered citations of Isidore, Bernard, the Gloss, Gorran, canon law, and Seneca.

[12] In L-25 he illustrates the evil effect of moral relapse with three similes ("Occurrit autem triplex exemplum ad detestandum hoc peccatum"): a child's returning to his evil ways after promising his father to be good; hurting oneself in the position of an old wound; and drinking poison again after one has been purged of it (ff. 88v–89).

Given his evangelical orientation, it is worth mentioning that among the saints' sermons are two for non-biblical saints, Nicholas and Agnes. The former does not mention the saint but speaks of aspects of the gospel reading for his feast (Matthew 25:14 ff., on pilgrimage and the talents). But the latter does mention St. Agnes extensively and praises her as our model.[13]

[13] The thema is Matthew 13:44 ff., "The kingdom of heaven is like a treasure hidden in a field." The sermon's first part deals with the lection very cursorily and concentrates on the kingdom of heaven, which St. Agnes is said to have sought as a virgin and martyr. It then turns to the saint and, using Judith 11:19, "There is no such woman on earth in her looks and beauty and sensible words," develops four spiritual virtues of St. Agnes.

17

Oxford, Bodleian Library, MS lat. th. d. 1 (Q)

The sermons in this volume represent a unified collection because we know the name of its collector. The volume is also written in a single hand and has a medieval foliation and index, and its sermons seem to be unique to this collection. The manuscript is made up of paper and parchment and was written in the 1430s.[1] Unfortunately the codex is in very poor physical condition: water damage occurs throughout and is so severe that from the opening leaves of the sermon collection, now ff. 5–29, only fragments remain. The medieval table at the end (f. 178r–v), however, gives some help by listing the themata of the sermons contained in the volume together with their occasions and the medieval folio numbers. It also shows that the traces of an alphabetical collection of theological articles that appear at the beginning and end of the volume were not part of it when the table was entered.[2]

The book is written in a single fifteenth-century Anglicana bookhand with some Secretary features. It contains sixty-two sermons[3] and several scattered *narraciones*; the latter and occasional non-sermon material are usually topically related to the sermon they follow, sometimes even with explicit references.[4] F. 43v

---

[1] For previous discussions, see: Owst, *Preaching*, p. 59 and passim; Little, "Fifteenth-Century Sermon"; Fletcher, "Sermon Booklets"; Wenzel, *Macaronic*, pp. 40–43 and 165–173; Wenzel, "Sermon Collections," pp. 12–15. In the following discussion as well as the inventory here I use a new numbering for the sermons, which differs from *Macaronic*; the latter was based on the inventory given by Fletcher, which lists not only sermons but also separate stories and notes.

[2] Ff. 1–4r, Abhominacio–Agonia; ff. 179–181v, Aaron–Amicicia. The latter entries contain some material.

[3] Since many pages are highly defective, especially at the beginning of the volume, and others are now almost entirely blank, an accurate and complete listing of individual sermons that are actually found in the codex is impossible. My count and inventory are based on the preserved text plus information provided by the table, which for the readable portions proves to be quite exact. The table lists the "processus" and the "antethema et introductio" for one and the same sermon *De gracia* separately (Q-21 and 22), and my inventory follows it in this.

[4] For instance, Q-42 ends with the usual closing formula, after which, following a blank line, the text continues: "Nota hanc historiam quia concludit predicta . . ." (f. 135r–v). This *narratio*

(the recto is blank), a smaller parchment leaf, begins a list of "Themata dominicalia," which extends to f. 45 and includes saints' feasts. It provides occasions and sermon themata (usually with biblical source) but no folio references. The occasions listed run through the Sundays and major feasts of the Church year, and then the saints' feasts in similar order. This is, therefore, an independent list of possible themata, not related to the sermons collected in this volume.

Although the sorry physical state of the manuscript does not allow a detailed collation, it is clear that the book comprises several booklets. At the bottom of the list of themata just mentioned (f. 43v, parchment) occurs an owner's note: "Quaternus Fratris Nicholai Phillypp. 1432. scriptus Lennie". F. 74 is likewise a parchment leaf and of smaller size; it has a catchword, which matches the beginning of f. 75. F. 75 again is parchment and of smaller size, and it matches f. 90. The latter contains the clue to a musical cipher and the cipher itself,[5] which reads "Liber fratris Nicholai Phillip de custodia Cantebrigie et conventus Lennie" and is followed by "Scriptus lichefilde 1436." This in turn is followed by three hexameters of cities, which give the "Ordo pro diffinitoribus prouincialis capituli," "ordo cursorum Londoniarum," and "circulus custodiarum pro capitulo provinciali" of the English Franciscans. F. 90v is blank. It would therefore appear that ff. 43 and 90 once were the outer leaves of a booklet that was evidently begun at King's Lynn in 1432 and finished at Lichfield in 1436. It has been suggested that the remainder of the volume consists of other booklets, though its present state makes it difficult if not impossible to say exactly how they are physically composed and whether they can be analyzed into smaller components.[6]

The booklet of ff. 43–90 contains thirteen sermons (13–25), of which seven bear the dates 1432 and 1435 as well as the place names of Oxford and Newcastle. In addition, the name forms "Nicholas," "Philip," or "Nicholas Philip" appear eight times in this section. These features extend to the remainder of the volume as well. Philip's name can be seen at least twenty-one times in it;[7] other places named are King's Lynn and Lichfield; and the dates range from 1430 to 1436. In addition, there are two sermons with the notation "Helbeche" or "Holbeche," and four more with the notation "Melton."

illustrates the Three Enemies of Man, which were mentioned at the very end of the sermon. Fletcher's account here (*Preaching*, p. 44) is inaccurate.

[5] Fletcher (*Preaching*, p. 56) thinks that "this melody appears to be the tenor part of a motet" and fails to understand the relation between clue and cipher. A correct account was given in Stainer and Stainer, *Early Bodleian Music*, 2:65; see also the facsimile in vol. 1, plate 29.

[6] On information from Jeremy Griffiths, Fletcher gives as "booklets": (1) ff. 5–29; (2) ff. 30–42; (3) ff. 43–90; (4) ff. 91–132; (5) ff. 133–156; and (6) ff. 157–177 (*Preaching*, p. 46, n. 2).

[7] They can be found in Fletcher's inventory (*Preaching*, pp. 42–46), though he misses the following: "nota Philipp" f. 74v margin; "Phillip dic" 129v (omitted in reprint); "Philip nota bene historiam . . ." f. 135v.

It is thus evident that the sermon collection has a strong connection with an otherwise unknown Franciscan Nicholas Philip of the convent at King's Lynn. But it is by no means clear whether Friar Philip was its scribe, collector, preacher, author, or any combination of these. For his authorship speaks one detail, the inscription at the top of Q-9: "Sermo quem predicaui Oxon'" (f. 30v).[8] This sermon is actually copied a second time as Q-14, where it addresses "Reuerendi." Philip could therefore have been a member of the university, though nothing more is known of such a connection. The sermons in this manuscript are clearly products of a well-educated man of some distinction, who also preached at visitations to Franciscan houses and at a synod in 1435. Whether the names "Helbech/Holbeche" and "Melton" refer to places or to preachers is unclear. A. G. Little and Alan Fletcher have opted for the latter, and Fletcher has gathered what clues the manuscript offers for "Melton" being a personal name.[9] If this is so, Philip would not have been the author of at least some of the sermons entered here.

The sermon style, too, may furnish evidence of multiple authorship. Though all sermons follow the scholastic sermon form, sermons 13–16 share some special features. Their introduction begins with a distinction, whose members are developed, followed by the sermon's main division and development. The preacher constantly proves a point with a *figura* ("in cuius figuram") which is then moralized ("moraliter"). At the end, he sums up his development with "Combinando iam dicta in sermone isto . . ." In contrast, the following sermons (Q-17 and following) often have a protheme leading to the invitation to pray; instead of "moraliter" they tend to say "spiritualiter ad propositum;" and they do not use the final *connexio partium*. Most of the sermons throughout the volume, however, have some English material, and a number of them are genuinely macaronic. There is no English in the synodal and visitation sermons.

The presence of place names and dates has caused Fletcher to call the manuscript a "sermon diary."[10] This may at first sight seem true, but closer analysis makes this designation problematic. A diary is a record of events or material entered in chronological order, and it may contain such personal remarks as, "I saw," "I heard," "I said," and so on. Both features are present in Richard FitzRalph's sermon collection as well as in the report of Cambridge university sermons preserved in MS Caius 356. But they do not appear in Friar Philip's volume. Apart from "The sermon I preached at Oxford" cited above, there are no further revealing personal remarks. More importantly, the dates that appear

---

[8] My reading of the title is shared by Fletcher (*Preaching*, p. 42). It is, however, just possible to read "predicauit."

[9] Little, *Franciscan Papers*, pp. 244–246; Fletcher, *Preaching*, pp. 50–51.

[10] Fletcher, *Preaching*, p. 41.

in the manuscript occur in a random sequence. While one must allow the possibility that here and there a later sermon was entered into the remaining blank leaves of an earlier booklet,[11] the general impression is that the dates appear in an erratic order; for instance, the sermons on the Passion occupying ff. 108–132v are dated 1436, 1436, 1434, no date, 1433, 1434.

But this erratic sequence suggests at once that these sermons are grouped together not by their dates but by their topic, here Christ's Passion. There is further evidence that, rather than being a diary, the manuscript gathers material that is organized by topical features. Thus, sermons 1–8 are for the Advent season. Sermons 31–34 form a sequence of sermons for visitation. Numbers 35–41 deal with the Passion, with strong thematic emphasis on the blood that Christ shed for us. Sermons 42–47 are for Rogationtide: 42–44 and 46 are so marked, while 45 deals with a major topic in Rogation sermons, petition, especially the Our Father, and 47 is marked for a procession. Again, the "Melton" sermons, 54–57, stand together in a group. This topical interest is further shown explicitly in several rubrics. Number 21 is a sermon "about grace on whatever thema" ("Processus de gracia pro quocumque themate," followed by an "Antethema et Introductio de gracia" in Q-22). Similarly sermon 48 is rubricated "on the blood [of Christ] for Passion and Palm Sunday and Good Friday" ("De sanguine pro dominicis pascionis et ramarum palmarum ac feria vi parasceu'") and is followed by different introductions for Palm Sunday (Q-49) and Good Friday (Q-50), while a third introduction deals likewise with the blood of Christ, though it does not indicate the occasion (Q-51). Finally, sermon 60, on "Qui custos est domini sui gloriabitur," ends with a reference to another sermon on the same key word *custodire* ("Custodi virum istum,") "for the same development" ("pro eodem processu"). The latter is sermon 62, the last in the volume, and to it the scribe has attached yet another related thema, "Custodite sicut scitis." The overall impression therefore is that this manuscript with its several booklets is a random collection of sermons, possibly by different authors, that were gathered following topical interests.

With one exception, a "sermo communis de beata Virgine" which is marked "Melton" (Q-55), all sermons in the collection are either *de tempore* or for such special occasions as Franciscan visitations (31–34), a synod (25), or the profession of a Franciscan novice (53). The *de tempore* sermons concentrate heavily on the seasons when preaching, especially by itinerant friars, was at a maximum: Advent, Lent, Holy Week, and Pentecost. There are several sermons for the Rogation Days (42–47) and one for Corpus Christi (61).

---

[11] I have discussed one such posssibility in "Sermon Collections," p. 13.

As stated earlier, the sermons in this collection seem to be unique. Only one, Q-50, is a very popular sermon by Michael of Hungary that has been preserved in several other English manuscripts.[12] Another piece, Q-56, shares its beginning and end with an item in Holcot's collection *Convertimini*, and closer comparison reveals that the author of Q-56 (perhaps Melton) used Convertimini-39 *in toto* for the second principal of a new sermon that, though it begins with *Convertimini*'s initial sentence, builds a larger structure with its own introduction, division, and first principal. Q-56 thus allows us to see a little more of the compositional technique of whoever wrote the sermons in this collection.

Though these sermons seem to have no explicit references to the Lollards, they can be confidently deemed orthodox because of their strong connection with the Franciscans and their conventional teaching about the Eucharist.

---

[12] *Quae utilitas in sanguine meo*, as CA/2-1 and in CUL MS Ii.6.3.

18

John Dygon (DY)

Another unified sermon collection made in the second quarter of the fifteenth century may be the work of a collector who is known to us by name and whose interests, as they are reflected in a number of manuscripts that he owned or wrote himself, included the collecting of sermons. John Dygon studied at Oxford, where he is attested as having earned bachelor degrees in both laws.[1] He must also have incepted as a master, probably of Arts, because in several subscriptions he calls himself "M[agister]."[2] From 1406 to 1435 he held appointments in several parishes in southern dioceses, the last one being St. Andrew's, Holborn, London. Then he was admitted as the fifth recluse to a cell at the recently founded Carthusian priory at Sheen in Surrey, where he lived from 1435 until at least 1449.[3]

Dygon has left various owner's notes and subscriptions in a number of manuscripts, many of which he gave to Magdalen College, Oxford. The notes are all written in the same hand, and this has been identified as Dygon's.[4] They can be separated into two types: in one, besides calling himself *Magister*, he titles himself only *presbiter*; in the other he also mentions that he is a *reclusus* at Sheen. If this distinction is meaningful, it indicates that books with the first form were owned and written before he entered the charterhouse. In this case, Dygon's activity of collecting books and writing them reaches back into his period as a parish priest. The following, then, are the books he owned or put together:

---

[1] *BRUO* 1:615–616.

[2] MSS Magdalen 60, flyleaf verso; Magdalen 79, f. 298v; Magdalen 93, ff. 226, 311v. One of the subscriptions in Magdalen 93 reads: "Scriptus per manus M. Johannis Dygon in vtroque iure Bacallarij . . . ," f. 226v. Likewise he is called "Magister" in his deposition in the canonization process of St. Osmund: *Canonization of St. Osmund*, p. 68.

[3] On the Charterhouse at Sheen see E. Margaret Thompson, *Carthusian Order*, pp. 238–246; and also Lawrence, "Role."

[4] Watson, *Catalogue of Dated*, no. 827: 1: 138, and vol. 2, plate 386.

No mention of Sheen:[5]

Magd. 60: William Peraldus, *Sermones dominicales*, and moralized exempla.
Magd. 79: a sermon collection, see below.

Mention of Sheen:[6]

Magd. 77: *Beatae Brigittae Revelationum libri ii*
Magd. 93: a notebook, see below.
Magd. 154: Thomas Docking, OFM, Commentary on the Epistle to the Galatians.
Magd. 156: an anonymous incomplete lecture course on the gospels for the feast days, see below.
Magd. 177: Haymo of Halberstadt, *Commentarius super epistolas Paulinas*, and other works.
Oxford, St. John's College, MS 77: a theological miscellany with some works on the spiritual life.[7]

In addition to these books that carry Dygon's ownership or bequest notes, his distinctive hand has been found in a number of other manuscripts, most of them now at Magdalen College. Several of these carry annotations in his hand, and these reveal a man who, besides other fields of learning,[8] was keenly interested in works of biblical exegesis,[9] treatises on the solitary life,[10] and sermons. In providing these books with rubrics and occasional corrections, Dygon is here revealed as a careful and often critical reader of this theological and devotional literature. His interest especially in sermons can still be seen in an earlier homiliary on the Sunday gospels (Magdalen MS 61), Peraldus's sermons on the Sunday gospels (MS 91), the *De sanctis* sermons by Januensis (MS 176),[11] and the *Distinctiones* by Nicholas de Byard, an alphabetical dictionary of topics for the use of preachers

---

[5] I.e., owner's note only: "Iste liber constat M. Johanni Dygoun presbitero."

[6] Donor's notes or subscriptions.

[7] Hanna, *Descriptive Catalogue . . . St. John's College, Oxford*, pp. 100–105.

[8] Magdalen MS 182 (astronomical works) and 188 (a Latin–French and English dictionary and other material).

[9] Magdalen MSS 57 (Grosseteste on Galatians), 113 (a thirteenth-century commentary on the Psalms), 150 (patristic expositions of the Old and New Testament), 154 (Thomas Dockyng on Galatians), and 177 (Haymo on the Pauline epistles).

[10] Magdalen MSS 67 (the *Ancrene Riwle* in Latin), 141 (see Doyle, "European Circulation," p. 138 n. 58), and Oxford, St. John's College, MS 77 (several). In this category also belongs Magdalen MS 93, which besides some sermons holds copies of and extracts from many works on the spiritual life, including the apparently earliest extant copy of Thomas a Kempis's *De imitatione Christi*.

[11] Dygon made corrections to the text of a sermon for St. James, f. 92v.

(MS 145). Beyond these annotations, Dygon himself also copied sermons into at least two volumes. Magdalen MS 60, written in Dygon's and perhaps some other hands, contains the cycle of Peraldus's Sunday sermons from 1 Advent to 2 Trinity. Apparently this work was done before his enclosure.

His copying continued at Sheen, as is witnessed by Magdalen MS 93 (**T**).[12] This is a notebook, written again by several different hands, among which Dygon's predominates. The volume gathers a number of excerpts and entire treatises, many of them of a devotional nature including Gerard van Zutphen's *De spiritualibus ascensionibus*[13] and Thomas a Kempis's *Imitatio Christi*, here called *Musica ecclesiastica*. Dygon indexed the contents of the manuscript on the front flyleaf. Among these excerpts and treatises occur ten more or less contemporary sermons. These include pieces for various occasions or unassigned, two funeral sermons (of which one mentions the deceased, Isabel Fullthorpe), and the popular Good-Friday sermon *Amore langueo* found in other collections.[14]

The first item in Magdalen MS 93 is of some interest in throwing light on one way in which sermon cycles could be composed. It is labeled *Exposiciones epistule*[15] *secundum Remigium Remensem archiepiscopum* (ff. 1–42) and written in Dygon's hand. Dygon or his exemplar clearly confused the sixth-century Remigius of Rheims with a later Remigius of Auxerre, who is elsewhere credited with a commentary on the Pauline epistles, which modern scholars tend to attribute to Haymo of Auxerre.[16] The *Exposiciones* in Magdalen 93 comprise twenty-three expositions of the epistle lections from 1 Advent to Palm Sunday.[17] What the unknown author, therefore, has done is to excerpt the relevant commentary on Paul's epistles and present it according to the official epistle lections. The result is a set of simple explanations or *postillationes* of the lection, phrase by phrase, most of them devoid of any non-biblical quotations other than those found in Remigius. The one exception is the fifth item, on *Gaudete* (Philippians 4:4), where the writer enriched the extracts from Remigius with further material on the Pauline text from "alius postillator" (identified in a marginal note as Gorran[18])

---

[12] Its contents are itemized in Coxe, vol. 2. A collation with newer foliation, discussion, and list of the ten sermons can be found in Wenzel, *Macaronic*, pp. 32 and 180–182. The concept of "notebook" is further discussed in Wenzel, "Sermon Collections."

[13] See Doyle, "European Circulation," p. 130.

[14] Inventoried here also with the siglum T.

[15] Thus in the title, f. 1. In the list of contents Dygon wrote "epistularum dominicalium," front pastedown.

[16] His commentary on the Pauline epistles appears in PL 117:361–938.

[17] The Sundays as well as Ember Saturday, Christmas Eve, Christmas, and St. Thomas Becket, but not Ash Wednesday.

[18] F. 7.

and one or two other authors.[19] The work, thus, is a late-medieval *postillatio* of the epistle lections, much like Repingdon's on the gospels or the English *Wycliffite Sermons* but considerably sparser than either. It lacks sermon or homiletic features altogether.

Finally, and for our survey most importantly, Dygon may himself have composed an entire sermon cycle, though I cannot prove his authorship beyond doubt. Magdalen College, MS 79 (DY) is a fifteenth-century paper codex of twenty-one quires bearing medieval signatures as well as a partial medieval foliation (to f. 124). The quires are mostly of sixteen leaves, with some variation.[20] Quire signatures H–P correct or replace earlier signatures A–H. What now is quire H was at one point clearly intended to be the beginning of the book, as it bears the inscription "In nomine Patris et Filii et Spiritus Sancti amen. Assit principio sancta Maria meo" in the opening top margin (f. 98). However, the actual sermon text continues from the preceding page, though in a different hand. The entire volume is written in a variety of hands, all of the first half of the fifteenth century. Two major hands alternate to some extent, while others are responsible for an occasional page or two and two entire quires (ff. 74–97v). The first major hand (A), which has been identified as Dygon's, also wrote "Iste liber constat M Johanni Dygon presbitero" at the end of the sermons (f. 298v).[21]

The book contains sixty-nine sermons for saints' feasts from the Annunciation to St. Martin, mixed with a number of sermons for various feasts from Easter to Corpus Christi in the proper places.[22] For many occasions, which are clearly marked at the head of each sermon, the author offers two or more pieces in order to accommodate his abundant material (see below). Several sermons have prothemes, one or two even with the expected prayer, but the majority open at once with a division of the thema that states that "pro materia sermonis" three things are *notanda* or *declaranda* or *tractanda* or *pertractanda* or

---

[19] "Archidiaconus," a thirteenth-century canonist, f. 7; "Cassiodorus," i.e. John Cassian, f. 7v; "Doctor de Lyra," f. 8.

[20] Collation based on the medieval and, after 124, the modern foliation: ii, I^{14} (1–14), II^{16} (leaf 14 excised, 15–29), III^{12} (30–41), IV^{16} (42–57), V^{16} (58–73), VI^{10} (74–83), VII^{14} (84–97), VIII^{16} (98–113), IX^{16} (114–129), X^{16} (130–145), XI^{16} (146–161), XII^{16} (162–177), XIII^{16} (178–193), XIV^{16} (194–209), XV^{16} (210–225), XVI^{14} (226–239), XVII^{14} (240–253), XVIII^{16} (254–269), XIX^{12} (270–281), XX^{12} (282–293), XXI^{6} (294–299), ii blank.

[21] On the following leaf begins "Exposicio epistule prima [!] ad corinthios 5 per doctorem de lyra" (modern 299r–b), which is seemingly continued on the remaining front flyleaves iii–iv. The hand on these folios is similar to A in its ductus but uses two-compartment *a*.

[22] It is possible that the collection may once have formed a complete cycle *de sanctis et de festis* whose beginning is now lost, but it should be noticed that apparently none of the various cross references to earlier sermons is to one before Rogation days (DY-14).

perstringenda.[23] Words denoting "brief" (*breuis* or *exilis*) are used with great regularity. In many cases the first part announced furnishes a phrase-by-phrase explanation of the lection (gospel or epistle), usually with glosses called *notule* from the Church fathers and doctors. Saints sermons are full of narrative material about the respective saint's life and miracles. Overall, the sermon writer has composed these sermons by drawing heavily on standard authorities, both for his exegesis of the readings (mentioning Bede, Jerome, Chrysostom, but not thirteenth-century commentators, unless they hide under an anonymous "postillator") and his moral matter. In the latter case, when he deals with topics that in other collections elicit references to specific contemporary social or moral abuses, such as nepotism, neglect of pastoral duties, or sexual failures, he normally discusses such topics with lengthy excerpts from Gregory the Great, Bernard, Peraldus,[24] or Grosseteste. The same is true of the author's attempt, normally made in the third principal part, to "excite" his audience to the practice of some virtue suggested by the respective saint's life, such as virginity (Mildred), fraternal love (Simon and Jude), willingness to die for Christ (Margaret, James, Lawrence), or the duty to censure public sin (Decollation of St. John the Baptist). Even here the substance and rhetoric of his words hardly ever goes beyond that of the prooftexts copied.

This scissors-and-paste work and the regular exegesis of the day's lection are reminiscent of such model-sermon collections as Repingdon's or Felton's, and they are here applied to the saints' feasts. But this cycle also contains features that betray a more individualized kind of work as well as a closer relation to actual preaching. Many sermons end after the first or second principal part and defer the remainder of the topics announced to another sermon, either for the same or for another feast. For example, sermon 28 ends with: "Here I omit dealing with the third principal point in order to avoid prolixity; but through God's help it will be made clear in the following sermon," and the point in question – the power of the keys given to St. Peter – is indeed taken up as the third principal of the next sermon.[25] Conversely, another sermon begins with, "Although I have dealt with some aspects [of the announced thema] in the preceding sermon but

---

[23] Normally the division comes at the very opening of the sermon, though several pieces start with an introduction of two or three sentences, and one or two temporal sermons have a regular protheme leading to prayer.

[24] For example, in the third sermon on the Decollation of St. John the Baptist, where the writer speaks of incontinence among the religious, he copies pages and pages from William Peraldus's *Summa de vitiis* on *luxuria*.

[25] "Et de tercio principali omitto hic tangere propter prolixitatem vitandam, sed per Dei graciam patebit in sermone proximo sequenti," DY-28, f. 109v, taken up at ff. 113–114v.

could not finish, three points are to be taken up in this present sermon."[26] In the sermon on St. Margaret, the third point – "Breuis excitacio ad martirium pro fide Christi vel obseruancia iusticie seu eciam caritatis" – is similarly "deferred until another time, in order to avoid prolixity, etc."; the collection does not contain another sermon on this saint, but martyrdom is indeed treated later in sermons on St. James and St. Lawrence.[27] Such remarks may well betray a concern with actual delivery to an audience whose limit of tolerance had to be kept in mind.

That this audience might be varied is shown in a rare instruction to the preacher. The sermon for the feast of the Annunciation, on "Behold the handmaiden of the Lord, let it be done to me according to your word" (Luke 1:38), begins by relating the five Marian feasts of the Church year to the Virgin's five major virtues. Then, after commenting on the entire lection at some length, the writer continues;

> For the moral instruction of the common people (*vulgarium*), develop these five virtues that have been set out in the beginning if your audience is capable [of understanding them]. And if lords (*domini*) are present, you could treat of their estate, and commend justice and right judgment and disparage pride, avarice, plunder, and lion-like tyranny.[28]

The sermon then develops the latter choice, the duties of lords.

Address forms seem to be lacking altogether, except for an occasional "Karissimi" within a quoted passage, but some direct appeals to the audience do occur. A fine case appears in sermon 7 for Corpus Christi. The entire sermon sets out three major requirements for receiving the sacrament worthily, of which the third is "a true confession of the belief in Christ's twofold nature, and devout prayer." The preacher then offers a lengthy model: "To make this confession and prayer in due form, pray devoutly as follows."[29] And he gives a sequence of thirteen short prayers built on the same format: invocation, an aspect of Christ's passion

---

[26] "Licet aliqua tetigi in sermone precedenti de beata Magdalena, quia tamen propter prolixitatem consummare non potui, ideo tria sunt aliqualiter declaranda in presenti sermone," DY-34, f. 134.

[27] "De tercio autem oportet differre vsque alias propter prolixitatem vitandam, etc." DY-32, f. 128v. Martyrdom is announced as the third principal of sermon 35, on St. James (f. 138), but deferred again (f. 144v) and finally developed as the third principal of sermon 36 on St. Lawrence (f. 150).

[28] "Pro morali instruccione vulgarium prosequere has quinque virtutes in principio declaratas si auditorium sit capax, et si domini sint presentes, poteris prosequi de statu illorum commendando iusticiam et iustum iudicium, detestando superbiam, auariciam, rapinam, et tirannidem leoninam," DY-1, f. 3.

[29] The prayer begins "Domine Iesu Christe, adoro te, qui es verus agnus Dei in ara crucis pro nobis immolatus ex caritate perpetua et infinita," but the sample quoted next in the text represents the format more precisely.

with scriptural testimonies, and prayer for forgiveness of sins in a particular area. For instance, the third prayer reads:

> Lord Jesus Christ, king of glory, I believe and confess that for our sins you were scourged by night and by day before your enemies in your whole body, from your head to the sole of your feet, as the gospel witnesses in Matthew 26, Luke 22, and Mark 15. I beseech you, Lord Jesus Christ, through that most dreadful scourging, forgive me, most pious Father of Mercies, all the sins I have committed in all my body or any of its members.[30]

This is the language of meditation on Christ's Passion and of affective piety, which in Dygon's period could be found in such meditative works as Rolle's *Meditations on the Passion* and in occasional sermons that were preached on Good Friday or Corpus Christi, as here, but not in systematic cycles made for preachers.

There are two further specific elements that may link these sermons to actual preaching. Sermon 8, for the feast of St. Ambrose, begins thus:

> Since this feast of blessed Ambrose sometimes occurs in the Easter season and then the gospel "I am the true vine," etc., is read, this gospel must therefore be treated somewhat for the spiritual edification of the audience here present.[31]

References to "the present audience" (*presens auditorium*) occur in at least four other sermons, which set out by declaring that "three things are to be shown to the present audience."[32] The texts reveal very little about the identity of that audience, but in at least one case it was clerical. The sermon for Tuesday after Pentecost, on "Who enters through the gate is the shepherd of the sheep" (John 10:2), speaks at length about the pastoral office and the good as well as the bad curate. "Censure of the bad prelate" is offered "to deter unfit ones from coming to the pastoral office . . . for the benefit of the present audience."[33] Another teasing element is the statement that a given text or topic is to be explained for

---

[30] "Domine Iesu Christe, rex glorie, credo et confiteor quod propter peccata nostra fuisti flagellatus nocte et die coram inimicis tuis in toto corpore a vertice capitis vsque ad plantam pedis, ut testatur euangelium Mathei 26, Luce 22, et Marci 15 capitulo. Obsecro, Domine Iesu Christe per illam dirissimam flagellacionem remitte michi, Pater piissime misericordiarum, omnia peccata que commisi in toto corpore meo seu aliquo membrorum," DY-7, f. 24.

[31] "Quia hoc festum beati Ambrosii quandoque contingit in tempore paschali et tunc legitur euangelium *Ego sum vitis vera*, etc., ideo hoc euangelium est parumper pertractandum propter spiritualem edificacionem / auditorii iam presentis," DY-8, f. 25r–v.

[32] "Tria sunt presenti auditorio breuiter declaranda," f. 72; similarly ff. 76v and 158v; "et de hiis membris poterit dilatari processus sermonis iuxta capacitatem auditorii presentis," f. 145.

[33] ". . . vituperacio mali curati ad deterrendum inhabiles accedere ad officium pastorale. Vt ergo ista tria valeam veraciter enodare ad honorem Dei et vtilitatem auditorii presentis . . . ," DY-20, f. 72.

the benefit of *minores* (or possibly *iuniores*). One occurrence opens a sermon that eventually discusses the fourth commandment, a context that would naturally concern instruction for children.[34] But two other occurrences have nothing to do with children or young people, and it remains unclear why these sermons should be of relevance to *minores*.[35]

That these *minores* could hardly be Franciscans is suggested by the sermon for Wednesday of Easter week, whose thema, "Cast your nets to the right of the boat" (John 21:6), is applied to the demand for manual labor among both monks and secular clergy.[36] The latter are admonished not only to work with their hands or learn a trade, but also to keep mendicants from sponging on their parishioners:

> For it does not seem befitting the estate of priests to admit religious, who in men's reputation are the most perfect, allowing them to "penetrate the houses of widows" and of other people, poor or powerful, to beg boldly, without shame, and needlessly, in order to gather for themselves worldly "dung" under the hue of poverty – those who sow lies and discord among their brethren and increase sins among the people for the sake of gain, and who blasphemously attribute this kind of clamorous mendicity to Christ and his apostles.[37]

Such antifraternal warnings continue later in the same sermon, when the preacher turns to an exposition of the third and fourth commandments (which follows the exposition of the first and second commandments in the preceding sermon, and in turn is followed by a similar one of the fifth commandment two sermons later).[38] For the commandment to honor father and mother the writer borrows several passages from Grosseteste's treatise on the Decalogue. Wedged in between two such excerpts is a passage that condemns "those modern religious who impiously

---

[34] DY-6, beginning "Primo breuiter tangenda est historia euangelii cum paucis notulis inde captis ad erudicionem minorum" (f. 18), though the fourth commandment is treated much later in the sermon; see the following discussion and note.

[35] In DY-4, *ad instruccionem minorum* introduces moral lessons drawn from Christ's appearing to the pilgrims to Emmaus (10v); in DY-9, *ad informacionum minorum* starts a longer development of the charge "So let your light shine before men," on virtues that priests ought to have (30 ff.).

[36] The sermon writer cites *Decretum*, Dist. 91 *per totum*.

[37] "Non igitur videtur decens statui sacerdotum inducere religiosos perfectissimos in reputacione hominum licenciando ipsos penetrare domos viduarum et aliorum pauperum et potencium ad mendicandum frontose et inverecunde et superflue, congregandum sibi ipsis [MS: ipsius] stercora mundana sub colore paupertatis, qui seminant mendacia et discordiam inter fratres et cumulant peccata in populo propter questum, et blaspheme imponunt Christo et suis apostolis huiusmodi mendicacionem [MS: meditacionem] clamosam," DY-6, f. 18v. For the two biblical quotations see 2 Timothy 3:6 and Philippians 3:8.

[38] DY-6, on *Mittite in dextram navigii rethe et invenietis*, begins on f. 18. The third commandment is discussed on ff. 19–20v, the fourth on ff. 20v–22v.

and cruelly steal children from their needy parents and send them to other countries under the color of religion."³⁹ These are called *fratrifactores*, and their offense is not simply condemned but argued against: "For without Christian faith there is no salvation of body or soul forever, but it holds true that without any private religion (*priuata religione*) a man can be saved and, further, serve the whole Church."⁴⁰ Though late fourteenth-century and fifteenth-century voices condemned this malpractice in all religious orders, traditionally the primary culprits had been the mendicants.⁴¹

The language of the sermon just quoted is strongly reminiscent of Wyclif,⁴² and other sermons in this collection bear a similar undeniably Wycliffite tone. Thus, the second principal part of sermon 17 brings a long "excitacio ad constanter predicandum euangelium," which includes such challenging statements as,

> As people run so much and bend their knees at a bishop's or priest's blessing at Mass, with how much love and desire should they run to hear the gospel and observe it constantly in their work and speech! For without it, even if they had a thousand human blessings, even papal bulls, these would not keep them from the punishment of hell . . . And a greater woe to those truant Antichrists who do not know or are not able to preach the word of God and yet prevent others who know, are willing, and are driven by the spirit of love to do this!⁴³

A few pages on, in dealing with the thema "Who enters through the gate is the shepherd of the sheep" (John 10:2), the writer says of true shepherds:

---

³⁹ "Hic timeant religiosi moderni qui impie et crudeliter furantur filios a parentibus egenis et ad alias terras transmittunt sub religionis colore," f. 21v.

⁴⁰ "Nam sine fide Christiana non est saluacio corporis vel anime in eternum, sed sine qualibet priuata religione stat hominem saluari et amplius proficere Ecclesie generali. Et talis fratrifactor nescit an induccio pueri in talem priuatam religionem cedat puero ad dampnacionem maiorem, eo quod non est acceptatus a Deo ad perfeccionem in ordine requisitam," f. 22.

⁴¹ See especially Szittya, *Antifraternal Tradition*, pp. 204–206; and *English Wycliffite Sermons* 4:137–138. See also Fowler, *Life and Times*, pp. 167–168. For the acceptance of adolescents and pre-adolescents into the Franciscan order, see Roest, *History*, pp. 238–243.

⁴² Another word that may have a connection with Wyclif is *missare*, "to say Mass": "tociens missantibus et tam raro predicantibus," f. 89.

⁴³ "Cum ergo homines tantum currunt et genua flectunt ad benediccionem episcopi vel sacerdotis in missa, quanto amore et desiderio currerent ad audiendum euangelium et seruandum [*MS* seruando] ipsum continue in opere et sermone. Nam sine hoc, etsi habeant mille benedicciones humanas, eciam bullas papales, non seruarent eos a supplicio iehenne. . . . Sed magis ve illis antechristinis discolis qui nesciunt vel nequeunt predicare verbum Dei et tamen impediunt ceteros scientes, volentes, et spiritu caritatis ad hoc faciendum libere commotos," DY-17, ff. 60v, 61. The apparent form *antechristinas* appears also on f. 73.

> Therefore it seems that a holy life and salutary teaching together with faithfully carrying out of the pastoral office make one a faithful curate or able prelate, not human election or sealed letters.[44]

As the next remarks in the same sermon derive from Grosseteste, it is probably correct to think that the two quotations were inspired by the great reforming bishop. But things become more unorthodox in a later sermon on "Blessed are the peacemakers for they shall be called children of God" (Matthew 5:9), where the sermon writer speaks with what seems straightforward Lollard sympathy:

> Here it is clear that simple Christians must not fear human reproach too much, even of the powerful of the world, and excommunications, however fearsomely they may be hurled forth in the words of their prelates, but rather bear them patiently where Christ is at issue, that is, where perverse men curse the simple because the latter defend or teach the gospel truth, or defend public justice or the common good. However, simple Christians should deeply grieve at the blindness of brothers (friars?) and prelates who in their blindness persecute Christ, that is, his truth or public justice. And they should the more humbly submit themselves to Christ, praying devoutly for their enemies who are blinded by the devil with pride, envy, or greed.

The sermon then continues with a careful and canonistic distinction between just and unjust excommunication, and counsels not to grumble against, but also not to fear the latter. Instead,

> Be fearful, however, of the vengeance that will fall on a blind prelate who excommunicates you unjustly, for perhaps they think they are doing God a service by spiritually killing the faithful for defending the gospel truth.[45]

All this is written in Dygon's hand. Yet in other passages the sermons show a clearly orthodox stand. Those for the saints, for instance, cover the whole spectrum of

---

[44] "Videtur ergo quod sancta vita et doctrina salutaris cum fideli implecione pastoralis officii, non eleccio humana seu litere sigillate constituunt quem fidelem curatum vel ydoneum prelatum," DY-20, f. 73, with "caue" in the margin.

[45] Following a quote from Chrysostom: "Hic patet quod simplices Christiani non debent nimium formidare opprobria hominum, eciam potentum seculi, et excommunicaciones quantumcumque horribiliter fulminatas verbis prelatorum, sed gaudenter tollerare vbi Christus est in causa, hoc est, vbi peruersi maledicunt simplices quia defendunt vel docent veritatem euangelicam, vel defendunt iusticiam publicam seu bonum commune. Debent tamen simplices vehementer dolere propter cecitatem fratrum et prelatorum qui ceci persecuntur Christum, quia veritatem eius seu iusticiam vulgarem, et tanto humilius submittent se Christo, deuotissime orando pro inimicis a diabolo superbia, inuidia, vel auaricia excecatis. . . Time tamen pro vindicta casura super cecum prelatum iniuste te excommunicantem, quia forsan arbitrantur obsequium se prestare Deo, interficiendo spiritualiter fideles pro defencione euangelice veritatis," DY-65, ff. 282, 283.

medieval saints and their worship; and sermon 51 affirms the traditional Church structure, from pope to parish priest.[46]

Even genuinely personal statements are not absent. In the sermon for Tuesday of Rogation Days "for peace" (DY-15), part three admonishes the audience not to trust in prayers devoid of devotion, which are invalid before God; and the writer confesses:

> I blush violently and am afraid in myself, for "my soul is weary of my life" [Job 10:1] because of the irreverent prayers I pour forth without devotion and love and attention to their meaning.[47]

The same passage also questions whether good church music "which is performed today" can be truly good if it detracts from prayers and devotion – though inspired by Augustine, the passage alludes to the present.[48] Finally, in dealing with St. Maurice, the writer quotes from the "Legenda sanctorum" and then adds: "In some old legend in the church of Adesham I have found far more plainly [?] what follows" and copies a page and a half from this *legenda antiqua*.[49] Another detail that brings the reader closer to the author's work of composition and writing than does any other collection I know are occasional references to the actual folios on which he had found his material:

---

[46] "Episcopi omnes catholici tenent locum et dignitatem apostolorum, secundum Gregorium, Ieronimum, Parisiensem et omnes doctores in hac materia loquentes. Inferiores sacerdotes, curati, et simplices sacerdotes tenent locum et dignitatem lxxii discipulorum Domini Iesu Christi, secundum Bedam et Glossam in Luce 10 et canones, XXI, distinccione *In nouo testamento*. Et quantum ad multas excellencias eciam infimi sacerdotes excedunt angelos bonos, vt patet in sermone precedente. Et hoc specialiter quantum ad dignitatem conficiendi eukaristiam, quantum ad potestatem ligandi et soluendi peccata, et quantum ad dignitatem martirii moriendo in caritate et paciencia pro fide catholica vel iusticia conseruanda," DY-51, f. 221v. The canonistic reference is to Gratian, *Decretum*, dist. 21, c. 1 (Friedberg 1:67).

[47] "Vehementer erubesco et timeo in me ipso, nam tedet animam meam vite mee propter irreuerentes preces quas fundo sine deuocione et caritate et sine aduertencia sentencie," DY-15, f. 51.

[48] "Videant ergo sapientes an subtilia dulciaque cantica hodie frequentata, que impediunt homines ab intelligencia scripture sacre et oracionum deuotarum et inducunt ad lasciuiam corporalem, edificent Ecclesiam sicut preces deuote et lacrime deberent. Et videant subtiliter an preferant minus bonum et postponant maius bonum," DY-15, f. 52, appparently not a quotation.

[49] "In quadam autem legenda antiqua in ecclesia de Adesham inueni longe planit [*sic*; planitus? planius?] in hunc modum," DY-58, f. 253v. "Adesham" must be Adisham in Kent. The preceding quote is from Jacobus de Voragine, *Legenda aurea*, pp. 628–630. Notice that there is another connection with Kent in the collection, the sermons for St. Mildred (DY-30 and 31), who was abbess at Minster-in-Thanet.

The Parisian [i.e., William of Auvergne], in his book *On the Sacraments*, in the treatise *On Confession*, on folio 90 of the entire book, writes as follows . . .[50]

One may ask whether the collection indeed belongs to the period with which we are concerned and, if so, whether the sermons were composed by Dygon himself. The former question can be confidently answered in the affirmative, since the collection cites Richard Rolle of Hampole at least four times. In three instances (ff. 17 and 251 twice) it quotes one or two sentences each from Rolle's commentary on the Psalms, and the quotations are fairly close to the text of the *Latin Psalter* as found in the fourteenth-century MS Lambeth 352. In the fourth instance, the sermon for the Exaltation of the Holy Cross, on the thema "I shall draw all things to myself," the preacher declares that God "also draws some with the sweetness of contemplation and prayer, such as Richard Hampole or the Hermit in our days, who excelled marvellously in these two."[51] It is as yet unclear at what time in Rolle's life the *Latin Psalter* was composed, but Rolle died in 1349, which would at least place these sermons within the century of our study. Furthermore, the use of *fratrifactor* – apparently a term coined by Wyclif[52] – and of similar terms and concerns mentioned earlier makes this work's composition after the 1370s more than likely. "Sweetness of contemplation" is of course very much a hallmark of Rolle's spirituality, as it would have been for a writer interested in the contemplative life. Dygon seems to have been very familiar with Rolle's work, since another of his manuscripts, Oxford, St. John's College, 77, which he gave to Exeter College, contains material from the English mystic.[53] It is therefore not improbable that the sermons in Magdalen 79 are Dygon's work.[54]

Taking all these factors into consideration, it would seem that this is essentially a systematic sermon cycle written with particular circumstances of delivery in

---

[50] "Parisiensis *De sacramentis* in tractatu *De confessione*, folio xc'mo tocius libri sic scribit . . . ," DY-34, f. 136v. A few lines later he says: "Idem in tractatu *De sacramento satisfaccionis* folio xcivi [*for* xcvi?] tocius libri" (136v); and, "Item in tractatu *De confessione* folio lxiii tocius libri Parisiensis sic scribit" (137).

[51] "Trahit eciam aliquos dulcedine contemplacionis et oracionis feruore, sicut Ricardum Hampul siue heremitam temporibus nostris, qui mirabiliter excellebat in hiis duobus," DY-48, f. 205.

[52] *Dictionary of Medieval Latin*, under "fratrifactor," gives only two loci for the word: Wyclif's *De apostasia* and *De blasphemia*. To these may be added *De religione privata* 2, in Wyclif, *Polemical Works* 2:526/10 and 527/1. Wyclif also uses *ordo Christianus*, as does the passage quoted above in note 39.

[53] *BRUO* 1:615–616.

[54] Cursory reading gives the impression that the text is relatively free of the usual scribal mistakes that occur in copying. However, I have found one instance of dittography, in a passage seemingly of the writer's own composition (f. 73).

mind. This is, finally, also revealed by occasional liturgical remarks made at beginning of sermons, among which the following is particularly interesting in that it further differentiates between writing and oral delivery:

> Since the vigil of the Assumption of the glorious Virgin often falls on a Sunday and then a sermon is customarily preached to the people in the vernacular, a short sermon ought to be written on the gospel of that vigil, by God's grace. In which three things are to be briefly developed.[55]

Whoever made these sermons deliberately poured relevant material from many sources into the mold of a sermon collection. If the author was not Dygon himself, the latter at least found the cycle worthy of copying.

One more manuscript should be considered in this connection, even if it was not written by Dygon but only belonged to him, bears his annotations, and was given by him to Magdalen College. MS 156, though called a "homiliary" by catalogers and recent students, is not at all a collection of homilies or sermons but an incomplete lecture series on the gospel readings for the feasts (not Sundays) of the Church year. The opening piece of the illuminated but heavily defaced book[56] is called "Prologus" by the rubricator, probably Dygon;[57] it forms in fact an opening lecture in which the speaker, presumably a new master of theology, eulogizes Scripture, here the gospels, and then announces that,

> in this lecture course (*lectura*), omitting superfluous elegant adornment, which I know nothing about, I intend first to divide the literal text into its units of meaning; second I will touch on other things that seem to me noteworthy; and third I will solve some other matters in the text that seem to be difficult. This mode and order I intend to continue according to my small skill to the end of this work.[58]

Before this, the speaker had paid a handsome compliment to "four reverend fathers present in this place and lecture" by likening them to the four evangelists

---

[55] "Quia Assumpcionis vigilia Virginis gloriose contingit frequenter in die dominica et tunc solet fieri sermo ad populum in vulgari, ideo de euangelio in vigilia ipsius, per Dei graciam scribendus est sermo breuis, in quo tria sunt breuiter perstringenda," DY-37, f. 150r–v. For another liturgical introduction of this kind see above, note 31.

[56] Alexander and Temple, *Illuminated Manuscripts*, no. 446, pp. 44–45.

[57] The running titles in the upper right corner of the rectos seem to be in Dygon's hand. The same hand also appears occasionally in marginalia, e.g. ff. 47v, 53.

[58] "In ista autem lectura vtrumque perficienda intendo omissis superfluis curiositatibus, de quibus nichil scio, primo vero [*or* volo] diuidere literam propter illa que sunt ibi sentencialia. Secundo volo tangere alia que michi videntur notabilia. Et tercio volo soluere quandoque alia que videntur in textu difficilia. Et istum modum et ordinem intendo continuare pro modulo mee paruitatis vsque in finem istius operis," f. 2vb. The immediately preceding text has apparently been excised.

and the four animals of Ezekiel 1:14, which was his thema. He actually mentions two of them by name with a pun, Bosworth and Arnaldus.[59]

The announced plan is faithfully carried out in the following seventeen pieces,[60] which are called "omelie," evidently so by the scribe.[61] They cover the feasts which have their "own gospel" from the vigil for St. Andrew to Good Friday.[62] The manuscript breaks off in the lengthy commentary on the Passion. In the individual pieces, the writer first divides the lection into significant parts. Next he takes up the text phrase by phrase and quotes a *notabile*, a noteworthy authoritative comment (often in fact several) for each. Finally, he goes through the text once more and reports or raises a number of *dubia*, questions about it, which again he answers by quoting other commentators. In both *notabilia* and *dubia* he adduces an astonishingly large number and variety of authorities. Major commentators on whom he relies are Bede, "sanctus" Thomas Aquinas, Nottingham, Nicholas of Lyra, Bertrand of Tours, Roger Bacon (whom he calls "inceptor"), Thomas Docking OFM, Januensis (i.e. Jacobus de Voragine), Peter John Olivi, and "quidam postillator" (hiding possibly more than one). Besides these, a host of other authorities occur with regularity, some quoted by the major commentators, others apparently gathered directly from the writer's own reading.[63]

---

[59] "Sed istud quoque pretereundum non puto quod quatuor animal mistica verbum Dei euangelizantes sunt quatuor reuerendi patres presentes in istis loco et lectura, vnde predecessores. Quorum vt pateat corespondencia ad quatuor animalia predicta, primus assimulatur leoni propter officii dignitatem. Secundus homini propter morum maturitatem socialem, et ideo vt alter Marcus [!, *for* Matheus] habet faciem quasi hominis propter virtutem mansuetudinis. Tercius assimulatur boui propter cognicionis conformitatem, cognominatur a boue Bosworth. Quartus assimulatur aquile propter vocalis conueniencie congruitatem; vocatur enim ab aquila Arnaldus. Et sic isti quatuor patres predicti instar quatuor animalium predictorum – tum propter sublimitatem fastii celsioris, tum propter soliditatem iudicii melioris, tum propter sanctitatem exercicii sanioris, tum propter subtilitatem ingenii alcioris – sunt diuinarum scripturarum misteriis multipliciter imbuti," f. 1vb. Arnaldus is likened to the eagle (St. John) because of Middle English *arn, ern* = "eagle." Such wordplay is common in academic sermons.

[60] The end of "homily" 6 and the beginning of 7 are wanting, due to missing leaves.

[61] At the head of the items and occasionally in the upper right-hand corner of the recto. The scribe was Thomas Colyngborne, who also wrote Magdalen College MS 154, dated AD 1448; see Parkes, *English Cursive*, p. 24 and plate 24(i).

[62] "Et ideo euangelia de principalibus festis Christi intendo tractare cum aliis euangeliis sanctorum aliorum," f. 15va. For "proprium euangelium" see ff. 8va, 13va.

[63] The quoted authorities, in alphabetical order, are: Adam de Marisco, Albertus, Albumazar, "Alchimus" (Alcuin?), Alexander Nequam, Alexander of Hales ("doctor primitiuus scilicet halys"), Alfarabius, Ambrose, Anselm, Aristotle, Athanasius, Augustine, Averroys, Avicenna, Bartholomaeus, Basil, Bernard of Clairvaux, Boethius, Bonaventura, Brito, canon law, Cassian, Cassiodorus, Chrysostom, Cicero ("Tullius"), Clemens, Clement of Llanthony, Council of Ephesus, Cyrillus, *De vita beate Virginis*, Dionysius, Eligius (*De mirabilibus mundi*), Fishacre

Though I cannot put a name to the writer, he clearly was a Franciscan, evidently learned though not necessarily a great thinker, and presumably a master of theology. He also left an interesting personal note. In commenting on the text "And Jesus walking by the sea of Galilee," etc. (Matthew 4:18), he raises the *dubium* whether Jesus walked shod or barefoot. The question may strike modern readers as a silly medieval conundrum, but of course it touched significantly on the whole controversy about the friars' claim that Christ was poor and that the mendicants' poverty is the highest state of perfection. Our anonymous writer reports:

> I have heard this question treated at greater length at Oxford when I was there as a student, from a certain modern doctor who is still alive and was very powerful in his ordinary lecture at our, that is Franciscan, place; whose name is Friar William Woodford. And this was question 28 in order on chapter 3 [!] of Matthew.[64]

("Fysceakyrensis"), FitzRalph ("Armachanus"), Franciscus de Mayronis, Fulgentius, Gameliel (titled "Venerandus"), Gervasius (*De ociis imperialibus*), Giles of Rome, *Glossa interlinearis*, *Glossa magistralis super Raymundum*, *Glossa ordinaria*, Gregorius Nazianzenus, Gregory the Great, Grosseteste ("Lincolniensis"), Haly ("commentator super *Centilogium Ptholomei*"), Heliandus, Higden ("Polichronicon," also "Cistrensis"), Hilarius, Hildefonsus, *Historia Alexandri magni*, *Historia tripartita*, Holcot ("Holcotes"), Hugh Brissyngham, Hugh of Saint Victor, Hugutius, Innocent III, Isidore, Jerome, Johannes Balbus ("Januensis," *Catholicon*), John Beleth, John Damascene, John of Abbeville, John of Wales ("Wallensis"), John Pecham (titled "Dominus Cantuariensis"), Josephus, *Legenda aurea*, *Legenda sanctorum*, Leo papa, *Liber de infancia Saluatoris*, *Liber de perfeccione spiritualis vite*, Liber qui intitulatur *Accenedon*, *Manipulus florum*, Marcius ("in cronica sua"), Martialis, Maximus, Mercurius ("in libro *De divinis*"), Origen, Orosius, Papias, Peter Auriol (*De conceptu virginali*), Peter Comestor ("Magister historiarum"), Peter Lombard ("Magister Sentenciarum"), Peter of Ravenna, Peter of Tarentaise, Philippus de Monte Kalerio, Plato, Pseudo-Boethius (*De disciplina scholarium*), Pythagoras, Rabanus, Raby Barathias, Raby Moyses, Raby Porcherius, Raby Salomon, Radulphus Ardens, Raymundus, Remigius, Richard of Mediavilla, Richard of St. Victor, Seneca, Severinus, Stanchawe, Suda ("Liber qui in greco vocatur S."), Theophilus, Thomas Ryngstede (titled "doctor," "episcopus Bangorensis"), Valerius, *Valerius ad Ruffinum*, *Vita beati Edmundi*, *Vita sancti Audoeni*, *Vita sancti Bertini abbatis*, *Vita sancti Eriaci*, *Vita sancti Olaui*, *Vitas Patrum*, William de Conchis, William de Montibus, William de Ware (titled "doctor"), William of Auvergne ("Parisiensis"), William of Auxerre ("Altissiodorensis"), William of Newburgh ("Neuburgensis in Cronica sua"), William Peraldus ("quidam auctor" without further identification), William Woodford.

[64] "Istam eciam questionem audiui tractari magis diffuse Oxon' quando eram ibi studens a quodam doctore moderno adhuc superstite satis valente in lectura sua ordinaria in loco nostro, scilicet minore, cuius nomen est Frater Willelmus Wodford, et fuit questio 28 in ordine super 3 capitulo Mathei," f. 6va. Dr. Jeremy Catto has kindly informed me that the cited *dubium* is from "Woodford's commentary on Matthew, actually Q.26 on chapter 3 (Cambridge UL MS Add 3571, fos 96ra–97rb)."

Woodford, also known as *Doctor fortissimus*, lectured on the Bible apparently in 1372–73 and died probably after the accession of Henry IV.[65] The quoted remark also suggests that its author did not write his commentary at Oxford.

Since this *lectura* breaks off at a point in the Church year before the sermons of Magdalen 79 begin, it is unfortunately not possible to tell whether the author of the latter, if it was Dygon, profited from the lectures in Magdalen 156. However, it is evident that John Dygon, before and during his enclosure at Sheen, was keenly interested in sermons. He studied and copied several cycles as well as individual sermons, and very probably composed a collection of his own.

[65] *BRUO* 3:2081–82; Catto, "Wyclif and Wycliffism," pp. 196–198.

19

Oxford, Magdalen College, MS 96 (CO)

One more unified collection originated about the middle of the fifteenth century, albeit an anonymous one. Magdalen College, MS 96, a fifteenth-century parchment codex,[1] contains in its entirety a curious sermon collection entitled *Tercia pars congestorum a festo pentecostes usque ad festum sancte Anne*[2] – the third volume of what must have been an entire cycle of mixed *de tempore* and *de sanctis* sermons named *Congesta*, of which the two preceding and the following parts are not known to have survived. On its 317 large folios the volume presents only twenty sermons, which cover the Sundays from Pentecost to the seventh Sunday after Trinity with some intervening ferial days[3] and saints' feasts[4] including Corpus Christi, all in correct liturgical order. The last sermon in this volume is for St. James, so that the feast of St. Anne mentioned in the title would have formed the beginning sermon of part 4 of *Congesta*. The occasions for the individual pieces are clearly marked, and the pieces are consistently called *sermones*, both in the rubrics and internally.

The word *Congesta* for a book-title is rather unusual, and if for a modern reader the notion of congestion has unpleasant connotations, this collection fully lives up to them. For one thing, the sermons are exceptionally long: the shortest here covers forty-five, the longest over ninety-seven tightly written columns of fairly large size.[5] This exceeds by far the longest sermons found elsewhere, and it

---

[1] Coxe, vol. 2, Magdalene College, p. 52. Folio size 350 × 260, written space 265 × 177+. Written in one clear and set Secretary hand with occasional long r's and two-compartment a's. The volume bears a medieval foliation. A decorated initial, color and gold, at the beginning of the first sermon; flourished initials (3–4 lines high) at beginning of prothemes and main parts.

[2] "Finitur tercia pars congestorum a festo pentecostes usque ad festum sancte Anne," f. 317b, in red, copying the scribal note in brown in bottom margin right corner.

[3] Monday through Wednesday after Pentecost. One sermon, CO-15, is for the "festum reliquiarum" and stands, with a sermon for the feast of St. Thomas (translation, July 7), between 4 and 5 Trinity.

[4] In order: John the Baptist, Peter and Paul (with a separate sermon for each), Thomas, Mary Magdalene, and James.

[5] Sermons CO-1 (ff. 1ra–12rb) and 7 (ff. 86rb–110vb) respectively.

would at once establish the collection as a reading text far removed from actual preaching. In addition, the unknown author has "thrown together" an abundance of material copied from a multitude of acknowledged sources. The material hangs together more or less notionally, but its collector does not make it easy to follow. Although he demonstrably had a thema in mind for all his sermons, and one that furnishes key words and notions for the protheme as well as the development, the thema is not always announced at the beginning of the sermon, and once or twice it is not even stated at the start of the sermon's main part. Moreover, while he generally follows the scholastic practice of dividing a topic and then developing its parts in numerical order, he does not begin with a division that announces all the parts to follow. Instead, he will, as for instance in his sermon on St. Paul dealing with the thema "He is to me a vessel of election" (Acts 9:15), say that a vessel must have four conditions, all of which could be found in St. Paul: "First, it must be clean; thus was the Apostle Paul . . ." (f. 194rb). But instead of learning at once what all four conditions are – as is customary in normal scholastic sermons – we have to wade through nearly five columns and many quotations to eventually and abruptly come across the next item: "Second it must be firm and solid through patience in tribulation" (f. 195va).[6] Add to this that in explaining a biblical phrase he often cites more than one author (with "vel sic"), and that very often his lengthy quotations lead him off the topic in directions that he cannot always resist following or else which force him to repeat points already made, and the result is a text that requires from its readers long and concentrated attention.

One may in fact doubt whether this is a collection of *sermons* at all. Yet all pieces are thus labeled, and in several of them occur such remarks as "in the epistle of this Sunday mention is made of . . ." or "after dealing with 'vessel' in four parts it remains to continue the sermon about 'election'," remarks that are typical of a preaching context.[7] Moreover, despite their length and poor streamlining, all

---

[6] "In verbis thematis tripliciter commendatur Apostolus: tangitur primo status eius penes conuersionem, ibi 'vas.' In vase requiruntur quatuor, que in ipso fuerunt. Primo quod sit mundum. Sic fuit apostolus Paulus . . . / Vnde Seneca in *Prouerbiis*: 'Auarus nisi cum moritur nichil recte facit.' Hec ille. Secundo quod sit firmum et solidum per pacienciam in tribulacione," CO-12, ff. 194rb–195va. Notice that after dealing with the four conditions of a vessel, the writer turns to "election," specifically "seven circumstances that exclude people from divine election" for the remainder of the sermon (ff. 197ra–203ra), and it is thus not clear what the third point in praise of the Apostle is ("tripliciter"). Further, the "Hec ille" may, as so often in this sermon, close not the Seneca quote but a longer, not clearly attributed excerpt.

[7] "Fit mencio in epistula presentis dominice de mundo humano generi inimico cum dicitur 'Nolite mirari . . .' [1 John 3:13]," CO-8, f. 110vb (similarly CO-17, f. 263rb; both in sermons on the gospel); "Pertracto de vase sub quadrifaria diuisione superest sermonem prorogare de eleccione," CO-12, f. 197ra.

pieces begin with a protheme that leads to an invitation to pray (often specifying an "Our Father" and the "Hail Mary"), followed by the main part with its long development, and ending with a closing formula. The address "Karissimi" occurs here and there, though not consistently.

The sermons' main parts reveal another peculiarity of the collection as a whole. A number of them furnish a sequential exposition of the day's lection, either from the gospel (CO-7, 8, 11, 13, 16, 17, 20) or from the epistle (9), and in doing so are very reminiscent of the ancient homily structure or the *postillatio* that we found earlier in Repingdon's cycle. But the anonymous author's aim is not to furnish homilies on the lection consistently, as was Repingdon's. While CO-18 begins by explaining the gospel of the multiplication of the loaves briefly (Mark 8:1–9), it then concentrates on seven kinds of bread, which are treated at length. Such enumerative amplification of a single term of the thema becomes the major form of development when the sermon's main part is entirely devoted to discussing the fifteen signs before the Last Judgment, eight feasts of the Jews, the twelve months of the year, sixteen *commendationes* of John the Baptist, twelve blessings of Thomas Becket (from Genesis 27:27–29), eight kinds of relics, or the seven Marys mentioned in Scripture.[8] With regard to its structure, between such amplification of a single term and the exegesis of the entire lection stands the Pentecost sermon, CO-1, whose main part announces that "today's sermon follows the sacred hymn 'Come, Holy Ghost'"[9] and then takes up the phrases of the hymn sequentially, thereby discussing the names and working of the Holy Spirit.

The work is clearly of English provenance, as the sermons contain a number of English words and phrases, not only in glosses, divisions, and proverbs but also in small genuinely macaronic structures.[10] Though I have not found any address form other than an occasional *Karissimi*, the sermons must have been directed to a clerical audience, for their compiler everywhere throughout the collection, in prothemes and main parts, addresses matters of priestly morals and the pastoral office, and he often does so in an academic manner. The most revealing sermon in this respect is CO-6, on Corpus Christi, which not only discusses the worthy reception of the sacrament from the celebrant's point of

---

[8] The sermons and the respective key terms are: 4 (*prodigia*), 5 (*dies Domini*), 6 (*mensis*), 10 (*Iohannes*, at Luke 1:60), 14 (*benedictionibus*), 15 (*reliquiae*), and 19 (*Maria*); see the themata listed in the inventory. The eight kinds of relics include not only bodies of saints but also the Eucharist and holy water, the word of Christ, peace, almsgiving, the name of Christ, etc.

[9] "Sermo presentis diei stabit in processu sacri ympni Veni creator spiritus," CO-1, f. 3vb.

[10] For instance: "Sed sicut bras et tyn nunquam bene sonant," CO-7, f. 86vb; or "Sicut enim piscator ponit bayte super hoke," CO-16, f. 260rb.

view but also takes up such topics as daily celebration of Mass and the nature of the Eucharist. The sermon quotes Wyclif and several of his opponents, together with the Council of Basel's discussion regarding the Eucharist.[11] This would put the date of composition beyond 1431 at least.[12]

The quotations form the collection's most interesting feature. Not only do they cover an unusually wide variety of authors, ranging from Aristotle to Francis Petrarch, but they include a number of important thirteenth- and fourteenth-century authorities that have few or no parallels in the other sermon collections here surveyed. In his exegesis the compiler relies very heavily on Hugh of St. Cher (consistently called "Hugo de Vienna"), Odo of Cheriton, Gorran, and Nicholas of Lyra, with some extracts from "Januensis," John of Abbéville, Nottingham, and the *Aurora* by Peter of Riga. With the Schoolmen Aquinas, Albertus Magnus, and Bonaventure come Henry of Ghent and Duns Scotus.[13] Of the major English theologians, Grosseteste and Holcot[14] appear frequently, as do more occasionally Alexander Nequam, FitzRalph, John of Wales, Walter Burley, Lathbury on Lamentations, and the rare William Wheatley on Boethius. The sermon for Corpus Christi (CO-6) counters the Lollards and especially Wyclif[15] on their views concerning the Eucharist and image worship and quotes a number of near contemporary English authors: Woodford, Dymmok, and Thomas Netter (here called "Walden"). Literally next to such theologians appear several late-medieval "classics" of the spiritual life: the *Stimulus amoris*,[16] the *Speculum spiritualium*, and especially St. Bridget's *Book of Revelations*, from which the author often copied individual visions and conversations at length.[17]

---

[11] "Ista que secuntur erant attitata in Consilio Basiliensi: Sciendum est quod sicut in scienciis naturalibus oportet fieri reduccionem [!] ad principia que per priora probari non possunt sed sunt indemonstrabilia et per se vera . . . ita in doctrina et sciencia fidei, que supernaturalis est, sunt quedam principia demonstratiua et persone [*read* per se] nota in lumine fidei que per alia se non probant, sed omnia alia que in doctrina theologie traduntur habent noticiam et manifestacionem per ipsam," CO-6, f. 77vb. *Attitata*, i.e. *actitata*, may refer to the council's procedures or transactions. The Council is mentioned again on f. 82vb: "Hoc in actu edito et in Consilio Basiliensi."

[12] Strictly speaking, the Council of Basel ended in 1438 and subsequently (1438–1449) moved to other locations.

[13] There are, further, citations of Durandus de Sancto Porciano, Peter Aureolis (both f. 69rb), apparently Franciscus de Meyronnes (f. 70va), and a "Johannes de Riuo Forti" (f. 14ra).

[14] Preponderantly his sermons, though the commentary on Wisdom is also quoted now and then.

[15] His name is usually abbreviated to "Wff."

[16] Citing book and chapter, hence what has been called the "Stimulus amoris maior."

[17] Again with identification of book and chapter.

If not all, at least the majority of these sources could be found in the library of Syon Abbey, including the classics on the spiritual life as well as the major biblical exegetes, theologians, and sermon cycles just mentioned.[18] Quite specifically, a volume left by John Pynchebek to the Syon library contained the works by Petrarch and Gerson that are quoted in CO-6.[19] If one adds to this information the fact that the sermons in CO are constantly concerned with priestly morals and the duty of preaching, the collection, though anonymous, points very strongly to a group of academic theologians of the mid-fifteenth century and later, many of whom, after holding important positions in the Church and the universities, joined Syon or a charterhouse. Some of them even engaged in such compilating work as one finds in CO.[20] Though anonymous, the collection may well have originated in this milieu, which included men like Pynchebek, John Dygon, and Thomas Gascoigne.[21]

[18] *Syon Abbey.* On the preaching by the priests attached to Syon Abbey, and the evidence for sermon literature in the abbey's library, see also Powell, "Preaching at Syon Abbey." It is interesting to note that the "sole English sermon extant indisputably attributed to a Syon brother" shares the abnormal length of the sermons in the *Congesta* (Powell, p. 233).

[19] *Syon Abbey*, pp. 281–282. Pynchebek held a D.Th. from Cambridge (by 1456) and served as rector in London, entering the London Charterhouse in 1459, then becoming a brother of Syon Monastery, and finally entering a Franciscan convent; see *BRUC*, p. 466.

[20] Typical is Gascoigne's collection of theological subjects in an alphabetical encyclopedia; see *Syon Abbey*, p. xliv, n. 39. Gascoigne says he had worked in the Syon library.

[21] See Catto, "Theology after Wycliffism," pp. 274–275.

20

Oxford, Balliol College, MS 149 (S)

As one turns from such unified sermon collections as Waldeby's or Brinton's or Dygon's to the miscellaneous one of MS Balliol College 149, one enters a different world. This impression begins at the visual level. The volume is made up of two booklets, both of the fourteenth century.[1] The first, with which alone we are concerned here (S, ff. 1–92v), contains twenty-three sermons.[2] These are written in two different hands that change in the middle of a gathering: a fourteenth-century Anglicana text hand, used by someone who apparently tried to imitate a gothic textura and who begins his sermons with rather homespun enlarged and flourished capitals, yields on f. 75v to a more regular Secretary hand (possibly even two) of the same period, which wrote two sermons running to f. 84 (with a renvoi back to f. 77). Evidently the second scribe was also responsible for many annotations throughout the booklet and for the corrections made in the sermons written by the first hand, which at times are quite heavy. Other codicological features draw similar attention. At the time of binding, two bifolia got exchanged (the fourth bifolium in gatherings 4 and 5), and the error was noticed by a fifteenth-century annotator. Some text is missing and is said to be found "in papiro," which is now lost. One sermon exists in two different versions. The flow of sermons is interrupted by an incomplete copy of Uhtred of Boldon's *Contra querelas fratrum*, in which the learned Benedictine monk from Durham held and defended a number of articles against the mendicants (cf. f. 64). Curiously enough, this antifraternal treatise is preceded by a sermon by a named Franciscan preacher. The last sermon in the booklet is followed by a complete treatise on the Decalogue. The manuscript itself, then, is a miscellany.

Uhtred of Boldon's treatise is followed, without break, by two pages of unrelated material, including memory verses and similar pastoral matter, notes on

---

[1] Mynors, *Catalogue . . . Balliol College, Oxford*, pp. 130–135.
[2] S-24 appears in the second booklet.

several historical events between 1361 and 1381, the name of John Richesdale, rector of Rodmarton (Glos.), and what seem to be two disconnected sermon notes. These were apparently copied without much discrimination from an exemplar in which Richesdale had left such notes.[3] It would thus appear that the entire booklet (ff. 1–92v) reflects the results of collecting a number of complete sermons that were deemed worth gathering, and beyond that it gives evidence that some of the texts were worked over. The latter is visibly shown by the corrections and annotation of several pieces, as well as the fact that a passage in sermon 1 is attributed to a named master whose quoted work appears later as sermon 20.[4] Whether the original collector was John Richesdale cannot be ascertained at this point. Since a number of the sermons are addressed to the clergy – as shown by the address forms they use, by such internal references as "nobis religiosis . . . nobis curatis et rectoribus Ecclesie Dei,"[5] and by their dealing with the priestly office in their prothemes –, and since they contain several references to "this university"[6] and to aspects of university study[7] including Uhtred's treatise which was drawn up at the university, their most likely place of origin is Oxford.

Of the twenty-three sermons, those that indicate their occasions are for major feast days of the Church year; however, they follow no particular recognizable order. The collection contains the names of two preachers. One is a Franciscan, "Iohannes de Scrata," who seems to be otherwise unknown (S-15); the other is a Master Chambron, whose work will be discussed in the following section. One Chambron sermon here, *Quare rubrum est idumentum tuum*, also occurs in several other manuscripts. Besides this, MS Balliol 149 contains several more sermons that also occur elsewhere. Among them are two remarkable Good-Friday sermons, which stand out by their length as well as the devotional tone with which they follow Christ's Passion. These are *Christus passus est vobis relinquens exemplum vt sequamini* – which may also be by Chambron –[8] and *Amore langueo*,[9] each extant in four copies altogether. Further sermons that Balliol shares with other collections are four pieces also extant in collection W (including the *Christus*

---

[3] See Mynors, *Catalogue . . . Balliol College*, p. 133.

[4] See the discussion of Chambron in the following section.

[5] Both in S-11, f. 49b.   [6] S-16.

[7] "Necesse est igitur michi facere secundum consuetudinem vsitatam in scolis theologorum, vbi responsales antequam respondeant ad questionem propositam solent invocare graciam Dei," S-19, f. 78; "sicut facit responsalis in scolis theologorum," S-20, f. 84v.

[8] S-1: also H-25, Z-19, and W-6.

[9] S-7, also in B/2-12, T-7, and Dublin, Trinity College, MS 277. Critically edited from S with translation in Wenzel, *Macaronic*, appendix B, pp. 212–267.

passus est already mentioned),[10] one that recurs in B and E,[11] and another in X.[12] Together with other features already discussed, such inclusion of shared material makes the sermons in Balliol 149 what I have labeled a "miscellaneous" collection.

Another differentiating feature of the Balliol sermons resides in their style and tone. Next to exclusively Latin sermons occur several that are fully macaronic, including two of the Good-Friday sermons, while yet others use English for their divisions as well as for non-structural phrases. They also vary considerably in length, ranging from less than three to as many as nearly thirty manuscript pages.[13] In contrast to the consistently devotional focus of Waldeby and the occasionally heavy social critique of Brinton, they show a certain sprightliness together with an occasionally strong academic flavor. Consider this opener:

> Dearly beloved, I find that nowadays three things are loved by many people: short skirts, short masses, and short sermons. It is their shortness that is loved, rather than their nature, for if they were loved for their nature, they would be loved no matter whether they are short or long. But this is not the case; so, they are loved because of their shortness. Now, it is fitting and useful to any preacher to adapt himself to his audience that he may be more profitable to them, after the good example of the great preacher Paul, who said of himself, "I have become all things for all persons, so that I may be profitable to all" [cf. 1 Corinthians 9:22]. And thus I will give you a short sermon inasmuch as I can.[14]

Of course the qualifier *quantum potero*, "inasmuch as I can," means exactly what it says, and so the anonymous preacher launches into a very long discourse, in which he demonstrates that in order to lead to eternal life, the word of God will have to be listened to for a while.[15] This academic, logical aura, as already evinced in the second sentence quoted above, also shows in the sermon's widely

---

[10] S-3: also in W-7; S-6: also in W copied as 10 and 32; S-16: also in W copied as 9 and 31. In all cases the versions show no more than individual scribal variation. On the whole, the copies in S are better than those in W, although both may have their individual errors including eyeskips.

[11] S-4: also B/2-57 and E-12. On the basis of eyeskips and other scribal errors, B and E stand against S, which has its own different eyeskips.

[12] S-11: also in X-5.   [13] S-10 (called "breuissima collacio") and S-1.

[14] "Karissimi, inuenio quod tria modernis temporibus diliguntur a multis, videlicet breues panni, breues misse, breues sermones. Et plus propter breuitatem quam rem in se. Quia si propter se diligerentur tunc vtrum essent breues aut longe diligerentur. Set nunc non est ita; ergo propter breuitatem diliguntur. Sed quia oportet predicatorem quemlibet \et/ expedit se conformare auditorio vt eos melius lucretur, ad bonum exemplum egregii predicatoris Pauli, qui de seipso dicit, 'Omnibus omnis sum factus vt omnes lucrifacerem,' et ideo quantum potero abbreuiabo sermonem." S-16, f. 65v. The copies of this sermon in S-16 and W-9 clearly read "panni"; W-31 has "penitencie."

[15] "Requirit tempus et moram non minus breuem," f. 66v.

argumentative style, when the preacher offers repeated syllogisms or draws distinctions, including whether it is legitimate to love a woman who is beautiful to look at (it is when done for the right reason).

While some of these stylistic features would argue for a popular milieu, others – such as their logical, argumentative tone that has just been mentioned – speak with equal strength for a clerical, even academic audience. Sir Roger Mynors described several of them as "addressed to 'predicatores'," presumably because they discuss features of preaching in their prothemes. Indeed, three sermons are explicitly addressed to *Reuerendi* (4, 13, 15), but two of these (4, 13) also contain addresses to *Karissimi*, and the latter address form occurs in a total of eight sermons in the collection. That some of these sermons intended a mixed audience is explicitly shown by S-2, given in Advent. Its protheme begins by explaining twice why the Son of God may be called "word." First the preacher constructs a simile between a human word and the Son of God: as a man's word is first conceived in his heart, second produced from his mouth, and third carried out in deed, so the Son of God was first thought in the heart of the Father, next made into speech through the prophets, and finally completed in deed in his incarnation. Then the preacher offers a second explanation "for the understanding of lay people" (*ad intelligenciam laycorum*), in which the Son of God is like a word for three reasons: a man's word passes outside yet remains inside; what is inside is taken outside; and a word is proper to humans and no other creature. It is hard to see how the second explanation could be more appropriate to, presumably, less intelligent layfolk than the first, especially since it relies on quotations from Scripture, Aristotle, Augustine, Seneca, Anselm, and Hugh of St. Victor. The difference between the two explanations seems to lie in that the first is based on theology and salvation history, whereas the second derives from everyday experience.

Lollards are not mentioned in this collection, but at least one sermon (S-16) discusses the need to confess one's sins to the ordained priest, giving orthodox answers to the objections why one should tell one's sins to a human being since God knows them already, and why one needs to confess at all since sorrow for one's sins is all that is needed.[16] An Easter sermon (S-9) similarly brings up and replies to questions concerning the Eucharist, in a manner that is clearly orthodox though not explicitly directed against Lollards.

[16] F. 71v.

21

Henry Chambron

The name of this Oxford Franciscan, of whom very little is known (but see below), is connected with six sermons that have been preserved in several manuscripts in a complicated relationship:

> *Christus passus est vobis relinquens exemplum* (?),
> *Corruit in platea veritas,*
> *Mundus crucifixus est,*
> *Percussa est tertia pars,*
> *Quare rubrum est indumentum tuum,*
> *Revertar in domum meam unde exivi* (?).

As already mentioned, MS Balliol 149 contains two sermons that are marginally ascribed in the text hand to "Chambron." The first is *Quare rubrum est indumentum tuum?* (Isaiah 63:2; S-20) with the rubric "Sermo chambron in die parasch" (f. 84). It is a long, complex sermon on Good Friday[1] and, judging by its relatively wide attestation in our period, evidently enjoyed great popularity. It also has a baffling textual history, for the Balliol manuscript itself contains a second version of it, S-19, which includes all of S-20, though with some important differences, and then adds a further development of the same thema, with a new division. This could of course mean that in S-19 the version of S-20 was expanded, or that perhaps a different sermon on the same thema was erroneously linked to the existing text of S-20. But there are several reasons to believe that, conversely, the shorter form S-20 is a redaction of the longer, more sprawling S-19, the most immediate being that in the Balliol manuscript the text of S-20 has been visibly corrected in light of S-19. But whatever the relation between the two versions might be, both have been preserved in multiple copies. A second copy of the shorter version S-20 appears in Padua, Biblioteca Antoniana, MS 515 (see below).

---

[1] It begins "Secundum sentenciam doctorum hec fuit questio angelorum" and ends "vt sui essemus et cum eo in perpetuum re[ma]neremus. Quod nobis concedat, etc. Amen."

The longer version, S-19, has similarly been preserved in four other collections: A-35; Z-20; P2-71; and Cambridge, University Library, MS Ee.6.27.[2] Thus, in one form or the other, Chambron's sermon *Quare rubrum* exists in seven known copies.

The second sermon that in Balliol 149 bears Chambron's name is *Revertar in domum meam unde exivi* (Luke 11:24), with the rubric "Sermo Chābron dominica 3 quadragesime" (S-23, f. 90), on which more needs to be said below. Chambron's name appears yet a third time in the Balliol manuscript. Sermon S-1, on *Christus passus est vobis relinquens exemplum vt sequamini* (1 Peter 2:21), asks in its development why God the Father struck his son in whom there was no guilt – why he struck God instead of man, his son instead of the slave, his friend instead of his enemy, heaven instead of earth, and the sun instead of the moon. In answer the preacher says: "Here God the Father can reply according to the imagination of that devout doctor who is called Chambernon."[3] The passage referred to occurs verbatim in *Quare rubrum* (S-20/S-19), which, as we have seen, is ascribed to Chambron.[4] *Christus passus est*, also a Good-Friday sermon, exists likewise in several other collections: H-25; Z-19; W-6; and Oxford, Christ Church MS 91 (ff. 122ra–132ra), thus bringing the number of known copies to five.

Another manuscript that ascribes sermons to Chambron is Padua, Biblioteca Antoniana, MS 515.[5] This is a curious parallel to the Dominican collection D, not only in that it has ended up in a non-English library but in that it preserves sermons by named fourteenth-century English theologians. The parchment codex

---

[2] The *initium* of S-19 is the same as that of S-20: "Secundum sentenciam doctorum hec fuit questio angelorum"; it ends incomplete with "manet vsque hodie sigillum infixum plaga lateris." The other four copies have the same initium. Of these, P2-71 and CUL Ee.6.27 are incomplete and break off long before the end of S-19. A-35 breaks off one word beyond S-19. Z-20 is the only version that ends with a closing formula ("in premii accepcione. Quod premium nobis concedat Iesus Christus, qui nos hodie redimebat. Amen, etc."), but its text, after the break-off point in S-19, does not continue the announced division. Notice that like the S-19 version, a different sermon in the same collection, S-16, has a similar shift in the development of the main division, after a long protheme and introduction.

[3] "Sed quare percussit eum pater suus, ex quo non potuit esse culpa in eo? Que racio exigit percutere deum pro homine, filium pro seruo, amicum pro inimico, celum pro terra, solem pro luna? Hic secundum ymaginacionem huius deuote [!] doctoris qui vocatur chamb*er*non potest respondere deus pater . . . ," f. 6v. Similarly in all other copies of *Christus passus est*, with the following spelling variants: Chamberon' (Christ Church MS 91, f. 126rb), Chauymon (W-6, f. 21v), chab'non (H-25, f. 88v), and Chamborn (Z-19, f. 55vb).

[4] In the longer version, S-19, ff. 78v–79. In the shorter version, S-20, the passage is present in a rather garbled form (f. 84v); thus also in Padua-48. The passage also appears in the sermon *Percussa est tertia pars solis*, see below.

[5] The manuscript has been brought to my attention by Tachau, who discusses it with a brief description in "Looking Gravely," pp. 342–345. Unfortunately, Tachau's account of this interesting collection is riddled with errors.

is written in a number of fourteenth-century hands, but in contrast to collection D all hands here employ forms of the Anglicana script with its characteristic features, and many English words and phrases, usually divisions, put the English provenance of the manuscript beyond doubt. Its seventy-two sermons, mostly addressed to the clergy, form a random collection. Noteworthy is the presence of at least eight pieces by Holcot, whose name appears three times next to them.[6] Four other names are found in the margins as well. "Frysbi" is thus marked as the author of a *collatio* on the third book of Peter Lombard's *Sentences*. This piece, an academic *principium*, is the second of four successive sermons or lectures (items 61–64) on the same thema, *Ubi spiritus Domini ibi libertas* ("Where there is the Lord's spirit, there is freedom," 2 Cor 3:17), of which the first (61) is labeled "Collacio finalis"[7] and the last (64), "Collacio in secundum librum Sentenciarum." It stands to reason that all four are by the same author. The title with Frysbi's name further tells us that this *collatio* comes as "reportacio Brok'." Another name outside the sermon texts is "Johannes Erduslowe," following the closing "Amen" of sermon 22. The fourth name is that of Chambron, which appears next to three consecutive sermons (48–50).[8] Based on the presence of Holcot material in the collection, Tachau assumed that the other named authors were Dominicans also and identified "Frysbi" with Ralph Frisby, "Johannes Erduslowe" with John de Erdesle, and "Chambr'" more tentatively with Robert de Chamberleyn. While the first two identifications may be correct,[9] there is some evidence that Chambron was a Franciscan (see below). The collection also contains other Franciscan traces: one sermon (57) praises St. Francis while criticizing failings in "nostra religione" (f. 115), and another (14) quotes Bonaventure (f. 29v), whose name appears several times in Chambron's sermons as well. Even though the Padua collection contains more material by Dominican authors than Tachau was able to identify,[10] the presence of Franciscan sermons in it may raise some doubt about considering the manuscript Dominican *tout court*.

---

[6] Holcot is named at sermons 43 (f. 78v), 47 (f. 81, "helcoth"), and 58 (f. 119). Other Holcot sermons, without his name, are 42, 59 (incomplete, complete in 68), 65, 69, and 70; see the inventory below. All can be found in Holcot's sermon collection in Cambridge, Peterhouse, MS 210.

[7] The closing lecture or speech for a university course. The lecturer praises his students' good academic behavior, introduces his successor (a Scotsman named Thomas), and warns his audience against the dangers of being idle during the coming vacation.

[8] *Quare rubrum est* (ff. 82v–87); *Mundus crucifixus est* (ff. 87–91); and *Percussa est tertia pars* (ff. 91–95), all three dealing with Christ's Passion.

[9] But notice that a (more famous) Franciscan Roger de Frisby and a secular priest by the same name lived in the 1380s, as did Chambron, though they were Cambridge men; see *BRUC* 244–245.

[10] At least five sermons by Jacobus de Losanna (30, 34, 36, 37, 38) and a highly abbreviated version of William Peraldus's second sermon for 4 Lent (45).

Two of Chambron's sermons in the Padua manuscript have also been preserved elsewhere, though without ascription. MS Bodley 859 is a compound manuscript made up of at least six booklets written by various hands in the fourteenth and fifteenth centuries.[11] One of these, booklet B (ff. 44–225v), preserves the only known copy of Bromyard's *Distinctiones*, with a note that it was written in 1409 (or 1410).[12] Booklet D (ff. 296–310) contains nine sermons for the feast of Mary's Purification (some are incomplete). Items 3–9, the core of these, are written in a quasi-humanistic hand and include at least two by Pope John XXII (items 7–8). Items 1–2, in contrast, are written in an ugly small cursive hand, which appears again on f. 310 with, apparently, the end of the second sermon. The following booklet, E, in two or three different Anglicana scripts (ff. 311–331),[13] contains another six sermons, which include *Percussa est tertia pars* (ff. 314v–319v, 322–325v) and *Mundus crucifixus est* (ff. 326–328v, 313–314, with renvois), both as we have seen also in the Padua manuscript. On f. 331v, a sewn-in leaf, appears a late-medieval list of seventeen sermon themata, of which only the first four are found in booklet E.

Curiously, the two sermons shared by Padua and Bodley 859 represent two different redactions: Bodley 859 has both sermons in a long form, Padua in a short one. The long forms in Bodley 859 are sprawling, interminable, and yet evidently incomplete; every time the reader thinks he has reached the end, the sermon writer takes up yet another topic and launches into a further development. As was noticed above, exactly the same differences distinguish the long and the short redaction of *Quare rubrum est*. As in that case, so it can be shown here, too, that the longer version appears to be the original one.[14] A comparison of all these sermons and their versions results in suggesting that Chambron wrote rather expansive and complex sermons and had some difficulty coming to an end; further, that his own work is preserved in the long forms of the three sermons; and finally, that the corresponding short forms are redactions, probably made by a different writer.

Yet another sermon bears Chambron's name, *Corruit in platea veritas* (Isaiah 59:14). This has all the marks of the sermons previously discussed: it deals with

---

[11] See *SC* 2:513–514, no. 2722.

[12] On this work see below, section 23 on manuscript CUL Kk.4.24 (B).

[13] The booklet was not written by "More," as the Bodley catalogue suggests. The word is *Mors* and notes a distinction on death in the sermon next to it (f. 311).

[14] The secondary nature of the short versions can be argued from the fact that the text is frequently garbled and meaningless (see above, note 4); that the long versions give correct source identifications; and that the short version of *Percussa*, in Padua, at one point (f. 94v, though this may be due to the scribe of the Padua manuscript) refers to a passage in *Quare rubrum* which the longer version of *Percussa*, in Bodley 859, uses in full (without reference to *Quare rubrum*).

Good Friday, it has many English elements, and it is confusing in structure and interminable in length. *Corruit* is extant in two collections which will be more fully discussed in later sections: Oxford, Trinity College, MS 42 (V-37) and Arras, Bibliothèque de la Ville, MS 254 (Z-1). The Trinity College version seems to have once been complete, but of the last folio the upper and lower thirds have been neatly cut out. At this point the preacher voices strong criticism of prelates who fail to preach true doctrine, and it is very likely that, while the sermon is hardly heterodox, this section might have offended pious ears later in the fifteenth century. In the Arras manuscript the sermon is acephalous and breaks off abruptly in mid-sentence with "Amen" at a point long before the Trinity version ends; it then adds: "Explicit sermo Magistri Henrici Chambron' predicatus Oxon' anno Domini MCCC82. Cuius anime, etc." (f. 4rb).

To this small detail about Chambron's date and place can be added some further information provided by yet another manuscript. Oxford, Christ Church MS 91 consists of at least two main parts, the first (ff. 1–194v) written in several fifteenth-century Secretary hands, the second (ff. 195–230v) in a late twelfth- or early thirteenth-century textura.[15] The first main part – which may have been put together from originally distinct booklets with medieval folio numbers – contains several discrete works, such as two pseudo-Augustinian treatises on visiting the sick; expositions of the Lord's Prayer, the Ave Maria, and the Creed (the latter two with references to Waldeby's similar treatises); and the entire temporal sermon cycle by Nicholas de Aquavilla (ff. 1–90v). In addition, it gathers excerpts from several other works: the *Vitas patrum*, the *Florarium Bartholomei*, Alexander Carpenter's *Destructorium viciorum*, and Holcot's commentary on the Book of Wisdom. This entire part, which has all the features of a notebook,[16] shows an academic hand at work that likes to identify the excerpts and provide them with topical indices. Many pieces from the lives of the Fathers, for instance, bear marginal annotations of a chronological nature or refer to other works about the same subject.

This part also contains a few scattered sermons. A group of seven numbered pieces (ff. 135–142ra) praise the Blessed Virgin and are written for the Saturdays of Lent and Easter Sunday; they come from Jacobus de Voragine's

[15] Kitchin, *Catalogus*, pp. 41–42. The second part collects copies of *De duodecim abusionibus*, here ascribed to Augustine; Innocent III's *De miseria condicionis humane*; several treatises by Augustine or else ascribed to him, on the dignity of human nature, lying, and penitence; and finally the *Derivationes* or *Panormia* by Osbern of Gloucester with its prologue that a medieval reader found "difficult to understand on account of the exotic words in which it is wrapped" (f. 222rb).

[16] For the difference between sermon collection and notebook see Wenzel, "Sermon Collections." Christ Church 91 is much like Oxford, Magdalen College, MS 93.

sermons for Lent. Other single sermons are devoted to the guardian angels (118va–121va), the feast of the Ascension (ff. 133ra–134ra), Palm Sunday (f. 193v, incomplete), and the Passion of Christ (ff. 122ra–132ra).[17] The last is the collection's most important piece for our purpose, because it is a copy of *Christus passus est*, and in this manuscript it comes with the following biographical note:

> Chambernowne quondam socius in Collegio Exon' et postea frater de ordine Minorum composuit et dixit hunc sermonem Oxon' et iacet apud Wttoun vnder haggie [*or* hoggie] et fuit ibi Oxon' in tempore Wodeford olim prioris sancti Johannis Exon'. ("Chambernowne, formerly a fellow of Exeter College and later a Franciscan friar, wrote and preached this sermon at Oxford. And he lies at Wotton under Edge [?]. And he was there, in Oxford, in the time of Wodeford, formerly prior of St. John's, Exeter.")[18]

The name Chambron/Chambernon was by no means uncommon, but Ralph Hanna has made a case that the biographical data here recited would fit the Henry Chambron who, as claimed in the Arras manuscript, preached a sermon at Oxford in 1382.[19] His being a Franciscan receives some, though admittedly not overwhelming, support from the fact that in one of his sermons he cites the example of St. Francis,[20] and that in *Percussa*, *Mundus*, and *Quare rubrum* he quotes Bonaventure by name and repeatedly.

But is *Christus passus est* really Chambron's work? The fact that in the body of this sermon Chambron is cited in the third person would argue against it. In addition, whereas the other sermons ascribed to Chambron make surprisingly little use of non-biblical quotations, *Christus passus est* uses them in much greater number and in a form that agrees more with run-of-the-mill sermons by authors other than Chambron. His authorship of *Christus passus est*, therefore, seems to me questionable. Such doubt receives support from the sermon on *Revertar in domum meam unde exivi*, which in S-23 is ascribed to Chambron. The text of S-23 is the same as sermon 65 in the temporal cycle ascribed to Robert Holcot in Cambridge, Peterhouse, MS 210 (ff. 96vb–99ra). A version of the same sermon,

---

[17] Ending with the "Charter of Christ" issued from the cross, to which two topically related texts have been added by a different and later hand, on the remainder of what is the last leaf of the quire. The first is a "Carta redempcionis humane" in verse (f. 132rb), which comes with a reference to book and chapter of *Fasciculus morum* where the gist of its contents can likewise be found. The second is a "Litera vel epistula Domino Iesu directa et dirigenda post eius ascensionem per modum oracionis anime suspirantis," also in verse (f. 132va).

[18] F. 122, top margin.

[19] Apparently Campus Arnoldi in Latin, a name that occurs in Exeter Cathedral records. I owe this information to Ralph Hanna.

[20] "Verus amor et feruens transformat amantem in similitudinem amati, vt patet in beato Francisco," in the long version of *Percussa*, MS Bodley 859, f. 319.

beginning at the division (i.e. lacking the introductory part) and containing the remaining text of Holcot and S-23, appears as Padua-70. While in this manuscript other sermons by Chambron are ascribed to him, this one is not. It would thus seem that Chambron was a well-known preacher whose name became easily attached to sermons of different origin. In that respect it should be mentioned that his name is also connected with a devotional treatise in English, preserved uniquely in a manuscript that belonged to the Oxford Franciscans.[21]

---

[21] Hereford, Cathedral Library, MS P.i.9, ff. 150v–151v; see Mynors and Thomson, *Catalogue . . . Hereford Cathedral*, p. 69.

22

Toulouse, Bibliothèque Municipale, MS 342 (D)

Like collection S, this Dominican manuscript, which has been carefully studied by Thomas Kaeppeli,[1] gathers a number of sermons by different authors who were connected with Oxford. The paper-and-parchment codex, which I believe is of the early fifteenth century, is written in one column by several hands, all of the Secretary type with different degrees of cursiveness but no Anglicana features. It contains ninety-one items, of which one occurs first incomplete and then, at the end of the collection, was copied complete with slight changes. The ninety sermons are *de tempore, de sanctis*, and for special occasions and stand in a random order. On the basis of changes in hand as well as blank folios, the volume seems to have been made up of several booklets. At the end of the first booklet, comprising four gatherings of sixteen, the scribe responsible for the catchwords wrote a table for the sermons in the entire volume, with folio numbers, listing them first in the order in which they occur in the manuscript (ff. 58–60v) and then (ff. 61–64) by their occasions ("ut decet ordinatorum"), where he gives first fifty-two temporal sermons by season (Advent through Trinity Sundays), next twenty-eight saints' sermons (which include Christmas and Easter), and finally four "sermones peregrini,"[2] two sermons "pro laude scripture" (i.e., academic *introitus*), and seven sermons "pro synodo."[3]

---

[1] Kaeppeli, "Sermonnaire." Before Fr. Kaeppeli's study the sermons were thought to be by Jean de Cardaillac; see Mollat, "Jean de Cardaillac," with a partial inventory of this manuscript at 118–121.

[2] Rather than denoting the name of the composer, "peregrini" may be an adjective indicating that these sermons could "wander about" in the liturgy. One (D-16) is labeled "pro accessu ad magnum dominum," two entries are for the repeated sermon 25/89, which discusses the Ten Commandments and whose thema "originaliter verumptamen non recitatur formaliter in aliquo euuangelio". The last, D-3, is on a thema which "recitatur in parte in epistula que legitur in quadragesima, scilicet feria quarta post dominicam terciam in quadragesima."

[3] 25 and 89, the two copies of the same sermon, are listed separately. 63 and 79 each are listed twice; see further below.

The most remarkable feature of this collection is that forty-one sermons are accompanied by preachers' names, and Fr. Kaeppeli has shown that these are all English theologians who were active from the 1330s to far into the second half of the century. In the order of their appearance in the volume they are:

William Bulwick: sermons 9–13, 58;
William Jordan (fl. 1350s and 60s): 16–22, 38–48, 53–56;
Henry (of Gloucester? fl. 1350s): 26;
John Languebeyrky: 27;
John Langley (fl. 1380s): 28–34;
John Segnew (fl. 1390s): 57, 70;
Holcot (died c. 1349): 59 (an academic *introitus*), 66.

The list shows that the sermons by named authors were not entirely copied *en bloc*; William Jordan's work, for instance, appears in three different booklets.

In listing these names I have given their suggested modern equivalents (except for "Languebeyrky," who remains unidentified). In the manuscript, the names, especially the less well-known ones, appear in several rather divergent forms. This would mean that the scribes were unfamiliar not only with the names but also with the English language. Fr. Kaeppeli speaks of the presence of eight different hands in the volume, two of which must have been of German and French origin respectively.[4] A third hand Kaeppeli thought was "without doubt that of an Englishman" who wrote the division for sermon 1 in the lower margin.[5] There are, however, many indications that all hands in the manuscript, including the first, belong to scribes who were unfamiliar with English. These include not only curious spellings of English words but equally curious reflexes in Latin spellings that must go back to an exemplar written in Anglicana. Clearly the English *w* and the long *r* gave the scribes some trouble.[6] That the original sermon makers themselves were English is shown beyond doubt by a number of English words

---

[4] Kaeppeli, "Sermonnaire," pp. 90–91.

[5] In the typical form: "In quibus ecce duo ostenduntur: Primo þat kepys in mynde thingis sere, quecumque scripta sunt; secundo þat makes vs syker suith [?] ovten were, ad nostram doctrinam" (f. 1). Written in the bottom margin, while in the text above, the line where it should appear has been erased. I assume that Kaeppeli thought that the hand of the insert is the same as that of the entire section, ff. 1–57, but there is room for some doubt that this is the case. Apart from the paleography, the insert itself shows that its scribe was not very familiar with English (cf. *suith ovten* for *with ovten*), and elsewhere in this section the name of an English preacher is rendered with great uncertainty.

[6] "Ewangelium" frequently appears as *evuangelium* (ff. 155, 173, 181v, 237); similarly the variant forms for Bulwick and *kyllkareby* for Kilwardby (170v). The name of Nicholas de Goran or Gorran here appears as *gosan*, the *s* evidently reproducing the Anglicana long *r* (f. 250).

and phrases throughout the manuscript, as well as such Latin calques as *permittere libros aliorum in pace* for "leave the books of others in peace."[7]

Various features establish that the collection and codex are of Dominican provenance, not least the presence of eight sermons in honor of St. Thomas Aquinas, including one for the feast of his translation (January 28), which was established in 1369.[8] The volume seems to have been written, at least in part, and put together in the fifteenth century. Apart from the hands and layout,[9] a curious passage speaks of the division in church and state because there are two popes, two emperors, and two kings each in France and Scotland. Kaeppeli wisely refrained from dating the passage more precisely than to the Great Schism.[10] But the passage continues with a reference to "the glorious victories and triumphs divinely granted to our lord king, through whom this country is nowadays honored everywhere in the world."[11] This sounds much like Henry V. Finally, in the table, sermon D-63, on *Docebat eos de regno Dei*, is listed twice: once as a temporal sermon for the Tuesday after the first Sunday in Lent,[12] and a second time as a saint's sermon in honor of Thomas Aquinas.[13] If this means that the two occasions fell on the same day, the year in question would have been 1346, 1419, or 1430. It thus seems that the collection, though containing earlier material, was put together not before the reign of Henry V. Sermons with address forms are about evenly divided between "Reverendi" (often with "patres" or "magistri") and "Karissimi," but the majority of the sermons if not all seem to have been destined for the clergy. One of the ninety sermons, D-20 for Easter, ascribed to William Jordan, also appears in collection E.[14]

---

[7] The passage is reproduced in Kaeppeli, "Sermonnaire," p. 107 n. 38.

[8] The table lists, among the saints' sermons, one for the translation of St. Thomas Aquinas and six "pro festo." In addition, D-90, on *Viam Dei in veritate doces*, is listed among the temporal sermons (for 23 Trinity), but it is exclusively in praise of St. Thomas. The maker of the table probably went by the sermon's thema, which indeed is from the gospel for 23 Trinity.

[9] Especially the habit of all scribes of writing the sermon thema in an enlarged textura, whereas the text is in Secretary script.

[10] Kaeppeli, "Sermonnaire," p. 109.

[11] "Orate pro pacis reformacione in Ecclesia. Vos videtis quod nunquam fuit magis necessarium quam est modo. Hodie namque vnitas Ecclesie per multos binarios est diuisa. Sunt duo pape, vnus realiter et alius [*canceled*] vocaliter. Sunt duo imperatores. Similiter duo reges Francie, duo reges Scocie. Et specialiter orate pro pace istius terre . . . Orate pro graciarum accione regraciando Deum toto corde pro gloriosis victoriis et triumphis concessis diuinitus domino nostro regi, per quem terra ista ubique per orbem hodie honoratur," D-69, f. 203.

[12] With marginal "et pro sancto Thomas de Aquino," f. 61v.

[13] As an insert between two lines; all by the same scribe.

[14] D-20 seems to be closer to the original.

I find no references to Lollard teaching or awareness of controversial topics in these sermons, which is a little surprising if my suggestion about the period in which the volume was put together is correct. There is no anti-Lollard stand on image worship in sermons 3, 82, and 89. But given the wide chronological spread of the sermons' composition, and the fact that they were apparently selected and certainly copied by Continental scribes, one can think of several explanations why this should be so.

23

Cambridge, University Library, MS Kk.4.24 (B)

This manuscript, of the early fifteenth century, presents a number of features that throw some light on how a sermon collection was made and actually utilized in the preaching in this period. I have examined these features in greater detail elsewhere, so that it will suffice here only to list them.[1] The volume contains two separate and very different series of sermons: a unique copy of the Dominican Bromyard's *Exhortationes* and a random collection of ninety-three sermons, perhaps of Franciscan origin. The two series were copied into this volume by a single hand and provided with an index, all of which would make this a "mixed" collection.[2] Other indications, especially in the numbering of quires and folios, allow us further to reconstruct the volume's genesis. In addition, a number of sermons are accompanied by marginal annotations, most of them erased but decipherable under ultraviolet light, that name some twenty villages and hamlets in south-western Bedfordshire and eastern Buckinghamshire, around modern Leighton Buzzard. These annotations evidently form a kind of record of the localities in which the respective sermons were preached, though in what years and by whom we do not know. That the sermons in the second collection are close to actual preaching is further shown in such remarks as, "I firmly believe that from the beginning of the year until now you have not had any preacher with such a blank soul as I am" or "You were more fully told of these things in Lent."[3]

Bromyard's literary output, to which the first of the two collections belongs (B/1), was produced before the period with which this book is concerned, but

---

[1] Wenzel, *Macaronic*, pp. 34–40. The sermons are listed ibid., pp. 140–156. Here I have separated the two sermon collections into B/1 (Bromyard, sermons 1–76) and B/2 and inventoried only the latter.

[2] In other words, Bromyard's *Exhortationes* forms a unified collection, by a known author; the second is a miscellaneous collection, with a number of pieces surviving in other, similar collections.

[3] "Vnde credo firmiter a principio anni vsque modo non habuistis aliquem predicatorem cum ita alba anima sicut ego sum," B/2-37, f. 193va ("alba anima," the preacher explains, means unlearned); "de quibus in quadragesima plenius informati fuistis," B-70, f. 264rb.

it is sufficiently important for preaching in England between 1350 and 1450 to merit some attention here. His life and work are still clouded by a good deal of uncertainty. For one thing, there were two fourteenth-century men by that name, both Dominicans and both of the Hereford convent. The younger John Bromyard studied at Oxford and eventually served as Chancellor of Cambridge University (1382) as well as prior of the Hereford convent (1391 and 1393); he was also a member of the Blackfriars Council in 1382. But it is his older namesake that we are here concerned with, who died before 1352.[4] This is the author of the great handbook for preachers, the *Summa praedicantium*, a lengthy alphabetical reference work on preaching topics larded with authoritative quotations, similes, *exempla*, and other illustrative material. Owst referred to him numerous times but confused him with his younger namesake. The older John Bromyard produced a second, equally large alphabetical reference work for preachers, which shares the *Summa*'s purpose of gathering material for use in the pulpit but in contrast draws on canon and civil law, as its medieval title declares: *Tractatus iuris ciuilis et canonici ad moralem materiam applicati secundum ordinem alphabeti.*[5] Both handbooks enjoyed much popularity, evidenced in the number of copies preserved and in quotations by English preachers in the later fourteenth and fifteenth centuries.[6]

In addition to these two encyclopedic handbooks for preachers, John Bromyard's name is linked to two extant sermon collections. One bears the contemporary title *Distincciones Magistri Johannis Bromyard* in the unique manscript, Oxford, Bodleian Library, MS Bodley 859, ff. 60–225v, written in 1409/10.[7] This is a series of 155 sermon outlines for all Sundays and feast days of the church year, in exact chronological order.[8] The title *Distinctiones* is quite accurate, because all the pieces begin by dividing their respective thema from the day's lection into four parts, which are then briefly developed with biblical and other authorities, similes, and occasional stories that are often homely and include references to contemporary Wales. All sermons bear indications of the occasion for which they were intended. These include 26 Trinity and the feast of the Crown of Thorns,[9] as

---

[4] For his dates, see Boyle, "Date." A survey of Bromyard's known writings has been given by Binkley, "John Bromyard."

[5] London, British Library, MS Royal 10.C.x, f. 9.

[6] For manuscripts see Kaeppeli, *Scriptores*, 2:392–94. For citations from the *Summa praedicantium* see below, note 11.

[7] "Finitur hec breuis compilacio in festo sancti Valentini, Anno Domini MCCCC nono," f. 225v. MS Bodley 859 was mentioned above in the section on Chambron, p. 135.

[8] Sermons for saints Stephen, John, Innocents, Thomas of Canterbury, and Silvester occur in both the temporal and saints' cycles; similarly, sermons for Christmas, Circumcision, Epiphany, and the Sunday after Epiphany appear in both cycles.

[9] "In festo corone Domini," f. 188v–189. For this feast in England see Pfaff, *New Liturgical Feasts*, pp. 91–97.

well as the feasts of major Franciscan and Dominican saints and of saints David, Chad, Cuthbert, Richard of Chichester, and Thomas of Hereford, whose cult has otherwise left few if any traces in the surviving sermon literature.[10] References to and quotations from these *Distincciones* appear in several collections studied here.[11]

Bromyard's other sermon collection is called *Exortationes fratris Johannis de Bromiard de ordine fratrum predicatorum*[12] and has, again, been preserved in only one known copy, the manuscript currently under discussion (CUL Kk.4.24, ff. 1–114va; collection B/1). It includes seventy-six numbered sermons *de tempore* and *de sanctis*, in the order of the Church year, which are followed by several indices. Their ascription to the older John Bromyard seems to be correct.[13] They are rather sparse in both structure and rhetorical texture, but were clearly intended as sermons for preaching, and in all likelihood served at least as base texts for preaching in the Midlands.

From Bromyard we turn to the sermon collection found in the second part of the same manuscript (ff. 121ra–301vb, collection B/2), which concerns us here more directly. This is a truly random collection: ninety-three sermons for Sundays and holy days, for saints' feasts, and for special occasions are mixed together without regard for their liturgical place; their structure shows much variation, and many remain incomplete, with blank spaces left where they break off; some are entirely in Latin, a few nearly entirely in English, and a good number in varying mixtures of the two languages; their audiences, apparently, are both clerical and lay; and although they all are anonymous, one can detect a strong Franciscan association, with one blatant exception in their midst, the anti-mendicant sermon that archbishop Richard FitzRalph gave at St. Paul's Cross on 26 February 1357 (FI-67).[14] The latter (B/2-82) occurs in a sequence of sermons for the first Sunday of Lent, and its presence here may mean no more than that the collector gathered sermons for a specific occasion from a variety of sources, including FitzRalph. Another source may have been the evidently Dominican collection that lies behind P1 (see above), whose sermon for the first Sunday of Lent (P1-27) appears

---

[10] MS Bodley 859 also contains a few sermons by Nicholas Orum, scattered in his lecture notes on Revelation; nine sermons for the Feast of the Purification, including several by Pope John XXII; and about half a dozen rather scrappy sermons of the later fifteenth century.

[11] See the section on Sheppey above, p. 29, and Part Three, chapter 46, pp. 322–324.

[12] F. 1ra, with flourished initial; similar explicit, f. 114va.

[13] For two references in sermon 48 to Bromyard's *Summa praedicantium*, and for other connections between the *Exhortationes* and the *Distinctiones*, see Wenzel, *Macaronic*, pp. 35–36 and n. 13.

[14] For supporting evidence for the points made in this paragraph and references, see *Macaronic*, pp. 37–39 and 148–156 (sermons B-77 to B-169). The FitzRalph sermon is briefly discussed in Walsh, *Fourteenth-Century Scholar*, p. 416.

here also, with slightly different opening words, as B/2-76. In addition to these two, at least four more sermons in B occur also in other collections.[15]

In spite of its overall randomness, the collection contains groups of sermons that, on some ground or another, show a certain unity, although in contrast to other collections they do not appear in separate booklets. Thus, the sermon by FitzRalph and the variant of P1 stand in a group of at least seventeen sermons for Lent that run in nearly entirely correct liturgical order (B/2-74 to 90). Before them, sermons 38–49 with two exceptions[16] are for Eastertide and deal repeatedly with the Easter Communion. Similarly, sermons B/2-52 to 54 are tied together through a number of cross references and shared material.[17] It would appear, therefore, that the collector copied his material in batches. He or the scribe was also aware of material he had copied earlier. This is shown rather neatly in B/2-69 where, in the middle of his text, he wrote: "Et nota in sermone *Elegit eam* ad tale signum +", with the numeral "149" added (evidently by the same hand) between the lines and in the margin (f. 262va). The sermon referred to is B/2-14, and the cross mark appears on the folio that bears the medieval foliation 149 (modern f. 154r).

The entire collection contains little to help us date it or its components. B/2-51 speaks of civil strife in England, of heavy taxation and wars; more specifically it then refers to "a general earthquake in England not many years ago," which could be the one of 1382.[18] What little social criticism these sermons contain echoes laments that were current in the later years of Richard II's reign or perhaps the early fifteenth century. They do not explicitly argue against Lollard teaching, but their orthodoxy seems assured by their insistence on confession and "right belief" as well as by their repeated retelling of eucharistic miracle stories.

---

[15] B/2-12 in D-2, S-7, and T-7 (the long Good-Friday sermon, edited in Wenzel, *Macaronic*, pp. 212–267); B/2-57 in S-4 and E-12; B/2-59 in H-22; and B/2-71 in O-32 and W-91.

[16] B/2-41 and 42. Both are in English and "de introduccione sentensie generalis," that is, the "great sentence" or excommunication, which was to be pronounced during the four Ember Days. Cf. Mirk, *Instructions*, ed. Kristensson, pp. 104–107.

[17] See Wenzel, *Macaronic*, pp. 39 n. 20. Further cross references occur in B/2-53 (to a sermon not in this manuscript) and B/2-85 (to 83).

[18] "Non sunt multi anni elapsi a tempore quo erat generalis terre motus per vniuersam Angliam" (B/2-51, f. 221vb). In addition, two sermons refer to a current pestilence: "Ista pestis iam regnans principaliter sit propter cupiditatem, sicut michi videtur" (B/2-8, f. 137rb); "in ista mortalitate" (B/2-54, f. 229va).

24

Cambridge, Jesus College, MS 13 (J)

This composite volume is made up of five different booklets, all of which contain sermons. They are as follows:[1]

(1) Quire A. Three folios extant. In two columns, written in an Anglicana bookhand of the first half of the fourteenth century. Two Marian sermons, J/1-1 and 2, the second ending incomplete.

(2) Quires B–F. Fifty-six folios extant. In two columns, written in an Anglicana hand much like (1) but more compressed laterally and with thinner strokes, becoming smaller later on. About 128 sermons *de sanctis* and *de tempore* in regular liturgical order, with medieval numbers 62–126 and 1–53.[2] I have inventoried them as J/2. The last saints sermon ends incomplete. All have the same format. Many *de sanctis* sermons correspond to the *Sermones de sanctis* of Bertrand de la Tour, OFM (died 1332).[3] Many *de tempore* sermons correspond to items in the Franciscan collection of Monte Cassino MS 213.[4] The two series are continuous, the second beginning on the verso of the same folio. They are followed by an alphabetical subject index for the *de sanctis* sermons, giving the sermon number and section (a–h). After the index, on the remaining verso and ultimate folio, a sermon has been added in one column and in a cursive fifteenth-century Anglicana hand; this is a visitation sermon on *Fratres tuos visitabis*, which also occurs elsewhere.[5]

---

[1] I follow the collation given by James, *Descriptive Catalogue . . . Jesus College*, pp. 11–12, with some necessary modifications.

[2] In several cases a numbered item is preceded by an unnumbered one, which presumably is intended as its protheme with a different text. I have inventoried these cases as separate sermons.

[3] See Schneyer 1:567–571.

[4] Cf. Schneyer 7:333–340. Jesus College, MS 13, however, seems to stand closer to whatever original lies behind these sermons.

[5] Aberdeen, University Library, MS 154, ff. 329–332, and X-309. Oxford, Merton College, MS 248, ff. 52rb–54va, gives several items on this thema that contain material similar to Jesus College 13.

(3) Quire G (medieval ff. 1–8). In two columns, written in an upright Angli-cana bookhand, different from (1) and (2), but apparently also first half of the fourteenth century. From here on a medieval hand has entered folio numbers. Four sermons, here inventoried as J/3; the last (*Ave Maria, gratia plena*) is incomplete in this manuscript but appears complete in V-40 and X-335.

(4) Quires H–I (medieval ff. 9–33). Same format and apparently same hand as (3), occasionally changing in quality. Thirty-five sermons, here invento-ried as J/4, forming a regular cycle for the Sundays from Advent through Pentecost. All have a peculiar structure which differs from those in (3) and elsewhere in this manuscript. They apparently correspond with anonymous Franciscan sermons in BN lat 18195[6] and in at least one instance use a thema according to the Franciscan use.[7] The first seventeen in this run also occur in collection X, where they are distributed in several different booklets (see below).

(5) Quires K–T (medieval ff. 34–[151]). In one column, written in a fifteenth-century Secretary (set cursive) hand. Forty-two sermons interspersed with prothemes and sermon notes, here inventoried as J/5 (ff. 34–149v).[8] The sermons are followed immediately by an alphabetical index in two columns, in a fifteenth-century bastard Anglicana (textura-like) hand. It lists topics as well as sermon themata (marked "t" marginally) that occur in booklets 3–5 and refers to folio and side (a–b) or column (a–d).

The entire volume is associated with Durham priory, in two different ways: it carries a Durham shelfmark (N/ii) on the front flyleaf, and in one of the sermons of part 5, on St. Benedict (J/5-13), the preacher asks for prayers for the soul of "bone memorie patris T. H. quondam episcopi huius loci et nostri collegii funda-toris."[9] The reference surely is to Thomas Hatfield, bishop of Durham (1345–81), who generously endowed the Benedictine Durham College at Oxford, whose foundation was completed c. 1389. A sermon in the first booklet, J/1-2, con-tains a story about a monk "de ordine nostro." But it is by no means clear that, apart from the cases just mentioned, the entire collection reflects Benedictine

---

[6] Schneyer 7:391–395.

[7] J/4-10: "Ecce agnus Dei, ecce qui tollit peccata mundi" (John 1:29) for the octave of Epiphany. Several discrepancies between the lection and the stated occasion in J/2 may also indicate Fran-ciscan use.

[8] A number of discrete items consist only of a thema followed by a brief moralizing exegesis of the key term or a distinction on it. I have not counted them as sermons.

[9] F. 68 of booklet 5.

preaching. In fact, it carries a number of features that would speak for Franciscan provenance. As indicated above, booklets 2 and 4 either are of Franciscan authorship or can be related to Franciscan collections. Further, many sermons in part 5 develop their points "by examples from nature, art, and Scripture" or a similar pattern reminiscent of mendicant preaching.[10] A major Franciscan handbook for preachers, the *Fasciculus morum*, is quoted in a note (f. 138), as are, more significantly, the lectures on Deuteronomy and on Isaiah by "Wallensis," presumably the Franciscan John of Wales.[11] In addition, there is an excerpt from the Psalms commentary by the Cambridge Franciscan Henry Costessey, a rarity in sermon books.[12] Finally, one sermon refers to "a sermon that was preached at Dunwich" (f. 97), where there was a Franciscan as well as a Dominican convent. None of this proves a Franciscan origin beyond doubt, but it strongly suggests it. But whatever their origin, the booklets must have been assembled when the Durham press mark was entered, because next to it is a very short list of the volume's contents that includes all booklets.[13]

The collection of sermons in the fifth booklet (J/5) – with which we are now exclusively concerned – is a rather mixed bag. The sermons do not follow any liturgical pattern and, with two exceptions, bear no indication of their occasion other than an internal reference here and there. Some are for major feasts including the Assumption and especially Rogation Days, others are for such special occasions as funerals or the dedication of a church. Among these is a remarkable sermon preached on the enclosure of Alice Huntingfield.[14] The collection closes with a correctly rubricated sermon preached by Richard FitzRalph at Avignon on Good Friday of 1342.[15]

[10] For this *modus procedendi*, see Wenzel, "Continuing Life," pp. 142–143.

[11] "Wallensis in lectura super Deuteronomio" (ff. 55v and 124v); "Wallensis in lectura super Ysaie capitulo 42" (f. 124v). Alternatively it could be the Dominican Thomas Waleys.

[12] "Costeci super illud Psalmi 20 'Quoniam declinauerunt in te mala' dicit sic: 'Declinauerunt, idest extorquebant, in te mala, idest peccata sua, ut sic inuenirent excusaciones . . .'," in a note on ff. 138v–139v. The same quotation appears within a sermon by Felton, FE-14.

[13] See James, *Descriptive Catalogue . . . Jesus College*, p. 11. More precisely, this index lists booklet 1 ("Sermones de sancta maria"), booklet 2 ("Sermones de sanctis et de tempore cum tabula") with the additional sermon in the same line ("sermo de visitacione non necgligenda"), and booklets 3–5 as one item ("Item sermones de tempore et de sanctis cum tabula"). Above this index, a strip has been cut out of the leaf; it probably bore a fifteenth-century *ex libris*.

[14] I have discussed this sermon in Wenzel, "Classics," pp. 135–142. An Alice was enclosed at St. Peter's Church, St. Albans, in the first quarter of the fifteenth century, but we do not know her last name; I thank Ann K. Warren for sharing this information with me (via a letter from Mary McLaughlin, June 29, 1991). The sermon thema, *Ingredere civitatem* (Acts 9:7), is said to be "in epistula hodierna," which could mean that the sermon was preached on the feast of the conversion of St. Paul, January 25.

[15] *Redemisti nos Deo in sanguine tuo*, ff. 145–149v (FI-73). See Walsh, *Fourteenth-Century Scholar*, pp. 206–207.

The sermons also vary greatly in length and texture. Typically, two Good-Friday sermons and one for Easter Monday are considerably longer (as much as over nine folios) than other full sermons, such as the one for Alice Huntingfield (about four folios). Other pieces occupy only one or two folios. The fuller sermons proceed along the normal lines of scholastic sermon structure and sometimes tend to ramble, a tendency that frequently shows in the sermon's syntax, as for example:

> Why does a physician want, when he comes to two sick people and in one sees hope for life and in the other not, why does he want to set the first, for whose life he has hope, why does he want to set him to abstinence and forbid him delicious food and drink?[16]

The preacher himself was not unaware of his rambling, as he comments later in the same sermon:

> Why have I been saying all this? Lots of people may want to think that it is far from the intention of my thema, far from the intended matter which I started to talk about, that is, strangers and pilgrims. But I don't think this is so. I think all this is very much to the point, because all I have been saying so far I have said to this end: you should care less about all worldly delights.[17]

With the full sermons occur a number of mere outlines, simple notes, or distinctions, which I have not included in my inventory; occasionally it is hard to distinguish such notes or outlines from genuine full sermons. This mixture is characteristic of a preacher's notebook, and other features of the collection place J/5 in a continuing preaching activity. For instance, one sermon for Rogation Days, *Nunquid pro pisce serpentem dabit?* (ff. 58v–59v), begins with the preacher saying,

> You know, dearly beloved, that last year I preached about the threefold loaf, which I gave you according to the grace that God had given me on that occasion.[18]

---

[16] "Quare wlt medicus quando venit ad duos infirmos et in vno videt specie [*read* spem] vite et in alio non, quare vult primum, de cuius vita sperat, quare wlt ponere eum ad abstinenciam et prohibere sibi deliciosos cibos et potus?" J/5-4, f. 49v.

[17] "Quare dixi omnia ista? Pluries homines vellent estimare quod esset longe a proposito mei thematis, longe a proposito materie de qua incepi loqui, idest de aduenis et peregrinis. Sed michi non apparet sic. Apparet michi quod est multum ad propositum, quia totum istud quod dixi iam vltimo dixi pro isto fine quod deberetis minus curare de omnibus mundialibus delectacionibus," f. 50. The sermon thema is *Peregrinus es in Ierusalem* (Luke 24:18).

[18] "Scitis, karissimi, quod anno preterito habui de triplici pane quem ministraui secundum graciam Dei pro eo tempore michi datam," J/5-7, f. 58v.

and summarizes that sermon and its structure. The sermon referred to, on *Amice, commoda mihi tres panes*, is indeed recorded before the reference (J/5-6, ff. 57–58v). Similarly, in an Easter Monday sermon, the preacher declares that he had preached on the same day and in the same place twice before.[19] Some of the longer sermons not only reuse material already employed but refer to other sermons by their respective themata. Of the more than a dozen sermons thus cross-referenced, some are present in this collection, but others are not, which suggests that the sermons in this manuscript were copied selectively from elsewhere. This impression is strengthened by a reference in a sermon on *Pueri mecum sunt*: "On these three [children found in scripture] see about sixteen folios above, at this sign." The reference has been crossed out by the scribe, and there is no *signe de renvoi*, nor is there a sermon sixteen folios earlier that contains material on the three meanings of "children."[20] In other words, the reference must have stood in the source book, was mechanically copied, and was then canceled. There are further indications that this booklet gathers material from various sources: besides the sermon by FitzRalph already mentioned, three successive sermons here have also been preserved in collection Z,[21] one comes from Felton,[22] and others occur also in E[23] and elsewhere.[24]

Among the sermons that are referred to but not present in the booklet is one said to have been preached at Oxford and another at Dunwich.[25] There are further references to the university. In one unassigned sermon the preacher laments that the faithful of the realm lack the bread (presumably of doctrine), but "God be praised, in this venerable university this bread is broken most abundantly," even if

---

[19] "Ego predicaui per prius bis in die isto hic in isto loco, vltimo anno et alia vice per ante, et vtraque vice accepi istud pro meo themate: *Mane nobiscum, Domine, quoniam aduesperascit et inclinata est iam dies*, Lord, with ous beleue, for now þe day goth doun and it waxit eue. Et vtraque vice rogaui istum bonum Dominum, istum peregrinum Christum Dei filium ex vestra omnium parte ita concorditer sicut sciui quod foret eius voluntas ad remanendum nobiscum stille. Et vlterius ostendi meo modo quomodo homines oportet facere ad faciendum eum remanere . . . " J/5-4, f. 48v. Sermons on the quoted thema were fairly common, though none occurs in this manuscript.

[20] "De hiis tribus require [supra quasi per 16 filia [*read* folia] ad hoc signum, *canceled*]," J/5-38, f. 136v.

[21] J/5-23 is Z-43; J/5-24 is Z-4; and J/5-25 is Z-6.   [22] J/5-36 is FE-23.

[23] J/5-22 is the same as E-39; it further occurs in Oxford, Magdalen College, MS 112, f. 221ra–va; see the discussion of Alkerton below.

[24] J/5-2, on *Confitemini* (James 5:16), beginning "Si quis peregre iturus esset," occurs in many other collections, e.g. Oxford, Bodley 857, Balliol 219, New College 305.

[25] "Et dic penas illas sub similitudine . . . personarum quas ponunt poete sicut habes in sermone *Vnusquisque sicut accepit* predicato [*MS*: predicare] Oxon', et infer auctoritatem Ezechielis 9" (f. 94; again at 97: "predicato Oxon'"); "tercio principaliter dixi quod deus arguet de peccato, et dic ut habes in sermone predicato Donewyc' *Arguet de peccato*" (f. 97).

it is not well eaten.[26] Elsewhere, a sermon division is introduced with references to scholastic customs.[27] And even the seedier side of life in a university town appears in references to university statutes against kicking balls against houses[28] and to swaggering undergraduates.[29] At one point the unknown preacher even summarizes for his audience what may have been a disputation: In a sermon for the Vigil of Ascension, on *Gratia magna erat in omnibus illis* (Acts 4:33), he quotes the verse "the multitude of believers had one heart and one soul" from the day's epistle (Acts 4:32) and reports that he had recently been asked whether more Christians were saved than damned. He had argued the former and replied to a number of biblical quotations alleged against him, including that "many are called but few are chosen," which he had defused by drawing a neat distinction between a general call to all men and a special one to Christians only.[30]

At least one sermon contains a direct address of the clergy: *attendite, vos curati*,[31] and like it, almost all the complete, longer sermons are addressed to *Reuerendi*.[32] Finally, the orthodoxy of the preacher or the collection is evinced by mildly anti-Lollard statements in two sermons. One, which deals with the first two commandments, takes issue with "some who believe there should be no images in God's Church,"[33] while another turns against those who believe confession to God alone is sufficient.[34]

---

[26] "In hac venerabili vniuersitate iste panis habundantissime frangitur, ymmo, ut timeo, longe plus quam adhuc bene commeditur," J/5-26, f. 111.

[27] "Mos est, karissimi, clericorum in scolis theologie exercitatorum quod quando questio proponitur sibi, conclusionibus respondere," J/5-17, f. 76v; similarly J/5-21, f. 95.

[28] In dealing with the third commandment, the preacher chastizes various people, including "isti lusores ad pilam super domos contra voluntatem dominorum earum." This is against the law of nature, Scripture, and "item contra legem et statuta vniuersitatis hoc prohibentis sub pena excommunicacionis," J/5-33, f. 124v.

[29] In a warning against dancing, using a curious moralization of the rape story of Judges 21:20–21, involving the sons of Benjamin and the daughters of Silo: "Beniamin interpretatur filius dextre et filius virtutis siue filius asininus. Per quos possunt intelligi *getturs* et *stretbetars* vniuersitatis, qui aliquando fuerant filii dextre, scilicet Dei, et filii virtutum, sed in quibusdam mutatus est color optimus, quia quidam eorum mutati sunt in filios asininos, *madards*. Et de talibus est maxime cauendum," J/5-34, f. 126.

[30] J/5-34, f. 125r–v.   [31] J/5-22, f. 99v.

[32] But at least one sermon may be directed to laypeople, in whose second part "ostenditur curatus vel persona cui dicetis vestram confessionem," J/5-14, f. 70v.

[33] *Amicus meus venit*, J/5-5, f. 55v. It also briefly justifies lay communion under one species only, ibid.

[34] "Vnde sciendum est quod non sufficit confiteri soli Deo, quod quidam heretici posuerunt," J/5-14, f. 71.

25

Worcester, Cathedral Library, MS F.126 (X)

As we have seen, a number of sermons in several booklets of Cambridge, Jesus College, MS 13 also occur in a major sermon collection from Worcester Cathedral Priory, made at about the same time and bearing the contemporary inscription "Liber Beate Marie Wigornie."[1] Worcester Cathedral MS F.126 is a large codex of thick parchment leaves written by several Anglicana hands with Secretary features, of the late fourteenth and early fifteenth century. It is fairly regularly constructed and has a medieval foliation.[2] The volume is essentially a very large sermon collection, one of the surprisingly great number of sermon books that were made for and stood in the medieval Benedictine priory at Worcester and can still be found in the cathedral library. Besides sermons it also contains what appears to be an academic lecture (f. 1ra–b),[3] the *Confessio Magistri et Fratris Iohannis Tyssyngtone de ordine minorum* (ff. 19ra–23rb), and a copy of the *Liber sextus decretalium* (ff. 280ra–294rb). Immediately after the sermons, on ff. 278–279, appears an index that lists the sermons in the order in which they stand in the codex, giving their occasion, thema, and folio. Earlier in the volume (ff. 235v–238rb) occurs a "Tabula de notabilioribus que continentur in presenti

---

[1] The manuscript is described in R. M. Thomson, *Descriptive Catalogue . . . Worcester Cathedral*, pp. 87–91. In *Macaronic* I listed twenty-three sermons that contain English material (pp. 200–203), and the manuscript is discussed ibid., pp. 58–60.

[2] The medieval foliation is irregular; see details in Thomson, *Catalogue*. Thomson uses a normalized modern foliation, which I follow here and in my inventory.

[3] The first sermon is preceded by a text beginning "Scio quod vox mea de fistula procedens exili forte nullatenus audietur," whose relation to X-1, if any, is hard to see. It begins with a prayer: "Rogo vt tua excellencia principium incepcionis mee instruat et informet, tuaque sapiencia progressum dirigat et exornet, incommutabilis bonitas compleat egressum ac consummet" and then speaks of jurisprudence: "Nec solum quero scienciam set eciam sapienciam que anthonomatice iurisprudencia nuncupatur." The first sentence, therefore, and the later discussion of a basic feature of study, make it likely that the piece is a *principium* or an opening lecture in the law faculty. The piece is not listed in the table of sermons at the end of the manuscript.

volumine," covering subjects from "Antethemata" and "Abstinencia" to "Ydria" and referring to folio and column (a–d) of the sermons that appear in the manuscript both before and after this table; its information seems to be generally based on marginal annotations.

The longer index at the end lists 328 sermons, but the collection in fact contains 336.[4] These are of all kinds: *de tempore, de sanctis,* and for special occasions, and they are largely grouped according to their liturgical occasion. In many quires the final columns or pages are left blank, and on occasion leaves have been excised, which would suggest that the codex is made up of a number of booklets. If not all, certainly the majority of these booklets can easily be seen to be unified by containing sermons that either belong to the same liturgical occasion or derive from the same source, as the following list will show:

Quires I–II	Nineteen sermons for the Advent season (1–19).		
	Shared:	X-4	= B/2-24
		X-5	= S-11
		X-8 and 9	= Boraston[5]
		X-17	= Worcester Q.63
		X-19	= Bonaventure
Quires IV–VI	Forty-one *temporale* sermons (28–68) in roughly seasonal order from Advent through Passion Sunday (without Ash Wednesday, for which see quire XIV).		
	Shared:	X-41 to 53	= J/4-1 to 13, same order; and Paris, BN lat. 18195[6]
Quires XI–XII	Eleven sermons for Good Friday and one for Holy Thursday (114–125).		
	Shared:	X-114	= Holcot 82
		X-117	= K-23
Quire XIII	Seven sermons "in pascali tempore" (126–132).[7]		
	Shared:	X-126	= A-11
Quire XIV	Nine sermons for Ash Wednesday (134–142).		

---

[4] The index misses eight items that are definitely separate sermons. Thomson speaks of 347 sermons (*Catalogue,* p. xxix), but on several occasions he lists prothemes and main parts separately, being in some but not all such cases misled by the scribe's beginning a sermon's main part with a new line and (intended) large initial.

[5] An Oxford Dominican, prior provincial in 1327; see *BRUO* 1:221. His sermons have been preserved in Merton College, MS 216.

[6] Schneyer 7:391–395.

[7] Thus in the index, f. 278va. The seven are followed by another sermon, *Mors illi ultra non dominatur,* for no specified occasion and not listed in the index.

Quire XV	*Collationes dominicales de evangeliis* by John Pecham, here numbered 1–55[8] but not identified (143–197). Of these, 52 are listed in Schneyer (3:669–672). At the end of the quire, three more sermons are added.

Shared: X-143 to 197 = Pecham, *Collationes*

Quire XVII	Twenty-two random sermons (237–258; but see below), of which a dozen are also found in a different order in Worcester MS F.10 (W).[9]

Shared:

X-237 to 239	= W-45, 46, 40
X-241	= W-47
X-245 to 250	= W-41, 48 to 53, 39
X-251	= F/5-56

Quire XX	Twenty-one sermons for random Sundays and saints' feasts, the last one crowded in (f. 217vb). According to the index (f. 279ra) these sermons are by Mr John Sene.[10]
Quire XXI	Five sermons for Corpus Christi (299–303).
Quire XXII	Five sermons for an election (304–308).

Shared: X-308 = Thomas de Lisle[11]

Quire XXIII	Eleven sermons for visitation or synod, dedication, or a religious profession (309–319).

Shared:

X-309 to 319	= Thomas de Lisle; X-309 also in J/2-128

Quires XXIV–V	Seventeen sermons for Marian feasts (320–336).

Shared: X-335 = J/3-4 and V-40

It should be noted that sermons for Ash Wednesday (XIV), Holy Week (XI–XII), Corpus Christi (XXI), and such special occasions as election (XXII), visitation, synod, dedication, and profession (XXIII) occur only in their respective booklets.

---

[8] *Collatio* 38 (f. 153vb) lacks the marginal number and is not listed in the manuscript's table.

[9] In my view W in general and this section in particular were copied later than X, so that both X and W may be derived from a common exemplar.

[10] They are bracketed in the index with his name next to them, f. 279ra. Sene was a monk at Glastonbury. He had received the D.Th. by 1360 and died before 1377, and there is some evidence that he was engaged in literary activity. See *BRUO* 3:1662–63; Pantin, *Documents* 3:30, 201, 202; and *Chronicle of Glastonbury*, pp. xxix–xxx. In addition to this booklet, Sene's name also appears marginally next to a sermon for the Translation of Saint Frideswide, the patron saint of Oxford, honored in X with four sermons.

[11] Aberdeen, University Library, MS 154 contains a collection of sixty-seven sermons which correspond to selected items in Schneyer's listing of the *Commune sanctorum* by Thomas de Lisle or Thomas Brito, supposedly a Dominican from Winchester convent and later bishop of Ely (died 1361); see Schneyer 5:631 and 663–670. Bataillon, however, in "Sermons attribués," argues that the sermons are by a Dominican contemporary of Aquinas, "un frère Thomas Lebreton dont nous ignorons tout par ailleurs" (p. 333). The Aberdeen manuscript is in an early fourteenth-century hand.

Quire XVII calls for some further comment. Thirteen of its twenty-two sermons (237–241, 243–250) form, with one exception (242), an uninterrupted series
on texts from John 1:6–11 in sequential order. Several among them are ascribed
to a specific occasion: several saints' feasts ranging from November 11 to December 6 and two sermons for Advent. Such a sequence of sermons written for a
liturgical season based on consecutive verses from a biblical book, verses that do
not form part of the official lections of the time, is unusual and may suggest a
university milieu. It is from this series that a number of sermons also appear in
collection W, and in discussing that collection I will pursue this phenomenon
further.[12]

I have been able to identify as many as one hundred sermons that X shares
with other collections. As the list above shows, groups of sermons in X are derived
from or shared with Thomas de Lisle's sermons, John Pecham's collations on the
Sunday gospels, and collections J and W. With them occur single or scattered
pieces that can also be identified in several other collections (A, B/2, F, J, K, S, V,
Boraston, Bonaventure, Holcot, Worcester Q.63), and to these must be added
further pieces not already included in the list above: another Holcot sermon
(X-100) and another by De Lisle (267), two sermons also in BL Add. 38818 (X-69
and 264), four more pieces shared by J/4 and BN lat. 18195 (X-87, 90–92), and
another two in F/1 (X-86 and 89, the latter also in BL Add. 38818), and finally
perhaps one sermon also preserved in Y/3 (X-101). What matters here is that in
X such cross-connections are unusually broad and numerous and pervade the
entire collection. They reflect an equally broad process of borrowing on the part
of the scribes of this collection.

It is, therefore, quite clear that whoever collected the sermons in MS X drew
on a variety of sources from which he or they frequently copied small batches of
sermons, collecting them into booklets that are unified by the occasions for which
the respective pieces had been written. The manuscript, thus, forms a genuine,
topically arranged sermon anthology, evidently made for the Benedictine monks
at Worcester Cathedral priory, whose library had and still has a surprisingly large
collection of sermon books.[13]

---

[12] The same phenomenon actually occurs a second time in X. The sermons by John Sene in booklet
XX are largely on verses from John 1:5–19 and beyond, but not in the same straight sequence as
those mentioned above. Most of them are on saints' feasts in November and early December
and on the first Sunday in Advent, but again not in as rigorous an order as the earlier series;
cf. the inventory for sermons X-279 to 299.

[13] See Greatrex, "Benedictine Sermons"; and R. M. Thomson, *Descriptive Catalogue . . . Worcester
Cathedral*, p. xxix. Evidence for the involvement of monks in the *cura pastoralis*, including
preaching *ad populum*, has been gathered by Greatrex, "Benedictine Monk Scholars."

Given the composite nature of the manuscript, the size of the collecting effort, and the participation of more than one hand, it is remarkable how little has gone wrong in compiling the book – in stark contrast to the other Worcester compilation that will be examined in the following section.[14]

Among the mostly Latin sermons occur nearly two dozen pieces with English material, even one fully macaronic sermon.[15] They have preserved interesting vernacular sayings, including a reference to the song "Maiden in the Moor Lay",[16] and some of them furnish intriguing clues to the use of both languages in actual preaching.[17] Such clues, together with other pieces of evidence, also indicate that, while a large number of sermons included were intended for a clerical audience, some were clearly directed to a lay or mixed audience.[18] Two sermons, without known parallels elsewhere, are each assigned to two occasions. If this information is trustworthy, their combined occasions would point to the year 1408.[19]

---

[14] The most blatant mistakes would be the index maker's missing some sermons and the scribes' occasional use of an enlarged initial at a point that is not the beginning of a new sermon, both noted above. Also, three sermons are copied twice.

[15] Sermons in this manuscript with significant amounts of English material are listed in *Macaronic*, pp. 201–203.

[16] See Wenzel, "Moor Maiden." The sermon refers to "a certain song, i.e. carol, 'þe mayde be wode lay'." For other examples of popular rhymes, see Wenzel, *Preachers*, Index of Manuscripts, p. 259.

[17] For instance, sermon 236 gives two divisions in sequence, the second for "people who are less educated" and written out in English; see Wenzel, *Preachers*, pp. 87–89.

[18] The address forms *Karissimi, Fratres*, or *Reverendi domini* (and similar titles) occur with regularity, and sometimes both *Reuerendi* and *Karissimi* occur in the same piece.

[19] According to the table, X-88 is for Septuagesima and the feast of St. Frideswide (translation on 12 February); the two days coincided in 1392, 1408, 1419, 1430. Similarly, X-200 uses as its thema a passage said to be "in euangelio dominicali," i.e. 2 Trinity, but in the table the sermon is listed as "De sancto Iohanne." 2 Trinity fell on 24 June in 1324, 1403, 1408, and 1487.

26

Worcester, Cathedral Library, MS F.10 (W)

In contrast to X, this volume, also a miscellaneous sermon collection and very probably made at Worcester, is considerably less neat in both form and contents.[1] It is a composite book, made up of paper and some parchment. It contains as many as eighteen separate booklets, some of one, many of two, and one of three quires. These are written in at least a dozen different hands, all fifteenth-century scripts, Anglicana with Secretary features or different grades of Secretary. The booklets also employ different layouts – one or two columns – and small decorative features, including different ways of indicating the beginning of a new sermon. Both layout and script occasionally change within the same quire. In all, I count over thirty changes of hand. Three different sets of quire signatures and a subsequent medieval foliation (beginning only at modern f. 18) indicate that the booklets were combined several times in different ways before reaching their present order. There is no table of contents.

Gathered here are 167 sermons (including the repeats)[2] occasionally inter-spersed with notes and pious stories. They are for Sundays and feast days, for saints' feasts, and for special occasions, and occur in a random mixture. It is hard to discern an organizing principle for the individual booklets and for the collection as a whole; there is certainly nothing like the neat arrangement found in collection X. But there is one important exception. Spread over booklets 4 and 5 (quires 6–9) are two runs of sermons, each with a curious internal coherence. The first, sermons 38–53, are on verses from John 1:6–12, though not in their

---

[1] The manuscript is described in R. M. Thomson, *Descriptive Catalogue . . . Worcester Cathedral*, pp. 10–13; see also Wenzel, *Macaronic*, pp. 182–183, with an inventory of its sermons ibidem pp. 183–200 and further discussion at pp. 55–58. The modern pencil foliation has counted f. 8 twice (8 and 8x) and there are other errors, which have now been corrected in a second modern foliation and in Thomson's catalogue. I follow the corrected modern foliation.

[2] For sermons copied twice in this manuscript see below. I have indicated repeated material with a slash between two numbers: 9/31, etc. Thomson speaks of 175 sermons (*Catalogue*, p. 10), but his count includes several sets of notes and in two instances lists prothemes separately from the main parts of a sermon.

original sequence. Of these sixteen sermons, twelve also appear in X, with similar ascriptions to occasions at the beginning of Advent. But W has three more pieces on John 1:12 (W-42 to 44) which are not found in X, and conversely X has one piece (X-240), on John 1:9, which is not in W. Hence, in this section X and W must have independently selected and copied material from the same source. As stated in the previous section on X, a sequence of sermons written for a liturgical season based on consecutive verses from a biblical book, verses that do not form part of the official lections of the time, is an unusual phenomenon and may suggest a university environment. This suggestion gains strength by W's having a second run of sermons with the same characteristics. Sermons 54–65 take as their themata verses from the book of Esther, from 1:2 to 15:3. These themata follow the biblical book exactly with one interesting exception. The first sermon, W-54, on Esther 1:2, is followed by one that uses as its thema a quotation from St. Jerome's prologue to the Book of Esther – at first glance a very unusual procedure. But the oddity is explained by the fact that W-54 is a sermon in praise of scripture and the study of theology, which was probably given at the beginning of a university course on the Book of Esther, and the following sermon, W-55, quite naturally utilizes a phrase from Jerome's prologue to the book. These sermons, therefore, seem to be intimately connected with a biblical lecture course. They are, however, not biblical exegesis but quite typical sermons addressing issues of common morality and exhorting the audience to penitence, though here and there one finds a definite tone from the academic life.[3] Three of these sermons are ascribed to saints' feasts in March,[4] and one further sermon is explicitly for Lent. In contrast to the earlier run (38–53), I know of no occurrence of the Esther sermons elsewhere.

The collection shares over twenty sermons (not counting the repeats) with other collections. Four of these (6, 7, 9/31, and 10/32 in W) also occur in S; and twelve almost successive sermons (39–41, 45–53 in W) also occur in X. In addition, W-91, labeled "sermo bonus," appears also as O-32 and B/2-71;[5] and three others (4, 83/92, and 163) appear in R, H, and A respectively. At least two, and possibly four, academic sermons here can also found in Worcester Cathedral

---

[3] For example, W-55, on Jerome's words "We do not strive for praise" ("Non affectamur laudes"), divides the thema into striving for praise for the goods of fortune, of nature, and of scripture. Contrary to what one might expect, the last part, with goods of scripture, is explained as deriving praise from teaching and arguing well and is condemned as an aspect of knowledge that "puffs up" (1 Cor 8:1).

[4] Gregory, Patrick, and Cuthbert = March 12, 17, and 20. For the sermon on St. Patrick, see Wenzel, "Saints and the Language of Praise," pp. 71–72. On St. Cuthbert, see Wenzel, "Preaching the Saints in Chaucer's England," p. 54.

[5] All three versions approach the status of redactions.

MS Q.56, of the beginning of the fifteenth century.[6] Finally, W-163 contains a reference to Alkerton, which will be discussed in a later section.[7] Spot-checking reveals that the versions in W and elsewhere derive independently from common ancestors. In particular, it seems highly likely that the shared material in W and X was independently copied from another exemplar or exemplars, and that W was made later than X.

The ongoing and somewhat haphazard scribal work that has produced this volume is also reflected in other ways. A number of sermons appear twice in the volume, in different booklets. Now and then one can observe that what must be the earlier copy was supplied with short marginal addenda in a corrector's hand, and that the second copy then incorporates the addenda in its text.[8] In other cases, part of a sermon is copied again and then canceled. In one instance, the corrector noticed a wrong sermon opening, replaced it with a new text, and ripped out the next three folios – this evidently after the medieval foliation had already been entered.[9] And a number of rubrics mark occasions that are clearly wrong.

But in spite of its occasional scrappiness this is a very important book. It preserves the names of several monastic preachers recorded at the head of sermons: Hugh Legat, monk of St. Albans, who left a very elaborate English sermon on the Passion (W-2, f. 8);[10] Folsham, apparently a monk of Norwich (W-16 and

---

[6] W-126 and 139, and perhaps 21 and 130 with different *initia*; see Thomson, *Catalogue,* under Q.56, article 10 (p. 155).

[7] See the section on Alkerton, pp. 169–170.

[8] Thus, several marginalia of sermon 19 appear in the text of the repeat, 96, and several of its eyeskips are corrected. Conversely, the second copy sometimes omits material no longer deemed relevant. For instance, sermon 93 has this reference: "Contra tales nota bonum exemplum in sermone Parasceue proxima precedente ad tale signum de domino Newgate in eodem sermone" (f. 177v). In sermon 112 the reference has been shortened to: "Contra tales nota bonum exemplum in sermone Parasciue de domino Neugat" (f. 213v). The sign mentioned in 93 is not in this manuscript, nor is the sermon before it on Easter.

[9] W-94, ff. 180v–182v. On f. 180v (medieval 162) the opening of sermon 21, "Veni ad me," is repeated (in the hand that wrote the preceding and following material), crossed out, and replaced, by the corrector's hand, in the lower margin, with the opening of sermon 94, "Ascendit in montem." Medieval folios 163–165 have been roughly ripped out. The text of "Ascendit in montem" then continues on medieval f. 166 (modern 181), the first line and a marginal insertion written by the corrector, the remainder by the main hand of this booklet.

[10] W-2, edited with W-13 and 14 in *Three Middle English Sermons.* For Legat, see also *BRUO* 2:1125–1126. In the otherwise English sermon, Legat ends each principal part with three Latin hexameters that recapitulate the subdivisions of the respective principal part. The use of hexameters for formal divisions and subdivisions also characterizes several academic sermons preached by the Carmelite John Haynton at Oxford in 1432; see London, British Library, MS Harley 5398, ff. 40–45 and 54–59v (a *sermo examinatorius*), and cf. *Formularies* 2:436–437.

17, ff. 55 and 58v);[11] and Master John Fordham, monk at Worcester (1396–1438), who held a D.Th. from Oxford and served as president of the general chapter 1420–1426 (W-71, f. 131rb).[12] An unidentified "Dominus Newgat" is mentioned in the body of a Passion sermon (W-93/112, f. 178v). In addition, a funeral sermon commemorates a Lady Blackworth (W-108), and another (W-83/92) was preached at the funeral of someone apparently named Simon.

Even more importantly, this collection is a significant witness to monastic and to university preaching in the early fifteenth century. Many sermons were given to a Benedictine audience at different monastic centers. At least four pieces were preached at a monastic visitation.[13] Two sermons are for the general chapter of the Black Monks, which in the fifteenth century met every three years and required at least two sermons, whose preachers were designated in advance.[14] Other pieces are seemingly the work of one or more young monk students, perhaps returning home from the university and humbly – one can almost hear them tremble – discharging their task of preaching a festive sermon to their elder brethren.[15] In all these, the virtues of the monastic profession are extolled and their current diminution is lamented.[16]

Next to such monastic sermons stand others that address a university audience and deal with *its* glories and vices. Some of these university sermons moralize and chastize the wrong ambition, greed, or negligence of masters as well as the immorality and unruliness of their students. One sermon furnishes a charming glimpse of the comforts of university life, in which an Oxford cleric who often attends the company of holy men invites one of them in for a drink at his rooms and praises the comfortable life of a master, with his pleasant chamber, fresh air, freedom to come and go as he pleases, plenty of good light, and a soft bed – only to be asked that, when he retires that night, he reflect on Isaiah 14, "Your pride is brought down to hell, your carcass is fallen down; under you shall the moth be spread, and worms shall be your covering."[17]

---

[11] In the 1440s; see *BRUO* 1:704.   [12] *BRUO* 2:705.

[13] Sermons 117, 130, 135, and 137.

[14] Sermons 28 and 71. W-28 has been edited by Pantin, "Sermon."

[15] At least one Worcester monk, John Wodeward, is on record as having ridden back to Worcester from Oxford, where he was studying at the time, in order to preach at Christmas in 1405/6 and on Good Friday. See Greatrex, *Biographical Register*, p. 894.

[16] I have discussed this aspect with quotations in Wenzel, *Monastic Preaching*, pp. 10–14.

[17] "Legitur quod erat clericus quidam Oxoniensis qui frequentans loca sanctorum hominum mouebatur ad sanctitatem. Qui [*MS* quia] aduertens quia, si sanctitatem intraret, oportet delicias et voluptates deserere quas habere solitus erat, nec loca sanctitatis voluit vlterius frequentare nec de Deo aliquid audire, ne per hec ad societatem sanctorum hominum / traheretur. Qui obuians cuidam sancto viro iuxta hospicium suum se inuitauit ad bibendum. Quo annuente duxit eum clericus in cameram recipiens 'Bene' inquit 'veneris, sub ista tamen

Other university sermons are in fact official academic exercises: several introductory sermons to courses on the Bible and on Peter Lombard's *Sentences*,[18]
and an address in praise of philosophy offered by a master of arts as part of his
inception.[19] Another piece, commending the example of St. Edmund, king and
martyr (feast day: November 20), and given on 25 Trinity, reads like a modern
commencement address, highlighting once more the priestly virtues to those
whom "this university has taught" and who are about to take on the pastoral
office.[20] Finally, several pieces contain rare citations of such scholarly authorities
as Duns Scotus and Henry of Ghent.[21] Given this environment and audience, it
is no wonder that a relatively large number of sermons speak of priestly morals
and pastoral duties, including the office of preaching. Their presence in this
collection furnishes evidence that some monks were indeed involved in the *cura
animarum.*[22]

But not all sermons here collected were for monastic or clerical ears. W-8/30
warns lay people ("tu ergo qui es laicus") against investigating the mysteries of
the Eucharist. W-14, addressing "Cristen peple," advises them to make their
confession to their own parish priest. In addition, at least three sermons reflect

condicione quod non loquaris michi de Deo.' Et concessit ille vir sanctus. Et clericus tempore
solacii quod sancto viro sibi dixit: 'Nonne tibi videtur hic quod habeo vitam solaciosam? Et
multiplici de causa. Vide si tamen pulcram cameram, quam bonus sit aer, satis de lumine, victus
sufficiens, lectus mollis,' quem sibi ostendit, 'libertas transeundi, solacium cordis. Nichil michi
triste. Et videtur michi quod vos et alii qui dant se penis, magne stulticie est et solacium mundi
tales relinquunt.' Cui post multa dixit ille vir sanctus: 'Ecce,' inquit, 'quod promisi feriam [!],
quia postquam necessarium non locutus sum tibi de Deo. Set iam peto pro honore Dei et
salute anime tue licencies me loqui vnum verbum de Deo.' Cui clericus concessit. 'Ecce,' inquit,
'multum commendas vitam propter cameram et istum mollem lectum et aerem et huiusmodi.
Et hec omnia vanitas et ostensio voluptatum tuorum et superbie tue contra Deum. Hoc est
quod peto pro honore Dei et salute anime tue, quod cito cum iacueris in lecto isto molli, cogites
de lecto isto de quo scribitur Ysaie 14: 'Determinata [for detracta] est ad inferos superbia tua,
concedit cadauer, te subter sternetur tinea, et vestimentum erit vermes.' . . . Clericus vero ad
lectum veniens hec omnia intime studuit et immediate post in societatem sanctorum hominum
intrauit," W-93, ff. 178v–179.

[18] Sermons 22, 26, 27, 54, and 80. They are discussed, with an edition of sermon 22, in Wenzel,
"Academic Sermons."

[19] Sermon 120, discussed and edited in Wenzel, "Sermon in Praise."

[20] "Vos quos erudiuit hec vniuersitas mater nostra in lege Domini . . . Vnusquisque vestrum,
cum sumpserit pastoris officium et sic[ut] rex preficiatur spiritualis huius regni, exhibeat se fidei
defensorem, doctorem, pastorem plebium, magistrum insipiencium, refrigerium oppressorum,
aduocatum pauperum, tutorem pupillorum, oculum cecorum, baculum seniorum, vltorem
scelerum, virgam potencium, et malleum tyrannorum," W-123, f. 232vb.

[21] "Doctor subtilis," f. 288ra; "doctor solempnis quodlibeto 7 questione 6 querit vtrum in patria
sit laus vocalis, et tenet quod sic, dicens . . . ," f. 322ra; "doctor solemnis in suo quodlibeto,"
f. 136va.

[22] Cf. Greatrex, "Benedictine Monk Scholars."

an ongoing preaching activity before the same congregation. Thus, the preacher of W-68, speaking to a lay or at least mixed audience, declares that he will pass over confession and satisfaction since "I understand one of our brothers taught you about these matters well and sufficiently a week ago."[23] Similarly, in W-13 the preacher, in English, passes over talking about charity "because our youngest brother taught it to you so well and openly a week ago."[24] And W-20 speaks of a *frater predicator* who on Palm Sunday preached on the thema "This chalice is the new testament" (I Corinthians 11:25).[25]

The diversity of the material brought together in this volume is also reflected in the dates to which individual sermons can be assigned. They range from the time of Richard II into the third decade of the fifteenth century. In one sermon the initial prayer includes "our king Richard, now recently crowned."[26] Another sermon (W-107/151) refers to political events of 1387.[27] Two sermons (W-13 and 14) include a prayer for pope Boniface IX (1389–1404), while a third (W-29/99) adds to Boniface King Henry, thus limiting its date to 1399–1404. On the other hand, the anonymous sermon for the general chapter (W-28) refers to what must be Henry V.[28] Finally, two sermons allow us to infer their dates from their liturgical position. One (W-123), in praise of St Edmund, takes its thema from the epistle for 25 Trinity, which would yield 1390, 1401, or 1412 as the year of preaching. The other (W-132), on the gospel for 2 Trinity, refers to "Petrus et Paulus, cuius triumphos hodie inuenimus"; 2 Trinity fell on 29 June in 1427 and 1432.[29]

---

[23] "De aliis duobus ramis penitencie, vt confessione oris et satisfaccione operis, quia intellexi quod quidam frater noster bene et sufficienter vos informauit de eis hodie ad septimanam, ideo transio," f. 126va. At the end, the preacher addresses "boni viri, vos qui habetis pueros ad custodiendum," f. 127va.

[24] *Three Middle English Sermons*, p. 49.

[25] "Frater predicator habuit istud thema in ramis palmarum, hoc scilicet 'Hic calix nouum testamentum est'," f. 69v. Another pointer to this ongoing preaching activity occurs in W-79, on *In nomine Patris et Filii et Spiritus Sancti* (Matthew 28:19). The preacher refers to a previous sermon he had given *ante nonam*, where he had spoken of the properties of the divine persons (f. 139vb). Now he will connect these properties with the clergy, the other members of the Church, and the bond of love between fathers and children. Only the first of these three parts has been preserved. The previous sermon referred to does not appear in W.

[26] "Pro rege nostro Richardo nunc nouiter creato [*read* coronato]," W-124, f. 232rb. Richard was crowned on July 16, 1377.

[27] I have edited the relevant passage in Wenzel, "Why the Monk?" p. 269 n. 24.

[28] See Pantin, "Sermon," p. 303. If indeed Henry V is intended, the sermon would have been preached in 1414, 1417, or 1420.

[29] F. 253vb. An additional tentative dating may be derived from a reference in W-102 to the Lollards – modern counterparts to the biblical dove-sellers and money-changers whom Christ drove from the temple: "Dicunt quod doctrina sua est comodifera regi et regno, sicut fecerunt

The entire volume contains several links to the cathedral priory of Worcester. In three instances the Worcester saints Oswald and Wulstan are invoked at the head of a sermon.[30] By the end of the century the book belonged to Thomas Meldenham, prior of Worcester (1499–1507). And one general-chapter sermon incompletely recorded in it was made by John Fordham, monk at Worcester 1396–1438 and president of the general chapter 1420–1426. However, these details do not conclusively prove that the volume was written at Worcester, since the material collected also includes sermons given at St. Albans (W-29/99), at a monastery dedicated to St. Peter,[31] and perhaps even at Canterbury,[32] and the book may have been written at Oxford.[33] That not all sermons collected here were preached at Oxford is clear from the preacher's remark in W-154 that "after Oxford, Cambridge, and London, there is no city in the realm that has more good sermons than this one, God save her!"[34]

The sermon just cited also contains a curious *exemplum* in which a man's basket with Love is stolen; when the town's mayor and his beadles look for it and cannot find it, they eventually go "ad locum fratrum," but it isn't there either. The moment the preacher says "ad locum fratrum," he protests that he is not talking about the venerable Friars Minor, and in his moralization solicitously includes "all who have received holy orders of priesthood in God's Church."[35] Barring irony, whether the anonymous preacher is using a pre-existing antifraternal story (he introduces it with "I have read"), or whether his point got changed between the sermon's delivery and its being written down, the remark betrays an interesting sensitivity to antifraternalism. Criticism of the friars is not so delicate in another sermon. W-145 includes, as its third principal, a longer development of "the harmful neglect of private religion" by abandoning the evangelical perfection one has vowed to pursue. This the preacher develops with a lengthy

---

in vltimo parliamento, / vbi mouebant regem et proceres vt spoliarent Ecclesiam possessionibus suis" (f. 194r–v). This may refer to the Disendowment Bill of 1410(?).

[30] Sermons 152, apparently 154 (barely legible), and 155, at ff. 288, 291rb, and 293vb.

[31] W-127 refers to "beato Petro apostolorum principe et huius sacri cenobii aduocato precipuo et patrono" (f. 242va). In *Macaronic*, p. 57, I suggested this was Gloucester, but other English monasteries were dedicated to St. Peter as well.

[32] W-121, in its initial prayer, commends "our elect" to the intercession of the Blessed Virgin, saints Peter and Paul, and "Saint Augustine and his companions": "Habentes ergo interuentricem Virginem gloriosam / cum beatissimis apostolis Petro et Paulo sanctoque Augustino et sociis eius nostroque electo vestris oracionibus primo specialiter commendato aliisque recommendandis commendatis," f. 227ra–b.

[33] Thomson says "probably made at Oxford," *Descriptive Catalogue . . . Worcester Cathedral*, p. 13.

[34] "Post Oxon', Cambrug, et Londoun non est aliqua ciuitas seu villa in regno que habet plures bonos sermones quam hec ciuitas, Deus eam salvet," f. 293rb; edited in Wenzel, *Macaronic*, p. 336.

[35] Edited in Wenzel, *Macaronic*, pp. 328–330.

quotation of "quidam modernus postillator" who criticized "three trangressions in the orders of the mendicants," namely, their precious clothing, sumptuous expenditures at their inceptions, and lack of fruitfulness in their preaching.[36] Less outspoken – as is to be expected in a sermon to the laity in the vernacular – yet clearly taking an antifraternal stand is W-14, which, in touching upon the common topic of the *proprius sacerdos*, recommends that its listeners go for their confessions to their parish priest or penitencer, "and to no ronners ouer cuntreys."[37]

This exhortation to auricular confession already reveals the collection's orthodoxy. Other features to the same effect are warnings against lay investigations of the nature of the Eucharist (sermons 8/30, 152), an argument in favor of venerating images and relics (143), and the disapproval of the disendowment bill already mentioned.[38] The Lollards are several times attacked as false teachers and hypocrites, whether by name (13, 14, 20) or not (102, 125), and the collection as a whole shares the opposition to Lollardy as well as the concern about national decay that characterized the monastic collections of O and R, although here in much less pronounced ways.

---

[36] Sermon W-145 is on the thema *Iudaea abiit in Galilaeam*, John 4:47, for 21 Trinity. I cannot tell who the preacher and his audience might have been; it addresses "amantissimi domini" but is not outspokenly monastic. It is fairly learned, and its criticism of the clergy would exclude a lay audience. The (rather poor) copy is hard to read. The third principal begins: "Tercio principaliter dixi et vltimo quod considerare poterimus in verbis tematis dispendiosum religionis priuate periculum fundamentaliter neclectum, cum dicitur *abiit*. Quam grande credimus est transgressionis delictum retrocedere ab euangelica perfeccione atque omittere Deo votum, et non solum debitum. Nempe permaximum est quia potissime faciunt religiosi necligentes debitum sue perfeccionis non implentes, sicud exemplificat quidam modernus postillator de tribus de tribus [!] transgressionibus in fratrum mendicancium ordinibus, idest de vestium preciocitate, de incepcionum su[m]ptuositate, et de predicacionum infructuositate," f. 276ra–b.

[37] *Three Middle English Sermons*, p. 60. Notice that W-147 contains a critique of canons who claim "distribuciones" in cathedrals though they do not participate in the required services (f. 280rb–va).

[38] In W-102; see above, note 29.

27

Hereford, Cathedral Library, MS O.iii.5 (E)

This fifteenth-century manuscript[1] contains a set of forty-one sermons (one appears twice)[2] and a version of the *Gesta Romanorum*, each in a different hand. The sermons form a random collection, mixing pieces for various Sundays, one or two saints' feasts, and various special occasions. Though their collector or indeed author remains anonymous, it seems that he was an Augustinian canon and doctor of canon law.

An unusally large number of these sermons, either according to their rubrics or by internal references, were delivered at visitations, at a synod, or to the clergy. Several visitation sermons were preached at an unspecified Augustinian house (16, 17, 32), and in them the preacher speaks of "our order," "our rule," and "our most blessed father Augustine."[3] In addition, on internal evidence E-18 also was preached at a visitation. It deals heavily with clerical duties and adduces a host of

---

[1] Described in Mynors and Thomson, *Catalogue... Hereford Cathedral*, pp. 19–20. The description contains a brief but good discussion of the sermon collection but no inventory of the sermons. The authors date the hand of the first article, the sermons, "c. 1400" (p. 20), but certain letter forms and the occasionally poor Latin spelling and grammar may, in my experience, point to a somewhat later date. Features of the collections are also discussed in Fletcher, *Preaching*, p. 126 and nn. 20–22.

[2] The contemporary index on f. i verso, barely legible, lists two more items, on *Sine sanguinis effucione non fit remissio peccatorum* and *Iudicabo eum peste et sanguine*, which appear at f. 30ra–b and 30va–b. They are at best sermon notes without address, division, etc.; I have not included them in my inventory.

[3] E-16: "Istius monasterii venerabilis [?] congregacio" (40ra); "beatissimus pater noster Augustinus quasi in capite regule nostre . . ." (40ra). – E-17: "Iuxta ordines [read ordinis] nostri constituciones" (41ra); "iuxta sentenciam sancti Augustini patris nostri" (41rb); "in hac terrena vita conuentuali" (41rb). – E-32: "Tam propter magistri mei reuerenciam hic personaliter visitantis cum propter venerabilis collegii vtilitatem et hic vnanimiter existentis" (85vb); "ad reformandum pacem, moresque, et vitam regularium canonicorum" (86ra); "quomodo fueritis sancti Augustini regulam vestramque professionem custodientes" (86rb); "ad solidius ordinis nostri regimen" (86rb).

canonistic citations.[4] Preaching at a synod is represented by three sermons that are linked by cross references and a common distinction: E-8, which is copied a second time as E-42, speaks of "in hac sacra sancta sinodo," and a later reference to this sermon reveals that it was preached at Easter. In it, the preacher begins with a threefold medieval etymology of the noun *sacerdos*: *sacra dans*, *sacer dux*, and *sacris deditus vel satis dans* (18va). He then uses the first and speaks of the seven sacraments and the sacerdotal office. In E-22 he refers back to E-8 as well as the threefold etymology and develops the third (which he now calls the second) in a critique of the clergy.[5] The following sermon 23 once again refers to the threefold meaning of *sacerdos* and now takes up the third etymology:

> As I have often repeated, a *sacerdos* is, by the word's etymology, defined in three ways. For a *sacerdos* is so called because he is *sacris deditus* [given over to holy things] or *sacra dans* [giving holy things] or *sacra docens* [teaching holy things]. First, let him be given over to holy things in his honest way of life, so that he may, like a burning lamp, shine rightly. Let him also be giving holy things, by ministering the sacraments of his ecclesiastical cure. And let him, thirdly, be teaching holy things, by sowing the spiritual seed of the gospels into his subjects . . . After I have gone over the first two with a somewhat superficial style, I am now content to dwell on the third.[6]

And with this he begins to speak of the preaching mission of priests. Sermons 22 and 23 bear no indication of being synodal sermons but clearly were preached to the clergy. The same audience may be posited for sermons 21, 24, and 36 (rubricated "in synodo"), which discuss matters of the pastoral office, though without the threefold "etymology."

The collection further contains a number of sermons not specifically destined for a clerical audience. As is shown by their rubrics or by internal references,

---

[4] Possibly E-40 also was intended for a visitation. It is on *Deus visitauit plebem suam* (Luke 7:16), and after citing the biblical source the text adds "et de cen per totum libro vi'o et in euangelio hodierno," which I interpret as referring to *Liber sextus* of Boniface VIII (of the *Decretals*), title 20, "De censibus, exactionibus et procurationibus." Chapter 1 there deals with visitation by an archbishop (Friedberg 2:1056–1057). The body of the sermon contains no references to visitation.

[5] "Dixi vobis alias vt in sinodo paschali . . . Sed primum principale aliquali modo pro tunc vt Deus dederat quodammodo declaraui. Ad secundum ergo pro iam me conuertam et sic finem ponam negocio speciali. Dico quod sacerdos sacris deditus aut sacer dux honestate morum vt lucerna lampadis luceat rutulando," f. 54vb.

[6] "Sacerdos ex vi nominis, prout sepius repetii, tripliciter insignitur. Dicitur nempe sacerdos sacris deditus vel sacra dans vel sacra docens. <Sit> primo sacris deditus honestate morum velud lampas ardens lucide rutilando. Sit eciam sacra dans sacramentorum cure ecclesiastice ministrando. Et tercio tercio sit sacra docens euangeliorum semen spirituales subditis seminando . . . Primis duobus principalibus quodam stilo superficiali primitus pertransitis in tercio pro presenti morari contentor," f. 58rb.

sixteen *de tempore* sermons are for Lent and Easter; five more are for Ascension, Pentecost, and two Sundays after Trinity, none of them standing in their due liturgical order. One sermon refers to an unspecified saint ("si autem attendamus ad vitam sancti quem hodie colit Ecclesia," f. 5va) and, thus, may be a general sermon for any saint. Another sermon is in fact called *Sermo generalis* and is elsewhere assigned to Easter. The label *sermo generalis* appears also with what could be a common sermon for a martyr,[7] unless it is a general sermon for a dead person; and there are two more funeral sermons in this manuscript.[8] Yet another sermon has the rubric *Sermo aureus et nobilis* and may have been preached in Advent.[9] Among the sermons appear notes on topics that often directly relate to the adjacent sermons; some of them may in fact have been intended as sermon outlines or prothemes.

If some of the sermons directed to the clergy are certainly of common authorship, the same cannot be claimed for the collection as a whole. Eight of its sermons occur, with various degrees of closeness, in one or more other collections. E-13 is a copy of sermon 115 in the thirteenth-century Dominican collection of Bodleian MS Laud misc. 511.[10] E-31 parallels a sermon that is elsewhere ascribed to the Dominican William Jordan (D-20). Three Hereford sermons appear in the more contemporary collection Z, and two more in yet other collections.[11]

The eighth shared sermon in the Hereford collection is a redacted anonymous version of a synodal sermon elsewhere ascribed to William of Rimington, who was a Cistercian monk and prior at Sawley (Sallay) Abbey in Yorkshire. One of the few members of his order that were privileged to receive a university education, he obtained a D.Th. at Oxford and served as chancellor of the university in 1372–1373. Besides his *Meditations* and some academic works, he also wrote two sermons, which he preached at the provincial synods of York in 1372 and 1373. These are extant with his name, occasion, and date of delivery in Paris, Bibliothèque de l'Université, MS 790, from which they have been edited.[12] Both

---

[7] The sermon refers to him as "gloriosus N." and "beatus N." and urges the preacher "hic narra de vita eius et quomodo transiit" (f. 25rb).

[8] E-26, a general sermon *pro defunctis*, and E-38, preached in the presence of the corpse ("de isto mortuo hic iacente," f. 105rb).

[9] E-37, on *Vox clamantis in deserto* (John 1:23).

[10] The two sermons have the same substance but differ in their quotations and wording. On Laud misc. 511 see O'Carroll, *Thirteenth-Century Preacher's Handbook*, p. 299.

[11] E-12 is the same as S-4 and B/2-57; and E-39, the same as J/5-22 and Oxford, Magdalen College, MS 112, ff. 221ra–va. E-38 is Z-2 and further exists in an English translation; see Fletcher, *Preaching*, p. 126. E-2 is closely related to Z-26 and H-8; see my remarks in "Prolegomena," pp. 5–6. E-40 may be a redacted form of Z-32 (or the reverse).

[12] O'Brien, "Two Sermons." McNulty, "William of Rymyngton," discusses Rimington's life and works, as well as the Paris manuscript (pp. 234–235).

are learned sermons, especially the earlier one, which draws on medieval optics. They also deal at length with the pastoral office and have much to say in criticism of the contemporary clergy's neglect of duties, including the study of scripture and preaching. The synodal sermon of 1373, *Luceat lux vestra coram hominibus* (Matt. 5:16), is of particular interest here. It begins with a protheme leading to the invitation to pray for the Church, pope, and clergy; for the diocese and its archbishop; for the peace and tranquillity of the realm and "the prince" and "the duke"; for Lord Percy and all other benefactors.[13] Its main part develops twelve properties of light and applies them to "all priests, especially if they have the cure of souls."[14] This sermon has also been preserved without attribution in three other English manuscripts including E. As I noted earlier with some detail, one of them is a copy, the other two are different redactions of Rimington's text.[15] E-14 reduces Rimington's original twelve points to four and reorders them as 1, 2, 5, and 3. Though it carries no rubric indicating the occasion, its text itself speaks of *in hac sancta synodo*.

But E-14 makes further changes to Rimington's synodal sermon of 1373. It occasionally alters the style, and it adds more authorities, especially references and quotations from canon law, a tendency that can be found in others of E's shared sermons.[16] That the author or collector of the Hereford sermons should quote canon law is in itself not very astonishing, as nearly all collections here surveyed contain at least a few canonical references or quotations,[17] especially when they discuss such matters as the priestly office or the Eucharist. But Hereford's quotations stand out for three peculiarities. First is the addition, already

---

[13] "Rogemus igitur in principio sermonis nostri ipsum qui candor est lucis aeternae et speculum sine macula, Sapientiae septimo: pro statu sanctae matris Ecclesiae, pro domino nostro summo pontifice cum toto clero sibi subjecto, et precipue pro statu hujus diocesis atque domini nostri archiepiscopi, ut Spiritus Sanctus irradiet eorum corda suis fulgoribus pariter et ardoribus, ad extirpandos excessus, errores, et haereses in Ecclesia modernis temporibus miserabiliter succrescentes. Rogemus eciam pro pace et tranquillitate hujus regni, pro domino principe, domino duce, cum omnibus eis fideliter adherentibus et subjectis. Et specialiter vestris orationibus recommendo dominum meum de Percy, fundatorem monasterii cujus professus sum, et singulos benefactores Ecclesiae sanctae Dei tam vivos quam defunctos, ut omnes vivos illustret gratia, et ipsa lux aeterna luceat animabus omnium fidelium defunctorum," O'Brien, "Two Sermons," p. 59. The concern about "excesses, errors, and heresies that are growing up in the Church in modern times" is curious for the sermon's date, 1373.
[14] "Proprietates duodecim sunt in luce quas habere tenentur singuli sacerdotes, presertim si curam habuerint animarum," O'Brien, "Two Sermons," p. 59.
[15] "Prolegomena," pp. 4–5.
[16] There are more canonistic references especially in E-12 against S and B, and in E-40 against Z.
[17] Closest to, and perhaps surpassing, the Hereford collection in the number of canonistic quotations are the sermons by Bishop Brinton; the 192 complete sermons in his collection contain about 287 citations. Brinton held a doctorate in canon law.

mentioned, of such references to sermons copied from elsewhere. The second peculiarity is that the Hereford author or compiler sometimes quotes canon law as the source of what is no more than a simple and fairly well-known proof-text. For example, when he affirms that "charity covers a multitude of sins," he refers, not to I Peter 4:8, but to "De penitencia, distinccione 3 in fine."[18] Lastly, beyond quoting the *Decretum* and *Decretals*, he also cites several glossators, such as "Arch[iadiaconus] in *Ro[sario]*,"[19] Johannes Andreae,[20] "B.,"[21] and "Teutonicus."[22] At one point he even corrects a wrong source identification.[23] All this would indicate a preacher who held an advanced degree in canon law. Who else but a canon lawyer would address the congregation before whom he gave the visitation sermon with, "When visitors come to the place they are to visit, they hold before the noses of those who understand them sweet-smelling citations of canon law"?[24]

Another peculiarity of this collection is the frequent discussion of the Eucharist. Five sermons, all marked for Easter (one is actually marked for "Easter or Corpus Christi"), speak at length about various features of the sacrament and about one's disposition to receive it worthily. In sermon 15 the preacher addresses such questions as, when and by whom the sacrament was instituted, what its material is, how it was made, and to whom it has been given, and derives his brief answers from the two basic texts of Matthew 26:26–28 and I Corinthians 11:23–25. In sermon 31 he explains at greater length how Christ can dwell within us, how he is hidden, and how his body gives eternal life to those who receive it worthily; and he touches on the conventional *mirabilia* of the Eucharist: how the immense body of Christ can be contained in a small piece of bread, how the entire body of Christ can be simultaneously in many different places, and so on. All this is standard medieval preaching on the Eucharist and remains far from speculative theology and heterodoxy.

The sermon E-24 just cited calls for some further comment. It is a rather long-winded though not uninteresting piece on "Jesus went over the sea" (John 6:1)

---

[18] E-4, f. 8rb. *De pen.*, dist. 3, c. 33, appears in Friedberg 1:1221.

[19] E-4, f. 10va.   [20] E-10, f. 21va.   [21] E-10, f. 22rb and va.

[22] E-38, f. 104vb. Hereford writes "Cantonicus" where Z-2 has, correctly, "Teutonicus."

[23] "Debet non incongrue actum visitacionis verbum precedere predicacionis, vt *Extra* De censibus, c. Romana Ecclesia, etc. Sane, Libro 6" (f. 85vb). The quoted passage occurs in the *Liber sextus* 3.20.1 (Friedberg 2:1056). The correct reference appears within the text.

[24] "Visitatores accedentes ad locum visitandum flores medicinales salutarium exortacionum proponunt visitandis, iura canonica naribus intelligencium odorifera administrant," f. 47va. Graduates in canon law were frequently used by bishops to preach their visitation sermon. Thus, Archbishop Courtenay used Mr Adam de Mottrum, licenciate in canon law, and Thomas Chyllynden, monk of Canterbury and a doctor of canon law; see *Metropolitical Visitations*, pp. 151–155, 202, and 159.

and marginally macaronic. It bears no indication of the occasion at which it was preached, but such remarks as "we churchmen who have the cure of souls" and others clearly point to a clerical audience. In the sermon's first part, the preacher utilizes the image of teaching grammar at some length and eventually says:

> Indeed, these schoolmasters (*magistri*), that is, curates, have teachers (*pedagogos*) ordained to alleviate their burden and for their relief. By these I understand the friars of the four orders, who are ordained in the Church especially for this purpose. Now, when these schoolmasters, that is, the curates, themselves taught the children of God and allowed their teachers, that is, the friars, to teach the literature of the divine law, then they grew in the knowledge of the divine law. But now some of these masters not only neglect to teach their students themselves but do not allow their teachers, that is, the friars, to teach them, by violently (*violenter*) taking from them the authority to teach and to preach which they have from the authority of our common mother, through that recently published statute. But, I ask, what is the cause? To be sure, their cupidity. For they believe that by teaching the pupils of these masters, these teachers take from these pupils their salary, for they believe they get from them a pound where in fact they don't get a penny. And as the masters want to have everything, they take from them whatever they can, and more than they may receive by law. And I have no doubt that, if this statute that has been published against the law lasts a long time, the children of Christ will be as ignorant in the literature of the divine law as the pagans are now.[25]

Since the preacher here laments withdrawing the right of preaching from the friars (not of teaching school, which is merely an analogy), the statute referred to may be Arundel's *Constitutions* promulgated in 1409.[26] Such outspoken sympathy

---

[25] "Reuera isti magistri, scilicet curati, ad alleuiacionem sui oneris et in eorum solacium habent pedagogos ordinatos, per quos intelligo fratres quatuor ordinum, quia propter hoc ordinantur principaliter in Ecclesia. Et quando isti magistri, scilicet curati, docuerint filios Dei in sua propria persona et permiserint suos pedagogos, scilicet fratres, docere eosdem literaturam legis diuine, tunc accreuerunt in sciencia legis diuine. Sed iam non solum necligunt saltem quidam istorum magistrorum docere suos condiscipulos in propria persona, verum eciam non permittunt suos pedagogos, scilicet fratres, docere <eos> violenter auferendo ab eis auctoritatem docendi et predicandi quam habent ab auctoritate communis matris per illud statutum nouiter editum. Sed que, rogo, est causa? Reuera cupiditas. Nam ipsi credunt quod isti pedagogi in docendo pueros istorum magistrorum auferunt ab illis pueris scolarium [*read* scolagium *or* salarium?] suum quia credunt quod habent ab eis li' vbi non <habent denarium>. Et quia vellent omnia habere, ideo auferunt ab eis in quantum possunt / et plus quam de iure possunt. Et non dubito quoniam si ho[c] statutum contra iura editum diu durauerit, quod pueri Christi erunt ita inscii in literatura legis diuine sicut iam sunt pagani," ff. 62vb–63ra.

[26] Mynors and Thomson, *Catalogue . . . Hereford Cathedral*, p. 19, think so, as does Fletcher, *Preaching*, p. 127, n. 22. But notice that in March 1409/10 Arundel made it clear that the constitution did not apply to the mendicants; see Kedar, "Canon Law," pp. 27–28. See also Spencer, *English*, pp. 363–368.

with the friars is rare in sermons of the period, and this sermon collection may, therefore, well have some connection with the mendicants.

At the same time, E-24 and the entire collection are clearly orthodox. Besides the standard teaching on the Eucharist noted above, the preacher of E-24 recommends pilgrimages and visits to shrines as penance for sins of the feet and in doing so links Lollards with heretics and hypocrites, calling them "masters of error."[27]

---

[27] "Et tunc debes consequenter mouere pinnulas tuas, videlicet þe fynys [*ms* synys] of þi fete, in pilgrimayge goyng, in holy corseyntis visityng . . . ," E-24, f. 64ra; "per doctrinam alicuius magistri erroris seu lollardi," f. 64vb.

28

Oxford, Trinity College, MS 42 (V)

Along with a number of theological treatises, some of which are incomplete, this composite manuscript[1] contains forty-five sermons which form a mixed collection. They begin with a brief prologue which contains a personal name associated with the college of canons at Chichester. Unfortunately, a hole in the page renders the name questionable, and the evidently garbled grammar of the sentence leaves it unclear whether the person named is the writer or the dedicatee of the sermons.[2] But the next sentences are clear about his intention:

> I have learned from your paternal report that you desire something delightful that may stimulate your mind to contemplate heavenly things, through which also your bodily mind – which, according to Holy Scripture, is commonly inclined to evil – may be called back from illicit things. As I wish to please Your Paternity's pious desire humbly and with complete devotion of my mind, I have tried to write up some deeds of the Romans together with words from Seneca, fittingly put into holy discourse as the occasion demanded it. With the

[1] See Coxe, vol. 2, Trinity College, pp. 16–17. A modern collation is desirable.

[2] The text reads: "In nomine Patris et Filii et Spiritus sancti Amen. [R]euerendo discrecionis viro dominus W. de C[.]kston sacri Collegii Cicestrie canonice siue sacris religionis professor, salutem et spem m[.]edis [*probably* mercedis] eterne. Domino adherere . . ." (f. 1). Hudson reads the name as "O[.]kston" and takes him to be the author of the sermons (*Two Wycliffite Texts*, p. xvi, n. 2). But the reading "C[.]kston" is equally possible. Further, while the nominative case in "dominus" and "professor" if correct certainly argues that the named person is the writer, the following "canonice" and "sacris" are syntactically problematic. In addition, the name is preceded by the address "Reuerendo discrecionis viro" without name and followed by the greeting and/or wish that he may have "salvation and the hope of eternal reward." In light of usual dedication forms, this should make the named person the dedicatee. A William de Chesterton was a canon at Chichester in 1391, though apparently not a magister; see Horn, *Chichester Diocese*, p. 59. I owe this reference to Professor R. W. Pfaff. In addition, Walter Eston has also been suggested as a possibility, who was vicar general of Bishop Polton, bishop of Hereford and later of Chichester; see O'Mara, *Study*, p. 39.

insistence of a young son I pray that you may accept, in your fatherly good will, such a small gift of modest value, as coming from a poor beggar.[3]

The program announced is carried out in sermons 1–27, which thus form a unified collection (ff. 1–27v). These are arranged in the order of the Church year ("as the occasion demanded") from 1 Advent to 21 Trinity; not every Sunday is represented, but those that are follow the liturgical calendar. Further, the sermons indeed make much use of the *Gesta Romanorum* as well as Seneca's *Declamationes*. They are relatively short and rhetorically sparse, but have all the same structure. They begin with a story that is briefly moralized ("in proposito" or "adaptacio"). Then the thema is repeated, and sometimes, after another sentence, repeated again. Next follows a division: "In quibus verbis duo occurrunt consideranda: primo . . . " dealing with two words of the thema. The parts announced may be confirmed and are then developed, usually with stories from pseudo-classical and other sources that are moralized ("adaptacio"). The transition from part 1 to part 2 is normally marked with: "Istud pro primo verbo thematis. Secundum verbum . . ." On the whole, these sermons are rather simple in structure, content, and rhetorical appeal, relying primarily on their stories. A number of them are, unusually, addressed to *Amantissimi*.

Though the hand continues on f. 27v (it changes several times later on), the following sermons 28–45 (ff. 72v–89v) differ markedly from the preceding ones and form a miscellaneous collection with varying structural features. As far as their occasions can be determined, they are intended for selected Sundays in the Christmas, Lent, and Easter seasons, as well as the feast of the Annunciation, but they do not follow the order of the calendar. In contrast to the earlier group, most have a protheme leading to the invitation to pray, and they are generally longer and rhetorically fuller. Among these random sermons are at least three pieces by known authors. One is Thomas Wimbledon's *Redde rationem vilicationis tuae*, here entered anonymously and entirely in Latin (V-33, ff. 47–56). The second, V-34, bears the rubric "secundum Alkertoun" (f. 56). Both Alkerton and Wimbledon will be further discussed in the following sections. The third, V-37, is Henry Chambron's *Corruit in platea veritas*, here anonymous (see the section on Chambron above). Besides the sermons by Wimbledon,

---

[3] "Vestro paterno relatu didici quod aliqua dilectabilia optatis que animum vestrum excitent ad celestia contemplanda, quorum eciam virtute mens carnalis, que, testante sacra scriptura, prona est comuniter ad malum, ab illicitis reuocetur. Volens igitur paternitatis vestre pio desiderio toto mentis affectu humiliter complacere, qu[e]dam gesta romanorum cum verbis Senece admixto conuenienter sacro eloquio prout exigit temporis aptido [!] conscribere studui, rogans instancia filioli vt tam modici valoris vestro paterno beneplacito velut mendici et pauperis munusculum admittatis," f. 1.

Alkerton, and Chambron, this miscellaneous group contains two more pieces that also occur elsewhere: V-39 in collection H, and V-40 in collections J and X.

Within this group of random sermons, items 40–44 may form a separate group. They stand in a new booklet whose handwriting seems to be earlier than the various hands of the later fifteenth century up to this point. They are also distinguished by different structural and stylistic features. Finally, the last item in the manuscript, sermon 45, is a sermon by Nicholas de Aquavilla.

This manuscript has a special interest for the consideration of the collections' orthodoxy. The warning, "Let no-one presume to preach unless he is sent by the Holy Spirit and ordained by the Church"[4] in the protheme of V-32, on *Paenitentiam agite*, and later on the statement that it is necessary to confess sins "to your curate or others according to the [Church] law,"[5] as well as the eucharistic sermon V-39 (also in H-23) clearly show the collector's orthodoxy. But apparently he was also willing to include material that to others may have smacked of Lollardy, such as Wimbledon's *Redde rationem* (V-33) and Chambron's *Corruit in platea veritas* (V-37). But of the latter, a later reader excised two thirds of f. 73, which contained strong criticism of preachers.[6]

[4] "Nemo eciam predicare presumat nisi missus a Spiritu Sancto et ab Ecclesia constitutus," V-32, f. 44.

[5] "Necessaria est confessio peccatorum sacerdoti uestro [*or possibly* nostro] curato uel aliis secundum formam iuris," f. 45.

[6] See above, the section on Chambron, p. 129.

29

Richard Alkerton

Alkerton (or Alkrynton) studied at Oxford in the 1370s and 1380s and had incepted in theology at Oxford by 1393.[1] Serving as rector of various parishes in Essex, Gloucestershire, and Sussex, he also held a canonry at Chichester until his death (after 1415). In 1406 he preached at St. Paul's Cross, London, and became involved in a public controversy against the Lollard William Taylor.[2] The text of this sermon has not yet come to light. The same is true of another sermon that he was asked to preach at St. Mary Spital, London, on 27 February 1415.[3] In contrast to these, an earlier sermon preached at St. Mary Spital on Easter Monday, April 12, 1406, has been preserved, in both English (incomplete)[4] and Latin. The latter, as was mentioned in the previous section, is V-34, where his name appears in the rubric. Though this sermon contains some lament at the evil times, it is essentially a devotional piece, developing the theme of pilgrimage on earth and giving a long speech of Christ at the Last Judgment.

In addition, Alkerton's name appears elsewhere and thus points to a fourth sermon of his homiletic work. A sermon on *Ecce nunc dies salutis*, which has been preserved as A-47 and W-163, develops the word "day" by dividing it into good (i.e., life in heaven), evil (the Last Judgment), and mixed (this present life). The third kind of day is given to us in order to gain spiritual health, and this can be done through six steps (*gradus*), which are likened to the signs of the zodiac through which the sun travels: hatred of sin, weeping for one's past sins, doing penance for them, and so on. Sermon A-47 develops all this fully. In contrast, W-163 introduces the analogy with the sun's course and then breaks off with the reference: "Nota sequencia in sermone Alkertoun qui incipit *Amice ascende*

---

[1] *BRUO* 1:25, and O'Mara, *Study*.

[2] The controversy surrounding William Taylor's sermon at St. Paul's Cross in November 1406 is reported in the *St. Albans Chronicle* and summarized in *Two Wycliffite Texts*, p. xiv, and in O'Mara, *Study*, pp. 28–32.

[3] O'Mara, *Study*, pp. 31–32.

[4] Edited ibid., pp. 57–80, with discussion of Alkerton and preaching at the Spital.

superius." A sermon on this thema with a substantively quite similar passage on the six *gradus* and the sun's course can be found in at least three manuscripts.[5] Though anonymous in all three, this might therefore be another surviving sermon by Alkerton.[6]

[5] E-39 (ff. 106vb–110rb), J/5-22 (ff. 97v–100v), and Oxford, Magdalen College, MS 112 (f. 221ra–va; the manuscript contains only a few scattered sermons). All three begin with "Reuerendi domini, cum princeps aliquis nobilis et graciosus venerit nouiter de terra guerre." The passage on the *sex gradus* alone occurs also in Felton's sermon 50 (ff. 89rb–91ra), which uses the same thema, *Amice ascende superius* but has a different *initium* and a substantially different text.

[6] There are, of course, other sermons on this thema, as well as a reference in Z "quere in sermone *Amice ascende superius*" (f.51rb) but no sermon on this thema in the collection.

30

Thomas Wimbledon, "Redde rationem"

Another sermon in collection V which can be linked to a named author is V-33, on *Redde rationem vilicationis tuae* (Luke 16:2), which calls for some special attention. It has been preserved in English and in Latin, both extant in several manuscripts, and thus clearly enjoyed much popularity which continued in several sixteenth- and seventeenth-century printed editions.[1] This long and complex sermon deals with the reckoning that the three estates – *sacerdotes*, *milites*, and *laborarii*, or priests, secular rulers, and everyman – must give on Judgment Day. In its first part it applies the three questions of how have you entered? how have you ruled? and how have you lived? to each of the estates. Then it turns to the questions of who shall call us to this reckoning, who shall judge us, and what our reward or punishment will be. In answering these the preacher tells us that for the special or individual judgment God sends three summoners: old age, sickness, and death. The coming general or universal judgment is similarly announced by the sickness and old age of the world and lastly by the final persecution by the Antichrist.[2] If this sermon thus shares a number of conventional topics,[3] which are developed with the usual array of authoritative quotations and biblical *figurae*, it also strikes a tone that is very unusual in the orthodox sermon collections of the period, an echo of the apocalypticism of the later fourteenth century: the sermon quotes "quidam doctor" who predicted the coming of the Antichrist for the year 1400.[4]

[1] Manuscripts and printed editions are described in *Wimbledon's Sermon* (ed. Knight), pp. 3–26.

[2] A more detailed analysis of the sermon may be found ibid., pp. 48–51, and a shorter schema in Horner, "Preachers at Paul's Cross," pp. 271–272.

[3] Besides the three estates, the summoners, and so forth, Wimbledon's basic schema of the three questions "How did you enter?" etc. is a commonplace in late-medieval preaching; see the following section, on collection A, note 10.

[4] *Wimbledon's Sermon*, lines 882–898. The same passage occurs in Latin in V-33, f. 54r–v, but not in A-48 or H-05. Cf. the earlier reference to the age of the world ibid., line 820 and Latin versions (with differing numerals); and the citations of Joachim and Hildegard ibid., lines 837 and 841 and in V-33. Notice that Wimbledon had earlier said, with reference to Acts 1:7, that we cannot know the exact time; *Wimbledon's Sermon*, lines 805–811.

The English version of *Redde rationem* exists in at least fourteen,[5] the Latin in at least four manuscript copies.[6] Though they maintain the substance and basic structure of the sermon, the Latin versions differ widely on the verbal level. To give a very brief illustration:

Knight, lines 380–85:	V-33, f. 50:	A-48, f. 141v:
Seynt Gregory seiþ: "He schal not take gouernayl of opere þat can not go byfore hem in good lyuynge." And whan any man stant byfore hym in dom, he most take hede tofore what Juge he shal stonde hymself to take his dom aftir his dedis.	Et beatus Gregorius dicit: "Ipse non susciperet regimen aliorum qui nescit antecedere in bona conuersacione." Et cum aliquis steterit coram iudice, necesse esset vt ipse iudex antecederet coram quo iudice ipsemet stabit recepturus iudicium secundum opera uel merita sua.	Gregorius 25 Moralium in fine: "Non debet homo ducatum accipere qui nescit homines bene viuendo preire." Cumque iudicanti ei assistitur vigilanti oculo aspiciat cui quandoque iudici ipse de hiis iudicandus assistet.

Knight, the editor of the English text, suggests that the sermon was first composed in English and then translated into Latin, perhaps even more than once.[7] In the passages cited the Latin version in V-33 reads very much like a direct translation of the English, but in contrast the Latin text of Z-48 differs from both the edited English and the Trinity Latin text considerably. For instance, A-48 quotes Gregory exactly, in contrast to the other two. It is therefore possible to think that *Redde rationem* first existed in a Latin version (A-48), was then translated into English, and finally retranslated from English into Latin (in V-33 and others).[8]

Three early English manuscripts bear a more or less contemporary inscription which ascribes the sermon to Thomas Wimbledon, and other inscriptions suggest that it was given at St. Paul's Cross, London, in 1387 or 1388.[9] A priest by that name, chaplain to Sir John Sandes, was licensed in 1385 by the bishop of Winchester to

[5] Knight lists and describes thirteen copies (*Wimbledon's Sermon*, pp. 3–18), to which should be added Durham Cathedral, MS Hunter 15, part 2, ff. 35–44v; see Ker, *Medieval Manuscripts in British Libraries* 2:493.

[6] A, H, V, and Caius 334. Knight lists and describes two, Caius and A (*Wimbledon's Sermon*, pp. 18–20). For all four, see the respective sections here.

[7] Ibid., p. 20.

[8] In H-05, f. 17, the Gregory quotation is the same as in A-48; but the Harley text appears to be abbreviated.

[9] The evidence is laid out in *Wimbledon's Sermon*, pp. 41–45.

preach throughout the diocese.[10] If this individual is the same as the writer and/or preacher of *Redde rationem*, a qualification expressed in the Winchester license gains some importance that has not yet been related to his sermon: it forbids Wimbledon to "assert or preach any heretical or erroneous opinions (*conclusiones*) that could subvert the state of our church at Winchester and the tranquillity of our subjects." The prohibition thus casts some suspicion of Lollardy on Wimbledon. There is little of a heterodox nature in *Redde rationem*, except for the concern with eschatology when Wimbledon discusses the end of the world, where he declares that the world will end in 1400,[11] quotes Joachim of Flora, and a few lines later says that "now the voice of the eagle is necessary so that God may be exalted, so that human traditions do not overcome and tread upon the gospel of Christ."[12] As we shall see, such sentiments occur in other sermons preserved with A-48 and may therefore point to a larger oeuvre of Wimbledon that has survived in collection A.

One *English* copy of Wimbledon's sermon appears in London, British Library, MS Royal 18.B.xxiii, which together with its English sermons edited by Woodburn O. Ross also contains two booklets of Latin ones.[13] The first run (ff. 1–23, two quires) holds eighteen sermons, most of which, according to Schneyer's *Repertorium*, appear elsewhere, notably in Paris, Bibliothèque Nationale MS lat. 3804, a twelfth-century codex of material from Carolingian homiliaries.[14] The second run (ff. 24–38, also in two quires), contains seventeen short sermon-like

---

[10] Owst, *Preaching*, Appendix V: "A Note on Thomas (or Richard) Wimbledon and His Sermon at Paul's Cross in 1388," pp. 360–362. See *Wimbledon's Sermon*, p. 43. Owen, "Thomas Wimbledon," has collected information about a number of Thomas Wimbledons from episcopal and Oxford records of the period; see also her edition in "Thomas Wimbledon's Sermon."

[11] There is some evidence that the belief that the end of the world was near may, in the 1380s and 1390s, have been linked to Lollardy. The Oxford sermon by Lychlade, for which Lychlade was banished from the university, begins with a similar sentiment; see Wenzel, "Robert Lychlade's Oxford Sermon," pp. 206–207.

[12] "Nunc ergo necessaria est vox aquile vt extollatur Deus ne humane tradiciones supergrediantur et calcent euangelium Christi," A-48, f. 143v; *Wimbledon's Sermon*, lines 963–965. Wimbledon is here expounding the opening of the fourth seal of Revelation 6:8 and the voice of the eagle of Revelation 8:13.

[13] *Middle English Sermons*. The manuscript is described and analyzed in Sir George F. Warner and Julius P. Gilson, *Catalogue of Western Manuscripts*, 2:295–297. The English sermons edited by Ross were copied selectively and from more than one source, including collections of Lollard sympathy; see *English Wycliffite Sermons* 1:188 and note 59; and, more fully, Spencer, *English*, pp. 278–311. Notice also Spencer's warning against considering the "Ross sermons" as a unified collection (p. 472 n. 22).

[14] Schneyer 9:150–156. For the Paris manuscript, see Bibliothèque Nationale, *Catalogue* 7: 220–226, with detailed references to Barré, *Homéliaires*. Some Latin sermons from Royal 18.B.xxiii can further be found in Oxford, Bodleian Library, MS Bodley 123; Cambridge, St. John's College, MS 133; and elsewhere.

pieces that are very similar to the sermons in the *Speculum sacerdotale* and its Latin forerunners. As these two series date from long before 1350, they have not been included in my inventories. Several of the Latin sermons further appear in Cambridge, St. John's College, MS 133, which was evidently written in the early fourteenth century. The latter manuscript contains a cycle of Sunday sermons followed by another of saints' sermons, of which many have parallels in Harley MS 2345 and related collections, and thus seem to belong to the same background that lies behind the *Speculum sacerdotale*.

31

Cambridge, University Library, MS Ii.3.8 (A)

One of the collections that contains a copy of Wimbledon's *Redde rationem vilica-tionis tuae* in Latin, Cambridge, University Library MS Ii.3.8, is a composite paper codex, written in a variety of hands that date from the early to the late fifteenth century.[1] Besides sermons of various lengths and degrees of completeness, it also contains free-standing *exempla*, commonplaces, and sermon outlines, as well as an entire *ars praedicandi* and three treatises on the Decalogue. Hence it presents itself as a preacher's notebook rather than a simple sermon collection. On its front flyleaves appears an index listing fifty-eight sermons with their themata and folio references. Many sermons are incomplete, and the copyists have left blank spaces together with such remarks as "vacat" and "non plus in copia," indicating that their exemplars were defective.[2] With one exception (St. Thomas the Apostle) the sermons are all *de tempore*, but do not follow the liturgical calendar. Sermons for Lent and Easter predominate.

After a series of rather unremarkable sermons, the manuscript preserves a number of pieces full of English material – not only short glosses, translations of quoted authorities, and divisions, but popular sayings and longer verse items, even genuinely macaronic structures. These vernacular items have repeatedly attracted the attention of literary scholars.[3] The popular style they create is further reflected in pious stories of, presumably, common-life experiences, such as the following:

---

[1] The manuscript was collated and its sermons inventoried in Wenzel, *Macaronic*, pp. 133–140; the collection is further discussed ibid. 44–46. The manuscript has since been refoliated, and the new folio numbers are, by quires: VII (69–78), VIII (80–89), IX (89–100), X (101–112), XI (113–124), XII (125–132), XIII (133–144), XIV (145–156), XV (157–166), XVI (167–177). In the following I use the new foliation.

[2] In my inventory I have followed the list of sermons given on the flyleaf. Thus I have included incomplete sermons but not pieces that are sermon notes, even though some of them address an audience and deal with a scriptural passage.

[3] For verse items see Erb, "Vernacular Material" and Stemmler, "More English"; further the indices in Wenzel, *Verses* and *Preachers*.

Notice what happened near King's Lynn to a woman left in great debt on account of her husband. As she once was in deep thought and by herself, the devil appeared to her in human shape. He asked her why she was so sad, and she told him her story. Then the devil promised to help her in everything if she trusted in him and gave him her child, which she was then carrying in her womb. And the woman consented readily and gave him her child. After she had gone home, she later went to the market with a cow. The devil appeared to her [again] and told her that she should return and she would find plenty. Which she did. But as the woman did not find anything, she grew afraid and went to the Franciscans of Lynn and confessed to the guardian of the place. He gave her a crucifix, which he had carried with him on his travels [or pilgrimage]. When the woman came back to her home, the devil appeared to her and threatened her and assured her that "no land-leaper of Lynn" should help her that the devil would not have her child. At the time of her delivery, the devil took the newborn away, but before he went out of the door, the aforementioned friar appeared, tore the child from the devil's hands, and gave it back to the woman. Two days later the friar came to the same place and claimed that this was the first time he had come to this place.[4]

In seeming contrast to this popular appeal, the preachers respresented in this volume also direct their words specifically to the clergy,[5] and in some instances popular style and address to preachers go hand in hand.[6]

Perhaps the most important aspect of this collection is its sharing individual sermons with similar other collections, including some by known authors:

[4] "Nota quid accidit iuxta Lenniam de muliere relicta grauiter indebitata pro viro. Cui semel sic cogitanti et sola sic existente diabolus in specie humana sibi apparuit, et querens ab ea causam quare sic tristis erat. Que sibi processum narrauit. Et ille promisit sibi in omnibus iuuare si sibi crederet et puerum cum quo tunc impregnata erat sibi daret. Et ipsa cito consenciens sibi puerum sibi concessit. Rediens mulier ad domum postea adiuit forum cum vacca. Cui apparens diabolus dicens ei quod rediret et satis inueniret. Quod et factum est. Et non inueniens aliquid tandem mulier sibi timens accessit ad fratres minores Lenn' et confessa est gardiano loci. Qui sibi tradidit crucem quandam quam secum portauerat peregrinando. Redeunte muliere ad locum proprium, apparuit sibi diabolus increpans illam et asserens quod ipsam non iuuaret no londleper of Lenne quin puerum sibi promissum haberet. Tempore partus breuiter nato puero assumpsit eum diabolus, sed antequam exiuit hostium apparuit iste frater predictus et rapuit puerum de manibus diaboli et restituit mulieri. Post duos dies accessit frater ad locum, qui asserens tunc primo ad locum illum venisse," f. 93. If this narrative paints a favorable picture of friars, a passage in A-29 seems to be anti-fraternal in its warning against false confessors: "Ante omnia igitur attende, karissime frater, quod non seducant te fatui confessores et ficti qui peccunie gracia vel aliqua cupiditate seducti inponunt penitencias nimis leues" (f. 95). Similarly a sentence in A-30 may be directed against mendicants: "Qualiter faciunt illi qui predicant principaliter vt mendicent" (f. 96).

[5] Sermon 42 is a little *ars pastoralis*. Sermon addresses "Reuerendi" occur in 22, 33, 41, 43, 44, 49, 54, 55, 56.

[6] Especially A-33.

Wimbledon's *Redde rationem vilicationis tuae* (A-48); a Lenten sermon that Bishop Thomas Brinton preached in 1374 (A-57), and Henry Chambron's *Quare rubrum est vestimentum tuum?* (A-35). Other sermons collected in A also appear in H (A-36), O (26 and 27), W (47), X (11), U (32), and Y (46). A-15 is a redaction of a sermon in Oxford, Merton College, MS 248 (ff. 131rb–132va).

In general, the sermons are orthodox; they speak of private confession and of the Eucharist in quite conventional terms.[7] But several items show an outspoken sympathy with Lollard concerns. These stand fairly closely together in the manuscript, in quires XIII–XVI, which comprise sermons 41–58 and are written in the same major Anglicana hand of the collection.[8] They may originally have formed a separate booklet. To this group belongs the perhaps original Latin version of Wimbledon's *Redde rationem* (A-48), and one may wonder whether other sermons here are by his hand as well. Owst certainly thought so but unfortunately did not make an argument for common authorship beyond rather vaguely noticing a common concern with pastoral duties and "the same vigorous style."[9] One can, indeed, point to more specific features that several sermons in this group share with Wimbledon's *Redde rationem*. The same pastoral concern and lament at its neglect appears in sermons A-41, 43, 48, 49, and 50. The major topic of Wimbledon's sermon: the three questions that pastors will have to answer on the day of final judgment, even if it seems to have been somewhat of a commonplace that was used by other preachers also,[10] appears concentrated and repeated in sermons 41, 42, and 48. The same three sermons also speak of the "Ecclesia militans." Even more specific is the peculiar tone of apocalypticism we noticed in Wimbledon: not only in A-48 but also in 42,[11] 49,[12] and 50 do we hear that the Church or the world has grown old and that Antichrist is very near. And Wimbledon's

---

[7] For instance, A-40 repeats much canonistic teaching about the Eucharist and discusses communion under one species, citing FitzRalph. It further says that, "other things being equal, it is safer for the salvation of souls to confess to one's own parish priest, as well as in greater accord with reason and more useful to our militant Church" ("Confiteri proprio curato cum ceteris paribus est saluti animarum securius, racioni conformius, ac nostre Ecclesie militanti expedicius," f. 131).

[8] The four quires are linked by continuous sermon texts. A-57, still written by the same Anglicana hand, is a sermon by Brinton (BR-36). A-58 is written in a later, more cursive Secretary hand, apparently to fill the quire. Of the sermons discussed in this paragraph, 41–43 and 49 address *Reverendi*; sermons 48 and 50 address *Karissimi*.

[9] Owst, *Preaching*, p. 362. Cf. *Preaching*, p. 33, n. 4; *Literature*, pp. 31 n. 2; 69 n. 8; 83 n. 1; 266 n. 5; and 314 n. 3.

[10] For instance, in BR-85 (p. 386), M/3-50 (and N-5), and *Stella clericorum*.

[11] "Ecclesia militante iam senescente" (f. 136v); "virgente mundi vespere et Ecclesia iam senescente" (f. 137). The phrase "virgente mundi vespere" is from the Advent hymn "Conditor alme siderum"; cf. also the beginning of a letter by Pope Innocent III written in 1199 (!) and later incorporated in the *Decretals* at 5.7.10: "Vergentis in senium saeculi corruptelam" (Friedberg 2:782).

[12] "Diabolus cum suis exercitibus iam fine mundi appropinquante forcius solito debacatur," f. 152.

quoting Joachim of Flora, in A-48, finds an echo in A-50, where, after listing the signs of the coming judgment, the preacher continues: "Abbot Joachim writes in his exposition of Jeremiah, and this is put into the *Speculum historiale*, book 32, chapter 17 as follows . . ."[13]

Sermon 50 is remarkable in one further respect. It is marked for the third Sunday in Lent, has as its thema *Quomodo stabit regnum*, and was evidently given by an itinerant preacher who had preached "here" before, as he says at the beginning of his third principal part:

> The last time I was here I spoke to you of Christ's castle, which is the faithful soul, and how it was besieged by the devil and his army.[14] But now I plan to call your attention to the castle of the devil, which he, with the help and support of these traitors, is building in our kingdom.[15]

Though the text tells us nothing about the exact place of its delivery, it is a little more informative about its date: "How great a dissension there has been we are now seeing and have seen since the beginning of this schism, that is, when pope Urban VI was elected, when a large part of the western Church abandoned him. And in the time of *this* pope an even greater dissension has taken place."[16] *This* pope would be a successor to Urban VI, and most likely Boniface IX, who held the office from 1389 to 1404. But dissension in the Church – as well as the realm – is only one evil of the times which the entire sermon laments. In his main division, the preacher declares that three things move him to ask the question of his thema,

---

13 "Scribit autem abbas Ioachim in exposicione Ieremie, et ponitur in *Speculo historiali*, libro 32, capitulo cvii, per hunc modum: 'Puto enim quod sicut olim Deus patres elegit senes, secundo apostolos ieniores [!], ita nunc tercio in litteratura eliget ad predicandum euangelium regni prelatis / adulantibus verbum Dei.' Hec Ioachim ibidem," f. 156r–v. The quotation can be found in Vincent of Beauvais, *Speculum historiale*, book 31, chapter 108; in *Speculum quadruplex* 4:1325. Notice that just before this passage in the *Speculum historiale* appears the Joachim quotation that Wimbledon used in *Redde rationem* (*Wimbledon's Sermon*, lines 837–840).

14 The soul as Christ's castle besieged by the sins is a fairly frequent sermon topic, and this reference alone is insufficient to identify the sermon here referred to. S-14 develops the image as well as the seven deadly sins at length.

15 "Vltimo quando eram hic loquebar vobis de castro Christi, quod est anima fidelis, et quomodo illa erat obsessa per diabolum et exercitum eius. Set modo intendo referre vobis de castro diaboli quod ipse cum auxilio et fauore istorum proditorum edificat in regno nostro," f. 157. Before this, the preacher had already referred to what I take to be another sermon: "Ostendi enim alias quod omnes falsi Christiani et spiritualiter falsi pastores Ecclesie sunt Christi proditores et tocius Ecclesie militantis," ibidem. There is another reference to his preaching in the same place on another occasion in A-49: "Quid autem sit penitencia al' dixi in isto loco" (f. 154).

16 "Et iam videmus et vidimus quanta fuit dissencio ab eo in principio istius scismatis, scilicet in creacione pape Vrbani VI, quando scilicet magna pars Ecclesie occidentalis dimisit ipsum. Et in tempore istius pape est adhuc maior dissencio facta," f. 156. I have added emphasis in my translation.

How shall the realm stand: "Fear of the threats of omnipotent God above us, horror at the division among us, and the fervent hostility of the devil who rages all around us."[17] Regarding the first point, he announces that "the Almighty threatens that he will make a quick end of us." These threats were predicted by Christ in Luke 21:9–19 and Matthew 24, speaking of wars, insurrections, pestilences, earthquakes, and famines. But such signs are not new, the preacher says, and have been with us for a long time,[18] whereas he can point to signs that – again according to biblical texts – are closer to the final judgment. These are four: signs in the sun, signs in the moon (cf. Luke 21:25 and Matthew 24:29), a revolt (from the Roman Empire; cf. 2 Thess 2:3), and, according to Christ's words, "this gospel of the kingdom shall be preached in the whole world . . . after which shall come the end" (Matthew 24:14). The preacher then continues to "show that these four signs, which are seen to be proximate to the Judgment, have all come to pass in our days."[19] The "signs in the sun and the moon" he interprets morally, referring to failings in the clergy (the sun) and the laity (the moon). The third sign, the predicted revolt or dissension, is seen in the schism. Concerning the fourth sign, the preacher's words become most interesting:

> Lo, we now see such a great spreading of the gospel that simple men and women, who in the public opinion are unlearned layfolk, write and teach the gospel, and as much as is in their power and knowledge, teach and spread the word of God. But whether, as the world is growing old, God has chosen such people to confound the pride of the wordly wise, I do not know – God knows.[20]

The speaker is evidently referring to the Lollards, though he waffles on whether their work is good or evil. But earlier in his sermon he had already mentioned them by name and had there taken a more definite stand. In his introduction, before reaching the main division, he had quoted a verse from Sirach to introduce his topic of national decay: "Kingdoms are transferred from one people to another on account of injustices and injuries, contumelies, and various deceits" (Sirach 10:8), and set out to interpret these terms. With regard to "contumelies," he cited the case of Rehoboam, who, when confronted by the request to relax

[17] "Terror minarum omnipotentis Dei supra nos, horror diuisionis existentis intra nos, et feruor inimicicie diaboli seuientis vndique circa nos," f. 155.

[18] "Hec signa non sunt noua set per multa tempora durauerunt," f. 155v.

[19] "Hec quatuor signa . . . omnia vt videtur veraciter sunt impleta in diebus nostris, vt intendo vobis ostendere," f. 155v.

[20] "Et quarto signo, scilicet disseminacio euangelii. Ecce iam videmus tantam disseminacionem euangelii quod simplices viri et mulieres et in reputacione hominum laici ydiote scribunt et discunt euangelium et quantum possunt et sciunt docent et seminant verbum Dei. Set nunquid tales senescente mundo elegerit Deus ad confundendum superbiam sapientum mundanorum nescio, Deus scit," f. 156.

the strictures his father had imposed, vowed that he would impose even greater ones. The preacher then continued:

> Certainly, many in this kingdom labor in this vice, and not only the common people but churchmen who should be examples of patience and holiness for the people. For you can very often hear, *in this high and venerable place*, that the one who stands here or should stand here to preach the word of God, through his entire sermon or at least for the most part, does nothing else but despise his neighbors. Now he reproves simple people who labor to learn the law of God and to live in accordance with it; then he despises faithful priests who preach Christ's lore without flattery and human regard. And in a high dudgeon they call such people "heretics" and "Lollards" and report of them many feigned lies which those people had never thought of. And where such a preacher should preach Christ, who is the Truth, he preaches himself and the lore of his father, the devil, that is to say, detractions and lies. He is a liar and his father. And what else is this, I ask, but that "abomination of desolation standing in the holy place" of Matthew 24 and Daniel 9? Such a person may be called Antichrist, for he stands in Christ's place and preaches against Christ.[21]

This certainly speaks for a genuine sympathy with the Lollards, to say the least.[22]

The "high and venerable place" in the passage just quoted may well be St. Paul's Cross, London, a place of fervent preaching by both orthodox preachers and Lollard sympathizers, which we have come across in the discussions of Alkerton and Wimbledon. Along with other shared features that have been examined, the preaching at St. Paul's Cross and the suspicion of Lollard sympathies, voiced in the one known documentary record that can be related to Thomas Wimbledon, thus make it likely that at least several sermons surrounding *Redde rationem* in this

---

[21] "Et certe in isto vicio nimis multi laborant in hoc regno, et non solum communis populus set viri ecclesiastici qui deberent esse in populo exempla paciencie et tocius sanctitatis. Potestis enim nimis sepe audire in isto alto et venerabili loco quod ipse qui hic stat vel stare deberet ad predicandum verbum Dei per sermonem suum vel saltem per magnam partem nichil aliud facit quam despicit proximos suos. Ibi reprobat simplices viros qui laborant vt addiscant legem Dei et viuant secundum eam, ibi despicit fideles sacerdotes qui absque adulacione et personarum accepcione doctrinam Christi predicant, vocando tales cum magno spiritu hereticos miseros et lollardos, et narrat de ipsis multa mendacia ficta que nunquam cogitabantur. Et sic vbi deberet predicare Christum, qui est veritas, predicat seipsum et doctrinam patris sui diaboli, scilicet detracciones et mendacia. Ipse enim est mendax et pater eius. Et quid queso aliud est quam 'abhominacio desolacionis stantis in loco sancto,' Matthei 25 et Danielis 9? Talis potest vocari Antechristus quia stat in loco Christi et predicat contra Christum," f. 155.

[22] Notice the similar remark about oppression of the gospel in Wimbledon's sermon: "Nunc ergo necessaria est vox aquile vt extollatur Deus ne humane tradiciones supergrediantur et calcent euangelium Christi," A-48, f. 150v; in *Wimbledon's Sermon*, lines 963–965. Wimbledon is here expounding the opening of the fourth seal of Revelation 6:8 and the voice of the angel of Revelation 8:13.

collection are by his hand as well. What might have exposed them to suspicion of Lollard tendencies would be their open critique of clerical failings as well as their apocalyptic tone, especially the notion that near the end of the century Satan rages ever more fiercely – both elements that also appear in a sermon preached by Robert Lychlade, for which he was banished from Oxford University in 1395.[23]

---

[23] See Wenzel, "Robert Lychlade's Oxford Sermon," pp. 206–207. Lychlade begins his sermon with "Cum diabolus . . . laboret fortiter ad subuersionem Ecclesie et . . . 'tanquam leo rugiens circuit querens quem deuoret,' oportet 'recistere fortiter in fide,' et specialiter iam contra finem mundi, quia in quanto propinquius / accedimus versus finem seculi, in tanto crudelius temptat hominem ut eum inpediat ne habeat vitam eternam," p. 206. Compare A-49: "Diabolus cum suis exercitibus iam fine mundi appropinquante forcius solito debacatur ["rages"]," f. 152.

32

Arras, Bibliothèque de la Ville, MS 184 (254) (Z)

Properly speaking, this volume, written entirely in one English Secretary hand of the early fifteenth century, is a preacher's notebook rather than a genuine sermon collection: its fifty-seven sermons are interspersed with notes, stories, excerpts, and longer treatises.[1] Often a sermon ends indeterminately and its subject is continued in one or two notes, and occasionally it is hard to distinguish between a sermon and a longer note. But all the non-sermon material contained in the book would have been of use to a preacher or curate.

Although here and there two or three successive sermons stand in their liturgical sequence, overall this is a random collection. Of the sermons that are or can be assigned to a specific occasion, about thirty-six are for selected Sundays of the Church year, from 1 Advent to 21 Trinity, with concentration on Lent, Good Friday, and Easter. Two sermons are for saints' feasts (Purification, All Saints; another sermon perhaps for St. John the Baptist), and one sermon is marked for the dedication of a church. Not all sermons have address forms, but of those that do, thirty-three address *Karissimi* and six *Reuerendi*.[2] In one sermon (44) the preacher states that in his audience he sees both clerics and lay people ("seculares") and that he will speak to both separately, which he then does. Another is addressed to *Fratres* and evidently directed to a university audience.[3] Several catechetical pieces are treated at some length,[4] even more than once; and several

---

[1] See the description of the manuscript and its contents in Wenzel, *Macaronic*, pp. 203–211, with further discussion ibid., pp. 47–49.

[2] In addition, one sermon addresses *Domini* and another *Amici*. *Fratres* occurs also in various combinations.

[3] Many students are more humble "quando primo veniunt ad istam vniuersitatem" than when they leave, f. 32rb.

[4] The Ten Commandments in sermon 16 (referred to in 18, 34, and 51); the seven deadly sins are frequently mentioned and more fully treated in 23, 24, 31 (referred to in 32), 35; the Pater Noster in 4 (the English treatise); the works of mercy are mentioned in 33, with a reference to a sermon for St. Lawrence, not preserved in this ms; beatitudes, gifts of the Holy Spirit, virtues, and vices in sermon 24.

sermons voice criticism of the clergy, though these are generally commonplaces shared with other sermons or derived from *Fasciculus morum* (see below).

The anonymous collector has taken his material from many different sources, going back in time as far as Grosseteste's address to the council of Lyons in 1250 (here a partial copy, Z-22). Closer to his own time, he has included a copy of the sermon which, according to its colophon, Robert Lychlade gave at Oxford in 1395, for which the latter was expelled from the university (Z-12, the only known copy).[5] Another sermon, also with a colophon, is attributed to Henry Chambron (Z-1), and two further sermons that elsewhere are ascribed to Chambron appear here as well, although anonymously (Z-19 and 20).[6] In all, the Arras manuscript shares fourteen sermons, and in several instances the shared sermon appears in more than one other manuscript.[7] Of particular interest in this respect are the sermons shared with MS Harley 331 (H). As will be noted in the section devoted to the latter, the relations between it and other manuscripts including Z are complex. A more detailed textual analysis will undoubtedly shed more light on them, but my impression is that both Z and H are independently derived from a common source collection.

Despite the fact that the collector of Z drew on a variety of sources, the collection possesses a certain partial unity. This is established by two features:

---

[5] Edited and further discussed in Wenzel, "Robert Lychlade's Oxford Sermon."

[6] The three Chambron sermons are *Corruit in platea veritas* with colophon, *Quare rubrum*, and *Christus passus est*. See the section on Chambron above, pp. 132–138.

[7] The shared sermons are as follows:

Z	E	H	J	S	V	Others
1					37	
2	38					
3		1				CA/2–03
4			5–25			
6			5–26			
14	7					
19		25		1		W-6
20					19	A-35, Ee.6.27
22						Grosseteste
24	10					
26	2	8				
32	40					
43			5–24			
56						Magd. 112

Oxford, Magdalen College, MS 112 is written in several fifteenth-century hands and contains only a few scattered sermons. On ff. 225ra–232vb it has a copy of the treatise which is also in Z (ff. 152rb–162vb), where it is called *Speculum sacerdotis* (Bloomfield, *Incipits*, no. 5269).

cross referencing and the repeated use of material from a Franciscan preaching handbook. At least fifteen sermons contain references to other sermons in the collection, which in all link twenty pieces together.[8] The references are generally accurate.[9] Some of these sermons also appear in collection H, and this feature once again suggests strongly that both Arras and H are independently derived from a common source. Many of these cross-referenced sermons, as well as some other in Zs, further contain the second unifying element: at least a dozen include passages from *Fasciculus morum* (= *FM*), a Franciscan preaching manual composed in the early fourteenth century and of great popularity.[10] These are mostly similes with moralization and include the famous Christ-Knight *exemplum*, the comparison of God to a nurse and her charge, the mother and her *filius freneticus*, pilgrims turning towards Scotland instead of the Holy Land, and others. There are at least eleven such passages that are, without acknowledgment, almost word for word derived from the *FM*. Several occur in more than one sermon, and conversely some sermons include more than one of them.[11] Such borrowings make it more than likely that the unknown composer was a Franciscan, which is further substantiated by sermon 3 (shared as H-1), which speaks of "beatus

---

[8] Sermons 11, 16, 18, 19, 24, 26–34, 37–41, 51. A sermon for St. Lawrence, which does not appear in the manuscript as it has survived, is referred to in Z-30 and 33.

[9] With an interesting exception: Z-26 mentions a very popular story from Étienne de Bourbon about a sinful woman who finally returned to God, "of whom the author of the work *On the Seven Gifts of the Holy Spirit* speaks, as is seen above (*supra*) in the sermon for the second Sunday of Lent." The Arras collection contains a sermon for 2 Lent (Z-38), but it occurs *after*, not before (*supra*) the cited reference. Moreover, Z-38 has only an introduction and then breaks off with listing the main parts to follow – contrition, confession, and satisfaction – whose treatment "can be found in the preceding sermon." It is, finally, Z-37, on 1 Lent, which contains the entire story with its source identified (f. 102va). A similar mistake (?) occurs in Z-24: "sicut patet in sermone Dominice 15 post Trinitatem" (f. 73va–b). The reference is to Z-40, which occurs *below*, on f. 88ra. There is no evidence that the respective quires were bound in the wrong order.

[10] The manuscripts are discussed in Wenzel, *Verses*, pp. 13–26; and in *Fasciculus morum*, pp. 1–23.

[11] The passages are as follows:
  (1) God and sinner are like a nurse and a child (*FM* V.vii.139–151, p. 440): Arras sermons 16, 24 (also H-10), 27, 35, 37, and 39.
  (2) The book of memory (*FM* V.xxi.15–32, p. 590): 5 and 16.
  (3) The Christ-Knight, with reference to Virgil and commentator (*FM* III.x.90–c.120, p. 204): 16, 30, and 40.
  (4) The falcon (*FM* V.vii, p. 438): 39.
  (5) Mother and her *filius freneticus* (*FM* III.x, p. 208): 28.
  (6) Pilgrims going to Scotland (*FM* V.xii, p. 474): 37 and 39.
  (7) Prelates suffer *accidia* (*FM* V.iii, p. 416): 49.
  (8) Adam's shield taken up by Christ (*FM* III.xv, pp. 234 f.): 50.
  (9) Gates of a delightful city close at night (*FM* V.viii, p. 454): 37.
  (10) The bird that flies up high is secure (*FM* III.xxi, p. 278): 41.

pater noster Franciscus in regula sua" in referring to the four standard topics of Franciscan preaching: vices, virtues, punishment, and glory (f. 5vb).[12] One may wonder whether Z or part of it is not a unified collection after all, but the irregular presence of sermons by known authors and the general random order (i.e., no grouping) speak against it.

If the collector of Z has thus drawn on a variety of sources, this may explain another peculiarity of the collection, its mixture of orthodox and seemingly Lollard elements. Where the sermons gathered here address doctrinally sensitive issues, they side with orthodoxy, as in dealing with the legitimacy of pilgrimages,[13] private auricular confession,[14] prayer for the souls in purgatory,[15] and image worship.[16] On one occasion the preacher warns his audience to "beware diligently of false teachers, counselors, flatterers, or backbiters, who try to deceive you and to poison your soul with the poison of heresy or of mortal sin."[17] To these elements may be added the presence in the codex of a small collection of the fables by Odo of Cheriton (ff. 181ra–190ra), sermon material that was under strong indictment from Wyclif and Lollard preachers.[18] However, the manuscript equally contains features that smack of Lollardy. These are, first of all, two Middle-English treatises,

---

[12] The partial homogeneity of the collection may also be seen in two additional features: six sermons have "Iesu mercy" at their head (35–37, 39–41), and several pieces begin like a homily by retelling the gospel lection and offering a moral exposition before turning to the sermon's main division with the formula "pro vlteriori processu" (e.g., 30, 32, 34, 35, 38, 51). The latter aspect will be discussed below in the chapter "The Preacher's Voice."

[13] Several sermons use pilgrimage imagery without doctrinal self-consciousness. More significantly, a note between sermons states that "a pilgrimage that is holy on account of its justice and usefulness must be done with much abstinence and good meditations, prayers, and almsgiving" ("Nota quod peregrinacio ex iusta et vtili causa sancta debet fieri in magna abstinencia cum bonis meditacionibus, oracionibus, et elemosinarum largicionibus, et non in ebrietatibus, commessacionibus, luxuriis, vaniloquio, et aliis viciis"), f. 129vb.

[14] Z-55 is a veritable treatise on confession; it discusses the conditions necessary in confessing one's sins, but also the necessary qualities of a prelate or confessor: "qui presentat regem regum et dominus dominancium: requiritur primo quod sit iustus iudicator, sanctus informator, et prudens cordium scrutator," f. 175rb.

[15] A funeral sermon, Z-2, speaks at some length about how good and necessary it is to pray for the dead.

[16] Z-16, on the Decalogue, in dealing with the first commandment, pays some attention to the worship of images. It argues the orthodox position that it is licit to worship the person represented by the image (*coram imagine*, not *ad imaginem*). The argument quotes Holcot and derives substantively from his commentary on the Book of Wisdom.

[17] In Z-18 on *Qui facit voluntatem patris mei qui in celis est* (Matthew 7:21), which begins: "Karissimi, in hoc euangelio precipit nos Saluator cauere et vitare consilium falsorum prophetarum dicens, 'Attendite a falsis prophetis,' hoc est, diligenter cauete a falsis doctoribus, consulatoribus, adulatoribus siue detractoribus, qui nituntur te decipere et animam tuam intoxicare veneno heresis siue peccati mortalis," f. 50vb.

[18] Cf. below, Part Three, chapters 50 (p. 393) and 47 (p. 343).

on the Pater Noster and on the Creed, which modern scholars have considered of Wycliffite origin. The copies in Z, though incomplete, agree in substance with the edited versions.[19] Second is the presence of a sermon by Lychlade, who was indeed expelled from Oxford for Wycliffite sympathies – though reinstalled four years later.[20] Thirdly, the manuscript bears indications that many folios have been excised after the medieval foliation had been entered, and at least some of the excisions occur at points where the preacher apparently indulged in criticizing the clergy.[21] Lastly, two sermons speak quite plainly about and to those who were being persecuted for preaching the gospel. Sermon 24, on "Your reward is very great in heaven" (Matthew 5:12), expounds the first seven beatitudes of the Sermon of the Mount and links them at some length to seven virtues and the seven deadly sins. The preacher then adds further comments on the eighth and ninth beatitudes, the last one being "Blessed are you when men revile you and persecute you . . . ," which contains the sermon's thema. "Here," the preacher declares, "Christ teaches us that we ought not to fear frivolous revilings (*maledicciones friuolas*) that are spoken out of the malice of falsehood." And he continues:

> Therefore, beloved, do not give up your good intent because of some such feigned excommunications, and especially you who have begun to preach the word of God, do not because of such things retreat, but for the love of the most sweet Jesus Christ preach the word of God always and faithfully. And if such people have persecuted you in one city, flee to another, and if they speak all evil against you, thereby lying, for Christ's sake do not fear them.[22]

---

[19] See Wenzel, *Macaronic*, p. 204.   [20] See above, n. 5.

[21] See especially after f. 99 and again after f. 166. In both cases there is visible evidence of excision, and the medieval foliation on the extant folios jumps from 119 to 121 and from 187 to 189.

[22] "Hic docet nos Christus quod non debemus timere maledicciones friuolas que fiunt pro malicia falcitatis. Malediccio enim talis uentosa non nocet bonis hominibus set redit ad animam toxicatam a qua procedit, cum hic dicat 'Beati eritis cum vobis maledixerint homines.' Et in Psalmo: 'Maledicent illi et tu benedices.' Igitur, karissimi, nolite dimittere bonum propositum pro aliquibus talibus fictis excommunicacionibus, et specialiter vos qui incipistis predicare verbum Dei, nolite pro talibus ire retrorsum, set pro amore dulcissimi Iesu Christi predicate continue et fideliter verbum Dei. Et si tales persecuti vos fuerint in vna ciuitate, fugite in aliam, et si dixerint omnem malum aduersum vos mencientes propter Christum, nolite eos timere. Nam vt dicit Crisostomus, 'qui concupiscit que sunt in celo, obprobria non timet in terris, nec cogitat que loquuntur homines per homines, set quid iudicet Deus de illo.' Qui enim letatur de laude hominum et quantum letatur, tristatur ille et de vituperacione hominum. Qui autem de laude hominum non extollitur nec de vituperacione humiliatur. Vnusquisque vbi gloriam querit illic timet confusionem: qui gloriam querit in terris, confusionem in terris timet, qui autem gloriam non querit nisi tantummodo apud Deum, confusionem non timet nisi tantummodo Dei. Similes [!] periculum belli sustinet dum sperat victorie predam, quanto magis vos opera mundi non debetis timere qui regni celestis premium exspectatis, set 'gaudete et exultate, quoniam merces vestra magna est in celis.' Quam mercedem vobis concedat qui sine fine viuit et regnat. Amen," Z-24, f.76ra.

A similar exhortation, using in part the same words, appears in Z-16, on "The door is closed" (Matthew 25:10), which the writer refers to in at least four other sermons.[23] Z-16, delivered after Lent, deals at length with the Ten Commandments, and in discussing the first raises the question of image worship, which, as noted above, it answers with Holcot quotations in an orthodox fashion. But it concludes with the observation that "those who call such images by the names of the saints who are now in heaven do wrong" and blames the higher clergy for such abuse:

> Such superiors of the Church, who ought to instruct the people in this fashion [i.e., to distinguish between worshiping an image and worshiping the person it represents], are so hardened in their sin of greed that they are afraid to teach the people how they should use images. [They fail do so] in order not to lose the offerings that are frequently made to such images in a diabolical fashion.[24]

Such an accusation was certainly raised by Wyclif and his sympathizers, but it was equally raised, and before Wyclif, by FitzRalph and in *FM*.[25] Yet the same sermon goes on to speak of another issue that strikes what sounds like a much more clearly unorthodox tone. Under the fifth commandment the preacher details sins that amount to killing physically or spiritually. Of the former he accuses false judges, false pardoners, oppressors of the people, and those who practice abortion; and of the sins of spiritual killing he accuses prelates who sin publicly and backbiters. Of the latter he says,

> Such are many nowadays who out of envy and malice falsely detract and most falsely impeach those who freely preach the word of God to the people and teach them spiritually.[26]

And under the eighth commandment he returns to backbiters and encourages his audience:

---

[23] *Clausa est ianua.* This sermon is referred to in Z-18, 30, 34, 51.

[24] "Ex quibus patet quod male faciunt qui appellant tales ymagines nominibus sanctorum qui sunt in celo . . . / Et tota causa est quia tales superiores Ecclesie, qui deberent populum informare taliter, sunt peccato auaricie obstinati quod timent populum informare qualiter debent [?] illis vti, ne perderent oblaciones que multociens talibus ymaginibus diabolice sunt contribute," f. 46rb–va.

[25] See the discussion of this issue and its appearance in *Piers Plowman* in Wenzel, "Eli," with the Wycliffite and orthodox passages referred to above given on pp. 149–150. In *FM*, bishops are accused of dressing up images with costly cloth while the poor go hungry (V.xxv.157–172, ed. cit. p. 552), in a quotation from Hugh of Folieto, *De claustro animae* I.1 (PL 176:1019).

[26] "Tales sunt multi hiis diebus qui propter invidiam et maliciam false detractant et falsissima eis imponunt qui libere predicant populo verbum Dei eis spiritualiter informanda," Z-16, f. 48ra.

Especially you who have begun to preach the word of God, do not retreat on their account but for the love of the most beloved Jesus Christ preach the word of God continually and faithfully. And if they persecute you in one town, flee to another.[27]

Whether these elements actually make the respective sermons Lollard productions is by no means certain. It is of course possible that whoever collected material for Z took what came to hand, whether it was orthodox or not. On the other hand, being persecuted for preaching need not necessarily point to Lollard origins. There is evidence from other collections that friars occasionally felt a similar constraint; and as we have seen, collection Z has a strong affiliation with the Franciscans. In this connection it may also be important to point out that Z-16 as well as Z-24 preach *pastoralia* (the Decalogue and the Seven Deadly Sins, respectively), not the gospel lection;[28] and further that the two quoted passages on persecution speak of "preaching the word of God" – not "the gospel," as might be more indicative of a Wycliffite language and position.[29] Perhaps it makes best sense to think of the collector as a Franciscan who shared with the Lollards, not their doctrinal positions but their critique of the contemporary clergy and concern for reform, as it had been expressed by Grosseteste at the Council of Lyons in 1250 and by Lychlade at Oxford in 1395.

[27] "Sic et vos, karissimi, sperate in Domino et nolite dimittere bonum proprium pro aliquibus talibus falsis detractoribus et testibus. Et specialiter vos qui incepistis predicare verbum Dei, nolite pro talibus ire retrossum set pro amore dilectissimi Iesu Christi predicate continue et fideliter verbum Dei. Et si tales persecuti fuerint vos in vna ciuitate, fugite ad aliam," Z-16, f. 48rb. The same passage is in Z-24, f. 76ra.

[28] Cf. below, Part Three, chapter 48.

[29] The common usage in canon law, synodal decrees, handbooks, and sermons is *praedicare verbum Dei*. The alternative *praedicare evangelium* occurs only very occasionally in some Church decrees and handbooks. A-50 and Dygon (DY-17 and 20), for example, use both forms, though *verbum Dei* prevails. Wyclif also uses both forms, but at the same time favors *evangelizare, evangelizatio* for "preaching." Of course, usage depends on how close the respective text stands to either Luke 8:11 and parallels ("semen est verbum Dei") or Mark 16:14 and its parallels ("praedicate evangelium omni creaturae").

33

London, St. Paul's Cathedral Library, MS 8 (Y)

This early fifteenth-century paper and parchment manuscript contains three separate booklets that were written in hands of the second half of the fourteenth and the early fifteenth century. It has been described in detail by N. R. Ker.[1] There seems to be no indication when and by whom the three booklets, Y/1-3, were joined, but all three contain sermons in random order.

Y/1 (ff. 1–197v) was written not long after 1404 (see below). Next to four homilies from St. Bernard's *Super Missus est* (ff. 139–149v), the Life of St. Brendan (ff. 166–175v), and a series of visions "de penis inferni et . . . de penis purgatorii" (ff. 188–197v), it contains close to a hundred items that mix sermons with articles on theological topics. The distinction between the two is not always easy to make, and this difficulty is enhanced by the fact that sometimes it is unclear where an item begins or ends. In addition, the ends of several sermons are copied in different parts of the booklet, with *signes de renvoi*. Pieces that can be considered to be sermons are themselves of two kinds. First there are items that have some or all of the normal parts of a scholastic sermon, such as thema, address, division, development of the principals, and closing formula. These parts are often carefully marked in the margins. There are roughly twenty-eight such items. But a much larger number come without thema. Instead, they usually – but not always – carry a keyword at their head, presumably taken from the intended thema or from the day's lection. Yet many of these thema-less items are clearly sermons, as they contain characteristic sermon elements. For example, an item on *Pax* begins with the address "Dilectissimi" and ends with a standard closing formula (ff. 46v–49v). It is where such elements in thema-less items are missing that one may suspect the item to be only a note or a longer article, but to repeat, such a distinction between notes and sermons is not always easy to draw. A number of items, about thirty-five, both with and without themata,

---

[1] Ker, *Medieval Manuscripts in British Libraries* 1:248–249.

mark their occasion in the margins. They are for Advent (seven), Christmas (seven), Epiphany, Passion Sunday, Good Friday, and Easter; for the feasts of Mary Magdalene, Peter's Chains, the Conversion of St. Paul, Matthew, and the Nativity and the Assumption of the Blessed Virgin; and for Masses for any virgin (apparently) and for the dead (three, marked *De morte*). These occur in absolutely random order, though several times a number of sermons for the same occasion are copied together. In one section of the booklet the occasion was originally written in the margin and has been erased (ff. 66–72). It is also interesting to note that in several cases the rubric marking the liturgical occasion includes a key term, thus bridging the difference between sermons with and without themata (for instance, "Stare. In die Pasche," f. 31v). Besides the unique occurrence of "Dilectissimi" noted above, the usual address form is "Karissimi" (in 46 items, plus one "Fratres karissimi") or a form including "Reverendi" (four); one sermon, on the Conversion of St. Paul, addresses "Reuerendi patres fratresque karissimi." On the basis of the page layout it is possible to discern at least three batches or runs of sermons that make up this series: folios 1–49v, 50v–77v, and 78–162.

This first booklet, Y/1, contains several pieces of information that connect it with a place and religious order. Ker noted the subscription "quod bannard in conuentu Wychie anno domini MCCCCIIII litera dominicalis d" (f. 20), which occurs after the explicit of a sermon on *Caritas non ficta* addressing "Reuerendi domini";[2] and the name of John Turuey, which appears twice in similar positions (ff. 88 and 149v). In fact, the latter name occurs yet another time in this booklet: "Per fratrem J. Turuay," after the sermon explicit on f. 121.[3] And there is still another name, this one definitely of a sermon writer rather than a scribe: "Istos duos sermones compilauit reuerendus Paulus Parden ordinis fratrum Carmelitarum Valarum. Qui si nimis prolixe videantur, possunt abbreuiari in quocumque membro sicut placet" (f. 43).[4] On the basis of the first subscription Ker suggested that this booklet was "possibly [written] at the convent of Austin friars at Droitwich."[5] As the other subscriptions show, the booklet clearly collects sermons by several hands, including a Carmelite friar. That Y/1 is a miscellaneous

---

[2] The Austin friar John Banard was at Oxford in 1402 and served as chancellor of the university in 1411–1422; see *BRUO* 1:102.

[3] The sermon is on *De morte transivit ad vitam*; it occurs also, without the name, as E-11. A Franciscan friar John Turvey is known to have been at Oxford in 1406; see *BRUO* 3:1981.

[4] The two "sermons" are on "Iudicium" (ff. 42v–43) and presumably the preceding piece marked "Soluere" for the feast of St. Peter's Chains (ff. 41–42v).

[5] Ker, *Medieval Manuscripts in British Libraries* 1:249.

sermon collection is further shown by the fact that at least six items in it also occur in other collections, including the popular series *Convertimini* by Holcot.[6]

The second booklet, Y/2 (ff. 176–187v), written in two Anglicana hands of the fourteenth century, contains ten (not eleven) numbered sermons.[7] Except for the first (on Ephesians 5:8), their occasions are marked, and they stand in proper liturgical sequence: two sermons each for Andrew, Nicholas, the Conception of the Blessed Virgin, and Thomas the Apostle, and an incomplete one for Christmas. One of these may also occur in some Continental collections.[8]

Y/3 (ff. 199–270v) was also written in the fourteenth century, in a more cursive Anglicana hand and somewhat later than Y/2. It ends with a list of forty-three sermon themata and references to the medieval pagination of this booklet. The original first quire, with its seven sermons, has been lost. The remaining thirty-six sermons[9] are interspersed with a number of notes on specified topics ("Rapina," 210v; "Gladius," 211; etc.) and on scriptural passages ("Vere langores nostros ipse tulit," f. 225; "Erat Iesus eiciens demonium," ff. 227–228; etc). In the latter case, one may wonder if these items were not also intended as sermons or parts of sermons, as seems to be particularly the case with a text on "Terra dedit fructum" (ff. 261v–262), which bears the marginal note "Introduccio" and has a regular division. But this and similar themata do not appear in the list on 270v; the maker of the list may have just followed annotations in the corner of the top margins. As a result, it is not always very clear whether a given item with thema is intended as a sermon or a note – a situation reminiscent of Y/1. Occasional rubrics indicate that the sermons are *de tempore* and *de sanctis* and stand in random order. Several of them occur also in other collections: two (Y/3-30 and 32) in P1 and a third (33) in the related manuscript P2; one (8) in A-46; and perhaps another (42) in X-101. Rather intriguingly, three of the seven themata found in the list whose texts are lost also appear in MS Toulouse 342, but the lack of *initia* and texts in Y/3 does not allow us to identify them with certainty. The extant sermons contain

---

[6] The two sermons from Holcot's collection *Convertimini* are *Convertimini* (here ff. 88–89; possibly also on f. 21) and *Qui vicerit* (ff. 82v–83v). Two other shared sermons in Y/1 (ff. 54v and 122) are W-19 and W-98; on f. 119v occurs a copy of E-11; and on f. 125v a sermon on *Tenere* also preserved as A-11 and X-126.

[7] Ker, *Medieval Manuscripts in British Libraries* 1:248, speaks of "eleven sermons," but his second item seems to be the main part of sermon Y/2-1, with a proper closing formula on f. 179v. The sermons are numbered 2–10 in the codex, although the scribe or rubricator made several mistakes. In the bottom margin of f. 176 the scribe has written a list of six occasions of these sermons.

[8] "Christo confixus sum cruci . . . Nauis in mari duobus indiget," on St. Andrew (ff. 180v–181v), has the same *initium* as a sermon Schneyer records for Jacobus de Losanna (Schneyer 3:89) and Michael de Furno (4:178).

[9] There is an additional sermon not listed in the table, Y/3-35A in my inventory.

a fair number of divisions, popular sayings, memorial verses, and the like, in English.

Examination of the codex *in situ* has not revealed any unorthodox traces, but the volume – which unfortunately cannot be microfilmed – calls for more extensive study.[10]

[10] I am very grateful to the current librarian of the Cathedral, Mr. Joseph Wisdom, for giving me access to the manuscript on several occasions and looking into the possibility of filming it.

34

London, British Library, MS Harley 331 (H)

This fragmentary paper manuscript, written about the middle and in the second half of the fifteenth century,[1] retains a miscellaneous sermon collection in which *temporale* and *sanctorale* sermons and pieces for unspecified and general occasions appear randomly without any apparent liturgical or thematic order and are interspersed with notes and some prothemes. Of its twenty-five sermons, ten occur elsewhere, some even in more than one other manuscript. Their distribution may be represented in tabular form:

H	A	B/2	S	V	W	Z	E	CA/2	Others
1 Iesus						3	3		
2 Miserere	36								
3 Quo abiit					83/92				
5 Redde	48			33				ff. 10v–18	
7 Surge et comede						14			
8 Surrexit						26	2		
10 Merces						24			
22 Surge qui		59						5	
23 Manhu				39					
25 Christus passus			1	6		19			Christ Church 91

[1] For a collation of the manuscript and an inventory of its sermons, see Wenzel, *Macaronic*, pp. 157–160. The first eighty-eight folios of the original manuscript are gone.

The main interest of this manuscript lies in what it tells us about the continued preservation into the later fifteenth century of sermons that were composed two or three generations earlier. It further presents a number of features that are characteristic of miscellaneous collections.

First of all, H preserves sermons by known authors together with others of unknown authorship. To the former belong H-25, a copy of the long and popular Good-Friday sermon on *Christus passus est pro nobis*, which is elsewhere ascribed to Chambron, and H-5, a copy of the Latin version of Wimbledon's *Redde rationem vilicationis tuae* (ff. 15–18) that, as I suggested earlier, seems to be based on the English text.[2] Next to these stand anonymous sermons that recur in as many as seven different other collections.

Second, the sermons shared by H and other collections are independent copies, deriving from a common and no longer known or extant ancestor. Some collation of H sermons with those in other manuscripts reveals that in no case can it be shown that one was directly copied from the other. For instance, the five sermons that H shares with Z (which include Z-3, quoting the four topics of Franciscan preaching taken from the Rule of "our blessed father Francis") are textually fairly much the same in both collections. Their differences, even where Z has smaller additions, can be considered scribal variations. Since in these texts each manuscript has its own eyeskips, neither is dependent on the other. In all five cases, thus, the shared sermons are what I have called separate copies. What emerges from comparing shared sermons in all miscellaneous collections here studied is a dense network in which the respective manuscripts are horizontally related but not vertically.

Such relationships can become more complicated where three or even more versions of the same sermon have been preserved. A good case in point is *Merces vestra copiosa est in celis*, extant in H-10 and Z-24. This sermon for the feast of All Saints has a fairly simple structure. After a brief introduction recalling that in his Sermon on the Mount Christ taught nine lessons, it devotes one section each to the first seven beatitudes, relating them to the gifts of the Holy Spirit and the seven deadly sins. In the end, the preacher declares that the eighth beatitude "confirms" all the preceding ones, and that the ninth is the same as the eighth. The two versions are substantively identical, with two interesting exceptions: (1) In dealing with pride, the preacher announces that he will show by an *exemplum* how foolish those are who wish to climb above others and have rule and cure over them. At this point H gives the entire narrative, whereas Z refers to a sermon for 15 Trinity.[3] Z's reference is accurate, as the respective passage occurs several

---

[2] See above "Wimbledon". H-5 patterns with A-48 but has an abbreviated text.

[3] "Sicut patet in sermone dominice 15 post Trinitatem," Z-24, f. 73vb.

folios later in that manuscript.[4] (2) The reverse happens in the section on the third beatitude: now Z has the complete text and H gives a cross reference, "as is shown in the sermon which begins *Amice, ascende superius* ('Friend, rise up higher')."[5] There is no such sermon in H, although there may once have been one on the original eighty-eight leaves that are now lost. Z does not have such a sermon either. But the sermon referred to, *Amice, ascende superius,* has been preserved elsewhere (E and J/5), with exactly the passage as in Z.[6] Since Z directly shares three other sermons each with E and J/5, one may expect that it is directly related to either or both. But such expectation is frustrated when one examines yet another sermon, *Surrexit Dominus vere.* Copies of it occur in H and Z, and there is a third version in E, but the latter is clearly a redaction.[7] Moreover, its version in Z-26 contains a cross reference that is not exactly right and may have thus been copied by the scribe of Z from his exemplar.[8] Instead of finding rock bottom on which he could build a relationship of clear derivation, the textual critic walks in a swamp of crisscrossing and changing rivulets.

The whole matter of cross references, however, leads to a more positive final observation about this and other miscellaneous collections. In many of them there is clear evidence that their collectors attempted to create something resembling a unified collection. Sometimes they grouped sermons on the same topic or belonging to the same liturgical season together. Sometimes they provided their manuscripts with an index. More frequently, and more obviously, they inserted cross references to other sermons in their collection. This technique has called our attention repeatedly in the preceding sections, and it appears again in the present collection H. In contrast to other collections, H does not refer to other sermons with *infra* or *supra,* nor does it use *signes de renvoi;*[9] but it does refer to seven sermons[10] either by their thema or their occasion, and of these at least two or three still occur in the defective codex.

The manuscript has some connection with a university milieu. Of the twenty-five sermons, fifteen are addressed to "Karissimi" and two to "Reuerendi," but more interestingly, among the sermons proper occurs a free-standing sermon

---

[4] In Z-31, f. 88rb.

[5] "Tales miseri inuidi et iracundi sponte sine voluntate [per]dunt animas suas, vt patet in sermone qui sic incipit: 'Amice, ascende superius'," H-10, f. 29v.

[6] E-39, ff. 108vb–109ra, and J/5-23, f. 99r–v.

[7] Discussed in "Prolegomena," pp. 5–7.

[8] See the section on Z, note 9. Absence of the sermon referred to in E and J/5 further proves that these cannot have been the exemplar of H.

[9] It does once say "ad tale signum" but there is no sign, either at f. 65v (margin defective) or at the possible places referred to.

[10] An eighth (H-9) speaks of the Ten Commandments and says "de quibus patet alibi," perhaps referring to H-19.

opener without thema addressed to "Reuerendi magistri, patres, atque domini" and asking them to pray for the state of the Church, the pope, cardinals, and entire clergy of England, the chancellor of this university and all masters regent or non-regent, King Henry with his queen and offspring, and so on. This is an example of the *commendatio* that was apparently customary in university sermons, as we saw earlier in collection C.[11]

[11] "Reuerendi magistri patres atque domini, in exordio huius sermonis breuissimi vostris deuotis precibus prosperum statum tocius Ecclesie militantis recommendo, dominum summum pontificem cum toto cetu cardinalium venerando et specialiter totum clerum prouincie Anglicane, dominum Cancellarium huius alme vniuersitatis matris nostre, ac omnes magistros regentes et non regentes, et singulos ceteros proficere volentes in eadem insuper recommendo vestris deuotis precibus tranquillitatem et pacem istius regni, illustrissimum principem dominum nostrum regem Henricum dominamque reginam cum illustri stirpe regali et ceteros huius regni tam proceres quam vulgares. Preterea recommendo vobis animas omnium fidelium defunctorum in pena purgatorii existentes et ibidem diuine misericordie auxilium prestolantes. Pro quibus omnibus et gracia vobis ac michi in hoc actu summe necessaria premittat quilibet vestrum si placeat mente deuota oracionem dominicam cum salutacione angelica," f. 79r–v. It is followed by another protheme leading to a prayer without thema.

35

Manchester, John Rylands Library, MS
Latin 367 (M)

This codex, containing a mixed collection of sermons, is made up of two separate, equally well written booklets that have the same layout in two columns and the same kind of initials and of careful rubrication, but are written by different hands.

(1) The first booklet, in a well-set Anglicana bookhand of the fifteenth century, contains a cycle of 123 *de tempore* sermons (ff. 1–111ra; = M/1) followed by another cycle of eighty sermons *de sanctis et de diversis* (ff. 112–197va; = M/2). They are preceded (f. 1ra) by a prologue "Cum in ecclesia mea quietus residerem." The two sets are called *partes* 1 and 2 by the rubricator, and the individual pieces are labeled *omelie* and numbered consecutively for each set. In the top margin of f. 1, written by the rubricator, next to "prima pars" and "omelia prima" appears the word "attoñ." The writer of the prologue indentifies himself as "Radulphus,"[1] and a colophon at the end of M/2 ascribes the two cycles to "Radulphus de Atton" or "Acton."[2] Hence bibliographers since Leland have posited an English sermon writer Ralph (of) Acton, who supposedly wrote in the early fourteenth century. But this is a bibliographical ghost, and the true author of the two sermon cycles, as has been known since at least 1937,[3] was the French theologian Radulphus Ardens, archdeacon of Poitiers (d. after 1101), whose work appears in print in PL 155.[4]

---

[1] The prologue has been edited by Wolf, "Préface," from Oxford, Lincoln College, MS 116.

[2] "Explicit expositorium omnium epistolarum euangeliorumque festiualium sanctorum secundum Radulphum de Atton'," f. 197va.

[3] *SC* 2:661, no. 3501, MS e Mus. 5.

[4] "Ralph Acton" or "of Acton" appears in many places, including the *Dictionary of National Biography* 1:68–69; Owst, *Literature*, p. 107, note, and passim; a correspondent quoted in *Medieval Sermon Studies Newsletter* 17 (Spring 1986): 6–7; and Wenzel, "Sermon Collections," p. 8. Taylor even identified him with Ranulf Higden (*Universal Chronicle*, p. 183). The ghost has been finally laid by Sharpe, *Handlist*, p. 443; for the corrected date see Sharpe's on-line "Additions, corrections and queries." Simon Forde, "Writings," 1. 137–162, discusses the manuscript in detail and Owst's use of it, but not the identity of "Ralph Acton."

(2) The second booklet begins on a new quire and is written in a Gothic textura, also of the fifteenth century. It holds a temporal cycle of fifty-four sermons (ff. 199–300rb; = M/3), which are identical with the series in MS Barlow 24, ff. 1–132 (see the following section). They, too, are called "omelie" and numbered. These fifty-four sermons are then followed without a break by a series of pieces that comprises sermons, prothemes, and simple excerpts (ff. 300rb–317vb; = M/4). The numbering of these pieces continues from the preceding cycle through 60 and then stops. A medieval reader evidently noticed that M/4 differed from the preceding sermon cycle and wrote "Hic desinit" in plummet in the margin of f. 300rb. Of these final pieces, only ten can be considered complete sermons. In so far as their occasions can be determined, three are for saints and one each for Christmas, Easter, perhaps 5 Easter, Pentecost, and 3 Lent. English divisions occur more frequently than in M/3. Four more pieces are sermon-like but very short and may have been intended as prothemes. Several pieces in this group contain references to other sermons *supra* and *infra*, including two to a sermon on *Christus passus est* "infra" that does not appear in this booklet.[5] In addition, this group of texts also includes two excerpts from Peraldus's *Summa de vitiis* on avarice, and further Anselm's *De custodia interioris hominis* (the Latin source for the *Sawles Warde*), none with attribution. In the manuscript these excerpts are numbered as if they were sermons. An alphabetical subject index for the entire volume, written in a smaller set Anglicana hand (ff. 318–321vb) and containing references to the part of the collection (1–3), homily number, and usually the principal part of a sermon, closes the collection.

This mixed collection shows, first of all, the continued interest among English preachers in a work made in the late twelfth century (i.e., M/1 and 2). In his opening prologue Radulphus speaks as a parish priest who has been preaching to his people regularly on Sundays and holy days and has been asked by his brethren to write down his work. After reflecting on four reasons why he should do so, he announces that he has

> yielded to the request of our brothers. But since I composed these little homilies for the benefit of simple people, I have tried to avoid allegorical obscurities, scriptural profundities, and rhetorical ornateness as much as possible and have everywhere looked for the moral truths that are more necessary to people's life.[6]

---

[5] The reference is: "De istis tribus [racionibus cantandi] require infra circa finem libri in sermone Christus passus est, primo principali," f. 308rb.

[6] "Quoniam autem ob vtilitatem simplicium omeliunculas istas composui, obscuritatem allegoriarum, profunditatem scripturarum, ornatumque sermonum euitare curaui pro posse meo, in vniuersis inquirens moralitatem vtpote vite hominum necessariorem," f. 1ra; in the edition by Wolf, "Préface," at p. 39.

The claimed sparseness goes in fact beyond rhetorical ornament: these pieces lack the *divisiones thematis* and in general the structure of scholastic sermons that by the end of the twelfth century were just beginning to enter the field. Instead, Radulphus's homilies explain the entire lection beyond the chosen thema, dividing the lection into several parts and then giving a moral commentary on each.

The basic homily structure of Radulphus's work continues in the fifty-four anonymous sermons of M/3. These are for the Sunday gospels from 1 Advent through 26 Trinity, omitting non-dominical feast days.[7] The individual sermons normally deal with the entire text of the lection and often quote it phrase by phrase, after which they extract its *sensus misticus* or *moralis* in a number of points. Frequently the sermon text makes it clear that the entire gospel lection was to be said in the course of the sermon, with the curious remark "et dicatur litera secundum quod iacet si placet," "let the literal text be quoted in its [literal] sequence, if it so pleases." Though here and there the preacher uses "karissimi," he hardly ever appeals to his audience directly.

It is this cycle, M/3, that furnishes the major interest of the entire collection. After the very last sermon in the manuscript and before the index, a different hand has written "Explicit doctor Rypyndon" in cursive script (f. 317v). On the basis of this ascription, recent students have included this manuscript (as well as Barlow 24, see below) among the codices that have preserved Repingdon's *Sermones super evangelia dominicalia*.[8] Comparison shows that indeed M/3 (ff. 199–300rb) – but not the subsequent random collection M/4 (ff. 300rb–317vb), at the end of which Repingdon's name appears – draws very heavily on Repingdon's work. Also, the sermons in M/3 correspond to Repingdon's expositions of the Sunday gospels with a few discrepancies.[9] One may well ask whether M/3 represents a "reworking" of Repingdon along the lines of contemporary preaching and for a different audience, and whether it was done by Repingdon himself.[10] Simon Forde, who has studied Repingdon's cycle in detail, comes to

---

[7] 1 Advent has an additional sermon based on the day's epistle. There are two sermons for 3 Advent, on the same gospel lection. Near the end, the medieval numbering goes wrong: sermon 50 is numbered "40," and the last four sermons bear the numbers 50–53.

[8] Forde, "Writings," 1: 109–192. He lists eight complete and genuine manuscripts of Repingdon's cycle. Similarly, Archer, "Preaching," pp. 14–31.

[9] M/3 has two sermons for 3 Advent (T03, *Cum audisset Johannes*); it divides Repingdon's sermon for the fourth Sunday after Epiphany (T13, *Cum descendisset*), which deals with two of Christ's miracles, into two separate sermons, both for the same Sunday (10–11); and it omits Repingdon's sermon for Easter Monday (T28/2, *Surrexit Dominus vere*). Further, M/3 adds a sermon on the epistle for 1 Advent (*Hora iam est*), and it has no sermon on the epistle for 20 Trinity (T61, *Videte quomodo*), which is present in some of the Repingdon manuscripts.

[10] See Forde, "Writings," 1:156.

the conclusion that M/3 "is an attempt to render material from the standard Repyngdon sermon-cycle into more digestible and practical form for preachers and according to the most popular format."[11] This is essentially correct.[12] M/3 thus demonstrates how biblical exegesis or *postillatio* in the order of the Sunday gospels is utilized in the creation of actual sermons. The process of *postillatio* even appears in the physical layout of the sermons, where the biblical text from the lection is underlined throughout the sermon, as if it were a sequence of lemmata.[13] In creating his sermons, the writer of M/3 first of all selected from Repingdon's *Sermones* what material he needed and thereby reduced Repingdon's material very drastically. In addition, he shaped the selected material into a structure that is basically homiletic but also contains features of the scholastic sermon. Its basic homiletic structure appears in that each sermon has two steps: first a literal exposition of the lection, and then a spiritual reading of it. As mentioned in the previous paragraph, the two steps are clearly indicated by the terminology used, *litera* and *sensus misticus* or *moralis*. Though consistently and explicitly distinguished, the two parts are not consistently given the same amount of space. While in some sermons the entire gospel text is recited at length with comments on its literal sense,[14] in others, after some introductory remarks, the sermon writer only declares "dicatur litera secundum quod iacet" and moves on to spiritual exegesis.[15] The latter, however, normally begins with a division into several, usually three, parts, which are then developed. Other features of the scholastic sermon structure that appear in many sermons of M/3 are address forms (*Fratres* or *Karissimi*) and the final closing formula. A number of these sermons also contain cross references to others in the collection, with precise indication of the respective principal parts.[16] None of these elements occur in Repingdon.

Yet another contrast between Repingdon and M/3 is that the latter utilizes material not found in the former. This usually concerns practical aspects of the

---

[11] Ibid., pp. 157–158.

[12] Forde's remark that in M/3 "the sources primarily used for scriptural exegesis on the literal level, William of Nottingham and Nicolas de Gorran, are absent" (ibid., p. 158) needs to be corrected: M/3 quotes Nottingham at least in sermon 52, and Gorran in 8, 14, 15, 54.

[13] This technique also appears in the English Wycliffite sermons, cf. *English Wycliffite Sermons* 1:134–136; and Hudson, "'Springing cockel'," p. 142 n. 49.

[14] A fine example is the sermon for the third Sunday of Lent, M/3-19, which will be discussed below, in Part Three, chapter 49, pp. 356–357.

[15] Thus in M/3-33.

[16] A particularly dense example occurs in M/3-20: "De contricione dicetur infra; de confessione nota illa que dicuntur supra in secunda dominica quadragesime, vltimo principali, et in tercia dominica primo principali. De ieiunio require in prima dominica quadragesime secundo principali. Item de oracione secunda dominica vltimo principali," f. 233va.

Christian life. For example, on 4 Lent both discuss the miracle of the multiplication of loaves, including the aspects of penance. Against Repingdon, M/3 includes a common, as it were catechetical, definition of contrition and explains it phrase by phrase.[17] It then, once more against Repingdon, follows this up with a longer excerpt from Grosseteste's *Dictum* 106. Similarly, in its sermon for 1 Lent, M/3 discusses fasting at some length, as does Repingdon. But to the material derived from the latter, M/3 adds that the weak and infirm as well as pregnant women and breast-fed babies are excused from fasting "sicut dicit W."[18] This concern for women, marriage, and family life appears in fact in other sermons of this series: for instance, marriage is discussed not only in sermon M/3-9 on *Nuptiae factae sunt*, as was standard in later medieval preaching,[19] but also in sermon 8, on Mary and Joseph finding the twelve-year-old Jesus in the temple; and a later sermon, in asking who should seek Christ, shows a rare gender consciousness in using both pronouns: "qui vel que."[20] There are even sermons in M/3 that after condensing material from Repingdon for their literal exposition then go entirely their own way.[21]

Very probably Repingdon himself was not the author of M/3. The sermon for 8 Trinity, M/3-38, on "Beware of false prophets" (Matthew 7:15), is of some interest in this regard. In his sermon cycle, Repingdon divides the "false prophets" into heretics, hypocrites, and bad Christians. The heretics he discusses at some length, though without reference to his contemporary situation. M/3-38 uses a similar initial distinction,[22] but when it turns to the heretics, it merely says: "The heretics I now bypass, because, I believe, they do not now abound in God's Church. And though there may be some in hiding, they are not now in evidence,

---

[17] "Contricio est dolor mentis formatus gracia voluntarie assumptus pro peccatis cum proposito ab eis abstinendi, confitendi, et satisfaciendi. Per hoc quod dicitur 'dolor mentis,' distinguitur a dolore ypocritarum, qui est in facie et non in corde. Et per hoc quod dicitur 'formatus gracia' distinguitur ab attricione, qui est dolor, non tamen sufficiens, quia non est acceptus a Deo propter aliquod inpedimentum Deo soli cognitum. Per hoc quod / dicitur 'voluntarie assumptus' distinguitur a dolore naturali, qui nec est meritorius nec demeritorius. Et ponitur 'pro peccatis' ad differenciam inuidie, que est dolor voluntarius de bono alieno. Set quia hec non sufficiunt sine confessione et satisfaccione si facultas assit, ideo additur 'cum proposito,' etc.," f. 234rb–va.

[18] M/3-17, f. 228ra.   [19] See d'Avray, "Gospel" and *Marriage*.

[20] M/3-22, f. 237va. Thus also in RE-19, f. 138ra.

[21] An example is M/3-21. It first explains the lection with material from Repingdon, giving it a logical rationale, and then develops independently six points in which "Jesus has instructed us in this gospel by his word and example."

[22] But a fourfold one: heretics, hypocrites, false Christians, and man's three spiritual enemies. Material for the fourth kind, however, is also derived from Repingdon.

as I believe."[23] This could have been written by Repingdon, but if so surely not until after Oldcastle's revolution (1414) or execution (1417). A closer comparative study of the two works may yet throw more light on the relationship.

In the final group, M/4, such features continue to some extent, and their partial carry-over may argue for common authorship of both sections. But in contrast to M/3 several pieces in M/4 begin with a protheme leading to prayer, and others introduce their division with the formula "pro processu (sermonis) . . . ," both typical elements of the scholastic sermon structure.[24] M/4 also contains a number of cross references, in fact proportionately more than M/3. One of them is to a sermon in M/3, another to one in M/4,[25] and two more to a sermon on *Christus passus est* "near the end of the book," which is not extant.[26]

---

[23] "De hereticis modo supersedeo eo quod modo in Ecclesia Dei non habundant ut spero; et quamuis sint aliqui occulti, non sunt ut credo presentes modo," f. 268vb.

[24] Prothemes occur in M/4-2, 4, 5, 8, 12, and 13; the formula "pro processu [sermonis]" in 5, 6, and 12. Neither element seems to be used in M/3.

[25] M/4-1 refers to M/3-22, and M/4-12 to M/4-3, both correctly with "supra."

[26] Ff. 308rb and 312ra.

36

Oxford, Bodleian Library, MS Barlow 24 (N)

The Repingdon-derived temporal cycle M/3 appears also in Oxford, Bodleian Library, MS Barlow 24, a late fifteenth-century paper manuscript.[1] To it has been added a set of fifty-five sermons for saints' days and for the non-dominical feast days (Christmas, Epiphany, Ascension, etc.; N-55 to 109 in my inventory) that are not represented in the temporal cycle (A), nor are they based on Repingdon's work. The two parts together, A and B, thus, form a systematic sermon collection for nearly all occasions of the Church year, including several common sermons for a martyr, confessor, virgin, and deceased person.[2] In this manuscript, neither cycle is ascribed to an author, but whoever may have written A and B and then combined them, the two cycles were put together to form one unified collection; evidence for this lies in at least one clear reference in B to a sermon in A.[3] The manuscript is written in one column by two distinct hands, both fairly cursive Secretary scripts of the second half of the fifteenth century. The first hand wrote A, then the two topical indices, and consecutively half of the first sermon of B, where the second hand took over (f. 142, in line 9).

Between A and B stand two alphabetical subject indices, one for each cycle. That for A is incomplete, as two leaves of the new quire have been ripped out. The second table, for B, is of some interest in that it yields the name of the compiler of at least the second set of sermons:

---

[1] *SC* 2:1059, no. 6470. A better description is given by Forde, "Writings," 1:176–178.

[2] More precisely: B contains sermons for three Sundays already covered in A (Easter, Pentecost, and Trinity). In addition, B brings sermons for Christmas, Circumcision, Epiphany, Ash Wednesday, Good Friday, Rogation Days, Ascension, and Corpus Christi; one sermon each for any saint, a martyr, a confessor, a virgin, dedication of a church, a priest's first mass (or ordination or visitation); five sermons for a dead person; and thirty-four sermons for saints' days, including the feasts of the Invention and the Exaltation of the Cross and All Souls. The sermons are indexed in Schneyer 9:13–22.

[3] N-107, "Ad quam misericordiam nos mouere debent tria; et nota processum dominica 4 post Trinitatem," f. 212, to N-34.

The form of quotation in this table is as follows. First are quoted the sermons by their numeral. Then their parts are quoted with the four letters of the compiler's name; for S indicates whatever precedes the development of the sermon, E indicates its first principal part, L its second principal part, and K its third principal part.[4]

This system is applied in the table as well as in the margins of the sermons in B. The name "Selk" has raised some speculation, for it is the same as one of the two names connected with the Franciscan handbook *Fasciculus morum*; and three sermons in B utilize material from that handbook, albeit without acknowledgment (N-91, 103, and 107). But whether the two Selks are the same person, and what their function in the respective two works is, remains undecided.[5]

The sermons of the *sanctorale* (i.e., B) are short and simple and, in contrast to the *temporale* cycle, deal only with the announced thema, not the entire lection. Their format is consistently the same: after a brief introductory section, which sometimes leads to a prayer, the thema is divided into three parts ("In quibus verbis"); this is followed by a second, closely related division "pro materia sermonis" or "pro processu," whose parts are then developed. In other words, the sermon writer consistently proceeded by following a *divisio ab intus* with another *ab extra*. A good example of this structure is the division in the sermon for St Mary Magdalene:

> *Many sins are forgiven her because she loved much*, Luke 7. . . . In these words three things are indicated, namely the deletion of sins, when the text says *Sins are forgiven her*; their large number, in *Many*; and the cause or reason for the deletion, *Because she loved much*. That great love is cause for the remission of sins is witnessed by 1 Peter 4: "Love covers a multitude of sins." Magdalene was forgiven many sins, etc. Beloved, the love of this Mary Magdalene was great for three reasons: she was most burning in her fervent conversion to Christ; most faithful in firmly adhering to Christ in his life; and most persevering in her diligent search for Christ. And this is the matter for our sermon.[6]

---

[4] "Incipit tabula super Sermones Sanctorum communiter festiualium per annum. Et huius tabule cotacio hec est. In primis quotantur sermones par [!] numerum algorismalem. Deinde quotantur partes ipsorum sermonum par [!] quatuor literas nominis compilatoris, nam S significat quidquid precedit sermonis processum, E significat primum principale, L secundum principale, et K tercium principale," f. 135.

[5] The matter has been discussed by Fletcher, "'I Sing'"; Powell, "Connections"; and Fletcher, "Authorship."

[6] "*Remittuntur ei peccata multa quoniam dilexit multum*, Luce 7. . . . In quibus notantur tria, scilicet culparum deletio [*ms* dilectio] cum dicit 'Remittuntur ei peccata'; earundem multitudinis numeracio, ibi 'multa'; et delecionis causa siue racio, 'quoniam dilexit multum.' Vnde quod dilectio multa est remissionis peccatorum causa testatur 1 Petri 4: 'Caritas operit multitudinem

In developing the principal parts announced, the preacher utilizes predominantly historical and legendary material. This is to some extent taken from "Januensis," that is, the *Legenda aurea*, but Januensis was by no means the only source and is certainly not used slavishly. In privileging narrative material at the expense of patristic quotations and doctrinal content, the Barlow sermons may be said to be similar to Mirk's *Festial*, but they do not share the latter's more sensationalist interest in miracle stories. Rather, they essentially praise the virtues of the saints and recommend their example to the audience. The introductory section now and then begins with a reference to the respective feast day, such as, "Today the Church celebrates the feast of . . . ," but again this does not take the form that Mirk uses. Many sermons end with a hexameter either before or after the closing formula. Another peculiarity of this cycle is that at the head of the sermons, together with the occasion, both the epistle and gospel lections are noted by their initial words. The thema is often not taken from the lections.

The same *sanctorale* cycle also contains a number of cross references. They point to other sermons by their number or occasion, and to the principal part where the material referred to appears (not, incidentally, to the marginal letters referred to above). Many such cross references are to sermons in the same cycle, notably to a sermon on St. Anne with its genealogical information. But several other references are to sermons outside cycle B. As already indicated, one of them refers correctly to a sermon in cycle A. Two more references are problematic. One is to the Articles of Faith "prout patet inter dominicas sermone 53 in primo principali" (f. 217v). There is a Sunday sermon in A that treats the Articles of Faith, *Erat quidam regulus* for 21 Trinity, but it is here numbered 51 and deals with the Articles of Faith in its second part (not called *principale*; ff. 124v–127). The other problematic but potentially more important reference occurs in B's sermon for All Saints, which ends with a reference to a *narracio* on the intercession of the saints, "quam require parte 2, sermone 80, in tercio principali" (f. 200). There is neither a "part 2" nor a "sermon 80" in the Barlow manuscript, and one may wonder whether the reference could not be to a sermon in MS Rylands 367, to which Barlow is clearly related. Rylands 367 does have an "omelia" 80 in its second part (M/2–80), but this contains no narrative on the intercession of the saints. It is possible that Barlow 24 once had a second part, though this is certainly not

---

peccatorum.' Remittuntur Magdalene peccata multa, etc. Karissimi, dilectio huius Marie Magdalene fuit magna propter tria, nam fuit ardentissima in feruente ad Christum conuersione, fidelisssima in firma Christo viuendi adhesione, et fuit perseuerantissima in diligente inquisicione. Et hec materia sermonis," N-85, f. 183r–v.

borne out by the subject indices.[7] There is, thus, little that can help us determine whether A and B were written by the same author.

Like its authorship, the date of B is equally open to speculation. A reference to Higden's "chronicles" and their report of Edward III criticizing his bishops for ordaining too many ill-educated priests who have become criminals and are filling the king's prisons, establishes a *terminus a quo* about the middle of the fourteenth century, but the report probably comes from a later version or continuation of the *Polychronicon* rather than Higden's original work.[8] Nonetheless, this peculiar reference would argue for a date well before 1400, which could be further seen in the absence of any sensitivity to doctrinal issues brought up by Wyclif and the Lollard movement. But again, this evidence is rather tenuous, since the sermons are so meager in content.

[7] The index for cycle B contains one reference to a sermon numbered higher than 55 (the last extant sermon), namely "58.L," as Fletcher pointed out ("'I Sing'," p. 107). But this must be a scribal error, since the subject ("Gradus sacerdocii quante est virtutis") appears in sermon "54.L" (f. 214) and the tabula has a second reference to "Sacerdocium quante dignitatis sit, 54.L."

[8] See Fletcher. "Authorship," with the crucial passage printed on 206. The MS reads "capitur" for "capiatur" and "quin de illa" for "quam de illa," and the reference is "in cronicis Cistrensis libro 7. c." The "c" must be an incomplete chapter reference, since earlier the scribe uses "libro 5, capitulo 2" in another quotation of Higden's work (f. 166v). The reported event does not appear in Higden, *Polychronicon*.

37

Cambridge, Corpus Christi College, MS 392 (K)

This paper manuscript of the later fifteenth century contains a number of different materials, which are all theological in nature and potentially related to preaching. They have been collected in what is basically a notebook, whose quires vary in size and are marked consecutively by a medieval hand.[1] Of interest here is the third main section of ten quires that range in length from eight to sixteen folios (ff. 209–323). This contains a random collection of sermons together with some theological extracts and *quaestiones* that are provided with subject headings (from f. 269 on; see below). It is the work of several fifteenth-century scribes. They tend to begin a sermon, and usually an extract, on a new page. Even where the material occupies only a few lines, the remainder of the folio is left blank. There are twenty-six sermons. The first eight, written by the same hand (ff. 209–224), are addressed to an academic audience and use such hyperbolic addresses as "Prehonorandi domini" or "Studiosissimi magistri." The first, for 2 Advent, bears the rubric "Samelyn Oxon'"; others are said to have been preached in Latin at Oxford (3) or Cambridge (4, 6),[2] and the last of this group presents itself as a *sermo examinatorius* (f. 222).[3] They all have a strong theological flavor and draw heavily on the fathers in long quotations. The group of eight is further characterized by invoking the Blessed Trinity at the head of several pieces (2, 3, 7, 8).[4] It is followed, in a different hand, by a sermon said to have been preached

---

[1] See James, *Descriptive Catalogue . . . Corpus Christi College*, 2:248–251.

[2] Rubrics: "Prima quadragesime Oxon' in latinis" (f. 214); "pro dominica in quadragesima in latinis et predicatus fuit cantebrigg'" (f. 217); "sermo in latinis pro 23'a post trinitatem predicatus cantebrigg'" (f. 219).

[3] In the text, after the protheme: "<Ideo> pro huius sermonis examinatorii, licet breuissimi et inculti, processu primordiali breuiter est annotandum" (f. 222).

[4] "Trinitas creatrix nobis sit auxiliatrix," f. 209; "Beatissima Trinitas, Pater et Filius et Spiritus Sanctus, miserere mei et vt vis adiuua me," ff. 212, 214, 220, 222.

on Christmas Eve 1435 in the chapter house of "Cant'." This sermon seems to be a later addition to the previous eight, probably to fill the quire.

From this point on the collection loses any coherence. Through the remaining eight quires there are many changes of hand, varying from a firm and large Secretary, which has also written the extracts, to nearly illegible cursive. Several times a single bifolium of smaller size or a quire containing an entire sermon has been inserted.[5] Some of these sermons also have a distinctly workbook-like appearance, in which the writer has canceled sections of several lines and marginally substituted a different and usually shorter text. Two sermons (10, 16) are for an election.[6] Several have possible monastic affiliations.[7] Two consecutive sermons (17–18) use material from *Fasciculus morum*, without acknowledgment. Sermon 19 is of unusual interest in that it deals with Hus and Jerome of Prague, the Hussites, and King Wenzel IV, and has an internal reference to "this sacred council."[8] The last piece (26) is a complete copy of Rimington's synodal sermon of 1373, and another sermon (23) is partially similar to X-117.[9] Ff. 317–325, in yet another fifteenth-century hand, contain a number of academic exercises in response to questions put by "pater meus et socius"[10] and signed, three times, by "Gherlacus Saxo." This final section of the manuscript begins with the date

[5] A good sense of how this section of the manuscript has been "thrown together" may be gained from the medieval quire A, ff. 285–297. Here the bifolia run as follows: 285–286/297-missing last folio; 287/296; 288/295; 289/294; 290–291/292–293 (the slash indicates the center of a bifolium or a set of bifolia). New sermons begin on 285, 287, 288, 289, 290 and continue on the respective conjoint leaves. Each is in a different hand. A renvoi on 287v is to the "third folio next," but the text continues only on 296.

[6] K-10 refers several times to "presentis collegii congregacio." *Collegium* here could refer to a monastic or conventual congregation as well as a university college (in the fifteenth century).

[7] K-23 (f. 289r–v) is similar to X-117 in the monastic collection X. K-17 invokes saints Thomas and Dunstan (f. 253).

[8] "Donet igitur Deus quod et nunc in isto sacro concilio Ecclesia Dei et sponsa sua precioso Christi sangwine redempta de manibus perfidorum hereticorum liberetur, et non dubium quin finaliter Ecclesia prevalebit" (f. 277v). The sermon refers to the Council of Constance and the execution of Hus and Jerome (ibidem), and King Wenzel is called "rex Bohemie maledicte memorie . . . fautor, tutor, et defensor fortissimus perfidorum hereticorum," who was exhumed and burned by the rebels after his death (f. 276). The Hussites are spoken of in both the perfect and present tenses. The sermon seems to lack its proper thema (perhaps 1 Cor 12:12?) as well as its division, though two parts are clearly marked and developed. The hand may very well be Continental or German; it uses the form "Bernhardus."

[9] The opening sentence is the same (except that K adds "Karissimi"), and the first paragraph is very similar, but from then on the two sermons go separate ways. I hesitate to call them even redactions.

[10] He is unnamed, but at one point the speaker says that he held a philosophical view "<quam> opinionem pater meus maxime nititur defensare cum aliis sequacibus illius Wiclyff" (f. 323).

"Anno Domini 1412" in the top margin of f. 317, and it is preceded, on f. 316v in the same hand, by a "Questio magistri Kerff. Vtrum rex pacificus geminus[?] gigas substancie sit deus deorum et dominus quem predicant prophecie, etc."[11]

The sermon booklet in this manuscript thus gathers sermons that clearly belong to the first half of the fifteenth century. It is another witness to the ongoing activity of collecting sermons of various kinds and provenance, including the university.

---

[11] William Corfe/Kerff held an Oxford MA by 1409 and was proctor of Archbishop Chichele at the Council of Constance, where he died in 1414; see *BRUO* 1:487.

38

On the margins

The preceding anonymous collections, together with the work of Dygon and the *Congesta*, have brought us to the end of the period with which this book is concerned. Yet a few words must be added about sermon collections that lie beyond its chronological boundaries of 1450 and of 1350, as well as about others that, although they contain Latin sermons, lie outside the concept of "sermon collection" that I explained earlier.

English preachers continued to produce sermons around and after 1450, and for the second half of the fifteenth century, the names of several famous preachers are known to us. But their work, if it was written up at all, seems to have disappeared.[1] What little has survived reveals that making sermon collections was considerably less original and vigorous than during the preceding one hundred years. To illustrate this I will discuss two collections of the later fifteenth century and then turn more briefly to others that are similarly marginal in terms of their date of composition.

Cambridge University Library, MS Gg.6.26 (G)

This odd, very irregularly constructed codex contains 167 paper leaves with parchments strips and some parchment folios. Besides sermons (ff. 5–118) it holds some scattered sermon material, a version of the *Gesta Romanorum* with *tabula*, and a second incomplete series of *Gesta Romanorum*.[2] The book has a medieval foliation of 1–78 for modern folios 4–80 (the medieval foliation skips the number 44 and does not count the column-wide strip that is modern f. 37). It is hard to say when it was assembled. The texts are written in several fifteenth-century hands, ranging from a well-set predominantly Anglicana or mixed hand to set Secretary. Originally blank spaces between major texts have been used to copy various documents, of which several are dated in the 1490s. These include a testimonial

---

[1] Cf. Catto, "Theology after Wycliffism," p. 266 and note 7, and p. 273.
[2] See *Catalogue . . . Library of the University of Cambridge*, 3:229–230.

addressed to the rector of the parish of N. on behalf of a husband Robert and his wife Joan, that they have made their annual confession and paid their tithes (f. 16, date omitted); another testimonial from the commissary of a bishop (of London?) on behalf of a group of pilgrims dated 1494 (f. 28v); and a papal document dated 1493 (f. 118v). Important specific data in these documents are omitted or replaced with "N." There are further the three main prayers from a Mass for a pregnant woman (f. 30v). The name of John Dotmotte from Lewes, County Sussex, occurs several times; on f. 4, the original opening leaf, he confirms a gift of twenty pounds to John Dayme.

The volume contains a total of seventy-nine sermons. The first forty-three, as far as their occasions can be determined, form an overall random collection, with sermons for Advent, Lent, and the Easter season. Many are addressed to "Reuerendi," and these include one sermon to an academic audience (G-6, also in W-123 but here lacking the third principal) and another for a monastic visitation (G-2). Some of these pieces are full, rhetorically developed sermons, others have a rather sparse text, and yet others consist of no more than a string of quotations, so that one must wonder whether the latter were indeed intended as sermons. Then, after an extract from the *Legenda aurea* on the Ascension (f. 73), follow another thirty-six sermons (G-44 to 79) for the period from Ascension to 10 Trinity, by the German Dominican Johannes Herolt (1380–1468).[3]

To judge by Schneyer's *Repertorium*, the earlier run of sermons, G-1 to 43, in addition to two sermons shared by English collections described above,[4] further shares material with half a dozen Continental collections, including those by Jacobus de Voragine, John of Abbéville, Rigaud, and Odo of Cheriton.[5] More interestingly, ten sermons in G, according to Schneyer, also occur in Toulouse, Bibliothèque municipale, MS 340.[6] In G they form a section of sermons that stand in an almost entirely regular liturgical sequence, from 3 Lent through 5 Easter. But they are interspersed with sermons from other sources. This would suggest that the collector of G drew material from various sources, often gathering two or three sermons for the same occasion. Despite its different Continental

---

[3] The scribe has copied the sectional letters from his exemplar as well as a German proverb (f. 105v).

[4] G-3 is W-123; G-28 is Z-13.

[5] Abbéville: 41, 42; Rigaud: 16, Odo: 36. G-6 is Jacobus's third sermon for 1 Lent, the first two principal parts, virtually the same though with one longer omission, which ruins the sermon's continuity.

[6] They are G-19 and 20, 22, 31–32, 34–35, 37–39. For details see my inventory. The Toulouse 340 sermons are listed in Schneyer 3:765–775, especially at 767–768. Why Schneyer connects this manuscript with John Sheppey is not clear. Several of these sermons also occur in Siena, Bibl. Com. F.ix.15 (Schneyer 9:497), and other sermons in G (18, 30) likewise appear in Siena but not in Toulouse 340.

connections, the volume itself is clearly of English provenance. It contains part of a Middle-English treatise on temptation, "The firste wile was."[7] In addition, the earlier sermons of the manuscript contain several English words and phrases as well as an entire sermon in Middle English, which has been recently edited,[8] and G-25 quotes a version of the popular Middle-English lyric "White was his naked brest."

London, University of London, MS 657 (U)

Much like G is this paper manuscript of the later fifteenth century. Various dates visible on strengthening strips establish that the codex was bound at some time after 1448.[9] It is a miscellany written in two columns in various fifteenth-century hands and bears a medieval pagination, which I will follow here. The volume comprises a number of theological and historical works including several batches of sermons. The first of these is a copy of the popular *Convertimini* by Holcot (pp. 1–74) with an alphabetical index of topics (pp. 86–88). Later, on pp. 227–234, come three sermons separated by notes. The first is a Christmas sermon that also occurs with some verbal differences as A-32; the second is specified as a sermon for a virgin; and the third, without a thema, is marked "for St. Mary or for St. James, whichever you will."[10] This small group is followed by a more interesting series of forty-three *de tempore* sermons (U-4 to 46). While these follow the liturgical order fairly well, with sermons on the epistles and gospels from the fourth Sunday after Epiphany to Good Friday, the series is less "regular" than Ker reports. For instance, several pieces are out of order, and there are sermons marked "Pro morte," "De dileccione," and even "Contra scotales in ecclesia." One or two Sundays are not provided for, while 1 Lent has eight and Good Friday nine sermons. Several sermons are interspersed with notes. But more importantly, half of these sermons occur also in **Cambridge, Pembroke College, MS 200.**

The latter manuscript, also written in the fifteenth century and in one hand, contains a regular and complete *de tempore* cycle of 120 numbered sermons,

---

[7] Here incomplete, beginning "It is nedeful to vnderstonde how þe fende deseyvith many men" and ending "þe weye of evirlestyng dampnacyoun. Amen. Iesus Christus," ff. 104–105v. On f. 104r–v the text is marked "Va-cat." The Latin text of the Herolt sermons continues in the wide bottom margins of the three pages. For the work see Jolliffe, *Check-List*, item K7(a), p. 120.

[8] The Middle-English sermon is G-7 (ff. 22v–23), edited by Galloway, "Confession Sermon." English words or phrases occur further at ff. 5 (thema), 5v (division), 34v (message verse), 40 (word), and 53 ("White was his naked brest").

[9] The manuscript has been described by Ker, *Medieval Manuscripts in British Libraries* 1:374–376.

[10] "De sancta Maria vel de sancto Iacobo vtrum volueris." It begins "Karissimi, quod hoc silere non debemus quod laudabilis memorie Hugo Cliniacensis[!] abbas solet narrare" (page 234, column b). Notice that the manuscript has a medieval pagination and is written in two columns.

ranging from 1 Advent to the following "Sunday nearest to Advent." They are followed by an alphabetical index of topics[11] with references to the sermons by number and marginal letters.[12] The sermons through Pentecost Tuesday have a structural peculiarity that sets them somewhat apart from the English collections so far surveyed: they begin with the phrase "pro ingressu sermonis accipio" followed by a biblical passage that is verbally or at least notionally related to the sermon's thema.[13] This introductory section is fully developed, often in two or three parts, and then gives way to the main division into three members, which are also developed in regular fashion.[14] While the introductory section could be considered as the development of a secondary thema, it is still notionally a part or aspect of the main thema. This structure is preserved in the sermons in collection U that correspond to the Pembroke cycle. In Pembroke 200, however, they are followed, from 1 Trinity on, by sermons that lack the "pro ingressu" formula, and many of the latter occur in the sermon cycle by Jacobus de Losanna and other, anonymous collections. Pembroke 200 itself, therefore, appears to be made up from several different sources. It is hard to say when and where it was made. The "pro ingressu" sermons also exist in a Munich manuscript, which the continuation of Schneyer's *Repertorium* attributes to a Friar Bartholomaeus Turgelow, with a reference whose relevance escapes me.[15] In fact, the sermon for 3 Advent in the Pembroke cycle speaks of "King Charles, the father of our lord king Robert, who was captured by the Aragonese and left his sons as hostages."[16] Robert of Anjou ruled as king from 1309 to 1343. Since other references in Pembroke 200 quote "Saint Thomas," its date of composition would therefore lie between 1323

[11] Abstinencia – Zinna, ff. 196–207ra, in two columns.

[12] Marginal letters given in the index appear in the sermon text only sporadically. Also, in parts of the cycle the sermon numbers do not agree with those in the index; hence, the index must be based on a different manuscript than this.

[13] Thus, the sermon for 3 Lent, on "When he had cast out the demon, the dumb man spoke" ("Cum eiecisset daemonium locutus est mutus," Luke 11:14), uses as its subsidiary thema "I cast out demons" ("Daemonia eicio," Luke 11:19; p. 199b). But more often than not the subsidiary thema is taken from a different biblical book than the thema. In fact, one sermon (U-11) uses a quotation from Seneca: "Pro ingressu sermonis accipio verbum dictum per Senecam quod est tale: 'Beneficiorum memoria labilis . . .'" (p. 253b).

[14] The transitions are consistently and clearly marked: "Hec pro primo. Secundo dico, etc. Circa quod sciendum est . . ." and so forth.

[15] *Repertorium der lateinischen Sermones für die Zeit von 1350–1500*, ed. L. Hödl and W. Koch, CD ROM edition. The database refers to Franz, *Magister Nikolaus*, which mentions a Polish theologian Bartholomaeus Turgelow at the university of Prague (D.Th. by 1390) without reference to these sermons (p. 39).

[16] "Sicut fuit factum de rege Karolo patre domini nostri regis Roberti quando fuit captus in mari et ductus ad regem Arragonum qui fuit dimissus missis filiis suis in obsidionem in loco eius," Pembroke 200, f. 12v.

and 1343.[17] Whatever the origin of the cycle, however, in Pembroke 200 it must have been copied in England. The manuscript's hand seems to be English, and in the occasionally massive annotations to the sermons, by several hands, occurs at least one English gloss as well as a quotation from "Stephanus Cantuarensis."[18]

As already stated, more than twenty sermons of this Pembroke cycle occur also in collection U, virtually in a block. Nor are these the only pieces U shares with other collections. U-1, as we have seen, occurs also in A-32; U-34 is similar to a sermon by Geoffrey Babion (died 1158; cf. PL 171:413); and U-38, according to Schneyer, occurs in several anonymous Continental collections.[19] A few sermons in U contain English words, phrases, memory verses, and even an entire stanza – the latter in a sermon shared with the Pembroke cycle, although there it has no English. Clearly, U is a collection made up of materials from a variety of sources.

These two collections, G and U, thus reveal a number of characteristic features of sermon collections made in the middle and during the second half of the fifteenth century as well as difficulties they present to historical research. It is often hard if not impossible to determine, on the basis of their handwriting alone, precisely when such manuscripts were put together. Their material comes from various earlier and often Continental sources that may even reach back to the thirteenth century. Yet now and then they also share individual sermons with some of the English collections that have been analyzed above. Their scribes evidently felt free to add bits of English material, in proverbial sayings and memory verses. Some of these collections also tend to hold a proportionately large number of sermons to the clergy or even an academic audience. These features recur in other collections besides G and U, and two or three of them deserve to be mentioned here.

Oxford, Bodleian Library, MS Bodley 123 was written about 1480–1490 by T. Urmston, chaplain of Lyme in Cheshire. It assembles various theological and liturgical pieces in Latin, including a treatise on the seven sacraments, the *Gesta Romanorum*, and a number of sermons on Sundays and feast days. These sermons also occur in anonymous Continental collections, from which one or two have found their way into BL MS Royal 18.B.xxiii.[20] **British Library, MS Harley**

---

[17] Notice further that the gospel thema for 4 Advent is Luke 3:3, according to the headnote "secundum consuetudinem quarundam ecclesiarum in euangelio hodierno" (f. 14v). This was the gospel reading for 4 Advent in the Franciscan and Roman *usus*. There is no other gospel sermon for this Sunday in this collection. On the different liturgical readings between Franciscans and Dominicans, see O'Carroll, "Lectionary."

[18] "Taxus one brok or one bagier," f. 22v; "super quo Stephanus Cantuar', 'Hoc facit qui propria potestat abutitur . . .'," a gloss on 1 Sam 31:5, "Saul irruit super gladium suum," f. 3v.

[19] Schneyer 3:767 (wrong attribution); 7:5; 8:151; 8:592; and 9:497. The sermon is on "En ego morior" (Gen 48:21), here marked for Good Friday.

[20] The sermons are inventoried in Schneyer 9:150–156.

2388 (I), a paper miscellany of some III folios, contains a variety of Latin and English treatises, including a variant version of the Middle-English treatise on temptation that appears in G.[21] At the end of one treatise appears the name of the monk Robert Selby, of whom little else is known;[22] at the end of another, the name of Thomas Auerey ("quod Thomas Auerey," f. 48), who held an Oxford BA (c. 1452) and MA (c. 1472), was a priest, and died after 1483.[23] Among these works and excerpts appear two fragmentary Latin sermons; and, more importantly, at the end of the codex, a run of perhaps as many as thirty-seven sermons, the last on severely damaged leaves (ff. 65–111). Many of these are incomplete, others at best sermon notes. They form a very random mixture of *de tempore* and a few saints sermons and two pieces for the dedication of a church. The majority of them are addressed to the clergy ("Reuerendissimi," "Prestantissimi domini," "Peritissimi animarum piscatores," etc.), and several may in fact be academic exercises. One at least had a clearly academic audience (I-13). It stipulates a prayer for the soul of Duke Humphrey (died 1447), the benefactor of "this university, our bountiful mother,"[24] which would place the collection around 1450 or later.

A very different kind of book, though seemingly from the same period, is **Oxford, Merton College, MS 236**. It is in its entirety written by one hand and follows throughout the same layout of presenting its texts in two columns, with a medieval foliation entered in the center of the top margin of the rectos. Some medieval quire signatures are still visible, and all the sermons begin with flourished capitals. On the front flyleaf occur two fifteenth-century lists of contents as well as a note that the book was left to the college in 1468 by Mr Henry "Seuer," professor of theology and warden of Merton. Sever had received his doctorate by 1438, was nominated as the first provost of Eton, and then served as chancellor of Oxford University (1442) and as chaplain to the king. He died in 1471.[25]

---

[21] See Jolliffe, *Check-List*, item 7(b), p. 120.   [22] *BRUO* 3:1665.   [23] See *BRUO* 1:80.

[24] "Quia sancta et salubris est cogitacio pro defunctis exorare vt a peccatis soluantur, specialiterque pro nostro Ioseph, anima hunfridi quondam ducis Glosesterie, qui velud alter Ioseph hanc almam matrem vniuersitatem optimo tritico litteralis disciplina contra famem interioris hominis liberatis distributor instaurit," f. 75. This passage occurs at the end of a long introduction leading to the request to pray especially for three modern equivalents to the biblical David (the Church Militant), Solomon (the king), and Joseph (Humphrey). The prayer for the king specifies that God "des nobis Salamonem regem pacificum, regem prudentem, et sapientem, qui sciat regere populum suum, quia volunt nos inimici nostri destruere et hereditatem / tuam delere" (74v–75). The sermon is on *Estote prudentes* (1 Peter 4:7) and given on the sixth Sunday after Easter. It addresses "Viri prudentissimi," "Vos venerabiles," and "Desideratissimi," and its three principal parts are directed to, respectively, pastors and rectors, graduates ("Vos itaque scienciarum laudibus laureati"), and undergraduates ("Postremo eciam de nostris iunioribus studentibus quiddam moris vellem dicere," 79). After the closing formula appears "Quod schyres" (79v).

[25] *BRUO* 3:1672–3; and Lovatt, "John Blacman," p. 419.

Whether he collected the sermons himself is not clear. Besides several treatises by the Franciscan theologian Francis of Meyronnes (died after 1328), the volume contains three distinct runs of sermons. The first (ff. 1–51rb) is entitled *Mendicus de tempore*, and its anonymous author explains in a prologue (f. 1) that, as he felt himself "noticeably lacking [or failing] in powers and memory," he has, "in lieu of a testament," extracted material from the sermon collections of "Januensis," i.e. Jacobus de Voragine, and composed a temporal cycle which he wants to be called *Mendicus*, "beggar," because "on account of my inexperience this little book has not been ashamed to beg from more experienced [writers]."[26] The resulting seventy-eight sermons cover the Sundays of the Church year. Their author has selected, reordered, and abbreviated material from several cycles of "Januensis," but he has also added some other material (as for instance the story of the Dancers of Colbek[27]) and has occasionally used a different thema from Januensis. This cycle is, thus, a genuine *rifacimento* of the work of the great Italian sermon writer. In its reliance on a much-used Continental collection, the cycle is joined by another run of sermons in the same manuscript (ff. 220ra–503rb), which begins with some Advent and Christmas sermons and then gives the saints sermons by Francis of Meyronnes (without acknowledgment). In between these two runs occurs yet another one (ff. 118–213) of fifty-seven sermons for Lent, from Ash Wednesday through all the days of Lent to Thursday in Easter week, giving for the Sundays sermons on both the epistle and the gospel lections. To my knowledge these are not copied from or modeled on any other collection. They have a peculiar structure, similar to but not identical with that of P1/P2, and are full of "classical" and learned references including Aristotle, Aquinas, Albertus, and "Vallensis." They also deal with several *pastoralia*, but they have no English elements. All in all, then, this large sermon book brings together three very different runs to form a complete collection of sermons *de tempore*, *de quadragesima*, and *de festis et sanctis*.

Such a combination of a well-known cycle of model sermons with another cycle can be found here and there in other fifteenth-century manuscripts as well.

---

[26] "Cum viribus et memoria notabiliter me deficere sentirem, ad honorem Dei et vtilitatem gratanter suscipiencium ac per me loco testamenti per totum annum de tempore singulis diebus de quadragesima opusculum sermonum compendiosum extrahere festinaui ex grandibus et in . . . [unum?] diffusis sed preciosis sermonibus Jacobi de Voragine ordinis fratrum predicatorum, qui passionale confecit . . . Et quia presens opusculum propter meam impericiam plerumque a pericioribus non erubuit mendicare, titulum eiusdem 'Mendicum' precor appellari . . . ," f. 1rb. Between these initial and final sentences the author briefly discusses the preacher's comportment (gesticulation, etc.) and adds that in preaching both *de tempore* and *de sanctis* it is good to explain the lection from which the thema has been taken fully.

[27] In sermon 22, ff. 14vb–15ra.

Thus, **Oxford, New College, MS 305**, written in 1467, combines the *Quadrages-imale* by Januensis with Felton's Sunday sermons, while in another manuscript from the beginning of the century the same *Quadragesimale* is followed by a cycle of undetermined provenance.[28] The collections by Januensis retained their popularity in England and continued to be copied separately throughout the fifteenth century,[29] as did those by Nicholas of Aquavilla, Nicholas de Gorran, Peraldus, Philip the Chancellor, Odo of Cheriton,[30] and others. These volumes are often very neatly written and provided with detailed indices, in contrast to the humbler collections by known or unknown English authors. The great model cycles were of course copied in England already in the thirteenth and early fourteenth centuries, and by the later fifteenth centuries they can be found in the libraries of many religious houses.[31] But with the coming of the printing press, interest in them seems to have waned, or more precisely, interest in printing them in England. Editions of the great Continental collections were produced before 1500, for example, at Brixen (Januensis), Augsburg (Januensis), Cologne (Gorran), Tübingen (Peraldus), Ulm (Peraldus), Paris (Peraldus), Lyons (Aquavilla), and Venice (Januensis), but not at Westminster, and this state of affairs continued throughout the following centuries. Whether for linguistic or ultimately confessional reasons, in England at some point in the later fifteenth century the influence of the great medieval model-sermon collections came to an end.

The other kind of marginality I spoke of concerns not the chronology but the genre of the literature with which this book has dealt. Whether unified, miscellaneous, or mixed, a sermon collection is essentially a sizeable group of individual sermons that stands by itself. But groups of sermons may also occur within, or as part of, works whose nature is defined by intentions or purposes other than that of collecting specifically sermons. Two types of such works are priests' notebooks and pastoral manuals. A priest's notebook gathers, often in a helter-skelter fashion, material that was deemed to be useful to a priest in

---

[28] British Library, MS Harley 755, written in one hand of the late fourteenth or early fifteenth century, in two columns. The first part, ff. 1–136v, contains the Lenten sermons by Jacobus de Voragine. After an alphabetical index and two expositions of the Decalogue, another cycle of *de tempore* sermons from Advent to All Saints follows (ff. 171ra–247vb), with shorter pieces on the epistle and gospel lections. They seem to have some connection with Hugh of St. Cher, but further study is needed.

[29] For example, Cambridge, Gonville and Caius College, MS 246.

[30] For example, Winchester College MS 11, written in England in the mid-fifteenth century. On the influence of Odo's model sermon collection see Spencer, *English*, pp. 296–297 and passim.

[31] See especially the catalogue of the magnificent library at Syon Abbey edited by Vincent Gillespie (*Syon Abbey*). Gillespie speaks of "the exceptionally strong holdings of sermons and sermon-aids" (p. xxxvii) and writes, "The single largest genre in the library's holdings of printed books is sermons" (p. lxiii).

his pastoral office: excerpts from the Fathers or canon law, pious stories, short summaries of the *pastoralia* often accompanied by memory verses and put into the vernacular, and more of the kind. Such a notebook may contain the name of its collector, but otherwise it is rather faceless and private. Among the useful material may also be one or more groups of sermons.

A good example is **Oxford, Bodleian Library, MS Bodley 857**, already discussed in an earlier section.[32] The book was written by "Castell de Wyroull" in the early fifteenth century and later belonged to William Marshall, chaplain of Peascholm, Yorkshire. Besides several treatises on the Pater Noster, the Decalogue (with some sermons), matters for hearing confession, the seven vices and virtues, and the *Gesta Romanorum*, it also contains the sermon cycle by Nicholas de Aquavilla (ff. 2–82, plus two more sermons by Nicholas) and, at its end, seventeen sermons of English provenance, a number of them shared with other collections. Another notebook from the same period, **Cambridge, University Library, Additional MS 5943**, is similarly written in a single hand and contains much pastoral material in Latin and English, including excerpts from the *Dieta salutis*, Grosseteste, FitzRalph, Richard Rolle, papal and synodal decrees, and much else including a "libellus qui dicitur vrbanus." In addition this manuscript holds a series of sermons (ff. 1–91) in random order and interspersed with notes and short excerpts.[33]

In contrast to these two manuscripts, two other priest's notebooks are clearly composite codices written by more than one hand. **London, British Library, MS Harley 2346** comprises at least three booklets, each written by a different hand of the later fourteenth and fifteenth centuries. The first and third contain material for catechetical teaching, in Latin and English, including a pastoral manual in Latin hexameters,[34] but the second booklet holds about a dozen sermons for major feast days including Ash Wednesday, Ascension, and Rogation Days. Some of these are also found in two manuscripts of an earlier date, Harley 2385[35]

---

[32] Section 12 above, pp. 79–80.

[33] The manuscript can be dated to 1409x1418; see Robinson, *Catalogue of Dated*, 1:43 and vol. 2, plate 199. The sermons seem to be by Jacobus de Voragine.

[34] Called *Speculum sacerdotum*, ff. 55v–72, and beginning "Ecclesie sancte regimen qui ducere sancte / Vis, hec metra lege de sacra condita lege." There is a printed copy of the work (Vienne, 1480?) in the British Library, IA 42732. In the printed edition the work is said to have been made in 1327. In the manuscript it follows the *Ten Comaundementes* (Lewis et al., *Index of Printed Middle English Prose*, no. 48) and a copy of the longer Charter of Christ. The first booklet (ff. 1–11) includes material on the sacraments, works of mercy, petitions, etc.

[35] MS Harley 2385, evidently a Dominican book, is made up of several booklets that date from the late thirteenth to the early fifteenth century. See *Catalogue of Romances*, 3:521. Several sermons also appear in Caius 52, one apparently is also D-89, and another is P1-37/P2-34. The sermons for Sundays and festivals on ff. 26–31v are in a late-thirteenth-century hand.

and especially Caius 52 (to be discussed further below). **MS Harley 7322** also is composed of several booklets, in fact more than ten, written in different hands that range through the fourteenth century. Several of them clearly come from other codices.[36] It is hard to say when, and even harder by whom, the volume was put together, but its contents would all have been useful to a preacher. They include two booklets of moralized tales, many of which can also be found in Holcot, the *Gesta Romanorum*, and the *Fasciculus morum*, with a large number of English verses.[37] Throughout, the booklets contain approximately ninety sermons of varied provenance, but not forming a genuine cycle. They include pieces by Nicholas de Byard and other Continental authors, as well as one of John Pecham's *Collationes* on the epistles (ff. 243–246). Both the identifiable sermons and the early-fourteenth century handwriting of the respective booklets indicate that some if not all of the sermon material comes from the later thirteenth century.

Next to such priests' notebooks stand pastoral manuals, that is, technical treatises written to instruct pastors in their duties, such as, how to say Mass, how to hear confession, what catechetical matters to preach to the people, etc. They often have a known author and a medieval name: the *Oculus sacerdotis* and the *Speculum praelatorum* by William of Pagula,[38] or the *Memoriale presbyterorum* by William Doune,[39] or the *Manuale sacerdotis* by John Mirk,[40] or the *Speculum curatorum* by Ranulph Higden (1340),[41] but others are anonymous. One or two of those made in England also contain a group of sermons, notably so the ***Speculum praelatorum*** by William of Pagula, written between 1320 and 1323. Its third part offers a series of sermon outlines, first for the Sundays and non-dominical feasts and then for saints' feasts, with several pieces for each.[42] These are quite short. They divide the lection into its two or three leading features or ideas, give a number of supporting scriptural authorities for each, and finally point out key words suggested by the lection. The key words, then, appear in alphabetical order after the sermon outlines (ff. 247–441), and these sections provide further material

---

[36] Medieval foliations visible: 1–151 (modern 1–151); 77–84 (modern 165–172); 77–92 (modern 180–195); 37–48 (modern 196–207); 74-c2 (i.e., 102, with some irregularities; there is second medieval foliation x-16) (modern 224–242). The whole volume has 246 folios plus two front flyleaves, the latter with sermon texts.

[37] The tales have been inventoried by Herbert in *Catalogue of Romances*, 3:166–179. For the relation between Harley 7322 and the *Fasciculus morum*, see Wenzel, *Verses*, pp. 116–119. Many of the English verses in Harley have been printed in *Political, Religious and Love Poems*, pp. 249–270.

[38] Boyle, "*Oculus sacerdotis*."   [39] Haren, *Sin and Society*.

[40] Fletcher, "Manuscripts." The work has been edited in an unpublished dissertation: Girsch, "Edition."

[41] Cf. Crook, "New Version"; and Crook and Jennings, "Devil."

[42] Oxford, Merton College, MS 217, ff. 179 ff. See also below, pp. 238–239.

and authorities for preaching on the respective matters. All this is explained in a prologue to this part of the *Speculum* (ff. 179ra–va), which also sets forth some moral and intellectual qualifications a preacher should have.[43]

This section of Pagula's *Speculum praelatorum*, thus, reads very much like an *ars praedicandi*, a technical treatise on how to preach and how to construct a sermon. The two most extensive arts of preaching made in England during the later Middle Ages – Robert of Basevorn's *Forma praedicandi* (1322) and Thomas Waleys's *De modo componendi sermones* (1340s) – both illustrate procedures of constructing a sermon with many examples in their text, examples that in length now and then approach a full sermon.[44] But in addition, Waleys's work, after its first part that deals with the qualities of a good preacher and with how to construct a scholastic sermon, was to contain two further parts that provide sample sermons.[45] Similarly, one manuscript of Basevorn's treatise includes a number of separate sermons. The fourteenth-century part of **British Library, Additional MS 38818**, has apparently suffered from errors in binding and losses, but it still contains a list of works beginning "De modo faciendi sermones" and adding a total of forty-two sermon themata (f. 261v). The title "De modo faciendi sermones" must refer to the text on ff. 256–260v, which is a defective copy of Basevorn's *Forma praedicandi* (beginning of prologue missing, and giving only twenty of the fifty chapters found elsewhere). Before that, on ff. 191–255, occur fifty sermons that correspond to the themata found in the list, many with the corresponding numbers. The sermons are in random order, of various forms, and written in a variety of hands, so that it is more likely that someone other than Basevorn collected and added them to this copy of his art of preaching. Several of them also occur elsewhere in the collections surveyed earlier,[46] and at least one of them contains English phrases. The practice of thus adding some exemplary sermons to the prescriptive treatise can also be found in other arts of preaching, such as that by the Augustinian canon Alexander of Ashby, who wrote about the year 1200.[47]

A different kind of preaching tool that similarly includes some model sermons is the alphabetical dictionary of topics that could be useful in sermons. The great

---

[43] This provision and disposition of sermon material is reminiscent of the "preaching machine" of the Dominican Guy d'Evreux; see Michaud-Quantin, "Guy d'Evreux," and d'Avray, *Preaching*, pp. 74–75.

[44] Both are discussed and partially edited in Charland, *Artes praedicandi*.

[45] See ibid., pp. 94–95. Waleys refers to these "exempla ponenda in secunda et tertia parte hujus opusculi" several times in part 1: see ibid., pp. 372, 379, and 384–385.

[46] Two in collection X and one in collection F; see the relevant sections above.

[47] Morenzoni, "Aux origines," with an edition of Alexander's *ars praedicandi* as well as the five model sermons.

Summa praedicantium by **Bromyard** (died by 1352), for example, contains not only lists of themata for special occasions but here and there fairly complete sermons.[48] A later example is **London, British Library, MS Harley 3130**, a paper manuscript of the fifteenth century. After some initial sermons mixed with notes, the first one acephalous, it contains two series of articles in alphabetical order.[49] Both contain references to Higden's ("Cestrensis") *Polychronicon*. Both also contain scattered full sermons, with divisions and addresses.

Pastoral manuals, especially shorter ones, were occasionally themselves included in priest's notebooks, where they came to find themselves in the company of collected sermons. Such is the case, for instance, of the ***Summa iuniorum*** by the English Dominican Simon de Hinton (died after 1261). A brief exposition of the *pastoralia* or catechetical pieces, it was enormously popular and survives in many copies.[50] In collection K it forms a booklet that has been joined with many others, written by various different hands, into a priest's notebook where it stands next to sermons.[51] Another copy of the *Summa iuniorum*, in British Library, MS Harley 586, is similarly accompanied by the sermons of Guibert de Tournai.

A very similar combination of priest's manual and sermon cycle appears in **Cambridge, Gonville and Caius College, MS 52**. The book begins with a copy of the *Speculum iuniorum*, by an anonymous English author, written in a thirteenth-century hand (ff. 1–43r). This is a fairly substantial *summa* of basic theological and pastoral knowledge.[52] Upon it follows a treatise on the Mass, "Loquimur Dei sapienciam in misterio" (ff. 43va–62rb), and then three runs of sermons. The first of these (ff. 62va–82vb) is a complete and regular *de tempore* cycle, mostly on the gospel lections, which I will call "Bis in anno."[53] This cycle, made in the thirteenth century, must have been very popular, as it has survived in at least eleven copies, ten of which are now in British libraries.[54]

---

[48] For example, the article on Visitation includes some fifteen *collaciones* that are complete model sermons.

[49] (1) Ff. 17–76v, Abstinere–Misericordia; (2) ff. 77–135, Ablactacio–Missa.

[50] See Bloomfield, *Incipits*, no. 0245, and additions in Sharpe, *Handlist*, pp. 615–616. The work is discussed in Boyle, "Notes."

[51] See above, section 37.　　[52] See Boyle, "Three English."

[53] For the characteristic *initium* "Hoc euangelium bis in anno legitur" of the sermon for 1 Advent, *Cum appropinquasset Iesus Ierusalem*. In Caius 52 it is followed by a cycle of temporal, saints, and special-occasion sermons (ff. 83ra–122va) that are apparently selected from Nicholas de Aquavilla; and another temporal cycle (ff. 122va–162vb). "Bis in anno" and the third cycle are inventoried in Schneyer 8:230–240, though very poorly. The last cycle contains a few phrases in French and English and an interesting remark about the English Church, f. 130vb (cf. Schneyer 8:236, no. 76).

[54] To the copies listed in Schneyer 8:452 should be added Caius 52 and Lambeth 352.

But the importance of this early collection goes beyond its popularity. In one manuscript, **Harley 2345**, "Bis in anno" is followed by a long series (if not several series) of saints sermons that is the Latin ancestor to the Middle-English *Speculum sacerdotale* and exists in at least three other manuscripts, as we saw in the discussion of Mirk's *Festial*. Since the *de sanctis* collection in Harley 2345 includes such rare British and Anglo-Saxon saints as Alphege, Frideswide, and Samson, the collection is likely to be of English provenance.[55]

"Bis in anno" also appears in **London, Lambeth Palace, MS 352.**[56] This, too, may be classified as a priest's notebook, which gathers works that are written by several hands of the fifteenth century and belonged to "Mr John May, rector of the church of All Saints the Greater in London," *ex dono* of Robert Norton, chaplain in the abbey of Malling, Kent.[57] Here "Bis in anno" is joined by a treatise on how to say Mass, John Waldeby's exposition of the Pater Noster (here called *Itinerarium salutis*), Richard Rolley's Latin commentary on the Psalms, and several meditative treatises. The latter show a pronounced interest in Christ's Passion, and this holds true of the final substantial item in the codex, a lengthy macaronic Good-Friday sermon on *Dilexit nos et lavit nos a peccatis nostris in sanguine suo* (Rev 1:5), written in a later fifteenth-century hand (ff. 216–224v).[58]

"Bis in anno" as well as the series of saints' sermons in Harley 2345 reach far back into the thirteenth century or perhaps even to before 1200 and may thus be an important bridge between pre-1200 "homiletic" preaching and the work of the great thirteenth-century makers of model collections as well as their successors in England. Both collections, whose traces appear in diverse forms and in many codices, call for closer investigation. Their transmission, interrelationship, and popularity will undoubtedly shed light on what still is a grey period in the history of medieval preaching. To this grey period before 1350 belongs the homiletic work of such English authors as John Pecham, Robert Holcot, Simon Boraston, the somewhat mysterious Thomas Lebreton, and others.[59] Next to them are other

---

[55] Before these saints sermons occur others including pieces for Cuthbert, Dunstan, Alban, Kenelm, Owald, Egwin, Oswald, and Godwald.

[56] See James and Jenkins, *Descriptive Catalogue . . . Lambeth Palace*, pp. 466–470; and Wenzel, *Macaronic*, pp. 33–34.

[57] "Pertinet liber iste Magistro Iohanni May rectori ecclesie omnium sanctorum maioris \London'/ ex dono domini Roberti Nortoun capellani in abbathia de Mallynge in comitatu kantie, etc.," back flyleaf. For a John May who was admitted as rector of All Hallows in 1470, see *BRUC* 398.

[58] Edited and translated in Johnson, "Preaching the Passion," pp. 51–177.

[59] For these authors and their sermon collections see Sharpe, *Handlist*. Pecham's *Collationes dominicales* (Sharpe p. 294) further appear in Cambridge, University Library MS Ii.1.26 (ff. 5–28v, gospels), my collection X (see section above), and London, British Library, MS Harley 7322 (ff. 243–246, epistles). Besides Robert Holcot's *Sermones dominicales* (Sharpe p. 557), his collection *Convertimini* enjoyed an even greater popularity; to Sharpe's listing (pp. 554–555) can be added

collections that remain anonymous. This being so, it is of course difficult to say whether their authors were indeed English. Yet they often stand in a net of complex relationships between manuscripts of English provenance. A good case is **Oxford, Merton College, MS 112.** It was written in the early fifteenth century, possibly by a single hand, and was chained in the college library in 1468.[60] With various theological works produced by English and Continental authors through the fourteenth century it contains a complete *de tempore* cycle with one sermon each for the epistle and gospel lections.[61] Over twenty of these also appear in **Cambridge, Trinity College, MS B.1.45** (ff. 25–41v), a miscellany of Latin and English works that was written in the thirteenth century.[62] Further study of such manuscripts that also contain sermons promises to reveal much about sermon making, the dependence of English authors and collectors on Continental models as well as their originality, the continued influence of older collections over centuries, and other matters that will enrich and extend our picture of preaching in medieval England, without however, I am convinced, denying the primary importance in this history of the century with which this study has been concerned.

BL MSS Harley 206, 5369, and 5396. On Thomas Lebreton, or de Lisle, see Sharpe, p. 665, and Bataillon, "Sermons attribués," pp. 332–333. Schneyer 5:631–670 lists under his name 599 sermons, in several cycles. See above, sections 25 (X) and 26 (W) with reference to Aberdeen University Library MS 154.

[60] See Powicke, *Medieval Books of Merton College*, p. 205, no. 963.

[61] 106 sermons. They are short and in the nature of outlines or skeletons, dividing the thema at once into three or four parts that are geared to the entire lection, and then developing the parts chiefly with biblical quotations. They lack address forms and closing formulas altogether. There is little if any rhetorical elaboration, although the preacher quotes "poeta" several times. With one or two exceptions each sermon begins with an enlarged and flourished initial. Rubrics at the head of the sermons indicate their occasion, from 1 Advent to 25 Trinity (with one or two skips).

[62] Cf. James, *Western Manuscripts . . . Trinity College*, 1:56–59. On the provenance of the manuscript see Reichl, *Religiöse Dichtung*, p. 53 n. 16. In addition to the sermons in the Trinity College MS, two sermons in Merton 112 can also be found in Bodley 50, and another among the sermons attributed to Thomas de Lisle.

PART II

Occasions of Preaching

39

Introduction

The first question anyone interested in medieval sermons normally has is, how much preaching was actually done: at every Mass? on every Sunday? in every church, small or large? by every ordained priest? Behind this question lie centuries-old and often vague convictions that medieval preaching on the whole was infrequent, often neglected, and mostly not very intelligent. Such convictions have been fed not only by the Protestant opposition to the medieval Church, with its own greater emphasis on the word of God, but also the Roman Catholic experience, for which, before Vatican II, a sermon at daily Mass was quite unusual, and the Sunday sermon something to be gotten over with quickly, on the part of both celebrant and congregation. But medieval voices themselves often criticized and even reviled priests for neglecting their duties of instructing their people, for failing to give the spiritual food of God's word to their flocks.

Part Two of this study will address the question of how frequent preaching was in the period covered, within the larger framework of the occasions when a sermon was, or was to be, given. To anticipate: although the sermon collections here examined furnish a few new insights, on the whole the question of how frequently sermons were actually preached will not find a new answer – Owst's "dry bones of an old controversy" will not gain new life.[1] But we shall notice that preaching was done at many other occasions than the weekly service in the parish church. This, again, is not a new insight, but the extant Latin sermon collections provide more and better evidence for it than previous studies have shown.

The following pages, then, will first discuss late-medieval preaching in general and in the parishes. They then turn to preaching by bishops in their cathedrals, in synods, on visitations, and on some other occasions. Next I will discuss preaching among and by monks, by the mendicants, and at the university. Finally, several special occasions, such as processions, parliamentary sermons, and sermons at St.

---

[1] Owst, *Preaching*, p. 25.

Paul's Cross, will be examined. In each case, I will follow a pattern of precept – practice – preserved texts. I first survey what the relevant Church legislation decreed about the respective type of preaching. Then I turn to what evidence about such preaching I have found in (mostly printed) records, such as episcopal registers, chronicles, and the like. Lastly, I survey what sermons from the extant collections belong to the respective type of preaching and discuss their characteristic features.

40

Preaching in the medieval Church
and in the parishes

It may be profitable to begin the examination of preaching in the later medieval Church, and in the parishes in particular, with relevant decrees issued by the Fourth Lateran Council of 1215–1216. Under the leadership of Pope Innocent III, the council enacted legislation that was to affect the universal Church at all levels and in very practical ways. Part of this wide-ranging effort was canon 10, which stated:

> Among other things that belong to the salvation of the Christian people, the basic food (*pabulum*) of the word of God is known to be absolutely necessary. For just as the body is nourished by material food, so is the soul nourished by spiritual food, because "man does not live on bread alone, but on every word that comes from the mouth of God." Now, it often happens that the bishops, because of their manifold business, or because of bodily infirmity, or because of attacks by enemies or other reasons – without mentioning their defect of knowledge, which in them must be altogether reproved and not tolerated at all – that for these reasons the bishops are unable by themselves to minister the word of God to their people, especially throughout large and widespread dioceses. We therefore ordain in this general constitution that the bishops take on capable men (*viros idoneos . . . assumant*) to profitably carry out the office of holy preaching, men powerful in deed and word, who are to visit their flocks in lieu of the bishops, when the latter cannot do so themselves, and edify them by word and example. And the bishops are to furnish them with what is necessary when they are in need, so that they are not compelled for lack of necessities to desist from what they have set out to do. We therefore command that both in cathedrals and in other conventual churches capable men be ordained, whom the bishops might use as their helpers and co-workers, not only in the office of preaching but also in hearing confessions and imposing penances and doing whatever else belongs to the salvation of souls. Whoever neglects to carry this out, shall undergo severe punishment.[1]

---

[1] Canon *Inter cetera*, taken into the *Decretals* of Gregory IX at 1.31.15 (Friedberg 2:192).

The canon highlights that by the year 1200, in the institutional Western Church as it was organized into parishes, dioceses, and provinces, preaching the word of God was first of all the obligation of the bishops, who then might delegate others to carry it out on various local levels, such as their cathedrals and the individual parishes. Further, canon 10 concerns itself specifically with preaching the word of God, not with celebrating "the divine mysteries." By 1200, the institution of a clergy charged with saying Mass and the Office and with the cure of souls, had been firmly in place in both legislation and social reality.[2] What is new in canon 10 is the attention given to the importance of preaching at the highest level of the Church, and to the obligation on the part of the episcopate to carry it out.[3]

Among the council fathers were a number of English bishops, including Richard Poore, who upon his return and subsequent installation at Salisbury (where he was bishop 1217–1228) issued constitutions that refer to canon 10 and repeat it almost verbatim.[4] Nor was Bishop Poore alone in this zeal to carry out what must have appeared to many churchmen as a breath of fresh air. In 1222, a synod held at Oxford decreed:

> As we wish to stir the minds of parish priests to carry out more eagerly the things that are most useful in our time, we have ventured to enjoin them, by the declaration of the present council, that they strive to teach (*informare*) the people committed to them with the food of God's word (*pabulo verbi Dei*).[5]

And another couple of years later, a synodal council at Winchester similarly declared:

> We order above all that parish priests frequently preach (*proponent*) the word of God to their parishioners . . . Whoever is found negligent in this, shall be at once suspended from his office.[6]

Preaching the word of God was joined by a second reforming effort stemming from Lateran IV, which has left much more numerous and tangible traces in the

---

[2] A succinct survey of the history of parish organization, especially in England, can be found in several booklets by Addleshaw, in the "St. Anthony's Hall Publication" series: *Beginnings*; *Development*; and *Rectors*. A good and more extensive account of the development of parishes and parish churches, albeit focused on the Continent, can be found in Feine, *Kirchliche Rechtsgeschichte*, and in Leclercq, "Paroisses rurales." Grégoire, in *Homéliaires*, pp. 11–18 ("Présence de la prédication"), discusses the office of preaching, its transition from bishop to parish clergy, and related aspects, on the Continent. For England see especially Godfrey, *Church*, ch. 9, pp. 310–330 ("The Origin and Development of the Parochial System"); and Barlow, *English Church*, pp. 183–208. A somewhat unsympathetic account is Pounds, *History*.

[3] For the immediate background of the concern with preaching at Lateran IV see Rouse and Rouse, *Preachers*, pp. 43–58.

[4] *Councils and Synods* 1:94. Cf. Gibbs and Lang, *Bishops*, pp. 122–129, especially at 125.

[5] *Councils and Synods* 1:110.   [6] Ibid., p. 130.

relevant documents of the thirteenth, fourteenth, and fifteenth centuries. This is the effort to educate the clergy, not by creating new institutions or providing means for clerics to attend university – this did not become Church law until the end of the century[7] – but by specifying a minimum of what a priest ought to know and to teach his parishioners. This minimum became at once formulated in a series of basic teaching units or set pieces which modern scholars refer to as *pastoralia*. They were spelled out and formulated, first in diocesan constitutions and then in numerous handbooks for priests, and so became the fundamental catechetical matter of the late-medieval Church. The very influential Constitutions of Bishop Robert Grosseteste of Lincoln (1235–53), issued probably in 1239, give a complete list:

> Since there can be no salvation of souls without the observation of the Decalogue, we exhort in the Lord and firmly command that every shepherd of souls and every parish priest know the Decalogue, that is, the Ten Commandments of the Mosaic Law, and that he frequently preach and expound them to the people in his care. He must also know that there are seven deadly sins (*septem criminalia*) and preach them likewise to the people, as things to be fled. But above all he must know the seven sacraments of the Church; and those who are priests must know above all what is necessary for the sacrament of true confession and penance. And they must often teach the baptismal formula to the laypeople, in their common language. Also, every one of them must have at least a simple understanding of the faith, as it is contained in the Symbol, both the greater and the lesser, as well as in the tract that is called *Quicumque vult*, which is daily recited at prime in the Church.[8]

This decree was repeated again and again in other diocesan constitutions through the thirteenth century, and later synods even added that priests were to be examined on how well they knew these matters.[9]

Some English bishops took an even more practical step and not only listed such catechetical units but had them written out in detail and copied for the use of simple parish priests.[10] Their work was in fact anticipated in the very popular, though today little known *Summa brevis* by Richard Wethersette (or Wethringset), compiled about 1220 and extant in many manuscripts.[11] Beginning with the scriptural verse "Let the priests that rule well be considered worthy of

---

[7] The constitution *Cum ex eo* of Boniface VIII (1298) permitted bishops to issue temporary dispensations to rectors and vicars to study, for as long as seven years, at university, supported by their parish income. Such dispensation was already an established custom at the end of the twelfth century. See Boyle, "Constitution."

[8] *Councils and Synods* 1:268.   [9] Cf. ibid., pp. 345, 403, 610.

[10] See Goering and Taylor, "*Summulae*," listing several such works on pp. 576–577 and notes; and Goering, *William de Montibus*, pp. 58–99. For evidence of such copies in medieval parishes, see Shinners, "Parish Libraries," pp. 209–210.

a twofold honor, especially those who labor in word and doctrine" (1 Timothy 5:17), the work outlines the following program:

> What belongs most basically to faith and morals and must be preached very frequently are: the Creed with its twelve articles of faith, the Lord's Prayer with its seven petitions, the general and particular gifts of God, especially the Seven Gifts of the Holy Ghost . . . The four cardinal . . . and three theological virtues. And above all the seven capital vices are to be preached . . . The Ten Commandments are to be preached . . . Also what the reward of the just in heaven is must be preached . . .

Wethersette then offers a respectable amount of such basic knowledge, replete with memory verses that not only summarize the individual units but connect them and their parts with relevant biblical figures.[12]

This basic catechetical matter, and the injunction for priests to know it and to teach it to their flocks, found its best known expression in the famous Lambeth Constitutions of Archbishop Pecham of 1281. Article 9, entitled "De informatione simplicium sacerdotum," declares that "the ignorance of the priests pushes the people into the pit of error, and the foolishness or stupidity (*stultitia vel ruditas*) of clerics who, by canonical decree, are commanded to instruct the children of the faithful, leads sometimes more to error than to true knowledge." To remedy this situation, each priest is now required to teach the *pastoralia*

> four times a year, that is, once in every quarter, on one or more solemn days, by himself or through someone else, in the common language (*vulgariter*), without any fanciful and subtle compositional art (*absque cuiuslibet subtilitatis textura fantastica*).

And that no-one might have reason to excuse himself out of ignorance, Pecham adds a précis of this catechetical matter, in a form that here and there goes well beyond a mere listing of the items.[13]

Pecham's Constitution was law for the entire province of Canterbury and some years later became similarly binding on the clergy of the province of York. Moreover, when Archbishop Arundel in 1407 established tighter rules concerning the licensing of preachers, he reaffirmed the catechetical material of *Ignorantia sacerdotum* as proper preaching matter for parish priests.[14] To preach these topics,

---

[11] See Goering, "Summa."   [12] Cf. Wenzel, *Sin of Sloth*, pp. 73–74.

[13] *Councils and Synods* 2:900–901.

[14] Wilkins, *Concilia* 3:315. The constitutions were originally drawn up at Oxford in 1407 and then promulgated on 14 January 1409. How well they were observed can be seen, for instance, in *Register Edmund Stafford*, pp. 41, 61, 84, 114, 116, 117, 222, 224, 238, 242, 247, 251, 263, 294, 317, 325, 327, 334, 335, 352, 355, 354, 360.

therefore, was an article of Church law for English priests through the period with which this book is concerned.[15]

By 1350, such constitutions issued by provincial synods, together with similar papal and conciliar pronouncements that had found their way into canon law, were available to simple parish priests in a number of pastoral manuals, of which William of Pagula's *Oculus sacerdotis* is the best known example.[16] These handbooks present the relevant material a parish priest needed to know in a form that is more clearly organized than it was in the *Decretum* and the *Decretals*, and they offer considerably more practical details for the administration of the sacraments. They also share the concern about ignorant priests that characterizes the reform efforts of Lateran IV. Thus, Pagula begins his *Oculus* by quoting Clement V:

> Churches that are ruled by persons/parsons who are little capable (*minus ydonei*) on account of their knowledge, morals, or age suffer serious detriments in temporal and spiritual matters.[17]

Through their negligence, he continues,

> they frequently lead their subjects to hell . . . , as I have learned from my own experience when I was a penitentiary, for I have many times known and found many parish priests to have made mistakes in hearing confessions and in imposing penances.[18]

In the three parts of his book,[19] Pagula then collects a large amount of information about a priest's work, particularly about his administering the sacraments, which includes detailed instruction on how to say Mass, how to hear confessions, how to baptize and to marry his parishioners, and so forth. This massive, and several times repeated, collection of information is sprinkled with remarks on what a priest must "preach" or "propose" or "expound" or "publish" or "instruct his parishioners in." As one scans what Pagula has to say about preaching in the

---

[15] For similar legislation in France, see *Statuts* 1:84.

[16] On manuals for parish priests of the fourteenth and early fifteenth centuries, see Pantin, *English Church*, pp. 189–219; the *Oculus sacerdotis* is analyzed on pp. 195–202. This and other works by William of Pagula are discussed by Boyle, "*Oculus sacerdotis*." Pagula died c. 1332.

[17] Quoting with reference Clementines I, tit. 6 (Friedberg 2:1139).

[18] "Frequenter suos subditos per suam necgligenciam ad infernum ducunt . . . provt experiencia didici in officio penitenciarii constitutus, nam multociens sciui et inueni quamplures sacerdotes parochianos errasse in modo confessionis audiende et in absolucione inpendenda, ac in penitenciis iniungendis et absoluentes parochianos suos de facto quos absoluere non possunt de iure, eneruantes ecclesiasticam disciplinam, et in multis casibus mittentes eos penitenciariis episcoporum, in quibus ipsi sacerdotes absoluere bene possunt." Prologue to the *Prima pars oculi*, London, British Library, MS Royal 8.C.ii, f. 52ra.

[19] They are called, respectively, *Prima pars oculi*, *Dextera pars oculi*, and *Sinistra pars oculi*.

parishes, one is overwhelmed by his repeated insistence on teaching, on inform-
ing the people in the faith. Emphasis on providing information – as opposed to
moral exhortation, or emotional appeal, or explaining the gospel – is a major
characteristic of what Pagula's and other pastoral manuals say about preaching.

As the quoted opening words of the *Oculus sacerdotis* have already shown,
the focus of Pagula's instructions for priests lies on the sacrament of Penance.[20]
We should recall, at this point, that in the medieval Church spiritual shepherds
were instituted to lead the souls committed to their care to salvation, as it is
also explicitly stated at the end of canon 10 quoted above. This *cura animarum*
involved a number of duties, all derived from Christ's words to Peter to "feed
my sheep": pastors were to feed their flock both physically (especially the poor,
from the parish income) and spiritually. The latter consisted in teaching, in
providing the sacraments, in giving an example of a holy life, and in ruling their
flock. In a written sermon read before the pope in 1250, which was later copied
into at least one fifteenth-century sermon collection, Grosseteste provided a fine
comprehensive statement:

> The work of pastoral care consists not only in administering the sacraments,
> saying the canonical hours, and celebrating Mass . . . , but in truly teaching the
> life of truth, in condemning vices by instilling fear, in correcting vices severely
> and with firm command where necessary and rigidly chastizing them . . . It also
> consists in feeding the hungry, in giving drink to the thirsty . . . , and especially
> so to one's own parishioners, to whom the temporal goods of the churches
> belong.[21]

To these aspects of the pastoral office should be added one more which is sounded
often in late-medieval sermons, that of answering questions concerning the faith
and morals – *dubia dissoluere et ad interrogata respondere*, in the words of a sermon
from the Hereford collection (E).[22]

---

[20] Boyle calls the first of part the work "in fact, a modest *Summa de Poenitentia*," "*Oculus sacerdotis*,"
  p. 86.
[21] "Opus curae pastoralis consistit, non solum in sacramentorum administratione et horarum
  Canonicarum dictione et missarum celebratione . . . , sed in veraci doctrina veritatis vitae, in
  vitiorum terrifica condemnatione, in vitiorum, cum necesse est, dura et imperiosa correptione et
  in rigida castigatione . . . Consistit etiam in pastione esurientium, in potatione sitientium . . . et
  maxime propriorum parochianorum, quorum sunt bona temporalia Ecclesiarum." Grosseteste,
  Sermon 14, printed in *Fasciculus rerum*, 2:253. Copied as Z-22.
[22] The entire sentence reads: "Sacerdotis nempe officium est subditorum mores componere, errores
  eorum effugare, dubia dissoluere, et ad interrogata respondere, sermones compositos et honestos
  ornate proferre, vt de eo verificetur illud Judith 8: 'Omnia que locutus es vera sunt, et non est
  in sermonibus tuis vlla reprehensio'," E-23, f. 58ra. For further discussion of the pastoral office
  see below, "Preaching and the pastoral office."

The way to salvation, for medieval Christianity, thus required two essentials: right belief and good morals. For both it was necessary to have a sufficient amount of basic knowledge: the fundamentals of Christian faith, as they are found and enunciated in the Apostles' and other Creeds, and the rule of good morality as found in the Ten Commandments, supplemented by standard lists of the major vices to be shunned and virtues to be striven for. As an essential act and exercise to ensure that all Christians had such knowledge and followed it in their daily lives, the medieval Church demanded that all men and women regularly examine their consciences and confess their sins to their established spiritual shepherd, do penance, receive absolution, and then receive the Eucharist. The famous canon 21 of the Fourth Lateran Council, *Omnis utriusque sexus*, demanded this to be done at least once a year,[23] and in order to do this well it was crucial to know the *pastoralia* discussed earlier. The latter, therefore, contained the basic necessary information at the simplest level that was required of both pastors entrusted with the *cura animarum* and all Christian men and women. This knowledge was to be presented by means of the regular sermon. The new emphasis on preaching that we found in the decrees of Lateran IV was, thus, intimately connected with the practices of confession and of receiving holy communion.[24]

It is therefore no wonder that the *Oculus sacerdotis*, written by a canonist who as penitentiary had been deeply involved with the sacrament of Penance, should insist so much on the parish priest's duty to inform his flock and to present to them the *pastoralia* as specified in article 9 of the Lambeth Constitutions, which Pagula quotes verbatim.[25] However, that does not mean that in the eyes of a canon lawyer preaching meant nothing but proclaiming the *pastoralia*. In a telling addition Pagula points out how the latter and "the word of God" may be combined and mutually accommodated:

> The priest who must preach the word [of God] to his parishioners can also inject (*intermittere*) and take some of these things that are described below [i.e. the *pastoralia*] as it pleases him in carrying out his purpose.[26]

How such a combination was effected, and whether it caused preachers any uneasiness as has been claimed, will be explored in a subsequent chapter.[27]

---

[23] Also taken into the *Decretals* of Gregory IX: 5.38.12 (Friedberg 2:887–888).

[24] This connection was fully recognized by D. W. Robertson, Jr., see n. 51.

[25] In part 2 of the *Oculus sacerdotis*, London, British Library, MS Royal 8.C.ii, f. 87ra.

[26] "Potest eciam sacerdos qui debet predicare parochianis verbum aliqua intermittere et accipere de hiis que ita [?] scribuntur secundum quod sibi placuerit ad suum propositum prosequendum," ibid., f. 87ra. The phrase *ad suum propositum prosequendum* could refer to the development of the sermon thema based on the day's lection.

[27] "The Word of God and *pastoralia*," pp. 346–353.

Yet despite its general insistence on providing basic information in the sermon, the *Oculus sacerdotis* pays hardly any attention to specific details of preaching. In contrast to its careful exposition of how the sacraments are to be administered, it says absolutely nothing about how a priest should address his congregation, what language and style he is to use, how long he may speak, and so on – matters that are more normally discussed in the *artes praedicandi*.[28] The impression that in these manuals for parish priests preaching does not command the same degree of detailed legislative attention as does the administration of the sacraments also emerges from other official Church documents. Thus, episcopal registers brim with regulations about church property, and cathedral customs are much concerned with how many candles should be lit on which occasions, but neither pay any attention to what sermons were to be preached on what occasions. Written official Church legislation, thus, might easily suggest that in the later Middle Ages the altar was more important than the pulpit; or as the Rouses put it, "the hearing of sermons was not, and has never quite become, a requirement for salvation."[29]

But to take this impression for the whole picture would be quite wrong. For one thing, twelfth-century authoritative pronouncements leave no doubt that preaching a sermon was part of the Church's main liturgical service, the Mass. We learn from them that, except for such special occasions as a visitation, or a synod, or an afternoon sermon,[30] the usual time for a sermon would have been during Mass after the Gospel had been read. Thus, an *Ordo Romanus* from before 1143 says that the archdeacon, deacon, and acolytes, after the gospel has been sung, "carry the gospel book in front of the bishop, and the bishop kisses it, ascends the pulpit, and preaches (*praedicat*) the Gospel," after which follows the Creed.[31] Later in the twelfth century Cardinal William Durandus gave more detailed prescriptions about preaching in his very popular manual for liturgical practices, the *Rationale divinorum officiorum*. He specified that after the gospel reading "preaching (*predicatio*) to the people takes place, as the exposition of the Gospel word and the Creed, whether of the New or the Old Testament . . . Commonly however, the Creed is sung after the sermon." He further stated that no one was to preach unless he had been commissioned to do so or unless this task belonged to him *ex officio*. The preacher should stand in a higher place (than

---

[28] The best study of the genre, with edition of two arts by English preachers, is Charland, *Artes praedicandi*. A brief and somewhat flawed survey was given by Marianne G. Briscoe in Briscoe and Jaye, *Artes praedicandi*.

[29] Rouse and Rouse, *Preachers*, p. 44.

[30] For Sunday afternoon sermons in our period see Spencer, *English*, pp. 71–72. Sermons *post prandium* or *post nonam* occur in collections B/1, C, DY, E, and Z.

[31] *Ordo Romanus XI*, PL 78:1033.

the congregation), and he should pronounce with humility what he teaches and refrain from entertaining his audience and from going into subtleties in order to show off his learning. "He who teaches and instructs must adapt himself to the understanding of those who are learning from him and order his words according to his audience's capacity, for he who teaches what his listeners cannot understand, does so not for their benefit but to display himself." Durandus based these details on biblical authorities and events (such as Ezra reading the Torah or Jesus preaching the Sermon on the Mount) as well as several fathers of the Church.[32] That the sermon was indeed given after the Gospel reading is shown in a fourteenth-century Dominican collection, where in opening his sermon the preacher refers to the "just read gospel."[33]

One of the patristic authorities quoted by Durandus is Gregory the Great's *Regula pastoralis*, a guide for spiritual shepherds which devotes about two thirds of its length to the art of preaching, particularly to the need for preachers to adapt their words to their audiences.[34] The sermon was thus explicitly an essential part of the *cura animarum* from the early Middle Ages on. Nor did later Church legislation, as we have seen, neglect the importance of preaching as a fundamental duty of parish priests.[35] The section of Gratian's *Decretum* that deals with the question whether monks may exercise pastoral functions, for instance, contains several statements of what rights and duties belong to this office.[36] These include "predicare, baptizare, penitenciam dare, debita miseris relaxare, decimarum, primiciarum, oblationum uiuorum et mortuorum portione iusta perfrui debere" and "clericorum offitia . . . predicare, baptizare, communionem dare, pro peccatoribus orare, penitenciam inponere, atque peccata soluere."[37] In fact, another often quoted canon even seems to privilege preaching over administering the sacraments when it declares that "priests must know Holy Scripture and the canons, and *all their work* must

---

[32] Cap. 27 "De predicatione," in Durantus, *Rationale*, p. 372.

[33] "In ewangelio statim lecto," D-45, f. 128v; also "in epistula statim lecta," D-19, f. 40v.

[34] A convenient summary of the *Regula* can be found in Murphy, *Rhetoric*, pp. 292–296. With Augustine's *De doctrina Christiana*, Gregory's *Regula* marks the early stages of treatises on the *ars praedicandi*. For the latter as a literary genre see above, note 28.

[35] Besides the basic texts already quoted, the *Decretum* speaks of preaching at Friedberg 1:90 (deacon is to "predicare euangelium et Apostolum," i.e. proclaim or read out the gospel and epistle lections); 91 (archdeacon: "ab ipso publice in ecclesia predicatur"); 153 (qualities of preacher, from Gregory); 156 (obligation to preach, and to do so in a way everyone can understand); 308 (bishop's obligation to preach); 333 (priest's obligations including preaching); 614 (neglect of bishops to preach); 625 (bishops' obligation to preach); 763, 765 (monks are not to preach to the people; but see the following remarks).

[36] On the question whether monks may have the cure of souls see Constable, "Monasteries." For a detailed examination of the involvement in parish work, including preaching, by monks of one English monastery, see Greatrex, "Benedictine Monk Scholars."

[37] C. 16, qu. 1, canons 21 and 24; Friedberg 1:766, 767.

consist in preaching and doctrine, and they must edify all, both in the knowledge of faith and in the discipline of works" (my emphasis).[38] That canon,
Ignorantia mater, had been issued at the Council of Toledo in 633 AD, and
it is one of the key texts that reflect the transition in which preaching was
extended from being the bishop's duty to becoming that of every parish priest
entrusted with the *cura animarum*.[39] Together with the *Oculus sacerdotis*,[40] sermons from the fourteenth and fifteenth centuries continue to echo this sentiment and indeed the very canon. Thus, Robert Rypon addresses his clerical
audience with, "You priests and curates, on whom it is incumbent by your office
to preach,"[41] and a somewhat later preacher actually quotes the canon in a sermon that is replete with extracts from Gregory's *Pastoral Care* and begins by
twisting Gregory's opening words into "the art of arts is *preaching*" (instead of
"the guidance of souls").[42] There can therefore be no doubt that the medieval
Church officially considered preaching a required part of the *cura animarum*
with which parish priests were entrusted and for which they received a benefice.
To neglect it meant to be unworthy of the Church's commission as well as the
benefice that went with it. As Robert Basevorn puts it in his *Forma praedicandi*, preachers *ex officio* (which includes those who have the *cura animarum*)
"at the risk of their own salvation are held to preach, by themselves or through
others, if necessary. If they do not do so, they sin mortally . . . If they are insufficient for this, they are in danger because by accepting a benefice they commit
themselves to something they do not know how to carry out."[43]

The Toledo canon quoted reappears not only in the *Oculus sacerdotis* but in
another large manual by the same writer, Pagula's *Speculum praelatorum*.[44] The

---

[38] "Sciant ergo sacerdotes scripturas sacras et canones, et omne opus eorum in predicatione et
doctrina consistat, atque edificent cunctos tam fidei scientia quam operum disciplina." D. 38,
c. 1; Friedberg I:141.

[39] A succinct account of the development of parish preaching in the early Middle Ages is given by
Zerfass, *Streit*, pp. 83–120.

[40] "Omne opus eorum debet esse in predicacione et doctrina" is quoted in *Oculus sacerdotis* at the beginning of both part 2 and part 3 (London, British Library, MS Royal 8.C.ii,
ff. 82rb and 116ra).

[41] "Vos sacerdotes et curati, quibus ex officio predicare incumbit," RY-3, f. 6v.

[42] "Ars arcium predicacio verbi Dei" (M/4-13, f. 313vb), an echo of Gregory, *Regula pastoralis* I.1, "ars
est artium regimen animarum." Gratian's canon *Ignorantia mater cunctorum errorum* is quoted
on f. 315ra, with identification.

[43] "Praedicatores ex institutione ordinaria . . . tenentur praedicare ex necessitate salutis, per se,
vel per alios, si oporteat. Quod si non faciant, peccant mortaliter. . . . Si insufficientes sunt,
periculosum est quod obligant se per acceptationem beneficii ad illud quod exsequi nesciunt."
Charland, *Artes praedicandi*, p. 240.

[44] "Et omne opus eius debet esse in predicacione et doctrina, et cunctos debet edificare tam fidei
sciencia quam operum disciplina," introduction to part 3 of the *Speculum praelatorum*; Oxford,
Merton College, MS 217, f. 179rb.

latter, written c. 1320 in three books, contains not only canonistic material for parish priests but devotes its entire third part to "predicacionibus verbi diuini et auctoritatibus sanctorum patrum." It is, in fact, a complete sermon cycle covering the Sundays and major feasts and saints' feasts of the church year, with often multiple sermons for gospel and epistle readings.[45] The sermons are, as Pagula admits, short,[46] but each has references to several key words organized in a huge alphabetical dictionary[47] where Pagula collected a wealth of preaching material.[48] Clearly, to this important canonist of the early fourteenth century, whose "first love was the parochial clergy,"[49] preaching in the parishes was a matter of great and practical concern.[50]

But to what extent were these precepts in fact carried out? The question has exercised modern scholars a good deal, and in a basic article D. W. Robertson, Jr., tried to show that, for the thirteenth century, the view that "a sermon was a rare event" is wrong.[51] In arguing his point, he used synodal legislation of thirteenth-century English bishops and closely related demands to the effect that preaching was to be frequent and to be done on every Sunday and major feast.[52] One might wonder whether beyond such legislation, in the later period of the fourteenth and fifteenth centuries, other records provide further information. Records of

---

[45] Ff. 179va–247rb. The volume has only a rudimentary modern foliation. See further Part One, section 38, p. 231.

[46] "Et licet predicaciones prima facie videantur breues, potest tamen lector eas facere satis longas recurrendo ad dicciones que ponuntur in fine cuiuslibet thematis assumpti, et multa que dicuntur in vna predicacione alteri congrue possunt adaptari. Et si predicator quodcumque aliud thema assumere sibi velit [*MS:* velud], ex diccionibus primum scriptis inueniat materias sufficientes per quas poterit suam predicacionem probabiliter consummare. Et qui suam predicacionem desiderat prolongare, videat ea que notantur supra in secunda parte . . . Nec lectori displiceat prolixitas et multiplicitas diccionum et predicacionum, quia de eis potest accipere ad suum propositum prosequendum quod sibi placuerit, prout ad vtilitatem audiencium et omnipotentis Dei laudem et honorem videret expedire," f. 179ra.

[47] Ff. 247rb–441ra, Aperire–Zelus.

[48] The alphabetical dictionary is followed by several *tabulae*, ff. 441rb–482.

[49] Boyle, "*Oculus sacerdotis*," p. 102.

[50] As Pagula specifies at the end of what I have called the alphabetical dictionary, his *Summa* is written "ad profectum prelatorum, episcoporum, religiosorum, rectorum, uicariorum, presbiterorum, et omnium clericorum," London, British Library, MS Royal 8.C.ii, f. 441ra.

[51] Robertson, "Frequency." The quotation is from Moorman, *Church Life*, p. 77. But notice that Moorman speaks of the thirteenth century; regarding the later medieval period he says: "Of the many thousands of sermons preached by the friars in the fifteenth century only the merest fragment is known to us now, and most of those not in the form in which they were delivered," ibid., p. 519.

[52] Of particular interest here are seven charters for private chapels issued by Grosseteste, to which Robertson called attention ("Frequency," in *Essays*, p. 126). They use the formula "singulis dominicis diebus et festivis quibus solempnes fiunt predicationes."

episcopal visitation could be expected to reveal how concerned bishops were about whether preaching duties were indeed carried out.[53] But both theoretical statements about episcopal visitations and the actual reports are, in this respect, remarkably silent. The summary of canonical pronouncements on visitations which will be cited below is a characteristic instance,[54] and it can be paralleled by visitation sermons that lay out what the visitor will inquire about; neither mention preaching. In records about visitations, one finds an occasional remark that a local bishop or archdeacon has been neglecting his statutory duties;[55] and later in the fifteenth century, here and there the preaching of an unlicensed person is reported.[56] But by and large such records are silent about preaching activity in the parish church.

One devoutly wishes, at this point, to have somebody's chronicle or diary that reports what sermons he or she heard when and where. *The Book of Margery Kempe* does this in a limited way.[57] Margery speaks of sermons she heard in Rome and Jerusalem, in York (by a monk, p. 123) and in her home town, King's Lynn. In the latter she went to hear a Franciscan friar, perhaps Melton (much to his annoyance), who preached there for seven years, in the chapel and yard of St. James (pp. 148–152). Margery also heard a parson who had taken a university degree and preached morning and afternoon (p. 165). A Dominican preached in the parish church when the order's provincial chapter was held in King's Lynn (p. 165). A doctor of divinity was assigned to preach in the parish church before all the people, and he did so in the morning of the feast of the Assumption (p. 166). During Lent, an Augustinian friar preached in his own house (p. 167), and on Good Friday the prior of St. Margaret's Church preached there on "Jesus is dead" (p. 167). In the same church Margery also heard Bishop Wakeryng of Norwich (p. 167). On Palm Sunday another doctor of theology gave a sermon (p. 185). And in a smaller village a famous friar preached to a large audience on "If God be with us, who shall be against us?" (p. 227). Though this is at best a very selective list giving us only a few clues about the frequency and regularity of preaching, it still furnishes a remarkable testimony about the variety of preachers available in a large English town in the 1420s and about their educational training – "many worschepful doctorys and oþer worthy clerkys, bothyn religyows and seculerys" (pp. 151–152).

---

[53] A thoughtful discussion of bishops' attitudes toward and involvement in preaching in the fifteenth century is Davies, "Episcopate."

[54] Chapter 41, "Bishops as preachers," p. 259.

[55] *Episcopal Register of Robert Rede*, 1:103, 116.

[56] Bishop Alnwick's visitation of the College of St Mary and All Saints at Fotheringhay, June 1442: *Visitations of Religious Houses*, 2:108 and 112; see also p. 184.

[57] *The Book of Margery Kempe*. The following references in parentheses are to this edition.

A somewhat different but more systematic record of preaching through the Church year has been preserved in a repertory of Cambridge university sermons for the years 1417 and 1424–1425 (collection C). Following the university calendar, the manuscript records sermons for every Sunday and major feastday excepting vacations. They were given at a number of different places in Cambridge and outside; hence the record is not one of the sermons delivered at a given place, but rather a personal memoir of the sermons the collector had heard. It is clear that he listened to one or more[58] on every Sunday and major feast. And one can assume that many if not all of these sermons were open to the public.[59]

Other sermon collections of the period offer some more hints about preaching in smaller and less academic places.[60] After he returned from Avignon to his diocese of Armagh in 1351, Richard FitzRalph preached sermons *ad populum* in various Irish parishes: Cowlrath (FI-35), Drumeskyn (36), Dundalk (37, 51, 54), Drogheda (39, 40, 45, 46, 53, 56), Trim (42, 47), Acrum Dei (41, 44), Athboy (43), Kell's (48), Grenok (49), Scryn (52), and Tarmfechym (55). The learned Augustinian friar John Waldeby preached on the Creed before the people of York and subsequently wrote up his sermon material as a treatise.[61] Over two generations later, a Franciscan friar, probably Nicholas Philip, preached at Oxford, Lichfield, Norwich, and Lynn, during the years 1430 to 1436. The two collections in Cambridge, University Library, MS Kk.4.24 (B/1 and B/2) come with several, now mostly erased, notations of places in modern Bedfordshire: Leighton Buzzard and nineteen neighboring villages. The eighteen sermons thus annotated (there may be more annotations which I have been unable to decipher) are for Sundays in the Advent season, Lent and Easter, and six scattered Sundays after Easter. Some Sundays carry more than one place name, as many as eight; conversely, Leighton Buzzard is mentioned ten times, but never more than once in a single inscription. I read these inscriptions as a record of where the respective sermons were preached, though unfortunately no dates are given. If this is correct, we find here a memoir of one or perhaps several preachers going out to small churches and chapels in the country and presumably using the material in the collection. And finally, about the middle of the fifteenth century the then former chancellor of Oxford, Thomas Gascoigne, tells us that he preached at Oxford ("in omnibus ecclesiis Oxonie,

---

[58] On many occasions he heard a second sermon *post nonam*.

[59] The major kind of university sermons required is called *sermo publicus*; see below, chapter 44. Certainly the sermons given by the chancellor were open to the laity; see p. 313, note 6. In about 1390 the vicar of the university church in Oxford, St. Mary's, preached on Corpus Christi "ad populum"; see Edden, "Debate," p. 120.

[60] For details see the discussion in the respective sections in Part One.

[61] See above, pp. 40–41.

et in comitatu Oxonie in diversis locis"), York, London, Pontefract, Doncaster, Leeds, Coventry, Nottingham, Evesham, Sussex, and Sheen.[62]

Although these records do not overwhelm us with their amount of information, taken together they yet speak of an ongoing preaching activity – more so, undoubtedly, in large town centers and university towns, but some also reaching to the smallest parishes. Precisely how frequent and regular such preaching in the parishes was can at this point only be guesswork; but it is clear that even people in smaller parishes heard some sermons, at least during the seasons of Advent, Lent, and Easter.

We can now turn to actual texts that have preserved preaching in the parish church. How many, and which, sermons in the collections here surveyed can be confidently assigned to just that milieu? The answer is, unfortunately, both more difficult to arrive at and more meager than one might hope. What sermons should be included? First and foremost, obviously, those that bear a rubric, or perhaps contain an explicit reference in their body, that they were given *ad populum*. In the entire corpus I have collected, less than two dozen carry that indication: twenty-one sermons by FitzRalph, one in the collection of Cambridge University sermons (C), and one by the Carmelite John Hornby.[63] This is an extremely small portion of the entire corpus, and surely there must be more parish sermons in the mass of preserved material. But how can we tell?[64] Besides their rubrics, a good number of sermons of course do contain clues about their intended audience in their address forms, contents, and style. It stands to reason that, negatively, sermons addressed to the clergy ("Reverendissimi domini," etc.), delivered at clerical assemblies (such as synods and visitations), or chastizing clerical failings were not given *ad populum*.[65] Moreover, individual sermons or entire collections that are full of quotations from such learned sources as St. Thomas Aquinas and canon law should at least be treated with diffidence. Even if, as I have argued earlier ("Prolegomena"), such learned references occasionally came into a sermon text only during its post-delivery composition, and even if a preacher occasionally may have striven to dazzle his audience by displaying his learning, by and large a plethora of learned quotations would *prima facie* argue against an audience of the common people.

---

[62] Gieben, "Thomas Gascoigne," p. 65.

[63] "Sermo Magistri Johannis Hornby carmelite ad populum de materia tangenti ordinem nostrum," Oxford, Bodleian Library, MS e Mus. 86, f. 219va (modern).

[64] See also the more fundamental remarks made in the "Prolegomena" above, pp. 9–10.

[65] It should be noticed that remarks about preaching per se, especially in the protheme, do not signal a clerical audience; many of them occur in sermons that bear clear indications of a lay or mixed audience. Further, switching from the vernacular to Latin in a sermon when clerical failures were discussed can indicate a mixed audience; see Wenzel, *Macaronic*, p. 121.

There remain stylistic elements that one would consider "popular" – not in the sense of being successful and having a wide appeal but rather of stemming from and relating to the lore, language, beliefs, and tastes of the common people, whoever those might have been. Though he never clearly defined his terms, Homer G. Pfander included as characteristic elements of the popular sermon vernacular verses of different kinds and used for different purposes, well-known exempla, and moralized "scientific" lore.[66] All of these, together with similes and narratives from everyday experience, can indeed be found in many sermons of our period that have been preserved in English or in Latin. But to infer from their presence a lay audience is a very slippery procedure. This can be neatly demonstrated with two contrasting sermons. In one, for the first Sunday of Advent, the anonymous preacher retailed a version of the widely used exemplum of Christ the Lover-Knight, from the *Gesta Romanorum,* complete with an English message verse.[67] In another sermon, perhaps for Passion Sunday,[68] a different

---

[66] Pfander, *Popular Sermon.*

[67] "Primo dixi, etc. In gestis Romanorum quomodo rex dedit filie sue hereditatem, set post deiectus per tirannum. vidit [*read* venit?] miles generosus, dixit sibi omnia. Dixit volo pugnare, quid vis dare michi? Dixit nichil habeo nisi corpus. Dixit miles, si esset mortuus in bello, mitteret scorthe [=shirt?] sanguineum ut recoleret. Habeo in memoria illum qui fuit kynde. Secundo, quando moueretur ad carnales delectaciones omnes tales ego renuo pro eius sake. Pugnabat cum tyranno et optinuit victoriam. Set post mortus de vulneribus. Respondit habeo semper in memoria pro illo generoso. omnes [*read* omne] peccatum renuo. [*blank*] Spiritualiter per imperatorem intelligo Patrem . . . ," C-13, p. 9. The text may be translated: "In *The Deeds of the Romans,* how a king gave his daughter her inheritance. But after he had been dethroned by a tyrant, a noble knight came, and [she] told him everything. [The knight] said: 'I will fight [for you], what will you give me?' [She] said: 'I have nothing but my body [i.e. myself].' The knight said, if he were to die in battle, he would send [her] his bloody shirt, so that she might remember him – 'I have in mind him who was kind.' Second, whenever she might be moved to carnal delights – 'All these I renounce for his sake.' He fought with the tyrant and gained the victory, but afterwords died of his wounds. She responded: 'I always have in mind for this noble [knight]. I renounce all sin.' Spiritually, by this emperor I understand [God] the Father . . ." Evidently the preacher had quoted a well-known message verse, parts of which the reporter jotted down. See for instance the close analogue in the English *Gesta* in BL Add. MS 9066, in *English Versions of the Gesta Romanorum,* p. 26. Here the verses are:

> While I haue in mynde
> The blode of hym that was so kynde,
> How shuld I hym forsake
> That the dethe for me wolde take?
> Nay, for sothe, I shall not so,
> For he brought me from mekill woo.

[68] *Quis arguet me de peccato?* J/5-21, ff. 94v–97v. No rubric. In this collection the preacher refers to a sermon preached at Oxford and another at Dunwich.

preacher likened the sinner to a man writing a letter to the devil, whose message is:

> My cristyndam I here forsake.
> The devyl of helle my sawle Y take.
> I forsake Crist and al hys loore.
> I take me to the feende foer euermore.'[69]

One might think that the latter story and its message verse are more "popular," more closely linked to the commoners, than the exemplum of Christ the Lover-Knight with its atmosphere of courtly romance. But such literary sociology turns out to be entirely wrong, because the sermon about Christ the Lover-Knight was given "in the church of Botulph in English" and is rubricated "ad populum," whereas the message to the devil, conversely, comes in a sermon that addresses "Reuerendi mei," quotes St. Thomas Aquinas twice, and begins its main division with "It is the scholastic mode, when a question is stated, to respond by giving conclusions."[70]

My aim here is not to cast radical doubt, let alone voice deep despair about the possibility that stylistic elements may give us at least tentative clues regarding popular preaching in the parishes in the absence of clearer indications. No-one who reads, for example, the macaronic sermons of O or other pieces preached on Good Friday,[71] Palm Sunday, or generally in Lent, would seriously question that these texts, which bear the marks of a "popular" style enumerated above, were preached before a parish congregation, even if their audience is not explicitly identified. But we need to exert a good deal of caution in using "popular" elements to determine sermon audience.[72]

Finally, in identifying sermons destined to be preached in the parishes we must also be aware that many sermons addressed to the clergy, at synods, visitations, or the university, were in fact meant to serve as models of what and how parish

---

[69] F. 96. The verses are introduced with: "Vnde quidam ymaginatur quod homo peccans mortaliter facit cartam dyabolo de quatuor uerbis siue proposicionibus."

[70] "Modus est scolasticus quando questio proponitur respondere per conclusiones," f. 95. The preacher had used the same idea in an earlier sermon for Corpus Christi, on the thema "What is this?" (Exodus 16:15, referring to the manna). That sermon, too, was addressed to "Reuerendi mei," ff. 76–79v.

[71] Good Friday would not have been a day for a clerical assembly, so that the chances that extant Good-Friday sermons were directed to a lay or at least mixed audience are *a priori* stronger. Good-Friday sermons also tend to brim with the putative "popular" elements mentioned above, including the Christ-the-Lover-Knight exemplum. See Johnson, "Preaching the Passion."

[72] Besides the difficulty of defining what elements may be popular by origin, it is equally difficult to say whether elements that intrisically belong to a lower or higher cultural level appealed to audiences of one level and not the other.

priests should preach in their parishes, so that even a good many pieces directed to "Reverendi" can be taken to reflect an intended preaching *ad populum*.

Trying to summarize the content of medieval preaching *ad populum* is much like filling a test tube with sea water and presenting it as a picture of the ocean. It can be done, but one may well wonder how representative the sample is and how well the proportions of its ingredients reflect those in the ocean. Nevertheless, an attempt must be made. To begin with, many sermons set their message in a narrative frame of *Heilsgeschichte*, the history of salvation. In the beginning, man was created in the image of God. Yielding to the temptation by Satan, chief of the fallen angels who envied man's exalted position, he lost his state of grace by sin and was ejected from Paradise and given over to the rightful power of the devil. But in his infinite mercy God wanted mankind to return to him, for which he first sent Moses and the Old Testament prophets; and as these were not universally heeded, God sent his own Son, who became man, called sinners to repentance, and died for mankind's salvation. Hence, although all men and women are born sinners and are most probably affected by some actual, personal sins, they may hope and trust in God's mercy, which during this life is available through repentance and the sacrament of Penance. At death, and again at the end of time, there will be judgment, when the condemned will go to eternal punishment and the saved to their glorious home with God.

This is the core message, and it is ever-present. But it comes in hundreds of different shapes formed by the many devices of medieval sermon rhetoric. The large topics[73] mentioned in the preceding sentences: sin and grace; God's justice and mercy; Christ's incarnation, exemplary life and teaching, passion, and redemption; the vices that beset us and the virtues we should strive for, which God's spirit can instil in us with his sevenfold gifts; the sacraments, particularly that of Penance with its three parts of contrition, confession, and satisfaction, are explained and clothed in the ever-changing garments of moral allegory, in which human life is likened to warfare, a sea voyage, and many other things. They are further developed with numerous authoritative prooftexts. These come primarily from sacred scripture, both Old and New Testaments – quite typically, a medieval preacher could not make a single statement without backing it up with a biblical "authority." Next to the Bible he would use quotations from the writings of the Church Fathers and teachers. Among them St. Augustine always holds pride of place, but he is followed by many others who lived through the

---

[73] Vices and virtues, punishment and glory were given as the main topics of preaching in the *Second Franciscan Rule* and quoted by many preachers including Benedictine monks and Wyclif; see Wenzel, *Verses*, pp. 9–10 and note 5. Sermon J/5-36, in short note form, similarly announces that "quinque sunt specialiter predicanda, scilicet: inferni supplicia, vicia, celi gaudia, uirtutes, et passio Christi," f. 126v.

centuries until the fourteenth (mostly Holcot and FitzRalph). Sacred writers are joined by secular ones: Aristotle and Avicenna, Seneca and Pliny, Ovid and Cicero, and many more. The basic message is then further illustrated with a host of images, similes, and stories (*exempla*). These are usually applied to the doctrine on hand by means of allegorization, frequently point by point. The treasury of such illustrative material available to the late-medieval preacher was very large and many-hued,[74] and a reader with an appreciation of rhetoric will find much to delight her or him in the way sermons are built and developed. To be sure, much of this material as it is found in preachers' handbooks of various sorts recurs with regularity and predictability; but the individual preacher's work of selecting details from it, combining them, and applying them to the specific thema of a given Sunday or feast was considerably more intelligent and original than "the scissors-and-paste method" that for some modern writers seems to constitute the essence of late-medieval preaching, a view that can hardly be based on wide and discriminating reading or careful attention to the construction of existing sermons.[75]

The various devices of sermon rhetoric always serve the purposes of instructing the faithful and of moving them, first of all to recognize their sinful condition and then to be contrite and resolve to turn or return to God. Hence arises the impression that much of medieval preaching deals with sinfulness and repentance, which is quite correct, though it must also be pointed out that nearly every complete sermon ends positively with a longing for eternal life and glory.

The message, in all these cases, was closely linked to the respective liturgical season, so that Christmas sermons, for example, tend to deal with Christ's incarnation, its theological contents as well as its joys. Lent is the time of penance and of preparation for Easter, and sermons during this season teach about sin and God's mercy and try to move their audiences to examine their conduct and to repent. Easter sermons then concentrate on the Eucharist, its worthy reception, and warnings not to relapse.

To illustrate what has been said about parish preaching and its contents, as well as other features discussed earlier, I will summarize a sermon on the thema "Do this in remembrance of me" (Luke 22:19) which has been preserved in two collections.[76] Elsewhere this thema is used on the feast of Corpus Christi,[77] but here it bears no rubric, and internal statements that "you will today receive this

---

[74] A good example is the Franciscan handbook *Fasciculus morum*. For a discussion of the breadth and variety of the devices of sermon rhetoric it offers, see Wenzel, "Vices, Virtues, and Popular Preaching," pp. 41–50.

[75] The main topics of this paragraph, use of authorities and variety of structure and style, are further developed in subsequent chapters on "An English theology" and "The Preacher's voice."

[76] Z-13 and G-28.   [77] DY-7, X-303.

sacrament" and that the audience's labors endured during "the entire preceding Lent" have now ended make it much more more likely that this sermon was given on Easter Sunday. The sermon begins with the address "Reuerendi domini" and later switches to "Karissimi," which may speak for a clerical audience, yet the sermon's emphasis on receiving communion on this day surely envisions what I have considered a parish community, not a clerical congregation, unless it be students at university. The anonymous preacher begins his fairly long protheme with the notion that true wisdom lies more in deeds than in words or writings, and that Christ had come on earth to show us "to carry out in deeds what he taught us to believe." Several authorities – biblical, pagan, and patristic – then lead to the point that in instituting the Eucharist Christ did not say "*believe* this" but "*do* this in remembrance of me." And so the preacher asks his hearers to say an Our Father and Hail Mary in order "that you may have true faith about this sacrament and receive it with devotion and live in accordance with it."[78]

Next he introduces his thema by explaining that "Christ is given us today in the sacrament for three reasons." First, as the fruit of our Lenten works. As a farmer who has bought a piece of land for a great price and after working it for a long time and planting good seed in it rejoices in its bringing a good harvest, so can we, who have, during the past Lent, not allowed our nature or our bodies, which Christ has bought with a great price, to lie idle but have toiled to eradicate sins and vices, now rejoice in receiving the reward for our work.

> By plowing this land you have worked well all through the past Lent, in fasting and other abstinences and other virtuous works. Now, then, rejoice and make great cheer, for all these labors have gone and your land carries the best fruit, namely Christ the only Son of God, whom you today will receive or have received under the form of bread.[79]

---

[78] "Hoc facite in meam commemorationem, Luce 22. Reuerendi domini, sicut patet ex processu sancti Ricardi *De sacramentis novi legis* et vera sapiencia pocius in factis quam in verbis consistit vel in scripturis. Vnde inquid Dei Filius de celo in terram venit ut exemplo suo monstraret factis se complendum quod ipse docuit esse credendum . . . [f. 38va] Cum igitur hoc venerabile sacramentum quod hodie recepturi estis . . . Et ideo merito Christus communicans discipulis in cena corpus suum et sanguinem suum ante passionem non dixit 'Credite hoc in meam commemoracionem' set 'Facite in meam commemoracionem.' . . . Quapropter, karissimi, ut possitis habere veram fidem de hoc sacramento et deuote id recipere et secundum id viuere, orabitis in principio dicendo Pater Noster et Aue," Z-13, f. 38rb.

[79] "Tribus de causis, ut testantur doctores, Christus hodie datur nobis in sacramentum. Primo ut sit fructus nostri laboris quadragesimalis . . . [f. 38vb] Hanc terram arando iugiter laborastis tota quadragesima precedente in ieiuniis aliisque abstinenciis et aliis operibus virtuosis. Nunc igitur gaudete et magnam gloriam facite, quia omnes isti labores transierunt et terra vestra portat fructus optimos, scilicet Christum Filium Dei vnigenitum, quem hodie in forma panis recipietis vel recepistis," f. 38va.

Second, receiving the sacrament is the cause of purity in our minds. Because in order to receive it worthily, one must be pure in perfect love of God and neighbor, and such purity is the result of the Lenten discipline. If Christians, therefore, did not take Communion "today," they would neglect to do penance during Lent and remain in their sins. Finally, and most importantly, we receive the sacrament so that it may become a "recent memorial of Christ's passion," which moves us to love God and brings comfort against the devil's temptations.[80]

The preacher then returns once more to the thema and now divides it into two parts: he finds that the words "Do this" signal "the prescription of an act," whereas the words "in remembrance of me" speak of "a continuing awareness." Since only the latter pertains to the Eucharist, he will focus on it alone. This he does by first explaining that through Adam's fall man has lost the original dominion over all creation that God had given him, as well as the right to enter the kingdom of heaven. But now, in the time of grace, that lost dominion can be ours again if we lead a good life, a dominion that includes friendship with the angels and freedom from the temptation of the devils. It further includes "the gift God has given to no other creature, namely himself, and this unique and highest gift every one of you will receive today under the form of bread." Reflecting on the richness of God's goods and gifts should make us rise to praise and love him as much as we can by constantly making remembrance of him. "Therefore remember through God's grace the beneficial gifts with which he has enriched you and love him from your whole heart, so that under the leadership of Christ you may come to the kingdom of heaven."[81]

---

[80] "Secunda causa quare Christus datur hodie in sacramento est ut recepcio sacramenti sit causa nostre mundicie mentalis. Si enim hodie Christum non reciperent Christiani, in quadragesima penitenciam non agerent nec curarent quamdiu iacerent in peccatis . . . [f. 39rb] Tercia et precipua causa quare nobis communicatur sacramentum est ut sit in nobis recens memoria passionis Christi, per quam mouetur maxime ad Dei dileccionem et precipue confortamur contra diaboli temptacionem," ff. 38vb–39rb.

[81] "In quibus verbis duo possunt considerari: operis determinacio, hoc facite; noticie continuacio, in meam commemoracionem. Set quia secundum verbum thematis pertinet ad propositum sacramenti, ideo de secundo tantummodo erit prosecucio sermonis . . . Vnde [*add* vt] arcius sui memoriam Deus cordi humano infigeret, larga dona et beneficia in principio creacionis mundi homini liberaliter exhibebat. In principio enim mundi creacionis homini dedit dominium omnium bestiarum et piscium et volatilium, et omnia sibi ad libitum sibi obediuissent si non peccasset . . . Set prodolor, tamcito seruus per peccatum qui homo est [?] ante peccatum habuit dominium omnium creaturarum, post peccatum fere quelibet alia creatura homini dominabuntur . . . [f. 39vb] Set videamus quomodo omnia que fuerant quandoque perdita per peccatum primi parentis iam in tempore gracie, si non ponamus obicem mundi, nostra sunt si fuerimus bone vite . . . Et [f. 42ra] certe Deus contulit totum donum pro redempcione nostra quem nunquam dedit pro aliqua alia creatura, quia semetipsum, et id solum summum donum recipiet quilibet vestri de manibus sacerdotis hodie in forma panis. Et melius donum et magis

The tone of the sermon is sober but not dry and almost devoid of imagery and narrative elements, except for the simile of the farmer cultivating his land and the story, quickly alluded to, of Moses making two rings when he was about to leave his wife (one of forgetfulness for her, the other of remembrance for himself).[82] Besides a proportionately large number of biblical quotations, the "Magister" (of the Sentences, Peter Lombard) appears a surprising seven times, and less often Augustine, Chrysostom, St. Richard (of St. Victor?), Aristotle, and Seneca.

Historians of medieval preaching often speak of *sermones ad status*, that is, sermons that are directed to specific social or professional groups, whose duties or failings they discuss.[83] Such sermons would have fulfilled the demand of theoreticians from Gregory the Great on, that preachers must adapt their discourse to the character and needs of their audience.[84] Medieval *artes praedicandi* often furnish material – themata, authorities, or even main ideas – that would fit a specific group of the clergy (popes, cardinals, monks, nuns, etc.) or the laity (married men and women, the sick, merchants, lawyers, etc.).[85] As far as actual sermons are concerned, one should perhaps distinguish between individual sermons that are in their totality directed to one specific group, whose duties of estate they outline, and more general sermons that only contain brief remarks about one or several such groups and usually take the form of social critique. The latter are commonplace. Of the former kind, that is, entire sermons addressing a particular group of society, we often find single sermons *ad clerum* or *ad monachos* in our collections, usually preached on such special occasions as visitations

proficuum non potuit nobis conferre quam semetipsum seu corpus suum preciosum . . . Pensando bonorum et donorum nobis a Deo adhibitorum affluenciam multum assurgere deberemus in ipsius laudem et amorem de ipso quam sufficimus continuam memoriam faciendo . . . Recole ergo Dei gracia beneficia quibus te ditauit, et ipsum ex toto corde tuo dilige, ut Christo ducente peruenias ad regnum celorum. Quod nobis concedat, etc." ff. 38ra–39vb, 42ra.

[82] Peter Comestor, *Historia scholastica*, on Exodus 6; PL 198:1144.

[83] Owst, *Preaching*, pp. 247–265; Spencer, *English*, pp. 65–67; Bériou, "Sermons latins," pp. 390–393.

[84] Especially in book 3 of his *Regula pastoralis* (PL 77:49–126), and similarly in his *Homilies on the Gospels* 1.17.18 (PL 76:1148–49).

[85] After reiterating the principle that the preacher must adapt his discourse to the condition of his audience, Alanus of Lille, in his *Summa de arte praedicandi*, gives brief directions of what to stress when one preaches to various social groups (ch. 39), followed by more extensive collections of commonplaces and authorities for these groups (chs. 40–48; PL 210:184–198). The Rouses call these chapters "model sermons" (*Preachers*, p. 71 and n. 14), but they are not sermons. A similar work is the *Ars praedicandi* by Grosseteste; cf. S. Harrison Thomson, *Writings*, p. 121. Robert Basevorn, in his *Forma praedicandi*, chapter 30, specifies "what themata may be used in matters that emerge, for example in visitations, elections, synods . . . / To various estates: the pope and cardinals . . ." But the only lay group here are merchants, and what Basevorn gives are only themata; see Charland, *Artes praedicandi*, pp. 267–268, omitting the themata (which can be found in Lincoln Cathedral MS 68, ff. 259–260).

or synods, as we shall see in the following section. But the English collections here surveyed do not contain any complete cycle of *ad status* sermons directed to virgins or married folk, merchants, physicians, lawyers, peasants, and the like.[86] Some complete cycles of this kind were indeed created by Continental authors, but they are quite few in number.[87]

A special case of preaching to a general audience are sermons on the saints.[88] Apart from Mirk's *Festial*, whose form and curious place in the tradition of late-medieval preaching was discussed earlier, the collections considered in this study contain about 360 sermons for individual or groups of saints.[89] Identification of the occasions is here made easier than in the case of *de tempore* sermons since, except in common sermons for a particular group of saints, the respective saint is usually mentioned by name, whether in a rubric or in the text.[90] The collections thus contain sermons for seventy feast days and two vigils.[91] These include several

---

[86] Notice also the reservations about the specificity of the implied audience, especially in vernacular sermons, that have been expressed by Mertens, "Der implizierte Sünder." I distinguish *sermones ad status* as a particular sermon genre from general sermons that deal with the customary three estates of medieval society. The latter topic of course occurs in many collections, especially O and Wimbledon. On this topic see Fletcher, *Preaching*, pp. 145–169 and 220–232. For medieval estates literature in general see Mann, *Chaucer*.

[87] See d'Avray, *Preaching*, pp. 80 and 127–128: for the thirteenth century d'Avray notes "only three or four" *ad status* collections, p. 127 n. 4., and at p. 278 n. 8, says, "I am not counting the *Communiloquium* of John of Wales as a sermon collection." Jean Longère is similarly negative about *ad status* sermons: *Prédication*, p. 147. The three main collections are discussed by Bériou, "Sermons latins," pp. 392–393. The Rouses' "a long line of collected *Sermones ad status*" seems to exaggerate (*Preachers*, p. 49). See also Gieben, "*Rudimentum*," p. 667 ("de modificanda praedicatione pro statuum et officiorum diversitate") and the "register" of thirty-five *status* with model sermons on pp. 668–671.

[88] See my discussion of saints' sermons with examples in Wenzel, "Preaching the Saints."

[89] Multiple copies have been counted only once. I have included individual sermons that may have originated before 1350, but not collections that in their entirety date from before 1350 (such as B/1 and J/1 to 3)

[90] I should add that many sermons in honor of the Blessed Virgin say so in a rubric or in their text, although they may leave the particular feast (Conception, Nativity, Annunciation, Assumption) unspecified. In my inventories they bear the siglum S86.

[91] These are, in liturgical order: Andrew, Birinus, Nicholas, BVM Conception, Thomas the Apostle, Stephen, John the Evangelist, Innocents, Thomas Becket, Antony, Vincent, Conversion of Paul, BVM Purification, Agatha, Frideswide translation, Chair of Peter, Matthias, Eleazar, Thomas Aquinas, Augustine of Canterbury translation, Gregory, Patrick, Cuthbert, Benedict, BVM Annunciation, Ambrose, Mark, Peter the Martyr, Philip and James, Invention of the Cross, Barnabas, Winfred translation, Etheldreda, John the Baptist, Peter and Paul, Thomas Becket translation, Mildred, Margaret, Mary Magdalene, James, Anne, Peter ad vincula, Dominic, Oswald, Lawrence, BVM Assumption, Louis of Anjou, Augustine, John the Baptist Decollation, BVM Nativity, Chrysostom, Exaltation of the Cross, Matthew, Maurice, Michael, Jerome, Francis, Denys, Luke, Frideswide, Ursula and the eleven thousand virgins, Simon and Jude, All Saints, All Souls, Martin, Edmund Rich, Hugh of Lincoln, Edmund King and Martyr, BVM

cycles: DY and N, as well as the respective booklets in X. Random collections may perhaps hold a greater interest in that they reflect the popularity of the respective saint and his or her feast more accurately.[92] Thus, the various feasts of the Blessed Virgin draw the largest number, and they are followed (in declining number) by those of Mary Magdalene, Thomas Becket, Holy Innocents, All Saints, Nicholas, John the Evangelist, John the Baptist, Katherine, Andrew, All Souls, Martin, Benedict, Thomas the Apostle, Mark, Augustine, Paul Conversion, and Luke, all represented by five or more sermons. As to their audience, saints sermons share the difficulties we observed in the case of *de tempore* sermons; what evidence they hold points to their being preached to lay, clerical, or even mixed audiences.

Saints sermons are characterized by two major elements occurring in a variety of combinations: praise of the saint and exhortation to follow his or her example. As an anonymous preacher says at midpoint in his sermon on St. Margaret: "This much serves as praise of this virgin; now let us apply it for our edification."[93] To praise their respective saints, some late-medieval preachers made use of a number of recurrent techniques and devices, including hyperbole, direct address, name etymology or *interpretatio nominis*, and – particularly in monastic sermons and sermons on the Blessed Virgin – the florid, convoluted, and highly decorated style that contemporaries called *florida venustas verborum* and later scholars have labeled "aureate diction" or "Euphuism."[94] In producing such eulogies, sermon writers drew on varying amounts of biographical and narrative data from their saints' lives. Some sermons barely mention their honorees and give no details from their lives; others adduce but one or two historical or legendary facts; and yet others carefully select a large number of biographical details and arrange them to prove the saint's excellence and exemplary qualities. In all cases, however, the biographical and legendary material is subordinated to the sermon's avowed purpose to hold up a model, and it is functionally integrated in the grid of the scholastic sermon structure. The example which the saints have given may stir the audience to a good, moral life in general, or it may give direction and impetus in very specific concerns of the day. The fascination with the sensational and even lurid details of saints' legends and their "racy anecdotes" that, at least according

Oblation, Katherine, BVM general. I have excluded from this listing the saints sermons in J/2, which are of earlier and apparently Continental origin.

[92] See Wenzel, "Preaching the Saints," pp. 49–50.

[93] "Hec ad virginis commendacionem; nunc ad nostram edificacionem applicemus," Merton 248, f. 135ra. The two fundamental purposes, praise and edification, are given by Thomas Waleys for any type of preaching: "rectum finem sermonis, ne videlicet ad sui ostentationem praedicet sed ad Dei laudem et proximi aedificationem," *De modo componendi sermones*, in Charland, *Artes praedicandi*, p. 330.

[94] Further discussion and examples can be found in Wenzel, "Saints and the Language of Praise," pp. 69–87.

to the accounts by some modern readers, characterize Mirk's *Festial* hardly appear at all in genuine saints' sermons.[95]

In concluding these remarks about preaching in the parishes, a few words may be added about pardoners or *quaestores*, that is, sometimes highly articulate special agents of hospitals and other charitable institutions sent to the parishes to solicit funds, who would explain their mission during Mass and mostly probably do so by way of preaching a sermon.[96] Despite the prominence that one member of this class and his performance holds in *The Canterbury Tales*, contemporary Church legislation took a rather negative view of their enterprise.[97] I have not found a single Latin sermon in the collections of this study that can even remotely be seen as an instance of such preaching.

---

[95] See Owst, *Preaching*, pp. 55, 245–247; and Heffernan, "Sermon Literature," p. 185.

[96] Bishop John Waltham of Salisbury (1388–1395), for example, stipulated that quaestors should explain the hospital's legitimate privileges and indulgences during Mass on Sundays and festival days; *Register John Waltham*, p. 4.

[97] Although the granting of pardons or indulgences was firmly anchored in medieval theology and Church law, late-medieval bishops and preachers were fully aware of abuses. See Kellogg and Haselmayer, "Chaucer's Satire"; and Wenzel, "Chaucer's Pardoner."

41

Bishops as preachers

In implementing the directions of Lateran IV and other papal decrees, bishops not only ordained priests, appointed parish clergy, and oversaw their life and activity but also did a fair amount of preaching themselves. They gave an occasional sermon at their cathedrals; they visited parishes and religious houses in their dioceses and preached on that occasion; they regularly called together their diocesan clergy and began the convocation with a sermon; and they might also say a few fitting words on less regular yet important occasions, such as ordinations of new priests and elections of some officials.

CATHEDRAL PREACHING

The primary function of a cathedral was to act as the liturgical center of a diocese, in which a specially appointed clergy would regularly celebrate Mass and perform the canonical office. Though in medieval England in all cases the bishop was the legal and administrative head of a diocese, his relationship to the primary church of the diocese, his "see," was usually not a very close one, and it varied from place to place. Of the seventeen cathedrals in late-medieval England nine were "secular," where the liturgical services as well as other items of cathedral business were carried out by a dean and chapter, including a number of canons.[1] The other eight were in the hands of a monastic order, either Benedictine (seven) or Augustinian Canons (one, Carlisle); here the liturgy was performed by the monastic congregation led by its prior or abbot.[2] Whatever public preaching at a cathedral occurred, therefore, would have involved either the bishop as titular head of the diocese, or the dean or prior as administrative official of the cathedral.

---

[1] On canons and their preaching at secular cathedrals see Lepine, *Brotherhood*, especially pp. 137–139.
[2] Two of the seventeen dioceses were joint secular and monastic: Wells (secular)/Bath (monastic) and Lichfield (secular)/Coventry (monastic).

Extant cathedral statutes call for a certain amount of regular preaching, usually making it the chancellor's office either to preach himself or to appoint others to do so. A particularly fine set of statutes has been preserved from Lincoln cathedral. In 1236 it was determined that

> it is the chancellor's business to rule the theology schools and to preach, either himself or through someone else whom he may choose from the church . . . There should be a sermon on the following days: to the people, on all Sundays; to the clergy in chapter, on the first three days of Christmas, Epiphany, the first three days of Easter, Assumption, the Nativity of Blessed Mary, All Saints, and Trinity. And this preaching should be done either by the canons or by other qualified men if such can be found who are willing and knowledgable. Further, on Ash Wednesday . . . on Palm Sunday, on the day of the major litany and the three Rogation Days, when there are solemn processions outside the church.[3]

Similarly at Lichfield it was the chancellor's duty to preach and/or arrange sermons, except for two days, 1 Advent and Ash Wednesday, when a sermon would be given by the dean.[4]

We can be reasonably sure that such statutory preaching was carried out, at both secular and monastic cathedrals. One piece of evidence comes from Bishop Alnwick's visitation of his cathedral at Lincoln in 1437, when it was reported that "the vergers fail to produce silence at the time the word of God is preached . . ."[5] Similarly, Bishop Reade, on his visitation of the cathedral in January 1403, heard that the archdeacon was not doing his duty of preaching on Ash Wednesday.[6] Even better evidence is provided by extant sermons. In the period here covered, two bishops, FitzRalph and Brinton, have left a number of sermons which they preached in their cathedrals. While dean of Lichfield, FitzRalph gave a fair number of sermons in the cathedral and other localities there,

---

[3] "Officium Cancellarii est scholas theologie regere, predicare vel per se vel per alium quem de ecclesia elegerit. Et hoc intelligendum est quando choro presente predicandum est; alias poterit cui voluerit officium iniungere memoratum. Est autem predicandum hiis diebus populo: singulis dominicis diebus. Clericis in capitulo per tres primas dies Natalis Domini, die Epiphanie item, per tres primas dies Pasche, die Assumptionis, die natiuitatis beate Marie, die Omnium Sanctorum, / die Sancte Trinitatis. Et hoc fiat vel per canonicos vel per alios viros autenticos si inueniantur qui velint et sciant. Item die Cinerum, per quinque dies apud locum stacionis, scilicet die Palmarum et maiores Letanie, et tribus diebus Rogationis, quando solempnes extra ecclesiam fiunt processiones." *Statutes of Lincoln Cathedral* 2A:158–159.

[4] Statutes of Roger Meuland, bishop of Lichfield, 1256–95, in *Monasticon* 6:1260. See also Edwards, *Secular Cathedrals*, pp. 136, 216, 250. Similar statutes for the monastic cathedrals have apparently not been preserved, or at least are not available in print. But see Greatrex, *Biographical Register.*

[5] "Virgarii non faciunt silencium tempore predicacionis verbi Dei, sicut in sermonibus et predicacionibus," *Statutes of Lincoln Cathedral* 2B:386.

[6] *Episcopal Register of Robert Rede*, 1:116.

including not only the two statutory sermons for 1 Advent and Ash Wednesday, but also those for Maundy Thursday, Pentecost, and the feasts of the Invention of the Cross, the Assumption, and Saint Katherine.[7] He continued the practice as archbishop of Armagh, at his "pro-cathedral" at Drogheda, where he is recorded giving sermons in Advent, Lent, and Palm Sunday.[8] Similarly, Bishop Brinton of Rochester, a Benedictine monk, preached through several years in his cathedral on Ash Wednesday,[9] Maundy Thursday, and Good Friday. One suspects that some of the many sermons preserved in the large collections from Worcester priory, particularly W, also contain statutory sermons preached in the cathedral by the prior, but the lack of rubrics leaves this speculative.

These cathedral sermons deal quite naturally with matters suggested or demanded by their liturgical occasions and are generally devotional, with an occasional bit of moral or social criticism added, much like the customary preaching in the parishes. Thus, Advent sermons would speak of the coming of Christ;[10] Ash Wednesday was an occasion to exhort to penance and expound the seven deadly sins;[11] Maundy Thursday might require a discourse on the priestly office (since the day commemorated, among other things, the institution of the priesthood) or on the Eucharist;[12] Good Friday suggested meditation on Christ's Passion;[13] and saints' feasts provided an occasion to praise the saint's virtues and recommend them to the audience.[14]

SPECIAL OCCASIONS

Among Bishop Brinton's sermons there is one said to have been given "in celebracione ordinacionis," at the ordination, evidently of young monks, in his cathedral at Rochester (BR-47). In it the bishop lays out three aspects of the life of holiness to which the ordinands have been called. Another sermon *in celebracione ordinum* has been preserved in W-147 and refers to the basic catechetical articles a priest must know and teach his people. Holy orders would be conferred by one or more bishops in the cathedral or else in some other church, and the ceremony was probably often, if not usually, accompanied by a sermon from the bishop or his delegate. But evidence for this is very scanty: though episcopal registers record ordinations, they usually do not mention sermons, and what sermons have survived may have done so by sheer chance. The collections of the period may

---

[7] See Walsh, *Fourteenth-Century Scholar*, pp. 221–232.   [8] Ibid., pp. 232–238 and passim.

[9] Though only three Ash Wednesday sermons are rubricated as having been given at Rochester cathedral (BR-32, 102, 105), four more (18, 49, 63, 79) may well have been given there, too.

[10] See especially FitzRalph's sermons 4, 13, and 15 given at Lichfield.

[11] Thus especially Brinton's sermons 32, 102 (addressing the clergy), and 105.

[12] FI-6 (Lichfield); BR-55 and 97.   [13] BR-56, 80, 104.

[14] Especially FI-3, 5, 24 (all on St. Katherine), and 11 (on the Blessed Virgin), all given at Lichfield.

in fact hide some further pieces, such as sermons 64 and 65 in MS Aberdeen 154 attributed to Thomas de Lisle, which share with Brinton's rubricated ordination sermon the topics of separation from the world and priestly duties[15] and stand in this regular sermon cycle at a point where ordination sermons would logically be found. Similar to ordination were the profession of a monk and the consecration of a virgin to the religious life. Q-53, in the fifteenth-century Franciscan collection made by Nicholas Philip, bears the rubric "in profescione nouicii" and apparently addresses a young friar after he has passed a year of probation. A similar sermon for the profession of a monk occurs in X-319, dealing with the thema "I am leaving the world" (John 16:28). It stands next to a sermon for the consecration of a virgin, "in consecracione virginis" (X-318), which is by Thomas de Lisle but does not occur in MS Aberdeen 154.[16] Yet another sermon, J/5-18, deals with the enclosure of a named woman, Alice Huntingfield; it is a rhetorical jewel of such preaching, with its interesting use of classical material and extensive punning on the woman's name.[17] In none of these cases, however, do we know who actually preached these sermons.

Another special occasion for an episcopal sermon was the election of a Church official.[18] Canonical elections were very important ecclesiastic events. Bishops in the medieval Church were normally elected by the cathedral chapter, as stipulated by canon law and, in England, guaranteed by King John's charter of 1214. The election followed a conventional procedure that began with a Mass of the Holy Spirit, recitation of the hymn *Veni, Creator Spiritus* and introductory prayers, and a sermon, after which the election proper was carried out.[19] This liturgical pattern was prescribed, and it was observed also on many other occasions, such as visitations, synods, and chapters. At a bishop's election, the sermon would be given by the cathedral dean, but elections of other officials were often graced by a sermon from the bishop. Brinton's collection contains one sermon which he preached before his fellow monks at

---

[15] Their themata are "These are they who come near the Lord to minister to him" (Ezekiel 40:46, sermon 64) and "God has separated you from the whole people and joined you to himself so that you may serve him" (Numbers 16:9, sermon 65).

[16] "Dilectus meus michi," see Schneyer 5:670, no. 599.

[17] The sermon has been analyzed in Wenzel, "Classics," pp. 135–140.

[18] For the election proceedings, including "a short exhortation," see Gibbs and Lang, *Bishops*, chapter 2, "Canonical Procedure in Elections, 1215–1272," pp. 55–68, esp. 64–65. At Canterbury, for instance, prior Henry Eastry preached at the election of a new archbishop in 1313 (Haines, *Ecclesia Anglicana*, p. 27), and the noted Benedictine preacher William Thornden similarly in 1454 (Stone, *Chronicle*, p. 60).

[19] See the treatise on canonical election of bishops by Lawrence of Somercotes (AD 1253–4), in *Statutes of Lincoln Cathedral* 2:cxxv–cxxxix. Here the dean (of Lincoln) "or someone else" preaches before the clergy assembled for the election.

the election of the Benedictine prior of Rochester, in which he exhorts them to choose a man who is humble, just, and holy.[20] Other collections include models for election sermons that do not indicate their precise occasion. Thus, the large Worcester collection X contains five successive sermons "de eleccione" (303–307), the last of which also occurs in MS Aberdeen 154 (62). The latter has preserved a second piece that, on internal evidence, also was written for an election (63). Both pieces set forth some generalities about election and what electors should be concerned with. The same is true of two anonymous sermons of the mid-fifteenth century preserved in collection K. It should perhaps be stressed that none of these pieces recommends or extols a specific candidate.

VISITATION

Much more important, and better represented in the extant collections, is the bishops' preaching that was carried out at visitations and synods. Lateran IV required all bishops to implement the new impetus of preaching the word of God and of educating priests and their flocks in the basics of Christian faith, not only by legislation but by direct action. Thus, the Legatine Council of London 1237 decreed that "bishops also should travel through their dioceses at opportune times and correct and reform, consecrate churches, and sow the word of life in God's field."[21] In a letter to his archdeacon, Bishop Robert Grosseteste of Lincoln (1235–1253) has left a record of how he carried out the mandate:

> Since we are obliged to preach the word of God to all in our diocese, and cannot fulfill the obligation with our own mouth because of the multitude of parochial churches and the immense number of people, we have no other remedy in this but, when we travel through the diocese, to preach the word of God to the rectors, vicars, and parish clergy in every deanery that have been assembled before us. There we teach them how to teach their subjects by word and instruct them by their exemplary life, so that in their ministry they somehow carry out what we cannot accomplish by ourselves. Therefore we command you to warn the deacons of your archdeanery to be ready to call together before you the rectors, vicars, and priests, at places and times that we will specify, so that we may find no hindrance in preaching and carrying out what belongs to our office.[22]

[20] BR-94. This seems to be related to BR-15, preached to the monks of Rochester after their electing a new prior. See Devlin's headnotes to both sermons.

[21] "Circumeant preterea dioceses suas temporibus oportunis, corrigendo et reformando, consecrando ecclesias et verbum vite in agro dominico seminando," *Councils and Synods* 1:255.

[22] Ibid., p. 263, my translation.

Elsewhere the great reforming bishop of Lincoln describes how he himself traveled through his diocese and preached to the clergy, while a Dominican or Franciscan friar did the same before the people.[23]

Though by 1350 this movement to educate clergy and laity may have lost some of its early impulse, there is sufficient evidence that throughout the fourteenth and fifteenth centuries individual bishops continued to visit their flocks and preach to them. The sermon diary of Richard FitzRalph furnishes a wonderful record of this learned and productive theologian's preaching not only before the pope and his cardinals at Avignon, before the bishop of London and at St. Paul's Cross, at processions and at provincial councils, but also in smaller rural parishes, both while he was dean of Lichfield (1337–1346) and later as archbishop of Armagh (1346–1360). The preaching activity of Bishop Brinton of Rochester, half a century later, cannot be localized with quite the same certainty; but it is clear that he, too, addressed not only the papal curia in Avignon and both civil and clerical rulers of England, but equally the people of his diocese.

In the period of this study, such episcopal activity can be said to have crystallized in two formal occasions: visitation and the synod. The visitation of diocesan churches and religious houses[24] was explicitly mandated by Church law, and preaching the word of God formed a requisite part of it.[25] William of Pagula's *Speculum praelatorum* states that

> in his visitation the bishop must observe this order: first he must preach the word of God, then inquire of trustworthy men of that parish, without coercion or requirement of an oath, about the life and behavior of the prelate and the clerics who minister there and of others ordained for the divine worship.[26]

---

23 Ibid., p. 265. Translation in Southern, *Robert Grosseteste*, p. 258.

24 On the visitation see Coulet, *Visites pastorales*, and Owst, *Preaching*, pp. 149–150. Visitation of religious houses was, with some exemptions, also the duty of the local bishop; for a historical survey see Knowles, *Religious Orders*, 1:78–112, and 2:204–218. For the form an episcopal visitation of a religious community took in the thirteenth century and the sermon that went with it, see Cheney, *Episcopal Visitation*, pp. 54–103. A list of what was to be examined at a visitation, "Videndum et inquirendum in visitacione ecclesiarum," appears in British Library, MS Harley 52, f. 26, a thirteenth-century anthology of English Church legislation.

25 The key text is Decretals, *Liber sextus*, 3.20.1, "Romana Ecclesia" (by Innocent IV). Paragraph 4 of the canon prescribes a sermon before the investigation: "proposito verbo Dei quaerat de vita et conversatione ministrantium" (Friedberg 2:1057). Though directed to archbishops, the decretal is cited in pastoral handbooks (see the following quotation) and at visitations conducted by prelates other than the archbishop; cf. BR-23 and E-32.

26 "Et hunc ordinem debet episcopus in sua visitacione seruare: primo debet proponere verbum Dei, deinde querere a viris fidedignis eiusdem parochie, absque coaccione et exaccione qualibet iuramenti, de vita et conuersacione prelati et clericorum ibidem ministrancium et aliis

Towards the end of the century, the pastoral manual *Floretum*, though Wycliffite in its associations,[27] furnishes a complete roster of legislative details concerning what should be done in a visitation. The visiting official must

> first preach the word of God . . . ; secondly correct the excesses of his subjects . . . ;
> thirdly console the faint-hearted . . . ; fourthly hear legal cases . . . And notice
> that the bishop must, either himself or, should he be prevented, visit his diocese
> through other well-intentioned men and make diligent inquiries about the
> life of his clergy, about the fabric and repairs. Likewise he must inquire about
> the state of the laypeople, if they are firm in the faith, if they flee from homicide,
> adultery, perjury, and similar sins, and if they believe in the resurrection . . .
> He must visit his diocese every year . . . In visiting the parishes, bishops must
> inquire more about the gain of souls than the gain of earthly things . . . Further,
> the archbishop, bishop, or any other prelate who visits the churches must first
> preach the word of God, then inquire about the life and behavior of the church's
> ministers . . .[28]

The chapter contains further instructions, even for such particulars as how many horses the bishop may have with him. All instructions are supported by either biblical or canonical references. Of particular interest in the passage quoted is the repeated demand that a visitation should begin with a sermon.[29]

Was this injunction carried out? Beyond the obvious response that some bishops (such as Robert Grosseteste earlier) were more diligent than others, it must be remembered that episcopal records did not always record the bishops' itineraries and inquiries in detail, or are lost, or still lie unedited. Yet

diuino cultui deputatis." *Speculum praelatorum ac religiosorum et parochialium sacerdotum*, part 2, title 14; Oxford, Merton College, MS 217, unfoliated.

[27] See Hudson, "Lollard Compilation"; and *Middle English Translation of the Rosarium Theologie*, pp. 19–42.

[28] "Visitator in sua visitacione debet quatuor facere: primo verbum Dei annunciare . . . ; secundo, excessus subditorum corrigere . . . tercio, pusillanimes consolari . . . quarto, causas audire . . . Et notandum quod episcopus per se uel per alios honestos, si ipse fuerit impeditus, debet dioceses suas visitare, de vita clericorum, de ornatu, et de reparacionibus diligenter inquirere . . . Item de statu laicorum, si in fide sunt stabiles, si homicidium adulterium periurium, et similia fugiant, et resurrexionem credant . . . Item omni anno tenetur diocesim visitare . . . Item episcopi visitando parochias plus debent inquirere de lucro animarum quam de lucro temporalium rerum . . . Item archiepiscopus, episcopus, uel alius prelatus visitans ecclesias primo proponunt verbum Dei, et querat de vita et conuersacione ministrancium ecclesie . . ." *Floretum*, Oxford, Bodleian Library, MS Bodley 448, f. 264va–b. I thank Professor Von Nolcken for the loan of a microfilm.

[29] A nicely detailed instruction about visitation from contemporary France is Gerson's *De visitatione praelatorum*. Visitation is to begin with a *commonitio brevis*. Among the questions the visitator must ask is "si fiant sermones apud eos [i.e. parochianos] et per quos et quando" (p. 51). Gerson also deals with visitation of mendicant houses, who are to be asked about "backbiting in their sermons and old wives' tales" ("detractiones in sermonibus, et fabulas aniles," p. 54). See Gerson, *Oeuvres* 8:47–55.

enough are available that record episcopal visitations, and these frequently mention that a sermon was given by the bishop or a designated cleric on his behalf (usually a man with university training in theology or canon law), and they often even list the themata of the visitation sermons. In the period with which this study is concerned, Archbishop William Courtenay of Canterbury (1381–1396) and Bishops Robert Reade of Chichester (1396–1415) and William Alnwick of Lincoln (1437–1449) stand out as prelates who took this obligation very seriously and about whose visitation sermons they or their delegates gave in cathedrals, parishes, and religious houses we are well informed.[30] Archbishop Simon of Sudbury (1375–1381), too, preached at visitations and convocation, or had someone else preach at his visitations.[31] Evidently, a visitation sermon was a very popular event: the laity was admitted to it and only after its delivery excluded from the subsequent official proceedings.[32] Failure to preach at a parish visitation occasionally caused angered frustration.[33]

The importance of visitation sermons is not only reflected in episcopal records but also in some features of their preservation. Regular sermon cycles of the period usually include one or more of them as models. In addition, handbooks were produced for the explicit purpose of instructing preachers on how to compose them. A fine example is a short treatise written in the thirteenth century that begins with the words "Illustris visitacio illustrando [*or* illustratur] triplici radio" and, after briefly developing the image of the three rays, continues:

> If anyone wishes to compose a visitation sermon, after choosing one of the themata here listed and dividing it as was mentioned, he then may select from any of the three rays one of the listed distinctions that he thinks to be most apt for his purpose.[34]

[30] See *Metropolitical Visitations*; Courtenay also visited Worcester in 1384 and preached on "I shall ascend and see," *Calendar . . . Henry Wakefield*, p. 131. Further: *Episcopal Register of Robert Rede*; and *Visitations of Religious Houses*. See also A. H. Thompson, *English Clergy*, pp. 171–181, on episcopal visitation of monastic houses.

[31] Marvin, "Diocesan Administration," pp. 83, 109, 123, 139, 140.

[32] Owst recreates a visitation and its sermon in *Preaching*, pp. 149–150.

[33] See Cheney, *Episcopal Visitation*, p. 64. Coulton, in *Five Centuries*, 2:245–246, prints a story reported by Étienne de Bourbon of a visiting prelate who fails to preach and thereby draws the anger of "certain noble ladies." See also Owst, *Preaching*, p. 168.

[34] "Si quis ergo componere voluerit sermonem de visitacione, assumpto aliquo presencium theumatum et distincto iuxta predictum modum eligat de quolibet radiorum vnam dictarum distinccionem quam proposito suo nouerit apciorem." Oxford, Bodleian Library, MS Bodley 677, f. 189va. The treatise occupies ff. 189va–210va. It is by the Cistercian John of Limoges (died 1270). Caplan knew of the work (but not of this manuscript): Caplan, *Artes praedicandi*, no. 560. It has been edited in John of Limoges, *Opera* 3:143–183, where it is followed by a similar treatise on composing sermons for an election, pp. 187–223.

This is followed by some twenty folios, first of possible themata for visitation sermons and then of distinctions for the terms found in these themata.[35] In a similar fashion, the Dominican John Bromyard, in his massive *Summa praedicantium*, listed appropriate themata for visitation sermons for a number of different venues and even developed some into model sermons.[36] The importance and frequency of visitation sermons can, finally, also be gauged from the fact that the episcopal records of Courtenay and Alnwick yield fifty-seven different themata, of which only five or six are matched by themata in the sermons preserved – surely a good measure of the vitality of actual visitation preaching as well as the low proportion of materials that has been preserved.

About two dozen visitation sermons have survived in the collections studied. Some are rubricated *in visitacione* or *pro visitacione* or *ad visitacionem*, while others lack such an explicit label but clearly belong with them because of internal references. For example, one of the model sermons by Thomas de Lisle that was copied into several collections has no rubric but declares in its body that the prelate is of necessity held to visit his subjects, and that "in this visitation which is conducted in the way of justice there must be a just cause, a just mind, and a just order."[37] Three were clearly preached by bishops: FitzRalph preached "in visitacione" at Trim on April 16, 1355 (FI-47), while Brinton's collection holds two sermons labeled "in visitacione." The first (BR-23), according to its rubric, was given to the clergy of Rochester cathedral, but the second (BR-75) lacks any indication of place and audience, in either rubric or content (which deals only with what the visitator should be like). A bishop's obligation to visit his cathedral and diocese also included visitation of religious houses under his jurisdiction,[38] while at the same time religious orders had their own internal systems of visitation by appointed members of their order. It is thus in many cases unclear who the preacher of a given visitation sermon was, especially when the community visited was a monastery or convent. Given this uncertainty, I have included in the two dozen sermons all visitation sermons I have found, whoever their preachers and whatever

---

[35] Thus the first thema listed is "*Ego scelera visitabo*, Leuitici 18," and the model distinctions begin with a threefold distinction on the word *Ego*, with schemata and biblical prooftexts.

[36] Bromyard, *Summa praedicantium*, "Visitacio," V.8,2, in British Library, MS Royal 7.E.iv, ff. 611va–620rb.

[37] "Dico primo quod prelatus ex necessitate tenetur uisitare subditos suos, quia precipitur ei . . . In ista uisitacione que fit per uiam iusticie debet esse iusta causa, iustus animus, iustus ordo," Aberdeen 154, ff. 329v–330 (with correction from the other MSS), on the thema *Fratres tuos visitabis*; also preserved as J/2-128 (as a filler), X-309, and perhaps partially in Merton 248, f. 52rb–va.

[38] Cf. Cheney, *Episcopal Visitation*. Courtenay and Alnwick visited many religious houses, as cited earlier; so did Simon Langham of Canterbury (1366–76), see *Registrum Simonis Langham*, pp. 229–238.

their audiences may have been. Besides the sermons by bishops FitzRalph and Brinton, the following collections have preserved visitation sermons: B/2,[39] E,[40] F/5,[41] G,[42] Q,[43] R,[44] W,[45] and X.[46] An interesting aspect here is that several visitators refer to their sermon as "collacio."[47]

Many visitation sermons can be considered business addresses. Their speakers recall that giving a sermon on this occasion is a well-established custom. "Reverend fathers and much beloved brethren," a Franciscan preacher says to members of his order,

> since according to a praiseworthy custom, in the beginning of any ordinary visitation, especially in public, the visitors usually preach something to their visitands by way of a collation . . .[48]

Another visitator begins addressing a monastic congregation with, "according to the praiseworthy custom of our order, a salutary sermon ought to precede the visitation."[49] Often the visiting prelate reminds his audience of his authority, of his obligation to undertake visitation, and of the qualities required of a visitator, which include firmness in correcting abuses as well as gentleness or leniency.[50] His business is to correct sinners, to console the weak, and to strengthen the perfect (B/2-5). Conversely, voluntary submissiveness and charitable affection are required of the flock he visits (ibid.). Visitors of religious houses, both monastic (R-18) and of mendicants (Q-34), will examine how the three vows are being kept. A sermon preached to a Benedictine community proposes a different agenda. It divides the visitands into three groups and specifies what the visitor will examine in each: administrative efficiency among the monastic officials, purity of life among the cloistered monks, and rule of and care for their subjects among the

---

[39] B/2-5.

[40] Sermons 16–19 and 32, given before a monastic audience, evidently Augustinian canons.

[41] F/5-5, perhaps given by a Worcester monk; and F/5-31, probably to a monastic community; it also occurs in Bodl 4-75 and elsewhere (cf. Schneyer 6:137 and 249, 7:68 and 78).

[42] G-2, monastic.   [43] Sermons 34–37, visitations of (Franciscan) *fratres*.

[44] R-18 addresses a Benedictine audience.

[45] Sermons 117–118, 130, 135, and 137. Several clearly address a monastic, Benedictine community.

[46] Sermons 309–315. They all occur in MS Aberdeen 154. Sermons 313 and 315 apparently were intended for a visitation and/or synod.

[47] As does Bromyard, see above n. 36. See further "Prolegomena," pp. 15–16.

[48] "Reuerendi patres fratresque predilecti, quia ante quamlibet visitacionem ordinariam saltem in publico laudabili consuetudine solent visitatores per modum collacionis aliquid visitandis proponere, igitur vt conformem me aliqualiter eisdem, sit hoc thema preuium," Q-34, f. 107. Quoted in Owst, *Preaching*, p. 150.

[49] "Reuerendi patres et domini, cum iuxta laudabilem ordinis nostri consuetudinem visitacionem precedere sermo debeat salutaris . . ." W-117, f. 222v.

[50] *Iusticia* and *misericordia* in X-309; *veritas* and *pietas* in X-310.

monastic prelates. If the members of these three groups do their jobs well, he says, the community will flourish and produce good fruit, which is what he hopes to find.[51]

COUNCILS AND SYNODS

At synods, also called councils or convocations,[52] bishops would call together their clergy to discuss Church business. By the later fourteenth and the fifteenth century, this may no longer have included so much moral reform and discipline as taxation, clerical complaints about the government or vice-versa, or disturbances caused by the Lollards. Like the visitation, such regular meetings were required by Church law.[53] In his sermon for the York synod of 1373, the learned Cistercian monk William Rimington announced the canonical injunction as well as the major concerns of contemporary synods directly:

> Churchmen should gather once annually in order to drive off the darkness of errors that are sprouting forth, to end controversies that have sprung up, to confute heretics and people who infringe upon the liberties of the Church, and to transmit grave causes to the Roman curia, with the counsel and assent of the whole clergy, as is decreed in canon law, Distinction 18 in its entirety.[54]

Apparently, in some places the annual synod was quite a show.[55] Another monk, Robert Rypon, said in the first of his synodal sermons:

> You know that it was an ancient custom, and in fact is a synodal constitution, that all rectors and vicars of this diocese should come in person or at least send in their place a priest and cleric in good standing to this monastery as to the foremost resting-place (*cubile*) once every year, namely in the week of Pentecost,

---

[51] W-130, on "Let us see if the vineyard flourishes" (Canticles 7:12). The vineyard and other agricultural images are frequently used for monastic visitation sermons: "I went down to the garden to see the fruits" (Cant 6:10, in X-310); "Flowers have appeared in our land" (Cant 2:12, in W-135); "I will seek my sheep and will visit them" (Ezekiel 34:11, in E-18); "From their fruits you shall know them" (Matthew 7:16, in Q-33).

[52] In the period of 1350–1450 the three words are roughly synonymous, though "synod" came to be used for diocesan gatherings and is thus used in surviving sermons. "Council" tended to mark a larger gathering, or a gathering of bishops, involving an entire province or the whole Church. "Convocation" signals that the clergy were called together; the verb *convocare* is frequently thus used in episcopal records. In modern English usage, "convocation" refers to the gathering of the bishops in the two English provinces of Canterbury and York.

[53] *Decretum*, Distinctio 18 (Friedberg I:53–58); this is evoked in the following quotation.

[54] O'Brien, "Two Sermons," pp. 58–59. O'Brien points out (n. 80) that the quoted section of the *Decretum* deals with the frequency of synods but not with the concerns mentioned by Rimington.

[55] Again, Owst recreates a synod and its sermon in *Preaching*, pp. 150–152.

with banners and crosses held up, so that they might walk in procession in order to pray devoutly to God, Blessed Mary, Saint Oswald, and Saint Cuthbert, patrons of this church, for the peace and tranquillity of the realm and especially of this region.[56]

Synods followed a more or less standard procedure. In the 1290s William Durandus left prescriptions in his *Pontifical* that a synod should begin with a Mass, initial prayers, litany, gospel reading, and the hymn *Veni Creator Spiritus*.

> When this has been done, all shall sit down in silence, and the bishop, if he wishes, addresses them thus: "Behold, my blessed and venerable fellow priests . . ." After this allocution or, even better, before it, there shall be a sermon dealing with Church discipline, the divine mysteries, and the correction of moral faults . . . And right after the sermon, complaints shall be heard, if there should be any.[57]

When synods went on for a number of days, a second sermon might be given later during the meeting.

English chroniclers often report the convening of Church councils and that on such occasions a sermon was preached. Now and then they even tell us what its thema was. At the provincial council of 1309, held at St. Paul's, London, first a Mass of the Holy Spirit was celebrated by the bishop of Norwich, "after which the archbishop preached the word of God in Latin, in which he reproved bishops who were illegally elected through prayers [i.e. intercession in their favor by influential people] or on account of their ambition, as well as those who hold office against Church law." After the sermon he gave an indulgence of

---

[56] "Constat vobis quod consuetudo erat antiqua, immo est constitucio sinodalis, quod cunti rectores et vicarii huius diocesis accederent personaliter aut saltem mitterent vice sua honestum sacerdotem et clericum ad istud monasterium tanquam ad principale cubile saltem semel in anno, videlicet in septimana Pentecostes, cum vexillis et crucibus erectis, vt processionaliter incederent, Deum, beatam Mariam, sanctum Osuualdum, sanctum Cuthbertum patronos huius ecclesie deuocius oraturi pro pace et tranquillitate huius regni et precipue huius patrie," RY-52, f. 194v. Rypon continues that nowadays this custom has been almost totally abandoned, as the diocesan priests, in their laziness, insolence, and pride, send laypeople in their stead who are often unfit (*inhonestas*) and have little or no devotion. For this section of the sermon see also Owst, *Preaching*, p. 216.

[57] "Quo expleto, omnes sedeant in silentio et pontifex, si velit, eos alloquitur ita dicens: Allocutio. 'Ecce, beatissimi et venerabiles consacerdotes . . .'. [9] Post allocutionem huiusmodi vel prius, quod est melius, fiat sermo, in quo tractetur de disciplina ecclesiastica, de divinis misteriis et de correctione morum in clero, secundum ea que in nostris Constitutionibus synodalibus, inter Instructiones, clarius demonstrantur. [10] Et mox post sermonem querele, si que sint, audiantur." Durand, *Pontifical*, p. 598.

40 days, and then explained the reasons for this council.[58] The archbishop's thema was "Take heed to yourselves and to your subjects" (Acts 20:28).[59] Over a century later, the custom was still kept and recorded. At the provincial council of York in 1426, "as is customary, the word of God was preached by the venerable and very learned man Master John Roxby, a famous doctor in theology, taking as his thema the words of Joshua: 'Joshua called together the elders'" (probably Josh 24:1).[60] And two years later, at the Canterbury convocation held again at St. Paul's, Robert Fitzhugh, chancellor of Cambridge, "gave a speech in favor of Cambridge University, on the thema 'Thus stand in the Lord' (Phil 4:1), which he developed with elegance, recommending first his university and then admonishing the lord [archbishop] and his brother bishops to defend the Catholic faith, by citing numerous authorities that fitted his matter well."[61] In a similar vein, the register of Archbishop Chichele (1414–1443) records a number of synodal sermons for the years 1415–1439 with the names of the preachers and their themata.[62]

From the century between 1350 and 1450 over thirty sermons have survived that are either rubricated *in synodo* or *pro synodo*, or else contain explicit internal indications that they were meant for such an occasion. As was the case with

---

[58] "Celebrata primitus missa de Sancto Spiritu per Norwicensem, archiepiscopo, et caeteris episcopis pontificalibus indutis; post finitam missam archiepiscopus proposuit verbum Dei in Latino, in quo reprehendit episcopos male per preces electos, vel ambitionem, necnon et eos, qui non stant pro jure ecclesiae. Finito autem sermone, dedit indulgentiam 40 dierum omnibus, qui eidem sermoni interfuerunt, confessis et contritis; et deinde exposuit in genere occasionem convocationis concilii." Wilkins, *Concilia* 2:304.

[59] *Councils and Synods* 2:1265.

[60] "Verbo Dei per venerabilem eximiae scientiae virum, magistrum Johannem Roxby, famosum in theologia doctorem, habentem pro themate istud Joshuae 'Vocavit joshue majores,' ut moris est praedicato." Wilkins, *Concilia* 3:487.

[61] "Quandam pro parte universitatis praedictae propositionem fecit solennem; sumpto quasi pro themate: 'Sic state in Domino,' quod eleganter prosequendo, facta primitus recommendatione dictae universitatis, dominum et confratres suos episcopos ad defensionem fidei catholicae, auctoritates nonnullas materiae multum convenientes allegando, exhortabatur." Wilkins, *Concilia* 3:495. Notice that the address here is called *propositio*; it need not have been a formal sermon, though it probably followed the sermon structure. Similarly, the noun *sermo* does not necessarily refer to a sermon. In a fifteenth-century chronicle, for instance, the term frequently denotes an address or speech: Amundesham, *Annales*, pp. 147–148, 212, 225, 233.

[62] The preachers include bishops (John of Llandaff, John [Langdon] of Rochester), theologians (Robert Gilbert, Henry Abingdon, Peter Partryche, Richard Praty, William Holmache, John Carpenter, John Pecock), lawyers (William Lyndwood, John Holand, Thomas Kyngton), friars (William Norham OP, John Courteys), and a monk (John Langdon); *Register Henry Chichele*, 3:3–279.

visitation sermons, two bishops, FitzRalph[63] and Brinton,[64] have left synodal sermons. However, as the two quoted cases of 1426 and 1428 show, bishops often sought or mandated the service of a learned preacher for the occasion. Thus, the Cistercian monk William of Rimington, who had been chancellor of Cambridge, preached at the provincial synods of York in 1372 and 1373. Another monk, Robert Rypon, wrote eight synodal sermons, presumably delivered by him. The collection in Hereford Cathedral MS O.iii.5 (E), which has affiliations with the Augustinian canons, similarly contains four, and possibly more, sermons for a synod. Another collection, by the Franciscan Nicholas Philip (Q), also contains at least one "sermo in synodo." The Dominican collection D, gathering sermons by several named English theologians, holds seven synodal sermons, including an earlier one by Holcot. One may be surprised that the surviving synodal sermons are so widely dominated by preachers from religious orders, including Brinton. This may be no more than an accident of preservation, and of course members of religious orders enjoyed a higher level of education and learning.

It seems not to have been a bishop's regular task to preach at provincial or general chapters of the religious orders; but Bishop Edmund Lacy of Exeter is on record for doing just that in 1441, and his sermon has been preserved in his register.[65]

SERMONS *AD CLERUM*

Our collections contain a number of further sermons that bear no indication of serving for visitations or synods yet were seemingly intended for clerical ears. This is clearly the case when they are marked *ad clerum* or *ad cleros*. Eleven sermons by Bishop Brinton bear this mark, to which can be added another four in other collections. But there are many more that address "reverendi" or even "vos curati," as has been noted in the previous descriptions of individual collections. These as well as sermons specified for synods characteristically deal with the pastoral office, extolling the dignity of priesthood, outlining its demands, and warning against moral failings among the contemporary clergy. In his fifth synodal sermon, on "The laborer is worthy of his hire" (Luke 10:7), Rypon devotes an entire section to the *quidditas* or nature of priesthood, which lies in an indelible

---

[63] FI-34 and 50, both delivered at the provincial council at Drogheda, in 1352 and 1355. The former is a complete sermon, the latter an abbreviated report. Both have been edited in Gwynn, "Two Sermons."

[64] BR-13 and 17. Neither is rubricated as a synodal sermon, but Devlin argues that they might have been preached at Canterbury convocations in 1373 and 1377 respectively; see her headnotes to the respective texts in Brinton, *Sermons*.

[65] At the general chapter of the Dominicans; *Register Edmund Lacy*, 2:241–6.

authority, in the *character* of the priestly order, "a certain indelible sign by which the ordained person is given spiritual power."[66] Earlier, in RY-54, Rypon had defined "the essence of the priestly office" as "dispensing the sacraments, announcing divine doctrine and the commandments, and pouring out devout and continual prayers for the people before God."[67] The systematic theologian's *quidditas* in RY-56 yields to a more memorable "etymological" definition when Rypon defines "priest," *sacerdos*, as *sacer dux, sacra dans*, and *sacra docens* ("a holy leader, giving holy things and teaching holy matters").[68] This etymological triad also receives some spotlight in the sermons by the anonymous Hereford preacher, who develops it in three separate but interlinked sermons. For him, the three terms summarize that by his sacred ministry a priest is to administer the sacraments of the Church to his subjects, to shine brightly like a lantern in the goodness of his behavior, and to preach to all the true doctrine of the gospels.[69]

Priesthood, then has a dignity that places its recipient high above any other human being, just as an angel is far above men, spirit above body, heaven above earth, and the sun above the moon (A-42). Indeed, priesthood is the degree closest to God himself (B/2-4: "gradus immediatissimus ipsi Deo"). "In the mystical body of Christ, he is the most perfect member, ordained for the most perfect and excellent office, namely, to offer gifts and sacrifices for men's sins."[70] Dygon expands this notion further: Christ gave priests the power to consecrate his body; to bind and to loose; he gave them the Holy Spirit more fully than others; they are God's angels and messengers, his ministers ordained to save the elect; they are Christ's legates or lieutenants sent to reconcile sinners, his mouth and eyes, who have the power to cast out devils from souls; they are spiritual fathers to the people; and they are to be heeded with reverence and be obeyed (DY-16). And in a later sermon Dygon specifies that

[66] "Quoddam signaculum indelebile, per quod spiritualis potestas traditur ordinato," RY-56, f. 205v.

[67] "Est enim de essencia sacerdotalis officii specialiter sacramenta dispensare, documenta et diuina precepta denunciare, pias et iuges oraciones coram Deo et [*read* pro?] populo fundere," RY-54, f. 200.

[68] RY-56, f. 205v.

[69] "Sacra scilicet dando per sacrum ministerium Ecclesie sacramenta subditis ministrando; sacris eciam deditus honestate morum vt lucerna lampadis lucide rutilando; tercio sacra docens euangeliorum dogmata veredica omnibus predicando," E-22, f. 54vb. The preacher here uses *sacris deditus* for *sacer dux*, though earlier he had employed the latter phrase. His usage in general is more fluid than Rypon's.

[70] "Sacerdos in corpore Christi mistico membrum sit perfeccius perfectissimo et excellentissimo officio deputatum, scilicet vt offerat dona et sacrificia de peccatis, et non dona carnalia vt olym in lege sed preciosissimam hostiam corporis et sanguinis Domini nostri Iesu Christi. O quali mundicia ad istud ineffabile sacramentum . . . accedendum est!" W-122, f. 230ra.

the pope properly holds on earth the place and office of Jesus Christ. All Catholic bishops hold the place and dignity of the apostles . . . The lower clergy, curates and simple priests hold the place and dignity of the seventy-two disciples of Our Lord Jesus Christ . . . Even the lowliest priests surpass the good angels in many excellent gifts . . . , especially in their privilege to confect the Eucharist, the power to bind and to loose, and the dignity of martyrdom in dying in charity and patience to preserve the Catholic faith or justice.[71]

As one sermon develops at length, a priest is thus like the tree of life planted in the middle of Paradise (W-16); or as several others declare, priests – not Christians in general – form "the chosen generation, the royal priesthood, the holy nation" of 1 Peter 2:9.

Naturally such a high calling makes high moral demands. A *sacerdos* must be *sacris deditus*, devoted to holiness. In himself, he must be sanctified and show forth purity in his life; with regard to his neighbor, he must shine with his knowledge and bring justice to his subjects; and with respect to God, he must be full of piety and devout prayers (Q-25). In every respect priests must "transcend the common way of living in the flesh with the goodness of virtue," as the Hereford preacher says, and they must be *viri heroici* and like the angels.[72] Priests carry God's temple in their reason, will, and memory, and therefore must keep their souls free of falseness, malice, and impurity, and must have the virtues opposed to the seven deadly sins (RY-52). Hence, sermons to the clergy constantly exhort their audiences to shun the seven deadly sins and particularly to practice chastity and modesty. Not only are they to refrain from any immoral contact with women but observe restraint in dress and bodily adornment, in gestures and in speech, and in such forms of conviviality as drinking at the tavern and rolling dice. Inward holiness must be reflected in a priest's outward comportment, through maturity, self-control, and soberness in his face, speech, and clothing.[73] Such demands had been frequently spelled out, and often with even

---

[71] "Nunc autem breuiter dicere sufficiat quod papa vel pontifex summus in terra gerit appropriate in terra vicem et officium Iesu Christi. Episcopi omnes catholici tenent locum et dignitatem apostolorum . . . Inferiores sacerdotes, curati, et simplices sacerdotes tenent locum et dignitatem lxxii discipulorum Domini Iesu Christi . . . Et quantum ad multas excellencias eciam infimi sacerdotes excedunt angelos bonos, vt patet in sermone precedente. Et hoc specialiter quantum ad dignitatem conficiendi eukaristiam, quantum ad potestatem ligandi et soluendi peccata, et quantum ad dignitatem martirii moriendo in caritate et paciencia pro fide catholica vel iusticia conseruanda," DY-51, f. 221v.

[72] "In dignitate sacerdotali Deo disposite constituti Domini sacerdotes in carne mortali communem hominum viuendi modum in virtutis bonitate transcendere deputantur . . . Vnde sacerdotes ne dumtaxat deberent viri eroyci appellari, sed propter magnam angelorum conformitatem angeli nominantur," E-23, f. 57rb–va.

[73] "Maturitatem in vultu, honestatem in gestu, sobrietatem in cultu," RY-52, f. 194.

greater concreteness, in thirteenth-century synodal decrees and pastoral hand-books,[74] and throughout the following two centuries they were voiced again and again in many sermons. Their breach is noted and chastized with equal frequency. To cite but one example: as he was nearing the end of his synodal sermon of 1355, FitzRalph said:

> It seems to me that our priests are defiled by the vices mentioned below, from all of which they are to be cleansed through the remedy of this sacred council. Among them some are lechers, others are drunkards, others are lazy, others are too much like laypeople, others are less hospitable than they ought to be; some are usurpers and thieves, namely the exempt mendicants who usurp the tithings of the land.[75]

Next to the call to personal holiness and to God's worship, priestly ordination leads, at least normally, to the cure of souls, and a good many sermons thus make it their aim to explain the duties that constitute the pastoral office. As one sermon has it: "This dignity [of the priesthood] was instituted in the Church for a threefold purpose: that priests may serve God inwardly through the devotion of their minds, that they may teach the people outwardly through spiritual *conversatio*, and that they may unite the people with God above through their spiritual mediation."[76] In detailing what the pastoral office demands, sermons quote and rely heavily on age-old standard texts, from Christ's threefold command to Peter to "feed my sheep" and his discourse on "I am the good shepherd"[77] through Gregory the Great's *Cura pastoralis* to Church legislation in canon law. The pastoral duties are usually specified in triads and often derived from the words of the sermon's thema. Thus the thema "Videte, vigilate, et orate" (Mark 13:33) leads to the threefold calling of priests to be watchmen of the Church, shepherds of the Lord's flock, and mediators between God and men.[78] Similarly, FitzRalph explains that the office consists in teaching the people, mediating between them and God, and spiritually ruling their subjects,[79] and Rypon declares that

---

[74] A good example is the Statutes of Salisbury I (1217×1219), in *Councils and Synods* 1:62–66. See further the entries "Priest – attire" and "misconduct," in the General Index ibid., 2:1436.

[75] Gwynn, "Two Sermons," p. 65.

[76] "Hec enim dignitas est in Ecclesia racione triplici instituta, vt scilicet sacerdotes Deo interius seruiant per mentalem deuotionem; exterius populum instruant per spiritualem conuersationem; et superius cum Deo populum vniant per sp[iritu]alem medicinam [*later:* mediationem]," B/2-4, f. 126va.

[77] "Pasce agnos meos," etc., John 21:15–17, the gospel for the vigil for the feast of Peter and Paul; "Ego sum pastor bonus," John 10:11 ff., the gospel for the second Sunday after Easter.

[78] "Speculatores domus Dei, pastores dominici gregis, and mediatores hominum et Dei," A-42, f. 135.

[79] "Notandum quod sacerdotes habent triplicem actum circa subiectos exercere, et ob hoc debent triplicem virtutem habere. Debent enim populum instruere, et ob hoc debent habere docendi

"the essence of the priestly office lies especially in dispensing the sacraments, preaching doctrine and the divine commandments, and pouring forth pious and continual prayers before God and men.[80] With mercy and charity a good pastor will teach his flock that is "struck with so much ignorance that they know nothing of what belongs to the salvation of their souls, not the Lord's Prayer, nor the Ave Maria, nor the Creed or the Commandments, the works of mercy, the seven deadly sins, or the five senses."[81] They even need to be taught how to make the sign of the cross (E-24). But a pastor is to teach not only in words but by his own example of holy living, for "God sent his apostles, namely churchmen, that through their good moral life and good example they might urge the laity to take the right way to heaven and withdraw from the darkness of their sins."[82] To teach them well he must know the Scriptures. As mediator he is to reconcile them to God by his prayers and by the sacraments of Penance and the Eucharist. He is to rule and defend them against spiritual dangers and attacks, by watching over his flock and keeping them from error, and by speaking out against sin, oppression, and injustice. Finally, he is also to feed them physically, sharing the resources of his parish with those who are poor and hungry.

Being a spiritual shepherd further increases the moral demands made on a priest. "It must not be enough for a priest to possess holiness in himself; his holinesss must be an example to others."[83] As in the Israelites' procession around the walls of Jericho, priests must "go in front . . . with the steps of virtue and a good life . . . But this is not enough . . . They must take the trumpet and blow it before the people . . . , the trumpet of the gospel, the word of God, the doctrine and preaching of Holy Church."[84] For that, the good pastor must have learning and

scienciam. Debent eciam inter deum et populum mediare, et ob hoc debent habere hominis utriusque mundiciam. Et debent subditos gubernare et ob hoc debent habere directricem iusticiam." FI-50; in Gwynn, "Two Sermons," p. 64.

[80] See above, n. 67.

[81] "Et ista miseria est maior pars populi, et precipue ruralium, et dolorose involuta, quid sacerdotum qui misericorditer et caritatiue ipsos informarent, informando releuarent . . . Isti sunt tanta ignorancia percussi quod nulla ad salutem anime sciunt pertinencia, nec oracionem dominicam nec salutacionem angelicam nec simbolum sciunt, et precepta et opera misericordie, septem peccata mortalia et quinque sensus ignorant." H-11, f. 34.

[82] "Deus misit apostolos suos, scilicet viros ecclesiasticos, vt ipsi vita honesta et bono exemplo excitarent laicos ad viam rectam versus celum et a peccatorum tenebris retraherent," P2–3, f. 7va.

[83] "Nec debet prelato sufficere quod in se habeat sanctitatem, sed oportet quod sua sanctitas sit aliis exemplaris," FI-34, in Gwynn, "Two Sermons," p. 55.

[84] "Oportet sacerdotes habere þe vawarde, oportet quod plebem precedant non passu pedum sed passu virtutis et bone vite. Si tu, sacerdos, fueris superbus in corde, elatus in responsis, in apparatu vt secularis ineptus, capis curuum passum, non recte incedis ante plebem. Si fueris negligens in seruicio, wild and rewle viuendo viuis non caste vt tuus expostulat ordo, vadis retorte [*ms* reterte],

knowledge, and the ability to pass these on and thereby to lead his flock. Thus, like the tree of knowledge in Paradise, a priest must be watered with salutary wisdom, bring forth virtuous learning, and be decked out with spiritual teaching (W-16). There is an absolute need for theological knowledge not only in preaching, as we shall see later, but also in hearing confessions and evaluating a parishioner's spiritual state – to "discern between leprosy and leprosy," as the standard canonical formula for the confessor's knowledge and ability declares.[85] And lastly, the good shepherd will have to rule his flock in mercy and charity and defend it against the wolf, not run away like a mercenary (cf. John 10:11–13). This involves standing up with zeal and decisiveness against public sin, doctrinal error and heresy, as well as the injustices and encroachments of the powerful on the rights of the Church, following thereby the great example of St. Thomas Becket. "Priests whose office it is to rule the people must be led by justice, so that they may not be broken by fear of a layman, nor bent by love of the flesh, nor corrupted by prayer or gifts . . ." They should keep in mind Eli, who was punished with a sudden death for not correcting his sons with the necessary severity.[86] FitzRalph sums it all up by saying that true prelates who are acceptable to God must have *sanctitas in vivendo, strenuitas in regendo,* and *sagacitas in docendo.* And in admitting a man to the priesthood, a bishop must make sure that the candidate indeed possesses such learning and is admitted by election and not through gifts or pressure from powerful relatives. FitzRalph even gives a little vignette of the bishop interrogating a candidate for the priesthood:

> "We ask you, beloved brother, in true charity, if you are willing to orient your whole moral life, in as much as this is possible in your nature, to the teachings of holy scripture?" Then the ordinand shall answer, "Yes, I will from my whole heart consent and obey in all things." When the bishop asks again, "Will you teach the people for whom you are to be ordained, in word and your example,

non debite precedis plebem, oportet te capere passum paciencie et humilitatis, castimon[i]e et sobrietatis; oportet precedere plebem in sanctitate et perfeccione, et per bonum exemplum in omni tua conuersacione. Sed hoc non sufficit. Non tibi sufficit qui habes curam animarum quod bonus sis in teipso. Oportet tubam capere et clangere coram plebe uel saltim alium qui tubare sciuerit exhibere. Quid est hec tuba? Tuba euangelica, verbum Dei, doctrina et predicacio sancte Ecclesie," O-2, f. 11.

[85] *Decretum* Dist. 20, introduction (Friedberg 1:65). The "scientia discernendi inter lepram et lepram" is one of the two keys given to Peter; the other is the power to bind and to loose. The formula was used several times by Grosseteste in his *Dicta* and sermons, and it appears in sermons RE-8, RY-56, Q-25, W-16, and W-23, often in Grosseteste quotations.

[86] "Sacerdotes qui habent populum gubernare debent habere directricem iusticiam: ita ut nec laicali timore frangantur nec carnali amore flectantur nec prece nec precio corrumpantur, quoniam e contrario faciendo sunt mercenarii, non pastores iuxta x. capitulo Johannis. Aut cum Hely sacerdote . . . ," FI-50; in Gwynn, "Two Sermons," p. 65. For the example of Eli in visitation and other sermons, see Wenzel, "Eli."

the things you learn from Holy Scripture?" the ordinand shall say, "I will." . . .
And when the consecrating bishop asks again, "Are you willing to withdraw
your behavior from all evil and, as much as you can, with God's help change it
to the good?" he shall answer, "I will."[87]

It is no wonder, then, that one preacher should exclaim that "to have the cure
and custody of souls is no child's play!"[88] Nor is it surprising that together with
injunctions to live up to the moral standards and duties of the pastoral office our
sermons should equally – if not more so – point out and chastize failures to do
so. Criticisms of the clergy occupy many an extant sermon; they form a major
locus for the complaint literature of the times and have been widely explored by
Owst. Indeed, preachers fulminated against their negligent and sinful brethren:

> Lo, now a days there is no tonsure on their heads, no religion in their dress,
> no modesty in their words, no temperance in their food, nor modesty in the
> signs they give nor even self-control in their deeds . . . Many are like laymen in
> gathering wordly riches, like merchants in having all sorts of dealings; many are
> like knights in the luxury of their garments and like women in the inconstancy
> of their minds . . . Our [spiritual] physicians do not direct their attention to the
> health of souls, nor do they give the sick healthy medicine according to what
> their sicknesses or sins require . . . We must fear, dearly beloved, that now a
> days the hearts of the Church's priests and ministers, through the pestilence of
> pride, ambition, and greed, have dried up; for want of the water of grace and
> devotion they have become so dry and cold that their prayers, petitions and
> loud cries are become inaudible to God.[89]

---

[87] "Interroganti enim ab episcopo consecrando consecratori ipsius hoc modo: Interrogamus te,
dilectissime frater, caritate sincera si omnem prudenciam tuam, quantum capax est tua natura,
divine scripture sensibus accommodare volueris: consecrandus ita respondet: Ita ex toto corde
volo in omnibus consentire et obedire. Item interroganti consequenter: Vis ea que ex divinis
scripturis intelligis plebem cui ordinandus es et verbo dicere et exemplo? sic respondet: Volo. Ymo
ut ad omne genus virtutum appareat ex sua professione esse episcopos obligatos, consecratori
interroganti ab episcopo consecrando: Vis mores tuos ab omni malo temperare, et quantum
poteris domino adiuvante ad omne bonum commutare: ita / respondet: Volo." FI-34; in Gwynn,
"Two Sermons," pp. 57–58.

[88] "Non est ludus puerilis habere curam et custodiam animarum," A-49, f. 152.

[89] "Ecce apud illos hiis diebus non est tonsura in capite, nec religio in ueste, non modestia in verbis,
non temperancia in cibis, nec pudicicia in signis, nec eciam continencia in factis . . . Multi eorum
sunt vt laici in temporalium congregacione, vt mercatores in omnimoda negociacione; sunt
autem vt milites in luxu vestium et vt mulieres in inconstancia animorum . . . / Medici nostri
saluti animarum non intendunt nec infirmis salutarem adhibent medicinam iuxta morborum
qualitatem uel culparum exigenciam . . . // Timendum est, karissimi, quod corda sacerdotum et
ministrorum Ecclesie sancte in tantum per pestem superbie, ambicionis, et auaricie hiis diebus
sunt arefacta et ex defectu humoris gracie et deuocionis arida facta sunt et frigida quod oraciones,
peticiones, et clamores eorum apud Deum inexaudibiles habeantur," A-42, f. 136v–138.

Or even more rhetorically:

> Oh grief and pain! Many priests of our time have cast off and scorned these
> most holy waters of Jordan through which the leprosy of their own iniquity and
> ignorance could be healed, and have instead chosen "Abana and Pharpar, the
> rivers of Damascus," that is, the occupations and pleasures of this world, where,
> the more thoroughly they wash themselves, the more fully do they get dirty,
> so that "As the people, so also the priest," or rather, "If the people are bad, the
> priest is worse." For in their gestures they are showmen, in their social behavior
> scoundrels; they are Ciceros in their affect, idols in their temples, thunderclaps
> in the courts, Argoses in their winnings, Tantaluses in their labors, Dedaluses in
> their cares, Sardanapalluses in their beds. But in meditating on and preaching
> the Scriptures you will find they are the most stolid.[90]

And worse, they have the temerity to excuse their failings with the Bible: when
one accuses them of striking other people, they reply, "So did Peter 'cut off the
ear of the servant of the high priest'" (Matthew 26:51). If they are blamed for
indulging in wine and gluttony, they say, "Christ, too, was called 'a glutton and
wine drinker'" (Matthew 11:19). And so on.[91]

Most pronounced among the personal failings are lechery and gluttony, which
one preacher finds allegorically in the two serpents placed by Juno in the cradle
of Hercules.[92] Next to these carnal vices stands greed, which in priests manifests
itself in many different ways: some rob the poor of what belongs to them by right
or oppress their parishes; others have become priests to enjoy a good income;
still others yearn for a more lucrative benefice, whether in the Church or in the
service of powerful magnates. "Whence is it," one preacher asks, "that churchmen
pay more attention to lucrative knowledge than to a speculative one? Whence
is it that they are more interested in pleading lawcases than in teaching their

---

[90] "Sed o luctus et dolor, plerique sacerdotes nostri temporis abiecerunt et spreuerunt has aquas
Iordanis sanctissimas. per quas sue iniquitatis et ignorancie lepra mundaretur, et elegerunt pocius
Abnar et Pharphar, fluuios Damasci [*cf. 2 Kgs 5:12*], ocupaciones videlicet et voluptates huius
seculi, in quibus quanto profundius lauerint, tanto amplius sordidantur, ita vt sicut populus, sic
et sacerdos <Quinymmo si malus populus, peior sacerdos>. In gestu namque sunt histriones,
in conuictu nebulones, in affectu Citherones, in templis simulacra, in curiis <tonitrua, in lucris
Argi, in laboribus Tantali, in curis> Dedali, in cubilibus Sardanapalli, sed in sacris scripturis
meditandis seu predicandis stolidissimos poteris intueri," W-16, f. 56.

[91] "Presertim cum ex eisdem scripturis defencionis sibi scutum assumant. Si obicias siquidem
quod quilibet talium insipiens est, respondit 'Per insipienciam mundi decreuit Deus saluare
credentes.' Dic quod iuuenis est, monstrabit seniores a Daniele puero condempnatos. Percussor
est? Sic Petrus serui principis sacerdotum auriculam amputauit. Vinolentus est et deditus gule?
Et Christus dictus est potator vini et carnium deuorator," W-16, f. 56.

[92] W-125, f. 237vb, with reference to Ovid, *Epistle 20*.

subjects by their preaching? Whence is it that they try with much greater zeal to understand canon and civil law than philosophy over which the knowledge of the gospel rules?"[93] It is avarice, he answers, the "inordinate desire for worldly goods." That urge also lies behind simony, the selling and buying of spiritual graces,[94] one of the major failings for which pastors will have to give an account when, at the Last Judgment, they will be asked, "how did you enter?": "Who brought you in [i.e. to the pastoral office], truth or deceit? God or the devil? Grace or money? The flesh or the spirit?"[95] Higher prelates specifically are often chastized for their nepotism, for providing benefices or funds for their relatives and concubines. FitzRalph apparently observed a good deal of it:

> Travel through the provinces and look at the cathedral churches: you will find them full of flesh and blood – I mean the bishops' nephews and great-nephews . . . I have heard of a certain prelate who gave a fat benefice to a young man among his relatives. When someone asked him why he did not confer that on a doctor, since he had several good ones in his diocese, he replied: "I cannot throw a heavy stone far, nor even lift it to my knees."[96]

In contrast, the lower clergy are accused of negligence and sloth in doing their spiritual work. In the ship of the devil called Vice, "the prelates of the Church row with the oar of simony, the lower clergy with the oar of sloth, and the religious, such as friars, monks, and others, with the oar of hypocrisy."[97] Neglect of pastoral duties, torpor in saying their prayers, pusillanimity in governing their flock,[98] and failure to speak out and announce the truth are all too common

---

[93] "Vnde queso est quod viri ecclesiastici plus vacant scienciis lucratiuis quam speculatiuis? Vnde est quod plus intendunt litigiis placitando quam sermonibus suos subditos informando? Vnde est quod diligenciori studio nituntur cognoscere iura canonica et ciuilis [!] quam philosophiam quam sciencia euangelica dominetur?" W-125, f. 238va.

[94] FI-34, in Gwynn, "Two Sermons," pp. 60–62.

[95] "Igitur questio prima querenda a primo villico, vicelicet a rectore animarum, erit ista: Qualiter intrasti. 'Amice, qualiter huc intrasti?' Mathei 22. Quis te introduxit, veritas vel dolus, Deus vel diabolus, gracia vel nummus, caro vel spiritus?" Wimbledon's Sermon in A-48, f. 141.

[96] "Transite per prouincias et considerate ecclesias cathedrales, et inuenietis eas plenas carne et sanguine: nepotes et pronepotes episcoporum intelligo . . . Audiui a quodam prelato qui vnum pingue beneficium dederat vni iuueni de suis nepotulis. Cum quidam ab eo quesierat cur illud non contulit vni doctori, cum in sua diocesi plurimos valentes haberet, ipse respondit: 'Grauem lapidem non possum ad remota proicere, set nec ad genua mea leuare,'" FI-70, f. 138.

[97] "Cum remo simonie remigant ecclesiastici prelati; cum remo accidie inferiores curati; cum remo ypocrisis religiosi, vt fratres, monachi, et alii," E-24, f. 67vb. A similar distinction between higher and lower clergy appears in Z-33, in a passage taken from *Fasciculus morum* V.iii (*Fasciculus morum*, p. 416), though here *accidia* is said to be a vice of both lower and higher clergy.

[98] See for example P1-3.

vices. Of course the fault does not always lie with the lower clergy. "Often a simple priest is not promoted just for his holiness but rather, if he can cheat others in computation and . . . to acquire goods the wrong way, then he will be deemed worthy of promotion."[99]

Such concerns with specific moral failings among priests echo thirteenth-century synodal decrees, and in that they are joined by another topic: their required knowledge and dissemination of catechetical matters. As we observed earlier, in the wake of Lateran IV English bishops were much concerned with stressing the need to preach basic Christian doctrine to the people and occasionally even promulgated useful summaries of the Ten Commandments, the seven deadly sins, the seven sacraments, and other catechetical units at a synod. There is some evidence that this practice continued into the later fourteenth and fifteenth centuries. Rimington's synodal sermon of 1372, for example, not only warns against unchastity, going to taverns, and *curiositas* in dress, hairdo, and behavior, but also exhorts priests to know Scripture, canon law, penitentials, and the differences between sins, and it then includes a listing of the seven deadly sins and aspects of Christ's passion against each. Similarly, the first synodal sermon by the Hereford preacher offers a brief exposition of the seven sacraments. In his sermon 43, directed to the clergy of London, Bishop Brinton discusses the first four commandments and then goes into the sacraments, singling out matrimony for more extensive treatment. And a sermon in Cambridge, University Library, MS Ii.3.8 (A-43), on "You teach the way of God in truth" (Matthew 22:16), addressing "Reuerendi domini" and dealing with "first how a curate of souls or a preacher of the word of God must teach the people, and secondly what he must teach," treats the seven beatitudes and the seven gifts of the Holy Spirit at some length.[100] As we shall see again in a later chapter, knowledge of and preaching the *pastoralia* was an integral part of the priestly office, and sermons *ad clerum* addressed the obligation repeatedly and sometimes in detail.

A final topic that is occasionally voiced in *ad clerum* sermons to be noted is their concern with political matters. Here the preacher goes beyond clerical duties and failings and addresses larger issues that concern the realm. Three sermons

---

[99] "Vnde simplex sacerdos raro promouetur solum propter sanctitatem; tamen si nouit in compoto defraudare alios et reddit dm' dm' iuuare et sic bona modo falso adquirere, tunc reputabitur dignus promocione," Z-3, f. 7ra. A good passage on the range of priestly failings occurs in Lychlade's sermon "for which he was banished" from the university of Oxford: Wenzel, "Robert Lychlade's Oxford Sermon," pp. 210–215; but the accusations he makes can be found in unquestionably orthodox sermons as well.

[100] A-43: "Primo qualiter curatus animarum siue predicator verbi Dei debet docere populum; secundo quid docere," f. 152. The seven beatitudes occupy ff. 152v–154v.

ad clerum by Bishop Brinton are particularly noteworthy. In BR-13, which he says he is preaching on the subject of peace "according to the mandate of my superior," he concludes with a reference to an embassy to be sent to the papal curia; hence its modern editor opined that the sermon was given at the provincial convocation meeting at St. Paul's in 1373.[101] Brinton here speaks against disunity among the higher clergy in face of secular encroachments on Church rights and property, and against those who run to the curia with letters from their (temporal) lords, divulging state secrets and pointing to ecclesiastic openings and "fat prebends," and then reporting back that the pope is French and does not like the English. Against such and similar abuses the clergy should stand firm. The latter point is made again in BR-85:

> Let us stand together, according to Isaiah 50:8, prelates, princes, clergy, and commons, resolving with one mind that nothing be received into the realm from the antipope that could contravene the right pope, favor the antipope, or separate us in any way from firm belief.

Brinton also complains that lay lords no longer submit themselves to their ordained pastors and ordinaries but seek out "someone who is completely inexperienced in the cure of souls"; and in their opposition to ecclesiastical censure and teaching, they collect "extraordinary masters who tickle their ears," particularly with respect to disendowing the Church.[102] These topics are sounded again in BR-92, preached on the Translation of St. Thomas of Canterbury and addressing "vos curati et precipue maiores prelati." It may be necessary, Brinton says, especially nowadays, to treat temporal lords with kid gloves rather than coercion, "but they should not be coddled to the permanent harm of the Church," as certain penitentiaries and confessors of temporal lords do with their false patience and considerateness.[103] Brinton's critique of weak-kneed pastors had already been sounded by FitzRalph in one of his synodal sermons:

> This is a great evil in God's Church: prelates do not dare defend the rights of the Church. Against them it behooves us, in my judgment, to establish some new penalty, for canons are made in vain lest they are observed by the pastors. Hence it is necessary that prelates have special courage.[104]

What is perhaps new in Brinton's preaching is the concern about disunity in the realm, a topic that occupied a major place in the political discourse in the period of, roughly, 1380 to 1420, in sermons as well as in secular works such as Gower's

---

[101] Brinton, *Sermons*, p. 49.   [102] BR-85, ibid., pp. 387–388.
[103] BR-92, ibid., pp. 422, 424.
[104] F-34; in Gwynn, "Two Sermons," p. 57.

poetry. Another collection that deals much with national unity and glory is the first, macaronic set of MS Bodley 649. Unfortunately it lacks any rubrics that might indicate the occasions of these sermons, but many use "Reuerendi domini" and similar titles as their address forms, and some speak directly to curates and deal with the priestly office.[105]

---

[105] Especially O-20 and 21, both entirely in Latin. See the previous discussion of that collection in Part I, section 14.

42

Monastic preaching

In the previous sketch of episcopal preaching we have noticed the occasional involvement of members of the religious orders – both monks and friars – as preachers at synods and visitations. We now turn to their preaching closer to home.

By the fourteenth century, Western monasticism could look back at a millennium of distinguished preaching and sermon-making, which, in the twelfth century, had reached its golden age with such figures as Isaac of Stella, Aelred of Rievaulx, Bernard of Clairvaux, the Victorines, and a host of others. By 1350, those glories were long past, and while Bernard's sermons on Canticles continued to be read and quoted, monks were no longer producing important sermon collections or well-known preachers. That achievement had passed on to the new mendicant orders, who, with their emphatic dedication to scripture studies and to public preaching, took the lead and breathed a powerful new life into preaching the word of God. As a sign of what monks lost in this development, we find, for instance, that major monastic houses had come to employ friars as lectors and as preachers in their cathedrals.[1] But at the same time, around 1350, monks were beginning to foster a new interest in preaching. Again the impetus can be located in directions from above: Pope Benedict XII, himself a Cistercian monk, issued a set of reforming constitutions for Cistercians (1336), Benedictines (1336), and Augustinian Canons (1339) that, among other things, called for the establishment of common houses of studies at the universities to which individual monasteries were to send a specified number of their members and support them with monetary contributions.[2] Their university study was explicitly oriented to the work of preaching. An English Benedictine provincial chapter enjoined that monk

---

[1] See the following chapter on Friars. Barbara Harvey has provided new evidence that the practice of "borrowing" friars as preachers in monasteries continued into the fifteenth century: "Novice's Life," pp. 53 and 70.

[2] Knowles, *Religious Orders*, 2:3–8. On the Augustinian Canons at Oxford, Forde has assembled a good deal of material in "Writings," 1:55–108 . On the three constitutions of Benedict XII see also McDonald, "Papacy."

students in philosophy and in theology and those sent from their monasteries to the university were to study

> not that they may reach the height of a master in theology or acquire the degree of bachelor, but rather that they learn there duly to preach the word of God to others and to become more able in disputing and preaching.[3]

Their teachers apparently continued to be friars. When the Benedictine John of Sheppey, who was to become bishop of Rochester, studied at Oxford in the 1330s, he collected at least two volumes of sermons, one of which contains a large number by named Dominican and Franciscan preachers, often forming entire booklets.[4] A few years later, Thomas de la Mare, before he became abbot of St. Albans (1349–1396), was prior at Tynemouth for nine years, three of which he spent

> in studying the preaching of the word of God, in both English and Latin. For which he always kept with him clerics and masters, both secular and mendicants, who also were to teach him in this work. Thus it happened that, when he became abbot, he was prepared and knew how to "bring forth new things and old" [Matthew 13:52] both to his monks and to people outside the monastery.[5]

De la Mare left no known record of his own preaching, but other monastic preachers did of theirs, and these collections are clear witnesses that Owst's view of "the actual dearth of fresh monastic sermon literature for the period under our examination" needs to be rectified.[6]

[3] "De hiis autem qui ad Universitatem mittuntur, non ob aliam causam nisi ut ibidem addiscant aliis rite proponere verbum Dei, statuimus ut illi, juxta dispositionem Prioris et saniorum studentium, in loco nostro communi Oxoniae, vel alibi, ubi Prior ipse et saniores decreverint, frequenter tam in lingua Latina praedicent, quam vulgari, ut sic id audacius, promptiusque, perficiant, cum eos ad sua Monasteria contigerit revocari." Constitutions of the Provincial Chapter of the English Black Monks, probably 1363; Pantin, *Documents* 2:75–76.

[4] See Part One, section 2.

[5] "In hujusmodi actibus, contiguisque profectibus, apud Tynemutham consummavit Prioris officium novem annis; e quibus, ut praemittitur, tres primos annos, necessarie placitando, transegit in magnis angustiis et labore; tres vero medios in studio praedicandi verbum Dei, tam in lingua Anglica quam Latina. Ac propter hoc, secum detinuit semper clericos et magistros, tam saecularis habitus, quam Ordinis Mendicantium, qui eum etiam in hoc opere informarent. Unde contigit quod expost factus Abbas in promptu habuit, atque scivit, unde proferret nova et vetera, tam suis monachis, quam externis. Nam cum factus esset Praesidens in Capitulis Generalibus, tam constanter praedicavit, tam constanter docuit, quid agendum monachis, ut favorem et gratiam sibi conciliaret omnium auditorum. Novissimis tribus annis quibus apud Tynemutham Prioris egit officium, murorum et domorum reparationibus, sive constructionibus, non segniter insudavit." Walsingham, *Gesta Abbatum*, 2:380.

[6] Owst, *Preaching*, p. 49. He continues to say that *sermones ad claustrales* or *ad religiosos* for the fourteenth century "are practically non-existent" (ibidem). Ironically, one of Owst's major sources, quoted again and again, is Robert of Rypon, Benedictine monk of Durham. See Horner, "Benedictines . . . in Fifteenth-Century England," and "Benedictines and . . . *Pastoralia*."

Walsingham's notice just quoted about Thomas de la Mare makes an interesting distinction between preaching "to his monks" and "to *externi*." The former very probably referred to the abbot's preaching at the daily chapter, while the latter seems to envision his addressing monks from other houses, and Walsingham in fact goes on to report De la Mare's preaching at the general chapter of the Black Monks.[7] The daily in-house chapter formed an essential part of a monk's life and formation and continuing strife for greater devotion and holiness. Held daily or, in smaller communities, at least once a week, it included reading of a section of the Rule of St. Benedict or other legislative texts of the order, an occasion for individual monks to confess their transgressions (or accuse others publicly) and be corrected, and an address given by the abbot or prior. In all likelihood, St. Bernard's *Sermons on Canticles* had originated in precisely this practice of daily monastic life.[8] That the practice continued, or at least was supposed to continue, in our period is shown by chapter directives in the monastic orders.[9] The collections studied here hold at least two chapter sermons of this kind. One has been preserved in the notebook of John Lawerne from the 1440s and bears the rubric "The first sermon of Dom John Lawerne, monk of the Blessed Virgin at Worcester, at the vigil of the Assumption of Blessed Mary, in the chapter house."[10] The other is anonymous and said to have been preached in 1435 "in domo capitulari Cant'."[11]

We are even better informed about the provincial and general chapters. The chapter acts of the English Black Monks especially yield a detailed picture of the preaching that went on at those occasions.[12] After 1336, their two English provinces were required to meet together every three years, usually in Northampton, and there they followed a set program which evidently had developed over a century.[13] As the chapter opened, all the abbots and priors and other clergy who had come to Northampton would, at the sign of a bell, assemble to

---

[7] See note 5 above. Walsingham also reports that De la Mare preached in Latin, English, and French, *Gesta abbatum*, 3:409–410.

[8] Holdsworth, "Were the Sermons."

[9] For the Black Monks see Pantin, *Documents* 2:40 (Statutes of provincial chapter, 1343); *Customary* 1:224. These directives only speak of expositions of the Rule, as do similar directions for the White Monks; but see Lekai, *Cistercians*, p. 366: "On more festive occasions the abbot was expected to deliver an appropriate sermon"; and *"Ecclesiastica Officia"*, p. 467 n. 243.

[10] "Primus sermo dompni Iohannis Lawarne monachi Beate Marie Wygornie in vigilia assumpcionis Beate Marie in domo capitulari," Oxford, Bodleian Library, MS Bodley 692, ff. 121–123v, at 121.

[11] K-9, ff. 224v–227, at 224v.

[12] Especially those of 1343; see Pantin, *Documents* 2:58–61.

[13] The following description is adapted from Wenzel, *Monastic Preaching*, pp. 3–4. Some of the practices described are also recorded for earlier chapters, both before and after the two provinces were united in 1336.

hear a Mass of the Holy Spirit. When Mass was over, the bell would ring again, and the attendants then proceeded to the chapter house, where they put on their monastic habits and listened to a sermon, which was preached in Latin "as it was fitting." When that was over, all secular clergy had to leave, and the business of the chapter began in earnest. Two days later, the chapter would close with another procession, Mass, and sermon, but this one was to be given "to the people in the vulgar tongue," presumably English. Just before these closing ceremonies, the chapter had already selected preachers who were to give these two sermons at the next provincial chapter three years later. Records of these chapters furnish the names of several preachers appointed to give chapter sermons, in Latin or English, and occasionally even mention their chosen thema.[14]

Other orders observed a similar program. The Augustinian Canons, about whose chapters, too, we are well informed, including the names of appointed preachers, had sermons at their general chapters from the early thirteenth century on. Of the recorded chapters, pride of place surely belongs to that held at Osney in 1445. Almost two hundred participants had gathered who, in the morning of the second Sunday after Trinity, moved in procession to the church of St. Frideswide.

> In the cemetery of this church the reverend president, the abbot of St. Osithe [Osney], offered a solemn sermon in English, elegantly composed, before the chancellor of the bountiful university of Oxford, the prelates of his order, doctors, masters, scholars, and others gathered in a great crowd.[15]

Then a Mass of the Holy Spirit was said. On the following day

> Dom Ralph Seyton, canon of Leicester and student at the university of Oxford, kneeled before the presidents of the chapter and received their blesssing to preach the word of God. After that he stood up, and standing next to the presidents he gave a sermon in Latin, very useful and not wanting in rhetorical art, to which he had been appointed in the preceding provincial chapter.[16]

---

[14] For some examples see Pantin, *Documents* 2:12–13, 15, 19–20, 23, 26, 97, 135, 155, etc.

[15] "In cuius ecclesie cimitorio prefatus Reuerendus dominus presidens abbas sancte Osithe solempnem sermonem in Anglicis coram Cancellario alme Uniuersitatis Oxonie, / prelatis eiusdem ordinis, doctoribus, magistris, scolaribus, et aliis in maxima multitudine tunc ibidem existentibus proposuit eleganter." *Chapters of the Augustinian Canons*, pp. 86–87.

[16] "Dominus Radulphus Seytone canonicus Leycestrie et scolaris Uniuersitatis Oxonie, prostratus coram presidentibus, acceptauit benedictionem ad pronunciandum uerbum dei, et accepta benedictione erexit se, et collocatus iuxta presidentes sermonem ualde utilem dictamine non carentem proposuit in Latinis, prout in capitulo prouinciali ultimo celebrato ad hoc fuerat deputatus," ibid., p. 88.

Finally, on Tuesday,

> at seven in the morning, when the presidents and others had come together in the chapter house as before, the most honorable father and president, the abbot of Osney, gave a well-composed solemn sermon in Latin, in which he, like a father, refreshed his brethren and all who were there like a father with the nourishment of God's word.

After which the chapter ended, having issued among other things a *forma capituli* which indeed speaks of three sermons.[17]

The Cistercians similarly held general chapters, and there is some evidence that here, too, sermons were given.[18] Even the Carthusians, not known for preaching orally, held a general chapter at the Grande Chartreuse, where after the customary initial rites the assembled abbots would hear a sermon, given either by the prior of the Grande Chartreuse or by a deputy.[19]

One feature of the regular business conducted at general chapters was to appoint brethren who were to visit the houses in a province. As did episcopal visitations, monastic visitations also included some preaching. Thus, in 1393 two monks from Ramsey Abbey, who had been commissioned by the General Chapter, arrived to visit St. Albans and preached a sermon before beginning the actual inquiry, and then, the next morning, another "brief collation in praise of the religious life and the men of the monastery."[20]

A particular form of monastic preaching relates to one of Henry V's religious foundations, the Bridgettine house at Syon (founded in 1415, first professions in 1420).[21] The double monastery, modeled after St. Bridget's own house at Vadstena, Sweden, and strongly influenced by the Benedictine order, especially St. Albans, was to hold sixty nuns and twenty-five men including twelve priests and four deacons. These priests were to "expound each Sunday the gospel of the day at Mass to all listeners in their mother tongue" and further "to preach openly" on solemn festivals.[22] Their listeners would have been primarily the nuns,

---

[17] "Mane hora septima, presidentibus et aliis in dicta domo capitulari ut supra insimul congregatis, prehonerandus pater et dominus presidens abbas sancte Osithe sermonem solempnem eleganter protulit in Latinis, fratres et omnes ibidem existentes paternaliter reficiendo pabulo verbi dei," ibid., p. 91.

[18] See *Statuta capitulorum generalium*, statute of 1389, § 32 (3:565) and of 1446, § 85 (4:601). The earlier *Carta caritatis* gives rules for attending the general chapter but does not mention a sermon; see Lekai, *White Monks*, Appendix II.

[19] E. M. Thompson, *Carthusian Order*, p. 252.

[20] Walsingham, *Gesta abbatum*, vol. 2, Appendix C, p. 409.

[21] On the founding of Syon and its library see now *Syon Abbey*, pp. xxix–lxv. The survival of sermons by brothers of Syon has been investigated by Powell, "Preaching at Syon Abbey."

[22] *Regula Saluatoris*; see *Syon Abbey*, p. xxxii.

although it is quite likely that religious and lay visitors were also present. Syon Abbey acquired a remarkable library, whose holdings were carefully and in detail catalogued at the beginning of the sixteenth century. This *Registrum* by Thomas Betson and several helpers or successors lists a large number of manuscripts and early printed books that contained sermon collections and preaching materials. I believe it is this library, and beyond it the particular spirituality of Syon and its twin foundation, the Carthusian house at Sheen, that are reflected in one collection of *sermones*, although these would hardly have been preached as they stand.[23]

Returning to Walsingham's distinction between "his monks" and "*externi*," one may wonder whether the latter could also refer to a non-monastic audience. Medieval canon law forbade monks the cure of souls,[24] but there is some evidence in monastic rituals that monks did deliver sermons *coram populo*. This would of course have been natural in the monastic cathedrals, and records tell us that such was indeed the case at Durham,[25] Worcester, and other cathedral priories.[26] And an entry in the expense accounts from Durham priory records Robert Rypon, evidently the well-known preacher whose sermons are extant, as preaching in neighboring villages.[27] But non-cathedral monasteries also had sermons to the people, as we know from Westminster,[28] St. Albans,[29] and Bury St. Edmunds.[30]

Such monastic preaching, whether before the congregation at home or more officially at chapters and visitations, has survived in a number of collections. Robert Rypon prepared a collection of sermons that are carefully worked out and evidently represent the fruit of his labors over more than a decade. He is only one of a number of Benedictine monks who can be linked to preserved sermons; in fact, his order's contribution to extant collections far outdistances that of the other monastic orders in our period. Thomas Brinton, during his episcopacy, continued to address his monks at Rochester. Monks from Durham priory seem to have authored at least some of the sermons in Cambridge, Jesus College,

---

[23] Collection CO; see Part One, section 19.   [24] See Constable, "Monasteries."

[25] An account of medieval monastic practices at Durham, written c. 1600, speaks of monks preaching to the people regularly: *Rites of Durham*, pp. 39, 46, 88.

[26] Greatrex, "Benedictine Monk Scholars" and "Benedictine Sermons."

[27] See above, p. 66, n. 1.

[28] See Barbara Harvey, *Living and Dying*, p. 158.

[29] When in 1452 John of Whethamsted was elected for a new term as abbot of St. Albans, he listed a series of complaints that called for reformation, including the preaching of the brethren in the pulpit, "since for several years there has hardly been a *confrater* who was willing to take this task upon him and to preach God's word there in Lent before the people (*coram populo*)," *Registrum Abbatiae Johannis Whethamstede*, p. 25.

[30] The Bury St. Edmunds *Rituale* orders that on Maundy Thursdy "fiat sermo populo coram magno altari" (MS Harley 2977); James, *On the Abbey*, p. 185.

MS 13 (J/5). At Worcester priory two major collections were made or housed, W and X. The latter is less a direct witness to Benedictine preaching than to the order's interest in making and keeping sermon collections, since it gathers material from various sources, some Benedictine, others mendicant.[31] In contrast, W clearly and beautifully reflects monastic preaching and mentions several monk preachers. Its texts cover the range from chapter sermons to preaching *ad populum*. Two further collections, O and R, equally come from and reflect Benedictine milieux. The first section of O was certainly composed by a Benedictine monk, a writer and preacher who cultivated very much his own style. He may have been John Paunteley, monk at Gloucester, whose name appears in the other collection, R, as the book's owner and preacher of a funeral sermon. He may well have collected the sermons in R while he was at Oxford.[32]

Collection R just cited also contains a sermon for the General Chapter of the Cistercians. A series of local chapter sermons given at Dore Abbey and dating from earlier in the fourteenth century have survived in two manuscripts.[33] Otherwise, the English White Monks are poorly represented by surviving sermons in our period;[34] only the two synodal sermons by Rimington can be linked to their order, which may come as a surprise, since the Cistercians could boast of a distinguished history of preaching and of writing and collecting sermon cycles as well as aids for preachers.[35] In contrast, the Augustinian Canons have left more texts: John Repingdon and John Mirk composed systematic sermon cycles, and at least some of the sermons in Hereford Cathedral MS O.iii.5 (E) are connected with an unspecified Augustinian house. The English Carthusians, lastly, are represented in the surviving collections by John Dygon, whose great interest in sermons we noticed earlier.[36]

Monastic contributions to the preaching at visitations and synods have already been discussed in connection with preaching by bishops. From the other important and genuinely monastic official occasion in our period, the general chapter, four sermons have survived: three from Benedictine chapters, and one from the general chapter of the Cistercians, which was traditionally held at Cîteaux,

---

[31] On sermon collections and preachers' aids in medieval monastic libraries, see Greatrex, "Benedictine Sermons," pp. 257–278. For the medieval sermon collections still extant in the Worcester Cathedral library, see R. M. Thomson, *Descriptive Catalogue . . . Worcester Cathedral*, p. xxix.

[32] The collections mentioned in this and the following paragraph were discussed above, Part One.

[33] British Library, MSS Royal 7.A.viii and 8.A.v. Sharpe, *Handlist*, p. 512, attributes them to abbot Richard Straddell (died 1346).

[34] An earlier manuscript of c. 1300, Cambridge University Library, Additional MS 2943, contains thirty-six sermons evidently of Cistercian origin: at least three are "De sancto Bernardo," and the saint is frequently referred to as "pater noster."

[35] Rouse, "Cistercian Aids."   [36] Part One, section 18.

though not during the Great Schism. All are distinguished by their heightened rhetoric. They are learned, and were composed and delivered *eleganter*. This is especially true of the chapter sermon given by Dr. John Fordham of Worcester, president of the general chapter from 1420 to 1426.[37] A second chapter sermon in the same manuscript is anonymous and has no address forms; it gives an interesting if sweeping survey of the development and history of monasticism.[38] The third sermon, preserved incomplete in a different manuscript, is said to have been given at Northampton and at one point addresses "pater pacientissime," which would mean that it was not spoken by the chapter president but by a monk assigned to this task.[39] All three sermons remind the abbots that they have assembled for the reform of errors and moral defects, and emphasize the need for an exemplary life in the prelates, for obedience in the monks, and for unity in the entire order. John Fordham points to the poor reputation of the monks among the people, while the other chapter sermon in W addresses especially the need to support monk students.

The Cistercian chapter sermon R-6 is considerably less concerned with monastic reform, and apart from the rubric "Sermo capitulo generali" and frequent references to "hoc sacrum collegium," it contains little that would link it to a monastic general chapter. Lengthy, learned, and essentially devotional, it unfolds its thema "Every one had four faces" (Ezechiel 1:6) into four kinds of unity, which are applied to the four liturgical occasions celebrated around the date of the General Chapter: the chapter itself, the Nativity of the Blessed Virgin (Sept. 8), the Exaltation of the Holy Cross (Sept. 14, the traditional date for the General Chapter), and the "Blessed Martyrs."[40] Each part is subdivided and developed at some length, and at the end of the first principal part the preacher shows how unity of consent, which establishes the dignity of monastic life and is manifested in "this sacred gathering," applies to the four daughters of Cîteaux: La Ferté, Pontigny, Clairvaux, and Morimond, who are mentioned seriatim with appropriate puns on their names.

---

[37] W-71. The beginning of this sermon is quoted and translated in Wenzel, *Macaronic*, pp. 128–129.

[38] Edited by Pantin, "Sermon."

[39] London, BL, Cotton MS Titus C.ix, ff. 26–27v. It asks the audience to pray for "illustrissimum principem regem nostrum ceterosque sub suo vexillo in armis militantes, quibus post datum triumphum annuente altissimo perpetua succedat cum felicitate tranquillitas duratura." If *post datum triumphum*, "after they have been given the triumph," refers to Agincourt, the sermon would have been preached between 1415 and 1422, or more precisely in 1417 or 1420. In 1417 the sermon in English was given by John Hynton of York; see Pantin, *Documents* 3:185 and 256. The sermon in the Titus MS is in Latin except for a single English verb form: "quod *parled* est" (f. 26v).

[40] The sermon does not specify who "the blessed martyrs" are, but it speaks of their coronation and triumph. The feast of the "Quattuor Coronati" was November 8.

Surviving sermons as well as reports, therefore, leave no doubt that a fair amount of in-house preaching on various occasions went on in English monasteries during our period. We are given a glimpse at this variety in the chronicle made by the Christ Church monk John Stone (1415–1471). He mentions a number of preachers by name, ranging from monks and bachelors in theology to abbots and archbishops, who preached at elections, visitations, funerals, and even before the people, and in several cases Stone records their themata.[41]

As was pointed out earlier, sermons in monastic collections for other than such official occasions often leave it unclear who the intended audience was, although sometimes address forms and internal references indicate whether they were addressed to a lay, or a clerical, or a monastic audience. Those addressing a lay audience are very much like general parish sermons. Sermons seemingly directed to a clerical audience (and here my identification becomes somewhat circular) speak of the pastoral office and of priestly morals and failings. But while in these two areas contents and tone are more or less identical with what they are in late-medieval preaching from any source, monastic sermons gain a more distinctive voice when they address monks themselves. Many speak of the monastic ideal, of the privileges of the monastic life, and reflect on its history, on the basic vows, especially obedience and the social unity that results from it. They call up the vision of an ordered harmony whose main parts have each its special function. Not surprisingly, they also lament the decay of those ideals and the failings of contemporary monks. But beyond the monastery walls is the larger society and its ideal harmony as well as the decadence that is there to see, and much monastic preaching deals with the glories of England's past, its present weakness including the subversive influence of the Lollards, and the new triumph that came with Agincourt. This larger consciousness of history and concern with the state of the nation is very typical of Benedictine preaching; it reflects, of course, the traditional interest in history and in record keeping for which the intellectual life in medieval monasteries is well known. Such concern for the welfare of the realm, itself anchored in the fact that many monastic houses were royal or noble foundations, shows also quite specifically in the *commendatio* at the opening of many sermons, where not only the preacher and his audience, and the living and the dead in general, but also the pope, bishop, king, magnates, and often specific members of the nobility are commended to the congregation's prayers.

Another feature of monastic preaching is its concern with the intellectual life. In addition to direct statements they make about the decline of learning

[41] Stone, *Chronicle.* For the period from the 1420s through the 1440s see pp. 13, 34–36; for post-1450 sermons see pp. 60–61, 78, 106, 109, 143.

and of book-making, many sermons are dressed in a cloak of unmistakable monastic erudition. This shows not only in their wealth of quotations from the Bible, the Fathers, Aristotle, theologians, and canon law, which one finds in non-monastic sermons as well, but also, and more specifically, in their use of classical material. Often a lament at social decay uses the trope of Fortune's wheel, with precise quotations from Boethius or Alan of Lille.[42] And in general, monastic sermons draw on a wide range of Classical authors with quotations that are not of the common run of the mill. Their authors share this custom with the "classicizing friars" of the fourteenth century, but there is a qualitative difference in that monastic sermons reach farther, and the borrowed learning becomes more intimately part of their verbal texture. That texture itself is highly wrought, especially when the pulpit discourse becomes a panegyric on learning, on monastic ideals, or on the Blessed Virgin; at these moments, these texts gain a syntactic complexity and lexical preciousness that are very reminiscent of the aureate diction in contemporary vernacular poetry.[43]

[42] See Wenzel, "Why the Monk?"

[43] I have not discussed the Premonstratensians, or "white canons," in this chapter because we lack documentation of their preaching in England. The order was permitted to hold parishes with, presumably, some cure of souls. See Gribbin, *Premonstratensian*, especially pp. 1–2. Gribbin's account is primarily based on visitation and other records from the second half of the fifteenth century. He discusses a collection of vernacular sermons on pp. 160–162.

43

The Friars

From the early thirteenth century on, the driving force behind the new effort to preach God's word were the mendicant orders. The Dominicans, whose order was founded specifically "for preaching and the salvation of souls," built an educational system to train future preachers;[1] and their example was followed in no time by the Franciscans,[2] Carmelites,[3] and Austin (or Augustinian) Friars (also called "Hermits," though they were sent into the world to preach).[4] By 1350 and into the next hundred years their work had been thoroughly integrated into the preaching mission of the Church. Beyond training their own successors in their conventual and provincial schools, their well-educated theologians would lecture at the universities, and many would produce basic handbooks on sermon making.[5] Many in fact also served as lectors to young members and priests in the older, monastic orders.[6] Monks and canons at major cathedrals are reported to have relied on Dominicans and Franciscans to preach the sermons demanded

[1] Mulchahey, "*First the Bow*"; the quotation, from the Constitutions of 1220, occurs on p. 3.

[2] A general survey of preaching among the medieval Franciscans was given by Moorman, *History*, pp. 272–277. In contrast to the Dominicans, the early Franciscans were rather secretive about their constitutions, but it seems clear that to a large extent they followed the Dominican example; see Brooke, *Early Franciscan*. Roest, *History*, offers a very useful summation and digest of older literature on the entire subject. He deals with the training of preachers especially on pp. 272–324 and expresses some caveats about the older view that the early Franciscans followed the Dominican model of education in chapter 1, esp. pp. 1–6.

[3] See Haren, "Friars," p. 512.

[4] Roth, *English Austin*, 1:142 n. 257, 196, 201–202.

[5] For Dominican aids to preaching, see Mulchahey, "*First the Bow*", pp. 400–479; for Franciscan works, Little, *Studies*. See also d'Avray, *Preaching*, pp. 64–90, to which should be added preaching encyclopedias such as Bromyard's *Summa praedicantium*. The more general studies of medieval preaching also have sections devoted to preaching tools: Longère, *Prédication*, pp. 177–202; and Schneyer, *Geschichte*, pp. 178–185.

[6] For Franciscan lectors at monasteries, see Little, *Grey Friars*, p. 47; and "Franciscan School," pp. 820–821. For the practice in the later fifteenth century, see chapter 42, p. 292 and n. 1.

by their statutes.[7] But most importantly, friars had their own churches, often impressive buildings with ample space for large audiences and located not far from the regular parish church. And beyond these, they would go through the country, usually in pairs, and preach, either in parish churches or in the open, on markets and cemeteries. This inevitably led to competition and a good deal of hostility from the secular clergy, which was already fully ablaze a mere generation after the orders' founding and continued through the later Middle Ages. Naturally many rectors were galled by the friars' right or privilege to come into the parishes and preach, to hear confessions, to bury the dead, and thereby to receive offerings from multitudes that were deeply impressed by a style of preaching more intelligent, more learned, and certainly more lively and entertaining than what their appointed rectors, let alone their ill-educated vicars, had to offer. Antifraternal sentiment ran high, and it has found its almost classical expression in the portraits, or perhaps caricatures, of friars that Boccaccio, Chaucer, Langland, and Gower have left us.[8]

In preaching in their convents[9] and at the university, friars gave examples of what a good sermon should be like. Like their monastic brethren, they also held visitations[10] and chapters,[11] at which a sermon may have been preached. But their fullest impact came in preaching *ad populum*. For this they had, early on, gained a papal mandate. The convoluted history of the friars' privileges has been often told; for our purposes and the period of this study it is enough to quote the relevant decree from the constitution *Super cathedram* of Boniface VIII (1300), renewed by Clement V (1312), and re-enacted in the *Decretals* (promulgated in 1314):

---

[7] At Exeter cathedral, "in the late fourteenth and late fifteenth century . . . the bulk of the preaching was done by the local Franciscan and Dominican friars," Lepine, *Brotherhood*, p. 138. See also Owst, *Preaching*, p. 51.

[8] The literature on antifraternalism is vast; a good survey is Szittya, *Antifraternal Tradition*. For a calendar of the main events in the controversy, see Congar, "Aspects," pp. 44–54. A good sketch appears in Dunbabin, *Hound of God*, pp. 57–59. The controversy had its theological and canonical center in the *proprius sacerdos* of Lateran IV; see further discussion in Part Three, chaper 50.

[9] For conventual preaching among the Dominicans, see Mulchahey, *"First the Bow"*, pp. 184–193. For the Franciscans, the Constitutions of Narbonne (1260) mandate that "fiat sermo fratribus in communi" at the renewal of their tonsure – fifteen times a year, later eighteen or even twenty times; see Bihl, "Statua," p. 58.

[10] The Franciscan constitutions apparently do not mention a sermon at visitation; Bihl, "Statuta," pp. 284–292. But collection Q contains two sermons "in (*or* pro) visitacione fratrum." Occasionally, friars were used by the bishop at his visitation; so Friar John de Monteacuto, DTh, preached at Bishop John Waltham's visitation of Salisbury in 1394; *Register John Waltham*, p. 208.

[11] For chapters general of the Austin friars see *Analecta Augustiniana* 3 and 4; bulletin on studies ibid. vol 5.

We order and ordain that the brethren of the said orders [i.e., Dominicans and Franciscans] may freely preach the word of God to the clergy and the people in their own churches and places as well as in public places, except at the time when prelates of these places want to preach or have a solemn sermon preached before them; at that time the brethren must stop preaching, unless it be the desire of the aforesaid prelates or by some special license. However, these brethren may and are allowed to preach freely in their own *studia generalia*, where by custom sermons to the clergy are given on those days on which it has been customary to preach solemnly; also at funerals and on feasts that are special and particular to these brethren; except at the time, in all these cases, when in order to preach the word of God to the clergy in those places, the bishop or a superior prelate calls the clergy in general together or has the clergy come together for some urgent reason or cause. In parish churches, however, the brethren must in no way dare preach or propose the word of God unless the brethren are invited or called by the parish priests and do so with the parish priests' good will and assent, having asked and received their permission, unless the bishop or a superior prelate mandates preaching to be done by the same brethren.[12]

Though *Super cathedram* did not require that friars be examined and licensed for preaching by the local bishop, through the fourteenth century and beyond, actual practice varied, with some bishops requiring that all itinerant priests be licensed for preaching in a given area.[13] But whatever controversies arose over the friars' privileges, and whatever limitations might be imposed on them, preach they did, and episcopal registers and contemporary chronicles are full of the names of friars who were licensed and preaching in their jurisdiction.

---

[12] "Statuimus et ordinamus, ut dictorum ordinum fratres in ecclesiis et locis eorum, ac in plateis communibus libere valeant clero et populo praedicare ac proponere verbum Dei, hora illa duntaxat excepta, in qua locorum praelati praedicare voluerint, vel coram se facere solenniter praedicari, in qua praedicare cessabunt, praeterquam si aliud de praelatorum ipsorum voluntate processerit ac licentia speciali. In studiis autem generalibus, ubi sermones ad clerum ex more fieri solent diebus illis, quibus praedicari solenniter consuevit, ad funera etiam mortuorum, et in festis specialibus sive peculiaribus eorundem fratrum, possunt iidem fratres et liceat eis libere praedicare, nisi forte illa hora, qua solet ad clerum in praedictis locis Dei verbum proponi, episcopus vel praelatus superior clerum ad se generaliter convocaret, aut ex aliqua ratione vel causa urgente clerum ipsum duceret congregandum. In ecclesiis autem parochialibus fratres illi nullatenus audeant vel debeant praedicare, vel proponere verbum Dei, nisi fratres praedicti a parochialibus sacerdotibus invitati fuerint vel vocati, et de ipsorum beneplacito et assensu, seu / petita licentia fuerit et obtenta, nisi episcopus vel praelatus superior per eosdem fratres praedicari mandaret." Decretals, Clementines 3, tit. 7, cap. 2, "Dudum" (Friedberg 2:1162–1163). *Super cathedram* further established rules about the friars' right to bury lay people who were not their parishioners in their churches and about their right to hear confessions. For the latter, friars needed to be licensed by the local bishop, but in the fourteenth century bishops occasionally combined license to hear confession with that of preaching; see Little, "Licence."

[13] See Kedar, "Canon Law," p. 20.

Given this powerful and often controversial role of the mendicant orders in medieval preaching, foremost the Dominicans and Franciscans,[14] one would like to know how their young members learned their trade. Modern scholars have unearthed much information about the friars' pursuit of higher studies in their *studia generalia* and at the universities, and have furnished ample lists of students' and professors' names and their works, including sermon collections and handbooks for preachers.[15] But we are considerably less well informed about the friars' study and training in sermon making. Of the four orders, only the Dominicans have left detailed information on how they organized their studies at the different levels. In a recent book Michèle Mulchahey has pieced together a finely differentiated picture of the Dominican educational system and includes some discussion of their learning how to preach.[16] For their study of sermon-making the friars had a number of preaching aids to hand, many written by fellow Dominicans: biblical concordances, encyclopedias of preaching matter, collections of model sermons and of *exempla*, and technical treatises on how to preach and make a sermon (the *artes praedicandi*). But beyond studying such preaching aids, "Dominic's sons learned to preach, in the main, by imitation."[17] In their churches and in the chapter houses of their convents they would hear numerous sermons, often given by well-trained and experienced preachers, and would thereby be not only edified but instructed in sermon rhetoric. The select few who were sent on to a *studium generale* to pursue university studies participated in the similar process of learning by hearing and eventually by doing that was part of the university formation in theology. Since by 1350 the other three mendicant orders had been largely imitating the Dominicans' devotion to preaching and their educational organization, we may, I think, assume that the way they trained young friars in preaching also followed the Dominican example.[18]

In the century from 1350 to 1450, all four orders in England left at least some sermons if not entire collections. MS 342 of the Bibliothèque Municipale of Toulouse, written probably at a large Dominican house in the late fourteenth

---

[14] Papal and episcopal legislation often speaks of the Dominicans and Franciscans together, not of all four mendicant orders; see the quotation from *Super cathedram* of Boniface VIII above, and similarly Arundel's *Constitutions* of 1407/1409.

[15] An excellent recent survey of the organization of education in all four orders in medieval England is Cannon, "Panorama" (in English), with older literature. For the Dominicans, see O'Carroll, *Thirteenth-Century Preacher's Handbook*; and Mulchahey, "*First the Bow*".

[16] Mulchahey, ibid., especially "The Making of the Preacher," pp. 184–193.

[17] Mulchahey, ibid., p. 184. For aids to preaching, ibid., pp. 400–479.

[18] For the Franciscans, see Roest, *History*, especially pp. 280–281. For the Austin Friars we have John Waldeby's statement that he composed a cycle of Sunday sermons for his students, presumably at York; see Part One, chapter 5.

and early fifteenth century (collection D), contains among its ninety sermons forty-one that are attributed to named English Dominicans active between the 1330s and the end of the century. The two collections P1 and P2, though devoid of external attributions, contain strong internal indications of Dominican provenance, including frequent citations of the thirteenth-century Dominicans Fishacre, Albertus, Aquinas, and Kilwardby. The work of another earlier Dominican, John Bromyard's *Exhortaciones*, appears in the first section of Cambridge, University Library, MS Kk.4.24.[19] The second part of this manuscript, however, shows Franciscan affiliations (B/2). Similar indications of a Franciscan origin appear in other random collections of the fifteenth century, H and Z. One sermon in S names a Franciscan, "Johannes de Scrata," in its rubric. There is evidence that Henry Chambron, whose name is connected with as many as half a dozen sermons, was a Franciscan. More impressively, the entire collection Q was made by a Franciscan friar, Nicholas Philip, and contains sermons addressed to Franciscan audiences on several different occasions including *in visitacione fratrum* and at the profession of a novice. From the Carmelite order, the names of many preachers are known,[20] but little if any sermon material has survived.[21] Collection Y/1 contains two sermons that are ascribed to a Carmelite friar, and elsewhere two academic sermons by John Haynton of the Cambridge convent, who was regent master at Oxford in 1432, are extant, one of which is marked *sermo examinatorius*.[22] Finally, preaching by the Austin friars is well represented by the work of John Waldeby, a very popular preacher in York and good friend of the abbot of St. Albans, Thomas de la Mare. He left several groups of sermons, some of them explicitly written for his own students.[23]

[19] B/1. For an even earlier Dominican collection of c. 1300 see Wenzel, "Dominican Preacher's Book." Further, some of the model sermons that once were attributed to Thomas de Lisle, OP (d. 1361) but seem to be by a contemporary of Aquinas appear in several later English collections.

[20] John Bale's notes in British Library MS Harley 3838 list many Carmelites from our period who wrote sermons. See now Copsey, "Carmelites." Older studies include Flood, "Carmelite," pp. 166–168; and Clark, "Thomas Maldon," with sermons attributed to him listed on pp. 196–197. See also Owst, *Preaching*, p. 66.

[21] Edden has claimed Carmelite authorship for the collections in Oxford, Bodleian Library, MS Auct. F. infra 1.3 ("Marian Devotion") and in British Library, Royal MS 7.B.i ("Carmelite"). But the latter has been shown to be sermons by Bertrand de la Tour (see Nold, "British Library Royal 7.B.I"). About the former collection, a sequence of 43 sermon-like items on Romans 16:6 and Luke 1:28 and 31, Edden herself is uncertain that they are sermons (as am I), and the Carmelite John Staunch, whose name appears in the colophon, only claimed to have made the *tabula*. For a genuine sermon cycle on the Ave Maria see the work by John Waldeby, Part One, section 5.

[22] In London, BL, MS Harley 5398, ff. 40–45 and 54–59v. See *Formularies* 2:435–438. In addition, Bodleian MS e Musaeo 86 contains, among academic material, a "Sermo Magistri Johannis Hornby Carmelite ad populum de materia tangenti ordinem nostrum" (modern ff. 219va–221vb); it is full of historical references and has been edited by Clark, "Defense."

[23] For the collections mentioned in this paragraph, see the sections in Part One.

As to the contents of mendicant sermons, there is very little that can be added to what has been said about preaching in the parishes in general or about sermons for visitation and general chapters. Regarding style and tone, however, the preaching of medieval friars has for a long time been perceived, in contrast to university and monastic preaching, as being more popular, more affective,[24] or more socially conscious;[25] and some critics would even distinguish different preaching styles that separate Franciscans from Dominicans.[26] There may be some truth in all of this, certainly for the preaching of St. Francis and plausibly for the thirteenth century as well as for the great mendicant preachers in fourteenth-century Italy. But the surviving texts from England during the period with which this study is concerned hardly support such broad claims, and for a more refined assessment we need critical editions and individual studies. Beyond referring the reader to characterizations I have given in the sections devoted to the individual collections, I would make one or two further comments. In extending her pioneering work on biblical exegesis into the fourteenth century, Beryl Smalley found herself "ambushed" to investigate the new interest in "ancient gods and heroes," fostered by seven Dominicans and Franciscans who taught in the second quarter of the century.[27] As a result, she could point to a great deal of material from classical and pseudo-classical sources that entered the mendicant schoolroom and, by implication, the pulpit. Foremost were the moralized *picturae* and images, putative statues or paintings that represented abstract qualities and their attributes. Were these devices in fact utilized in sermons after 1350, and if so, to what extent?[28] They do indeed appear in collections made by mendicant authors or collectors, such as Nicholas Philip, Waldeby (but not Chambron), the two collections I believe are of Dominican provenance (P1 and P2), and D. But these account for only eight or nine out of three dozen instances, and even if we were to attribute further sermons to mendicant authors, their use of moralized *imagines* and *picturae* is relatively small. On the other hand, such images appear in equal or even greater proportion in monastic collections: especially O, but also W, RY, and even E, which is connected with Austin Canons. And what is perhaps more interesting, the monastic author of O brings a pseudo-classical *imago* he found in Ridevall up-to-date by applying it to the contemporary Lollards (O-3). To say the least, then, by the end of the fourteenth century and later, pseudo-classical

---

[24] For example, John V. Fleming speaks of "the emergence throughout Europe of a pervasive and durable 'Franciscan' style in which the conscious manipulation of vicarious emotional experience has become an important element," *Introduction*, p. 186.

[25] See especially Lesnick, *Preaching*.

[26] See my discussion of several such claims as they affect the Middle English lyric, in Wenzel, "Dominican Presence," pp. 322–327.

[27] Smalley, *English Friars*, especially p. 1.

[28] I have previously posed this question and given a tentative answer in Wenzel, "Classics."

lore and the moralized *picturae* had become part of the *koiné* of pulpit rhetoric and were no longer a distinguishing feature of mendicant preaching.

The same holds true of another device of pulpit rhetoric: to prove a point by a series of arguments that are taken in order from human reason, natural law, art, and scripture (in either authoritative quotations or *figurae*).[29] Thus the Austin friar Waldeby proves that God is merciful and compassionate "primo per naturam, secundo per picturam, tercio per scripturam."[30] Another mendicant sermon is entirely built on a similar succession of proofs *per scripturam, picturam,* and *figuram* which show that Christ was a lamb.[31] This technique, which can be found with some variation but always strings together three or more sources of authoritative proof, may be thought to be characteristic of mendicant preaching. One can find its beginnings in the *Summa de vitiis* by the thirteenth-century Dominican William Peraldus, and two major handbooks by English authors that collected and ordered commonplaces for preachers in this way – the *Summa iusticie* and *De lingua* – can be related to the friars.[32] While in our sermon texts this rhetorical pattern occurs but rarely,[33] its most frequent user is not a friar but the secular priest John Felton, who in a fair number of instances declares that a moral point "ostenditur natura, arte, et figura" and then copies such proofs.[34] Limited though this evidence may be, it strongly suggests that by the end of the early fifteenth century this argumentative pattern, too, had become a common feature.

It remains, in this connection, to say a word about affective preaching. In a general way, of course, any preaching is directed not only to the audience's

[29] The pattern exists in a variety of forms; some representative appearances are in B/2-15 ("quod ostenditur natura, racione, et figura"), Bodley 859-1 and parallels ("in natura, arte, sacra scriptura, et exemplo"), J/5-37 ("in natura, arte, figura, et exemplo"), BR-6 and passim ("in natura, scriptura, et figura," p. 11), Z-10 ("natura, ratio, et scriptura"), Felton passim ("natura, arte, et figura"), Q-58 ("per scripturam, per picturam, et per figuram"). Basevorn recommends it in his *Forma praedicandi*, in Charland, *Artes praedicandi*, pp. 269–270 and 315–316 ("in natura, in arte, in historia" and "in natura, in figura, in historia").

[30] WA-42, f. 107v. The *pictura* Waldeby adduces is that of *Jupiter deus amoris*, from *Fulgentius metaphoralis*.

[31] "Hoc ostendo per scripturam, per picturam, et per figuram," Q-58, f. 167; the terms are then repeated at the beginnings of the principal parts. The *pictura* here is that of Christ as lamb commonly depicted in churches (f. 170v).

[32] See Wenzel, "Continuing Life," pp. 142–143, with the prologue of the *Summa iusticie*, ibid., p. 155. The author of the *Summa iusticie* refers to *De lingua* as *tractatus noster* (ibid.). Whether the *Summa iusticie* is by John of Wales, OFM (died perhaps 1285) is not certain. For the *De lingua*, the second half of the thirteenth century and influence from the school of Grosseteste have been recently suggested: Casagrande and Vecchio, *Peccati della lingua*, pp. 141–174.

[33] I have found it in J/3-1 and H-25.

[34] For example, in sermons 1, 19, 21, 30, and others.

understanding but also to their feelings and emotions. A lecture may offer information and new insights, but a sermon must move the heart to reverence, fear,
trust, longing, compassion, love. And a good preacher himself must speak with
some feeling. As William of Auvergne, philosopher, theologian, and bishop of
Paris (died 1249), says of preachers who take great pains to speak of marvelous and
new things with lovely words and try to unravel difficult questions: "Preaching
of this kind without feeling and charity, which is spoken like an assertive and
continuous lecture, leads to sleep rather than sorrow."[35] Instead, William recommends that the preacher use specific *gestus et verba* to arouse fear, compassion,
and other emotions. For the modern reader, the *gestus* of course are lost,[36] but
some *verba* may still be present. In our collections such an affective preaching
style can indeed be found in mendicant sermons. A good example is a Palm
Sunday sermon given in Newcastle in 1435. The preacher, probably Nicholas
Philip himself, begins by explaining that he will combine the gospel of Christ's
entry into Jerusalem and the Passion story, which were both read at Mass on this
day, in his chosen thema of "Laughter shall be mingled with sorrow" (Proverbs
13:14). As he turns to announce the division, he says, "But that I may *move* your
mind and feeling the more . . ." (my emphasis).[37] What may move his audience,
presumably, is first his subject matter: aspects of Christ's passion, here specifically
the honor Christ received from the people at his entry into Jerusalem, which on
Good Friday turned into contempt and condemnation. But the sermon text also
contains some rhetorical devices clearly employed to engage and move the listeners, such as rhetorical questions ("But one may ask: Brother, why did he want
to be honored today and hardly at any other time?")[38] and exclamations ("Oh
how unlike was that 'Take him, take him, crucify him!' to that 'Blessed is he
who comes in the name of the Lord'!").[39] Such appeals to the listeners' compassion, particularly in preaching Christ's Passion, have been seen as hallmarks of
Franciscan preaching. In our collections, they can indeed be found in a number
of sermons of mendicant provenance, especially those in Q. But whether they
may be called *characteristic* of mendicant preaching in our period remains, again,
questionable. A number of "affective" sermons for Passion Sunday and Good
Friday have been preserved in clearly non-mendicant collections or else are hard

[35] Poorter, "Manuel," p. 202.
[36] But see Schmitt, *Raison des gestes*, pp. 279–284 and 400–401.
[37] "Sed vt magis vestram mentem et affectum moueam," Q-41, f. 130.
[38] "Sed posset interrogari: 'Frater, quare hodie et vix vnmquam in aliis temporibus voluit honorari?'"
f. 129v.
[39] "O quam dissimile 'Tolle, tolle, crucifige eum' et 'Benedictus qui venit in nomine
Domini'!" (f. 132); also "Sed heu, aliqui sunt qui nolunt vestimenta sua sternere sed semper
in dorso tenere . . ." (f. 131) and many similar exclamations.

to affiliate with the friars. And the two rhetorical devices mentioned, rhetorical questions and exclamations, occur equally in definitely monastic collections.[40]

It would therefore seem that, in our period, mendicant preaching continued to exist and perhaps even flourish, but it did so *pari passu* with that of monastic and secular preachers.

[40] For example, rhetorical questions in O-14 and particularly 16; exclamations in R-29, W-4 and W-129.

44

University preaching

In the medieval university, giving sermons represented one of the basic academic actitivies, together with lectures and disputations. As Peter the Chanter put it famously near the end of the twelfth century, the graduate in theology had to be proficient in the acts of *legere, disputare, praedicare*.[1] This highlights the fact that in the medieval university, preaching was the end to which all higher study of theology led. But not all university students worked to become full-blown theologians by incepting as masters. We have seen that, from the early fourteenth century on, monks were sent to the university primarily to learn how to preach; and recent studies of the educational organization of the mendicant orders point out that many friars similarly spent some time at the university, not to gain a higher degree but to receive the necessary theological training for their use as future lectors in convents and study houses. To the secular clergy, too, the possibility of some university study had opened up with the constitution *Cum ex eo* of Pope Boniface VIII in 1298, which made it possible for beneficed clergy to take a leave of absence in order to study at the university for a shorter or longer period;[2] and episcopal records of the fourteenth and fifteenth centuries are full of such dispensations. But whether a degree candidate or a priest who simply meant to deepen his theological knowledge, all students were exposed to a good deal of preaching.

Candidates for an advanced degree in theology, then, took an active part in all three academic exercises. As the Oxford University Statutes in the fourteenth century put it:

> Those who are about to incept in theology, before they are admitted to inception, must throughout all theology schools oppose in public, preach in public, and read in public some book from the biblical canon or the *Sentences*.[3]

[1] Peter the Chanter, *Verbum abbreviatum*, PL 205:25; see Baldwin, *Masters*, 1:90 and 107–116.
[2] Boyle, "Constitution."
[3] "Qui / incepturi sunt in theologia, antequam admittantur ad incipiendum in eadem, per omnes scolas theologie publice debent opponere, et respondere, et publice predicare; et aliquem librum

Their preaching comprised several different kinds. First, all bachelors and masters in theology were to give a *sermo publicus* at least once a year. This was scheduled and announced in advance, and a copy of it had to be deposited with the university officials for the benefit of theology students. At both Oxford and Cambridge, this public sermon was held in the respective university church,[4] where there would have been at least one sermon on every Sunday and on a number of feast days, the *dies non legibiles*.[5] Attendance of all students was required, and it was open to the public. Apparently the chancellor himself, too, was required to preach on major feasts.[6] Second, a *sermo examinatorius* was demanded of all candidates before being admitted to their inception as masters. The third type is a sermon with which a bachelor or master would begin his course in either the Bible or the *Sentences*. This was a speech in praise of the text the speaker was to lecture on – either the Bible or Peter Lombard's *Sentences*. It was called *introitus* or *principium* (the latter mostly by modern scholars). It also formed part of the master's inception, as the beginning of his course of lectures which represented a part of his newly acquired rank and duties.

One can safely assume that what the university statutes required in this respect was in fact carried out. Although apparently no copies of the university registers that were to preserve public and examinatory sermons are known to exist, the collections here surveyed do contain a number of actual sermons of all three types. Several examinatory sermons, in the manuscripts identified as such, appear

---

de canone Biblie uel sentenciarum Oxonie in scolis theologie publice legant," *Statuta antiqua*, pp. 49–50. Gibson gives a well documented summary of the requirements in the faculty of theology ibid., pp. cix–cxxii. For further discussion of university preaching, including documents and further literature, see Wenzel, "Academic Sermons." Notice that in 1994 Maieru wrote: "Sermons are the least studied part of university literary production. In this area we must wait for results of further research"; *University Training*, p. 71.

[4] Before 1303 the Oxford Franciscans and Dominicans apparently had their Sunday sermons at their own houses; after that, at St. Mary's. See Forde, "Nicholas Hereford," pp. 208–211. Probably in 1321, Richard de Bury wrote to the pope asking for indulgences "in order to spur the devotion of the faithful on account of the sermons that are preached by a doctor of theology or a bachelor every Sunday at the church of St. Mary the Virgin in Oxford, to the fruitful study of Holy Scripture and the inestimable benefit of the students," item 63 in the *Liber epistolaris Ricardi de Bury*, in *Formularies* 1:75. For Cambridge, see *History of the County*, p. 153.

[5] See the list in Little and Pelster, *Oxford Theology*, p. 175.

[6] In 1382, Robert Rygge of Oxford was accused by the archbishop of delegating known followers of Wyclif to preach in his stead "diebus solemnioribus, quibus ejus incumbebat officio sermones in populo facere," Walsingham, *Historia anglicana*, vol. 2, p. 60. For Cambridge, the chancellor is reported to have preached on the fourth Sunday of Lent (C-45) and on Corpus Christi (C-70). In the thirteenth century, the chancellor of Oxford University, Nicholas of Ewelme (1268 A.D.), preached publicly before clergy and laity; *Munimenta Academica* 1:36; as did Chancellor Simon de Gandavo on Ash Wednesday 1293, whose sermon is preserved in Oxford, New College, MS 92, ff. 94–95v, and has been edited by Pelster in Little and Pelster, *Oxford Theology*, pp. 205–215.

in London, British Library, MS Harley 5398,[7] in the repertory of Cambridge university sermons (C),[8] and in Cambridge, Corpus Christi College, MS 392 (K).[9] *Introitus* similarly tend to be identified as such, and from our period several examples have survived in collection W.[10] Also the notebook of the Worcester monk John Lawerne (1440s) contains his *introitus* to the books of Lombard's *Sentences*.[11] And the Dominican collection D contains two sermons "pro laude sacre scripture," one by Holcot.[12] The academic public sermon, however, is harder to identify. Here one has to rely on address forms that typically include *magistri* and on internal references to the university or its town and perhaps to aspects of student life. Even with a margin of uncertainty it is remarkable how many of the sermons that have been preserved in the century covered by this study are university-related and thus, without having the marks of formal *introitus* or examinatory sermons, must have been given as the required public sermons. Of course not every sermon of this kind needs to have been the required *sermo publicus* preached at the university church. The various religious orders would have had a good many in-house sermons, since we know, for instance, that Benedictine monks were urged to "preach frequently in Latin as well as in the vernacular,"[13] and much preaching must have been done in the Oxford and Cambridge *studia* of the mendicant orders as well. In any case, our sermon collections hold a surprisingly large number of sermons that may be considered to have been delivered at the university.[14]

One must wonder whether an academic speech in praise of scripture or of Peter Lombard's *Sentences* may in fact be considered to be a genuine sermon, whose main concern was to proclaim the word of God as found in the Bible. In their form, *introitus* in our period followed the model of the scholastic sermon

---

[7] First identified by Owst, *Preaching*, pp. 259–62. For the manuscript, see further *Formularies* 2:436–38.

[8] Sermons C-9, 63, 71, 99, 128, 138, 145, and perhaps 73.

[9] K-8, f. 222, an internal reference: "pro huius sermonis examinatorii, licet breuissimi et inculti, processu."

[10] Two sermons rubricated *Introitus Sentenciarum* and three unmarked sermons in praise of Scripture and theology; see Wenzel, "Academic Sermons," with edition of W-22.

[11] Oxford, Bodleian Library, MS Bodley 692, ff. 6v, 10v–11, 11v, 12v–14. On Lawerne see Catto, "Theology after Wycliffism," pp. 268–269; and Dobson, "The Religious Orders 1370–1540," pp. 574–575.

[12] D-59 (Holcot) and 77. See further the university sermons in Padua, Biblioteca Antoniana, MS 515.

[13] Provincial constitutions of 1363; in Pantin, *Documents* 2:76.

[14] See the discussion above of the following collections: C, probably D (Dominican), J/5 (Benedictine), K, Q (Franciscan), R. and W. The material in S is probably by secular preachers. An earlier Dominican collection is Oxford, New College, MS 88; see Wenzel, "Dominican Preacher's Book," p. 190.

structure exactly, with a scriptural thema that is introduced and divided into parts
that are then developed; and they begin with an address and end with the typical
closing formula of a sermon. Now, the practice of beginning a course on the
Bible or the *Sentences* with a eulogy of the subject in sermon form seems to have
spread from theology to other faculties. At Continental universities, *introitus* and
other academic sermons are known to have been preached also in the faculties
of arts and philosophy and of law.[15] From the English universities of our period,
an *introitus* to the study of Aristotle has been preserved,[16] as well as a series of
similar sermons in praise of canon law.[17] Some speeches for these occasions use a
non-biblical thema,[18] while others begin with a text from scripture,[19] but all of
them follow the structure of the scholastic sermon precisely. It would thus appear
that late-medieval preaching and especially the scholastic sermon form provided
a powerful model for many different kinds of public speech-making, both at
the university and elsewhere.[20] Students of course were exposed to a good deal
of regular preaching, whatever their future careers were to be, and it seems that
university regulations that *all* students must hear the weekly university sermon[21]
paid off handsomely.

One other required academic speech, the presentation of degree candidates and
their commendation as persons of knowledge and moral standards, was similarly
shaped by the scholastic-sermon model. In the thirteenth century, such exercises
seem to have been simple presentation speeches, as in the four *commendationes*
for Masters of Arts dating from c. 1270–1310.[22] But in the fifteenth century such
speeches are definitely built as scholastic sermons, beginning with a thema which
is then divided into parts and developed, just as in a characteristic scholastic

[15] For some evidence with further references see Wenzel, "Sermon in Praise," pp. 253–254.

[16] Discussed and edited in Wenzel, ibid.

[17] Logan, "Cambridge Canon Law Faculty." Another case is Oxford, New College, MS 192, the
notebook of Robert Heete (died 1433; see *BRUO* 2:901–902) given by him to the college. It
contains at least one sermon in praise of legal studies, notes for lectures on the *Decretals* (given
1415–16), and other speeches and academic material; see Coxe, vol. 1, New College, p. 73. It is,
thus, a lawyer's parallel to the notebook of Lawerne discussed below. Further, the first item in
collection X (f. 1), titled "Antethema," may be an academic speech or sermon given by a lawyer
("Rogo vt tua excellencia principium incepcionis mee instruat").

[18] For instance, the speech edited in Wenzel, "Sermon in Praise," or some of those discussed and
edited in Fioravanti, "Sermones."

[19] For instance, three of the sermons noted by Fioravanti, ibid., use as their thema *Sapientia foris
predicat* (Prov 1:20, for a speech in praise of grammar and another of logic) and *Bibe aquam de
cisterna tua* (Prov 5:15, in praise of grammar).

[20] See the following chapter on "Other Occasions."

[21] According to the *Statuta aularia*, "all [students] are required to hear mass daily and to attend
university sermons"; Rashdall, *Universities*, 3:374. See also Glorieux, "Enseignement," p. 149.

[22] Lewry, "Four Graduation Speeches."

sermon. But the tone differs. Oxford, Magdalen College, MS 38, for example, contains several examples of academic speeches, including a presentation of three candidates for the doctorate (*inceptores*). This speech begins with a thema from Aristotle's *Metaphysics*, "The sign of a knowledgeable person is the ability to teach," which the anonymous speaker then, in very florid language, formally introduces and divides into three parts, all confirmed with other passages from Aristotle. The first two principals are then developed at length, beginning with a praise of the seven liberal arts and leading to a detailed humorous characterization of the three *inceptores*. The first is a man by the name of Dobbys, and from his name the speaker deduces his character: since his name begins with "Dob," has two syllables, contains a geminated consonant, and end in "bis," this individual is unquestionably a man of duplicitous character. Things then get even worse when poor Dobbys is described as having a large head held high, which shows him to be undisciplined and stolid; large black eyes, which show him to be an imbecile, a fool, and totally without virtue. And so on. The portrait ends with an anecdote of how one evening Dobbys returned to his room drunk, looked through his astrolabe, and thought the sky was falling. This wonderful picture of Oxford life and its inhabitants continues with the other two candidates – all good fun, but clearly not a proper sermon.[23]

Such varied academic sermons and speeches are neatly reflected in an academic notebook written by John Lawerne, a Benedictine monk from the Worcester priory, who studied at Oxford in the 1440s and became a doctor in theology. The notebook, Bodleian Library, MS Bodley 692, is a paper codex of 163 leaves, many of which are unfortunately defective or stained.[24] It presents itself as "Liber M[agistri] I[ohannis] Lawerne" (f. 3v, in a large hand), and Lawerne's name occurs through the volume. With some other matters, such as letters and documents relating to Worcester, the volume covers the range of academic activities in their regular order, from "actus scolastici" (f. 4 top margin) to "lectiones ordinarie."[25] In these folios are included *quaestiones* of Lawerne's teacher, material for the disputation to be held at inception, *introitus* to the four books of Peter Lombard's

---

[23] Oxford, Magdalen College, MS 38, ff. 39v–42v. The three men were Merton scholars receiving the MA in the 1420s. The manuscript was used by Gibson in *Statuta antiqua*, Appendix C ("The Order of Disputations"), pp. 643–647; and the personal parts of the speech were translated in Gibson, "Order of Disputations," pp. 107–108.

[24] *SC* 2:402–403.

[25] "Expliciunt lecciones ordinarie M. Io. Lawerne sacre pagine professor, edite et publice lecte in scolis theologie Oxon' anno Domini millesimo CCCC'o XL'o octauo [et nono, *added*]," f. 163. This section begins on f. 42 with the heading "In nomine Patris et Filii et SS. Incipiunt lecciones ordinarie et disputaciones J. Lawerne in scolis theologicis Oxon'." For the academic material, especially the *quaestiones* recorded, see Catto, "Theology after Wycliffism," pp. 268–269, and Dobson, "Religious Orders," pp. 574–575.

Sentences with brief outlines (*replicaciones*), *introitus* to lectures on the Bible with, apparently, notes for lectures, and other academic documents. Several of these discourses take the form of scholastic sermons as described above: a number of *introitus* for the *Sentences*[26] and the Bible,[27] an inception sermon, various pieces called *Benediccio inceptoris* held at the Divinity School (*in scolis theologicis*),[28] and one *commendacio inceptoris* given at the university church of St. Mary the Virgin.[29] The latter takes as its thema *Propheta magnus surrexit in nobis* ("A great prophet has arisen among us," Luke 7:17). As a *commendatio* the speech praises the doctoral candidate, and it does so by showing that the unnamed candidate is both *magnus* and *propheta*: great – or rather, as it turns out, big – both in character and even more so in body, to whom the words about John the Baptist may be easily applied, "No greater one has arisen among those born of women" (Matthew 11:11) – "none fatter or thicker or more solid or more round/jocund . . ., or heavier in his body passing all others in gravity."[30] About his standing as a prophet we learn that once, when he had prepared a sermon which in part strongly criticized monks, he had a vision in which St. Bernard appeared to him and gave him a hard beating. To this monastic wit and piety Lawerne joins what must be monastic discretion, because in his written text he only calls him "N," though not without the usual punning.[31] This exercise of monastic wit in sermon form ends with a little story about the candidate:

> He does not like to run, and to swim he hates and denounces highly. For he once was going for a swim, but his heaviness did not let him float but drove him like a rock to the depth of the water, so that he hardly escaped death. This becomes clear in a story I must tell you. Once his companions invited him to bathe in a river or deep pool. As he saw them swimming hither and thither, he took off his clothes except for his cap under which he was hiding his tonsure. As he jumped into the water, he sank to the bottom of the water. His companions came near and with effort took him out of the water. One of them asked: "Master N, do you want to swim?" Our inceptor said yes. Right away his companion put his hand to the inceptor's forehead and said, "Kick up your feet!" And kicking up his feet he got his stomach pointing to the sky

[26] Ff. 6v–12v.   [27] Ff. 12v, 24v, 26v.   [28] Ff. 34, 34v, 37.

[29] "Commendacio inceptoris in ecclesia Beate Virginis," ff. 37v–38v.

[30] "Et sic prophecia de beato Johanne Baptista de nostro inceptore secundario adinpletur: "Sic inter natos mulierum non surrexit maior" [Matt 11:11], et sic de .N., quia nec crassior nec grossior nec solidior nec rotundior/iocundior, et quamuis rot/iocundissimus, non in corpore ponderosior precellens alios grauitate," f. 38v. In Lawerne's script, the letters j and long r are often indistinguishable.

[31] "Et sic ex suis meritis propheta magnus surrexit in nobis, magnus corpore, magnus robore, quod suum nomen connotat et designat, quia viribus et robore refertus .N. congrue nuncupatur. Ac de villa patrie seu de villa in patria cognominatur. Vnde .N. est nostri inceptoris cognomen, ad similitudinem maxime ville que in patria situatur," f. 38.

and his back toward the deep water. And the hand of his teacher that was lying on his forehead pushed him deep into the water, so that our inceptor's head struck a stone and hurt his crown. Whence traces can still be seen on his head. And so, as I have heard from many people, our inceptor would have died if his companion had not swum to him and quickly lifted him up and blamed him: "You tried to swim on your back before you could swim on your belly!" To which our inceptor replied: "Why did you tell me to kick up my feet instead of kick them back?" Thus both were deceived through the lack of communication in their languages, for one – master John N – was a Welshman and the other an Englishman from N. And so, may our inceptor never again descend, but let him ascend from the lower lectern to the higher one and receive the degree of doctor among the theology masters next Monday, for the praise and honor of God to the profit and strength of our college. Which he may grant him and us who lives and reigns without end. Amen.[32]

Naturally, serious academic exercises – the *introitus* and *sermones examinatorii* – are more academic in their tone and deal with weightier matters than students' antics on the Isis. Not only do they speak of serious matters, such as the liberal arts or the structure of Peter Lombard's *Sentences* or the superiority of theological knowledge, but they fairly bristle with learned authorities. In contrast to them, the public university sermons lean more towards moral exhortation and the tone of popular preaching, with illustrations taken from everyday life and exempla. Their contents also tend to be less academic and instead focus on the office

---

[32] "Pretextu cuius non libenter currit sed natare summe odit et rennuit, quia iste dominus quondam natare volens sed grauitas ipsum supernatare non permisit sed ad aquam locum profundissimum quasi lapis inpulit, sic quod mortem vix evasit. Quod satis liquebit in narranda istoria. Nam dum socii ad balneandum in fluuio seu in stangno profundo istum dominum inuitarunt, et videns suos socios huc et illuc natantes, sua vestimenta deposuit excepto capicio quo coronam sacerdotalem absconderet, et saltare in aquam nitens ad fundum aque cecidit. Ad quem sui socii concurrentes nostrum inceptorem vix de aqua eleuarunt. Quorum vnus sibi dixit: 'Magister .N., vis tu natare?' Ad quod noster inceptor consenciit. Et statim socius manum ad frontem nostri inceptoris apposuit dicens: 'Protende pedes tuos.' Et pedes suos protendens ventrem versus celum et dorsum versus fundum aque extendit. Et sic manus docentis apposita fronti ipsum pepellit ad aque abyssum, sic quod nostri inceptoris capud super lapidem cecidit et contactus ipsius ad lapidem in coronam contigit. Vnde in corona eius satis parent vestigia. Et sic iste dominus, vt audiui a pluribus, expirasset nisi suus socius natando ipsum cicius eleuasset, nostrum inceptorum reprehendens: 'Quasi incepisti natare super tergum antequam scires natare super ventrem.' Ad quod noster inceptor respondit: 'Quare michi dixisti 'protende seu pretende pedes tuos?' Et sic ex defectu communicacionis linguarum fuit vterque deceptus. Nec mi .N. quia vnus mere Wallicus, videlicet magister Johannes .N., et alius mere Anglicus de .N. oriundus. Et sic noster inceptor non descendet de cetero, sed ascendet de cathedra inferiori ad superiorem, statum doctoratus inter doctores theologie in die lune proximo adepturus, in laudem Dei et honorem ad in profectu nostri collegii et vigorem. Quod sibi et nobis concedat qui sine fine viuit et regnat. Amen," f. 38v.

and duties of pastors and preachers, and on the failings of priests and university students.[33] John Lawerne also mastered the medium of such genuine sermons, and once more his notebook gives fine testimony in that it has preserved, besides the more playful praise of degree candidates, sermons in praise of scripture and the *Sentences*, and in addition two pieces that are clearly not academic exercises. One is a sermon he preached to his fellow monks on the vigil of the feast of the Assumption "in the chapter house," presumably at the Worcester priory, a piece distinguished mostly by the florid monastic style of the time. And at the very beginning of his notebook occurs a somewhat more startling sermon preached "before the king at Christmas in Oxford."[34] At its head Lawerne is called "the king's prophet," and in the text, which again deals with "A prophet has arisen among us" (Luke 7:16), he likens himself to Ezechiel and warns his "most serene prince" against his seneschal, against his secretary (*scriba*) named Bernard, and against false prophets in the realm. The notebook thus furnishes an interesting witness of sermon writing, and of preaching, that ranges from academic exercises to contemporary social critism at the highest level.

---

[33] For some examples see the discussions of collections J/5, R, S, and W in Part One.

[34] At the head of the sermon, in the top margin of f. 1, appears his name, "J. Lawarn'," with a string of saints' names whose help he invokes. Then, in a frame, "coram rege natali oxonie" and "albon rex"; followed by "Johannes lawarn' propheta regius." The string of saints' names also appears on ff. 55v and 121 and always includes Oswald and Wulstan. The sermon occupies ff. 1–2v. After some English lines on 2v, it is followed (ff. 3r–v) by a *Proposicio excusatoria de antedictis penes Bernardum scribam eadem natali per Johannem Lawarn' monachum*, which also uses a thema ("Pro iniquitate vidi tentoria," Habakuk 3:7) and a characteristic closing formula followed by "quod lawarn'." These three folios stand outside the strictly academic matter ("Incipiunt actus scolastici," f. 4 top margin) and may have been added later.

45

Other occasions[1]

Throughout the fourteenth and into the fifteenth century a good number of English prelates visited Avignon and participated in the customary preaching there, either at the papal curia or at various religious houses, and in several cases their sermons have been preserved in our collections. Thus FitzRalph, on his occasionally very extended visits, gave sermons before the pope and the cardinals and to the Franciscans, Dominicans, and Carmelites. Brinton similarly left at least two sermons that must have been preached in Avignon. Another important figure was the English Benedictine Adam Easton, a great scholar who got enmeshed in papal politics and nearly lost his life, but ended up as cardinal priest of Santa Cecilia in Trastevere, where he lies buried. He must have given many sermons, but none seem to have survived.[2] In its final stages, the Great Schism also drew several Englishmen to the councils. Thus, Richard Fleming, bishop of Lincoln and founder of an Oxford college, is known to have preached at Constance (1417) and at Siena (1423), and several of his sermons are extant.[3] Other English prelates were with him there or later attended the council of Basel, though only one or two of their sermons seem to have been preserved.[4]

Closer to home, sermons likewise graced major public events beyond the normal liturgical life of the Church. We know from Thomas Walsingham's *Historia anglicana* that Bishop Brinton preached on the day after the coronation of Richard II, in the course of "a general procession for the king and the peace of the realm." Walsingham even summarizes the sermon:

---

[1] In a chapter entitled "Wandering Stars" Owst includes pardoners and hermits (*Preaching*, pp. 96–143). There are historical references to the preaching of both, but we have no surviving sermons, let alone collections.

[2] On his life see *BRUO* 1:620–621, and Margaret Harvey, *English in Rome*, pp. 188–237.

[3] *BRUO* 2:690. See Nighman, "Accipiant."

[4] Robert Hallum of Salisbury (died 1417); Henry Abingdon, warden of Merton College, at Constance (died 1437), one sermon extant; the Carmelite provincial of England preached at Basel in 1432: *Concilium basiliense* 2:300.

The bishop of Rochester exhorted the people that the dissensions and discords that have risen and continued for a long time between the people and the lords, be put to rest, proving with many arguments that such dissensions highly displease God. He exhorted especially the lords that they should no longer impoverish the people with so great taxations without cause. He further admonished them, if there is a reasonable cause why they should in every respect help the king and the realm, they should do what is necessary patiently and without murmuring and the least threat of sedition. And further, he exhorted those in general who were close to the king, a young and innocent child, to leave the vices they were practicing, namely fornication and adultery, and instead to try to conform themselves to the king's purity and innocence . . .[5]

Brinton further preached a eulogy on Edward, the Black Prince, after his death in 1376 (BR-78), and other panegyrics in our period similarly eulogize Blanche of Lancaster at a memorial service, Henry IV at his enthronement, the Duke of Gloucester at his reburial, or the Earl of Huntingdon on his death.[6]

Another occasion for a panegyric sermon was victory in war. In 1346 the "profound doctor" of theology and future archbishop Thomas Bradwardine, then still chancellor of St. Paul's cathedral in London, had preached a sermon that celebrated the English victory at Crécy,[7] and after Agincourt his example was followed by Bishop Henry Beaufort when he, in his capacity as chancellor of England, preached "on the triumphs of our king" at the parliament of March 1416.[8] Military concerns led to another kind of preaching as well. In earlier times, the call to a crusade and the recruitment of crusaders had been made through preaching.[9] The report of Giraldus Cambrensis in 1188 is well known.[10] In our period the bishop of Norwich, Henry Despenser, agitated for and conducted a crusade against the supporters of the anti-pope, Clement VII (that is, the French), for which he drummed up support by means of a preaching campaign in England and France;[11] and we hear that the bishop and his chief captain instilled courage in their troops by "preaching that all who were to fall in this cause would become martyrs."[12] But their preaching has left no evident traces in the orthodox sermon

[5] Walsingham, *Historia anglicana*, 1:338–339. Whether this sermon as reported by Walsingham is indeed BR-44 remains, to my mind, an open question; see above, p. 46 and n. 6.

[6] Walsingham, *Gesta abbatum*, 3:277 (Blanche); *Historia anglicana*, 2:237 (Henry IV); *Chronicle of Adam Usk*, pp. 84 (reburial) and 88 (Huntingdon, a letter in sermon form).

[7] Discussed and edited in Oberman and Weisheipl, "*Sermo Epinicius*." The sermon has been recently re-edited with further discussion by Offler, "Thomas Bradwardine's 'Victory Sermon'."

[8] *Gesta Henrici Quinti*, pp. 122 and 123, note 3.

[9] See Tyerman, *England*, esp. chapter 7, pp. 152–167.   [10] Ibid., 156–159.

[11] Perroy, *Angleterre*, pp. 186–187 and 235–236. In 1383 Archbishop Courtenay mandated masses, sermons, and processions for the bishop of Norwich in his crusade against the schismatic French (Wilkins, *Concilia* 3:177).

[12] Walsingham, *Historia anglicana*, 2:89.

collections. For other military enterprises, as well as in times of danger or distress, public prayers and processions were frequently solicited by the king or the archbishop of Canterbury and then promulgated by local bishops, and often these processions were to be accompanied by a sermon.[13] Along with procession sermons given at normal liturgical occasions, such as Palm Sunday, Rogation Days, or academic processions,[14] the collections have preserved a number of sermons given at processions for secular rulers and concerns. In 1345 FitzRalph preached "in processione facta pro rege et principibus" (FI-10) and again, perhaps a year later, "in processione London facta pro rege" (FI-23). The following year he preached again in London "in processione generali" and repeated the same sermon at Dundalk in 1348 (FI-26). Though this sermon may have been given at a more liturgical procession, FitzRalph says that "for many reasons the lord our king needs the prayers of the devout more than usual."[15] At a different venue, the repertory of Cambridge university sermons includes one given at a *Processio pro belli victoria in Francia* (C-76), probably in 1424. Where a procession is not thus specified in the rubrics, other sermons may yet have been pronounced on such occasions and now hide behind a simple marginal "pro pace" or "in tempore belli."[16]

Another occasion of state was the opening of parliament. The *Modus tenendi parliamentum* prescribes that

> an archbishop or bishop or another high clergyman who is prudent and eloquent, after being chosen by the archbishop in whose province the parliament is being held, should, on one of the first five days of parliament, preach (*praedicare*) in full parliament and in the presence of the king, and this while the parliament has met and gathered for its greater part. In his sermon he must then submit to the whole parliament that they humbly adore God with him and pray for peace and tranquility of king and realm.[17]

---

[13] For some examples see Wilkins, *Concilia* 2:42 (1359, Edward III asks for "processiones, praedicationes, aliasque Deo placabiles hostias"), 2:79 (1368, "sermones publici"), 3:195 (1386, to pray for Admiral Arundel's expedition against the French who intend to invade England); or *Register John de Grandisson*, 2:1159 (1348, the king asks for prayers, sermons, and processions, for his wars in France), 1069–1070 (masses, sermons, and processions against the Black Death); etc.

[14] Perhaps at Corpus Christi processions, too. Rubin, *Corpus Christi*, in discussing "Preaching on Corpus Christi" (pp. 213–232), finds only one Latin Corpus Christi sermon from England marked for the feast; the collections here analyzed contain over twenty more that are clearly rubricated, and some further possibilities. But where exactly these were preached is unclear. That the Corpus Christi *plays* were accompanied by a sermon is not likely.

[15] For an appraisal of these sermons see Walsh, *Fourteenth-Century Scholar*, pp. 227–231.

[16] "In tempore belli" at B/2-30 and 31. Rogation Day sermons are often marked *pro* or *de pace*.

[17] *Select Charters*, p. 509. The *Modus* has also been preserved in French and English; for the latter, see Hodnett and White, "Manuscripts."

After this sermon, the Chancellor or the Chief Justice of England was to "pronounce" the causes of the present parliament. Judging by extant reports, the two – *praedicatio* or *sermo* and *pronuntiatio* – were usually combined. Especially if the chancellor of England was a clergyman – frequently the archbishop of Canterbury – his *pronuntiatio* included, or was preceded by, or was given in the form of, a (scholastic) sermon, whose thema and divisions are often recorded in the *Rotuli parliamentorum* and elsewhere until at least the mid-fifteenth century. Thus, in Richard II's first parliament of October 1377, the archbishop of Canterbury "had the words of the *pronuntiatio*" and used as his thema *Rex tuus venit tibi*, which he divided into three parts "as if it were a sermon."[18] Half a century later the chancellor of England, Bishop John Stafford of Bath and Wells, opened the parliament of 1433 in the same fashion with a discourse on "Let the mountains receive peace for the people, and the hills justice" (Ps 71:3). Brinton's famous sermon 69, which retells the fable of Belling the Cat, also is connected with parliamentary business, though the sermon itself was preached before the clergy who met in convocation, as it often did, simultaneously with the king's parliament. The themata for a number of parliamentary sermons have been recorded, and now and then their reporters also furnish a summary of their contents. Not surprisingly, often "the biblical verses provided a peg for a statement of royal rights and duties."[19]

A final special occasion for a public sermon was "preaching at the cross," presumably outdoors and not strictly connected with the liturgy. Nicholas Hereford preached the Ascension Day sermon in 1382 "at the cross in the cemetery of St. Frideswide's, Oxford," in which this follower of Wyclif attacked the friars and possessioners in sometimes rather inflammatory words and thereby caused alarm and some unhappiness between Oxford and Canterbury. An official eyewitness has left a detailed report of the sermon.[20] Three weeks later Philip Repingdon, while still an adherent of Wyclif, preached the Corpus Christi sermon in the same place.[21] Another venue for such public sermons, and one that naturally would lead to wider repercussions, was St. Paul's Cross in London.[22] According to Millar Maclure,

---

[18] *Rotuli parliamentorum* 2:3. Similarly, at Richard's last parliament, Edmund Stafford, bishop of Exeter, "gave the *pronuntiatio* of the parliament in form of a sermon" ("facta pronunciacione parliementi ad modum sermonis per Edmundurn Stafford episcopum Exon'"); *Chronicle of Adam Usk*, p. 20.

[19] R. N. Swanson, *Church and Society*, p. 93. Swanson discusses parliamentary sermons on pp. 93–94, with pertinent references in the *Rotuli parliamentorum*.

[20] Forde, "Nicholas Hereford." See also Hudson, "'Poor Preachers'," pp. 50–51.

[21] *Fasciculi zizaniorum*, pp. 299–300. For Corpus Christi preaching, mostly by Wycliffites or insurgents, in 1381–1382, see Aston, "Corpus Christi."

[22] For a review of the medieval history of preaching at St. Paul's Cross and a discussion of sermons by Brinton, Wimbledon, William Taylor, and Alkerton and their engagement with current

the earliest documentary evidence of its use dates from 1214, when Henry III met the citizens of London there to consult with them about a projected visit to Gascony . . . When the Cross is first mentioned in surviving documents, it is rather a place of assembly for the hearing of proclamations than a preaching place."[23]

In 1387 Archbishop William Courtenay could say that "at the high cross in the greater cemetery of the church of London . . . it has been customary to preach the word of God to the clergy and the people, as it were in a more public and outstanding locale."[24] Actual sermons given at St. Paul's Cross are recorded from about 1330 on. According to their rubrics, two sermons by John Sheppey, OSB, were given at that location in 1336 and 1337, and both are extant.[25] Later in the century FitzRalph used this locale as a platform to preach against the mendicants.[26] By the 1380s the Cross had become a place "where the word of God is habitually preached, both to Clergy and Laity,"[27] and in 1382 this pulpit was used to publicize a miracle against the Lollards.[28] It continued to be a place for important political announcements. Thus, in 1417 Henry V sent the archbishop a liturgical book defaced by Lollards, asking him to have it displayed "in sermonibus faciendis ad Crucem Sancti Pauli Londoniis."[29] Again, in the same place in 1431, "the archbishop of Canterbury with ten bishops around him with lighted tapers in their hands, flung the sentence [of excommunication] against the heretic Lollards, their supporters, and usurers."[30] More happily, in 1420 St. Paul's Cross witnessed a sermon about the king's marriage to Katherine and his new seal.[31] One of the Cambridge university sermons still extant was preached in 1425 "apud crucem Londoniarum." Its summary records nothing more inflammatory than that "people of London are newfangled."[32] And

---

political issues, see Horner, "Preachers at Paul's Cross." See also *English Works of John Fisher*, pp. 42–47.

[23] Maclure, *Paul's Cross Sermons 1534–1642*, p. 5.

[24] "Cum itaque Crux Alta in majori cimiterio Ecclesiae London, ubi verbum Dei consuevit clero et populo praedicari, tanquam in loco magis publico et insigni . . . ," *Documents . . . St. Paul's Cathedral*, p. 7.

[25] Oxford, New College, MS 92, ff. 173–176v ("Ad crucem sancti Pauli anno Christi 1336") and ff. 180, 177–178 ("In ecclesia sancti Pauli ad crucem in die conuersionis sancti Pauli anno Christi 1337").

[26] See Walsh, *Fourteenth-Century Scholar*, pp. 415–420.

[27] Maclure, *Paul's Cross Sermons*, p. 6, quoting Archbishop Courtenay, 1387.

[28] Aston, "Corpus Christi," pp. 38–39.

[29] Walsingham, *Historia anglicana*, 2:326.   [30] *Chronicon rerum gestarum*, 1:59.

[31] Walsingham, *Historia angliana*, 2:335.

[32] "Item homines Lond' sunt newefangul," C-151, p. 142.

much later in the fifteenth century an Austin Friar student offered preaching at St. Paul's Cross as part of the requirements for his baccalaureate.[33]

The fifteenth century also saw a huge increase in the founding of chantries, and occasionally the founders required their chaplains not only to say prayers and masses but also to preach a determined number of sermons. But this seems to have been a development of the later fifteenth century, and to my knowledge no clearly marked chantry sermons survive.[34]

A final occasion for a sermon would have been the funeral or anniversary of an important cleric or lay person. Thus, for example, in January of 1392 Bishop John Waltham of Salisbury wrote to the dean and chapter of his cathedral requesting that they intercede for the soul of the recently deceased Countess Margaret of Devon, in masses, prayers, sermons, and processions.[35] Sermons for the feast of All Souls form part of regular *de sanctis* cycles, and a number of those have been preserved. Funeral and anniversary sermons for individuals, who are often mentioned by name, can also be found in several collections and have been called attention to in the previous sections.[36]

---

[33] Roth, *English Austin Friars*, 2:388*.

[34] See now Wabuda, *Preaching*, especially pp. 163–168.   [35] *Register John Waltham*, p. 20.

[36] Sermons for All Souls day are inventoried as S80; for individual funeral and anniversary sermons I have used the siglum C21.

PART III

Orthodox Preaching

46

An English theology

In the late-medieval Church, preaching was very closely linked to academic theology. The entire range of theological studies, whether they were offered and pursued at universities, monastic houses, or the *studia* of religious orders, aimed in essence at the training of future preachers. We can safely assume that all authors of the sermons here surveyed had enjoyed some formal training in theology, at least at the undergraduate level. A number of them advanced to the doctorate in theology, where, as formed bachelors, they would have had to lecture on the Bible and on the *Sentences*, and then, after inception as masters, again give more advanced courses. Thus, of the known sermon writers between 1350 and 1450, FitzRalph, Sheppey, Waldeby, Rimington, Repingdon, Alkerton, and Rypon were all doctors in theology, whereas Brinton held a doctorate in laws.

It is therefore not surprising that sermons could and did occasionally serve as vehicles in which specific theological doctrines might be developed and, as it were, published in full academic form. Thus, FitzRalph together with other theologians preached on the nature of the Beatific Vision before the pope and cardinals at Avignon, and he similarly preached on the Immaculate Conception and on the hotly disputed matter of friars' privileges both at Avignon and in London. His preaching at St. Paul's Cross in London seems to have marked the beginning of a flourishing use of that pulpit to air theological positions with rational argumentation, proof, and attack on opposite views. But such sermons were really lectures in sermon form and quite different from the more usual preaching that happened during the liturgy or on the various occasions that have been surveyed in the preceding part. An example might illustrate the differences.

A sermon on the Blessed Virgin, "whose conception we celebrate today," divides its thema, *Ego quasi vitis fructificavi* ("Like a vine I have brought forth," Sirach 24:23), into three parts: Mary was elevated with a unique worthiness (her sinlessness), enlarged in her natural copiousness (her virtues), and laden with spiritual fruitfulness (in bearing the Savior). The anonymous preacher certainly had some learning, as he quotes Alexander Nequam throughout the sermon, together with Anselm, Bernard, Isidore, Palladius, and Ovid; and his audience was clerical. In developing his first point, on Mary's sinlessness, he simply states:

> In her such a unique worthiness and excellence shone forth that she was preserved from any sin, original and actual. For if God conferred so great a grace on the prophets John the Baptist and Jeremiah that, sanctified in the womb, they were born of a womb as saints, against the common order, we should devoutly and rationally believe that an even greater gift of grace was conferred on the ruler of the world and queen of heaven and future mother of God, that not only her birth was pure but also her conception in the womb was pure and free from all infection of sin. Take as witness blessed Anselm . . .[1]

And next to Anselm he adduces Scripture and Alexander Nequam to prove his statement that Mary was conceived without sin.[2] In contrast to this essentially panegyric sermon with prooftexts, FitzRalph offered a much more academic argument on why the feast of the Immaculate Conception should be observed in the Church (which implies the belief that Mary was conceived immaculate). Preaching before the Carmelites at Avignon he first, like a good Schoolman, lined up a series of authorities against Mary's sinlessness, some even with objections and rebuttals, and then gave his reasons in favor, though not without protesting that

> I am not one who should, in this or in any other question, affirm anything; and therefore I declare that in what I am going to say on this matter I do not intend to boldly assert as true but only to state what seems to me more probable, under the correction of our most Holy Father and my lords the cardinals here present, and the prelates and doctors as well as anyone who is wiser than I am, for I am not ashamed to learn from anyone.[3]

---

[1] "Tanta in ipsa refulsit singularis dignitas et excellencia quod ab omni originali peccato et actuali erat preseruata. Si enim Johanni Baptiste et Jeremie prophetis Deus tantam graciam contulit vt preter communem legem in vteris sanctificati sancti ex vtero nascerentur, pie et racionaliter credendum est amplioris gracie munus dominatrici [*MS*: dominatrice] orbis ac regine celorum ac matris Dei future fuisse collatum, vt non solummodo natiuitas eius munda esset sed eius concepcio in vtero et munda esset et ab omni peccati infeccione preseruata, teste beato Anselmo in tractatu eiusdem Virginis . . . ," W-106, f. 201v. Anselm's testimony is his autobiographical account, which can be read in Burridge, "Immaculée Conception," p. 593 n. 3.

[2] Note however that even so he had at least one objection in mind, as he says after the quoted passage: "Nor is it a counterargument that she was conceived between sinners and in fleshly concourse from sinners" ("Nec obstat quod inter peccatores ipsa et de peccatoribus in carnali copula fuerit procreata," f. 200v).

[3] "Ego vero non sum talis qui debeam in ista questione aut alia aliquid affirmare, et ob hac protestor quod in hiis que sum dicturus in ista materia nichil intendo pertinaciter astruere sed tantum illud recitare quod michi probabilius videtur sub correccione sanctissimi patris nostri et sub correccione dominorum meorum cardinalium hic presencium ac prelatorum et doctorum ac

In a similar vein, "Magister Ricardus Kilwyngton" preached a sermon *de aduentu Domini*, in which he, too, asked whether the Church may rightly celebrate Mary's Immaculate Conception "on the morrow,"[4] marshaled authorities *pro* and *con*, and like FitzRalph concluded in the affirmative, though ending with a rather waffling quotation from Augustine.[5] Although these sermons do not reach the learning and logical toughness of genuine academic disputations, they yet have an argumentative theological edge to them that is missing in simpler panegyrics for the same feast day, such as the sermon in collection N which, in its major division (*ab extra*), simply declares that "this Blessed Virgin Mary was today conceived without Original Sin, and this for three reasons: that she might bear the Son of God from her flesh, that she might reign in glory as the queen of heaven, and that she might prepare eternal life for a lost world."[6]

This argumentative edge goes beyond merely taking up an abstract theological or philosophical topic, or raising a question or objection,[7] or marshaling authorities to prove a point. As illustrated, FitzRalph and Kilvington set up arguments both against and for a theological statement and then committed themselves to one position. That such sermons are extremely rare in the collections here studied[8] would, I think, indicate that in essence theological disputation and preaching were considered separate activities. This difference can be further seen in that the laudatory speeches given as academic exercises, whether *introitus* (the opening sermons to a course on the Bible or Peter Lombard's *Sentences*) or

eciam / cuiuscumque melius sapientis, quia non vereor a quocumque addiscere," FI-85, f. 225r–v. The arguments *contra* appear on ff. 224v–225, FitzRalph's answer on 225v–228v. See also Walsh, *Fourteenth-Century Scholar*, pp. 208–210.

4 Both name and occasion are given in the rubric to a sermon on *Erunt signa in sole*, F/4-2. The reference "quam cras celebrabit mater Ecclesia" appears in the text f. 292rb. Together with patristic authorities, Kilvington quotes Alexander (evidently Nequam), Nicholaus de Sancto Albano *De concepcione Uirginis gloriose*, Hostiensis, and "Raynaldus."

5 "'Cum,' inquit Augustinus, 'de peccatis agitur, nullam de Beata Uirgine propter honorem Domini volo facere questionem.'" f. 292va. The quotation is from *De natura et gratia*, 36.42.

6 "Hec beata Virgo Maria fuit hodierna die concepta sine originali peccato, et hoc propter tria, scilicet vt Dei Filium ex sua carne procrearet, vt regina celi effecta gloriosa regnaret, et ut mundo perdito vitam eternam prepararet," with reference to St. Anselm's *De concepcione beate Virginis* (N-57, f. 143v). Other examples are W-52, W-106, B/1-75.

7 A good example is P1-14 on *Verbum caro factum est*. Here the preacher begins by listing three heretical opinions that Christ was not true man and gives reasons and authoritative statements against them. The entire passage (f. 64va–b), taken with acknowledgment from Aquinas, *De Christo*, quaestio 16, serves as no more than a prooftext for the thema which it introduces.

8 One example is Repingdon's handling of the question why Christ said, "If I do not go away, the Holy Spirit, the Paraclete, will not come to you" (John 16:7): he begins with "It seems that Christ had not been a spirit" and then makes a statement *contra* followed with *respondeo dicendo* (RE-24, f. 179vb). Another case is RY-9, on *Dominum Deum tuum adorabis* (Matthew 4:10); see below p. 382.

sermones examinatorii, follow the structure and general characteristics of normal sermons, not disputations.[9] In a general way, then, it is quite true to claim with H. Leith Spencer that in late-medieval preaching the "habit of persuasive reasoning [was] by means of similitudes" rather than logical or theological arguments.[10] For example, when preachers came to address the question of why God chose to redeem mankind through the incarnation of the Son, they usually did not marshal the arguments developed by Anselm and others but instead told a little extended simile taken from the chivalric world, the custom observed at celebrating the Round Table.[11] Anselm was not forgotten, and we shall see another instance at the end of this chapter, but the prevailing mode in preaching was not that of theological argumentation.

Before that, however, we must look at another aspect of the interface between preaching and academic theology, for the "habit of persuasive reasoning" in medieval preaching was not just by similitudes but even more so by means of "authorities." Late-medieval sermons are filled with quotations from authoritative sources offered as proof, and their authors very often identify these sources, whether from a sense of scholarly accuracy or to impress their audiences. Naturally, the density of such quotations varies from author to author, but it can reach remarkably high degrees. The range of the quoted material would presuppose access to libraries and to lectures, and hence reveals an important aspect of the diffusion of academic theology. Of course, more often than not the preachers probably did not consult the originals but drew on intermediaries.[12] Many even acknowledged such intermediary sources, as did Philip Repingdon and Felton in their temporal cycles, and similar acknowledgments occur in almost any anonymous collection. A fifteenth-century preacher, for instance, will quote Gregory of Nazianzus or Chrysostom as "alleged" by Januensis,[13] or Ambrose as quoted in Gorran.[14] Other exegetical works that admittedly served as

---

[9] See Wenzel, "Academic Sermons." The *sermones examinatorii* in London, British Library, MS Harley 5398 noted there (p. 306, n. 11) contain no discussion of academic questions or matters.

[10] Spencer, *English*, p. 81.

[11] See Wenzel, *Preachers*, p. 234, n. 68; and Warner, "Jesus the Jouster." A different example of the same procedure is a late fifteenth-century sermon in Cambridge, Corpus Christi College, MS 423. Here, too, the preacher raises the question why the Son was incarnated rather than the Father or the Holy Spirit. After mentioning four different opinions he concludes with a simile "in experiencia": when three persons clothe one young woman, each of them does the same as the others, and yet only one is being clothed (p. 259).

[12] For quotations of the Fathers in several large medieval texts, see the collection of essays in *Reception of the Church Fathers*, especially the contributions by Matter on the *Glossa ordinaria* (1:83–111) and by Bougerol on the *Sentences* (1:113–164).

[13] "Posuit Gregorius Nazanzenus, ut dicit Januensis," M/3-5; "sic dicit Crisostomus super Matheum, quem allegat Januensis," M/3-12.

[14] "Sicut dicit Gorram et allegat pro se Ambrosium," M/3-54.

intermediaries are Nottingham[15] and Holcot's lectures on the Book of Wisdom.[16] Similarly acknowledged is the major theological textbook of the later Middle Ages, Peter Lombard's *Sentences*.[17] Other large treatises and encyclopedic works likewise gathered vast amounts of historical and other information and handed it on to later preachers, ranging from Augustine's *City of God* with its historical and mythological tidbits[18] to Vincent of Beauvais' *Speculum historiale*,[19] the *Golden Legend*,[20] John of Wales,[21] and the *Manipulus florum*.[22] Pastoral handbooks, too, transmitted earlier authoritative material; sermon Z-12, for instance, acknowledges the popular *Oculus sacerdotis*.[23] Even the medieval collections of canon law served as repositories of quotable patristic authorities and are frequently thus acknowledged.[24]

Whether derived directly or through an intermediary, the quotations in these collections are from a vast number of authors and works. These range in time from ancient classical writers to near contemporaries,[25] and they cover all major

---

[15] For example: "Iohannes de Rvpella quem allegat Notingham," RE-24 (f. 92ra).

[16] For example: "Sextus Iulius refert libro 3, vt recitat Holcote *Super Sapientia*," O-5, f. 29.

[17] For example: "Secundum Ambrosium, ut eum allegat Magister *Sentenciarum* libro 3, capitulo 18," R-7; "quod bene probat beatus Ambrosius, et ponitur 1 *Sentenciarum*, distinccione 9," J/5-16; "Augustinus *De doctrina Christiana* capitulo 6, et eum allegat Magister *Sentenciarum*, libro 3, distinccione 29, dicens . . . ," S-1.

[18] For example, O-45 gives a series of "wondrous works of demons by which humans are led away from their faith," which includes: "Recitat quod Apuleius in libro qui [*MS* quod] intitulatur *De caseis aureis* [!] dicit de seipso quod accepto quodam veneno, humano animo perdurante, fiebat asinus," f. 223. Similarly, R-10: "Narrat Ouidius *De Transformatis*, et recitat Augustinus *De ciuitate Dei*, libro 18, capitulo 17, quod erat quedam maga [*MS* magna] in Grecia nomine Circe" (f. 56).

[19] For example: "Scribit autem abbas Ioachim in exposicione Ieremie, et ponitur in *Speculo historiali*, libro 32, capitulo cvii," A-50, f. 156; the source is book 31, chapter 108 of the *Speculum historiale*, in Vincent of Beauvais, *Speculum quadruplex* 4:1325.

[20] For example: "Beatus Augustinus secundum quod allegat Ianuensis in *Legenda*," N-60, f. 148v. Other patristic quotations taken from the *Golden Legend* with acknowledgment in collection N are of Jerome, Ambrose, Richard of St. Victor, and Bernard.

[21] For example: "Narrat Trogus Pompeius libro 3, et Valensis allegat in *Breuiloquio philosophorum*," WA-24, f. 56v.

[22] "Loquitur beatus Ambrosius in libro suo *De Ioseph*, et ponitur in *Manipulo florum*, capitulo de libertate," RY-30, f. 112v.

[23] "Sicut testatur Jeronimus, ut recitat eum *Pars oculi sacerdotis*, parte secunda, capitulo primo," Z-12, f. 37vb.

[24] See the discussion of collection E in Part One, section 27, pp. 172–173. Similar acknowledged borrowings from canon law occur in C-105, A-36, DY, and elsewhere.

[25] Near-contemporaries or contemporaries to the sermon collections are: St. Bridget of Sweden (quoted in CO, J/5-3, O-14), Walter Burley (W-167), the councils of Constance and Basel (K-19, CO-6), Henry of Costessey (FE-14, J/5), Henry of Ghent (D-6, P2-50, W-76, Bodley 857-5 and 17), Ranulph Higden (N, RE, WA, FE-25), Nicholas of Lyra (frequent), Mandeville *(De mirabilibus mundi*, RY-31), Marco Polo (F/1-30, R-8), John de Burgh (*Pupilla oculi*, M/4-2),

disciplines, from grammar and history to theology. Even if some authors, such as Augustine and Peter Lombard, furnished material in more than one field – biblical exegesis, theology and matters of faith, ancient history and mythology, and natural science – such fields tend to be dominated by their respective major authorities.[26] Pride of place belongs to the Bible, both Old and New Testaments. To the medieval preacher, preaching the word of God meant not only basing his entire discourse on a biblical text and explaining it, but further "proving" every statement he made with at least one verse from Scripture. As a result, biblical quotations are ubiquitous in our sermons, and they come from all parts of the Bible. Several major fourteenth-century theological figures and preachers have impressed modern students with their deep and wide-ranging knowledge of the Scriptures. Thus, Walsh speaks of "an impressive knowledge of the Bible" that FitzRalph displayed in his sermons from 1338 onwards, and in a very personal prayer FitzRalph himself confesses to having been illumined by Holy Scripture after spending years in the darkness of philosophy.[27] A similar intense turn to Scripture-based theology has been seen in Bradwardine.[28] This impressiveness is fully shared by the sermons in our collections, whether random or in systematic cycles.

Often a preacher will use a biblical text not merely to prove his point but further to develop the sermon by means of its exegetical exposition and moralization. In order to explain a biblical word or concept or an entire lection, our collections draw with some regularity on the standard patristic exegetes, including Origen, Gregory the Great, pseudo-Chrysostom on Matthew, and Cassiodorus on the Psalms. From the post-patristic age, Bede, Haimo, Rabanus, Remigius on Matthew, and the Gloss are often cited by name. So are such later exegetes and makers of model sermon collections as Nottingham, Nicholas of Lyra, Jacobus de Voragine ("Januensis"), Gorran, Peraldus ("Parisiensis"), and John of Abbéville. In contrast, Odo of Cheriton appears considerably less frequently in the Latin collections than he apparently does in English ones.[29]

Richard Rolle (DY), Thomas Ringstead (O, Q-13, Z-3), Nicholas Trevet (A-39), and Thomas Waleys (J/5, O-37, Q-37). See also the sections in Part One on the respective collections.

[26] "Major authorities" are those that appear at least in five different collections.

[27] Walsh, *Fourteenth-Century Scholar*, pp. 174, 176. The entire passage is translated in Pantin, *English Church*, pp. 132–133; also in Courtenay, *Schools*, p. 321.

[28] Robson, *Wyclif*, pp. 38–39. Like FitzRalph, Bradwardine also left an autobiographical passage on this matter, which has been printed in Workman, *John Wyclif*, 1:120–121.

[29] Odo is mentioned by Felton as a main source of his sermon collection and apparently was utilized a good deal in Middle-English sermons (see Spencer, *English*, pp. 81–88 and passim; and Hudson, "Wycliffite Scholar," p. 307), but in Latin material his name appears very rarely: E-30, A-30, and passim in CO. For the close connection between university lectures on the Bible and preaching see d'Avray, *Preaching*, pp. 188–190, with references to the basic studies by Smalley.

Biblical studies in medieval schools were closely linked to the reading of, and drawing material from, the *Historia scholastica* by Peter Comestor (usually called "Magister historiarum"), which consequently furnished the collections with much historical information offered with acknowledgment. Beyond it appear Josephus for Jewish history and Sextus Julius and Valerius with material from the Classical world, as well as the *Historia tripartita*. Much of this information the preachers may well have found in the thirteenth-century *Speculum historiale* by Vincent of Beauvais, which itself is directly quoted a good many times. For the lives of saints and their miracles, the *Legenda aurea* by "Januensis" is the main quoted authority.[30] With historical material it was mythology and pseudo-historical anecdotes that held an enormous attraction for medieval preachers, and thus together with Virgil and Macrobius appear various collections created both before and after the exegetical work by the "classicizing friars" of the fourteenth century that has been studied by Beryl Smalley. A major source in this field is John of Salisbury, usually referred to as "Carnotensis." His large work, the *Policraticus*, gathers many anecdotes suitable for moral instruction. In the sermons it is usually called "Policraticon," sometimes also "De nugis curialium" or "De nugis philosophorum," and quoted very frequently.[31] Next to it, many other authors and collections of entertaining and morally instructive tales are quoted, among which Vegetius' *De re militari*, Jacques de Vitry's and John of Wales's *exempla* collections, Ovid's *Metamorphoses* for classical myths and fables, and the *Vitas Patrum* for the wisdom of the desert monks occur with some frequency.

Anecdotes about historical characters, myths and customs of pre-Christian peoples, and particularly depictions of abstract virtues and vices in the form of *picturae* or *imagines* all became vehicles of detailed moralization and served to impress a sermon's major points vividly on the audience's mind and memory for later recall and reflection. So did many aspects of "science" or natural lore, such as the properties of things and the strange behavior of beasts. Here again, a wide array of names and works are quoted, ranging in time from Aristotle's *Naturalia* and Pliny's *Historia naturalis* through several Arabic scientists to Roger Bacon. The primary authority in this field is Bartholomew the Englishman, whose *De rerum proprietatibus* occurs nearly everywhere in the sermon collections. Two earlier encyclopedias are also frequently quoted, Isidore's *Etymologies* and Alexander Nequam's *De naturis rerum*. So are the exegetical works on the six days of Creation (*Hexameron*) by Basil and by Ambrose. Galen's name appears in several collections, together with Avicenna's and Albumasar's; and Albert the

---

[30] The *Legenda aurea* itself has the structure of a *de sanctis et festis* cycle; see d'Avray, ibid., pp. 70–71.
[31] In addition, John of Salisbury's *Entheticus* appears in W-27; and his letters are quoted in BR-10.

Great, too, is quoted as a major authority on a large variety of natural phenomena. Another medieval work that gathered natural lore and human activities to illustrate moral points and is frequently cited in the sermon collections is the *Similitudines* attributed to Anselm.

While moral and ethical behavior is thus illustrated by similes and anecdotes, it is equally often taught directly in the pronouncements of wise teachers. Thus Aristotle and Seneca are quoted very frequently, as are Cicero and Boethius. The popular *De duodecim abusivis*, attributed to Cyprian and other patristic authors, as well as the *Secreta secretorum* and the sayings of the philosopher Secundus belong in this category of prudential ethics, as do remarks by Alan of Lille, Hugh of St. Victor, and "Aegidius" or Giles of Rome. For a more specifically Christian morality, Gregory the Great is the greatest authority, while Origen, Bernard of Clairvaux, Peter of Blois, and William Peraldus also appear next to him to teach good moral behavior.

As Christian wisdom finds its fulfillment in devotion and ultimately mysticism, a number of spiritual teachers are likewise quoted with some regularity. Pride of place here belongs to Bernard of Clairvaux; but Cyprian, Isidore's *De summo bono*, Peter Chrysologus ("Ravennatensis"), Peter of Blois, Innocent III, and Bonaventure, too, provide authoritative teaching on the devout life. In liturgical matters the two major authorities quoted are John Beleth and William Durandus. And for all aspects of Christian life and Church organization, canon law is cited very frequently, together with somewhat less frequent quotations from civil law.

Finally, for theological doctrines and matters of faith the overwhelming authority is Augustine, whose name and works appear in practically every sermon. His authority is followed at some distance by the other Latin Church Fathers: Gregory the Great above all, and then Jerome and Ambrose. Several compendia of theological teaching, from John Damascene's *De fide orthodoxa* to Peter the Chanter's *Verbum abbreviatum*, are likewise drawn upon frequently. With the latter we approach, chronologically, the rise and flourishing of systematic theology in Scholasticism. Many collections represented in this study draw heavily on Thomas Aquinas, normally called "sanctus Thomas," a fairly wide range of whose works are quoted with surprising regularity.[32] Aquinas is closely matched by Peter Lombard (the "Magister Sententiarum"). Of other scholastic predecessors, Dionysius, Anselm of Canterbury, and William of Auvergne ("Parisiensis") also appear fairly often. With Aquinas some half dozen other theologians of the thirteenth and early fourteenth centuries are named here and there, though not

---

[32] Including theological and philosophical commentaries, treatises, the *Summa theologiae*, and the *Compendium theologicae veritatis* attributed to him.

as major authorities. These are Fishacre,[33] Bonaventure,[34] Kilwardby,[35] Henry of Ghent ("Doctor solempnis"),[36] Richard Middleton ("Doctor de Mediavilla"),[37] Duns Scotus ("Doctor subtilis"),[38] Henry Cossey (or Costesey),[39] and Bradwardine (also cited as "Doctor profundus").[40]

Such authoritative quotations, taken from a wide range of works from the Bible and formal theology to collections of illustrative stories (*exempla*), served a number of purposes. Foremost is the evident need of medieval preachers to support every statement with an "authority." This urge reached a certain climax in a pattern of proof that adduces illustrations or arguments taken in regular order from nature, reason, art, and Scripture, a pattern that may have originated among mendicant preachers but by the fourteenth century had been accepted by others as well.[41]

It may be worth pointing out that often a biblical *figura* invoked in the sermon text does not merely look back at the doctrinal matter to be proven but at the same time points forward and provides the ground for further amplification. Especially where a *figura* involves an entire narrative passage, its details may be moralized to carry on the development of the sermon. For example, a sermon on the gospel of Jesus bringing the son of the widow of Naim back to life (Luke 7:11–16) explains that the dead man may signify a sinner because sinners become spiritually blind. "For this," the preacher says, "we have a figure in 1 Samuel 11," and he briefly tells the story of the men of Jabes who, being attacked by the Ammonite Naas, offered to make a covenant with him and become his subjects. Naas is agreeable, but on the condition that he will pluck out all their eyes. So the men of Jabes send messengers to Saul, and Saul in anger comes and rescues

---

[33] P1-1, 23 (twice), 27; P2-57 (several times); and C-30. References are to his commentaries on the *Sentences* and on biblical books.

[34] J/5-3, 17, and W-18 contain quotations from his commentary on the *Sentences*; S-9 and 19 from the *Compendium theologiae*.

[35] Quoted with Fishacre in P2-57 and D-57.

[36] In D-6, P2-51, W-76 and 164. References are to his *Quodlibetum*.

[37] J/5-3, a devotional passage on Christ's Passion.

[38] W-152, apparently from his *Sentences* commentary: in God wisdom, mercy, and justice exist more perfectly than in any temporal ruler. Repingdon incorporates a number of references to his *Sentences* commentary in a lengthy argument that sinful priests confer sacraments validly (RE-28).

[39] An English Franciscan active in the 1330s. FE-14 quotes from his commentary on Psalm 20: eight ways of excusing one's sin and their rebuttals. The same passage appears as a note in D, ff. 138v–139v.

[40] D-18, O-8 and 11, R-14 and 15, RE-18, and W-123; from *De causa Dei*. Repingdon and O-8 say the material comes from the Talmud.

[41] See Part Two, chapter 43, p. 294.

them (1 Samuel 11). In the story's spiritual meaning Naas stands for the devil, who "has already entered the realm of man's soul"; and the preacher can call out, "Let us emend our life and leave behind our sins," and God "will send us Saul, who signifies security in temptation and the Holy Spirit," and God will spare the city as he once spared Niniveh.[42] To find an appropriate biblical *figura* – in this case, one that lies rather off the beaten path – and weave it meaningfully into the verbal texture of the sermon surely requires skill and intelligence, and the writer of collection E was not the only one to possess them.[43]

Where biblical *figurae* lack this careful and detailed integration, however, the result may indeed read like a rather lifeless chain of authorities. Individual sermons, of course, vary widely in their density of prooftexts, from having no authorities other than a few biblical verses to the equivalent of a card index on a given topic, combining classical and modern, pagan and Christian material. A good example of a fairly well-provided text is the Latin version of Wimbledon's sermon *Redde rationem*. In about 6,800 words, it contains approximately ninety quotations, of which some sixty-three – in addition to the thema – are from the Bible,[44] six from Gregory the Great, four from Augustine (including the spurious *De conflictu viciorum et virtutum*), two each from the Gloss, Pseudo-Chrysostom, Hugh of St. Victor, Bernard of Clairvaux, and Bartholomew the Englishman; and one each from Isidore, Ambrose, Rabanus, Innocent III, Martin of Poland, Aristotle, and Valerius Maximus.[45]

In the ranks of these authorities, English writers rub shoulders with Continental ones. Of course, many English authors themselves enjoyed a wide international reputation and use, such as Bede, Anselm, John of Salisbury, Bartholomew the Englishman, Roger Bacon, John of Wales, FitzRalph, and others. But three English authors deserve some special attention here for the frequency with which they appear in later sermons: Robert Grosseteste, John Bromyard, and Robert Holcot. Of these, the Dominican John Bromyard is probably best known to medieval historians and literary scholars because Owst quoted from his *Summa praedicantium* very widely, even if he identified Bromyard incorrectly and placed the *Summa* half a century too late. How and for what purposes Bromyard was utilized is shown nicely by the very first sermon writer studied here, John Sheppey. His sermon for Ash Wednesday 1353, *Flebitis vos* ("You shall weep"), refers the

---

[42] E-40, ff. 111ra–va.

[43] Another writer who used such developed *figurae* constantly is the author of the macaronic sermons in collection O. An example appears in Wenzel, *Macaronic*, pp. 272–274 (sermon O-7, with translation), and in Wenzel, "Preaching the Seven Deadly Sins" (sermon O-2, discussion only).

[44] The figures are approximate because the sermon quotes other biblical phrases or clauses, and refers to biblical stories and characters, without identification.

[45] These figures are based on A-48.

reader to the second member of Bromyard's *Distinctio* 97.[46] The context indeed agrees with a point made in Bromyard's sermon collection as indicated: anyone who helps a sinner to commit a sin or to conceal it shares himself in that sin.[47] This is hardly a homiletic commonplace, and Sheppey must have read Bromyard's work very carefully. The same Ash Wednesday sermon further contains two marginalia with other references to Bromyard. In one, Sheppey (the marginalia are written by the same hand as the text, both probably Sheppey's) sends the reader to further material on the subject treated at this point in the sermon: "If you want more on Compassion, see in Bromyard C.12."[48] The reference is to section C.xii, on Compassion, in Bromyard's *Summa praedicantium*. The other marginal notation refers again to Bromyard: next to the sermon division Sheppey wrote: "For these note in Doctor Bromyard *Distinction* 55."[49] A look at the distinction reveals that Sheppey not only took the fourfold division but in addition borrowed heavily from Bromyard's second and third parts, writing in fact a redacted, expanded version of his source. In a different sermon, on *Qui manducat hunc panem vivet in aeternum* ("He who eats this bread shall live forever," John 6:59) and probably intended for Corpus Christi, Sheppey once more refers several times to Bromyard, now to the article on the Eucharist in his *Summa praedicantium*.[50] Bromyard thus furnished homiletic material, including *exempla*, for proof and elaboration, for structural distinctions, and even for theological doctrine.

In our collections, including Sheppey's, these various uses of Bromyard can be found in some twenty named quotations. Thus "Brom3erd" is mentioned in one of the Cambridge academic sermons, on the dedication of a church (C-74), whereas R-1 alludes to "auctor in *Summa predicancium*" and E-30 quotes "Bromiardus in Summa," all on moral matters. Brinton, too, may have drawn on the *Summa* extensively and repeatedly, although he never mentions Bromyard or the title of his work.[51] But the most significant use of the *Summa* with identification was made by another of Sheppey's fellow Benedictines, Robert

---

[46] "Quere de hoc in D[octore] Bromard d[istinccione] 97, membro 2, ad hoc signum o-o." Oxford, New College, MS 92, f. 158v. The copy of *Distincciones*, in Bodley 859, has no such sign.

[47] Oxford, Bodleian Library, MS Bodley 859, f. 174v, in a sermon for St. Cedd on *Ecce quomodo amabat eum*.

[48] "Si velis plus de compassione vide in Brom3ard C.12," f. 158v.

[49] "De istis nota in D[octore] Brom3ard d[istinccione] lv," f. 156v.

[50] "Nota illam [i.e. narracionem] que scribitur E.6 articulo 6, et totum quod sequitur usque ad articulum 7" (New College, MS 92, f. 171); "nota E.6.13 ... ibidem 21 ... ibidem 17" (f. 171). In the *Summa praedicantium*, article E.vi deals with the Eucharist.

[51] Of the seventy references to Bromyard the editor gives in her index, some thirty passages occur in Bromyard with varying degrees of closeness, of which – as is usual with Brinton – a number are in more than one sermon; Brinton, *Sermons*, pp. 514–515.

Rypon, who often refers to him as "doctor Brum3ard". I have counted at least thirteen instances in his sermons. Modern scholars often speak of Bromyard's work simply as a collection and treasure trove of *exempla* and pious stories, but in effect it is much more than a florilegium, for together with the illustrative material for the theological and moral topics that it provides in its 189 alphabetical articles, it also discusses the topics themselves by defining them, explaining major issues, raising objections, and so forth. Rypon clearly read and utilized Bromyard for this totality of what the learned Dominican had to offer. Thus he quotes little stories to illustrate a point, such as the anecdote about a devil named Gerard, who helped a miller grind his grain. One day the master gave him a new coat. When Gerard looks at himself so neatly attired, he refuses further help, saying, "Should such a proud man grind grain?" Apparently one of Bromyard's favorite tales, it appears at least twice in the *Summa*; and Rypon quotes it with acknowledgment against bad priests who, once they have received a benefice, refuse to serve God and men diligently.[52] Elsewhere, *exempla* from Bromyard have not merely an illustrative but a probative function. Thus, several stories from Bromyard's article on believing in dreams are quoted to argue that such belief is erroneous (RY-9). Similarly, Rypon borrows a simile from the *Summa praedicantium* to show that in the mystical body of the Church, while some members are at rest, others always are at prayer (RY-39). Later in the same sermon, Rypon returns to Bromyard's article on *Oratio*, discussing distraction during prayer and the efficacy of prayer for the person who prays for others, and at this point he relies on distinctions and explanations from Bromyard without any *exempla*. In the same way, in a sermon on Temptation he borrows a listing of seven kinds of help one may receive in temptation (RY-8), and in yet another sermon, on witchcraft, he rebuts the argument that witches bind devils through the power of God's name with a quotation from Bromyard, to which he adds that "St. Thomas teaches the same" (RY-9).

If Rypon thus makes frequent and varied use of Bromyard's *Summa*, he gives no evidence of having known Bromyard's contemporary and fellow Dominican Robert Holcot at all. Yet Holcot appears in the other sermon collections even more frequently than Bromyard: I have found over sixty references with his name. Of the quotations that identify Holcot's works, many come from his sermons, one from his commentary on Ecclesiasticus, one from his *Distinctiones*, and the remainder (thirty) from his commentary on the Book of Wisdom. The latter is a sequential series of lectures on the Old Testament book that enjoyed a great and

---

[52] RY-15, f. 55. In Bromyard's *Summa* at D.11.17 (MS Royal 7.E.iv, f. 134va) and G.4.12 (f. 218ra).

international reputation.[53] Holcot is quoted in eighteen of the collections that are here surveyed.[54]

Holcot's commentary on Wisdom is of course a very different book than Bromyard's *Summa*. As a series of lectures, it follows the biblical text, divides and interprets it, and then treats relevant theological and moral issues raised by the text in the mode employed by an academic lecturer. But the commentary also addresses future preachers and their needs, and thus is filled with material for possible use in preaching, from distinctions to prooftexts and illustrative similes and narratives; and an alphabetical index of key terms provides easy access to major topics.[55] As with Bromyard, the sermon collections display the whole range of this material. Thus a later preacher will use a few words from Holcot's commentary to support his own point: "As Holkot says in his *On the Book of Wisdom*, such is the progression of falling into sin: first to neglect small matters and thus not paying attention to Christ's words in Luke 16, 'He who is faithful in what is least, is also faithful in what is greater.'" And he continues to borrow from Holcot by quoting the subsequent simile of hoops that hold a barrel together.[56] Another preacher takes over Holcot's comparing the world to an innkeeper and men to wayfarers who stay for a night and are then forgotten, and elaborates the image with several of the points made by Holcot.[57] *Exempla* are similarly borrowed with acknowledgment, such as the two dragons in Armenia who prevent travelers from passing through the mountains and thus illustrate pride,[58] or several tales of ancient heroes.[59] But the borrowing goes beyond short probative and illustrative quotations to longer citations that teach and develop some theological issue, such as the three kinds of harm a perjurer does,[60] or the signs by which a person can know whether he or she has the Holy Spirit;[61] or

[53] Holcot incepted as DTh at Oxford in 1332 and died probably in 1349. He may have given the course on Wisdom at Cambridge. See *BRUO* 2:946–947.

[54] C (seven), CO (twenty-one), D (one), DY (at least one), E (two in the same sermon), FE (at least two), H (two), J (four), N (one), O (three), P2 (one), Q (five), R (three, including an English sermon), RE (at least one), S (one), W (two), Z (two).

[55] For instance, the "Tabula . . . Holkoth super librum Sapiencie" in Lincoln Cathedral, MS 68, ff. 190–199v. This follows upon a similar alphabetical subject index to Grosseteste's *Dicta* (see below), on ff. 181v–190.

[56] H-2, from Holcot's *lectio* 36. References to Holcot's lectures on Wisdom are to Holcot, *Super libros Sapientiae*.

[57] J/5-53, from Holcot's *lectio* 67.

[58] H-119, from lection 141, which however illustrates lust.

[59] C-2; O-4; O-5; P2-53.

[60] DY-2 (f. 6r–v), with material from Augustine, Bernard, and canon law copied between points 2 and 3.

[61] N-77, from Holcot's commentary on Sirach.

reasons for and the efficacy of praying for the souls in purgatory;[62] or Mary's privileged status of sinlessness;[63] or Holcot's views on image worship.[64] The range of borrowings from Holcot is nicely reflected in a sermon on *Venite ascendamus ad montem Domini* ("Come, let us go up to the mountain of the Lord," Isaiah 2:3). It mentions Holcot's name three times: once in a short authoritative quotation that "a little play is sufficient," and twice in a longer exegesis of the story of the drunken Noah, which shows four evil effects of intoxication and includes the moralization of an image of Drunkenness. Beyond that, the same preacher has evidently also borrowed Holcot's four kinds of *invitatoria* that can be found in Scripture and used this as his major sermon division, albeit now without giving Holcot credit.[65]

The last passage just referred to is also utilized by a second preacher, and this time with acknowledgment. Z-54 deals with the thema *Psallite Domino qui ascendit* ("Sing a psalm to the Lord who ascends," Ps. 67:5) and speaks at some length of singing, using several musical terms. Embedded in this development is Holcot's entire passage on the four *invitatoria*, which provides approximately a third of the entire sermon. Another passage from Holcot, his development of the seven properties of boys, *pueri*, which are summarized in two Latin hexameters and then applied to the seven deadly sins, similarly became somewhat of a commonplace. In J/5-49 this material forms practically the entire sermon.[66] Exactly same text, with the same variations from Holcot's text, occurs again in Felton's sermon 11, though here the passage on *pueri* forms only the second part of the sermon, which deals with the second part of the gospel lection, the healing of the boy, *puer*, of the centurion (Matthew 8:5-13). Clearly, Holcot was a great favorite with English preachers, and the same is evidenced by the fact that

---

[62] J/5-32, a longer extract from Holcot on Wisdom, *lectio* 42.

[63] W-104: "Nam secundum doctorem Holkote post Verbi incarnacionem tanta Spiritus Sancti superaddita fuit gracia que flexibilitatem libiri [*read* liberi] arbitrii solum determinauit ad bonum, sic quod ex tunc nullo modo potuit in malum sed sic in vita stabilita ac confirmata fuit quod deinceps peccare non potuerit," f. 199, from Holcot's *lectio* 160.

[64] Z-16 copies a passage on image worship from Holcot, *lectio* 157, in two parts, reversed, the second with Holcot's name. O-18 refers to the same *lectio* and quotes a shorter sentence.

[65] E-30. "Eodem modo est secundum Hiscolte [!] *Super Sapienciam* de ludo: Modicus sufficit," f. 81vb, from *lectio* 59. The two quotations on drunkenness come from *lectio* 20. The four *invitatoria* are biblical passages beginning "Venite . . ." attributed respectively to greedy, lustful, mischievous, and virtuous people, and are borrowed from *lectio* 19. Holcot on *invitatorium* is also quoted in FE-6, which is a more distant paraphrase; see Fletcher, *Preaching*, pp. 86–90, especially lines 99–101.

[66] From Holcot's *lectio* 118. In the sections on several sins F omits material from Holcot and adds some of its own.

in several collections extracts or entire chapters from *In Sapientiam* appear next to proper sermons.[67]

If Bromyard and Holcot were used extensively and widely, they are far outshone by an earlier English theologian. Robert Grosseteste, bishop of Lincoln from 1235 to 1253, left a varied and internationally esteemed oeuvre ranging from translations from the Greek, to commentaries and treatises on philosophical, theological, and scientific matters, to letters, sermons, and pastoral writings. Judging by the incidence of his quotations, his influence on English preachers of the fourteenth and fifteenth centuries was huge. I have found him quoted in nearly all the collections analyzed here, in over 165 different sermons (not counting multiple copies), many of them with more than one and up to seven citations (Chambron's *Mundus crucifixus est*).[68] A particular fondness for Grosseteste is shown by Dygon, Rypon, Repingdon, the Repingdon-derived sermons in M/3, and the academic sermons in collection C. Where the works quoted are identified, as most of them are, the borrowed material comes predominantly from his *Dicta* and from a number of his sermons.[69] His commentaries on the works of Dionysius have also furnished some material, as have his longer treatises on the Decalogue (*De decem mandatis*),[70] his *Exameron*, and the *De cessacione legalium* (both in W-129). Several times he is quoted for explaining a biblical passage, while his scientific works appear twice and his letters once. Some other treatises that went under his name but are today considered of dubious or different authorship also occur with some regularity, such as the *Summa iusticie*, *De lingua*, *De venenis*, and *De septem noctibus*.[71] References to "De corde" and "De spirituali paradiso" may or may not be to actual titles.[72] Finally, the *De oculo morali*, by

---

[67] Several lectures from Holcot's *In Sapientiam* were copied into the sermon collection F/4; similarly a sermon in collection M/4 refers to "abstracta de Hulkot" earlier in the codex which are now lost. Extracts from Holcot also appear in sermon notebooks, such as Z. Individual sermons by him, too, were copied into later collections, as for instance CA/2, S, Y/1, X, and Padua Antoniana 515.

[68] Apparently without Grosseteste quotations are the sermons by FitzRalph (FI) and Brinton (BR).

[69] The distinction between sermon and *dictum* is fluid, as Grosseteste himself says, and is reflected in his manuscripts as well as the quotations; see below, n. 79. For the medieval table to the *Dicta* see above, n. 30.

[70] Dygon borrows heavily from *De decem mandatis*; shorter quotations appear in J/5-12, H-11, and RY-9.

[71] *Summa iusticie*: FE-18, 20, and 50; *De lingua*: three different quotations in J/5-34 and J/5-14 (two), also FE-19 and 30; *De venenis*: J/5-7 and J/5-35, two each, also FE-37; *De septem noctibus*: RY-8.

[72] In J/5-14, and C-42 and 120, respectively. Sermons in D quote him on "De investigacione summarum causarum," "De discrecione spirituum," and "De forma pura."

Peter of Limoges, is consistently attributed to Grosseteste and quoted at least half a dozen times, in four collections.[73]

From Grosseteste's genuine works the preachers frequently borrow short similes, explanations of biblical passages, and definitions. Some of the latter clearly were commonplaces to be appropriated by more than one preacher; thus his definitions of sin as the devil's progeny,[74] of mercy as the desire to relieve a wretch of his misery,[75] and of the king as a ruler[76] all appear in several sermons. Beyond these, longer passages are directly copied or else quoted implicitly (*sententialiter*), whether in answer to a question raised by the preacher, or to develop part of the sermon, or to furnish authoritative teaching on a point of faith or morality. Dygon especially engages in this practice frequently, copying long passages from Grosseteste; but Robert Rypon, too, draws heavily on Grosseteste's works, particularly his *De decem mandatis*. It is clear that Grosseteste was a cherished authority for teaching unusual matters, such as the notion that a higher degree of perfection is reached when one adds bodily poverty to one's poverty of the spirit (N-67). It may also be that many a Grosseteste quotation was used not only for its substance but its elegant style, as in this passage:

> Vnde Lincolniensis in quodam sermone quasi loquens in persona Domini sic ait: "O auare, lucrum quere, da et recipies. Da terrena et celestia sume. Da temporalia et sume eterna. Da mea et meipsum sume. Quod si non feceris, michi es contrarius et omnibus operibus meis, et inimicus nature et gracie aduersarius." Hec ille.[77]
>
> ("Whence the bishop of Lincoln says in some sermon, as if he were speaking in the person of the Lord: 'O greedy man, seek gain: give and you shall receive. Give earthly things and receive heavenly ones. Give temporal things and receive eternal ones. Give things [you have] from me and receive my own self. If you do not do so, you are against me and all my works, an enemy to nature and an opponent to grace.' Thus Grosseteste.")

---

[73] In C-61, C-72, H-14, R-30 (English), RY-12 and 13. The editor of *De oculo morali*, Professor Richard Newhauser, confirms that the quotations are from Peter's work.

[74] "Peccatum est diaboli progenies, mortis parens, nature corruptio, boni privatio, anime captivatio," from Grosseteste's *Sint lumbi vestri precincti* (in *Fasciculus rerum* 2:272), appears (with variants) in DY-3, E-39, FE-50, M/3-20, P2-14, RE-19, W-149.

[75] "Misericordia est amor siue voluntas releuandi miserum a miseria," from Grosseteste's *Dictum* 2, appears in H-10 and 11 (the latter without acknowledgment), M/3-31, M/4-8, and RY-19.

[76] "Rex a regendo dicitur, ideo rex recte nominatur qui regiminis sibi commissi gubernacula recte moderatur," from Grosseteste's *Rex sapiens stabilimentum* (*Fasciculus rerum* 2.258), quoted in M/3-51, RE-49, and RY-1.

[77] A-50, f. 157.

Such sentences have a rhetorical ring reminiscent of Augustine and Bernard of Clairvaux, and in fact Grosseteste is often linked with the latter. In one sermon a work by Grosseteste is even wrongly ascribed to Bernard.[78]

His doctrinal matter quoted by later preachers covers a wide range of faith and morals, including such topics as the ugliness of sin (P2-14), judgment (M/3-34), tribulation (DY-4), qualities of prayer (DY-16), right fasting (RY-12, 13, 31), perfect love (RY-38), how Adam could fall for the devil's promise "You will be like gods" although he knew God and all creatures (S-19), why Christ died on a cross (N-74), whether a perverse sinner deserves pity (Q-30), why we must confess our sins to a priest (M/3-17), whether one should give alms to *histriones* (M/3-39), and much else. Evidently a favorite was his exposition of the Ten Commandments, *De decem mandatis*, from which both Dygon and Rypon copied large blocks of material. But Grosseteste's most important contribution to preaching in the later fourteenth and the fifteenth centuries comes from his teachings about the priestly office and his criticism of negligent pastors. At least six sermon collections, including Dygon's, Rypon's, and CO, derive substantial amounts of relevant material from the bishop's well-known sermons and *Dicta* that deal with such pastoral matters.[79] As one might suspect, a number of these sermons are addressed to the clergy and were made for synods and visitations.[80] But others are designated for various Sundays throughout the Church year and even the Tuesday after Pentecost[81] and may thus have had mixed audiences. Their mode of integrating Grosseteste material also varies considerably, ranging from Dygon's verbatim copying to Rypon's selective quotation and paraphrase from more than one Grosseteste text. It is quite clear that Rypon did not simply copy fitting authoritative quotations (as did Dygon) but utilized Grosseteste's

---

[78] DY-48: "Vnde Bernardus in tractatu orandi qui sic incipit 'Deus est quo nichil melius cogitari potest' . . ." (f. 205). In DY-16 Dygon quotes the same work correctly as *Quomodo examinandus est penitens* and attributes it to "Lincolniensis" (f. 58). The quotations come from Grosseteste's "Deus est": see Wenzel, "Robert Grosseteste's Treatise," pp. 256–257.

[79] The two categories overlap in the sermon quotations as well as the tradition of Grosseteste manuscripts, and the lack of a clear distinction seems to go back to Grosseteste himself; see S. Harrison Thomson, *Writings*, p. 214. Thomson lists sermons and *Dicta* at pp. 160–191 and 214–232, with brief notes on their content. Grosseteste wrote and evidently preached a number of sermons on the pastoral office, some of which were edited in *Fasciculus rerum* 2:250–307. Especially popular were *Ego sum pastor bonus* (with the six parts of the pastoral office based on John 10:11; quoted in M/3-24, RY-3, and RY-54), *Exemplum esto* (developing a mirror of priestly behavior based on 1 Timothy 4:12; quoted in M/3-21, M/4-20, and RY-54), *Scriptum est de levitis* (quoted in DY-20 and E-8), and *Vae pastoribus* (quoted in O-20, W-16, and RY-56). Other sermons of a similar nature are Grosseteste's *Beati pauperes, Beatus Paulus, Dominus noster Iesus Christus, In libro Numerorum*, and *Natis et educatis*.

[80] E-8 and 9; RY-54 to 57; possibly O-20 and W-16.

[81] Dygon in DY-20; RY-3; O-27; M/3-21, M/3-24; M/4-8. The occasion is undetermined for M/4-2.

thoughts and words meaningfully as a basis for his own teaching and sermon structure.[82]

Grosseteste's writings thus had a major impact on preaching in the later fourteenth and fifteenth centuries – not only on Wyclif and his followers but on their orthodox contemporaries as well. This interest in "Lincolniensis" can still be seen, for instance, in marginal annotations in the unique manuscript of Brinton's sermon. In MS Harley 3760 several medieval and later readers have left occasional notes in the margins, mostly concerning sources and important points. One reader, writing an upright, fine cursive Anglicana, mentions "Lincolniensis" at least three times.[83] And in the 1450s, Thomas Gascoigne, theologian and chancellor of Oxford, still quotes Grosseteste (together with FitzRalph) in support of his own criticism of abuses in the contemporary Church and reports that he had seen Grosseteste's commentaries on the Psalms and the Pauline epistles, written in Grosseteste's own hand, in the library of the Oxford Franciscans.[84]

Given the frequency with which Grosseteste, Bromyard, and Holcot are quoted, one may thus speak of an "English theology." As I showed at the beginning of this chapter, the sermons in the collections under consideration are no equivalent to academic theological discourse in their level of analysis and academic form.[85] Nevertheless, a good number of them are certainly theologically informed. Likewise, these sermons do not pursue abstract or philosophical topics that were current among systematic theologians of the time, such as whether God has foreknowledge of future contingents, or whether charity is required for every meritorious act, or whether the substance of bread is annihilated in the Eucharist, or whether the Bible can and may legitimately be translated into the vernacular. Where they do address larger issues of theological speculation, these tend to be questions debated in an earlier age. A good case is a sermon in the theologically weighted collection of Cambridge, Pembroke College, MS 199 (P1-23). The sermon is addressed to the clergy and begins in English but soon shifts to Latin. In it, the anonymous preacher, probably a Dominican, develops his thema – "I know a man in Christ" (2 Corinthians 12:2) – by showing that a man

---

[82] I have not included Repingdon in the collections that quote Grosseteste on the pastoral office at some length because, while in his sermon 22 Repingdon does copy Grosseteste's popular passage on the six parts of the pastoral office (in *Ego sum pastor bonus*), he seems to do so because he is essentially giving an exegesis of his own thema, *Ego sum pastor bonus*. The same process can be observed in RE-50, where he extracts material from Grosseteste's sermon on *Rex sapiens* in his exegesis of the word *regulus* from the lection.

[83] Ff. 143v, 172, and 186. The first two mention Holcot together with Grosseteste. The second note refers to "in primo mandato," the third to *Dictum* 2.

[84] Gascoigne, *Loci*, pp. 103, 126–127, 129, 138, 142, 170, 192. See also Gieben, "Thomas Gascoigne."

[85] The exception is collection CO, which is unusual in other ways as well. But the texture of its "sermons," too, is not the same as that of quodlibets or *quaestiones*.

can be in Christ through the power of the Father, the science of the Son, and the grace of the Holy Spirit. The power of the Father is shown in the Son, and the preacher addresses the old question of how sinful man could be saved from the devil's bondage:

> He absolutely had to show this power if he wanted to free nature reasonably from the power of the devil and save it. Anselm proves this in book 1 of *Why God Became Man*, where he puts this question: "Who could give satisfaction for the sin that had been committed and thus bring man back to his original standing?" To which Anselm answers saying that God could do so but this was not fitting; man ought to do have done so but he was unable. Hence it was necessarily to be God and man: God who could and man who ought to. For this reason God the Son, who is God and man, came into this world and took on our nature. Surely that was a great power, for no creature could have shown it. Anselm proves this in the same place: "If man," he says, "had been redeemed by another, he would have become the servant of him who redeemed him and thus would have had another lord than the true God, and in consequence would not have been restored to his original standing." And so God had to show this power altogether if he wanted to redeem human nature and set the whole order of creation in perfect order, as Fishacre shows in his commentary on book 1 of the *Sentences*. His reason is this: "As long as the beginning and the end of a circle are not fitted together, the circle is imperfect. But God and man are the circle of the whole creation, because God is its beginning and man its end. Therefore, before these two natures became united there was no perfect union, but through God's power, in the union and conjunction of the two the circle was perfected, for through God's power divinity and human nature are in one person, the beginning and end of the circle so joined and united that they can never again be separated from each other." As the Athanasian Creed has it: "Perfect God and perfect man, consisting in a rational soul and human flesh."[86]

---

[86] "Istam potenciam oportuit ipsum omnino ostendisse si voluisset naturam de potestate diaboli racionabiliter liberasse et saluasse. Hoc probat Anselmus 1 *Cur Deus homo*, vbi querit istam questionem: Quis potuit pro peccato commisso satisfacere et sic hominem ad pristinum gradum reparare? Ad quam respondet dicens quod Deus potuit sed non decuit; homo debuit sed non potuit. Oportuit igitur quod fuisset Deus et homo, Deus qui potuit et homo qui debuit. Propter quam causam Filius Deus [!], qui est Deus et homo, in hunc mundum venit et nostram naturam assumpsit. Ista potencia certe [*or iuste*] erat magna, quia istam potenciam nulla creatura potuit ostendisse. Quod probat Anselmus ibidem: 'Si homo, inquit, per alium fuisset redemptus, seruus fuisset illius redimentis, et sic habuisset alium dominum quam Deum verum, et per consequens non fuisset restitutus ad gradum pristinum.' Et ideo istam potenciam oportuit eum omnino ostendisse si voluisset humanam naturam redemisse et totum / ordinem creaturarum perfecte operasse, sicut probat Fyschaker super 1 *Sentenciarum*, et racio sua est hec: 'Quamdiu principium uel finis circuli non coniunguntur, tamdiu circulus est imperfectus. Sed Deus et homo sunt circulus omnium creaturarum, quia Deus est principium, homo est finis. Ergo

This is an unusually "theological" passage in the sermons here studied, particularly by its quoting Fishacre; and yet the argumentation belongs to the twelfth and thirteenth centuries and is free from the refined Aristotelian logic and dialectic of the fourteenth.

Much more commonly than such issues of speculative theology, these collections reflect practical and ecclesiological concerns that were debated in the contemporary schools. Jeremy Catto has said about Oxford theology in our period: "Above all, the period of Oxford history which lasted from 1356 to 1430 was an era of controversy, focussing on the apostolic mission of the clergy . . . In the century after Fitzralph pastoral duty would be a constant theme of debate in the Oxford schools, diverting the masters' attention from philosophical questions to issues of immediate and universal concern."[87] What "theology" one finds in the sermon collections is precisely of this nature, such as: concern with the dignity and demands of the pastoral office, the privilege of mendicants and especially whether confession made to a friar must be repeated before one's *proprius sacerdos*, the legitimacy of image worship, or the disendowment of the clergy. Of these, the concern about preaching and the pastoral office especially merits closer attention.

---

ante vnionem istarum duarum naturarum non erat vnitas perfecta sed in potencia vnionis et coniunccionis illarum erat circulus perfectus, quia in vna persona sunt per potenciam Patris deitas et humanitas, que sunt principium et finis circuli coniuncti et vniti, quod nunquam possunt deinceps ab inuicem separari.' Vt in symbolo Athanasii habetur: 'Perfectus Deus, perfectus homo, ex anima racionali et humana carne subsistens'," P1-23, f. 84ra–b.

[87] Catto, "Wyclif and Wycliffism," pp. 180–181. Similarly Courtenay, *Schools*, p. 379: "What late fourteenth-century Oxford exported was not its current logic, epistemology, or scholastic theology but its practical, eucharistic, and penitential theology, both Wycliffite and anti-Wycliffite."

47

Preaching and the pastoral office

"A priest's office is to regulate the moral life of his subjects, to drive off their errors, to solve their doubts and answer their questions, *and to preach elegantly well-constructed and moral sermons.*"[1] These words of the anonymous Hereford preacher emphasize that within the range of pastoral duties that sermons *ad clerum* praise and whose neglect they sharply criticize, preaching takes a very important place. Whereas we had occasion to observe that in Church legislation and official registers, administering the sacraments seems to push preaching somewhat to the side, the situation in actual sermons is quite the reverse.[2] Virtually all collections here surveyed contain observations about preaching and preachers. Some may only have a passing remark, usually in their protheme,[3] where a preacher is frequently identified with a term from the sermon's thema: he is God's mouth, Moses, the sower, light and a lamp, the wielder of a sword, and so forth. But others go beyond such similes and speak at greater length about the office of preaching, the qualities of a good preacher, and a preacher's failings. Some do so in their protheme, others throughout the entire development.[4]

Where this occurs, preaching is held to be a major part of a priest's duties. The sermons in collection E that are directed to the clergy and deal with the threefold etymology of *sacerdos* as *sacris deditus*, *sacra dans*, and *sacra docens* place "sowing

---

[1] "Sacerdotis nempe officium est subditorum mores componere, errores eorum effugare, dubia dissoluere, et ad interrogata respondere, sermones compositos et honestos ornate proferre," E-23, f. 58ra.

[2] See above, pp. 236–237.

[3] In scholastic sermons, the protheme was traditionally the locus to discuss the office of preaching; see Schneyer, *Unterweisung*. In addition to Brinton, prothemes often include a remark about the preacher's office in FE, J/5, RY, S, W, X, and other collections.

[4] Longer discussions of preaching in prothemes occur especially in Brinton; see his sermons 7, 20, 59, 66, 69, and 72. An entire sermon devoted to the preaching office is A-49, on *Viam Dei in veritate doces* and directed to the clergy. Its two main principals that are developed answer the questions how and what the *curatus animarum siue predicator verbi Dei* must preach to the people. Other cases are quoted in the following paragraphs.

the seed of the gospels among their subjects" (*euangeliorum spirituale semen subditis seminando*) next to leading an exemplary saintly life and to administering the sacraments (E-23). "Pastors and curates must frequently offer the souls of their subjects spiritual seed, the bread of the word of God,"[5] says the anonymous preacher, and then devotes much of his sermon to this office, which involves preaching the words of the gospel clearly and without obscurity, being faithful to it, and seeking the audience's good with sweetness and compassion. If this serious concern for preaching the word of God might tempt modern readers to detect a tone of Lollardy, I should point out that the same preacher explicitly turns against

> heretics, hypocrites, and Lollards, who with their wretched doctrine hardly ever cease to deceive the meek and the simple in the Church. Against them the faithful shepherd must fight strongly with the keenness of the words of sacred scripture and, given his pastoral staff, with the threat of censure.[6]

Since priests are obliged to preach, and preaching was the most important activity of Christ, the office of preaching is the most important.[7] It is the rudder in the ship of the Church, says one preacher; and another, in a twist of Gregory the Great's famous saying, declares that preaching – not the cure of souls – is "ars arcium."[8] In one of his major documents on the pastoral office, a sermon on "I am the good shepherd," Grosseteste had, on the basis of that text, divided the pastoral office into six parts. The first part, entering through the door (John 10:2), the bishop had interpreted as entering the ears and minds of the audience through preaching the word of God:

> First, he who is installed in the pastoral office must preach the word of Christ or Christ the Word, and thus through preaching Christ enters as if through the door (for Christ himself is the door) into the minds of his subjects, as if into the sheepfold.[9]

---

[5] "Frequenter tenentur pastores et curati spiritualem semen, panem verbi Dei, subditis sibi animabus porrigere," E-23, f. 58rb.

[6] "Heretici, ypocrite, et lollardi designantur, qui per prauam doctrinam mites ac simplices in Ecclesia decipere minime cessant, contra quos fidelis pastor asperitate verborum scripture sacre baculoque pastorali censurarum fulminacione cum sancto pastore Dauid fortiter dimicaret eosque a subditis sibi fidelibus vsque ad sanguinis effusionem constanter fugaret," E-23, f. 59va.

[7] "Officium prelatorum stat in predicacione, est maximus actus Christi, ergo officium prelatoris est maximum," C-137, p. 122.

[8] Rudder: O-10, f. 62v. Gregory spoke of *regimen animarum* as the *ars artium* in his *Regula pastoralis* 1.1 (PL 77:14), although of course he was dealing with pastoral instruction and preaching, too. The phrase is applied to *predicacio verbi Dei* in M/4-10 and 13 (ff. 311vb and 313vb).

[9] *Fasciculus rerum* 2:261. Grosseteste's remarks on preaching have been collected by Gieben, "Robert Grosseteste."

This unusual interpretation, and with it Grosseteste's exegesis of *Ego sum pastor bonus*, appears in several sermons that discuss the preacher's office at greater length.[10]

Given this importance, it is not astonishing that some preachers might declare preaching and hearing the word of God to be as important as, if not more important than, celebrating Mass and receiving Communion. An English sermon declares:

> þerfor, for soþe, it is more nedful and spedful þe pepul to haue prechyng and techyng þan it ys to haue masse or matyns; and þat is most nedful schuld raþer be done. þerfor prestis ben more bounden to preche or to say masse or matyns.[11]

Such a statement may strike us as reflecting a Lollard milieu, and collection Z, where it appears, seems indeed to stand on the borderline between orthodox and Lollard preaching. But another, undoubtedly orthodox preacher of the early fifteenth century similarly declared that "the word of God seems to be greater than the Body of the Lord," in expanding a sentence of the *Decretum* that "he who lets the Lord's Body fall on the ground sins no less than he who hears the word of God with negligence."[12] The same notion was expressed already earlier in the same collection and apparently by the same preacher: "Whoever hears the word of God negligently does not sin less than he who treads the Body of Christ in the sacrament under foot."[13] Ranking preaching as equal to the sacraments was not new to Gratian; long before the twelfth century Caesarius of Arles had said in one of his sermons, "Which seems to you greater, the word of God or the Body of Christ? If you want to speak the truth, you must say that the word of God is not less great than the Body of Christ."[14] The relative priority of the word

---

[10] E-22; M/3-24; RY-03 and 54.   [11] Z-15, f. 41vb.

[12] "Dicit Canon I questione I, / *Interrogo*, quod non minus peccat qui corpus dominicum permittit in terram cadere quam qui verbum Domini necgligenter audit. Nonne verbo Domini celi firmati sunt, spiritu oris eius omnis virtus eorum? Nonne et ipsum corpus dominicum ministerio sacerdotis in altari factum est sub specie panis per verbum Domini? Maius ergo videtur verbum Domini quam corpus Domini. Sic ergo peccatum est necgligenter sentire corpus Domini et tam grande vel maius est necligenter audire verbum Domini," S-14, f. 57r-v. The canonical reference is to Friedberg 1:391.

[13] "Et ideo dicit *Decretalis* quod non minus peccat qui verbum Dei necgligenter audit quam qui corpus Christi in sacramento pedibus conculcat, <I, q. 1, Interrogo>" S-2, f. 15bis, verso.

[14] "Quid vobis plus esse videtur, verbum Dei an corpus Christi? Si vultis verum respondere, hoc utique dicere debetis, quod non sit minus verbum Dei quam corpus Christi," *Sermo* 78.2 (CCSL 103:407). On other pre-fourteenth-century expressions of the same notion see Rouse and Rouse, *Preachers*, pp. 61–64. Notice also the story about St. Louis trying to dampen Henry III's fervor to hear and serve at several masses a day reported in Rishanger, *Chronica*, pp. 74–75. I owe this reference to Professor Joseph Goering.

of God or the sacrament is nicely handled by Robert Rypon, basing himself on a distinction that St. Thomas Aquinas drew with his customary evenhandedness. In dealing with the question of how much learning different groups of the clergy must have, Aquinas distinguished between two different acts of priesthood: one regarding the true Body of Christ (i.e. the sacrament of the Eucharist), the other – which is secondary – regarding the mystical body of Christ (i.e. the Church). Some, Aquinas says, receive priestly orders to carry out the first act, that is, to administer the sacraments; these are the religious and simple priests who have no cure of souls, and they need to know only as much as is necessary to administer the sacraments correctly. Others, however, receive priestly orders to carry out the second act, and they need to have the knowledge of God's law in order to teach the people. To this distinction Rypon adds:

> From these words it is very clear that religious and simple priests who do not have the cure of souls are held to know only what belongs to the Church's sacraments. But curates are held to have knowledge of Holy Scripture, with which they are to preach the word of God to the people. And the higher clergy are held to know the law so well that they may be able to give answers to all difficult questions of the law when it becomes necessary.[15]

Preaching is therefore, as Brinton says, the most awesome of human activities,[16] whose neglect merits God's wrath and eternal death.[17] But when done conscientiously, it not only leads its hearers to God but is most meritorious for the preacher, even when his efforts remain fruitless.[18] His first task is to instruct his flock in the faith. But that is not all: besides preaching the faith, he must "instruct them to have good morals, reprehend their vices, and stir them to penance."[19] Or as another preacher has it,

> To the preacher's office belongs first to ascend the mountain of virtues. Then he must, with alluring exhortations, efficiently invite the people to

---

[15] "Ex quibus euidet luculenter quod religiosi et simplices sacerdotes curam animarum non habentes tenentur scire solum ea que pertinent ad Ecclesie sacramenta, sed curati tenentur habere scienciam scripture sacre, qua predicent populo verbum Dei. Sed superiores prelati taliter legem scire tenentur quod ad omnes difficiles questiones legis valeant cum opus fuerit respondere," RY-53, f. 197. The passage referred to is Thomas Aquinas, *Super 4 Sentenciarum*, dist. 34, c. 12 [or 13?], responsio. For a similar ranking in Stephen Langton, see Quinto, "Influence," p. 64.

[16] "Magis terribile et premiosum," BR-59, p. 268; similarly BR-69, p. 315 (Devlin prints "periculosum," later the text has "preciosum"), and BR-72, p. 330 ("arduum et terribile").

[17] Thus Rypon in his sermon 58 (f. 214v), quoting Gregory's exegesis of Exodus 28:35 from *Regula pastoralis* 2.4 (PL 77:31).

[18] BR-59, p. 269, and BR-66, p. 299.

[19] "Fidem predicare, ad mores instruere, vicia reprehendere, et ad penitenciam excitare," RY-34, f. 129v.

give a sympathetic hearing to God's word, praise the virtues, inflame his audience to [strive for] the mountain of our heavenly home, reprove loudly errors and arrogance, reproach sins and crimes with an effective outcry, and condemn them with the witness of Holy Scripture.[20]

What thus stands very much in the foreground of what our sermons themselves have to say about preaching *ad populum* is their moral aim, their appeal to the will rather than to reason: "This is the office of preachers, that they try in every way as best they can to invite the people to penance and to grace. For it is better that a preacher have stimulating words . . . than one useless authoritative quote," and he will have done his duty when he has drawn people to fight against vices and consort with the virtues.[21] A more comprehensive definition declares that "the office of a priest is to order well the moral life of his subjects, to drive away their errors, to lay their doubts at rest and answer their questions, and to deliver well-constructed sermons of integrity."[22] A gospel that lent itself easily to being allegorized as the preacher's office was Christ's entry into Jerusalem, read on the first Sunday of Advent as well as on Palm Sunday (Matthew 21:1–9). Rypon, for instance, interprets the lection as teaching us that preachers, who are sent by Christ "to the village that is over against you," that is, sinful people, are to loose souls from the bonds of sin and lead them to Christ, so that he may dwell in their hearts.[23] Similarly, the gospel for 1 Lent, on Christ's temptation in the desert, teaches that "there are three things to which a preacher's intention must be directed: first that he inform sinners how they must rise from their sins; second that he teach those turned away from sins how they must progress in the virtues; and third that he teach everybody how they must resist temptation."[24]

---

[20] "Ad predicatoris siquidem officium primo pertinet virtutum ascendere montem, etc. Pertinet populum congruenter ad audiendum verbum Dei aleciis extortacionibus [!] ad benignam audienciam efficaciter inuitare, virtutes commendare, eosque ad montem celestis patrie inflammare, errores et insolencias increpare, peccata et facinora vtili clamore reprobare eademque sacre scripture testimonio detestari," A-30, f. 96.

[21] "Hoc est officium predicatorum, quod omni modo studea[n]t quomodo melius p[ossun]t populum ad penitenciam et graciam inuitare. Melius est enim quod predicator habeat verba excitatiua . . . quam vnam inutilem auctoritatem." S-16, f. 66v; "trahere audientes ad litem viciorum et ad concordiam virtutum," S-01, f. 1v.

[22] "Sacerdotis nempe officium est subditorum mores componere, errores eorum effugare, dubia dissoluere, et ad interrogata respondere, sermones compositos et honestos ornate proferre," E-23, f. 58ra.

[23] RY-01, f. 1r–v. Similarly M/3-01.

[24] "Tria sunt circa que versari debet intencio predicatoris: primum est ut informet peccatores quomodo debeant a peccatis resurgere; secundum est ut doceat a peccatis conuersos qualiter debeant in virtutibus proficere; tercium est ut doceat omnes quomodo debeant temptacionem resistere. Et hec triplex informacio in presenti euangelio continetur." M/3-17, f. 226va–b.

In order to "teach, move, and please" the people, the preacher needs to have "holiness of life, purity of learning, and *gravitas* of eloquence."[25] Together with holiness of life and charity towards his parishioners, then, it is especially knowledge and learning that are emphasized as primary requirements in the preacher. "We clerics," says one preacher, "who ought to be intercessors for the people, must not only not turn our ears away from God's law but also turn our eyes to studying and meditating on God's law, because a person will meditate on the law of him whose servant he is," and he supports this with quotations from canon law and Gregory the Great.[26] With similar support from Gregory another sermon in the same manuscript declares that "he who has received the office and cure of souls must always and for the greater part [of his life] study in Holy Scripture." This sermon deals with the miracle of feeding the four thousand (Mark 8:1–9) and stresses that Jesus gave bread to his disciples, which the disciples then distributed to the multitude: "In the disciples who distribute the loaves and collect the fragments lies an exemplary teaching for curates, whose task it is to distribute the bread of the word of God to their subjects and to diligently lay up the leftovers of Scripture in the treasure chest of their memory." The latter, he explains, means that preachers should "examine carefully the subtleties of Holy Scripture which laypeople do not understand, for their own use and that of the Church."[27]

Consequently, what sermons criticize most frequently in preachers is their lack of knowledge. Rypon reproaches priests who let others do their preaching for them with the excuse taken from civil law that "what someone does through another person, he is considered doing himself":

[25] "Docere, monere, placere," W-129, f. 244rb, with reference to Augustine, *De doctrina Christiana*; "vite sanctitas, sciencie puritas, eloquencie grauitas," B/2-06, f. 128va.

[26] "Nos clerici, qui essemus intercessores populi, non solum non declinaremus aures nostras a lege Dei, set eciam declinaremus oculos nostros ad studendum et meditandum in lege Dei, quia cuius est minister, eius et legem meditabitur" (M/4-13, f. 315ra), followed by citations of the canon *Ignorantia mater cunctorum errorum*, from Gratian, *Decretum*, Dist. 38, cap. 1 (Friedberg 1:141), and of Gregory's *Regula pastoralis* 2.11 (PL 77:48).

[27] "In discipulis panes distribuentibus et fragmenta colligentibus est exemplaris informacio curatorum, quorum interest panem verbi Dei subiectis distribuere et reliquias scripture in armariolo memorie diligenter recondere . . . / Et ut sacerdotes officium predicacionis conueniencius possint implere, debent reliquias mense Domini cum discipulis eius attencius colligere, idest subtilitates scripture sacre quas laici non intelligunt ad suam et Ecclesie vtilitatem perscrutare," M/3-37, f. 268ra–b. It may be worth pointing out that this and many other remarks of similar intent urge the centrality of Scripture, not of the Fathers or handbooks of theology, for a pastor's ongoing study.

Such a man I ask whether he knows how to preach or not. If he says, "I don't," then I say: The principal and necessary office of a curate is to inform the people in his care in the way of life that agrees with that of Christ and the apostles according to Holy Scripture and all holy doctors. And he is obligated foremost to carry out this principal office. So, if he does not know how to preach, he does not know how to carry out his office. From whence it follows that he is not worthy to hold that office.

And Rypon continues: if a priest has the knowledge as well as the power to preach and does not use it, "knowing that it is the will of his lord Jesus Christ that he should do so, what else is there to say but that 'the servant who knows the will of his lord and does not do it, will be beaten with many stripes' [Luke 12:47]?"[28] Elsewhere, inspired by Gregory and Grosseteste, Rypon laments "that many today, led by the spirit of ambition, assume this office but do not know how to preach nor want to learn."[29] Thus, next to ignorance it is neglect of preaching that is constantly chastized. To such priests another preacher applies the words of Isaiah 56:10: "His watchmen are blind" through ignorance, and "dumb dogs not able to bark," for they will not open their mouths to teach.[30] To illustrate this dumbness, the anonymous preacher of collection E uses twice a story from Alexander Nequam, about a sea bird whose cries warn animals living near the water of an imminent tide. But when this bird finds an oyster and tries to eat it, the oyster gets caught in his beak, the bird cannot cry, and the animals on the seashore perish in the tide.[31] The oyster, of course, signifies worldly values, and avarice is commonly blamed for causing priests to preach poorly, or rarely, or not at all. Another cause of failing to preach is fear of losing rank and possessions: "Where is now found the prelate or preacher who dares to speak the truth plainly?" asks one preacher, and continues:

---

[28] "Quero a tali vtrum scit predicare vel non. Si dicit 'Nescio,' tunc sic: Principale officium et necessarium curati est informare populum sibi subiectum in modo viuendi conformi vite Christi et apostolorum secundum sacram scripturam et omnes sacros doctores, et ad suum principale officium faciendum principaliter obligatur. Si ergo nescit predicare, nescit suum officium implere. Ex quo sequitur quod non est dignus ipsum officium occupare. Si sciat predicare, aut ergo potest aut non potest. Si non potest, tunc regula iuris supraposita habet locum. Si potest et non vult et bene nouit quod voluntas sui domini Iesu Christi est vt hoc faciat, quid restat nisi 'quod seruus sciens voluntatem domini sui et non faciens plagis vapulabitur multis'?" RY-43, f. 161.

[29] "Sed quod dolendum est, nonnulli moderni spiritu ambicionis ducti super se dictum assumunt officium qui predicare nesciunt nec discere volunt," RY-59, f. 216.

[30] "De quibus loquitur Dominus signanter per prophetam Ysaiam 56 sic dicens: 'Speculatores eius ceci,' scilicet per ignoranciam, 'canes muti non valentes latrare,' quia os suum aperiri nesciunt ad docendum," R-17, f. 84v.

[31] E-6 and 41; from Neckam, *De naturis*, p. 150. Also used in Q-37.

The reason is only, I suppose, the loss of temporal things. For in the early Church, when the apostles were poor, they were martyrs for the truth. Today there is none who will open his mouth to speak up for the truth, and this is the reason why so many evils rule in the world.[32]

And where friars may occasionally accuse the secular clergy of neglecting to preach,[33] conversely the parish clergy will blame friars for preaching for gain, "as do those who preach mainly to beg and not to lead souls back to Christ's sheepfold who have been redeemed through Christ's precious blood and are submerged in sin."[34] These accusations of ignorance, avarice, and neglect are now and then joined by those of preaching about matters that go over the head of both preacher and congregation,[35] or else of preaching without permission, the latter evidently a charge against the Lollards.

Several sermons in our collections also deal with the content and form of preaching. Where this is more than "the word of God" or the Church's doctrines in general, they specify basic catechetical matters, from making the sign of the cross to the Decalogue and the Creed – the *pastoralia*, in other words, that priests with the cure of souls were officially required to preach regularly, a subject to be pursued further in the next chapter. But preachers also speak occasionally about the style of preaching. Such remarks invariably hark back to Augustine and Gregory. Thus, one preacher begins his sermon with a reference to the former: "According to blessed Augustine's *De doctrina Christiana*, the office of a church doctor or preacher is to teach the people, move the people, and please the people," and continues:

> Since he needs to teach, he must speak openly and wisely; since he needs to move the people from vices to virtues, he must speak sharply and censoriously; and since he needs to please, he must speak in a lovely and goodly fashion, so that the people may see that his sermon aims at praising God and saving their

---

[32] "Vbi iam inuenitur prelatus / uel predicator qui audet dicere veritatem plane? Et causa est solum vt suppono rerum temporalium perdicio; nam in primitiua Ecclesia, quando apostoli erant pauperes, tunc erant martires pro veritate. Iam non est aliquis qui vult aperire os suum ad loquendum pro veritate, et hec est causa quare tot mala regnant in orbe," P1-22, f. 83ra–b.

[33] For instance, Q-37, f. 115v.

[34] "Qualiter faciunt illi qui predicant principaliter vt mendicent et non vt animas Christi precioso sanguine redemptas peccato submersas ad ouile Christi reducant . . . ," A-30, f. 96. Similarly, J/5-4 declares that preaching must be *generaliter* (to everybody), *liberaliter*, and *utiliter* (f. 46). The second quality condemns preaching for money, as done by *questores* (pardoners) and mendicants, and for pride, as done by heretics.

[35] R-30. For the topos of "not hewing above one's head," see Fletcher, *Preaching*, pp. 239–248.

souls, nor must he say anything whereby anybody may be reasonably offended or perturbed.[36]

The three features are then taken up and developed with specific details. Thus, under the first heading, the preacher observes that many of his colleagues are satisfied with "fables, stories, and commonplace matters and sayings," so that many listeners believe this is all there is to divine scripture and hence think less of their sermons and of theology altogether. In order that these people may understand that in Holy Scripture are many things that go beyond their understanding, the good preacher must "sometimes recite such in his sermons." Others blame the sermons when they cannot grasp all of their contents, because the subject matter is either too abstract or too manifold, and these people are like those who blame the king's banquet when they are not able to eat it all.[37] Next, to move his audience the preacher must speak "fervently and with weight":

> Some people praise sermons and preachers when they speak sweetly and peacefully, without commotion or excitement or outcry. Then they say, "He has preached beautifully and well." But when preachers use the opposite tone, they say "he is perturbed and angry and melancholy."[38]

Of course, a preacher cannot but speak according to the grace he has been given and his own aptitude. But if he has the grace and a fervent spirit, when he deals with the causes for Christ's death, with the injury the sinners do to God, or with God's condemnation, he must indeed speak with fervor like someone in

---

[36] "Est autem notandum secundum beatum Augustinum *De doctrina Christiana* quod officium doctoris ecclesiastici seu predicatoris est docere populum, mouere populum, et placere populo. Si debeat docere, oportet quod loquatur opynliche and wysliche. Si debeat mouere populum de viciis ad uirtutes, oportet quod loquatur acute and charganliche. Et si debeat placere, oportet quod loquatur loueliche and godliche, ita quod populus possit videre quod sermo suus tendit ad laudem Dei et salutem animarum, nec debet aliquid dicere vnde deberet aliquis racionabiliter offendi vel turbari," W-129, f. 244rb.

[37] "Multi sunt sermones et communiter quiescant in fabulis et narracionibus et communibus materiebus et dictis. Multi credunt quod nichil aliud est in thezauro diuine scripture nisi talia, et ideo minus reputant de sermonibus et de tota theologia. Vt ergo sciant quod in scriptura diuina sunt multa que transcendunt intelligenciam illorum, talia / sunt aliquando recitandi in sermonibus. Isti autem qui uituperant sermones quia non possunt reportare totum aut propter altitudinem materie aut propter multitudinem materiarum sunt similes homini qui culpat festum regis quia non potest totum commedere, et culpat forum quia non potest omnia venalia emere," W-129, f. 244rb–va.

[38] "Sed hic est notandum quod aliqui commendant sermones et predicatores quando loquuntur suauiter et pacifice absque aliqua commocione vel turbacione vel clamore. Tunc dicunt quod 'pulchre et bene predicauit.' Sed quando habent modum contrarium, tunc dicunt quod 'est turbatus et iratus et malencolicus [!],'" ibid.

anger.[39] And lastly, the preacher should not personally offend his audience but rather "touch upon their vices in general, as well as the virtues, punishment, and glory."[40]

These concerns: of preaching solid doctrine, even where it goes beyond the hearers' capacity, instead of merely entertaining them; of using rhetoric to stir them up; and yet of not becoming personal, appear fairly consistently in sermons that devote some attention to style and rhetoric. Repingdon's Sexagesima sermon, on the sower who went out to sow his seed (Luke 8:4–15), is perhaps the most detailed case in point, almost an *ars praedicandi*. He lists twelve requirements of a good preacher, ranging from living a praiseworthy life to making sure that his teaching is useful. Several of these refer to matters of style: the preacher should love learning and knowledge more than words (requirement 4), he should observe restraint in making divisions (7), and he should take the middle way between slow and precipitate delivery (8).[41] On the priority of substance over words, Repingdon quotes Augustine and Seneca, and at one point, where Augustine warns to "take care, when one adds number in divine and grave pronouncements, that one does not take off from their weight," Repingdon clarifies: "Understand that 'number,' as it is here used, includes the proportion of syllables, meters, and rhetorical colors."[42] Similarly, on restraint in making divisions, Repingdon observes that "many modern preachers pay more attention to elegant divisions than to fruitful pronouncements; indeed, they take such pains about their divisions that they

---

[39] "Vnum tamen scio, quod si quis haberet graciam et spiritum feruentem quando loqueretur propter quod Christus mortuus est et de iniuria quam faciunt peccatores Deo peccando et de dampnificacione Dei quando dampnant seipsos, tunc debet loqui cum feruore tanquam iratus et deuotus contra peccatum," ibid.

[40] "Sed in generali tanget eius vicia et uirtutes, penam et gloriam secundum graciam a Deo sibi datam," ibid. Notice that *vitia et virtutes, poena et gloria* are the traditional four preaching topics of Franciscans. They are also mentioned in E-33.

[41] "De predicatoribus et auditoribus aliqua sunt dicenda, quorum primum est que sunt requisita in predicatore ad hoc quod debite seminet verbum Dei, et sunt duodecim. Quorum primum est vt ipse laudabiliter viuat . . . Secundum requisitum in predicatore est vt auctoritatem magisterii Deo non sibi attribuat . . . Tercium est vt doctrine oracionem premittat . . . Quartum est vt scienciam plus amet quam verba . . . Quintum est vt in scripturis auctorum sensus requiratur . . . Sextum est vt in scriptura sacra non vbique misterium requirat . . . Septimum est vt in diuidendo mediocritas seruetur . . . Octauum est inter tarditatem et precipitacionem medium in proferendo seruare . . . Nonum est vt docendo veritatem non deserat . . . Decimum est vt doctrina facilis sit et aperta . . . Undecimum est vt doctrina sit breuis . . . Duodecimum est vt doctrina sit vtilis," RE-12, ff. 79ra–80va.

[42] "Item: 'Cauendum est ne in diuinis grauibusque sentenciis dum numerus additur pondus detrahatur.' Ad numerum prout hic sumitur intelligas pertinere proporcionem sillabarum, metrorum, et colores rhetoricos," ibid., f. 80ra.

rarely work towards charity and unity."[43] Repingdon's wariness of rhetorical devices, of course, stands in the wake of centuries of warnings against letting the substance of Christian doctrine fall prey to an exaggerated concern for form that shows itself in the over-use of subtleties, rhetorical decoration, and fables, warnings voiced by theologians, councils and synods, *artes praedicandi*, and even poets.[44] They appear equally in other orthodox sermons of Repingdon's time. Thus the preacher of the Hereford sermons (E) speaks against those who, instead of opening up the words of the gospel, "wrap and hide the divine word in the ornamentation of their sermon."[45] And another preacher explains Christ's words "He that speaks from himself seeks his own glory" (John 7:18) with,

> he speaks from himself who tries too hard to show his learning in subtleties, such as elegant introductions of his thema, or elegant divisions of his sermons, or the strange telling of poetic fables.[46]

And still another anonymous preacher begins the main part of his discourse with, "I will not make any divisions but proceed plainly, for he who teaches what cannot be understood by his audience seeks not their benefit but his own ostentation."[47] Brinton shares the same sentiment.[48]

Nonetheless, the collections at the same time emphasize the need for eloquence in order to please the audience, because "what does not please is easily despised."[49]

---

[43] "Sed certe multi modernorum predicatorum plus ad curiosas diuisiones quam ad sentencias fructuosas attendunt. immo tantum circa diuisiones laborant quod caritatem et vnitatem raro edificant," f. 80rb.

[44] For some examples see Wenzel, *Preachers*, pp. 64–65, to which may be added the demand to preach "absque cuiuslibet subtilitatis textura fantastica" (*Councils and Synods* 2:901), though this is said about preaching the *pastoralia*.

[45] "Requiritur cuilibet seminanti semen verbi Dei dictorum apercio. Pro quo dicitur 1 Corinthiorum 9: 'Si incertam vocem det tuba quis se preparabit ad pugnam?' Sunt qui verbum diuinum inuoluunt \et abscondunt/ in decore sermonis, qui procul dubio maledicti sunt, testante propheta . . . ," E-23, f. 58va.

[46] "Ille enim a seipso loquitur qui nimis nititur ostendere scienciam suam in subtilitatibus, sicut sunt curiose introducciones thematum siue curiose diuisiones sermonum, uel extranea narracio fabularum poeticarum," M/4-13, f. 314ra. Similarly in the protheme of S-1: "Homo a seipso loquitur quando nimis nititur ostendere scienciam in tenebris figurarum, in subtilitatibus introduccionum et diuisionum, in multitudine auctoritatum literalium. Et vere multi nituntur ostendere suas subtilitates quod fructus sermonum multum subtrahitur," f. 1.

[47] "Non faciam divisiones set plano modo pro[c]edam, quia qui ea docet que ab auditoribus intelligi non possunt, non eorum vtilitatem querit set sui ostensionem facit, XLIII di. c. vltimo," A-2, f. 44; the reference is to Gratian's *Decretum* (Friedberg 1:156).

[48] "That I may shape my sermon for your edification and forego an elegant introduction," BR-45, p. 201.

[49] "Quod non placet faciliter despicitur," B/2-6, f. 128vb.

At Pentecost the Holy Spirit was sent to the young Church in the form of different tongues "as a sign that eloquence is necessary to the preacher, so that his audience may understand him and that he may not offend anyone in his speech."[50] Both knowledge and eloquence are thus necessary in order to reach diverse audiences, as Gregory the Great had already explained at some length in his *Pastoral Rule*. An early fifteenth-century successor elaborates that "not every way of preaching is equally pleasing to all," for

> some people want sermons about refined matters, and if the preacher talks of light and plain things, they think little of it . . . Others in contrast want solid and graspable [*grossos et palpabiles*] sermons about matters they know . . . And there is a third group of people who scorn any way of preaching and never want to hear a sermon at all . . .[51]

So, preachers are advised to consider the disposition of their audience and modify their approach accordingly, for as the same food is not equally good for healthy and sick people, so "must one vary one's sermon matter according to the varying disposition of one's audience, if preaching is to be salutary to them."[52] The demands to vary one's preaching style according to the audience and to please them clearly clash with the demand not to sacrifice the weight and substance of a sermon to its appeal. Hence a Lenten sermon, evidently directed to a lay audience, can raise the question whether it is allowed to quote sayings of non-Christians in one's sermon. The extant text is not quite clear on what answer the preacher gave, but he does eventually announce that "it is the preacher's office to see in every way how best he can invite his audience to penance and grace."[53]

---

[50] "In forma diuersarum linguarum missus est in signum quod predicatori necessaria est eloquentia vt audientes eum intelligant et ne offendat aliquem in loquendo," B/2-37, f. 193rb.

[51] "Nec omnis modus predicandi est omnibus / eque placens. Quidam enim vellent habere sermones de materia curiosa, et si predicator predicat leuia et plena, paruipendunt. De hiis dicitur Numeri: 'Anima nostra nauseat super isto cibo leuissimo' [21:5]. Alii econtra vellent habere sermones grossos et palpabiles de materiis sibi notis. Isti figurantur Numeri 11, qui dixerunt: 'Quis dabit nobis escas carnium' [11:18]. Sed sunt tercii qui omnem modum predicandi contempnunt et nunquam vellent audire sermonem," S-3, ff. 19v-20.

[52] "Sic in verbo Dei predicando vel comunicando primo consideranda est disposicio comedentis. Non enim infirmis et sanis est idem cibus eque salutaris, vt constat. Conformiter secundum diuersam disposicionem audiencium oportet diuersificare materiam predicandi si predicacio erit eis salutaris," S-3, f. 19v.

[53] "Sed forte hic queritur vtrum liceat inmiscere dicta gentilium sermonibus . . . Et hoc est officium predicatorum, quod omni modo studea[n]t quomodo melius p[ossun]t populum ad penitenciam et graciam inuitare," S-16, f. 66v.

One assumes that if moralizing an Ovidian fable was the way to achieve this, then let him go ahead. Extant sermons are of course full of divisions, fables, and rhetorical devices; but in theory preachers were evidently as much concerned with their abuse as was Wyclif.[54]

---

[54] See further the chapter "Orthodox and heterodox" below, p. 393.

48

The word of God and *pastoralia*

In the fourteenth and fifteenth centuries, preachers in England were by Church law required to preach a number of basic catechetical pieces, the *pastoralia*, including the Ten Commandments, Creed, Our Father, seven deadly sins, and other sets, which every priest was to know well and to explain to his parishioners regularly.[1] These catechetical pieces did not merely represent theoretical knowledge but had a very practical application, for at least several of them furnished patterns in which one might examine one's conscience before going to confession, as is evident from penitential handbooks as well as from Lenten sermons.[2] What light

---

[1] The present chapter expands on what has been said above, Part Two, chapter 40, pp. 231–233.

[2] S-10, on *Illi soli servies* for 1 Lent, is a good example. In its third part, the preacher calls his audience to "turn to God in this Lent through true contrition of heart, true confession of mouth, and complete penitence in mind. But if you want to confess well, you must begin by pondering in your heart how you have offended God through pride" and the other deadly sins; "also, if you have sinned in your five senses . . . ; if you have not carried out the works of mercy." Because, he goes on, whoever wants to serve God and please him must have true humility in his heart so that by that virtue he may push back pride; and the Christian virtues opposed to several other deadly sins follow. Finally, "he will also observe God's commandments, which are ten." "Conuertatis vos ad Dominum in ista quadragesima per veram cordis contricionem, veram oris confessionem, et penitencie in mente complecionem. Sed si velis bene confiteri, precogites in corde tuo quomodo Deum offendistis [!] per superbiam, iram, inuidiam, gulam, luxuriam, accidiam, et auariciam, et ostende sacerdoti qualiter deliquisti in aliquo istorum, quo genere superbie, ire, vel inuidie, et sic de ceteris. Item quociens deliquisti in tali peccato vel tali, quo die, solempni vel non solempni, et an tempore solennis ieiunii. Item de persona cum qua deliquisti, vel contra quam deliquisti. Item quamdiu iacuisti in tali peccato vel in tali. Item an prebuisti causam vel malum exemplum alicui ad peccandum, et sic de omnibus aliis circumstanciis que multum aggrauant peccatum, solummodo precogites qualiter deliquisti contra decem precepta Dei non obseruando ea sicut teneris. Item si deliquisti in quinque sensibus tuis, videlicet in visu, auditu, gustu, odoratu [*MS* adoratu], et tactu. Item non inplesti septem opera misericordie, que continentur hiis versibus:

     Vestio, poto, cibo, tectum do, visito, \soluo,/
     Et sepellio mortuos ut Thobias fecit.

can the Latin sermon collections throw on the relation between preaching these *pastoralia* and preaching the "word of God"?

Archbishop Thomas Arundel's *Constitutions* of 1407 established – or perhaps better, consolidated and updated – laws about who could officially preach, with or without examination and special license,[3] and then determined that priests and temporal vicars who were not regular incumbents or privileged to preach (as were Franciscans and Dominicans) could preach only the *pastoralia* as decreed by John Pecham. A regular parish priest, therefore, was quite free to preach anything, though he was still required to deal with the *pastoralia* at regular times. About the relation of the two – the word of God and *pastoralia* – Spencer, in her study of sermons in the English language, finds "a basic incompatibility between the preaching of the gospel and the preaching of pastoralia," because

> the integral nature of such teaching [i.e. the *pastoralia*] made it hard to accommodate within the framework of Sunday sermons on the lections, even though both kinds of preaching were traditionally considered of equal importance. This posed a dilemma which was (and is) incapable of easy resolution . . . A number of the fourteenth- and fifteenth-century English sermon collections attempted to combine the two, but the results are idiosyncratic and even a little forced.[4]

I have shown elsewhere that, at least with respect to one of the *pastoralia*, the seven deadly sins, there is no incompatibility between preaching them and preaching on the lection for the day, nor is their combination "forced" beyond the allegorical interpretation of scripture that was quite normal in medieval preaching.[5] Extant Latin sermons manage very nicely to integrate the seven deadly sins fully with their themata, both notionally and verbally. The same is true of other set pieces, such as the Creed, the Lord's Prayer, the virtues, the gifts of the Holy Spirit, or the works of mercy.

A number of extant sermons show an awareness that priests were required to preach these catechetical pieces to their people. A sermon in E, for instance, directed to the clergy and evidently preached after Arundel's *Constitutions* had been issued, uses imagery from grammar teaching to detail what a pastor should do and teach. After showing parishioners how to make the sign of the cross, the preacher is to begin by teaching the letters of the alphabet and to give for each letter a Christian virtue, dividing the latter into three groups that are respectively

---

/ . . . Qui vult Deo seruire et complacere ei oportet quod habeat veram humilitatem in corde, vt per illam virtutem repellat superbiam . . . Item quod seruet Dei precepta, que sunt decem," S-10, ff. 45v–46.

[3] Arundel's legislation and difficulties of interpretation are discussed in Spencer, *English*, pp. 163–177.

[4] Ibid., p. 208.   [5] Wenzel, "Preaching the Seven Deadly Sins."

related to childhood, adulthood, and old age. Next the preacher is to teach how to "syllabify," that is, to put the letters together to make them all into one virtue – evidently a reference to the chief virtue, charity, expressed in the two greatest commandments. Then the students are ready to "read" the Lord's Prayer with its seven petitions, the Hail Mary, and the Creed, which the pastor is to "construe" for them.[6] Another sermon, on "Blessed are the merciful" (Matthew 5:7), delivered on All Saints' Day, laments that the people, and especially *rurales*, "are struck with such great ignorance that they do not know anything that pertains to the salvation of their souls: not the Lord's Prayer, not the Ave Maria, nor the Creed, the Commandments, the works of mercy, the seven deadly sins, or the five senses." To teach them is a spiritual work of mercy, which properly belongs to the clergy, though any Christian also is by the law of brotherly love and the law of nature obliged to do so.[7] These two sermons thus echo what synodal decrees had demanded from the early thirteenth century on. They do not explicitly refer to Church law, but another preacher, Robert Rypon, at one point says that the Lord's Prayer, Hail Mary, and Creed "are ordained by Christ and the Church."[8]

There is ample evidence in the collections here studied that the *pastoralia* were indeed preached. FitzRalph's sermon diary is of some interest because it contains several remarks that he spoke about catechetical set pieces on various occasions. For example, on the vigil of the Ascension in 1345 he preached a sermon "in the vernacular to the people" in the churchyard of the hospital of St. John in Lichfield, where he said:

> Sometime I explained to you the Lord's Prayer and promised I would explain to you the Hail Mary, which I did on the first Sunday of Advent. And I also promised I would teach you to understand your faith. I will gladly preach this sermon on the articles of the faith contained in the Creed.[9]

---

[6] E-24.

[7] "Et ideo isti sunt tanta ignorancia percussi quod nulla ad salutem anime sciunt pertinencia, nec oracionem dominicam nec salutacionem angelicam nec simbolum sciunt et precepta et opera misericordie, septem peccata mortalia et quinque sensus ignorant . . . / Et quamuis istud officium conueniat specialiter clericis cum quibus bonus Christianus ad hoc tenetur ex lege caritatis fraterne et ex lege nature . . . Et ad talem correctionem fraternam et spiritualem misericordiam pene subditos obligantur stricte omnes habentes in domibus suis subditos, vt puta filios vestros vel seruientes," H-11, f. 34r–v.

[8] "Sunt ordinate a Christo et Ecclesia," RY-37, f. 145.

[9] "Quia al' exponendo vobis oracionem dominicam promisi expon[er]e vobis salutacionem angelicam, quod et feci dominica prima aduentus, et eciam docere vos intelligere fidem vestram, ideo gratis de articulis fidei contentis in simbolo volo facere hunc sermonem," FI-8, f. 9v. Similar references made before his audience occur in FI-26 and 28.

MS	Deadly sins	Virtues	Beat	Decalg	Creed	Pater	Gifts	Sacramts	Senses	Works
A	(49)	(49)	49	2			49			
B/2	16, 22, (58),¹⁰ 80,89	16, 80		76, 77	75			42 (English), (12)		
BR	10, 12, 28, 32, 45			(43)	27, 69, 93	34		(43)		(102)
DY	6	6	63 to 65	(5 to 8)						4, 64
E	34, 37, 40, 41							(10), 22		
F/5	13									
FE	6, 11, 23, 33, (45), 54			51	54			54	23	
FI	29, 73			55	8, 31	26		(37)		
G	15, 17									
H	10, 14,¹¹ 19	10, 19	10				10			
J/5	4, 7, 19, 35, 36, 38	7		11						
K	16									
M/3	1, 10, 19, 51				51		1	8		
M/4	12			8						
N	55, 82, 68				109	109				
O	2, 4, 37, 42				(6), 17, 19		29			
P1	15, 26, 37			27						
P2	(33), 26, 35			25			53, 64			
Q	38, 40, 66			61		50				(44)
R	(20, English)				28					

¹⁰ Mentions three followed by "etc., de quibus si placet tangat singillatim" (242ra).
¹¹ Contains a reference to the seven sins which were treated in the sermon for Christmas, which is missing in the codex as it stands.

MS	Deadly sins	Virtues	Beat	Decalg	Creed	Pater	Gifts	Sacramts	Senses	Works
RE	(13), 16, 42, 51			(51)	49		21			
RY	2, 3, 4, 7, 11, 14, 23, 24, 25, 26, 27, 29, 32, 34, 45, 48, 51, 55	3		15, 18, 19, 20	20		51		34, 44, 49	19, 20, 31, 44
S	10, 11, 14	10, 14		16					10	10
T	5									
V	26, 35	29		29, 36						
W	16, 67, 72, 167			9, 67						
WA[12]	3, (36)			4	8					
X	18, 100,	18								
Z	(5), 8, 10, 23, 24, 29, 30, 31, 35, 42, 55	24	24	16, (30)			24, 29			33

FitzRalph was not the only one to do so. The table above shows what catechetical pieces appear in individual sermons.[13]

The table reveals that, first of all, some of these set pieces were evidently more popular – or felt by the preachers to be more needful – than others, particularly the seven deadly sins, the Ten Commandments, and the articles of faith. Secondly, although in most cases a sermon deals with only one of the set pieces, here and there a sermon does discuss or at least list two or three of them. Thus,

---

[12] Besides the sermons here included Waldeby also wrote treatises on the Pater Noster, Ave Maria, and Creed, based on his preaching. See Part One, chapter 5.

[13] I list only sermons that detail the members of the respective set piece ("pride, wrath, . . ."), not those that merely mention them as a group ("the seven deadly sins"). Items in parentheses list members only partially. I have excluded lists that, for the virtues, give only the four cardinal or the three theological ones. Several sermons in C must have mentioned the *pastoralia*, but their abbreviated state leaves this uncertain. The set pieces may appear in the sermons listed in a variety of forms, ranging from mere enumeration to extensive treatment, even with a rationale (RY). Individual sermons that appear in several collections are here given in each of them.

Felton's sermon 54 lists and deals with the seven deadly sins (in part 2), the articles of faith (in part 3), and the seven sacraments (under believing in the "Holy Church" of the Creed). Quite remarkable in this respect is a sermon for All Saints' Day, on "Your reward in heaven is abundant" (Matthew 5:12), preserved in two collections. Its thema is taken from the Sermon on the Mount (the day's gospel reading), where Christ is said to have given nine lessons, which can be reduced to seven, which are the traditional seven beatitudes. Each is discussed at some length, and the preacher connects it with a deadly sin, a chief virtue, and a gift of the Holy Spirit.[14] Thus, Christ's first lesson was "Blessed are the poor in spirit, for theirs is the kingdom of God," in which he teaches us humility, which springs from the first gift of the Holy Spirit, the fear of God, and which shuts out pride, the first of the seven deadly sins.[15] Another preacher found a different way to incorporate several catechetical set pieces into his Palm Sunday sermon on "They offered him green branches and palms" (2 Maccabees 10:7). He first expounds the seven deadly sins and then, near the end, quotes Canticles 7:8, "I will climb up into the palm tree and gather its fruits," and develops this quotation with the image of a ladder that has thirty-six steps, which combine the Ten Commandments, theological and cardinal virtues, articles of faith, works of mercy, and again the seven deadly sins.[16]

One may query whether the appearance of one or even several catechetical set pieces in an actual sermon indeed means that the preacher treated them so as to comply with episcopal legislation. I do not know of any instance where a preacher announced that he was doing just that. Further, I do not know any sermon which in fact goes through *all* catechetical pieces specified by Pecham. Are then the sermons listed above at best coincidental to the question of how preachers fulfilled their obligation to preach the *pastoralia*? That is a possibility. However, it should be pointed out that some pastoral handbooks were seemingly aware of the difficulty of preaching all *pastoralia* at once and therefore allowed preachers to take up only one or two at a time. The very popular *Oculus sacerdotis*, for instance, begins its discussion of "the things which a priest must preach to his subjects" with a reference to Pecham's Lambeth Constitutions and the required catechetical

---

[14] "Hic iam ostendi septem lecciones virtutum que originantur a septem donis Spiritus Sancti, per quas vt ostendi excluduntur septem peccata mortalia," Z-24, f. 75vb; also in H-10.

[15] "Prima leccio Christi sequitur in hiis verbis: 'Beati pauperes spiritu, quoniam ipsorum est regnum celorum.' In ista leccione docet nos Christus humilitatem, que oritur a primo dono Spiritus Sancti, scilicet timore Domini, quia timor Domini facit hominem humilem siue pauperem spiritu . . . Et per istam humilitatem excluditur superbia, que est primum peccatorum mortalium. Que traxit suum originem a Lucifero in celo . . . ," ibid., f. 73va.

[16] V-29, f. 33; the seven deadly sins were listed earlier in the sermon, f. 31. A similar ladder of perfection appears in A-49, with the seven virtues/beatitudes, seven gifts, and some of the seven deadly sins, ff. 152v–154v.

351

set pieces: "the fourteen articles of faith, the seven sacraments of the Church, the seven works of mercy, the seven chief virtues, the Ten Commandments, the two commandments of the gospel, namely those regarding the twofold charity, and the seven deadly sins with their offspring." Before the author deals with each of these at some length, he counsels that "they are to be preached to the layfolk in the easiest way they can, for he who preaches what cannot be understood by his audience does so not to their usefulness but his own ostentation . . . And thus he who teaches and instructs uneducated souls (*animas rudes*) must adapt himself to what his audience can understand and order his words according to their capacity." And then, which is of particular relevance to the present discussion, the handbook advises: "The priest who must preach to his parishioners the word [of God], may mix with it and accept some of the things written below, according to what pleases him to carry out his intention."[17] Selecting material from the catechetical syllabus and incorporating it into his preaching the word of God is precisely what the preachers represented in the table above did.

There is, however, another aspect regarding the preaching of the *pastoralia*. Preachers who did not have the necessary skill to construct sermons that incorporated some of the *pastoralia*, and after Arundel's Constitutions certainly vicars or deacons not officially entrusted with the cure of souls, may have simply read out a list of the catechetical items, with at best minimal explanations. When English bishops in the early thirteenth century began to require that their clergy know the catechetical set pieces and preach them to their flocks, several of them also wrote and published short treatises that contained the relevant information, sometimes in connection with instructions regarding confession: especially Alexander of Stavensby of Lichfield, perhaps Robert Grosseteste of Lincoln, Walter de

---

[17] "Nunc videndum est de hiis que presbiter debet predicare subditis suis et que quilibet sacerdos plebi presidens quater in anno, hoc est semel in qualibet parte anni, vna die solempni uel pluribus diebus, per se uel per alium exponere debet vulgaliter, populo absque subtilitate: xiiii articulos fidei, septem Ecclesie sacramenta, septem opera misericordie, septem virtutes principales, decem mandata, duo precepta euangelii scilicet gemine caritatis, septem peccata moralia cum sua progenie, vt in Constitucione prouinciali de Lam[b]eth Pecham, 'Cum ignorancia.' Et nequis curatus habens curam animam a predictis per ignorancia se excuset, omnia predicta per ordinem hic pertracto summaria breuitate. Et sunt predicta laycis predicanda modo quo poterint faciliori, quia qui ea docet que ab auditoribus non valent intelligi, non eorum vtilitatem sed sui ostentacionem facit, XLIII distinccione, paragrapho ultimo. Et ideo oportet eum qui docet et instruit animas rudes esse talis ut pro ingenio audiencium possit se aptare et verborum ordinem pro ipsorum capacitate dirigere. Debet ergo ille qui predicat verbum Dei esse eruditus et doctus, irreprehensibilis et maturus, VIII, q. 1, 'Oportet.' Potest eciam sacerdos qui debet predicare parochianis verbum [Dei] aliqua intermittere et accipere de hiis que infra scribuntur secundum quod sibi placuerit ad suum propositum prosequendum," William of Pagula, *Oculus sacerdotis*, *pars dextera*, MS Royal 8.C., f. 87ra. On this work see Part Two, chapter 40, pp. 233–234. The two canonical references are to Friedberg 1:156 and 594.

Cantilupe of Worcester, Roger Weseham of Coventry and Lichfield, and Peter Quinel of Exeter.[18] In addition, parish priests would have found such lists, albeit with longer explanations, in pastoral handbooks.[19] A simple handbook of this kind has actually made its way into a random sermon collection. This is W-77, beginning with the words, "Although eminent knowledge is desirable in pastors, a competent one is tolerable." The writer then deals with the (twelve) articles of faith, the five senses, the sacraments, the Ten Commandments followed by the two commandments of love, the Pater Noster, the seven virtues (which are said to be found in the seven petitions), the seven deadly sins, and the seven works of mercy. All set pieces come with short explanations and borrow material from the *Catholicon* of Johannes Balbi of Genoa. The little treatise ends with advice on how to bear with tribulation, as many other pastoral handbooks do, too. As it stands in the midst of regular and complete sermons, the work quite plausibly served as a text to be read from the pulpit.

Thus, in considering the relation between preaching the word of God and preaching the *pastoralia*, it makes, on the available evidence, more sense to think, not of incompatibility, but of two parallel forms of preaching whose use depended on the skill, preparation, and – after Arundel – precise rank of the preacher.[20] Well educated preachers, whether parish clergy or mendicant friars, seem to have satisfied episcopal requirements by skilfully incorporating one or several catechetical set pieces into their preaching on the day's lection or a related thema. Less well-educated curates, and in agreement with Arundel's Constitutions non-beneficed priests, would have simply read a list of the relevant items. Such lists evidently have largely disappeared, since they were at best quires rather than books, although some traces have indeed been preserved in sermon collections.

---

[18] See Part Two, chapter 40, pp. 230–232.

[19] For a good survey of fourteenth-century pastoral handbooks see Pantin, *English Church*, pp. 189–219 and 277–280. Add: W-77, dealt with below. Oxford, Bodleian Library MS Bodley 857, which belonged to William Marshall, chaplain of "Pesholme," probably Peaseholm, Yorkshire; it contains sermons by Nicholas of Aquavilla and seventeen anonymous sermons; see above, p. 218. Similarly, Oxford, Trinity College, MS 7, of the early fifteenth century, contains, after some scattered sermons, Pecham's canon in Latin and then the *pastoralia* in English (ff. 165–174); the final section contains some material collected from "the teachings of our fathers which priests can safely preach to their people . . . These I have written down in an uncultivated [*rudi*] style and as it were in childish words [*puerilibus verbis*] so that no-one may excuse himself through not understanding them," (ff. 177–181v, at 177). Further English manuals of this kind can be found in Raymo, "Works of Religious," pp. 2270–2274. For evidence of such copies in medieval parishes, see Shinners, "Parish Libraries," pp. 209–210.

[20] Compare d'Avray's remarks about two tiers of preaching in the thirteenth century, in *Preaching*, p. 6, point 6, and pp. 82–90.

49

The preacher's voice

It has become customary to speak of late-medieval sermons as texts of unrelieved monotony and dullness. Here is how the pioneer of English sermon studies put it:

> The same fatal influence of the past seems to creep onward through the discourse: the same allegorical turns of exposition, the same "figurae" from animals or things, the same old sayings of "the great clerks," the same anecdotes, where anecdotes are to be found. The landscape is barren and monotonous . . . a decaying art . . . such tedious stuff.[1]

And Owst is echoed by a more recent scholar speaking of

> a startling unoriginality in most sermons, because there is no concern to offer experiences from the preacher's own life . . . Academic preaching is not an individualizing act, but one judged successful by the skillful manipulation of the rules of composition – the scissors-and-paste method . . .[2]

Foolish though it may seem to look for some life in "these dry bones, that whiten the road,"[3] I wish to argue that the collections surveyed here reveal that English preachers between 1350 and 1450 did in fact create works with an astonishing degree of variety and individuality, that hardly deserve the judgments just quoted. My argument will center on the choice preachers had in selecting the structure of their sermons as well as their verbal texture.

To illustrate this choice, sermons for the third Sunday in Lent will serve as a good case,[4] whose gospel (Luke 11:14–28) tells of Jesus casting out a demon and then arguing with the crowd:

[1] Owst, *Preaching*, pp. 238–239.   [2] Coleman, *English Literature*, p. 193.
[3] Owst, *Preaching*, p. 239.
[4] Compare Bataillon, "Early Scholastic," who used the same gospel lection to focus on biblical quotations in thirteenth-century sermons. His results yield a fine parallel to the following discussion for an earlier phase in scholastic preaching.

(14) And he was casting out a demon, and that was mute, and when he had cast out the demon, the mute man spoke, and the crowds were astonished. (15) But some among them said, "He casts out demons in Beelzebub, the prince of the demons," (16) while others tempted him and asked for a sign from him. (17) But he, as he saw their thoughts, said to them: "Every realm divided against itself comes to ruin, and house will fall upon house. (18) But if Satan is divided against himself, how then shall his realm stand? You say I cast out demons in Beelzebub. (19) But if I cast out demons in Beelzebub, in whom do your sons cast them out? Therefore they will be your judges. (20) But if I cast out demons in the finger of God, the kingdom of God has indeed come among you. (21) When a strong armed man guards his court, everything he owns is at peace. (22) But when someone stronger than he falls on him and overcomes him, he takes all his weapons in which he had confided from him and distributes his spoils. (23) He who is not with me is against me, and he who does not gather with me scatters. (24) When the unclean spirit goes out of a man, he walks about waterless places seeking rest, and as he does not find it, he says, 'I will return to my house from where I have left.' (25) And when he comes, he finds it cleaned with brooms, (26) and then he goes and takes seven other spirits with him that are worse than himself, and they enter and dwell there, and the new condition of that man is worse than his former one." (27) As he said these things, it happened that a woman of the crowd raised her voice and said, "Blessed is the womb that bore you and the breasts you drank from." (28) But he said, "To be sure, blessed are those that hear the word of God and keep it."

Biblical commentators from Bede through the *Glossa ordinaria* and William of Nottingham developed a fairly standard exegesis of the miracle and its spiritual meaning, Christ's argument against the Pharisees, his little parable about recidivism, and the praise of the woman from the crowd. They generated a number of topics that recur in many sermons of the fourteenth and fifteenth centuries. The more important ones, which appear in RE-16, are:

1. The gospels for 1–3 Lent deal with four ways of temptation and overcoming it.
2. According to Matthew and Chrysostom, the demoniac was not only mute but also deaf and blind; and Jesus achieved several miracles: the devil is driven out, a blind man sees, a mute man speaks, and a deaf man hears.
3. Four reasons for expelling someone from one's house.
4. The devil acts like a thief.
5. The devil catches man as a wolf catches a lamb, by his throat.
6. Three functions of speech, which the mute (i.e. sinners) neglect.
7. Muteness: seven impediments to confession.

8. Seven reasons for penance and confession.
9. Etymology of Beelzebub, from Belus, the father of Ninus.
10. The seven biblical devils signify the seven deadly sins.
11. They are to be driven out like a serpent, in four ways.

As one studies the treatment of this gospel in the various collections, one is at once compelled to distinguish between two very different kinds of "sermon," a distinction I have spoken of before: sermons that use the process of *postillatio*, and "real" sermons.[5] The former tend to go through the entire text of the lection phrase by phrase and add whatever explanation is deemed necessary and useful. They occur in systematic *de tempore* cycles and clearly aim at furnishing as much exegetical material on the lection as possible. The richness of their substance, their wealth of information, and their academic concern with scriptural details, all make it highly doubtful that they were preached in this form; more plausibly, they were produced in order to be be studied by would-be preachers at their desks. The material they gather is taken from earlier biblical exegetes and tends to come in large excerpts. For example, Repingdon's sermon on 3 Lent (RE-16) begins with an introductory quotation from "Januensis," i.e. Jacobus de Voragine, and then divides the lection into six parts (against Jacobus's four) for verses 11–14, 15–16, 17–23, 23–26, 27, and 28 of the lection, quoting the biblical text successively and commenting on it. In doing so, Repingdon copies relevant sections from a number of earlier exegetes: predominantly Bede and Januensis, but also William Peraldus (here called "postillator"), Nottingham, Gorran, and Hugh of St. Cher (likewise called "postillator"). As a result, Repingdon's "sermon" is a progressive exegesis of the gospel lection for the day, in the course of which he develops the topics listed above. His entire work could thus be called a biblical commentary organized by the Sunday gospels. In contrast to "real" sermons, it lacks such standard features as address, protheme, or (in most cases) closing formula. Several subdivisions occur, normally taken from Nottingham; likewise, there are a number of similes, usually taken from a major source, but there are no narrative exempla.

This difference of *postillatio* from "real" sermons stands out immediately as one compares Repingdon's work with a cycle that is closely derived from it, M/3.[6] In the sermon for 3 Lent (M/3-19), the anonymous redactor begins by dividing the entire gospel lection into three parts: the expulsion of the demon and Jesus's argument with the Jews, the little parable of the return of the expelled demon, and the unnamed woman's praise. He then quotes the gospel text phrase by phrase and adds some comments on its literal meaning. Next, with no other

[5] For my use of the label "real sermon" see "Prolegomena," p. 3.
[6] See Part One, section 35, pp. 197–202.

structural marker than saying "about this gospel we should notice," he returns to the beginning of the lection, links it to the gospels for 1 and 2 Lent, and then once more goes through the three parts mentioned at the very outset of his sermon, but now speaking of their moral meanings. He does so by way of a number of questions: why is that demon called mute? how is that demon to be expelled? who are the seven evil spirits? and so on. By the end, he has covered topics 1, 6–7, 10–11. His sermon is considerably shorter than Repingdon's discursive exposition,[7] and instead of commenting on the lection verse by verse, he has created a structure in which the gospel text is first quoted with some literal comments ("Hoc euangelium ad sensum literalem potest diuidi . . .") and then explained spiritually ("Circa hoc euangelium notandum . . ."). In other words, he has changed a linear commentary on the gospel (*postillatio*) into a two-part structure that is reminiscent of the ancient homily and has organized his moralization into several points.

The distinction between homily and scholastic sermon represents an important issue in the history of medieval preaching.[8] In the homily, which was in use mostly before the thirteenth century, the preacher would cite the entire text of the lection and then give an allegorical or moral commentary on it verse by verse. In contrast, the scholastic sermon is based on a relatively short string of words, the thema, taken from either the lection or another biblical text, from which it derives its subject matter by a division. One could say that, while all late-medieval preachers were committed to preaching "the word of God," some extracted a few major points from a short string of words from the lection, while others in contrast presented and expounded the lection in its entirety. Medieval commentators, especially authors of *artes praedicandi*, were aware of this difference, and Thomas Waleys mentions that in his time the homily structure was being used in Italy.[9] In fact, in our period several English writers called their works not sermons but homilies. The outstanding example is Repingdon, whose expositions of the Sunday gospels are, in the manuscripts, called *omelie*.[10] M/3 likewise lists its

---

[7] RE-17 is over three times as long as M/3-19: nearly 10,700 words as against 3,060.

[8] See also "Prolegomena," pp. 11–15.

[9] "In aliquibus partibus, puta in Italia, communiter, quando praedicatur non clero sed populo, non accipitur breve thema; sed totum evangelium quod legitur in missa accipitur pro themate, et totum exponitur, et in ejus expositione multa pulchra et devota dicuntur," Thomas Waleys, *De modo componendi sermones*, in Charland, *Artes praedicandi*, p. 344.

[10] For instance, in Lincoln Cathedral MS 10 the sermons are marked "omelia [number]" in the upper right hand corner of the rectos. Similarly in Oxford, Bodleian Library, MS Laud misc. 635; in addition, the entire cycle is here called "Omelie Repyngton super euangelia dominicalia" in a medieval hand (f. 396rb). In other manuscripts, the title is *sermo/sermones*. The scribe of Oxford, Corpus Christi College, MS 54 does not give any title, but in the alphabetical subject index he uses *omelia* regularly (ff. i recto a–xviii verso b).

sermons as "omelie," and the entire manuscript may in fact be considered an attempt to collect sermons in that form.[11] Similarly, Waldeby refers to his five sermons on the Ave Maria as "omelie." The fifteenth-century BL MS Harley 3126 contains a complete *de tempore* cycle which presents itself as "Omelie de diuersis tractatibus."[12] And in Oxford, Magdalen College, MS 156, a series of lectures on the gospels is likewise called "omelie."[13]

It has been said that the later Middle Ages witnessed a return to the ancient homily structure.[14] For England, the primary witness would be the English Wycliffite Sermons, which basically deal with the respective lection (gospel or epistle) sequentially, phrase by phrase. This, in my view, would place them with the simple *postillatio* form used by Repingdon rather than with "real" sermons written in a form suited to actual preaching. Better evidence for such a revival – if it was indeed a revival – may be found in other orthodox sermons besides M/3 which, in some form or another, include the entire text of the lection.

In the Cambridge university sermons of 1417 and 1425–1426 (collection C), most items definitely follow the scholastic sermon form, yet several items have a structure that was of sufficient interest to the reporting scribe to note that they were given as a *postillatio*. Of one he says that the preacher "dealt with the whole gospel exegetically,"[15] and of another that "the whole sermon consisted in a *postillatio*."[16] These remarks are too brief to give us a full view of the respective sermon structures. But another sermon, for the first Sunday in Lent, on Christ's temptations in the desert (WA-28), is more revealing, and it is consciously built like an ancient homily. The preacher, probably John Waldeby, begins with a lament that in contrast to ancient virtues, nowadays people prefer their sermons, like garments, to be short and tight:

[11] The title then carries over into the fourth series of sermons, ff. 300rb–317vb, in the top margins; see above, p. 198.

[12] Nearly all the pieces are individually called *omelia*, and many cite Bede as their source. The sermons follow the entire gospel lection and occasionally explain the text "mistice." I find only one or two in Schneyer.

[13] See Part One, chapter 18, pp. 114–117. But notice that, while the *de tempore* pieces in collection CO have a right to be called homilies, they are consistently labeled *sermones* in the manuscript; see Part One, chapter 19.

[14] For instance, Forde says: "By the start of the fifteenth century the revival in vernacular preaching in the 'ancient' form in England had come about" ("Writings," 1:267.) Forde sees this revival in several Middle English collections: the Wycliffite sermons, Robert de Gretham's *Evangile des domnees*, the *Filius matris*, and the cycle in Longleat MS 4. Spencer discusses the question at some length (*English*, pp. 228–268) and arrives at a more nuanced view (265–268).

[15] "Postillauit totum euangelium," C-23; a few lines earlier he remarked that this sermon did not have much rhetorical splendor: "Incipit p'o [postillacio?] licet iste sermo non splendet rethoricis, etc."

[16] "In ista postillacione stetit totus sermo," C-104. Other sermons that were or included *postillatio* are 28, 112, 154, 155.

> Whereas in the early Church doctors used to expound the entire gospel as material for their sermon, nowadays they are hardly heard to expound a very short word taken as their thema to its very end.

In contrast to current practice, he will expound "the *complete* gospel for today" (my emphasis).[17] He apparently had already spoken the entire lection as his thema,[18] and then divides the lection into four parts, much as Repingdon, other model sermon cycles, and M/3 had done.[19] In the following discourse he goes through the pericope clause by clause, from beginning to end, quoting the relevant verses and commenting on their moral teaching. Such a sequential exposition of the gospel lection together with moral interpretation is precisely the mode of the ancient homily, and as we saw, this preacher was conscious of it. But at the same time he has, in contrast to the *postillacio* of Repingdon, made it into a "real" sermon with address ("Karissimi"), a protheme leading to prayer ("Oremus, etc."), and a closing formula ("Deo gracias").

Similar attempts to follow the characteristic feature of the pre-thirteenth-century homily, i.e. preaching on the entire lection, can be found in other Latin sermons from the period of 1350–1450, and in a variety of ways. One of them is H-19, a sermon for Quinquagesima Sunday. Here the preacher chooses for his thema only the words "Jesus, Son of David, have pity on me" (Luke 18:38) but then covers the entire lection (Luke 18:31–43).[20] After reciting all of it at the beginning of his sermon, he divides the gospel into two parts, Jesus's prediction of his passion, death, and resurrection, and his healing the blind beggar on the way to Jericho. For each part, the preacher takes one element of the text after another and applies it morally to the human condition. This long sermon thus furnishes a moral exegesis of the entire gospel lection, in the course of which the preacher manages to deal with the seven deadly sins at some length (ff. 58–62). Though the sermon is divided into two parts, according to the two constituent narrative elements of the gospel, it lacks the division of the thema that is characteristic of the scholastic sermon form.

---

[17] "Vbi in primitiua ecclesia solebant doctores pro materia sermonis exponere totum euangelium, modo vix audiuntur ad finem exponere breuissimum verbum pro themate sumptum. Sed triplex racio me mouet iam exponere totum euangelium hodiernum . . ." WA-28, f. 64. Apparently the sermon was delivered in two separate sessions: "Et materiam iam inchoandam post prandium morosius terminabo," ibid.

[18] The initial statement of the thema has: "Ductus est Iesus in desertum, et reliqua vsque ad finem euangelii, Mathei 4," f. 64.

[19] "In hoc euangelio patent quatuor articuli ordine satis serioso: primo magestas ineffabilis deitatis eterne; secundo veritas immutabilis humanitatis assumpte; tercio elicitur diabolica calliditatis sagacitas in vario temptacionis inuolucro; quarto concluditur angelica viuacitas in sedulo consolacionis obsequio," f. 64v.

[20] "Jesus fili Dauid miserere mei," H-19, ff. 54v–62v.

The same pattern with one slight difference occurs in the Epiphany sermon H-13. It, too, announces only one verse as its thema, "And having opened their treasures, they offered him gold, incense, and myrrh" (Matthew 2:11), and then retells the entire lection (Matthew 2:1–12) interspersed with some literal comments. Then it continues "for the spiritual understanding of this gospel" to divide the lection into three parts, raising such questions as, who were those three kings, or what does it mean that they opened their treasures, and answers them in terms of moral allegory: the three kings are the three faculties of the soul, opening their treasures signifies confession, and so on. What distinguishes H-13 from H-19 is that, instead of covering the entire lection, it derives three topics from it which it announces and then develops. This pattern can be found in other collections as well.[21] To give one more example: Z-32 has the thema "God has visited his people" (Luke 7:16). It begins by retelling, with a few comments, the gospel story of Jesus bringing a young man, the only son of a widow in Naim, back to life (Luke 7:11–16). Then, "for the further development with respect to the moral understanding of this gospel," the preacher outlines three topics: "first, what is understood by this dead youth, second who are the bearers that carried him, and third how or by what power he was raised from death."[22] In connection with these sermons and their structural relation to the entire gospel lection one should also mention the Wycliffite sermons of collection L. As analyzed earlier, their themata are the complete lections, which they first interpret in moral allegory, and from which they then derive two or three major points for further development. In doing so, they – and other sermons like them – reveal the preacher's desire to combine the thematic concerns of scholastic preaching with attention to and interpretation of the entire gospel lection.

Deriving two or three or four major topics from the *entire* lection is fundamentally different from deriving such topics from a short phrase in the lection – the thema of the sermon – by means of dividing it into two or three or four parts – the major division. To demonstrate the difference I will cite another sermon on "Jesus was led into the desert," which can be compared with the Waldeby sermon mentioned above (WA-28). J/4-20 begins by stating its overall subject matter: "In order to prove against coming heresies that he possessed a human nature, Jesus was led into the desert to fast, so that he might there experience our infirmity." Then the anonymous preacher uses an image to introduce his thema: Worldly champions are often presumptuous by entering fights without being invited; they

---

[21] For example: H-12, 13, 21; Z-30, 35, 51; E-41; WA-13. Also very frequently in M/3.

[22] "Sed pro vlteriori processu quantum ad intellectum moralem huius euangelii tria sunt principaliter declaranda. Primum quid per istum adolescentem mortuum significatur; secundum est qui sunt portatores a [*ms* et] quibus efferebatur; tercium est quomodo siue qua virtute suscitabatur," Z-32, ff. 90vb–91ra; similarly in E-40, where the sermon has a protheme.

are weak by succumbing in battle; and they seek public acclaim. In contrast to them, Christ is to be praised for three virtues: humility, for he did not enter on his own but *was led*; strength, for he is *Jesus*; and disregard for public acclaim, for he was led to a place far from public notice, namely *into the desert*. The remainder of the sermon then deals with Christ's humility, strength, and disregard for public acclaim, and omits everything else narrated in the lection.[23] This is the genuine scholastic sermon form.

Other preachers use the scholastic structure by similarly basing their division on a short thema and concentrating on it in the body of their sermons, but in addition they also recite – or at least the surviving texts preserve – the entire lection at the beginning. A good example is A-49, on the thema "You teach the way of God in truth" (Matthew 22:16). After a one-sentence invitation to pray, the sermon recites the entire gospel lection (Matthew 22:15–21). But then it leads to a division of the stated thema into three parts:

> the preacher of the word of God must *teach in truth* . . . , he must teach the *way* of perfection . . . , and . . . his reward will be *God*.

Instead of preaching on the entire lection, this preacher speaks exclusively about matter verbally derived from the thema alone.[24] His recitation or retelling of the entire lection before the division could be considered as the conventional *introductio thematis*, leading to the chosen thema and putting it into its biblical context. If this is this case, the gospel lection here would share this function with other narratives, both biblical and secular ones, which in the *introductio thematis* could be and often were moralized in some detail.[25] The difference between this type of reciting the day's lection and the genuine homily form, once more, lies in that the latter develops, or preaches on, the entire lection. Using the day's lection merely as an introduction to the thema may have served quite simply to

---

[23] "Ut probaret Iesus contra insurgentes hereses se habere humanitatem, in deserto ieiunaturus ductus est vt ibi nostram experiretur infermitatem [!]. Propter quod dicitur *Ductus est Iesus in desertum*. Cum mundanos pugiles considero, tria in ipsis reperio, videlicet: temeritatem, et debilitatem, apparatum popularis fauoris uel lucri cupiditatem. Propter presumpcionem non inuitati se litibus ingerunt; propter debilitatem vigoris in litibus sepius succumbunt; propter appetitum lucri et fauoris ram [*English* "ram"?] et tumultum requirunt. Contra hec tria a cuilibet redemptorem nostrum commendat euangelista: primo ab humilitate, quia *ductus est*, non se ingessit; secundo a virtuositate, quia *Iesus est*; tercio a loci congruitate quo ductus est, quia *in desertum* vbi bellum ingeritur," J/4-20, f. 23vb.

[24] Other cases are E-5, H-2, J/5-8, Z-6, 10.

[25] Thus, many of the macaronic sermons in O begin by retelling a biblical story ("Lego in sacra scriptura") and moralizing it (O-1, 3, 4, etc.); for an example, see below, pp. 370–371. Others begin with a bit of natural lore that is similarly moralized (O-9, 14). Elsewhere, a block of sermons in V begin with a non-biblical story, which they, too, moralize.

announce the gospel to a vernacular audience in their own language, after it had been read in Latin in the Mass.

In order to claim that these various ways of incorporating the entire gospel lection in the scholastic sermon structure constitute a conscious revival of the ancient homily form one would need further statements of intent from preachers. In their absence, the cases I have discussed at least show a *de facto* concern on the part of some preachers to deal with the entire lection, to present the whole gospel reading to their audiences. The sermon collections of this period, therefore, represent in their structure not a simple opposition of homily versus scholastic sermon, but a sliding scale with nothing but exposition of the gospel and its moralization on one end and, through various forms of mixture, the scholastic sermon form without any mention of the gospel narrative on the other. These many varieties existed in English preaching simultaneously, and it is thus clear that fourteenth- and fifteenth-century preachers in England could and did use a fairly wide range of structural possibilities. It is interesting to note that a similar variety, with a strong influence of biblical exegesis and *postillatio* on the scholastic sermon form, has been noticed among some preachers in Italy.[26]

Structure, then, was one area in which variety and individuality could be achieved. Another is the preacher's freedom to select part of the reading which he would use as his thema and subject matter. Here it is instructive to compare John Felton's with Repingdon's cycle of sermons on the Sunday gospels.[27] Like Repingdon, in his sermon for 3 Lent Felton copies material from earlier model sermon collections. He draws on Jacobus de Voragine ("Januensis") and Peraldus, with acknowledgment. In addition, he copies blocks of material, also with acknowledgment, from *De lingua*, a treatise that gathers much illustrative material from scripture, reason, art, and nature and was frequently attributed to Robert Grosseteste, as it is in Felton. And he adds a number of references to pious stories, some of them set in England. But instead of covering the entire gospel lection as Repingdon's *omelia* does, Felton selects a short thema, "The mute man spoke" and focuses on it to the exclusion of other parts of the lection. While his sermon lacks a division and instead simply puts material on spiritual muteness and its healing together, it begins with an address ("Amici") and ends with the customary closing formula ("Quod nobis concedat Christus. Amen"). In doing this, Felton manages to include topics 1–3, 6, 8, 5, and 4, in this order. He, thus, worked with traditional material and used the scissors-and-paste method, but selected only a part of the lection and wrote a sermon on it.

This selection of thema and subject matter is paralleled in other sermons for the third Sunday in Lent. The twenty-nine found in the Latin collections made

[26] Delcorno, "Predicazione."   [27] See Part One, section 8.

between 1350 and 1450[28] that are genuine sermons, and not *postillationes* on the entire lection,[29] have the following short phrases or single words as their thema:

Erat Iesus eiciens daemonium (RY-28, X-60)
Erat Iesus eiciens daemonium et illud erat mutum (B/2-86)
Locutus est mutus (FE-19, R-17, RY-27)
Signum de caelo quaerebant ab eo (WA-30)
De caelo quaerebant (O-7)
Quomodo stabit (A-50, C-44, E-7, P1-32, R-1, R-25, X-106)
In digito Dei eicio daemonia (X-218)
Eicio daemonia (P1-33 and parallel)
Pervenit in vos regnum Dei (BR-20)
Cum fortis armatus custodit atrium suum in pace sunt omnia quae possidet (S-14)
Fortis armatus custodit atrium (C-114, C-115, O-6)
Armatus custodit atrium suum (BR-81)
Revertar in domum meam unde exivi (S-23 and parallel, sermon by Holcot)
Revertar in domum meam (V-18)
Revertar (B/2-71 and parallels, J/3-1, P2–33 and parallel)
Beati qui audiunt verbum Dei (W-18).

All twenty-nine concentrate on their themata, whether in the literal or spiritual sense, and pay little attention to the remainder of the pericope, even if they may slip in some of the topics listed above. Several speak about the selected part of the lection and apply it to the spiritual or moral life. Thus, B/2-86, on *Erat Iesus eiciens daemonium et illud erat mutum*, after a protheme and introduction, divides its thema into three parts based on the chosen text, in which "we can contemplate a name of excellent worthiness, an act of incomparable power, and the hiding of truth."[30] The preacher then speaks of the holiness and power of the name of Jesus, devotion to it, and taking it in vain; further, of Christ's power, manifested chiefly in forgiving sins and healing; and finally of the devil's attempt to render sinners mute in confession and of the qualities a good confession must

---

[28] Excluded are collections G, U, and Mirk, and further W-75, which is by Peraldus, but I have included a sermon by Holcot copied in collections S and Padua 515. In the Latin collections there are also ten sermons for the third Sunday in Lent on the epistle reading. No sermons clearly marked for 3 Lent are based on other biblical texts than the gospel and epistle lections according to Sarum use.

[29] RE-17, M/3-19, and L-25, as discussed above.

[30] "In quibus verbis tria possumus contemplari: Nomen eximie dignitatis, 'erat Iesus'; actus incomparabilis potestatis, 'eijciens demonium'; occultatio veritatis, quia 'illud erat mutum,'" B/2-86, f. 293ra.

have. All of this is rather briefly done, in the manner of expounding the biblical text selectively and morally.

A greater distance between gospel story and sermon text appears in Rypon's sermon 28, on *Erat Iesus eiciens daemonium*. Although the lengthy protheme sharply focuses on a word that is not even in the official lection, the copula *et*, which, as Rypon rather laboriously explains, connects this lection with the preceding text in Luke's gospel, he then derives from the chosen thema the sermon's two major parts: evil (in *daemonium*) and its remedy (in *Erat Iesus eiciens*). These are developed at greater length and with subdivisions. Thus, the first section on evil treats the questions, what is evil, how it begins with sin, and how sin is signified by the *daemonium*. In the course of this section, Rypon not only quotes Aquinas and other theologians but lists the seven deadly sins, in connection with the biblical names for the devil. Then, in the second major part, he similarly explains "how the help and remedy against all evil is expressed in our text by the antecedent words 'Jesus was casting out'."[31] Here he speaks, first, of the name of Jesus, and second about the forgiveness of sins, enumerating eleven requirements for a valid confession. Although Rypon utilizes some traditional topics (10 and 9), it is clear that the thema from the lection is but a springboard for him to preach about sin and repentance, the major topics of sermons in Lent.

Another major topic and concern that derives from this gospel is spiritual muteness, inspired by the words *Locutus est mutus*. In traditional exegeses, spiritual muteness is the inability or unwillingness to use speech for the various purposes it was given in creation (topic 6), and it was thus taken by Repingdon, his predecessors, and others. But several preachers handle *mutitas* in uncommon, original ways. Rypon, for instance, extends *mutitas* from speech to thought and deeds. His first sermon on 3 Lent (RY-27) begins with a lengthy protheme on two kinds of speech, *per linguam* and *per propheciam*. The following *introductio thematis* locates the thema in the entire lection and makes several references to the gospel story, using topics 2 and 10. His division then works with three kinds of *mutitas* and speech, and combines the analyzed parts of the verbal thema into a complex division:

> You who are mute in evil thought, speak like the Father through true contrition.
>
> You who are mute in evil speech, speak like the Son through true confession.

---

[31] "Quomodo contra omne malum iuuamen et remedium exprimitur in peccati euacuacione, cum premittitur 'Erat Iesus eiciens.' Peccati iuuamen et remedium est in 'Iesu' interpretacione, nominacione, et signacione, et secundo in peccati euacuacione, cum dicitur 'eiciens'," RY-28, f. 105.

And you who are mute in evil action, speak like the Holy Spirit through fitting satisfaction.[32]

Despite its seeming complexity, the division combines three very conventional triads (sins of thought, speech, and deed; the three persons of the Holy Trinity; and the three parts of Penance), though the entire discourse is by no means simple and easy to grasp, especially the connection that Rypon draws between the three kinds of muteness and the three persons in the Holy Trinity.[33] In developing it, Rypon again weaves in several references to the gospel story as well as to the day's epistle, and manages to preach not only about sins of speech but also about the five senses, the seven deadly sins, the parts of penance, and even sins of several social classes – once again, common aspects of Lenten preaching.[34]

The connection with the gospel reading, and especially its meaning of muteness, is even more tenuous in another sermon on *Locutus est mutus*, which was given on 3 Lent, evidently to a clerical audience. After some initial remarks about Christ's healing the mute man, the preacher applies the thema to "nos ecclesiastici et religiosi" and bases his division on the terms *mutus* and *locutus*. But in complete contrast to the gospel story, *mutitas* is here a positive quality, namely inner stillness. Thus, a priest or religious grows silent through inner contemplation in order to praise and thank God; he grows silent in discretion in order to correct his erring neighbor; and he grows silent in true wisdom in order to confess his own failures and admonish others to confess.[35] The three parts are then developed at some length.

---

[32] "Tu qui mutus es in praua locucione [*read* cogitacione] loquere ad similitudinem Patris per cordialem contricionem; et tu qui mutus es in praua locucione, loquere ad similitudinem Filii per veram confessionem; et tu qui mutus es in praua accione, loquere ad similitudinem Spiritus Sancti per aptam satisfaccionem," RY-27, f. 98v.

[33] The relationship is taken from Anselm's *Monologion*, with acknowledgment. For example: Speech of the heart corresponds to contrition. As God the Father is the cause, *principium*, of the Son and the Holy Ghost, so is speech of the heart the *principium* of actual speech and of deeds: "Est locucio in cogitacione correspondens contricioni; est locucio in verbo correspondens confessione; est locucio in opere correspondens satisfaccioni. Prima locucio Patri in diuinis, secunda Filio, tercia Spiritui Sancto. Quia sicut est principium Filii et Spiritus Sancti, sic locucio cordis est principium verbi exterioris et operis, quia verbum exterius et opus sunt nisi signa verbi interioris," ibid., f. 98.

[34] Near the end Rypon details some specific sins of merchants, craftsmen, and hired servants, ff. 100v–101.

[35] "Propter quod ecclesiasticus seu religiosus obmutescens per internam contemplacionem loqui debet reuerenter Deo suo laudes et gracias referendo. Secundo obmutescens per bonam discrecionem loqui debet frequenter errantem proximum corrigendo. Et tercio obmutescens per veram sapienciam loqui debet prudenter per confessionem propria crimina reuelando et principaliter ad confessionem alios admonendo." Thus the division of R-17, f. 82v. The sermon also uses topics 2 and 6.

The variety that is achieved by selecting a small part from the lection for one's thema and handling it in very different, individual ways could be further demonstrated with other sermons for the same third Sunday in Lent that select for their themata *Quomodo stabit regnum?* or *Fortis armatus custodit atrium suum.* As one might expect, the former leads to a consideration of conflict and dissension in the soul or in the nation, and indeed one sermon speaks of the danger that threatens the realm from France.[36] The thema *Fortis armatus custodit atrium suum,* again not unexpectedly, takes the preacher to speak of guarding the castle of the soul and of the Christian's spiritual warfare. In all these cases, the sermons' connection with the gospel story is indeed tenuous if it exists at all. But enough has been said to show that, in making his selection from the official reading of the day and interpreting it, the preacher had a good deal of choice that could lead him to a wide variety of subjects.

This claim can be extended to the use of the structural features that make up the standard scholastic sermon form. "There are almost as many different forms of preaching as there are able preachers," Robert of Basevorn observed in his treatise on sermon form; and Thomas Waleys echoed him: "You can hardly find two people who preach sermons they themselves composed who agree with each in every respect in their form of preaching."[37] The surviving collections do indeed bear these contemporary observers out: in describing the collections, I noted several times significant variations in the basic scholastic sermon model. Besides the radically different structure used by Mirk, a group of sermons in V regularly begins with a narrative that is moralized and eventually followed by the main division, while in contrast a group in Q begins with a distinction whose members are developed and then followed with the regular division and development. We also noticed that the sermons in P2 and related manuscripts fall into two parts, each with a division based on the thema and developed at equal length. Brinton often utilized a similar structure that slightly deviates from the normal scholastic sermon form. For example, his sermon 17 has the following structure:

Thema: *Humiliamini sub potenti manu Dei*
Protheme leading to prayer (60–61)
Thema repeated
Division: the hand of God is spiritually powerful to do three things: to
    subdue the proud, to lift up the fallen, and to sustain the weak (61–64).

---

[36] R-1, f. 1.

[37] "Fere quot sunt praedicatores valentes, tot sunt modi distincti praedicandi," and "Vix inveniantur duo, sermones a seipsis compositos praedicantes, qui in forma praedicandi quoad omnia sint conformes;" in Charland, *Artes praedicandi,* pp. 243 and 329.

Under the first item Brinton gives biblical examples and discusses three particular groups of proud people (61–63).
Thema repeated
Division of the thema ("In quibus verbis," 64):

> Salubris informacio vnitatis, *humiliamini* (64–66),
> Stabilis quietacio securitatis, *sub potenti manu Dei.*

Development: Brinton develops only the first part, saying he has already developed the second earlier, i.e. under the first division.[38]

This is in essence the normal structure of a scholastic sermon, in which the first division and its development would function as the *introductio thematis*. However, that section of Brinton's sermon does not really introduce the thema in the way the writers of *artes praedicandi* describe it; the whole section is disproportionately long; and it already develops a topic that forms part of the following main division, as Brinton then acknowledges.[39]

To this wide range of possibilities that lie in selecting a thema and structuring the discourse based on it must be added an at least equally wide range of possibilities to create the texture of the sermon and to employ rhetorical means for its development. As is well known, handbooks on sermon-making, the *artes praedicandi*, taught a large variety of ways in which the chosen thema and its divisions could be developed, dilated, or amplified, and it suffices here to say that it was indeed employed in the extant sermons (or, if one prefers, the use of such variety in actual preaching was what the *artes praedicandi* codified). As a result, some preachers rather relentlessly pursued a point by further divisions and subdivisions, whereas others preferred illustrating it with biblical *figurae*, similes from nature, and pious stories. And of course there are varieties of discourse: exegetic, expository, exhortatory or parenetic, persuasive, illustrative, emotive, inspirational, panegyric, and any combination of them. Detailed consideration of the texture and rhetoric in individual sermons and collections will often allow one to identify the characteristic style of an individual preacher, whether he is known by name or not. I have elsewhere given some examples of very different

---

[38] "Secundo in precedentibus expedito, de primo breuiter est sciendum . . . ," Brinton, *Sermons*, p. 64. Brinton uses this "expedito" formula similarly in other sermons that are built on this structure.

[39] See the previous note. Notice also that in sermon 24, preached to the clergy probably at convocation 1377, Brinton says that the archbishop had asked him to be brief and he therefore will preach "omitting a lengthy introduction which, even though it be carefully crafted (*curiosa*), is usually tedious to the audience" (p. 68; cf. p. 201). He then divides his thema into three parts and develops them in due order.

individual styles found in early fifteenth-century sermons[40] and will here add only one more case. A sermon for St. Mark, on the thema "Lord, save us, we are perishing" (Matthew 8:25), eventually concentrates on the word and notion of "salvation" and applies it to three stages of life (youth, maturity, and old age) and to being saved from the flesh, the world, and the devil. But before that, the preacher had briefly retold the gospel lection of Jesus calming the storm (Matthew 8:23–27). But when he turned to his expected moral commentary, he did not do so with a conventional "moraliter" or "mistice" but instead used a rhetorical question: "This is the text of the gospel. Lord God, can we draw from this text some spiritual fruit, some spiritual understanding to edify man's soul? Yes, certainly. As Augustine says . . ."[41] The result is a loosened-up style that is remarkably close to spoken discourse. In marked contrast to the relentless sequence of division/distinction – explanation – prooftext, some preachers could utilize such devices of orality as exclamations, rhetorical questions, and appeals to the audience – "But I ask, aren't there some Christians who disturb this peace? Why, yes, and especially so temporal lords who should preserve the peace before all others" – to fill tired bones with new life.[42]

Such variety and individuality of style, texture, and overall structure clearly exists throughout the corpus of late-medieval sermon texts, and it is not restricted to English preachers of the period.[43] Whether one can go further and speak of "originality" is a question of definition. Some modern readers would categorically deny it, as Janet Coleman does in the passage quoted at the outset of this chapter. But looking for "experiences from the preacher's own life" surely misunderstands the *raison d'être* of the homiletic genre altogether. One cannot measure the qualities of the medium whose declared purpose it was to instruct Christian people in the faith and lead them to virtue, with standards derived from St. Augustine's *Confessions* or Dante's *Vita nuova*, let alone post-Romantic poetry. To be sure, late-medieval preachers did use the scissors-and-paste method. Repingdon and Dygon copied large blocks of material, and Brinton used entire paragraphs of his own again and again. Beyond this, the sermons constantly draw on a common fund of topics, prooftexts, and illustrative material that was collected in a variety

---

[40] Wenzel, *Macaronic*, pp. 101–104, 125–127, and 128.

[41] "Discipuli videntes periculum timuerunt valde et pre timore mortis excitauerunt Iesum dicentes: 'Domine, salua nos, perimus.' At Iesus surgens imperauit ventis et mari, et vterque sibi obediuit, et statim cessauit tempestas. Iste est textus euangelii. Domine Deus, possumusne de isto textu elicere aliquem spiritualem fructum, aliquem spiritualem intellectum ad edificacionem anime humane? Et certe. Vt dicit Augustinus . . ." O-16, f. 97.

[42] "Sed rogo non sunt aliqui Christiani qui hanc pacem perturbant? Certe sic, et precipue domini temporales, qui pre ceteris pacem conseruare deberent," Q-35, f. 110v. See also the example from J/5-4 given in Part One, chapter 24, p. 145.

[43] See Bataillon, note 4 above.

of sermon aids – material whose occurrence a modern reader with some experience in this genre can easily predict. A sermon on penance, for instance, is bound to present the sacrament's three parts (contrition, confession, and satisfaction), quote biblical verses that contain words like "convert" or "return," adduce well-known biblical *figurae* of repentance, such as Peter and Mary Magdalene, and tell favorite stories about the blessed effect of contrition, such as that of the woman who committed incest, killed her parents as well as her offspring, and yet was finally converted and saved through a preacher's words. But as this chapter has tried to show, by selecting their topic, shaping it in a structure of their choosing, and expressing it with means they deemed appropriate and fruitful, late-medieval preachers could and did present their message in ways that a modern reader who is sensitive to the medium's horizon and truly familiar with the corpus of Latin sermons might be willing to call original.

50

Orthodox and heterodox

With only one exception, the Latin sermon collections made during the decades in which Wyclif and the Lollards greatly affected Church life in England including preaching were, as their descriptions earlier in this book have shown, orthodox. We can now inquire what image of the Lollards they present, what controversial topics they raise, and at what level they do so.[1]

The most outspoken texts in this respect are the macaronic sermons in O, which deal with the Lollards with regularity and condemn their teaching with fervor. All twenty-five pieces mention them by name[2] and warn against their doctrines. The most outstanding sermon in this collection, both for commenting on the Lollards in detail and for its historical perspective, is O-6. Evidently destined for the third Sunday in Lent, it uses as its thema "A strong man armed guards his court" (*Fortis armatus custodit atrium suum*, Luke 11:21). It begins by retelling a story from 2 Maccabees: When King Antiochus had oppressed the Jews for a long time, God sent them a knight from heaven, seated on a horse, clothed in a white garment, armed in gold, and shaking a spear in his hand (cf. 2 Maccabees 11:8). This account is then moralized twice. First, Antiochus stands for the devil, and the heavenly knight for the Son of God, riding on the Cross, clothed in human flesh, armed with divinity, and shaking the spear of his passion and death to overcome the devil. To this the preacher adds a second allegorization, in which he applies "this story [or literal sense, *historia*] to the world as it is today." Now Antiochus is "the devil, who has for a long time oppressed the Church in this realm, has stirred up wars and dissensions among us, and has been the cause of death for many, both spiritually and bodily."[3] Like Antiochus, he has hired and attracted many to his side and "has given them all the livery of the Lollards, has armed them all with malice and bad faith, and has gathered a great army

---

[1] Morrison, "Lollardy," raises similar questions but limits himself to vernacular sermons.

[2] This includes the two sermons that are entirely in Latin, O-20 and 21, directed to the clergy.

[3] "Diabolum qui diu grauauit super Ecclesiam in isto regno, qui mouit bella et dissenciones inter nos, et est causa plurium mortis tam spiritualiter quam corporaliter," O-6, f. 35.

against God and his ministers." This war has been going on since the time of Wyclif, "who was armed in heresy in every way and was the leader and captain of the devil's war." Since then, many sharp assaults have been launched against the Church.

> First these Lollards shot many evil words against the poor friars; they slandered their poverty and their order, which the Church approves and in which there are many great clerics and good men. Then they undermined the column of the monks; they dug deep for the treasure of the Church and devised temporal means to capture our possessions. They labored beyond human strength to ravish our livelihood. They did not care about excommunication or ecclesiastical censures; they threw their conscience to the wind and didn't give a fig for the pope and his power.[4]

Thus they have grown in both number and error, until of late they rose against the king in order to destroy him. In this grave danger God sent the English a knight from heaven, "our liege lord, the king, whom God has sent to defend the Church and to save the whole realm."[5] The attributes of this heavenly knight mentioned in Maccabees are then moralized. The white garment is his clear conscience and purity of life. His golden armor is God's grace, which has shown especially in his victory at Agincourt. And finally, the lance he has shaken is "the sharp sentence against the Lollards by which they are given over to fire and death."[6] Thus this strong knight has been guarding the court of the Church. With this the preacher has returned to his initial thema, and especially the word *atrium*, which he now continues to read spiritually rather than politically. God's special *atrium*, that is, his home or house, on earth is the human individual, where it is surrounded and attacked by mankind's three enemies – the devil, the world, and our flesh.

---

[4] "Iste Anthiocus hathe sowdid plures homines, plura milia fel to him quam scio referre, omnibus contulit liberaturam lollardrie, omnes armauit malicia et mala fide, et magnum congregauit exercitum aduersus Dominum et eius ministros. Ista guerra non durauit per vnum uel duos dies sed a tempore Wiclif, qui fuit armatus in heresi ad omnem partem et erat dux et capitaneus diabolici belli. In medio tempore multus populus hath be spied, plures acuti insultus fiebant in atrium Dei, Ecclesiam sanctam. Primo isti lollardi sagittauerunt plura praua verba ad pauperes fratres, deprauarunt eorum pauperiem et ordinem quos Ecclesia approbat, in quo plures magni clerici et boni viri sunt. Deinde þai castonn a myn ad columpnam pocessionatorum, profunde foderunt pro thesauro Ecclesie, fecerunt media ad temporalem manum ad capiendum nostras possessiones. Ultra vires laborabant ad rapiendum nostrum victum, non ponderabant excomunicacionem aut censuras Ecclesie, iecerunt conscienciam ad gallum, þai set not vnum cirpum per papam et totam eius potestatem," f. 35. The passage is repeated in O-24, f. 125.

[5] "Iste celestis miles est qui celice viuit, ligius Dominus noster rex, quem Deus misit nobis in defensionem Ecclesie et saluacionem tocius regni," f. 35.

[6] "Per lanceam quam miles vibrauit in manu intelligitur acuta sentencia contra lollardos per quam traduntur igni et morti," f. 35v.

Against these man must arm himself and do battle with the shield of faith, the helmet of hope, and the armor of love.

These three features of spiritual battle now form the sermon's main part, and in their development the Lollards appear once more. As ancient warriors had their heroic deeds engraved on their shields, so must the Christian warrior carry the twelve articles of faith on his shield. But the articles have been attacked and shot at by various heretics, and as Arrius and Sabellius once fought against the article of belief in the Holy Trinity, so modern Lollards fight against that of the remission of sins.[7] For

> they despise the oral self-accusation which is part of Penance; they hate hearing about it; they disparage this sacrament, which is a necessary and safe remedy against actual sin. For it is not enough for one's salvation to confess to God only in one's heart, as the Lollards assert. One must also confess with one's mouth to the priest who stands in God's place. Such oral confession is so necessary that, if there is the opportunity for making it, no one can be saved without it.[8]

And the preacher adds that confession saves a sinner not only from death of his soul but sometimes even from that of his body, as is shown in a miracle story reported by Caesarius of Heisterbach – "But tell that to a Lollard, and he will laugh!"[9] Similarly, Lollards put little stock in other remedies against sin, such as indulgences, pilgrimages, and prayers to the saints. The last of these they despise so much that "they have erased all the names of saints in the litany from their books."[10] "What shall we do with such people without grace?" the preacher then asks, and he replies with the story of Joshua who is commanded by God to lift up his shield against the city of Ai and who then burns the city. Now King Henry V enters the sermon again and is seen as a new Joshua who has lifted the shield of faith through the death of the Lollards, "and especially their captain who was recently burned."[11]

---

[7] "Et sicud scutum erat tactum olim et plures errabant in articulo Trinitatis, ita tactum est iam, plures errant in articulo sacramentorum," f. 37.

[8] "Despiciunt vocalem defensionem que est pars penitencie, odiunt audire de illa, vilipendunt illud sacramentum quod est necessarium remedium et securum contra actualem peccatum. Est necessarium remedium. Non sufficit ad salutem corde soli Deo confiteri, vt lollardi asserunt, sed oportet eciam ore confiteri sacerdoti in loco Dei. Ista vocalis confessio est adeo necessaria quod habita oportunitate sine illa nequis saluari," f. 37.

[9] "Virtus huius sacramenti saluat peccatorem non solum a spirituali morte sed eciam aliquando a corporali . . . / . . . Narra istud lollardo et faciet inde derisum," f. 37r–v.

[10] "Et in signum quod [non] desiderant istud medium, non cupiunt oraciones sanctorum, vt dicitur raserunt omnia sanctorum nomina in latenia extra suos libros," f. 37v.

[11] "Quid faciemus cum istis ingraciosis? . . . Nostrum scutum multum eleuatur, fides multum roboratur / per mortem lollardorum, et specialiter capitanei ipsorum qui tarde erat combustus. Deus ex sua misericordia fortificet nostrum specialem Iosue in omnibus bellis," ff. 37v–38.

The strong sentiments of national pride (the faithful English are God's special temple on earth, as one sermon claims), of deep worry about dissension and spiritual decay in the realm, and of triumphant exultation in the victories of King Henry V are all characteristic of this collection, as is its condemnation of the Lollards. While the grim call to destroy them, based on Old Testament precedent, is somewhat unusual,[12] the views of the Lollards expressed in O-6 recur throughout this collection and are to some extent echoed by other sermon writers. First of all, Lollards are seen not only to hold errors in the Christian faith but to spread them to others and thereby pervert true Christians and destroy Holy Church (O-16). In that they do the devil's work, becoming "false preachers" or "false prophets" and heretics. Specifically, they hold and teach wrong "opinions" about the two major sacraments, Penance and the Eucharist.[13] For the former they claim that auricular confession to a priest is not necessary, and for the latter they deny the doctrine of transubstantiation, maintaining that "it is a fiction and phantasm, and [the host] remains bread after the words of consecration as it was before."[14] Lollards similarly despise other customs of the Church through which grace may be obtained: the intercession of saints, worship of images, and pilgrimages.[15] They likewise despise the established clergy, from pope to parish priest, whose spiritual power they deny;[16] prelates are hateful to them, and the religious are a speck of dust in their eyes.[17]

Frequently orthodox preachers recognize that Lollards lead what appears as a holy life. For instance, "they do many good deeds, many of them give sizeable alms, they pay their debts, they abstain from great oaths and from the custom of swearing. These are good deeds in themselves." But, the preacher continues, "under these good deeds they hide their false errors; they do these deeds so that

---

[12] It recurs, however, in another collection (W-143) and is paralleled in O-18 by the demand to stone Lollards to death (with reference to Achan, Joshua 7; the writer or scribe speaks of "Achor," confusing Achan with the Vale of Achor).

[13] For Lollard teaching on these subjects, especially in the Wycliffite Sermons, see *English Wycliffite Sermons*, 4:41–56.

[14] "Et non solum de istis materiis se intromittunt, sed eciam de venerabili sacramento altaris quod Christus constituit ante passionem suam et dedit solum presbiteris potestatem conficiendi. Isti dicunt quod est ficticium et fantasma, et remanet panis post verba consecracionis sicut antea," O-18, f. 102v.

[15] "Non vult adorare ymagines, he forbarryt suas oblaciones; non vult offerre ipsemet nec pati alium si possit impedire," O-10, f. 64; "dicentes quod nostra mater Ecclesia nimia habundat peccuniarum copia, etc.," W-20, f. 69v.

[16] "Papam appellant antichristum, episcopos et Ecclesie prelatos scribas et phariseos," O-10, f. 64.

[17] "Destruere nitebantur [*ms* nitabantur] sacramenta Ecclesie et prelacie ac sacerdocii potenciam annullare . . . Prelati erant eis valde odiosi, religiosus erat malus attomus in oculo lollardi," O-15, f. 93.

simple people may give greater faith and credence to their false opinions."[18] In this, Lollards are "poison mongers," "pope-holy men," "wrapped in holiness" (O-3) to deceive. Like a limping man they have one leg shorter than the other:

> The legs that should support them are holiness and excellence of life. One of their legs is very long: they know how to read and understand the scriptures, many of them are very literate. But their other leg is shorter: the holiness and perfection they show outwardly is nothing but hypocrisy; it is not done for the love of God, it is not rooted in charity.[19]

Hypocrisy is thus a constant accusation hurled at the Lollards. Like the lion they hide their tracks with their tails:

> Thus it is with hypocrites, Lollards, and pope-holy men. They leave tracks of holiness, they give alms, they do not swear, they fast, they look modestly, and they always speak of perfection. These are signs of a good life, traces of holiness. But they erase them with their tail. Why do they do so? You think for God? No, but that they may be appreciated and elevated in the world and praised by the people. With this tail they erase their [true] merit.[20]

One sign for orthodox preachers that Lollards are not as truly holy as they might appear is that they work no miracles: "Those who die in this Lollardry never come back; no miracle is shown by them; God works none for them. Once they are gone, we hear of them no more."[21] Hence, "Words alone without works are not to be believed. Where are the miracles . . .? Where are the dead they have raised? Where are the lepers they have healed?"[22]

---

[18] "Lollardi plura bona opera faciunt, plures ex illis dant magnam elemosinam, soluunt bene debita, abstinent se a magnis iuramentis et consuetudine iurandi. Ista sunt bona opera in se, sed sub istis bonis operibus colorant suos falsos errores. Ista opera faciunt vt simplex populus det maiorem fidem et credenciam suis falsis opinionibus. Est de illis sicut de istis poyswunmongeres . . . ," O-10, f. 64v.

[19] "Claudus ex natura habet vnam tibiam alteri breuiorem. Sic est de illis. Tibie que ipsos supportarent sunt sanctitas vite et [exellencia sciencie, *canceled*] excellens vita. Vna tibia est satis longa. Sciunt legere scripturas et intelligere. Plures illorum sunt multi literati. Sed alia tibia est minus curta, sanctitas et perfeccio quam demonstrant exterius, nichil est nisi ypocrisis, non fit pro amore Dei, non radicatur in caritate," O-13, f. 80.

[20] "Leo delet propria vestigia sua cauda. Sic est de ipocritis [*MS*: ipocrisis] lollardis and popholi men. Vestigia ostendunt sanctitatis, dant elemosinam, non iurant, ieiunant, respiciunt simpliciter, et loquuntur de perfeccione totaliter. Ista sunt signa bone vite, ista sunt vestigia sanctitatis. Delent sua cauda. Sed quare hec faciunt? Credis propter Deum? Non, sed vt exaltentur et magnificentur in mundo, vt commendentur a plebe. Cum ista cauda detergunt suum meritum," O-12, f. 74v.

[21] "Qui moriuntur in ista lollardria numquam reueniunt, nullum miraculum ostenditur per eos, Deus nullum operatur pro eis. Be þai ones go, non plus audimus de eis," O-10, f. 64.

[22] "Sed nuda verba sine operibus non sunt credenda. Vbi sunt miracula facta per virtutem anuli eorum? Vbi sunt mortui quos suscitaverunt? Vbi sunt leprosi quos mundauerunt?" O-3, f. 19v.

Lollards have been spreading their harmful teaching throughout the land. In likening them to the moneylenders Christ drove from the temple, W-102 says "they go throughout the country sowing false doctrine and teaching the people errors and heresies;"[23] and O-16, dealing with the gospel of Jesus calming the storm, interprets the boat as England and tells us that "in every shire of England are some of this sect."[24] In another sermon, the university (presumably Oxford) is singled out as the "chief seat of heretics and Lollards."[25] Given their spread, devoted activity, and evil intent, it is no wonder that the Lollards should be accused of causing national disasters, both physical and spiritual. "As soon as the sect of the Lollards grew in our realm, honor began to wane, shame to grow; subjects turned into rebels, our enemies became bold, and poverty and pestilence fell upon us at the same time."[26] Hence "the good ship of England is at the point of perishing,"[27] a state of peril only less grievous than that found "at Prague in the kingdom of Bohemia."[28] Had it not been for King Henry V, "our ship would have been likely to have gone to wreck."[29] Thus the king is praised for overcoming "Oldcastle and his sect, who were joined and bound together in their malice against the Lord God, against our gracious king, and against the servants of the Church."[30]

The reference to the *anulus* derives from a story, told and moralized by the preacher, of a ring with a precious stone left by a rich lord; his elder son diligently searches for and finds it, while the younger one fabricates a false one.

23 "Isti sunt qui circueunt patrias et seminant falsas doctrinas, et docent homines errores et herises," W-102, f. 194. The same interpretation of the moneylenders appears in O-15: "Qui sunt isti nummularii qui circueunt patrias et seminant falsas doctrinas? Docent homines hereses et errores, et faciunt eos linquere meritoriam legem Dei. Et sicut falsus monetarius ponit falsa nummisma regis, þe print denarii uel grossi, super falsam materiam sicut super cuprum, plumbum, uel alkinoniam, sic isti noui monetarii ponunt þe coyn regis celi, signum crucis, super falsam eorum doctrinam," f. 92v. For the connection between Lollards and counterfeiters, see Strohm, *England's Empty Throne*, pp. 128–152.

24 "Ista tempestas lollardrie adeo creuit quod nauis Anglie fere operitur fluctibus fidei peruerse. In qualibet patria, in qualibet schira Anglie sunt quidam de ista secta, plurimi vacillant in fide, tam mares quam femine, tam eruditi quam laici," O-16, f. 97v.

25 "Sicut hec vniuersitas fuit olim verus fons fidei et virtutis, sic reputatur iam a chef [*blank*] hereticorum et lollardorum," O-8, f. 49.

26 "Quamcito secta lollardorum creuit in regno, honor incepit euanescere, dedecus crescere, subditi wex rebel, inimici toke boldnes, pouert and pestilens ceciderunt super nos simul," O-9, f. 55.

27 "Bona nauis Anglie est in puncto pereundi," O-16, f. 98v.

28 "Sed multo peius circa Prage in regno Boemie, vt asseritur," O-24, f. 125.

29 "Nostra nauis fuit in tanto periculo quod nisi noster graciosus rex set honde on þe raþer and stirid nostram nauem tempistiuius, nostra nauis had schaplich to a go al to wrek," O-25, f. 130.

30 "Oldcastel et eius sectam, qui era[n]t connexi et confederati in malicia contra Dominum Deum, contra graciosum regem nostrum et ministros Ecclesie," O-22, f. 113. The same passage recurs in O-24, f. 125. Another reference to "the captain" of the Lollards and his being burnt appears in O-6; see above, note 6.

A good deal of the blame for the perils posed by the Lollards falls on negligent pastors. Their "devotion is slacker than usual, their heart and mind is not as much fixed upon God as it used to be, our way of life is not what it once was . . . As to their preaching and teaching, God knows how they are doing their job . . ."[31] Many curates themselves have fallen prey to Lollard teaching, as two sermons in this collection, spoken to the clergy in a very rhetorical style and entirely in Latin, declare.[32] Instead, in the words of a synodal sermon from another collection, the true shepherd must "fight with the harshness of the words of Scripture and his shepherd's staff by threatening ecclesiastical censure."[33] But the laity, too, are at fault for the spread of heresy. O-1 once again allegorizes a story of Joshua's fight for the Israelites, this time against Amalek. As told in Exodus 17, during the fight Moses stood with his arms extended in prayer, and his arms were held up by Aaron and Hur. The two men signify the clergy and the laity, and both are needed in the struggle. The preacher's comment about Aaron, the clergy, was quoted a moment ago. He then continues,

> But is Hur without fault, you think? In no way. In many of them [i.e., the laity] there is very little goodness. Their faith is weak, their devotion very short, many of them put little stock in the divine service and the teaching of the Church . . . I don't wish to speak any more about this, the facts speak for themselves.[34]

---

[31] "Spiritualitatis deuocio est multo remissior solito, cor et mens non est ita fixum vt consueuit in Deo, nostra conuersacio et modus viuendi non est sicut fuit, pannus est alterius coloris, non est similis vite antiquorum patrum. Quantum ad predicacionem et doctrinam, nouit Deus quomodo faciunt debitum. Nimia falsa heresis et lollardria ventilatur inter nos, lollardorum accrescit numerus, plura alia iam regnant peccata, et nulla fit correxio uel modica," O-1, f. 2.

[32] "Sed nostris vilescit temporibus fidei firmitas, articulorum gemma palescit luciditas. Ideo belli terribilis infremit dolor, pestis martifere [!] inualescit langor, diuineque vlcionis insta[t] tempestas [*blank*], eo quod nedum plebeia cecitas, verum et curatorum serenitas lollardrie motiuis in fide vacillet. O igitur vasa Domini . . ." O-20, f. 109v. "Plurimi vero in sacre fidei vacillantes articulis, pestiferis lollardrie viciantur doctrinis," O-21, f. 111; the context makes it clear that *plurimi* refers to members of the clergy.

[33] The passage occurs in a moralization of the shepherd David's report of killing a lion and a bear, in 1 Samuel 17:34: "'Pascebat seruus tuus gregem patris sui, et veniebat leo et vrsus et tollebat arietem de medio gregis, et persequebar eos et percuciam eos.' . . . Quid per vrsum, animal versutum et callidum, nisi heretici ypocrite et lollardi designantur, qui per prauam doctrinam mites ac simplices in Ecclesia decipere minime cessant? Contra quos fidelis pastor asperitate verborum scripture sacre baculoque pastorali censurarum fulminacione cum sancto pastore Dauid fortiter dimicaret eosque a subditis sibi fidelibus vsque ad sanguinis effusionem constanter fugaret, idest 'bonus pastor animam suam dat pro ouibus suis,' Iohannis 10," E-23, f. 59va.

[34] "Sed estne Vr, creditis, inculpabilis? Nequaquam. Exilis bonitas est in eorum pluribus. Eorum fides est debilis, deuocio valde breuis, plures istorum diuinum paruipendunt seruicium et doctrinam Ecclesie . . . De hoc plus loqui non cupio, demonstrat ad oculum res gesta," O-1, f. 2.

Of the doctrinal positions Wyclif's followers held against orthodox beliefs it is especially those on auricular confession (to a priest) and on the Eucharist that are countered in orthodox sermons. The latter often do so even without mentioning Lollards by name. On these issues, however, orthodox sermons as a rule do not engage in explicit controversy but content themselves with reaffirming basic Catholic faith and practice. In fact, the emphasis in such matters is decidedly on practical aspects. Thus, auricular confession is taught to be absolutely necessary (as are the other two parts of Penance, contrition and satisfaction) when a priest is available,[35] and our sermons will show this importance by stories that tell of the benefits of a good confession and conversely of the harm that comes from neglecting it. While an occasional sermon may cite biblical passages on which the institution of the priesthood for the forgiveness of sins rests,[36] a medieval audience was much more likely to hear about the requirements for a good confession, including the need to prepare themselves well, like a governor of a castle or a bailiff who has to render a yearly account (A-37; also Q-19).

The same is true of the other major controversial issue, the Eucharist. The most "theological" passage on its nature that I know from a "real"sermon is short enough to be quoted in full. Sermon J/5-36 uses "Who eats this bread will live forever" (John 6:59) as its thema and is marked *De corpore Christi*. After a short protheme leading to prayer, the preacher gives the following introduction:

> About the Manna, which was a prefiguration of this bread, the question was asked, "What is this?" Exodus 16. How much more can this question be asked about *this* bread! In the schools of theology a question is usually answered by means of conclusions. And thus I choose three conclusions that answer this question. The first is this: Although [in the sacrament] appears material bread, this is not truly the case, but there is the flesh and blood of Christ . . . The first part of this conclusion [i.e., that in the Eucharist is Christ's flesh] is evident from the determination of the Church, the second [i.e., that there is the blood of Christ] from the sequence. "Christians have been given the dogma that bread turns into flesh," etc.[37] Likewise, this is evident from Christ's words in John 6,

---

[35] An example is J/5-15, which stresses the need for auricular confession without mentioning the Lollards in particular: "Non sufficit confiteri soli Deo, quod quidam heretici posuerunt, sed si habeatur copia confessorum, necesse est ut ei fiat [con]fessio in tempore necessitatis. Et hoc probatur auctoribus, figuris, et exemplo . . . ," f. 71.

[36] Including the gospel of Jesus healing the ten lepers, who were asked to show themselves to the priests (Luke 17:14), in A-40.

[37] A good example of this "dogma" from a contemporary sermon is this: ". . . firmiter credendo quod per virtutem verborum Dei a sacerdote prolatorum ille panis ante consecracionem fuit panis materialis, post consecracionem est vere et racionaliter [!] ille idem Christus, qui natus erat de Virgine, passus in cruce, tercia die resurrexit a mortuis, in die iudicii venturus est iudicare viuos et mortuos," E-2, f. 4ra. The other two copies of this sermon, *Surrexit Dominus vere*,

"He who eats my flesh and drinks my blood," etc. . . . The second conclusion is this: Although there appears [material bread, this is not truly the case] but it is the body of Christ that was put on the cross . . . The first part [i.e., that it is the body of Christ] is evident [i.e., from the preceding conclusion], and the second part is evident from what Augustine said in his letter, which is put in the *Decretum*, "De consecratione," distinction 2, "Not this body." There it is said that the same body of Christ is taken invisibly by the faithful that was placed visibly on the Cross. The third conclusion is: Although there appears [material bread, this is not truly the case] but here it is spiritual nourishment and food . . . The first part is evident [i.e. that it is spiritual food], and the second part is proven by the thema [of this sermon]. Therefore, I say that there [i.e., in the Eucharist] is Christ's flesh and blood.[38]

This is, at least stylistically, fairly heavy going and unlikely to have been thus preached to the people. A similar case is S-9. It is a sermon for Easter, the major feast when late-medieval Christians were expected to fulfill the Church's decree to receive Holy Communion at least once a year and when preachers tended to prepare their audiences for it.[39] Against the Lollard doctrine that after

express the need for faith differently: one must have "fidem et discrecionem de humanitate Christi ac eciam de deitate, que sunt vere et r'aliter in hoc venerabili sacramento secundum fidem scripture sacre et eciam secundum omnes doctores fideles Ecclesie catholicos," H-8, f. 24v. For *r'aliter* (= realiter) Z-16 reads *racionabiliter*, f. 79va.

[38] "De manna, quod fuit figura huius panis, fuit hec questio facta 'Quid est hoc?' Exodi 16. Quanto magis potest talis questio fieri de isto pane! Sed ad questionem communiter in scolis theologie respondetur per conclusiones. Vnde tres elicio michi conclusiones huic questioni responsiuas. Quarum prima sit hec: Licet ibi apareat panis materialis, tamen ibi non est, sed est ibi caro et sanguis Christi. Anglice: þof þer seme materiale brede, 3et þer es non bot þer es Cristis fleys and his blude. Prima pars huius conclusionis patet ex determinacione Ecclesie, secunda ex insequenter 'Dogma datur Christianis quod in carnem transit panis,' etc. Item ex dictis Christi Johannis 6: 'Qui manducat meam carnem et bibit,' etc. Hic nota quod solum sacerdotes sumunt hoc sacramentum sub specie vini, quia qui sumit corpus Christi, ipse sumit tam carnem quam sanguinem Christi. Vnde insequenter: 'Manet tamen Christus totus sub vtraque specie.' Secunda conclusio sit hec: Licet ibi apareat, etc., sed est ibi corpus Christi quod positum fuit super crucem. Anglice: þof seme, etc., bot þer es Cristis body þat doyn was in þe rude. Prima pars patet, et secunda ex dicto Augustini in epistula, et ponitur in canone *De consecratione*, dist. 2, *Non hoc corpus*. Ibi habetur quod hoc idem corpus Christi sumitur invisibiliter a fidelibus quod visibiliter positum fuit super crucem. Tercia conclusio: Licet ibi appareat, etc., sed est ibi spirituale nutrimentum et cibus. Anglice: þof þer seme, etc., bod þer es gostly fude. Prima pars patet, et pro secunda allegatur thema. Ideo dico quod ibi est caro Christi et sanguis, etc.," J/5-36, f. 126v. The canonistic authority quoted is *Decretum*, De cons., 2.45 (Friedberg 1:1330–1331). The sequence referred to ("insequenter") is *Lauda Sion*.

[39] Canon 21 of the Fourth Lateran Council, *Omnis utriusque sexus*, established what became known as the "Easter duty": to confess all one's sins at least once a year, to fulfill the imposed penance, and to receive Communion at least at Easter; see above, p. 235. Sermons usually deal with the Eucharist and Holy Communion on Easter and Corpus Christi, and occasionally on Maundy Thursday, and now and then quote the canon, as does A-40.

consecration the substance of bread remains, this and other orthodox preachers declare:

> This bread is the true body of Christ, which is truly contained in the sacrament of the altar under the species of living bread. Therefore you must firmly believe and in no way doubt that in the sacrament of the altar Christ's true body, taken from the Virgin and offered up on the cross, and his true blood shed from his side, is not merely signified by but truly contained under a twofold species, that is, bread and wine, as in one sacrament, not two.[40]

The preacher then brings in conventional sacramental theology, on the distinction between *res* and *sacramentum*,[41] which, given the incidence of scribal corruption, seems to have been a little above the scribe's head. The same is true of the following section, where with the help of Bonaventure he explains that the sacrament can be perceived by faith alone, not with our human senses.[42] But this is as much systematic theology as one finds in "real" sermons of the period, and it is a far cry from the technical debates about the nature of the Real Presence held during Wyclif's time.[43] Most popular preaching on the Eucharist thus consists of simple assertions about the *verum corpus Christi sub forma panis*, often presented as answers to questions: that God, who created the world *ex nichilo*, surely can change bread into human flesh; that Christ's body is present in every fragment of the consecrated host; and that he is simultaneously present in many different locations. These tenets of faith appear in a range of *mirabilia* of the consecrated host and in several other standard topics.[44] Thus, sermon J/5–36 shows how the seven liberal arts are helpless before this mystery; how there are seven qualities in the host that oppose the seven deadly sins; how with respect to this sacrament

---

[40] "Iste panis est verum corpus Christi quod veraciter continetur in sacramento altaris sub specie panis viui. Quapropter firmiter debetis credere et nullatenus dubitare quod in sacramento altaris verum corpus Christi emptum de Vi[r]gine et oblatum in cruce, et verus sanguis effusus de eius latere non tantum signatur sed veraciter continetur sub dupplici specie, scilicet panis et vini, tanquam sub vno non dupplici sacramento." S-9, f. 42v.

[41] See for instance Peter Lombard, *Sentences*, 4.8.6, in Petrus Lombardus, *Sententiae*, 4:284.

[42] He quotes Bonaventure's "Conpendium theologie," i.e. *Breviloquium*, 5.7.3: S-9, f. 43.

[43] The sermons surveyed here seem to avoid the terminology of substance and accidents. A very rare exception is S-3: "Hic sunt accidencia sine subiecto cui inherent" with repeated mention of *subiectum/substanciale* and *accidens* in a discussion of three *mirabilia in hoc sacramento*, ff. 22v–23.

[44] A convenient list appears in the *Compendium theologicae veritatis* 6.14, in Albertus, *Opera* 34:212. In sermons the topos appears in E-31 (with reference to the *Compendium*), FE-24, FI-6, G-26, J/5-17, Merton 236/2-49, Q-61, S-3, and W-8, and Z-14 (at end, without development). It should be distinguished from the so-called "Virtues" or "Meeds of the Mass," which lists a number of benefits to the person who looks upon the consecrated host: he will not die that day, etc. Another related topos is "The Properties of the Host." All these, with a popular treatment of the Eucharist, can be found in *Fasciculus morum* V.ii; see *Fasciculus morum*, pp. 404–417.

all human senses err except hearing (since, as Scripture says, "faith comes by hearing," Romans 10:17), and how "this admirable transubstantiation or super-natural conversion"[45] may be illustrated with examples from nature, "art" (here chemistry), biblical figures, and pious stories.[46]

Similarly constant in orthodox preaching is the warning not to engage in theological speculation.[47] The macaronic sermons in O repeatedly exhort priests and the laity not to investigate matters that are too high for their understanding – not to hew above their heads lest the chips fall in their eyes, as a vernacular proverb puts it.[48] A sermon in another collection recommends David, who, despite his great wisdom, after reciting the wonders of Creation refrained from probing more deeply into God's works (*substitit et vlterius pertransire noluit*) and instead exclaimed, "Oh Lord, your works are great and wonderful, and you have made all things in your high wisdom" (Psalm 103:24). "Oh," the preacher adds, "that people and especially illiterate ones nowadays would imitate the footsteps of this wise man."

> But it is a great harm when someone, the more illiterate he is, the more he tries
> to investigate the secrets of God's works and to prove with his natural reason
> what incomparably transcends the whole course of nature, such as the articles
> of our faith, the sacraments of the Church, and especially the sacrament of the
> precious body and blood of Christ. But as is commonly said: if someone hews
> above his head, the pieces will fall into his eyes. Thus people of this kind who
> put their hand on such high and secret works of God often become blind and
> fall into divers errors and heresies.[49]

[45] "Euidencia de hac admirabili transubstanciacione siue supernaturali conuersione panis in corpus Christi," f. 128v.

[46] "Circa vlteriorem processum est sciendum quod intendo primo ostendere qualiter circa hoc sacramentum errant omnes sciencie liberales, et quomodo in hoc sacramento sunt septem proprietates opposite septem mortalibus peccatis. Secundo, qualiter circa hoc sacramentum omnes sensus hominis preter auditum errant, et quomodo cognoscetur cibus incognitus. Tercio intendo aliqualiter ostendere in natura, arte, figura, et exemplo qualiter hec mirabilis conuersio fit, scilicet panis in Corpus Christi, et quomodo eadem res vni est tiriaca et alii venenum," J/5-36, f. 126v, the main division of the sermon. The final point is not treated.

[47] See also Fletcher, "Faith."

[48] O-10, 13, 16; see Wenzel, *Macaronic*, p. 92; the expression is proverbial in Middle English.

[49] "Et ideo substitit ibi et vlterius pertransire noluit, sed dixit: 'Quam magnificata sunt opera tua, Domine; omnia in sapiencia fecisti.' O lord, he seyþ, þy werkus been grete and wondurful, and al þyng þu madest yn hy wysdome. Et vtinam homines et specialiter illiterati viri vellent modernis diebus imitari vestigia huius viri sapientis. Set maius dampnum est, quanto magis illiteratus quis fuerit iam, tanto secreciora Dei opera nititur perscrutari et fundari naturali racione quod incomparabiliter transcendit omnem cursum nature, sicud sunt articuli fidei, sacramenta Ecclesie, et specialiter sacramentum preciosi corporis et sanguinis Christi. Set sicud communiter dicitur, siquis secauerit [*MS*: occauerit] supra capud, pecie cadent in suos oculos. Sic huiusmodi homines qui ponunt manum sic alte ad secreta operum Dei, cecantur pluries

Closely connected with sacramental theology was the question whether sacraments administered by a priest in the state of sin are valid. Orthodox teaching from at least Augustine on had answered in the affirmative, but Wyclif and his followers strongly denied this. Their view is reflected in Brinton's sermons that give a short list of Wycliffite errors. There the bishop precedes his denunciation of those who teach that "if anyone is duly contrite, any external confession is superfluous and useless" and that "in the sacrament of the altar the substance of material bread and wine remains after consecration" with condemning those as "pseudo-prophets"

> who preach and affirm falsehoods about the Church's sacraments, and particularly about baptism, saying that if a bishop or priest is in mortal sin, he does not confect [the sacrament] nor baptize.[50]

Brinton replies to all three errors with very brief citations from canon law. A much deeper engagement with this controversy appears in Repingdon's very long sermon for Trinity Sunday, on "There was a man of the Pharisees named Nicodemus" (John 3:1). This is really a treatise on baptism, which contains a discussion of whether baptism (to which Repingdon later adds the Eucharist) administered by an unworthy priest is a valid sacrament. The discussion is developed in genuine scholastic form, with a detailed argument against validity, counter argument pro, objections, and Repingdon's determination in the affirmative, though he adds that in administering the sacraments an unworthy priest is guilty of a greater sin, as is a lay person who receives them in the state of sin. Not only does Repingdon here use the form of a scholastic disputation, but he also quotes a wide array of authorities ranging from Augustine through Grosseteste to Thomas Aquinas and Duns Scotus (quoted several times).[51]

But Repingdon's discussion of this question is a rarity that has, except for Brinton's brief references, no parallel in other orthodox sermons. This is different with another major controversial topic, the veneration of images. By Wyclif's time, attacks against image worship and its defense had had a long history in the western Church, and the last two decades of the fourteenth century as well as the following generations witnessed a sharp revival of the controversy.[52] A

---

et cadunt in diuersos errores et hereses," W-152, f. 288va. W-8 similarly exhorts lay people to "believe faithfully as the Church believes," no matter how much and in what ways clerics "investigate the truth and make subtle arguments about this sacrament in order to demolish the errors of infidels and bad Christians," ff. 29v–30.

[50] BR-101, p. 466. The passage recurs in BR-107, p. 495.

[51] RE-28. He presents a similar argument for the validity of Penance in RE-21.

[52] For the issue of image worship in Lollard teaching and practice see Aston, "Lollards and Images"; and Hudson, *Premature*, pp. 301–309; see also ibid., p. 208 note 193. Academic disputations of this topic in the 1390s are discussed ibid., pp. 92–94.

good deal of it is also reflected in the late-medieval Latin sermon collections. Rypon's sixth sermon for 1 Lent, on the thema "You shall adore the Lord your God" (Matthew 4:10), deals with the first commandment. In doing so, Rypon says that "the bishop of Lincoln [i.e., Grosseteste] raises the common question if it is allowed to make images and place them in churches for veneration, which all Lollards and many others deny." Instead of just saying yes or no, Rypon reports two reasons against the legitimacy and six reasons for it, followed by responses to the two reasons against. "In this way the bishop of Lincoln answers the question about worshiping images in the affirmative."[53] Throughout this scholastic form of handling a question and beyond, Rypon credits his material to Grosseteste.[54] An equally scholastic discussion of the issue had been given by Holcot in his commentary on the Book of Wisdom, with reasons against and for, and a final determination in favor of, the legitimacy of image worship. But Holcot used very different authorities, pitting John Damascene and Thomas Aquinas against the prohibition of Exodus 20:4. His position and argument are taken over in a sermon on *Clausa est ianua* (Matthew 25:10), evidently given after Easter. The anonymous preacher deals with the Ten Commandments, and under the first he declares that "against this commandment act all idolaters, and especially all those who adore some image of wood or stone."[55] But then he qualifies the prohibition and, after citing John Damascene and Aquinas, concludes with Holcot (whom he mentions by name) that "it seems to me that I do not worship the cross of Christ because it is wood, nor his image, but I worship Christ in front of his image, because it is the image of Christ and stirs me to pray to Christ."[56] The difference between idolatry and legitimate worship thus turns on the notion of representation.[57]

---

[53] "Mouet Lincolniensis commune dubium an licet facere ymagines et statuere in ecclesiis ad colendum, quod omnes Lollardi \et alii/ nonnulli negant . . . / Igitur istam questionem de adoracione ymaginum modo quo dicam affirmat Lincolniensis," RY-9, ff. 31v–32.

[54] In the sermon, the question proper is followed by another paragraph beginning "Vlterius doctor distinguit" which cites several biblical prohibitions against venerating irrational creatures, f. 32. I cannot find any parallels to any part of this argument in Grosseteste's *De decem mandatis*.

[55] "Contra istud mandatum faciunt omnes ydolatre, et specialiter omnes tales qui adorant aliquam ymaginem ligniam vel lapideam," Z-16, f. 46ra.

[56] "Videtur, inquit [i.e., Holcot], mihi quod nec adoro ymaginem Christi quia lignum nec quia ymago sed adoro Christum coram ymagine Christi, quia est ymago Christi et excitat me ad orandum Christum," Z-16, f. 46rb, quoting Holcot, *In Sapientiam*, lectio 157 (see Holcot, *Super libros Sapientiae*, f. 170va).

[57] Another sermon that mentions the Lollards in discussing the first commandment is J/5-5: "Credunt quidam quod non deberent esse ymagines in ecclesia Dei," then giving several standard authorities and reasons in favor of image worship and ending up reaffirming that pious gestures before an image are done not to the image but to what it stands for; J/5-5, ff. 55v–56.

The same preacher of Z-16 continues that "from this it is clear that those do wrong who call such images by the names of the saints who are in heaven"; and he further assigns a cause for such mispractice:

> The whole cause is that the higher clergy, who ought to inform the people about this, are so obstinately given to the sin of avarice that they are afraid to inform the people how they should use these images correctly, so that they may not lose the offerings that are made to these images.[58]

It is not impossible that this could be coming from a Wycliffite preacher, especially since collection Z contains a number of similar pointers.[59] But we should notice that the two points of this last quotation: that simple people give statues the name of saints, and that their offerings are welcome to greedy prelates who are unwilling to teach them better, occur likewise in an earlier sermon by an undoubtedly orthodox if not universally liked churchman, Archbishop FitzRalph. In his sermon for All Saints' Day in 1356, FitzRalph developed three reasons why we should honor the saints. As he reports in his sermon diary, he spoke about dangers in the veneration of images, because some people cannot or do not clearly distinguish between the physical image and the person imaged therein; hence they speak of "Blessed Mary of Lincoln, Blessed Mary of Walsingham, Blessed Mary of Newark, and so of others, whereas Blessed Mary the Mother of God is always in heaven and never in those places or others like them here on earth," and thus some faithful indeed worship an image of stone or wood. Moreover, the cause of this abuse is greed for the offerings made to such images because of "the fabricated and feigned miracles of the ministers of the Church."[60] It would seem that Z-16 is indebted to FitzRalph, whose indignation was similarly picked

---

[58] "Ex quibus patet quod male faciunt qui appellant tales ymagines nominibus sanctorum qui sunt in celo . . . / Et tota causa est quia tales superiores Ecclesie, qui deberent populum informare, taliter sunt peccato auaricie obstinati quod timent populum informare qualiter debent illis vti, ne perderent oblaciones que multo[ciens?] talibus ymaginibus diabolice sunt contribute," Z-16, f. 46rb–va.

[59] But see my remarks in the final paragraph of this chapter.

[60] "Dicta fuerant aliqua pericula de veneracione ymaginum quas communiter nomine ymaginatorum appellant et male, videlicet 'sanctam Mariam de Lincoln,' 'sanctam Mariam de Walsyngham,' 'sanctam Mariam in Nouo Opere,' et ita de ceteris, cum sancta Maria mater Dei sit semper in celo, numquam in locis illis aut aliis illis similibus hic in terra . . . Non solum ymaginem tanquam ymaginem, scilicet solum ymaginatum, adorant, set parcialiter propter ipsam ymaginem. Vnde non dubium quin racionale obsequium trunco exhibent aut picture propter picturam. Et est supersticio reprobanda . . . Istam ydolatriam introducit cotidie cupiditas oblacionum que offeruntur talibus ymaginibus propter fabricata ac ficta miracula ministrorum Ecclesie, ymmo verius Sathane. Super quo excessu expedit per prelatos remedium adhiberi," FI-64, f. 92.

up and shared by Wyclif in his Bible commentary[61] and seems to have found a strong echo in the C text of *Piers Plowman*.[62]

Holcot's discussion of image worship was evidently well-known in the early fifteenth century, since it is again referred to in collection O. Sermon 18 here speaks of

> these Lollards who look into Holy Scripture and only take the letter and not the sense. In their great presumptuousness they lean more on their own reasoning than on the authorities of the saints, and lurking in corners they teach not to go on pilgrimages and not to worship images, whose worship was introduced by the apostles, as Holcot declares in his commentary on Wisdom.[63]

Another sermon, O-17, exhorts its audience to look at Christ on the cross: "Let us bend our knees before the cross and adore the good Lord with our whole heart who has redeemed us with his blood." But, the preacher continues,

> perhaps you say as the Lollards have been teaching, "Why should I bend my knee before the cross, since this is stone or wood?" To which I say that, although the image of the Crucified which you see with your bodily eyes is made of stone or wood, it yet represents to you the sufferings he bore on the cross ... Therefore, whatever the Lollards may have said, do not believe them but honor the images in your prayers and offerings.[64]

Yet another preacher of the same time speaks against the Lollards, not so much condemning them as putting them in their place. His English sermon, R-30, deals largely with pride, and he criticizes the laity for their pride and scornful indignation that has caused them to withdraw their due reverence for the clergy. To illustrate his point, he tells of an image of Pride painted in the city of Athens. "Is this image not painted in our realm?" he asks, and then answers,

---

[61] See Benrath, *Bibelkommentar*, pp. 34–35 n. 78.

[62] C, prologue, lines 95–102; in Langland, *Piers Plowman*, pp. 202–204. Cf. Wenzel, "Eli."

[63] "Isti lollardi qui inspiciunt sacram scripturam et solum capiunt literam et non sensum. Isti ex magna presumpcione magis innituntur suis ingeniis quam auctoribus sanctorum, et latentes in angulis docent peregrinaciones non fieri, ymagines non adorari quarum r [*blank*] inducebatur ab apostolis adorandi, vt Holkote recitat *Super librum Sapiencie*," O-18, f. 102v.

[64] "Flectamus vtrumque genu ante crucem et toto corde adoramus bonum Dominum qui suo sanguine te redemit. Sed forte dicis sicut lollardi docuerunt per prius, 'Quare / deberem genuflectere ad crucem ex quo sit lapis uel trunctus?' Ad hoc dico quod licet imago crucifixi quam vides oculis corporeis fiat ex lapide uel ligno, tamen representat penas tibi quas pertulit in ligno, et sic quelibet imago illum cuius est, et quod qui es laicus videres passionem Christi et meritoriam vitam aliorum sanctorum, et cicius moueri ad deuocionem. Et ad hoc apostoli introduxerunt vsum ymaginum. Ideo quicquid dixerint lollardi, ne credatis eis, sed honorate ymagines in precibus et oblacionibus, quia voluntas Dei est vt honoretur in talibus imaginibus," O-17, f. 101r–v.

Yes, truly, and it is held in such great reverence and worship that I dare well say that, if half as much worship were done to the images that are painted in the church, we should have only a few Lollards in this realm . . . Let your own eyes be judge whether I speak the truth or I not . . . You will agree with me that there is more idolatry, more maumetry done to this cursed image of Pride than due worship or meritorious pilgrimages to Our Lady of Walsingham, to our glorious patron St. Alban, or to the holy martyr St. Thomas of Canterbury.[65]

From a similar monastic environment comes still another sermon that voices the same sentiment, now in Latin, with greater fierceness, and in an elevated style. It, too, reiterates John Damascene's teaching that "according to the tradition of the Church we should venerate the cross of Our Lord and other relics of the saints," the cross in which, "by kneeling before it, we venerate the memory of the one crucified for us." Consequently, he who forbids the veneration of relics is outside the faith, *infidelis*, "and thus is deservedly judged to be burned by fire."[66]

Image worship and pilgrimage together with the nature of the Eucharist and the necessity of auricular confession are, thus, the main controversial topics between orthodoxy and the Lollards that are reflected in orthodox sermons of the late fourteenth and fifteenth centuries. It should be added that apart from condemning the Lollards for their errors in these matters, orthodox sermons vary in the degree of emphasis they themselves give to the same topics. The need to confess one's sins to a priest appears constantly in exhortations during Lent and at other times. Likewise exhortations to receive communion with the right disposition, as well as explanations of the sacrament and its beneficial effects, are constant ingredients in sermons for Easter and Corpus Christi. But the other,

---

[65] "Lord God, whether thys image be naw3t peydyd in the cyte of thys reme? 3es, truly, and hathe in so great reuerens and worshep that Y der wel sey, and alfe so myche worschep were do to ymagis that be depeydyd in holy churche, we schulde haue bot a fewe lollardis in thys reme . . . And late 3owre oune eyin be iuge whether y sey soth or y do now3t . . . 3e wyl acorde wth me and sey ther ys more ydolatrie, more maumetri do to thys cursed ymage of pride than dow worshep or merytory pylgrymage to howre lady of Walsyngham, owr gloryous patroun synt Albone, or to the holy Martyr synt Thomas of Cawterbury," R-30, f. 149v. Another sermon that blames the Lollards' opinions on pride is W-154, edited in Wenzel, *Macaronic*, pp. 308–345, at 334–336, lines 429–440.

[66] "Sed secundum eundem in eodem libro capitulo 3, crucem Domini consecratam ceterasque sanctorum reliquias ex traditione Ecclesie debemus venerari, cum per nullum aliud primi parentis exilium fuerat euacuatum, peccatum solutum, infernus depredatus, filii Dei et heredes facti sumus, nisi per crucem Domini, quam procidentes veneramur nostri memoriam crucifixi. Est ergo sacrarum reliquiarum venerationis prohitor [!] infidelis per consequens et hereticus, et sic censatur ecclesiastica igne merito concremandus," W-143, f. 2. The reference is to John Damascene, *De fide orthodoxa*, 4.3 (John Damascene, *De fide orthodoxa*, pp. 299–304). Before this passage the preacher had quoted John Damascene 4.2: "Qui non credit secundum traditionem Ecclesie catholice aut comunicat per inconvenientia opera diabolo infidelis est" (p. 298).

more external religious practices, which exercised Lollards so much, hardly ever form subjects of exhortation. The orthodox sermons from England that have come down to us do not "advertise" pilgrimages or the veneration of images.

Of other controversial topics one finds little or no mention. I have discovered no traces of the subject of dominion, which was so fundamental in Wyclif's career as a polemicist.[67] The related issue of disendowment of the clergy, however, does occur here and there, primarily in sermons from a monastic milieu. We already noticed that in O-6 the Lollards are said to have "dug deep for the treasure of the Church and devised temporal means to capture our possessions." The point is almost literally repeated in O-24, whose speaker is a possessioner who in the beginning of the sermon prays "particularly for the venerable college and chapter of St. Francis."[68] In the development he says that "Oldcastle and his sect . . . first shot the arrows of evil words against the poor friars, slandered them and reproved their poverty"; later they undermined the tower of the possessioners and "appealed to the temporal lords to take away our livelihood."[69] Similarly the Worcester sermon W-102, clearly spoken by a monk and addressing curates,[70] speaks against the Lollards, who go through the country teaching errors and heresies: "They say that their doctrine of Christ is profitable to king and country, as they did in the last parliament, where they moved the king and his magnates to despoil the Church of her possessions."[71] Another sermon in the same collection mentions that "nowadays many desire to rise illegally; whence they slander churchmen in everything they do or propose to take away the goods they have."[72]

---

[67] An apparent exception occurs in DY-1: "Ordinata est a Deo potestas dominii," f. 3v, but Dygon here copies from Grosseteste's sermon *Unguentum effusum nomen tuum* (cf. MS Bodley 830, f. 146ra).

[68] "In speciali venerabile collegium et capitulum sancti Francisci sacre professionis," O-24, f. 124v.

[69] "Per castellum quod erat in fieri et stare nequiuit intelligo castrum peccati et miserie, castrum diaboli, Oldcastell et suam sectam . . . Primo sagittauerunt plura praua verba ad pauperes fratres, deprauabant et reprobabant eorum pauperiem et ordinem quam Ecclesia approbat et de quo plures excellentes clerici, plures perfecti sacerdotes et virtuosi viuent . . . Postea þai cast a myne ad turrim possessionatorum, foderunt alte pro thesauro Ecclesie, fecerunt media ad dominos temporales ad auferendum nostrum victum, vltra vires laborabant ad rapiendum nostras possessiones," O-24, f. 125.

[70] "Reuera, domini, vos qui habetis curam animarum et manucepistis Deo edificare bonum templum," W-102, f. 194. On the following page the preacher again addresses "vos curati, qui habetis curam templi Dei."

[71] "Dicunt quod doctrina sua est comodifera regi et regno, sicut fecerunt in vltimo parliamento, / vbi mouebant regem et proceres vt spoliassent Ecclesiam possessionibus suis," W-102, f. 194r–v.

[72] "Hiis diebus plures illicite exaltari appetunt propter quod in omni quod faciunt viris ecclesiasticis detrahunt aut bona que habent auferre proponunt," W-105, f. 200v. *Bona* could conceivably refer to spiritual, not temporal goods.

A somewhat more complex issue in the orthodox sermons is hostility to the friars, which, as was noted earlier, the two sermons in O included in their critique of the Lollards. By the early fifteenth century, the clash between secular clergy and the mendicant orders over the latter's privileges to preach in the parishes, to hear confession, and to bury the dead had been a matter of fierce controversy, involving theologians, canonists, and the papacy.[73] The precise theological and canonistic root of the struggle lay in the Church's requirement that every Christian was to make his or her confession at least once a year. In the canon *Omnis utriusque sexus*,[74] the Fourth Lateran Council stated that this was to be done to the *proprius sacerdos*, that is, one's own parish priest, to whose office belonged the spiritual guidance and sacramental cure of all Christians within his area of jurisdiction, for whom he would have to give a reckoning at the Last Judgment. The actual work of hearing confessions and giving absolution, especially near the end of Lent, was often more than a single parish priest could manage and thus required the help of additional priests. This need was quickly supplied by the mendicant orders. But the friars' vigorous involvement in pastoral work – hearing confessions as well as preaching – led to strong opposition from the secular clergy, who both resented mendicants as intruders and questioned their legitimacy as preachers and confessors in the parishes. The ensuing struggle led to several papal decrees, and while *Omnis utriusque* remained in effect and was quoted in sermons of the later fourteenth and fifteenth centuries,[75] its application continued to be debated and refined. Of primary importance was the question to what priest a person could lawfully make his or her confession; in addition, theologians and canon lawyers asked whether a penitent who had confessed to another priest was to repeat his or her confession to the *proprius sacerdos*. The resulting polemic between secular clergy and mendicants eventually also touched on the friars' claim of following the ideal of poverty while holding property and relying on contributions from parishioners for their livelihood. By the 1350s, Church leaders, canonists, and the mendicants themselves were hoping that these issues had been satisfactorily settled, and they were therefore disturbed when FitzRalph stirred them up again in the last decade of his life, from his *Proposicio* of 1350 preached at

---

[73] Among recent studies are helpful: Haren, "Friars" and Haren, "Bishop Gynwell." R. N. Swanson follows the topic into the early fifteenth century, for England as well as the Continent, in "'Mendicant Problem'." Avril, "A propos," traces the background from Carolingian Church legislation to Lateran IV. Congar, "Aspects," surveys the controversy through its critical period and provides a handy calendar. Kedar, "Canon Law," examines the varying practice among English bishops to license friars for preaching and hearing confessions.

[74] Included in the *Decretals* at 5.38.12 (Friedberg 2:887–888).

[75] It is cited in the four Brinton sermons considered below; also in A-40, J/5–14, P2–22, and in *Middle English Sermons*, p. 287. In addition, it is referred to in the late-fifteenth-century collection in Cambridge, Corpus Christi College, MS 423, p. 161.

Avignon through the sermons he gave in London in 1357–1358.[76] By the latter date FitzRalph had further "introduced into the smouldering poverty controversy a fresh complicating factor, the theory of dominion founded on grace."[77] His sermon 67, given at St. Paul's Cross on the first Sunday of Lent in 1357, deals with confession and states firmly that confession is safer if it is made to one's regularly instituted priest (*persona ordinarii*), such as "capellanus parochialis, vicarius, rector, episcopus, vel eius penitenciarius generalis."[78] He further declares that anyone who had confessed to an "extrinsic" priest had to repeat his confession to his parish priest (though without repetition of the absolution).[79] As a result of FitzRalph's sermon, representatives of the four mendicant orders met a few days later, drew up a list of twenty-four errors they found in his teaching, and presented the list to him. FitzRalph reacted at once with his sermon 68, preached again at St. Paul's Cross on 3 Lent, in which he replied to twenty-one assertions one by one. But apparently his voice was soon silenced.[80] However, his teachings quickly found new fertile ground in Wyclif, first in his view that true dominion is based on grace, with its corollary that a person not in the state of grace could not have any spiritual or material rule, and later in his arguments against the mendicants' exalted claims of poverty.[81]

FitzRalph's opposition to the friars surfaces also in later orthodox sermons. Bishop Brinton, for instance, gives several times a comprehensive list, with proper citations of canon law, of the priests to whom one can lawfully make

---

[76] Walsh, *Fourteenth-Century Scholar*, pp. 348–451, gives an authoritative account in chronological order.

[77] Ibid., p. 377.

[78] FI-67, f. 109. A few lines later FitzRalph cites *Omnis utriusque* and glosses "suo proprio sacerdoti" as "ordinario confitentis." And again: "Persona ordinarii ad audiendum confessiones subditorum suorum est persona securior quam quis persona extrinseca" (f. 110v) and "Ex istis racionibus videtur probabiliter posse inferri quod iste confessiones facte fratribus ab alienis parochianis sunt magis secure cum fiunt ordinariis quam cum fiunt solis fratribus" (f. 112).

[79] "Videtur quod quisque confessus cuicumque extrinseco tenetur iterum de suis peccatis suo ordinario confiteri, non dico ab eo absolui," f. 110.

[80] In sermon 38 (the sermons in the manuscripts are not in strict chronological order), given on March 25, 1357, FitzRalph refers back to sermons 67 and 68; but he preached it at St. Mary's Newchurch, London, not at St. Paul's Cross.

[81] With respect to FitzRalph's stirring up the controversy about friars' privileges, Catto writes: "Though the phase of sharp public controversy in the university was probably over by the end of 1358, it rankled through the next / decade particularly between monks and friars, and must have exacerbated the quarrel between Uhtred of Boldon OSB and his mendicant critics in 1368. More significantly, it turned the attention of theologians to questions with an ecclesiological aspect: the nature of property and dominion, the state of man before the fall, and the public implications of individual sin . . . These would be the great issues of the next twenty years," Catto, "Wyclif and Wycliffism," p. 184.

confession: the *proprius sacerdos*,[82] mendicant friars admitted by general license or privilege, and extraordinary confessors to whom individual Christians may make their confession by a permission issued in "letters from the Curia" for three years.[83] But Brinton also noticed that this system led to abuses:

> I am much grieved by the common error that very many subjects contemptuously leave their curates and *proprii sacerdotes* and make their confession to priests that are out of the common, strangers, and *ignoti*, who themselves assert both publicly and privately (*occulte*) that they are more capable of effecting the conversion of the people than curates.[84]

And he adds, with special attention to friars: "Against their assertion I say, other things being equal, that a confession made to the *proprius sacerdos* is safer than one made to a friar."[85] A similar listing of priests to whom valid confession may be made and Brinton's *securior* position against friars appear in the sermon collection from Worcester. W-136, a Lenten sermon directed to university students, has this to say:

> But nowadays great strife has arisen among doctors of the Church concerning the *proprius sacerdos*. Whence some say that the pope, bishop, and anyone admitted by the bishop, a friar or someone else, is the *proprius sacerdos*. In this matter we should act after the counsel of St. Augustine, given in a sermon that begins "Poenitentes," at whose end he says: "Leave what is uncertain and hold what is certain." Thus, if you would be on the safe side, confess to your rector, vicar, or parish priest![86]

---

[82] This concept includes the pope and his penitentiary, the bishop and his penitentiary, the archbishop at the time of his visitation of his province, and the parish priest (*rector*) and his vicar, both perpetual and temporary.

[83] This outline appears in sermons 19, 54, 86, and 99; Brinton, *Sermons*, pp. 75–76, 244–245, 393–394, and 455.

[84] BR-86, ibid., pp. 393–394; similarly in the other three sermons.

[85] Ibid. Brinton then gives three reasons why confession to one's parish priest is safer: fulfilling the decree of Lateran IV, supporting the parish to which one belongs, and fostering the virtue of humility by confessing to the ordained local priest. In sermon 99 Brinton seems to add that his antifraternal stand in this respect was promulgated through his diocese: "Nam licet per diocesem sit veraciter proclamatum quod confessio facta proprio sacerdoti sit securior quam confessio facta fratri," but the edited text appears to be garbled or at least badly punctuated (ibid., p. 455).

[86] "Sed iam istis temporibus magna altercacio inter doctores ecclesie oritur de proprio sacerdote. Vnde quidam dicunt quod papa, episcopus, et quilibet admissus ab episcopo frater vel alius est proprius sacerdos. Ideo in isto faciendum est secundum concilium Augustini in sermone qui sic incipit 'Penitentes,' vbi dicit in fine: 'Dimitte insertum et tene certum.' Si vis igitur esse securus, confitearis tuo rectori, vicario vel parochiali sacerdoti," W-136, f. 260vb. The reference is to Augustine, *Sermon 393* (PL 39:1715). The *securior* view appears likewise in A-40: "Confiteri

Another sermon in the collection makes the same point in English: "The schalt, more-ouer, whan þe schriueste te, go to him þat hath cure o þi sowle, as to þi paro prest, þi person, or þi pentauncer, and to no ronners ouer cuntreys".[87] It is interesting to note that antifraternalism in this matter should come, not from seculars but from monastic preachers. One may wonder whether the macaronic sermons in O also share this position, at least by implication, for while they do not mention the friars as confessors, they rather insistently exhort the faithful to "go to *your curate*" (my emphasis) and "tell him the whole burden of your conscience."[88]

Nonetheless, as one might imagine, not all orthodox sermons of this period share such antifraternal sentiments but instead object to them. A collection of evidently Dominican origin claims that restricting confession to one's *proprius sacerdos* is caused by envy,[89] and another, after giving curates and friars equal power, stresses that it is not mandatory to repeat one's confession. Thus, confession

> is to be made to a priest who has the power and knowledge, that is, the regular curate, and also to friars admitted by the bishop, who have an equal power to absolve. Nor are those that have confessed to a friar held to confess the same sins again to their *proprius sacerdos*. Saying the opposite is erroneous, nor does anyone do so except from ignorance or malice.[90]

The question of *proprius sacerdos* was only one aspect of the wider controversy between mendicants and the secular clergy (and to some extent the monastic orders), which also encompassed the mendicants' privileges to preach in the parishes and to bury the dead, as well as, ultimately, their claiming to follow the ideal of poverty while they were holding property and begging for contributions from parishioners for their livelihood. In these matters FitzRalph's outspoken hostility is not matched in later orthodox sermons, although here and there one can at least sense some tension. The academic sermons given at Cambridge

proprio curato cum ceteris paribus est saluti animarum securius, racioni conformius, ac nostre Ecclesie militanti expedicius," f. 131; this sermon, incidentally, quotes FitzRalph on the Eucharist.

[87] W-14, f. 50; in *Three Middle English Sermons*, p. 60.

[88] "Vade in hoc sacro tempore ad curatum tuum," O-9, f. 59; "clama ad curatum per veram confessionem, quod possis intrare, enarra sibi totum grauamen consciencie," O-12, f. 77; and similar exhortations in O-1, 3, 6, 9, 10. Repingdon similarly stresses "tuum proprium curatum," in RE-14, f. 99va.

[89] "Alii qui per inuidiam oblocuntur aliis dicentes quod parochiani sui tenentur et debent suis curatis confiteri et nullo modo aliis," P1-38, f. 130vb.

[90] "Que facienda est potestatem habenti et scienciam, videlicet curato ordinario, fratribus eciam ab episcopo admissis, qui equalem auctoritatem absoluendi habent; nec eis confessi tenentur eadem peccata iterato confiteri proprio sacerdoti, quia dicere oppositum est erroneum, nec aliquis dicit oppositum nisi ex ignorancia vel malicia," P1-33, f. 115vb.

report two remarks about friars (or perhaps monks) and seculars calling each other Pharisees.[91] A Lenten sermon in collection A criticizes those who "preach chiefly in order to beg, not to bring souls back to Christ's flock."[92] And one monastic sermon in W preaches against the friars' precious clothes, expensive celebration of their inception, and fruitless preaching,[93] while another tells a little allegory that may or may not contain a gentle slap at the friars.[94] On the other hand, occasionally an orthodox sermon speaks up in favor of the friars. O-44 thus defends the poor Friars Minor against churchmen who criticize them.[95] More remarkable is E-24, which laments that the four mendicant orders are held back by Church decrees from helping the parish priest in his task of teaching his flock.[96]

All these remarks, whether in favor of or against the mendicants, firmly stand in the tradition of antifraternalism and have little to do with controversies between orthodoxy and the Lollards. The same I believe is true of an aside Repingdon makes in his sermons on the Sunday gospels, where he criticizes friars – as well as monks – for bending Scripture to their own desires:

> If a mendicant friar interprets the scriptures and they suggest anything against his mendicancy . . . , he will either pass it over entirely in silence or obfuscate it with a gloss that goes against the text.

Monks, he adds, will likewise not willingly hear or lay open scriptural truths that speak against defects of their order.[97] But Repingdon's aside brings us closer

---

[91] "Hic nota quod frater comparauit prelatos Phariseis quia diuisi sunt ab illis in vit' quia vnus secularis dixit ante quod Iudas post vendicionem Christi ibat ad Phariseos et non venit ad templum," C-64, p. 58; "Hic dixit secularis de Phariseo per multas auctoritates quod fuit religiosus," C-67, p. 61.

[92] "Qualiter faciunt illi qui predicant principaliter vt mendicent et non vt animas Christi precioso sanguine redemptas peccato submersas ad ouile Christi reducant," A-30, f. 96.

[93] W-145, see above, pp. 159–160.

[94] W-154, see ibid., and Wenzel, *Macaronic*, pp. 328–331.

[95] See above, p. 87.   [96] See above, pp. 165–167.

[97] "Si enim frater ordinis mendicantium interpres fuerit scripturarum, si qua forte contra eius mendicacionem sonuerint uel eorum temporale emolumentum in aliquo iuste retrahere poterit, vel ea omnino silebit uel ea cum glossa textui contradicente obscurabit. Sic possessionatus qui contra sui graduum defectus veritates scripturarum manifeste sonantes nec voluntarie audiet nec reserabit," RE-50, f. 366vb. The remark was caused by Repingdon's quoting "Woe to you, Scribes and Pharisees, who shut the kingdom of heaven" (Matthew 23:14) with the commentary by Pseudo-Chrysostom. In the redacted version M/3-52 this passage reads: "Si enim clericus secularis uel religiosus in officiis secularitatis occupatus, et per hoc prebens exemplum subditis cupiditatis uel superbi ornatus, interpres fuerit scripturarum, si qua forte contra eius voluntatem uel emolumentum sonuerint in aliquo, uel omnino silebit uel eam cum glossa textui contradicente subdole obscurabit. Sic et valide mendicans textus scripture sacre sue spontanee mendicacioni repugnantes, ut est illud Deuteronomii 15 . . . uel omnino silebit uel subdole glosabit" (f. 297rb).

to the heart and "centrepiece" of the Lollard creed, the primacy of Scripture. The principle of *Scriptura sola*, of the Bible as "the single validating law"[98] for Christian belief and practice, clearly lay at the heart of Wyclif's and his followers' beliefs. In the orthodox sermons I have surveyed I have found only one remark that takes some issue with the Lollard position. It occurs in Felton's sermon for the fourth Sunday in Lent, in which he preaches on the five loaves of the gospel (John 6:9). He distinguishes the five as material, doctrinal, sacramental, penitential, and heavenly bread and divides each into three parts. Those of the doctrinal loaf of bread are "the Old Testament, the New Testament, and the expositions or pronouncements of the doctors [of the Church]."[99] To confirm this, he curiously quotes from the story of the good Samaritan (Luke 10:33–35) who left the inn-keeper two pence with the promise, "and whatever you spend over and above, I will repay you." In Felton's exegesis, the two pence stand for the two testaments, and the additional money for "the exposition of Holy Scripture," because Scripture needs an exposition – "which is against the Lollards." And Felton ends by including in the "over and above" "all good exhortations and exempla and stories, which are medicine for the soul."[100]

It would, then, seem that *Scriptura sola* was a topic for formal theology, not for preaching, at least not in the orthodox camp. As far as the actual use of the Bible in sermons is concerned, the surviving texts show that in their density of biblical quotations orthodox preachers were in no way left behind by Lollard preachers. This should not astonish us at all, because both orthodox and Lollard preachers held on firmly to the traditions of medieval preaching, more precisely to the tradition of privileging the biblical text as the foundation of the sermon in its thema and as the predominant source for proof within its development. Thus it is no wonder to observe that the sermon on the third Sunday in Lent by a Wycliffite preacher has considerably fewer biblical quotations, apart from the thema, than a comparable orthodox work.[101]

---

[98] Hudson, *Premature*, p. 228. See also her discussion on pp. 228–277, 280–281, 375–378, and passim.

[99] "Secundus panis est doctrinalis et habet tres partes, scilicet vetus testamentum et nouum et exposiciones uel dicta doctorum," FE-20, f. 34va.

[100] "Duo denarii possunt dici duo panes, et opera supererrogacionis tria, quia sacra scriptura indiget exposicione. Trenorum 4: 'Paruuli pecierunt panem et non erat qui frangeret eis.' Ecce quod scriptura sacra indiget exposicione. Hoc est contra Lollardos et hereticos. Immo omnes bone exortaciones et exempla, narraciones que sunt medicine anima sunt quasi opera supererrogacionis," ibid.

[101] The Wycliffite L-25 is a little over 6,000 words long and has sixty-five biblical quotations apart from its thema. The orthodox M/3-19 contains fifty quotations in just over half the same length. Wyclif's sermon for T21 has only eight biblical references besides the thema, whereas an orthodox sermon of comparable length, R-25, has eighteen. Of course density of biblical

What then about Wyclif's and the Lollards' deep concern that the word of God be preached often and with a purity that would avoid such rhetorical tinsel as rhymes, fables, and meretricious stylistic adornment?[102] The reformers surely must have had cause to be concerned about and to reject abuses they observed. But as we saw in an earlier chapter, the same concerns and rejections are voiced in orthodox sermons, which not only exhort priests constantly to preach the word of God, and threaten neglectful pastors with eternal punishment, but also warn against an excessive interest in rhetorical decoration.[103] One may wonder whether this warning from orthodox preachers of the 1380s and 1390s as well as the fifteenth century came as a positive response to the biblical and pastoral seriousness of their counterparts. Such an influence is possible but rather difficult to assess. We should remember that declarations that a pastor's primary duty is to teach his flock and preach the word of God, as well as warnings against excessive concern with rhetorical effect and against watering down the gospel through too much care for popular appeal, were heard in the Church long before FitzRalph and Wyclif.

In clashing with Lollardy, then, orthodox sermons address clear differences on a small number of specific issues, such as the nature of the Eucharist, the necessity of confession to a priest, and such devotional practices as image worship and pilgrimages. But at the same time they share the other side's moral earnestness and desire to reform abuses. In this latter respect, it is often impossible to tell the difference between orthodox and Lollard, and in particular to assign an anonymous text to one camp or the other. In discussing the sermon collection that was probably made by John Dygon – trained lawyer, parish priest, and recluse at a Carthusian house – I pointed at the presence of Wycliffite views and

---

quotation varies much according to a preacher's style and other factors, but it seems clear that an orthodox preacher's audience could have heard, quantitatively, as much if not considerably more of the Bible than Wyclif's. For thirteenth-century sermons on the same gospel and their biblical quotations see Bataillon, "Early Scholastic," pp. 165–198. And see Walsh, "Preaching."

[102] For a brief survey of the use of stylistic ornaments in preaching see Spencer, *English*, pp. 242–247. A primary locus for Wyclif's and his followers' condemnation of superfluous rhetoric in preaching is an entire sermon in Wyclif's *Quadraginta Sermones*, in which he complains: "Nowadays, if anyone speaks, he will preach, not as it were the words of God, but – for the sake of illustration – stories, poems, or fables from outside Scripture; or in his preaching he will divide up Scripture into smaller segments than is natural and then bind them up like weeds with rhetorical colors until the text of Scripture can no longer be seen, and instead the words of the preacher as the first author and inventor. And from this diabolical affectation, in which everyone desires to have these things from himself and not from anyone else, stems the whole vicious novelty of this world. For it is on its account that the divisions of sermons and the divisions of the ornaments and other tricks exist, beyond what has been customary," in Wyclif, *Sermones* 4:265.

[103] See above, pp. 343–345.

terminology.[104] One sermon in the otherwise orthodox collection A expresses sympathy with the Lollards, who are, as the preacher says, denigrated and slandered, presumably at St. Paul's Cross.[105] Similarly, the anonymous collection in Z contains sermons that in regard to such major controversial topics as auricular confession and pilgrimages are unquestionably orthodox yet stand, in the manuscript, next to Wycliffite treatises, a sermon by Lychlade, and an expression of sympathy with preachers of the word of God who are threatened with excommunication.[106] While in most of our orthodox sermons that reflect the clash between orthodoxy and Lollardy the dividing line on specific doctrinal points is clear, there are some that in their religious and moral seriousness stand in an area that is shared by both. After examining the sermon cycle by the former Wyclif sympathizer turned bishop of Lincoln, Repingdon, with respect to controversial matters, Simon Forde cannot do more than claim "a common cultural phenomenon and religious temperament to have existed in the late fourteenth-century."[107] And similarly Margaret Aston has said that "historians who once saw orthodoxy and heresy more or less in terms of white and black are now more keenly aware of the varying shades of greyness in contemporary religion."[108] This would apply to the preaching of the period as well.

[104] Part One, section 18, pp. 108–110.
[105] See above, Part One, section 31, pp. 180–182. The collection also contains Wimbledon's sermon in English, another case of possible Wycliffite sympathies.
[106] See above, Part One, section 32, pp. 187–190. One should also recall here that the learned orthodox theologian and chancellor of Oxford Thomas Gascoigne reports that Arundel "before his death was so stricken in his tongue that he could not swallow or talk for days before his death. And thus he died, and, as people believe, he was thus stricken in his tongue because he thus tied down the word of God from the mouth of preachers," Gascoigne, *Loci*, pp. 61 and 181.
[107] Simon Forde, "Writings," 1:326.
[108] Aston, "Were the Lollards," p. 164, with further references to the work of John Thomson as an indicator of this shift.

Final reflections

The preceding chapters have surveyed thirty-two major and some additional collections of Latin sermons made in England in the century between 1350 and 1450.[1] Of these, seven or eight are by named authors (Sheppey, FitzRalph, Waldeby, Brinton, Repingdon, Felton, Rypon, and perhaps Philip), the others are anonymous, although some of them contain one or more pieces by a named author (Chambron, Alkerton, Wimbledon, Lychlade, the Dominican preachers in D). All together, these collections contain over 2,100 individual sermons.[2] In light of Schneyer's *Repertorium*, this may be a far cry from sermon production during the previous two centuries, especially on the Continent.[3] It reflects the absence of major model collections composed in England during our period, with the exception of Repingdon's and Felton's.[4] But the number of texts tells us little about the actual orthodox preaching that was done in that century. In all likelihood, all the preserved sermon texts, whether they stand in diaries, notebooks, or repertories intended for a preacher's own use or else were "published" for the use of others, could have served as models and therefore been used on more than one occasion.

---

[1] I have described 32 major collections (in sections 2–8, 10–20, 22–28, 31–37) with additional collections in Caius 334 (sect. 5); Bodley 857 (sect. 12); Magdalen 93 (sect. 18); Bodley 859, Padua Antoniana 515, and Christ Church 91 (sect. 21); Rimington's two sermons (sect. 27); and several minor collections mentioned in section 38. Mirk's *Festial* is excluded from these statistical reflections.

[2] Included in this count are the thirty-two major and additional collections mentioned in the previous note. Multiple occurrences are counted only once.

[3] On the basis of Schneyer's *Repertorium*, Bériou has estimated that for the period of 1150–1350 about 60,000 Latin sermons by named authors have been preserved, of which only 5% are from before 1200. To these can be added some 44,000 more that are anonymous. There is, of course, a good deal of overlap; see Bériou, "Sermons latins," p. 363 and note.

[4] Even here the quantitative difference is remarkable. While Repingdon wrote 52 sermons for the Sunday gospels, the production of Nicholas de Gorran, in several cycles, for example, runs to almost a thousand items (Schneyer 4:255–321)

Of these Latin collections, several have in their entirety survived in more than one manuscript: FitzRalph, Waldeby, Repingdon, Felton, and to some extent the Wycliffite preacher of L. The others have come to us only in single copies. Unless new information emerges, I think it is useless to speculate whether further copies of Brinton's or Rypon's sermons, for example, did at one time exist. On the other hand, many individual sermons – a few by named authors, but most anonymous – appear in more than one manuscript. I have drawn attention to such shared or multiple copies in the respective sections. There are over a hundred such sermons that have been preserved in two or more places.[5]

The religious status of a known author or else some dominant characteristics found within an anonymous collection allows us to say that the thirty collections are distributed among a fairly wide spectrum of religious affiliation, including secular clergy (FitzRalph, Felton, Dygon?, and presumably the Wycliffite author of L), Benedictines (Sheppey, Brinton, Rypon), Augustinian Canons (Repingdon), Franciscans (Q), Dominicans (P1, P2, D), Austin Friars (Waldeby), and perhaps Carmelites. What may surprise us is the absence of sermon collections by Cistercians, who in the century under consideration could look back to a distinguished history of preaching and sermon-making. Less surprising is the virtual absence of collections made by Carthusians, who by their rule were not allowed to preach orally, even though in the fifteenth century they played an important role in the spread of religious literature. Only one collection can be linked to their order, John Dygon's, and his interest in collecting and making sermons may well stem from before his enclosure at Sheen. The curious collection CO seems to belong to the same milieu of Sheen and Syon, though the precise nature of the relationship is as yet unclear. What is more surprising, however, is the statistical imbalance between Benedictine and mendicant sermon writers. While the latter had made an enormous impact on preaching in the thirteenth century, in our collections their predominance has, statistically, given way to the older monastic order of Black Monks.

The period from about 1380 to about 1440 clearly formed the peak in the history of preaching in medieval England after the much earlier flourishing of Aelfric and Wulfstan. Not only is it graced with the names of important and original preachers, but its production shows a vitality in sermon style and in the engagement with contemporary concerns that are absent from the half centuries before and after. Further research into English preaching from the late thirteenth century to about 1350 may still bring to light some rhetorical achievements that

---

[5] I count 113 individual sermons that occur in two or more of the collections analyzed above. To these can be added another eighteen that occur in one collection plus one or more other English manuscripts, and another twenty in one collection plus one or more Continental authors or manuscripts (including Thomas de Lisle).

have so far gone unnoticed. For the second half of the fifteenth century, on the other hand, the field of new sermon literature strikes me as quite fallow, and while I cannot claim to have studied surviving manuscripts of that period with equal care, I would doubt that much fresh material may yet emerge. Around mid-century and later, English bishops and theologians certainly voiced strong and serious concerns for a well-informed and committed preaching to the people,[6] but direct written evidence that such was in fact carried out does not seem to exist.[7] Whether this apparent decline in the production of new sermon cycles should be blamed upon the simple loss of manuscripts,[8] or on the more casual nature of the preaching and a new preaching style,[9] or on the restrictive limitations that Archbishop Arundel imposed on preaching[10] remains an open question. Arundel's constitutions surely had no immediate negative effect on making and collecting sermons, as can be seen from our collections O/1, FE, Q, and DY. In contrast to these, the few collections made around the middle of the century

---

[6] See especially the fine, balanced account by Davies, "Episcopate," especially pp. 78–79; and Ball, "Opponents." Pecock had made himself obnoxious to reform-minded churchmen by declaring, among other things, that bishops are not bound to preach and that they can work more usefully for the souls of Christians in other ways; see Ball, ibid., p. 233.

[7] Catto has said the same in reverse: "*Though it cannot be traced directly*, the impact of Oxford theologians through the pulpit *is likely* to have been no less in the later fifteenth century than it had been in the time of Richard Fitzralph," "Wyclif and Wycliffism," p. 273 (my emphasis). For two collections that may be linked to the serious concern of Oxford and Cambridge theologians with preaching and the pastoral cure, see DY and CO; but the "sermons" contained in the latter cannot possibly be considered to be a reflection of actual preaching.

[8] The surviving catalogue of the Syon library allows us to see that sermon collections made in the second half of the fifteenth century were "de-accessioned" in the early sixteenth century; Gillespie, "Syon and the New Learning," p. 86; and p. 93 on the changing tastes of the Syon brethren.

[9] According to Gascoigne, writing at mid-century, Richard Fleming had introduced a more flexible method of preaching at Oxford around 1420; see Gascoigne, *Loci*, pp. 182–185. His remarks are summarized in Catto, "Wyclif and Wycliffism," pp. 257–258, but they remain insufficiently clear so that, in the absence of illustrative texts, not much can be learned about this putative new style of preaching. Gascoigne's main point seems to be that in developing his sermon a preacher should follow the order of natural inquiry and not an artificial, rhetorical one ("Forma enim debita in sermone est quando res declaratur et manifestatur et ordo dicendi sequitur ordinem essendi in rebus," *Loci*, p. 179), and hence Gascoigne recommended preaching without a thema (p. 180). But in this he was apparently not thinking of the "ancient" sermon form of the homily. In the sermons I have read I find nothing similar to the example Gascoigne gives (pp. 182–185).

[10] Commenting on the decline of preaching in fifteenth-century England, Kedar remarks: "The restricting 'laws and statutes' of Arundel's time, aimed primarily at the Lollards, silenced the orthodox preachers as well . . . the virtual cessation of preaching," "Canon Law," p. 32. Gascoigne, whose deep concern about preaching is well known, retails a story that Arundel "before his death was so stricken in his tongue that he could neither swallow nor speak for days before his death; and thus he died, and as people believe, he was stricken in this way because he thus bound the word of God from the mouth of preachers," *Loci*, p. 61.

and later that I have included here show that the effort to write new sermons (O/1, Q) or to compile bits and pieces from an earlier tradition into new sermons (FE, DY) gave way to merely collecting older pieces, often of Continental origin. It would seem that, just as a person's emotional and intellectual life has its ups and downs, so homiletic efforts around and after 1450 hit a valley, for whatever concrete causes.[11]

In the sections that dealt with individual collections I have called attention to the relatively high proportion of sermons addressing the clergy. In retrospect, the extant Latin sermon literature of 1350–1450 will surprise modern readers by containing far more pieces directed to a clerical audience than one might have expected. It would therefore seem that statistically this literature can hardly reflect what actual preaching must have gone on at all levels and throughout the country, Sunday after Sunday and saint's feast after saint's feast. This apparent disproportion, however, should keep us alerted to the fact that much of the sermon literature preserved was written down in order to give instruction and examples to the clergy who were directly involved with preaching to the people. This is no mere speculation – a good many sermons *ad clerum* or delivered at visitations and synods make it clear that what they say should be passed on to their flock. Modern attempts to discern what a common English audience heard from the pulpit in the age of Chaucer and Langland are thus made more difficult, not only by the difference in language (Latin vs. English) and medium (written vs. spoken discourse) but also by this deliberately intermediate function of the sermons that have been preserved.

While the intended audience of most of this literature can be more or less easily divided into clerical (*ad clerum*) and lay (*ad populum*), one may wonder whether there is not a further vertical division that should be considered, especially with regard to lay audiences. It is now commonly accepted that the period with which this book has been concerned witnessed the growth, if not of lay literacy *tout court*, certainly of a literate and cultivated laity.[12] Whether at court or among the middle classes, this new audience was addressed by the greatest poets medieval England produced: Chaucer, Langland, and the *Pearl*-poet, whose works they read and presumably responded to. Can one discern such an implied cultivated audience, trained not so much in theology as in secular literature, in our sermons as well? Answering this question is hampered by the notorious difficulty of knowing the real or intended audience of a given sermon. Though a more detailed analysis

[11] Marshall, *Catholic Priesthood*, has brought together some evidence for such aspects as the frequency of preaching, preaching and the priestly office, priestly ignorance, the *pastoralia*, and the Bible in English, for the late fifteenth and early sixteenth centuries; see especially the section "The Priest in the Pulpit," pp. 86–96. See further above, p. 286 and p. 210, n. 1

[12] See the succinct discussion by Courtenay, *Schools*, pp. 19–20 and note 25, and p. 374.

of preaching style and contents may still be able to detect finer differences in sophistication, my impression is that what dividing line between a higher and lower level of sophistication one may find seems to separate the common folk from an implied *academic* one (in contrast to literary or humanistic), and that would most likely be the clergy. Typical in this respect are, on the one hand, the macaronic sermons in O, which teach only the basic truths and warn the laity against going beyond them, albeit with much invention and richness in their imagery, language and structure; and on the other, the sermons by Robert Rypon (RY) with their often extremely fussy academic interests. It is hard to imagine that the latter could have appealed to, or would have been understood by, even the most literate and sophisticated lay person.

One element that unites these preachers and collections is their demand for moral reform. At the most basic level it calls individual Christians to conversion, to a turning from vices to virtues. Whether in the form of a bare exposition of the Decalogue and the seven deadly sins, or else shaped into a rhetorically sophisticated structure that applies the day's reading to the Church's seasonal themes and concerns – penitence during Lent, for instance, or the worthy reception of Holy Communion at Easter – these sermons directly instruct and exhort to lead the good life. If they raise doctrinal issues at all, such as why the Son rather than the Father or the Holy Spirit was incarnated, they tend to do so with easy-to-grasp imagery rather than logical arguments, and always lead to the implications such doctrines have for our moral life. In a different form they may address the traditional three estates of society and set forth what the correct moral behavior of magnates, priests, and commoners should be. The latter is very frequently done negatively by pointing at or fulminating against common failings among bishops and priests, the nobility, merchants, and laborers. Here again one finds important and often individual differences of tone and themes, and one may fruitfully compare the macaronic sermons in O with those of Brinton's discourses that must have been addressed to a lay audience or at least to one in which layfolk sat or stood next to the clergy. But one will also have to remain aware of the fact that Brinton's text suppresses what may have been his most direct and personal remarks of this kind with a summary injunction to "tell how" and hardly more than a pointer to the recipients of his social criticism.

One aspect of this moral concern that should be stressed once more is the outspokenness and force with which preachers in this period criticized and condemned failures in their own class, from simony, nepotism, and absenteeism, through neglect in studying scripture and in preaching, to misplaced personal ambition, greed, and sexual sins. At first glance one may be tempted to think that this feature could have been influenced by Wyclif and his followers. But chronology speaks against it. FitzRalph, Waldeby, and Brinton preached and condemned before Wyclif made his impact on the theological world, and before his followers came to the pulpit in the early 1380s. The first of these, FitzRalph, was the most outspoken and vehement of them all, and with the much earlier figure of Robert Grosseteste he provided the major inspiration for moral-reform concerns that were shared by both orthodox and heterodox preachers. And we have seen that an occasional orthodox sermon would even voice strong sympathy for ideals and activities that we normally associate with the Lollards.

Finally, are these sermons rhetorical masterpieces? I have on various occasions claimed that at their best individual sermons or entire collections can indeed be said to make an inventive and often sophisticated use of structural approaches, imagery, and linguistic devices to give their message effectiveness and appeal. As they stand on their written pages, the sermons on the whole appeal to their audience's reason and understanding rather than to their emotions. Some of the Good-Friday sermons, by leading their audience to reflect on Christ's sufferings or to identify with Mary beneath the cross, do indeed issue a strong emotional appeal. But even here the habit of rationally dividing, subdividing, and enumerating generally prevails. This feature of scholastic mentality, of course, has its advantages, in that it causes a sermon to rest on a clear structure that is adhered to from the first announcement of its thema to its closing formula. Some modern readers may find this barren, but I think they would admit that, with very few exceptions that I have noted, these preachers do not lose their way in the kind of repetitive and undisciplined ramble that occasionally comes from modern pulpits. To what extent this clarity of exposition and development was in fact followed in actual preaching, we will of course never know. But at least it was presented as a model. And as I showed in a previous chapter, working within a strong tradition that determined the content, purpose, and form of preaching did by no means fetter talented preachers and prevent them from creating their own style.

To illustrate the art and wide variety of preaching styles that are found in this period I will quote two more examples, both from sermon openings:

> Reuerendi in Christo patres atque domini, celestis imperii piissime impera-
> tor eterne claritatis lumine naturaliter circumfulsus humanam nuper cernens
> naturam, extincta quasi sue racionis lampade, sorde multipliciter peccatorum
> turpiter denigratam in miserabili nostri incolatus Egipto, a recto tramite veri-
> tatis per deserta et inuia heresum et errorum sepius delirare, tamquam bonus
> pastor suas oues quas redemit ad catholice caritatis [W: veritatis] ouile reducere
> disponebat. Et ne in nostre peregrinacionis itinere viarum ambiguitas et cecitas
> ignorancie de nostri laboris premio nos redderet desperatos, destructo primi-
> tus Pharaone, principe videlicet tenebrarum, talem nobis ductricem constituit
> hic in via qualem sibi in patria sponsam assumere non veretur. O magna nostri

redemptoris dileccio. O erga nos immense diuine caritatis affeccio, que in huius festiuitatis solempniis non Moysen suum famulum ut olim in veteri testamento sed suam propriam genitricem ac natura mirante matrem simul et virginem castitatis floribus vnda redimita ad montem fulgentis Olimpi, ad montem Dei Oreb [voluit] conuocare, vbi diuinis plenissime illustrata fulgoribus et super omnes choros angelorum dignissime exaltata Deum facie ad faciem assidue contemplatur.

(Reverend fathers and lords in Christ: The most pious emperor of the heavenly empire, who is in his nature surrounded by the light of eternal clarity, having seen that human nature, after the light of its reason had been almost extinguished, has become blackened with the stain of manifold sins and is, in the Egypt of our wretched dwelling, often wandering off the straight path of truth through the deserts and wastelands of heresies and errors, took it in mind, like a good shepherd, to lead the sheep he has redeemed back to the fold of the Catholic truth. And in order that in our pilgrimage the confusion of ways and the blindness of our ignorance might not render us despairing about the reward of our labors, after he had first destroyed Pharaoh, the prince of darkness, he has given us as leader on our pilgrimage that person whom he does not hesitate to take up as his spouse to the heavenly home. Oh great love of our redemption! Oh immense affection of divine love for us, which on this solemn feast wanted to call this person to the shining mount Olympus, to Oreb, the mountain of God – not his servant Moses, as once in the Old Testament, but his own mother, who in the face of astounded nature was both mother and virgin, wreathed in waves of flowers of chastity. There, illumined to the fullest in divine radiance and most worthily exalted above all the choirs of angels, she is eagerly contemplating God face to face.)[13]

And the second example:

Karissimi, bene videtis ad oculum et verum est quod si aliqua comunitas, ciuitas, uel villa scholde falle in a daunger erga regem, et nameliche si forefecerit contra coronam et audierunt quod rex est myspaide þerwith et wlt punire eos qui hauen forfetyd contra eum, quod pro dolore et timore þat ipsi habent in cordibus suis colligunt se mutuo et quilibet petit consilium ab alio. "Allas, quid faciemus?" dicit vnus; "quid est melius faciendum?" dicit alius; "quod est consilium tuum?" dicit tercius. Iam spiritualiter loquendo, recte sic it farith inter Deum et genus humanum, quod iam stat ita quod non solum vna ciuitas uel villa set totus mundus, hoc est dictu totum genus humanum, is fallyn in danger erga illum qui est rex regum et dominus dominancium, et omnes forefecimus erga coronam regni celestis, in as muchel as we han brokyn et dispoylyd thesaurum of God almyti. Quia debetis intelligere quod þe moste derworthy tresour quod

---

[13] R-5, f. 27, for the feast of the Assumption; also in W-4.

pertinet ad regem celestem est anima humana, quam noster Dominus Iesus Christus redemit ita care cum suo benedicto sanguine super lignum crucis. Hunc thesaurum tradidit ipse in custodiam nostram, tibi vnam, michi vnam, et cuilibet homini vnam ad custodire.

(Beloved, you see with your own eyes – and it is true – that, if some community, town, or village should fall into some disgrace before the king, and especially if they had committed a crime against the crown and have heard that the king is displeased by it and will punish those that have transgressed against him – that for the pain and fear they have in their hearts they will come together, and each asks the other for his counsel. "Alas, what shall we do?" says one. "What is best to do?" says another. "What is your advice?" says a third. Now, speaking spiritually, it is same between God and man. Right now it is the case that not only one city or village but the whole world, that is to say, the entire human race, has fallen into disgrace before him who is the king of kings and lord of lords. We all have transgressed against the crown of the heavenly kingdom, in so far as we have broken and despoiled the treasure of almighty God. For you must know that the most precious treasure that belongs to the king of heaven is man's soul, which our Lord Jesus Christ has redeemed so dearly with his blessed blood on the cross. This treasure he gave into our custody – one to you, one to me, and one to every human person.)[14]

To be sure, the two pieces were directed at very different audiences, but what concerns us now is the great stylistic range, from the syntactically highly wrought panegyric of the first to the more homely appeal of the second that then leads to teaching basic Christian truths and to a call to penance. If one adds to these two examples others that employ a more academic style, such as the exposition of a grammatical point by Rypon, or the combination of appeal to common sentiment with a logical distinction ("Nowadays three things are loved by many people: short skirts, short masses, and short sermons. It is their shortness that is loved, rather than their nature . . ."), both quoted in earlier sections,[15] or else the judicious use of natural lore, observations from everyday experience, and pious or astounding tales that appears in many places, one can hardly deny these literary texts, which were ultimately destined for oral presentation, a rather amazing degree of stylistic variety and craftsmanship. The rhetoric of preaching in England between 1350 and 1450 thus forms one aspect of the mass of literary texts traced in this study whose further exploration, together with questions of audience, favorite themes, moral concerns, and other matters, still promises many rewarding insights.

[14] Q-19, f. 66, for 1 Lent.
[15] In the sections on Robert Rypon, pp. 70–72, and on Balliol 149, p. 125.

Inventories

The following inventories give information about the individual sermons in the collections in the following order and form:

1. Consecutive **number** of the sermon in the collection.
2. **Occasion**. I use the sigla established by Schneyer with some modifications. The sigla are:

(a) Sermons *de tempore*:

T01	1 Advent
T02	2 Advent
T03	3 Advent
T04	4 Advent
T05	Vigil of Christmas
T06	Christmas
T07	Sunday in octave of or after Christmas
T08	Circumcision
T09	Vigil of Epiphany
T10	Epiphany
T11	Sunday after Epiphany
T11a	1 Sunday after octave of Epiphany
T12	2 " " "
T13	3 " " "
T14	4 " " "
T15	5 " " "
T16	Septuagesima
T17	Sexagesima
T18	Quinquagesima
T18/4	Ash Wednesday
T19	1 Sunday of Lent

T20	2 Sunday of Lent
T21	3 Sunday of Lent
T22	4 Sunday of Lent
T23	Passion Sunday
T24	Palm Sunday
T25	Holy Thursday
T26	Good Friday
T27	Vigil of Easter
T28	Easter
T29	1 Sunday after Easter
T30	2 Sunday after Easter
T31	3 Sunday after Easter
T32	4 Sunday after Easter
T33	5 Sunday after Easter
T34	Rogation Days
T35	Vigil of Ascension
T36	Ascension
T37	6 Sunday after Easter
T38	Vigil of Pentecost
T39	Pentecost
T40	Trinity Sunday
T41/5	Corpus Christi
T42	1 Sunday after Trinity
T43	2 after Trinity
T44	3 after Trinity
T45	4 after Trinity
T46	5 after Trinity
T47	6 after Trinity
T48	7 after Trinity
T49	8 after Trinity
T50	9 after Trinity
T51	10 after Trinity
T52	11 after Trinity
T53	12 after Trinity
T54	13 after Trinity
T55	14 after Trinity
T56	15 after Trinity
T57	16 after Trinity
T58	17 after Trinity

T59	18 after Trinity
T60	19 after Trinity
T61	20 after Trinity
T62	21 after Trinity
T63	22 after Trinity
T64	23 after Trinity
T65	24 after Trinity
T66	25 after Trinity

(b) Sermons *de sanctis* as found in the collections, including J/2:

S01	Nov 30	Andrew
S02a	Dec 3	Birinus
S03	Dec 6	Nicholas
S04	Dec 7	Ambrose
S05	Dec 8	Conception of the Blessed Virgin Mary
S07	Dec 13	Lucy
S08	Dec 21	Thomas the Apostle
S09	Dec 26	Stephen
S10	Dec 27	John the Apostle
S11	Dec 28	Innocents
S12	Dec 29	Thomas of Canterbury
S16	Jan 17	Antony
S18	Jan 21	Agnes
S19	Jan 22	Vincent
S20	Jan 25	Conversion of Paul
S20a	Jan 28	Thomas Aquinas, translation
S21	Feb 2	Purification of the Blessed Virgin Mary
S22	Feb 5	Agatha
S22a	Feb 12	Frideswide, translation
S23	Feb 22	Peter in Cathedra
S24	Feb 24	Matthias
S24a	Feb 27	Eleazar
S24f	Feb 28	Augustine, translation
S24e	Mar 7	Thomas Aquinas
S25	Mar 12	Gregory the Great
S25a	Mar 17	Patrick
S25b	Mar 20	Cuthbert
S26	Mar 21	Benedict
S28	Mar 25	Annunciation of the Blessed Virgin Mary

S28b	Apr 4	Ambrose
S30	Apr 25	Mark
S31	Apr 29	Peter the Martyr
S32	May 1	Philip and James
S33	May 3	Invention of the Cross
S35	May 6	John ante portam latinam
S39	May 25	Francis, translation
S39a	May 26	Augustine of Canterbury
S40	Jun 11	Barnabas
S41	Jun 13	Anthony of Padua
S43a	Jun 22	Winefride, translation
S43b	Jun 23	Etheldreda
S44	Jun 24	John the Baptist, nativity
S46	Jun 29	Peter and Paul
S46b	Jly 7	Thomas of Canterbury, translation
S46c	Jly 13	Mildred
S47	Jly 20	Margaret, virgin and martyr
S49	Jly 22	Mary Magdalene
S50	Jly 25	James
S50a	Jly 26	Anne
S52	Aug 1	Peter ad vincula
S54	Aug 4	Dominic
S54a	Aug 5	Oswald, king and martyr
S56	Aug 10	Lawrence
S57	Aug 12	Clare
S59	Aug 15	Assumption of the Blessed Virgin Mary
S59a	Aug 19	Louis of Anjou
S60	Aug 20	Bernard
S61	Aug 24	Bartholomew
S63	Aug 28	Augustine
S64	Aug 29	John the Baptist, decollation
S65	Sep 8	Nativity of the Blessed Virgin Mary
S65b	Sep 13	Chrysostom
S66	Sep 14	Exaltation of the Cross
S67	Sep 21	Matthew
S68	Sep 22	Mauritius
S70	Sep 29	Michael, Holy Angels
S71	Sep 30	Jerome
S73	Oct 4	Francis

S74	Oct 9	Dionysius
S75	Oct 18	Luke
S75a	Oct 19	Frideswide
S77	Oct 21	Ursula and the 11,000 virgins
S78	Oct 28	Simon and Jude
S79	Nov 1	All Saints
S80	Nov 2	All Souls
S81	Nov 11	Martin
S81a	Nov 16	Edmund Rich, archbishop
S81b	Nov 17	Hugh of Lincoln
S82a	Nov 20	Edmund, King and Martyr
S82b	Nov 21	Oblation of the Blessed Virgin Mary
S83	Nov 22	Cecilia
S84	Nov 23	Clement
S85	Nov 25	Katherine
S86		Blessed Virgin Mary in general

(c) Sermons for special occasions:

Co4	One martyr
Co5	Several martyrs
Co6	One confessor
Co8	One virgin
Co9	Several virgins
C11	Dedication of a church
C14	Synod, chapter, to clergy
C15	Election
C16	Orders
C18	Consecration of virgin, etc.
C19	Visitation
C21	Funeral, anniversary
C22	University sermon
C23	Pro pace; in tempore belli

I distinguish between different kinds of evidence for the occasion of a given sermon, in the following form:

Too = occasion is indicated in rubric at head of sermon or margin.

Too+ = the sermon is rubricated as for an entire season, such as Lent or Christmas.

Too* = occasion is indicated in text or inferred. This includes several possibilities:

(a) the occasion is mentioned with the biblical source of the thema ("Hebre-orum 9 et in epistula hodierna");

(b) the occasion is mentioned in the body of the sermon ("Hoc festum est festum quia est de sacramento altaris"; "Ecclesia isto die agit . . ."; "Hodie recolit sancta Ecclesia . . . ," etc.);

(c) the occasion is noted in the table to the sermons;

(d) the occasion may be inferred from a shared sermon where it is men-tioned;

(e) a sermon that is clearly directed to the clergy and deals with the clerical office, or a university sermon, or a sermon on the monastic life and duties (C14*);

(f) a sermon that deals substantially with a named saint or is clearly in praise of Mary (S86*);

(g) a sermon that refers to "isto sacro tempore," i.e. Lent, and whose thema places it clearly in the liturgy of the season.

Too? = occasion inferred from the sermon's lection and its position in the calendar, in cycles whose sequence is regular (e.g., P1 and P2, etc.).

? = occasion not specified or inferred.

3. **Thema**. I use the spelling of the Latin Vulgate Bible but retain substantive differences in wording and word order as they appear in the sermons.

4. **Biblical source**. According to the Latin Vulgate Bible, regardless of the presence and form which these references take in the manuscript. Late-medieval texts normally indicate the chapter but not the verse, which I supply. Occasionally the manuscripts indicate more than one biblical source for a sermon thema, which I reproduce here without the number of the verse.

5. **Initium**. The opening words of the sermon, in the spelling found in the manuscript.

6. **Explicit**. The final words of the sermon before the normal closing formula ("qui vivit et regnat cum Patre et Spiritu Sancto" or similar). Items 5–6 are separated by ellipsis and hyphen (". . .-. . .").

7. **Folios** where the sermon appears in the given collection. Some manuscripts are paginated ("Pp."). "Inc" indicates that the sermon is incomplete in the manuscript.

8. **Author's or preacher's name** where known.

9. **Other occurrences** of a given sermon, with "Also . . ."

10. **Edition** where applicable.

A – Cambridge, University Library, MS Ii.3.8

1. ?. *Apprehende arma et scutum et exsurge in adiutorium* (Ps 34:2). Si debilis quisquam bellum inire debeat cum aduersario forti et astuto . . .-. . . pro hereditate nostra ciuitate, scilicet celesti. Ad quam etc. Ff. 41–43v.

2. T19*. *Hortamur vos ne in vacuum gratiam Dei recipiatis* (2 Cor 6:1). Karissimi, ista dicitur dominica in quadragesima. Est quadragesima dies quadraginta dierum incipiens ab hac dominica . . .-. . . qui similes estis sepulcris dealbatis. . Ff. 43v–45v inc.

3. T26. *Christus passus est pro nobis* (1 Pet 2:21). Racio potest assignari quare hodie sancta Ecclesia a Spiritu docta . . .-. . . in iusticia vero mortis adquisicio. Ff. 46–47 inc.

4. S08*. *Lapis solutus calore in aes vertitur* (Job 28:2). Ista verba, dilectissimi, si ad literam intelligantur, veritatem habent, sed spiritualiter . . .-. . . imetemur [!] ergo beatum Thomam in hiis et consimilibus, vt tandem peruenire possimus ad gloriam, etc. Ff. 47v–48.

5. ?. *Veni, Domine Iesu* (Rev 22:20). Scitis quod vnumquodque naturaliter sanitatem corporis diligit . . .-. . . in gloria collocabitur, vbi videbimus Deum sicut est. Ad quam visionem. . . . Ff. 49–50.

6. ?. *Paenitentiam agite* (Matt 3:2). Dilectissimi, sapiens rex Salomon qui scienciam docet . . .-. . . penitenciam agamus et Deum rogemus vt concedat nobis finem bonum et post hunc finem nos perducat. . . . Ff. 50–51.

7. ?. *Parce, Domine, parce populo tuo* (Joel 2:17). Karissimi, quando aliquis populus verberibus opprimitur grauioribus, tanto idem populus ad Deum calmat [!] feruencius . . .-. . . in quibus duxerunt dies suos in mundo etc. Ff. 52–53 inc.

8. ?. *Ultra non serviamus peccato* (Rom 6:6). Wlgariter dicitur, Stultus est qui potest eligere et capit partem peiorem . . .-. . . pro nostro fideli seruicio in celesti gloria mercedem habere mereamur. Quam. . . . Ff. 53–54.

9. ?. *Orate, ut non intretis in temptationem* (Matt 26:41). In quibus Saluator duo facit: primo ad ipsum interueniendum nos inuitat . . .-. . . regnum quod vobis paratum est ab origine mundi. Ad quod. . . . Ff. 54–55.

10. ?. *Hortamur vos, ne in vacuum gratiam Dei recipiatis* (2 Cor 6:1). Hec gracia est remissio peccatorum . . .-. . . nisi enim dolor pudorem vincat, non est iste dolor contricio vera. Ff. 55–56.

11. T28*. *Tene quod habes* (Rev 3:11). Karissimi, magne virtutis est amicum adquerere [!], set maioris est amicum adquesitum [!] retinere. Set tu, quicumque Christiane, hodie in ecclesia . . .-. . . tradatur sepulture et

anima cum Filio Dei assendat [!] ad celum. Quod. . . . Ff. 56–57v. Also X-125; Y/1, f. 125v.

12. T19. *Ecce nunc dies salutis* (2 Cor 6:2). Karissimi, infirmis [!] multiplicibus egritudinibus laborant' maxima materia consolacioni quando veniens ad eum . . .-. . . et tunc sunt dies desiderandi. Ff. 58–59 inc.

13. ?. *Christus passus est pro nobis vobis relinquens exemplum ut sequamini vestigia eius* (1 Pet 2:21). Christus de mundo transiens multas angustias et tandem mortem sustinuit . . .-. . . relinquendo ex hiis patet quod passio Christi fuit necessaria etc. Ff. 59–60.

14. T20. *Haec est voluntas Dei, sanctificatio vestra* (1 Thess 4:3). Scribitur, karissimi, Luce 12, Seruus sciens voluntatem Domini et non . . .-. . . que perfecte habebitur et plenius in gloria. Quam nobis. Ff. 62r–v.

15. T41/5*. *Panem de caelo praestitisti eis omne delectamentum in se habentem* (Wisd 16:20). Boni et mali hic sine gracia Dei et eius adiutorio et eius misericordia nichil possumus agere . . .-. . . Deus det nobis graciam suam sic manus et cetera membra nostra et sensus exteriores et interiores sic custodire. . . . Ff. 66–71. Also in Merton 248, f. 131rb.

16. ?. *Memorare testamenti Altissimi* (Sir 28:9). Valerius libro suo 1 capitulo narrat quod maiores natu Romanorum opera predecessorum suorum egregio carmine . . .-. . . ad illum diem te para in quo gloria huius mundi finienda est. Ad quam. . . . Ff. 71–74v.

17. ?. *Benedictus qui venit in nomine Domini* (Matt 21:9). Karissimi, secundum philosophos et eciam astrologes [!] inter omnes planetas sol precellit . . .-. . . de quolibet sensu vel membro que nos ad peccatum alliciunt. <non plus in copia>. Ff. 74v–76 inc.

18. T24*. *Ecce rex tuus venit tibi mansuetus* (Matt 21:5). Introduccio fuit de breui honore hodie Christo collato . . . Rex iste mansuetus Christus est . . .-. . . et ideo demonibus traditur eternaliter crucianda. <non plus in copia>. Ff. 76v–77 inc.

19. T26. *Per proprium sanguinem introivit semel* (Heb 9:12). Karissimi, in principio debetis scire sicut docet beatus Anselmus *Cur Deus*, quod creatura racionalis . . .-. . . Pater omne iudicium dedit Filio etc. Ff. 77v–79.

20. T19+. *Dominus hiis opus habet* (Matt 21:3). Karissimi, sum nuncius ad vos arduis negociis et missus ex parte regis et tocius consilii ad notificandum vos de vna magna taxacione . . .-. . . sic et vos confitemini alterutrum peccata vestra etc. Ff. 79v–81.

21. T28*. *Panem nostrum cotidianum da nobis hodie* (Matt 6:11). þe bred þat fedeȝ vs eueri day þou graunte vs lord þis esterday. Karissimi, qualiter hec

verba sunt ad propositum aduertamus . . .-. . . redemisti me, Domine Deus veritatis. Ff. 81v–82v.

22. ?. *Luna mutatur* (Sir 27:12). Reuerendi mei, ut directe descendam ad materiam sermonis, scire debemus secundum Ysodorum *Ethimologiarum* quod luna mutatur variis temporibus . . .-. . . sed luna perfecta in eternum et testis in celo fidelis. Vnde tota die predicaui de inconstancia, iam intendo vobis predicare de constancia et quare tenebimus nobiscum illum reuerendum Dominum quem accepimus. Tene inquit. . . . Ff. 82v–84v.

23. ?. *Tene quod habes, ne alius accipiat a te coronam* (Rev 3:11). Non est enim magnum bonum amicum adquirere, set pocius magnum est amicum adquesitum tenere. Pro quo scire debemus, si tenere voluerimus hunc regem regum . . .-. . . per piissimam mortem tuam mane nobiscum, Domine. Quod. . . . Ff. 84v–85.

24. ?. *Heu, heu, heu* (Ezek 6:11, or rather 9:8?). Heu, casus accidit dolorosus: punctus qui erat in circuli medio non contentus tali loco tam abcessit rupto circulo . . .-. . . heu inicium misero cognita tela michi parce patrie nec memor huius o si etc. [= "heu nimium misero cognita tela mihi Parce pater patriae ne nominis inmemor huius olim placandi spem . . . ," Ovid, *Tristia* 2.180–181]. <non plus in copia>. Ff. 85–88v inc.

25. T41/5. *Sic honorabitur quem rex voluerit honorare* (Esther 6:9). Pro processu sermonis debetis scire quod quatuor personas in mundo isto video honorari . . .-. . . in me manet et ego in illo etc. Quod. . . . Ff. 89–90v.

26. T19. *Ecce nunc dies salutis* (2 Cor 6:2). Prima dies exploracio sue culpe, secunda culpe deploracio, tercia eiusdem explicacio. . . .-. . . teipsum fedum et quod deum offendisti. Ff. 90v–91 inc. Also O-39.

27. ?. *Caritas operit multitudinem peccatorum* (1 Pet 4:8). Karissimi, quatuor sunt experimenta per que literas priuatas potest homo legere . . .-. . . gaudia varia et ine[na]rrabilia que. Ad que. . . . Ff. 91v–92. Also O-30.

28. ?. *Lacrimis coepit rigare pedes eius* (Luke 7:38). Vbi describitur vt desolata ut humiliata. Narra de muliere meretrice quam desponsauit imperator quidam . . .-. . . ad locum illum venisse non magis complete in narrando. Ff. 92–93 inc.

29. T20*. *Iesu, fili David, miserere mei* (Matt 15:22). Karissimi fratres, Hester 3 scribitur quod cum filii Israel grauiter . . .-. . . latere erit inpossibile, apparere intollerabile. Ff. 93v–95v inc.

30. T22. *Clama quae non parturis* (Gal 4:27 and Isa 45:10). Karissimi, solent clamatores publici et precones ad promulgandum leges seu edicta regum

et principum . . .-. . . primo oportet þat þou crye to hym etc. Nota in proximo sermone etc. Ff. 96r–v.

31. To1+. *Veniens veniet et non tardabit* (Hab 2:3). Notandum, karissimi, quod secundum veritatem et Ecclesie consuetudinem triplicem recitamus Christi aduentum . . .-. . . cum venerit Filius in magestate in sede magestatis sue et cum eo omnes angeli, tunc sedebit super. Et dicatur exposicio huius euangelii etc. Ff. 96v–97v.

32. To6*. *Gloria in altissimis Deo, et in terra pax hominibus bonae voluntatis* (Luke 2:14). Hodie recolit sancta Ecclesia, fratres karissimi, prerogatiua gaudia que humiliter angeli de natiuitate . . .-. . . istam pacem triplicem concedat nobis etc. Ff. 97v–99. Also U-1.

33. T20. *Haec est voluntas Dei, sanctificatio vestra* (1 Thess 4:3). Reuerendi mei, sicut dicit beatus Gregorius in *Registro* . . .-. . . et sciencia in viuendo quoad mancionem celi. Quam etc. Ff. 99–100v.

34. T19+*. *Paenitentiam agite* (Matt 3:2). Karissimi, quia per totum hoc sacrum tempus quadragesimale est dedicatum hominibus ad agendam penitenciam . . .-. . . sic ergo penitenciam veram agere nobis ipse concedat . . . Ff. 101–105v.

35. T26*. *Quare rubrum est indumentum tuum?* (Isa 63:2). Secundum sentenciam doctorum hec fuit questio angelorum in die Ascencionis Domini . . .-. . . et manet vsque hodie sigillum infixum in plaga lateris Christi. Ff. 106–114v. Also P2-71, S-19, Z-20, and CUL Ee.6.27, f. 73.

36. T20*. *Miserere mei, Domine* (Matt 15:22). Karissimi, sicud testatur sacra scriptura 2 Regum 12, cum rex Dauid suggestionem [!] diaboli fedasset . . .-. . . et corrigere se et bonis hominibus vitam et gloriam sempiternam. Quam . . . Ff. 115–118. Also H-2.

37. ?. *Cum ieiunasset quadraginta diebus et quadraginta noctibus, postea esuriit* (Matt 4:2). Pulcrior modus et nobilior docendi est quod magister prius faciat documentum . . .-. . . quoad conscienciam, modestam quoad carnem etc. Ff. 118–119v.

38. ?. *Cum ieiunas, ungue caput tuum et faciem tuam lava* (Matt 6:17). Dignitas ieiunii multipliciter commendatur: a loco . . .-. . . qui est fons aque salientis in vitam eternam. Amen. Ff. 120–121v.

39. T23*. *Ipse vulneratus est propter iniquitates nostras, et eius livore sanati sumus* (Isa 53:5). Crist ys wounded for oure wikkednesse . . . Tractaturi de passione Domini secundum quod modo solempnizat Ecclesia . . .-. . . causa vero finalis erat sanitas nostra, et tangitur ibi Et sanati sumus. Ff. 121v–128.

40. T41/5*?. *Probet seipsum homo et sic de pane illo edat* (1 Cor 11:28). Applicando materiam collacionis ad circumstancias huius festi, notandum, karissimi, quod quisquis reficere debet amicum suum . . .-. . . vt ad montem Dei possimus peruenire nobis concedat. Amen etc. Ff. 128–132.

41. T16. *Quid hic statis* (Matt 20:6). In principio huius collacionis recommendatis omnibus . . . Reuerendi, secundum mortem [!] laudabilem Ecclesie diucius approbatam solet filius post decessum patris . . .-. . . quod non vidit oculus nec auris aud[i]uit nec in cor homins ascendit etc. Ff. 133–134v.

42. C14*. *Videte, vigilate, et orate* (Mark 13:33). Summus sacerdos noster Iesus Christus, qui de celis descendit vt seipsum hostiam viuam Deo Patri . . .- . . . quod humano ore dicimur, in tuis oculis esse valeamus. Quod . . . Ff. 134v–138v.

43. T23. *Quare non creditis* (John 8:46). Reuerendi mei, inuenio scriptum Exodi 4 quod cum Pharao rex Egipciorum fuisset rebellis voluntati diuine . . .- . . . et dabo tibi coronam glorie. Ad quam. . . . Ff. 138v–140v.

44. ?. *Declina a malo et fac bonum* (Ps 36:27). Gracia omnipotentis . . . Reuerendi domini, sicut nos dococet [!] experiencia, siquis habens dominum cum in alico offenderit, si ei de reco[n]siliacione . . .-. . . videbimus et cognoscemus omnem veritatem ad minus necessariam ad salutem. Ad istam mercedem. . . . Ff. 141–143.

45. T06. *A, a, a* (Jer 1:6). Pro introduccione notandum quod propter tres proprietates que inveniuntur in Christo et eciam in hac littera a conuenienter potest a assumi pro themate . . .-. . . to wel and blisse also, hoc est gaudium sempiternum. Ad quod. . . . Ff. 143–144.

46. T36. *Sedet a dextris Dei* (Mark 16:19). Dicitur communiter quod boni rumores letificant corda, etc. Set optimos . . .-. . . vbi eternaliter sedet a dextris dei. Ad quem . . . Ff. 144–145. Cf. Y/3-8.

47. T19. *Ecce nunc dies salutis* (2 Cor 6:2). Istud verbum vobis veraciter prolatum supponit quod perdidistis optimum diligibile . . .-. . . ad hunc diem festum ascendent omnes anime iuste, vbi in secula seculorum manebunt in splendoribus suis. Amen. Ff. 145–147. Also W-163.

48. T50*. *Redde rationem vilicationis tuae* (Luke 16:2). Noueritis, Karissimi mei, quod Christus autor veritatis et doctor in libro suo de euangelio Mathei 20 assimulans regnum celorum patrifamilias . . .-. . . cecidit corona capitis nostri, ve nobis quia peccauimus. Ff. 147–151. Wimbledon. Also H-5, V-33, Caius 334. English version in *Wimbledon's Sermon* and in Nancy Owen, "Thomas Wimbledon's Sermon."

49. T64 / C14*. *Viam Dei in veritate doces* (Matt 22:16). In principio huius colacionis recommendatis omnibus qui deberent hic recommendari . . . Reuerendi domini, refert euangelium hodiernum quod Pharisei consilium inierunt . . .-. . . hereditas et premium et gaudium in celo sine fine. Ad quod. . . . Ff. 151v–154v.

50. T21*. *Quomodo stabit regnum* (Luke 11:18). In principio huius collacionis recommendo . . . Karissimi, sicut dicit Sapiens Ecclesiastici 10, regna perduntur . . .-. . . quod stabit eternaliter in prosperis et honore. Ad quod. . . . Ff. 154v–157v.

51. ?. [*Loquimini veritatem* (Eph 4:25).] Sciendum est quod cum Moyses duceret populum . . .-. . . ita depauperatur quod vix vnum optinet. F. 161r–v, inc, and thema missing.

52. ?. *Clama ne cesses, exalta vocem tuam quasi tuba* (Isa 58:1). Hic precipit Dominus clamare . . .-. . . quod predicta accidere poterunt dicat quilibet Pater, Aue. F. 161v. Only 8 lines, marked "Antethema" but referred to in table. Followed by another short piece marked "Antethema": "Licet homo aliquando habeat raucam vocem . . ."; and perhaps another one: "Si aliquis esset in via tenebrosa."

53. ?. *Beati qui audiunt verbum Dei* (Luke 11:28). Tria sunt que a multis maxime desiderantur: sanitas corporis, diuicie temporales, et vita prolixa . . .-. . . non fiant participes gaudii sed meroris. F. 162.

54. T19*. *Ductus est Iesus in desertum a spiritu ut temptaretur a diabolo* (Matt 4:1). Gracia . . . Reuerendi mei, in exordio nostre collacionis . . . Reuerendi, verba . . . Iesu was lad, etc. Karissimi, testante beato Gregorio omnis Christi accio . . .-. . . peccatorum veniam consequeris in presenti graciam et in futuro gloriam. Quam. . . . Ff. 164v–166.

55. T06. *Unus est et secundum non habet* (Qoh 4:8). þer is on and swsch anothur was neuer non. Reuerendi mei, fuit vnum genus hominum qui voluit libenter audire . . .-. . . þat dere hath vs bowth. Qui. . . . Ff. 166v–168.

56. T28/4*. *Venite, benedicti Patris mei* (Matt 25:34). Reuerendi domini, nouerunt iuris periti, homo qui habet magnam causam . . .-. . . quod vobis paratum est a principio mundi. Ad quod . . . Ff. 168–171.

57. T22*. *Laetare* (Gal 4:27). Quantus est dolor et tristicia cum quis a suo solo exulat naturali . . .-. . . ut adquiratis quartam gloriam, scilicet eternalem. Ad quam. . . . Ff. 171–173v. Also BR-36.

58. ?. *Comedite* (Matt 26:26). Auicenna primo canone docet quod iter agens debet precipue esse sollicitus de nutrimento . . .-. . . virtutum et graciarum in presenti et in futuro delectabimur in omni bono. Quod. . . . Ff. 174–176.

B/2 – Cambridge, University Library, MS Kk.4.24

1. C11. *Mulier sapiens aedificat sibi domum, mulier insipiens destruit constructam* (Prov 14:1). Multe benedictiones fiunt in dedicatione ecclesie et altarium et omnes pertinent . . .-. . . vt perueniamus ad celi societatem, gaudium, requiem, et in vertatis cognicionem. Quod . . . F. 121ra–va.

2. C11. *Sanctificavi domum hanc* (1 Kings 9:3). Karissimi, decens est et conueniens regie magestati vt non solum habeat aulam . . .-. . . agite penitenciam et appropinquabit regnum celorum. Ad quod . . . Ff. 121va–123rb.

3. C11. *Sanctifica te*; vel sic: *Haec est voluntas Dei, sanctificatio vestra*; vel sic: *Sanctificavi domum hanc* (Acts 21:24, or 1 Thess 4:3, or 1 Kings 9:3). Karissimi, quatuor genera domorum inuenio in sacra scriptura que dedicantur . . .-. . . aut debet subito mori aut aliquod membrum a casu vulnere perdet. . Ff. 123rb–125vb, inc?

4. C14. *Custodite sacerdotium vestrum* (Num 18:7). Domini reuerendi mei, res in se nobilis ac eciam preciosa aliis vtilis et fructuosa . . .-. . . propter consequendum premium eterne vite vestrum sacerdotium custodite. Quod . . . Ff. 125vb–127rb.

5. C19. *Glorificent Deum in die visitationis* (1 Pet 2:12). Reuerendi patres et domini, in principio nostre breuissime collationis premittamus suffragium orationis . . .-. . . et sic attingentes finem debitum sue operationis glorificent deum in die visitationis. Ff. 127rb–128va.

6. T23. *Qui ex Deo est verba Dei audit* (John 8:47). Reuerendi domini et amici, tria videntur michi esse necessaria cuilibet qui verbum predicaret . . .-. . . qui elucidant me vitam eternam habebunt. Ad quam . . . Ff. 128va–129vb.

7. T23 or T24. *Apertus est liber* (Rev 20:12). Est liber vnus de quo fit mensio in sacra scriptura quem vidit Iohannes in tipo . . .-. . . testamentum Altissimi et agnitio veritatis, Ecclesiastici 24. Quo libro nos faciat inscribi . . . Ff. 129vb–134vb.

8. T23 or T24. *Ortum est bellum satis durum* (2 Sam 2:17). Karissimi, inuenio in sacra scriptura Exodi 17 semel populum Israeliticum . . .-. . . nisi dulcia et suauia et si quod de floribus. Ff. 134vb–138rb, inc.

9. T23. *Veritatem dico* (John 8:45). In sacra scriptura plura inueniuntur exempla quomodo sancte et iuste viuentes . . .-. . . post huius vite transitum transuexhit [!] ad gloriam sempiternam. Ad quam . . . Ff. 138va–139ra.

10. T23 or T26. *Secundum legem debet mori* (John 19:7). Karissimi, scribitur Ad Galatas, 'Propter transgressores [!] lex posita est' . . .-. . . in quacumque hora ingemuerit peccator saluus erit. Ff. 139ra–142vb.

11. T26 or T23. *A, a, a dicite quia prope est dies Domini* (Joel 1:15). Si quis mirabilia audiret vel videret qualia nunquam audierat . . .-. . . . reduxit erroneum ad patriam claritatis eterne. Ad quam . . . Ff. 142vb–143vb.

12. T23 or T26. *Amore langueo* (Cant 2:5). Prolatiue potest dici sic: Karissimi, sicut manifeste videtis . . .-. . . Graunt vs þy blysse withowte ende. Ad quam . . . Ff. 143vb–150ra. Also S-7, T-7, Dublin Trinity College 277. Edited in Wenzel, *Macaronic,* pp. 212–267.

13. C14. *Videte* (Luke 21:8?). Ista congeries literarum *videte* potest esse una dictio et tunc sermo . . .-. . . ad interitum sed viuens lucem videbit. Quam . . . Ff. 150ra–153va.

14. S86*. *Elegit eam in habitationem sibi* (Ps 131:13). In his mundanis principum et dominorum dominiis video quod secundum cursus . . .-. . . a damnatione et aliorum periculo malorum suis meritis eruat et saluet. Amen. Ff. 153va–155rb.

15. T41/5. *Hoc est corpus meum* (1 Cor 11:24). Teste Seneca in suis *Prouerbiis* quietissime viuerent homines si hec duo . . .-. . . corpus meum est pro multorum vita. Quam . . . Ff. 155rb–157va.

16. T06. *Natus est vobis hodie salvator* (Luke 2:11). Karissimi, domini terreni in die natalis sui solent esse gratiosi . . .-. . . in magni Dei reconciliatione summa gloria. Ad quam . . . Ff. 157va–159ra.

17. S09. *Stephanus plenus gratia* (Acts 6:8). Auxilium et gratia Dei omnipotentis per gloriosam intercessionem . . .-. . . pro sua paciencia erat accepturus, quod premium [?] est vita eterna. Ad quam . . . Ff. 159ra–160ra.

18. S10. *Diligebat Jesus sequentem* (John 21:20). Reuerendi patres et domini, Saluator noster nos instruere desiderans . . .-. . . vbicumque manet Deus, ibi gloria. Ad quam . . . Ff. 160ra–161rb.

19. S12. *Hic perfectus est vir* (James 3:2). Reuerendi domini et amici, si loquamur de isto nomine Thomas videtur totaliter . . .-. . . et diuitie in domo eius etc. Ff. 161rb–162rb.

20. T08. *Nomen eius Iesus* (Luke 2:21). Karissimi, secundum Ysodorum *Ethimologiarum* 7, quod recte nominatum est sortitur nomen . . .-. . . nomina eorum in libro vite. Ad quam . . . Ff. 162rb–163vb.

21. T10. *Venimus adorare eum* (Matt 2:2). Karissimi mei, hec fuerunt verba regum qui adorauerunt Filium Dei . . .-. . . quia eius seruitus est vita perhennis. Ad quam . . . Ff. 163vb–165rb.

22. T01. *Exulta, filia Sion, iubila, filia Ierusalem. Ecce rex tuus venit . . . pullum asine* (Zech 9:9). Voluntas terreni regis in diuersis ciuitatibus scitur per suas

literas . . .-. . . ad ordines angelorum vt fruamur eterna iocunditate in patria celesti. Amen. Ff. 165va–166va.

23. T02. *Christus suscepit vos in honorem* (Rom 15:7). Vbi tria notantur: Redemptoris benignitas in confortando . . .-. . . quod paratum a constitutione mundi. Amen. Ff. 166va–168rb.

24. T03. *Tu quis es?* (John 1:19?). Puer tener et iuuenis sub matris custodia delicate nutritus non libenter . . .-. . . tu semper mecum es et omnia mea tibi sunt etc. Ff. 168rb–171rb. Also X-4.

25. T40. *In tribus complacitum est spiritui meo* (Sir 25:1). Sapientissimus Salomon Prouerbiorum 30 capitulo ait, Tria michi deficilia [!] . . .-. . . gloriosam Trinitatem, Patrem et Filium et Spiritum Sanctum. Ad quam . . . Ff. 171rb–172vb.

26. T41/5. *Hic est panis* (John 6:50). Karissimi, legitur in libro Regum quod Joab, qui princeps exercitus Dauid fuit . . .-. . . ex hoc pane viuet in eternum, Iohannis. Quam . . . Ff. 172vb–175ra.

27. T54. *Quid faciendo vitam aeternam possidebo?* (Luke 10:25). In quanto quis appetit aliquam rem quam non habet, diligentius inquirit . . .-. . . fac hoc et viues, scilicet vita eterna. Ad quam . . . Ff. 175ra–176ra.

28. S65. *In me spes vitae* (Sir 24:25). Ieronimus de Beata Virgine dicit sic: Si omnia membra essent lingue . . .-. . . qui elucidant me, vitam eternam habebunt. Ad quam . . . Ff. 176ra–vb.

29. S59. *In plenitudine sanctorum detentio mea* (Sir 24:16). Reuera summa felicitas est cuilibet illam rem possidere quam summe diligit . . .-. . . in plenitudine sanctorum detentio mea. Quam plenitudinem . . . Ff. 176vb–177vb.

30. C23 "In tempore belli". *Adiuva nos, Deus* (2 Chron 14:11). Necessitas et miseria homines compellit vt auxilium inuocent a potente . . .-. . . ipsorum est regnum celorum, Mathei 5. Ad quod . . . Ff. 177vb–179ra.

31. S22. *Iste est amicus meus* (Cant 5:16). Karissimi mei, signum magnum amicicie est quod vnus libenter audiat bona de alio . . .-. . . magnificauit illum, in gloria scilicet eterna. Quod . . . Ff. 179ra–180va.

32. T19*. *Ecce nunc tempus acceptabile* (2 Cor 6:2). Istud tempus, Karissimi, vocatur a clericis ver, hoc est tempus vernale . . .-. . . cor tuum non sit lapideum. Ff. 180va–184vb, inc.

33. T36. *Relinquo mundum et vado ad Patrem* (John 16:28). Anglice: Al þys wordyl Y forsake, and to my fader þe wey Y take. Videmus enim in natura . . .-. . . gaudium vestrum nemo tollet a vobis. Quod . . . Ff. 185ra–186ra.

34. T36. *Ascendit Deus in iubilo* (Ps 46:6). Anglice: God ys went into heuene . . .
Reuerendi, pro processu nostri sermonis . . .-. . . quia mitis sum et humilis
corde etc. F. 186ra–vb.

35. ?. *Convertimini ad Dominum* (Hos 14:3?). Pro processu debetis scire quod
quatuor inconuenientia siue incomoda sequuntur peccatum . . .-. . . a veritate quidem auditum auertent, ad fabulas autem conuertentur. Ff. 186vb–
189ra, inc.

36. T56. *Dum tempus habemus operemur bonum* (Gal 6:10). Karissimi, sicut
dicit beatus Augustinus super illud Psalmi, Incensa et suffossa . . .-. . . ita
amabiles sicut pietas viscerosa. Ff. 189rb–193ra, inc.

37. T39/2. *Lux venit in mundum, et dilexerunt homines magis tenebras* (John
3:19). Into þys wordel ys ycome lyȝth . . . Karissimi, in predicatione verbi
Dei si ex verbis predicatoris . . .-. . . quos videt deuotos et contemplatiuos
nutrit et ducit ad celestia. Quo . . . Ff. 193ra–196ra.

38. T28. *Alleluia* (Rev 19:1). Narrat, karissimi, Giraldus historiographus de
quodam rege qui Persis . . .-. . . et vos apparebitis cum Christo in gloria.
Quam . . . Ff. 196ra–198vb.

39. T28. *Verus panis dat vitam* (John 6:33). Karissimi, debetis intelligere quod
preter panem materialem duplex inuenitur . . .-. . . in celo, vbi est gaudium
sine fine. Ad quod . . . Ff. 198vb–201ra.

40. T28. *Custos domini sui gloriabitur* (Prov 27:18). Karissimi, vt dicit Augustinus *De ciuitate Dei* 13, Omnes homines cupiunt et desiderant . . .-. . . to
euery man þat workyth goodnesse. þe whyche blys . . . Ff. 201ra–203rb.

41. T34. "De introductione excommunicacionis/sentensie generalis quatuor
temporibus anni." *Securis ad radicem posita est* (Matt 3:10). Anglice: þe axe
ys set at þe rote. Leue syrys, ȝe weteþ wel þat a man . . .-. . . venite, benedicti
patris mei, possidete regnum. Quod . . . Ff. 203rb–205ra.

42. T34. "Item alius bonus modus introducendi casus sentencie generalis."
Coepit colere terram et plantavit vineam (Gen 9:20). Good men, þese wordys
byth þus moche to sey yn englysch: He began . . . ȝe wetyþ wel þat a good
hosbund . . .-. . . wyt þe holy sacrament and vere frute of blysse. Quod . . .
Ff. 205ra–209ra.

43. T28. *Probet seipsum homo et sic de pane illo edat* (1 Cor 11:28). Karissimi,
videmus ad oculum quod si corporalis medicina sumatur . . .-. . . ad futuram
gloriam que reuelabitur in nobis. Ad quam . . . F. 209ra–va.

44. T28. *Custodite sicut scitis* (Matt 27:65). Quanto res est melior in se et quanto
maius damnum prouenit ex eius perditione . . .-. . . qui est custos domini
sui gloriabitur. Ad quam . . . Ff. 209va–211rb.

45. T28. *Comedite panem* (Prov 9:5). Homo ex duplici natura componitur, scilicet ex corpore et anima, et ideo . . .-. . . qui hodie sua carne propria et sanguine pascet et potabit. Amen. Ff. 211rb–213rb.

46. T28. *Venias hodie ad convivium quod paravi* (Esther 5:4). Videtis quod quando filius regis magni desponsatur, post desponsationem . . .-. . . et ego resuscitabo in nouissimo die. Quod . . . F. 213rb–vb.

47. T28/2. *Mane nobiscum, Domine, quoniam advesperascit* (Luke 24:29). Anglice: Wone wyth vs, lord ful of myȝth. . . . Genesis 19 habetur quod Abrahe sedenti . . .-. . . et vtilior, tanto amplius diligatur. Ff. 213vb–215ra, inc.

48. T28. *Custodi partem tuam* (2 Macc 1:26). Scitis, karissimi, quod homo est creatura composita ex duabus partibus . . .-. . . dabo illi stellam matutinam. Quam . . . Ff. 215ra–217rb.

49. T30. *Peccatis mortui iustitiae vivamus* (1 Pet 2:24). Fiat oracio. Si lex condita sit super duobus articulis, oportet obligatos illi legi . . .-. . . serenitas sine nube et gloria sine fine. Ad quam . . . Ff. 217rb–218rb.

50. T10. *Obtulerunt ei munera: aurum, tus, et murram* (Matt 2:11). Karissimi, in verbis propositis tanguntur duo, videlicet magorum oblatio . . .-. . . oportet quod tecum portes quemdam lapidem preciosum. Ff. 218rb–219ra, inc.

51. T56. *Dum tempus habemus, operemur bonum* (Gal 6:10). Worke we þe goode faste . . . Karissimi, debetis scire quod tempus diuiditur . . .-. . . nollem habere locum angeli si possem habere locum debitum homini. Ff. 219vb– 223va, inc.

52. T18/4. *Revertimini et vivite* (Ezek 18:32). Karissimi, secundum communem famam nunquam fuerunt homines ita maliciosi . . .-. . . quamuis sint aliis alia gaudia, illis tamen talia. Hec ille. Ff. 223va–226va, inc.

53. ?. *Vocati estis* (1 Peter 3:9). Scitis, Karissimi, quod quatuor modis solet quis vocare amicum suum . . .-. . . quousque reddidit vniuersum debitum et cetera. Ff. 226vb–229va, inc.

54. C21. *Memento finis* (Sir 36:10). Karissimi, sicut videtis nunquam fuerunt homines ita dediti mundo luxurie . . .-. . . recordatio ardoris gehenne ardorem extinguit luxurie. Hec ille. Ff. 229vb–232va, inc.

55. T19. *Illi soli servies* (Matt 4:10). To god and to no mo . . . Reuerendi domini, secundum beatum Gregorium omelia 10 *Super Ezechielem* in omni quod cogitamus . . .-. . . vt iudicaret sed vt saluaret mundum. Hec ibi. Ff. 232vb– 234va, inc.

56. T01+. *Ecce venio cito* (Rev 22:12?). Reuerendi mei, debetis scire quod de quadruplici aduentu Christi in isto sacro tempore . . .-. . . cum genuflectione

et muneribus Esau, Christus antequam Abraham fieret etc. Ff. 234vb–238ra.

57. T28. *Tene quod habes* (Rev 3:11). Reuerendi mei, sicut scribit Discoriades libro 2 capitulo 57, in India inferiori est arbor . . .-. . . ipse est a ledere qui te ducet ad regnum suum þat ys endles welþ wythoute wo. Quod . . . Ff. 238ra–240rb. Also E-12, S4.

58. T40. *In nomine Patris et Filii et Spiritus Sancti* (Matt 28:19). Sancta Trinitas, cuius memoria generaliter per totam Ecclesiam hodierna die recolitur . . .-. . . in eterna tabernacula celorum, que preparabunt diligentibus se. Ad que etc. Ff. 240rb–242ra.

59. ?. *Surge qui dormis* (Eph 5:14). Karissimi, in tribus periculis solent homines in lecto dormientes euigilare . . .-. . . nec in cor hominis ascendit. Quo . . . Ff. 242rb–243vb. Also H-22, CA/2–5.

60. S65*. *Quae est ista quae progreditur sicut aurora consurgens, pulchra ut luna, electa ut sol?* (Cant 6:9). Reuerendi mei, quia prerogatiua Virginis benedicte non possunt sufficienter . . .-. . . et ideo ad visionem claram illius benedictus filius suus nos omnes perducat . . . Ff. 243vb–247rb.

61. T41/5. *Qui manducat vivet* (John 6:58). Karissimi, beatus Bernardus dicit et eciam Philosophus quod ignis . . .-. . . a muliere que est laqueus venatorum et sagena. Ff. 247rb–248rb, inc.

62. ?. *Exiit qui seminat seminare semen suum* (Luke 8:5). Seminat Christus, seminat diabolus, seminat homo . . .-. . . et metite in ore misericordie, scilicet in ore Dei, vitam eternam. Amen. Ff. 248va–249rb.

63. T16. *Voca operarios et redde illis mercedem* (Matt 20:8). Multi sunt vocati in vineam, sed quidam venire noluerunt. Vnde in Prouerbiis . . .-. . . digni simus recipere denarium diurnum, idest eternam beatitudinem in mercedem. Amen. Ff. 249rb–250rb.

64. ?. *Qui est ex Deo, verba Dei audit* (John 8:47). Ergo ad destructionem consequentis: qui non audit verbum Dei, non est ex . . .-. . . concupiscentiis mundialibus valeamus peruenire ad eternam beatitudinem. Ff. 250rb–251rb.

65. ?. *Cum venerit spiritus veritatis, docebit omnem veritatem* (John 16:13). Sciens Iesus discipulos de absentia eius dolentes, consolabatur eos . . .-. . . mente celestia in presenti contemplemur et in futuro facie ad faciem Deum videamus. Amen. Ff. 251rb–253ra.

66. T19. *Vivit homo* (Matt 4:4). Ex sacra scriptura patet quod sepius per deuote oracionis instantiam . . .-. . . ex fine pensant habere, 7 *Morum* capitulo 2. Qui finis est deus omnipotens, quem . . . Ff. 253ra–256ra.

67. ?. *Vexatur qui non respondit* (Matt 15:22–23). Vt comuniter ratione vtentibus exprimitur quod quanto quis dure . . .-. . . quos leuiter possent superare et vincere. Quam victoriam . . . Ff. 256ra–258ra.

68. ?. *Orate pro invicem ut salvemini* (James 5:16). Impotentes virtute orationis a periculis se defendunt, quod viribus naturalibus . . .-. . . vos in dilectione seruate expectantes misericordiam Domini nostri Iesu Christi in vitam eternam. Amen. Ff. 258ra–261rb.

69. ?. *Ubi est Deus?* (Joel 2:17?). Inter omnes questiones in sacra scriptura motas assumpta pro themate . . .-. . . vbi nec erugo nec tinea demolitur. Ad quod . . . Ff. 261va–263rb.

70. ?. "Tres sunt . . .". *Tres sunt qui testimonium dant* (1 John 5:7). Sacra scriptura approbante inueni quod quatuor pro processu sermonis . . .-. . . ad memoriam omnes reducant, quoniam tres sunt etc. Ff. 263rb–265ra.

71. T21. *Revertar* (Luke 11:24). Inter clementiam et vindictam naturalis ordo statuit vt prius attemptetur . . .-. . . reuertere ad me quoniam ego redemi te, scilicet ad vitam eternam. Amen. Ff. 265ra–268rb. Also O-32, W-91.

72. T10. *Ortus est sol, congregati sunt* (Ps 103:22). De nocte quamdiu solis absentia durat, tria incomoda sequuntur . . .-. . . iste qui fuit natus reduceret homines ad pacem sempiternam. Quam . . . Ff. 268rb–269rb.

73. ?. *Voca operarios et redde illis mercedem* (Matt 20:8). Vita hominis sicut ferrum est. Nam sicut ferreum instrumentum non vsitatum . . .-. . . super omnia bona sua constituet. Quorum bonorum participes nos faciat . . . Ff. 269va–273vb.

74. T18/4. *Convertimini ad me in toto corde vestro* (Joel 2:12). Karissimi, loquitur 3 Regum 20 quod cum rex Ezechias egrotaret vsque ad mortem . . .-. . . et in cor hominis non ascendit, quam preparauit deus diligentibus se. Ad quam . . . Ff. 273vb–274va.

75. T18. *Fides, spes, caritas, tria haec* (1 Cor 13:13). Quam necessarium est cuilibet ad eternam salutem festinanti scire . . .-. . . et nos in ipso quid graciosius. Ad suam ergo mansionem et gloriam . . . Ff. 274va–276rb.

76. T19. *Dominum Deum tuum adorabis* (Matt 4:10). Ratio edocet naturaliter quod quilibet deberet illud libenter facere per quod . . .-. . . qui adorat, in oblatione suscipietur. Quod . . . Ff. 276rb–279va. Also P1-27 with slightly different opening words.

77. T22. *Filii promissionis sumus* (Gal 4:28). Cum Saul rex Israel preuaricatus esset legem Dei, statim malignus spiritus . . .-. . . per consequens ipsius heredes, coheredes autem Christi. Ad quam . . . Ff. 279va–281ra.

78. T19. *Exhibeamus nos Dei ministros in patientia* (2 Cor 6:4). Minister escas apponere potest, sed edentibus saporem dare non potest . . .-. . . honorificabit eum pater meus qui est in celis. Quod . . . Ff. 281ra–282vb.

79. T19. *Nunc dies salutis* (2 Cor 6:2). Karissimi, secundum Augustinum *De verbis Apostoli* omelia 88, ex quo Adam lapsus . . .-. . . a peccatis per penitentiam et a morte ad vitam eternam. Ad quam . . . Ff. 283ra–284vb.

80. T19. *Dominum Deum tuum adorabis* (Matt 4:10). Iob: Quam mutationem dabit homo pro anima sua. Abraham ait pueris suis . . .-. . . in suo seruitio perseuerare, vt cum eo sine fine valeatis regnare. Amen. Ff. 284vb–285rb.

81. T19. *Si filius Dei es, dic* (Matt 4:3). Crisostomus in *Imperfecto* omelia 13, Filii carnales si similes sint . . .-. . . heredes autem Dei, coheredes autem Christi. Quod . . . Ff. 285rb–286rb.

82. T19. *Dic ut lapides isti panes fiant* (Matt 4:3). Iuxta illud quod Apostolus dicit Ad Thimotheum 2 capitulo, Obsecro ergo primum omnium . . .- . . . tota sua merces sibi reddetur in felicitate eterna. Ad quam . . . Ff. 286rb–289ra. FitzRalph, FI-67.

83. T20. *Miserere mei, fili David* (Matt 15:21). Reuerendi et amici karissimi, duabus de causis potest Filius Dei filius Dauid appellari . . .-. . . coronam, per quam designatur vita et gloria sempiterna. Ad quam . . . Ff. 289ra–290vb.

84. T20. *Domine, adiuva me* (Matt 15:25). Debilis et impotens, pauper et indigens, pauidus et timens habent materiam auxilium inuocandi . . .- . . . inopem et de stercore erigens pauperem. Quam . . . Ff. 290vb–291vb.

85. T20. *Filia mea a daemonio male vexatur* (Matt 15:22). Cum rex Saul preuaricatus esset legem Dei ac mandata, spiritus malus . . .-. . . Si predictis hostibus locum dederis peribis; si illos superaueris saluus eris. Exemplum de peregrino vt supra. Hoc eodem in sermone Miserere mei fili Dauid etc. Ff. 291vb–292vb.

86. T21. *Erat Iesus eiciens daemonium, et illud erat mutum* (Luke 11:14). Karissime [!], hoc nomen Iesus vocabulum est eximie pietatis ac dulcedinis . . .- . . . in cor hominis non ascendit, quam preparauit deus diligentibus se. Quam . . . Ff. 292vb–294rb.

87. T21. *Christus dilexit nos* (Eph 5:2). Ratio edocet quod homo paruipendat ea que vilia sunt, sed ea que preciosa . . .-. . . coronam vite, quam repromisit Deus diligentibus se. Quam . . . Ff. 294rb–295rb.

88. T21. *Estote imitatores Dei* (Eph 5:1). Secundum artem medicine contraria contrariis curantur. Aqua et ignis . . .-. . . vt ita faciatis vt eciam possitis ad gaudium eternum peruenire. Amen etc. Ff. 295rb–296rb.

89. T22. *Signa faciebat super his qui infirmabantur* (John 6:2). Triplex est infirmitas corporalis: quedam extra corpus vt in manibus et pedibus . . .-. . . adiuuisti me et consolatus es me. Quod auxilium . . . Ff. 296rb–297va.

90. T22. *Quid dicit Scriptura?* (Gal 4:30). Karissimi, Apostolus 2 Corinthiorum 3 dicit quod non sumus sufficientes cogitare . . .-. . . misericordiam consequetur quoad graciam in presenti et gloriam <in futuro> sine \fine/. Quam . . . Ff. 297va–298vb.

91. ?. *Ecce ascendimus*, etc. (Matt 20:18 etc.). Iste ascensus Domini in materialem Hierusalem signat nostrum ascensum spiritualem . . .-. . . manu precedente et pede subsequente ascendamus. Ad quam . . . Ff. 298vb–300ra.

92. ?. *Gratia super gratiam mulier sancta et pudorata*. Et in eodem: *Narratio fatui quasi sarcina in via, in labiis sensati invenitur gratia* (Sir 26:19). Sensatus est cui res sapiunt prout sunt. Item notandum quod Beata Virgo comparatur cristallo . . .-. . . qui perseuerauerit vsque in finem, hic saluus erit. Ad quam salutem . . . Ff. 300ra–301ra.

93. T23. *Emundabit conscientiam nostram ab operibus mortuis ad serviendum Deo viventi* (Heb 9:14). Karissimi, si reducamus ad memoriam humani generis principium et consequenter . . .-. . . vt seruiamus Deo viuenti, timendo penas et premia expectando. Que . . . F. 301ra–301vb.

Oxford, Bodleian Library, MS Bodley 857

Discussed in Part One, pp. 80–81 and 218.

1. T34?. *Confitemini* (James 5:16). Si quis peregre iturus esset versus terram sanctam, scilicet Ierusalem . . . Ff. 153–154. Also J/5-2, Balliol 219, New College 305.

2. T66?. *Rex faciet iudicium in terra* (Jere 23:5). Reuerendi mei, secundum scripturam expositoresque eiusdem tria requiruntur ad regem quando habet iudicium facere . . . Ff. 154–155.

3. T03. *Quaeritur quis fidelis inveniatur* (1 Cor 4:2). Reuerendi mei, provt docet scriptura, triplici questione [*read* racione?] queritur questio . . . Ff. 155–156v. Also P1-9 and C-21 (outline).

4. T20?. *Miserere mei, Domine* (Math 15:22). Reuerendi mei, secundum scripturam tria genera hominum clamant pro misericordia . . . Ff. 156v–157v.

5. ?. *In diebus suis placuit Deo* et vel *Placuerunt tibi, Domine* (Sir 44:16 (or 48:25?) and Wisd 9:19). Reuerendi mei, prout testatur scriptura, per tria homo placet Deo in vita ista . . . Ff. 157v–159.

6. T21?. *Scitote quod immundus non habet hereditatem in regno Dei* (Eph 25:5). Reuerendi mei, prout docet sacra scriptura et communia iura, tria excludunt hominem ab hereditate paterna . . . Ff. 159–161. Also P1-34 and P2-31.

7. T63?. *Oro ut caritas vestra magis abundet; Dominus dirigat corda nostra in caritate* (Phil 1:9; 2 Thes 3:5). Reuerendi mei, prout docet sacra scriptura, propter tria solent homines Dominum Deum adorare . . . F. 161.

8. T47?. *Ultra non serviamus peccato* (Rom 6:6). Reuerendi mei, tria hominem impediunt ne alteri seruiat . . . F. 161r–v.

9. ?. *Homo tu quis es?* (Rom 9:20). Reuerendi mei, prout docet scriptura, propter tria queritur questio per hanc diccionem quis . . . Ff. 161v–162v. Also P2-8.

10. T03. *Pax Dei custodiat corda vestra* (Phil 4:7). Reuerendi mei, duo reperio prout docet scriptura . . . Ff. 162v–163v. Also P1-11 and P2-7.

11. T02. *Deus repleat vos gaudio et pace* (Rom 15:13). Reuerendi me, duo sunt quibus solent homines desiderare repleri . . . Ff. 163v–164v. Also P1-5.

12. ?. *In Christo Iesu* (?). Karissimi, bene scitis quod quanto quis grauatur, siue per lesionem in corpore siue per dolorem in corde, statim ad talem confugeret . . . Ff. 164v–166.

13. ?. *Gaudeamus et demus gloriam Deo* (Rev 19:7). Reuerendi mei, secundum scripture testimonium tria genera hominum solent gaudere et dare gloriam Deo . . . Ff. 166–167v. Also P1-13 and P2-10.

14. ?. *Verbum caro factum est* (John 1:14). Prout docet sanctus Thomas *De Christo*, questione 16, triplex fuit opinio hereticorum . . . Ff. 167v–168v. Also P1-14.

15. ?. *Convertere ad Dominum et relinque peccata* (Sir 17:21). Reuerendi mei, prout docet Aristoteles 8 *Ethicorum* quod animal naturaliter fugit tristia . . . Ff. 168v–169v.

16. S28?. *Maria, invenisti gratiam* (Luke 1:30). Reuerendi mei, docente sacra scriptura propter tria inuenit quis graciam coram Deo . . . Ff. 169v–171.

17. ?. *Sperate in Deo, quia adiutor noster est* (Ps 51?). Reuerendi mei, propter tria solent homines in alium sperare et ab eo adiutorium petere . . . Ff. 171–172v.

Oxford, Bodleian Library, MS Bodley 859

Discussed in Part One, p. 130. Besides Bromyard's *Distinctiones* (ff. 44–225v), the codex contains the following sermons:

1. S21*. *Impleti sunt dies purgationis* (Luke 2:22). Karissimi, hodierni ewangelii series . . . F. 296.

2. S21*. *Parasti lumen* (Luke 2:31–32). Karissimi, festum celebre hodierne diei vulgari nomini candelaria . . . Ff. 296–297.

3. S21. *Veni, ut docerem te* (Dan 10:14). Karissimi, hodie sancta Mater Ecclesie agit diem festum . . . Ff. 297–299.

4. S21. *Ecce Dominus Deus noster, exspectavimus eum et salvabit nos* (Isa 25:9). Videmus quod quando aliqua comunitas diu desiderauit . . . Ff. 299–300v.

5. S21. *Postquam impleti sunt dies purgationis Mariae*, etc. (Luke 2:22). Secundum quod dicit Augustinus quarto libro *De Trinitate* capitulo 13, in qualibet oblacione . . . Ff. 301–302.

6. S21. *Ecce Dominus Deus noster, istum expectavimus et salvabit nos* (Isa 25:9). Karissimi, sicud scitis, tria consueuerunt presenciam alicuius domini reddere gaudiosam . . . Ff. 302–304v.

7. S21 ("Sermo domini pape in purificatione domine nostre"). *Cum autem apparuit benignitas et humanitas salvatoris . . . regenerationis Spiritus Sancti* (Tit 3:4–5). Carissimi, istis diebus sacratissimis audiuimus quod fecit mencionem sancta mater Ecclesia de triplici apparitione . . . Ff. 304v–306. Pope.

8. S21 ("Sermo domini pape in purificatione beate Marie"). *Suscepit Israhel, puerum suum* (Luke 1:54). Sicut Sapiens dicit, Desiderium suum iustis datur . . . Ff. 306v–308. Pope.

9. S21. *Columba venit ad Noe portans ramum olivae virentibus foliis* (Gen 8:11). Karissimi, sicut dicit Dyonisius 4 capitulo 77, diuinitatis lex immobilis . . . F. 308r–v, inc.

10. T24. *Dispone domui tuae et morieris* (Isa 38:1). Dilectissimi filii, triplicem legimus mortis necessitatem . . . F. 311r–v, inc.

11. T19. *Filius Dei es, mitte te deorsum* (Matt 4:6). Deuotorum moribus insidiantes peruersi falsitatis . . . F. 312r–v, inc.

12. T26. *Percussa est tertia pars solis* (Rev 8:12). Dicunt astrologi quod sol est propinquior terre in hyeme . . . Ff. 314v–319v, 322–325v. Also Padua-50.

13. T26*. *Mundus crucifixus est* (Gal 6:14). Scribit Apostolus vbi thema sic: Michi autem absit gloriari . . . Ff. 326–328v, 313–314, with renvoi. Also Padua-49.

14. ?. *Diligite inimicos vestros, benefacite hiis qui vos oderunt, et orate pro persequentibus vos, ut sitis filii altissimi* (Matt 5:44). Nostri enim inimici nobis multipliciter aduersantur . . . F. 329v, inc.

15. ?. *Buccellam panis* (Gen 18:5). Solent potentes et nobiles in suis conuiuiis copiose panem apponere . . . F. 331, inc.

BR – Thomas Brinton

The inventory is based on *The Sermons of Thomas Brinton, Bishop of Rochester (1373–1389)*, edited by Mary Aquinas Devlin, O. P., Camden Third Series, vols. 85–86 (continuous pagination; London, 1954), with some corrections from the manuscript. Page references are to the edited text.

4. S12. *Nec quisquam sibi sumit honorem nisi qui vocatur a Deo* (Heb 5:4). Si reuerencia et honor qui matri defertur filio . . .-. . . certe moderni non . . . Pp. 1–6, inc.

5. S24a*. [Acephalous] . . . quot sanis doctrinis . . .-. . . cum eo perpetuo coronati. Quod etc. Pp. 7–8, inc.

6. T03. *Meipsum iudico* (1 Cor 4:3). Dicunt iura vbi aliquis accusandus est de crimine coram iudice . . .-. . . gremium redeunti, Extra. *De hereticis.* Pp. 8–14.

7. T02. *Uno ore honorificetis Deum* (Rom 15:6). Inter cetera membra corporis humani predicator verbi Dei poterit ori comparari triplici racione . . .-. . . quia ad dexteram filii tui honorifice collocata. Pp. 15–22.

8. T03. *Mortui resurgunt* (Luke 7:22). Si communiter omnis sermo soleat incipere ab oracione . . .-. . . post resurrectionem erit sibi gloria. Ad quam etc. Pp. 22–28.

9. S59. *Exaltata sum* (Sir 24:17). Inter multa que personam bene meritam exaltant, magnificant, et extollunt . . .-. . . quia exaltabitur. Hac exaltacione dignos nos efficiat. Pp. 28–32.

10. S12. *Bonus pastor animam suam dat pro ovibus suis* (John 10:11). Si omne datum optimum . . . a patre luminum, Iacobi 1, ad Mariam virginem . . .-. . . veritas in promisso, vita in premio. Quod etc. Pp. 32–37.

11. C14. *Sic currite ut comprehendatis* (1 Cor 9:24). Quia cursus presentis vite secure dirigere . . .-. . . qua omnia penetrat subtilitate. Hanc caritatem . . . Pp. 38–42.

12. T31 ("apud sanctum Paulum"). *Regem honorificate* (2 Pet 2:17). Secundum Remigium super illud Matthei 2 Optulerunt . . . , magi regi regum aurum, thus, et mirram optulerunt . . .-. . . et etate regem honorificate. Pp. 43–48.

13. C14. *Gratia vobis et pax multiplicetur* (1 Pet 1:2). Quia secundum Gregorium in *Registro* frustra laborat lingua exterius predicatoris . . .-. . . sanctificet vos per omnia. Quod . . . Pp. 49–54.

14. C14. *Filii, oboedite* (Eph 6:1). Quia secundum beatum Bernardum in sermone de ascensione securum habemus accessum . . .-. . . inter filios Dei eternaliter computari. Quod . . . Pp. 55–58.

15. C14. *Ecce quam bonum et quam iucundum habitare fratres in unum* (Ps 132:1). Quia vnitas Ecclesie consistit in multorum per dilectionem connexione . . .-. . . vnus accepit brauium. Quod bravium . . . Pp. 58–60.

16. T44. *Humiliamini sub potenti manu Dei* (1 Pet 5:6). Videtis exemplariter in natura quod auis se ordinans ad volandum . . .-. . . ad quam cum aues accedunt eas rapit, etc. Pp. 60–66.

17. T65 / C14. *State in Domino* (Phil 4:1). Liquet ex serie scripturarum quod vniuersorum Dominus est singulariter adorandus . . .-. . . in omnibus stare perfecti. Quod . . . Pp. 67–71.

18. T18/4. *Convertimini* (Joel 2:12). Sicut diuine faciei auersio creaturas adnichilat et conturbat . . .-. . . efficiamini, intrabitis in regnum celorum. Quod etc. Pp. 71–74.

19. T19. *Ecce nunc tempus* (2 Cor 6:2). Licet omni tempore obligemur ad bonum operandum, dicit Apostolus . . .-. . . in gloria quantum ad regnum. Ad quod perducat. Pp. 75–79.

20. T21. *Praevenit in vos regnum Dei* (Luke 11:20 and Matt [12:28?]). Potest elici ex scripturis quod regnum Dei debet esse primum in predicacione . . .-. . . paratum est ab origine mundi. Ad quod, etc. Pp. 80–84.

21. T23. *Emundabit conscientiam vestram*, suple sanguis Christi (Heb 9:14). Sicut ad emundacionem templi materialis tria requiruntur principaliter, videlicet aqua . . .-. . . transeamus ad gloriam sempiternam. Ad quam, etc. Pp. 84–87.

22. T26. *Exivit sanguis* (John 19:34). Si homocide qui sanguinem filii crudeliter effuderunt accedant . . .-. . . meam carnem habet eternam. Ad quam, etc. Pp. 88–94.

23. C19 ("apud Roffam"). *Adpropinquaverunt visitationes urbis* (Ezek 9:1). Narrat Valerius libro 7, capitulo 6, rex Iudeorum in turribus vrbium fortes posuit canes . . .-. . . det nobis tamquam capiti talem visitandi graciam vt visitacio nostra . . . Pp. 94–96.

24. T46. *Vocati estis* (1 Pet 3:9). Patet ex serie scripturarum quod Deus tripliciter suos elegit . . .-. . . de tenebris in admirabile lumen suum. Quod, etc. Pp. 97–99.

25. T47. *In novitate vitae ambulemus* (Rom 6:4). In sacra scriptura describitur triplex vita, quarum prima est temporalis . . .-. . . et dabo tibi coronam vite. Ad quam. Pp. 99–101.

26. T55. *Spiritu ambulate* (Gal 5:16). Licet quis non possit se probare Spiritum Sanctum certitudinaliter possidere . . .-. . . innocens manibus et mundo corde. Ad quem montem, etc. Pp. 102–104.

27. T18. *Fides tua te salvum fecit* (Luke 18:42). Volenti a Deo per oracionem aliquid impetrare neccesse est in fide firmiter stare . . .-. . . pro premio eternaliter possidendo. Quod, etc. Pp. 104–109.

28. T58 / S74*. *Solliciti servare unitatem* (Eph 4:3). Triplex sollicitudo commendabilis elicitur a scriptura . . .-. . . vnum locum eterne mansionis, quia regnum. Ideo simus ita vnanimes . . . Pp. 109–117.

29. T42 [?]. *Induite novum hominem* (Eph 4:24). Ad innouacionem hominis interioris, idest anime purioris, tria . . .-. . . induimini Dominum Iesum Christum. Quod . . . Pp. 117–119.

30. S12 / C14. *Laus eius in ecclesia* (Ps 149:1). Si iubemur in sanctis suis Dominum collaudare, Extra. *De reuerencia* . . .-. . . quia inter benedictos benedicetur. Quam benediccionem, etc. Pp. 119–125.

31. T06. *Apparuit gratia Dei* (Tit 2:11). Quia secundum Gregorium in *Registro* frustra laborat exterius lingua predicatoris . . .-. . . benedixit te Deus in eternum. Quam benedictionem . . . Pp. 126–130.

32. T18/4 ("apud Roffam"). *Scindite corda vestra* (Joel 2:13). Ad finem quod oracio debeat exaudiri duo spiritualiter requiruntur . . .-. . . gracia stabiliri cor, Ad Hebreos 13. Quam graciam . . . Pp. 130–135.

33. T19. *Exhibeamus nosmetipsos sicut Dei ministros* (2 Cor 6:4). Inter cetera ministeria exhibita a populo Christiano, ministerium Deo exhibitum est magis honorabile . . .-. . . in gloria quoad regnum. Quod regnum . . . Pp. 135–140.

34. T20. *Vocavit nos Deus* (1 Thess 4:7). Positi in tribulacionibus et dolore solent eius protectionem et auxilium deuocius inuocare . . .-. . . in hoc vocati estis vt benedictionem hereditate possideatis. Pp. 140–145, inc?

35. T21. *Fructus lucis est in omni bonitate* (Eph 5:9). Ad oculum innotescit quod terra de se sterilis et arida non potest fieri fructuosa . . .-. . . et in omni opere bono fructificare. Quod . . . Pp. 145–151.

36. T22. *Laetare* (Gal 4:27). Quantus est dolor et tristicia cum quis a suo solo exulat naturali . . .-. . . vt adquiratis quartam gloriam, scilicet eternam. Quam, etc. Pp. 151–157. Also A-57.

37. T23. *Per proprium sanguinem introivit* (Heb 9:12). Ad oculum videmus quod si crudeles et homicide qui sanguinem filii inhumaniter effuderunt . . .- . . . habet vitam eternam. Ad quam, etc. Pp.156–162.

38. S28 ("apud Eylisforde in domo Carmelitorum coram Domino de Grey"). *Nomen virginis Maria* (Luke 1:27). Naute in maris periculis constituti, si diligenter respexerint stellam maris . . .-. . . nomina vestra scripta sunt in celis. Quod . . . Pp. 163–168.

39. T26. *Filius regis mortuus est* (2 Sam 18:20). Quia secundum Bernardum in sermone de quadragesima filii nostri sunt bona opera . . .-. . . preciosa in conspectu Domini est mors sanctorum eius. Quam, etc. Pp. 169–176.

40. T28. *Iesum quaeritis* (Mark 16:6). Quia scribitur per Ysaie 50 Querite Dominum dum inueniri potest . . . , sciendum est quod qui mane . . .-. . . remuneratorem inuenire poteritis. Quod . . . Pp. 177–180.

41. T31. *Deum timete* (1 Pet 2:17). Quia plenitudo sapiencie est timere Deum, Ecclesiastici primo, pueri timere Deum ab infancia sunt docendi . . .-. . . fiducialiter agam et non timebo. Pp. 180–185.

42. S49. *Dilexit multum* (Luke 7:47). Cum dicat Augustinus in *Soliloquiis*, Nichil potuit Deum de celo ad terram trahere . . .-. . . finaliter comprehendere valeatis. Quod nobis, etc. Pp. 185–190.

43. C14 ("London'"). *Honorificetur Deus* (1 Pet 4:11). Cum dicat scriptura in persona Christi, Inuoca me in die tribulacionis, eruam te et honorificabis me, et honor que matri defertur filio . . .-. . . in sanctificacione et honore, 1 Ad Thessalonicenses 4. Pp. 190–193.

44. ?. *Simul in unum dives et pauper* (Ps 48:3). Sicut ab vno mari manant diuersi riuuli, ab vna luce diuersi radii . . .-. . . habitare fratres in vnum. Quod vobis, etc. Pp. 194–200.

45. ?. *Videte* (Eph 5:15). Si iuxta sentenciam Saluatoris Luce 10 beati sunt oculi . . .-. . . salua facta est anima mea. Ad quam visionem . . . Pp. 200–206.

46. C21*. *Miserere animae* (Sir 30:24). Cum sit sancta et salubris cogitacio pro defunctis exorare . . .-. . . de penis grauissimis ad gloriam sempiternam. Pp. 206–209.

47. C16 ("apud Roffam"). *Sancti estote* (Lev 19:2). Cum dicat scriptura Ad aliquem sanctum convertere, Iob 5, ad Mariam . . .-. . . ad sancta sanctorum mereamur finaliter introire. Quod nobis, etc. Pp. 209–212.

48. T12. *Domino servientes* (Rom 12:11). Positi in periculis et dolore ad illum dominum confugiunt . . .-. . . ita digne sibi ministrare vt cum eo mereamini eternaliter conregere. Quod, etc. Pp. 212–217.

49. T18/4. *Quid superbit terra et cinis?* (Sir 10:9). Si terra de se sterilis debeat fieri fructuosa, duo precipue requiruntur . . .-. . . graciam in presenti et gloriam in futuro. Pp. 218–222.

50. T19 ("apud Derteford"). *Angeli accesserunt* (Matt 4:11 and Luke 4). Accedente presencia maioris vel eciam forcioris cessant virtus . . .-. . . super vno peccatore penitenciam agente. Ad quod gaudium, etc. Pp. 222–227.

51. C14 / T? ("dominica)". *Quod bonum est tenete* (1 Thess 5:19). Vt verbum Dei digne audire et auditum tenere firmiter valeamus . . .-. . . pro premio Ecclesie triumphantis, vt est conclusum. Quam vobis, etc. Pp. 227–229.

52. S28. *Maria, invenisti gratiam* (Luke 1:30). Dicit Origenes in quadam omelia quod tria precipue faciunt hominem graciam inuenire . . .-. . . semper in me manet, quoad tercium. Cuius gracie . . . Pp. 230–234.

53. T22. *Promissionis filii sumus* (Gal 4:28). Si ciuitas vel communitas grauiter deliquerit contra principem . . .-. . . vt mereamini in iudicio finali inter filios Dei eternaliter computari. Pp. 234–240.

54. T23. *Per proprium sanguinem introiuit* (Heb 9:12). Si homicide qui sanguinem filii crudeliter effuderunt accedant ad patrem . . .-. . . ita a falsis iuramentis abstineatis ne pretextu bonorum temporalium animas, que sunt precium sanguinis Christi, amittatis. Pp. 241–247.

55. T25 ("in ecclesia cathedrali Roffensis"). *Corpus meum dedi* (Isa 50:6). Licet contra singula temptamenta dentur virtutum singula dona . . .-. . . et in custodito tam perseueranter persistere vt ad gaudia eterna meriamur peruenire. Pp. 248–251.

56. T26 ("in ecclesia cathedrali"). *Respice in faciem Christi tui* (Ps 83:10). Inter ceteras visiones quas vidit Ezechiel . . .-. . . et vos apparebitis cum ipso in gloria. Ad quam nos, etc. Pp. 252–260.

57. C21* ("apud Pepinbury"). *Manus Domini tetigit me* (Job 19:21). Positi in periculis et dolore ad illum dominum confugiunt pro salute . . .-. . . quoad triumphum, in gloria quoad regnum. Quod, etc. Pp. 260–265.

58. C21* ("apud Wrotham"). *Post tenebras spero lucem* (Job 17:12). Inter sanctos Dei in Maria matre virgine specialiter est sperandum . . .-. . . in spe glorie filiorum Dei. Pp. 266–268.

59. C21. *Opera enim illorum sequuntur illos* (Rev 14:13). Inter opera que audet humana industria acceptare . . .-. . . merces operi tuo, Ieremie 31. Quam mercedem nobis, etc. Pp. 268–272.

60. S49. *Vade in pace* (Luke 7:50). Tanta est dignitas vere pacis quod a Christo iubetur generaliter predicari . . .-. . . cum pacis principe mereamini eternaliter conregnare. Quod, etc. Pp. 273–278.

61. S01. *Secuti sunt eum* (Luke 5:11 and Matt 4:20). Ad oculum videmus quod communiter Christiani vel secuntur carnem . . .-. . . non dixit discite . . . Pp. 278–280, inc.

62. C21 ("apud C[h]elesfeld"). *Mortui qui in Christo sunt resurgent* (1 Thess 4:16). Ex quo formaliter ab oracione debeat incipere omnis sermo, pro mortuis orare principaliter duo monent . . .-. . . sarcina, post resurrectionem erit sibi gloria. Quam, etc. Pp. 280–284.

63. T18/4. *Sanctificate ieiunium* (Joel 1:14). Potest elici ex scripturis quod ieiunii corporalis quatuor sunt effectus . . .-. . . sanctificet vos per omnia, 1 Timothei 5. Quod . . . Pp. 285–289.

64. T19. *Gratiam Dei recipiatis* (2 Cor 6:1). Si ciuitas vel communitas grauiter deliquerit contra principem . . .-. . . graciam scilicet in presenti et gloriam in futuro. Ad quam. Pp. 290–294.

65. T21. *Ambulate in dilectione* (Eph 5:2). Cum dicat Hugo in *Soliloquiis*, Nichil potuit Deum de celo ad terram trahere . . .-. . . vt sitis filii patris vestri qui in celo est. Quod, etc. Pp. 295–299.

66. T23. *Qui est ex Deo, verba Dei audit* (John 8:47). Cum dicat Apostolus Ad Romanos 10, Omnis . . . , igitur requiritur . . .-. . . fructum afferunt in paciencia. Quem fructum facere . . . Pp. 299–304.

67. T25. *Laventur pedes vestri* (Gen 18:4). Quia cena Domini est priuilegiata in multis . . .-. . . laui pedes meos quomodo coinquinabo eos. Quod . . . Pp. 305–306.

68. T26. *Requiescite sub arbore* (Gen 18:4). Positi in tribulacione vel egritudine, si possint saluari herba . . .-. . . vt possitis hic cum Christo requiescere per graciam et in futuro per gloriam. Quod vobis. Pp. 307–314.

69. T33. *Factor operis hic beatus* (James 1:25). Inter opera que audet humana industria attemptare . . .-. . . dicente Patre ad Filium, Voca operarios et redde illi mercedem. Pp. 315–321.

70. T? ("dominica") / C14*. *Vigilate* (1 Pet 5:8). Quia secundum Apostolum 1 Ad Thimotheum 5, Oportet . . . , dominus rex in suis literis petit . . .-. . . vt de presenti vigilia transiatis ad festum eternaliter mansurum. Quod, etc. Pp. 322–326.

71. T47*. *Offeres munus tuum* (Matt 5:23). Si infideles in arduis attemptandis deos solebant deuocius inuocare . . .-. . . premium sempiternum, 16 q. 1, *Decime*. Quod . . . Pp. 326–330.

72. T16. *Voca operarios et redde illis mercedem* (Matt 20:8). Spiritualiter inter cetera que solet humana industria attemptare . . .-. . . est quieta carens omni perturbacione. Ad quam, etc. Pp. 330–335.

73. T29. *Pax vobis* (John 20:19). Tanta est dignitas vere pacis quod a Christo iubetur generaliter predicari . . .-. . . ad pacem eternam finaliter attingatis. Quod vobis, etc. Pp. 336–339.

74. C21. *Moriemini* (Ps 81:7). Ex quo formaliter ab oracione incepere debeat omnis sermo . . .-. . . cum Christo eternam merearis mansionem. Pp. 340–343.

75. C19. *Visitabo in virga* (Ps 88:33). Fratres amantissimi, quia inter arbores fructuosas vinea frequencius visitatur . . .-. . . et virga discipline fugabit eam. Pp. 343–345.

76. T19. *Ecce vivimus* (2 Cor 6:9). Cum anima fuerit mortua per peccatum . . .-. . . et dabo tibi coronam vite. Ad quam, etc. Pp. 346–349.

77. S49. *Laudent eam in portis opera eius* (Prov 31:31). Licet os humanum ad laudandum Deum sit specialiter ordinatum . . .-. . . vt laudem hic inceptam continuemus in futuro. Quod . . . Pp. 350–353.

78. C21 ("apud Roffam, pro domino Edwardo principe Wallensis[!]"). *Laudabile nomen Domini* (Ps 112:3). Positi in periculis et tribulacione solent eius nomen deuocius inuocare . . .-. . . essencia veritatis quoad tercium. Quod, etc. Pp. 354–357.

79. T18/4. *Memoria vestra comparabitur cineri* (Job 13:12). Videtis exemplariter in natura quod auis, cuius proprium est volare . . .-. . . in memoria eterna erunt iusti. Quam memoriam . . . Pp. 357–361.

80. T26 ("apud Roffam"). *Laboravi clamans* (Ps 68:4). Rege in actibus milicie viriliter laborante, si miles eius . . .-. . . et ego vos reficiam. Quam refectionem . . . Pp. 361–368.

81. T21. *Armatus custodit atrium suum* (Luke 11:21). Sicut miles terrenus habens exterius quantumcumque pulcrum indumentum . . .-. . . vt in virtute Dei custodiamini per fidem in secula seculorum. Pp. 368–372.

82. S28. *Benedicta tu in mulieribus* (Luke 1:28). Si communitas vel ciuitas contra principem grauiter deliquerit . . .-. . . vt benedictionem hereditate possideatis. Ad quam, etc. Pp. 372–376.

83. S49. *Remittuntur tibi peccata* (Luke 7:48). Inter cetera ad remittendum peccata ordinauit Deus tria . . .-. . . cum Magdalena mereamur eternam mansionem. Ad quam . . . Pp. 376–380.

84. S59a / C14. *Erat cotidie docens in templo* (Luke 19:47). Si templum materiale describitur ex artifice speciosum . . .-. . . in quo templo omnes dicent Gloriam, in Psalmo. Ad quam gloriam, etc. Pp. 381–385.

85. C14 ("ad clerum Londonie"). *Stabunt iusti* (Wisd 5:1). Cum stare sit proprie perfectorum, prelati et predicatores tamquam ceteris perfectiores . . .-. . . reddet michi Dominus in illa die iustus iudex. Quam coronam . . . Pp. 386–391.

86. T23. *Obtulit semetipsum* (Heb 9:14). Licet pura oracio offerenda thuri congrue comparatur . . .-. . . indulgenciam peccatorum et premium sempiternum, 16, q. 1, *Decime.* Quod . . . Pp. 391–396.

87. T25. *Vos mundi estis* (John 13:10). Si magna mundicia cordis requiritur in laicis . . .-. . . mundam serua animam meam. Quod . . . Pp. 396–399.

88. T42. *Diligamus Deum* (1 John 4). Cum secundum Augustinum in *De cat-echizandis rudibus* nulla est maior . . .-. . . que promisit deus diligentibus se. Ad que promissa . . . Pp. 400–403.

89. T48. *Habetis fructum vestrum in sanctificationem* (Rom 6:22). Ad oculum innotescit quod terra de se sterilis et arida non potest . . .-. . . vos sanctificet per omnia, 1 Ad Thessalonicenses 5. Quod . . . Pp. 403–407.

90. S49. *Fides tua te salvam fecit* (Luke 7:50). Cum dicat Apostolus 1 Ad Corinthios 10, Vigilate, state in fide, volenti a Deo orando aliquid impetrare . . .-. . . firmiter teneamus fidem et eius opera, vt mereamur premia eternaliter repromissa. Quod nobis, etc. Pp. 407–412.

91. S46b. *Placuit Deo et translatus est* (Sir 44:17 and Heb [11:5?]). Quia mansuetorum et humilium semper Deo placuit deprecacio, Iudith 9 . . .-. . . et a carcere transferat ad regnum, qui . . . Pp. 412–419.

92. C14 / T? ("Ad Clerum, dominica post . . ."). *Probatio fidei vestrae patientiam operatur* (James 1:3). Quia secundum Bernardum . . .non fidei sed perfidie . . .-. . . quam repromisit Deus diligentibus se. Quam coronam . . . Pp. 420–425.

93. T20. *Magna est fides* (Matt 15:28). Volenti aliquid a Deo viuendo impetrari necesse est in fide . . .-. . . pro regni premio eternaliter hereditando. Ad quod, etc. Pp. 426–433.

94. C15 ("apud Roffam, in electione prioris Roffensis"). *Eligite ex vobis virum* (1 Sam 17:8). Si apostoli Mathiam in suum collegium electuri . . .-. . . et timens Deum, quoad tercium. Quod . . . Pp. 434–435.

95. T31. *Fraternitatem diligite* (1 Pet 2:17). Cum dicat Hugo in *Soliloquiis,* Nichil potuit de celo Deum trahere . . .-. . . celestem hereditatem perpetuo possidere. Quod . . . Pp. 436–440.

96. T19. *Illi soli servies* (Deut 6:13, Matt 4:10, and Luke 4:9). Ad finem quod seruicium humanum debeat Deo esse acceptabile . . .-. . . omnibus diebus vite nostre, ecce tercium. Quod . . . Pp. 440–445.

97. T25 ("apud Roffam"). *Homo de pane illo edat* (1 Cor 11:28). Prelati et curati qui sunt in Ecclesia positi subditos ad pascendum . . .-. . . manducabit panem in regno celorum. Ad quod, etc. Pp. 445–448.

98. S28 ("apud Hoo"). *Missus est Gabriel angelus a Deo* (Luke 1:26). Positi in periculis et dolore solent a Deo petere angelum . . .-. . . super vno peccatore penitenciam agente. Ad quod gaudium, etc. Pp. 448–453.

99. T22. *Erumpe et clama* (Gal 4:27). Dicunt naturales quod homo vel animal positum in tribulacione . . .-. . . vt ad dexteram Dei mereamur eternaliter consedere. Quod . . . Pp. 454–458.

100. T37. *Vigilate* (1 Pet 4:7). Inter cetera Christus legitur discipulos docuisse tria notabilia documenta . . .-. . . secure ad festum eternaliter permansurum. Quod . . . Pp. 458–462.

101. S49 ("apud Cobham"). *De nocte surrexit* (Prov 31:15). Potest elici ex scripturis quod quantum ad animam . . .-. . . post resurrectionem esset sibi in gloria. Qua nobis, etc. Pp. 462–466.

102. T18/4 ("apud Roffam"). *Misereris omnium, Domine* (Wisd 11:24 "et in officio misse hodierne"). Si filius Dei et hominis in tremendo iudicio cum angelis . . .-. . . venite, benedicti Patris mei, etc. Quod. Pp. 467–470.

103. T23. *Emundabit conscientiam nostram* (Heb 9:14). Si magna mundicia consciencie requiretur in laicis . . .-. . . post mortem de gloria consciencie transeamus ad gloriam sempiternam. Quam . . . Pp. 471–475.

104. T26 ("apud Roffam in ecclesia cathedrali"). *Christus passus est pro nobis* (1 Pet 2:21). Quia secundum Ambrosium in quodam sermone omnia habemus in Christo . . .-. . . fuerimus socii passionum, erimus eciam consolacionum. Quod, etc. Pp. 476–482.

105. T18/4 ("apud Roffam"). *Oculi mei semper ad Dominum* (Ps 24:15 "et in officio misse hodierne"). Si iuxta sentenciam Saluatoris Luce 10 beati sunt oculi . . .-. . . vt finaliter acceptetur, quoad quartum. Quam . . . Pp. 482–486.

106. T23. *Gloria mea nihil est* (John 8:54). Quantus dolor est et tristitia quando exulans expellitur . . .-. . . passiones huius temporis ad futuram gloriam. Ad quam . . . Pp. 487–491.

107. T28. *Resurrexi* (Ps 138:18, "Sumptum . . . et recitatum in officio misse hodierne"). Iuxta ordinacionem matris Ecclesie duobus precipue temporibus surgimus . . .-. . . debet esse perfecta sine recidiuacione, etc., vbi supra in sermone 101, De nocte surrexit. . Pp. 492–496.

108. ? ("apud sanctum Paulum Londonie"). *Veritas liberabit* (John 8:31). Existentes in tenebris indigent lucerna vel ductore . . .-. . . cum Deo veritatis possimus eternaliter conregnare. Quod . . . Pp. 496–501.

C

C – Cambridge, Gonville and Caius College, MS 356

The highly abbreviated form of these university sermons makes it impractical to give initia and explicits. For a complete record of the rubrics see Wenzel, "Sermon Repertory."

1. T58 (Bury). *Si licet sabbato curare* (Luke 14:3). P. 1. Hyn[wood?].
2. T58/2 (Bury). *Similis est homini aedificanti domum* (Luke 6:47). Pp. 1–3.
3. T57 (Bury). *Miserere mei, Deus, secundum magnam misericordiam tuam* (Ps 50:3). P. 3. Melton, OFM.
4. T60 (Resumption). *Ambuletis ut sapientes* (Eph 5:15). P. 3.
5. T61. *Quoscumque inveneritis vocate ad nuptias* (Matt 22:9). P. 3.
6. C14. *Luceat lux vestra* (Matt 5:16). Pp. 3–4.
7. T62. *Redde quod debes* (Matt 18:28). P. 4.
8. S79 ("Cotoun"). *Gloria haec est omnibus sanctis eius* (Ps 149:9). Pp. 5–6.
9. T63. *Princeps unus accessit* (Matt 9:18). P. 6.
10. T64. *Veni et impone manum* (Matt 9:18). P. 6.
11. T66. *Regnabit rex* (Jere 23:5). P. 7.
12. T01. *Hora est iam nos de somno surgere* (Rom 13:11). P. 8.
13. T01 (Botulph). *Ecce rex tuus venit* (Matt 21:5). Pp. 8–10.
14. T01 ("Post nonam"). *Induamur arma lucis* (Rom 13:11). Pp. 10–12.
15. T01/6 (procession). *Levate in caelum oculos et videte* (Isa 51:6). P. 12.
16. T02. *Adpropinquat redemptio vestra* (Luke 21:28). P. 13.
17. T02 ("Post nonam"). *Venturus est* (Matt 3:11). Pp. 13–14.
18. S05. *Ego mater pulchrae dilectionis* (Sir 24:24). Pp. 14–15.
19. S05 ("Post nonam"). *Ego quasi vitis fructificavi* (Sir 24:23). Pp. 15–17.
20. T03. *Pauperes evangelizantur* (Matt 11:5). P. 17.
21. T03 ("Post nonam"). *Quaeritur quis fidelis inveniatur* (1 Cor 4:2). Pp. 18–19. Also Bodley 857-3 and P1-9.
22. T04. *Dirigite viam Domini* (John 1:23). Pp. 19–20.
23. T12. *Manifestavit gloriam suam* (John 2:10). Pp. 20–19bis.
24. S20. *Conversus est ad Dominum* (Acts 11:21). P. 19bis.
25. T13. *Domine, salva nos, perimus* (Matt 8:25). P. 19bis.
26. S21. Notetaker was out of town. P. 19bis.
27. T14. *Si Dominus donavit vobis, ita et vos* (Col 3:13). P. 20bis.
28. T15. *Nonne bonum semen seminasti in agro tuo?* (Matt 13:27). P. 21.
29. T15 ("Collacio ad clerum in ecclesia Beate Marie"). *Vocati estis* (Col 3:15). P. 22.
30. T16. *Acceperunt singulos denarios* (Matt 20:9). Pp. 22–23.

31. T16 ("Post nonam"). *Currite ut comprehendatis* (1 Cor 9:24). Pp. 23–25.
32. T17. *Vobis datum est nosse mysterium regni Dei* (Luke 8:10). Pp. 25–26.
33. T17 ("Post nonam"). *Sufficit tibi gratia* (2 Cor 12:9). Pp. 26–27.
34. S24f. *Radices superborum arefecit et plantavit humiles* (Sir 10:18). P. 28.
35. T18. *Iesu, miserere mei* (Luke 18:38). Pp. 28–29.
36. T18 ("in ecclesia Beate Virginis"). *Caecus sedebat secus viam mendicando* (Luke 18:35). Pp. 29–30.
37. T18 ("Post nonam"). *Nunc videmus per speculum in aenigmate* (1 Cor 13:12). Pp. 30–31.
38. S24e. *Transivi ad contemplandam sapientiam* (Sir 2:12). P. 31.
39. T19. *Ecce nunc dies salutis* (2 Cor 6:2). P. 32.
40. T19 ("Post nonam"). *Illi soli servies* (Matt 4:10). Pp. 32–33.
41. T20. *Ambulatis* (1 Thess 4:1). Pp. 34–35.
42. S28. *Virtus Altissimi in te* (Luke 1:35). P. 35.
43. S28 ("Post nonam"). *Invenisti gratiam apud Deum* (Luke 1:30). Pp. 35–37.
44. T21. *Quomodo stabit regnum* (Luke 11:18). Pp. 37–38.
45. T22. *Hierusalem servit cum filiis* (Gal 4:25). Pp. 38–39. Chancellor.
46. T22 ("Post nonam"). *Sequebatur eum multitudo magna* (John 6:2). Pp. 39–40.
47. C20 (procession). *Aperuit oculos caeci nati* (John 9:32). P. 41.
48. T23. *Veritatem dico* (John 8:45). Pp. 41–42.
49. T23 ("Post nonam"). *Quare non creditis?* (John 8:46). Pp. 42–44.
50. T24. *Hosanna* (John 12:13). Pp. 44–45.
51. T25. *Hodie rex est, cras morietur* (Sir 10:12). P. 45.
52. T26. *Occiditur in sanctuario sacerdos et propheta* (Lam 2:20). Pp. 45–47.
53. T29. *Adfer manum tuam* (John 20:27). P. 47.
54. T26 ("alibi"). *Oblatus est quia voluit* (Isa 53:7). P. 47. "Doctor" (?).
55. T30 (after Resumption). *Ego sum pastor bonus* (John 10:11). Pp. 48–49.
56. T30 ("Post nonam"). *Sequamini vestigia eius* (1 Pet 2:21). Pp. 49–50.
57. T31. *Conversationem vestram inter gentes habentes bonam* (1 Peter 2:12). P. 50.
58. T31 ("Post nonam"). Sermon in English, not recorded. P. 50.
59. T32. *Veritatem dico vobis* (John 16:7). P. 51.
60. T32 ("Post nonam"). *Omne datum optimum et omne donum perfectum descendens est a patre luminum* (James 1:17). Pp. 51–52.
61. C11. *Sanctificavi domum istam quam aedificavi* (1 Kings 9:3). Pp. 53–54.
62. C20 (procession). *Orate* (Matt 26:41?). Pp. 54–55.
63. T33. *Estote factores verbi* (James 1:22). Pp. 55–56.
64. T34/2. *Videte, vigilate, et orate* (Mark 13:33). Pp. 56–58.

65. T34/3. No sermon, on account of rain. P. 58.

66. T35. *Adsumptus est in caelum et sedet a dextris Dei* (Mark 16:19). Pp. 58–59.

67. T36. *Quis ascendet in montem Domini?* (Ps 23:3). Pp. 59–61.

68. C21 (Funeral of the master of King's Hall). *Amicus noster dormit* (John 11:11). Pp. 61–63.

69. T39. *Emitte spiritum tuum et creabuntur, et renovabis faciem terrae* (Ps 103:30). P. 63.

70. T41/5. *Qui manducat hunc panem, vivet* (John 6:59). Pp. 64–65.

71. T42. *Recordare quia recepisti bona* (Luke 16:25). P. 65.

72. C11. *Fecerunt dedicationem domus Domini in gaudio* (1 Esdr 6:16). Pp. 66–67. Same preacher as of C-61.

73. T43. *Homo quidam fecit cenam magnam* (Luke 14:16). P. 67.

74. C11 / S26?. *In domo tuo oportet me manere* (Luke 19:5). Pp. 68–69. Same preacher as, apparently, of C-72.

75. C11. *Fecerunt dedicationem* (1 Esd 6:16). Pp. 69–70. Same preacher as before.

76. C20 (procession for victory in France). *Laudate, pueri, Dominum* (Ps 112:1). Pp. 70–71.

77. C21. *Mementote quia mors non tardabit* (Sir 14:12). P. 72.

78. T58 (after Resumption). *Vocati estis cum omni humilitate* (Eph 4:1–2). P. 72.

79. S43b. *Virgo cogitat quae Dei sunt* (1 Cor 7:34). Pp. 72–73.

80. T59. *Diliges Dominum Deum tuum* (Matt 22:37). 73–74.

81. T60. *Operemini manibus vestris* (1 Thess 4:11). P. 74.

82. T61. *Venite ad nuptias* (Matt 22:4). P. 74.

83. T62. No sermon recorded. P. 74.

84. T63. *Caritas abundet in scientia* (Phil 1:9). P. 74.

85. T66. *Accepit panem, et cum gratia egisset, distribuit* (John 6:11). P. 75.

86. S01. *Unus ex duobus erat Andreas* (John 1:40). P. 75.

87. T01/6 / C20 (procession). *Nisi abundaverit iustitia vestra plus quam*, etc. (Matt 5:20). P. 75.

88. T01 (Botulph). *Hora est nos de somno surgere* (Rom 13:11). Pp. 75–76.

89. T01. *Ambulate* (Gal 5:15; Eph 5:2,8; Col 2:6; 4:5; etc.). Pp. 76–77.

90. T01 ("Post nonam"). *Ambulemus honeste* (Rom 13:13). P. 77.

91. S05. *Concepit filium* (Luke 1:36). Pp. 77–78.

92. S05 ("Post nonam"). *In me omnis spes vitae* (Sir 24:25). Pp. 78–79.

93. T03 [!] ("Post nonam"). *Erunt signa in sole et luna* (Luke 21:25). Pp. 79–80.

94. T03. *Qui iudicat me, Dominus est* (1 Cor 4:4). Pp. 80–82.

95. T05. *Fili, quid fecisti?* (Luke 2:48). P. 82.

96. T13? (Sunday after Resumption). *Filii regni eicientur in tenebras* (Matt 8:12). P. 82.

97. S19. *Quasi ignis effulgens et thus redolens in igne* (Sir 50:9). P. 83.

98. S20. *Vas electionis est iste* (Acts 9:15). P. 83.

99. T13. *Domine, si vis, potes me mundare* (Matt 8:2). Pp. 83–84.

100. S21. *Erunt offerentes sacrificia in iustitia* (Mal 3:3). P. 84.

101. S21 ("Post nonam"). *Placebit Deo sacrificium* (Mal 3:4). Pp. 84–86.

102. T16. *Voca operarios et redde illis* (Matt 20:8). Pp. 86–87.

103. T16 ("Post nonam"). *Ite in vineam* (Matt 20:4). Pp. 88–89.

104. T17. *Vobis datum est nosse mysterium regni* (Luke 8:10). Pp. 89–90.

105. T17 ("Post nonam"). *Veritatem dicam* (2 Cor 12:6). Pp. 90–92.

106. T18. *Maior horum est caritas* (1 Cor 13:13). P. 92.

107. T18 ("Post nonam"). *Caecus qui sedebat per viam clamabat: Miserere mei, Iesu, filii David* (Luke 18:35–38). Pp. 92–93.

108. T19. *Ecce nunc tempus* (2 Cor 6:2). Pp. 93–94.

109. T19 ("Post nonam"). *Illi soli servies* (Matt 4:10). Pp. 95–96.

110. S24f. "De Augustino". *Fratres, translati sumus* (1 John 3:14). P. 96.

111. T20. *Domine, adiuva me* (Matt 15:25). Pp. 97–98.

112. T20 ("Post nonam"). *Domine, miserere mei* (Matt 15:22). P. 98.

113. S24e. *Inspice et fac secundum exemplar quod tibi in monte monstratum est* (Exod 25:40). P. 99.

114. T21. *Fortis armatus custodit atrium* (Luke 11:21). Pp. 99–100.

115. T21 ("Post nonam"). *Fortis armatus custodit atrium* (Luke 11:21). Pp. 100–101.

116. T22. *Facite homines discumbere* (John 6:10). P. 101.

117. T22 ("Post nonam"). *Quomodo tunc, ita et nunc* (Gal 4:29). Pp. 102–103.

118. C20 (procession). *Magister adest et vocat te* (John 11:28). Pp. 103–104.

119. T23 / S28 ("hora 8"). *Invenisti gratiam* (Luke 1:30). P. 104.

120. T23 / S28. *In te virtus Altissimi* (Luke 1:35). Pp. 104–105.

121. T23 / S28 ("Post nonam"). *Quare non crediditis mihi* (John 8:46). Pp. 105–107.

122. T24. *Respice et vide fera pessima, etc.* (Gen 37:20?). P. 107.

123. T29. *Ostendit manus* (John 20:20). Pp. 107–109.

124. T30. No sermon given. P. 109.

125. S30. *Marcus similis est leoni* (? cf. Rev 4:7). Pp. 109–110.

126. T31 (after Resumption). *Modicum et videbitis me* (John 16:16). Pp. 110–111.

127. T31 ("Post nonam"). *Karissimi, obsecro vos tamquam advenas et peregrinos, etc.* (1 Pet 2:11). Pp. 111–113. "Doctor."

128. T32. *Omne donum perfectum descendens est a patre luminum* (James 1:17). P. 114.

129. T32 ("Post nonam"). No sermon recorded. P. 114.

130. T32/6 / C20 (procession). *Petite ut gaudium vestrum sit plenum* (John 16:24). P. 114.

131. T33. *Quicquid petieritis Patrem in nomine meo, dabitis vobis* (John 16:23). Pp. 115–116.

132. T33. *Comparabitur viro consideranti vultum nativitatis in speculo* (James 1:23). P. 116.

133. T33 ("Post nonam"). *Usque modo non petistis quicquid in nomine meo, petite et accipietis* (John 16:24). Pp. 116–117.

134. T34/2. *Rogate quae ad pacem sunt Hierusalem* (Ps 121:6). Pp. 118–120.

135. T34/3. *Petite et accipietis* (John 16:24). Pp. 120–121.

136. T35. *Ascendit ut adimpleret omnia* (Eph 4:10). Pp. 121–122.

137. T36. *Reversus est Ionathas in Hierusalem* (1 Macc 10:67). Pp. 122–126.

138. T37. *Estote prudentes et vigilate* (1 Pet 4:7). P. 126.

139. T39/4 ("in ecclesia Beate Virginis"). *Si Spiritum Sanctum accepistis* (Acts 19:2). Pp. 127–128.

140. T40. *Crede in Dominum Iesum et salvus eris* (Acts 16:31). Pp. 128–130.

141. C14. *Pasce oves meas* (John 21:17). P. 131.

142. T41/5. *Accipite et manducate, hoc est corpus meum* (Matt 26:26). Pp. 131–133.

143. T42. *In hoc apparuit caritas* (1 John 4:9). P. 133.

144. T43. *Homo quidam fecit cenam magnam* (Luke 14:16). Pp. 134–135.

145. T44. *Vocavit nos Deus in aeternam gloriam* (1 Pet 5:10). Pp. 135–136.

146. S46. *Estote misericordes* (Luke 6:36). Pp. 136–137.

147. T45 (last Sunday in academic year). *Pater vester misericors est* (Luke 6:36). P. 137.

148. T46 ("et in festo reliquiarum apud Bery"). *Beati misericordes* (Matt 5:7). Pp. 137–138.

149. C11. *Vere Dominus est in loco isto* (Gen 28:16). Pp. 138–140.

150. C21. *Memor esto iudicii mei* (Sir 38:23). Pp. 140–142.

151. T50 (St. Paul's Cross, London). *Quantum debes Domino tuo?* (Luke 16:5). P. 142.

152. C21. *Cuius est imago haec?* (Matt 22:20). Pp. 142–144. "Doctor."

153. T60 (after Resumption). *Renovamini et induite novum hominem in iustitia* (Eph 4:23–24). P. 144.

154. T61. *Simile est regnum caelorum homini qui fecit nuptias filio suo* (Matt 22:2). P. 144.

155. T62. *Descende priusquam moriatur filius meus* (John 4:49). P. 145. Prior of Colchester.

156. S79. *Iesus ascendit in montem* (Matt 5:1). P. 146.

CA – Cambridge, Gonville and Caius College, MS 334/727 (Waldeby?)

Besides the three major treatises by John Waldeby, as well as a copy of Wimbledon's sermon in Latin, the manuscript contains two runs of sermons.

CA/1

1. ?. *Quomodo stabit regnum* (Luke 11:18). Karissimi, sicut scitis, qui regnum possidet temporale, totis certat uiribus . . . Ff. 1–2.

2. ?. *Christus dilexit nos* (2 Thess 2:16). Karissimi, si quis pauper esset infirmus et peteret aquam fontis . . . Ff. 2–3.

3. ?. *Paenitentiam agite* (Matt 4:17). Karissimi, dicit Augustinus libro suo *De uera et falsa penitencia*, tercio capitulo: fides fundamenum est penitencie . . . Ff. 3r–5v.

4. ?. *Diliges proximum tuum* (Matt 22:39). Karissimi, legitur in naturis rerum quod est quedam arbor in India . . . Ff. 5v–7v.

5. T20*. *Domine, adiuva me* (Matt 15:25). Carissimi, necessitas, miseria, et defectus virtutum compellunt hominem ut ad auxilium aliorum confugiat . . . Ff. 7v–8.

CA/2

1. ?. *Quae utilitas in sanguine meo* (Ps 29:10). Karissimi, sicut nouerunt homines scole qui fuerunt Oxon' uel Cantebryg', quando magister . . . Ff. 172va–176rb. Michael of Hungary. Also Q-50.

2. ?. *Paenitet me fecisse hominem* (Gen 6:7). Karissimi, thema istud potest dici duobus modis . . . Ff. 176va–177ra, perhaps inc.

3. ?. *Iesus* (Matt 10:5). Tria me mouent accipere hoc thema, scilicet dede, nede, and spede . . . Ff. 177ra–179va. Also H-1 and Z-3.

4. ?. *Si revertamini et quiescatis, salvi eritis* (Isa 30:15). Karissimi, in euangelio Luce 2 tres Magi . . . Ff. 179va–181ra.

5. ?. *Surge qui dormis* (Eph 5:14). Karissimi, in tribus periculis solent homines euigilare . . . Ff. 181ra–182va. Also H-22 and B/2-59.

6. ?. *Non regnet peccatum in vestro mortali corpore* (Rom 6:12). Karissimi, quilibet subditus minor est domino . . . Ff. 182va–183rb.

7. ?. *Ambulate in dilectione* (Eph 5:2). Karissimi, Augustinus in epistula Ad Macedonium . . . Ff. 183rb–185vb. Also S-17.

8. ?. *Nolite conformari huic saeculo* (Rom 12:2). Karissimi, quia Iohannes 1 canonica sua dicit Omne quod est in mundo . . . Ff. 185vb–187va. Perhaps also W-76.

9. ?. *Videte* (Luke 12:15). Gregorius 1 *Morum* capitulo 28 dicit quod omnia opera nostra . . . Ff. 187va–188vb. Holcot, sermon 114.

10. ?. *Melior est mors quam amara vita* (Sir 30:17). Karissimi, sanctus Iob qui transiit personaliter passum tam uite quam mortis . . . Ff. 188vb–189vb.

11. ?. *Intravit Iesus in quoddam castellum* (Luke 10:38). Pro materia sermonis triplex est castellum . . . Ff. 189vb–193ra. Also H-15.

12. ?. *In Hierusalem potestas mea* (Sir 24:15). Hec uerba conuenienter sunt Beate Uirginis . . . Ff. 190va–192ra.

13. ?. *Veni sponsa mea* (Cant 4:8). Karissimi, nouistis quod quandocumque est grandis et magna dissencio . . . Ff. 192ra–193rb.

14. ?. *Paenitet me fecisse hominem* (Gen 6:7). Anglice: Mercy and truthe togedere han met . . . Tunc Pater dixit Filio: Fili mi, contra te ista forisfactura . . . Ff. 193rb–195rb.

15. ?. *Dies mali sunt* (Eph 5:16). Deus creator omnium, qui hominem plasmauerat . . . Ff. 195rb–198ra.

CO – Oxford, Magdalen College, MS 96

In most cases, the thema appears only at the beginning of the sermon's main part, which is usually set off by a space and enlarged capital. The following list reflects this peculiarity, indicating also the folio on which the main part begins.

1. T39. *Non permanebit spiritus meus in homine in aeternum quia caro est* (Gen 6:3). Quia sumus pondere peccatorum pregrauati . . . [2va:] Vnde Beda libro 3 et primo super Actus . . .-. . . persecucionem pacientibus promissum secure peruenient. Quod. . . . Ff. 1ra–12rb.

2. T39/2. Karissimi, cum Christus misit discipulos suos ad predicandum insufflauit et dixit, Accipite . . . [14va:] *Omnis qui male agit odit lucem* (John 3:20). Male agere cum lucis odio est actualiter peccare . . .-. . . renascimur ad beatitudinem celesterm. Quam . . . Ff. 12rb–24va.

3. T39/3. Luce 24, Vos autem sedete donec . . . [25vb:] *Ego sum ostium; per me si quis intraverit salvabitur* (John 10:9). Notandum quod hostium materialiter

dicitur . . .-. . . de aliquibus secretis diuinorum. Hec Thomas. Quo lumine nos illustret. . . . Ff. 24va–35vb.

4. T39/4. Item in Deuteronomio legitur quod est animal quod comedere debetis . . . [38va:] *Dabo prodigia in caelo sursum et signa in terra deorsum* (Acts 2:19). Vnde Holcot sermone *Erunt signa in celo*, etc., ostendit que sunt signa saluandorum . . .-. . . ab omni miseria segregati et postremo in paradiso collocati. Quod annuat pater misericordiarum. Amen. Ff. 35vb–52va.

5. T40. Est prouerbium penes omnes in anglicis . . . [55va:] *Comedite pinguia et bibite mulsum, quia dies Domini est* (Neh 8:10). Hec sunt uerba Neemie sacerdotis magni . . .-. . . primo celebrant festum, deinde vigilam, idest, hic prosperant et post cruciantur. Ff. 52va–67ra.

6. T41/5. Omnes naturales tractantes de lege nature . . . [68vb:] *Decima die mensis tollat vnusquisque agnum* (Exod 12:3; the thema is given only in the body of the sermon, whose main part begins:) Scriptum est: Quemadmodum desiderat ceruus ad fontes aquarum, ita desiderat anima mea ad te, Deus. Quoniam igitur cerui in solitudine serpentes pluras gluciunt . . .-. . . Sic sumens corpus Christi debet conuerti a vicio in virtutem, ut finaliter sic conuersus possit transferri seu conuerti a viatore ad comprehensorem, vbi quantum meruit, tantum fruetur Deo trino et vno. Quo frui . . . Ff. 67ra–86rb.

7. T42. Beda super Prouerbia capitulo audiens sapiens sapiencior erit . . . [87va:] *Homo quidam*, etc. [erat dives?] (Luke 16:19?). Homo quidam, idest instabilis. Secundum Plinium est bestia que vocatur hiena . . .-. . . intelligite ergo qui obliuiscimini Deum, ut peruenire poteritis ad finem beatum. Amen. Ff. 86rb–110vb.

8. T43. Fit mencio in epistula presentis dominice de mundo humano generi inimico cum dicitur Nolite mirari . . . [113ra:] *Homo quidam fecit cenam magnam* . . . (Luke 14:16–24). Sic vero cum Deus a principio ordinauit quandam cenam . . .-. . . passiones huius temporis ad futuram gloriam, que reuelabitur in nobis, Romanorum 8. Ad quam gloriam. . . . Ff. 110vb–132rb.

9. T44. Quia in hodierno sacro euangelio specialis fit mencio de peccatore penitente cum dicitur Gaudium est angelis . . . [135rb:] *Humiliamini* etc. [*sub potenti manu Dei*] (1 Pet 5:6). In iure ciuili capitulo De rei vendicione libro 2, cuius est inferius . . .-. . . et presbiter episcopi officium ipsi gloriam in secula. Ad quam. . . . Ff. 132rb–154va.

10. S44. Iohannes antequam legatur baptizasse uel predicasse . . . [157rb:] *Elisabeth impletum est tempus pariendi* (Luke 1:57). Hugo de Vienna sermone

Johannis baptiste: Est autem multiplex partus . . .-. . . ideo nolite diligere mundum neque ea que in mundo sunt. Hec Holcot sermone 91. Sed cum Johanne mundum contempnere Deoque frui beato fine. Amen. Ff. 154va–170ra.

11. S46. Legitur Mathei 14 quod Petrus nauigans in mari . . . [172rb:] [*Venit autem Iesus in partes Caesaraei Philippi* (Matt 16:13 ff., inferred from body of the sermon)]. Venit Iesus tanquam saluator vbique lumen doctrine spargens . . .-. . . dum viuerent seducebant. A quorum seduccionibus liberet nos Deus, qui in suis sanctis extat gloriosus. Amen. Ff. 170ra–190ra.

12. S46. Uyllelmus in *Racionali diuinorum*: Propter tres causas ymago Pauli stat in sigillo pape . . . [193rb:] *Vas electionis mihi est iste* (Acts 9:15). Primo sic: Vas eleccionis, quia electus fuit a Deo . . .-. . . Hec Holcot. A quibus, scilicet pena et culpa, eruat nos Deus manu sua dextera. Amen. Ff. 190ra–204vb.

13. T45. Moris est in regionibus vbi guerra est quod custos . . . [207rb:] *Estote misericordes,* etc. (Luke 6:36). Magna est virtus misericordie . . .-. . . iuste meretur penam perpetuam per perpetuitatem sue praue voluntatis. Quam euitare concedat. . . . Ff. 204vb–222vb.

14. S46b. Secundum nomen tuum, o Thoma sanctissime . . . [225rb:] *Dabis eum in benedictionibus in saeculum saeculi* (Ps 20:7). Numeri 6: Hec erat benediccio super Nazareos et eciam super filios Israel . . .-. . . et bonis ascribamur in via, ut cum celestibus conscripti simus in patria. Quod. . . . Ff. 222vb–234va.

15. T45, "Sermo in festo reliquiarum." *Reliquiae cogitationis diem festum agent tibi* (Ps 75:11). Ad diem festum in veteri testamento . . . [236ra:] *Reliquiae cogitationes diem festum,* etc. Nota hic quod apud Iudeos erant septem festa . . .-. . . Hec Holcot. Quam misericordiam ipse Pater misericordiarum et Deus tocius consolacionis nobis in extremo vite annuat et ad regnum eternum perducat. Amen. Ff. 234va–248ra.

16. T46. Romanos 10: Quomodo ergo inuocabimus eum etc. Multa expediunt predicatori seu doctori catholice veritatis . . . [249vb:] *Cum turbae irruerunt,* etc. (Luke 5:1). Ecce impetus deuocionis turbarum . . .-. . . diues et pauper in vnum dico Deum et trinum. Cui laus et gloria per seculorum secula. Amen. Ff. 248ra–262va.

17. T47. Multi propter timorem hominum parcunt dicere . . . [264ra:] *Amen, amen, dico vobis* (Matt 5:20). In quo erudimur euitare iuramenta ociosa . . .-. . . ut hic temporalibus in via et post spiritualibus fruantur bonis in patria. Quibus perfruicionibus nobis annuat qui in trinitate viuit et regnat. Amen. Ff. 262va–279va.

18. T48. Cum fit mencio in euangelio de conuiuio per Christum celebrato . . . [281va:] *Cum turba* etc. [*multa esset*] (Mark 8:1). Videns Christus multitudinem hominum . . . Sic cum Christus in deserto huius mundi multos videat . . .-. . . . pascite verbo, pascite exemplo, ut de pascuis solicitudinis trahat nos ad pascua sacietatis Iesus Christus etc. Ff. 279va–292va.

19. S49. *Maria sedebat secus pedes Domini et audiebat verbum illius* (Luke 10:39). In quo euangelio notatur quod Iesus et Maria erant in domo Simonis . . . [294rb:] *Maria sedebat,* etc. Pro sermonis dilacione est annotandum quod de pluribus deuotis mulieribus legimus nomine Maria . . .-. . . nec in cor hominis ascendit, quam consolacionem preparauit Deus diligentibus se. Amen. Ff. 292va–308rb.

20. S50. Helias repperit Helizeum arantem inter duodecim iuga boum . . . Istud potest allegari ad apostolos . . . [309va] *Accessit ad eum* (Mattt 20:20), auiditate feminea cupiens pro se et filiis presencia immemor futurorum . . .-. . . dum tempus ergo habemus, operemur bonum usque in finem per felicem perseueranciam, ut meritis sancti Iacobi percipiamus immarcessibilem eterne glorie coronam. Amen. Ff. 308rb–317rb.

D – Toulouse, Bibliothèque Municipale, MS 342

1. T02. *Quaecumque scripta sunt, ad nostram doctrinam scripta sunt* (Rom 15:4). Moyses volens de aliquo dubio certus esse . . .-. . . in tempore autem illo saluabitur omnis populus qui inuentus fuit scriptus in libro vite, Danielis 12. Ad quam vitam. Ff. 1–3v.

2. T12*. *Exhibeatis corpora vestra hostiam viventem* (Rom 12:1). Reuerendi et venerabiles domini, vt et scripture testimonio et experienciarum patrocinio . . .-. . . multiplicamur vt absque. Ff. 3v–5, inc.

3. T21/4*. *Non habebis deos alienos* (Exo 20:3). Vt docet Augustinus libro 10 *De ciuitate Dei,* et eciam Tullius libro 2 *De natura deorum,* Romani . . .-. . . in dileccione Dei seruate expectantes.m. d. ix. in.vi. etc., Johannis primo. Ad quam. . . . Ff. 5v–8.

4. T18*. *Iesu fili David, miserere mei* (Luke 18:38). Reuerendi domini, cecus iste de quo fit mencio isto die . . .-. . . consolatur nos in omni tribulacione nostra. Quam consolacionem etc. Ff. 8–9v.

5. S59. *Super caelos gloria eius* (Ps 112:4). Karissimi, iam sciatis quod tronum deifice maiestatis intemerata virgo con[s]cendit . . .-. . . et deliciis affluatis ab omnimoda gloria eius. Ad quam gloriam . . . Ff. 10–12v.

6. S79. *In plenitudine sanctorum detentio mea* (Sir 24:16). Vniuersaliter vnumquodque in adepto termino detencione finali sistitur et tenetur . . .- . . . honorabunt sanctos et gloria est omnibus sanctis. Ad quam gloriam . . . Ff. 12v–14v.

7. S86. *Mulier sancta es* (Judith 8:29). Reuerendi patres mei, quia Iob 5 capitulo consulitur quod quisquis in necessitatibus constitutus . . .-. . . pro nobis orando quia mulier sancta es. Ff. 14v–17.

8. S31*. *Fortitudo et decor indumentum eius* (Prov 31:25). Sciendum Ysidorus *Ethimologiarum* 20 capitulo dicit sic: Est quoddam sacerdotale vestimentum . . .-. . . vt vitam eternam cum eo consequi mereamur. Quam vitam . . . Ff. 17–19v.

9. T17*. *Si gloriari oportet* (2 Cor 12:1). Reuerendi domini et patres mei, dum prefigitur modus enti opportet et affigitur actus menti . . .-. . . sic et ambuletis vt habundetis magis, 1 Ad Thessalonicenses 4. Quod vobis concedat omnis bonitatis permanens plenitudo, in qua oportet finaliter gloriari, Christus Iesus filius Marie. Amen. Ff. 19v–21v. "Frater Guillelmus de Bolenkycr'."

10. T21*. *Fructus lucis est in omni bonitate* (Eph 5:9). Reuerendi domini et patres, cum singula queque specie, modo et ordine vt suis regulis contenta sint . . .-. . . ad letandum in leticia gentis tue, Psalmo 105. Ad quam lucem. . . . Ff. 21v–24. "Fr. Willelmus de Bulky'."

11. T22*. *Quae sursum est Hierusalem libera est* (Gal 4:26). Reuerendi domini et patres, cum ipsum bonum testantibus doctoribus et philosophis triplici modo mentem alliciat . . .-. . . illa attingendo que sursum est Ierusalem et libera est. Quod. . . . Ff. 24v–26. "Frater Guillelmus de Bolenc'."

12. T23*. *Est qui quaerat et iudicet* (John 8:50). Reuerendi domini et patres, cui competat actus ierarchicus, in *De ecclesiastica ierarchia* capitulis 2 et 5 a beato Dionisio patenter edocetur . . .-. . . pertingere valeatis vbi videbimus sicuti est, 1 Iohannis 3. Quod. . . . Ff. 26–28v. "Fr. Guillelmus de Bolen'."

13. T63*. *Caritas vestra magis abundet* (Phil 1:9). Reuerendi domini et patres, cum verbum propositum vim totam legis inplicet . . .-. . . quod in vita presenti vobis mereatur caritas nostra vt cum Iesu nostro in statu beatifico magis habundet. Qui. . . . Ff. 28v–31. "Fratris Guillelmi de Bay'lewyk."

14. T26*. *Respice in faciem Christi tui* (Ps 83:10). In Glossa 2 Machabeorum 3 dicitur quod facies est lingua cordis . . .-. . . et tunc dicent boni illud Psalmi: Ostende faciem tuam et salui erimus. Amen. Ff. 31–32v.

15. T06*. *Factum est verbum Domini super Iohannem* (Luke 3:2). Factum Domini pensantes verbum superuenerantes quod adhuc est in conclaue . . .- . . . et ita habebimus illius summe Trinitatis cognicionem. Quam. . . . Ff. 32v–34v.

16. ?. *Gratia vobis et pax* (?). Prelati maiores Ecclesie, puta archiepiscopi et episcopi, in epistolis suis hoc modo salutant . . .-. . . quod testatur Apostolus, vbi supra, cum dicit: Gracia Dei sum id quod sum. Ff. 34v–35. Jordan.

17. S49*. *De fructu manuum suarum laudent eam* (Prov 31:31). In officio matutinali huius festi Ecclesia sic decantat: Laudemus opus Dei in Maria genitrice sed virgine . . .-. . . et cum gloria sucepisti [!] me, gloria videlicet eterna. Quam gloriam . . . Ff. 35–38. Jordan.

18. T19*. *Illi soli servies* (Mat 4:10, Luke 4:9). Scribuntur hec verba originatiue a Moyse legislatore Deuteronomio 6. Ponuntur transsumptive a Christo . . .- . . . et lucem habitat inaccessibilem. Cuius lucis participes. . . . Ff. 38–40v. Jordan.

19. S03*. *Invenit gratiam* (Sir 44:27). In epistula statim lecta verumptamen non habentur hec uerba Ecclesiastici 44 capitulo vnde epistula est accepta, sed scribuntur Gen 6 et sepe alibi in scriptura. Hanc autem seriem vt in epistula Inuenit graciam coram Domino nusquam repperi in scriptura. Tamen . . .-. . . de quo Ad Romanos 6, Gracia est vita eterna. Ad quam . . . Ff. 40v–43v. Jordan.

20. T28*. *Vere tu es deus absconditus* (Isa 95). Hec verba huic diei sacratissime dupplici ratione conuenire videntur. Sollempnisat Ecclesia hodie de Christi resurrectione . . .-. . . notas facere diuicias glorie sacramentis huius. Quam gloriam . . . Ff. 43v–46. Jordan. Also E-31.

21. S28* or S65*. *Sapientia aedificavit sibi domum* (Prov 9:1). Videmus quod rex uel alius magnus princeps . . .-. . . in domo tua, Domine, in secula seculorum laudabunt te. Quod. . . . Ff. 46–48. Jordan.

22. S24e*. *Sedet in cathedra sapientissimus* (2 Sam 23:8). Ex more antiquo necnon et moderno percipimus tria fore hominum genera qui [!] pre ceteris dignius cathedrales sedes merentur . . .-. . . cathedra iam regalis quam reuerenter [?] promeruit in gloria consummata. Ad quam . . . Ff. 48–50v. Jordan.

23. T20*. *Miserere* (Ps 50:3 "et quasi in locis scripture sacre innumeris"). Augustinus 18 *De ciuitate Dei* capitulo 8 tangit quomodo iuxta fabula figmenta Archas . . .-. . . quia tu mulier sancta es, cuius sanctitatis participes efficere nos dignetur . . . Ff. 50v–52.

24. S10. *Dabo tibi coronam vitae* (Rev 2:10). Dicit Ysidorus libro 18 *Ethimologiarum* capitulo 2 quod duces Romanorum . . .-. . . inmarcessibilem eterne glorie coronam et coronam vite eterne. Quam percipere . . . Ff. 52–55.

25. ?. *Si vis ad vitam ingredi, serva mandata* (Mat 19:17). Quicumque debet aliquam ciuitatem multum remotam intrare . . .-. . . primo sic quod nullus debet periurare, idest scienter falsum dicere. F. 55r–v, inc; a complete version as D-89.

26. T64*. *Expectamus Dominum qui reformabit* (Phil 3:20–21). Patet ex fidelissima policitacione que neminem defraudabit . . .-. . . fient plenius per consumantem gloriam. Quam . . . Ff. 56–57v. Henricus.

27. T63*. *Caritas vestra magis ac magis abundet* (Phil 1:9). Sacra scriptura in laudem caritatis sepius se diffundens ipsam inter cetera quatuor comparat misticeque describit . . .-. . . seruare vnitatem spiritus in vinculo pacis. Quam vnitatem . . . Ff. 65–67v. "Frater Iohannes Languebeyrky."

28. T15a*. *Pax Christi exultet in cordibus vestris* (Col 3:15). Create nature inclinacione apercius ostendente et sacre scripture assercione perfeccius approbante . . .-. . . que exsuperat omnem sensum custodiat corda vestra et intelligencias vestras in Christo Iesu Domino nostro. Amen. Ff. 67v–70v. "Iohannes angloys."

29. T33*. *Gaudium vestrum sit plenum* (John 16:24). Seneca epistula <6> ad Lucilium querit que est causa quare non potest nos replere vlla felicitas temporalis . . .-. . . locutus sum vobis ut gaudium vestrum plenum sit. Quod . . . Stant hart, laz dich melken. Ff. 70v–73. "Johannes langolis."

30. T29*. *Venit per aquam et sanguinem* (1 John 5:6). Sicut scribitur in *Collacionibus patrum*, collacione 1, agricola nunc torridos solis radios, nunc pruinas et glacies . . .-. . . mansionem apud eum faciemus. Cuius perpetuam mansionem . . . Ff. 73v–76v. "Johannes langeley."

31. T62*. *Induite vos armaturam Dei* (Eph 6:11). Karissimi, sicut ex Genesis testimonio comprobatur, parens primus honore dominii excellentis prelatus . . .-. . . percipere valeamus coronam glorie per triumphum. Quod . . . Ff. 76v–79v. "Johannes langeloy."

32. T02. *Scitote quia prope est regnum Dei* (Luke 21:31). Karissimi, sicut apostolica predicacio nos informat, vnusquisque propriam mercedem accipiet . . .-. . . paratum vobis regnum ab origine mundi. Quod . . . Ff. 79v–82v. "Johannes Langel'."

33. T59*. *Sede a dextris meis* (Matt 22:44). Reuerendi mei, quamquam hec uerba thematis sint verba Dei Patris ad Filium . . .-. . . quem confirmasti tibi in

vinculo caritatis. Cuius dextre nos participes etc. Ff. 82v–86. "Johannes Langel'."

34. T18*. *Caecus clamabat, Miserere* (Luke 18:39). Reuerendi mei, in hoc ceco lucis solacio destituto sed vocis auxilio exaudito . . .-. . . qui coronat te misericordia et miseracionibus. Cuius miseracionibus coronari in celestibus nos . . . Ff. 86–89. "Johannes langeley."

35. T19*. *Nunc dies salutis* (2 Cor 6:2). Humane condicionis infirmitas perdelata spe consolacionis impliciter est priuata . . .-. . . salus et virtus et regnum Dei nostri. Ad quod regnum . . . Ff. 89–93.

36. T65*. *Veni, impone manum* (Matt 9:18). Sacra scriptura sinceriter intellecta nobis proponit ternario numero manum Dei . . .-. . . Oremus ergo ad honorem trium manuum predictarum cum Psalmista: Opera manuum nostrarum dirige. Quod . . . Ff. 93–95v.

37. T31*. *Sic est voluntas Dei* (1 Pet 2:15). Beatus Augustinus voluntatem diuinam regulam infallibilem manifestans . . .-. . . ipse intrabit in regnum celorum. Quod . . . Ff. 95v–98v.

38. T36*. *Ascendebat e terra* (Gen 2:6). Homo in profunda valle constitutus si debeat montem excelsum ascendere . . .-. . . ut sic tandem ad eum ascendamus, quia tunc dicet nobis istud Luce 14, Amice, ascende superius. Tunc erit tibi gloria. Ad quam . . . Ff. 98v–103. Jordan.

39. T42*. *Recordare* (Luke 16:25). Remigius in commento super Marcianum *De nupciis* ita dicit: Omnia que uel auditu uel visu percipimus . . .-. . . et misertus est hereditatis sue. Cuius misericordie nos participes . . . Ff. 103–106v. Jordan.

40. T28. *In domo tua oportet me manere* (Luke 19:5). Homo qui per-diderit domum suam per maliciam inimici sui . . .-. . . in domo tua, Domine, in secula seculorum laudabunt te. Ad quem . . . Ff. 106v–110v. Jordan.

41. T61. *Dies mali sunt* (Eph 5:17). Testante poeta libro *De fastis*, liquet Romanos illis diebus quibus eis subditus erat orbis . . .-. . . dies bonos indubitanter videbit. Sic igitur a malo diuertere et bonum perficere . . . Ff. 110v–115. Jordan.

42. T21*. *In digito Dei eicio daemonia* (Luke 11:20). Verum est quod Dominus Iesus Christus, cuius hec sunt uerba, videtur ea condicionaliter expres-sisse . . .-. . . minor digitus meus grossior est dorso patris mei, scribitur 3 Regum 10. Ff. 115–120v. Jordan.

43. T01. *Induimini* (Rom 13:14). Inconueniens magnum esset nudum de modo induendi, pauperem de via ditandi, fatuum de arte sciendi alios

informare . . .-. . . hoc induere immortalitatem, glorie scilicet sempiterne. Ad quam . . . Ff. 120v–124v. Jordan.

44. S44. *Iohannes est nomen eius* (Luke 1:63). Sicut dicit auctor *De interpretacionibus nominum*, hoc nomen Iohannes tres habet interpretaciones . . .- . . . gloriam magnam et nomen eternum. Quam gloriam . . . Ff. 124v–128. Jordan.

45. S10*. *Domine, hic autem quid?* (John 12:21,22). Reuerendissimi patres et domini, causa quare vestre reuerencie proposui uerba thematis preaccepti . . .-. . . et misericordiam a Deo salutari suo. Quam nobis meritis sancti Iohannis . . . Ff. 128v–132. Jordan.

46. T31?. *Vado ad Patrem* (John 16:16 etc.). Crisostomus omelia 14 *Operis inperfecti* super illo Matthei 6, Pater noster qui es in celis: Patrem, inquit, se maius quam dominum voluit dici . . .-. . . in qua est gloria sempiterna. Ad quam . . . Ff. 132–136. Jordan?

47. T43*. *Adhuc locutus est* (Luke 14:22). Secundum doctrinam Philosophi 4 *Phisicorum*, vnumquodque naturaliter fertur et tendit ad suum locum . . .- . . . et in muris meis locum. Ad quem . . . Ff. 136–139. Jordan.

48. T19. *Quasi morientes et ecce vivimus* (2 Cor 6:9). Gloriosissimam matrem Dei, quam ob sui prerogatiuas multiplices . . .-. . . ut cognoscant te solum verum Deum. Ad quam . . . Ff. 139–143. Jordan.

49. T19*. *Quasi morientes et ecce vivimus* (2 Cor 6:9). Sequitur: Verba que ego loquor spiritus et vita sunt. Si custodita sint offerunt vitam . . .-. . . si mortui sumus et conuiuemus, vita scilicet eterna. Quam etc. Ff. 145–148.

50. T23*. *Gloria mea nihil est* (John 8:54). Karissimi, facere aliquid ex nichilo potenciam exigit infinitam . . .-. . . capiat gaudium suum, quomodo erit capax tot et tantorum gaudiorum. Ad que gaudia . . . Ff. 148–149v.

51. T22*. *Non erit heres filius ancillae* (Gal 4:30). Quia ut scribitur Ioannis 1, Deus dedit potestatem filios Dei et heredes regni sui fieri . . .-. . . delectabor in Domino in presenti per graciam, in futuro per gloriam. Quam vobis etc. Ff. 149v–151.

52. T20*. *Haec est voluntas Dei* (1 Thess 4:3). Sicut tam catholicorum quam philosophorum euidentibus patet testimoniis . . .-. . . voluntatem Dei facientes reportetis promissionem. Quem . . . Ff. 151–155.

53. S28. *Ave, gratia plena* (Luke 1:28). Vasis plenitudinem liquoris quem continet infallibiliter tria probant . . .-. . . et gloria Domini plenum est opus eius. Ad quam nos etc. Ff. 155–156v. Jordan.

54. C14. *Exaltavi te de medio populi* (1 Kings 14:7). Sacra scriptura luculencius exprimente ac rerum natura euidencius exigente . . .-. . . ad faciem videbitis

Deum nostrum qui est gloria sempiterna. Ad quam . . . Ff. 156v–161 (no f. 157). Jordan.

55. S10. *Exaltavit eum apud proximos suos* (Sir 15:4). Propheta David, Psalmo 98, precepit nobis dicens bina vice: Exaltate Dominum Deum vestrum . . .- . . . vnusquisque cum proximo suo ita salute eterna. Quam . . . Ff. 161v–164v. Jordan.

56. C14. *Videte vocationem vestram, fratres* (1 Cor 1:26). In librorum continencia sepius reperitur et factorum evidencia cercius experitur quod res clara . . .- . . . ad brauium superne vocacionis Dei in Christo Iesu. Quod brauium eterne beatitudinis comprehendere . . . Ff. 164v–169v. Jordan.

57. T02. *Deus repleat vos omni gaudio* (Rom 15:13). Reuerendi domini, prout scitis, in omni peticione debite ordinata tria sunt principaliter requisita . . .- . . . in vobis omnem saciet appetitum et sic repleat vos omni gaudio. Ad quod . . . Ff. 169v–173. "Fr. Ioh' Segno."

58. T63*. *Redde quod debes* (Matt 18:28). Reuerendi domini et patres, teste Dyonisio 3 *De celesti ierarchia*, infimi per medios ad primum reduncuntur . . .-. . . mercedem laborum premium beatorum. Quod . . . Ff. 173–176v. "Fr. Guillelmus Bolew'."

59. C22*. *Venite audite et narrabo* (Ps 65:16). Quamuis omnis sciencia secundum Aristotelem 1 *De anima* de numero bonorum et honorabilium sit censenda, sacra tamen theologia diuinitus inspirata . . .-. . . et ideo istius narracionis fiat hic finis. Amen. Ff. 176v–179. Holcot.

60. S65*. *Nova lux oriri visa est* (Esther 8:15). Cum mentis humane curiositas inexhausta rerum nouitate naturaliter delectetur . . .-. . . cum ipsa est anima exaltata in montem sanctum tuum et in tabernacula tua. Ad que . . . Ff. 179–181v.

61. T20*. *Clamavit miserere mei* (Matt 15:22). Reuerendi domini et magistri, considerate in tripplicem fore statum generis humani . . .-. . . exspectantes misericordiam Dei in vitam eternam. Ad quam . . . Ff. 181v–184.

62. T21*. *In digito Dei eicio daemonia* (Luke 11:20). Diuine operacionis effectus secundum Rabanum . . .-. . . in digito Dei eiecta sunt demonia. Cuius benediccionis nos omnes participes . . . Ff. 184–186v.

63. S24e*. *Docebat eos de regno Dei* (Luke 9:11?). Quia secundum Senecam *De liberalibus artibus* liberalibus studiis filios enutrimus, non quia virtutem dare possunt . . .-. . . et persistentem entitatem quod non corrumpetur. Ad quod regnum . . . Ff. 186v–189.

64. S05*. *Spes vitae et virtutis* (Sir 24:25). Secundum varias auctorum sentencias tria reperio summo opere necessaria predicanti . . .-. . . ecce coronacio eternalis, videbitur Deus. Ad quam . . . Ff. 189–192.

65. S05*. *Electa ut sol* (Cant 6:9). Peritissimus astrologus \Alfraganus/ intuens disposicioues omnium planetarum . . .-. . . in amenum verteretur paradisum. Ad istud gaudium . . . Ff. 192–193v.

66. C14. *Attendite, popule meus, legem meam* (Ps 77:1). Reuerendi domini, scriptum est thema istud de Psalmo 77, et hoc pro tanto est quia numerus iste est mirabiliter misticus et moralis . . .-. . . non populus meus vos et ego non certe Deus vester etc. Ff. 194–195v. Holcot.

67. C14. *Videte, vigilate, et orate* (Mark 13:33). Videte mundi maliciam, vigilate contra dyaboli nequiciam . . .-. . . et in eternum regnabis cum Christo. Quod . . . Ff. 195v–198.

68. T19*. *Gratiam Dei recipiatis* (2 Cor 6:1). Sicut ex communi hominum consuetudine satis patet, in quaque curia . . .-. . . gracia Dei et vita eterna. Ad quam . . . Ff. 198–199v.

69. C14*. *Videte, vigilate, et orate* (Mark 13:33). Magna confusio est cuicumque persone statum assumere cuius officium nesciat excequi [!] . . .-. . . vt saluemini in presenti per graciam et in futuro per gloriam sempiternam. Ad quam . . . Ff. 199v–203.

70. C14*. *Elegit sacerdotes sine macula* (1 Macc 4:42). Christus Iesus immunis ab omni culpa qui falli non potest . . .-. . . iustos facit, Numeri 16 capitulo, sicut dictum. Ff. 203v–206v, inc. "Frater Joh' Sechne."

71. S20a. *Discipuli eius tulerunt corpus* (Matt 14:12). Considero euidenter ex testimoniis scripturarum quod antiqui fideles . . .-. . . ante translacionem testimonium habuit placuisse Deo. Cui nos placere concedat . . . Ff. 207–208v (modern foliation).

72. T02*. *Tunc videbunt Filium Hominis venientem in nube cum potestat magna et maiestate* (Luke 21:27). Intellexi tam in iure canonico quam ciuili reum posse quatripliciter in sua causa iudicium <declinare> . . .-. . . nota tunc de iudicio bonorum venite etc. Ad quam gloriam . . . Ff. 208v–211v.

73. T34*. *Petite et dabitur vobis* (Luke 11:9). Seruientes humiliter et subiecti, assistentes vtiliter et electi . . .-. . . et erit merces vestra multa. Quam mercedem etc. Ff. 211v–213v.

74. S24e*. *Venit in me spiritus sapientiae* (Wisd 7:7). Karissimi, tria sunt que alliciunt spiritum sapiencie . . .-. . . concupiscencia sapiencie deducit ad regnum perpetuum. Quod . . . Ff. 213v–216.

75. S24e*. *Datus est mihi sensus* (Wisd 7:7). Ex modernorum experiencia [?] viuaciter percipitur . . .-. . . vt in omnem plenitudinem impleatur in omnes generaciones seculi seculorum. Ad cuius plenitudinem etc. Ff. 216–219.

76. S24e*. *Repletus est spiritu sapientiae* (Deut 34:9). Reuerendi patres et domini, secundum sentenciam huius sancti doctoris, *De Christo* questione 7 articulo 10 . . .-. . . et dedit illi scienciam sanctorum. Quod regnum . . . Ff. 219–221v.

77. T22*. *Quid dicit scriptura?* (Gal 4:30). Reuerendi patres et domini, racione triplici solent homines querere questiones . . .-. . . vt credatis et vt credentes vitam habeatis. Quam . . . Ff. 221v–223v.

78. T06*. *Simul in unum dives et pauper* (Ps 48:3). Beatus Augustinus *De verbis Domini* sermone 35 dicit quod si essent uere diuicie . . .-. . . omnia in te simul vno habentes. Ad quem . . . Ff. 223v–224v.

79. C14 / T64*. *Sic state in Domino* (Phil 4:1). Reuerendi magistri, patres et domini, quamquam [!] secundum Tullium in libro suo *De facto virtutis sencibilis* . . .-. . . vt humiliter subiecti cum spe firma quiescendi in Domino, in quo eternaliter nos quiescere concedat etc. Ff. 225–227v.

80. T20*. *Miserere mei, Domine* (Matt 15:22). Perscrutanti in singulas peticiones positas in scriptura . . .-. . . in misericordia et ueritate redimetur inquietas. Cuius expiacionem. . . . Ff. 227v–229.

81. T18/5. *Homo sum* (Matt 8:9). Tradunt doctores varii, ymmo expertes, innotescit homini . . .-. . . flecto genua mea ad Patrem Domini mei Iesu Christi, vt det vobis secundum diuicias glorie sue . . . Ff. 229–231.

82. T64*. *Cuius imago haec?* (Matt 22:20). Consuetudo humana planius protestatur et ex diuina scriptura planius confirmatur . . .-. . . sic Dei ymaginem poterit reuocare siue in se renouare. Quod . . . Ff. 231–233.

83. T14*. *Domine, salva nos* (Math 8:25). Reuerendi domini, si uerba thematis contemplemur et eorum sentencias vt expedit perscrutemur . . .-. . . de corde puro et consciencia munda, terminos in themate positos d. Domine salua nos. Cuius salutis hered' etc. Ff. 233–234v.

84. T30*. *Iustitiae vivamus* (1 Pet 2:24). Triplex malum considero, cuius contrarium desidero . . .-. . . iustus Dominus et iusticias dilexit. Cuius dileccionis participes . . . Ff. 235–236v.

85. S24e*. *Inextinguibile est lumen illius* (Wisd 7:10). Sicut experimentaliter satis liquet quod sine lumine . . .-. . . in lumine tuo videbimus lumen, scilicet glorie. Quod . . . Ff. 237–240v.

86. T18/4. *Ubi est Deus?* (Joel 2:17). Humana experiencia crebrius attestatur et diuina sapiencia planius protestatur . . .-. . . vbi fures non effodiunt nec furantur, Mathei 6. Ad hanc mansionem . . . Ff. 241–242v.

87. T21*. *Eicio daemonia* (Luke 11:19). Triplici de causa aliquis aliqua eicit . . .-
. . . intra in gaudium Domini tui. Hec Augustinus. Quod gaudium . . . Ff.
243–245v.

88. T22. *Clama* (Gal 4:27?). Tribus dici solet comuniter moueri homines ad
clamandum . . .-. . . glorificabo eum, gloria scilicet sempiterna deifice
visionis. Quam . . . Manu fratris egidii de manso. Ff. 245v–251.

89. ?. *Si vis ad vitam ingredi, serva mandata* (Matt 19:17). Quicumque debet
aliquam ciuitatem multum remotam intrare . . .-. . . Johannis 12: Mandatum
eius vita eterna est. Ad quam . . . Ff. 251v–256. Repeats D-25, with changes;
perhaps also Harley 2385, see Morton W. Bloomfield et al., *Incipits of Latin
Works on the Virtues and Vices, 1100–1500 A.D.* (Cambridge, MA: Mediaeval
Academy of America, 1979), no. 5654.

90. T64* or S24e*. *Viam Dei in veritate doces* (Matt 22:16). Reuerendi patres et
domini, quamquam sint multiplices vie domini . . .-. . . Prouerbiorum 13:
Doctrina dabit graciam, scilicet in presenti, et in futuro gloriam. Amen.
Ff. 257–258.

91. T64*. *Reddite quae sunt Dei Deo* (Matt 22:21). Reuerendi patres mei et
domini, illa operacio complacenter admitti debet . . .-. . . cuius sunt beneficia potiora et promissa certiora. Ff. 258r–v, inc.

DY – Oxford, Magdalen College, MS 79 (Dygon)

1. S28. *Ecce ancilla Domini, fiat mihi secundum verbum tuum* (Luke 1:38). Sicut
Beata Virgo Maria mater Iesu Christi habet quinque solempnitates . . .-
. . . hanc humilitatem, iusticiam, misericordiam, pacem, et caritatem mul-
tiplicet Christus Iesus in omni statu Christianorum, vt possimus consortes
fieri glorie sempiterne. Amen. Ff. 1–4v.

2. S28. *Ecce virgo concipiet et pariet filium et vocabit nomen eius Emmanuhel*
(Isa 7:14). Sanctus propheta Ysaias repletus Spiritu Sancto dixit per multos
centenarios . . .-. . . et eius glorie fieri participes per eterna secula. Quod . . .
Ff. 4v–6v.

3. T28. *Mane nobiscum, Domine* (Luke 24:29). Cum Dominus Iesus Christus,
verus Deus et verus homo, iam nobiscum est . . .-. . . mane nobiscum,
Domine. Quam mansionem . . . Ff. 7–10v.

4. T28/2. *Oportuit Christum pati et ita intrare in gloriam suam* (Luke 24:26).
In primis est notanda sentencia euangelii sub compendio perstingenda,
quomodo duo discipuli . . .-. . . gloriam possidere perfectam tam corporis
quam anime sine fine. Quod . . . Ff. 10v–14v.

5. T28/3. *Pax vobis* (Luke 24:36). Pro antethemate pax bona multipliciter est commendanda . . .-. . . a quibus periculis preseruet populum suum misericordissimus redemptor anime. Amen. Ff. 14v–18.

6. T28/4. *Mittite in dextram navigii rete et invenietis* (John 21:6). Primo breuiter tangenda est historia euangelii cum paucis notulis inde captis ad erudicionem minorum . . .-. . . et inuenietis requiem anime et corporis et gaudia sempiterna. Quod . . . Ff. 18–22v.

7. T41/5. *Hoc facite in meam commemorationem* (Luke 22:9 and 1 Cor 11:4). Licet Matheus et Marcus exprimant formam consecracionis . . .-. . . ad quam Christus resurexit immortalis et beatus. Ad quam . . . Ff. 22v–25.

8. S28b. *Si manseritis in me, et verba mea in vobis manserint, quodcumque volueritis petetis et fiet vobis* (John 15:7). Quia hoc festum beati Ambrosii quandoque contingit in tempore paschali . . .-. . . optinebimus a patre misericordie et consolacionis perfecte. Quod . . . Ff. 25–30.

9. S28b. *Sic luceat lux vestra coram hominibus ut videant vestra bona et glorificent Patrem vestrum qui in caelis est* (Matt 5:16). Quia festum beati Ambrosii contingit frequenter in quadragesima et tunc legitur euangelium Vos estis sal terre . . .-. . . ut sic luceat \lux/ vestra coram hominibus etc. Quod. . . . Ff. 30–32v.

10. S28b. *Qui fecerit et docuerit, hic magnus vocabitur in regno caelorum* (Matt 5:19). Qui fecerit mandata Dei et concilia Christi et docuerit . . .-. . . et sequelam veracem mereamur beatitudinem eternam. Quam . . . Ff. 32v–35v.

11. S30. *Manete in me et ego in vobis* (John 15:4). Quia exposicio literalis huius euangelii patet aliquantulum in festo beati Ambrosii . . .-. . . in caritate perfecta erga amicos et inimicos propter amorem et reuerenciam Iesu Christi. Quam caritatem . . . Ff. 35v–38v.

12. S32. *Ego sum via, veritas, et vita* (John 14:6). Christus Iesus, Deus et homo, est via qua venitur ad beatitudinem . . .-. . . hanc vindictam et potissime finalem auertat Deus a nobis . . . Ff. 38v–41v.

13. S33. *Sicut Moses exaltavit serpentem in deserto, ita exaltari oportet Filium Hominis* (John 3:14). Quia totum euangelium propter eius prolixitatem et difficultatem exponere non sufficimus, pauca eius uerba exiliter perstringimus . . .-. . . et auditorium ad celestia confortare. Ff. 41v–44v.

14. T34/2. *Petite et dabitur vobis* (Luke 11:9). Quia hiis diebus ex institucione Ecclesie et deuocione fidelium solent fieri rogaciones . . .-. . . vel excitare homines ad deuote orandum per historias noui et veteris testamenti, de quibus patebit per Dei graciam in proximo sermone. Ff. 45–48.

15. T34/3. *Haec locutus sum vobis, ut in me pacem habeatis* (John 16:33). Ad rogandum pro pace tria sunt breuiter declaranda: primum est exilis transcursus euangelii hodierni . . .-. . . vt pacem veram eternam habeamus in Domino Iesu Christo. Quod . . . Ff. 48–53v.

16. T35. *Ego pro eis rogo, non pro mundo, sed pro hiis quos dedisti mihi, quia tui sunt* (John 17:9). Tria sunt tangenda breuiter pro pace veraci inter homines optinenda: primum est breuis explanacio euangelii hodierni . . .-. . . ad optinendum graciam ampliorem in presenti et maius premium in futuro. Quod . . . Ff. 53v–58v.

17. T36. *Dominus Iesus adsumptus est in caelum et sedet a dextris Dei* (Mark 16:19). Circa hec verba pauca, tria sunt tangenda: primum est exposicio succincta euangelii cum paucis notulis sanctorum doctorum . . .-. . . donec videatur Deus deorum in Syon. Quod . . . Ff. 58v–63.

18. T39. *Si quis diligit me, sermonem meum servabit* (John 14:23). Signanter dicit Christus sermonem meum, non sermones . . .-. . . de qua patebit per Dei graciam in sermone sequenti. Ff. 63–67v.

19. T39/2 ("in feria 2 septimane pasche[!]"). *Sic Deus dilexit mundum ut filium suum unigenitum daret* (John 3:16). Circa hec pauca verba tria sunt breuiter declaranda. Primum est exposicio euangelii ad literam . . .-. . . et omnium sanctorum ad inuicem in eternum. Quod . . . Ff. 67v–72.

20. T39/3. *Qui intrat per ostium, pastor est ovium* (John 10:2). Circa hec verba pauca cum Dei gracia et vestra supportacione benigna tria sunt presenti auditorio breuiter declaranda. Primum est literalis exposicio . . .-. . . amplitudinem celestium gaudiorum. Sic intrare per hostium . . . Ff. 72–76.

21. T39/4. *Nemo potest venire ad me nisi Pater, qui misit me, traxerit illum* (John 6:44). Iudeis ingratis et murmurantibus contra Christum quia dixit se esse panem . . .-. . . vt possimus ipsum videre beatifice in regno celorum. Quod . . . Ff. 76v–79.

22. T40 ("Sermo de trinitate ante nonam"). *Gratia Domini nostri Iesu Christi et caritas Dei et communicatio Sancti Spiritus sit cum omnibus vobis* (2 Cor 13:12). Vbi Glosa sic exponit: Gracia Domini nostri Iesu Christi, idest Christus gratis . . .-. . . indubie ipsa nos perducet ad beatitudinem celestem. Quam . . . Ff. 79–83.

23. T40 ("Sermo de trinitate post nonam"). *Benedicamus Patrem et Filium et Spiritum Sanctum* (Canticle based on Dan 3:57). Hoc canticum, scilicet Benedicite omnia opera Domini Domino etc., a principio . . .-. . . teneamus veraciter caritatem triplicem, scilicet Dei et proximi et specialiter inimici. Quod . . . Ff. 83–87v.

24. T41/5. *Qui manducat meam carnem et bibit meum sanguinem in me manet et ego in illo* (John 6:55). Quia vero ut patet ex textu precedenti Christus multipliciter inuitauit Iudeos . . .-. . . vt digne valeamus conficere et suscipere hoc uenerabile sacramentum. Amen. Ff. 87v–93.

25. S40. *Hoc est praeceptum meum, ut diligatis invicem sicut dilexi vos* (John 15:12). Circa hoc thema tria sunt breuiter declaranda: primum est exilis et breuis exposicio euangelii hodierni . . .-. . . in manibus inimicorum meorum. Hec Parisiensis ibidem. Sic ergo diligamus inuicem . . . Ff. 93– 97.

26. S44. *Iohannes est nomen eius* (Luke 1:63). De Iohanne Baptista precursore Christi sunt tria breuiter declaranda: primum est de ingressu eius in mundum . . .-. . . Iohannes est nomen eius. Sic nos sequi hunc Iohannem . . . Ff. 97–100.

27. S44 ("post nonam"). *Iohannes est nomen eius* (Luke 1:63). Circa hoc thema tria sunt breuiter perstringenda. Primum est de ingressu Iohannis . . .- . . . Iohannes est nomen eius. Sic nos viuere doceat et mori doceat Altissimus . . . Ff. 100v–104v.

28. S46. *Beatus es, Simon Bar Iona* (Matt 16:17). Simon interpretatur obediens, Bariona interpretatur filius columbe . . .-. . . patebit in sermone proximo sequenti. Ff. 104v–109v.

29. S46b. *Homo quidam nobilis abiit in regionem longinquam accipere sibi regnum et reverti* (Luke 19:12). Hic homo secundum doctores est Iesus Christus, verus Deus et verus homo . . .-. . . pertingens per hec media ad regnum celorum. Quod . . . Ff. 109v–114v.

30. S46c. *Vigilate quia nescitis diem neque horam* (Matt 25:13). Secundum Gregorium in omelia super illo Luce 12 Sint lumbi vestri precincti: Ille vigilat . . .-. . . pro commendacione virginitatis sincere. Ff. 114v–119v.

31. S46c. *Vigilate, quia nescitis diem neque horam* (Matt 25:13). Pro materia huius sermonis tria sunt breuiter declaranda: primum est literalis exposicio euangelii . . .-. . . det nobis virginitatem mentis cum fideli obseruancia mandatorum suorum quatinus mereamur ingredi gaudia celorum . . . Ff. 119v–123v.

32. S47. *Inventa una pretiosa margarita abiit et vendidit omnia quae habuit et emit eam* (Matt 13:45). Circa hoc thema tria sunt breuiter perstringenda: primum est exilis exposicio euangelii . . .-. . . propter prolixitatem vitandam etc. Ff. 123v–128v.

33. S49. *Remittuntur ei peccata multa, quoniam dilexit multum* (Luke 7:47). Circa hoc thema tria sunt \breuiter/ perstringenda: primum est aliqualis

declaracio euangelii cum exposicione succincta . . .-. . . vt ad regna celorum cum beata Maria Magdalena et sanctis omnibus conscendamus. Quod . . . Ff. 128v–134.

34. S49. *Dimissa sunt ei peccata multa, quoniam dilexit multum* (Luke 7:47). Licet aliqua tetigi in sermone precedenti de beata Magdalena . . .-. . . ut de quolibet nostrum dicatur cum Magdalena, Dimissa sunt ei peccata multa, quoniam dilexit multum. Quod nobis etc. Ff. 134–138v.

35. S50. *Potestis bibere calicem quem ego bibiturus sum?* (Mark 20:22). Est calix vindicte seu dampnacionis quem bibunt reprobi . . .-. . . supersedeo propter prolixitatem vitandam. Ff. 138v–144v.

36. S56. *Si quis mihi ministrat, me sequatur* (John 12:26). Quilibet Christianus ex nomine et ex religione vel ex obligacione tenetur . . .-. . . et martirio perfecto quatinus mereamur introire in regnum celorum. Amen. Ff. 145–150.

37. S59 vigil. *Beati qui audiunt verbum Dei et custodiunt illud* (Luke 11:28). Quia Assumpcionis vigilia Virginis gloriose contingit frequenter in die dominica . . .-. . . quatinus per intercessionem sue piissime matris et omnium sanctarum feminarum et tocius curie celestis obtineamus benediccionem Dei in presenti et gloriam sempiternam. Amen. Ff. 150–154.

38. S59. *Optimam partem elegit sibi Maria quae non auferetur ab ea* (Luke 10:42 "in sentencia et in seruicio hodierno"). Circa hoc euangelium tria sunt breuiter declaranda: primum est exilis declaracio euangelii . . .-. . . sic ergo eligamus constanter bonam partem Marthe per actiuam, meliorem partem Marie per contemplatiuam, et optimam partem, scilicet actiuam et contemplatiuam simul, cum beata Virgine, Christo, et apostolis quatinus mereamur fieri consortes glorie sempiterne. Amen. Ff. 154–158v.

39. S59. *Assumpta est Maria in caelum; gaudent angeli, laudantes benedicunt Dominum* ("In seruicio Ecclesie in hoc festo"). Circa hoc thema propositum tria occurrunt breuiter presenti auditorio declaranda: primum est mors et sepultura beate Virginis . . .-. . . et securi erimus de gaudio sempiterno. Quod . . . Ff. 158v–163v.

40. S61. *Vos estis qui permansistis mecum in temptationibus meis* (Luke 22:28). Circa hoc thema propositum tria sunt breuiter declaranda: primum est exposicio euangelii . . .-. . . hee meditaciones specialiter facient vos victores in omni temptacione carnis, diaboli, siue mundi. Quam victoriam . . . Ff. 163v–168v.

41. S63. *Quis putas est fidelis servus et prudens quem constituit dominus suus super familiam suam et det illis cibum in tempore?* (Matt 24:45). Quia proprium

euangelium vnius doctoris, scilicet Vos estis sal terre, expositum est in festo beati Ambrosii . . .-. . . propter prolixitatem vitandam oportet complere residuum in sermone sequenti. Ff. 168v–173.

42. S63. *Quis putas est fidelis servus et prudens*, etc. (Matt 24:45). Circa hoc thema secundo propositum oportet primo succincte ipsum declarare . . .- . . . hec ibi et multa alia de commendabili vita eius, que oportet alium sermonem tractare. Ff. 173–177v.

43. S63. *Quis putas est fidelis seruus et prudens*, etc. (Matt 24:45). Circa hunc sermonem tria sunt breuiter pertractanda, scilicet aliqua omissa de laudabili vita sua . . .-. . . Lira plenissime pro hac questione ex textu Christus Iesus . . . Ff. 177v–182.

44. S64. *Misit Herodes et tenuit Iohannem et vinxit eum in carcere propter Herodiadem* (Mark 6:17 and Matt 14:3). Circa thema propositum tria sunt breuiter declaranda: primum est exposicio breuis euangelii . . .-. . . et constanter predicauit regnare perhenniter in celis. Quod . . . Ff. 182–187.

45. S64. *Non licet tibi habere uxorem fratris tui* (Mark 6:17 and Matt 14:3). Quia tercium principale sermonis precedentis non potuit ibi tangi propter prolixitatem vitandam, ideo hic . . .-. . . cum sua excusacione blasphema, a qua nos preseruet Altissimus per intercessionem beati Johannis Baptiste et omnium sanctorum. Amen. Ff. 187–192v.

46. S64. *Volo ut protinus des mihi in disco caput Iohannis Baptistae* (Mark 6:25). Circa thema propositum tria omissa in sermone precedenti sunt aliqualiter explananda . . .-. . . et faciat vere continentes in corpore atque mente. Amen. Ff. 192v–198.

47. S65. *Nativitas est hodie sanctae Mariae Virginis, cuius vita inclita cunctas illustrat ecclesias* ("In antiphona huius festi," i.e. antiphon for Lauds). Nota in primis quod Ecclesia sancta celebrat tres natiuitates in anno . . .-. . . ut ipsa pro nobis intercedat ad Dominum Iesum Christum quatinus . . . Ff. 198–203v.

48. S66. *Omnia traham ad me ipsum* (John 12:32). Circa thema propositum sunt tria breuiter perstringenda: primum est exilis declaracio euangelii hodierni . . .-. . . sic ergo, Pater misericordie, trahe nos ad te tractu gracie, misericordie, et caritatis, vt tecum . . . Ff. 203v–208v.

49. S67. *Non veni vocare iustos sed peccatores* (Matt 9:13). Circa thema breue propositum tria sunt breuiter pertractanda: primum est exilis exposicio euangelii quoad literam et sensum misticum . . .-. . . quam lingua mortalis non sufficit enarrare. Quam penitenciam . . . Ff. 208v–213.

50. S65b. *Multae tribulationes iustorum, et de omnibus hiis liberabit eos Dominus* (Ps 33:20). Circa thema propositum tria sunt breuiter declaranda: primum est vita et excellencia beati Johannis . . .-. . . pro sana doctrina et martirio glorioso coronatur in patria celesti. Ad quam . . . Ff. 213–217.

51. S70. *Angeli eorum semper vident faciem Patris mei, qui in caelis est* (Matt 18:10). Circa pauca verba proposita tria sunt breuiter declaranda: prima [!] est exposicio literalis huius euangelii . . .-. . . vt finaliter cum suis gregibus valeant ascendere ad regna celorum. Quod . . . Ff. 217–221v.

52. S70. *Angeli eorum semper in caelis vident faciem Patris mei, qui in caelis est* (Matt 18:10). Circa hoc thema secundo propositum tria sunt breuiter pertractanda: primum est aliqualiter declarare nouem ordines . . .-. . . debite ergo et deuote venerentur angelos beatos, quatinus mereamur . . . Ff. 221v– 227v.

53. S71. *Euge, serve bone et fidelis, quia super pauca fuisti fidelis, supra multa te constituam; intra in gaudium domini tui* (Matt 25:21). Circa thema propositum tria sunt breuiter declaranda: primum est exposicione [!] huius euangelii . . .-. . . ideo oportet claudere sermonem super primo principale [!] et residuum complere in sermone sequente [!]. Ff. 227v–234.

54. S71. *Euge, serve bone et fidelis,* etc. (Matt 25:21). Circa thema propositum tria sunt breuiter declaranda: primum est bonitas moralis beati Jeronimi . . .- . . . nos miseros et peccatores esse fideles et prudentes summe Trinitatis, quatinus . . . Ff. 234–238.

55. S75. *Ecce ego mitto vos sicut agnum [!] inter lupos* (Luke 10:3). Circa thema propositum tria sunt aliqualiter pertractanda: primum est exilis declaracio euangelii . . .-. . . duo principalia proficere [!] in sermone sequenti. Ff. 238–241v.

56. S75. *Ecce ego mitto vos sicut agnos inter lupos* (Luke 10:3). Circa hoc thema secundo propositum tria sunt breuiter pertractanda: primum est vita et predicacio et paciencia prelatorum . . .-. . . complebitur in sermone sequente [!]. Ff. 242–246.

57. S75. *Ecce ego mitto vos sicut agnos inter lupos* (Luke 10:3). Circa hoc thema tercio propositum tercium principale ad excitandum primo omnes curatos in genere ad execucionem officii spiritualis . . .-. . . verbum Dei ad salutem Christianorum; vt sic pertingere . . . Ff. 246–251v.

58. S68. *Omnis turba quaerebat Iesum tangere, quia virtus de illo exibat et sanabat omnes* (Luke 6:19). Circa thema propositum tria sunt breuiter pertractanda: primum est quomodo turba querebat Christum tangere corporaliter . . .-

. . . per veram castitatem mentis et corporis queramus Iesum et tangere spiritualiter, quatinus . . . Ff. 251v–256.

59. S74. *Ego dabo vobis os et sapientiam cui non poterunt resistere et contradicere omnes adversarii vestri* (Luke 21:15). Circa thema propositum tria breuiter sunt perstringenda: primum est exposicio aliqualis huius euangelii . . .-. . . vt fideliter imitemur beatum Dionisium cum sociis suis in vita et doctrina et martirio si oportet, quatinus . . . Ff. 256–261.

60. S77. *Mulier quae innupta est et virgo cogitat quae Domini sunt, ut sit sancta et corpore et spiritu* (1 Cor 7:34). Circa thema propositum tria sunt breuiter declaranda: primum est exposicio literalis epistule plurimarum virginum . . .-. . . mancipauimus nos seruicio diuino in suscepcione ordinis sacramenti. Quod . . . Ff. 261–265v.

61. S78. *Haec mando vobis, ut diligatis invicem* (John 15:17). Circa thema propositum tria sunt breuiter declaranda: primum est breuis exposicio euangelii . . .-. . . ideo respiciat ibi qui voluerit dilatare materiam caritatis. Ff. 265v–270v.

62. S79. *Omnes sancti Dei, orate pro nobis* (Liturgy of all saints). Circa breue thema propositum tria sunt breuiter declaranda: primum est ponere noticiam quare beati orant pro viatoribus . . .-. . . orate pro nobis miseris in tot periculis constitutis . . . Ff. 270v–274.

63. S79. *Beati pauperes spiritu, quoniam ipsorum est regnum caelorum* (Matt 5:3). Hoc euangelium continens virtutes et beatitudines legitur . . .-. . . nostrum regnum est celorum ex promissione fidelissima Iesu Christi. Ad quod . . . Ff. 274v–278.

64. S79. *Beati qui esuriunt et sitiunt iustitiam, quoniam ipsi saturabuntur* (Matt 5:6). Circa thema propositum, quod est quarta beatitudo, tria sunt aliquantulum perstringenda: primum est breuis exposicio thematis . . .-. . . simus misericordes et mundi corde, quatinus . . . Ff. 278–280v.

65. S79. *Beati pacifici, quoniam filii Dei vocabuntur* (Matt 5:9). Circa thema propositum, quod est septima beatitudo, tria sunt breuiter pertractanda: primum est exposicio thematis . . .-. . . dileccione inimicorum mereamini percipere gaudia celorum. Quod . . . Ff. 280v–283.

66. S80. *Resurget frater tuus* (John 11:22). Circa thema propositum tria sunt breuiter explananda: primum est breuis recitacio huius euangelii . . .-. . . et postmodum in corporibus et animabus eternaliter copulatis. Quod . . . Ff. 283v–285v.

67. S80. *Consolamini invicem in verbis istis* (1 Thess 4:18). Circa thema propositum tria sunt breuiter perstringenda: primum est exposicio

epistule hodierne . . .-. . . et feliciter euolent ad gaudia celorum. Quod . . . Ff. 286–289v.

68. S80. *Audient mortui vocem Filii Dei, et qui audierint viuent* (John 5:25). Circa thema propositum tria sunt breuiter perstringenda: primum est exposicio breuis euangelii in feria quarta pro defunctis . . .-. . . a pena transibunt ad gaudia sempiterna. Quod . . . Ff. 289v–294.

69. S81. *Beati sunt servi illi quos cum venerit dominus invenerit vigilantes* (Luke 12:37). Quia euangelium proprium in die sancti Martini, scilicet Homo quidam peregre, etc., exponitur in sermonibus precedentibus, ideo euangelium in communi plurimorum confessorum exponetur in festiuitate presenti. Circa thema propositum tria sunt aliqualiter pertractanda: primum est exilis declaracio huius euangelii . . .-. . . foris palacii sibi claui fecit. Ff. 294–298v.

E – Hereford, Cathedral Library, MS O.iii.5

1. T28*. *Intravit Iesus in quoddam castellum* (Luke 10:38). Venerabiles amici, sicut refert Valerius *De gestis Alexandri magni* . . .-. . . ista domus taliter edificata debet mundari etc. Ff. 1–2rb.

2. T28. *Surrexit Dominus vere* (Luke 24:34). Karissimi, sicut medicina corporalis si fuerit conueniens compleccioni . . .-. . . et ineffabili bonitate istum benedictum cibum sic nos concedat spiritualiter manducare . . . Ff. 2rb–5ra. Also Z-26, H-8.

3. ?. *Quid facietis in die festivitatis?* (Hos 9:5). Hec questio queritur in sacra scriptura triplici de causa . . .-. . . quoniam ipsi Deum videbunt in eterna gloria. Ad quam . . . Ff. 5ra–7rb.

4. T19+*. *Anima quae peccaverit, ipsa morietur* (Ezek 18:4). Karissimi, sicut repereo in sacra scriptura Ieremie 22, quod quando sanctus propheta . . .- . . . recipiam ad me, scilicet per graciam et misericordiam hic in presenti et per gloriam et gaudium in futuro. Que . . . Ff. 7vb–11ra.

5. T56. *Nemo potest duobus dominis servire* (Matt 6:24). Karissimi, dicunt doctores, et scriptura eciam cum hoc concordat, quod verbum Dei speculo comparatur . . .-. . . tunc erit coronatus cum gloria \in/ regno celesti. Ad quod . . . Ff. 11va–14va.

6. S09*. *Sanguis iustus effusus est super terram* (Matt 23:36). Karissimi, legitur in quadam historia quod ostendit nobis Alexander Nekham 3 *De naturis rerum* . . .-. . . omnes electi filii Dei transibunt secum ad vitam eternam. Quam . . . Ff. 14va–17rb.

461

7. ?. *Quomodo stabit regnum* (Luke 11:18). Vnde satis docet experiencia, propter tres causas multociens queruntur questiones in sacra scriptura . . .-. . . tendere debemus, vbi lex est veritas, rex est caritas, possessio eternitas. Ad quod etc. Ff. 17rb–18va.

8. C14*. *Audite* [ms Attendite] *haec, sacerdotes* (Hos 5:1). Reuerendi magistri et domini, sacra nobis testatur assercio . . .-. . . Ideo vt premittitur, Audite hec sacerdotes. Ff. 18va–19rb. Repeated as 42.

9. C14*. *Bonus pastor animam suam dat pro ovibus suis* (John 10:12). Reuerendi magistri, domini, atque patres. In exordio huius collacionis breuissime vestris deuotis precibus recommendo statum vniuersalis Ecclesie . . . Teste beato Augustino in epistula ad Valerium, et ponitur in canone, 40 D., ante omnia in hac vita nichil difficilius . . .-. . . viciorum humores efficacissime euacuant atque purgant. Ff. 19rb–21rb.

10. T28 or T41/5. *Qui manducat hunc panem vivet in aeternum* (John 6:59). Omnipotens et misericors Deus, qui vult omnes homines saluos fieri et neminem perire, videns . . .-. . . vt esset vno die in gaudio illo. Ad quod . . . Ff. 21va–24rb.

11. S00?, "Sermo generalis". *De morte transit ad vitam* (John 5:24). Sicut dicit Philosophus 3 *Phisicorum*, omnis transitus siue motus est de contrario in contrarium . . .-. . . ad vitam soliditatis sine terminacione. Ad quam . . . Ff. 24rb–26ra.

12. T28. *Tene quod habes* (Rev 3:11). Reuerendi mei, sicut scribit Diascorides libro 2 capitulo 97, in Iudea inferiori est arbor . . .-. . . þat is endeles welth wyth outen wo. Quod . . . Ff. 26ra–28vb. Also S-4, B/2-57.

13. T28*. *Si consurrexistis* [ms surrexistis] *cum Christo*, etc. (Col 3:1). Homo ex duabus naturis constans duplicem mortem habet . . .-. . . tenui eum nec dimittam. . F. 31ra–va, inc? Also Laud misc. 511–115.

14. C14*. *Luceat lux vestra coram hominibus* (Matt 5:16). Reuerendi magistri, patres, et domini, sicut sol materialis sue lucis radios in hec inferiora defundens . . .-. . . et Deus tuus in gloriam tuam. Quam gloriam . . . Ff. 33ra–35vb. Rimington's synodal sermon of 1373; also K-25 and in Harley 1615. Edited from Paris, Université, MS 790, in O'Brien, "Two Sermons."

15. T28. *Hoc est corpus meum* (Matt 26:26). Vnde primo quero quando fuit hoc sacramentum factum . . .-. . . in tua dulcedine tibi me cum meis commendo sine fine. Ff. 35vb–38rb.

16. C19*. *Videbo templum* (Jonah 2:5). Reuerendi domini, patres et magistri, vt constat philosophis, nemo potest sine lumine aliquid corporale videre . . .-

. . . cognoscendi facultatem et requiescendi felicitatem. Ad quam . . . Ff. 38rb–40vb.

17. C19*. *Oboedite praepositis vestris* (Heb 13:17). Patres reuerendi et fratres in Christo karissimi, vt nos informat scriptura diuinitus inspirata 1 Regum 17 . . .-. . . prepositis vestris. Sic nos propositis nostris obedire . . . Ff. 40vb–42vb.

18. C19*. *Requiram oves meas et visitabo eas sicut pastor visitat gregem suum* (Ezek 34:11–12). Scribitur in canone, Nihil illo pastore miserius . . .-. . . vt ministros Christi et dispensatores ministeriorum [!] Dei. Vt sic . . . Ff. 42vb–45ra.

19. C19*. *Unus accessit* or *Unum est necessarium* (Matt 9:18 or Luke 10:42). Secundum Fulgencium *De ornatu vrbis,* cohabitancium presidium ac singulare solacium . . .-. . . egrotum non sanastis sed cum potencia et austeritate. Ff. 45rb–48ra. Parallels with F/1-7.

20. T19+. *Paenitentiam agite* (Matt 3:2). 3e þat singhyn bewar of gyle, doth now penaunce a lytyll qwyll'. Pro processu . . .quatuor sunt que mouere debent quemlibet Christianum . . .-. . . sic penitere quod ad illud gaudium poterimus peruenire. Quod . . . Ff. 48ra–50rb.

21. C14*. *Pasce oves meas* (John 21:17). Notet caritas vestra quod ista verba sunt verba Christi dicta et prolata beato Petro . . .-. . . felix et suauis est refeccio animarum ille pastor nobis concedat . . . Ff. 50vb–53vb.

22. C14*. *Benedicite, sacerdotes Domini, Domino* (Dan 3:84). Secundum beatum Ambrosium in *Officiis* d' sacerdotis officium est nulli nocere . . .-. . . sacri duces exemplo bone vite. Vt sic valeamus . . . Ff. 53vb–56vb.

23. C14*. *Benedicite, sacerdotes Domini, Domino* (Dan 3:84). Mulier volens querere dragmam perditam lucernam accendit . . .-. . . qui eum totis visceribus amare dedicerunt. Sic nos amare concedat etc. Ff. 57ra–60va.

24. C14*. *Abiit Iesus trans mare* (John 6:1). Reuerendi domini, inuenio quod de triplici mari in scriptura sacra fit mencio . . .-. . . scilicet celestem Ierusalem, quod est celum. Ad quod . . . Ff. 60va–68rb.

25. T28. *Panis quem ego dabo caro mea est* (John 6:52). Reuerendi mei, secundum quod dicit euangelium omnis Christi solicitudo tam in doctrinis quam in factis ad hoc tendebant [!] . . .-. . . sunt verba decreti. Sic ergo hoc sacramentum . . . Ff. 68va–70ra.

26. C21. *Morieris* (?). Nullum est verbum in scriptura sacra vt estimo quod ita exitaret hominem ad cognoscendum se ipsum . . .-. . . in vita beati Laurencii manus pauperum deporta [uerunt, *catchword*!]. Ff. 70vb–71va, inc.

27. T24. *Humiliavit semetipsum* (Phil 2:8). Si terrenus rex vel princeps pro proprio delicto pauperem statum assumeret . . .-. . . et sic pro nostra salute humiliauit se ipsum. Ff. 73ra–75va.

28. T22*. *Christus nos liberavit* (Gal 4:31). Secundum seriem veteris testamenti et epistulam huius diei, tot fuerunt sacrificia, ritus, et obseruancie . . .-. . . merito inferri potest quod Christus nos liberauit. Ff. 75va–77rb.

29. T39. *Emitte spiritum* (not stated at beginning; Ps 103:30). Secundum doctorem de Lira super euangelium istius diei, obediencia in opere denotat . . .-. . . proficitur ad supernacturlia. Ff. 77rb–78ra, inc?

30. T36*. *Venite, ascendamus ad montem Domini* (Isa 2:3). Reuerendi domini, Dominus noster Iesus Christus, qui vt dicitur Luce 19 Venit querere . . .-. . . persequentibus vos benedicere, venite etc. Ad quod . . . Ff. 78rb–83ra.

31. T28*. *Vere tu es deus absconditus* (Isa 45:15). Hec verba huic diei sacratissime duplici racione conuenire videntur. Solemnizat Ecclesia hodie de Christi resurreccione . . .-. . . quibus Deus voluit notas facere diuicias glorie sacramenti huius. Quam gloriam . . . Ff. 83ra–85va. Jordan in D-20.

32. C19*. *Visitabo in virga iniquitates eorum* (Ps 88:33). Reuerendi mei et fratres karissimi, quia modus et consuetudo . . .-. . . sed ipsos secum ducat ad gaudia celorum. Quod . . . Ff. 85vb–86vb.

33. T28. *Exsurrexi* [MS Resurexi] *et adhuc tecum sum* (Ps 138:13). Anglice potes dici I am resyn vpe on he and ʒit my dwellyng is with ʒe. Vbi pro introduccione est notandum quod quilibet predicator verbi Dei debet tria principaliter considerare . . .-. . . manducauerit ex hoc pane, viuet in eternum. Quid . . . Ff. 86vb–88rb.

34. T19+ ("Iste sermo potest competenter predicari per totam quadragesimam quacumque die placet"). *Miserere mei, Domine, quoniam infirmus sum* (Ps 6:3). Karissimi, sicut scitis, ille qui est pauper et infirmus, si vellet curari . . .-. . . contra has septem infirmitates septem peccatorum mortalium <Deus> ipse de sua misericordi det nobis tales medicinas . . . Ff. 88rb–90rb.

35. T28. *Alleluia* (Rev 19:1 etc.). Et i[bi]dem scribitur quod Iohannes audiuit duos cantus cantari in celo; vnus erat of sorow et off weping, et alter of joy and of laʒyng [*later* halwyng] . . .-. . . cantabunt Alleluia, canticum gaudii et risus. Quod . . . Ff. 90rb–93rb.

36. C14. *Amen* (?). Vbi plurimorum [?] affecciones in aliquid vnum inprecandum conueniunt, in premissam vocem libenter prosiliunt . . .-. . . quod velis retinere. Hec canon. Ff. 93rb–96rb.

37. ? ("Sermo aureus et nobilis"). *Vox clamantis in deserto* (Isa 40:3 and John 1:23). Cum tante esset sanctitatis beatus Ioannes et Christus putaretur . . .- . . . iuxta illam denominatur peccatum mortale. Ff. 96rb–104va.

38. C21. *Mortuus vivet* (John 11:25). Reuerendi, ante omnia opera misericordie primum et principale <est> orare . . .-. . . et sicut stelle in perpetuas hereditates, Danielis 12. Quam vitam . . . Ff. 104va–106vb. Also Z-2; and English translation in Sidney Sussex 74.

39. T36. *Amice, ascende superius* (Luke 14:10). Reuerendi domini, cum princeps aliquis nobilis et gloriosus venerit nouiter de terra querere . . .-. . . sanctam requiem et beatam celi que nunquam finietur. Ad quam requiem . . . Ff. 106vb–110rb. Also J/5-22; Oxford Magdalen College 112, f. 221ra; and cf. A-47, W-163.

40. T57. *Deus visitavit plebem suam* (Luke 7:16). Karissimi, triplex genus peccati occidit animam . . .-. . . de seruitute diaboli et ad restituendum ad gaudia regni celestis. Quod . . . Ff. 110rb–114va.

41. T24. *Benedictus qui venit in nomine Domini* (Matt 21:9). Karissimi, sicut ostendit Alexander in quodam libro *De naturis rerum* quod quedam erat auis . . .-. . . offerimus palmas cruci siue sacerdoti. Taliter nos transire . . . Ff. 114va–117va.

42. C14*. *Audite haec sacerdotes* (Hos 5:1). Reuerendi magistri et domini, sacra nobis testatur assercio 4 Regum capitulo 4 quod cum vir Dei Heliseus . . .- . . . ascendit quod Deus preparauit diligentibus se. Ad quod gaudium . . . Ff. 117va–119va. Repeats E-8.

F – "Collectarium," Oxford, Bodleian Library, MS Auct. F. infra 1.2

F/1

1. ?. *Dilectio sine simulatione* (Rom 12:9). Hugo de Sancto Victore in principio cuiusdam libelli sui qui intitulatur *De arra anime* sic dicit: Loquar in secreto anime mee . . .-. . . ecce finis gloriacionis et causa. Ff. 85ra–87ra.

2. T24*. *Vigilate* (Matt 26:41). Secundum medicos pessimum signum in homine est quando freneticus conuertitur in litargicum . . .-. . . semper in Domino viuamus, Thessalonicensium 5. Quam vitam . . . Ff. 87ra–89vb.

3. ?. *Arguet mundum de peccato* (John 16:8). Tullius *De officiis* libro 1 volens ostendere sit necessaria futurorum prouidencia . . .-. . . sanctificacionem, finem vero vitam eternam. Quam . . . Ff. 89vb–91vb.

4. T02*. *Prope est regnum Dei* (Luke 21:31). Beatus Gregorius 5 *Morum* super illud Iob 3 quod effodientes aurum etc. dicit sentenciam talem: Effodientes . . .-. . . cuius regni nos coheredes efficiat qui . . . Ff. 91vb–93vb. Also X-28.

5. T14. *Imperavit ventis et mari* (Matt 8:26). Beatus Augustinus 3 *De ciuitate Dei* capitulo 4 recitans sentenciam Uarronis dicit sic: Vtile . . .-. . . qui crediderit et baptizatus fuerit, saluus erit. Quod . . . Ff. 93vb–96ra. Also X-86.

6. T17*. *Gloriabor in infirmitatibus meis* (2 Cor 12:15). Basilius magnus in quodam sermone dicit sic: Pro summo beneficio . . .-. . . gloriam que reuelabitur in nobis. Quam gloriam . . . Ff. 96rb–97vb. Also London, British Library, Additional MS 38818, f. 193 (Basevorn?), and X-89.

7. ?. *Unus accessit* (Matt 9:18). Fulgencius in libro *De ornatu vrbis* virtutem vnitatis et concordie sic depingit . . .-. . . accessum habemus per fidem in graciam. Quam . . . Ff. 97vb–100va. Parallels E-19.

8. ?. *Sic state in Domino* (Phil 4:1). Vegecius *De re militari* . . . militantem in acie instruit in hec verba . . .-. . . sic semper cum Domino erimus. Quod . . . Ff. 100va–103ra.

F/2: *short* antethemata

1. *Ad te levavi oculos meus qui habitas in caelis* (Ps 122:1). Ad hoc quod aliquis auditor proficiat . . . F. 231ra.

2. *Cognoscetis veritatem et veritas vos* (John 8:32). Tanguntur tria que debet predicator facere . . . F. 231ra.

3. *Corruisti iniquitate tua* (Hos 14:2). Corruisti enim a gracia in culpam . . . F. 231ra.

4. *Orabat ad te omnis sanctus in tempore oportuno* (Ps 31:6). In quibus uerbis tria tanguntur que debet facere predicator: primo debet monere . . . F. 231rb.

5. *Sapientia proposuit mensam, misit ancillas suas ut vocarent ad arcem* (Prov 9:2–3). Solet esse quod quando aliquis aliquem graciosa comestione cibare requirit . . . F. 231rb.

6. *Venite, filii, audite me, timorem Domini docebo vos* (Ps 33:12). Tanguntur tria que debet facere predicator respectu auditorum . . . F. 231rb.

7. *Vita vivet, quia annuntiasti ei et animam tuam liberasti* (Ezek 3:21). Tria que debet predicator facere: primo enim debet peccata reprehendere . . . F. 231va.

8. *Emundabo eos et erunt mihi populus* (Ezek 37:23). In quibus verbis tanguntur tria que sermo Dei facit in anima . . . F. 231va.

9. *Aperuit illis sensum ut intelligerent scripturas* (Luke 24:45). In quibus verbis describuntur tria que in omni doctrina sunt necessaria . . . F. 231vb.

10. *Ioseph lota facie egressus est* (Gen 43:31). In quibus uerbis tria tanguntur que debent esse in predicatore . . . F. 231vb.

11. *Domine, vociferabor ad te vim patiens* (Hab 1:2). In quibus verbis tanguntur tria que solent facere homines quando nolunt rogare . . . F. 231vb.

12. *Sanctificatur aliquis per verbum Dei [et] orationem* (1 Tim 4:5). In quibus uerbis tria tanguntur que sunt predicatori necessaria . . . F. 231vb.

13. *Vas pretiosum labia scientiae* (Prov 20:15). In quibus verbis tanguntur tria necessaria ad hoc quod aliquis sit bonus predicator . . . F. 232ra.

14. *Beati qui audiunt verbum Dei et custodiunt illud* (Luke 11:28). Tria solet facere doctor quando uult inducere auditorem . . . F. 232ra.

15. *Vir oboediens loquitur victorias* (Prov 21:28). In quibus verbis tanguntur tria cuilibet predicatori necessaria . . . F. 232ra–b.

16. *Audite me, qui loquimini [!] quod iustum est* (Isa 51:1). Ad hoc quod aliquis ad aliam perfeccionem perueniat . . . F. 232rb.

17. *Peregrino et advenae qui intra portas tuas est [da] ut comedat* (Deut 14:21). In quibus uerbis tria tanguntur que debet facere predicator . . . F. 232rb–va.

18. *Audite disciplinam meam et estote sapientes* (Prov 8:33). Prouerbiorum 19: Audi consilium et suscipe disciplinam . . . F. 232va.

19. *Sit splendor Domini mei super nos et opus manuum nostrarum* (Ps 89:17). In quibus uerbis tria tanguntur que docent predicatorem . . . F. 232va.

20. *Super excelsum montem ascende tu qui evangelizas Sion, exalta in fortitudine vocem* (Isa 40:9). In quibus uerbis tanguntur tria que competunt predicatori . . . F. 232va.

21. *Cor prudentis [!] posside[bit scie]ntiam et auris sapientium quaerit doctrinam* (Prov 18:15). Tria tanguntur que necessaria sunt ad hoc quod aliquis proficiat in doctrina . . . F. 232va–b.

22. *Spiritu inspirati locuti sunt sancti Dei homines* (2 Pet 1:21). Tria tanguntur que sunt predicatori necesssaria . . . F. 232vb.

23. *Amice, accommoda mihi tres panes* (Luke 11:5). Tria tanguntur que facere debet predicator . . . F. 232vb.

24. *Diligite lumen sapientiae* (Wisd 6:23). Tanguntur tria que debent esse in predicatore . . . F. 232vb.

25. *Mors et vita in manibus linguae* (Prov 18:21). Tria tanguntur que facere debet predicator . . . Ff. 232vb–233ra.

26. *Vigilantes ad praedam preparant panem laboris* (Job 24:5). Qui mane vigilaueri[n]t ad me . . . F. 233ra.

27. *Vocavit nos Deus per evangelium nostrum in adquisitionem Domini nostri Iesu Christi* (2 Thess 2:14). Describuntur tria, scilicet primo quod Deus est . . . F. 233ra.

28. *Aperis tu manum tuam et imples omne animal benedictione* (Ps 144:16). Tanguntur tria que dant audaciam indigenti . . . F. 233ra–b.

29. *Dedit Deus palam facere* (Rev 1:1). Tria tanguntur que congruunt predicatori . . . F. 233rb.

30. *Caleph testificatus est in ecclesia et accepit hereditatem* (1 Mach 2:56 [ms Sir 33]). Tria esse debent in predicatore . . . F. 233rb.

31. *Venit a finibus terrae audire sapientiam Salomonis* (Luke 11:31). Tria in predicacione esse debent ad hoc quod predicacio sit efficax . . . F. 233rb–va.

32. *Praecipit tibi Dominus: vade et duc exercitum in montem* (Judg 4:6). Tria tanguntur conueniencia predicatori . . . F. 233va.

33. *Acceptus est minister regi et intelligens* (Prov 14:35). Tria in hiis uerbis notantur que debent in quolibet predicatore reperiri . . . F. 233va.

34. *Ego veni ut iudicarem tibi, quia vir desideriorum es* (Dan 9:23). Tria tanguntur que in predicatore esse debent . . . F. 233va.

35. *Ego autem mendicus sum et pauper, Dominus sollicitus est mei* (Ps 39:18). Tria tanguntur que debent competere predicatori . . . F. 233va–b.

36. *Spiritus sanctus Domini induit Abisai [!]* (1 Chr 12:18). Tria tanguntur que conueniunt predicatori . . . F. 233vb.

37. *Audi me, et quod vidi narrabo tibi* (Job 15:17). Tria notantur pro predicatore . . . F. 233vb.

38. *Conforta me, rex sanctorum principatum tenens, et da mihi sermonem rectum et bene sonantem in os meum* ("Hest' 14"). Notantur tria que primo debet predicator appetere . . . Ff. 233vb–234ra.

39. *Ego sum Dominus Deus tuus docens utilia* (Isa 48:17). Solent esse tria que mouent scolares . . . F. 234ra.

40. *Nubes rore concrescunt* (Prov 3:20). Tria sunt necessaria in predicatoribus . . . F. 234ra.

41. *Invocavi et venit in me spiritus sapientiae* (Wisd 7:7). Hic tanguntur tria que in predicatore debent esse . . . F. 234ra–b.

42. *Haurietis aquas in gaudio de fontibus salvatoris* (Isa 12:2). Scitis quod sicut aqua est mundatiua . . . F. 234rb.

43. *Oportet solem praevenire ad benedictionem* (Wisd 16:28). Tria solent adiuuare ad hoc quod peticio exaudiatur . . . F. 234rb.

44. *Nescio loqui, quia puer ego sum* (Jer 1:6). Prescitis quod intendi ad negocium arduum . . . F. 234rb–va.

45. *Misit servos suos vocare invitatos ad nuptias* (Matt 22:3). In quibus tria tanguntur predicatori necessaria . . . F. 234va.

46. *Quomodo audiet me Pharao, praesertim cum circumcisus sim labiis* (Exod 6:12). Scitis quod tria solent ardua proponentem desolari . . . F. 234va.

47. *Misit Moses nuntios ad regem* (Num 20:14?). In quibus describuntur tria que in quolibet ad predicandum destinato reperiri . . . F. 234va–b.

48. *Venite, filii, audite me*, etc. (Ps 33:12). Videamus [!] naturam in mutacionibus ordinate procedere . . . F. 234vb.

49. *Intravit sapientia cor tuum, et scientia animae tuae consilium custodiet* (Prov 2:10–11). In quibus verbis notantur tria que vnicuique ad capiendum . . . Ff. 234vb–235ra.

50. *Respexit in orationem humilium et non sprevit preces eorum* (Ps 101:18). In quibus uerbis primo innuit . . . F. 235ra.

51. *Auferte malum cogitationum vestrarum ab oculis meis, quiescite agere perverse, discite benefacere* (Isa 1:16–17). In quibus uerbis tria tanguntur que predicator debet specialiter facere . . . F. 235ra.

52. *De plenitudine eius accepimus omnes gratiam* (John 1:16). In quibus uerbis tria tanguntur que solent petentem quemque consolari . . . F. 235ra.

53. *Elegit Dominus per os meum audire gentes euangelii* (Acts 15:7). In quibus tanguntur tria que conueniunt predicatori . . . F. 235ra–b.

54. *Orate pro nobis, ut sermo Dei currat* (2 Thess 3:1). Tria iuuant predicatorem ad complendum sermonem . . . F. 235rb.

55. ?. Tria sunt conueniencia predicatori verbi Dei, primum est sciencie veritas . . . F. 235rb.

56. ?. Scitis quod Iacob supplantator interpretatur et signat predicatorem . . . F. 235rb.

57. ?. Secundum quod dicit beatus Bernardus, vnicum in dubiis remedium . . . F. 235rb–va.

58. *Vinea mea coram me est* (Cant 8:12). Vinea mea, idest talis sanctus uel ipsius vita . . . Ff. 235va.

59. ?. Triplex gracia nobis desuper collata esse dinoscitur . . . F. 235va–b.

60. ?. Sicut nos videmus quod corporaliter quod inter omne terre nascencia . . . F. 235vb.

61. ?. Secundum quod dicit Augustinus 14 *De ciuitate Dei* capitulo 2, corrupcio . . . Ff. 235vb–236ra.

62. ?. Sicut dicit Lincolniensis super 1 *Posteriorum*, nec uox . . . F. 236ra.

63. ?. Dicunt scribentes de naturis rerum quod pantera . . . F. 236ra.
64. ?. Sicut dicit Lincolniensis 1 *Posteriorum*, nec vox . . . F. 236rb; repeat of F2/62, slightly expanded.
65. *Dominus dabit verbum evangelizantibus virtute multa* (Ps 67:12). Karissimi, quemadmodum arbor corporalis per influenciam radii solaris . . . F. 236rb–va.
66. *Audite verbum Dei, et veniet vobis lucrum sine labore* (?). Dilectissimi patres et fratres, necessarium est audire ea que mores edificant . . . F. 236va–b.

F/3: Thirteen sermons by FitzRalph

1 = FI-65, ff. 237ra–240vb.
2 = FI-66, ff. 240vb–245vb.
3 = FI-69, ff. 246rb–250ra.
4 = FI-70, ff. 250ra–254ra.
5 = FI-71, ff. 254ra–257r.
6 = FI-72, ff. 257ra–260ra.
7 = FI-73, ff. 260ra–263rb.
8 = FI-74, ff. 263rb–266va.
9 = FI-75, ff. 266va–270va.
10 = FI-83, ff. 270va–273ra.
11 = FI-84, ff. 273ra–275ra, inc. (ends "in hac mortali vita consistere").
12 = FI-67, ff. 276ra–279vb.
13 = FI-68, ff. 279vb–287vb.

F/4

1. ?. *Dolentes quaerebamus te* (Luke 2:48). Karissimi, querere ab extra quod apud nos est in copia surperfluum est . . .-. . . sic igitur oues vestras querere Deus faciat, qui sine fine viuit et regnat. Amen. Ff. 288ra–290ra.
2. T02. *Erunt signa in sole* (Luke 21:25). Karissimi, Christo Domino in terris cum hominibus conuersante signa . . .-. . . sol utique, qui tunc malis preparabit penam et bonis gloriam. Quam, etc. Ff. 290ra–293vb. "Sermo magistri Ricardi Kilwyngton."
3. C15 "Incipiunt sermones et materie diuerse de eleccione." *Eligite meliorem de filiis* (2 Kgs 10:3). Reuerendi domini, sicut sacra scriptura testatur Christus de mundo transiturus . . .-. . . quod ut melius faciatis, inuocetis primo graciam Spiritus Sancti, qui semper assistat et hunc actum ad optatum finem perducat. Amen. Ff. 293vb–294vb.

4. C15*. *Facite iter et eligite* (Isa 62:10). Amantissimi patres et domini mei reuerendi, antequam iter nostrum iam inceptum progrediamur . . .-. . . istam eleccionem bene incipere et optime proficere nobis concedat . . . Ff. 294vb–296ra.

5. C15*. *Tu autem elegisti me regem populo tuo et iudicem filiorum tuorum et filiarum . . .praeceptis tuis* (Wisd 9:7–9). Postquam Salomon supplicauerit pro sapiencia impetranda et racionem . . .-. . . et dispensacione que ab optimo rege fieri possunt. Ff. 296ra–297rb. Holcot, *Super Sapienciam*, lectio 119 (in the edition of Hagenau 1494).

6. C15*. *Mitte illam de caelis sanctis tuis et a sede magnitudinis tuae, ut mecum sit . . .apud te* (Wisd 9:10). Posita supplicacione deuota pro sapiencia . . .- . . . beati qui habitant ibi et laudant Deum in secula seculorum. Quod . . . Ff. 297ra–298rb. Holcot, *Super Sapientiam*, lectio 120.

7. C15*. *Scit enim omnia illa . . . dignus sedium patris mei* (Wisd 9:11–12). Postquam Salomon declarauit quod per sapienciam quam optauit intendebat se regere . . .-. . . errare facit eos quasi ebrios. Ff. 298rb–299va. Holcot, *Super Sapientiam*, lectio 121.

8. C15*. *Quis enim hominum poteri scire . . . multa cogitantem* (Wisd 9:13–15). Postquam Salomon deuote supplicauit . . .-. . . quasi aque dilabimur in terram que non reuertentur, etc. Ff. 299vb–301ra. Holcot, *Super Sapientiam*, lectio 122.

9. C15*. *Et difficile aestimamus quae in terra sunt . . . a principio* (Wisd 9:16–19). Postquam Salomon allegauit . . .-. . . ad te conuertantur. . Ff. 301ra–302va. Holcot, *Super Sapientiam*, lectio 123.

10. C15*. *Haec illum qui primo formatus est . . . continendi omnia* (Wisd 10:1– 2). Hic signatur decimum capitulum . . .-. . . dimicantem parat eternitatis coronam. Quam . . . Ff. 302va–303va. Holcot, *Super Sapientiam*, lectio 124.

11. C15*. *Ab hac ut recessit . . . iustum gubernans* (Wisd 10:3–4). Postquam Salomon declarauit gubernacionem tam utilem . . .-. . . ambules cum uiro furioso. Ff. 303va–304rb. Holcot, *Super Sapientiam*, lectio 125.

12. C21. *Morior* (Gen 25:32 and Dan 13:43). Scitis quod pauperes et infirmi quando volunt facere homines sibi compati . . .-. . . ibunt hii in supplicium eternum, iusti autem in vitam eternam. Ad quam, etc. Ff. 304va–307vb.

13. C05. *Fortes facti sunt in bello* (Heb 11:34). Karissimi, de virtutibus ad virtutes gradatim ascendere cupientes . . .-. . . suo imperio facit esse tranquillos . . . Ff. 307vb–309ra.

14. S12* *In occursum pergit armatus, contemnit pavorem, nec cedit gladio* (Job 39:21–22). Dicitur Thimothei 2, Non coronabitur nisi qui legitime

certauerit. Vnde omnis triumphus . . .-. . . ascendit superius inter primos in patria, vbi est gloria per infinita seculorum secula. Ad quam gloriam . . . Ff. 309ra–310rb.

15. S12*. *Calix meus inebrians quam praeclarus est* (Ps 22:5). Sicud narratur inter miracula illius sancti, quod quedam fuit auis edocta loqui . . .-. . . fac nos, Christe, scandere quo Thomas ascendit, Amen. Ff. 310rb–313rb.

16. C06 (?). *Sapiens abstinebit se a peccatis et in operibus iustitiae successus habebit* (Sir 3:33). Beatus Augustinus super Psalmum 36 tempora viatoris distinguens . . .-. . . in libro *De vita Christiana*. Non hec a Christiano solum queritur. Ff. 313rb–314ra.

17. S63*. *Armatus custodit atrium* (Luke 11:21). Recitat Seneca 4 libro *Declamacionum*, declamacione 4, de accione violati sepulcri . . .-. . . de qua domo sequitur gloria et diuicie in domo eius. Quam gloriam . . . Ff. 314ra–316rb.

18. S39a*. *Enoch placuit Deo et transitus est in paradisum, ut det gentibus sapientiam* (Sir 44:16). Karissimi, cum predicator verbi Domini ex inminenti officio habeat aliquid . . .-. . . et ideo transeo et finem facio. Rogabimus, etc. Ff. 316rb–318vb.

19. C06 (?). *Labora sicut bonus miles Christi* (2 Tim 2:3). Job 7 scribitur quod milicia est vita hominis super terram. Super quo dicit Gregorius . . .-. . . ergo ut videtur non oportet laborare. Ff. 318vb–319vb.

20. C06 (?). *Fecit illum vas alterum* (Jer 18:4). Mens humana, karissimi, que capax est veritatis et vicii, efficitur vas honoris . . .-. . . statim receptum est vas in celum. Ad quod . . . Ff. 319vb–322ra.

21. C06 (?). *Factus sum uelut aes* (1 Cor 13:1). Karissimi, Gregorius *Super Ezechielem*, omelia 3, dicit eris metallum ualde sonorum est . . .-. . . per quam sit homo commensalis in celi palacio. Ad hoc palacium . . . Ff. 322ra–324va.

22. C06. *Vigilate* (1 Pet 4:7). Karissimi, sicut dicit beatus Bernardus in *Meditacionibus* suis, Nichil in hac vita dulcius sentitur . . . .-. . . faciet illos discumbere in regno celesti. Quod regnum . . . Ff. 324va–328ra.

23. S19*?. *Vincenti dabo edere de ligno vitae* (Rev 2:7). Pugil aggrediens bellum pro alio uult esse certus de salario pro victoria . . .-. . . pendentis in ea Iesu Christi, cui sit honor et gloria. Ff. 328ra–328va.

24. C06. *Vincenti dabo edere de ligno vitae* (Rev 2:7). Omissis introductis et diuisione, agendum est de prosecucione. Karissimi, instat nobis multiplex pugnacio . . .-. . . edent pauperes et saturabuntur, etc. Quod . . . Ff. 328va–329va.

25. C06. *Sacerdos magnus circuivit* (Jdt 4:11). Secundum iura, vbi maius periculum est, caucius est agendum . . .-. . . Iob 1: Circuiui terram et perambulaui eam, etc. F. 329va–b.

26. C03*. *Opus fac evangelistae* (2 Tim 4:5). Karissimi, sicut dicit Philosophus in *Ethicis*, ex non operando nullus efficit bonus . . .-. . . hec gloria erit in patria sempiterna. Ff. 329vb–330vb.

27. S54*. *Effulsit in templo Dei* (Sir 50:7). Secundum Ysidorum celum diuiditur in tres partes . . .-. . . propter quod dicit Apostolus, Omnia in gloriam Dei facite, etc. Ff. 330vb–331vb.

28. C06, perhaps S73*. *Redde quod debes* (Matt 18:28). Meditantibus dupliciter sunt debita onerosa, predicantibus imponuntur onera laboriosa . . .-. . . ut hanc caritatem Christo creatori nostro nubia, ut sic propter eam coronemur in patria. Amen. Ff. 331vb–333va.

29. C06. *Egredere et clama* (?). Duo: expressa locucio confitentis, clama, compunccio vetustatem reicit delictorum, locucio integritatem reficit iam lapsorum . . .-. . . quoniam infirmus sum et vere miserebitur nostri Deus. Ff. 333va–334rb.

30. C06, perhaps S25*. *Transfiguratus est ante eos* (Matt 17:2). Karissimi, Saluator noster Iesus in euangelio Luce 8 assimilat illum qui predicat Dei verbum uiro que seminat semen . . .-. . . talia monachis seu clericis indigna et inhonesta. Ff. 334rb–337rb.

1. T06 or rather T05*. *Dominus vobiscum* (Ruth 2:4). Karissimi, quamuis ex proposito themate in presenti solempnitate . . .-. . . dominus virtutum, ipse est rex glorie. Ad quam . . . Ff. 340ra–341rb.

2. T06. *Exiit sermo inter fratres* (John 21:23). Deuocio exterior signum est euidens deuocionis interioris . . .-. . . populum suum faciat intrare qui de ista gloria inter fratres uoluit exire. Amen. Ff. 341rb–342ra.

3. T06. *Homo ad laborem nascitur* (Job 5:7). In verbis proponitur [!] describitur ydoneus predicator . . .-. . . ad laborem voluntarie passionis nascitur. Huius ergo mediator . . . Ff. 342ra–343va.

4. T06. *Sol egressus est super terram* (Gen 19:23). Karissimi, exigente peccato primi parentis omnia elementa in vindictam . . .-. . . beata Virgo hodie fructum suum. De cuius fructus dulcedine nos repleat . . . Ff. 343va–344ra.

5. C19. *Visita nos, Domine* (Ps 105:4?). Karissimi, tres sunt condiciones hominum precipue indigentes . . .-. . . Filius Hominis descendet de celo et filius Dei crucifixus est. F. 344ra–b.

6. T06 or rather T05*. *Vos estote parati* (Matt 24:44 or Luke 12:40). Sicut humana tenet consuetudo et scripturarum tradit certitudo. tria adsumit ad que homines se prepare solent . . .-. . . a summo celo egressio eius et occursus eius vsque ad summum eius. Ff. 344rb–345ra.

7. T06. *Haec est dies boni nuntii* (2 Kgs 7:9). Sic clamat regula duplicis artis, rhetorice scilicet et po[e]tice . . .-. . . dulcis erit et consula [?] et paruula melodia. Quem . . . F. 345ra–vb.

8. ?. *Media nocte egrediar in Aegyptum* (Exod 11:4). Humanum genus propter peccatum primorum parentum . . .-. . . spiritualiter sanati ad visionem istius mereatur peruenire . . . Ff. 345vb–346rb.

9. S86. *Benedicta tu in mulieribus* (Luke 1:28). Karissimi, sicud preceptis salutaribus monitis et diuina institucione . . .-. . . percipite regnum quod uobis est paratum ab origine mundi. Quod regnum . . . Ff. 346va–347rb.

10. S86*. *Solem nube tegam* (Ezek 32:7). Qui sunt isti qui vt nubes volant, Isaie v.s. [=60:8]. In hiis verbis Ysaias per nubes dat nobis intelligere predicatores . . .-. . . sed recurramus igitur ad hanc vmbram dum peregrinamur in via et fructu illius arboris fruamur in patria. Quod . . . Ff. 347rb–348va.

11. S28*. *Haec est dies boni nuntii* (2 Kgs 7:9). Sicut haberi potest de beato Dionisio in *Ecclesiastica ierarchia*, illa que sunt in ierarchia celesti . . .-. . . in patria ex diuina visione et fruccione feliciter deriuatur. Cuius visionis . . . Ff. 348va–350rb.

12. S86. *Solem nube tegam* (Ezek 32:7). Commentator super *Angelicam ierarchiam* quinto capitulo id sensibilium symbolorum . . .-. . . similes vespertilioni qui omnia[?] pant[?]. F. 350rb.

13. T18/4. *Quid superbis, terra et cinis* (Sir 10:9). Dominice sapiencie inscrutabilis altitudo, indescibilis plenitudo . . .-. . . memento quoniam mors non tradat. Rogabimus, etc. Ff. 350va–351ra.

14. T36. *Civitatem fortium ascendit sapiens* (Prov 21:22). Quia Filius, qui de celo descenderat cum humilitate, hodie de terra sursum ad celos ascendit . . .- . . . quando in tuba et voce descendet, sibi obuiam venientes semper cum ipso regnemus. Qui . . . F. 351ra–b.

15. S86. *Dilectus meus descendit in hortum suum* (Cant 6:1). In sillogisticis ita est quod secundum condicionem medii . . .-. . . et de futuris cautelam et prouidenciam. Et tandem nos perducat . . . Ff. 351rb–352va.

16. T19. *Quasi morientes et ecce vivimus* (2 Cor 6:9). Prouerbiorum 18 [:21] dicitur mors et vita in manu lingue . . .-. . . ibunt hii in supplicium eternum, iusti vero in vitam eternam. Quam vitam . . . Ff. 352va–353va.

17. ?. *Est qui quaerat et iudicet* (John 8:51). Tria inveniuntur in hiis qui presunt quamplurimum que prebent suis subditis . . .-. . . quod vobis paratum est ab origine mund, Mathei 25. Hanc acceptacionem . . . Ff. 353va–354va.

18. T23. *Sanguis Christi emundabit conscientiam nostram* (Heb 9:14). Secundum Philosophum 2 *De anima,* animalia que carent sanguine . . .-. . . non adquieui carni et sanguini, etc. Ff. 354va–355ra.

19. T23?. *Sanguis Christi emundabit conscientiam nostram* (Hebr 9:14). Secundum Philosophum 2 *De anima,* omnia animalia que carent sanguine . . .-. . . gloria hec est omnibus sanctis eius. Ad quam . . . F. 355ra–vb.

20. ?. *Vidi finem* (Ps 118:96). Apud philosophos et sapientes est finis animi concepcio . . .-. . . que non est in potestate voluntatis; ergo, etc. F. 356ra–vb.

21. S59. *Puella non est mortua sed dormit* (Matt 9:24, Mark 5:39, Luke 8:52). Concorditer scribuntur in tribus ewangeliis . . .-. . . inspirauit, quem Beata Virgo tam habunde recepit. Qui . . . Ff. 357ra–358va.

22. S59. *Hodie incipiam exaltare te coram omni Israel* (Josh 3:7). Sicut dicit Augustinus *Super Johannem* omelia 31, nichil aliud in hac vite nostre peregrinacione meditemur . . .-. . . Maria se humiliando exaltata est, non solum ad locum paradysi celestis, vt corregnet filio suo in secula seculorum. Amen, etc. Ff. 358va–359rb.

23. S65. *Dixit Deus: Fiat lux, et facta est lux . . . tenebras* (Gen 1:3). Verba ista optime conpetunt natiuitati Beate Virgini, nam sicud Deus in mundi creacione . . .-. . . tenebre eam non comprehenderunt, etc. Ff. 359rb–359va. Cf. Valencia, Biblioteca del Calbildo, MS 284 (Schneyer 6:211).

24. T39. *Lux venit in mundum* (John 3:19). Dilectissimi, quedam est lux exterior corporalis . . .-. . . et luminose vl'r et spaciose, etc. Amen. Ff. 359va–360va.

25. T06. *Apparuit Filius Dei,* etc. (1 John 3:8). Quem Filium Dei, qui hodie mundo apparuit, in carne inuenimus in sacra scriptura . . .-. . . veritas sine errore, felicitas sine perturbacione. Ad quod regnum . . . Ff. 360va–362ra.

26. T06. *Egressus est a filia Sion omnis decor eius* (Lam 1:6). Verba magne dulcedinis diuine benignitatis . . .-. . . decepisti me temporaliter, decepta es eternaliter. Ff. 362ra–364ra.

27. ?. *Sic currite ut comprehendatis* (1 Cor 9:24). Fratres, orate vt sermo Dei currat et clarificetur. Scribuntur Tessa 4. Secundum doctrinam beati Pauli debemus orare . . .-. . . ad Iesum, qui saluat nos in presenti [per] graciam, in futuro per gloriam, etc. Amen, etc. F. 364ra–vb.

28. S21*. *Laetus moriar, quia vidi faciem tuam et superstitem te relinquo* (Gen 46:30). Hodie Filii Dei presentacionem, matris Dei purificacionem, serui

Dei exspectacionem . . .-. . . vidi igitur faciem tuam. Quam faciem . . . Ff. 364vb–366ra.

29. ?. *Virtus in infirmitate perficitur* (2 Cor 12:9). Sedete in ciuitate quoadusque induamini virtute ex alto, in Luca. Karissimi, os predicatoris verbi Dei est instrumentum Creatoris . . .-. . . requies transquilla purus te terrene finis. Ad quem . . . F. 366ra–vb.

30. T01*. *Rex tuus venit* (Matt 21:5). Aduentus Domini per quatuor septimanas agitur ad signandum . . .-. . . exultabunt sancti in gloria. Ad quam . . . Ff. 366vb–368ra.

31. C19*. *Visita vineam istam* (Ps 79:15). Sicud ab omnipotente omnia producuntur originaliter et eciam [ad] ipsum reducuntur . . .-. . . nec rerum temporalium amor subuertat . . . F. 368ra–va. Also Bodley 4 and elsewhere (Schneyer 6:137, 6: 249, 7:68 and 78).

32. ?. *Crucifixus est ut destruatur corpus peccati* (Rom 6:6). Vltra non seruiamus peccato . . . Karissimi, duo proposita predicator verbi Dei debet assumere . . .-. . . vt peccatis mortui iusticie viuamus. Quam vitam . . . Ff. 368va–369vb.

33. S79 vigil*?. *Beati viri tui* (1 Kgs 10:8). Karissimi, in sacra scriptura multiplex legitur beatitudo . . .-. . . exultabunt sancti in gloria. Ad quam . . . Ff. 369vb–371va.

34. ?. *Visita vineam istam* (Ps 79:15). Sicud ab omnipotente omnia producuntur originaliter et eciam [ad] ipsum reducuntur finaliter . . .-. . . quia tibi mentaliter obtemperantes. Ad hos viros bonos . . . Ff. 371va–b. See above no. 31.

35. ?. *In omnibus divites facti estis* (1 Cor 1:5). Facti sumus paruuli in medio vestrum, Tessalonicensium 2. In verbis, karissimi, secundo propositis tria breuiter notari poterunt . . .-. . . facti sumus letantes. Ad quam leticiam . . . Ff. 371vb–373rb.

36. S81a*. *Perambulabam in innocentia cordis mei in medio domus meae* (Ps 100:2). In medio multorum laudabo eum, in Psalmo [108:30]. Vbi prohennnatur [=prophecialiter] proponuntur duo que, vt credo, meam insufficienciam possunt confortare . . .-. . . induit eum aureola, videlicet virginalis mundicia, et coronauit debita sue innocencie. Quam . . . Ff. 373rb–374rb. Also Oxford, New College, MS 92, f. 53v.

37. T31*. *Arguet mundum de peccato* (John 16:8). Ego elegi uos de mundo et posui vos ut eatis et fructum afferatis, scribuntur in Iohanne [15:16]. Saluator noster in Johanne loquitur de eleccione apostolorum . . .-. . . tota

Trinitas vos recipiat et ad gloriam perducet. Ad quam . . . Ff. 374rb–375vb. Also Oxford, New College, MS 92, f. 114, and Worcester Q.46.

38. S81*. *Scidi pallium meum* (Ezra 9:2). Ista verba vno modo possi[n]t esse verba predicatoris . . .-. . . illud pallium glorificacionis feliciter induet. Quod pallium . . . Ff. 375vb–377va.

39. ?. *Genuit nos verbo veritatis,* etc. (James 1:18). Et in eodem capitulo iubet dictus apostolus in mansuetudine verbi Dei . . . In quibus verbis tria notantur, scilicet effectus diuini verbi . . .-. . . hec est omnibus fauctis[?] eius. Ad quam gloriam . . . Ff. 377va–378rb.

40. ?. *Misit ignem in ossibus meis et erudivit me* (Lam 1:13). Inter cetera, ymo pre ceteris, tria predicatori sunt necessaria: primo quod sit eloquens . . .- . . . Dominus Iesus Christus in gloria Dei Patri est. Ad quam . . . Ff. 378rb–379va.

41. T30*. *Conversi estis nunc,* etc. (1 Pet 2:25). In Psalmo: Nisi conuersi fueritis, gladium suum vibrabit. De quo dicitur in Ezechielis 33 . . .-. . . finem habetis vitam eternam contra tercium. Ad quam . . . Ff. 379va–380rb.

42. T37*. *Estote prudentes et vigilate in orationibus* (1 Pet 4:7). Karissimi, verbum diuinum vult suptiliter interrius [!] inteligi . . .-. . . ibi eciam dignitas, sanctitas, vita, eternitas. Ad quam . . . Ff. 380rb–381rb.

43. ?. *Spiritus meus erit in medio vestri, nolite timere* (Hag 2:6). Nolite timere eos . . . in jehennam, Mathei 10 . . .-. . . alius diuicie et gloria vsque lignum vite, etc. Ff. 381rb–383va.

44. ?. *Orietur vobis timentibus nomen meum sol iustitiae* (Mal 4:2). In verbis istis duo notantur principaliter: primo Christi aduentus . . .-. . . super nos lumen wltus tui, Domine. Ad quod lumen . . . F. 383va.

45. S85*. *Nigra sum et formosa* (Cant 1:4). Secundum beatum Augustinum *Super Iohannem* sermone vltimo, duas vitas mater Ecclesia . . .-. . . in regno celorum tripplici diademate coronat. Ad quod regnum . . . Ff. 383va–384ra.

46. ?. [*Dominum Deum Iesum Christum?*] (?). Gracia Dei necessaria est in quolibet opere, quia est ignorancie documentum . . .-. . . clamans voce magna emisit spiritum sanctum [!], etc. F. 384ra–b.

47. S82a*. *Beata terra cuius rex nobilis est* (Qoh 10:17). Beatus homo quem tu erudieris . . . In quibus verbis ostenditur nobis Deus vt lex . . .-. . . quod seminatum est [*blank*] surget in gloriam. Ad quam . . . Ff. 384rb–385va. Also New College 92, f. 45, and Worcester Q.46.

48. T01*. *Veni, Domine Iesu* (Rev 22:20). Sicud dixerunt mundi sapientes et eciam sancti doctores, prius debet homo orare quam probare . . .-

. . . perseuerantes perducet ad hereditatem eternam. Ad quam . . . Ff. 385va–386vb. Also New College 92, f. 61, and Q.46.

49. T42*. *Diligamus Deum, quoniam ipse prior dilexit nos* (1 John 4:19). Inter plura signa dileccionis tria sunt principalia . . .-. . . suauitas atque dulcedo de Dei visione. Ad quam . . . Ff. 386vb–388rb. Also Worcester Q.46.

50. S12*. *Quare rubrum est indumentum tuum* (Isa 63:2). Secundum Johannem [!] super Ysaiam libro 17, vox ista vox angelorum fuit videncium Dominum celos ascendere . . .-. . . et sic fuit ornatus omni lapide precioso, etc. Ff. 388rb–390ra. Also New College 92, f. 77, and Q.46.

51. ?. *Tres unum sunt* (John 4). In Luca scribitur: Amice, commoda michi tres panes. Amicus de quo hic fit mencio secundum Glossam Deus est . . .-. . . vnde soli veraces ad eum accedunt. Ad quam [!] accessum . . . Ff. 390ra–391ra. Also Q.46.

52. S85*. *Gloria Libani data est ei, decor Carmeli et Saron* (Isa 35:2). Dicit in acccione naturali non potest inpassio forma . . .-. . . habentes passiones indomitas non possunt bene intelligere. Ff. 391ra–392rb.

53. ?. *Ecce morior, cum nichil horum fecerim quae isti malitiose composuerunt adversum me* (Dan 13:43). In sermone eius conposita sunt omnia, Ecclesiastici 43, et licet dicta sint de sermone interiori . . .-. . . eius incarnacione magnificemur. Ff. 392rb–394rb.

54. S82a*. *Videte regem* (Cant 3:11). Loquiturus, fratres karissimi, de rege quondam terreno sed iam celesti . . .-. . . cum hoc rege in celesti regno eternaliter coregnet. Quod . . . Ff. 394va–395vb.

55. T21*. *Ambulate in dilectione* (Eph 5:2). Reuerendi patres et domini, inter vias condicionis humane tres uideo pertinentes . . .-. . . et caritas eius in nobis perfecta est. Ad quam . . . Ff. 395vb–397rb.

56. S10*. *Veni dilecte mi* (Cant 7:11?). Domine, labia mea aperies, in Psalmo. Ad hoc quod aliquis verbum concipiat . . .-. . . pro tua humilitate ad gradum ineffabilis excellencie. Ad quam coronam . . . Ff. 397rb–399rb. Also X-251 without the protheme.

57. S31*. *Ambulavit pes meus iter rectum* (Sir 51:20). Recti diligunt te, Canticorum 1. Karissimi, in verbis secundo propositis predicatores verbi Dei commendantur a tribus, videlicet a statu, actu, et obiecto . . .-. . . adducet directum ad illum et letificabit illum. Ad quam leticiam . . . Ff. 399rb–400vb. Also Worcester Q.46.

58. T43. *Homo quidam fecit cenam magnam* (Luke 14:16). Nos videmus per experienciam fi's et vale'a prandium vel cenam ad sustentacionem

corporis . . .-. . . que omnia sunt in illa cena, hoc est felicitas superna. Ad quam . . . Ff. 400vb–401vb.

59. ?. *Conversus Petrus vidit discipulum quem diligebat Iesus* (John 21:20). Nos videmus in regno terrestri quod inter probos . . .-. . . et dabo ei coronam vite et subditur. F. 401vb, inc.

FE – Felton

Inventory based on Lincoln Cathedral MS 204.

1. T01. *Dicite filiae Sion, Ecce rex tuus venit tibi* (Matt 21:5). Sciendum est quod gracia Dei est nobis necessaria . . .-. . . iudicabo uos. Sic recipere Christum in primo aduentu et secundo, quatenus ipse nos recipiat per misericordiam suam in tercio, ipse idem Christus concedat. Amen. Ff. 1ra–4vb.

2. T02. *Tunc videbunt Filium Hominis venientem* (Luke 21:27). Nota de duabus tubis argenteis, Numeri 10, quarum officium secundum Magistrum Historiarum . . .-. . . iusti autem in vitam eternam. Ad quam . . . Ff. 4va–6ra.

3. T03. *Cum audisset Iohannes in vinculis opera Christi*, etc. (Matt 11:2). Legitur in *Alphabeto predicancium* de quodam habente paruum beneficium . . .-. . . tu vero felici consummacione transibis ad regnum. Quod . . . Ff. 6ra–7ra.

4. T04. *Ego vox clamantis in deserto: dirigite viam Domini* (John 1:23). Dicit sanctus Paulus Romanorum 13, Hora est iam . . .-. . . oportet nos intrare in regnum celorum. Et ad illud . . . Ff. 7ra–9va.

5. T04. *Gaudete in Domino* (Phil 4:4). Legitur 1 Regum 16 quod quando malignus spiritus . . .-. . . omnem gradum humilitatis. Sic nos . . . Ff. 9va–11ra.

6. S11. *Sequuntur agnum* (Rev 14:4). Diceret forte quis quod agnus, scilicet Christus, secutus est eos . . .-. . . quatenus verificetur de omnibus nobis Hii sequuntur agnum. Quod . . . Ff. 11ra–12vb. Edited from Oxford, Oriel College MS 10, with translation in Fletcher, *Preaching*, pp. 86–99.

7. T07. *Ecce positus est hic in ruinam*, etc. (Luke 2:34). Crisostomus super Matheum *Opere imperfecto* omelia 30 [*read* 20] assimilat predicacionem pluuie . . .-. . . habens multas possessiones. Nos sic iusticiam Dei formidare . . . Ff. 13rb–14ra.

8. T11. *Ecce agnus Dei* (John 1:29). Sciendum est quod in veteri testamento quando populus Dei transiturus erat . . .-. . . agnus Dei. Sic in hac vita Deum et proximum diligere . . . F. 13rb–vb.

9. T11a. *Remansit puer Iesus in Ierusalem* (Luke 2:43). Dicit Augustinus in quodam sermone quod quilibet homo habet duos homines . . .-. . . vt videant, etc. Nos sic Christum recuperare . . . Ff. 14vb–15vb.

10. T12. *Nuptiae factae sunt in Cana Galilaeae* (John 2:1). Dicit Christus Luce 11, Beati qui audiunt verbum Dei . . .-. . . et anime in limbo. Nos sic desponsari . . . Ff. 16ra–17va.

11. T13. *Secutae sunt eum turbae multae* (Matt 8:1). Vnde ad literam cum Iesus descendisset de monte . . .-. . . se gladiis interficientes. Nos ergo a lepra . . . Ff. 17va–19rb.

12. T14. *Ascendente Iesu in naviculam, secuti sunt eum discipuli eius* (Matt 8:23). Augustinus 4 libro *De doctrina Christiana*, capitulo 30, hortatur hominem qui vult sapienter loqui . . .-. . . caueant ne cadant. Nos sic pericula maris . . . Ff. 19rb–20rb.

13. T15. *Semen bonum seminasti in agro tuo* (Matt 13:27). Dicit Salvator Iohannis 8, Qui est ex Deo . . .-. . . ita habebunt graciam in huius vite via et gloriam in celesti patria. Quod . . . Ff. 20rb–21vb.

14. T16. *Redde illis mercedem* (Matt 20:7). Legitur Numeri 22 quod angelus qui missus fuerat ad prohibendum Balaam . . .-. . . et ipse reddet nobis mercedem in patria. Quod . . . Ff. 21vb–24rb.

15. T17. *Exiit qui seminat seminare semen suum* (Luke 8:5). Sciendum est quod Sapiencie 16 habetur quod Dominus prestitit populo suo panem de celo . . .- . . . accendendum in infernum procientur. Dominus noster sic dignetur . . . Ff. 24rb–26ra.

16. T18. *Caecus sedebat secus viam* (Luke 18:35). Sciatis, amici, quod si quis in nocte peregre iturus esset per viam incognitam . . .-. . . desideria eternorum. Nos sic euitare cecitatem spiritualem . . . Ff. 26rb–27ra.

17. T19. *Ductus est Iesus in desertum* (Matt 4:1). Sciendum est quod omnis homo fit ex duabus substanciis . . .-. . . et tu tempteris. Nos sic vincere . . . Ff. 27ra–28vb.

18. T20. *Miserere mei, Domine* (Matt 15:22). Dicit Lincolniensis in libro *De summa iusticia* quod gracia Dei est necessaria tam predicatori quam verbum Dei audienti . . .-. . . humiliter exorabant. Nos sic precibus sanctorum . . . Ff. 28vb–30vb.

19. T21. *Locutus est mutus* (Luke 11:14). Amici, gracia Dei est nobis necessaria. Hoc ostenditur in arte . . .-. . . caput, idest potestatem, eius amputare. Quod . . . Ff. 30vb–33vb.

20. T22. *Est puer unus hic qui habet quinque panes* (John 6:9). Karissimi, gracia Dei est nobis necessaria. Hoc ostenditur per exemplum et

figuram . . .-. . . perfruamur hoc pane semper in patria. Quod . . . Ff. 33vb–36ra.

21. T23. *Exivit de templo* (John 8:59). Sciendum est, karissimi, testante sacra scriptura 1 Machabeorum 3, cum nephandissimus ille rex Antiochus . . .- . . . eius hereditatem, scilicet regnum celorum. Quod . . . Ff. 36ra–38rb.

22. T24. *Straverunt vestimenta sua in via* (Matt 21:8). Narratur de quodam habente beneficium paruum . . .-. . . Ff. 38rb–[39vb]. In Lincoln Cathedral MS 204 several folios are wanting here; they may have contained the following sermons:

23. T28. *Qui manducat hunc panem vivet in aeternum* (John 6). Augustinus 4 libro *De doctrina Christiana* cap. 17 ostendit quod qui vult illa suadere . . . In University of Pennsylvania MS lat. 35, ff. 66v–69. Also J/5-35.

24. T28. *Acceperunt corpus Iesu* (John 19:40). Dicit Augustinus in sermone quod cuilibet incipienti opus bonum gracia Dei est necessaria . . .-. . . poterimus ad eternum brauium peruenire. Hoc . . . In University of Pennsylvania MS lat. 35, ff. 69–72v. Ending in Lincoln Cathedral MS 204 at f. 40va. Also Bodley 687, ff. 74v–76v.

25. T29. *Venit Iesus et stetit in medio* (John 20:19). Dicit Cistrensis in distinccionibus suis quod predicator debet ante sermonem orare vt sermo Dei currat et fructificet in auditoribus . . .-. . . malis penam et bonis premium eternum. Quod . . . Ff. 40va–42rb.

26. T30. *Ego sum pastor bonus* (John 10:11). Dicit Christus Iohannis 8: Qui est ex Deo, verba Dei audit. Vnde sciendum est . . .-. . . condempnatus in aduentu Domini. Dominus Iesus Christus, qui est essencialiter pastor bonus, concedat omnes pastores inferiores sic pascere . . . Ff. 42rb–44ra.

27. T31. *Tristitia vestra vertetur in gaudium* (John 16:20). Legitur in *Gestis Romanorum* quod Theodosius imperator summe dilexit venacionem . . .- . . . liberari a tormentis. Nos sic pati . . . Ff. 44ra–45va.

28. T32. *Ille arguet mundum de peccato* (John 16:8). Legitur 2 Regum 13 quod Absolon interfecit fratrem suum . . .-. . . semel vidisse est omnia scire. Ad quod collegium . . . Ff. 45va–47va.

29. T33. *Si quid petieritis Patrem in nomine meo, dabit vobis* (John 16:23). Sciendum est quod ista dominica dicitur dominica Rogacionum . . .-. . . vera obediencia est celestis via. Nos sic scalam . . . Ff. 47va–49rb.

30. T37. *Absque synagogis facient vos* (John 16:2). Legitur 4 Regum 2 quod Helias assumendus in paradisum dixit Helizeo . . .-. . . domum non manu factam eternam in celo. Quam . . . Ff. 49rb–51rb.

31. T39. *Si quis diligit me, sermonem meum servabit* (John 14:23). Sciendum est quod predicatores specialiter vocantur ministri Dei . . .-. . . fons eius est amor mundi. Sic maneat nobiscum Spiritus Sanctus . . . Ff. 51rb–53ra.

32. T40. *Quod scimus loquimur, et quod vidimus testamur, et testimonium nostrum non accipitis* (John 3:11). Dicit sanctus Iacobus Iacobi 1, Siquis autem indiget sapiencia . . .-. . . iusti fulgebunt sicut sol in regno patris eorum. Quod . . . Ff. 53ra–55rb.

33. T42. *Mortuus est dives* (Luke 16:22). Dicit Apostolus 2 Corinthiorum 3 quod non sumus sufficientes . . .-. . . habet nomen quod os Domini nominauit Ysaie 62. Hoc nomen . . . Ff. 55rb–58vb.

34. T43. *Homo quidam fecit cenam magnam et vocavit multos* (Luke 14:16). Dicit Ecclesia Christo Canticorum 5: Anima mea liquefacta est . . .-. . . vocauit nos Dominus ad cenam suam. Ad quam . . . Ff. 58vb–60va.

35. T44. *Gaudium est angelis Dei super uno peccatore paenitentiam agente* (Luke 15:10). Legitur Malachie 3: Ecce ego mitto angelum meum et preparabit . . .-. . . tunc coronaberis corona glorie eterne. Illam coronam . . . Ff. 60va–61vb.

36. T45. *Estote misericordes sicut et Pater misericors est* (Luke 6:36). Sciendum est quod Apostolus orauit specialiter pro Colocensibus . . .-. . . suffragia pro existentibus in purgatorio, vt ipsi a penis liberati et in celo collocati nobis impetrent veniam in presenti et in futuro vitam sine fine. Amen. Ff. 61vb–63vb.

37. T46. *Relictis omnibus secuti sunt eum* (Luke 5:11). In hoc euangelio fit mencio de piscacione; quapropter ego ad presens venio ad capiendum pisces pro cena Domini . . .-. . . benedicti Patris mei, percipite regnum, etc. Istud regnum . . . Ff. 63vb–65vb. Edited from Oxford, Oriel College MS 10, with translation in Fletcher, *Preaching*, pp. 100–113.

38. T46. *Praeceptor, per totam noctem laborantes nichil coepimus* (Luke 5:5). Predicatores Dei vocantur piscatores, venatores, et vindemiatores . . .-. . . cum sint negociatores regni, Luce 18. Quod regnum . . . Ff. 65vb–67ra.

39. T47. *Nisi abundaverit iustitia vestra plus quam Scribarum et Pharisaeorum*, etc. (Matt 5:20). Sciendum est quod quilibet homo fit ex duobus substanciis . . .-. . . heredes erimus regni eterni. Quod regnum . . . Ff. 67rb–68va.

40. T48. *Misereor super turbam, quia ecce iam triduo sustinent me* (Mark 8:2). Verbum enim Domini necessarium est omni volenti seruari . . .-. . . quod preparasti expectantibus te. Istud gaudium . . . Ff. 68va–70ra.

41. T49. *Attendite a falsis prophetis* (Matt 7:15). Dicit Christus 14 Luce: Quis rex iturus committere bellum . . .-. . . bonorum laborum gloriosus est fructus. Istum fructum . . . Ff. 70ra–72va.

42. T50. *Facite vobis amicos* (Luke 16:9). Verbum Dei necessarium est saluare animas suas volentibus . . .-. . . venite, benedicti, in regnum patris mei, etc. Illud regnum . . . Ff. 72va–74rb.

43. T51. *Videns civitatem flevit super illam* (Luke 19:41). Legitur Iohannis 11 quod Christus in resuscitacione Lazari primo fleuit, secundo orauit, tercio clamauit . . .-. . . vsque hic saluus erit. Hoc . . . Ff. 74rb–77vb.

44. T52. *Omnis qui se exaltat humiliabitur*, etc. (Luke 18:14). Karissimi, si quis spargerit aurum vel argentum . . .-. . . ad Christum venire meriamur. Quod . . . Ff. 77vb–79ra.

45. T53. *Adducunt ei surdum et mutum* (Mark 7:32). Sciendum est quod aduersarius noster continue pugnat contra nos cum tribus exercitibus . . .-. . . multos quos Conditor non agnoscit. Nos sic credere . . . Ff. 79vb–80va.

45a. T53. *Adducunt ei surdum et mutum* (Mark 7:32). Dicit Theophilus quod omnia que in corpore Christi fuerunt sancta et diuina fuerunt siue vestimenta eius siue digiti eius siue sputum eius . . . A second sermon for T53, not in Lincoln MS 204. In University of Pennsylvania MS lat. 35 at ff. 133v–135.

46. T54. *Homo quidam descendebat ab Hierusalem in Hiericho*, etc. (Luke 10:30). Sciendum est quod oracio est necessaria pugnaturo cum diabolo . . .-. . . habentur vita gracie in presenti et vita glorie in futuro. Quam vitam . . . Ff. 80va–82vb.

47. T55. *Occurrerunt ei decem viri leprosi* (Luke 17:12). Sicut dicit Augustinus, De celo venit magnus medicus . . .-. . . et ille habebit vitam eternam. Quod . . . Ff. 82vb–84vb.

48. T56. *Scit enim Pater vester quia hiis omnibus indigetis* (Matt 6:8). Sciendum est quod gracia Dei est necessaria tam predicatori quam audientibus . . .-. . . vbi vera sunt gaudia. Quod . . . Ff. 84vb–86va.

49. T57. *Defunctus efferebatur*, etc. (Luke 7:12). Sciendum est quod oracio est quasi columba que reuersa est ad archam . . .-. . . et veni, scilicet ad gaudia paradisi. Ad illa . . . Ff. 86va–88ra.

50. T58. *Amice, ascende superius* (Luke 14:10). Dicit Lincolniensis in libro *De summa iusticia* quod gracia Dei est necessaria tam predicanti quam audienti verbum Dei . . .-. . . requiem celi, que nunquam finietur. Ad quam . . . Ff. 88ra–91rb.

51. T59. *In duobus mandatis tota lex pendet et prophetae* (Matt 22:40). Gracia Dei predicatori est necessaria. Hoc ostenditur in arte. Sicut agricola potest agrum suum diligenter exercere . . .-. . . sicut teipsum, scilicet ad graciam in presenti et ad gloriam in futuro. Ad illam . . . Ff. 91rb–92vb.

52. T60. *Ait Dominus paralitico: Tolle lectum tuum, et vade in domum tuam* (Matt 9:6). Gracia Dei predicatori est necessaria. Hoc ostenditur in figura. Exodi 35 et 36 Deus impleuit Beselleel spiritu sapiencie . . .-. . . gloria et diuicie in domo eius. Ad istam domum . . . Ff. 92vb–95ra.

53. T61. *Amice, quomodo huc intrasti non habens vestem nuptialem?* (Matt 22:12). Dicunt doctores quod in cuiuslibet boni operis principio debemus mittere ad Deum oracionem . . .-. . . gaudebit super te Deus tuus. Ad illas nupcias . . . Ff. 95ra–96vb.

54. T62. *Erat quidam regulus cuius filius infirmabatur Capharnaum* (John 4:46). Misericordia Dei nobis est necessaria . . .-. . . alii in opprobrium. Sciendum est quod hic ponuntur articuli fidei dati ab apostolis et autoritates prophetarum qui conueniunt in articulis. Ff. 96vb–100ra.

55. T63. *Redde quod debes* (Matt 18:28). Augustinus *De spiritu et anima* tractans illud verbum Petite et accipietis ait: Nunquam tantum ortaretur . . .-. . . ad suam misericordiam possimus peruenire. Quod . . . Ff. 100ra–101vb.

56. T64. *Obtulerunt ei denarium* (Matt 22:19). Dicit Apostolus 1 Timothei 2: Obsecro primo omnium fieri . . .-. . . saluus erit, scilicet in eterna gloria. Quam . . . Ff. 101vb–103va.

57. T65. *Confide, filia Sion [!], fides tua te saluam fecit* (Matt 9:22). Scitis, karissimi, quod si rex tradidisset vni ex militibus suis castrum ad custodiendum . . .-. . . reficiam vos, scilicet pane glorie. Illam [!] panem . . . Ff. 103va–105rb.

58. T66. *Est puer unus hic qui habet quinque panes* (John 6:9). Sciendum est quod in veteri testamento, quando populus Dei transitus erat ad bellum . . .-. . . gloria, laus, requies, amor, et concordia dulcis. Ad illa gaudia . . . Ff. 105rb–106vb.

FI – FitzRalph

Based on Oxford, Bodleian Library, MS Bodley 144. I have added, as item 93, FitzRalph's *introitus* found in Oxford, Oriel College MS 15. For the dates I have followed Gwynn, who also gives the complete headnotes to the sermons: Aubrey Gwynn, SJ, "The Sermon-Diary of Richard FitzRalph, Archbishop of Armagh," *Proceedings of the Royal Irish Academy* 44 C (1937): 1–57, at 48–57.

1. T18/4 (1353 or 1354). *Cum ieiunas, unge caput tuum et faciem tuam lava* (Matt 6:17). Per caput mentem intellige . . .-. . . si ergo sic ieiunauerimus, habebimus graciam in presenti et gloriam in futuro. F. 1r–v.

2. C19*. *Videte, vigilate, et orate* (Mark 13:33). Prelati aut quicumque curam aliorum gerentes . . .-. . . sedulitate actuosa erit et vtilitas fructuosa. Ff. 1v–2.

3. S85 (Lichfield, 1345). *Ecce quattuor rotae iuxta Cherubin* (Ezek 10:9). Primo fiebat oracio. Resumpto themate . . .-. . . qui est Deus verus et summus, benedictus in secula seculorum. Amen. F. 2r–v.

4. T01 (Lichfield, 1344). *Ave, Maria, gratia plena, Dominus tecum . . . Iesus* (Luke 1:28). Sparsim introduccio per hoc quod philosophi dicunt qui vult maius . . .-. . . absque malediccione materni doloris, quam omnes alie incurrebant. F. 2v.

5. S85* (1344 or 1345). *O mulier, magna est fides tua, fiat tibi sicut vis* (Matt 15:28). Katerina post Mariam dulcissima atque sanctissima . . .-. . . ex auersione faciei eius ab ea fuit ammonitus. Ff. 2v–3, inc.

6. T25 (Lichfield, 1345). *Hoc est corpus meum . . . commemorationem* (1 Cor 11:24 and Luke 22:19). Christus noster Dominus et magister ista die cibauit . . .- . . . a tuo domino et magistro graciam in presenti et gloriam in futuro. Quam . . . Ff. 4–7v.

7. S30 (Lichfield, chapel of St. John, 1345). *Marcum assume* (2 Tim 4:11). Christus in ewangelio huius diei Patrem suum vocauit agricolam . . .- . . . quod siquis fecerit, consequitur graciam in presenti et gloriam in futuro. Quam . . . Ff. 7v–9.

8. T35 (Lichfield, hospital of St. John, 1345). *Credentium erat cor unum* (Acts 4:32 "et in epistulari leccione huius diei"). Sanctus Iohannes ewangelista refert in ewangelio hodierno nostrum Dominum et magistrum Iesum Christum Dei Filium sic orasse . . .-. . . spiritus tuus inueniet vitam eternam. Quam . . . Ff. 9–13v.

9. T39 (Lichfield, choir, 1345). *Paraclitus Spiritus Sanctus, quem mittet Pater in nomine meo, ille vos docebit omnia* (John 14:26). Verba ista Saluatoris sunt verba dicta suis discipulis . . .-. . . ut in eius nomine det salutem eternam. Ad quam . . . Ff. 13v–17.

10. C20 (1345). *Orate pro invicem ut salvemini* (James 5:16). In ewangelio huius ebdomade legitur qualiter Christus, noster Dominus et magister, ascendit in Petri nauiculam . . .-. . . sed semper eritis cum summa securitate beatissimi atque felices. Quod gaudium . . . Ff. 17–20.

11. S59 (Lichfield, 1345). *In plenitudine sanctorum detentio mea* (Eccli 24:16). Hec verba ad litteram dicta sunt de summa sapiencia . . .-. . . filio suo ostendit, eum amantissime requirens ut hac saltem. Ff. 20–22, inc.

12. S74 (Brewood, 1345). *Beati qui nunc fletis, quia ridebitis* (Luke 6:21). Verba ista sunt Christi, nostri Domini et magistri, que ipso predicando docebat . . .-. . . sine fine hoc risu, hoc gaudio perfruemur. Quod . . . Ff. 22v–24.

13. T01 (Lichfield, 1345). *Dominus ad iudicium veniet* (Isa 3:14). Premittebatur oracio, resumptum fuit thema et versum in linguam vulgarem. Premittebatur quod quatuor erant Dei aduentus . . .-. . . et de ipso verbali iudicio fuit expositum. Ff. 24–25.

14. T16 (1346). *Simile est regnum caelorum homini patrifamilias* (Matt 20:1). Primo fuit repetitum totum ewangelium in vulgari et expositum quod Deus trinitas in sensu parabole est paterfamilias . . .-. . . ut premissum Deum percipiatis. Que nobis omnibus . . . Ff. 25–26.

15. T18/4 (1346). *Bona est oratio cum ieiunio et elemosyna* (Tob 12:8). In quibus verbis instruimur de duobus: quid hac quadragesima agere debeamus . . .-. . . et sic oracio nostra nos ducet ad celum. Quod . . . Ff. 26–27.

16. T22 (Brewood, 1346). *Laetare, sterilis, quae non paris* (Gal 4:27 and Isa 54:1). Duplicem habent sensum hec verba . . .-. . . sterili hic letanti in Domino et quare de illa leticia fiet ibi summa securitas. F. 27r–v.

17. T24 (Burton, 1346). *Hoc sentite in vobis quod in Christo Iesu* (Phil 2:5). Quia officium est prolixum, congruit loqui breuiter; quia video laicum populum congregatum, conuenit loqui leuiter; et quia trino hic populum multum expediret loqui vtiliter . . .-. . . intra in gaudium Domini tui, Mathei 25. Quod gaudium . . . Ff. 27v–30.

18. T18/4 (Lichfield, 1346). *Exemplum dedi vobis ut, quemadmodum ego feci vobis, ita et vos faciatis* (John 13:15). De duobus Dominus noster et magister in hiis verbis nos instruit . . .-. . . si hec scitis, beati eritis si feceritis ea. Quod . . . Ff. 30–31v.

19. S33 (Lichfield, 1346). *Ostendit ei lignum quod, cum misisset in aquam, in dulcedinem versae sunt* (Exod 15:25). Premissa oracione pro gracia obtinenda expositum fuit thema . . .-. . . nobis ostensi fructus ligni vite carpamus. Quod . . . Ff. 31v–32v.

20. T33 (Cannock, 1346). *Estote factores verbi, non auditores tantum fallentes vosmetipsos* (James 1:22). Premissa oracione duo iste sanctus apostolus in hiis verbis propter nos agit . . .-. . . et gaudium vestrum impleatur. Ad quod . . . Ff. 32v–33v.

21. T34/2 (Lichfield, chapel of St. Nicholas, 1346). *Petite et accipietis, ut gaudium vestrum sit plenum* (John 16:24). Hic primo exponebantur ea que fiunt hac die, scilicet quare hec letania . . .-. . . vbi eadem materia lacius pertractata habetur. Ff. 33v–34.

22. T34/4 (cemetery of hospital of St. John, 1346). *Petite et accipietis, ut gaudium vestrum sit plenum* (John 16:24). Tria in hiis verbis aut quatuor libertatem Christi . . .-. . . vt gaudium vestrum sit plenum. Quod . . . Ff. 34–36v.

23. C20 (London, 1346). *Offerant oblationes Deo caeli orentque pro vita regis* (1 Esdra 6:10). Primo reddebantur tres cause quare nolui uti latino . . .-. . . et fiebat finis commendando presentes illi qui est rex alpha et omega principium et finis viuens et regnans per omnia secula seculorum. Amen. Ff. 36v–37v.

24. S85 (Lichfield, 1346). *Deus meus, exaltasti super terram habitationem meam* (Sir 51:13). Premissa oracione dati erant duo sensus thematis iuxta duplicem sensum huius preposicionis super . . .-. . . vt per hoc ostenderetur eam plene legem implesse. Ff. 37v–38v.

25. T01 (Lichfield, 1346). *Ecce rex tuus venit tibi* (Zach 9:9). Premissa oracione fiebat distinccio de triplice nostri summi nostri regis aduentu . . .-. . . et introitum regni celestis, et fiebat ibi finis sermonis. Ff. 38v–39v.

26. C20 / T29/4 and T29+ (London, 1347; and Dundalk, 1348). *Pater noster, qui es in caelis, sanctificetur nomen tuum,* etc., oracionis dominice usque in finem (Matt 6:9). Premissa fuit oracio dominica cum adieccione salutacionis angelice, et suasum fuit quod Deus exaudiret . . .-. . . si quis in eam incidat, vt sic liberati a pena ad gloriam deducamus, prestante . . . Ff. 39v–41v.

27. T10? (Burford, 1347). *Procedentes adoraverunt eum* (Matt 2:11). Preparacio fiebat de miraculo couersionis aque in vinum . . . Duo nobis vtilia . . .-. . . plus prodest parum dare in vita quam mille milia talenta auri facere, idest dari post mortem, sicuti habetur in sermone. F. 42r–v.

28. T28/5 (Dundalk, 1348). *Pater noster qui es in caelis,* etc., vsque in finem oracionis dominice (Matt 6:9). Duplex causa fuit assignata . . .-. . . sicuti in illo sermone. F. 42v.

29. T29 (Louth, 1348). *Cum sero esset die illo una sabbatorum et fores essent clausae,* etc., usque in finem ewangelii dominicalis (John 20:19). Expositum fuit ewangelium quoad tria . . .-. . . haberent vitam in nomine eius, sicut dicit euangelium. Quam . . . Ff. 42v–43.

30. T29/3 (Acrum Dei, 1348). *Vide* (Mark 13:37). Introducto themate distinccio sic fiebat: Videte quid interius habeatis . . .-. . . cuncta que possidentur in terris. Ad quam beatitudinem . . . Ff. 43–44.

31. T30 ("apud Pontem," 1348). *Qui crediderit et baptizatus fuerit, salvus erit* (Mark 16:16). Premissa oracione et eius introduccione . . .-. . . in vigilia Ascensionis. F. 44r–v.

32. T31 (Mansfieldstown, 1348). *Tristitia vestra vertetur in gaudium* (John 16:20). Fiebat introduccio oracionis de gaudio sponsi in nupciis . . .-. . . propter pulcritudinem et delectabilitatem obiecti, et fiebat finis. Ff. 44v–45v.

33. S28 (Drogheda, Carmelites, 1349). *Ave Maria, gratia plena,* . . . *mulieribus* (Luke 1:28). Verbum Marie non ita inuenitur in serie, sed ante et post ibi exprimitur . . .-. . . per hominem sui generis et nature redimi omnino non debuit hoc modo ostenditur. Ff. 45v–49.

34. C14 / T16 (Drogheda, provincial council, 1352). *Viri pastores sumus, servi tui* (Gen 46:34). Pro edificacionis gracia nobis communiter impetranda . . . Reuerendi patres et fratres et amici carissimi, in epistula huius dominice ac huius diei hortamur ad pugnam . . .-. . . et de ceteris erroribus, quibus poterit prouide obuiari. Quod ut per istud consilium . . . Ff. 49–51v. Edited in Gwynn, "Two Sermons."

35. S65 (Coleraine ["Cowlrath"], 1351). *Egredietur virga de radice Iesse* (Isa 11:1). Legimus in ewangelio Iohannis 2 quod Iesus vocatus erat ad nupcias . . .- . . . tam potenti, tam grate, et tam clementi patrone cotidie deuote efferent; et fiebat finis indulgencia eis d. a. ta. Ff. 51v–53v.

36. T02 (Dromiskin, 1351). *Venit iudicare terram* (Ps 95:13). Vbi iudex noster describitur vt socialis, vt curialis, et vt regalis. Aduentus exprimit eum . . .- . . . et gaudium vestrum nemo tollet a vobis. Quod . . . Ff. 53v–55v.

37. S03 (Dundalk, 1351). *Ecce sacerdos magnus* (Sir 44:17). Premissa fuit oracio. Beatus Augustinus 6 libro *De Trinitate* dicit quod in hiis rebus . . .-. . . dixi tercio quod sacerdoti congruit sciencia ad conuersandum. Ff. 55v–56v, inc.

38. S28 (London, St. Mary's Newchurch, 1357). *Ave Maria, gratia plena, Dominus tecum* (Luke 1:28). Adieci Maria quia sic vtitur et vti docet Ecclesia salutacione angelica . . . Cum Mariam mente considero . . .-. . . plena erat gracia ad gaudia transiens angelorum. Quod . . . Ff. 56v–58.

39. T04 (Drogheda, 1351). *Gaudete in Domino semper* (Phil 4:4). Pater et Aue premittamus corde deuote vt ad Dei laudem . . . Carissimi mei fratres atque filii, sorores ac filie, anima racionalis sic ab omnium artifice est creata . . .- . . . quod sic debes sine fine gaudere. Quod . . . Ff. 58–62v.

40. Toi (Drogheda, 1352). *Induimini Dominum Iesum Christum* (Rom 13:14). Introducta fuit oracio dominica et similiter salutacio angelica, quia munera preparant viam hominis . . .-. . . habent lineum pannum Domini Dei non induunt. Ff. 62v–63v.

41. T33 (Acrum Dei, 1354). *Vado ad eum qui misit me* (John 16:5). Et fuit thema singulis nostrum adaptatum de incensu spirituali, et diuisum fuit thema in tria, que exprimuntur in verbis in ingressu, Misit me. Qui omnes sumus peregrini et nuncii in incensum vado quia. F. 63v, inc.

42. T20 (Trim, 1352). *Ambuletis ut abundetis magis* (1 Thess 4:1). Premissa oracione termini thematis exponebantur. Primo quia amor est pes mentis . . .-. . . vade prius reconciliare fratri tuo et tunc veniens offeres munus tuum. Ff. 63v–64.

43. Toi (Athboy, 1354). *Rex tuus veniet tibi iustus* (Zach 9:9). Ad introducendum oracionem pro gracia edificacionis inpetranda . . .-. . . in vita eius vsque finem legende; et fiebat sic finis sermonis. Ff. 64–65.

44. S24 (Acrum Dei, 1355). *Innocens contra hypocritam suscitabitur* (Job 17:8). Et fuit thema introductum per illud Ecclesiastici 34, Contra malum bonum . . . Et fuit thema tripliciter expositum. Primo . . .-. . . facta erant statuta in precedenti parum ante in concilio generali. F. 65r–v.

45. T21 (Drogheda, 1355). *Nemo vos seducat inanibus verbis* (Eph 5:6). Et fiebat totus sermo de constitucionibus factis in concilio parum ante, sicut duo precedentes sermones . . .-. . . propter solucionem decimarum omnium que habebat, Luce 18. F. 65v.

46. T22 (Drogheda, 1355). *Eice ancillam hanc et filium eius* (Gen 21:10). Primo fuit oracio introducta per quinque panes ordaceos . . .-. . . Ysmael vir auditus Deo vel assumens audicionem Dei. Ff. 65v–66.

47. C19 / T32 (Trim, 1355). *Tristitia vestra vertetur in gaudium* (John 16:20). Pro gracia sermonis sciencie impetranda . . . dicta fuit oracio dominica . . . Introductum fuit thema per hoc quod sunt duo genera hominum . . . , ciues siue burgenses mundum pro Deo colentes, et peregrini . . .-. . . vt gaudium vestrum sit plenum; et sic finis fiebat. Ff. 66–67v.

48. T36 (Kells, 1355). *Dominus Iesus, postquam locutus est eis, adsumptus est in caelum* (Mark 16:19). Premissa oracione dominica . . . introductum fuit thema per similacionem Christi ad doctum medicum . . .-. . . pro nobis aduocandum et fuerant ex scripturis ostensa; et fiebat finis sermonis. Ff. 67v–69.

49. T42 (Greenoge, 1355). *Mandatum habemus a Deo ut qui diligat Deum, diligat et fratrem suum* (1 John 4:21). Premissa dominica oracione . . . expositum

fuit verbum fratrem, et ostensum fuit quod omnis homo debet frater intelligi . . .-. . . non debuit sicut homo per hominem; et fiebat finis sermonis.
Ff. 69–70.

50. C14 (Drogheda, 1355). *Mundati sunt sacerdotes et levitae et mundaverunt populum* (Neh 12:30). Premissa oracione . . . introductum fuit thema per materiam caritatis de preferenda dileccione . . .-. . . et testibus falsis qui minus recipiunt; et sic fuit sermo conclusus. F. 70r–v. Edited in Gwynn, "Two Sermons."

51. T19 (Dundalk, 1355). *In omnibus exhibeamus nosmetipsos sicut Dei ministros in multa patientia* (2 Cor 6:4). Diuisio fuit ordine construccionis, quod ibi instruimur et suademur, vt hoc sacro tempore habeamus temperanciam . . .-. . . grauius crimen et magis impugnans legem nature predictam. F. 71r–v.

52. T43 (Screen, 1355). *Erant adpropinquantes ad Iesum publicani* (Luke 15:1). Introductum fuit thema per parabolas duas istius euangelii . . .-. . . tamquam collectores tolneti diaboli fuit factus sermo moralis. Ff. 71v–72.

53. T44 (Drogheda, cemetery of St. Mary, 1355). *Vanitati creatura subiecta est* (Rom 8:20). Premissa oracione introductum fuit thema describendo condiciones nostre miserie . . .-. . . in toto aut in parte ipsius; igitur etc., et fiebat finis sermonis. Ff. 72–73.

54. T22 (Dundalk, 1356). *Erumpe et clama, quae non parturis* (Gal 4:27 and Isa 54:1). Christus Dominus Deus noster apud nos predicando opera trine condicionis exercuit . . .-. . . et palmam duplicem promeretur in celo. Qualem . . . Ff. 73–75v.

55. T23 (Termonfechin, 1356). *Qui est ex Deo, verba Dei audit* (John 8:47). Premissa oracione . . . distincta fuit triplex audicio: solius auris percepcio . . .-. . . capellano existente in peccato mortali. Ff. 75v–77v.

56. T24 (Drogheda, 1356). *Humiliavit semeipsum, factus est oboediens usque ad mortem* (Phil 2:8). Propter prolixitatem officii et pluralitatem laicorum presencium et multitudinem populi fuit oracionis instancia introducta sicut in sermone de isto festo Hoc sentite in vobis quod in Christo Iesu. Et thema fuit hic sicut ibi introductum atque diuisum per responsionem ad tres questiones . . .-. . . precipitur grata subieccio. De quibus duobus fuit tractatum . . . et finis fiebat vt ibi. Ff. 77v–80.

57. T28 (Episcopal chapel, 1356). *Sitis nova conspersio* (1 Cor 5:7). Fuit primo notatum quam prudenter Apostolus sua verba aptauit . . .-. . . recipietis ex hoc immarcessibilem glorie eterne coronam. Quam . . . Ff. 80–81.

58. T39 (Coventry, 1356). *Paraclitus, Spiritus Sanctus, quem mittet Pater in nomine meo, docebit vos omnia* (John 14:26). Sermo fiebat iuxta sermonem

sub eodem themate [*blank*], set pauca fuerant que tangentur in secundo sermone sequente sub thematis isto: Qui diligit Deum . . .-. . . priuilegia impetrantes vt possint confessiones audire. F. 81.

59. T41/5 (London, nuns in the East End, 1356). *Qui manducat meam carnem et bibit meum sanguinem, in me manet, et ego in illo* (John 6:36). Premissa oracione fiebat introduccio, quod post lapsum primorum nostrorum parentum . . .-. . . et deus in eo. Et predicare intendebam . . . volui differre illam materiam et sermoni finem imposui. Ff. 81–82.

60. T42 (London, St. Paul's Cross, 1356). *Qui diligit Deum, diligat et fratrem suum* (1 John 4:21). Paulus apostolus dona graciarum enumerans . . .- . . . iuxta regulas supratactas in simili de dileccione Dei; et fiebat finis sermonis. Ff. 82–86.

61. T43 (London, St. Paul's, 1356). *Vanitati creatura subiecta est* (Rom 8:20). Dicta oracione . . . introduccio fiebat in sermone eiusdem thematis . . . et diuisio fiebat quasi similiter, set materia huius sermonis fuit ita descripta, scilicet quod ex primo verbo . . .-. . . in gaudium in fine, et in sermone Dominus Iesus postquam locutus est, etc., imediate; et fiebat finis. Ff. 86–87.

62. S75 ("Dacmexton" =? Deddington, 1356). *Ubi erat spiritus impetus, illuc gradiebantur et non revertebantur* (Eze 1:12). Premissa oracione cum introduccione ipsius oracionis . . . introduccio thematis facta fuit per hoc quod per multa annorum curricula . . .-. . . et fuerant dicta aliqua pauca inpertinencia, quia videbantur vtilia; et fiebat finis sermonis. Ff. 87–88v.

63. T58 (Deddington, 1356). *Diliges Dominum Deum tuum ex toto corde tuo* (Luke 10:27). Premissa oracione introductum fuit thema hoc modo, quod non fuit necessarium vt diligerent preceptum . . .-. . . in melius commutata vsque in finem sancta permansit. Quod . . . Ff. 88v–91.

64. S79 (Deddington, 1356). *Audivi numerum signatorum* (Rev 7:4). Premissa oracione introductum fuit thema per tria genera signatorum . . .-. . . tales se facere vellent concessa, finis fuit sermoni impositus. Ff. 91–92v.

65. T04 (London, bishop's *aula*, 1356). *Dirigite viam Domini* (John 1:23). Pro gracia obtinenda Pater et Aue. De duplici via Domini hodie est loquendum . . .-. . . indulgenciam tamen exhibere, quam nos prelati conferre valemus . . . Ff. 92v–98v. Also F/3-1.

66. T12 (London, St. Paul's Cross, 1357). *Quodcumque dixero vobis, facite* (John 2:5). Nostis huius leccionis historiam, qualiter nupcie facte sunt . . .-. . . sic penitus reuocata iuxta hec verba domini pape Johannis. Ff. 98v–106. Also F/3-2.

67. T19 (London, St. Paul's Cross, 1357. *Dic ut lapides isti panes fiant* (Matt 4:3). Iuxta id quod Paulus apostolus dicit . . . Obsecro . . . Primo vos hortor in Domino . . .-. . . tota sua merces sibi reddetur in felicitate eterna. Ad quam . . . Ff. 106–112. Also B/2-82 and F/3-12.

68. T21 (London, St. Paul's Cross, 1357). *Nemo vos seducat inanibus verbis* (Eph 5:6). Hoc loco hodie in quindecim dies non solum oraciones . . .-. . . erit igitur quisque securus quod sua felicitas perpetuo permanebit. Quam . . . Ff. 112v–127. Also F/3-13.

69. S79 (Avignon, chapel of vice-chancellor, 1358). *Qui diligit Deum, diligat fratrem suum* (1 John 4:21). Pro edificandi gracia impetranda . . . Ante tres dies aut quatuor desuper mandatum accepi quod essem in isto sermone breuis et clarus . . .-. . . et totum renuens quod molestat. Hanc visionem . . . Ff. 127–134v. Also F/3-3.

70. S12 (Avignon, "in audiencia causarum," 1341?). *Princeps maximus cedidit hodie in Israel* (2 Sam 3:38). Reuerendi patres et domini, circa nostri thematis intellectum tria michi premittenda videntur . . .-. . . et in leticia delectantur. Hec Bernardus. Hanc leticiam . . . Ff. 134v–141. Also F/3-4.

71. S16 (Avignon, Franciscans,?). *Invenit gratiam in deserto* (Jer 31:2). Videtur michi iuxta sacre scripture ac sanctorum doctorum sentenciam . . .-. . . gloriosa dicta sunt de te, ciuitas Dei. Hec Bernardus. Ad hanc ciuitatem . . . Ff. 141–145v. Also F/3-5.

72. T18/4 (Avignon, papal chapel, 1338). *Aspergite vos cinere, optimates gregis* (Jer 25:34). Maria, mater sublimis et virgo humilis, recordare . . .-. . . in terra viuencium duplicia possidebitis sine fine. Quod . . . Ff. 145v–150. Also F/3-6.

73. T26 (Avignon, chapel of vice-chancellor, 1342). *Redemisti nos Deo in sanguine tuo* (Rev 5:9). Reuerendissimi patres et domini, videtur michi circa reparacionem humani generis . . .-. . . qui redemisti nos Deo in sanguine tuo. Amen. Ff. 150–155v. Also J/5-42 and F/3-7.

74. S46b (Avignon, Dominicans, 1335). *Transtulit illum Dominus* (Hebr 11:5). Reuerendi patres et domini, ex quatuor causis translacionem sanctorum reputo . . .-. . . ne captiuos ferant ad infera hostis, mundus, vel carnis opera. Quod . . . Ff. 155v–161. Also F/3-8.

75. C14 / S54 (Avignon, Dominicans, 1341). *Crevit in vineam latiorem* (Eze 17:6). Reuerendi patres et domini, michi videtur quod duplex vinea spiritualis . . .-. . . late foris luces et intus suauiter ardes, prestante . . . Ff. 161–168v. Also F/3-9.

76. S65 (Avignon, papal chapel, 1342). *Nomen virginis Maria* (Luke 1:27). Verbum supplens sensum thematis precedit statim sic: Cui nomen . . . Bernardus in sermone de hoc festo . . .-. . . pro hiis quos liberauit Deus pius et potens, qui est . . . Ff. 168v–175.

77. S81 (Avignon, Franciscans, 1338). *Vir Dei sanctus est iste* (2 Kings 4:9). Beatus Ambrosius, sicut refert Seuerius in suo dialogo de beato Martino . . .-. . . angelica societas ympnis celestibus honoratur. Ad quam societatem . . . Ff. 175–179v.

78. S85 (Avignon, Franciscans, 1338). *O mulier, magna est fides tua* (Matt 15:28). Reuerendi patres mei et domini, Apostolus ad Hebreos 11 pro ingenti preconio . . .-. . . nobis apperiat et effectum sue propiciacionis exhibeat Dominus noster . . . Ff. 179v–187.

79. S46b (Avignon, papal audience, 1344). *Contemnit timorem nec cedit gladio* (Job 39:22). Reuerendi patres et fratres, legimus de nostro Thoma martire et presule Cantuariensis ecclesie, de quo nobis est sermo . . .-. . . intra in gaudium Domini tui. Hec Augustinus. Hoc gaudium . . . Ff. 187–193.

80. S73 (Avignon, Franciscans, 1349). *Mihi mundus crucifixus est et ego mundo* (Gal 6:14). Quia accepi a pluribus quod sermonum prolixitas dominos hic sepe attediat . . .-. . . et inuenietis requiem animabus vestris. Hanc requiem . . . Ff. 193–199v.

81. S03 (Avignon, papal palace, 1349). *Vigilate* (Matt 24:42). Paulus apostolus Ad Corinthios 1 epistula capitulo 12 dicit quod diuisiones graciarum sunt . . .-. . . et ita nullus poterit eum destituere. Quod stipendium . . . Ff. 199v–205.

82. T19 (Avignon, papal chapel, 1350). *Iesus ductus est in desertum a spiritu, ut temptaretur a diabolo* (Matt 4:1). Vt spiritus ductor Iesu, in qua datur sermo sciencie qui eciam scienciam habet vocis in presenti sermone . . . Iesus paruulus natus est nobis . . .-. . . et aduentum glorie magni Dei et Saluatoris nostri Iesu Christi, cui est honor . . . Ff. 205–212v.

83. T01 (Avignon, chapel of vice-chancellor,?). *Veni, Domine Iesu* (Rev 22:20). Cum venerabili Ancelmo primo libro *Cur Deus homo* capitulo 1 dico quia materia . . .-. . . gaudium vestrum nemo tollet a vobis, Johannis 16. Ad istud gaudium . . . Ff. 212v–217. Also F/3-10.

84. T02 (Avignon, chapel of vice-chancellor, 1338). *Venit iudicare terram* (Ps 95:13). Propheta Osee 4 capitulo sui libri, Audite, inquit . . .-. . . sicut certi erunt si ea numquam spontanee deserturos. Hec ille. Ista bona . . . Ff. 217–222v. Also F/3-11.

85. So5 (Avignon, Carmelites, 1342). *Ave* (Luke 1:28). In exordio nostri sermonis ad eam mentis oculos dirigamus . . .-. . . non peccasset, futuri essemus. Hec Ancelmus. Hoc regnum . . . Ff. 222v–231.

86. To3 (Avignon, chapel of vice-chancellor, 1341). *Gaudete in Domino semper* (Phil 4:4). Reuerendi patres et domini, michi videtur quod in personis triplici condicione preditis solent homines gaudere . . .-. . . leticia sine fine. Hec Bernardus. Ad hoc gaudium . . . Ff. 231–236.

87. S46b or S12 (Avignon, "in audiencia causarum," 1340). *Bonus pastor animam suam dat pro ovibus suis* (John 10:11). Michi videtur quod vnicuique pastori gregis dominici tria debent precipue conuenire . . .-. . . dicit Gregorius et ego sic dico cum ipso, prestante inquam hoc nobis . . . Ff. 236–241.

88. T10 (Avignon, papal chapel, 1359). *Videntes stellam gavisi sunt gaudio magno valde* (Matt 2:9). O Maria, stella maris, mater stelle solaris, si non precessisset . . .-. . . ac pietatis reuertetur in regionem suam eternam. Quam . . . Ff. 241–246v.

89. *Propositio* in papal consistory, 1349. *Domine, salva nos, perimus* (Matt 8:25). Pater sanctissime, nos sanctitatis vestre deuoti filii insulares . . .-. . . in gaudio de fontibus Saluatoris, quod vestre sanctitatis sacro ministerio nobis ille prestare . . . Ff. 246v–251v.

90. *Propositio* in papal consistory, 1350. *Unusquisque in quo vocatus est frater, in hoc maneat apud Deum* (1 Cor 7:20). Pater sanctissime, loqui prohibior et tacere non possum . . .-. . . in hoc maneat apud Deum. Cetera que ad predicta pertinent . . .propalabit. Ff. 251v–255. Edited in Hammerich, "The Beginning."

91. *Propositio* in papal consistory, 1357). *Nolite iudicare secundum faciem, sed iustum iudicium iudicate* (John 7:24). Pater sanctissime, in principio mei sermonis protestor quod non intendo aliquid asserere . . .-. . . per me tacta iuxta peticionem quam feci: Nolite iudicare secundum faciem set iustum iudicium iudicate. Ff. 255–271.

92. "Responsiones Domini Ardmachani ad obiectus [!] contra materiam de mendicitate et paupertate". Quia in proposicione nuper facta . . .-. . . ad statum sanctum sue institucionis primarie reuocentur. Quod . . . Ff. 271–279.

93. C22. *Luminis impetus laetificat civitatem Dei* (Ps. 45). Postquam primus parens in paradyso deliciarum constitutus, vbi competencium commodorum inerat affluencia . . .-. . . et iocunda visione sui principis eternaliter perfruatur. Quam visionem . . . Unique copy in Oxford, Oriel College, MS 15, f. 1ra–va.

G

G – Cambridge, University Library, MS Gg.6.26

1. ?. *Dominus in caelo paravit sedem suam,* etc (Ps 102:19). He þat is lord of all thing' in hevyn hath rayid hys syttyng'. Sicut testatur Augustinus super Johannem, Humilitas est optima . . .-. . . in tabernaculis fiducie in requie opulenta. Quod . . . Ff. 5–8.

2. C19*. *Sanctifica bellum* (Jere 6:4?). Reuerendi fratres, sentencia doctorum satis declarat . . .-. . . spiritus, anima, et corpus sine querela in aduentum Domini seruetur. Quod . . . Ff. 8v–12.

3. T66*. *Regnabit rex* (Jere 23:5). Reuerendi magistri, patres, et domini, Ier-archa suppremus, rex omnipotens, Deus noster mundi minoris regimen regulam atque regnum . . .-. . . tanquam reges regnant patet per beatum Augustinum. Ff. 12–16, inc. Also W-123.

4. T01. *Scientes quia hora est iam nos de somno surgere* (Rom 13:11). Preparare in occursum Dei tui, Israel, Amos 4 . . . Per sompnum designatur peccatum propter quinque . . .-. . . honeste ibimus obuiam regi nostro. Quod . . . Ff. 16v–18.

5. T03. *Dirigite viam Domini* (John 1:23). Ista sunt verba sancti Iohannis Bap-tiste, in quibus docet nos tria quomodo caute ambularemus . . .-. . . oremus ad Deum cum matre nostra sancta Ecclesia, vt istam viam sic dirigamus . . . Ff. 18–20v.

6. ?. *Et cum ieiunasset quadraginta diebus et quadraginta noctibus, postea esuriit* (Matt 4:2). In isto euangelio mencio fit de tribus, scilicet de Christo ieiu-nante . . .-. . . interitum sempiternum, vnde Psalmo: mors depascet eos. Ff. 21–22, inc.

7. ?. *Confitemini Domino et invocate nomen eius* (Ps 104:1). Fre[n]dis, ther be many thyngis the whiche shulde move men to hye them to confessioun . . .-. . . to blisse þat neuer shall haue ende. Ff. 22v–23. Edited in Galloway, "Confession Sermon."

8. T19*. *Ecce nunc dies salutis* (2 Cor 6:2). Karissimi, in curriculo siue in anni circulo diuersa dierum genera invenio . . .-. . . vnde ecce nunc tempus. F. 23, canceled.

9. T17. *Aliud cecidit in terram bonam et ortum fecit fructum* (Luke 8:8). In quibus verbis docet nos Dominus noster Iesus Christus quomodo debemus verbum Dei audire . . .-. . . consistit tota beatitudo celestis. Ad quam . . . Ff. 23–25v.

10. ?. *Ecce sanus factus es, iam noli peccare* (John 5:14). Christus dicit Luce 11 quomodo spiritus immundus exiit ab homine . . .-. . . aliquid fetidum vel lutum poneret infidelis. F. 26r–v, inc.

11. ?. *Vidit Iacob scalam cuius summitas caelum tangebat* (Gen 28:12). Gorham:
Angeli per scalam ascendentes et descendentes euangeliste sunt et predicatores . . .-. . . humilitatem eligamus et in humilitate Deo seruiamus, vt
cum eo regnare possimus in eternum, idest sine fine. Amen. Ff. 27–28.

12. ?. *Nocte os meum perforatur doloribus, et qui me comedunt non dormiunt*
(Job 30:17). Verba ista representant nobis triplicem miseriam animarum in
purgatorio existencium . . .-. . . absoluuntur tam a culpa quam a pena, etc.
Ff. 28v–29.

13. ?. *Miseremini, miseremini,* etc. (Job 19:21). Due sunt cause quare dicitur
bis "miseremini" . . .-. . . eadem mensura qua mensi fueritis, etc. Taliter
facere . . . F. 29r–v.

14. ?. *Paterfamilias curam habet suae familiae* (?). Ecclesiastici 7: Pecora tibi
sunt, attende illis, et si sunt vtilia, perseuerent apud te . . .-. . . receperunt.
Hec ille. Plus vbi euangelium. F. 30.

15. ?. *Vidi bestiam de mare ascendentem habentem capita septem et cornua decem*
(Rev 13:1). Bestia ista, secundum librum *Ethimologiarum* a vastando sic
dicta, est . . .-. . . tercia racio est quod peccatum est vita diaboli et eius
delectacio, sicut dicitur quando [homo delectatur, *catchword*]. F. 31r–v, inc.

16. ?. *Sic currite ut comprehendatis* (1 Cor 9:24). Quoniam, karissimi, ad audiendum verbum diuinum aliqui currunt per affeccionem . . .-. . . scilicet
coronam felicitatis eterne. Ad quam . . . Ff. 32–35.

17. T19. *Ductus est Iesus in desertum a spiritu ut temptaretur a diabolo* (Matt
4:1). Amici, alias notaui tria in hoc euangelio: primo quem Christus in
deserto habuit ductorem . . .-. . . sic tu et aliter non poteris habere. Quam
misericordiam nobis concedat. Ff. 38–46v.

18. ?. *Ecce mulier Chananea a finibus illis egressa clamabat dicens: Miserere mei, fili
David* (Matt 15:22). In quibus verbis spiritualiter intellectis anima penitens
in tribus comendatur . . .-. . . inuentus est. Ad illud conuiuium. Ff. 46v–47.
Also in Siena, Bibl. comm. F.ix.15 (Schneyer 9:497).

19. ?. *Erat Iesus eiciens daemonium, et illud erat mutum . . . locutus est mutus*
(Luke 11:14). Karissimi, in verbis propositis tanquam quoddam miraculum
a Saluatore nostro factum . . .-. . . erat mutum. Ab hoc demonio defendat
nos Deus. Amen. Ff. 47–48. Also in Toulouse 340 (Schneyer 3:767).

20. ?. *Sequebatur eum multitudo magna, quia videbant signa quae faciebat Iesus
super hiis qui infirmabantur* (John 6:2). In istis verbis duo ostenduntur,
scilicet sequencium deuocionem [!] . . .-. . . per penitenciam et postea
ad ipsum peruenire per suam magnam graciam. Amen. F. 48r–v. Also in
Toulouse 340 (Schneyer 3:767).

21. ?. *Per proprium sanguinem introivit semel in sancta aeterna redemptione inventa* (Heb 9:12). Quia modo Iudei inceperunt tractare de passione et de morte Christi . . . Sunt autem in verbis istis tria consideranda. Primum est quam crudeliter pro nobis Christus passus est . . .-. . . de tali redempcione benedicamus Deo, qui est benedictus in secula. Amen. Ff. 48v–49v.

22. T24*. *Plurima autem turba straverunt vestimenta sua in via . . . filio David*, etc. (Matt 21:8–9). Sancta mater Ecclesia portanto ramos hodie rememorat honorem . . .-. . . vsque in finem saluus erit. Hanc perseueranciam . . . Ff. 49v–50v. Also in Toulouse 340 (Schneyer 3:767) and Siena F.ix.15 (Schneyer 9:497).

23. T24*. *Ecce rex tuus venit tibi mansuetus* (Matt 21:5). Quibus verbis tria possunt notari, scilicet Christi dignitas . . .-. . . regnum quod vobis paratum est ab origine mundi. Ad quod. Ff. 50v–51v.

24. ?. *Adferam vobis pauxillum aquae et laventur pedes vestri* (Gen 18:4). Volentibus digne accedere ad sanctum corporis sacramentum . . .-. . . ex hoc pane, viuet in eternum. Ad hanc vitam etc. Ff. 51v–52.

25. T28*. *Mortuus erat et revixit* (Luke 15:24). Legimus in quadam historia, scilicet Hester I, quod rex Assuerus grande fecit conuiuium . . .-. . . digne habet vitam eternam. Quam . . . Ff. 52v–55v.

26. ?. *Escam dedit timentibus se* (Ps 110:5). O quam mirabilis cibus est corpus Christi in specie panis . . .-. . . visio Christi eterna, peruenire valeamus. Ad quam . . . Ff. 55v–56v.

27. ?. *Tene quod habes* (Rev 3:11). In presenti vita quasi in via sumus . . .-. . . ducite caute per operacionem, vt pertingere valeatis ad gloriam, etc. Ff. 56v–58.

28. ?. *Hoc facite in meam commemorationem* (Luke 22:19). Reuerendi, sicut patet ex processu Ricardi *De sacramentis noue legis*, vera pocius consistunt in factis . . .-. . . vt Christo duce peruenias ad regnum celorum. Quod . . . Ff. 58–60v. Also Z-13.

29. ?. *Resurrexit a mortuis* (Acts 10:41). Dicitur in Prouerbiis Salamonis: Indignacio regis nuncius mortis . . .-. . . ne a celesti gloria repellatur. Ad quam etc. Ff. 60v–61v.

30. T26*. *Dignus est agnus qui occisus est accipere virtutem* (Rev 5:12). In quibus verbis ostenduntur tria, scilicet Christi conuersacio . . .-. . . clauem crucis, per quam possimus venire ad regnum. Quod . . . F. 62r. Also in Siena F.ix.15 (Schneyer 9:497).

31. ?. *Surge, Domine, in requiem tuam, tu et archa sanctificationis tuae* (Ps 131:8). Et possunt esse verba matris Ecclesie . . . Vnde in verbis istis tria possunt notari: primo enim sancta mater Ecclesia proponit suam peticionem . . .-

. . . surge, Domine, in requiem tuam. Ad quam requiem . . . Ff. 62v–63. Also in Toulouse 340 (Schneyer 3:767).

32. ?. *Venit Iesus et stetit in medio discipulorum suorum et dixit: Pax vobis* (John 20:19). In quibus ostenditur benigna humilitas Saluatoris . . .-. . . vt det nobis illam pacem que est in celo, etc. Ff. 63r–v. Also in Toulouse 340 (Schneyer 3:767) and Siena F.ix.15 (Schneyer 9:497).

33. T34*. *Rogate quae ad pacem sunt* (Ps 121:6). Karissimi, beatus Mauricius Vidunie ciuitatis episcopus anno Domini millesimo, etc . . .-. . . vt possimus in eius seruicio sustentari, etc. Ff. 63v–64v.

34. C14*. *Ego sum pastor bonus; bonus pastor animam suam dat pro ouibus suis* (John 10:11). Verba ista scripta sunt in Iohanne et sunt verba Saluatoris nostri nos ad suum amorem benigniter attrahentis. Est enim triplex beneficium per quod nos trahit . . .-. . . ego sum pastor bonus. F. 65. Also in Toulouse 340 (Schneyer 3:767).

35. ?. *Plorabitis et flebitis vos, mundus autem gaudebit* (John 16:20). Ex quibus verbis possumus colligere quedam signa, et notant diuersa . . .-. . . et gaudium paradisi querendum. Ad quod nos perducat. F. 65v. Also in Toulouse 340 (Schneyer 3:767) and Siena F.ix.15 (Schneyer 9:497).

36. ?. *Modicum et iam non videbitis me* (John 16:19). Dominus noster duos solempes fecit sermones . . .-. . . iterum modicum et videbitis me. Hec ille. Ff. 65v–66v.

37. ?. *Cum venerit paracletus, ille arguet mundum de peccato, de iustitia, et de iudicio* (John 16:8). Sunt autem verba Filii Dei mouencia peccatores ad penitenciam . . .-. . . fugere argucionem diuinam et secure stare ante Deum. Quod . . . F. 66v. Also in Toulouse 340 (Schneyer 3:768).

38. ?. *Vos testimonium perhibebitis, quia ab initio mecum estis* (John 15:27). In quibus verbis ostenditur quod ad confermacionem [!] iustorum . . .-. . . vt possimus esse cum ipso regnante in celo. F. 67. Also in Toulouse 340 (Schneyer 3:768) and Siena F.ix.15 (Schneyer 9:497).

39. ?. *Petite et accipietis, ut gaudium vestrum sit plenum* (John 16:24). Hec sunt verba Iesu Christi suam dileccionem manifestantis . . .-. . . gaudium vestrum sit plenum. Ad quod gaudium. F. 67r–v. Also Toulouse 340 (Schneyer 3:768).

40. ?. *Petite et accipietis* (John 16:24). Consuetudo est diuitum scolarium, quamdiu manserint in loco vno . . .-. . . item eterna beatitudo ad consummacinem vtriusque. Ff. 67v–69.

41. T29*. *Omne quod natum est ex Deo vincit mundum* (1 John 5:4). In precedente dominica agebatur de vtraque resurreccione; in hac prima dominica

post Pascha agitur de statu vtriusque resurreccionis . . .-. . . esse in testimonium filii. Januensis. F. 69r–v, inc. Also Abbéville (Schneyer 3:515) and in Hatton 101 (Schneyer 9:31).

42. T20. *Egressus Iesus secessit in partes Tyri et Sidonis* (Matt 15:21). Qualiter peccator victus a temptacione sancte matris Ecclesie suffragio liberetur . . .- . . . pro constancia salutem proculdubio optinebimus. Quam . . . Ff. 70–71. Also Abbéville (Schneyer 3:513).

43. T20. *Egressus Iesus secessit in partes Tyri et Sidonis, et ecce mulier Chananea ante illum egressa,* etc. (Matt 15:21–22). In isto autem euangelio de quinque personis fit mencio . . .-. . . illa petite a Domino que et vobis expediant et illum deciat [!] dare, etc. Ff. 71–72v.

44 to 79 (ff. 73v–118): sermons by John Herolt, OP., from Ascension to 10 Trinity.

H – London, British Library, MS Harley 331

1. T19*. *Iesus* (Matt 4:7 etc.). Tria mouent me istud thema accipere: dede, nede, and spede–opus meum, necessitas Ecclesie, et bona expedicio presentis populi. Reuerendi mei, predicacio potest assimilari . . .-. . . misisti Iesum Christum, qui semetipsum nobis donet et vitam eternam concedat, qui sine fine viuit et regnat, Amen. Ff. 1–5. Also Z-3, CA/2-3.

2. T20. *Miserere mei, Domine* (Matt 15:22). Karissimi, sicut testatur sacra scriptura 2 Regum 12, cum rex David suggestione diaboli fedasset adulterio uxorem alterius viri, scilicet Vrie . . .-. . . corrigere se et bonis omnibus gloriam sempiternam. Quam . . . Ff. 5–9v. Also A-36.

3. C21*. *Quo abiit Simon?* (1 Mach 5:21). Reuerendi mei, Christus Dei Filius loquens suis discipulis in parabolis Luce 19 sic inquit: Homo quidam nobilis abiit in regionem longinquam accipere . . .-. . . iam euasit et ad futuram et perpetuam gloriam securus Symon abiit. Amen. Ff. 9v–13. Also W-83/92.

4. S28*. *Maria* (Luke 1:27). O gloriosa domina, excelsa supra sydera, inebriare nos digneris tanquam infantulos suggentes ubera matris sue ab uberibus consolacionis tue . . .-. . . ad inuocacionem sui nominis Maria perduxit et sicut quamplura alia miracula, etc. Ff. 13–15.

5. ?. *Redde rationem vilicationis tuae* (Luke 16:2). Noueritis, karissimi mei, quod Christus auctor veritatis et doctor in libro suo de euangelio Mathei 28 assimulans regnum celorum patrifamilias . . .-. . . de gaudio electorum cui te remitto, et sic finem istius sermonis faciendo. Amen. Ff. 15–18.

Wimbledon's sermon in Latin. Also A-48 and V-33. English version edited in *Wimbledon's Sermon* and in Owen, "Thomas Wimbledon's Sermon."

6. ? ("Sermo generalis"). *Si secundum carnem vixeritis, moriemini* (Rom 8:13). Istud taliter declaratur: Notandum est cuicumque quod quilibet existens in mundo tres habet capitales inimicum [!] . . .-. . . Deo placebitis et regnum eternum possidebitis. Quod . . . Ff. 18–21.

7. T28. *Surge et comede* (1 Kings 19:5). Dicit Gregorius in *Morum* quod qui Deo loqui desiderat, de nulla re confidere debet nisi de gracia Dei . . .- . . . cum Deo poteritis continue viuere in celesti gaudio. Quod . . . Ff. 21–23. Also Z-14.

8. T28*. *Surrexit Dominus vere* (Luke 24:34). Karissimi, sicut medicina corporalis, si fuerit conueniens complexioni recipientis, multociens cum bona gubernacione est causa salutis . . .-. . . reuertimini in regionem vestram, scilicet in regionem gaudii et glorie sempiterne. Quod . . . Ff. 23v–26v. Also Z-26 and E-2.

9. ?. *Dirigite viam Domini* (John 1:23). Karissimi, in hoc euangelio ostenditur quomodo Iudei audientes mirabilem nativitatem et excellentem sanctitatem et predicacionem Iohannis Baptiste . . .-. . . quinque sensus, que sunt partes anime, de quibus patet in sermone de circumcisione Domini, etc. Amen. Ff. 26v–27v.

10. S79. *Merces vestra copiosa est in caelis* (Matt 5:12). Karissimi, sicut legitur in euangelio Mathei 4, Christus ante passionem suam circuibat Galileam predicans euangelium regni Dei . . .-. . . merces vestra magna est in celis. Quam mercedem . . . Ff. 27v–31v. Also Z-24.

11. S79. *Beati misericordes, quoniam ipsi misericordiam consequentur* (Matt 5:7). Pro processu sermonis debetis notare quod misericordia est amor siue voluntas releuandi miserum a sua miseria . . .-. . . obiurgando ad custodiam, si necesse sit tradendo flagellis et cedendo. Amen. Ff. 32–35.

12. S12. *Euge, serve bone* (Luke 19:17). Karissimi, in euangelio hodierno Christus Redemptor noster ostendit nobis per parabolam . . .-. . . venite benedicti, etc. Quod . . . Ff. 35–38.

13. T10. *Apertis thesauris suis obtulerunt ei munera: aurum, tus, et murram* (Matt 2:11). Karissimi, in hoc euangelio ostenditur quomodo nato Saluatore nostro in Bethelem Iude in tempore Herodis Astolonite regis tres magi venerunt ab oriente . . .-. . . per viam mandatorum Dei rediat ad regionem suam, scilicet ad regionem regni celestis. Quod . . . Ff. 38–41.

14. T08. *Circumcidimini Domino* (Jer 4:4). Karissimi, hodie celebrat Ecclesia festum de circumcisione Domini, qui circumcisus fuit in octaua die a sua

natiuitate . . .-. . . a seruitute corrupcionis in libertatem glorie filiorum Dei. Quod . . . Ff. 41–43.

15. *S59. Intravit Iesus in quoddam castellum, et mulier quaedam,* etc. (Luke 10:38). Karissimi, erat quondam rex nobilis habens duos filios et quatuor filias, quorum iunior filius deliquit contra seniorem volens eum surripere dignitatem . . .-. . . castrum of resoun, scilicet castrum celi. Ad quod castrum . . . Ff. 43–47. Also WA-11 (without protheme).

16. *S44. Praeibis enim ante faciem Domini parare vias eius* (Luke 1:76). Verba ista fuerunt data prophetice de sancto Baptista per Zachariam patrem eius . . .-. . . venite, benedicti Patris mei, ad regnum quod . . . Ff. 47–49.

17. *S44. Tu, puer, propheta Altissimi vocaberis* (Luke 1:76). Sanctus Iohannes Baptista fuit sanctificatus in vtero matris sue et prophetice prenunciatus ab eodem angelo a quo sancta Maria salutatur . . .-. . . et translati erimus ab hoc mundo ad vitam eternam. Quam vitam . . . Ff. 49v–52.

18. ? ("Sermo generalis"). *Videte, vigilate, et orate* (Mark 13:33). Reuerendi mei, testante scriptura sacra solebant sancti se dare oracioni et iugiter eidem assistere insistere [!] pro timore inimicorum . . .-. . . apud summum Deum taliter. Igitur nos orare . . . Ff. 52–54v.

19. *T18. Iesu fili David, miserere mei* (Luke 18:38). Karissimi, antequam Christus passus fuit suam passionem dolorosam quasi prophetice ostendebat suis discipulis . . .-. . . ita graciose illuminando. Ideo nos taliter illuminari . . . Ff. 54v–62v.

20. *S65. Ego quasi vitis fructificavi suavitatem odoris* (Sir 24:23). Karissimi, Christus in euangelio Iohannis 14 vocat seipsum vitem . . .-. . . a seruitute diaboli et effecti heredes regni celestis. Ad quod . . . Ff. 62v–65.

21. *S66. Qui ambulat in tenebris nescit quo vadit* (John 12:35). Karissimi, euangelium hodiernum ostendit quomodo Christus ante passionem suam manifestauit Iudeis quod per suam passionem diabolus priuaretur sua potestate . . .-. . . vel tempus in quo potestis illam lucem adquirere, credite in lucem, vt filii lucis sitis. Ff. 65–66.

22. *T19+* ("Sermo generalis pro tota quadragesima"). *Surge qui dormis* (Eph 5:14). Karissimi, in tribus periculis solent homines euigilare in lecto dormientes: in periculo ignis, et in periculo aque crescentis, et in periculo latronum . . .-. . . nec auris audiuit \nec/ in cor hominis ascendit, etc. \Ad quod/ . . . Ff. 68–69v. Also B/2-59 and CA/2-5.

23. *T28/2*. Manhu* (Exo 16:15). Karissimi, sacra scriptura nos docet sicut legitur in veteri testamento quod filii Israel exeuntes Egyptum . . .-. . . quasi post

cruciat eum passio miseri quam ipsum miserum compassio sui. Ff. 70–71v. Also V-39.

24. S30*. *Ego sum vitis, vos palmites* (John 15:5). Karissimi, ut experimentum docet, multociens quando aliquis dominus uel paterfamilias conducit operarios in vineam . . .-. . . et fiet vobis. Ideo, karissimi, sic petere et sic in Christo manere . . . Ff. 72–75.

25. T26*. *Christus passus est pro nobis, vobis relinquens exemplum ut sequamini* (1 Pet 2:21). Anglice: Crist in his passion reliquit exemplum vobis quomodo vos schuden. Quamvis hec verba dicantur generaliter omnibus Christianis . . .-. . . sic iuste poteris vendicare eius hereditatem, scilicet regnum celorum. Quod . . . Ff. 80–99. Also W-6, S-1, Z-19, and Oxford Christ Church 91. Edited in Johnson, "Preaching the Passion," pp. 178–287.

I – London, British Library, MS Harley 2388

1. ?. *Attendite, popule meus, legem meam* (Ps 77:1). Unusquisque \magis/ timeret de dissolucione legis Dei quam legis alicuius . . .-. . . tot demones fuerunt in vno homine, vt dicitur Mathei 8. F. 52r–v.

2. S05* or S65*. [Acephalous. *Quam pulchra est?* Wisd 4:1] [pulcra ab in]mundicia peccati originalis, peccati venialis, et tandem fuit pulcra ab inmundicia peccati mortalis . . .-. . . operari precipitur, ibi Fac mecum. Ff. 53–54, acephalous and inc?

3. ?. *Frange esurienti panem tuum* (Isa 58:7). Prestantissimi domini, superne sapiencie panibus indies emittitur quo interior homo exteriorem dignitatem antecedit . . .-. . . premissa quatuor sequentur questiones, quarum hec est prima. F. 65r–v, inc.

4. ?. *Doctrina bona dabit gratiam* (Prov 13:15). Doctissimi viri, quos gloria litterarum inter ceteros mortales amplius in honorem prouexit . . .-. . . hec in ordine est prefixa, videlicet, etc. Ff. 66–67, inc.

5. ?. *In verbo tuo laxabo rete* (Luce 5:5). Peritissimi animarum piscatores, Petrum ac ceteros coapostolos meminimus per totam noctem laborasse . . .-. . . procedit doctoris conclusio prima, scilicet. F. 67r–v, inc.

6. ?. *Fratres, renovamini spiritu mentis vestre*, etc. (Eph 4:23). Ista epistula diui[di]tur in tres partes, scilicet in mentis renouacionem . . . Pro processu istius sic incipio. Carissime [!], peroptime noscitis . . .-. . . sed Filii Altissimi, etc. Renouamini, fratres. Ff. 68v–69.

7. ?. *Estote imitatores mei, sicut et ego Christi* (1 Cor 11:1). Fratres, non vos latet quod vnusquisque scolaris siue discipulus bene dispositus sequeretur suum

magistrum in illa facultate in qua ab ipso legitur . . .-. . . exibicio operis est probacio dileccionis. F. 69v, inc?.

8. T19. *Illi soli servies* (Matt 4:10). In ista scriptura [?] resurgunt plures dubita-ciones propter istum terminum soli . . .-. . . non sis seruus illius stando de hoc peccato, etc. F. 70r–v, inc?

9. ?. *Catelli edunt de micis* (Matt 15:27). Fuit una mulier pulcra et decora, iniqua et viciosa . . .-. . . ab illo vicio et deducere ipsum ad vitam, etc. F. 71.

10. ?. *Ecce morior, cum nihil horum fecerim* (Dan 13:43). Anglicum eiusdem [?]: Behald my lyffe I lese and I am gylylles in ony off þes . . .-. . . ? F. 72v. Possibly only notes.

11. ?. *Sanguis Christi emundabit conscientiam nostram* (Heb 9:14). Nisi miseri-cordie Domini essent multe, nos essemus destructi . . .-. . . ? F. 73. Notes only?

12. T03. *Fratres, sic nos existimet homo ut ministros Dei et dispensatores mysterio-rum Dei, etc.* (1 Cor 4:1). Reuerendissime [!], vnusquisque Christianus est vel esset minister Dei. . . .-. . . scitis \vere/ ministros Dei et dispensatores, etc. F. 73.

13. T37*. *Estote prudentes* (1 Pet 4:7). Viri prudentissimi, collata homini racio asserit quantum omnia quelibet vita, sensu, vel racione carent . . .-. . . Deus pacis erit vobiscum. Amen. Quod Schyres. Ff. 74–79v.

14. C11. *Sanctificavi domum hanc, quam aedificavi, ut ponerem nomen meum in sempiternum* (1 Kings 9:3). Hec domus sancta est, ideo sibi competit sanctitudo . . .-. . . que est infima in comparacione. F. 79v, inc.

15. ?. *Unus accipit bravium* (1 Cor 9:24). Reuerendi magistri et domini, ad hoc quod aliquis voluerit accipere brauium, idest requiem celorum . . .-. . . et orando vt vnus accipiat brauium. Ad quod . . . Ff. 80–81.

16. T19*. *Ecce nunc tempus acceptabile* (2 Cor 6:2). Cryst crose gud me sped and saue. Reuerendissimi, in omni ordine unus precedit et melius subse-quitur . . .-. . . adqueret gloriam eternam. Ad quam . . . Ff. 82–83v.

17. T04*?. *Fratres, gaudete in Domino semper* (Phil 4:4). Idest, vos qui estis servi Christi, ut determinatum est in dominica precedente . . .-. . . per suam mortem et resureccionem, etc. Ad quam . . . F. 84v.

18. T13(?). *Nuptiae factae sunt* (John 2:1). Pro quibus verbis notandum est quod tripliciter dicuntur nupcie . . .-. . . quamplures iam dierum ad oppositum, etc. F. 85r–v, inc.

19. T21. *Estote filii carissimi* (Eph 5:1). Anglice: Be ȝe þe dere chylder off Cryste. Legitur in libro *Poleticorum* [!] quod sunt due condiciones . . .-. . . vt possitis regnum Dei adquerere. Ad quod . . . Ff. 86–87v.

20. T23. *Sanguis Christi emundabit conscientiam nostram* (Heb 9:14). Reuerendissimi patres et domini, sunt tria requisita ad Dei predicatorem . . .-. . . and a merrure þat ys dredffull. Ff. 88–89, inc.

21. T10. *Surge, inluminare, Hierusalem* (Isa 60:1). O tu, anima, que es operta cum caligine et tenebris . . .-. . . malum culpe et malum pene, etc. F. 89v, inc.

22. ?. *Vidi sanctam civitatem* (Rev 21:2). Reuerendissime [!], sunt plures cause \siue condiciones/ quibus mediantibus unusquisque potest deffendere se a peccato . . .-. . . in qua nichil depingitur. F. 90r–v, inc.

23. ?. *Oblitus est qualis fuit* (James 1:24). Reverendissime [!] magistri, peroptime scitis quod verbum Dei enunciabitur per \eius/ predicatores . . .-. . . potestatem super nos, etc., erimus filii Dei, etc. Ff. 91–93.

24. ?. *Quaerite, et invenietis* (Matt 7:7). Reuerendissime [!] patres et fratres, predicator Dei secundum Crisostomum potest assimilari lucerne ardenti . . .-. . . in pace factus est locus eius, etc. Ad quam pacem . . . Ff. 93v–95v.

25. ?. *Estote factores verbi Dei et non auditores tantum* (James 1:22). Reuerendissime [!] fratres, sunt tria necessaria ad vitam et ad saluacionem . . .-. . . erit nobis vita et gloria sempiterna. Ad quam gloriam . . . Ff. 96–97.

26. T36. *Ascendisti in altum, captivam duxisti captivitatem, dedisti dona hominibus* (Ps 67:19; *ms*: duxit, dedit). Reuerendissimi, est magna differencia inter scolam Domini et diaboli . . .-. . . sufficienter radicata per sacram scripturam, vsum, et huiusmodi. Ideo, etc. F. 97v.

27. S49. *Confidit in ea cor viri* (Prov 31:11). Anglice: þe hert off a man trystus in a strong woman. Reuerendissime [!], sunt tria in quibus homo non poneret suam spem . . .-. . . hic potest induci narracio de isto peccato et eciam figura, etc. Ff. 98–99.

28. C11. *Salus huic domui facta est* (Luke 19:0). Cum est ita, fratres, quod quevis natura tam animata quam inanimata desiderat salutem . . .-. . . nec auris auidiuit nec, etc. Ad quod gaudium . . . Ff. 99v–100.

29. S79. *Docebat eos* (Matt 5:2). Reuerendissimi patres atque domini, quiscumque informaret aliquos vel moneret aliquos ad Dei amorem . . .-. . . timor iudicii et delectacio eternalis glorie. Ad quam gloriam, etc. Ff. 100v–101.

30. T34. *Rogate quae ad pacem sunt* (Ps 121:6). Scribitur Luce 10 quod Christus dixit discipulis suis quod vbicumque intrauerint . . .-. . . que est pax pacis. Ad quam pacem, etc. F. 101r–v.

31. T21. *Omne regnum in seipsum divisum desolabitur* (Luce 11:17). Secundum Philosophum in 2 *Phisicorum*, finis debet esse primum in intencione . . .-

... numquam dolor, etc. De aliis dilatando materiam si tempus permitterit. Ad quod regnum ... Ff. 102–103.

32. T22. *Distribuit discumbentibus* (John 6:11). Anglice: Cryst haþe mayd þe pepyll a grett fest. Reuerendissimi, in eo quod hodierna die mencio specialis facta est de cibariis distributis ... .-. ... sic Deus pacis et dileccionis maneat semper nobiscum, etc. Ff. 103v–104.

33. ?. *Per proprium sanguinem introivit in sancta* (Heb 9:12). Reuerendissimi, est consuetudo antiqua quod ad hoc quod aliquis procedat ad aliquam materiam ... .-. ... custodieris te ab hoc peccato. Ad quod gaudium ... Ff. 104v–105.

34. T21. *Locutus est mutus* (Luke 11:14). Fratres, Petrus apostolus desideravit ambulare super mare ... .-. ... ecce vox sanguinis fratris tui clamat, etc. F. 105r–v, inc.

35. T63. *Simile est regnum caelorum homini regi qui voluit rationem ponere cum servis suis* (Matt 18:23). Iste homo rex est Christus Iesus, in scripturis rex regum ... .-. ... sed quam iocundum Venite. Ad quod Venite ... F. 106r–v.

36. T22. *Erumpe* (Gal 4:27). Reuerendissimi in Christo, omne peccatum semper est vitandum propter plura ... .-. ... ? Ff. 107–108v? (folio defective).

37. T66. *Cum sublevasset oculos Iesus et vidisset multitudinem* (John 6:5). Scribitur Luce 10 quod peccator est vulneratus, semiuiuus, et a vestimentis spoliatus ... .-. ... ? F. 109r–v? (folio defective).

38. T01. *Hora est iam nos de somno surgere* (Rom 13:11). In ista epistula vna cum ewangelio sequenti sunt tres nuncii ... .-. ... antiquorum patrum, etc. F. 110r–v.

39. T02. *Non congregabo conventicula eorum de sanguinibus* (Ps 15:4). In dominica precedente, fratres karissimi, dictum fuit de tribus nunciis ... .-. ... ? Ff. 111–? (folios defective).

J – Cambridge, Jesus College, MS 13

For the five sermon booklets, their affiliations, and their dates, see the section on this manuscript in Part One.

J/1

1. S86*. *Flos de radice eius ascendet* (Isa 11:1). Est intuenti sacram scripturam et sanctorum et sapiencium sentenciam quomodo ... .-. ... possimus reponi in tabernaculo eternitatis. Quod. ... Ff. 1ra–2va.

2. S86*. *Missus est* (Luke 1:26). Inter omnia bona missa de celo in veteri lege legimus . . .-. . . ad istam virginem Mariam mittam spiritum meum super. Ff. 2vb–3vb, inc.

J/2

Many *de sanctis* sermons are apparently by Bertrand de la Tour (see Schneyer 1:567–71); many *de tempore* sermons also occur in the Franciscan collection of Monte Cassino MS 213 (see Schneyer 7:333–40).

1. S01. *Ascendam in palmam et apprehendam fructum eius* (Cant 7:8). Uerba ista secundum sensum anagogicum intellecta sunt ipsius Ecclesie ad beatitudinis palmam . . .-. . . in fructus eius dulcedine pene euasio et glorie collacio. Ad quam nos, etc. Booklet not foliated; medieval sermon numbers in upper margin.

2. S03. *Ab infantia crevit mecum miseratio* (Job 31:18). In uerbis istis literaliter et historice intellectis commendatur Job . . .-. . . apponit vinum confortacione subuencionis.

3. S04. *Examen apium in ore leonis erat et favus mellis* (Judg 14:8). Uerba proposita secundum literam intellecta plena sunt . . .-. . . in beato Ambrosio, sicut patet in legenda sua.

4. S07. *Luce splendida fulgebis* (Tob 13:13). In verbis istis hystorice intellectis Thobias in spiritu . . .-. . . hec tria habuit beata Lucia, sicud patet ex legenda sua. Rogemus etc.

5. S08. *Scio quod cum caecus essem, modo video* (John 9:25). Verba proposita historice sumpta sunt verba ceci . . . set allegorice intellecta verba sunt beati Thome apostoli . . .-. . . et ideo bene dicebatur in themate assumpto, Scio, etc.

6. T06. *Cum incaluerit sol, nobis salus* (1 Sam 11:9). Verba ista secundum sensum ystoricum sumpta verba sunt Saulis . . .-. . . quia constituens te in gloria. Amen.

7. S09. *Ruben primogenitus meus principium doloris mei* (Gen 49:3). Verba proposita secundum sensum hystoricum intellecta sunt uerba Iacob . . .- . . . vnde dicebat Ne statuas, etc.

8. S10. *Vulnerasti me, sponsa mea, in uno oculorum tuorum et in uno crine colli tui* (Cant 4). Verba proposita spiritualiter intellecta sunt verba Christi sanctam matrem Ecclesiam dulciter alloquentis . . .-. . . propter informacionem consciencie. Amen.

9. S11. *Ambulabunt mecum in albis, quia digni sunt* (Rev 3:4). In verbis propositis spiritualiter intellectis describit nobis beatus Iohannes sanctorum innocencium collegium . . .-. . . . datur eis fiducia plenissime iocunditatis. Amen.

10. S12. *Usque ad mortem certa pro iustitia* (Sir 4:33). In verbo proposito sapiens consilium de veritatis perfeccione suscipit . . .-. . . et ideo mors eius fuit dispendiosa. Rogemus, etc.

11. T08. *Oleum effusum nomen tuum* (Cant 1:2). Quoniam presens festum ab inposicione nominis Iesu Christi recepit ab Ecclesia digne reuerenciam et honorem . . .-. . . gutta sanans et saluans in operacione.

12. T10. *Quaerite et invenietis* (Matt 7:7). Licet verbum istud possit exponi de sanctis regibus . . .-. . . quia prestans soliditatem paciencie. Rogemus ergo, etc.

13. S18. *Fortitudo et decor indumentum eius, et ridebit in die novissimo* (Prov 31:25). In uerbis propositis spiritualiter intellectis describitur beata Agnes . . .-. . . perfruicione et delectacione indicibili. Rogemus, etc.

14. S19. *Vincenti dabo edere de ligno vitae* (Rev 2:7). Uerba proposita spiritualiter intellecta sunt verba Christi beatum Vincentium alloquentis . . .-. . . quia ibi est omne sine corrupcione. Amen.

15. S20. *Lapis solutus calore in aes vertitur* (Job 28:2). In verbis propositis hystorice intellectis est mira diuersorum translacio . . .-. . . es metallum commune et copiosum.

16. S21. *Columba portans ramum olivae venit ad Noe* (Gen 8:11). In verbis propositis literaliter intellectis rexitur hystoria de columba . . .-. . . inpleuit gracia in ascencione. Amen.

17. S22* (ms: S81). *Nigra sum sed formosa, Ierusalem* (Cant 1). Uerba proposita spiritualiter intellecta sunt verba Agathe . . .-. . . veni ad possessionem eterne securitatis.

18. S23. *Iudicabit nos rex noster* (1 Sam 8:20). Cum verba proposita spiritualiter intellecta sunt uerba Ecclesie . . .-. . . contra lanceam eius carnem reprimendo. Amen.

19. S24 (ms: S67). *Surge, aquilo, et veni, auster, perfla hortum meum* (Cant 4:16). Uerba proposita spiritualiter intellecta sunt uerba Dei Patris . . .-. . . cum perflata fuerunt austro, idest predicacione. Amen.

20. S25. *Anima mea liquefacta est ut dilectus locutus est* (Cant 5:6). Uerba proposita spiritualiter intellecta sunt verba sancte matris Ecclesie . . .-. . . per libertatem voluntarie supererrogacionis. Amen.

21. S26. *Fugit Matthathias in montem et reliquit quaecumque habebat in civitate* (1 Macc 2:28). In verbis propositis literaliter intellectis commendatur Mathatias . . .-. . . ponitur aliis in exemplum et euidenciam. Amen.

22. S28. *Signum magnum apparuit in caelo* (Rev 12:1). Iohannes in exilium relegatus quanto magis a mundano tu[m]ulto et strepitu separatus . . .-. . . fecundat fructum bonarum operacionum. Amen.

23. T25. *Panis quem ego dabo caro mea est pro mundi vita* (John 6:52). Can' hod' die sacramentum eucharistie institutum, ideo pro presenti solempnitate congrue assumitur istud verbum . . .-. . . et omnem saporem suauitatis. Amen.

24. T26. *Fel eius valet ad unguendos oculos* (Tob 6:9). In uerbis istis historice intellectis describitur cecitas corporalis . . .-. . . per donorum et virtutum multiplicacionem. Amen.

25. T26. *Ego morior et Dominus est nobiscum* (Gen 48:21? ms: Acts 18). In verbis istis allegorice intellectis describitur benedicta Christi passio . . .-. . . quomodo hec omnia sunt completa. Rogemus ergo, etc.

26. T26. *Lacrimabatur mater eius irremediabilibus lacrimis dicens, Heu me, fili mi* (Tob 10:4). Presens auctoritas historice intellecta inducit nobis Annam . . .-. . . omnes amici eius spreuerunt eam, propter tercium.

27. T26. *Vitulus et leo simul morabuntur* (Isa 11:6). In verbo isto describit nobis Ysaias Dei Filium incarnandum . . .-. . . per angeli ruine reparacionem. Amen.

28. S30. *Factus est sicut catulus leonis rugiens in venatione sua* (1 Macc 3:4). Uerbum propositum allegorice intellectum commendat nobis tripliciter beatum Marchum . . .-. . . fidelem predicacionem. De hiis omnibus quere in legenda eius. Rogemus, etc.

29. S32. *Isti sunt duae olivae et duo candelabra lucentia lucem* (Rev 11:4). Cernens Johannes in Apocalipsi sanctos apostolos Philippum et Iacobum . . .-. . . et supportantes inuicem in caritate.

30. T34/2. *Aer congregatur in aquas et ventus transiens fugabit eas* (Job 37:21). Letanie ad hoc sunt a sanctis patribus institute, ut in eis fiant . . .-. . . mortem spiritualem et amittunt iusticie libertatem.

31. ? ("Pro pluuia impetranda"). *Loquimini ad petram et ipsa dabit vobis aquas* (Num 20:8). In verbis istis hystorice intellectis iubentur Moyses et Aaron aquam de petra elicere . . .-. . . ad bonorum omnium consummacionem.

32. ? ("De Christo quantum ad diuersa facta"). *Saliet sicut cervus claudus, et aperta est lingua mutorum* (Isa 35:6). Describit nobis Ysayas hic

Christum quantum ad quatuor . . .-. . . aromatum regum possidendo et aliis acquirendo. Amen.

33. T39? ("De sancto Spiritu"). *De excelso misit ignem in ossibus meis et erudivit me* (Lam 1:13). Spiritualis [!] sunt verba sancte matris Ecclesie . . .-. . . speciositatem spiritus vite, preciositatem, et vtilitatem. Amen.

34. S33*. *Tria sunt mihi difficilia, et quartum penitus ignoro . . . in adolescentia* (Prov 30:19–20). Iste numerus fuit completiuus beneficiorum omnium monachorum, euangelistarum, prophetarum, crucis effectus, beatus Franciscus, Iohannes Euangelista, Iohannes Baptista. Et propterea Sapiens . . . horum quatuor festorum scienciam singularem multipliciter commendat . . . Ista quatuor festa communiter ordinantur et in simul celebrantur . . .-. . . tercia pars moritur per gehennam.

35. S35. *Via aquilae in caelo difficilis* (Prov 30:19). Diuidatur sicud supra. Circa hoc notandum quod per aquilam signatur Johannes . . .-. . . propter bonorum omnium perfectam integritatem.

36. S39*. *Via colubri super petram difficilis* (Prov 30:19). Sicut dictum est superius. Commendatur beatus Franciscus a muneris singularitate et preciositate . . .-. . . detestacionem et omnium bonorum acumulacionem.

37. S44. *Viam viri in adolescentia penitus ignoro* (Prov 30:19). Sicud distinctum et dictum est de aliis. In hoc verbo Iohannes Baptista commendatur . . .- . . . per ignoranciam et seduccionem.

38. S40. *Praebebis equo fortitudinem et circumdabis habitum collo eius* (Job 39:19). In verbis istis allegorice intellectis ad Christum directis describitur beatus Barnabas . . .-. . . per pacienciam in sustinendo.

39. S41. *Quis dedit gallo intellegentiam?* (Job 38:36). In verbis istis literaliter intellectis miratur sanctus Iob galli prudenciam . . .-. . . et doctrine quantum ad instruccionem conuersorum. Amen.

40. S41*. *Columba cum non inveniret ubi requiesceret pes eius, reversa est ad Noe in archam* (Gen 8:9). Spiritualiter in verbis istis describitur beatus Antonius . . .-. . . decora per venustatem et conuersacionem.

41. S46. *Numquid coniungere valebis micantes stellas Pliades* (Job 38:31). Literaliter in predictis verbis miratur beatus Iob . . . .-. . . quia erunt sine inpuritate. Rogemus, etc.

42. S46a. *Habet argentum venarum suarum principia [ms: precipium], et auro locus est in quo conflatur* (Job 28:1). In verbis istis methaphorice intellectis quantum ad quatuor describitur beatus Paulus . . .-. . . quoad puritatem innocencie. Rogemus, etc.

43. S49. *Pro urtica myrtus crescet* (Isa 55:13). In verbis istis methaphorice intellectis Ysayas in spiritu prophetico constitutus . . .-. . . lignum pulcherimum amenitatem in visu. Amen.

44. S50. *Locus sapphyri lapides eius, et glebae illius aurum* (Job 28:6). Quoniam beati Iacobi in Ecclesia festum maxime veneratur . . .-. . . quantum ad multiplicacionem operum bonorum. Amen.

45. S52. *De carcere catenis interdum quis egreditur ad regnum?* (Qoh 4:14). Verbum hoc potest intelligi de carcere pene, culpe, et miserie . . .-. . . ideo efficiuntur validi. Amen.

46. S54. *Ecce ego mitto angelum meum qui praeparabit viam meam ante faciem tuam* (Mal 3:1). Sicud beatus Johannes Baptista preparauit viam . . .-. . . cum auaricia immutatur.

47. S56. *Quasi tus redolens in diebus aestatis, sic iste refulsit in templo Dei* (Sir 50:7–8). Verba hec secundum sensum historicum dicta sunt in laudem . . .-. . . ideo dicit odium suscitat rixas.

48. S57. *Quasi rosae plantatae secus rivos aquarum fructificate* (Sir 39:17). In verbis propositis methaphorice intellectis inuitat Sapiens vniuersos fideles . . .-. . . per ipsorum predicacionem et scripturarum apercionem. Amen.

49. S59. *Quasi cedrus exaltata sum in Libano* (Sir 24:17). Quoniam, ut pie creditur, beatissima Christi mater hinc in corpore et anima est assumpta . . .-. . . purpura splendidam puritatem. Amen.

50. S60. *Mel et lac sub lingua tua* (Cant 4:11). Quoniam beatus Bernardus lac suxit de beata Virgine . . .-. . . hoc spectat ad euitacionem supliciorum. Amen.

51. S61. *Posuit vineam meam in desertum, et ficum meum decoriavit* (Joel 1:7). Hystorialiter verba sunt destruccionem populi Israeliti deplangentis . . .-. . . et deuocionem. De omnibus istis inuenies in legenda sua.

52. S63. *Refulsit sol qui prius erat in nubilo* (2 Macc 1:22). Uerbum istud hystorialiter sumptum refert miraculum de Ecclesie illuminacione . . .-. . . conuersus est illustrando cognicionem.

53. S64. *Quaerunt scintillam meam extinguere quae relicta est . . . super terram* (2 Sam 14:7). Uerbum istud hystorialiter sumptum est mulieris . . .-. . . pungenti predicacionis eloquio. Amen.

54. S65. *Sicut lilium inter spinas, sic amica mea inter filias* (Cant 2:2). In verbis propositis ad laudem Virginis recitantis . . .-. . . et ante filium matrem mater opponit, etc.

55. *S66. Quasi cypressus exaltata sum in monte Sion* (Sir 24:17). In verbis istis allegorice intellectis describitur beata crux . . .-. . . filie Ierusalemitarum quantum ad futuram gloriam beatorum. Amen.

56. *S67. Nubecula parva quasi vestigium hominis quae ascendit de mari* (1 Kings 18:45). Verbum propositum literaliter intellectum refert nobis corporalis [!] materiam . . .-. . . cecitatem in possidendo. Rogemus Dominum, etc.

57. *S70. Angeli autem proeliabantur cum dracone* (Rev 12:7). In visione ista, quam vidit Iohannes in spiritu . . .-. . . et multiplicabitur eius affliccio siue pena.

58. *S71. Ponam solitudinem eius quasi hortum Deo* (Isa 51:3). Quoniam beatus Ieronimus in epistola Ad Eu[s]thocium de se dicit . . .-. . . quantum ad virtuosas et salubres operaciones.

59. *S73. Dedi te in lucem gentium, ut sit laus mea usque ad extremum terrae* (Isa 49:6). In uerbis propositis spiritu prophetico mirabilia beati Francisci . . .-. . . castitatem, que est ornamentum mentis.

60. *S73. Quis est pluviae pater, aut quis genuit stillas roris* (Job 38:28). In verbis istis historice et literaliter intellectis describitur aeris impressio . . .-. . . Iob, quia plena sunt admiracione. Amen.

61. *S73. Numquid per sapientiam tuam plumescit accipiter expandens alas suas ad austrum?* (Job 39:26). In verbis istis spiritualiter intellectis describit nobis Iob beatum Franciscum quadrupliciter . . .-. . . caro liuens plagarum proprietate. Amen.

62. *S75. Disciplina medici exaltabit caput illius* (Sir 38:3). Verbum propositum secundum faciem litere intellectum est verbum Sapientis beati Luce medici . . .-. . . iecur sanguinem mirabiliter generat.

63. *S78. Duo ubera tua sicut duo hinnuli gemelli* (Cant 4:5). Verba proposita spiritualiter intellecta verba sunt Christi sponsam . . .-. . . temperanciam que reprimit desideria.

64. *S79. Stellae dederunt lumen in custodiis suis* (Baruch 3:35). In verbis propositis spiritualiter intellectis Baruch propheta cupiens . . .-. . . conformes fulgentis iusticia paupertatis quasi dicet sic. Amen.

65. *S81. Vide arcum et benedic qui fecit illum* (Sir 43:12). Quoniam de beato Martine legitur quod oculis . . .-. . . pacificet et concordet nostras contenciones.

66. *S83. Brevis in volatilibus apis, et dulcoris habet fructus eius* (Sir 11:3). Quoniam in ecclesiastica hystoria beata Cecilia propter multiplicem eius virtutem . . .-. . . honorant Deum per reuerenciam graciarum accionis. Amen.

67. S84. *Agnus stabat supra montem Sion* (Rev 14:1). Quoniam de beato Clemente dicitur in legenda sua . . .-. . . percipiens dulcedinem diuine benediccionis. Amen.

68. S85. *Collum tuum sicut turris eburnea* (Cant 7:4). Verba ista spiritualiter intellecta sunt verba ipsius Christi beatam Katerinam sponsam familiariter alloquentis . . .-. . . in saphiro humilitas consciencie. Amen.

69. S46*. *Ascendit Loth de Segor et mansit in monte* (Gen 19:30). Istud posset esse thema de presenti sollempnitate apostolorum Petri et Pauli . . . In quibus verbis duo possunt notari: meritum passionis . . .-. . . in cuius figura Numeri 33 dicitur. Inc.

70. T01. *Mitte agnum, Domine, dominatorem terrae . . . Sion* (Isa 16:1). In verbis propositis Ysayas virtute preclarus prophecia precipuus . . .-. . . qui ad cenam nupciarum agni vocati sunt. Ad quam . . .

71. T01?. *Hora est iam nos de somno surgere* (Rom 13:11). In verbis propositis clamat preco vigilantissimus ut excitet peccatores . . .-. . . suplex quod sit per opera virtuosa. Quod . . .

72. T02. *Deus autem spei repleat vos omni gaudio* (Rom 15:13). Appostolus ardenter desiderans animas nostras gracie munere adornari in uerbis propositis tria facit . . .-. . . collacione que est in illa Ierusalem. Quod . . .

73. T03. *Caeci vident* (Matt 11:5). In verbis istis spiritualiter intellectis excellenti beneficio . . .-. . . stantem a dexteris Dei. Amen.

74. T04. *Pax Dei, quae exsuperat omnem sensum, custodiat corda vestra* (Phil 4:7). In hiis verbis optans Apostolus fidelibus beneficium . . .-. . . subleuemur; dic' igitur pax Dei, etc. Amen.

75. T07. *Ecce positus hic in ruinam et in rationem multorum . . . contradicetur* (Luke 2:34). Uerba sunt venerabilis Symeonis in spiritu prophetico . . .-. . . in eterne vite resurreccione suscitabit. Ad quam . . .

76. T11a. *Fili, quid fecisti nobis? sic ego et pater tuus dolentes quaerebamus te* (Luke 2:48). Verba sunt Virginis gloriose ad suum filium . . .-. . . apparuit illi homini, ecce tercium. Rogemus. etc.

77. T12. *Nuptiae factae sunt in Cana Galilaeae et . . . discipulis eius* (John 2:1). In verbis istis tria notantur . . .: recommendant scilicet coniugii . . .-. . . ad quartas ut iudices. Amen.

78. T13. *Ecce leprosus veniens adorabat eum dicens, Domine, si vis potes me mundare* (Matt 8:2). In verbis propositis sub methaphora leprosi [*ms*: reprosi] a Deo curati . . . .-. . . ecce castitas in signo et in verbo. Rogemus, etc.

79. T14. *Qui diligit proximum, legem implevit* (Rom 13:8). In hac breui verborum serie s. [duo?] tangit Appostolus essencialia caritatis . . .-. . . soluentur, ecce spes venie. Rogemus, etc.

80. T15. *Sicut Deus donavit vobis, ita et vos* (Col 3:13). In verbis propositis intendens Apostolus reducere nos . . .-. . . inuicem, sicut et Christus donauit uobis. Amen.

81. T16. *Voca operarios et redde illis mercedem suam* (Matt 20:8). Uerba ista spiritualiter intellecta possunt esse Christi . . .-. . . ecce remuneracionum indistinccio. Rogemus, etc.

82. T17. *Exiit qui seminat seminare suum semen* (Luke 8:5). Verbum istud trepost' interpr' predicatori potest esse . . .-. . . et oblaciones ad reuerenciam sanctorum. Amen.

83. T18. *Confestim vidit et sequebatur magnificans dominum* (Luke 18:43). In uerbo isto spiritualiter intellecto tria possunt congrue assignari . . .-. . . regni optentus per remuneracionem. Amen.

84. T19. *Ductus est Iesus a spiritu in desertum, ut temptaretur a diabolo* (Matt 4:1). Nota quod in verbo proposito spiritualiter intellecto quatuor que concurrunt . . .-. . . ecce appetitus excellenciarum. Rogemus Dominum, etc.

85. T20. *Levantes autem oculos suos neminem vident nisi solum Iesum* (Matt 17:8). In uerbis propositis literaliter intellectis describitur visio . . .-. . . propter triplicem causam supradictam. Rogemus igitur. etc.

86. T21. *Cum eiecisset Iesus daemonium, locutus est mutus, et admiratae sunt turbae* (Luke 11:14). In verbo proposito tam literaliter quam spiritualiter intellecto tria . . .-. . . noticia sciendorum, credendorum, agendorum, sustinendorum. Rogemus igitur, etc.

87. T22. *Suscepit Iesus panes . . . discumbentibus* (John 6:11). In verbo proposito et regulariter intellecto triplex . . .-. . . in quo habemus redempcionem et remissionem, ecce absolucio. Rogemus igitur Dominum, etc.

88. ?. *Nolite cogitare quomodo aut quid . . . loquamini* (Matt 10:19). Quoniam due sunt que predicacionem faciunt uiciosam . . .-. . . scilicet copiose et virtuose.

89. T21. *Locutus est mutus* (Luke 11:14). Quoniam duo sunt in quibus consistit informacio vite nostre . . .-. . . crimina mundat, penam dimittit, sis' ad patriam que reiuertit [?]. Ad quam, etc.

90. ?. *Cibavit illum Dominus pane vitae* (?). Intellectus quem predicator siue doctor secundem beatum Augustinum *De doctrina Christi* laborare debet ut . . .-. . . rogemus igitur Dominum vt ipse michi tribuat ista tria, etc.

91. T22. *Suscepit Iesus panes et cum gratias egisset, distribuit discumbentibus* (John 6:11). Secundum illam regulam theologie que docet exponere de membris . . .-. . . ad gloriam et remuneracionem quam acquirit. Amen.

92. T23. *Multi sunt qui persequuntur me; a testimoniis tuis non declinavi* (Ps 118:157). Duo sunt que predicacionem maxime inficiunt . . .-. . . Rogemus ergo ut in nobis non sit lingua odibilis . . . sit forma commendabilis predicatoris. Perhaps protheme of the following.

93. ?. *Multiplicati sunt qui tribulant me; multi insurgunt . . . in Deo eius* (Ps 3:2–3). In uerbis propositis, ut prouocet nos predicator . . .-. . . ad acerbitatem flagelli.

94. T23. *Per proprium sanguinem introivit semel in sancta aeterna redemptione inventa* (Heb 9:12). In verbo proposito tripliciter describitur passio . . .-. . . ideo regnabunt mecum in patria. Rogemus, etc.

95. T24. *Gaudium et laetitia invenietur in ea* (Isa 51:3). Duo sunt que predicacionem faciunt congruentem . . .-. . . ex sapida refeccione verborum. Perhaps protheme to the following.

96. T24*. *Extrema gaudii luctus occupat* (Prov 14:13). In verbis istis tropologice intellectis describitur status . . . .-. . . ad mortem pene ad quam sunt obligatoria. Amen.

97. T24. *Acceperunt ramos palmarum et processerunt . . . David* (John 12:13). Colligitur ex uerbis propositis honoris illius . . .-. . . ecce inuocacio pietatis. Rogemus igitur, etc.

98. T26. *Loquere, Domine, quia audit servus tuus* (1 Sam 3:9). Quatuor sunt que predicatorem ad spontaneam . . .-. . . propter quartum, seruus tuus. Perhaps protheme to the following.

99. T26*. *Convenerunt in unum adversus Dominum et adversus Christum eius* (Ps 2:2). Tangit hic propheta crimen lese maiestatis . . .-. . . sufficienter patent ex euangelio. Rogemus Deum, etc.

100. T29. *Gavisi sunt discipuli viso Domino* (John 20:20). In uerbis propositis literaliter intellectis describitur ipsius Christi a suis discipulis visio corporalis . . .-. . . scilicet in consolacione uerborum. Rogamus, etc.

101. T30*. *Ego sum pastor bonus et cognosco oves meas. et cognoscunt meae me* (John 10:14). Uerba ista possunt exponi uel de capite . . .-. . . eas prioribus viuendo, ecce vnitas. Amen.

102. T31. *Tristitia vestra vertetur in gaudium* (John 16:20). In uerbis istis literaliter intellectis premittit Christus . . .-. . . nemo tollit a uobis, quia eritis in firma possessione. Amen.

103. T32. *Abicientes omnem inmunditiam et abundantiam . . . verbum*, etc. (James 1:21). In uerbis istis beatus Jacobus intendens nos sufficienter instruere . . .-. . . iniuste ad iudicium protrahendo. Rogemus, etc.

104. T33. *Exivi a Patre et veni in mundum . . . Patrem* (John 16:28). Uerba hec si exponantur in sensu quo fiunt . . .-. . . in celis per eternam duracionem. Quod . . .

105. T37. *Estote prudentes et vigilate in orationibus* (1 Pet 4:7). In uerbis propositis informat beatus Petrus triplex genus militancium . . .-. . . scilicet perficiendo sine diminucione.

106. T42. *Diligamus Deum, quia ipse prior dilexit nos* (1 John 4:19). Tria facit Iohannes apostolus in hiis uerbis . . .-. . . processionem tam laicos quam clericos. Rogemus igitur, etc.

107. T43. *Estote misericordes sicut Pater vester misericors est* (Luke 6:36). Quoniam tunc est vera aqua cum originali suo pr'n'o continuatur . . .-. . . misericordia exemplaris et exemplata. Quam . . .

108. T44. *Translati sumus de morte ad vitam, quoniam diligimus fratres* (1 John 3:14). In uerbis propositis quatuor exprimuntur. Primum est actus penitencie . . .-. . . pro salute mutua moriendo. Amen.

109. T44. *Humiliamini sub potenti manu Dei . . . visitationis* (1 Pet 5:6). In uerbis propositis inuitat nos beatus Petrus ad tria . . .-. . . propter bonorum omnium perfectam aggregacionem. Amen.

110. T46. *Relictis omnibus secuti sunt eum* (Luke 5:11). Hec est conclusio tocius euangelii, in quo exemplariter habetur perfeccio . . .-. . . non declinaui ex ea, quantum ad secundum. Rogemus etc.

111. T46*. *Praeceptor, per totam noctem laborantes nihil coepimus; in verbo autem tuo laxabo rete* (Luke 5:5). In uerbis istis spiritualiter intellectis ostendit beatus Petrus . . .-. . . preceptorum exequcionem in opere. Rogemus Dominum, etc.

112. T46. *Si quid patimini propter iustitiam, beati* (1 Pet 3:14). Quoniam consideracio premii minuit vim flagelli . . .-. . . in die corporis pudicicia. Amen.

113. T47. *Omnis qui irascitur fratri suo, reus est iudicio*, etc. (Matt 5:22). In isto euangelio prohibet Dominus mecum [! = motum] ire . . .-. . . minuunt dies et ante ire huiusdam uitale. Rogemus, etc. Amen.

114. T48. *Misereor super turba, quia ecce iam triduo sustinent me* (Mark 8:2). In verbis propositis literaliter intellectis quatuor assignantur . . .-. . . condensatur cum durescit in fructu, sic penitens. Amen.

115. T48. *Accipiens Iesus panes, gratias agens fregit* (Mark 8:6). Secundum illam theologie regulam que docet . . .-. . . et uox laudis pro bonis collatis etc. Amen.

116. T49. *Arbor bona bonos fructus facit* (Matt 7:17). Verbum istud licet possit exponi [de] quolibet uiro iusto . . .-. . . propter quadruplex beneficium utilitatis. Amen.

117. T50. *Facite vobis amicos de mammona iniquitatis . . . tabernacula* (Luke 16:9). Quoniam sicut dicitur Ecclesiastici 6, Amico fideli . . .-. . . modicum recipientem per fidem. Rogemus Dominum, etc.

118. T51. *Domus mea domus orationis est . . . latronum* (Luke 19:46). Hec sunt uerba Domini, in quibus spiritualiter intellectis tria facit . . .-. . . ad altum diuine contemplacionis penetratur. Amen.

119. T52. *Qui se humiliat exaltabitur* (Luke 18:14). Hec est conclusio tocius euangelii, in qua . . .-. . . amicos docebat sapienciam. Amen.

120. T52. *Deus, propitius esto mihi peccatori* (Luke 18:13). Formam tenens penitentis publicanus . . .-. . . exuendo ab iniquitate. Amen.

121. T52. *Christus mortuus est pro peccatis nostris* (1 Cor 15:3). Apostolus in uerbis istis, ut alcius inprimat affectum . . .-. . . caro spiritus [!] erit subdita et ipse spiritus Deo. Quod . . .

122. T54. *Beati oculi qui uident quae vos videtis* (Luke 10:23). Et si uerba ista historialiter intelligantur de apostolis . . .-. . . historialiter quam spiritualiter intellectis introducit nobis euangelista.

123. T53*. *Mutos fecit loqui* (Mark 7:37). Quod [*read* quoniam?] olim quatuor ad curacionem cuiuslibet egritudinis . . .-. . . nescientes loquere sa. doc.

124. T55*. *Ostendite vos sacerdotibus* (Luke 17:13). In uerbis istis literaliter intellectis describitur corporalis curacio . . .-. . . ne peccent, quantum ad cauenda. Amen.

125. T56*. *Volatilia caeli non seminant neque metent neque congregant . . . pascit illa* (Matt 6:26). In uerbis istis literaliter intellectis ostenditur quod creature irracionales . . .-. . . recongnoscat in laudibus et graciarum accione. Amen.

126. T57*. *Resedit qui prius erat mortuus et coepit loqui* (Luke 7:15). In uerbis istis naturaliter intellectis describitur per Christum facta recussitacio . . .- . . . quoad edificacionem. Rogemus, etc.

127. T58*. *Amice, ascende superius* (Luke 14:10). Istis literaliter intellectis refertur ad sensum quomodo propter humilitatem subsidencie . . .- . . . pinguedo releuacionis in facto. Rogemus Dominum nostrum Iesum Christum. Amen, amen, amen, amen.

128. C19*. *Fratres tuos visitabis si recte agunt, et cum quibus ordinati sunt, disce* (1 Sam 17:18). Vnde verbum communiter dicitur, et est verum, velit nolit . . .-. . . diliciis affluens. Thomas de Lisle, in Aberdeen University 154, f. 329; also X-309 and Merton 248, f. 52rb.

J/3

1. T21*. *Revertar* (Luke 11:24). In principio cum Tobia, Thobiae 12, Reuertar ad eum qui me misit; vos autem benedicite Deum, quasi dicerem reuertar ad Deum qui me misit pro impetranda gracia . . .-. . . cuius bonitas fine caret nec habuit principium. Quod . . . Ff. 1ra–2vb.

2. S46*. *Transeuntes primam et secundam custodiam venerunt ad portam fer-ream quae ducit ad civitatem.* (Acts 12:10). Inter ceteras festiuitates sanc-torum, vel verius supra ceteras post Christi et matris eius Marie, magis sicud scitis et celeberimus est dies iste, quem duorum tam magnorum et excellencium, Petri videlicet et Pauli . . .-. . . <introducatur> narracio de clerico et cane suo, etc. Ff. 3ra–6va.

3. T28/2*?. *Hoc est corpus meum.* (Mark 14:22). Karissimi, Sigibertus in *Cronicis* manifeste declarat quod olim in castro Emaus, in quo Chris-tus hodierna die se ostendit . . .-. . . ad hanc finem resurreccionis et glorie pariter veniemus. Quem . . . Ff. 6va–8va.

4. S28*. *Ave Maria, gratia plena, Dominus tecum, benedicta tu in mulieribus* (Luke 1:28). Aue inquiunt saluta[n]tes, de pleno accipiunt exorantes . . .-. . . per illud Aue habemus incarnacionem. F. 8va–b, inc. Also V-40 and X-335.

J/4

1. T01*. *Abiciamus opera tenebrarum et induamur arma lucis; sicut in die hon-este amubulemus.* (Rom 13:12). Defige[n]s Apostolus oculorum intuitum interiorum in auctorem fidei venientem . . .-. . . cum finali bonorum operum execucione. Abiciamus ergo opera tenebrarum, etc. Ff. 9ra–vb. Also X-41.

2. T02*. *Levate capita vestra, ecce adpropinquat redemptio vestra.* (Luke 21:28). Sicut qui claudit oculos non potest videre, sic qui demittit oculos semper deorsum non potest respicere que sunt sursum . . .-. . . lauate [!] capita vestra, etc. Ff. 9vb–10vb. Also X-42.

3. T04*. *Pax Dei que exsuperat omnem sensum custodiat corda vestra*, etc. (Phil 4:7). In quibus ostenditur doctrine apostolice auctoritas . . .-. . . secundum

omnem temporis mensuram pax dei que exsuperat etc. Ff. 10vb–11rb. Also X-43.

4. T03*. *Quid existis in desertum videre* (Matt 11:9). Verba proposita sunt verba Redemptoris, et secundum sensum in quo ponuntur . . .-. . . dicatur ergo Quid existis videre, etc. Ff. 11rb–12ra. Also X-44.

5. T04*. *Vox clamantis in deserto* (John 1:23). Verba proposita allegorice sumpta propter aduentum Filii Dei . . .-. . . fructificacionem, dic' ergo Vox clamatis in deserto. F. 12ra–va. Also X-45.

6. T04*. *Dirigite viam Domini, sicut dicit Esaias propheta* (John 1:23). Quam-plures sunt hodie qui contendunt . . .-. . . diffidencia et trepidacione, Dirigite ergo viam Domini, etc. Ff. 12vb–13rb. Also X-46.

7. T06*. *Videamus hoc verbum quod factum est* (Luke 2:15). Quia enim facilius et forcius homo credit visui quam auditui . . .-. . . distribucione premiorum. Dic' ergo Videamus hoc verbum quod factum est, etc. Ff. 13rb–14ra. Also X-47.

8. T07*. *Misit Deus filium suum factum ex muliere, factum sub lege, vt eos qui sub lege erant redimeret* (Gal 4:4). In verbis propositis scriptis Galatarum 3 exprimitur nobis Filii Dei excellencia . . .-. . . nisi redimi profuisset, Gregorius. Ideo misit . . . F. 14ra–vb. Also X-48.

9. T10*. *Intrantes domum invenerunt puerum*, etc. (Matt 2:11). In hiis verbis Matthei 2 scriptis et hodie in Ecclesia recitatis innuit nobis sermo diuinus quia omnis qui petit accipit . . .-. . . iocunditate interminabile, Intrantes . . . Ff. 14vb–15va. Also X-49.

10. T11*. *Ecce agnus Dei, ecce qui tollit peccata mundi* (John 1:29). Quanta sit Redemptoris nostri benignitas, quanta sit efficacia . . .-. . . peccata abstulit. Propter quod Iohannes Ecce . . . Ff. 15va–16ra. Also X-50.

11. T11a*. *Post triduum invenerunt eum in templo in medio doctorum* (Luke 2:47). In verbis propositis scriptis [*blank*] 2 innuit nobis sermo ewangelicus quod qui Iesum bene querunt bene inueniunt . . .-. . . de confitentibus Iesum querentibus dic' Post . . . Ff. 16ra–17rb. Also X-51.

12. T12*. *Spiritu ferventes, Domino servientes, non alta sapientes, sed humilibus consentientes* (Rom 12:11). Defigens beatus Apostolus acie[m] intelligencie in contuitum hominum mundanorum . . .-. . . in obseruacione preceptorum, vt sic simus Spiritu feruentes . . . Ff. 17rb–18ra. Also X-52.

13. T13*. *Extendens Iesus manum tetigit eum dicens, Volo, mundare* (Matt 8:3). Visitacio siue presencia boni medici solacium et remedium est infirmi . . .- . . . a macula turpium accionem per satisfaccionem. Dicat ergo Exten-dens . . . F. 18ra–va. Also X-53.

14. T14*. *Surgens imperavit ventis, et facta est tranquillitas magna,* etc. (Matt 8:26 et Mark 4:39). Sicut presencia medici cedit egrotantibus et male habentibus in solacium et remedium . . .-. . . tranquillitas glorie. Dicit ergo Surgens . . . Ff. 18va–19ra. Also X-87.

15. T15?. *Pax Christi exultet in cordibus vestris, in qua vocati estis* (Col 3:15). Videns Apostolus mundanos homines prauos et promptos ad iram . . .- . . . peremptorie citando, vt dicatur viris perfectis Pax Christi, etc. F. 19rb– vb. Also X-91.

16. T16*. *Voca operarios et redde illis mercedem suam* (Matt 20:8). In verbis propositis Matthei 20 introducturus Deus Pater loquens ad Vnigenitum de mercede . . .-. . . redde mercedem sempiternam. Dic' ergo Voca, etc. Ff. 19vb–20va. Also X-92.

17. T17?. *Libenter gloriabor in infirmitatibus meis, ut inhabitet in me virtus Christi* (2 Cor 12:9). Intuens Apostolus Spiritu Sancto repletus homines valde promptos ad inaniter gloriandum . . .-. . . inhabitet in me per remuneracionem, dic' ergo Libenter . . . Ff. 20vb–22ra (no f. 21). Also X-90.

18. T18?. *Caecus vidit et sequebatur eum* (Luke 18:43). In verbis propositis scriptis Luce 18 datur nobis intelligi quod qui non cognoscit non diligit . . .-. . . ideo sequebatur eum perseueranter. Cecus ergo vidit. Ff. 22ra–23ra.

19. ?. *Memor esto unde excideris et age paenitentiam, et prima opera fac* (Rev. 2:5). In verbis propositis scriptis Apocalipsis 2 innuit nobis sermo diuinus quod sicut ille qui morbo medicinam non querit . . .-. . . opus compassionis qua regnum eternum acquiritur Memor esto . . . F. 23ra–vb.

20. T19?. *Ductus est Iesus in desertum* (Matt. 4:1). Ut probaret Iesus contra insurgentes hereses se habere humanitatem . . .-. . . ab eterna penalitate, propter quod dicitur Ductus . . . Ff. 23vb–24rb.

21. ?. *Levantes oculos neminem viderunt nisi solum Iesum* (Matt. 17:8). In hiis verbis designatur status perfectorum ad contemplanda celestia assumptorum . . .-. . . et super excelsa mea deducet me victori in psalmis. Dicit ergo Leuantes . . . Ff. 24rb–25ra.

22. T21?. *Eratis aliquando tenebrae, nunc autem lux in Domino, ut filii lucis ambulate* (Eph. 5:8). Quia malorum perpessorum recognicio est frequenter adipiscendorum occasio . . . .-. . . in honestate conuersacionis, ut merito dicatur eis Eratis . . . F. 25ra–vb.

23. T24?. *Illa quae sursum est Hierusalem libera est mater nostra* (Gal. 4:26). Beatissimus Apostolus vsque in tercium celum raptus fuerat . . .-. . . libera in passagiis, quia iure bona [?] conseruatis et continens. Dicit igitur Illa, etc. Ff. 25vb–26ra, 26vb–27ra.

24. T23?. *Si veritatem dico vobis, quare non creditis mihi?* (John 8:46). Vnicuique in propria facultate creditur et quia Christus medicus animarum repellitur . . .-. . . quare non creditis, vt resipiscatis? Dic' igitur Si veritatem dico, etc. Ff. 26ra–vb, 27ra–vb.

25. T24?. *Ecce, rex tuus venit tibi mansuetus* (Matt. 21:5). Inuestigator cordium et cognitor siue conditor omnium, Iesus Christus . . .-. . . vt te duceret ad eternitatem homo siue femina te propria diligenter, quia Ecce . . . F. 27rb–vb.

26. T27?. *Si consurrexistis cum Christo, quae sursum sunt quaerite* (Col 3:1). In verbis propositis scriptis innuit nobis beatus Apostolus quod anima que Deum diligit . . .-. . . querite in illa colacione que incipit Illa que sursum est Ierusalem, etc. F. 28ra–rb.

27. T29?. *Gavisi sunt discipuli viso Domino* (John 20:20). Post illam apparicionem qua Iesus se ostendit . . .-. . . repromissione glorie, ut merito de ipsis dicatur Gauisi . . . Ff. 28rb–29ra.

28. T30?. *Bonus pastor animam suam dat pro ovibus suis* (John 10:11). In hiis verbis renuit nobis ipsa eterna veritas qualis esse debeat spiritualis pastor . . .-. . . pascendis et custodiendis, propter quod de ipso merito dicitur Bonus pastor, etc. F. 29ra–va.

29. T31?. *Tristitia vestra vertetur in gaudium* (John 16:20). Verba ista sunt Christi ad discipulos . . .-. . . conuertitur in gaudium comprehensionis premiorum, etc. Ff. 29va–30ra.

30. T32?. *Cum venerit spiritus veritatis, docebit vos omnem veritatem* (John 16:13). Quanta in Spiritu Sancto sit equitas, quanta vtilitas . . .-. . . tercio ut doceat veritatem iusticie, Cum venerit . . . F. 30ra–b.

31. T33? *Petite et accipietis, ut gaudium vestrum plenum sit* (John 16:24). In quibus verbis innuit sermo ewangelicus quod petentes . . .-. . . fruicione et tencione ipse est qui ait Petite . . . Ff. 30rb–31ra.

32. T36?. *Ascendisti in altum, accepisti captivitatem, dedisti dona hominibus* (Ps. 67:19). Multa redemptore [!] nostri gesta fuerunt sanctis patribus reuelata . . .-. . . dona perfectissima et sufficientissima. Dic' ergo Ascendisti, etc. Ff. 31ra–32ra.

33. T37?. *Estote prudentes et vigilate in orationibus* (1 Pet 4:7). Videns Apostolus multiplicem dolum et fallacia . . .-. . . bonis operibus finaliter persistatis. Dicit ergo Estote prudentes, etc. F. 32ra–b.

34. T39*. *Spiritus ubi vult spirat, et vocem eius audis, sed nescis unde veniat aut quo vadat* (John 3:8). Verba prophetica aduentum Spiritus Sancti recolencia seu representancia, et ideo presenti solempnitati conueniencia, scripta sunt

Iohannis 3. In quibus verbis sunt tria . . .-. . . aut quo vadat propter cordis infirmitatem. Dicit ergo Spiritus . . . Ff. 32rb–33va.

35. ?. *Cum venerit spiritus veritatis, docebit vos omnem veritatem* (John 16:13). Quia Dei Filius ex sui absencia corda discipulorum fore conturbanda . . .- . . . et hoc est quod dicitur Danielis. F. 33va–b, inc.?

1. S49*. *De nocte surrexit* (Prov 31:15). Karissimi, videtis quod quilibet homo componitur ex duobus, scilicet ex corpore et ex anima. Et sicut corpus exterius deficit . . .-. . . et sic de nocte surrexit. Nos cum ea sic consurgere Christus concedat. Ff. 34–35v.

2. T34*. *Confitemini* (James 5:16). Si quis peregre iturus esset versus terram sanctam, scilicet Ierusalem, causa indulgenciarum, necesse haberet primo confitere . . .-. . . sequitur quod confessio precessit baptismum Christi. Nos sic confiteri . . . Ff. 35v–37v. Also Bodley 857–1, Balliol 219, New College 305.

3. ?. *O ante quorum oculos Christus Iesus proscriptus est et crucifixus* (Gal 3:1). Quia, reuerendi mei domini, ista uerba sumpta pro themate sunt uerba maxime lamentacionis, eciam mornyngis . . .-. . . sed eciam quod eius mortem non vindicabant, etc. Ff. 37v–46.

4. T28/2*. *Peregrinus es in Ierusalem?* (Luke 24:18). Christus, Dei Filius, qui ut isto tempore surrexit de morte . . .-. . . et societatem Dei et omnium suorum angelorum et omnium aliorum sanctorum ille vos perducat . . . Ff. 46–55.

5. ?. *Amicus meus venit* (Luke 11:6). Dicit Parysiensis in sermone qui sic incipit: Facite vobis amicos, quod in eleccione amici quatuor sunt attendenda . . .- . . . glorie quia perfecti habebunt centuplum fructum. Ff. 55–57.

6. T34*. *Amice, commoda mihi tres panes* (Luke 11:5). Secundum Goram amicus iste Christus est, tum quia prius dilexit . . .-. . . qui manducabit panem in regno Dei ille concedat . . . Ff. 57–58v.

7. ?. *Numquid pro pisce serpentem dabit?* (Luke 11:11). Scitis, karissimi, quod anno preterito habui de triplici pane quem ministraui secundum graciam Dei pro eo tempore michi datam. Vnde dixi quod est triplex panis . . . Sed quamuis quis quis [!] habeat panem valde delicatum, nisi habuerit aliquod eduleum, non tenet se bene contentum. Sed eduleum conuenientissimum huic diei est piscis. Ideo, etc. Sed quia pisces ad presens non habeo, ideo dico cum Petro, Iohannis vltimo, Vado piscari. Dicit Ianuensis in sermonibus

dominicalibus. . . .-. . . ut tunc ascendamus in anima et in die iudicii in corpore et anima ad celum. Quod . . . Ff. 58v–59v.

8. ?. *Hodie salus domui huic facta est* (Luke 19:9). Dictis precibus anglizetur thema, pro cuius introduccione dicitur euangelium usque ad thema. Moraliter quilibet nostrum debet esse Zacheus . . .-. . . Deus in domibus eius cognoscetur. Ff. 59v–61.

9. ?. *Erat autem proximum pascha Iudaeorum* (John 6:4). Pascha transitus interpretatur, et est dies festus non quorumcumque sed Iudeorum, idest peccata sua vere confitencium . . .-. . . Deus vitam meam audiet etc. humilis. Ff. 61v–62v.

10. T36*. *Ascendit* (Ps 67:34?). Boneventura in *De vita Christi,* capitulo penultimo, comendat istud festum vltra omnia festa . . .-. . . si scirem homines ignoraturos et deos ignoscituros, non peccarem. Ff. 62v–63v.

11. ?. *Diliges Dominum Deum tuum* (Luke 10:27). Pro antethemate nota Paulum 1 Ad Thimotheum 2: Obsecro primo . . . Pro induccione nota processum ewangelii. . . .-. . . solare, remitte, fer, ora. Ff. 63v–66v, inc.

12. S49*. *Attulit alabastrum unguenti* (Luke 7:37). Hec uerba possunt dici de tribus personis secundum triplicem sensum sacre scripture. Primo de Maria Magdalena . . .-. . . de vidua paupercula que obtulit duo minuta. Ff. 66v–67v.

13. S26 vigil*. *Cor tradet ad vigilandum* (Sir 39:6). Sapientissimi Platonis sanxit auctoritas in Thimeo quod in cuiuslibet actus exordio diuinum congruit auxilium precibus inprecari . . .-. . . euge, serue bone et fidelis, etc. Ff. 67v–70.

14. T34*. *Confitemini alterutrum* (James 5:16). Scitis, karissimi, quod isti dies dicuntur dies rogacionum cicius quam ieiuniorum [a]ut elemosinarum, et causa est . . .-. . . et emundet nos ab omni iniquitate. Quod . . . Ff. 70–71v.

15. ?. *Revertentur ad Dominum* (Isa 19:22). Nota Crisostomum *De pluuia et vento,* etc . . . Karissimi, experiencia docet quod si filius regis uel magni domini eiectus esset de terra . . .-. . . in uerbis thematis habetur res quam debemus amare et timere, scilicet Dominus. Pro quo nota alibi, etc. Ff. 71v–73v.

16. ?. *Verbum caro factum est* (John 1:14). Reuerendi mei, dicit beatus Gregorius . . .-. . . et invariabile. Cuius premii participes nos efficiat qui . . . Ff. 73v–76.

17. ?. *Quid est hoc?* (Exo 16:15). Reuerendi mei, verba ista fuerunt uerba filiorum Israel quando collegerunt manna . . .-. . . non moriatur sed habeat vitam eternam. Ad quam . . . Ff. 76–79v.

18. C18*, perhaps S20*. *Ingredere civitatem* (Acts 9:7). Reuerendi mei, dicit Egidius . . .-. . . Et habitacio huius ciuitatis optima est. Ad quam . . . Ff. 79v–83v.

19. T26*. *Quid fecit, quare morietur?* (1 Sam 20:32). Wat hath ys man do . . . Karissimi, narrat Augustinus . . . de Codro rege Atheniensium . . .-. . . ut dicitur in tercio principali. Cuius hereditarii iuris participes nos efficiat qui . . . Ff. 83v–90v.

20. ?. *Tu es qui venturus es?* (Matt 11:3). Karissimi, Virgilius 6 *Enidorum* docet quod tria principaliter requiruntur in rege uel principe . . .-. . . nescitis qua hora Dominus vester venturus sit, Mathei 24. Ff. 90v–94v.

21. ?. *Quis arguet me de peccato?* (John 8:46). Reuerendi mei, peccatum tante est malicie quod destruit in homine tria meliora homini pertinencia . . .-. . . de peccato pro primo; de iusticia, supple in purgatorio, pro secundo; de iudicio pro tercio. Ff. 94v–97v.

22. T36*. *Amice, ascende superius* (Luke 14:10). Reuerendi domini, cum princeps aliquis nobilis et graciosus venerit nouiter de terra guerre . . .-. . . in istam sanctam requiem et beatam celi que nunquam finietur. Ad quam . . . Ff. 97v–100v. Also E-39 and Magdalen 112, f. 221ra.

23. T26*. *Hic est Iesus rex* (Matt 27:37). Scitis quando pauper qui haberet magnum negocium pertractandum cum rege uel cum domino . . .-. . . omnia ita fecit ut nos saluaret. Quod . . . Ff. 100v–104. Also Z-43.

24. T34*. *Petite et dabitur vobis* (Luke 11:9). Secundum Walensem *De penitencia*, volens orare et aliquid a Deo petere debet seipsum diligenter considerare . . .-. . . vbi tam corporis quam anime erit perfecta beatitudo. Ad quam . . . (As in Z-4, this is followed by "Sicut dicit Glossa super illud 'Apud me oracio vite' . . . Sequitur quid Christus docuit orare, quia Pater noster," ff. 106v–107v.). Ff. 104–106v. Also Z-4.

25. C11*. *In domo tua oportet me manere* (Luke 19:5). Scribitur 2 Paralipomenon 6 de prima Ecclesia, templo scilicet Ierusalem, quod rex Salomon edificauit Domino templum . . .-. . . nobis vitam et gloriamque sempiternam tribuendo. Ad quos . . . Ff. 107v–110v. Also Z-6.

26. ?. *Colligite quae superaverunt fragmenta ne pereant* (John 6:12). Karissimi, sicud dicit beatus Ieronimus epistula 37, totum quod legimus in libris diuinis nitet quidem et fulget . . .-. . . cognoscat voluntatem illius quem temptat. Ff. 110v–111v, inc?

27. ?. *Petite et accipietis, ut gaudium vestrum sit plenum* (John 16:24). Karissimi, instante tempore quo Helias celum aereum ascensurus erat, dixit

ad Helizeum: Postula . . .-. . . sed toti gaudentes intrabunt in gaudium. Quod . . . Ff. 111v–114.

28. T17*. *Libenter gloriabor in infirmitatibus meis* (2 Cor 12:9). Uerba proposita sumpta sunt de epistula hodierna et sunt uerba Apostoli Cor 12. Et est sciendum quod mater Ecclesia videns filios suos multis infirmitatibus et miseriis oppressos et non valens eos ad plenum liberare . . .-. . . qui humiliatus fuerit, erit in gloria. Ad quam nos, etc. Ff. 114v–116v.

29. ?. *Libenter gloriabor*, etc. (2 Cor 12:9). Egregius predicator Paulus sic loquitur auditoribus suis, scilicet Corinthiis in principio epistule sue: Nos inquit sumus gloria vestra . . .-. . . ut possim aliquod uerbum sic proferre et vos audire, etc. Ff. 116v–117.

30. ?. *Unus pro omnibus mortuus est* (2 Cor 5:14). Patet Iohannis 11 ex prophecia Spiritus Sancti dicta per Caypham quod post resuscitacionem Lazari et ostensionem miraculorum expediens erat Christum mori . . .-. . . hoc facere debuit ut redimeret quod fecit, etc. Ff. 117–118v, inc?

31. C21*. *Amicus noster dormit* (John 11:11). Reuerendi, sicut videmus quod in rebus ad corpus pertinentibus communiter est causa quadruplex . . .-. . . nobis impetrent veniam in presenti et in futuro vitam sine fine etc. Ff. 119–122.

32. ?. *Sponsabo te* (Hos 2:19). Intendo ad presens Deo dante primo declarare quasdam questiones quas mulier possit interrogare de sponso accipiendo . . .-. . . de Egipto 600000 pugnatorum. De qua materia nota in sermone Amicus meus venit. Ff. 123–124.

33. T34*. *Orate* (James 5:16). Nota de duobus tubis argenteis ductilibus, Numeri 10, quarum officium secundum Magistrum *Historiarum* erat ad quatuor . . .-. . . in quarto mandato honora patrem tuum etc. F. 124r–v.

34. T35*. *Gratia magna erat in omnibus illis* (Acts 4:33). Nota de Helya, 4 Regum 2, qui transiit Agalgal. . . .-. . . nota de seruo blasphemo mortuo in die Pasche lingua corrupta, etc. Ff. 124v–126.

35. ?. *Ascendit in arborem* (Luke 19:4). Nota de aquis Marath, Exodi 14, quas populus Israel transiens . . .-. . . ut notatur in sermone Dic verbo etc. F. 126r–v.

36. T41/5. *Qui manducat hunc panem, vivet in eternum* (John 6:59). Augustinus *De doctrina Christiana* libro 4, capitulo ultimo, hortatur hominem . . .-. . . et post hanc vitam in celo vita glorie. Quod . . . Ff. 126v–128v. Also FE-23.

37. ?. *Plenitudo legis est dilectio* (Rom 13:10). Lex quidam consistit in decem mandatis . . .-. . . colloquium mulieris quasi ignis exardescit. Ff. 133v–135.

38. ?. *Pueri mei mecum sunt* (Luke 11:7). Dictis precibus repetatur thema. Ista sunt uerba Christi . . . Possunt eciam dici de quolibet Christiano fideli cui tres primi [= pueri] sunt necessarii: primus in Egiptum cum matre portandus . . .-. . . hic in gracia et in futuro erunt secum in gloria. Quam . . . Ff. 136v–138.

39. ?. *Hierusalem libera est* (Gal 4:25). Homo ponitur in libertate ad eligendum quod vult . . .-. . . sumitur anagogice pro Ecclesia trihumphante, idest pro celo. F. 138r–v.

40. S59*. *In hereditate Domini morabor* (Sir 24:11). Notandum est de triplici habitacione siue mora hominis . . .-. . . in hereditate Domini morabor, que est gloria sempiterna. Ad quam . . . Ff. 141v–143.

41. S59*. *In hereditate Domini morabor* (Sir 24:11). Pro processu huius colacionis est notandum secundum iuristas quod volenti habere hereditatem paternam tria sunt necessaria . . .-. . . sic nos ista tria habere dum viuimus . . . Ff. 143–144v.

42. T26. *Redemisti nos Deo in sanguine tuo* (Rev 5:9). Reuerendissimi patres et domini, videtur michi circa reparacionem humani generis triplex . . .- . . . detur ista perfeccio, qui redemisti nos Deo in sanguine tuo. Amen. Ff. 145–149v. FitzRalph, FI-73; also F/3-7.

K – Cambridge, Corpus Christi College, MS 392

1. T02 ("Samelyn, Oxon'"). *In eum gentes sperabunt* (Rom 15:12). Prehonorandi domini, patres, et magistri, ex gencium actuali liberacione . . .- . . . et in futuro gloriam. Sic igitur nos hic regi per spem . . . Ff. 209–210v.

2. T16*. *Ite in vineam* (Matt 20:4). Studiosissimi magistri, patres, atque domini, < . . . set> vnunquisque quid agat et <consideret>si in vinea Domini laboret . . .-. . . vt ad agrum requiei peruenire valeatis, vbi floret Christus vera vitis nostre spei. Amen. Ff. 212–213v.

3. T19 ("Oxon' in latinis"). *Ecce nunc tempus acceptabile* (2 Cor 6:2). Studiosissimi magistri, patres, atque domini, cum verbum predicacionis et salutis . . .-. . . operemur bonum, Ad Galatas 6. Igitur vt sic agamus . . . Ff. 214–215v.

4. T18 ("in latinis et predicatus fuit Cantebrigg'"). *Iesu, miserere mei* (Luke 18:38). Studiosissimi magistri, patres, atque domini, veluti sacrarum scripturarum mellea fantur eloquia . . .-. . . Iesu miserere mei. Ipsam misericordiam dignetur . . . Ff. 217–218.

5. T65 ("Fundamentum sermonis in latinis"). *Impleamini agnitione voluntatis Dei* (Col 1:9). Reuerendi magistri, patres, atque domini, ex oculata praxi lucidius contemplamur . . .-. . . ob amissum iam diu visum. F. 218v.

6. T64 ("predicatus Cantebrigg'"). *Magister, scimus quod verax es* (Matt 22:16). Honorandi magistri, patres, atque domini, illibate veritatis magisterium . . .- . . . verax es. Cuius veritatis participes . . . F. 219r–v.

7. T32*. *Suscipite verbum quod potest salvare animas vestras* (James 1:21). Honorabiles domini, patres, et magistri, provt euidet ex beatissimo Augustino libro suo *De mendacio*, capitulo 27, sanctitatis causa . . .-. . . simul gaudeat et qui metit. Quod . . . Ff. 220–221v.

8. T31*. *Servi estote,* scilicet Domino (1 Pet 2:18). Doctissimi magistri, patres, atque domini, <[*cut off, top margin*]> quarum habeat homo potestatem certificamur, inquid Augustinus . . .-. . . conuertit in securitatem, 2 Esdre 1. Ad quam . . . Ff. 222–224.

9. T05 ("in domo capitulari Cant'," 1435). *Filius datus est nobis* (Isa 9:6). Prehonorandi domini, patres, fratresque dillectissimi, ad hoc quod sermo diuinus effectum habeat in mente humana . . .-. . . cum Spiritu Sancto seruiamus securi. Quod . . . Ff. 224v–227.

10. C15*. *Vos autem cognoscetis eum, quia apud vos manebit et in vobis erit* (John 14:17). Reuerendi patres et domini, triplici ex affectu viantibus Dei verbum proponitur hic in via . . .-. . . animam suam ponentem pro ouibus suis. Quem . . . Ff. 229–231v.

11. T23*. *Gloria mea nihil est* (John 8:54). Grisostomus *De opere imperfecto* comparat hominem mortalem ad condiciones . . .-. . . et sic intrare in gloriam. Ad quam gloriam . . . F. 233r–v.

12. T06*. *Evangelizo vobis gaudium magnum* (Luke 2:10). Karissimi, usitata consuetudo hoc declarat quod quando nascuntur filii regum . . .-. . . ut vere filii pacis dici mereantur. Hanc pacem . . . Ff. 234–235v. Perhaps protheme to the following, though it has division and development.

13. T06*. *Evangelizo vobis gaudium,* vt supra (Luke 2:10). Unde advertendum est quod materia sermonis quod inter omnia festa Saluatoris festum natiuitatis est festum gaudii . . .-. . . accipietis ut gaudium vestrum sit plenum. Quod . . . Ff. 235v, 238–239v, with renvoi.

14. T30. *Iustitiae vivamus* (1 Pet 2:25). Videmus in natura, et concordat Psalmista, quod quando humiditas . . .-. . . et quod perfectissimum in . . . semper erit. Istam vitam nobis. Ff. 236–237.

15. T26*. *Quid fecit, quare morietur?* (1 Sam 20:32). Magnifici domini patresque precelsi, textum almi codicis diligencius exaranti eminenter euidet et

aperte . . .-. . . si non vultis foras eiectum diabolum intro interum reuocare. Ff. 245–247, 250–251v.

16. C15*. *Eligite hodie quod placet* (Josh 24:15). Reuerendi mei, beatus pater Ieronimus in libro *De mirabilibus mundi* sic dicit: Apud Eracleam in regis eleccione . . .-. . . in viam pacis talem pastorem nobis eligere concidat . . . Ff. 248–249.

17. T24*. *Invenietis asinam alligatam* (Matt 21:2). Reuerendi, legimus in ewangelio hodierno quod Dominus noster Iesus appropinquans ciuitati Ierusalem premisit . . .-. . . per consequens inueniet azinam alligatam. Ff. 253–257v. Followed by a folio in English, in a different hand: *O quam dissimile*, etc. O lord, how dyuers and onlych were þe pepul wordes <dedes> in þese too processyones. In þe fyrst þei cried on hy . . .-. . . þe first property of þe asse is þat she is a vyle best. So is euery synful vyle be dedly synne. þerfore seiþ þe wyse man: Quasi a facie colubri, etc. <De tercio principali.> Ad hoc verbum Corpus coruptibile fouere sic procedatur: þus wiþ fonnednes and foly al men be i-bounde . . .-. . . to blys of heuen þer to be euerlastyng. Ad quod. . . .

18. T22*. *Non sumus ancillae filii* (Gal 4:31). Reuerendi mei, a dominica Septuagesime, in qua planctus in Ecclesia incepit pro humana miseria . . .-. . . in presenti bene viuere et gloriam in futuro. Quam . . . Ff. 262–267v.

19. ?. *Aperiantur ergo labia mea, ut recte predicem* (Prov 8:6). Vbera huius corporis sunt vino fragrancia, et hec sunt sacre doctrine . . .-. . . excipiat tutissimum portum salutis. Ad quem . . . Ff. 274–278.

20. ?. *Gratia Dei gustavit mortem* (Heb 2:9). Reuerendi mei, \egregius doctor beatus/ Dionisius 3 *De diuinis nominibus* ymaginatur quod Deus sit quasi summum celum . . .-. . . gracia eius semper in me manet, et tantum de principali. Ff. 285–286v?.

21. ?. *Exivit sanguis et aqua* (Matt 19:34). Secundum scripture processum non solum Deus totum mundum creauit ad hominis obsequium . . .-. . . eo fons aque salientis in vitam eternam. Quam, etc. Ff. 287r–v, 296r–v, with renvoi.

22. ?. *Est puer unus hic* (John 6:9). Karissimi, beatus Augustinus *Super Iohannem* omelia 12, super illo verbo Nemo assendit in celum nisi qui descendit de celo, Filius Hominis, qui est in celo, loquens . . .-. . . tales regunt totam patriam in qua sunt. F. 288r–v.

23. T26*. *Iesus Nazarenus rex Iudaeorum* (John 19:19). Beatus Bernardus, monastice vite eximius executor et nominis Iesu deuotissimus predicator . . .-. . . ex mortuis primicie dormiencium in Ap'. F. 289r–v. Also X-117.

24. ?. *Diligamus Deum, quoniam ipse prior dilexit nos* (1 John 4:19). Reuerendi domini, ex sentencia beati Bernardi *Super Cantica* omelia 20, precipua et principalis causa quare Deus voluit ab hominibus videri . . .-. . . ad terram promissam facilius valeamus peruenire. Ad quam terram . . . Ff. 290–292v.

25. T24* or T26*?. *Christus factus est oboediens usque ad mortem* (Phil 2:8). Reuerendi patres et domini, secundum sentenciam Sapientis, Deus de terra creauit . . . , Ecclesiastici 17, et si magna erant sibi ista . . .-. . . venit igitur aliquis etc. . Ff. 305–307.

26. C14*. *Luceat lux vestra coram hominibus* (Matt 5:16). Reuerendi domini, sicut materialis sol sue lucis radios in hec inferiora diffundens patefacit omnia . . .-. . . erit tibi Dominus in lucem sempiternam et Deus tuus in gloriam tuam. Quam . . . Ff. 314–315v. Rimington's synodal sermon of 1373; also E-14 and Harley 1615, f. 5v. Edited from Paris, Université, MS 790, in O'Brien, "Two Sermons."

L – Oxford, Bodleian Library, MS Laud misc. 200

1. T01. *Cum adpropinquasset Iesus Hierosolymis et venisset Bethfage*, etc. (Matth 21:1). Appropinquacio Christi versus Jerosolimam signat moraliter eius aduentum in personam hominis . . .-. . . et dabo tibi coronam uite. Hanc coronam. . . . Ff. 2–5v.

2. T02. *Erunt signa in sole et luna et in stellis*, etc. (Luc. 21:25). In hoc euangelio fit mencio de aduentu Christi ad judicium finale . . .-. . . ibi ab origine mundi. Ad hanc paratam gloriam. . . . Ff. 5v–8v.

3. T03. *Cum audisset Iohannes in vinculis opera Christi, misit duos . . . an alium expectamus* (Matth 11:2). Non autem propter hoc quod Johannes dubitavit . . .-. . . in eternum non peccabis, et sic venies ad gloriam. Quam. . . . Ff. 8v–12v.

4. T04. *Miserunt Iudaei ab Hierosolymis sacerdotes et levitas*, etc. (John 1:19). Hoc euangelium testificatur quomodo Iudei perfidi miserunt sacerdotes suos . . .-. . . miseraciones eius super omnia oper eius. Ff. 12v–15v, inc.

5. T06. *Exiit edictum a Caesare Augusto*, etc. (Luke 2:1). Moraliter hoc edictum signat Filium, qui est verbum Patris altissimi . . .-. . . beati pacifici, quoniam filii Dei uocabuntur. Ff. 16–18v.

6. S09. *Ecce, ego mitto ad vos prophetas sapientes et scribas*, etc. (Matt 23:34). Hoc euangelium facit mencionem de persecucione et tribulacione . . .- . . . stantem a dextris uirtutis Dei. Ad quem . . . Ff. 18v–20v.

7. S10?. *Dixit Iesus Petro: Sequere me* (John 21:19). Christus antequam dixerat Petro: Sequere me, quesiuit ab eo, numquid eum dilexerat in corde . . .-

... hec secta Christi ducit homines de uirtute in uirtutem ad gloriam, ubi uidebitur Deus deorum in Sion. Ff. 20v–22v.

8. S11. *Angelus Domini apparuit in somnis Ioseph dicens: Surge et accipe puerum et matrem eius . . .dum dicam tibi* (Matt 1,20). Moraliter potest iste angelus signare racionem hominis . . .-. . . qui perseuerauerit usque in finem, hic saluus erit. Ff. 22v–24v.

9. S12. *Homo quidam nobilis abiit in regionem longinquam accipere regnum et reverti* (Luke 19:12). Homo iste nobilis est Dominus Iesus Christus, qui est nobilissimus in potencia . . .-. . . et hiis dictis ascendit Christus in celestem Ierusalem. Quo . . . Ff. 24v–27.

10. T07. *Erant Ioseph et Maria mater Domini mirantes super hiis quae dicebantur de illo* (Luke 2:33). Ioseph interpretatur augmentum et signat uerum prelatum aut curatum . . .-. . . dabit primo graciam ad merendum et post gloriam ad fruendum. Ff. 27–29.

11. T08. *Postquam consummati sunt dies octo . . . in utero conciperetur* (Luke 2:21). Notum est fidelibus quomodo Christus, qui est finis legis ueteris . . .-. . . saluauit eos in uita eterna. Ad quam . . . Ff. 29–31v.

12. T10. *Cum natus esset Iesus in Bethlehem Iudaeae in diebus . . .qui natus est rex Iudaeorum* (Matt 2:1). Natiuitas Christi in Bethleem Iude potest signare spiritualiter manifestam ostencionem scripture sacre . . .-. . . propria regio anime racionalis. Ad quam . . . Ff. 31v–35.

13. T11. *Vidit Iohannes Iesum venientem ad se . . . peccata mundi* (John 1:29). Hoc euangelium narrat quomodo Baptista fuit propheta predicando futura de Christo . . .-. . . iniciat in uia et permanet eternaliter in patria. Ff. 35–36v.

14. T11. *Venit Iesus a Galilaea in Iordanem ad Iohannem, ut baptizaretur ab eo* (Matt 3:13). Solempnitas Epiphanie commendatur propter quatuor . . .-. . . quod os Domini locutum est. Ad quam gloriam . . . Ff. 36v–38v.

15. T11a. *Cum factus esset Iesus annorum duodecim . . . non cognoverunt parentes eius* (Luke 2:42). Christus docens exemplum sufficiens tam iuuenibus quam senibus . . .-. . . saluos nos fecit, primo per graciam et demum per graciam [!]. Ff. 38v–41v.

16. T12. *Nuptiae factae sunt in Cana Galilaeae* (John 2:1). Constat ex processu euangelii quomodo Christus affuit nupciis . . .-. . . vertetur in gaudium sempiternum. Ad quod gaudium . . . Ff. 41v–43v.

17. T13. *Cum descendisset Iesus de monte, secutae sunt eum turbae multae* (Matt 8:1). Cum autem Iesus descendisset in montem ad predicandum perfeccionem . . .-. . . et in futuro per suam mundam vitam gloriam eternam. Ff. 44–47v.

18. T14. *Ascendente Iesu in naviculam, secuti sunt eum discipuli eius* (Matt 8:23). Hoc euangelium docet Christianos quomodo facere debent in tempore tribulacionis . . .-. . . que purgat peccata et facit inenire vitam eternam. Ad quam . . . Ff. 47v–50.

19. T15. *Simile est regnum caelorum homini qui seminavit bonum semen in agro suo* (Matt 13:24). Christus in hoc euangelio assimilat regnum celorum, scilicet Ecclesiam catholicam . . .-. . . et vitam concordie et vitam eterne glorie. Ad quam . . . Ff. 50–52v.

20. T16. *Simile est regnum caelorum homini patrifamilias qui exiit primo conducere operarios in vineam suam* (Matth 20:1). Iste paterfamilias qui exiit primo mane conducere operarios . . .-. . . o piger, et considera uias eius, et disce sapienciam. Ff. 52v–58.

21. T17. *Cum turba multa convenirent et de civitatibus properarent exiit, qui seminat,* etc. (Luke 8:4). Paterfamilias iste ad seminandum semen suum est Dominus Iesus Christus . . .-. . . per nullam predicacionem restaurantur. De cecitate spirituali quere in proximo sermone sequenti. Ff. 58–64v.

22. T18. *Adsumpsit Iesus duodecim discipulos suos et ait illis: Ecce ascendimus Hierosolyma,* etc. (Luke 18:31). Ascensus Christi et suorum discipulorum ad Ierosolimam signat ascensionem eorum ad celum . . .-. . . et si omnia munda, tunc oculus mundus; ideo respice. Ff. 64v–69v.

23. T19. *Ductus est Iesus in desertum a spiritu, ut temptaretur a diabolo* (Matt 4:1). Ductio ista in desertum, qua Christus inducebatur a Spiritu Sancto . . .-. . . Dominum Deum tuum adorabis et illi soli seruies, ut sic peruaeniatur ad gloriam, etc. Ff. 69v–75v.

24. T20. *Egressus Iesus secessit in partes Tyri et Sidonis* (Matt 15:21). Moraliter Iesus egressus est quando fuit incarnatus . . .-. . . qui fidem suam nunquam mutant ab eo. Hanc uitam . . . Ff. 75v–82.

25. T21. *Erat Iesus eiciens daemonium, et illud erat mutum,* etc. (Luke 11:14). Mutus iste signat omnem hominem qui per mortale peccatum . . .-. . . per dignam penitenciam, et sic peruaeniamus ad gloriam eternam. Amen. Ff. 82–89v.

26. T22. *Abiit Iesus trans mare Galilaeae* (John 6:1). Transitus Iesu ultra mare Galilee signat suam laboriosam conuersacionem . . .-. . . ut cum anima munda possitis intrare mundiciam regni celorum. Amen. Ff. 89v–94v.

27. T23. *Quis ex vobis arguet me de peccato?* (John 8:46). Hoc euangelium narrat quomodo Christus, qui non potuit peccasse . . .-. . . quasi holocausta hostie accipiet eum in eternum. Ff. 94v–101.

28. T25. *Hic est calix novi testamenti in meo sanguine* (Luke 22:20). Et pertinenter ad propositum passionis Christi tria possunt racionabiliter tangi super isto textu . . .-. . . ut subleuemur per sanguinem redempcionis ad sancta sanctorum. Amen. Ff. 101–106v.

29. T26?. *Stabant juxta crucem Iesu mater eius et soror . . . Magdalene* (John 19:25). In istis uerbis possunt tria intelligi ad utilitatem Christianorum . . .-. . . Et vos, domini, eadem facite illis sic stare in fidem [!] et crucem penitencie tollerare, ut predicitur illis statibus, Deus concedat . . . Ff. 106v–111v.

30. T28. *Maria Magdalene et mater Iacobi et Salome*, etc. (Mark 16:1). Iste tres mulieres possunt moraliter signare tres potencias . . .-. . . cum Christo, sole iusticie, regnemus in eternum. Quod . . . Ff. 111v–115.

31. T28/2. *Duo ex discipulis Iesu ibant ipsa die in castellum*, etc. (Luke 24:13). Isti duo discipuli Lucas et Cleophas significant corpus et animam . . .-. . . De tercia dicit Psalmista Saciabor cum apparuerit gloria tua. Ad quam gloriam . . . Ff. 115–118v.

32. T29?. *Cum sero factum esset in die illa vna sabbatorum et fores essent clausae . . . et stetit*, etc. (John 20:19). Sero signat finem mundi et specialiter tempus Antechristi . . .-. . . et perducit ad domum Ecclesie triumphantis. Ff. 118v–121v.

33. T30. *Ego sum pastor bonus*, etc. (John 10:11). Christus Iesus ostendens se esse Deum manifestat deitatis nomen . . .-. . . vnus pastor, Christus, pascens eos visione beatifica deitatis. Ff. 121v–124.

34. T31. *Modicum et non videbitis me, et iterum modicum et videbitis me, quia vado ad Patrem* (John 16:16). Hec verba protulit Christus suis discipulis in nocte qua tradendus erat . . .-. . . sunt incomprehensibilia, que preparauit Deus diligentibus se. Ff. 124–127.

35. T32. *Vado ad eum qui me misit, et nemo ex vobis interrogat me, Quo vadis?* (John 16:5). Christus ostendens se esse Deum, cui omnia sunt presencia . . .-. . . ad vindictam malefactorum, laudem vero bonorum. Ff. 127–131.

36. T33. *Amen, amen, dico vobis, si quid petieritis Patrem in nomine meo, dabit vobis* (John 16:23). Euangelista Iohannes habens specialem reuelacionem de humanitate . . .-. . . dat seipsum nobis et Spiritum Sanctum et graciam in presenti et gloriam in futuro. Amen. Ff. 131–134.

37. T36. *Recumbentibus Christi discipulis apparuit illis Iesus et exprobravit incredulitatem illorum et duritiam cordis*, etc. (Mark 16:14). Christus in hoc euangelio ad exemplandum opus prelati et veri predicatoris ordinate procedit in docendo . . .-. . . ipse est in celo et non timet inimicos. Ad quem . . . Ff. 134–139v.

38. T37. *Cum venerit paracletus quem ego mittam vobis a Patre meo, spiritum veritatis, qui a Patre procedit*, etc. (John 15:26 [ms 16]). Christus in hoc euangelio informat suos apostolos de Spiritus Sancti missione . . .-. . . . remunerabit hereditate celesti et eterna. Ad quam . . . Ff. 139v–142.

39. T39?. *Si quis diligit me sermonem meum servabit* (John 14:23). Quasi diceret: Obseruancia sermonis mei est verum signum dileccionis mee . . .-. . . in cor hominis ascendit, que preparauit Deus diligentibus se. Ff. 142–146v.

40. T40. *Erat homo ex Pharisaeis Nicodemus nomine, princeps Iudaeorum . . . nocte* (John 3:1). Hoc euangelium docet Christianos venire ad Jesum in nocte tribulacionis . . .-. . . non pereat sed habeat uitam eternam. Ff. 146v–151.

41. T41/5. *Caro mea vere est cibus, et sanguis meus vere est potus* (John 6:56). Christus in hoc euangelio declarans verum modum essendi sui corporis . . .- . . . vos in me et ego in vobis. Ff. 151–155.

42. T42. *Homo quidam erat dives qui induebatur purpura et bisso* (Luke 16:19). Iste dives signat quemlibet auarum aut diuitem . . .-. . . datis a Deo, et ista exprobracio. Ff. 155–158, inc.

43. S01. *Ambulans Iesus iuxta mare Galilaeae*, etc. (Matt 4:18). Hoc euangelium est satis planum quoad literam . . .-. . . sanitas tua, idest saluacio eterna cicius orietur. Ff. 162–165v.

44. S03. *Homo quidam peregre proficiscens vocavit*, etc. (Matt 25:14). Homo iste signat Iesum Christum, qui profectus . . .-. . . facit totum corpus operum bonorum lucidum, hic per graciam et in futuro per gloriam sempiternam. Ff. 165v–169.

45. S05. *Liber generationis Iesu Christi . . . Abraham* (Matt 1:1). In hoc euangelio declaratur generacio Christi carnalis . . .-. . . et sic sumus liber generacionis Christi. Ff. 169v–174.

46. S08. *Quia vidisti me, Thoma, credidisti; beati . . . et crediderunt* (John 20:29). Thomas iste, qui dicitur Didimus, spiritualiter signat tales qui dubitant . . .- . . . hic scilicet beatus per graciam, et in futuro per gloriam. Ff. 174–176v.

47. S18. *Simile est regnum caelorum thesauro abscondito in agro*, etc. (Matt 13:44). Hoc euangelium grauidatur cum tribus parabolis . . .-. . . si in uirtutibus finaliter discedamus. Ff. 176v–179a, verso.

48. S20. *Dixit Simon Petrus ad Iesum: Ecce, nos reliquimus omnia . . . erit nobis* (Matt 19:27). Hoc euangelium perfecte declarat tam meritum . . .- . . . regnum quod paratum est ab origine mundi. Ff. 179b–180b, verso.

49. S21. *Postquam impleti sunt dies purgationis Mariae . . . Domino* (Luke 2:22). Hoc euangelium docet quomodo Beata Uirgo et ceteri . . .-. . . semper

constans per immortalitatem. Hoc templum inhabitare . . . Ff. 180b, verso-185.

50. S24. *Confiteor tibi, Pater, Domine caeli et terrae, quia abscondisti haec . . . parvulis* (Matt 9:25). Hoc euangelium legitur in festo Sancti Mathie Apostoli . . .-. . . corde optimo disposuit nobis vitam eternam. Ff. 185–189.

51. S28. *Missus est angelus Gabriel a Deo in civitatem Galilaeae*, etc. (Luke 1:26). Moraliter iste angelus Gabriel, qui Dei fortitudo . . .-. . . sed perfectissime quantum ad eternam glorificacionem. Quam . . . Ff. 189–193v.

52. S30. *Ego sum vitis vera et Pater meus agricola est*, etc. (John 15:1). Christus in hoc euangelio ante passionem . . .-. . . et post eternaliter per eternam saluacionem. Ff. 193v–197.

53. S32. *Non turbetur cor vestrum; creditis in Deum, et in me credite* (John 14:1). Christus in hoc euangelio consolatur discipulos . . .-. . . saciabor cum aparuerit gloria tua. Ff. 197–202v.

54. S33. *Mihi autem absit gloriari nisi in cruce Domini nostri Iesu Christi* (Gal 6:14). Hec uerba sunt dicta ab apostolo Paulo ad hunc sensum: Procul . . .-. . . et incorrupcionem querentibus vitam eternam. Ad quam nos perducat, etc. Hec Lincolniensis dicto 119. Ff. 202v–207.

55. S44?. *Elisabeth impletum est tempus pariendi et peperit filium* (Luke 1:57). Elizabeth, que interpretatur Dei mei saturitas, signat . . .-. . . quia nemo de cognacione tua. F. 207r–v, inc.

M – Manchester, John Rylands Library, MS Latin 367

M/1: Radulfus Ardens (died after 1101), Homiliae dominicales
(*PL 155:1667–2118*)

M/2: Idem, Homiliae in Epistolas et Evangelia sanctorum (*PL 155:1301–1626*)

M/3

1. T01 "Dominica 1 aduentus Domini" head. *Cum adpropinquasset Iesus Hierosolymis*, etc. (Matt 21:1; Mark 11; Luke 19; et Iohannis 12 "in sentencia"). Hoc euangelium potest sic introduci: Karissimi, tempus presens dicitur adventus Domini . . .-. . . raro desiderant ut gaudia percipiant in excelsis. Ad que gaudia . . . Ff. 199ra–200rb.

2. T01. *Hora est iam nos de somno surgere*, etc. (Rom 13:11). Karissimi, in euangelio hodierno fit mencio . . .-. . . nisi in cruce Domini nostri Iesu Christi. Cui sit honor . . . Ff. 200rb–201va.

3. T02. *Erunt signa in sole*, etc. (Luke 21:25). In hoc euangelio huius dominice secunde fit mencio de secundo aduentu . . .-. . . quia tunc reddit vnicuique secundum opus suum. Cui sit gloria . . . Ff. 201va–203ra.

4. T03. *Cum audisset Iohannes in vinculis opera Christi*, etc. (Matt 11:2). Karissimi, in hoc sacro tempore recitantur que pertinent . . .-. . . erunt commendandi a Christo cum Iohanne, ut dixi primo. Quod . . . Ff. 203ra–204vb.

5. T03 [gutter]. *Cum audisset Iohannes in vinculis*, etc. (Matt 11:2). Iohannes interpretatur gracia uel in quo est gracia . . .-. . . oportet nos intrare in regnum celorum. Ad quod . . . Ff. 204vb–205va.

6. T04. *Miserunt Iudaei ab Hierosolymis sacerdotes*, etc. (John 1:19). Pro declaracione principii huius euangelii . . .-. . . peccatum cum quo nemo intrabit in regnum celorum. Ad quod . . . Ff. 205va–207va.

7. T07. *Erant pater et mater Iesu mirantes super hiis quae dicebantur de illo*, etc. (Luke 2:33). Litera huius euangelii potest diuidi in duas partes . . .-. . . procedit et crescit usque ad perfectum diem glorie. Ad quam . . . Ff. 207va–209va.

8. T11a. *Cum factus esset Iesus annorum duodecim*, etc. (Luke 2:42). In litera huius euangelii instruimur . . .-. . . set transibit de morte ad vitam. Ad quam . . . Ff. 209va–211va.

9. T12. *Nuptiae factae sunt in Cana Galilaeae*, etc. (John 2:1). In hoc euangelio ad literam ostenditur Iesus Nazarenus esse Deus per miraculum . . .-. . . impleamini vino glorie mee. Ad quam . . . Ff. 211va–213va.

10. T13. *Cum descendisset Iesus de monte, secutae sunt ei turbae multae*, etc. (Matt 8:1). Pro aliquali literali declaracione . . .-. . . mundi corde, quoniam ipsi Deum videbunt. Qui viuit, etc. Ff. 213va–215va.

11. T13*. *Puer meus iacet in domo paralyticus*, etc. (Matt 8:6). Ut supra in proximo sermone, et exponatur literaliter ut ibi expositum est. Moraliter per istum paraliticum peccator . . .-. . . sermo tuus qui sanat omnia. Ad quam sanacionem . . . Ff. 215va–216va.

12. T14. *Ascendente Iesu in naviculam, secuti sunt ei discipuli eius*, etc. (Matt 8:23; Mark 4, and Luce 8 "in sentencia"). In isto euangelio hodierno Christus ostendit se esse dominum maris . . .-. . . cum probatus fuerit, accipiet \a Deo/ coronam vite. Qui . . . Ff. 216va–218va.

13. T15. *Simile est regnum caelorum homini qui seminat bonum semen in agro suo*, etc. Et dicatur litera secundum quod iacet, si placet (Matt 13:24). Hoc euangelium potest diuidi in quinque partes . . .-. . . qui manducabit panem in regno celorum. Ad quod . . . Ff. 218va–220rb.

14. *T16. Simile est regnum caelorum homini patrifamilias qui exiit primo mane,* etc. (Matt 20:1). Karissimi, tempus Septuagesime, quod modo instat, representat . . .-. . . portam que ducit ad vitam. Ad quam . . . Ff. 220va–222va.

15. *T17. Cum turba plurima convenirent,* etc. (Luke 8:4). Karissimi, modo, ut scitis, instat tempus seminandi . . .-. . . ecce enim agricola, etc. Ad illum fructum . . . Ff. 222va–224va.

16. *T18. Adsumpsit Iesus duodecim discipulos,* etc. (Luke 18:31). Hoc euangelium diuiditur in duas partes . . .-. . . hic gracia et postea gloria. Ad quam . . . Ff. 224va–226va.

17. *T19. Ductus est Iesus in desertum,* etc. (Matt 4:1). Karissimi, tria sunt circa que versari debet intencio predicatoris . . .-. . . in presenti graciam et in futuro ministrabit gloriam. Ad quam . . . Ff. 226va–228vb.

18. *T20. Egressus Iesus secessit in partes Tyri et Sidonis,* etc. (Matt 15:21). Karissimi, inter omnia desiderabilia huius mundi sanitas . . .-. . . humilem spiritu suscipiet gloria. Ad quam . . . Ff. 228vb–230vb.

19. *T21. Erat Iesus eiciens daemonium, et illud erat mutum,* etc. (Luke 11:14). Hoc euangelium ad sensum literalem potest diuidi in tres partes . . .- . . . spiritualibus operibus est magis detentus ad honorem Dei. Cui est honor . . . Ff. 230vb–232vb.

20. *T22. Abiit Iesus trans mare Galilaeae, quod est Tiberiadis,* etc (John 6:1, Matt 14, Mark 6, Luke 9). Notandum primo quod hec dominica dupliciter nominatur . . .-. . . per multas tribulaciones oportet nos intrare regnum Dei. Ad quod . . . Ff. 233ra–235ra.

21. *T23. Quis ex vobis arguet me de peccato,* etc. (John 8:46). In principio hic notandum secundum Januensem quod dominica in qua legitur hoc euangelium vocatur . . .-. . . graciam in presenti et gloriam in futuro. Ad quam . . . Ff. 235ra–237ra.

22. *T28. Maria Magdalena et Maria Iacobi et Salome emerunt aromata,* etc. (Mark 16:1). Fratres, in processu euangelii istius diei describitur manifestacio . . .-. . . facie ad faciem perpetuo videbunt. Ad quam visionem . . . Ff. 237rb–239ra.

23. *T29. Cum esset sero die illa una sabbatorum et fores essent clausae,* etc. (John 20:19). Hic primo notandum est quod Christus post resurreccionem suam . . .-. . . oportet nos intrare in regnum Dei. Ad quod . . . Ff. 239ra–241ra.

24. *T30. Ego sum pastor bonus,* etc. (John 10:11[-16]). Karissimi, princeps peregre proficiscens et gregem ouium sibi carum habens, balliuum . . .-. . . sanguinem suum super crucem fundendo. Cui sit honor . . . Ff. 241ra–243ra.

25. T31. *Modicum et non videbitis me,* etc. (John 16:16). Karissimi, veri amici cupiunt quasi mutua visione perfrui . . .-. . . cum apparuerit, videbimus eum sicuti est. Ad quam visionem . . . Ff. 243ra–245ra.

26. T32. *Vado ad eum qui misit me,* etc. (John 16:5). Solent homines peregrinaturi predicere familie sue recessum . . .-. . . habere omnia que vult et nichil mali velle. Ad quam . . . Ff. 245ra–247ra.

27. T33. *Amen, amen, dico vobis, si quid petieritis patrem in nomine meo, dabit vobis,* etc. (John 16:23). Karissimi, die Iouis proximi sequentis erit dies Ascensionis . . .-. . . manifestabo ei meipsum in celesti gloria. Ad quam . . . Ff. 247ra–249ra.

28. T37. *Cum venerit paracletus quem ego mittam vobis,* etc. (John 15:26). Karissimi, hodie ad septimanam erit festum Pentecostes . . .-. . . habemus eternam in celis. Ad quam edificacionem . . . Ff. 249ra–251ra.

29. T39. *Si quis diligit me, sermonem meum servabit,* etc. (John 14:23). In hac dominica recolit Ecclesia illam habundantem donacionem . . .-. . . custodiat corda vestra et intelligencias vestras. Ad hanc pacem . . . Ff. 251ra–253ra.

30. T40. *Erat homo ex Pharisaeis Nicodemus nomine,* etc. (John 3:1). In principio huius euangelii est notandum quod in hoc euangelio . . .-. . . inplebit splendoribus animam tuam. Ad quod . . . Ff. 253ra–255rb.

31. T42. *Homo quidam erat dives et induebatur purpura et bisso,* etc. (Luke 16:19. "Et dicatur litera secundum quod iacet si placet. Et tunc dicatur:"). Karissimi, in hoc euangelio ponit Christus speculum diuitum . . .-. . . et in requie opulenta. Ad illam requiem . . . Ff. 255rb–257va.

32. T43. *Homo quidam fecit cenam magnam,* etc. (Luke 14:16). Nobilis enim dapifer, si habeat in domo sua delicatum morcellum . . .-. . . ad cenam Dei que prius in hoc euangelio declaratur. Ab hac cena infernalis nos eruat . . . Ff. 257va–259rb.

33. T44. *Erant adpropinquantes ad Iesum publicani et peccatores, ut audirent illum,* etc. (Luke 15:1). Mos est periti medici corporalis volentis nomen magnum habere . . .-. . . penitenciam agite et appropinquabit regnum celorum. Ad quod . . . Ff. 259rb–261rb.

34. T45. *Estote misericordes sicut Pater vester misericors est* (Luke 6:36). In serie huius euangelii tria tanguntur . . .-. . . tunc laus erit vnicuique a Deo. Ad quam . . . Ff. 261rb–263rb.

35. T46. *Cum turbae irruerent in Iesum,* etc. (Luke 5:1). Secundum Crisostomum *Operis imperfecti* omelia 29, signum studiosi agricole . . .-. . . videre bona Domini in terra viuencium. Ad quam . . . Ff. 263va–265ra.

36. T47. *Nisi abundaverit iustitia vestra plus quam Scribarum et Pharisaeorum, non intrabitis in regnum caelorum* (Matt 5:20). Secundum Ianuensem solent magistri scolarum, potissime grammaticalium, tres ordines scolarium optinere . . .-. . . Phariseorum intrabimus in regnum celorum. Ad quod . . . Ff. 265ra–266va.

37. T48. *Cum turba multa esset cum Iesu,* etc. (Mark 8:1 and Matt 15 "sentencialiter"). <Fratres,> Matthei 6 dicit Iesus discipulis suis: Primum . . .- . . . super beatitudinem celestem, vbi est congregacio omnium bonorum. Ad quam . . . Ff. 266va–268va.

38. T49. *Attendite a falsis prophetis qui veniunt ad vos,* etc. (Matt 7:15). Si quis iturus esset ad terram sanctam uel ad aliam remotam regionem, valde timendum esset ei de malo consorcio . . .-. . . ipse intrabit in regnum celorum. Ad quod . . . Ff. 268va–271ra.

39. T50. *Homo quidam erat dives qui habebat vilicum,* etc. (Luke 16:1). Fratres, si quis sciret se infra breue a domo propria et cognatis et amicis exulaturum . . .-. . . sunt cause quare recipiemur in celestem gloriam. Ad quam . . . Ff. 271ra–272vb.

40. T51. *Cum adpropinquaret Iesus Hierusalem, videns civitatem flevit super illam,* etc. (Luke 19:41). Dicitur vulgariter, Quod oculus non videt, cor non dolet . . .-. . . in templo suo, idest in anima auditorum. Cui sit honor . . . Ff. 272vb–275ra.

41. T52. *Dicebat autem Iesus ad quosdam qui in se confidebant,* etc. (Luke 18:9). Si quis mitteret aliquod exennium alicui magno domino . . .-. . . postea gloriam, que est gracia consummata. Ad quam . . . Ff. 275ra–277ra.

42. T53. *Exiens Iesus de finibus Tyri,* etc. (Mark 7:31). Fratres, si esset in aliqua ciuitate uel patria medicus corporalis . . .-. . . seruos suos premiabit misericorditer. Cui sit honor . . . Ff. 277ra–278va.

43. T54. *Beati oculi qui vident quae vos videtis,* etc. (Luke 10:23). In processu huius euangelii commendauit nobis Christus triplicem virtutem . . .- . . . quoniam ipsi misericordiam consequentur. Ad quam misericordiam . . . Ff. 278va–281rb.

44. T55. *Cum iret Iesus in Hierusalem,* etc. (Luke 17:11). Quia enim propter nos et propter nostram salutem . . .-. . . et fluenta gracie. Hoc ergo vicium auertat a nobis . . . Ff. 281rb–283rb.

45. T56. *Nemo potest duobus dominis servire* (Matt 6:24). In euangelio hodierno Dominus nititur repellere ab affeccione hominis inordinatam solicitudinem . . .-. . . gracia in presenti et gloria in futuro. Ad quam, etc. Ff. 283rb–285rb.

46. T57. *Ibat Iesus in civitatem quae vocatur Naim,* etc. (Luke 7:11). Notandum quod inter omnia miracula a Christo humanitus perpetrata . . .-. . . gracias agere ei. Vide supra dominica in Quinquagesima, secundo principali. Ff. 285rb–286vb.

47. T58. *Cum intraret Iesus in domum cuiusdam principis Pharisaeorum sabbato manducare panem,* etc. (Luke 14:1). Fratres, sapiens Salomon dicit Ecclesiastes 3: Omnia tempus habent . . .-. . . exaltabitur in futuro ad gloriam. Ad quam . . . Ff. 286vb–289ra.

48. T59. *Pharisaei autem audientes quod Iesus silentium inposuisset Sadducaeis,* etc. (Matt 22:34). Hic primo notandum quod in hoc euangelio fit mencio de tribus questionibus . . .-. . . difficile quiescere. Quod quidem venenum auferat . . . Ff. 289ra–290va.

49. T60. *Ascendens Iesus in naviculam,* etc. (Matt 9:1). Venit in ciuitatem suam, scilicet Capharnaum, que dicitur ciuitas Christi . . .-. . . secundum exigenciam meriti sui. Ad quam . . . Ff. 290va–291vb.

50. T61. *Simile est regnum caelorum homini regi qui fecit nuptias filio suo* (Matt 22:1). Karissimi, in euangelio hodierno Christus nos informat . . .-. . . placuit Patri vestro dare vobis regnum celorum. Ad quod . . . Ff. 291vb–293vb.

51. T62. *Erat quidam regulus, cuius filius infirmabatur,* etc. (John 4:46). Karissimi, in hoc euangelio describitur quoddam miraculum . . .-. . . a quo igne Iesus Christus pro benedicta sua passione nos liberet et . . . Ff. 293vb–296va.

52. T63. *Simile est regnum caelorum homini regi qui voluit rationem ponere cum servis suis* (Matt 18:23). Karissimi, duo sunt circa que potissime intencio racionalis creature debet occupari . . .-. . . eternaliter premiabit. Sic igitur offensas remittere . . . Ff. 296va–298rb.

53. T64. *Reddite quae sunt Caesaris Caesari,* etc. (Matt 22:21). In hiis verbis commendatur nobis virtus iusticie . . .-. . . aput Dominum est merces eorum. Ad quam mercedem . . . Ff. 298rb–299ra.

54. T65. *Mulier quae sanguinis fluxum patiebatur duodecim annis,* etc. (Matt 9:20, Mark 5, Luke 8). Pro declaracione istius miraculi ponatur talis conclusio . . .-. . . retribuetur tibi in resureccione iustorum. Ad quam retribucionem . . . Ff. 299rb–300rb.

M/4

1. S49*. *Fides tua te saluum fecit, vade in pace* (Luke 7:50). Ista verba dicta fuerunt a Christo ad Magdalenam ut dicunt aliqui . . . Karissimi, notum

est omnibus fidelibus quod tres capitales inimicos spirituales habemus . . .-
. . . et in pace ibimus ad celum. Quod . . . Ff. 300rb–301ra.

2. ?. *In patientia vestra possidebitis animas vestras* (Luke 21:19). Karissimi, si quis peregrinaretur versus terram sanctam . . .-. . . in hac vestra peregrinacione versus celestem Ierusalem. Ad quam . . . Ff. 301ra–302va.

3. ?. *Memor esto iudicii mei; sic enim erit et tuum* (Sir 38:23). Dicitur vulgariter quod pulcre se castigat qui per alterum se castigat. Ideo introducit Ecclesia loquentem . . .-. . . sic deprehensus in quam partem se premet. Ff. 304ra–305ra.

4. S44. *Iohannes est nomen eius* (Luke 1:63). Karissimi, ista verba fuerunt scripta primo per Zachariam . . .-. . . gracia que est arra glorie. F. 305ra–vb, inc?

5. S64*. *Non licet tibi habere uxorem fratris tui* (Mark 6:18). Karissimi, sanctus Augustinus super epistolam canonicam Iohannis sermone 3 comparat predicatorem seminanti . . .-. . . menciuntur super illos. Contra quod notetur factum Christi supra, dominica in passione, tercio principali. Cui addend' exposicio Iohannis Crisostomi super verbis Beati pacifici, etc., omelia 9. Ff. 306vb–307vb.

6. T06*. *Evangelizo vobis gaudium magnum*, etc. (Luke 2:10). Dicitur vulgariter quod non potest nimis tarde venire qui malos affert rumores. Ita per contrarium . . .-. . . eius natiuitatem annuncians, Euangelizo vobis, etc. Ff. 307vb–309ra.

7. ?. *Comedite, amici, et bibite, et inebriamini, karissimi* (Cant 5:1). Secundum Lincolniensem *Dicto* 27, consuetudo curialis est in conuiuiis . . .-. . . eritis michi karissimi, inebriamini a clara visione Dei. Ad quam . . . Ff. 309ra–310ra.

8. ?. *Estote factores verbi et non auditores tantum* (James 1:22). Secundum sentenciam Parisiensis notandum est quod sunt quidam qui verbum Dei nec audiunt . . .-. . . spiritualiter curabit et curatos in sanitate conseruabit. Ff. 310ra–311vb, inc.?

9. T39*. *Apparuerunt apostolis dispartitae linguae tanquam ignis* (Acts 2:3). Karissimi, scribitur Hester 1 et 2 capitulis quomodo rex magnus Assuerus . . .-. . . apparuerunt apostolis. Pro sermone require ut supra. F. 311vb.

10. ?. *Pacem relinquo vobis, pacem meam do vobis* (John 14:27). Karissimi, in omni artificio siue sciencia oportet discipulum . . .-. . . a meipso non loquor, etc. Vide infra in sermone Christus passus est, in principio. Ff. 311vb–312ra.

11. CII*. *Hodie salus huic domui facta est* (Luke 19:9). Fratres karissimi, ut dicit [*blank*] in legenda hodierna, quociescunque altaris uel templi dedicacionem

colimus . . .-. . . ex quibus partibus constat ecclesia materialis. Require infra folio. Ff. 312ra.

12. ?. *Si quis diligit me, sermonem meum servabit* (John 14:23). Dicit Gregorius omelia 30 *Euangeliorum*: Ecce si vnusquisque vestrum requiratur an diligat Deum . . .-. . . ipse manebit nobiscum in patria per gloriam. Ad quam . . . Ff. 312rb–313vb.

13. ?. *Haec locutus sum vobis, ut in me pacem habeatis* (John 16:33). Karissimi, racio et experiencia docent quemquam apprenticium volentem . . .-. . . corda vestra et intelligencias vestras, Philippensium 4. Ad quam pacem . . . Ff. 313vb–315vb.

14. T21*. *Estote imitatores Dei* (Ephe 5:1). Recommendatis omnibus viuis et defunctis, repetatur thema, etc. Reuerendi domini, nouistis quod in negocio magni ponderis . . .-. . . ducet ad celum in celesti gloria secum regnaturos. Ad quam gloriam . . . Ff. 315vb–317vb.

Oxford, Merton College, MS 236

Between a run of *de tempore* sermons based on Jacobus de Voragine ("Sermones mendici de tempore," ff. 1ra–51rb) and a run of *de sanctis* sermons by Francis de Meyronnes (ff. 220ra–503rb) occur the following quadragesimal sermons:

1. T18/4?. *Cum ieiunas, unge caput tuum et faciem tuam lava* (Matt 6:17). Secundum sentenciam Ieronimi *Contra Iouinianum*, beatitudo in paradiso . . .-. . . In toto corde meo quesiui te. Quod nobis concedat. Ff. 118ra–119rb.

2. T18/5. *Ego veniam et curabo eum* (Matt 8:7). Inter agens et passum secundum Philosophum oportet quod fiat debita approximacio . . .-. . . filii mei mecum in cubili sunt. Quod . . . Ff. 119va–121rb.

3. T18/6. *Cum facis elemosynam, noli tuba canere ante te* (Matt 6:2). Origenes dicit quod aliquod iustum potest iniuste fieri . . .-. . . ostende faciem tuam et salui erimus. Quod . . . Ff. 121rb–122vb.

4. T18/7. *Vidit eos laborantes in remigando* (Mark 6:48). Salomon dicit quod homo nascitur ad laborem . . .-. . . Emitte manum tuam de alto. Quod . . . Ff. 122vb–124va.

5. T19. *Gratiam Dei recipiatis* (2 Cor 6:1). Secundum sentenciam Philosophi omne incipiens naturam ad suam imprimit disposicionem . . .-. . . quecumque voluit absque eo quod obtulit munere regio. Cuius munerum, etc. Ff. 124va–126ra.

6. T19? *Ductus est Iesus in desertum a spiritu, ut temptaretur a diabolo* (Matt 4:1). Seneca ad Lucillum de prouidencia loquens . . .-. . . et dabo tibi coronam vite. Quam . . . Ff. 126ra–127vb.

7. T19/2. *Ibunt hii in supplicium aeternum* (Matt 23:46). Secundum sentenciam beati Augustini, nullum malum impunitum . . .-. . . Angelus Domini coartans eos, etc. Ff. 127vb–129va.

8. T19/3. *Relictis illis abiit* (Matt 21:17). Secundum Philosophum motus est acquisicio partis . . .-. . . Estote ergo prudentes. Quod . . . Ff. 129vb–131va.

9. T19/4. *Paenitentiam egerunt in praedicatione Ionae* (Matt 12:41). Secundum quod ait Lactancius libro *De falsa religione,* nullus suauior anime cibus . . .-. . . et in cinerem reuerteris. Quod . . . Ff. 131va–133rb.

10. T19/5. *Unum patrem habemus, Deum* (John 8:41). Secundum quod ait Lactancius libro 5, nemo apud Deum seruus est . . .-. . . consolatus est igitur Dominus populum suum. Quod . . . Ff. 133rb–135ra.

11. T19/6. *Vis sanus fieri?* (John 5:6). Secundum quod dicit Lactancius, sanitas proprie non consistit . . .-. . . Magnificate Dominum mecum. Ff. 135ra–137ra.

12. T19/7. *Bonum est nobis hic esse* (Matt 17:4). Omnis potencia naturaliter quietatur in suum obiectum . . .-. . . ad illud bonum insemitum assequendum. Quod . . . Ff. 137ra–138vb.

13. T20. *Sciat unusquisque suum vas possidere* (1 Thess 4:4). Homo a duobus compositus est ex anima et corpore . . .-. . . vasa a Deo electa in vitam eternam. Ad quam, etc. Ff. 138vb–140ra.

14. T20. *Magna est fides tua, fiat tibi sicut vis* (Matt 15:28). Seneca dicit quod egre fortune sunt sana consilia . . .-. . . ideo dicitur: Ignis ardorem extinguit aqua. Ff. 140ra–141vb.

15. T20/2. *Moriemini in peccato vestro* (John 8:21). Beatus Anselmus in suis *Meditacionibus* loquens de culpa primi parentis . . .-. . . Eruat a morte animas eorum. Quod nobis. Ff. 141vb–143rb.

16. T20/3. *Qui se humiliat exaltabitur* (Matt 23:13). Beatus Augustinus *De verbo Domini* loquens de humilitate . . .-. . . et hic maior est in regno celorum. Quod . . . Ff. 143rb–144vb.

17. T20/4. *Accessit ad eum mater filiorum Zebedaei . . . aliquid ab eo* (Matt 20:). Philosophus dicit: Signum scientis est posse docere . . .-. . . caro et sanguinis non possidebunt regnum Dei. Ff. 144vb–146rb.

18. T20/5. *Factum est autem ut moreretur mendicus* (Luke 16:22). Et licet hominum genus arte et racionibus uiuat . . .-. . . Ingrediatur putredo in ossibus meis. A qua nos liberet . . . Ff. 146rb–148ra.

19. T20/6. *Reddant illi fructum temporibus suis* (Matt 21:41). Beatus Ieronimus *Ad Rusticum* exhortando ipsum ad penitenciam . . .-. . . fructum labiorum confitencium nomini eius. Quod . . . Ff. 148ra–149vb.

20. T20/7. *Peccavi in caelum et coram te* (Luke 15:18). Ieronimus *Super Exodum*, et habetur *De penitencia* distinccione 1, volens innuere . . .-. . . et sicut onus graue grauate sunt super me. Rogemus, etc. Ff. 149vb–151ra.

21. T21. *Fructus autem lucis est in omni bonitate* (Eph 5:9). Secundum sentenciam Sexti Pictag', Deus in bonis actibus lux est . . .-. . . Iustorum semita quasi lux splendens. Quod . . . Ff. 151ra–152vb.

22. T21. *Armatus custodit atrium suum* (Luke 11:21). Homo tenetur rem suam custodire et conseruare . . .-. . . Induamini ergo virtute ex alto. Amen. Ff. 152vb–154rb.

23. T21/2. *Fac hic in patria tua* (Luke 4:24). In *Prouerbiis sapientum* dicitur quod expedit vt patriam interdum quis negligat . . .-. . . sed permanet in vitam eternam. Quod . . . Ff. 154rb–155va.

24. T21/3. *Si peccaverit in te frater tuus, vade et corripe eum inter te et ipsum solum* (Matt 18:15). Secundum sentenciam Saluatoris nostri, homo debet diligere . . .-. . . et magnum beneficium prestat. Rogemus, etc. Ff. 155va–157rb.

25. T21/4. *Quare et vos transgredimini mandatum Dei?* (Matt 15:3). Psalmista dicit secundum Ieronimi sentenciam seu literam quod lex Domini . . .-. . . beati qui audiunt verum Dei et custodiunt illud, etc. Ff. 157rb–158vb.

26. T21/5. *Imperavit febri et dimisit illam* (Luke 4:40). Secundum sentenciam Salomonis, Non est census super censum . . .-. . . et sic tandem morte eterna extinguntur. A qua morte, etc. Ff. 159ra–160va.

27. T21/6. *Hora est quasi sexta* (John 4:6). Ieronimus *De naturalibus questionibus* dicit quod oppinio fuit Calles philosophi . . .-. . . Omnes ad quos venit aqua ista salui facti sunt. Quod nobis, etc. Ff. 160va–162ra.

28. T21/7. *Nec ego te condemnabo; vade, et noli amplius peccare* (John 8:11). Seneca *De clemencia* dicit quod verecundiam peccandi facit ipsa clemencia . . .-. . . quia stipendia peccati mors. Quam . . . Ff. 162ra–163va.

29. T22. *Eice ancillam et filium eius . . . cum filio liberae* (Gal 4:30). Verbum est Sixti philosophi in suo *Morali*: Omnia tibi auferenti concede . . .-. . . vt celestem hereditatem habere possimus. Quod . . . Ff. 163va–164vb.

30. T22 "Dominica 4 quadragesime[?]" margin. *Cum sublevasset oculos Iesus et vidit*, etc. (John 6:5). Saluator noster dicit quod nemo potest venire ad statum salutis . . .-. . . et in vltimo per gloriam. Ad quam . . . Ff. 164vb–166va.

31. T22/2. *Solvite templum hoc, et in tribus diebus excitabo illud* (John 2:19). Ecclesiastici [34] dicitur quod est vnus destruens et alius edificans . . .- . . . sacrificium iusticie et sperate in Domino. Quod . . . Ff. 166va–168ra.

32. T22/3. *Qui autem quaerit gloriam eius qui misit illum . . . in illo non est* (John 7:18). Salustius in *Cathelinario* dicit quod gloriam et honorem . . .-. . . terra nostra dabit fructum suum, scilicet gloriam. Quam . . . Ff. 168ra–169va.

33. T22/4. *Caecus cum essem, modo video* (John 9:25). Per dicta sacre scripture habemus quod status peccati est status tenebrosus . . .-. . . et non viderunt solem. A quo igne liberet nos Christus. Ff. 169vb–171ra.

34. T22/5. *Adolescens, tibi dico, surge* (Luke 7:14). Saluator dicit quod non venit vocare iustos . . .-. . . habeant graciam et vltimo gloriam. Quam . . . Ff. 171ra–172vb.

35. T22/6. *Domine, si fuisses hic, frater meus non fuisset mortuus* (John 11:21). Natura et ars docent quod idem est causa contrariorum . . .-. . . ite, maledicti, in ignem eternum. A quo . . . Ff. 172vb–174vb.

36. T22/7. *Ego sum lux mundi* (John 8:12). Salomon dicit quod homo sapiens in sapiencia manet sicut sol . . .-. . . et lux venit in mundum. Quam lucem . . . Ff. 174vb–176rb.

37. T23. *Christus adsistens pontifex futurorum bonorum* (Heb 9:11). Regula Philosophi est in libro *De generacione et corrupcione* quod corrupcio vnius . . .-. . . vitam amisit, vt nobis vitam inueniret. Quam . . . Ff. 176rb–177vb.

38. T23. *Arguit me de peccato* (John 8:46). Secundum sentenciam Cathonis, turpe est doctori cum culpa redarguit ipsum . . .-. . . Misertus est Dominus timentibus se. Quem, etc. Ff. 177vb–180ra.

39. T23/2. *Vos non potestis venire* (John 7:34). Seneca dicit: Numquam deueniet qui quot videt sequitur calles . . .-. . . estimabamus vitam eorum insaniam. A qua . . . Ff. 180ra–181va.

40. T23/3. *Tempus autem vestrum semper est paratum* (John 7:6). Psalmista dicit quod tempus vite nostre est tempus benefaciendi . . .-. . . Quasi a facie colubri fuge peccatum. Quod . . . Ff. 181va–183ra.

41. T23/4. *Opera quae ego facio in nomine Patris mei, haec . . . de me* (John 10:25). In quolibet iudicio secundum omnia iura eciam Ysidorus . . .- . . . ornamenta sunt quos generamus filios, opera scilicet virtuosa. Que opera . . . Ff. 183ra–184va.

42. T23/5. *Remittentur ei peccata, quoniam dilexit multum* (Luke 7:47). Seneca ad Lucilium dans modum vt aliquis ametur . . .-. . . et facit inuenire vitam eternam. Quam . . . Ff. 184va–186rb.

43. T23/6. *Collegerunt pontifices et Pharisaei concilium . . . quid facimus?* etc. (John 11:47). Seneca dicit quod inter cetera que habent amiciciam et benevolenciam causare . . .-. . . sed in dampnacionem mortis eterne. A qua . . . Ff. 186rb–188ra.

44. T23/7. *Misisti Iesum Christum* (John 17:3). Salomon dicit quod sapiencia vincit malum . . .-. . . et ad vitam perduxit eternam. Quam . . . Ff. 188ra–189vb.

45. T24. *Hoc enim sentite in vobis quod in Iesu Christo* (Phil 2:5). Seneca in *Prouerbiis* dicit quod optimum est malorum vestigia . . . .-. . . Sacrificium sanctificacionis et mundicie offeres Domino. Quod . . . Ff. 189vb–191va.

46. T24. *Rex tuus venit tibi mansuetus* (Matt 21:5). Beatus Anselmus libro *Cur Deus homo* loquens de causa Filii Dei in carnem . . .-. . . Iusticia iusti super eum erit. Quod . . . Ff. 191va–193rb.

47. T24/2. *Si autem mortuum fuerit, multum fructum adfert* (John 12:25). Beatus Augustinus in suo *Enchiridion* dicit quod cum Deus summe bonus sit . . .-. . . Ego veni vt vitam habeant. Quam . . . Ff. 193rb–195ra.

48. T24/3. *Tradidit Iesum flagellis caesum ut crucifigeretur* (Mark 15:15). Omnis effectus habet causam suam efficientem . . .-. . . Paratum cor meum, Deus, etc. Ff. 195ra–196vb.

49. T24/4. *Instabant autem vocibus magnis postulantes ut crucifigerent* (Luke 23:23). Salomon dicit quod mors et vita sunt in manibus lingue . . .-. . . Est confusio adducens gloriam. Quam . . . Ff. 196vb–198va.

50. T24/5. *Quod ego facio tu nescis modo, scies autem postea* (John 13:7). Quamquam Filius Dei omnes virtutes docuerit in vita sua . . .-. . . in sacramento scilicet altaris sta in timore Dei. Quod . . . Ff. 198va–200va.

51. T24/7. *Angelus autem Domini descendit de caelo* (Matt 28:2). Ysidorus *Ethimologiarum* dicit quod hoc nomen angelus est nomen officii . . .-. . . penetrabo inferiores partes terre. Ff. 200va–202rb.

52. T28. *Pascha nostrum immolatus est Christus* (1 Cor 5:7). Diebus solemnibus precipuis et festiuis consueuerunt homines laute commedere . . .-. . . Replebit splendoribus animam tuam. Quod faciat, etc. Ff. 202rb–204rb.

53. T28. *Surrexit, non est hic* (Matth 28:6). Racionabile est quod qui condidit legem, seruet eam . . .-. . . Ero illi in patrem, etc. Ff. 204rb–206rb.

54. T28/2. *Hunc Deus suscitavit tertia die et Deum eum <dedit> manifestum fieri* (Acts 10:40). In sacra scriptura fit questio vbi sit sapiencia . . .-. . . Ecce nunc tempus acceptabile, etc. Ff. 206rb–208ra.

55. T28/3. *Surrexit Dominus vere et apparuit Simoni* (Luke 24:34). Saluator noster dicit quod necesse est vt veniant scandala . . .-. . . Cum hiis conuersare qui possunt te facere meliorem. Ff. 208ra–209vb.

56. T28/4. *Stetit Iesus in medio discipulorum suorum . . . Pax vobis* (John 20:20). Seneca dicit quod decet magnum dare magna . . .-. . . seruare vnitatem spiritus in vinculo pacis, etc. Quam . . . Ff. 209vb–211rb.

57. T28/5. *Stetit Iesus in medio discipulorum* (John 20:19). Saluator noster volens ostendere suis discipulis quantum intersit inter mundo adherentes . . .- . . . Dominus custodiat corda vestra, etc. Deo gracias. Amen. Ff. 211rb–213ra.

N – Oxford, Bodleian Library, MS Barlow 24

1 to 54 (ff. 1–132) are the same as M/3–1 to 54.

55. S01. *Sustinuit crucem confusione* (Heb 12:2). Carissimi, ut dicit beatus Barnardus [!] sermone apostolorum Petri et Pauli: Tria sunt . . .-. . . mortuos suscitauit submersos. Ff. 140–142.

56. S03. *Puer crevit et ablactatus est* (Gen 21:8). Karissimi, hec verba quondam dicta fuerunt de Ysaac . . .-. . . ipsi misericordiam consequentur. Quam . . . Ff. 142–143v.

57. S05. *Iam concepta eram* (Prov 8:23). Karissimi, hodie sancta Ecclesia facit mencionem de concepcione sancte Marie Virginis . . .-. . . sine ipsa saluari non possumus. Ff. 143v–145.

58. S08. *Quia vidisti me, Thoma, credidisti* (John 20:29). Karissimi, secundum Januensem Thomas interpretatur abyssus uel geminus . . .-. . . qui non viderunt et crediderunt. Ff. 145–146.

59. T06. *De Maria natus est Iesus* (Matt 1:16). Karissimi, secundum Eusebium Christus fuit natus anno ab origine . . .-. . . vt te vsque ad celum exaltaret. Quod . . . Ff. 146–147v.

60. S09. *Stephanus plenus gratia et fortitudine* (Acts 6:8). Karissimi, hac die Ecclesia solempnizat festum . . .-. . . quem Syon occidit nobis Bisancia misit. Quam . . . Ff. 147v–149.

61. S10. *Hic est discipulus ille quem diligebat Iesus* (John 21:24). Karissimi, hac die Ecclesia solempnizat festum beati Iohannis euangeliste . . .-. . . diligentes me diligo, scilicet per graciam in presenti et gloriam in futuro. Ff. 149–150v.

62. S11. *Pueri mei mecum sunt* (Luke 11:7). Karissimi, videtis quod inter pueros est talis nature amicicia . . .-. . . si cum puero Iesu voluerimus gaudere. Quod . . . Ff. 150v–152v.

63. S12*. *Homines impii interfecerunt hominem innoxium in domo sua* (2 Sam 4:11). Karissimi, etsi verba predicta secundum fidem historie dicta fuerunt de filio Saul . . .-. . . quam sibi concessit pro labore. Quam . . . Ff. 152v–153v.

64. T08. *Vocatum est nomen eius Iesus* (Luke 2:21). Karissimi, hunc diem, que dicitur prima dies anni . . .-. . . de quodam Lumbardo qui consueuit iurare per nomen Dei, etc. Nota narracionem. Ff. 153v–155.

65. T10. *Venimus adorare eum*, idest Dominum (Matt 2:2). Karissimi, hec verba scripta sunt in euangelio hodierno sed possunt esse ad propositum presentis sollepnitatis que Epiphania . . .-. . . oportet quod oracio sit cum caritate. Quam . . . Ff. 155–156v.

66. S21. *Obtulit mater puerum viro Dei* (secundum antiquam translacionem) (1 Sam 1:25). Karissimi, hec verba presenti festiuitati satis conueniunt . . .-. . . Per lichnum lumen luminisque deitatis cacumen. Ff. 156v–158.

67. S24. *Dominus Deus tuus elegit te hodie* (Deut 26:2). Karissimi, hec verba dici possunt de isto beato Matthia . . .-. . . beati Mathie animam in celo exaltauit. Ff. 158–159v.

68. T18/4. *Convertere ad Dominum et relinque peccata tua* (Ezek 18:30). Karissimi, secundum prophetam Ezechielis 33 Dominus non vult mortem . . .-. . . sanabo vos graciam tribuens in presenti et gloriam in futuro. Ff. 159v–160v.

69. S28. *Nomen virginis Maria* (Luke 1:26). Karissimi, tria communiter inuenio que personam quemcumque [!] efficiunt nominatam . . .-. . . gloriosa que inueniet gloriam, Prouerbiorum 11. Quam . . . Ff. 161–162v.

70. T26. *Christus mortuus est pro peccatis nostris* (1 Cor 15:3). Karissimi, Seneca *De beneficiis* dicit: Beneficium acceptum est eterne memorie infigendum . . .-. . . filio cuiusdam magni et de camisia, etc. Ff. 162v–164.

71. T28. *Iesus meus cibus est* (John 4:34). Karissimi, secundum Philosophum omne animal indiget alimento . . .-. . . domini sui gloriabitur. Quam . . . O precium predo cibus et iudex tibi me do. Ff. 164–165v.

72. S30. *Similis factus est leoni in operibus suis* (1 Macch 3:4). Karissimi, hec verba quondam erant dicta de Iuda Machabeo . . .-. . . quod ipse iam est in eterna gloria in celo. Quam . . . Ff. 165v–166v.

73. S32. *Computati sunt inter filios Dei* (Wisd 5:5). Karissimi, hec verba sunt Sapientis et possunt ad presens dici de istis beatis apostolis . . .-. . . hereditas vite eterne. Quam . . . Horum per meritum da Christe regnum petitum. Ff. 166v–168v.

74. S33. *Mihi absit gloriari nisi in cruce Domini* (Gal 6:14). Karissimi, hodie Ecclesia festum facit de invencione sancte crucis Christi . . .-. . . dissolui et

esse cum Christo. Quod . . . In crucis auctorem totum tendamus amorem. Ff. 168v–169v.

75. T34. *Orate pro invicem ut salvemini* (James 5:16). Karissimi, habetur in vita Gregorii pape quod hoc tempus Rogacionum . . .-. . . orate pro invicem ut saluemini, scilicet per graciam in presenti et gloriam in futuro. Versus: Quod iustum est petito uel quod videatur honestum. Ff. 169v–171.

76. T36. *Ascendit Christus super omnes caelos* (Eph 4:10). Karissimi, videtis enim quod quando via aliqua non est bene vsitata . . .-. . . super omnes celos ut nobis daret dona, scilicet graciam in presenti et gloriam in futuro. Quod . . . Ff. 171–172v.

77. T39. *Accipite Spiritum Sanctum in vos* (John 20:22). Karissimi, antiquum est prouerbium quod omne promissum ab ore fidelis est debitum . . .-. . . signum est quod Spiritum Sanctum accepit. Quod nobis etc. Ff. 172v–174.

78. T40. *Pater et Filius et Spiritus Sanctus, et hii tres unum sunt* (1 John 5:7). Karissimi, ut dicit Rabanus, Quicumque occupat ingenium suum circa quatuor . . .-. . . adquirit eternum bonum, quia celi gaudium. Quod . . . Ff. 174–175v.

79. T41/5. *Sanctificati sumus per oblationem corporis Christi* (Heb 10:10). Karissimi, sicut Christus secundum fidem Ecclesie est fons omnis sanctitatis . . .-. . . vt in principio dixi Sanctificati sumus, etc. Ff. 175v–176v.

80. S39a. *Qui fecerit et docuerit, magnus vocabitur in regno caelorum* (Matt 5:19). Karissimi, hec verba Christi de isto beato Augustino Anglorum apostolo verificari possunt . . .-. . . sic nec merces ista vmquam habebit finem. Quam . . . Ff. 177–178.

81. S40. *Erat Barnabas vir bonus et plenus Spiritu Sancto* (Acts 11:24). \Karissimi,/ ad literam hec verba dicta erant de beato Barnaba . . .-. . . ipse in celis glorificatus est. Quod . . . Ff. 178–179.

82. S44. *Non surrexit maior Iohanne Baptista* (Matt 11:11). Karissimi, debetis intelligere quod sancta mater Ecclesia tres . . .-. . . non est inventus similis illi in gloria. Quam . . . Ff. 179–180v.

83. S46. *Fecit Deus duo luminaria magna* (Gen 1:16). Karissimi, Ecclesiastici 11 [!] scribitur quod in manu artificis opera laudabuntur . . .-. . . magna lucencia ante Deum in vita eterna, etc. Ff. 180v–181v.

84. S46b. *Ante translationem suam testimonium habuit placuisse Deo* (Heb 11:5); item thema *Placuit Deo et translatus est* (Sir 44:16). Karissimi, hec verba dicta fuerunt quondam de sancto Ennok et possunt ad propositum dici de sancto Thoma Cantuariensi . . .-. . . translatus est in paradisum, idest

eternum gaudium. Quod . . . Versus: Carne pater cleros hostes sibi flecte seueros. Ff. 181v–183.

85. S49. *Remittuntur ei peccata multa, quoniam dilexit multum* (Luke 7:47). Karissimi, quanta sit virtus dilectionis patet in Christo . . .-. . . exemploque meo vos preparate Deo. Quod . . . Ff. 183–184v.

86. S50. *Adsumpsit Iesus Iacobum* (Matt 17:1). Karissimi, hec verba dicta fuerunt quondam de isto beato Iacobo . . .-. . . quare merito ab omnibus est diligendus. Ff. 184v–185v.

87. S50a. *Annam diligebat Dominus* (1 Sam 1:5). Karissimi, debetis scire quod Anna secundum sui nominis interpretacionem . . .-. . . repromisit Deus diligentibus se, Iacobi 1. Quam, etc. Ff. 185v–187.

88. S56. *Igne me examinasti* (Ps 16:3). Karissimi, solet consuetudo omnium discretorum aurifabrorum . . .-. . . suffert temptacionem, quoniam cum probatus, etc. Ff. 187–188.

89. S59. *Tu supergressa es universas*, idest creaturas (Prov 31:29). Karissimi, tanta est excellencia gloriose Virginis Marie . . .-. . . assumpta est in gloriam. Quam . . . Ff. 188–189v.

90. S61. *Rursum circumdabor pelle mea* (Job 19:26). Karissimi, hec verba quondam erant dicta a beato Job, quando fuit in desolacione . . .-. . . cum corpore septipliciter clariorem solis. Quod . . . Ff. 189v–190v.

91. S65. *Multi in nativitate eius gaudebunt* (Luke 1:14). Karissimi, debetis scire quod tres nativitates precise sollempnizat Ecclesia . . .-. . . to þe blysse þat ys euerlastyng. Quod . . . Marie festum pellet procul omne molestum. In te spes tota, miserorum suscipe vota. Ff. 191–192.

92. S66. *Exaltavi lignum humile* (Ezek 17:24). Karissimi, quamuis hec verba dicta erant secundum glossam de Christo . . .-. . . Crucis hoc signum fugiat procul omne malignum; et per idem signum saluetur quodque benignum. Quod . . . Ff. 192–193v.

93. S67. *Surgens secutus est Iesum* (Matt 9:9). Karissimi, hec verba dicta fuerunt de isto beato apostolo et euangelista . . .-. . . ostendit eum esse verum Dei Filium. Vnde metrice de eis scribitur: Est homo Matheus, vitulus Lucas, Leo Marcus; estque Johannes auis, quatuor ista deus. Ff. 193v–195.

94. S70. *Adiutor meus in omnibus Michahel* (Dan 10:21). Karissimi, secundum Januensem in istius archangeli festo . . .-. . . qualiter angeli boni sunt adiutores nostri. Quod . . . Ff. 195–196.

95. S75. *Salutat vos Lucas medicus carissimus* (Col 4:14). Karissimi, hec verba fuerunt beati Pauli dicta ad commendacionem beati Luce euangeliste . . .- . . . Nos meritis Luce vera deus instrue luce. Ff. 196v–197v.

96. S78. *Isti homines servi Dei sunt* (Acts 16:17). Karissimi, hec verba quamuis dicta fuerunt literaliter . . .-. . . qui seruos suos ditat in gloria. Ff. 197v–198v.

97. S79. *Gloria haec est omnibus sanctis* (Ps 149:9). Karissimi, hec verba sunt prophete Dauid . . .-. . . Visio fit victus opus laus lumen amictus. Ff. 199–200.

98. S80. *Animae in manu Dei sunt* (Wisd 3:1). Karissimi, tria sunt genera bonorum . . .-. . . sine fine, quia in manu Dei sunt. Quod . . . Ff. 200–201v.

99. C04. *Pro iusto moritur* (Rom 5:7). Karissimi, hec verba Apostoli de isto beato N. martire . . .-. . . vnde iam cum ipso viuit in gloria. Quam, etc. Ff. 201v–202v.

100. C06. *Est fidelis servus et prudens* (Matt 24:45). Karissimi, Christus in hiis verbis, que isto sancto N. confessori applicari possunt . . .-. . . intra in gaudium Domini. Quod nobis. Nobilis antistes, seruos tuos respice tristes. Ff. 202v–204.

101. C08. *Ora pro nobis, quoniam sancta es* (Jth 8:29). Karissimi, hec verba que quondam erant dicta de nobili muliere . . .-. . . qui cum mulieribus non sunt, etc. Ff. 204–205.

102. S00 ("Cuiuscumque sancti vel sancte sermo generalis"). *Data est ei corona* (Rev 6:2). Anglice sic: A crowne of joy . . . Karissimi, vt enim dicit Almagestus libro *De consulibus* I: Imperatores antiquitus . . .-. . . carnalis integritas immo'ta. Require supra sermone 47 in processu tercii principalis. Versus: Virgo Deo digna prece nobis esto benigna. Ff. 205–206.

103. C21 ("Vnius viri mortui"). *Homo nobilis abiit in regionem longinquam* (Luke 19:12). Karissimi, vt mihi videtur, tria sunt motiua precipua quare huc congregati sumus . . .-. . . transiet de morte ad vitam. Quam sibi . . . Ff. 206–208.

104. C21 ("Sermo generalis vnius femine defuncte"). *Mulier gratiosa inveniet gloriam* (Prov 11:16). Karissimi, ut mihi videtur, triplex est causa quare predicacio fit in sepulturis mortuorum . . .-. . . in eternum premiabuntur in celo, etc. Set quilibet homo adiscet hanc lectionem, nota in sequente sermone 53 in tercio principali. Ff. 208–209.

105. C21 ("Cuiuscumque defuncti viri aut mulieris"). *Transit de morte ad vitam* (John 5:24). Karissimi, ut dicit Gregorius in communi omelia vnius martiris: Temporalis vita . . .-. . . que sit merces quam exspectamus. Quam mercedem N. et nobis omnibus concedat, etc. Dum viuis viuunt, moriens moriuntur amici. Ff. 209–210v.

106. C21 ("Sermo generalis in anniversario cuiuscumque defuncti"). *Memento mei cum tibi bene fuerit* (Gen 40:14). Karissimi, hec verba que iam dixi, ut mihi videtur, sunt verba longoris [!], doloris, et pudoris . . .-. . . quamuis mors nulli parcit, quod erat principium. Ff. 210v–212.

107. C21 ("Sermo generalis pro omni defuncto"). *Miseremini mei saltem, vos amici mei* (Job 19:21). Karissimi, dicit Magister *Sentenciarum* libro 4 distinccione 45 quod tria sunt per que iuvantur anime . . .-. . . beati mortui qui in Domino, etc. Ff. 212–213v.

108. C17 / C16 / C19 ("Sermo in celebracione prime misse sacerdotis vel in ordinibus aut visitacionibus"). *Elegit sibi Dominus sacerdotes sine macula* (1 Macc 4:42). Karissimi, Paulus 1 Corinthiorum 4: Sic, inquit, nos existimet homo . . .-. . . numquam elegit Dominus, quia non sunt digni, etc. Ff. 213v–214v.

109. C11. *Domum tuam, Domine, decet sanctitudo* (Ps 92:5). Karissimi, quamdiu homo vivit in hoc mundo . . .-. . . sequitur dicere qualiter sit consecrata. Ff. 214v–217v, inc.

O – Oxford, Bodleian Library, MS Bodley 649

1. T19?. *Nunc dies salutis* (2 Cor 6:2). Anglice: Alle seke and woful come to weele, now is a day of gostle hele. Lego in scriptura sacra Exodi 17 quod quando crudelis tirannus Amalec . . .-. . . campus tunc erit noster et celum nostrum erit premium. Sic nos perfecta penitencia armare et campum contra demones tenere in breui solari die gracie quod in eterna requiei die habere possimus pro premio coronam glorie, Iesus vobis annuat et michi, qui pro humana salute pugnauit et occubuit in cruce. Amen. Ff. 1–8.

2. T19?. *Adsumpsit eum in civitatem* (Matt 4:5). Deus qui fudit suum sanguinem pro humano peccato et sustulit mortem in cruce ad saluandum ciuitatem anime humane rede, etc. Assumpsit . . . Anglice: He toke . . .- . . . in ciuitate celesti habebis benediccionem Dei, felicitatem eternam. Ad gloriam huius ciuitatis . . . Ff. 8–13v.

3. T20?. *Magna est fides* (Matt 15:28). Lego in sacra scriptura Danielis 4 quod magnus ille rex Nabogodonosor vidit . . .-. . . mirthe sine tristicia, et gaudium sine fine. þus to kepe sapienter manumissionem fidei . . . Ff. 14–19v.

4. T20*. *Domine, adiuva me* (Matt 15:25). þe help and þe comfort Domini nostri Iesu Christi intercessione sue gloriose matris . . . Vt lego in sacra scriptura Apocalipsis, 5 þe evangelista Iohannes inter ceteras . . .-. . . iste

Dominus, qui paciebatur mortem for mannys help and sauacioune, help ʒow and kep ʒow in þis perilous abidinge . . . Ff. 19v–27.

5. T20*. *Iesus* (Matt 15:21). þe gracius comfort omnipotentis Domini Iesu intercessione sue misericordissime matris Marie . . . Reuerendi domini, sicut lego in sacra scriptura Apocalipsi 10 quod sanctus euangelista Iohannes vidit . . .-. . . quia sue dulcedine deitatis pascuntur, sicut dixi in tercio. þus to loue and drede þis worthi Lorde . . . Ff. 27–34. Also R-13.

6. T21?. *Fortis armatus custodit atrium* (Luke 11:21). Anglice: A myʒti werrour and a wyʒt kepes his halle armed briʒt. Lego 2 Machabeorum XI quod quando maledictus rex Anthiocus . . .-. . . lorica caritatis sine duplicitate, pro tercia. Sicque armari fide, spe, et caritate . . . Ff. 34–40v.

7. T21*. *De caelo quaerebant* (Luke 11:16). Gracia and comfort benedicte Trinitatis intercessione beate Domine Christi matris . . . Venerandi domini, verba que sumpsi pro themate . . . þai soʒt fro heuon. Domini, specialis vinea . . .- . . . et misericordiam de suis peccatis pro tercio. Istam misericordiam . . . Ff. 40v–48.

8. T22*. *Videbant signa* (John 6:2). Lego in scriptura sacra Apocalipsis 12 quod sanctus euangelista Iohannes vidit magnum et mirabile signum in celo . . .- . . . videbunt my ioy and blis in heuoun sine fine. þus to lokon in speculo mundane vanitatis . . . Ff. 48–54.

9. T22?. *Abiit Iesus* (John 6:1). Reuerendi domini, autores qui tractant de naturis dicunt quod est naturale odium, inimicicia inter regem auium, aquilam, et venenosum serpentem . . .-. . . et securus de sua eterna hereditate. þus abire peregrinacionem in deserto mundiali . . . Ff. 54–60v.

10. T22?. *Abiit trans mare* (John 6:1). Reuerendi domini, acerbum mare quod Christus transiit et quod nos omnes oportet superuelificare . . . .-. . . and ouerseiled þe see of synne to blis sine fine. þus to gouerne vs infra nauim . . . Ff. 60v–68.

11. T22*. *Videbant signa* (John 6:2). Lego in sacra scriptura Apocalipsis 12 quod sanctus euangelista, sanctus Iohannes, vidit magnum mirabile signum in celo . . .-. . . In quat mischef vos sitis, confidite in eius misericordia. þus videre signa vindicte . . . Ff. 68v–74.

12. T23*. *Pontifex introivit in sancta* (Heb 9:11–12). Anglice: þe bischop hath entred þe temple of blis þoroo þe blod he schad [for] mannys mys. Lego 2 Paralipomenon quod gloriosus rex Salamon fecit sibi statlich trone . . .- . . . habebis mercedem eterne hereditatis. Ad illud beatificum templum . . . Ff. 74–79v. Also R-2.

13. T23?. *Christus introivit in sancta* (Heb 9:12). Lego in sacra scriptura Exodi 20 quod postquam omnipotens Deus descenderat in sacrum montem . . .- . . . benedicite Dominum qui moriebatur voluntarie ad reducandum [!] vos ad eternam felicitatem. Summus pontifex Christus Iesus vos omnes benedicat . . . Ff. 79v–85.

14. T24?. *Ecce rex venit* (Matth 21:5). Anglice: Synful man behold and se, a blisful rex comus to þe. Vt auctores nature dicunt, Bartholomei 12 *De naturis*, est quoddam genus virtuosorum lapidum, magnetes . . .-. . . dabit nobis celum pro mercede. Dominus omnis virtutis, qui est rex glorie, vobis omnibus benedicat . . . Ff. 85–91.

15. T23*. *Exivit de templo* (John 8:59). Summus celi pontifex, qui isto sacro tempore paciebatur passionem et mortem pro humano peccato . . . In huius sermonis exordio . . . Speciale templum . . .-. . . gracia que fuit diu in exilio demum reuersa est. Sic nostrum graciosum regem se regere . . . Ff. 91–96v. Also R-12.

16. S30*. *Domine, salva nos, perimus* (Matt 8:25). Non miremini quod sumpsi ista verba pro themate, quia isto die quidam habent missam principalem de ieiunio, quidam de sancto M . . .-. . . potestatem absoluendi. Legimus in euangelio Luce. Ff. 97–100, inc.

17. ?. *Fructus iusti lignum vitae* (Prov 11:30). þe holi crosse, þe liuelich tre, est þi frute if þou riȝtful be. Secundum doctores iusticia est virtus reddens vnicuique quod suum est . . .-. . . videbis fructum consolacionis et fortitudinis etc. Ff. 100v–102, inc.

18. T58*. *Sanavit eum* (Luke 14:4). Lego in sacra scriptura Iosue 7 capitulo tempore quo magna ciuitas Iericho destrueretur manu omnipotentis Dei . . .- . . . He hath sine fine made him hol, sicut dixi in principio. þus to euerlastinge ioy and welthe . . . Ff. 102v–105v.

19. S02a*. *Vestivit pontificem* (Lev 8:7). Scriptura sacra Exodi 28 et Leuitici 8 et Magister *Historiarum* super illis locis dicunt quod summus pontifex veteris legis erat vestitus tribus solennibus ornamentis . . .-. . . ostende ergo michi veraciter [*read* veritatem] huius sacramenti, vt veraciter credere et saluari queam. Ff. 106–107v, inc. Also R-28.

20. C14*. *Sacerdos est angelus* (Mal 2:7?). Reuerendi patres et domini, in gloriosissimo templo celestis Ierusalem ab arca fecundissima paternalis glorie [canc] memorie manna profluit . . .-. . . vt in celesti gloria angelorum frui gaudiis possitis perhennibus ipse vobis concedat qui . . . Ff. 108–109v.

21. C14*. *Quasi flos rosarum in diebus veris* (Sir 50:8). Increate splendor sapiencie ab eterni solis cardine progrediens sui ortus fulgore temporanee nostre

552

mortalitati serenus illuxit . . .-. . . concedat florescere flos florum Iesus prodiens de virgula Iesse. Qui . . . Ff. 110–111.

22. T19*. *Statuit eum supra pinnaculum templi* (Matt 4:5). Deus qui statuebatur supra pinnaculum crucis pro hominis peccato et effudit sanguinem suum super illud ad sanctificandum templum anime humane, rede vs . . .-. . . in mundicia ab omni pollucione et feditate peccati mortalis. þus to clense templum consciencie . . . Ff. 112v–119.

23. C21*. *Dies mei transierunt quasi navis* (Job 9:26). Deus qui fecit diem et noctem pro hominis succur . . . rede us, etc. Dies hii cito complentur . . .-. . . fro þe woful wawis mundi ad portum felicitatis eterne. Ad istum portum . . . Ff. 119v–124.

24. S59*. *Intravit castellum* (Luke 10:38). þe souerayne lord celi et terre, qui per portam misericordie intrauit castellum nostre nature . . . reede . . . Anglice: Moder and maiden that neuer did mysse . . .-. . . ad sublime castellum et turrim perpetue leticie et felicitatis. Ad illud felix castellum . . . Ff. 124–128v.

25. ?. *Qui navigat mare enarrat pericula* (Sir 43:26). Suppremus princeps celi et terre, Deus, qui creauit solum et mare pro socour humani generis, rede vs, etc. Anglice: Qwo sailet . . . vel sic: Vr maryner . . . Magnum mare quod Dominus noster . . .-. . . quod we mow passe pericula maris and saile rectum cursum ad portum celi. Ad istum portum. Amen. Ff. 128v–133. Edited in Haines, "'Our Master Mariner'."

26. ?. *Ascendens Iesus in naviculam transfretavit* (Matt 9:1). Beati homines in hac peregrinacione langore cruciantur, timore consternantur, fauore demendantur . . .-. . . magis preciosum erubescencia in fronte, et perfice vltra questiones secundum alphabetum. Ff. 145–148.

27. T62*. *Induite vos armaturam Dei* (Eph 6:11). Intelligatis quod armatura fidelium debet esse oracio . . .-. . . primum genus armorum idest scutum fidei de quo in epistula hodierna. Ff. 148–150, inc.

28. ?. *Videte quomodo caute ambuletis* (Eph 5:15). In hiis verbis docet nos Apostolus subtilem theoricam et vtilem practicam . . .-. . . considera ista et reuera caute ambulabis. F. 150.

29. T39*. *Dedit dona hominibus* (Eph 4:8). Karissimi, si consideremus vniuersorum dominum, eum tam auidum humani amoris inueniemus . . .-. . . eternam beatitudinem toto desiderio concupiscas. Quam . . . Ff. 150v–157v.

30. ?. *Caritas operit multitudinem peccatorum* (1 Pet 4:8). Quatuor sunt experimenta per que literas priuatas potest homo legere . . .-. . . quid magis varium, quia ibi erunt varia gaudia etc. Ff. 157v–159. Also A-27.

31. T26*. *Amore langueo* (Cant 2:5). Karissimi, septem signa amoris et langoris considero que isto die humano generi acciderunt, nam isto [die] primus homo fuit creatus . . .-. . . esse sponsa Christi, oportet quod abtrahat [!] affecionem ab istis terrenis etc. Ff. 159–164, inc. Cf. B/2-12, etc.

32. T21*. *Revertar* (Luke 11:24). Inter clemenciam et vindictam ordo struitur vt preacceptetur clemencia, postea sequatur vindicta . . .-. . . et sic tandem per confessionem Christum inueniet quem per peccatum amisit. Ff. 164–168v, inc. Also B/2-71 and W-91.

33. ?. *Veni et vide* (John 1:45). Ante incarnacionem genus humanum fuit lanceatum tribus lanceis . . .-. . . tabula de oliua, de cuius liquor vulnera sanat. Ff. 168v–169v, inc.

34. S81. *Non potest civitas abscondi supra montem posita* (Matt 5:14). Solent homines commendare ciuitates propter quatuor condiciones . . .-. . . vt cadentem flebiliter et ideo tenet eliotropum. Ff. 169v–174v, inc.

35. S82a. *Ecce rex vester* (John 19:14). Karissimi, regna solent distingui per arma et per regem, per loquelam et per legem . . .-. . . sic errata corrigere et correcta finaliter tenere. Ff. 174v–177v, inc.

36. S32. *Statuit duas columnas in porticu templi* (1 Kings 7:21). Dicit Augustinus *De verbis Apostoli* quod templum Dei istis duobus columpnis, que sunt bona operacio et contemplacio . . .-. . . nullus istorum debuit ministrare in templo. Ff. 177v–178v, inc.

37. S08. *Deus meus et Dominus meus* (John 20:28). Secundum commentarium Boecii *De consolacione*, tres fuerunt vite famose . . .-. . . a primo ad vltimum Dominus meus et Deus meus, etc. Ff. 178v–183. Also Merton 248 f. 97vb.

38. ?. *Vade* (John 4:16 or 50). Narrat di'i Agellius in quodam libello *De bellis Armenie* de quodam rege generoso, formoso, et famoso . . .-. . . vade et lauare sepcies in Iordano, etc. Ff. 188v–189, inc?

39. T19*. *Ecce nunc dies salutis* (2 Cor 6:2). Prima dies exploracio sue culpe, secunda culpe deploracio, tercia eiusdem explicacio, quarta Dei imploracio, scilicet per oracionem, quinta in bono expedicio, sexta contricio in bono . . .-. . . superius et inferius que circa te et intra te. Ff. 192–194, inc. Also A-26.

40. S85. *Quasi si sit rota in medio rote*, suple: apparuit beata Katerina (Ezek 1:16). Refert historia 3 Regum 1 quod rex Dauid senuerat habebatque etatis plurimos annos . . .-. . . nostra supportans onera et nostra consumans opera, vt per eam peruenire possimus ad regna celestia. Amen. Ff. 194–201v.

41. S79. *Beati qui per portas intrant civitatem* (Rev 22:14). Karissimi, ista verba scribuntur in ultimo loco sacre scripture et possunt esse verba Ecclesie.

In quibus videtur loquitur sicut loquebatur homo . . .-. . . cuius modus iocunditas, cuius nodus eternitas. Amen. Ff. 201v–206.

42. S80. *Libera nos a malo, Amen* (Matt 6:13). Karissimi, anime defunctorum penis purgatorii deputate duplici malo inuoluuntur . . .-. . . sed libera nos a malo, amen, et concede nobis vitam eternam. Ad quam . . . Ff. 207–213.

43. S44*. *Ipsum elegit ab omni vivente* (Sir 45:20). Karissimi, scitis quod primus parens in mundi primordio se cum suis subiugauit multiplici obproprio . . .-. . . ducitur ad celi capitolium, vt eternam capiat gloriam. Ad quam . . . Ff. 213–217.

44. S40. *En morior* (Gen 25:32). Karissimi, Barnabas interpretatur filius concludens. Sed quid isto die verius sibi concludere poterat adhuc non vidi. Nam isto die martirium . . .-. . . non solum mementote principii vestri sed et medii in quo corpus, etc. Ff. 217–220v, inc.

45. S01. *Crucifixus sum* (1 Cor 1:13?). Secundum Varronem hec fuit tragedia peccati mortalis quod reclinabatur in lectulo ad similitudinem hominis letaliter vulnerati . . .-. . . inuitam mortem commutauit et patriam perditam recuperauit. Ad quam . . . Ff. 220v–227.

P1 – Cambridge, Pembroke College, MS 199

1. T01*. *Abiciamus opera tenebrarum* (Rom 13:12). Philosophi sentencia proclamat duplicem proprietatem esse tenebrarum . . .-. . . in stola glorie Ecclesiastici 6. Ad quam . . . Ff. 41ra–43rb. Also P2–1.

2. T01?. *Abiciamus opera tenebrarum* (Rom 13:12). Reuerendi, propter tria abiciunt homines rem aliquam . . .-. . . et facit inuenire uitam etc. Quam . . . Ff. 43rb–44va.

3. T01?. *Abiciamus opera tenebrarum et honeste ambulemus* (Rom 13:12). Reuerendi mei, super isto textu mouentur tria dubia . . .-. . . digni sunt Apocalipsis 3 scilicet in regno celorum. Ad quod . . . Ff. 44va–45vb.

4. T02*. *Deus repleat vos gaudio et pace* (Rom 15:13). Reuerendi mei, secundum Glosam ordinariam super eodem textu duplici de causa scripsit Apostolus ista uerba Romanis . . .-. . . repleat vos gaudio et pace. Ad quod . . . Ff. 45vb–48ra. Also P2–2.

5. T02?. *Deus spei repleat vos gaudio et pace* (Rom 15:13). Reuerendi mei, duo sunt quibus solent homines desiderare repleri . . .-. . . in gaudium domini tui Mathei 25. Ad quod gaudium . . . Ff. 48ra–49va. Also Bodley 857–11.

6. T02?. *Unanimes honorificetis Deum* (Rom 15:6). Reuerendi mei, inuitus nemo bene facit secundum Augustinum . . .-. . . et vnanimes honorficetis deum. Sic eum vos honorare . . . Ff. 49va–51va.

7. T03?. *Iam quaeritur fidelis quis* (1 Cor 4:2). Reuerendi, dominus ad long-
inquas partes exiturus . . .-. . . dabo tibi coronam uite. Quam . . . Ff.
51va–54ra.

8. T03?. *Qui iudicat me Dominus est* (1 Cor 4:4). Reuerendi mei, tria requiruntur ad Dominum qui habet iudicare . . .-. . . iudicat me dominus est. Sic
enim nos iudicare . . . Ff. 54ra–55vb. Also P2–4.

9. T03?. *Quaeritur quis fidelis inveniatur* (1 Cor 4:2). Reuerendi mei, prout
docet scriptura sacra triplici racione queritur questio . . .-. . . fidele coram
te Neemie 9. Sic ergo fideles . . . Ff. 55vb–57vb. Also C-21.

10. T04?. *Tu quis es?* (John 1:19). Racione triplici questio solet queri . . .-. . . tu
quis es. Ff. 57vb–60rb.

11. T04?. *Pax Dei custodiat corda vestra* (Phil 4:7). Reuerendi mei, duo reperio
prout docet scriptura que indigent custodiri . . .-. . . in pace illius erit pax
vestra. Quam . . . Ff. 60rb–61vb. Also P2–7.

12. T04?. *Gaudete in Domino semper* (Phil 4:4). Reuerendi mei, tria genera
hominum solent de alio gaudere . . .-. . . intra in gaudium domini tui. Ad
quod . . . Ff. 61vb–63ra.

13. ?. *Gaudeamus et demus gloriam Deo* (Rev 19:7). Reuerendi, secundum scripture sacre testimonium triplex genus hominum solet gaudere . . .-. . . demus
gloriam Deo. Quod sic facere . . . Ff. 63rb–64va. Also P2–10.

14. T06?. *Verbum caro factum est* (John 1:14). Reuerendi mei, prout recitat sanctus Thomas de Christo questione 16, triplex fuit opinio hereticorum . . .-
. . . propiciacionem pro peccatis nostris. Sic eum honorare . . . Ff. 64va–66ra.
Also Bodley 857–14.

15. T06?. *Parvulus natus est nobis* (Isa 9:6). Reuerendi mei, vt claret per scripturas, quilibet hic mortalis cum incommodo triplici . . .-. . . qui nos ditabit
in celis. Quod . . . Ff. 66rb–68vb.

16. T08*. *Iuste vivamus in hoc saeculo* (Tit 2:12). Reuerendi mei, tria excitant
hominem ad aliquod opus operandum . . .-. . . iuste viuamus in hoc seculo.
Quod nos facere . . . Ff. 68vb–70rb. Also P2–12.

17. T10*. *Venimus adorare eum* (Matt 2:2). Reuerendi mei, sicut in hodierno
euangelio legitur, magi, idest tres reges . . . Tria enim sunt quare quis
racionabiliter adoratur: . . .-. . . adorare eum. Eum nos adorare . . . Ff.
70rb–72ra.

18. T16?. *Quod iustum fuerit dabo vobis* (Matt 20:4). Docet Seneca *De beneficiis*
quod in dacione muneris debet homo respicere . . .-. . . ille scilicet habitabit
in domo dei. Vbi nos habitare . . . Ff. 72ra–73vb. Also P2–17.

19. T16?. *Quid hic statis otiosi?* (Matt 20:6). Quilibet homo optat pro suo labore for to have mede and for to have help in nede . . .-. . . mercedem habebitis in celo. Quam . . . Ff. 74ra–76va.

20. T16?. *Multi sunt vocati, pauci vero electi* (Matt 20:16). Reuerendi mei, prout docet scriptura postquam primus parens . . . vocauit nos ad tria . . .-. . . in bonitate electorum tuorum Psalmo 105. Ad quam visionem . . . Ff. 76va–78vb.

21. T17?. *Sitis ipsi sapientes* (2 Cor 11:19). Reuerendi, tria genera hominum reperio que sapiencia multum indigent . . .-. . . sitis ipsi sapientes. Sic vos fieri sapientes . . . Ff. 78vb–81rb. Also P2–21.

22. T17?. *Veritatem dicam* (2 Cor 12:6). Reuerendi mei, prout dicunt doctores sacra scriptura attestante, tria debet quilibet predicator uerbi Dei dicere sue docere . . .-. . . sum via veritas et vita. Ad quam . . . Ff. 81rb–83vb.

23. T17?. *Scio hominem in Christo* (2 Cor 12:2). Reuerendi mei, havyng reward to haly wryt and to þe techyng of owr doctours, ilk man in qwhat stat he be . . . Nam testante scriptura . . .-. . . sufficienter scire nos ipsos. Hanc scienciam . . . Ff. 83vb–85vb.

24. T18?. *Nihil sum* (1 Cor 13:2). Sicut ex philosophia et scriptura canonica satis patet, quelibet creatura ex nichilo est et ex Deo . . .-. . . vsque in finem sine crimine. Hanc graciam . . . Ff. 86ra–89va.

25. T18?. *Iesu fili David, miserere mei* (Luke 18:38). Sicut sacra scriptura testatur et uariis exemplis demonstratur, nunquam indigebat aliquis miseria nisi racione . . .-. . . quoniam in seculum misericordia eius. Quam . . . Ff. 89va–93va.

26. T19*. *Illi soli seruies* (Matt 4:10). Reuerendi mei, prout docet sacra scriptura, tria precipue inter alia mouent hominem alteri seruire . . .-. . . quoniam Dominus illuminabit eos et regnabunt in secula seculorum. Amen. Amen. Ff. 93va–96rb. Also P2–26.

27. T19?. *Dominum Deum tuum adorabis* (Matt 4:10). Reuerendi mei, homines libenter faciunt illud per quod possunt fugere penas . . .-. . . in bono suo scilicet in gloria. Ad quam . . . Ff. 96rb–99va. Also P2–25 and B/2–76.

28. T19*. *Illi soli servies* (Matt 4:10). Lactancius libro 3 *Diuinarum Institucionum* capitulo 8 dicit: Si quis hominum interrogetur . . .-. . . finem vero vitam eternam. Ad quam . . . Ff. 99va–102ra.

29. T20?. *Domine, adiuva me* (Matt 15:25). Reuerendi mei, triplex hominum genus solet adiutorem implorare . . .-. . . Domine, adiuua me. Sic hic nos adiuuet . . . Ff. 102ra–105rb. Also P2–30.

30. T20?. *Gentes ignorant Deum* (Thess 4:5). Karissimi, sanctus Thomas libro 3 *Contra gentiles* capitulo 156: Deus, inquit, quantum in se est paratus est . . .- . . . quem misisti Iesum Christum. Quam vitam . . . Ff. 105rb–108rb. Also Y/3-32.

31. T20*. *Miserere mei, Domine* (Matt 15:22). Tria mouent homines ad petendum misericordiam, videlicet vel quia sunt pauidi . . .-. . . miserere mei, Domine. Quam misericordiam . . . Ff. 108rb–111rb.

32. T21?. *Quomodo stabit regnum?* (Luke 11:18). Ysidorus *Ethimologiarum* dicit quod regnum dicitur a regibus . . .-. . . in eternum regnum Domini nostri Iesu Christi. Quod . . . Ff. 111rb–113vb.

33. T21?. *Eicio daemonia* (Luke 11:20). Triplici de causa aliquis aliqua eicit; primo dominus seruos . . .-. . . non eiciam foras. Sic nos sibi venire . . . Ff. 113vb–116ra. Also Y/3-30.

34. T21?. *Scitote quoniam immundus non habet hereditatem in regno Dei* (Eph 5:5). Reuerendi mei, prout docet sacra scriptura et communia iura, tria excludunt hominem ab hereditate paterna . . .-. . . paratum est ab origine mundi. Quod regnum . . . Ff. 116ra–117vb. Also P2-32.

35. T22? [4 Lent]. *Quid dicit scriptura?* (Gal 4:30). Reuerendi mei, racione triplici queritur questio per hanc diccionem quid . . .-. . . et viues scilicet vita eterna. Quam . . . Ff. 117vb–120va. Also P2-34.

36. T22?. *Christus nos liberavit* (Gal 4:31). Karissimi, propter primorum parentum delictum incurrebat humanum genus triplex malum . . .-. . . in exitu vite habebitis vitam sine fine. Quam etc. Ff. 120va–124rb.

37. T22*. *Dicit scriptura, Eice* (Gal 4:30). Tria solent homines a se eicere . . .- . . . dicit scriptura eice. Sic eicere vos . . . Ff. 124rb–127va. Also P2-35.

38. T23?. *Quis ex vobis arguet me de peccato?* (John 8:46). Duo maxime decent illum qui habet alium arguere de delicto . . .-. . . in sanctificacionem, finem vero uitam eternam. Ad quam . . . Ff. 127va–131ra.

39. T23*. *Iesus abscondit se* (John 8:59). Reuerendi domini, ex scriptura sacra elicio pro presenti quod aliqui se abscondunt racione pudoris . . .-. . . exultabo in Deo Iesu meo. Quod . . . Ff. 131ra–133rb.

40. T23?. *Gloria mea nihil est* (John 8:54). Beatus Augustinus super illud Psalmi Dormierunt sompnum suum et nichil inuenerunt omnes viri diuiciarum, etc . . .-. . . et annos suos in gloria. Ad quam . . . Ff. 133va–136rb.

41. T26?. *Ecce morior, cum nihil horum fecerim* (Dan 13:43). Debetis scire quod quanto aliquis minus reus patitur, tanto magis naturaliter sibi alii compaciuntur . . .-. . . propter gloriam nostram fratres, Corinthiorum 15. Ad quam gloriam . . . Ff. 136rb–139ra.

42. T26?. *Videte dolorem meum* (Lam 1:18). Karissimi, sacram scripturam diligencius intuenti aperte ostenditur quod causa triplici homini vt aliquid videat precipitur . . .-. . . vite eterne heredes efficeremur. Quam vitam . . . Ff. 139ra–141ra.

43. T26?. *Expedit unum mori* (John 18:14). Of thre maneris I may say opynly þat is spedeful one to dye . . .-. . . Ambrosius et allegat eum Magister. F. 141ra–vb, inc.

P2 – Cambridge, Pembroke College, MS 257

1. T01. *Abiciamus opera tenebrarum* (Rom 13:12). Communis sentencia proclamat duplicem proprietatem . . .-. . . in obiectacionem in scola glorie, Ecclesiastici 6. Quam gloriam. . . . Ff. 1ra–4a. Also P1-1.

2. T02. *Deus repleat vos omni gaudio et pace* (Rom 15:13). Vt testatur sacre scripture eloquium, duplici generi hominum adoptatur gaudium et pax . . .-. . . omni gaudio et pace, hic scilicet in presenti sic ut in futuro ad pacem eternam et gaudium sine fine mereamus peruenire. Amen. Ff. 4ra–7rb. Also P1-4.

3. T02?. *Respicite et levate capita vestra* (Luke 21:28). Tria excitant homines ut sursum leuant capita atque respiciant . . .-. . . et leuate capita vestra etc. Ff. 7rb–9vb.

4. T03?. *Qui iudicat me Dominus est* (1 Cor 4:4). Reuerendi mei, tria requiruntur ad eum qui debet iudicare . . .-. . . iudicat me Dominus est. Sic eum iudicare dignetur. Ff. 9vb–12ra. Also P1-8.

5. T03?. *Tu es qui venturus es?* (Matt 11:3). Reuerendi mei, propter tria solet aliquando questio queri . . .-. . . quod nobis paratum est ab origine mundi. Quod. . . . Ff. 12ra–13vb.

6. T04?. *Gaudete in Domino semper* (Phil 4:4). Reuerendi mei, docet scriptura quod de tribus solent homines gaudere . . .-. . . gaudete in Domino semper. Quod gaudium . . . Ff. 13vb–15rb.

7. T04?. *Pax Dei custodiat corda vestra* (Phil 4:7). Duo reperio prout docet scriptura que indigent custodiri . . .-. . . in pace illius est pax vestra. Quam . . . Ff. 15rb–17ra. Also P1-11.

8. T04?. *Homo tu quis es?* (Rom 9:20; or rather John 1:19?). Secundum sacram scripturam propter tria queritur questio per hanc diccionem quis . . .-. . . in eternum non peccabis. Sic facere . . . Ff. 17ra–19rb. Also Bodley 857–9.

9. T06. *Verbum caro factum est* (John 1:14). Reuerendi mei, prout docent histr' euangelice, propter tria Uerbum Dei factum est homo . . . .-. . . fines terre salutare Dei nostri, Ysaie 72. Quod . . . Ff. 19rb–21ra.

10. ?. *Gaudeamus et demus gloriam Deo* (Rev 19:7). Secundum scripture testimonium triplex genus hominum solet gaudere et dare gloriam Deo . . .- . . . gaudeamus et demus gloriam Deo. Quod sic facere . . . Ff. 21ra–22va. Also P1-13.

11. T06?. *Gloria in altissimis Deo* (Luke 2:14). Duplici generi hominum datur gloria . . .-. . . gloria in altissimis Deo. Fiat processus de gloria. Ff. 22va– 23rb.

12. T08. *Iuste vivamus in hoc saeculo* (Tit 2:12). Tria excitant hominem ad aliquod opus operandi . . .-. . . iuste viuamus in hoc seculo. Sic nos viuere . . . Ff. 23rb–25va. Also P1-16.

13. T13?. *Cum omnibus hominibus pacem habentes* (Rom 12:18). Docet Aristoteles 8 *Eticorum* quod omne animal per viam nature fugit nociuum . . .- . . . Deus pacis et dileccionis erit semper vobiscum. Sic fieri . . . Ff. 25vb– 27va.

14. T13?. *Ego homo sum* (Matt 8:9). Secundum sentenciam beati Gregorii 14 *Moralium* ex causa tripharia in scripturis quempiam hominem conuenit appellari . . .-. . . tandem Deo perhenniter perfruamur. Quod . . . Ff. 27va–31rb.

15. T14. *Domine, salva nos* (Matt 8:25). Docet scriptura quot [!] tria genera hominum optant saluari . . .-. . . beatus vir qui sperat in eo. Quod . . . Ff. 31rb–32va.

16. T16?. *Quod iustum fuerit dabo vobis* (Matt 20:4). Reuerendi mei, prout docet scriptura tria genera hominum tenentur et debent esse iusti . . .- . . . ideo dicit Christus ut prius quod iustum fuerit [dabo vobis, *canceled*]. Ff. 32va–35ra.

17. T16?. *Quod iustum fuerit dabo vobis* (Matt 20:4). Docet Seneca: Dabo vobis [!] De beneficiis . . .-. . . qui operatur iniusticiam, qui iurat proximo suo et non decipit. Ff. 35ra–36va. Also P1-18.

18. T16?. *Amice, non facio tibi iniuriam*(Matt 20:13). Sicut patet Johannis 14 Christus loquitur isto modo: Qui credit in me . . .-. . . Vos amici mei estis si feceritis que ego precipio vobis. Quod facere etc. (followed by another division of the same thema). Ff. 36va–39va.

19. T16?. *Pauci sunt electi* (Matt 20:16). Tria genera hominum debent elegi . . .- . . . quod est vinculum perfeccionis vite eterne. Ad quam . . . Ff. 39va– 42ra.

20. ?. *Circumdederunt me dolores mortis* (Ps 17:4). Beatus Augustinus 13 *De civitate Dei* capitulo 11 de triplici morte loquitur . . .-. . . et optinebunt gaudium et leticiam. Ad quod gaudium . . . Ff. 42ra–48ra.

21. T17?. *Sitis ipsi sapientes* (2 Cor 11:19). Reuerendi mei, tria genera hominum reperio que sapiencia mulum indigent . . .-. . . principantes in gradibus suis sic in homine. F. 48ra–va, inc. Also P1-21.

22. T19. *Ecce nunc tempus acceptabile* (2 Cor 6:2). Propterea precepit homo alteri rem aliquam prospicere . . .-. . . ecce nunc dies salutis. Ff. 49ra–52vb.

23. T19?. *Nunc dies salutis* (2 Cor 6:2). Reuerendi magistri, prout dicunt doctores, dies dicuntur boni . . .-. . . ad habendum huius salutem dicit Apostolus in verbis premissis. Ff. 52vb–55rb.

24. T19*. *Scriptum est* (Matt 4:4). Reuerens [!] mei, prout docet procressus [!] euangelii hodierne dei'te diabolus . . .-. . . intra in gaudium Domini tui, Mathei 24. Ad quod gaudium . . . Ff. 55rb–59ra.

25. T19?. *Dominum Deum tuum adorabis* (Matt 4:10). Homines libenter faciunt illud per quod possunt vitare penas . . .-. . . qui adorat Dominum in oblacione sussipietur [!]. Quam . . . Ff. 59ra–63va. Also P1-27 and B/2-78.

26. T19?. *Illi soli servies* (Matt 4:10). Testante scriptura tria inter alia mouent hominem alteri seruire . . .-. . . quem Dominus illuminabit et regnabit in secula seculorum. Quod . . . Ff. 63va–67vb. Also P1-26.

27. T20. *Gentes ignorant Deum* (1 Thess 4:5). Testante scriptura tria genera hominum solent Deum ignorare . . .-. . . impleatur in cognicionem Domini nostri. Quod . . . Ff. 67vb–70va.

28. T20*. *Miserere mei, Domine* (Matt 15:22). Tria genera hominum solent misericordiam implorare . . .-. . . quoniam ipsi misericordiam consequentur. Quam misericordiam etc. Ff. 70va–72vb.

29. T20. *Domine, adiuva me* (Matt 15:25). Reuerendi mei, prout docet Boycius 3 *De consolacione* prosa 11, Omne animal tueri propriam salutem laborat . . .-. . . hoc deuote: Domine adiuua me. Sic fieri . . . Ff. 72vb–75vb.

30. T20?. *Domine, adiuva me* (Matt 15:25). Triplex genus hominum solet auxilium implarare [!] . . .-. . . assequi quod promisit, vitam scilicet eternam. Quod . . . Ff. 75vb–79vb. Also P1-29.

31. T21*. *Estote imitatores Dei* (Eph 5:1). Reuerendi mei, prout docet scriptura tria mouent hominem alium imitare . . .-. . . estote imitatores Dei. Sic imitari . . . Ff. 79vb–81va.

32. T21?. *Scitote quoniam inmundus non habet hereditatem in regno Dei* (Eph 5:5). Docet sacra scriptura et communia iura quod tria excludunt hominem ab hereditate . . .-. . . preparatum electis percipere merebitur. Quod . . . Ff. 81va–83ra. Also P1-34.

33. T21. *Revertar* (Luke 11:24). Istud tema potest tribus modis verificari; primo si quis incederit . . .-. . . ad principalius bonum meum. Ad quod bonum etc. Ff. 83ra–87ra. Also Y/3-33.

34. T22?. *Quid dicit scriptura?* (Gal 4:30). Reuerendi mei, triplici racione queritur per hanc diccionem quid . . .-. . . in lege quid scriptum est, Luce. Ff. 87ra–90rb. Also P1-35.

35. T22?. *Dicit scriptura, Eice* (Gal 4:30). Reuerendi mei, tria solent homines a se eicere . . .-. . . quod dicit scriptura eice. Sic eicere . . . Ff. 90rb–92vb. Also P1-37.

36. T22?. *Promissionis filii sumus* (Gal 4:28). Sacre scripture auctoritas protestatur et nostre nature auiditas attestatur . . .-. . . voluntate[m] Dei facientes reportetis promissionem gracie in presenti et glorie in futuro. Ff. 93ra–97rb.

37. T22?. *Christus nos liberavit* (Gal 4:31). Docente scriptura cum testimonio doctorum post peccatum primi parentis . . .-. . . inuenire vitam eternam, Tobie 12. Quam . . . Ff. 97rb–99va.

38. T22?. *Christus nos liberavit* (Gal 4:31). Tria genera hominum a statu suo indigent liberari . . .-. . . in sanctificacionem, finem vero vitam eternam. Quam vitam . . . Ff. 99va–103vb.

39. T23. *Sanctificat sanguis Christi* (Heb 9:13–14). Debetis aduertere quod tripliciter contingit aliquid sanctificari . . .-. . . sumus factura creati. In illis ergo ambulare . . . Ff. 103vb–109ra.

40. T23. *Sanctificat sanguis Christi* (Heb 9:13–14). Triplex est causa propter quam aliquis dicitur sanctificare . . .-. . . quia sanctus ego sum, Ieremie 3. Quam sanctitatem . . . Ff. 109ra–114ra.

41. T23. *Qui est ex Deo, verba Dei audit* (John 8:47). Tria solent homines libenter audire . . .-. . . hic saluus erit, Mathei 10. Quam salutem . . . Ff. 114ra–116vb.

42. T24. *Christus humiliavit semetipsum* (Phil 2:8). Reuerendi mei, tria ostendunt humilitatem veram alicuius rei . . .-. . . humiliatus fuerit, esset in gloria. Ad quam gloriam . . . Ff. 116vb–123rb.

43. T28. *Beatus qui habet partem in resurrectione prima* (Rev 20:6). Reuerendi mei, inter cetera que hominem ad beatitudinem disponunt . . .-. . . qui habet partem in resurreccione. Quam beatitudinem . . . Ff. 123va–129rb.

44. T28*. *Amicus meus venit ad me* (Luke 11:6). Reuerendi mei, tria reperio que inter aliquos ostendit [!] amiciciam . . .-. . . habebit amicum regem, scilicet Deum. Quem vobiscum manere . . . Ff. 129rb–133va.

45. T28/2?. *Mane nobiscum, Domine* (Luke 24:29). Cum addiscione Ecclesie teste sacra scriptura solent homines rogare aliquem secum manere precipue

propter tria . . .-. . . Dominus virtutum nobiscum. Sic fieri . . . Ff. 133va–136vb.

46. T28/2?. *Surrexit Dominus vere* (Luke 24:34). Prout dicit scriptura, tria sunt signa quod aliquis a morte ad vitam resurgat . . .-. . . hic saluus erit, Mathei 24. Quod . . . Ff. 136vb–138vb.

47. ?. *Recordare quia recepisti bona*, etc. (Luke 16:25). Secundum scripture doctrinam triplex genus hominum necesse est recordare . . .-. . . recordare quia recepistis bona. Quod . . . Ff. 138vb–142rb.

48. T29. *Quis est qui vincit mundum?* (1 John 5:5). Triplici de causa in scripture sacre sorie [*read* serie] quare questio queritur per hanc diccionem quis . . .-. . . sedere mecum in trono meo, Apocalipsis 3. Ad quod tronum . . . Ff. 142rb–146rb.

49. T29?. *Pax vobis* (John 20:19 etc.). Prout docet scriptura tribus generibus hominum optatur pax . . .-. . . pacis non erit finis. Quam . . . Ff. 146rb–149ra.

50. T30?. *Iustitiae vivamus* (1 Pet 2:24). Bernardus libro 3 *De consideracione ad Eugenium* dicit quod in omni operacione . . .-. . . secundum consilium Apostoli faciamus et iuste viuamus. Sic nos iuste viuere concedat. Ff. 149ra–152vb.

51. T31?. *Militavit adversus animam* (1 Pet 2:11). Hec verba ad litteram verificare [!] possunt de sermonibus Dei . . .-. . . et honorabile nomen eorum coram illo. Hinc [!] honorem nobis etc. Ff. 152vb–157ra.

52. T31?. *Deum timete* (1 Pet 2:17). Tria faciunt hominem timere . . .-. . . in sermonis fine Deum timete. Sic eum timere etc. Ff. 157ra–160rb.

53. T32?. *Spiritus veritatis docebit vos* (John 16:13). Secundum scripture sentenciam tria requiruntur ad bonum doctorem . . .-. . . non solum eum ad vitam corporalem reduxit sed ad vitam glorie. Nobis concedat etc. Ff. 160rb–162ra.

54. T32?. *Omne donum perfectum desursum est* (James 1:17). Reuerendi mei, ad donum perfectum duo requiruntur: scilicet liberalitas conferentis . . .-. . . perfectus inuentus est, erit illi gloria eterna. Quam . . . Ff. 162ra–165va.

55. T32. *Omne donum perfectum desursum est* (James 1:17). Reuerendi mei patres et domini, ut michi apparet, duplici de causa Apostolus proponit nobis verba preaccepta . . .-. . . et sumus, si filii, heredes. Quam hereditatem . . . Ff. 165va–168ra.

56. T33?. *Oblitus est qualis fuerit* (James 1:24). Testante Seneca *Epistula 40* ad Lucillum, cibus corpori non prodest . . .-. . . obliuissi [!] me fecit Deus omnium laborum meorum. Ad istam ciuitatem . . . Ff. 168rb–175va.

57. T33?. *Qui in lege perfectae libertatis permanserit, hic beatus in facto suo erit* (James 1:25). Glosa legem perfecte libertatis vocat legem gracie . . .-. . . perfecte quare etc. Vnde recapitula et fac finem. Cuius finis sit thema. Ff. 175va–180vb.

58. T34/2. *Quis vestrum habebit amicum* (Luke 11:5). Tripliciter mouentur homines ad quirendum [!] de alico per istam diccionem quis . . .-. . . iam non dicam vos seruos sed amicos. Quam amiciciam . . . Ff. 180vb–183va.

59. T34?. *Multum valet deprecatio* (James 5:16). Propter tria solent homines rem propriam commendare . . .-. . . multum placet est deprecacio iusti. Sic eum . . . Ff. 183va–185rb.

60. T34?. *Multum valet deprecatio iusti* (James 5:16). Secundum sacre scripture historias triplicem rem solent homines comendare . . . .-. . . vindictam et grandem punicionem. In huius exemplum nota in tercia parte sermo precedit [!] etc. Ff. 185rb–187ra.

61. T36. *Ascendit in Ierusalem* ("Matt 13"). Reuerendi domini, secundum naturales vnumquodque naturaliter fertur ad suum locum naturalem . . .-. . . ascendam in palmam et apprehendam fructus eius. Quem fructum etc. Ff. 187ra–190va.

62. ?. *Ascendit super Cherubin et volavit* (Ps 17:10). Carissimi, ut uos breuiter expediam dico sic . . . .-. . . habitauit in nobis hic per graciam et in futuro per gloriam. Sic nos ascendere concedat. Amen. Ff. 190va–195rb.

63. T37?. *In omnibus honorificetur Deus* (1 Pet 4:11). In quantum quis bene operatur, in tantum meretur honorem . . .-. . . quia vera iudicia et iusta eius sunt etc. Ff. 195rb–197rb.

64. T39?. *Spiritus sanctus docebit vos* (Luke 12:12; or rather John 14:26?). Docente sacra scriptura tria pertinent ad doctorem . . .-. . . docebit vos. Fiat processus ut in sermone Spiritus veritatis docebit. Ff. 197rb–198rb.

65. T40. *Omnia operatur Deus tribus* (Job 33:29). In qualibet re sensibili aliquale relucet vestigium Trinitatis . . .-. . . recipietis retribucionem, scilicet eternam, Ad Colossenses 3. Quam nobis etc. Ff. 198rb–200rb.

66. ?. *In tribus placitum est spiritui meo* (Sir 25:1). Docet Aristoteles 5 *Politice* capitulo 2 quod similitudo est causa dileccionis . . .-. . . in tribus placitum est spiritui meo. Ff. 200rb–201ra.

67. T41/5. *Memoriam fecit mirabilium suorum* (Ps 110:4). Docet post miranda opera et mirabilia gaudia relinquere . . . .-. . . dolores non recordentur amplius. Quod . . . Ff. 201ra–205rb.

68. T41/5. *Sacramentum magnum hoc est* (Eph 5:32). Teste scriptura res aliqua solet uocari magna propter tria . . .-. . . estis hodie sicut stelle celi. Quod . . . Ff. 205rb–206vb.

69. ?. *Circumdederunt me dolores mortis* (Ps 17:4). Secundum postillam super thema, dolores mortis sunt penalitates . . .-. . . with hard engynyng circumdederunt me, etc. Ff. 206vb–208ra.

70. T24*. *Vere Filius Dei erat iste* (Matt 27:54). Tria secundum sacre scripture historias ostendunt aliquem vere filium Dei esse . . .-. . . quod vere Filius Dei erat iste. Sic nos esse concedat. Amen. Ff. 208ra–210rb.

71. T36*. *Quare rubrum est indumentum tuum?* (Isa 63:2). Secundum sentenciam doctorum hec fuit questio angelorum . . .-. . . questio cuiuslibet Christiani, scilicet quare rubrum est indumentum tuum? Ff. 210rb–211va, inc. Also A-35, S-19, Z-20, and CUL Ee.6.27, f. 73.

72. ?. *Salvatorem expectamus, Dominum nostrum Iesum Christum, qui reformabit cor humanitatis nostrae* (Phil 3:20). Quoniam sicut dicitur vulgariter Mount annui [?] a qui attent'. spes enim que differtur affligit animam . . .-. . . et ideo de eo nichil amplius ad presens dicetur. Rogemus ergo etc. Ff. 212–213v. Guillelmus de Malliaco, see Schneyer 2:489.

73. ?. *Omnis qui se humiliat exaltabitur* (Luke 18:14). Quamuis homo in infimo loco quia in terra conditus sit, tamen ad alta et sublimia creatus est . . .-. . . magnifice honorabit et exaltabit. Ad quam exaltacionem etc. Ff. 213v–214v, 225r–v, with renvoi. Guillelmus de Malliaco.

74. ?. *Videte quomodo caute ambuletis* (Eph 5:15 [T61?]). Quoniam vita nostra non est nisi quidam cursus uel quedam via ad mortem . . .-. . . qui perseuerauerit vsque in finem, hic saluus erit. Ad quam salutem . . . Ff. 225v–226v. Guillelmus de Malliaco.

Padua, Biblioteca Antoniana, MS 515

References to Holcot's sermons are to Cambridge, Peterhouse MS 210.

1. T01. *Erunt signa in sole et luna* (Luke 21:25). Secundum Lincolniensem super thema dupliciter dicitur signum . . .-. . . que laborat hec in terra, erunt signa in sole. Ff. 1–8.

2. T01. *Erunt signa in sole et luna,* etc (Luke 21:25). Ad habendum noticiam de Christi aduentu et per noticiam perfectam . . . notandum quod quatuor sunt aduentus Christi . . .-. . . Prouerbiorum 8: Delicie mee esse cum filiis, etc. Ff. 8–9v.

3. ?. *Ecce tabernaculum Dei* (Rev 21:3). Quatuor genera tabernaculorum legimus in scriptura . . .-. . . melius est dies tua in atriis tuis super milia. Quo . . . Ff. 10–12.

4. T19. *Omnis arbor quae non facit fructum bonum excidetur et in ignem mittetur* (Matt 7:19). Pro quo est notandum quod erat olim rex quidam habens regnum latissimum . . .-. . . amenitatem in vmbra, integritatem in cortice. Ff. 12–16v.

5. T61*? *Multi sunt vocati, pauci vero electi* (Matt 22:14). Pro cuius prime partis introduccione est aduertendum quod quatuor sunt cause que communiter excitant quemlibet vocatum . . .-. . . in hoc vocati estis vt benediccionem hereditate possideatis. Quam benediccionem . . . Ff. 16v–19.

6. ? [No thema, perhaps *Multi sunt vocati pauci vero electi*] (). Scribit Hugo de Sancto Victore in tractatu *De oracione* quod oracio est conuersio . . .-. . . et pro omnibus qui solebant uel merito deberent hic recommendari, dicendo Pater Noster et Ave Maria. F. 19. Protheme for the preceding.

7. T17*. *Libenter gloriabor in infirmitatibus ut inhabitet in me virtus Christi* (2 Cor 12:9). Super illud Psalmi 42, Confitebor tibi in cithara, Deus, Deus meus, et sic scribitur cithera . . .-. . . prorsus despexit et ideo reposita est sibi corona iusticie. Quam . . . Ff. 19–22.

8. T17?. [*Libenter gloriabor in infirmitatibus* etc., mentioned in text]. Reuerendi domini et magistri, iuxta consuetudinem non minus amabilem quam laudabilem, nec minus necessarium quam vtilem, verbo predicacionis [p]remittendum est verbum deuote oracionis . . .-. . . pro gracia inpetranda dicetis si placet PN et Aue Maria. F. 22r–v. Protheme for the preceding.

9. T17*. [*Libenter igitur gloriabor in infirmitatibus meis ut inhabitet in me virtus Christi*]. Reuerendissimi [*or* Reuerendi domini], Sexagesima, cuius hodie celebratur dominica qua cantatur "Exurge quare obdormis Domine," cuius terminus est feria quarta in ebdomada pasche . . .-. . . Gloriabor libenter vt in inhabitet in me virtus, etc. F. 22v. Probably the *introductio thematis* for item 7.

10. T25*?. *Sic Deus dilexit mundum* (John 3:16). Reuerendi domini et magistri, ex festo presenti celebrato in memoriam humilitatis Iesu . . .-. . . Qui vero digne manducat hunc panem, viuet in eternum. Ff. 22v–25.

11. T25*?. *Sic Deus dilexit mundum* (John 3:16). In quibus verbis ecce oracionis premittende motiuum . . .-. . . pro gracia inpetranda et pro omnibus qui solent, etc. F. 25.

12. T06. *Sol in ortu suo splendet* (Judg 5:31). Reuerendi mei, efficienter intuenti actus astronomorum ac perspicaciter prospicienti processus philosophorum clarebit solem . . .-. . . non esse lumina sed hunc dicit ducem et principem, etc. Amen. Ff. 25–27.

13. T04*. *Dominus prope est* (Phil 4:6). Reuerendi mei, celsitudo dominicalis cunctis sublimata, Dominus . . .-. . . vt sibi simus proximi in gloria permansura. Quam . . . Ff. 27v–29v.

14. T17*. *Sufficit tibi gratia* (2 Cor 12:9). Reuerendi mei, satis liquet ex serie epistule instantis dominice Apostolum pro temptacionibus . . .-. . . ad quodcumque bonum volueris sufficit tibi gracia, etc. Ff. 29v–30.

15. T17*. *Sufficit tibi gratia* (2 Cor 12:9). Reuerendi mei, secundum quod potest elici ex sacra scriptura est enim gracia triplici virtute decorata . . .-. . . donacionis accipientes in vita eterna, Romanorum 5. Quam vitam . . . Ff. 30–32.

16. ?. *Tolle quod tuum est et vade* (Matt 20:14). Karissimi, notandum est quod omnis est . . .-. . . et rapinas quas faciunt in pauperes suos. Ff. 32–33.

17. ?. *Melius est mihi mori quam viuere* (Sir 40:29). Karissimi, quod mors sit appetenda patet multiplici racione . . .-. . . spes erit de eterna salute, et hoc . . . Ff. 33–34.

18. ?. *Caro mea vere est cibus* (John 6:56). Sicut dicit Gregorius 24 *Morum* super illud Iob Stulti despiciant me . . .-. . . peiores sunt tales quam gentiles. Ff. 34–35.

19. C22 ("Principium theologie"). *Fons sapientiae verbum Dei* (Sir 1:5). Sacratissima sciencia theologie facultatem . . .-. . . in lumine tuo videbimus lumen. Quod lumen . . . Ff. 35–37v.

20. C22 ("Principium in theologia"). *Lex sapientiae est fons vitae* (Prov 13:14). Sacratissima sciencia domina Theologia altissimam inmensitatem considerans . . .-. . . quem misisti, Iesum Christum. Ad quam . . . Ff. 37v–39.

21. ?. *Dabo laudem* (Isa 42:8). Consequenter ad thema prius acceptum dedi te in lucem gencium . . .-. . . vt impleat quem omnis creatura magnificat atque laudat. Ff. 39–40v.

22. S44. *Tamquam flos agri sic efflorebit* (Ps 102:15). Patet secundum sentenciam Iob sanctissimi quilibet homo comparatur flori . . .-. . . et in operibus suis benedicunt Dominum, qui . . . Ff. 40v–42v. Johannes Erduslowe.

23. T30*. *Sequamini vestigia eius qui peccatum non fecit* (1 Pet 2:21–22). Reuerendi mei, sicut apostolus Petrus, caput Ecclesie et dux constitutus a Christo . . .-. . . in tenebris scilicet inferni, sed habebit lumen vite. Quam vitam . . . Ff. 43–46v.

24. T19. *Ductus est Iesus* (Matt 4:1). Saluator noster Christus Dei Filius omnium ducum primus olim Dei populum duxit . . .-. . . in montem excelsum et bene ex. .um ne facile residiuent. Ff. 47–49.

25. ?. *Levemus corda nostra cum manibus ad Deum in caelos* (Lam 3:41). Teste Gregorio frustra laborat lingua predicantis si non assit gracia . . .-. . . et nullus de Romanis fuit wlneratus, etc. F. 49r–v.

26. T01. *Erunt signa in sole et luna et stellis* (Luke 21:25). Reuerendi domini et magistri, consideranti diligenter signacionem triplicem per solem et lunam . . .-. . . in perpetuas eternitates, Danielis 12. Ad quam eternitatem . . . Ff. 49v–53.

27. ?. *Ubi spiritus Domini est, ibi libertas* (2 Cor 3:17). Reuerendi domini, certitudo[?] formalis qua . . .-. . . ubi ego sum et ille sint mecum, de quorum numero nos deficiat, etc. Ff. 53v–55.

28. T01. *Erunt signa in sole*, etc. (Luke 21:25). Tangit autem Saluator in isto euangelio s. signi multiplicis precessionem, erunt signa . . .-. . . ab istis secularibus negociis ad veram gloriam. Quam . . . Ff. 57–59.

29. T01. *Quoniam appropinquavit redemptio vestra* (Luke 21:28). Karissimi, vulgo dicitur quod homines viuentes modo in isto seculo sunt peiores . . .-. . . est eterna redempcio et eterna vita. Ad quam . . . F. 59r–v.

30. T01. *Prope est regnum Dei* (Luke 21:31). Secundum iura regnum elongatum amissum quantum ad successionem . . .-. . . ministrabitur vobis introitus in regnum Domini nostri Iesu Christi. Ff. 59v–61. Jacobus de Losanna (Schneyer 3:56).

31. T02. *Tu quis es?* (John 1:19). Puer tener et iuuenis sub matris custodia delicate nutritus non libenter recipit munus uel dona ab ignoto . . .-. . . omnia mea tua sunt. Ad quem . . . Ff. 61–63v. Also B/2-24 and X-4.

32. T06*. *Lignum attulit fructum* (Joel 2:22). Karissimi, hodie tres misse celebrantur sicut audistis . . .-. . . gauderet plus non tribulato. Ff. 63v–64v.

33. T06*. *Quod in ea natum est de Spiritu Sancto est* (Matt 1:20). Opus omne commendat artificem . . .-. . . bonum depositum custodi per Spiritum Sanctum. Quod. Ff. 64v–65v.

34. T06*. *Verbum caro factum est* (John 1:14). Secundum Philosophum aquila est rex animalium, vnde alcius volat . . .-. . . vidimus gloriam eius quasi vnigeniti a Patre. Ad quam gloriam . . . Ff. 65v–67. Jacobus de Losanna (Schneyer 3:58).

35. T05?. *Filius Dei in virtute* (Rom 1:4). Karissimi, teste Suetonio in tractacione *De veneracione* . . .-. . . verus Deus in premium finalem nobis promissus. Quo nobis plene frui . . . Ff. 67–69.

36. T07. *Heres parvulus est* (Gal 4:1). Karissimi, cui non sufficiunt verba, solent suadere exempla . . .-. . . heredes simus vite eterne secundum spem. Ad quam . . . Ff. 69–70v. Jacobus de Losanna (Schneyer 3:59).

37. ?. *Vocatus est Iesus et discipuli eius ad nuptias* (John 2:2). Volens contrahere matrimonium sine periculo et offensa . . .-. . . replebantur gaudio et Spiritu Sancto concedat qui cum . . . Ff. 70v–71v. Jacobus de Losanna (Schneyer 3:61).

38. ?. *Potes me mundare* (Matt 8:2). In morbis incurabilibus per naturam solet haberi recursus ad Deum . . .-. . . meretur habere beatitudinem consequentur. Quam . . . F. 72r–v. Jacobus de Losanna (Schneyer 3:62).

39. ?. *Iesu, fili David, miserere mei* (Luke 18:38). Karissimi, in hiis verbis innuuntur tria cuilibet predicatori necessaria . . .-. . . quia infirmus sum. Ad sic loquendum et vos audiendum . . . Ff. 72v–73. Some similarity with Schneyer 8:466–7, # 25 (London, British Library, MS Royal 7.A.viii).

40. T18*. *Iesu fili David miserere mei* (Luke 18:38). Karissimi, verba ista de euangelio hodierno sumpta ad literam sunt verba cuiusdam ceci . . .-. . . sed perpetua mansione in celestibus. Ad hanc ergo mansionem . . . Ff. 73–75.

41. ?. *Misericordia tua magna est super me* (Ps 85:13). Karissimi, legitur 13 quod apparuit Dominus Salomoni nocte per seipum . . .-. . . graciam inveniamus in auxilio oportune. Quam . . . Ff. 75–76v.

42. T20*. *Miserere mei* (Matt 15:22). Karissimi, quamuis Dei misericordia videtur a nobis multum elongata . . .-. . . et ideo tu peccator modo fiducialiter. Ff. 76v–78v, inc. Holcot, sermon 53.

43. T16*. *Voca operarios et redde illis mercedem* (Matt 20:8). Sicut hec exponit Glossa, verba hec erant Dei Patris ad Filium . . .-. . . et pax omni operanti bonum. Quod . . . Ff. 78v–79. Holcot, sermon 32.

44. ?. *Abiit Iesus trans mare* (John 6:1). Karissimi, multe sunt cause quare aliquis recedit de vno regno ad alium regnum . . .-. . . quam si non sanus factus esses et peccasses. Ff. 79–80, inc?.

45. T22*. *Laetare sterilis quae non paris* (Gal 4:27). Spiritus Sanctus, a quo ordinatum est officium Ecclesie, hodie mouet Ecclesiam ad leticiam in missa . . .-. . . que dicta sunt michi, in domum Dei ibimus. Quod nobis etc. F. 80r–v. Peraldus, second sermon for T22, highly abbreviated.

46. T19. *Si Filius Dei es, dic* (Matt 4:3). Karissimi, cum ad me pertineat hac vice dicere verbum Dei . . .-. . . dicat in principio Pater et Aue Maria. F. 80v, inc.

47. ?. *Per proprium sanguinem introivit semel in sancta* (Heb 9:12). Propinquior amicus facit oblacionem pro se et quanto est maioris honoris . . .-. . . et

iniquitatem miseriis pauperum etc. Ff. 81–82v. Marginally attributed to "Helcoht," but not in Holcot's sermons.

48. T26*. *Quare rubrum est indumentum tuum* (Isa 63:2). Secundum sentenciam doctorum hec fuit questio angelorum in ascencione . . .-. . . in perpetuum essemus sui et cum eo. Quod . . . Ff. 82v–87. Chambron. Also S-20.

49. T26*. *Mundus crucifixus est* (Gal 6:14). Karissimi, scribit Apostolus vbi thema sic: Michi autem absit gloriari . . .-. . . et bonis vitam eternam. Ad quod. . . . Ff. 87–91. Chambron. Also Bodley 859–13.

50. T26*. *Percussa est tertia pars solis* (Rev 8:12). Dicunt astrologi quod sol est propinquior terre in hyeme quam in estate . . .-. . . dicentes Aue, Rabi. Et sic prosequere de passione. Ff. 91–95. Chambron. Also Bodley 859–12.

51. T21/?* ("in euangelio dominice subsequentis"). *Ergo Iesus* (John 6:10). Reuerendi magistri, patres, et domini. Teste Petro Rauennacensi in quodam sermone de apostolis Christi . . .-. . . eruat ab omnibus malis et confirmet in bonis. Quod . . . Ff. 95–97.

52. T44/?* ("in epistula dominice precedentis"). *Unianimes in oratione estote* (1 Pet 3:8). Reuerendi magistri et domini, teste Ricardo de Sancto Victore tractatu quodam siue libello de mundo et ornatu eius nichil amplius commendat Ecclesiam . . .-. . . ideo et vos ad domum eiusdem beate Virginis et fratrum eius, scilicet ad ecclesiam fratrum Ordinis b. m.s. ibitis cum processione deuote psallentes Domino Salua[tori?], qui . . . Ff. 97–98v.

53. ?. *Per proprium sanguinem introivit* (Heb 9:12). Karissimi, sapientes philosophi, doctores catholici, et omnes deuoti religiosi vna voce clamant quod prius debet homo esse orator quam doctor . . .-. . . per portas glorie suos electos sibi vniendo. Quam vnitatem . . . Ff. 99–101.

54. T02*. *Honorificetis Deum* (Rom 15:6). Reuerendi mei [*or* magistri], vulgo dicitur quod magna incurialitas et beneficium ab alico scienter accipere . . .-. . . glorificabo eum, scilicet in celorum habitaculo. Ad quod regnum . . . Ff. 101v–107.

55. S59. *Tu autem, Domine, susceptor meus es, gloria, et exaltans caput meum* (Ps 3:4). Reuerendi domini, ad laudem benedicte Virginis Dei matris, et specialiter sue venerande Assumpcionis . . .-. . . dedit gloriam qualem nullus ante habuit. Ad quam . . . Ff. 107v–110.

56. ?. *In tribus bene placitum est spiritui meo* (Sir 25:1). Reuerendi domini, summus pontifex matris Ecclesie prebendarum celestium paradisi dispensator . . .-. . . nec archangelus sed precipue homo. Ad quam visionem . . . Ff. 110–113v.

57. ?. *Attendite ad petram unde excisi estis* (Isa 51:1). Ad sensum videmus quod error hominis in via corporali est aliquando lassatiuus . . .-. . . oculis poterit aspicere. Quod . . . Ff. 113v–117v.

58. T19. *Ecce nunc dies salutis* (2 Cor 6:2). Sicut vulgariter dicitur, omni negocio tempus est . . .-. . . consilia et habebitis vitam eternam. Quam . . . Ff. 119–120. Holcot, sermon 48.

59. T19. *Dic ut lapides isti panes fiant* (Matt 4:). Karissimi, quanto diucius hic viuimus, tanto peior est mundus. Hoc autem gentiles . . .-. . . poma mirtices. F. 120, inc; full copy in No. 68. Holcot, sermon 50. Also X-100.

60. T64?. *Dic nobis quid tibi videtur* (Matt 22:17). Reuerendi patres, ex quadruplici causa que relucet in verbis predicti thematis ars sermonandi quadrupliciter redditur commendabilis . . .-. . . et gloriam, suple eternam. Ad quam . . . Ff. 120v–123v.

61. C22 ("Collacio finalis"). *Ubi spiritus Domini, ibi libertas* (2 Cor 3:17). Reuerendi patres, auditorii assistentis caritas specialis appropriata spiritui . . .-. . . nostra corda sint fixa vbi vera sunt gaudia. Quod . . . Ff. 123v–126v. Frisby.

62. C22 ("Collacio Frysbi in librum 3 Sentenciarum. reportacio Brok' "). *Ubi spiritus Domini, ibi libertas* (2 Cor 3:17). Reuerendi domini, teste beato Paulo doctore gencium, 2 Thimothei 1, omnis scriptura diuinitus inspirata vtilis est . . .-. . . vbi est spiritus Domini. Quam . . . Ff. 126v–128v. Frisby.

63. C22*. *Ubi spiritus Domini, ibi libertas* (2 Cor 3:17). Beatus Augustinus *De ciuitate Dei* libro 8 capitulo 4 Platonem commendat eo quod uim moralem racionalem ac naturalem scienciam . . .-. . . intrauit ibi vbi est spiritus Domini. Ad quem . . . Ff. 128v–130.

64. C22 ("Collacio in 2m librum Sentenciarum"). *Ubi spiritus Domini, ibi libertas* (2 Cor 3:17). Reuerendi domini, teste bono [!] Augustino *De doctrina Christiana*, libro 4, capitulo 4, sicut docet doctorem eloquentem . . .-. . . plene ibi vbi est spiritus Domini. Quam refeccionem . . . Ff. 130r–v, 117v–118v, with renvoi. Frisby.

65. ?. *Super hanc petram aedificabo Ecclesiam meam* (Matt 16:18). Karissimi, cum racione firmitas edificium fundamenti [?] reddatur indissolubile . . .-. . . vbi se sperat sine fine gaudere. Ad quam . . . Ff. 131–132.

66. S25*. *Virgam vigilantem ego video* (Jer 1:11). De isto sancto benedicto Gregorio lego quod fuit monachus optimus . . .-. . . thesauri sapiencie et sciencie Dei. Ad quam . . . Ff. 132–133v.

67. S21 "In purificacione Domine" top margin. *Impleti sunt dies purgationis Mariae* (Luke 2:6). Karissimi, vt ait Remigius in exposicione *De Fastis* libro

2, olim fuit modus aput Romanos quod sacerdotes . . .-. . . cuius meritis dies nostros in bono hic compleri faciat qui . . . Ff. 134–136.

68. T19*. *Dic ut lapides isti panes fiant* (Matt 4:3). Quanto diucius hic viuimus, tanto peior est mundus. Hoc autem gentiles ostendere . . .-. . . que in presenti et in perpetuum perseuerat. Quam . . . Ff. 136–140v. Holcot, sermon 50. Also X-100 and Padua-59.

69. T20*. *Haec est voluntas Dei sanctificatio vestra* (1 Thess 4:3). Karissimi, dicit Seneca *Epistula* 2 docendo hominem debere habere vnum virtuosum hominem . . .-. . . sanctificacio vestra. Quod . . . Ff. 140v–141v. Holcot, sermon 52.

70. T21?. *Revertar in domum meam unde exivi* (Luke 11:24). Karissimi, predicta verba possunt esse Dei de fideli anima . . .-. . . sponsabit te Christus in vita eterna. Ad quam . . . Ff. 141v–143v. Part of Holcot, sermon 65; also S-23 (ascribed to Chambron).

71. ?. *Estote imitatores Dei* (Eph 5:1). Karissimi, sacra scriptura vocat predicatorem verbi Dei et omnem hominem . . .-. . . totaliter homo in Deo quietatur. Ad quem . . . Ff. 143v–146.

72. ?. *Gratiam Dei recipiatis* (2 Cor 6:1). Karissimi, quia verbum predicatoris meritorie inicium sumere debet ab oracione . . .-. . . ut peruemiat ad celeste gaudium. Quod . . . Ff. 146–150.

Q – Oxford, Bodleian Library, MS Lat. th. d. 1

Based on the texts as preserved in the codex and the table of sermons on f. 178r–v. For the first four items the themata and folio references are hypothetical, as the respective folios are very defective and what handwriting has been preserved is faded or illegible. Separate stories and notes have been omitted.

1. T01+* (Newcastle, 1432). *Ecce rex tuus venit* (Matt 21:5). F. 5r–v.

2. T02. *Tunc videbunt filium hominis venientem* (Luke 21:27). Dicit Hugo de Sancto Victore . . . Ff. 5v–?.

3. T01?. [?*Benedictus qui venit*]. F. 7.

4. T01?. *Venit Iesus?* F. 7r–v?.

5. T07?. [*Expectabant redemptionem Israel*] (Luke 2:38). . . .-. . . exspectamus. Quam gloriam nobis ille concedat . . . F. 8r–v.

6. ?. [*Praeparate corda vestra*] (1 Sam 7:3). . . .-. . . ?. Ff. 9–11?

7. T02 / T03 / T04*. *Quaecumque scripta sunt* (Rom 15:4). Anglice: Alle thyng . . .-. . . ?. Ff. 14–?

8. T02*. *Unianimes uno ore honorificetis Deum* (Rom 15:6). . . .-. . . Amen. Ff. 17v–18v.

9. T19* (Oxford). *Gratiam Dei recipiatis* (2 Cor 6:1). Karissimi, secundum Boecium in suis *Distinccionibus* recepcio gracie diuine in nobis tria facit. Primo reprimit . . .-. . . Ff. 30v–33. "Sermo quem predicaui [?] Oxon'" (30v). Repeated as Q-14.

10. T08*. *Est nomen Iesus* (Luke 2:21). Ff. 34–36v.

11. T06*. *Hoc vobis signum* (Luke 2:12). Ff. 36v–38v.

12. T06+*. *Mementote mirabilium eius* (Ps 104:5). Reuerendi, Thomas *De veritatibus theologie* . . .-. . . Ff. 39–41.

13. T22*. *Sequebatur eum multitudo magna* (John 6:2). Reuerendi mei, dicit enim Boicius in suis *Distinccionibus* quod ad sequendam aliquam predam absentem tria sunt que iuuant hominem . . .-. . . inuenietis uitam, iusticiam, et gloriam. Ad quam gloriam . . . Ff. 45–48.

14. T19* (Oxford, 1432). *Gratiam Dei recipiatis* (2 Cor 6:1). Reuerendi mei, secundum Boicium in suis *Distinccionibus* recepcio gracie diuine in nobis tria facit. Primo reprimit temptacionem . . .-. . . et gloriam dabit Dominus. Ad quam . . . Ff. 48–51. Repeats Q-9.

15. ? (1432). *Dominus est* (1 Cor 4:4). Reuerendi, secundum Holket in postilla sua *Super Sapienciam* tria requiruntur ad hoc quod aliquis sit verus dominus . . .-. . . protector vite mee a quo trepidabo, pro tercio. Quam proteccionem . . . Ff. 51v–54.

16. ? (Oxford, 1432). *Pater meus glorificat me* (John 8:54). Karissimi, quamuis ista verba dicantur de Patre in diuinis et Christo eius filio . . .-. . . qui consolatur nos in omni tribulacione nostra, pro tercio. Quam consolacionem . . . Ff. 54v–57.

17. T01+. *Salvator tuus veniet* (Isa 62:11). Karissimi, videtis bene ad oculum et verum est quod quando est ita quod rex vel aliquis dominus veniet ad vnam ciuitatem, comuniter vnus nuncius veniet . . .-. . . veni, benedicte Patris mei, percipe regnum. Quod . . . Ff. 57v–61.

18. T06. *Natus est nobis hodie Saluator* (Luke 2:11). Karissimi, videtis bene ad oculum quod homines huius mundi habent lykyng and will ad audiendum thre maner of thydinggis. Primo habent delectacionem . . .-. . . istud gaudium est gaudium celi. Ad quod . . . Ff. 61–65v.

19. T19+ (1432). *Paenitentiam agite, appropinquabit enim regnum caelorum* (Matt 3:2 and 4:17). Auxilium et gracia, etc. Karissimi, bene videtis ad oculum, et verum est, quod si aliqua comunitas, ciuitas, vel villa scholde falle in a daunger erga regem . . .-. . . et tunc appropinquabit regnum celorum. Ad quod . . . Ff. 66–69.

20. T28 (1432). *Dii estis. Ecce constitui te deum. Quocumque die comederitis, ex eo eritis sicut dii* (Ps 81:6; Exod 7:1; Gen 3:5). Karissimi, dicit Glosa super

illo textu "Siquidem sunt dii . . ." quod iste termino deus intelligitur tribus modis in sacra scriptura . . .-. . . and endelesse blisse with sikirnesse. Ad istam . . . Ff. 69v–74.

21. T19+* ("Processus de gracia pro quocumque themate"). [See the following item.] Domini, pro processu debetis intelligere quod sicut diuersi doctores dicunt qui tractant de ista materia, gracia accipitur duobus modis. Primo . . .-. . . schal ʒeuen þe grace in isto mundo et gloriam in beatitudine celi. Quam graciam et gloriam . . . Ff. 74v–78v.

22. T19+* ("Antethema et Introduccio de gracia") (Newcastle, 143?). *Gratiam Dei recipiatis. Unicuique vestrum data est gratia. Dabit Dominus gratiam populo suo* (2 Cor 6:1; Eph 4:7; Exod 11:3). Auxilium et graciam, etc. Karissimi, debetis intelligere sicut dixit vnus magnus clericus, et est venerabilis Beda *De ymagine mundi*, iste clericus dicit quod est vna insula . . .-. . . wey et recipiatis graciam Dei . . . Ff. 78v–80.

23. T28. *Dii estis omnes* (Ps 81:6 [ms: Sapiencie 80]). Glosa dicit erga [*read* super] octavum capitulum prime epistule ad Corinthios sic: iste terminus deus, inquid, tripliciter accipitur in scriptura . . .-. . . and þis day wyth hys precyuus body fed vs. Qui . . . Ff. 80–84.

24. T28*. *Custodite sicut scitis* (Matt 27:65). Karissimi, secundum beatum Augustinum super Psalmum 7, duo sunt effectus medicine . . .-. . . custos Domini sui gloriabitur. Quam gloriam . . . Ff. 84–86v.

25. C14 (1435). *Sacerdotes sanctificentur* (Exod 19:22). Reuerendi domini patresque amantissimi, cum secundum commentatorem super Dionisium *De diuinis nominibus* sanctificacio sit ab omni immundicia pura . . .-. . . in aduentum Domini nostri Iesu Christi seruetur, 1 Ad Thessalonicenses vltimo. Quod nobis sacerdotibus . . . Ff. 87–89.

26. T19+*. *Ecce nunc tempus* (2 Cor 6:2). Karissimi, inter omnia que perdimus, iactura temporis est maxima . . .-. . . et perducet te ad celi gaudium. Quod gaudium . . . Ff. 91–93v.

27. T19+. *Ecce nunc tempus* (2 Cor 6:2). Dicit Ianuensis . . . tria proprie visum corporalem impedire possunt. Primo si homo . . .-. . . venite, benedicti. Et tunc fiet combinacio, etc. Qui . . . Ff. 94–96.

28. T24. *Ecce* (Matt 25:1 or John 12:15). Karissimi, rogatus breuem sermonem facere ideo breue verbum assumpsi quod est nisi due sillabe, scilicet ecce . . .-. . . quia Deus est in gloria Dei Patris. Ad quam . . . Ff. 96v–99.

29. T19 (1430). *Gratiam Dei recipiatis* (2 Cor 6:1). Karissimi, Apostolus in epistula hodierna hortatur nos ne in vacuum graciam Dei recipiatis. Ille in

vacuum graciam Dei recipit . . .-. . . Romanorum 6, Gracia Dei vita eterna. Quam . . . Ff. 99v–100v.

30. T20 (14??). *Miserere mei, fili David* (Matt 15:22). Karissimi, dicit Philosophus 2 *De celo et mundo* quod omne graue naturaliter appetit descendere . . .-. . . et postmodum perducet ad gloriam. Ad quam gloriam . . . Ff. 100v–102.

31. T29 / C19 ("pro visitacione fratrum"). *Tres sunt qui testimonium dant* (1 John 5:7). Karissimi patres, sicut scitis, vnumquodque principiatum de quanto similius, propinquius, ac conformius existit primo principio, de tanto dignius, melius, et nobilius . . .-. . . celeritatem in correccione pro tercio. Hanc autem triplicem citatem [!] . . . Ff. 102v–103v.

32. T32 / C19 ("In visitacione fratrum"). *Spiritus veritatis docebit vos omnem veritatem* (John 16:13). Tribus modis, karissimi, secundum Magistrum *Sentenciarum* et doctores, peccatum committitur . . .-. . . cauebo michi satis de vtroque. Sed istam triplicem veritatem vitando . . . Ff. 103v–104v.

33. T47 / C19 ("In visitacione fratrum"). *Ex fructibus eorum cognoscetis eos* (Matt 7:16). Karissimi, rector et redemptor generis humani assimilando hominem arbori iuxta illud dictum philosophi Secundi, Homo est arbor euersa . . .-. . . si perseuerauerimus in vocacione qua vocati sumus. Quod . . . Ff. 104v–107.

34. C19 ("In visitacione fratrum"). *Relictis omnibus secuti sunt eum* (Luke 5:11). Hec verba ad literam dicuntur de beatis apostolis qui propter Deum reliquerunt recia . . .-. . . et gaudii perhennitatem, quia vitam eternam possidebunt. Ad quam . . . F. 107r–v.

35. T26 (Lichfield, 1436). *Quae utilitas in sanguine meo?* (Ps 29:10). Karissimi, hec verba sic dici possunt: Qwhat profy3te is heere in myn blode? Doctor Crisostomus . . .-. . . vt virtute sanguinis eius intrare poterimus vitam eternam. Quod . . . Ff. 108–113.

36. T26* (Lichfield, 1436). *Redempti estis sanguine Iesu* (1 Peter 1:18–19). Karissimi mei, secundum Crisostomum in *Imperfecto* omelia 1, Christus habuit tres dignitates, nam erat rex . . .-. . . sanguis Christi aperuit nobis ianuam paradisi, etc. Amen. Ff. 113v–115, 102, with renvoi.

37. T26* (1434). *Exivit sanguis et aqua* (John 19:34). Karissimi, viri ecclesiastici laicis [tenen]tur doctrinam salutarem prebere principaliter propter duas causas: primo quia sine tali doctrina . . . .-. . . eratis aliquando longe, facti estis prope in sanguine Christi. Amen. Ff. 115v–118v.

38. T26* (Newcastle,?). *Extra portam passus est* (Heb 13:12). Karissimi, Ieremie 7 habetur et dicitur predicatori, Sta in porta . . . Karissimi, ad presens in

nostro proposito per portam domus Domini . . .-. . . sustinebit paciens et postea ibit ad eternam iocunditatem. Ad quam . . . Ff. 119v–123, 119, with renvoi.

39. T26 (Newcastle, 1433). *Vae mihi, mater mea* (Jer 15:10). Quare rubrum est indumentum tuum. Gentes videntes nouam rem et inconsuetam multum mirantur . . .-. . . de morte vocati sumus ad vitam. Ad quam . . . Ff. 123v–126v. Edited in Little, "Fifteenth-Century Sermon."

40. T26*. *Vidi librum scriptum intus et foris* (Rev 5:1). Karissimi, videtur michi quod est de nobis et de Saluatore nostro sicut de magistro et eius discipulis . . .-. . . Nota historiam Iude et Pilati in *Legenda aurea*. Amen. Ff. 127–129v.

41. T23* (Newcastle, 1434). *Risus dolore miscebitur* (Prov 14:13). Karissimi, in predicto themate continetur plenarie quid legit Ecclesia et canit in presenti sollempnitate . . .-. . . laudem, confessionem, et Patris sui glorificacionem. Quam . . . Ff. 129v–132v.

42. T34*. *Nunc clamemus in caelum et misereatur nostri Deus* (1 Macc 4:10). Karissimi{?}, ista fuerunt verba Iude Machabei, pugnatoris strenui, et sicut videmus per exemplum quod modus est pauperum cum venerint ad portas . . .-. . . dabit nobis graciam in presenti et gloriam in futuro. Ad quam . . . (f. 135). Nota historiam que concludit predicta. Narratur quod duo fratres . . .-. . . miserebitur nostri Deus, vt prius. Quam misericordiam . . . Ff. 133–135v.

43. T34/3. *Nunc clamemus*, vbi supra (1 Macc 4:10). Karissimi, habetur in euangelio hodierno quod quando Christus predicauit hic in terra dixit inter alia sic: Si quis vestrum habebit amicum . . .-. . . þat we mow hafe in heuen oure dwellyng. Amen. Ff. 136–137v.

44. T34/4 (1430). *Nunc clamemus*, etc. (1 Macc 4:10). Karissimi, Dominus Iesus Christus cum discipulis suis post resurreccionem aliquantulum commoratus instante iam tempore quo corporaliter ab eis erat recessurus . . .-. . . vobis paratum est ab origine mundi. Quod . . . Ff. 137v–139.

45. ? (1430). *Petite et dabitur vobis* (Luke 11:9). Karissimi, in principio huius sermonis due possunt hic queri questiones. Prima est, quis est ille . . .- . . . regna celorum dabuntur vobis. Igitur vt sic petere . . . Ff. 139v– 142.

46. T34 ("Helbech," 1430). *Orate pro invicem ut salvemini* (James 5:16). Reuerendi, sicut docet Hugo de Sancto Victore in libello suo *De virtute oracionis*, duo sunt que precipue nos ad orandum videntur excitare . . .-. . . et facit invenire vitam eternam, Tobie 12. Quam . . . Ff. 142v–143v.

Q

47. ? ("Sermo processionalis). *Unianimes estote in oratione* (1 Peter 3:8). Dicit Ysidorus *De summo bono* quod seruus Dei quocienscumque aliquo vicio tangitur . . .-. . . instabile quia modo cogitat de vno peccato. F. 144r–v, inc.

48. T23 / 24 / 26. *Sanguis Christi emundabit conscientiam nostram* (Hebr 9:14). Reuerendi, quia vt dicit Augustinus et ponitur in canone 28, questione i, *Ex hiis*, quilibet iudicabitur secundum conscienciam . . .-. . . quod sic iustificati in sanguine ipsius salui erimus. Quod . . . Ff. 145–149.

49. T24. *Sanguis meus effundetur in remissionem peccatorum* (Matt 26:28). Reuerendi mei, sicut testatur Apostolus Ad Hebreos 9, in antiqua lege sine sanguinis effusione non fiebat peccati remissio . . .-. . . Pro processu sermonis dic si placet sicut in precedenti sermone, scilicet Sanguis Christi emundabit, etc. F. 149v.

50. T26. *Quae utilitas in sanguine meo?* (Ps 29:10). Karissimi, sicut sciunt scolastici qui fuerunt in vniuersitatibus, vtputa Oxon' vel Cantebrig', quando magister debet incipere . . .-. . . ad questionem ergo respondendum est per processum sermonis illius in passione, scilicet Sanguis Christi emundabit conscienciam, etc. F. 150. Michael of Hungary. Also CA/2-1.

51. ? ("De sanguine"). *Quanto magis sanguis Christi* (Heb 9:14). Nota quod in veteri testamento reperiuntur sex genera animalium . . .-. . . pes tuus in sanguine Christi, in Psalmo. F. 150r–v, inc? Followed by two notes, the second "pro sermone predente bonam figuram," f. 150v, Lichfield.

52. T37 (Lichfield, 1436). *Mittam vobis spiritum veritatis* (John 15:26). Karissimi mei, in huius sermonis exordio secundum laudabilem consuetudinem necessarium est ad Deum preces deuotas effundere . . .-. . . si sic vitam nostram correxerimus. Quod . . . Ff. 151v–154v.

53. C18 ("In profescione nouicii"). *Ecce agnus Dei* (John 1:29). Quamuis, karissimi, ista verba historialiter et ad litteram dicantur de nostro Saluatore, nihilominus tamen moraliter dici poterunt de suo sectatore presenti ordinis professore . . .-. . . vtinam quilibet nostrum sit illius meriti quod vere dici possit Agnus dei. Quod . . . Ff. 155–156.

54. ? ("Sermo Melton de x preceptis," 1430, 1431). *In duobus mandatis tota lex pendet* (Matt 22:40). Karissimi, racio dictat et experiencia probat quod omne . . .-. . . tota lex pendet. Quibus hec sic custodire valeamus vt cum Deo poterimus conregnare . . . Ff. 157–159.

55. S86 ("Melton," 1431). *Ora pro nobis, quoniam mulier sancta es* (Jth 8:29). Anglice: As þou . . . Karissimi, racio dictat et exemplo confirmatur quod quando malefactores timent castigari propter demerita sua . . .-. . . invenit gloriam vbi glorificabit Dominum suum. Quod . . . Ff. 159–161v.

56. ? ("Sermo de misericordia. Melton," 1431). *Expectat Dominus, ut misereatur nostri* (Isa 30:18). Anglice: Oure Lord . . . Karissimi, audi, peccator, Dei benignitatem. Qui iuste poterit punire exspectat . . .-. . . expectat Dominus, vt miseriatur nostri. Quam misericordiam . . . Ff. 162–164v. Related to Holcot, Convertimini-39.

57. ? ("Sermo generalis de conuersione peccatorum. Melton," 1431). *Convertimini ad me in toto corde vestro* (Joel 2:12). Anglice: With all . . . Karissimi, videmus ad oculum quod quando pater videt filium suum male morigeratum . . .-. . . assumam vos, scilicet ad gloriam meam. Ad quam . . . Ff. 165–166.

58. T26 (King's Lynn, 1431). *Agnus qui in medio troni est reget eos*, etc. (Rev 7:17). Karissimi, quando Deus fecit hominem, constituit eum dominum mundi . . .-. . . ad perducendum te ad vitam eternam. Quam . . . Ff. 166v–170v.

59. T26. *Sustinuit crucem confusione contempta* (Hebr 12:2). Karissimi, inter omnia annualia Romanorum habetur quod Rome inventa fuit vna mensa aurea . . .-. . . and bryng vs all to good endyng. Amen. Ff. 171–173.

60. T28 (1431). *Qui custos est domini sui gloriabitur* (Prov 27:18). Karissimi, si enim ita esset quod rex Anglie vel Francie traderet custodiam ciuitatis vnius cuidam in terra sua . . .-. . . ad sui honorem et tui gloriam. Ad quam . . . Ff. 173–175.

61. T41/5 (Holbeche). *Iste est panis quem dedit vobis Dominus ad vescendum* (Exod 16:15). Karissimi, debetis intelligere quod triplex est panis quibus indigemus vt vescamur . . .-. . . digne manducetis, ad vitam eternam peruenietis. Quam nobis, etc. Ff. 175v–176v.

62. T28*. *Custodi virum istum* (1 Kings 20:39). Karissimi, sic in Anglico: Kepe . . . Karissimi, ista est dies in qua omnes debemus venire ad mensam Domini et ipsum recipere in forma panis . . .-. . . primo ergo quod requiritur. Nota in sermone Qui custos est domini sui, gloriabitur. F. 177v.

R – Oxford, Bodleian Library, MS Laud misc. 706

Folio references are to the modern foliation.

1. T21*. *Quomodo stabit regnum* (Luke 11:18). Sicut testatur Sapiens, Sapiencie 6 capitulo, sapiencia et obseruancia preceptorum Dei faciunt regna in perpetuum durare . . .-. . . et queritur a te quomodo stabit regnum, respondebis: cum suo principe Christo Iesu in perhenni gloria. Ad quam . . . Ff. 1–5v.

2. T23*. *Pontifex introivit in sancta* (Heb 9:12). Anglice: þe bischope . . . Libro 2 Paralipomenon est scriptum quod gloriosus rex Salamon fecit sibi a statelich trone . . .-. . . habebis mercedem eterne hereditatis. Ad illud beneficium . . . Amen. Ff. 5v–12v, 63, with envoi. Also O-12.

3. C21 (funeral of Walter Frouceter, abbot of Gloucester, 1412). *Fluvius egrediebatur de loco* (Gen 2:10). Anglice sic: Water is went out of the reuer. Totus iste mundus potest dici magnus fluuius . . .-. . . aut inedia sine fine. Ad quod balneum beatitudinis . . . Ff. 13–20. John Paunteley. Edited in Horner, "Edition," pp. 180–215, and Horner, "John Paunteley's Sermon."

4. T24 ("coram quodam episcopo, sermo de sancto Bernardo"). *Pater, dimitte illis* (Luke 23:34). Karissimi, celestis magister ea quibus indigemus quomodo assequi debeamus edocens, Petite, inquit, et accipietis . . .-. . . tue pietati innixi illius ine . . . participes esse possimus, tete prestante qui . . . Ff. 20–27.

5. S59*. *Ascendit aurora, ascendit aurora* (Gen 32:26). Reuerendi in Christo patres atque domini, celestis imperii \celice regionis/ piissime imperator eterne claritatis lumine naturaliter . . .-. . . ut post huius vite occasum eterne beatitudinis dulcedine mereamur finaliter premiari, nobis ipse concedat . . . Ff. 27–30. Also W-4.

6. C14. *Quattuor facies uni erant* (Ezek 1:6). Karissimi, beatus Gregorius 8 *Morum* de predicatoribus loquens dicit quod vis et summa loquencium quadr[i]faria qualitate distinguitur . . .-. . . Christi dilectores per tormenta auolant ad sibi paratum gaudium. Ad quod, etc. Ff. 30–39.

7. ?. *Ego propono animam meam* (John 10:15). Beatus Augustinus sermone de fide conuenientem modum nostre redempcionis insinuans dicit sic: Sicut ille . . .-. . . fulgor inobuscabilis, vigor interminabilis. Ipsi honor et gloria per infinita secula. Amen, etc. Ff. 39–44. Followed by introductory prayer: "In principio istius sermonis recommendo vobis dominum papam . . .-. . . mente pia Pater Noster et Aue Maria, etc."

8. ?. *Clamavit: miserere mei* (Matt 15:22). Sicut narrat Macrobius in *Saturnalis* libro 2, consuetudo Romanorum fuit quando obsidebant ciuitatem hostium, clamarent ad Deum tutorem istius . . .-. . . potest Deus dicere, Dilexi te et attraxi te miserans. Quam misericordiam . . . Ff. 44–49v.

9. S28*. *Maria* (Luke 1:27). In principio nostre collacionis breuissime, ut impetremus graciam, curramus ad nostram Mariam. Bernardus dicit: Si queris inuenire graciam . . .-. . . affugantur demones sicut inuocato hoc nomine Iesu, etc. Ff. 49v–52v.

10. T39*. *Accipite Spiritum Sanctum* (John 20:22). Consuetudo erat apud milites circa obsidionem Troie commorantes omni die quo ad bellum procederent . . .-. . . dignus est ut ad eternam vitam ingrediatur. Ad quod . . . Ff. 52v–57v.

11. C14*. *Benedicta tu* (Luke 1:28). Reuerendi et domini, sicut 3 Regum 10 legitur, illustris rex Salamon habuit in mari classem magnam . . .-. . . et in fratre suo ut detur vobis benediccio sed rerum muneracio precantibus fit san[i]or. Ff. 57v–62v.

12. T23*. *Exivit de templo* (John 8:59). Summus celi pontifex, qui isto sacro tempore paciebatur passionem et mortem pro humano peccato . . .-. . . qui quinque pertulit vulnera in suo templo corporeo in ligno crucis. Qui . . . Ff. 63–70v. Also O-15.

13. T20*. *Iesus* (Matt 15:21). The gracowsus comfort omnipotentis Domini Iesu intercessione . . . Reuerendi domini, sicut lego in sacra scriptura Apocalipsis 10, quod sanctus ewangelista . . .-. . . mulier Cananea, idest mater nostra sancta Ecclesia. . F. 71r–v, inc. Also O-5.

14. C21. *Pulcritudo agri mecum est* (Ps 49:11). Karissimi\mei,/ secundum Gwidonem et alios dictatores, idem est dicta pulcritudo agri et pulcher ager . . .-. . . et quelibet singularis persona per se in eterno gaudeo [!] et beatitudine. Quam . . . Ff. 72–80. Edited in Horner, "Edition," pp. 216–249, and Horner, "Sermon on the Anniversary."

15. T41/5. *Probet seipsum homo* (1 Cor 11:28). Non inueniuntur in aliqua ciuitate seu villa regni tot acute argumentaciones seu arguentes. Sed timendum . . .-. . . tanto magis eius acc[r]escet gloria et famosior predicabitur prestante Christo. Amen. Ff. 80–82.

16. T28/2. *Redde quod debes* (Matt 18:28). Introduccio istius thematis isto modo fiebat, scilicet quod duo sunt que maxime quemlibet hominem obligant ad reddendum . . .-. . . et qualiter probetur per auctoritates et sufficientes et pertinentes, etc. F. 82.

17. T21 / C14*. *Locutus est mutus* (Luke 11:14). Reuerendi, etc., inmensa Dei bonitas cuncta que ab inicio creauit et fecit ad salutem et profectum hominis tam corporaliter quam spiritualiter ordinauit . . .-. . . terrentes de futuris tormentis, promittentes de futuris premiis. Ad que premia . . . Ff. 82–86v.

18. C19. *Venio quaerens fructum* (Luke 13:7). Reuerendi patres et domini, qualiter ad reuelacionem [!] nostre indigencie in principio cuiuslibet nostri operis oracionem permittere [!] debeamus . . .-. . . iuxta opera manuum suarum retribuetur ei, Prouerbiorum 12. Quo fructu . . . Ff. 86v–89v.

19. T20. *Vocavit nos Deus* (1 Thess 4:7). Venerandi domini, secundum doctores causa quare Apostolus scripsit hanc epistulam erat ista: gentiles in primitiua ecclesia reputabant simplicem . . .-. . . inter quos lucetis siue luminaria in mundo verbum vite continentes. Ad quam vitam . . . Ff. 89v–98.

20. T21. *Venit ira Dei* (Eph 5:6). Gentil Iesu, in whom ys comprehendit my3th, wit, comfort, and vertu, be medyacioun . . . Cristis pepul, þe most opun knowynge experience scheuyth . . .-. . . the wrathe of God come therefore. Qui . . . Ff. 98–109. Edited in Horner, "Edition," pp. 72–110.

21. T24. *Hoc sentite in vobis, quod et in Christo Iesu* (Phil 2:5). Karissimi, hoc nomen Iesus nomen est dignitatis regie; ideo debet adorari precipue . . .-. . . ego enim stigmata Domini mei Iesu in corpore in porto. Ff. 109–118, inc.

22. S28*. *Dominus tecum* (Luke 1:28). Reuerendi magistri et domini, sicut legitur in quodam sermone quem beatus Bernardus fecit de sancto festo, omnipotens Deus quando creauit hominem . . .-. . . te deducet ante conspectum Filii sui, qui in eterna sedet gloria. Ad . . . Ff. 119–123v.

23. C14*. *Magna est fides tua* (Matt 15:28). Teste scriptura sacra Genesis 2 capitulo, Deus fecit paradisum voluptatis in quo plantauit omne lignum pulcrum . . .-. . . iustificatus est ante Deum et modo participat coronam glorie. Quam . . . Ff. 123v–129.

24. ?. *Veritatem dico* (John 8:46). Iesus via, veritas, et vita: via ad patria ducens, veritas realiter existens, et vita indeficiens, sit . . . Venerandi mei, perpendens ego talis . . .-. . . gloriam et graciam dabit Dominus. Ad quam . . . Ff. 129–130v, 133–134. "Quod frater Ricardus Cotell."

25. T21*. *Quomodo stabit regnum* (Luke 11:18). Quamuis a seculis in regibus magna fuerit gloria, machina multiplex et regna varia . . .-. . . Huius lucis bonitatis, iusticie, et veritatis participes nos [*ms* non] efficiat et ad regnum eternum perducat qui . . . Ff. 132, 135–136.

26. T04. *Tu quis es?* (John 1:19). Peregrinus ingrediens terram extraneam multas solet de statu ab indigenis questiones recipere . . .-. . . et ad saluandum mediatorem. Cuius salutis nos participes efficiat qui . . . Ff. 134v, 131r–v.

27. ?. *In principio erat verbum* (John 1:1). Reuerendi patres et domini, in principio huius sermonis breuissimi recommendatis omnibus . . . Eternitatem omnipotentis uerbi eternaliter apud Deum . . .-. . . vos inquit moneo dilectissimi reuerenter ac. Ff. 139–140, inc.

28. S02a*. *Vestivit pontificem* (Lev 8:7). Scriptura sacra Exodi 28 et Leuitici 8 et Magister *Historiarum* super illis locis dicit quod summus pontifex veteris

legis erat vestitus tribus solempnibus . . .-. . . vt veraciter credere et saluari queam. Ff. 140v, 137–138v, inc. Also O-19.

29. T05*. *Sol egressus est super terram, sol egressus est super terram* (Gen 19:23). In Christo merito recolendi patres atque domini, ante radios matutinos fulgentis aurore duo prenotande signorum indicia solis ortum visibilis . . .-. . . gloria mentalis sit nobis lux facialis, in uidendo solem. Quod . . . Ff. 141–143v.

30. T21?. *Estote sicut filii* (Eph 5:1). Sextus Iulius *De bello Cesaris* refert quod fuit venerabilis princeps . . . Beth 3e as gode childur . . . Be thys worthy prince I vndurstond at this tyme Crist . . .-. . . when thow comyst to confessiun of alle [*catchword*:] thy synys. Ff. 144–152v, inc. Edited in Horner, "Edition," pp. 111–146.

31. S43a*. *Coronavit eum in die laetitiae* (Cant 3:11). Venerandi patres et magistri, triumphantis milicie princeps coronatus residens in excelsis ineffabilem sue diuinitatis magnificenciam uolens . . .-. . . dabit leticiam et gaudium in longitudine dierum, Ecclesiastici 1. Ff. 153–156, inc.

32. T21*. *Fructus lucis est in bonitate* (Eph 5:9). Venerandi patres et amici, as þe famwes clerk Lincolniensis rehersit in his tretis that he made *De spera celesti*, sex signes þer be . . .-. . . the herbe of thy confessioun [*catchword*:] for the more. Ff. 156–163v, inc. Edited in Horner, "Edition," pp. 147–179.

33. S28*. *Invenisti graciam apud Deum* (Luke 1:30). [Acephalous] Gabriel racionabilis est . . .-. . . in domo ventris eiusdem gloriose Virginis hodierna die incarnatus est. Qui . . . Ff. 164–171, acephalous.

RE – Philip Repingdon, *Sermones Super Evangelia Dominicalia*

Inventory based on Oxford, Corpus Christi College, MS 54.

1. T01. *Cum adpropinquasset Iesus,* etc. (Matt 21:1). Euangelium autem istud in duabus dominicis solet legi . . .-. . . et reuelasti ea paruulis, idest humilibus et pauperibus. Ff. 1rb–6va.

2. T02. *Erunt signa in sole,* etc. (Luke 21:25). In precedente dominica recoluit Ecclesia aduentum Saluatoris in carnem . . .-. . . et contra eos testimonium iustum ferant. Ff. 6va–10vb.

3. T03. *Cum audisset Iohannes in vinculis opera Christi* (Matt 11:2). Herodes Antipas Iohannem Baptistam in vinculis posuit . . .-. . . oportet intrare in regnum celorum. Ff. 10vb–15va.

4. T04. *Miserunt Iudaei ab Hierosolymis sacerdotes,* etc. (John 1:19). Pro huius declaracione in principio notandum secundum doctorem de Lira . . .-. . . nisi ad pauperculum, idest humilem, etc. Sic igitur humilari et conteri . . . Ff. 15va–22ra.

5. T07. *Erant pater et mater Iesu mirantes de hiis quae dicebantur de illo,* etc. (Luke 2:33). In principio huius euangelii notandum secundum Januensem . . .-. . . voluntate nostra pro sensu et voluntate Dei. Ff. 22ra–30ra.

6. T11a. *Cum factus esset Iesus annorum duodecim, ascendentibus illis Hierosolymam* (Luke 2:42). Hic sciendum secundum Iohannem de Abbatis[villa] . . .-. . . vt videant vestra bona opera et glorificent patrem vestrum, etc. Ff. 30ra–37vb.

7. T12. *Nuptiae factae sunt in Cana Galilaeae* (John 2:1). In principio huius exposicionis primo videndum est quando fuerunt . . .-. . . amplius confirmata et roborata fuit. Ff. 37vb–48ra.

8. T13. *Cum descendisset Iesus de monte, secutae sunt eum turbe multae,* etc. (Matt 8:1). Inmediate quasi ante hoc euangelium principalior sermo ponitur quem Dominus Iesus fecerat in hoc mundo . . .-. . . qui eciam iacendo in domo adquirunt. Ff. 48ra–58va.

9. T14. *Ascendente Iesu in naviculam, secuti sunt eum discipuli eius,* etc. (Matt 8:23–27, Mark 4:36, and Luke 8:22, "in scntentia"). In principio huius euangelii notandum secundum Jeronimum . . .-. . . longior est terra mensura eius et lacior mari. Ff. 58va–65vb.

10. T15. *Simile est regnum caelorum homini qui seminavit bonum semen in agro suo,* etc. (Matt 13:24). Istam parabolam de seminante exponit ipsemet Christus . . .-. . . in horreum Christi, idest in celum empireum. Quo nos . . . Ff. 66ra–71vb.

11. T16. *Simile est regnum caelorum homini patrifamilias qui exiit primo mane conducere operarios in vineam suam* (Matt 20:1). In hac parabola a Saluatore ad nostram informacionem prolata sex se offereunt intellectui breuiter declaranda . . .-. . . leticiam operis in peccati satisfaccionem. Ff. 71vb–78va.

12. T17. *Cum turba plurima convenirent et de civitatibus properarent ad Iesum,* etc. (Luke 8:4). Pro declaracione huius euangelii notandum primo quod sicut ex graciositate . . .-. . . si fructum fecisset de prima. Ff. 78va–89ra.

13. T18. *Adsumpsit Iesus duodecim discipulos,* etc. (Luke 18:31). Sicut dicit Gregorius in omelia: Redemptor noster preuidens ex passione sua . . .-. . . in illo nullo modo augetur ingrato. Ff. 89ra–98vb.

14. T19. *Ductus est Iesus in desertum* (Matt 4:1). Tria sunt circa que versatur intencio predicatoris: primum vt informet peccatores . . .-. . . post suam quadragesimam celebratam. Ff. 98vb–106vb.

15. T20. *Egressus Iesus secessit in partes Tyri et Sidonis* (Matt 15:21). Reprobato errore Phariseorum qui discipulos Christi increpabant . . .-. . . ad modum cere se a Christo duci permisit. Ff. 106vb–112rb.

16. T21. *Erat Iesus eiciens daemonium, et illud erat mutum* (Luke 11:14). Secundum Januensem, quia diabolus in sacro tempore quadragesimali non desinit . . .-. . . graciam videlicet in presenti et gloriam in futuro. Ad quam . . . Ff. 112va–121rb.

17. T22. *Abiit Iesus trans mare Galilaeae quod est Tiberiadis*, etc. (John 6:1). In principio huius euangelii notandum primo quod miraculum in hoc euangelio recitatum . . .-. . . flectere vt moueat ad agendum. Ff. 121rb–128ra.

18. T23. *Quis ex vobis arguet me de peccato*, etc. (John 8:46). In principio hic notandum secundum Ianuensem quod dominica in qua legitur hoc euangelium . . .-. . . tollat crucem et sequatur me. Ff. 128ra–138ra.

19. T28. *Maria Magdalene et Maria Iacobi et Salome emerunt aromata*, etc. (Mark 16:1). In processu huius euangelii sunt quatuor in grosso consideranda . . .-. . . surgens Christus mane prima sabbati. Ff. 138ra–147rb.

20. T28/2. *Surrexit Dominus vere et apparuit* (Luke 24:13). In principio huius sermonis notandum secundum Lincolniensem *Dicto* 20 . . .-. . . surrexit Dominus vere et apparuit. Ff. 147rb–157rb.

21. T29. *Cum esset sero die illa una sabbatorum et fores essent clausae*, etc. (John 20:19). Pro intellectu istius euangelii hic in principio notandum secundum quemdam postillatorem . . .-. . . qui creditis in nomine Filii Dei. Ad hanc vitam . . . Ff. 157rb–163vb.

22. T30. *Ego sum pastor bonus*, etc. (John 10:11). In principio huius\euangelii/ notari expedit, cum hoc euangelium . . .-. . . in pascuis vberrimis pascam eas. Et in hiis pascuis nos pasci . . . Ff. 163vb–171ra.

23. T31. *Modicum et non videbitis me, et iterum modicum et videbitis*, etc. (John 16:16). Ius vere amicicie satis dictat quod ab amicis quasi inseparabile est . . .- . . . per processum de manifestacione post hanc vitam, etc. Ff. 171ra–177va.

24. T32. *Vado ad eum qui me misit, et nemo ex vobis interrogat me quo vadis*, etc. (John 16:5). Solent homines peregrinaturi predicere familie sue . . .- . . . eadem sunt Patris et Filii et Spiritus Sancti. Ff. 177va–185ra.

25. T33. *Amen, amen, dico vobis, si quid petieritis Patrem in nomine meo, dabit vobis* (John 16:23). Secundum Januensem, si quis in curia alicuius

imperatoris haberet aliquem sapientem aduocatum . . .-. . . Deus a Deo, manens ab inmutabili et semper permanente, etc. Ff. 185ra–191ra.

26. T37. *Cum venerit paracletus quem ego mittam vobis*, etc. (John 15:26). In euangelio isto recolit Ecclesia hac dominica specialem promissionem . . .- . . . confitentur enim se nosce Deum, factis autem negant. Ff. 191ra–195va.

27. T39. *Si quis diligit me, sermonem meum servabit* (John 14:23). In hac dominica recolit Ecclesia in euangelio illam habundantem et excellentem donacionem Spiritus Sancti . . .-. . . vt nos efficeremur iusticia in ipso, etc. Ff. 195va–226va.

28. T40. *Erat homo ex Pharisaeis Nicodemus nomine*, etc. (John 3:1). In principio huius euangelii est notandum quod in hoc euangelio, quod legitur in festo beatissime Trinitatis, quelibet persona . . .-. . . intelligi de fide que per dileccionem operatur. Ff. 206va–226va.

29. T42. *Homo quidam erat dives*, etc. (Luke 16:19). In processu Luce precedente hoc euangelium monuit Dominus ad cauendum malum pene . . .-. . . sufficit intueri rerum exitus prudencia metitur. Ff. 226va–236ra.

30. T43. *Homo quidam fecit cenam magnam*, etc. (Luke 14:16). In hac parabola Saluatoris, in qua instruit Dominus penitenciam inchoandam . . .-. . . erit plena completo numero electorum. De quo numero . . . Ff. 236ra–244rb.

31. T44. *Erant adpropinquantes ad Iesum publicani et peccatores* (Luke 15:1). In presenti euangelio quatuor occurrunt principaliter declaranda . . .-. . . facite dignos fructus penitencie, etc. Ff. 244rb–251rb.

32. T45. *Estote misericordes, sicut Pater vester misericors est* (Luke 6:36). In principio huius euangelii hic notandum quod quamuis Deus sit omnipotens . . .- . . . cum baculo viam prius palpat. Ff. 251rb–261va.

33. T46. *Cum turbae irruerent in Iesum* (Luke 5:1). Secundum Crisostomum super Mattheum *Opere imperfecto* omelia 29, signum studiosi agricole est messis fecunda . . .-. . . quoniam ipsi consolabuntur. Ad hanc consolacionem . . . Ff. 261va–273vb.

34. T47. *Nisi abundaverit iustitia vestra plus quam Scribarum et Pharisaeorum, non intrabitis in regnum caelorum* (Matt 5:20). Secundum Ianuensem solent magistri scolarum, potissime gramaticalium, tres ordines scolarium optinere . . .-. . . redde ei que abstulisti. Ff. 273vb–283rb.

35. T48. *Cum turba plurima esset cum Iesu*, etc. (Matt 8:1 and Matt 15:). Recolit Ecclesia in hodierno euangelio vnum de conuiuiis solempnibus a Saluatore in hoc mundo factis . . .-. . . vel temporaliter temporalia multiplicando. Ff. 283rb–289vb.

36. T49. *Attendite a falsis prophetis qui veniunt ad vos,* etc. (Matt 7:15). Cum secundum Bernardum *Super Psalmum Qui habitat,* in sentencia, quatuor sunt impedimenta Ecclesie . . .-. . . non intrabit in regnum celorum. Ff. 289vb–297vb.

37. T50. *Homo quidam erat dives,* etc. (Luke 16:1). In hac parabola multiplicis edificacionis spiritualis nobis materia ministratur . . .-. . . magis proprie benefacit bono quam malo. Ff. 298ra–301vb.

38. T51. *Cum adpropinquasset Iesus, videns civitatem,* etc. (Luke 19:41). In hoc euangelio de clemencia Saluatoris . . .-. . . erat cotidie docens in templo. Ff. 301vb–304vb.

39. T52. *Dixit Iesus ad quosdam,* etc. (Luke 18:9). Bernardus: Quoniam fundamentum omnem virtutem supportans et munimentum . . .-. . . in gloria videlicet sempiterna. Ad quam . . . Ff. 304vb–308va.

40. T53 "Dominica 12 post Trinitatem" at head and top. *Exiens Iesus de finibus Tyri, etc.* (Mark 7:31). In euangelio isto, quod de curacione surdi et muti agit secundum sensum literalem . . .-. . . mutos, claudos, et cecos curauit, etc. Ff. 308va–312ra.

41. T54. *Beati oculi qui vident,* etc. (Luke 10:23). In processu huius euangelii commendat triplicem virtutem . . .-. . . quid enim ad infirmum de cantu medici, etc. Ff. 312ra–317rb.

42. T55. *Cum iret Iesus in Ierusalem,* etc. (Luke 17:11). Recolit Ecclesia in presenti euangelio vnum de miraculis . . .-. . . iam in spe, tandem in re. Ff. 317rb–322ra.

43. T57. *Ibat Iesus in civitatem quae vocatur Naim,* etc. (Luke 17:11). Pro huius euangelii intellectu sciendum quod inter omnia miracula a Christo humanitus perpetrata . . .-. . . quod spiritualiter resuscitati sumus, etc. Ff. 322ra–319vb [! medieval foliation: 322(and 313 crossed out)–325, 317–319].

44. T56. *Nemo potest duobus dominis servire,* etc. (Matt 6:24 et Luke 12). Reuerendi, in processu euangelii Mathei paulo supra quam ponitur hoc euangelium prohibet Christus in terra thesaurizare . . .-. . . pereunt afflictione pessima, etc. Ff. 319vb–327rb.

45. T58. *Cum intraret Iesus in domum cuiusdam principis Pharisaeorum sabbato manducare panem,* etc. (Luke 14:1). In processu huius euangelii, preter sensum literalem qui in suis locis breuiter declarabitur, duo principaliter sunt attendenda . . .-. . . amice, ascende superius. Quo ascendere . . . Ff. 327rb–333ra.

46. T59. *Audientes Pharisaei quod Iesus silentium inposuisset Sadducaeis,* etc. (Matt 22:34). Sicut dicitur in historia, tres erant secte inter Iudeos ab

aliis differentes . . .-. . . sed difficile posse quiescere, etc. Ff. 333ra–339ra.

47. T60. *Ascendens Iesus in naviculam*, etc. (Mark 2, Luke 5, and Matt 9:1). Secundum sentenciam Januensis sermone 1, Deus in principio omnia creauerat satis munda . . .-. . . in stupencia corda conuertuntur. Ff. 339ra–344va.

48. T61. *Videte, fratres, quomodo caute ambuletis*, etc. (Eph 5:15). Secundum Glosam videre est diligenter considerare et ambulare . . .-. . . vt dictum est prohibitum est insipiencia. Ff. 344va–351ra.

49. T61. *Simile est regnum caelorum homini regi qui fecit nuptias filio suo* (Matt 22:2). Secundum Januensem, quia sumus sensibilibus assueti . . .-. . . per caritatem est electa. Ff. 351ra–357vb.

50. T62. *Erat quidam regulus, cuius filius infirmabatur*, etc. (John 4:46). Sicut dicit Theophilus, iste regulus interfuit miraculo facto . . .-. . . contra illos qui sunt in purgatorio. Ad quam vitam . . . Ff. 357vb–365va.

51. T63. *Simile est regnum caelorum homini regi qui voluit rationem ponere cum servis suis* (Matt 18:23). Reuerendi, duo sunt cirac que racionalis creature versari debet intencio . . .-. . . eternaliter premiabit. Sic ergo offensas dimittere . . . Ff. 365va–370rb.

52. T64. *Abeuntes Pharisaei consilium inierunt ut caperent Iesum in sermone*, etc. (Matt 22:15, Mark 12, and Luke 20). Eo tempore quo Cesar Augustus vniuersum mundum describi fecit . . .-. . . factus est omnius reus. Ff. 370rb–375rb.

53. T65. *Loquente Iesu ad turbas ecce princeps unus*, etc. (Matt 9:18, Luke 8, and Mark 5). Agitur in hoc euangelio de Christo lapide angulari . . .-. . . mordent enim animum cure dum inquietant. Ff. 375rb–380va.

RY – Robert Rypon, *Sermones*: London, British Library, MS Harley 4894

1. T01. *Ecce rex tuus venit tibi* (Matt 21:5, from and Zach 9:9). Ista verba euangelii et prophete triplici de causa in hac prima aduentus dominica possunt capi . . .-. . . Omnis qui videt Filium et credit in eum habet vitam eternam. Ad quam . . . Ff. 1–4.

2. T04. *Tu quis es?* (John 1:22). Ista fuerunt Phariseorum missorum a Iudeis ad Iohannem Baptistam . . .-. . . in collibus supremis, vbi leticia et pax eterna. Ad quam . . . Ff. 4–6v.

3. T11. *Notas facite in populis adinventiones* (Isa 12:4). Epistula hodierna secundum morem Ecclesie cotatur leccio Ysaie, que tamen epistula non habetur

ad verba in aliquo capitulo Ysaie . . .-. . . et spem sui amoris reciproci cum ipso eternaliter conuiuendi. Quod . . . Ff. 6v–9.

4. T19. *Ne in vacuum gratiam Dei recipiatis* (2 Cor 6:1). Gracia Dei capitur hic pro habilitate ad regnum celorum . . .-. . . Vnde scribitur in Psalmo: Graciam et gloriam dabit Dominus. Quam . . . Ff. 9–12.

5. T19. *Ne in vacuum gratiam Dei recipiatis* (2 Cor 6:1). Omne donum datur principaliter propter duo . . .-. . . scilicet gracia consummante, que est vita eterna. Quam . . . Ff. 12v–17.

6. T19. *Tempore accepto audivi te* (2 Cor 6:2). Ista verba capit Apostolus a propheta Ysaie 49 . . .-. . . et dabit Dominus nobis mercedem in tempore suo. Quam mercedem, etc. Ff. 17–22.

7. T19. *In die salutis adiuvi te* (2 Cor 6:2 and Isa 49). Apostolus capit ista verba a propheta Ysaie 49, que in persona Patris de Filio suo pro salute humani generis incarnando prophetauit . . .-. . . operatus est salutem hic in presenti et anime et corporis pro perpetuo. Quam . . . Ff. 22–25v.

8. T19. *Mitte te deorsum* (Matt 4:6). Ista sunt verba scripture sacre in euangelio hodierno, que verba dixit diabolus Christo Iesu . . .-. . . Hic inquit est verus Deus et vita eterna. Ad quam . . . Ff. 25v–31.

9. T19. *Dominum Deum tuum adorabis* (Matt 4:10). Ista verba euangelica allegauit Christus diabolo ipsum temptanti . . .-. . . que debentur humanitati Christi. Ff. 31–35.

10. T19. *Quasi morientes et ecce vivimus* (2 Cor 6:9). Secundum beatum Gregorium omelia 17 libri 1, vita mortalis est prolixitas mortis . . .-. . . verum eciam vita gracie et vita glorie eternaliter conuiuemus. Quod . . . Ff. 35–38.

11. T19. *Quasi morientes et ecce vivimus* (2 Cor 6:9). Aliud est hominem esse morientem et aliud esse mortuum . . .-. . . videlicet hic vita gracie in presenti et vita glorie perpetue post decessum. Ff. 38–41v.

12. T19. *Reliquit eum diabolus* (Matt 4:11). Omnis Christianus habet hoc nomen a Christo . . .-. . . et in fine vite animas suscipiendo et ad celestia deportando. Quod . . . Ff. 41v–45v.

13. T19. *Reliquit eum,* diabolus suple (Matt 4:11). Tria sunt que faciunt diabolum relinquere Christum . . . .-. . . et tandem deducent in gaudium sempiternum. Ff. 46–50.

14. T19. *Accesserunt angeli et ministrabant ei,* suple Christo (Matt 4:11). Memorat processus euangelii vbi thema quomodo Christus Iesus ductus est a Spiritu, scilicet Sancto . . . .-. . . Mali ad penam, boni ad gloriam sempiternam. Quam, etc. Ff. 50v–52v.

15. T19. *Exhibeamus nosmetipsos sicut Dei ministros* (2 Cor 6:4). Queri potest quare Apostolus interponit hoc aduerbium similitudinis sicut . . .-. . . Intra in gaudium Domini tui. Quod . . . Ff. 52v–56.

16. T20. *Accepistis a nobis quomodo vos oporteat ambulare* (1 Thess 4:1). Apostolus dicit hec verba ad literam de se ipso . . .-. . . regio viuorum est paradisus celestis. Ad quam, etc. Ff. 56–60v.

17. T20. *Vocavit nos Deus in sanctificationem*, idest, ut sancte vivamus (1 Thess 4:7). Ista verba dicit Apostolus de seipso et aliis Christianis quos Dominus . . .-. . . vt puri et inmaculati laudemus in gaudio sine fine. Ad quod . . . Ff. 60v–65v.

18. T20. *Scitis quae praecepta dederim vobis* (1 Thess 4:2). Apostolus inter cetera dedit Thessalonicensibus ista precepta . . .-. . . qui te inmitantur in terra, etc., scilicet viuencium. Quam terram, etc. Ff. 65v–69.

19. T20. *Sic et ambuletis ut abundetis magis* (1 Thess 4:1). In ambulacione corporali, precipue in via tenebrosa diuerticulis plena . . . .-. . . que valet centuplum omnibus bonis corporalibus huius mundi. Quas graciam et vitam . . . Ff. 69–72v.

20. T20. *Fiat tibi sicut vis* (Matt 15:28). Hec sunt verba Christi dicta ad mulierem gentilem egressum de partibus Tiri et Sydonis . . .-. . . beatitudo finis vltimus voluntatis, scilicet gloria sempiterna. Quam, etc. Ff. 73–75.

21. T20. *Gentes ignorant Deum* (1 Thess 4:5). Beatus Paulus apostolus in epistula vbi thema ipsos Thessalonicenses isto modo fuerat allocutus . . .-. . . Hic est verus Deus et vita eterna. Quam nobis. Ff. 75–79.

22. T20. *Vocavit nos Deus in sanctificationem* (1 Thess 4:7). Consuetudo est predicatorum et auditorum verbi Dei in principio sermonum diuinum auxilium implorare . . .-. . . in conspectu Dei cuntis diebus, idest in sanctificacione superna sine fine. Ad quam . . . Ff. 79v–83v.

23. T20. *Mulier egressa clamavit* (Matt 15:22). Tria sunt necessaria clamanti ad hoc quod bene audiatur . . .-. . . Penitenciam agite et appropinquabit regnum celorum. Ad quod . . . Ff. 83v–86v.

24. T20. *Mulier erat in civitate peccatrix* (Luke 7:37). Ista verba scribuntur in euangelio sancti Luce quod legitur isto die in sacra Ecclesia, et dicuntur specialiter de Maria Magadalena . . .-. . . sanitas sine infirmitate. Ad quod gaudium . . . Ff. 86v–89v.

25. T21. *Omnis inmunditia nec nominetur in vobis* (Eph 5:3). Sanctus Iacobus apostolus in epistula sua capitulo 1 auditores verbi Dei instruit . . .-. . . Igitur penitenciam agite et appropinquabit regnum celorum. Ad quod . . . Ff. 89v–92.

26. T21. *Ut filii lucis ambulate* (Eph 5:8). Carissimi, reperio tres proprietates in luce . . .-. . . et habet totam hereditatem Patris sui, regnum scilicet celorum. Ad quod . . . Ff. 92–96v.

27. T21. *Locutus est mutus* (Luke 11:14). Sanctus Paulus apostolus Corinthiorum 14 tractat de duobus modis loquendi . . .-. . . vt sic a luce boni operis ad lucem que Deus est transeatis. Amen. Ff. 96v–101.

28. T21. *Erat Iesus eiciens daemonium* (Luke 11:14). Ista verba mediante hac coniunccione et copulantur processui euangelii precedenti . . .-. . . et septem pro anima cum confessione laudis diuine ad veram beatitudinem pertinente. Quam . . . Ff. 101–106v.

29. T22. *Abraham duos filios habuit* (Gal 4:22). Ista verba sunt principium epistule, in quibus includitur totus processus epistule . . .-. . . coheredes <Christi> autem, quia cum ipso corregnabimus in gloria. Quod . . . Ff. 106v–110v.

30. T22. *Hierusalem libera est* (Gal 4:26). Capio ista verba duplici de causa: primo quia nomen Ierusalem notat michi historiam signantem totum tempus a Septuagesima . . .-. . . nouissima cumulum iocunditatis. Ad quam . . . Ff. 110v–114.

31. T22. *Impleti sunt* (John 6:12). Hec verba includunt miraculum factum a Christo quod recitatur in euangelio hodierno . . .-. . . secundum diuicias suas in gloria in Christo Iesu. Quam . . . Ff. 114–119v.

32. T23. *Sanguis inquinatos sanctificat* (Hebr 9:13). Dicit Iohannes in prima epistula sua, capitulo 5, quod tres sunt . . .-. . . in quam tanquam in sancta sanctorum introibimus ad gloriam perpetuo duraturam. Quam, etc. Ff. 119v–124.

33. T24. *Processerunt ei obviam* (John 12:13). Gaudium et dolor, gaudium et dolor, et tercio gaudium et dolor in verbis nostri thematis includuntur . . .- . . . et ad gaudium maximum a parte iustorum. Quod . . . Ff. 124–128v.

34. T24. *Quid faciam de Iesu?* (Matt 27:22). Ista verba fuerunt Pilati, qui adiudicauit Iesum cruci . . .-. . . vt glorificemur, videlicet cum eo in gloria sempiterna. Ad quam . . . Ff. 129–133v.

35. T28. *Pascha nostrum immolatus est Christus* (1 Cor 5:7). De duplici immolacione seu oblacione legitur in scriptura . . .-. . . si quis habuerit, viuet in ea vita gracie in presenti et glorie in futuro. Ad quam, etc. Ff. 133v–138v.

36. T28. *Epulemur* (1 Cor 5:8). Cibus de quo fiet sermo non est tantum corporalis set pocius spiritualis . . .-. . . qui de vno pane et de vno calice participamus. Quem panem, etc. Ff. 138v–143v.

37. T34. *Obsecro orationes fieri pro omnibus hominibus* (1 Tim 2:1). Apostolus Paulus in epistula hodierna precipit generaliter . . .-. . . omnia impetrantur bona tam presentis vite necessaria quam future. Quam . . . Ff. 144–146v.

38. T34. *Quis ex vobis homo* (Matt 7:9). Scitis, karissimi, quod huc conuenimus ad orandum principaliter pro remisione peccatorum . . .-. . . et tandem bona glorie quoad hominem compositum. Que . . . Ff. 146v–149.

39. T34. *Multum valet deprecatio iusti assidua* (James 5:16). Beatus Gregorius in suis *Moralibus* <inquit>: Quanto grauiori carnalium tumultu premimur . . .-. . . a pio iudice mercedem consequetur, suple leticiam sempiternam. Quam . . . Ff. 149–152.

40. T34. *Dabit spiritum bonum petentibus se* (Luke 11:13). Ista sunt verba euangeliste de Deo Patre, que inducit . . .-. . . et heredes, vt hereditatem possideamus sanctuarium Dei. Quod . . . Ff. 152–155.

41. T34. *Pueri mei mecum sunt in cubili* (Luke 11:7). Gorham super Lucam exponit clare euangelium vbi thema . . .-. . . et letabuntur in cubilibus suis, idest in requie sempiterna. Quam . . . Ff. 155–157v.

42. T34. *Pueri mei mecum sunt in cubili* (Luke 11:7). Scitis quod huc venimus processionaliter ad orandum. Ideo super materiam oracionis sunt quatuor questiones vestre audiencie declaranda [!] . . .-. . . in cubilibus suis, vbi Christus dicet eternaliter Pueri mei, etc. Ad quam. Ff. 157v–160v.

43. T40. *Homo venit ad Iesum nocte* (John 3:2). In hiis verbis breuiter quantum ad meum propositum cerno duo . . .-. . . et introibimus in tabernacula sempiterna. Ff. 160v–169.

44. T50. *Redde rationem vilicationis tuae* (Luke 16:2). Dicunt doctores super euangelio vbi thema quod Dominus per parabolam villici excitauit suos apostolos . . .-. . . et corona iusticie in seculum seculi, scilicet imperpetuum. Quam . . . Ff. 169–172.

45. S44. *Erat Iohannes* (John 1:28). Vbicumque dicuntur ista verba in scriptura sacra, notantur de sancto Iohanne Baptista cum certis addicionibus quas recitabo posterius in processu . . .-. . . et tunc dicetur de te Fuit homo missus, etc. Ff. 172–174v.

46. S49. *Fortitudo et decor indumentum eius* (Prov 31:25). Sanctus Beda dicit super hunc textum quod hec verba concordant in sentencia cum illis verbis dictis de Domino . . .-. . . finaliter perseuerando et tunc regna eternaliter iubilando. Quod . . . Ff. 174v–177v.

47. S49. *Confidit in ea cor viri sui* (Prov 31:11). Salamon in suis Prouerbiis vbi thema comparat Ecclesiam mulieri forti . . .-. . . et possidebit montem sanctum meum, scilicet celum, etc. Ff. 177v–180.

48. S49. *Mulier erat in civitate peccatrix* (Luke 7:37). Ista verba ad literam dixit sanctus Lucas de beata Maria Magdalena, de qua memorat Ecclesia . . .- . . . in plenam remissionem suorum omnium peccatorum. Quam . . . Ff. 180v–182v.

49. S54a. *In brevi explevit tempora multa* (Wisd 4:13). Dicit commentator *Phisicorum*, et experiencia docet idem, quod ille [!] qui facit opus delectabile apparet tempus breue . . .-. . . et sublimis erit valde cum choris angelorum in celesti gloria sine fine. Ad quam, etc. Ff. 183–186.

50. S54a. *Hic homo coepit aedificare* (Luke 14:30). Sanctus Lucas in isto euangelio loquitur secundum doctores spiritualiter de edificacione sancte conuersacionis . . .-. . . gradus hominum predicti in habitaculum Dei in Spiritu Sancto, etc. Ff. 186–190.

51. S54a. *Aetas senectutis vita inmaculata* (Wisd 4:9). In istis verbis duo video necessaria nedum predicatoribus set auditoribus verbi Dei . . .-. . . Iocunditas enim cordis vita hominis, Ecclesiastici 30. Quam . . . Ff. 190–192v.

52. C14. *Dicite: Pax huic domui* (Luke 10:5). Secundum Glosam illius textus Apostoli Thimothei 2, Obsecro primum omnium fieri obsecraciones . . .- . . . dicitur congrue habere plenitudinem realem cum dicere [?] Spiritus Sancti. Quam pacis plenitudinem . . . Ff. 193–195v.

53. C14. *Ite* (Luke 10:3). Secundum processum euangelii vbi thema Saluator noster Christus Iesus mittens 72 discipulos verbum Dei predicaturos . . .- . . . mercedem dispensacionis a Domino, scilicet gloriam in futuro. Quam gloriam . . . Ff. 195v–198v.

54. C14. *In eadem domo manete* (Luke 10:7). De domo triplici reperio in scriptura . . .-. . . vt amicos in domo supernaturalis patrie, vbi viuit cum Patre et Filio sine fine. Amen. Ff. 198v–202.

55. C14. *Operarii autem pauci* (Luke 10:2). Christus Iesus in euangelio vbi thema 72 discipulis indicens officium predicandi . . .-. . . premium superadditum pro meritis subditorum nostrorum finaliter saluatorum. Quod premium . . . Ff. 202–205.

56. C14. *Dignus est operarius mercede* (Luke 10:7). Cum secundum doctores hec verba dicantur ad literam de sacerdotibus et curatis in vinea Domini operantibus . . .-. . . eciam est in perpetua largitate, quia multa. Quam mercedem, etc. Ff. 205–208v.

57. C14. *Misit illos binos* (Luke 10:1). Pro processu collacionis est notandum quod hec tria, scilicet dignissima auctoritas, specialissima personalitas, et gratissima societas, ostendunt . . .-. . . et colligit fructum meritorum, scilicet premium perpetuo duraturum. Quod nobis, etc. Ff. 208v–212.

58. C14. *Pax vestra ad vos revertetur* (Luke 10:6). Christus Iesus 72 discipulos predicare missurus ad thematis propositum eis dixit . . .-. . . et aspectus mentis informabitur tocius pulcritudinis perpetua visione. Quam visionem, etc. Ff. 212–214v.

59. C14. *Ecce ego mitto vos* (Luke 10:3). Pro fundamento processus breuiter est notandum quod hoc aduerbium ecce in scriptura sacra, sicut et hoc pronomen ego, tripliciter est acceptum . . .-. . . scilicet sudario, orario, et planeta, idest manipulo, stola, et casula. Ff. 214v–216v, inc.

S – Oxford, Balliol College, MS 149

1. T26*. *Christus passus est, vobis relinquens exemplum vt sequamini* (1 Peter 2:21). Anglice sic: Crist in hys passion reliquit vobis quomodo schil doun, etc. Quamuis hec verba dicantur generaliter Christianis omnibus . . .-. . . poteris vendicare hereditatem, scilicet regnum celorum. Quod . . . Ff. 1–15v. Also H-25, W-6, Z-19, and Oxford Christ Church 91, f. 122ra. Edited from H-25 in Johnson, "Preaching the Passion," pp. 178–287.

2. T01/7. *Factum est verbum Domini super Iohannem* (Luke 3:2). Iohannes euangelista Filium Deum Christum comparat verbo . . .-. . . hos et omnes tales emendet Dominus Iesus. Qui . . . Ff. 15v–19v.

3. T41/5. *Memoriam fecit mirabilium suorum misericors Deus: Escam* (Ps 110:4–5). Secundum sanctos Gregorium, Augustinum, et alios doctores, verbum comparatur cibo . . .-. . . qui edit me non esuriet. Vt finaliter saturemur . . . Ff. 19v–23. Also W-7.

4. T28. *Tene quod habes* (Rev 3:11). Reuerendi mei, sicut scribit Dyascorides libro 2, capitulo 97, in India inferiori est arbor cuius fructus tam intus quam extra est rubeus . . .-. . . quia ipse est a leder qui te ducet ad regnum suum þat is endles. Quo . . . Ff. 23–25v. Also B/2-57 and E-12

5. T28. *Gaudere oportet, quia frater tuus revixit* (Luke 15:32). þe by-ouys to be glad and fayne, for þi broþer is on liue agayne. Sicut dicit scriptura sacra, Christus est frater noster . . .-. . . qui manducat me, ipse viuet propter me. Quam vitam . . . Ff. 25v–28.

6. ?. *Ministri Christi sunt* (2 Cor 11:23). Secundum beatum Bernardum quatuor sunt quibus seruitur in hoc mundo: mundus, caro, demon, et Deus . . .-. . . Pater meus qui est in celis. Ad quos celos . . . Ff. 28–31. Also W-10/32.

7. T26*. *Amore langueo* (Cant 2:5). Prolatiue potest dici sic: Karissimi, sicut manifeste videntes . . .-. . . grant vs þi blisse wyþoute ende. Ad quam . . . Ff. 31–38v. Also B/2-12, T-7, and Dublin Trinity College 277. Edited in Wenzel, *Macaronic*, pp. 212–267.

8. T24. *Ite, solvite, et adducite* (Matt 21:2). In hiis verbis exprimit triplex misterium apostolorum prelatorum . . .-. . . finaliter saluos faciat Christus ipse, qui . . . Ff. 38v, 51r–v, 40–41, with renvoi.

9. T28. *Panis cor hominis confirmet* (Ps 103:15). Inter ceteras peticiones quas posuit Dominus in oracione dominica . . .-. . . quoniam digni sunt habiti sunt pro nomine, etc. Amen. Amen. Ff. 41–43v, 56r–v, with renvoi.

10. T19. *Illi soli servies* (Matt 4:10, from Deut 6:13). Carissimi mei, esset voluntas mea hac vice aliquem sermonem vobis dicere ad presens ad honorem Dei . . . Quilibet homo in toto mundo deberet . . .-. . . illuc et minister meus erit, Iohannis 12, in [*ms* et] gloria eterna. Ad quam gloriam . . . Ff. 45–46.

11. T01. *Parate viam Domini* (Mark 1:3). Sicut in primo parente per diabolum via nobis patuit ad mortem . . .-. . . \graciam/ in presenti et gloriam in futuro. Quam . . . Ff. 46–50v. Also X-5.

12. T18/4. *Convertimini ad me in toto corde vestro* (Joel 2:12). Quia totaliter auerti a Deo est dampnabile, et solum parcialiter reuerti ad Deum est culpabile . . .-. . . securissime tenet Deum. Et sic nos Deum querere . . . Ff. 50v, 39r–v, 52r–v, with renvoi.

13. T18/4*. *Homo in cinerem revertetur* (Job 34:15). Reuerendi patres, ex natura corumptiua racione regulata, vt homo . . .-. . . corpus terre et animam celo. Ad quod . . . Ff. 52v–55.

14. ?. *Cum fortis armatus custodit atrium suum, in pace sunt omnia quae possidet* (Luke 11:21). Anglice: Wyle the stronge yarmyd keputh his holde or his halle . . . Ad hoc quod firma sit custodia . . .-. . . est michi reposita corona iusticie quam etc. Ad quam . . . Ff. 55r–v, 44r–v, 57–59, with renvoi.

15. ?. *Suscitare super pastorem meum* (Zech 13:7). Patris [!] mei, reuerendi domini, et magistri, iuxta sentenciam Saluatoris michi deccorantis imperantis n[u]nc predicator habeo existere veritatis . . .-. . . viri beatitudinis misericordiam consequentur. Quam misericordiam . . . Ff. 59–63. Johannes de Scrata, OFM.

16. T21. *Ambulate in dilectione sicut Christus dilexit* (Eph 5:2). Karissimi, inuenio quod tria modernis temporibus diliguntur a multis . . .-. . . gaudium habebimus quod suis dilectoribus ordinauit. Ad quod . . . Ff. 65v–72. Also W-9/31.

17. ?. *Ambulate in dilectione* (Eph 5:2). Sicut Augustinus in *Epistula ad Mecedones* [!], bonos vel malos mores non faciunt nisi boni et mali amores . . .-. . . si vultis venire ad regnum celeste, Ambulate in dileccione. Quam dileccionem . . . Ff. 72–75. Also CA/2-7.

18. ?. *Exiit qui seminat seminare semen suum*, etc. (Luke 8:5 and Matt 13:3). Verba ista sunt bene exposita a Christo Saluatore nostro et ideo non indigent nostra. . . .-. . . benedictus fructus ventris tui. Quem fructum . . . Ff. 75v–77.

19. T26*. *Quare rubrum est indumentum tuum?* (Isa 63:2). Secundum sentenciam doctorum hec fuit questio angelorum in die Assencionis Domini, et erit questio iudicandorum in die finalis iudicii . . .-. . . sigillum infixum plaga lateris. Ff. 77v–83v, 77, inc?. Chambron. Also A-35, P2–71, Z-20, and CUL Ee.6.27, f. 73. Shorter version in S-20.

20. T26. *Quare rubrum est vestimentum tuum?* (Isa 63:2). Secundum sentenciam doctorum hec fuit questio angelorum in Ascensione \uel in die Ascencionis/ Domini. Et erit questio iudicandorum in die iudicii <finalis> . . .-. . . vt sui essemus et cum eo in perpetuum re[ma]naremus. Quod . . . Ff. 84–86v. Chambron. Short version of S-19. Also Padua-48. Edited in Johnson, "Preaching the Passion," pp. 288–322.

21. T15 / T16 / T62. *Simile est regnum caelorum homini* (Matt 13:24; 20:1; and 18:23). Inuenio quod regnum celorum aliquando vocatur sancta Ecclesia . . .-. . . usque ad messem, idest consummacionem seculi. Et tunc agricola. Ff. 86v–87, inc.

22. ?. [*Miserere mei*, beginning missing] (?). Supra caput scripsit: Hic est deus pietatis et misericordie . . .-. . . qui proximo misericors est, beatus erit. Quam beatitudinem . . . Ff. 87–90, acephalous.

23. T21. *Revertar in domum meam unde exivi* (Luke 11:24). Karissimi, presenti dominica de muto a demonio vexato tractatur, ad designandum duplicem effectum predicandi . . .-. . . et sic sponsabit te Christus in vita eterna. Quam . . . Ff. 90–92v. Chambron. = Holcot sermon 65!

24. T10*. *Quaerite et invenietis* (Matt 7:7 and Luke 11:9). Hodie sancta mater Ecclesia recolit magos ab oriente uenisse et Christum natum diligenter inquisisse . . .-. . . et idcirco infatigabilis in nouitate perdat. Querite igitur . . . Ff. 219–220v.

SH – John Sheppey

For his various collections see Part One, section 2, pp. 26–28. Inventoried here are his own sermons as preserved in booklet 3 of Oxford, New College, MS 92 (medieval nos. 49–67). Occasions are given as indicated in rubrics or in the table, f. 40v.

1. T18/4. *Domine, parce populo tuo* (Joel 2:17).? . . .-. . . quod adipisci mereamur tuam gloriam in futuro. Quam . . . Ff. 139–141. Edited in Mifsud, "John Sheppey."

2. T25 (Rochester, 1343). *Dilexit nos* (John 4: and Rev 1). Karissimi, inter alia secreta que vidit beatus Iohannes ewangelista vidit bestiam . . .-. . . in remissionem peccatorum secundum diuicias glorie eius. Ad quam gloriam . . . Ff. 141v–144v. Edited in Mifsud, ibidem.

3. ?. *Exi cito*. [Illegible]. F. 145.

4. ?. *State*. In primo membro nota . . . F. 145.

5. ?. *Per Spiritum Sanctum optulit semetipsum immaculatum Deo* (Heb 9:14). In isto sermone . . . F. 145.

6. ?. *Estote factores verbi* (James 1:22).? F. 145.

7. ?. *Ambuletis digne Deo* (Col 1:10). Vbi nota tres vias . . . F. 145.

8. ?. *In te virtus* (Luke 1:35?). Vbi nota Beatam Virginem quomodo in ea sunt 4 virtutes . . . F. 145.

9. C21 ("In exequiis domini Nicholai Malameyn, 1349"). *Certamen forte dedit illi, ut vinceret* (Wis 10:12). Negocium non debet committi illi qui nescit nec potest ipsum ad finem debitum deducere . . .-. . . fortitudo sua, idest gaudium ipse. Quod . . . Ff. 148v–151.

10. C21 ("Iste sermo fuit ordinatus pro exequiis domine de Cobham, anno Christi 1344"). *Ecce ancilla Domini* (Luke 1:38). Tunc cognoscitur esse morigerata et obsequiosa ancilla . . .-. . . pro sua misericordia perducat eam ad gaudium sempiternum. Quod . . . Ff. 152–155. Edited in Mifsud, ibidem.

11. C18. ("In eleccione abbatisse"). *Electa ut sol* (Cant 6:9). In ewangelio Marci capitulo 3 legimus quod omne regnum in se diuisum desolabitur . . .-. . . augmentum gaudii vestri in hoc seculo et futuro. Quod . . . Ff. 155v–156. Edited in Mifsud, ibidem.

12. T18/4 (?, 1353/54). *Flebitis vos* (John 16:20). Karissimi, si inspiciamus generaliter ad totum genus humanum . . .-. . . sicud magister flet propter discipulum degradandum. Ff. 156v–159v, inc? Edited in Mifsud, ibidem.

13. C21 ("In exequiis Stephani"). *Stephanus plenus gratia et fortitudine* (Acts 6:8). Karissimi, debetis intelligere quod nullus . . .-. . .? Ff. 160–162. Edited in Mifsud, ibidem.

14. C21. *Ascendit super Cherubin et volavit* (Ps 17:10). Secundum sentenciam beati Gregorii 4 *Dyalogorum*, licet in vita eterna sit communis remuneracio bonorum . . .-. . . in tercio finale premium operacionis meritorie consummate. F. 164r–v, inc.

15. T41/5*. *Qui manducat hunc panem, vivet in eternum* (John 6:59). . . .-. . . ?.
Ff. 169v–?.

16. T33* (St. Paul's Cross, 1336). *Consideravit se et abiit* (James 1:24). Karissimi,
in loco et aere periculoso et sue complexioni contrario constitutus . . .-
. . . venite, benedicti Patris mei, percipite regnum. Ad quod . . . Ff. 173–176v.
Edited in Mifsud, ibidem.

17. S20 (St. Paul's Cross, 1337). *Vocavit eum de medio caliginis* (Exod 24:16). Si
quis teneret candelam accensam inter manus suas bene clausam . . .-. . . de
suis secretariis in gaudio perpetuo. Quod . . . Ff. 180, 177–178. Edited in
Mifsud, ibidem.

18. ?. *Esto firmus in via Domini et in veritate sensus tui, et prosequatur te verbum
pacis et iustitiae* (Sir 5:12). Trescher et tres redoubtie s' mons' de ourealme,
ad bien et sagement moustre . . .-. . . pur vous noz seignurs et profitable a
voz deus roialiues. Amen. Ff. 181–183. Probably not a sermon.

19. ?. *Spiritus veritatis docebit vos* (John 16:13). Ad sensum frequenter videmus
quod homines \vni/ domino seruientes . . .-. . . fulgeatis sicud \stelle/ in
perpetuas eternitates. Quo . . . Ff. 184v–187. Also Merton 248, f. 176rb.

T – Oxford, Magdalen College, MS 93 (Dygon)

The manuscript contains the following late-medieval sermons:

1. C21*. *Mortuus viuet* (John 11:25). Lincolniensis *Dicto* 25 dicit et ponit tres
mortes: corporis, anime, et gehenne . . .-. . . si mortuus fuerit viuet. Dic
hic narracionem Egesippi et ibi fac finem+. Ff. 130–132.

2. C21*. *Mortuus viuet* (John 11:25). Graciam Domini nostri Iesu Christi, etc.
Apostolus scribens 1 Ad Thimotheum 2.a. petit ante omnia fieri oraciones
et obsecraciones . . .-. . . non potest male mori qui bene vixit, et vix bene
moritur qui male vixerit. F. 136v.

3. S28. *Salutate Mariam* (Rom 16:6). Karissimi, in isto festo sacratissimo Deus
tria mirabilia fecit . . .-. . . et in hora mortis ad te nos suscipe. Amen. Ff.
140–143v.

4. S28. *Concipies et paries filium* (Luke 1:31). Karissimi, in omni actu tria
requiruntur, scilicet tempus, modus, et causa . . .-. . . quod filius et heres.
Quam hereditatem . . . Ff. 144–147.

5. T21*. *Ambulate* (Eph 5:2). Karissimi, homo existens de paupertate magna,
sequuntur eum multe miserie . . .-. . . qui timent Dominum, qui ambulant,
etc. Ff. 148–149.

6. ?. *Ecce morior, cum nihil horum fecerim* (Dan 13:43). Karissimi, in hiis verbis Christus pro nobis in cruce pendens ostendit se suis amicis conqueri . . .-. . . . per consequens heredes regni celorum. Quam hereditatem . . . Ff. 149–151.

7. T26*. *Amore langueo* (Cant 2:5). Probatiue [!] potest dici: Karissimi, sicut manifeste videtis, in isto themate non sunt nisi duo verba . . .-. . . graunte vs thy blis withouten ende. Ad quod . . . Ff. 152–157. Also B/2-12, S-7, and in Dublin Trinity College 277, p. 185; variant in O-31. Edited from S-7 in Wenzel, *Macaronic*, pp. 212–267.

8. ?. *Credite* (Mark 11:24). Gracia Domini nostri Iesu Christi, etc. Karissimi, si aliquis imperator vel rex mandaret populo cui preest legem . . .-. . . concipies in vtero et paries. Ff. 168–169, inc.

9. T60. *Ascendens Iesus in naviculam transfretauit . . . qui dedit potestatem talem hominibus?* (Matt 9:1–8; Mark 2; Luke 5). In isto euangelio declaratur nobis miraculum per quod Dominus noster Iesus Christus ostendit potenciam sue deitatis . . .-. . . duplicem curacionem, scilicet spiritualem et corporalem. Ff. 172–174, inc?

10. T01. *Rex tuus venit* (Matt 21:5). Primo est considerandum quid est quod Iesus appropinquans Ierosolimis . . .-. . . eum desuper sedere fecerunt. Ff. 174–175v. inc.

11. T14. [*Invicem diligatis*] (Rom 13:8). In epistula hodierna informat nos Apostolus vt diligamus, scribens Romanis. <Sed pro introduccione materie obsequentis> hic nota in principio quod Paulus in partibus Grecorum existens . . .-. . . debes Domino Deo tuo ministrare. F. 197.

U – London, London University, MS 657

Most if not all of sermons 4–31 also occur in Cambridge, Pembroke College, MS 200, and elsewhere; see discussion in Part One, section 38, p. 212.

1. T06*. *Gloria in excelsis Deo, et in terra pax hominibus bonae voluntatis* (Luke 2:14). Fratres karissimi, hodie recolit sancta Ecclesia prerogatiua gaudi . . .-. . . violenter attraxerat, sed idem homo ad illum se sponte contulerat. Hec ille. Pp. 227a–229b. Also A-32.

2. Co8. "De vna virgine" marg. *Domine Deus, liberasti me de perditione* (Sir 51:16). Sed ob processu huius thematis, sicut vos intelligetis, per tria precipue genera viciorum temptatur homo . . .-. . . et ita venietes ad regnum celeste. Quod . . . Pp. 229b–233a.

3. S86 or S50. ? (?). Karissimi, quod hoc silere non debemus quod laudabilis memorie Hugo Cliniacensis[!] abbas solet narrare . . .-. . . visit deuotus in seruicio dei cui sit laus. Amen. P. 234b.

4. T14*. *Secuti sunt discipuli eius eum* (Matt 8:23). Pro ingressu sermonis accipio illud Iohannis 8: Ego sum lux . . .-. . . per eum habetur gracia in presenti et gloria in futuro quam . . . Pp. 235a–238a.

5. T15. *Induite vos sicut electi Dei* (Col 3:12). Pro ingressu sermonis accipio illud Proverbiorum 30: Fortitudo et decor. . Vbi innuitur quod aliis vestimentis est induenda puella que debet alicui nobili desponsari . . .-. . . ecce habere Deum scilicet gloriam paradisi quam . . . Pp. 238a–240b.

6. T15. *Bonum semen seminasti in agro tuo* (Matt 13:27). Legantur remissiue et sunt verba Christi ad penitentem. Pro ingressu sermonis accipio illud Prouerbiorum 24: Diligenter excerce agrum tuum . . .-. . . confert in presenti graciam et gloriam in futuro. Quam . . . Pp. 240b–243a.

7. T16?. *Sic currite ut comprehendatis* (1 Cor 9:24). Pro ingressu sermonis accipio illud Psalmi: Sine iniquitate cucurri . . .-. . . in terra promissionis scilicet in celo per gloriam. Quam . . . Pp. 243b–245b.

8. T16*. *Ite et vos in vineam meam . . . vobis* (Matt 20:4). Pro ingressu sermonis accipio illud Zacharie 8, Vinea dabit fructum. . . .-. . . Dedit illis decem mnas, que possident in gloria. Quam . . . Pp. 245b–248a.

9. T18*. *Iesu, fili David, miserere mei* (Luke 18:38). Pro ingressu sermonis accipio illud Psalmi, Clamauit . . . Karissimi, homo per senectutem peccati perdit saporem . . .-. . . in presenti contulit graciam que disponit ad gloriam. Quam . . . Pp. 248a–251a.

10. T18/4. *Convertimini ad me in toto corde vestro* (Joel 2:12). Pro ingressu sermonis accipio illud Thobie 12, Conuertimini . . . Karissimi, dictum est quod Deus tenet archum paratum . . .-. . . gracie que disponit ad graciam et ad gloriam. Quam . . . Pp. 251a–253b.

11. T18/4. *Memor esto unde excideris, et age paenitentiam* (Rev 2:5). Pro ingressu sermonis accipio verbum dictum per Senecam quod est tale: Beneficiorum memoria labilis . . .-. . . de qua victoria recipiet penitens honorem in gloria. Quam . . . Pp. 253b–255b.

12. T19*. *Nunc dies salutis* (2 Cor 6:2). Pro ingressu sermonis accipio illud Iohannis 2: Conuertimini ad me . . .-. . . in Deum credentibus per veram fidem dicitur Ad Hebr 4: Ingrediemus in requie qui credimus. Ad quam . . . Pp. 255b–258b.

13. T19. *Ductus est Iesus* (Matt 4:1). Pro ingressu sermonis accipio illud 1 Petri 5, Aduersarius sicut leo . . .-. . . graciam pro presenti et gloriam pro futuro. Quam . . . Pp. 258b–261a.

14. T19. *Ductus est Iesus* (Matt 4:1). Pro ingressu sermonis accipio illud Iob 14, Cunctis diebus . . .-. . . per graciam et tandem introducet ad gloriam. Quam . . . Pp. 261a–263a.

15. T19. *Nunc tempus* (2 Cor 6:2). Karissimi, sicut attestatur sanctum euangelium Mathei 10 quando Dei Filius . . .-. . . ut nostra loquela directa sit in honorem Dei, cui sit honor et gloria nunc et semper. Amen. Pp. 263a–267a.

16. T19. *Nunc tempus* (2 Cor 6:2). Karissimi, sicut attestatur sacra scriptura 2 Machabeorum vltimo capitulo quando Iudas Machabeus . . .-. . . proficere, et ita intrabitis regnum celeste. Quod . . . Pp. 267a–270b.

17. T19. *Gratiam Dei recipiatis* (2 Cor 6:1). Et pro processu huius thematis, sicut vos intelligitis, qui graciam diuinam voluerit recipere, oportet illum ad tria oculum habere . . . Karissimi, qui habet negosium fiendum . . .-. . . idcirco graciam Dei recipiatis in tempore gracie. Quam . . . Pp. 270b–274a.

18. T19. *Gratiam Dei recipiatis* (2 Cor 6:1). Reuerendi mei, ista sunt verba Apostoli in epistula hodierna, in quibus verbis potestis videre a gret profere . . .-. . . et tunc in isto templo recipies graciam in presenti et gloriam in futuro. Quam . . . Pp. 274a–276a.

19. T20. *Miserere mei, Domine, fili David* (Matt 15:22). Tres sunt [?] . . . et licet ponantur hic multa exempla, attingo tamen vnum . . .-. . . viuere nos facit in presenti per graciam et in futuro per gloriam. Quam . . . Pp. 276a–278b.

20. T20. *Miserere mei, Domine, fili David* (Matt 15:22). Pro ingressu sermonis accipio illud Jeremie 17, Sana me . . .-. . . flagellas et saluas in presenti per graciam et in futuro per gloriam. Quam . . . Pp. 278b–280b.

21. T20. *Misere mei, Domine* (Matt 15:22 "vbi supra"). Homo qui habet magnam famem et paruam partem de pane . . .-. . . spiritualiter hic graciam et in futuro gloriam permanentem. Quam . . . Pp. 280b–282b.

22. T20. *Non vocavit nos Deus in inmunditiam sed in sanctificationem* (1 Thess 4:7). Pro ingressu sermonis accipio illud Apocalipsis 1, vbi dicitur de Christo, primogenitus (!) mortuorum et princeps regum terre . . .-. . . ex quibus graciam in presenti et gloriam in futuro nobis concedat . . . Pp. 282b–291a.

23. T18/4. *Paenitemini et convertimini, ut deleantur peccata vestra* (Acts 3:19). Scribitur in Iob 5: Nichil in terra sine causa fit . . .-. . . per quam meruit graciam hic in presenti vita et gloriam in futuro. Ad quam . . . Pp. 291a–293b.

24. ?. *Nunc tempus acceptabile* (2 Cor 6:2). Scribitur in Psalmo: Tempus bene placiti . . .-. . . Syba vero confessio gracie interpretatur. Ideo ad Deum perfecte conuerti per penitenciam. Pp. 294a–296b.

25. T21. *Ut filii lucis ambulate* (Eph 5:8). Pro ingressu sermonis accipio illud Ecclesiastici 41, Ambulatuit pes . . . Nota inter hominem et bruta animalia . . .-. . . ut maneatis in gracia et tandem in gloria. Quam . . . Pp. 296b–299b.

26. T21. *Cum eiecisset daemonium, locutus est mutus* (Luke 11:14). Pro ingressu sermonis accipio illud [*blank*] Demonia eicio . . .-. . . beneficium victorie habuit diabolo per graciam ei collatam in presenti, et tandem recipiet gloriam in futuro. Quam . . . Pp. 299b–303a.

27. T21. *Fortis armatus* (Luke 11:21). Pro ingressu sermonis accipio illud Deuteronomii 4, Custodi temetipsum . . . Racio autem huius hortacionis . . .-. . . euadat dampnacionis iudicium et meruetur graciam in presenti et gloriam in futuro. Amen. Pp. 303a–306b.

28. T22. *Christus nos liberavit* (Gal 4:31). Pro ingressu sermonis accipio illud Psalmi, Emitte manum . . . Racio vero dicte peticionis est quia quando aliquis graui carcere detinetur . . .-. . . super omnem terram, in presenti vita per graciam et in futuro per gloriam. Ad quam . . . Pp. 306b–310a.

29. T22. *Illa quae sursum est Hierusalem* (Gal 4:26). Pro ingressu sermonis accipio illud Iob 7, Milicia . . . Vbi satis innuitur quod licet quoad mundum non sit miles quilibet . . .-. . . ancille filii [!], idest carnis, sed libere, idest celetis patrie. Ad quam . . . Pp. 310b–315b.

30. T22. *Subiit in montem Iesus* (John 6:3). Pro ingressu sermonis accipio illud Psalmi, Requiescet in monte . . . scilicet penitencie, vbi est quies a malo culpe . . .-. . . positus est in monte hoc, scilicet paradisi glorie. Ad quam . . . Pp. 315b–320a.

31. T23. *Christus existens pontifex* (Heb 9:11). Pro ingressu sermonis accipio illud Ysaie 19, Mittet eis . . . Que promissio fuit per Christum . . .-. . . mundemur a peccatis et demum participare partem cum sanctis in gloria eterna. Amen. Pp. 320a–323b.

32. C21. *Circumdederunt me dolores mortis* (Ps 114:3 [or 17:4?]). In uulgari prouincialico dicitur tale prouerbium . . .-. . . factus es michi in salutem. Ad quam . . . Pp. 323b–333a.

33. ?. *Plorans ploravit in nocte, et lacrimae eius in maxillis eius. Non est qui consoletur eam ex omnibus caris eius* (Lam 1:2). Sicut enim propheta historice deplorauit domum Iude, sic modo alegorico modo quilibet deuotus potest plangere domum Ecclesie . . .-. . . suggestione diaboli prorumpat

iusticia oracionis, qua concedat vti filius incarnatus Virginis Marie. Amen. Pp. 333a–337a.

34. T10. *Cum natus esset Iesus in Bethlehem Iudaeae . . . adorare eum* (Matt 2:1–2). Cum Creator omnium, fratres karissimi, formam serui accipiens . . .-. . . qui iterant peccata postquam Christi sanguine sunt redempti. Ideo caueamus, etc. Pp. 337b–339b. Geoffrey Babion.

35. ?. *Singula autem alter alterius membra* (Rom 12:5). Vnde sic omnes vnum corpus sumus in Christo, videmus enim in membris vnius hominis . . .-. . . custodiamus usque ad separacionem aninme a corpore. Amen. Pp. 340b–341b.

36. ?. *Nemini quicquam debeatis nisi ut invicem diligatis* (Rom 13:8). Sciendum est, karissimi, quod ista leccio est dileccionis . . .-. . . omnia bona pariter cum illa, bona inquam gracie in presenti et glorie in futuro. Amen. Pp. 341b–342b.

37. ?. *Nemini quicquam debeatis,* etc. (Rom 13:8). Sciendum est quod summe debeamus cauere ne simus debitores carni . . .-. . . Bonum est ergo, diabolum et omne peccatum de corde expellere, ut inhabitet ibi Christus, qui est benedictus in secula. Amen. Pp. 342b–343b.

38. T26. *En ego morior, et erit Dominus vobiscum . . . terram patrum,* etc. (Gen 48:21). Verba sunt Iacob patriarche ad filios suos, et secundum alegoriam conueniunt saluatori . . .-. . . postquam autem ille obierit homicida reuertitur, etc. Pp. 345a–347a. Also in several anonymous Continental collections.

39. T26. *Et acceperunt triginta argenteos,* etc. (Matt 27:9). Precium appreciati a filis. Hec verba sunt in Ieremia 31. In quibus quatuor insinuantur . . .-. . . empti estis nolite fieri serui hominum, quasi dicat sed serui Dei. Pp. 347a–348a.

40. T26. *Filius hominis tradetur ut crucifigatur* (Matt 26:2). In hiis verbis propositis tria notantur de Christi passione . . .-. . . sustulit crucem confusione contempta. Pp. 348a–349b.

41. T26. *Reus est mortis* (Matt 26:66). In hiis verbis, karissimi, duo possunt notari, scilicet crudelis et concors Iudeorum acclamacio . . .-. . . vt vite eterne efficeremur heredes. Ad quam . . . Pp. 349b–350b.

42. T26. *O vos omnes qui transitis per viam . . . meus* (Lam 1:12). Quod Christi passio seu dolor fuit maior omni dolore quam passus erat vnquam aliquis in hac vita . . .-. . . de pena vero redempcionis non est compassio mentis. Pp. 350b–352b.

43. T26. *Iesus autem clamans voce magna expiravit* (Luke 23:46?). Et est sciendum quod in hiis verbis exprimuntur tria, scilicet Filii Dei ad redimendum

ydoneitas . . .-. . . ex quo Filius Dei pro peccato primi hominis satisfacere dignatus est. Pp. 352a–353a.

44. T26. *Exaudiet te Dominus in die tribulationis, protegat te nomen Dei Iacob* (Ps 19:2). Et nota quod Christus in sua passione dedit septem voces vel sonos . . .-. . . sed ex quo Christus Iesus homo [?] insonuit pendens in cruce, aliis omnibus exemplum tribuit. Pp. 353a–354b.

45. T26. *Peccavi tradens sanguinem iustum* (Matt 27:4). In hiis verbis, karissimi, possunt duo notari . . .-. . . tres sunt qui testimonium dant . . . Pp. 354b–357a.

46. T26. *Tunc apprehendit Pilatus Iesum* (John 19:1). Circa passionem Christi, de qua agitur in presenti, quatuor sunt consideranda . . . P. 357a, inc.

V – Oxford, Trinity College, MS 42

1. T01. *Venio cito* (Rev 22:20). Karissimi, legitur in gestis philosophorum quod cum venisset quo[n]dam Demetricus philosophus ad regem Hyspannye . . .-. . . vt mediante eius consilio transire mereamur ad gaudia sempiterna. Ff. 1–2.

2. T02?. *Videte ficulneam* (Luke 21:29). Quidam philosophus quondam quesiuit ab alio que fuit ultima virtutum . . .-. . . viriliter inherendo, vt ad celestia regna pertingere mereamur. Ad illa. . . . F. 2r–v.

3. T03?. *Pauperes evangelizantur* (Matt 11:5). Karissimi, legitur de Deogene paupere quod vi tanta dilexit paupertatem suam quod fecit sibi dolium . . .-. . . erit sibi collata perpetuo possidenda. Ad quam . . . Ff. 3–4.

4. T04?. *Gaudete in Domino* (Phil 4:4). Karissimi, licet vnus homo posset totum gaudium mundi huius amplecti, adhuc sine tristicia non esset . . .-. . . de manibus diaboli liberatum est et ad sempiternum gaudium restitutum. Ad quod . . . Ff. 4–6.

5. T06?. *Parvulus natus est nobis* (Isa 9:6). Dilectissimi, legitur in *Gestis Romanorum* quod ante Christi natiuitatem quoddam templum Rome extitit fortissime fundatum . . .-. . . qui fecit nos liberos, ut secum manere perpetuo valeamus. Qui . . . Ff. 6–7v.

6. T08*. *Hodie abstuli obprobrium* (Josh 5:9). Legitur in vita beati Benedicti quod cum esset ellectus a monachis in abbatem et vellet subditos suos ad religionis obseruancias prouocare . . .-. . . ad gloriam Saluatoris hodie circumsisi valeat peruenire. Qui . . . F. 8r–v.

7. T10*. *Adoraverunt eum* (Matt 2:11). Dicit Augustinus in quodam sermone: Nuper celebrauimus diem quo ex Iudeis natus est . . .-. . . et si sic fecerimus, Deus ostendet nobis faciem suam et salui erimus. Ff. 8v–10.

8. T11a?. *Dolentes quaerebamus te* (Luke 2:48). Dilectissimi, ista sunt verba Marie cum dolore querentis quem supra modum dilexit . . .-. . . tradidit vitam suam preteritam corrigens prestante Domino nostro . . . Ff. 10–11.

9. T12. *Quodcumque dixerit vobis, facite* (John 2:5). Amantissimi, beata Virgo Maria, que semper fuit humilis et deuota . . .-. . . facite, et sic poterimus ad celestia gaudia peruenire. Que . . . Ff. 11v–13.

10. T13. *Vince in bono malum* (Rom 12:21). Legitur in *Gestis Romanorum* quod quidam rex nobilis expugnauit quondam vnam magnam ciuitatem . . .- . . . poterimus eterna tabernacula feliciter introduci. Vbi nos introducat qui . . . Ff. 13–14.

11. T14. *Non concupisces* (Rom 13:9). Dilectissimi, concupiscencia concistit in omni illicito desiderio . . .-. . . illuc et minister meus erit. Quo . . . Ff. 14–15v.

12. T15?. *Seminavit bonum semen* (Matt 13:24). Seminanti agricole tria conue- niunt. Primum est quod terra aperiatur . . .-. . . patrem nostrum et semini eius in secula. Ad quam . . . Ff. 15v–16.

13. T16. *Ite et vos in vineam meam* (Matt 20:4). Karissimi, Saluator refert parabolice quod cultores vinee dominice in vltimo venientes . . .- . . . vt peruenire mereamur ad Ecclesiam triumphantem. Ad quam . . . Ff. 16–17.

14. T17. *Gloriabor in infirmitatibus* (2 Cor 12:9). Karissimi, scribitur inter quos- dam gestus antiquorum philosophorum quod Ypocras misit ad Aristotilem ymaginem . . .-. . . curet infirmitates nostras spirituales et ducat nos ad glo- riam sempiternam. Ad quam . . . Ff. 17–18.

15. T18. *Miserere mei* (Luke 18:28). Amantissimi, multi homines hiis diebus singularem habentes opinionem dicunt: Non curo quantumcumque pec- cauero . . .-. . . Miserere mei, et sic perueniemus ad gloriam sempiternam. Ad quam . . . Ff. 18–19.

16. T19. *Si Filius Dei es, dic* (Matt 4:3). Dilectissimi, videmus ad sensum quod filius iuuenis adhuc puer, licet familia domus credit ipsum . . .-. . . ideo, fratres karissimi, confiteamur integre et perueniamus ad gloriam sempiter- nam. Ad quam, etc. F. 19r–v.

17. T20. *Domine, adiuva me* (Matt 15:25). Dilectissimi, adiutorium hominum transitorium est, ipsius omnipotentis Dei manet . . .-. . . nunquam virgo pariet in futuro. Ad hoc templum . . . Ff. 19v–20v.

18. T21. *Revertar in domum meam* (Luke 11:24). Karissimi, domus sicut scitis nullo modo erigitur sine fundamento . . .-. . . et letabimus in eternum in Ecclesia triumphante. Ad quam . . . Ff. 20v–21v.

19. T22. *Impleti sunt* (John 6:12). Fratres dilectissime [!], videmus comuniter quod diues aut nobilis commendatur ex hoc quod dat cibum vel potum . . .- . . . Deus ostendet nobis faciem suam, et salui erimus. Ad hanc ostensionem . . . Ff. 21v–22v.

20. T23. *Lavit nos a peccatis nostris in sanguine suo* (Rev 1:5). Dilectissimi fratres, ille prophetarum eximius Dauid salutarem locucionem quondam ab alto desiderans . . .-. . . Translati sumus de morte ad vitam. Ad quam . . . Ff. 22v–23v.

21. T24. *Exaltatus autem humiliatus et conturbatus* (Ps 87:16). Amantissimi, si diligenter consideramus in Domino Saluatore primam exaltacionem . . .- . . . vt mereamur in eterna tabernacula feliciter introduci. Quo nos miserando perducat qui . . . Ff. 23v–24.

22. T28. *Surrexit Dominus* (Luke 24:34). Dilectissimi, in veteri testamento legimus de propheta Helya quod surgens a dormicione . . .-. . . a profundissimo carcere peccatorum, vt in altissimo palacio cum Christo viuamus in secula seculorum. Amen. Ff. 24–25.

23. T37. *Vigilate in orationibus* (1 Pet 4:7). Dilectissimi, dicit Bartholomeus quod diabolus nunquam dormit . . .-. . . ad ipsum venire mereamur qui non auertit faciem suam ab oracionibus peccatorum. Quod . . . F. 25r–v.

24. T39. *Misit Dominus spiritum* (Gal 4:6). Karissimi, hodie legitur in sancta Ecclesia de aduentu Spiritus Sancti . . .-. . . post peregrinacionem vite huius ad eternam requiem cum beata virgine Lucia poterimus introduci. Quam . . . Ff. 25v–25bis.

25. T40. *Tres sunt qui testimonium dant* (1 John 5:7). Scitis, dilectissimi, quod in ore duum uel trium stat omne testimonium . . .-. . . ad contemplacionem sancte et indiuidue Trinitatis feliciter exaltari. Quod . . . Ff. 25bis, verso-26.

26. ?. *Deus, propitius esto mihi peccatori* (Luke 18:3). Amantissimi, Saluator noster volens nos per exempla salutaria erudiri . . .-. . . ut premisi Deus, propicius esto michi peccatori, etc. Ff. 26–27.

27. ?. *Filius tuus vivit*, etc. (John 4:50). Dilecti fratres, naute cum fuerint in medio mari aut mercatores cum viderint . . .-. . . mox mitteret ministros quod tubis clamarent. F. 27r–v, inc?

28. T11a. *Puer Iesus proficiebat aetate* (Luke 2:52). Karissimi, pueri a parentibus ad scolas cum eis necessariis transmissi . . .-. . . puerorum et paruulorum sapientissimus et humilissimus. Qui . . . Ff. 27v–30.

29. T24*. *Frondes virides et palmas offerebant ei* (2 Mach 10:7). Karissimi, Iohannis 6 scribitur Veri adoratores adorabunt Patrem . . .-. . . hic est Christus,

Marie filius, cui sit honor et gloria sine fine, qui est benedictus in secula seculorum. Amen. Ff. 30–33.

30. T26. *Sumetis fructus arboris pulcherrimae* (Lev 23:40). Karissimi, ortolanus in vinea sua excolenda habens diuersorum fructuum arbores . . .-. . . perduceret ad societatem ciuium supernorum. Cui sit honor . . . Ff. 33–40.

31. ?. *Cantate Domino canticum novum* (Ps 95:1). Karissimi, solent in tempore gaudii et leticie vniuersaliter letari . . .-. . . sex autem note sunt iste. Ff. 40–43v, inc.

32. ?. *Paenitentiam agite, adpropinquabit enim regnum caelorum* (Matt 3:2 and 4:17). Dominus ac Saluator noster, Iesus Christus, sicut euangeliste scribunt, postquam baptizatus est a Iohanne . . .-. . . tota Christi doctrina semper et opera referuntur. Ff. 44–47, inc.

33. ?. *Redde rationis vilicationis tuae*, etc. (Luke 16:2). Karissimi, notum sit vobis quod Iesus Christus, auctor et doctor veritatis . . .-. . . pro eterna gloria, quam habent in conspectu Dei, cui sit honor et gloria in secula seculorum. Amen. Ff. 47–56. Wimbledon in Latin, also A-48 and H-5. English version edited in *Wimbledon's Sermon*; and in Owen, "Thomas Wimbledon's Sermon."

34. T28/2. *Mane nobiscum, Domine, quia advesperascit* (Luke 24:29). Reuerendi domini, nouistis quod si quis debet transire viam daungeriis et periculis plenam . . .-. . . nec manus scribere nec cor cogitare. Ad quod gaudium . . . Ff. 56–59. Alkerton. English version in London, British Library, MS Additional 37677, ff. 57–61, edited in O'Mara, *Study*, pp. 57–66.

35. T26*. *Percussa est tercia pars solis* (Rev 8:12). Secundum astrologos sol materialis est propinquior terre in hyeme quam in estate. Sic sol iusticie . . .-. . . hodie quando, vt predictum est, Percussa est tercia pars solis, etc. Ff. 59–62. Chambron.

36. T19*. *Unum Deum tuum adorabis et illi soli servies* (Matt 4:10). Karissimi, adorare volentes tria debent attendere: primo personam . . . .-. . . ymmo plus offenderetur, et Fili, prebe michi cor tuum, Prouerbiorum 20, etc. Ff. 63–65.

37. T26. *Corruit in platea veritas* (Isa 59:14). Anglice: In þe hye strete of þe tounne Sothenesse ys falle a-downe. Reuerendi mei, quia ista dies est dies penitencie . . .-. . . reprobare ab homine quam a Deo . . . Non sic, karissimi mei, sed si volu-. Ff. 65–73 (defective), inc. Chambron. Also Z-1.

38. ?. *Plenitudo legis est dilectio* (Rom 13:10). Beatus Augustinus in quodam sermone dicit sic: Esto similis medico . . .-. . . qui vera est dileccio peruenire finaliter valeamus. Quod . . . Ff. 74–75.

39. T28/2*. *Manhu* (Exo 16:15). Karissimi, sacra scriptura nos docet, sicut legimus in veteri testamento, quod filii Israel exeuntes . . .-. . . plus cruciat eum compassio miseri quam ipsum compassio sui, etc. Ff. 77–78v. Also H-23.

40. S28. *Ave, gratia plena, Dominus tecum, benedicta tu in mulieribus* (Luke 1:28). Aue inquiunt salutantes; de pleno accipiunt erorantes [!] Domino . . .-. . . in anima et corpore post Deum summa dote glorie. Ad quam . . . Ff. 79–80v. Also J/3-4 and X-335.

41. T26. *Domine, quid multiplicati sunt qui tribulant me?* (Ps 3:2). Rectum est vt ad Dominum recuratur cum simus tribulatur [=tribulati?], cum tribulacio multiplicatur . . .-. . . percipite regnum celorum ab eterno nobis paratum. Ad quod . . . Ff. 80v–82v.

42. T06. *Cantate Domino canticum novum, quia mirabilia fecit* (Ps 97:1). Solent homines in solempnitate ista multa habere noua . . .-. . . iusti autem in vitam eternam. Ad quam. Ff. 82v–84v.

43. T06. *Verbum caro factum est et habitavit in nobis* (John 1:14). In istis verbis duo principaliter possunt attendi: primum eius Filii Dei incarnacio . . .-. . . veniemus et mancionem apud eum faciemus. Ad quam . . . Ff. 84v–86.

44. T19. *Hortamur vos, ne in vacuum gratiam Dei recipiatis* (2 Cor 6:1). Hec gracia secundum Glosam est peccatorum remissio, et merito . . .-. . . ad graciam, per quam ad perfectam peruenitur gloriam. Ad quam . . . Ff. 86–87.

45. T26 [but surely T19?]. *Ductus est Iesus in desertum a spiritu, ut temptaretur, et cum ieiunasset . . . esuriit*, etc. (Matt 4:1–2). In isto euangelio tria dicuntur de Christo. Primum est quod in desertum a Spiritu Sancto ductus fuit . . .-. . . vere esurientes gloriam sempiternam implebit Dominus bonis gracie hic in presenti et bonis glorie in futuro. Ad illam gloriam . . . Ff. 87–89v.

W – Worcester, Cathedral Library, MS F.10

1. T20*. *Magna est fides tua* (Matt 15:28). O altitudo incomprehensibilis bonitatis et pietatis Domini Dei nostri, cuius bonitatis non est numerus, pietatis non est terminus . . .-. . . et sic proprietatem Spiritus Sancti. Sic ergo per fidem hostium nostrorum sublata formitudine . . . Ff. 5v–8. Repeated as W-34.

2. T23 ("Sermo Hugonis Legat in Passione Domini"). *Accipiant repromissionem vocati* (Heb 9:15). The help . . . I rede in Genesi . . . þat God thorw þe heȝe loue . . .-. . . with scharpe þorne was crowned vp o þe rode tre.

Qui . . . Ff. 8–14v. Hugh Legat. Edited in *Three Middle English Sermons*, pp. 1–21.

3. T36*. *Dominus in caelo paravit sedem suam* (Ps 102:19). Sicut testatur Ysydorus *Ethimologiarum* libro 18, inter omnia que debent preparari ad hoc quod aliquis excercitus pugnet . . .-. . . quod tamen fieret si faceret mandatum. Ff. 14v–15v, inc.

4. S59*. *Ascendit aurora* (Gen 32:26). Reuerendi in Christo patres atque domini, celestis imperii piissimus imperator humanam nuper cernens naturam . . .-. . . eterne beatitudinis dulcedine mereamur finaliter premiari nobis ipse concedat qui . . . F. 17r–v. Also R-5.

5. T05. *Protulit terra herbam virentem* (Gen 1:12). Reuerendi patres et domini, postquam genus humanum nostri primi parentis Adam exigente demerito a paradisi deliciis . . .-. . . possimus fructus felicitatis perpetue, nobis annuat flos Iesus, quem protulit virga Iesse. Amen. F. 18r–v.

6. T26*. *Christus passus est vobis relinquens exemplum ut sequamini* (1 Peter 2:21). Anglice sic: Cryst in hiis passyone reliquit exemplum vobis quomodo . . .-. . . vendicare hereditatem eius, scilicet regnum celorum. Quod . . . Ff. 19–27v. Also H-25; S-1; Z-19; Christ Church 91, f. 122ra. Edited from H-25 in Johnson, "Preaching the Passion," pp. 178–287.

7. T41/5*. *Memoriam fecit mirabilium suorum misericors Dominus, escam* (Ps 110:4–5). Secundum sanctos Gregorium, Augustinum, et alios doctores, verbum comparatur cibo . . .-. . . non esuriet. Vt finaliter saturemur isto pane per gloriam . . . Ff. 28–30v. Also S-3.

8. ?. *Panis dat vitam* (John 6:33). Karissimi, verbum Dei frequenter dicitur verbum vite, quia sicut panis corporalis dat homini vitam corporalem . . .- . . . et tandem optinebitis vitam eternam. Quam . . . Ff. 30v–32. Repeated as W-30.

9. T21*. *Ambulate in dilectione sicut Christus dilexit* (Eph 5:2). Karissimi, inuenio quod tria modernis temporibus diliguntur a multis . . .-. . . et gaudium habebimus quod suis dilectoribus ordinauit. Ad quod . . . Ff. 32–37. Repeated as W-31. Also S-16.

10. ?. *Ministri Christi sunt* (2 Cor 11:23). Secundum beatum Bernardum, quatuor sunt quibus seruitur in hoc mundo: mundus, caro, demon, et Deus . . .-. . . honorificabit eum pater meus, qui est in celis. Ad quos . . . Ff. 37–39v. Repeated as W-32. Also S-6.

11. ?. *Flos de radice ascendet et requiescet* (Isa 11:1–2). Experimur naturaliter, karissimi, quod arbores et herbe naturaliter producunt folia ante florem . . .-

. . . et festinemus ingredi illam requiem, Hebreorum 4. Ad quam, etc. Amen. Ff. 39v–42v. Repeated as W-33.

12. T39*. *Accipite Spiritum Sanctum* (John 20:22). Karissimi, scitis quod est vulgare et commune dictum quod omne promissum est debitum . . .- . . . hoc donum Spiritus Sancti discipulis suis hoc [*catchword*: die fuit missum]. F. 42v, inc.

13. T22*. *Liberavit nos* (Gal 4:31). The helpe . . . Crysten peple, thier wordis that I af take . . .-. . . sched his blod o þe rode tre. Qui . . . Ff. 43–48va. Edited in *Three Middle English Sermons*, pp. 22–50.

14. T23*. *Christus semetipsum optulit Deo* (Heb 9:14). The help . . . Cristen peple, þes wordes þat ich ha take to prech of . . .-. . . offre himsilf to þe vader of heuene. Qui . . . Ff. 48va–53vb. Edited in *Three Middle English Sermons*, pp. 50–80.

15. T24?. *Acceperunt ramos palmarum* (John 12:13). Seneca libro secundo *De beneficiis* capitulo 20, þis clerk tellyt þat þer was . . .-. . . Fulgencius in his methus *Meth'* þis clerk feyngt þat. Ff. 53vb–54vb, inc. Edited in C. E. M. Glover, PhD dissertation, Birmingham University, 1977, pp. 42–47.

16. C14*. *Lignum vitae in medio paradisi* (Gen 2:9). Reuerendi patres, in glorio-sissimo paradiso orbis architipi, quem inmensa magestate solus inhabitat rex regum et dominus dominancium . . .-. . . sic igitur vestrum quemlibet exequi curam pastoralis officii concedat . . . Ff. 55–58v. Folsham. 28 lines repeated on fol. 73va–b and canceled.

17. ?. *Accipite armaturam Dei* (Eph 6:13). In quibus verbis includuntur tria necessaria in omni sermone. Quiscumque predicaret, oportet eum habere quibus predicaret . . .-. . . post accipere eternam requiem in alio. Ipse concedat . . . Ff. 58v–63v. Folsham.

18. T21*. *Beati qui audiunt verbum Dei* (Luke 11:28). In quibus verbis, quia virtuosa operacio consulitur vobis in audiendo verbum Dei . . .-. . . humane debilitati spiritualis cibacio. Sic ergo audire verbum Dei ipse, etc. Ff. 63v–67v.

19. ?. *Requiescet pax* (Luke 10:6). Karissimi, Mathei 12 legitur quod postquam Christus iecisset demonium ab uno ceco et muto . . .-. . . in contemplacione diuina, per quem optinebit gaudium celeste. Ad quod . . . Ff. 67v–69v. Repeated as W-96.

20. ?. *Iesus exivit de templo* (John 8:59). Primo in antetemate qualiter sol habuit quoddam templum, cuius templi descripcio habetur in Ouidio *De*

transformatis libro 2 . . .-. . . Tercia pars est ciphus, scilicet corpus Christi rubeo sanguine cruentatum. F. 69v.

21. S59*. *Veni ad me* (1 Sam 17:44). Sicut iudicio naturali cognoscimus quod quando aliquis artifex presumptuosus suscipit aliquod opus arduum operandum . . .-. . . in trono glorie sue secum eternaliter coronando. Ad quam . . . Ff. 70–74va. 17 lines repeated at fol. 179v and canceled. Perhaps also in Worcester Q.56.

22. C22 ("Introitus sentenciarum"). *Lignum vitae in medio paradisi* (Gen 2:9). Reuerendi magistri, patres, et domini, fons sapiencie, verbum Dei, in orto anime racionalis scaturiendo emanaciones . . .-. . . sic igitur de fructu istius ligni gustare pro statu vie, vt mereamur eterna refici dulcedine pro statu patrie . . . Ff. 75ra–76va. Edited in Wenzel, "Academic Sermons," pp. 321–329.

23. C14*. *Multi sunt vocati* (Matt 20:16). Reuerendi patres et magistri, vt vinea Domini Sabaoth, Ecclesia militans, sponsa Christi, in triplici actu scilicet actu purgandi, actu illuminandi, et actu perficiendi . . .-. . . durius excandescit sunt enim fornicatus est ire cum. F. 76vb, inc.

24. T26*. *Abundant passiones Christi* (2 Cor 1:5). Summus rerum pontifex solo sue bonitatis intuitu cuncta esse producens naturalem boni amorem . . .- . . . sic igitur Christi vulnerum et eius passionis recordari ille nobis concedat . . . Ff. 77ra–78rb.

25. ?. *Erumpe et clama* (Gal 4:27). Reuerendi domini, pro materia huius sermonis diligenter est notandum quod tria precipue faciunt hominem clamare . . .-. . . erumpe et clama, vbi supra. Sic ergo clamare . . . Ff. 78va–79vb.

26. C22?. *Ego Iohannes vidi civitatem* (Rev 22:8). Reuerendissimi magistri, patres, et domini, princeps philosophorum Aristoteles . . .-. . . Ad illam que sole et luna non indiget, Apocalipsis 21, Iesus Christus nos perducat . . . Ff. 79vb–81ra.

27. C22 ("Introitus sentensiarum"). *Semper laus in eius ore* (Ps 33:2). Reuerendi domini, patres, et magistri, secundum beati Augustini doctrinam, maior est sacre scripture subtilitas . . .-. . . et sic semper laus eius in ore. Quam laudem . . . Ff. 81ra–82rb.

28. C14 ("in conuocacione uel in capitulo generali") . . . *Principes populorum congregati sunt* (Ps 46:10). Qui autem nunc prelati vocantur, olim [*add* principes] populi dicebantur. Ideo dicit Iohannes Crisostomus . . .-. . . sicut promisisti Pachomio requiem sorciamur eternam. Amen. Dico etc. Ff. 82rb–84rb. Edited in Pantin, "Sermon."

29. C14 / S43a*. *Speciosus est in splendore* (Sir 43:12). Oriens sol iusticie et splendor lucis eterne ab interius penetralibus celestis archani mundum foras voluit euocare . . .-. . . in hoc quod dicitur Speciosus est in splendore, etc. Ff. 84rb–85va. Repeated as W-99.

30. T41/5. *Panis dat vitam* (John 6:33). Karissime [!], verbum Dei frequenter dicitur verbum vite, quia sicut panis corporalis dat homini vitam corporalem . . .-. . . optinebitis vitam eternam. Quam vitam . . . Ff. 85vb–87ra. Repeats W-8.

31. T21*. *Ambulate in dilectione sicut Christus dilexit* (Eph 5:2). Karissimi, inuenio quod tria modernis temporibus diliguntur a multis . . .-. . . gaudium habebimus quod suis dilectoribus ordinauit. Ad quod, etc. Ff. 87ra–91rb. Repeats W-9. Also S-16.

32. ?. *Ministri Christi sunt* (2 Cor 11:23). Secundum beatum Bernardum, quatuor sunt quibus seruitur in hoc mundo: Mundus, caro, demon, et deus . . .-. . . pater meus qui est in celis. Ad quos celos . . . Ff. 91rb–93va. Repeats W-10. Also S-6.

33. ?. *Flos de radice ascendet et requiescet* (Isa 11:1–2). Experimur naturaliter, karissimi, quod arbores et herbe naturaliter producunt folia . . .-. . . festinemus ingredi istam requiem, Hebreorum 4. Ad quam, etc. Amen. Ff. 93va–96rb. Repeats W-11.

34. T20*. *Magna est fides tua* (Matt 15:28). O altitudo incomprehensibilis bonitatis et pietatis Domini Dei nostri, cuius bonitatis non est numerus, pietatis non est terminus . . .-. . . sic proprietatem Spiritus Sancti. Sic ergo . . . Ff. 96va–98vb. Repeats W-1.

35. S59*. *In gloria requiescet* (Sir 14:26). Reuerendi patres et domini, triplici radio virtuali exigitur operator spiritualis verbum Dei seminaturus . . .- . . . abundanter affluamus ipsius deliciis glorie prestante eius filio . . . Ff. 98vb, 286rb–v, 3–5v, with renvois.

36. ?. *Petite* (Luke 11:9). Karissimi, legitur in *Vitis Patrum* quod petenti a quodam sancto verbum Dei respondit ille se verbum non habere . . .-. . . et qui potens est omnia facere habundanter quod petimus. ipsi gloria. Amen. Ff. 99ra–100vb.

37. T35*. *Est vita aeterna ut cognoscant te* (John 17:3). Fratres, sicud homo constans ex duplici natura, corporali videlicet et spirituali . . .-. . . in ipsum, non pereat sed habeat vitam. Ff. 101ra–102vb.

38. S81*. *Ut testimonium perhiberet de lumine* (John 1:7). Solent testes veridici ad testimonium ducti de scitis deponere et testificari . . .-. . . nos lumen vultus tui, Domine. Ad quem, etc. Ff. 102vb–103ra.

39. ?. *Venit* (John 1:7 or 11?). Solent duces et reges incliri [!], principes potentes et strenui . . .-. . . quia coronaberis. Hanc coronam . . . F. 103ra–b. Also X-250.

40. ?. *Non* (John 1:11?). Duo loc[cuc]ionum sunt genera, et due sunt species diuinitus accepte sermonum . . .-. . . .vt cum Domino regnare possimus in celis. F. 103rb–vb. Also X-239.

41. S82a but rather S85*. *Erat lux vera quae illuminat,* etc. (John 1:9). Karissimi, prout omnium mortalium laborat fama et auctoritas, tria sunt precipua [!] . . .-. . . hec virgo coniuncti habere noscatur. Ff. 103vb–104va. Also X-243.

42. ?. *Dedit* (John 1:12). Inter liberales et prodigos sic solet plurimum variari condicio ut illiberales aliqui presto recipere et nichil e contrario donare disponunt . . .-. . . animam suam dedit pro redempcione pro multis. Cuius redempcione . . . Ff. 104va–105ra.

43. ?. *Dedit,* vbi prius (John 1:12). Secundum sentenciam Philosophi 4 *Ethicorum,* generalium personarum condicio sic in accepcione . . .-. . . de pinguedine terre habundanciam, quam optinuit quasi per instructa [?] posteriora secula seculorum. Amen. F. 105ra–va.

44. ?. *Potestatem* (John 1:12). Motus continui mundi, carnis, et diaboli sic corda hominum ventilant . . .-. . . vt vos a mundi fallaciis et a carnis molestiis et a hostis insidiis preseruare dignetur qui . . . Ff. 105va–106ra.

45. ?. *Fuit homo* (John 1:6). Primus parens, cum dati sibi premii dignitate reiecta . . .-. . . diligenter pensemus, vitabimus penam et perueniemus ad palmam. F. 106ra–vb. Also X-237.

46. S81a* and S81b*. *Omnes* (John 1:7?). Karissimi, beatus Bernardus *De gracia et libero arbitrio* capitulo 8 probare videtur quod . . .-. . . manifestari oportet ante tribunal Christi. Vtinam sic ibi manifestari valeamus . . . Ff. 106vb–107rb. Also X-238.

47. ?. *Venientem* (John 1:9). In aduentu regis et principis domini eximii et potentis ad ciuitatem aliquam siue regnum solent premitti veridi nuncii . . .- . . . ante aduentum ergo Christi sic penitere valeamus . . . Ff. 107va–108ra. Also X-241.

48. S01*. *Hominem* (John 1:9). Karissimi, licet prophecie ac sacre pagine detractatores . . .-. . . merito Christi passionis tam Andree quam Christi peruenire poterimus ad gaudia paradisy. Amen. F. 108ra–va. Also X-244.

49. ?. *In mundo erat* (John 1:10). Karissimi, tam fide quam scripturis testantibus . . .-. . . et ad vitam eternam perducat. Amen. F. 108va–b. Also X-245.

50. ?. *Mundus* (John 1:10). Karissimi, sicut dicit Crisostomus omelia 18 *Operis imperfecto* [!], Non est in mundo sic quod . . .-. . . mundam seruaui animam meam ab omni cupiditate. Hanc animam mundam sic seruare possumus vt Deo eternam beatitudinem habeamus. Amen. Ff. 108vb–109rb. Also X-246.

51. S03. *Eum* (John 1:10). Karissimi, sicut dicit beatus Augustinus *De perfeccione iusticie*, Dominus, inquit . . .-. . . egressi de naui continue cognouerunt eum. Sic eum in terris venerari . . . F. 109rb–va. Also X-247.

52. S05. *Non cognovit* (John 1:10). Princeps seculi, princeps mundi, princeps tenebrarum . . .-. . . Hic cognitus est ab eo. Sic meritis virginis gloriose cognosci . . . Ff. 109va–110rb. Also X-248.

53. S86*. *Cognovit eum* (John 1:10). Coram sapiente et iudice qui negocia sua sunt facturi . . .-. . . dum paruulus versaretur inter brachia, penderet ad vbera. Ff. 110rb–111rb. Also X-249.

54. C22*. *Sedit in solio regni sui* (Esther 1:2). Solebant magne potencie dignitate prefecti, vt reges illustres et domini . . .-. . . concupiscencia sapiencie deducit ad regnum perpetuum. Quod nobis. Amen. Ff. 111rb–112va.

55. ?. *Non affectamur laudes.* ("Ieronimus in prologo libri Hester"). Karissimi, vt dicit Gregorius 2 *Morum*, laus humana oculis oblata mortalibus mentem operantis immutat . . .-. . . vnicuique erit laus a deo, 1 Ad Corinthios 4. Quam . . . F. 112va–b.

56. ?. *Cuncta faciebat consilio* (Esther 1:13). Mundi sapiens architectus cunta disponens numero, pondere, et mensura . . .-. . . in sapiencia vtique increata. Sic nobis consulat . . . Ff. 112vb–113va.

57. ?. *Invenit gratiam in conspectu illius* (Esther 2:9). Multos et in multis legimus Christum Dominum quesiuisse quem multos in multis legimus inuenisse. Magdalena Christum inuenit . . .-. . . in conspectu agni amicti stolis albis. Ita hoc . . . Ff. 113va–114rb.

58. T19+*. *Flectebant genua et adorabant* (Esther 3:2). Multos constat coram Deo indies genuflectere, proni in terram Dominum adorare . . .-. . . adorauerunt viuentem in secula. Sic adorare . . . F. 114rb–vb.

59. S25. *Hoc honore condignus est* (Esther 6:11). Karissimi, sanctos multos quos ad honoris fastigium non ambicio popularis set spectata inter bonos moderacio provehebat fuisse legimus . . .-. . . quod suscipiet a Deo Patre honorem et gloriam, 2 Petri 1. Quam . . . Ff. 114vb–115va.

60. ?. *Stabat in ministerio regis* (Esther 7:9). Secundum quod dicit August 11 *De ciuitate Dei* capitulo 12, omnes de suo perseuerancie premio certi . . .-. . . hii enim foris apparent humiles. Ff. 115va–116ra.

61. ?. *Quid vis fieri?* (Esther 9:12; cf. 7:2). Sicud dicit Hugo de Sancto Victore, capitulo de oracione, Dei beneficia ad memoriam reuocemus . . .-. . . perueniamus ad patriam eterne claritatis. Quod . . . F. 116ra–va.

62. S25a. *Fecit signa multa* (Esther 10:9). Solent magni et magnifici regum precipue fulti subsiduis non exigua facere . . .-. . . Hic homo signa multa facit. Cuius sanguis nos adiuuari . . . Ff. 116va–117rb.

63. T19+*. *Humiles exaltati sunt* (Esther 11:11). Sicut Augustinus 4 *Contra Iulianum* capitulo 22, et capit a Tulio *De re publica*, sicut dicit ibidem Tullius, inquit Augustinus, hominem . . .-. . . vos exaltet in tempore tribulacionis. Quam exaltacionem . . . Ff. 117rb–118ra.

64. S25b. *Eius imperio subiecti sumus* (Esther 13:1). Augustinus dicit, *Questionum* questione 63, duabus personis, viz. sacerdotali et regina [!], ad quas sacrosancta vnccio pertinebat . . .-. . . nec interius intrare presument. Huius sancti . . . F. 118ra–vb.

65. ?. *Nunc invoca Dominum* (Esther 15:3). Sicut dicit Augustinus in libello suo *De miseria hominis*: Quicquid vident, quicquid splendit, quicquid pulcherrimum est . . .-. . . dominus sit vobiscum in futuro gloriam conferendo. Quam . . . Ff. 118vb–119va.

66. T26*. *Amore langueo* (Cant 2:5). Induite, Ad Ephesios 4. Rex sanctorum conforta me principatum tenens et da sermonem rectum et bene sonantem . . .-. . . nisi ipse ab eis occideretur. Ff. 119va–122vb, inc.

67. T24*. *Rex tuus venit tibi* (Matt 21:5). In quibus verbis ostenditur iocundissimum matrimonium vnquam factum inter potenciam et misericordiam Dei . . .-. . . et in die iudicii erit iustissimus iudicando. Qui . . . Ff. 123ra–125va.

68. T24*. *Secundum gloriam eius multiplicita est ignominia eius* (1 Macc 1:42). In quibus verbis potestis videre duo tangencia Christi personam. Primum est magnum servicium . . .-. . . et dabit delicias anime tue. Amen, Amen. Ff. 125va–127va.

69. ?. *Existis in desertum* (Matt 11:7). Reuerendi magistri, patres, et domini, nostri thematis verba tam historice quam allegorice diligenter indaganti occurret triplex esse desertum . . .-. . . illico sanabatur. Sic reuera spiritualiter. F. 127va–b, inc.

70. T19+*. *Sanguis Christi emundabit conscientiam nostram* (Heb 9:14). Tria inuenio in sacra scriptura que mundant humanam conscienciam. Primum est sermo divinus . . .-. . . ad beatitudinem sanctorum. Sic virtute istius sanguinis . . . Ff. 128ra–131ra.

71. C14. ("Sermo magistri Joh. Ford in capitulo generali"). *Congregate vos in domum disciplinae* (Sir 51:31). Amantissimi patres et domini, oriens splendor solis iusticie candorque lucis eterne et speculum sine macula deifice maiestatis, ipsa videlicet sedium divinarum assistrix sapiencia . . .-. . . illuminare debent Dei precepta publice edocendo. Ff. 131rb–132rb, inc. John Ford.

72. T18/4*. *Convertimini* (Joel 2:12). Reuerendi domini, duos dominos I rede of in sacra scriptura qui continue . . .-. . . ducam in meam beatitudinem, vbi regnabitis mecum in eternum. Ad quam . . . Ff. 132rb–133v.

73. T19?. *Ductus est Iesus in desertum a spiritu ut temptaretur a diabolo* (Matt 4:1). Ad literam iam post lapsum [*read* baptismum] suum recessit in desertum et ibi temptatus est a diabolo . . .-. . . vel addiendo [?] delectabilia et vana, etc. F. 134ra–b.

74. T20. *Domine, adiuva me* (Matt 15:25). Tria sunt circa que versatur intencio predicatoris: primum ut informet peccatores . . .-. . . vt in bono perseuerantes Christus Deus dignetur in suo regno coronare. Amen. Ff. 134rb–135va.

75. T21*. *Erat Iesus eiciens daemonium et illud . . . locutus est mutus* (Luke 11:14). Hoc euangelium octo continet. Primo Saluator miraculum operatur . . .-. . . quod precepta Dei opere seruauit et compleuit, etc. Ff. 135va–136va. Peraldus.

76. T11a*. *Nolite conformari huic saeculo* (Rom 12:2). Reuerende [!] magistri, patres, et domini. In principio huius colacionis nolite confirmari [!] huic seculo. Reuerendi domini, quia testant beato Iohanne in sua epistula . . .-. . . voluntas dei bona bene placens [?] et perfecta. Qua . . . Ff. 136va–137va.

77. [No thema]. Quamvis eminens sciencia desideranda sit in pastore, tamen competens tolleratur, secundum Apostolum Ad Corinthios octavo: Sciencia inflat . . .-. . . per multas tribulaciones oportet vos intrare in regnum celorum. Ad quod. . . . Ff. 137vb–139rb. A pastoral manual.

78. T25*. [No thema]. Adueniente iam et iminente tempore miseracionum et misericordiarum Domini Iesu quo disposuerat saluam facere plebem suam . . .-. . . quia omnes pariter intingebant. F. 139va, inc.

79. ?. *In nomine Patris et Filii et Spiritus Sancti* (Matt 28:19). Quanta sit dignitas humane condicionis patescit dum ad ymaginem et similitudinem suam . . .- . . . Per virga Aaron sacerdotalis potestas designatur. Ff. 139vb–140ra, inc.

80. C22*. *Seminavit bonum semen in agro* (Matt 13:24). Patres et domini reuerendi, ager veteris sinagoge quem a publica via gencium

ceremoniarum <pluralitas> clausura notabili circumserit . . .-. . . diligenter inquit excerce agrum. Sic ergo excitari in hoc agro . . . Ff. 140rb–141va.

81. ? ("Sermo de morte"). *Sic est omnis qui natus est* (John 3:8). Ad ea que sunt de iure nature omnis creatura particeps obligatur . . .-. . . et debet quod habuerit bonam mortem. Quam . . . Ff. 141va–142vb.

82. T34. *Orate pro invicem ut salvemini* (James 5:16). Scitis quod quando aliquis aduocatus est iturus ad curiam in breui . . .-. . . ostende faciem tuam et salui erimus. Quod . . . Ff. 142vb–143va.

83. C21. *Quo abiit Simon?* (1 Macc 5:21). Reuerendi mei, Christus Filius Dei loquens discipulis suis dicens in parabolis Luce 19 sic inquit: Homo quidam nobilis abiit . . .-. . . iam euasit et ad futuram et perpetuam gloriam securus iam Symon abiit. Amen. Ff. 143va–145rb. Repeated as W-92. Also H-3.

84. T34. *Clamemus in caelum, et miseretur nostri Deus noster* (1 Macc 4:10). Karissimi mei, Cristus Iesus Mathei 5 dat nobis vnum sanum consilium . . .-. . . in felyng in hus owyn body. Medicus iste [*catchword*: qui nouit]. F. 145rb–vb, inc.

85. ?. *Sitis ipsi sapientes* (2 Cor 11:19). In has [!] verbis notantur diuersa necessaria homini. Primo vita secundum racionem seu racionalis, ibi sitis . . .-. . . vera sapiencia, que stat in bene operari. Ff. 146ra–151rb.

86. ?. *Quid hic statis tota die otiosi?* (Matt 20:6). In quibus verbis comprehendi possunt duo conueniencia predicatoribus verbi Dei: primum est consideracio humana vite . . .-. . . bona continuacio premium meretur, quod est gaudium eternum. Ad quod . . . Ff. 151rb–154vb.

87. ?. *Probet seipsum homo, et sic de pane edat* (1 Cor 11:28). In quibus verbis duo sunt consideranda: primum est discussio seu consideracio cuiuslibet hominis in seipso . . .-. . . et homines iustos temptacio tribulacionis. Ff. 155va–159va.

88. T25*. *In finem dilexit* (John 13:1). Karissimi, sicut dicit beatus Iohannes euangelista, Dominus noster Iesus Christus appropinquante die passionis pro redimenda anima humana, cum dilexit homines . . .-. . . auidius bibatur suauissimum poculum caritatis. Ff. 159va–163rb.

89. T16*. *Sic currite ut comprehendatis* (1 Cor 9:24). Karissimi, ad disponendum et preparandum nos ad currendum siue ad faciendum cursum nostrum versus celum . . .-. . . illum honoret nobis concedet qui . . . Ff. 163rb–167rb.

90. ?. *Audiat terra verba oris mei* (Deut 32:1). Ecce iam videmus quomodo celum et terra et omnia elementa accusantur de morte . . .-. . . tunc occides peccato et viuere facis cum Christo. Quod . . . F. 170r–v.

91. T21*. *Revertar* (Luke 11:24). Naturalis ordo fatetur vt prius attemptetur clemencia et postmodum sequatur vindicta . . .-. . . respondent quod eum non. Ff. 171–174, inc. Also B/2-71 (complete) and O-32 (inc.).

92. C21. *Quo abiit Simon?* (1 Macc 5:21). Reuerendi mei, Christus Filius Dei loquens discipulis suis dicit in parabolis Luce 19 sic inquit, Homo quidam nobilis abiit in regionem longinquam . . .-. . . gloriam securus iam Symon abiit. Amen. Ff. 174v–177.

93. T34, T22, but rather T23*. *Veritatem dico vobis, quare non creditis?* (John 8:46). Domini et amici, hec verba fuerunt Christi ad Iudeos et possunt esse predicatorum populo . . .-. . . eicerat septem demonia, idest septem genera peccatorum mortalium. Amen. Ff. 177–180v.

94. T36. *Ascendit in montem* (Matt 5:1). Karissimi, sicut sacra commemorat scriptura, dum Christus fuit in hoc mundo tribus vicibus ascendit in montem . . .-. . . firmissimo habitaculo tuo quod operatus es, Domine. In quem montem nos ascendere. . . . Ff. 180v–182v, see above, p. 155.

95. ?. *Omnis lingua confiteatur* (Phil 2:11). Karissimi, secundum Ysidorum *Ethimologiarum* libro 9, capitulo 1, sicut sunt tres lingue principales . . .- . . . þat synful man þorow his beleue haþ lyf þat lastut ay. Confiteatur. Ff. 182v–184v.

96. ?. *Requiescet pax* (Luke 10:6). Karissimi, Mathei 12 legitur quod postquam Iesus eiecisset demonium ab vno ceco et muto . . .-. . . per quam optinebimus gaudium celeste. Ad quod gaudium no perducat. Amen. Pur charyte. Ff. 184v–186.

97. T26. *Quid faciam de Iesu?* (Matt 27:22). Hec verba dici possunt a beata Virgine Maria vel sancta Ecclesia et a peccatrice anima . . .-. . . sepeli et custodes adhibe, vt tecum habitare dedignetur. Quod . . . Ff. 186–188v.

98. T26. *Occiditur Christus* (Dan 9:26). Hec verba prophecie per multa curicula annorum ante Christi aduentum et mortem spiritu prophetico erant prenunciata . . .-. . . ita pauperem sicut vnquam fuit Iob. Ff. 188v–189v, inc. (see below, W-113).

99. S43a*/C14*. *Speciosus est in splendore* (Sir 43:12). Oriens sol iusticie et splendor lucis eterne ab interius penetralibus celestis archani mundum foras voluit euocare . . .-. . . estote prudentes, scilicet vos prelati et superiores exemplum. F. 190v, inc. Repeats W-29.

100. ?. *Oculi mei semper ad Dominum* (Ps 24:15). Nota quod diabolus laqueum parat vt animas quasi aues capere queat. Nota historiam . . .-. . . spaciosa est via, etc. Diabolus ibi venatur et predam capit. F. 191. Holcot, *Convertimini*, sermon 5.

101. T62*. *Descende priusquam moriatur filius meus* (John 4:49). Reuerendi magistri, patres, et domini, primi hominis miseria et pii redemptoris misericordia in serie presentis euangelii pariter includuntur . . .-. . . premisi sepius Descende, etc. Sic igitur Christum ad nos descendere . . . Ff. 191v–193v.

102. C14*. *Venit* (Matt 21:5). Reuerendi domini, speciale templum et habitacio quod Christus, Filius Dei, habet hic in terra est multitudo et congregacio fidelium . . .-. . . Filius hominis non venit ministrari sed ministrare, etc. Ff. 193v–196.

103. T17*. *Fructum afferunt* (Luke 8:15). Reuerendi magistri, patres, et domini, in agro dominico fructeficantes [!] in triplicem solent statum distingui, incipiencium . . .-. . . in statu perfectorum, pro tercio principali. Finem . . .eternam vitam. Quam . . . Ff. 196–197v.

104. S65. *Lux orta est* (Isa 9:2). Reuerendi patres et domini, fons et origo sapiencie virtutum largitor et remunerator meritorum, Dominus . . .-. . . vnde merito de ipsa dicitur thema Lux, etc. Cuius claritatem . . . Ff. 197v–199v.

105. S26*. *Abite, liberi, ad patrem* (Gen 44:17). Reuerendi patres et domini, postquam primus parens de patria libertatis in locum miserabilis servitutis per esum pestiferum suggestione corruerat serpentina . . .-. . . sed vt feliciter iocundemini et cum gloria coronemini secundum thematis sentenciam Abite liberi ad patrem. Ad quem . . . Ff. 199v–201v.

106. S05* / S65. *Ego quasi vitis fructificavi* (Sir 24:22). Reuerendi domini, que, qualis, et quanta sit benedicta Virgo, cuius concepcionem hodie celebramus . . .-. . . superni ciues celorum. Ad quorum desiderabile consorcium . . . Ff. 201v–202v.

107. T24*. *Ite in castellum* (Matt 21:2). Reuerendi patres, in primeua creacione generis humani graciosa bonitas omnipotentis Dei dedit prothoparenti nostro Ade pro se et omnibus suis castellum . . .-. . . fistulacionem illam faciet nos obdormire et totum castrum ibit in prodicionem [!]. Ff. 202v–208, inc? Repeated partially in W-151.

108. C21*. *Nigra sum et formosa* (Cant 1:4). Solet esse assercio popularis colorem nigram indelectabilem esse atque(?) indiligibilem ac inter ceteros colores magis deformem. Sue sentencie videtur Aristoteles consentire . . .-. . . aut schrunke and scorchyd per solis calorem. Ff. 208–211, inc.

109. C22*. *Cooperatores simus veritatis* (3 John 8). Honorabiles magistri, patres, atque domini, teste beato Aug *De vita beata* capitulo 27, illa est plena satietas animorum, hec vita est beata pie perfecteque cognoscere . . .-

. . . omnis gracia vite et veritatis. Vt ergo cooperatores simus . . . Ff. 211–212v.

110. S86*. *Dicit Dominus: Lauda, filia Sion* (Zeph 3:14). Hiis verbis Dominus filiam Syon ad laudem invitat. O Beata Virgo potest dici filia Syon, scilicet Dei . . .-. . . et de infecundo creature ad plenitudinem Creatoris. Ff. 212v–214.

111. S86*. *Ecce nubecula parva quasi vestigium hominis ascendebat de mari* (1 Kings 18:45). Legitur Genesis 32 de Iacocob [!] qui luctabatur cum angelo. Cui dixit angelus: Dimitte . . .-. . . qualiter ascendit. F. 214r–v, inc.

112. T23*. *Veritatem dico, quare non creditis mihi?* (John 8:46). Domini, hec verba fuerunt Christi ad Iudeos, et possunt esse predicatorum populo . . .-. . . quod Christus eiecit septem demonia idest septem genera peccatorum mortalium, etc. Amen. Ff. 215–217. Repeats W-93.

113. S26. *Surgam et ibo ad Patrem* (Luke 15:18). Reuerendi magistri, patres, atque domini, grauis offensa peccatoris et grandis clemencia Redemptoris in hodierna Christi parabola innuuntur . . .-. . . ad patrem quoad tercium. Sic surgere . . . Ff. 217–219v. End repeated after W-98 and canceled.

114. C14*. *Conversi estis nunc ad pastorem* (1 Peter 2:25). Quamdiu oues non sunt sub manu pastores [!], tamdiu sunt in periculo . . .-. . . a quo patre habebimus hereditatem sempiternam. De qua . . . Ff. 219v–220v.

115. T06. *Natus est hodie Salvator* (Luke 2:11). Reuerendi patres mei, hodie vt solempnizat Ecclesia dum vox angelica sonuit qua frangitur ira . . .-. . . quia natus est hodie saluator. Christus ergo, qui natus pro peccatoribus . . . Ff. 220v–221.

116. T23. *Graviter vulneratus sum* (1 Kings 22:34). Karissimi, predicator verbi Dei debet sic vilescere ut vulneret superbos exemplo sue humilitatis . . .-. . . vbi si locus vllus fuerit optinendi, nullus erit admittendi. Ad quod, etc. Ff. 221–222v. Repeated as W-148.

117. C19*. *Pax vobis* (Luke 24:36 and John 20:20). Reuerendi patres et domini, cum iuxta laudabilem ordinis nostri consuetudinem visitacionem precedere sermo debeat salutaris . . .-. . . pacem habete, et Deus pacis et dileccionis erit vobiscum. Quod . . . Ff. 222v–223v.

118. C19*. *Videte vocationem vestram* (1 Cor 1:26). Reuerendi patres et domini, triplicem inuenio in sacra scriptura vocacionem. Prima est signi exterioris . . .-. . . et ego faciens finem dico cum eodem apostolo, scilicet Ipsi gloria et imperium per omnia secula seculorum. Amen. Ff. 224–225.

119. S26*. *Benedictus es in templo* (Dan 3:53). Benedictus Deus in donis suis et sanctus in omnibus operibus suis. Benediccionis qua bonus erat . . .-

. . . frueris beatissima visione et beatus eris in templo glorie. Cuius glorie nos det . . . Ff. 225–226.

120. C22*. *Purum diligenter monstrat* (Aristotle, *De insomniis* 2). Reuerendi mei, quia nouerit vestra discrecio quod inter consuetudines quas mater nostra venerabilis . . .-. . . quia Dominus superbis resistit, etc. F. 226r–v. Edited in Wenzel, "Sermon in Praise of Philosophy."

121. C14*. ("De castitate"). *Timentibus Deum orietur sol iustitiae* (Mal 4:2). Reuerendi mei, quia secundum Philosophum anima in sua prima creacione est tabula nuda . . .-. . . et caritate feruidi perducamur ad premium eternum, supple quod . . . Ff. 227ra–229va.

122. T64* / C14* ("De bono exemplo alii proponendo"). *Expectamus Dominum* (Phil 3:20). Iustissimi iudicis sentencia diffinitiua exigentibus parentis nostri demeritis in hanc insulam deportati . . .-. . . et pro instabilitate inconcussa securitas. Hec nobis concedat . . . Ff. 229va–231rb.

123. T66* and S82a. *Regnabit rex* (Jer 23:5). Reuerendi magistri, patres, et domini, ierarcha suppremus rex, omnipotens Deus noster, mundi minoris regimen . . .-. . . cum eo imperpetuum et beatifice rex regnabit. Quod . . . Ff. 231rb–233ra. Also G-3.

124. S59*. *Hodie incipiam te exaltare* (Josh 3:7). Reuerendi patres et domini, sine gracia specialis influencia ipsius fontis misericordie celestium atque terrestrium conditoris . . .-. . . et eterne beatitudinis claritate nos eciam per infinita secula premiet et coronet. Amen. Ff. 232ra–237ra.

125. C14*. *Ut filii lucis ambulate* (Eph 5:8). Reuerendi domini et magistri, tria conspicio necessaria cuilibet viatori que fideles animos ad spiritualem progressum dirigunt indefessos . . .-. . . factus est nobis via temporalis per humilitatem, que mansio nobis eterna per diuinitatem. Ad quam mansionem . . . Ff. 237ra–239ra.

126. S59. *Data est ei corona* (Rev 6:2). Reuerendi patres et domini, secundum quod dicit Eustachius 8 *Ethicorum* capitulo 23, Dare est quoddam honorificum et diuinum . . .-. . . fructoque [!] benedicto refici. Et sic ad celi gaudia introduci . . . Ff. 239ra–241ra. Also in Worcester Q.56.

127. C14*. *Aedificavit domum suam super petram* (Matt 7:24). Reuerendi patres et domini, ad hoc precipue debet quilibet pronuncians verbum Dei se habere vt audientes retrahat a peccati consuetudine . . .-. . . temporalia propter ipsum relinquere. Vt valeamus cum eo . . . Ff. 241ra–242va.

128. C14*. *Qui humiliatus fuerit, erit in gloria* (Job 22:29). Reuerendi patres et domini, tria considerantur in sacra scriptura de quibus viatori cuilibet

conuenit gloriari . . .-. . . concludatur thematis nostre [!] veritas declarata: Qui humiliatus fuerit, erit in gloria. Ad quam . . . Ff. 242va–244rb.

129. T26*. *Intelligite haec qui obliviscemini Deum* (Ps 49:22). Est autem notandum secundum beatum Augustinum *De doctrina Christiana* quod officium doctoris ecclesiastici seu predicatoris est docere populum, mouere populum, et placere populo . . .-. . . Deus, Deus meus, respice in me, quare me dereliquisti, etc. Ff. 244rb–248vb.

130. C19*. *Videamus si floruerit vinea* (Cant 7:12). Reuerendi patres ac domini, in predicatore verbi Dei tria specialiter requiruntur, scilicet sapiencia sermonis . . .-. . . scilicet contemplatiui, hic scilicet cum gracia in presenti et gloria in futuro. Quam . . . Ff. 248vb–250va.

131. S26*. *Labora ut bonus miles Christi* (2 Thim 2:3). Reuerendi magistri, patres, et domini, sicud miles mundialis militare habet in defensione regni populumque precedere ac ipsum excitare hostes . . .-. . . saciabor inquit cum apparuerit gloria tua. Quam gloriam . . . Ff. 250va–252vb.

132. T43*. *Vocavit multos* (Luke 14:16). Infelix morsus fructus prohibiti, quem divina primis parentibus interdixit autoritas, vere felicitatis carenciam . . .-. . . quod fuit secundum principale. Quam quidem sanctitatem [!] sanctificari in via . . . Ff. 252vb–255ra.

133. T26*. *Amore langueo* (Cant 2:5). Reuerendi patres et domini, in hiis verbis duo possumus intueri que preces orancium cicius faciunt exaudiri . . .-. . . que preparauit Deus diligentibus se. Ad quod . . . Ff. 255ra–257rb.

134. ?. *Elegit vos Deus* ("2 Tim 2" = 1 Cor 1:27? Eph 1:4?). Discretor cogitacionum et cordium, Deus noster, cuius inuestigabiles vie, cuius occulta concilia, cuius consilia abissus multa . . .-. . . ecce secundum. Istum igitur fructum afferre . . . Ff. 257rb–258va.

135. C19*. *Flores apparuerunt in terra* (Cant 2:12). Reuerendi patres et domini, secundum beatum Ambrosium in *De paradiso* fons ineffabilis bonitatis, rerum omnium conditor et creator sue bonitatis . . .-. . . in terra. Sic ergo veluti flores nos apparere . . . Ff. 258va–259vb.

136. T19+*. *Ecce nunc dies salutis* (2 Cor 6:2). Beda super Apocalipsim in principio inter diuersas condiciones de audiendo verbum Dei duas recitat . . .-. . . miserere anime tue. Secunda consistit in. Ff. 259vb–261vb, inc.

137. C19*. [Acephalous]. In pacis, vnitatis, et dileccionis firma obseruacione . . .-. . . sed salus in celesti patria perpetuo permansura. Quam salutem . . . F. 262ra–va, acephalous.

138. S59* vigil. *Data est ei corona* (Rev 6:2). Reuerendi patres et domini confratresque karissimi, vt refocilletur fames interior anime ne dum sufficit

lepos diuini verbi venustus solum aures . . .-. . . quibus tu saginaris quam sepe ieiuni. Ff. 262v–263v, inc.

139. S59*. *Requiem quaesivi* (Sir 24:11). Reuerendi patres et domini, indigens alieno presid[i]o ad ipsius concurrit clemenciam qui verisimiliter sue indigencie voluerit ac poterit gaciosius subuenire . . .-. . . Requiem quesiui. Sic cum Uirgine in celi palacio faciat nos commescere . . . Ff. 264–266. Also in Worcester Q.56.

140. ?. *Nunc bene* (1 Macc 12:18). Karissimi, ex dictis sancti Augustini 12 *De ciuitate* capitulo 1 patet quod bene esse et male cuiusdam racionalis creature est penes accessum et recessum . . .-. . . Cantate ei canticum angelicum, videlicet Gloria in excelsis Deo. Ad hanc gloriam . . . F. 266r–v.

141. ?. *Regnum surget* (Luke 21:10). (Acephalous; text begins:) per medicinarum sumpcionem . . .-. . . spumat in libidinem nec vacat a misterio quod hec. Ff. 267–268v, acephalous and inc.

142. T18/4*. *Praeparate corda vestra Domino* (1 Sam 7:3). Karissimi mei, triplici instante causa solemnitatis huius diei nobis merito congruit corda Domino preparare . . .-. . . ita impossibile est hominem saluari sine humilitate. Ff. 269v–271, inc?

143. C14*. *Florete, flores* (Sir 39:19). Venerandi patres et domini, rosa refulgens ciuitatis superne, pater ille suppremus et rector Olimpi . . .-. . . vt vinee sitis efflorentes in huius mundi viridario iam Florete, flores, etc. Ff. 271r–v, 1–2, with renvoi.

144. T26*. *Lavit nos in sanguine suo* (Rev 1:5). Reuerendi domini, secundum Hugonem 4 *Super Angelicam Ierechiam* capitulo 4, mundum esse oportet qui alios mundare debet . . .-. . . participes effici valeatis glorie celestis regni. Quod . . . Ff. 272ra–274va.

145. T62*. *Iudaea abiit in Galilaeam* (John 4:47). Amantissimi domini, sicut scribit Remigius in suis *Interpretacionibus,* hec diccio Iudea secundum ebraicam accepcionem triplicem habet interpretacionem . . .-. . . diuitibus blandientes. Deus autem omnipotens sic nobis . . . Ff. 274vb–276rb.

146. ?. *Gentes ignorant Deum* (Thess 4:5). Attestante sentencia patrum et doctorum, tria sunt que ignoranciam causant Dei. Primum est necligencia proprie consideracionis . . .-. . . vita eterna, vt cognoscant te solum verum Deum. Quod . . . Ff. 276va–278va.

147. C16 ("In celebracione ordinum"). *Illi soli servies* (Matt 4:10). Karissimi, dicit Philosophus 3 *Ethicorum* quod aliter iudicat studiosus, aliter prauus . . .-. . . in finali iudicii districtissimo examine. Ff. 278va–280va, inc.

148. T23*. *Graviter vulneratus sum* (1 Kings 22:34). Karissimi, predicator verbi Dei debet sibi vilescere vt vulneret superbos exemplo sue humilitatis . . .- . . . voluntas nulla delinquendi potestas, etc. Ff. 280va–282ra, inc. Repeats W-116.

149. ?. *Vade et noli amplius peccare* (John 8:11). Ista verba dixit Iesus cuidam mulieri deprehense in adulterio . . .-. . . post istam vitam manebis seor[s]um in celo. Quod . . . Ff. 282ra–283va.

150. ?. [Acephalous]. (?). Sumus cum Christo per baptismum in mortem . . .- . . . veritas in promisso et vita in premio sempiterno. Quod . . . F. 284ra–b.

151. T24*. *Ite in castellum* (Matt 21:2). Non erunt nisi quasi flores sine fructu, quia sicut Apostolus dicit 1 Ad Corinthios 13, Si linguis . . .- . . . fistulacionem illam faciet nos obdormire et totum castrum nostrum ibi in prodicionem. Ff. 284rb–287ra, inc. Repeats W-107 without its beginning.

152. T25*. *A Domino corripimur, ut non cum hoc mundo damnemur* (1 Cor 11:32). Domini, lego in scriptura sacra 3 Regum 18 capitulo quod sanctus propheta Helias, cum offerret sacrificium ad placitum Domini Dei sui, tulit illud quod foret suum . . .-. . . exultacio, quantam nec lingua potest dicere nec cor cogitare. Ad quod . . . Ff. 288ra–290ra.

153. T26*. *Ecce quomodo amabat* (John 11:36). Reuerendi patres et domini, in huius exilis collacionis exordio Patris potenciam, Filii sapienciam, ac Spiritus Sancti benignissimam clemenciam . . .-. . . qui vt instrueret quomodo nos amauit, diram pro nobis mortem hodie tollerauit. Amen. Ff. 290ra–291rb.

154. T23*. *Quem teipsum facis* (John 8:53). Ista verba primitus recitata . . . Domini, si consideracionem habere vellemus ad statum . . .-. . . hic scilicet viuere in gracia et goodnes, et in celo eternaliter in blys and gladnes. Quo . . . Ff. 291rb–293va. Edited in Wenzel, *Macaronic*, pp. 308–345.

155. T26*. *Vulnerasti cor meum, sponsa* (Cant 4:9). Reuerendi patres et domini, in huius exilis collacionis exordio, inuocato Sancti Spiritus auxilio in omni bono opere necessario requisito . . .-. . . tuta habitacio paradisi. Huius gloriose habitacionis . . . Ff. 293vb–294vb.

156. S59*. *In civitate sanctificata requievi* (Sir 24:15). Reuerendi domini, sicut ciuium societati firma sit proteccio, in ciuitate, de qua sceleris et peccati plena fit eieccio, per sanctificacionem . . .-. . . secundum quod in tercio principali tactum est, verba thematis recitari In ciuitate sancta requieui. Ff. 295–297v.

157. C21?. *Transiet de morte ad vitam* (John 5:24). Secundum Philosophum a fine denominandum est vnumquodque . . .-. . . <protractans> concludit sic ibidem: Qui verbum meum audit et credit, etc. Ff. 309va–310rb.

158. C21. *Cuius est imago haec?* (Luke 20:24). Videmus quod quando quis debeat alteri obligari pro aliqua certa re, tunc faciunt tales inter se vnam indenturam cum creditis signis . . .-. . . tunc intrabit rex noster Christus Iesus et suum castrum possidebit in honore et gloria, etc. Ff. 310rb–311vb.

159. S65. *Lux orta est* (Isa 9:2). Reuerendi patres et domini, fons et origo sapiencie, virtutum largitor, lux et remunerator meritorum, Dominus Iesus Christus . . .-. . . thema Lux, etc. Cuius claritatem . . . Ff. 311vb–315rb. Repeats W-104.

160. S26*. *Abite, liberi, ad patrem* (Gen 44:17). Reuerendi patres et domini, postquam primus parens de patria libertatis in locum miserabilis seruitutis per esum pestiferum suggestione corruerat serpentina . . .-. . . secundum thematis sentenciam Abite, liberi, ad patrem. Ad quem . . . Ff. 315rb–318rb. Repeats W-105.

161. S05*. *Ego quasi vitis fructificavi* (Sir 24:23). Reuerendi patres, que, qualis, et quanta sit Beatissima Virgo, cuius concepcionem hodie celebramus . . .-. . . recreantur, pascuntur, sociantur superni ciues celorum. Ad quorum . . . Ff. 318rb–319vb. Repeats W-106.

162. ?. *Iesus faciebat signa* (John 6:2). Solent signa triplici de causa dari aut fieri, videlicet supereminencia et potestate . . .-. . . de Petro qui Christum negauit. F. 320ra–vb.

163. T19*. *Ecce nunc dies salutis* (2 Cor 6:2). Karissimi, istud verbum veraciter vobis prolatum supponit quod perdidistis optimum diligibile . . .-. . . ascendent omnes anime iuste, vbi in secula seculorum manebunt in splendoribus suis. Amen. Ff. 320vb–321rb. Also A-47.

164. ?. *Psallite Deo qui ascendit* (Ps 67:34). Karissimi, musica seu melodia adeo est naturalis secundum Boecium in prologo *Musice* quod impossibile est hominem melodiam bene sonantem sine delectacio . . .-. . . cum triumphatore Christo celos ascendit. Hic igitur sit finis, benedictusque Marie filius. Amen. Ff. 321vb–322vb.

165. T28/2*. *Regressi sunt in Hierusalem* (Luke 24:33). Reuerendi domini, vos intelligetis, secundum quod dicunt clerici, quod Ierusalem accipitur multipliciter . . .-. . . sic abstulerunt et satisfaciant pro illis. Ff. 322vb–323va.

166. ?. *Exaltavi lignum humile* (Ezek 17:24). Reuerendi patres et domini, cum secundum Apostolum 2 Ad Corinthios 3 capitulo infirma nature nostre condicio tanta langueat debilitatis impotencia . . .-. . . cornibus nexibus

videlicet spi- [*catchword*: narum atque tribulorum]. F. 323va–b, inc. with renvoi.

167. T62*. *Induite vos armatura* (Eph 6:11). Reuerendi domini patresque conscripti, quamdiu in valle miserie simus, mundi humana versatur mortalitas . . .-. . . sic pugnemus in via vt pro triumphali victoria nobis reddatur corona in patria. Quam . . . Ff. 336–338.

WA – John Waldeby, *Novum opus dominicale*

Based on Oxford, Bodleian Library, MS Laud misc. 77.

1. ? (Prologue to the following sermons). *Praedicate evangelium omni creature* (Mark 16:15). Ad oculum cernitis quod in successione hereditaria . . .-. . . repleti fructu iusticie per Iesum Christum in laudem et gloriam Dei, cui sit honor et gloria in secula seculorum. Amen. Ff. 1–2v.

2. T54. *Quaerite regnum Dei* (Matt 6:33). Videtis quod peregrini, cum per partes . . .-. . . illud solum est perpetuum. Cuius participes non efficiet qui. . . . Ff. 2v–3v.

3. T55. *Resedit qui erat mortuus* (Luke 7:15). Historialiter potest introduci thema per processum euangelii hodierni, Ibat Iesus in ciuitatem que vocatur Naym, etc., set moraliter sic: Christus, postquam fuit suscitatus a mortuis, stetit in medio discipulorum . . .-. . . facit inuenire vitam eternam. Quam . . . Ff. 4–5v.

4. T57. *Magister, quod est magnum mandatum in lege?* (Matt 22:36). Loqui de mandatis legis est ad propositum . . .-. . . eterna serua mandata. Que conseruare . . . Ff. 5v–7.

5. T56. *Amice, ascende superius* (Luke 14:10). Karissimi, \natura,/ ars, et Christi doctrina concorditer nos docent . . .-. . . ascendamus ad montem Domini. Cui honor . . . Ff. 7–9.

6. T58. *Offerebant ei paralyticum* (Matt 9:2). Karissimi, videtis ad oculum quod quando aliquis famosus artifex in arte aliqua transit per patriam . . .-. . . infirmos curare possit Dominus Iesus Christus. Cui honor . . . Ff. 9–11v.

7. T59. *Nuptiae quidem paratae sunt, sed qui invitati erant, non erant digni* (Matt 22:8). Karissimi, quando aliquis magnus nupcias contrahit cum aliqua puella . . .-. . . inuenit dignos se. Cui sit . . . Ff. 11v–13.

8. T60. *Nisi signa et prodigia videritis, non creditis* (John 4:48). Videtis quod quando rex declinat ad aliquam partem regni . . .-. . . in festo vel cena regis eterni. Cui honor . . . Ff. 13–16.

9. T61. *Oportet te misereri conservi tui, sicut et ego tui misertus sum* (Matt 18:33). Predicare de misericordia est ad propositum et aliunde est valde necessarium . . .-. . . inueniat graciam et gloriam. Quam . . . Ff. 16–18.

10. T62. *Reddite* (Matt 22:21). Karissimi, qui multa recipit sine suo merito, multa reddere tenetur ex debito . . .-. . . a nouissimis vsque ad primos. Hanc mercedem . . . Ff. 18–20.

11. T63. *Confide, filia* (Matt 9:22). Ieronimus in epistula dicit quod Christiani celebribus nominibus . . .-. . . in futuro per firmitatem glorie. Quam . . . Ff. 20–22v.

12. T64. *Misereor super turbam* (Mark 8:2? Matt 15:32? John 6:15 ff.?). Karissimi, Dominus Iesus in sua incarnacione . . .-. . . et sanabat omnes. Virtutis huius et gracie nos participes . . . Ff. 22v–26.

13. T01. *Cum adpropinquaret Iesus Hierosolymis,* etc. (cf. Matt 21:1). Euangelium est laycis exponendum et predicandum triplici de causa . . .-. . . cotidie, idest in aduersis, in prosperis. Huic Domino . . . Ff. 26–28v.

14. T02. *Erunt signa in sole* (Luke 21:25). Karissimi, legimus in veteri testamento de tribus magnis vindictis Dei . . .-. . . a signis celi nolite metuere. Ad hunc aduentum . . . Ff. 28v–33v.

15. T03. *Mortui resurgunt* (Matt 11:5 and Luke 7). Videtis quod ille expertus esset medicus . . .-. . . a mortuis suscitare potens est Deus. Cui honor . . . Ff. 33v–36.

16. T04. *Ego vox clamantis in deserto* (John 1:23). Cum preco clamat et puplicat decretum et voluntatem regis . . .-. . . vocem fletus mei. Hanc vocem . . . Ff. 36–38v.

17. T06. *Gloria in excelsis Deo et in terra pax hominibus bonae voluntatis* (Luke 2:14). Videtis quod rex, quando de nouo venit ad regnum . . .-. . . sicud in celo et in terra. Quam voluntatem . . . Ff. 38v–41.

18. T07. *Gratia Dei erat in illo* (Luke 2:40). Karissimi, quoniam rex aliquis terrenus contra populum sibi superbum, rebellem, et proteruum statuit legem duram . . .-. . . in electos illius ipsius. Quam graciam . . . Ff. 41–44.

19. T11a. *Remansit puer Iesus in Ierusalem* (Luke 2:43). Quando seruus aliquis habet negocium . . .-. . . sursum est Ierusalem libera est. Quam . . . Ff. 44–46.

20. T12. *Nuptiae factae sunt* (John 2:1). Karissimi, in hac dominica, que prima est post natalem Christi completum, fit mencio de nupciis . . .-. . . sicud rex in magna gloria. Quam . . . Ff. 46–48v.

21. T13. *Domine, si vis, potes me mundare* (Matt 8:2). Istud euangelium cito post natale Christi . . .-. . . repentina calamitas. Quam deus auertat . . . Ff. 48v–50v.

22. T14. *Motus magnus factus est in mari* (Matt 8:24). Karissimi, quamuis motus continuus fluxus et refluxus mari . . .-. . . in primo principali sermonis Confide filia . . . Ff. 50v–52v.

23. T15. *Spiritus Domini super me* (Luke 4:19). In euangelio super illo textu Marci 2 Vidit Iohannes spiritum sanctum descendentem super eum . . .-. . . et spiritu principali confirma me. Huic spiritui . . . Ff. 52v–54.

24. T16. *Voca operarios et redde illis mercedem* (Matt 20:8). Karissimi, solent domini terreni, cum laboratores de sero . . .-. . . merces tua magna nimis. Hanc . . . Ff. 54–56v.

25. T17?. *Exiit qui seminat seminare semen suum* (Luke 8:5). Karissimi, videtis quod paterfamilias prouidus exit primo mane portans secum diuersa semina . . .-. . . bona domini in terra viuencium. Ad quam . . . Ff. 56v–59v.

26. T18. *Iesu, fili David, miserere mei* (Luke 18:38). Legimus quod mulier Chananea frequenter . . .-. . . misertus est Dominus timentibus se quoniam ipse . . . Ff. 59v–61v.

27. T18/4. *Faciem tuam lava* (Matt 6:17). Karissimi, sicud corporalis honestas hoc exigit . . .-. . . facies tua plena graciarum. Cuius aspectum . . . Ff. 62–64.

28. T19. *Ductus est Iesus in desertum*, et reliqua vsque ad finem euangelii (Matt 4:1–11). Karissimi, eodem modo videtur iam de sermonibus sicud de vestibus. Olim homines vtebantur vestibus longis et latis . . .-. . . adiutorio angelorum ex mandato Dei. Cui sit honor, etc. Deo gracias. Ff. 64–70.

29. T20. *Miserere mei, Domine* (Matt 15:22). Tradunt auctores de bellorum titulis tractantes . . .-. . . maxima pro transitoriis eterna recompensare, etc. Ff. 70–73.

30. T21. *Signum de celo quaerebant ab eo* (Luke 11:16). Legitur Iudicum 6 quod filii Israel erant sub seruitute Madian . . .-. . . in inferno hii qui peccauerunt. Igitur queramus a Deo modo predicto signum . . . Ff. 73–77.

31. T22. *Abiit Iesus trans mare* (John 6:1). Secundum Gregorium mare est presens seculum . . .-. . . quoad omnes satisfacientes. Quam graciam . . . Ff. 77–80v.

32. T23. *Tulerunt lapides ut iacerent in eum* (John 8:59). Karissimi, videtis quod quando artifex debet facere pontem securum . . .-. . . in filiis Abrahe per gloriam. Quam . . . Ff. 80v–84v.

33. T24. *Cum adpropinquaret Iesus Hierosolymis*, etc. (Matt 21:1). Require dominica prima aduentus. F. 84v.

34. T24. *Tristis est anima mea usque ad mortem* (Matt 26:38). Hec verba tripliciter exponi possunt . . .-. . . gaudium vestrum nemo tollet, etc. Amen. Ff. 84v–87v.

35. T26?. *Exivit Iesus portans coronam spineam et purpureum vestimentum* (cf. John 19:2). Dicitur frequenter in scriptura, et verum est, quod Christum per suam passionem erat remedium . . .-. . . manebit in gloria celesti. Quam . . . Ff. 87v–91.

36. T28*. *Epulari et gaudere oportebat, quia frater tuus hic mortuus erat et revixit* (Luke 15:32). Karissimi, ista fuerunt verba patris de filio suo prodigo . . .-. . . et vitam vsque in seculum. Quam nobis, etc. Ff. 91–94v.

37. T29. *Pax vobis* (John 20:19). Videtur quod qui ad aliam terram vadit ut inhabitet, expedit sibi ydioma patrie scire . . .-. . . et qui erat et qui venturus est. Cui honor, etc. Amen. Ff. 94v–98.

38. T30. *Vocem meam audient* (John 10:16). Sicut dicit Aristoteles in *Problematibus* suis . . .-. . . ceruus ad fontes aquarum, etc. Ad hoc potest adduci exemplum aliquod de vita vel doctrina sancti de quo fit predicacio, etc. Concluditur sermo. Ff. 98–99v.

39. T31. *Tristitia vestra vertetur in gaudium* (John 16:20). Karissimi, vita hominis in hoc mundo . . .-. . . gaudium vestrum nemo tollet a vobis. Quod . . . Ff. 99v–101v.

40. T32. *Ille arguet mundum* (John 16:8). Dicunt naturales quod quando fortiter due nubes . . .-. . . propterea odit vos mundus. Ff. 101v–104v.

41. T33. *Petite et accipietis, ut gaudium vestrum sit plenum* (John 16:24). Sicud dicit Augustinus super illud Matthei 16, Vidit aliquos in foro stantes . . .- . . . peticiones vestre innotescantur apud Deum. Cui honor . . . Ff. 104v–106v.

42. T34*. [*Petite et accipietis, ut . . . plenum* (John 16:24)]. Accipiet homo prosequens aliquam possessionem temporalem tripliciter . . .-. . . qui vocati sunt eterne hereditatis, quasi, etc. Amen. Ff. 106v–107v.

43. T34?. *Gaudium vestrum sit plenum* (John 16:24). Est triplex gaudium, scilicet [vanum?] auarorum . . .-. . . gaudere oportebat, in secundo principali; et concluditur sermo. Ff. 107v–108.

44. T36. *Dominus Iesus, postquam locutus est eis, adsumptus est in caelum* (Mark 16:19). Cum in hoc mundo tria sunt opera . . .-. . . de celo venit super omnes. Cui honor . . . Ff. 108–111.

45. T37. *Reminiscamini* (John 16:4). Karissimi, tria sunt que reddere debent homini tribulacionem . . .-. . . ne reminiscaris, Domine, delicta mea; et finiatur sermo. Amen. Ff. 111–113v.

46. T39. *Vadit et assumit septem spiritus* (Matt 12:45 and Luke 11:25). Verba ista in serie euangelii . . .-. . . pietatem in Spiritu Sancto. Cui honor . . . Ff. 113v–116.

47. T39*. *Spiritus Domini super me* (Luke 4:19). Require totum sermonem dominica quinta post Epiphaniam, et est totus sermo de Sancto Spiritu et ad propositum de festo. Ff. 116.

48. T41. *Estote misericordes, sicud Pater vester caelestis misericors est* (Luke 6:36). Sicud dicit Augustinus in quadam omelia, filiorum condicio esse debet . . .- . . . memoratus sum misericordie tue. Quam . . . Ff. 116–117v.

49. T42. *Homo quidam fecit cenam magnam et vocavit multos* (Luke 14:16). Karissimi, quando multi simul per viam peregrinantur . . .-. . . ad cenam nupciarum vocati sunt. Ad quam cenam nos, etc. Ff. 117v–119.

50. T43. *Quaerit diligenter donec inveniat* (Luke 15:8). Scribitur Ecclesiastici 5: Contra malum bonum est . . .-. . . iudex Dei sedens. Cui honor . . . Ff. 119–121v.

51. T44. *Per totam noctem laborantes nihil cepimus* (Luke 5:5). Communiter dicitur quod quilibet vadum sic describit secundum quod ipsemet pertransit . . .-. . . dormierunt sompnum suum et nichil inuenerunt, etc. Ff. 121v–123v.

52. T45. *Nisi abundaverit iustitia vestra plus quam Scribarum et Pharisaeorum, non intrabitis in regnum caelorum* (Matt 5:20). Karissimi, obseruantibus legem Moysaicam Deus promisit solum temporalia . . .-. . . quoniam ipsorum est regnum celorum. Quod . . . Ff. 123v–125v.

53. T46. *Misereor super turbam, quia ecce iam triduo sustinent me nec habent quod manducent* (Mark 8:2). Karissimi, sicut dicit Augustinus in omelia super illud Duo homines ascenderunt . . .-. . . manducabit panem in regno celorum. Quod . . . Ff. 125v–127.

54. T47. *Qui facit voluntatem Patris mei qui in caelo est, ipse intrabit in regnum caelorum* (Matt 7:21). Karissimi, triplex extitit opinio de introitu in regnum celorum . . .-. . . per multas tribulaciones oportet intrare in regnum Dei. Quod, etc. Ff. 127–129v.

55. T48. *Filii huius saeculi prudentiores filiis lucis in generatione sua sunt* (Luke 16:8). Karissimi, cum in sacra scriptura per filios huius seculi intelligantur homines mali . . .-. . . inaccessibilem, suple per eternam gloriam. Quam, etc. Ff. 129v–131.

56. T49. *Domus mea domus orationis vocabitur* (Luke 19:46). Karissimi, quamuis omnes domus palacii regii sint domus regis . . .-. . . conserua in eternum inpollutam domum istam . . . Ff. 131–133v.

57. T50. *Qui se exaltat, humiliabitur . . . exaltabitur* (Luke 18:14). Karissimi, videtis quod in statera . . .-. . . et sublimis erit valde. Hanc sublimitatem . . . Ff. 133v–135.

58. T51. *Surdos fecit audire et mutos loqui* (Mark 7:37). Karissimi, secundum phisicos et omnes naturales, arterie et meatus per quos transit auditus . . .- . . . surdos fecit audire et mutos loqui. Cui honor . . . Ff. 135–137.

59. T52. *Diliges Dominum Deum tuum ex toto corde tuo* (Luke 10:27). Sicut dicit Augustinus, dilectio est vita anime . . .-. . . dedit nobis consolacionem eternam. Hanc . . . Ff. 137–138v.

60. T53. *Surge et vade* (Luke 17:19). Perfectus medicus non solum egrotum curat . . .-. . . in domum tuam, idest in eternam gloriam. Quam nobis, etc. Ff. 138v–140.

X – Worcester, Cathedral Library, MS F.126

Occasions as given in rubrics or in the table. Due to the poor quality of the microfiche provided, my recording of explicits is incomplete.

1. T01. *Venit in nomine Domini* (Matt 21:9). Karissimi, sancta mater Ecclesia hodie celebritatem facit de adventu . . .-. . . venit in nomine Domini. Ff. 1rb–3va.

2. T02. *Mitte angelum tuum bonum ante nos* (2 Macc 15:23). Fratres, sapiencie vnigenitum Dei verbum . . .-. . . ? Ff. 3va–4rb.

3. T03. *Tunc laus erit* (1 Cor 4:5). Karissimi, tota sacra scriptura certis quasi leuiter ponderatis . . .-. . . ad istam laudem audiendam et Saluatori nostro sine fine reddendam precordia nostra apperiat Iesus Christus Dominus noster qui. . . . Ff. 4va–7ra.

4. T04. *Tu quis es?* (John 1:19). Puer tener et iuuenis sub matris custodia delicate nutritus . . .-. . . fili, tu semper mecum es et omnia mea tua sunt. Ad quem. . . . Ff. 7ra–8vb. Also B/2-24 and Padua-31.

5. T01. *Parate viam Domini* (Mark 1:3). Sicud in primo parente . . .-. . . et in viis Domini ambulantes impetrare poterimus graciam in presenti et gloriam in futuro. Quam. . . . Ff. 8vb–11ra. Also S-11.

6. T02. *Erunt signa in sole et luna et stellis* (Luke 21:25). Vegecius *De re militari* libro 3 capitulo 5 dicit quod inter reliqua . . . .-. . . . in quo signati estis,

signati inquam in presenti per graciam, in futuro consequamur gloriam. Ad quam . . . Ff. 11ra–12ra.

7. T01. *Benedictus qui venit in nomine Domini* (Matt 21:9, etc.). Karissimi, humana natura in primo parente per peccatum quasi infecta . . .-. . . pax sine discordia. Ad illam pacem . . . Ff. 12ra–13ra.

8. T01. *Hora est iam nos de somno surgere* (Rom 3:11). Volentibus transire mare est necessarium considerare . . .-. . . et displicencie tradidit . . . F. 13ra–b. Boraston, in Merton 216 (Schneyer 5:449); cf. Forte, "Simon of Boraston."

9. T03. *Caeci vident* (Matt 11:5). Augustinus libro *Confessionum* [?] . . . super illicitas cupiditates . . .-. . . suscepit graciam plurimas defert ad,,, semen. F. 13rb–vb. Boraston, in Merton 216 (Schneyer 5:450).

10. T04. *Gaudete in Domino* (Phil 4:4). Karissimi, status presentis vite videtur . . .-. . . Ff. 13vb–15rb.

11. T01. *Nox praecessit, dies autem appropinquabit* (Rom 13:12). Karissimi, noctis dieique temporum vicissitudine rerum . . .-. . . ? F. 15rb–va.

12. T02. *Levate capita vestra ecce appropinquabit redemptio vestra* (Luke 21:28). Mult' per quod. .atur infirmit' [?] . . .-. . . ? F. 15va.

13. T03. *Tu es* (Matt 11:3). In quibus verbis asserendo prolatis Christi perfeccio . . .-. . . vt conueniunt isti. Tu es, etc. F. 15vb.

14. T04. *Dominus prope est* (Phil 4:5). Karissimi, omnes in aduentu domini sui habens [?] sibi qui sunt de familia . . .-. . . prope est Dominus omnibus invocantibus eum in veritate . . . F. 15vb.

15. T04. *Gaudete in Domino* (Phil 4:4). Numquid . . . sequitur acceptabile quod de iure . . .-. . . propter hec et alia similia nos monet apostolus Gaudete. Ff. 15vb–16ra.

16. T04. *Vox clamantis in deserto* (John 1:23). Karissimi, diuersa ministeria diuersimodo designantur, sed hic . . .-. . . beatus Iohannes vox clamantis. F. 16ra.

17. T02. *Erunt signa in sole et luna* (Luke 21:23). Karissimi, hec verba sic allegorice exponantur misterium reparacionis humane . . .-. . . verba prius proposita iam veraciter esse completa: Erunt signa in sole et luna. F. 16rb–va. Also in Worcester Q.63.

18. T02. *Respicite et levate capita vestra, ecce appropinquabit redempcio vestra* (Luke 21:28). Karissimi, verba ista sub vno intellectu exposita denotant quedam precipua . . .-. . . et in illis plus elementa. Ff. 16va–17vb, inc.

19. T01. *Veniet desideratus cunctis gentibus* (Hagg 2:8). Quoniam ad miseri[cordi]am pertinet desolatos et afflictos consolari . . .-. . . omnis

corrupcio siue passibilitas. Quod . . . Ff. 17vb–18vb. Bonaventura (Schneyer 1:653; cf. 1:779).

20. To1. *Veni, Domine Iesu* (Rev 22:20). Desiderium antiquorum patrum . . .-. . . serotinus terre ymber terram fructificare facit. F. 24ra–b.

21. To2. *Erit radix Iesse et qui exsurget regere gentes, et in eum gentes sperabunt* (Rom 15:12). Cor hominis quadrupllici affeccione mouetur . . .-. . . sed caritati succedit possessio eterne glorie. Ad quam . . . Ff. 24rb–25ra.

22. To4. *Promiserat per prophetas suos de filio suo in scripturis sanctis* (Rom 1:2). Aduentus, karissimi, Domini nostri Iesu Christi in mundum per natiui-tatem . . .-. . . celestium possessores in superna curia. Ad quam . . . F. 25ra–b.

23. To4. *Qui factus est ei ex semine David secundum carnem* (Rom 1:3). Diuini-tas colenda humilitas stupenda dignitas preferenda . . .-. . . sanctus est secundum carnem natus prius . . . F. 25rb–vb.

24. To1. *Benedictus qui venit*, etc. vbi prius (Matt 21:9, etc.). Karissimi, Celum, terra, mundus totus, angeli, demones . . .-. . . via proximior ad regnum celorum scilicet via caritatis. Quam viam . . . Ff. 26ra–27ra.

25. To2. *Respicite et levate capita vestra* (Luke 21:28). Homines autem miseros et confusioni proximos . . .-. . . pallium laudis pro spiritu meroris. Quo nobis . . . Ff. 27ra–28ra.

26. T24. *Extrema gaudii luctus occupat* (Prov 14:13). Karissimi, ista verba que nunc dixi in latinis possunt sic dici in Anglico: Worliche blysse . . . Quia si consideremus gaudium. . . .-. . . et terremotus factus est, etc. Nota in ewangelio. Ff. 28rb–30rb, inc.

27. To1. *Veni, Domine Iesu* (Rev 22:20). Karissimi, testante commentatore super *Angelicam ierarchiam* capitulo [*blank*], cuius operacio ab alieno . . .-. . . ire et furoris ad conterendos peccatores de terra. Ff. 30rb–31vb, inc.

28. To2. *Prope est regnum Dei* (Luke 21:31). Beatus Gregorius 5 *Moralium* capit-ulo super illud [Iohannis?] . . .-. . . cuius regni nos coheredes efficiat qui . . . Ff. 32ra–33ra. Also F/1-4.

29. To1. *Venit tibi*, idest veniet tibi (Matt 21:5). Karissime [!], scitis quod duo sunt motiua . . .-. . . nisi fuerit Deus cum eo. F. 33rb–va.

30. To2. *Appropinquat* (Luke 21:28). Karissimi, scire debetis quod totum genus humanum ante Christi aduentum fuit quadruplici miseria inuolutum . . .-. . . erat lux vera usque in hunc mundum. F. 33va.

31. To3. *Iudicat me Dominus*, idest, iudicabit me Dominus (1 Cor 4:3). Licet Christi potestas in diuersis diuersimodis causis . . .-. . . ad celestem gloriam transierunt. F. 33va.

32. T04. *Prope est* (Phil 4:5). Karissimi, scitis quod quilibet solet multum gratulari . . .-. . . homo erat Deus nec Deus erat homo etc. F. 33va–b.

33. T06 ("In prima missa natiuitatis"). *Exiit* (Luke 2:1). Karissimi, videmus ad sensum quod solent reges et principes . . .-. . . fecit angelorum. F. 33vb.

34. T06 ("in prima missa Natiuitatis"). *Invenerunt Mariam* (Luke 2:6). Karissimi, legimus in ewangelio quod duo genera hominum sollicite querentes . . .-. . . tanquam filium tali exibere matri. A[d] quam, etc. Ff. 33vb–34vb.

35. T06 ("In tercia missa"). *Venit* (John 1:7). Pro breui processu sermonis est aduertendum quod tria mala in mundo habundant valde . . .-. . . quia a Deo venisti, etc., usque cum eo. F. 34ra.

36. T01. *Induimini Dominum* (Rom 13:14). Sciens, karissimi, apud exercitum Christianorum . . .-. . . dat graciam ita in [!] hic in presenti et gloriam in futuro. Ad quam . . . Ff. 34vb–35ra.

37. T01. *Rex tuus venit* (Matt 21:5). Sicud dicit Gregorius 4 *Moralium* capitulo 19, reges quippe . . .-. . . ad paradysi gaudia pie reduxit. Ad quem . . . Ff. 35ra–36ra.

38. T04. *Ego vox clamantis* (John 1:23). Mathei 2 dicit et Saluator recitat in euangelio Ecce ego mitto angelum . . .-. . . veniet angelorum equalitas et veniet Christi hereditas. Ad quam . . . Ff. 36ra–37rb.

39. T02. *Levate capita vestra, quoniam appropinquabit redemptio vestra* (Luke 21:28). Ex verbo salutifero predicacionis non tantum predicatoris verum verbi Dei . . .-. . . ? Ff. 37rb–39va.

40. T04. *Dirigite viam Domini, sicut dixit Esaias propheta* (John 1:23). Sicut dicit Gregorius in quadam omelia . . . illud Mathei 3 Vox clamantis . . .-. . . in eadem auctoritate Ysaie 40. Ad quam . . . Ff. 39vb–40ra.

41. T01. *Abiciamus opera tenebrarum . . . ambulemus* (Rom 13:12). Defigens Apostolus oculorum intuitum . . .-. . . cum finali bonorum operum execucione Abiciamus ergo opera tenebrarum etc. F. 41ra–va. Also J/4-1 and BN lat. 18195-1 (see Schneyer 7:391–395).

42. T02. *Levate capita vestra, ecce appropinquat redemptio vestra* (Luke 21:28). Sicut qui claudit oculos non potest videre . . .-. . . dicit sicud Leuate capita vestra, etc. Ff. 41va–42ra. Also J/4-2 and BN lat. 18195-2.

43. T04. *Pax Dei, quae exsuperat omnem sensum, custodiat vestra corda*, etc. (Phil 4:7). Verba proposita scripta sunt in epistula Ad Philippenses 4, in quibus ostenditur doctrine apostolice auctoritas . . .-. . . omnem temporis mensuram pax Dei exsuperat, etc. F. 42ra–b. Also J/4-3 and BN lat. 18195-4.

44. T03. *Quid existis in desertum videre?* (Matt 11:7). Uerba proposita sunt uerba Redemptoris, et secundum sensum . . .-. . . quid existis videre, etc. F. 42rb–va. Also J/4-4 and BN lat. 18195-3.

45. T04. *Vox clamantis in deserto* (John 1:23). Uerba proposita allegorice sumpta . . .-. . . dic' ergo Vox clamantis in deserto. Ff. 42va–43ra. Also J/4-5 and BN lat. 18195-5.

46. T04. *Dirigite viam Domini* (John 1:23). Quamplures sunt qui contendunt exequi . . .-. . . sine diffidencia et trepidacione Dirigite ergo viam Domini, etc. F. 43ra–b. Also J/4-6 and BN lat. 18195-6.

47. T06. *Videamus hoc verbum quod factum est* (Luke 2:15). Quia enim facilius et forcius homo credit visui quam auditui . . .-. . . distribucione premiorum dic' ergo Videamus hoc verbum quod factum est. F. 43rb–vb. Also J/4-7 and BN lat. 18195-7?

48. T07. *Misit Deus filium suum ex muliere factum sub lege . . . reduceret* (Gal 4:4). In uerbis propositis scriptis Galatarum 2 exprimitur nobis Filii Dei excellencia . . .-. . . ideo Misit deus filium factum ex muliere factum sub lege, etc. Ff. 43vb–44ra. Also J/4-8 and BN lat. 18195-8.

49. T10. *Intrantes domum invenerunt puerum,* etc. (Matt 2:11). In hiis verbis Mathei 2 scriptis et hodie in Ecclesia recitatis innuit nobis sermo dominicus quod omnis qui petat accipit . . .-. . . puerum iocunditate interminabilem. Intrantes . . . F. 44ra–va. Also J/4-9 and BN lat. 18195-9.

50. T11. *Ecce agnus Dei, ecce qui tollit peccata mundi* (John 1:29). Quanta sit nostri redemptoris benignitas . . .-. . . ideo peccata abstulit quod ideo Ecce agnus Dei, etc. F. 44va–b. Also J/4-10 and BN lat. 18195-10.

51. T11a ("dominica 2 post natiuitatem Domini"). *Post triduum invenerunt eum in templo in medio doctorum* (Luke 2:46). In uerbis propositis scriptis Luce 2 innuit nobis sermo euangelicus quod qui Iesum bene querit, bene inuenit . . .-. . . querentibus dicatur Post triduum inuenerunt eum etc. Ff. 44vb–45rb. Also J/4-11 and BN lat. 18195-11.

52. T12. *Spiritu ferventes Domino sequentes, non alta sapientes sed humilibus consentientes* (Rom 12:11). Defigens beatus Apostolus aciem intelligencie in contuitum hominum . . .-. . . vt sic simus spiritu feruentes et Domino seruientes, etc. F. 45rb–vb. Also J/4-12 and BN lat. 18195-12.

53. T13. *Extendens Iesus manum tetigit eum dicens, Volo* (Matt 8:3). Visitacio siue presencia boni medici solacium . . .-. . . per satisfaccionem, dic' ergo Extendens Iesus manum, etc. Ff. 45vb–46ra. Also J/4-13 and BN lat. 18195-14.

54. T19. *Ecce nunc dies salutis* (2 Cor 6:2). In uerbis istis tangitur intencio principalis cuiuslibet predicatoris . . .-. . . penitenciam agite, appropinquabit enim regnum celorum. Quod . . . Ff. 46ra–48ra.

55. T19. *Ductus est Iesus a spiritu in desertum, ut temptaretur a diabolo* (Matt 4:1). Qui voluerit esse Iesus, idest sui Saluator, imitetur . . .-. . . et corruet et non erit qui suscitet eum. Ff. 48ra–va.

56. T19/5. *Servus non manet in domo in aeternum, filius autem manet in aeternum* (John 8:35). Secundum duas partes iusticie que notantur in Psalmo Declina a malo . . .-. . . heredes dei coheredes autem Christi. F. 48va.

57. T19/7. *Surgite et nolite timere* (Matt 17:7). Anima racionalis in ymaginem Dei creata . . .-. . . ? Ff. 48va–49ra.

58. T20. *Domine, adiuva me* (Matt 15:25). Verba proposita recitata sunt in ewangelio instantis dominice quoad vsum secularium. Videns Saluator hominem errantem per culpam . . .-. . . ? F. 49rb.

59. T20. *Miserere mei, Domine, fili David* (Matt 15:22). In principio sermonis debet predicator premittere laudem . . .-. . . ipse tribuit vnde placetur. Cui honor et gloria. Amen. Ff. 49va–50va.

60. T21. *Erat Iesus eiciens daemonium* (Luke 11:14). Oblatus est demonium habens cecus et mutus . . .-. . . expectantes beatam spem, idest spem eterne beatitudinis. Ad quam . . . Ff. 50va–51ra.

61. T21. *Estote imitatores Dei* (Eph 4:32). Apostolus Paulus, doctor gencium egregius et predicator bonorum morum . . .-. . . imitantur Christum integritate animi et corporis. F. 51ra–b.

62. T21. *Christus dilexit nos et tradidit semetipsum pro nobis* (Eph 5:2). Apostolus Paulus intente considerans et mente deuota . . .-. . . ipsum pro nobis. F. 51rb–va.

63. T22. *Non sumus ancillae filii sed liberae* (Gal 4:28). Quamuis homines secundum Apostolum de synagoga et ecclesia misticam habeant intelligenciam, possunt tamen . . .-. . . filii libere. F. 51vb.

64. T22. *Colligite fragmenta ne pereant* (John 6:12). Beatus Ieronimus epistula 37 dicit: Totum quod legimus in diuinis libris . . .-. . . ? Ff. 51vb–52va.

65. T22. *Eice ancillam et filium eius* (Gal 4:30). Dominica ista est 4[?] ab illa in qua incepit . . .-. . . qui sancto suo dixit Eice ancillam . . . Ff. 52va–54vb.

66. T22. *Quae sursum est Ierusalem, quae est mater* (Gal 4:26). Duo vehementer mouent desiderium . . .-. . . per racionem, vt valeamus peruenire ad istam conclusionem. Amen. Ff. 54vb–57ra.

67. T22. *Quae sursum est Ierusalem, libera est* (Gal 4:26). Increata sapiencia Patris eterni innata . . .-. . . requiescet secura in Ierusalem. Quam gloriam . . . Ff. 57ra–59vb.

68. T23. *Sanguis Christi emundabit conscientiam* (Hebr 9:14). Karissimi, propter mundiciam quam Dominus in anima racionali . . .-. . . gloriam intrabunt electorum. Ad quam . . . Ff. 59vb–6ova.

69. T06. *Lux oriri visa est* (Esth 8:16). Reuerendi domini, lux increata est indeficiens errantibus . . .-. . . spiritualibus oculis videbimus in futuro. Quod . . . Ff. 66ra–67vb. Also BL Additional 38818, f. 209v.

70. T05. *In sole posuit tabernaculum suum* (Ps 18:6). Karissimi, propter peccatum primi parentis sumus expulsi ex habitacione paradisi . . .-. . . oculis, suple meis, videre solem, etc. Ff. 67vb–68va.

71. T05. *Et in terra pax hominibus* (Luke 2:14). Sicud dicunt isti clerici qui varia instituta inspexerunt . . .-. . . seruare vnitatem spiritus in vinculo pacis. Quod . . . Ff. 68va–69vb.

72. T08. *Ecce nova facio omnia* (Rev 21:5). Reuerendi mei, rex vniuerse creature in principio fundauit . . .-. . . esto memor quod puluis es et eris esca vermium etc. Amen. F. 74ra–va.

73. T09. *Accipe puerum* (Matt 2:13). Rabanus super illud Mathei 7, Omnis . . . , dicit quod Deus peccatoribus misericordiam . . .-. . . secundum est meritum, tercium est premium. Ad quod, etc. Ff. 74va–75ra.

74. T10. *Quod natum est ex Deo vincit mundum* (1 John 5:4). Reuerendi mei, constat quod ipsa mundi constitucione mundum sub triplici tempore concurrisse . . .-. . . et post eorum mortem in regionem celestem. Ad quam nos, etc. F. 75ra–b.

75. T11a. *Quaerebamus te* (Luke 2:48). Reuerendi domini, multi multipliciter Iesum querebant . . .-. . . regnare possimus. Quod . . . F. 75rb–vb.

76. T11a. *Fili, quid fecisti?* (Luke 2:48). Karissimi, licet Spiritus Sanctus sit doctor nobilissimus . . .-. . . vt sitis filii eius. Quod . . . Ff. 75vb–76rb.

77. T12. *Implete hydrias aquae* (John 2:7). Beatus Bernardus super hunc locum euangelii dicit sic: Omnes vos . . .-. . . surgamus purissimi ad purissimam perfeccionem. Ff. 76rb–77vb.

78. T16. *Quod iustum fuit dabo vobis* (Matt 20:4). Karissimi, secundum [quod] dicit Crisostomus super Matheum in *Inperfecto* capitulo 37, quod omnes nos . . .-. . . nolite timere pusillus grex, etc. Quod regnum . . . Ff. 77vb–78rb.

79. T17. *Tempore temptationis recedunt* (Luke 8:13). Reuerendi domini, scitis quod in hiis qui grauis [!] corporis infirmitate . . . .-. . . retro cor nostrum Psalmo 43. Istam contemplacionis perfeccionem . . . Ff. 78va–8ora.

80. T17. *Gloriabor in infirmitatibus meis* (2 Cor 12:5). Ex processu Tullii 2 *De officiis,* a capitulo 8 vsque ad 13 inclusiue, patet quod nullus ad perfectam gloriam . . .-. . . erunt adinuicem amicabiliter sociata, quoad tercium iam premissum. Quod . . . Ff. 80ra–82rb.

81. T18. *Si tradidero corpus meum,* etc. (1 Cor 13:3). Noua libenter auditur [!], caritas est quoddam nouum, ergo . . .-. . . venerunt michi bona omnia pariter cum illa . . . F. 82rb–vb.

82. T18. *Caritas benigna est* (1 Cor 13:4). Sicud patet de variis scripture locis est caritas . . .-. . . hominum et angelorum associetur. Ad quam . . . Ff. 82vb–84vb.

83. T18*. *Caecus quidam sedebat secus viam* (Luke 18:35). Legitur in ewangelio hodierno quod iste cecus, de quo assumptum est thema . . .-. . . in fine non carebit diuina visione. Quam . . . Ff. 84vb–85va.

84. T17. *Fructum afferunt in patientia* (Luke 8:15). Iacobus in epistula capud 1 Paciencia opus perfectum habet. Racio istius . . .-. . . purgare vt amplius fructificet etc. F. 85va–b. Repeated as X-95.

85. T18. *Fides tua te salvum fecit* (Luke 18:42). Crisostomus super Matheum dicit: Si fornicatus fuerit homo vel adulteratus . . .-. . . probare qui essent fideles Christiani etc. Amen. F. 85vb. Repeated as X-96.

86. T14. *Imperavit ventis et mari* (Matt 8:26). Beatus Augustinus 3 *De ciuitate Dei* capitulo 4 recitans sentenciam Varronis . . .-. . . qui crediderit et baptizatus fuerit saluus erit. Quod . . . Ff. 86ra–87rb. Also F/1-5.

87. T14. *Surgens imperavit ventis et mari, et facta est tranquillitas magna* (Matt 8:26 and Mark 4). Sicut presencia medici cedit egrotantibus, idest male habentibus, in solacium . . .-. . . ? F. 87rb–va. Also J/4-14 and BN lat. 18195-15.

88. T16 / S22a. *Sic currite ut comprehendatis* (1 Cor 9:24). In quibus verbis duo breuiter designantur, scilicet strenuitas excercenda in opere . . .-. . . vinculis pacis. Per eum . . . Ff. 87vb–88vb.

89. T17. *Gloriabor in infirmitatibus meis, ut inhabitet in me virtus Christi* (2 Cor 12:5). Basilius magnus in quodam sermone dicit . . .-. . . ad futuram gloriam que reuelabitur in nobis. Quam gloriam . . . Ff. 89ra–90ra. Also F/1-6 and BL Additional 38818, f. 193.

90. T17?. *Libenter gloriabor in infirmitatibus meis, ut in habitet in me virtus Christi* (2 Cor 12:5). Intuens apostolus Spiritu Sancto repletus homines valde promtos ad inaniter gloriandum . . .-. . . virtus autem Christi hominem mundat, hominem ligat, hominem continuat, etc. F. 90ra, inc. (the explicit

agrees with the catchword in J/4-17, f. 20vb!). Also J/4-17 and BN lat. 18195-18.

91. T15? ("De pace"). *Pax Christi exultet in cordibus vestris, in qua vocati estis* (Col 3:15). Videns Apostolus mundanos homines pronos et promptos ad iram et discordiam . . .-. . . peremptorie citando vt dic' viris perfectis Pax Christi, etc. F. 90rb–va. Also J/4-15 and BN lat. 18195-16.

92. T16. *Voca operarios et redde illis mercedem suam* (Matt 20:8). In verbis propositis Mathei 20 introducturus Deus Pater loquens ad vnigenitum de mercede . . .-. . . dic' ergo Voca operarios et redde illis mercedem, etc. Ff. 90va–91ra. Also J/4-16 and BN lat. 18195-17.

93. T16. *Voca operarios et redde illis mercedem suam* (Matt 20:8). Aliqui operarii conducuntur secundum mensuram temporis . . .-. . . talis saccus, sicut scitis, nichil retinet infra se. F. 91ra–b.

94. T16. *Voca operarios et redde illis mercedem* (Matt 20:8). Istud tempus Septuagesime, quod usque ad Sabbatum in Albis septuaginta diebus . . .- . . . merces nostra copiosa est in celis, Mathei 9. Quam . . . Ff. 91rb–93ra.

95. T17. *Fructum afferunt in patientia* (Luke 8:15). Jacopus in sua epistula capitulo 1: Paciencia perfectum habet . . .-. . . purgare ut amplius fructificet etc. F. 93rb. Repeats X-84.

96. T18. *Fides tua te salvum fecit* (Luke 18:42). Crisostomus super Matheum dicit: Si fornicatus fuerit homo uel adulteratus . . .-. . . probare qui essent fideles Christiani etc. F. 93va.

97. T18. *Ascendimus Hierosolyma* (Luke 18:31). Karissimi, secundum quod dicit beatus Augustinus 19 *De ciuitate Dei* capitulo 14 in principio, Deus naturarum omnium sapientissimus conditor . . .-. . . tanto mercedem recipiat ampliorem. Quam . . . Ff. 93vb–96ra.

98. T19. *Illi soli servies* (Matt 4:10). Quatuor sunt secundum beatum Bernardum quibus seruimus . . .-. . . et quem misisti, Dominum Iesum Christum. Ad quem . . . Ff. 96rb–97rb.

99. T19. *Ecce nunc tempus* (2 Cor 6:2). Deuota necessitas excogitauit antiquitus et vtilis consuetudo obseruauit . . .-. . . nemo nos separabit a caritate Christi . . . Ff. 97rb–98vb.

100. T19. *Dic ut lapides isti panes fiant* (Matt 4:3). Secundum omnes doctores quanto diucius viuimus, tanto peior est mundus . . .-. . . qui in presenti et in perpetuum perseuerat. Ad quam . . . Ff. 99ra–100vb. Holcot, sermon 50 (Cambridge, Peterhouse MS 210, f. 64vb). Also Padua-59.

101. T19. *Dum tempus habemus, operemur bonum* (Gal 6:10). Omnia tempus habent, et est tempus laborandi et tempus quiescendi . . .-. . . memoria

istius passionis in corde cuiuslibet nostrum accendere deberet amorem. Ff. 101ra–102ra. Cf. Y/3-42.

102. T19. *Quasi morientes, et ecce vivimus* (2 Cor 6:9). Prouerbiorum 18 dicitur: Mors et vita in manibus lingue. Istud patet Ezechielis 3 . . .-. . . tunc dicere possumus, Translati sumus de morte ad vitam etc. Amen. F. 102ra–va.

103. T19. *Quasi morientes, et ecce vivimus* (2 Cor 6:9). Mors, karissimi, quasi morsus dicitur, quia quamcito . . .-. . . cum Deo beatifice copulatus fui mortuus et ecce sum viuus in eo. Ad quam vitam . . . Ff. 102va–104ra.

104. T19. *Ecce nunc tempus* (2 Cor 6:2). Ecce nunc tempus idoneum, medicina peccaminum quibus Deum offendimus . . .-. . . multas mercedes. A quibus . . . F. 104ra–va.

105. Soo ("De quocumque sancto"). *Magnus vocabitur in regno caelorum* (Matt 5:19). Secundum Boecium 3 *De consolacione philosophie* 4, magna potestas . . .-. . . post ipse peior quam prius efficitur. F. 104va–b.

106. T21. *Quomodo stabit regnum?* (Luke 11:18). Reuerendi, scitis quod terra sterilis fructum non facit . . .-. . . recogitabo tibi omnes annos meos in amaritudine anime mee. Quod . . . Ff. 104vb–105ra.

107. T22. *Erumpe et clama* (Gal 4:27). Reuerendi mei, secundum quod dicit Ouidius *Methamorfoseos* libro 1, quod rex quidam habuit . . .-. . . et ideo a peccato erumpe et clama. In quibus verbis vt superius est dictum. F. 105ra–va, inc?

108. T22. *Christus nos liberavit* (Gal 4:31). Nota quod Christus vnctus interpretatur, quia per totum guttis sanguineis vngebatur . . .-. . . hunc ingressum et sanctum progressum et vltimo securum egressum glorie nobis concedat etc. Ff. 105va–106ra.

109. T22. *Christus nos liberavit* (Gal 4:31). Tyranni ac eciam terminarii est condicio pro tempore [?] . . .-. . . sapienciam que sua morte nos liberauit, ipsi honor et gloria cum . . . Ff. 106ra–107rb.

110. T23. *Gloria mea nihil est* (John 8:54). Karissimi, sicut ex verbis Pros[peri?] recoligi [?] potest quod diuini verbi,,,, . . .-. . . vt Deus omnibus graciam concedat et gloriam. Quam . . . Ff. 107rb–108ra.

111. T24. *Factus est oboediens usque ad mortem* (Phil 2:8). Reuerendi mei, scitis quod si nubes texerint solem, aer . . .-. . . fortitudo mea et laus mea Dominus etc. Quam . . . F. 108ra–va.

112. T24. *Abscondit me in umbra* [!] (Ps 26:5). In principio pro gracia impetranda . . .-. . . sub vmbra manus sue protexit me. Quam vmbram . . . Ff. 108va–109ra.

113. T24. *Ut quid dereliquisti me?* (Matt 27:47). Reuerendi, multi cotidie ad predicaciones veniunt set paruum perficiunt . . .-. . . tales diuicie nichil valent . . . F. 109ra–vb.

114. T26. *Eamus et moriamur cum illo* (John 11:16). Ieronimus *Contra Iovinianum* tangit libro primo quamdam historiam . . .-. . . hanc mortem necesse est preuidere. F. 110ra–vb. Holcot, sermon 82 (Cambridge, Peterhouse MS 210).

115. T26. *Rex Israel mutavit habitum suum et ingressus est proelium* (1 Kings 22:30). Dicunt isti poete quod consuetudo erat antiquorum regum . . .- . . . illum introduxit in celum, quod est vita eterna. Ff. 110vb–111rb.

116. T25. *Cum dilexisset suos qui erant in mundo, in finem dilexit eos* (John 13:1). In hoc euangelio duo principaliter tanguntur: Christi caritas . . .-. . . vt hec mulieris quatuor considera etc. Ff. 111va–112rb.

117. T26. *Iesus Nazarenus rex Iudaeorum* (John 19:19). Karissimi, beatus Bernardus, monastice vite eximius executor et nominis Iesu deuotissimus predicator . . .-. . . ? Ff. 112rb–113vb. Also K-23.

118. T26. *Deus meus, Deus meus, ut quid dereliquisti me?* (Matt 27:46). In principio exoramus Christum, et si quis auderet . . .-. . . ab omni peccato custodiat et a potestate diaboli . . . Ff. 113vb–114vb.

119. T26. *Iesum quaeritis* (Matt 28:5). Reuerendi mei, licet omnes Iesum querere curant et licet iste puelle, scilicet iste Marie, in tumulo . . .-. . . et vobis ianua aperietur celestis. Quod nobis etc. Ff. 114vb–115rb.

120. T26. *Ego dormio et cor meum vigilat* (Cant 5:2). Karissimi, inter tam [*or* cetera] diuine maiestatis beneficia humano generi exhibita . . . .-. . . vt impleatur quod scribitur: Cinis es et in cinerem reuerteris, etc. Ff. 115rb–117va.

121. T26. *Versa est in luctum cithara mea* (Job 30:31). In verbis istis moraliter intellectis . . .-. . . in mensuram etatis plenitudinis Christi. Ff. 117va–118vb.

122. T26. *En ego morior* (Gen 48:21). Primus parens diuina bonitate [?] sic in naturalibus et gratuitis fuerat creatus . . .-. . . in qua dampnandi auctoritas robora. Ff. 118vb–119ra.

123. T26. *Filius regis mortuus est* (2 Sam 18:20). Reuerendi patres et fratres amantissimi, sicud dicit Apostolus Ephesiorum 3, Deus qui diues est in miseri[cordi]a . . .-. . . in gloria est Dei Patris, Philippensium 2. Ad quam gloriam . . . Ff. 119ra–121rb.

124. T26. *Fili mi, quis mihi det ut moriar pro te?* (2 Sam 18:33). Sicud colligi potest ex verbis Crisostomi omelia 42 *Inperfecti,* quamuis sentencia

mortis . . .-. . . scies quia ego Dominus saluans te. Quam glorificacionem . . . Ff. 121rb–123ra.

125. T26. *Rex mutavit habitum suum et ingressus est bellum* (1 Kings 22:30).
Solent reges quando procedunt . . .-. . . est virgo. F. 123ra–va, inc.

126. T28+. *Tene quod habes* (Rev 3:11). Karissimi, magne virtutis [*add* est]
amicum adquirere, sed maioris est . . .-. . . cum Filius Dei ascendat ad
celum. Quod . . . F. 126ra–vb. Also A-11 and Y/1-76.

127. T28+. *Manducavimus et bibimus cum eo* (Acts10:41). In quibusdam
regionibus mos est quod in festis magnis . . .-. . . cum illo in gloria
semper erimus. Quod . . . Ff. 126vb–127va.

128. T28+. *Christus surrexit a mortuis* (Rom 6:4). Karissimi, tanta est conueniencia inter corpus Christi sacramentaliter sumptum in [=et?] verbum
salutis predicatum . . .-. . . sequitur tercium principale cum dicit A mortuis. Ff. 127va–129vb, inc.

129. T28+. *Viderunt revolutum lapidem* (Matt 28:17). Karissimi, omnium auctorum vnanimis sentencia in hoc concordat quod quando diucius mundus
durat . . .-. . . de crabbe [?], etc. Ff. 130rb–131ra. See Wenzel, "The Moor
Maiden: a contemporary view."

130. T28+. *Tristitia vestra vertetur in gaudium* (John 16:22). Reuerendi mei,
quia malis propriis . . .-. . . gaudium vestrum nemo tollet a vobis. Quod . . .
Ff. 131ra–132vb.

131. T28+ / T36. *Sedet a dextris Dei* (Mark 16:19). Wlgariter dicitur: Cum
poteris quod vis, probat accio tua quid sis. Wan þou . . .-. . . cor nostrum
inquietum est donec etc. etc. Ff. 132vb–133vb.

132. T28+. *Spiritus eius ornavit caelos* (Job 26:13). Sicud dicit beatus Bernardus
in quodam sermone, Spiritus Sanctus multiplex dicitur . . .-. . . mundiales
quibus confertur ornatus fortune. Ff. 133vb–134vb.

133. T47?. *Mors illi ultra non dominabitur* (Rom 6:9). Karissimi, si sponsa
intense diligat maritum suum . . . .-. . . ad penam, electis ad gloriam
sempiternam. Ad quam . . . Ff. 134vb–135vb.

134. T18/4. *Revertar* (Luke 11:24). Animam humanam quatuor solicitari non
desistunt, scilicet caro, mundus, diabolus, et Deus . . . .-. . . pro peccatis
expleturus et sic sit Reuertar. F. 136ra.

135. T18/4. *Ad me* (Joel 2:12). Et [in?] singulis qui cum rege nostro et domino
ac principe illustrissimo quidquam h'm [= habent?] facere uel negocia
ardua volunt expedire . . .-. . . conuertimini ad me et salui eritis. Hanc
salutem . . . Ff. 136ra–137rb.

136. T18/4. *Convertimini ad Deum, quia benignus est* (Joel 2:13). Secundum Augustinum sermone de quadragesima: Exhortacio nostra, fratres, debemus ut sermo Dei per nostrum officium ministretur . . .-. . . et in futuro in gloria. Quam . . . Ff. 137va–139va.

137. T18/4. *Quod abiectum erat, requiram* (Ezek 34:16). Sicud in naturalibus transmutacionibus non introducitur forma . . .-. . . Deus illuminabit eos et regnabunt in secula seculorum. Amen. Ff. 139vb–140rb.

138. T18/4. *Agite paenitentiam* (Job 21:2). Karissimi, in omnibus que vtiliter agere debemus . . .-. . . satisfaccio consistit in oracione, ieiunio, et elemosina. F. 140rb–va.

139. T18/4. *Revertar* (Luke 11:24). Karissimi, oportet predicatorem verbi Dei efficaciter esse . . .-. . . vt eum videre valeamus. Quod . . . Ff. 140va–141ra.

140. T18/4. *Revertere, dilecte mi* (Cant 2:17). Thobie 12 scribitur, Tempus est vt reuertar . . .-. . . ? Ff. 141ra–142va.

141. T18/4. *Cum ieiunas, unge caput tuum et faciem tuam lava* (Matt 6:17). Secundum Augustinum in quodam sermone, oracio et ieiunium congrue . . .-. . . sedere ociosi . . . Ff. 142vb–144rb.

142. T18/4. *Loquar ad Dominum meum cum sim pulvis et cinis* (Gen 18:27). Scitis, karissimi, quod quando pauper et maxime mendicus loquitur cum magno domino . . .-. . . paratum vobis regnum ab origine mundi. Quod . . . Ff. 144va–146va.

143. T02. *Levate capita vestra* (Luke 21:28). Sciens Saluator genus humanum ante suum aduentum diutino merore confectum . . .-. . . visiones capiti mei conturbauerunt me. F. 148ra. Pecham-49. Sermons X-143 to 197 are the *Collationes dominicales de evangeliis* by John Pecham, OFM, here unidentified but numbered 1–55. I give the numbers as in Schneyer 3:669–672 (items numbered 00 are not listed by Schneyer).

144. T03. *Caeci [vident]* (Matt 11:5). Licet hec verba per seriem historie dicantur de ceco . . .-. . . quamcito transituram. F. 148ra. Pecham-50.

145. T04. *Medius autem vestrum stetit* (John 1:26). Beatus Iohannes Baptista volens nos. . . .-. . . et Iesum stantem a dextris Dei. F. 148rb. Pecham-52.

146. T04. *Praeparate viam Domini* (Luke 3:4). Hec verba protulit Iohannes Baptista . . .-. . . per vias rectas, etc. F. 148rb–va. Pecham-51.

147. T07. *Gratia Dei in illo erat* (Luke 2:40). In quibus verbis beatus Lucas sciens quoniam sine dono sciencie . . .-. . . vt in optimo feliciter quiescant. F. 148va–b. Pecham-00.

148. T11. *Dolentes quaerebamus te* (Luke 2:48). Vt Christum necessario corde queramus beata Virgo . . .-. . . et orabunt coram te, Domine. F. 148vb. Pecham-53.

149. T12. *Crediderunt in eum discipuli eius* (John 2:11). Vt veram fidem teneamus . . .-. . . vere discipuli mei eritis . . . F. 148vb. Pecham-54.

150. T13?. *Veniens adorabat eum* (Matt 8:2). Ne Domino inueniamur ingrati . . .- . . . pro tercio Venite filii audite, etc. Ff. 148vb–149ra. Pecham-55.

151. T14. *Salva nos* (Matt 8:25). Scientes discipuli a Christo tamquam saluatore salutem esse querendum . . .-. . . a te queramus salutem, etc. F. 149ra. Pecham-56.

152. T15. *Accesserunt servi* (Matt 13:27). Vt in Dei obsequio fideles inueniamur . . .-. . . contractando vt de nobis dicatur, etc. F. 149ra–b. Pecham-57.

153. T16. *Voca operarios et redde illis mercedem* (Matt 20:8). Et possunt esse verba Dei Patris filium pro redempcione generis humani in mundum missum alloquentis . . .-. . . redditurus dicat pro vobis Voca, etc. F. 149rb–va. Pecham-58.

154. T17. *Cum gaudio suscipiunt verbum Dei* (Luke 8:13). Benedictus Saluator volens nos salu [*blank*] hortamenta suscipere . . .-. . . suscipite insitus verbum. Ff. 149va. Pecham-59.

155. T18. *Sequebatur eum magnificans Deum* (Luke 18:43). Licet hec verba dicantur de ceco . . .-. . . ob felicitatis [?] amorem. F. 149va–b. Pecham-60.

156. T19. *Vivit homo* (Matt 4:4). Karissimi, sicud patet in fine [?] euangelii, Saluatori facta suggestione vt de lapidibus panem faceret . . .-. . . vt viuat caritate que concupiscibilem inflammat. Ff. 149vb–150ra. Pecham-61.

157. T18/7. *Ipsum audite* (Luke 9:35). Quoniam genus humanum ex primi parentis preuaricacione multiplici languebat miseria . . .-. . . Ipsum audite. F. 150ra. Pecham-00.

158. T21. *Locutus est mutus* (Luke 11:14). Quia secundum Augustinum omnis Christi accio nostra est instruccio . . .-. . . ? F. 150ra–b. Pecham-63.

159. T22. *Sequebatur eum* (John 6:2). Vt perfecti Christi ymitatores inueniamur . . .-. . . Sequebatur illum, etc. F. 150rb–va. Pecham-64.

160. T22/7. *Ego sum* (John 8:58). Volens benedictus Saluator vnumquemque nostrum ad suam deuenire noticiam . . .-. . . Ego sum qui sum. Ff. 150va. Pecham-65.

161. T24. *Solvite, adducite mihi* (Matt 21:2). In hiis verbi spiritualiter intellectis pius Saluator integritatem . . .-. . . implebitis quod hic dicit Dominus. F. 150va–b. Pecham-66.

162. T24. *Rex tuus venit* (Matt 21:5). Ne desperare posset genus humanum dominico merore confectum . . .-. . . quia noster rex, etc. Ff. 150vb–151ra. Pecham-67.

163. T28. *Cum videbitis* (Mark 16:7). In hoc promisso angelico secundum intellectum spiritualem . . .-. . . dicentis Videbitis eum. F. 151ra. Pecham-69.

164. T28. *Iesum quaeritis* (Mark 16:6). Licet per fidem historie hec fuerunt verba angeli mulieres . . .-. . . Iesum queritis etc. F. 151ra–b. Pecham-68.

165. T28. *Christus est veritas* (John 18:38?). Beatus Iohannes in hiis verbis nostrum describit reparatorem . . .-. . . quod Christus est veritas. F. 151rb. Pecham-00.

166. T28/3. *Pax vobis* (Luke 24:36). Sciens benedictus Saluator discipulis inter mundi procellas nauigantibus . . .-. . . ? F. 151rb–va. Pecham-70.

167. T29. *Iesus est filius Dei* (John 20:31). Volens Iohannes nos ad memoriam reducere nostre salutis et reparacionis beneficium . . .-. . . est filius Dei. F. 151va. Pecham-00.

168. T30. *Ego cognosco oves meas* (John 10:14). In hiis verbis benedictus Saluator Deus personam . . .-. . . ego sum pastor etc. F. 151va–b. Pecham-71.

169. T31. *Gaudebit cor vestrum* (John 16:22). Sciens benignus Saluator discipulos non sine graui merore . . .-. . . promissum quoniam gaudium etc. Ff. 151vb–152ra. Pecham-72.

170. T32. *Docebit vos omnem veritatem* (John 16:13). Volens benedictus Saluator discipulis ostendere vtilitatem . . .-. . . hic dicitur Docebit vos. F. 152ra–b. Pecham-73.

171. T33. *Petite et accipite* (John 16:24). In hiis verbis benignus Saluator volens nobis munifice sua dona . . .-. . . veraciter Dominum Petite. F. 152rb. Pecham-74.

172. T37. *Locutus sum vobis* (John 16:4). Quia secundum beatum Gregorium minus iacula feriunt que preuidentur . . .-. . . quia Locutus sum vobis. F. 152rb–va. Pecham-75.

173. T39. *Si diligeretis me, gauderetis utique* (John 14:28). Sciens benedictus Saluator ex. . . .-. . . dicit ergo Si diligeretis, etc. F. 152va–b. Pecham-76.

174. T45. *Pater vester misericors est* (Luke 6:36). Volens pius Saluator nos ad misericordie opera [inui]tare . . .-. . . senciatis quod Pater vester misericors est. Ff. 152vb–153ra. Pecham-80.

175. T43. *Fecit coenam magnam* (Luke 14:16). Sciens benignus Saluator et [in?] . . . cultura desudantibus . . .-. . . quidam Fecit cenam magnam. F. 153ra. Pecham-78.

176. T44. *Gaudium erit in caelo* (Luke 15:7). Volens pius Deus electos [?] sub penitencie iugo laborantes . . .-. . . in celo vbi est per luce' radi'. F. 153ra–b. Pecham-79.

177. T46. *Descendebant et lavabant* (Luke 5:2). Cum due sint partes iusticie . . .- . . . reportabunt vnde dicitur, etc. etc. F. 153rb–va. Pecham-81.

178. T47. *Offeres munus tuum* (Matt 5:23). Nolens Deus electos suos vacuos in conspectu suo apparere . . .-. . . Offer munus tuum. F. 153va–b. Pecham-82.

179. T48. *Dimisit eos* (Mark 8:9). Hec sunt verba Marci de Domino nostro . . .- . . . Dimisit eos. F. 153vb. Pecham-83.

180. T49?. *Arbor bona fructus bonos facit* (Matth 7:17). Vt reparatori nostro gracias agamus in his verbis . . .-. . . quod veraciter a Saluatore dictum est. Ff. 153vb–154ra. Pecham-84.

181. T50. *Homo quidam erat dives* (Luke 16:1). Vt pro certaminis labore certi simus . . .-. . . quia Homo quidam erat diues. F. 154ra–b. Pecham-85.

182. T51. *Domus mea domus orationis vocabitur* (Luke 19:46). Vt ad celeste palacium iugiter [?] suspiremus . . .-. . . ergo Domus mea, etc. F. 154rb. Pecham-86.

183. T52. *Descendit hic* (Luke 18:14). Vt per viam vite in . . .-. . . Descendit. F. 154rb–va. Pecham-87.

184. T53. *Deprecabantur eum* (Mark 7:32). Quoniam per instanciam deuenitur ad graciam . . .-. . . Deprecabatur eum. F. 154va–b. Pecham-88.

185. T54. *Fac et vives* (Luke 10:28). Quoniam Dei electus meritis bene operandi accumulat . . .-. . . dicitur Fac et viues. F. 154vb. Pecham-89.

186. T55. *Cum irent, mundati sunt* (Luke 17:14). Beatus euangelista per curacionem leprosorum statum designans . . .-. . . dicitur Cum irent. Ff. 154vb–155ra. Pecham-90.

187. T56. *Quaerite regnum Dei* (Matt 6:33). Volens benedictus Saluator nos abstrahere ab amore . . .-. . . dicitur Querite, etc. F. 155ra. Pecham-91.

188. T57. *Ibant cum illo* (Luke 7:11). Optans beatus Lucas nos esse perfectos Christi imitatores . . .-. . . perducendo Ibant ergo, etc. F. 155ra–b. Pecham-92.

189. T58. *Amice, ascende* (Luke 14:11). Volens benedictus Saluator erga nos benevolenciam suam increscere . . .-. . . dicitur Amice, ascende. F. 155rb–va. Pecham-93.

190. T59. *Diliges Dominum Deum tuum* (Matt 22:37). Vt per viam deueniamus ad gloriam felicitatis, in his verbis duo facit . . . .-. . . dicitur Diliges Dominum. F. 155va. Pecham-94.

191. T60. *Surge et ambula* (Matt 9:5). Quoniam due sunt partes iusticie . . .-
. . . dicitur Surge. F. 155va–b. Pecham-95.

192. T61. *Misit servos suos* (Matt 22:3). Volens benedictus Saluator in diuinis
obsequiis vigilanter insistere . . .-. . . dicitur Misit seruos suos. Ff. 155vb–
156ra. Pecham-96.

193. T62. *Domine, descende* (John 4:49). Vt ordinate discamus petere que
desideramus . . .-. . . clamatis Domine descende. F. 156ra. Pecham-97.

194. T63. *Oportuit te misereri* (Matt 18:33). Volens pius Dominus ad inpendenda [?] . . .[misericordie] opera nos excitare . . .-. . . illud euangelicum
Oportuit te misereri. F. 156rb. Pecham-98.

195. T64. *In veritate doces* (Matt 22:16). Licet hec verba fuerunt Phariseorum
Christum fallaciter alloquencium . . .-. . . dicere possumus Saluatori In
veritate doces. F. 156rb–va. Pecham-99.

196. T65. *Fides tua te salvam fecit* (Matt 9:22). Benedictus Saluator hic describit
mulierem . . .-. . . dicitur Fides tua, etc. F. 156va. Pecham-100.

197. T66. *Congregabunt electos* (Matt 24:31). Volens Dominus iustos nos . . .-
. . . quia per ipsos congregabit Dominus electos. Amen. F. 156va–b.
Pecham-101.

198. T63. *Omne debitum dimisi tibi, quoniam rogasti me* (Matt 18:32). Karissimi,
sicut Thomas recitat super Luce 7 capitulo quod Glosa dicit . . .-. . . bonum
est solus Deus cui sit honor et gloria in secula seculorum. Amen. Ff.
156vb–158ra.

199. T18/5. *Homo sum sub potestate* (Matt 8:9). Adelardus in libro suo qui intitulatur *Dialogus Adelard de naturalibus questionibus* . . .-. . . transtulit
in regnum Filii dileccionis sue. Ad quam regnum, etc. Ff. 158ra–
159rb.

200. S44. *Servus nuntiavit* (Luke 14:21). Primo inducatur qualiter iuxta diuersa
officia diuersa nomina inponit Deus seruis suis . . .-. . . ? F. 159rb–
vb.

201. T14. *Plenitudo legis est dilectio* (Rom 13:10). Hec que breuiter illata sed
grauiter inpregnata quatinus set facilis . . .-. . . plenitudo legis est dileccio,
etc. F. 160ra.

202. T15? *Pax Christi exultet in cordibus vestris* (Col 3:15). Karissimi, signum
habitus est ex dileccione et faciliter agere . . .-. . . exoritur Pax Christi
exultet etc. F. 160ra–b.

203. T16. *Sic currite ut comprehendatis* (1 Cor 9:24). Labor fidelibus inducitur
quo admodum exercicii et finem negocii . . .-. . . quod latet in absconditis,
etc. F. 160rb–va.

204. T16. *Ite in vineam meam* (Matt 20:7). Karissimi, secundum Apostolum Ad Romanos, qui preest in sollicitudine . . .-. . . et sic ite in vineam, etc. F. 160va.

205. T16. *Voca operarios et redde illis mercedem* (Matt 20:8). Situs [?] ordo iusticie seruari debet inter dominum et famulum . . .-. . . dicat igitur paterfamilias Voca operarios, etc. F. 160va–b.

206. T17. *Raptus est in paradisum* (2 Cor 12:4). In raptu isto considerare possumus motum . . .-. . . Raptus est in paradisum. Ff. 160vb–161ra.

207. T17. *Semen est verbum Dei* (Luke 8:11). In locucione parabolica possumus attendere sentenciam vmbratam . . .-. . . et sic semen est verbum Dei. F. 161ra.

208. T18. *Scientia destruetur* (1 Cor 13:8). Illud idem quod vi n'e [nature or necessarie?] appetitur . . .-. . . dicentes verba proposita. F. 161ra–b.

209. T18. *Quando factus sum vir, evacuavi quae erant parvuli* (1 Cor 13:11). Sicud etas puerilis et virilis non compaciuntur se . . .-. . . vnde factus sum etc. F. 161rb.

210. T18. *Adsumpsit Iesus duodecim* (Luke 18:31). Per . . . ad Ierusalem ascenditur . . .-. . . pro quibus Assumpsit Iesus duodecim. F. 161rb–va.

211. T18. *Miserere mei, fili David* (Luke 18:38). Omnis oracio ad aliquem dirigitur pro alico . . .-. . . ergo Miserere mei fili Dauid. F. 161va–b.

212. T19. *Ecce nunc tempus acceptabile* (2 Cor 6:2). Media redduntur [*or* medicina redditur?] appetibil' si sit presens et valens . . .-. . . sic dicitur Ecce nunc tempus acceptabile. Ff. 161vb–162ra.

213. T19. *Accesserunt angeli et ministrabant ei* (Matt 4:11). In quibus verbis custus latrie soli Deo debitus describitur . . .-. . . Angeli ergo accesserunt et ministrabant ei, etc. F. 162ra.

214. T20. *Ambuletis ut abundetis* (1 Thess 4:1). Cum in via Dei non progredi sit regredi . . .-. . . propter hoc Ambuletis, etc. F. 162ra–b.

215. T18/7. *Duxit illos in montem excelsum* (Matt 17:2). Sub huius nouitate [?] miraculi transfiguracionis dominice . . .-. . . ? F. 162rb–va.

216. T18/7. *Hic est Filius meus dilectus in quo mihi complacui; ipsum audite* (Matt 17:5). In quibus verbis ostenditur quod generacio in diuinis . . .-. . . Filii dilecti et sic facite, etc. F. 162va–b.

217. T21. *Estote imitatores Dei* (Eph 5:1). Ars ymitatur naturam . . .-. . . ? F. 162vb.

218. T21. *In digito Dei eicio daemonia* (Luke 11:20). In [omni cura?] considerare possumus medium . . .-. . . ergo In digito Dei eicio demonia. Ff. 162vb–163ra.

219. T22. *Non sumus ancillae filii sed liberae* (Gal 4:31). Karissimi, secundum Philosophum de quolibet affirmacio et negacio . . .-. . . possimus dicere, Nos scilicet sumus ancille, etc. F. 163ra–b.

220. T22. *Quae sursum est Ierusalem libera est, quae est mater nostra* (Gal 4:26). In quibus verbis differencia non eleg' ad veterem ostenditur . . .-. . . dicatur ergo Que sursum est Ierusalem, etc. F. 163rb–va.

221. T22. *Est puer unus hic* (John 6:9). Vnum est quod est in se indiuisum . . .- . . . dicatur ergo Est puer vnus hic, etc. F. 163va.

222. T23. *Per proprium sanguinem introivit semel in sancta* (Heb 9:12). In quibus verbis iuxta literam et intentum Apostoli describitur . . .-. . . propter hoc ergo Per proprium sanguinem, etc. F. 163va–b.

223. T23. *Vidit et gavisus est* (John 8:56). Dicitur de patre fidei nostre Abraham, in cuius persona . . .-. . . de quietacione seculi Vidit et gauisus est. Ff. 163vb–164ra.

224. T31. *Vado ad Patrem* (John 16:17 etc.). Verba proposita imminenti Christi ascencione ab Ecclesia recitantur . . .-. . . propter hec talia Vado ad Patrem, etc. etc. F. 164ra.

225. T33. *Exivi a Patre et veni in mundum* (John 16:28). Due sunt Christi emanaciones: eternalis et temporalis . . .-. . . Exiui a Patre et veni in mundum, etc. F. 164ra–b.

226. T61*. *Caute ambuletis* (Eph 5:15). Karissimi, ductor malorum doctor bonorum . . .-. . . Caute ambuletis, etc. etc. F. 164rb.

227. T64. *Magister, scimus quod verax es* (Matt 22:16). Karissimi, veritas quandoque confessionem recipit . . .-. . . in iudicio, etc. etc. F. 164rb–va.

228. T65. *Confide, filia* (Matt 9:22). Karissimi mei, teste scriptura oportet accedentem credere v'i animam languidam . . .-. . . verba proposita, Confide, filia, etc. F. 164va–b.

229. ?. *Habemus redemptionem* (Eph 1:7, Col 1:4). Karissimi, sicud scribitur Prouerbiorum 13, spes que differtur affligit animam . . .-. . . pro quibus omnibus Habemus redempcionem, etc. F. 164vb.

230. T20. *Domine, adiuva me* (Matt 15:25). Karissimi, iuxta sentenciam beati Augustini . . .-. . . ad tercium. Ff. 164vb–165ra.

231. T22. *Christus nos liberavit* (Gal 4:31). Karissimi, proximi sunt [?] vobis in hoc tempore . . .-. . . redemit deus Iacob et liberauit eum. F. 165ra–b.

232. T23. *Semetipsum optulit* (Hebr 9:14). Et si queratur quis, etc., respondeo Iesus . . . Dilectissimi mei, Filius Dei uolens habere hominem . . .-. . . graciam contulit Semetipsum obtulit, etc. F. 165rb.

233. T29. *Pax vobis* (John 20:19). Karissimi, Gigas gemine [*add* substancie?] mediator Dei et hominum, homo Iesus Christus pro nobis miseris peccatoribus mortem subiit . . .-. . . seruauit haȝt him vnrichtfulliche. F. 165rb–va.

234. T21?. *Ut filii lucis ambulate* (Eph 5:8). Karissimi, Paulus apostolus, quem Deus fecit magistrum tocius Ecclesie . . .-. . . per eterni gaudii aspiracionem. F. 165va.

235. T50. *Redde rationem* (Luke 16:2). Karissimi mei, dicit Plato in *Timeo* bene post principium sic: Cum, inquid, omnibus mos sit et quasi quedam religio . . .-. . . intra in gaudium Domini tui. Salus interpretatur abeunde [?] consilio, et illud consilium scribitur 1 Petri 5: Humiliamini sub potenti manu Dei. Isto consilio abutebatur quando superbiuit. Ff. 165va–167ra.

236. T30. *Fiet unum ovile et unus pastor* (John 10:16). Karissimi, Ysaie 53: Omnes quasi oues errauimus . . . Certe, karissimi, pro tanto dicitur . . .-. . . dilatare materiam. Ff. 167ra–168ra.

237. ?. *Fuit homo* (John 1:6). Primus parens cum dati sibi premii dignitate . . .- . . . vitabimus et perueniemus ad palmam. Amen. F. 170ra–va. Also W-45.

238. ?. *Omnes* (John 1:7). Karissimi, beatus Bernardus *De gracia et libero arbitrio* 8 probare videtur . . .-. . . ? F. 170va–b. Also W-46.

239. ?. *Non* (John 1:8?). Karissimi, duo locucionum sunt genera . . .-. . . vt cum illo finaliter regnemus in celis, Iesus Christus, qui . . . Ff. 170vb–171rb. Also W-40.

240. S82a. *Erat lux* (John 1:9). Karissimi domini, sicut virtus clausa . . .-. . . cuius precibus nos adiuuari concedat qui . . . F. 171rb.

241. T01. *Venientem* (John 1:9). In aduentu regis et principis, domini eximii et potentis . . .-. . . ante aduentum Christi sic penitere . . . F. 171va–b. Also W-47.

242. T06. *Nomen eius Iesus* (Luke 2:21). Reuerendi patres, ex insignibus et vtilibus actibus . . .-. . . nomina nostra scripta sunt in celis. Quod . . . Ff. 171vb–172rb.

243. S85. *Erat lux vera quae illuminat* (John 1:9). Karissimi, prout omnium mortalium laborat fama et auctoritas, tria sunt precipue . . .-. . . ? F. 172rb–vb. Also W-41.

244. S01. *Hominem* (John 1:9). Karissimi, licet philosophie et sacre scripture tractatores videantur asserere . . .-. . . tercium principale, sed merito passionis tam Andree quam Christi peruenire poterimus ad gaudia paradisi. Amen. Ff. 172vb–173rb. Also W-48.

245. ?. *In mundo erat* (John 1:10). Karissimi, tam fide quam scripturis sacris testantibus, dum in presenti seculo . . .-. . . et ad vitam eternam nos perducat. Amen. F. 173rb. Also W-49.

246. ?. *Mundus* (John 1:10). Karissimi, sicud dicit Crisostomus omelia 18 *Operis inperfecti,* non est in mundo . . .-. . . vt cum Deo eternam beatitudinem habeamus. Amen. F. 173va–b. Also W-50.

247. S03. *Eum* (John 1:10). Karissimi, sicud dicit beatus Augustinus *De perfeccione iusticie,* Dominus, inquit . . .-. . . sed eum in terra venerari possimus, ad eum vt perueniamus. F. 173vb. Also W-51.

248. S86. *Non cognovit* (John 1:10). Princeps seculi, princeps mundi, princeps tenebrarum . . .-. . . hic cognitus est ab eo. Sic meritis Virginis gloriose agnosci possimus . . . Ff. 173vb–174va. Also W-52.

249. S86. *Cognovit eum* (John 1:10). Coram rege sapiente et iudice qui negocia sunt facturi . . .-. . . dum paruulus versaretur inter brachia, penderet ad vbera. Ff. 174va–175ra. Also W-53.

250. T10 / T01. *Venit* (John 1:11). Solent duces et reges incliti, principes potentes et strenui . . .-. . . honoratus gloriosius quia coronaberis. Hanc coronam . . . F. 175ra–b. Also W-39.

251. S10. *Veni, dilecte mi* (Cant 7:11). Karissimi, prouerbialiter dicitur omne promissum est debitum . . .-. . . pro tua humilitate ad gradum ineffabilem excellencie. Ad quam coronam . . . Ff. 175rb–177rb. Also F/5-55, without protheme.

252. S24. *Sedeat cum principibus et solium gloriae teneat* (1 Sam 2:8). Consideraui opiniones philosophorum et collegi quod post [?] consummata bellorum certamina incipiunt . . .-. . . legem pone michi, Domine, etc. Quam legem . . . F. 177va–b.

253. S63. *Resplenduit facies eius* (Matt 17:2). Karissimi, sicud ex literis scriptis philosophorum liquet . . .-. . . vt Deum in facie videre valeatis. Quod . . . Ff. 177vb–178rb.

254. S63. *Transfiguratus est* (Matt 17:2). Per verba preassumpta intelligo tres figuraciones . . .-. . . ? Ff. 178rb–179ra.

255. S19. *Nomini tuo da gloriam* (Ps 113:9). Karissimi mei, quis [inten]se cogitans et aduertens . . .-. . . hec est victoria que vincit mundum. Quam victoriam etc. F. 179rb–va.

256. S75a. *Vidi mulierem* (Rev 17:3?). Reuerendi mei, in principio originis humani generis . . .-. . . misericordiam facere, vt cum eo regnare possitis. Quod . . . Ff. 179va–180rb.

257. S?? (Thomas). *Ego sum pastor bonus* (John 10:11). Karissimi, videmus quod nec cleri nec laici erubescunt habere pannos dissutos . . .-. . . ? F. 180rb–va.

258. S25. *Hic magnus vocabitur in regno caelorum* (Matt 5:19). Reuerendi, iuxta consilium Ecclesiastici 40 [*read* 44] laudemus vires gloriosis . . .-. . . sanguis, qui fuit vna probacio trium. F. 180vb.

259. S81. *Hoc honore condignus est* (Esth 6:11). Reuerendi mei, sicut patet ex sentencia beati Augustini 4 *De doctrina* . . .-. . . in bono finaliter perseuerare. Ad istud regnum . . . Ff. 182ra–184rb.

260. ?. *Nolite diligere mundum* (1 John 2:15). Karissimi, cor humanum non potest simul capere duos amores . . .-. . . vt non cum hoc mundo dampnemur. Ff. 184va–185rb.

261. ? ("De quolibet prelato"). *Diligite iustitiam*, etc. (Wisd 1:1). Vbi breuiter docet prelatos tria, videlicet qualiter sint affecti . . . digne sunt electi . . . que sunt eis subiecti . . .-. . . caritas sine inuidia, felicitas sine miseria. Ff. 185rb–186va.

262. S22a. *Vidi mulierem* (Rev 17:3). Reuerendi mei domini et magistri, vas eleccionis et ecclesie doctor, summus apostolus Dei Paulus . . .-. . . cum nostra muliere in terra viuencium bona dei videre. Amen. Ff. 186va–188rb.

263. ?. *Gratiam Dei recipiatis* (2 Cor 6:1). Exigit et hortatur sacra doctorum professio . . .-. . . illam graciam que glorificat comprehensores. Quam . . . Ff. 188rb–190rb.

264. T03? *Praeparabit viam tuam* (Matt 11:10). Reus lese maiestatis apparere coram principe irato non audet . . .-. . . et quartum penitus ignoro. Ff. 190rb–191ra, inc. Also BL Additional 38818, f. 196v.

265. S26. *Ecce* (Matt 10:16). Ecce nescio loqui quia puer sensibus s. ego sum. Confidens . . .-. . . quam benediccionem meritis et precibus beati Bernardi nobis concedat . . . Ff. 191ra–192va.

266. S65 / S44? *Terra dedit fructum* (Ps 66:7). Reuerendi domini, tocius mundi machine eligans architectus . . .-. . . et sic in terra fructum dantes. Vt nostrorum mediantibus fructibus meritorum peruenire . . . Ff. 192va–193va. Repeated as X-332.

267. C04. *Non coronabitur nisi qui legitime certaverit* (2 Tim 2:5). In istis verbis ostendit Apostolus quibus datur beatitudo . . .-. . . ? F. 193va–b. Thomas de Lisle, in Aberdeen 154, f. 274.

268. S20? *Fecit illud vas alterum* (Jere 18:4). Vasis nomine, karissimi, predicator verbum Dei non [inconuenienter?] accipitur . . .-. . . ? Ff. 194ra–195rb.

269. S11. *Sine macula sunt ante thronum Dei* (Rev 14:5?). Karissimi, sicud milites et armigeri in magnis festis . . .-. . . laus illius opus nostrum in ista vita beata. Ad quam, etc. Ff. 195rb–197rb.

270. S03. *Ab infantia crevit mecum miseratio* (Job 31:18). Sicut Spiritus Sanctus vbi vult spirat, sic quando vult . . .-. . . iam coronatus est in celo in misericordia et miseracionibus. Quam coronam . . . Ff. 197rb–199ra.

271. S11. *Tempus nascendi et tempus moriendi* (Qoh 3:2). Karissimi, si labilitatem humane condicionis seu nature consideremus . . .-. . . illa in oculo. Ad propositum de facie interiori applica sicud scis. F. 199ra–b.

272. S26. *Non quaero gloriam meam* (John 8:50). Karissimi, sanctus iste mundi vanitates reliquit et ideo bene dicere potui . . .-. . . michi inquit absit gloriari. Quem nos diligere . . . Ff. 199rb–200rb.

273. S10. *Qui vicerit dabi ei sedere mecum* (Rev 3:21). Secundum quod dicit quidam doctor super Psalmum, Melius vincit . . .-. . . in regno celesti. Ad quod . . . F. 200rb–va.

274. C05. *Sancti per fidem vicerunt regna, operati sunt iusticiam, adepti sunt repromissiones* (Hebr 11:33). Dilectissimi, fides sanctorum commendatur hic in tribus . . .-. . . in die visitacionis . . . Ff. 200va–201va.

275. S12. *Data est gratia* (Eph 3:8). Cum omne donum optimum et omne datum . . .-. . . nobis sit data gracia. Amen. Ff. 201va–202ra.

276. ?. *Veritas per Iesum Christum facta est* (2 Cor 7:14?). Iuxta beatum Augustinum 2 *De libero arbitrio* cap. 2 veritas intus docens est . . .-. . . certitudine veritatis. F. 202ra–b.

277. S22a. *Est in sinu Patris* (John 1:18). Fugienda defectiua, contempnenda infectiua . . .-. . . ? Ff. 202va–203ra.

278. T10. *Vidimus stellam eius in oriente et venimus adorare* (Matt 2:2). Magi causam proponunt . . .-. . . ? Ff. 206ra–207va.

279. S09. *Lux in tenebris lucet* (John 1:5). In principio creans Deus celum et terram . . .-. . . quam repromisit Deus diligentibus se. Hanc coronam nos habere . . . Ff. 207va–208ra.

280. S11. *Tenebrae eam non comprehenderunt* (John 1:5). Si lux dicat humane menti quicquid gracie uel fauoris . . .-. . . ? F. 208ra–va.

281. S10. *Fuit homo missus a Deo cuius nomen Iohannes erat* (John 1:6). Si consideramus [?] dictum Domini nostri ad hominem . . .-. . . per consequens ad gloriam, que est Patri et Filio et Spiritui Sancto. Quam . . . Ff. 208va–209ra.

282. S78. *Fuit homo missus a Deo* (John 1:6). Iuxta Iohannem Carnotensem in suo *Policratico* libro 2 in prologo, post preclaros arcium scriptores . . .- . . . saluate uos a tenebris putei altissimi. Amen. F. 209ra–va.

283. S79. *Dedit eis potestatem filios Dei fieri* (John 1:12). Aduertens [*or* Benedictus?] Deus in donis suis et sanctus in omnibus operibus . . .- . . . gloria hec est omnibus sanctis eius. Quam . . . Ff. 209va–210ra.

284. S80. *Qui credunt in nomine eius* (John 1:12). Cum tuba fidei Christiane auribus meis intonat strepitusque . . .-. . . quasi vnigeniti a patre. Quam . . . F. 210ra–va.

285. S81. *Erat lux vera* (John 1:9). Dominus illuminacio mea et salus sicut auribus nostris . . .-. . . sed vera in doctrine sanitate. Hunc nobis Christe concede ducem . . . Ff. 210va–211rb.

286. S81a. *Et mundus per ipsum factus est* (John 1:10). In huius mundi exilio peregrinantibus . . .-. . . de sanctitate sicut libet. Que prosequi et assequi donet Saluator . . . F. 211rb–vb.

287. S82a. *Hic venit in testimonium* (John 1:7). Sicuti inquisiciones . . . con-sultaciones . . .-. . . in testimonium felicitatis. Ad quam Iesus Saluator mundi per preces martiris . . . Ff. 211vb–212va.

288. S82b. *Illuminat omnem hominem venientem in hunc mundum* (John 1:9). Surge illuminare Ierusalem . . .-. . . regia via est etc. Per quam eternam gloriam post tenebrarum miseriam . . . Ff. 212va–213ra.

289. S85. *Habitavit* (John 1:14). Domine, quis habitabit in tabernaculo . . .- . . . fecit in tabernaculo suo vbi prius. Huius vite mare dat nobis Deus habitare. Amen. F. 213ra–va.

290. T01. *Habitavit in nobis* (John 1:14). Ecce quam bonum et quam iocun-dum . . .-. . . dominus uirtutum nobiscum susceptor noster deus Iacob. Quis nos in celo suscipiat . . . Ff. 213va–214ra.

291. T01+. *Verbum caro factum est* (John 1:14). Verbum supernum prodiens a Patre olim exiens . . .-. . . qui mortem nostram moriendo destruxit et vitam resurgendo reparauit, etc. Ff. 214ra–215va.

292. S79. *Omnes accepimus gratiam* (John 1:16). Boni principis siue ducis excercitus est tirones . . .-. . . sanctificacio Sancti Spiritus sit semper cum omnibus nobis. Amen. F. 215va–b.

293. T04?. *Tu quis es* (John 1:19). Venite et videte opera Domini . . .-. . . cuius salutis nos participes efficiat qui . . . Ff. 215vb–216ra.

294. S03. *Recordati sunt discipuli* (John 2:17). Scitis quod quanto magister [fuerit in] gestu dileccior, in doctrina . . .-. . . in eterno libro vite erit vestra recordacio. Amen. F. 216rb–va.

295. ?. *Vidimus gloriam eius* (John 1:14). Visionum distincciones [?] esse multiplices nullus negat . . .-. . . possunt dicere tales sancti Vidimus gloriam eius. Ff. 216va–217ra.

296. S21. *Vidimus gloriam eius* (John 1:14). Nostis, domini reuerendi, quod Purificacionis solempnitas matri dedicatur et virgini . . . .-. . . accipiens hanc sacratissimam. F. 217ra–b.

297. S08. *De plenitudine eius accepimus* (John 1:16). Domini est terra et plenitudo eius . . .-. . . sed glorie partem accipere de plenitudine eius. Amen. F. 217rb–vb.

298. S24. *Ecce agnus Dei* (John 1:29). Ecce nunc benedicite Dominum . . .- . . . agnus Dei. Amen. F. 217vb.

299. T41/5. *Hoc est signum foederis* (Gen 9:12). Quando dilecti recedunt, inuicem solent aliquod preciosum donarium relinquere . . .-. . . ? Ff. 218ra–220va.

300. T41/5. *Accipite et manducate* (cf. 1 Cor 11:24). Beatus Gregorius 18 *Moralium* dicit Inuocare Deum omni tempore . . .-. . . visum illum et cognicionem. Illam . . . Ff. 221ra–222rb.

301. T41/5. *Sacramentum hoc magnum est* (Eph 5:32). Sacramentum secundum vnam nominis interpretacionem . . .-. . . est hoc sacramentum percipiendum etc. Ff. 222va–224va.

302. T41/5. *Panis quem ego dabo caro mea est pro [mundi] vita* (John 6:52). I'o premium [?] pre [*blank*] mittitur digne recipientibus corpus Christi . . .- . . . de celebracione missarum ex'a etc. Ff. 224va–226rb.

303. T41/5. *Hoc facite in meam commemorationem* (Luke 22:19 et 1 Cor 11:24). Omnia facta nostra sunt in Dei gloriam facienda . . .-. . . hunc panem viuit in eternum. Quod . . . Ff. 226rb–228rb.

304. C15. *Eligite* (?). Dilectissimi mei, sicud dicit Philosophus 1 *Ethicorum* in principio quod omnis ars et doctrina . . .-. . . qui diligit nos, etc. F. 230ra–b.

305. C15. *Quis erit electus* (Jere 49:19). Scitis quod in quibusdam regnis non solum . . .-. . . Spiritus Sancti gracia talis eligatur, qui nobis omnibus iter salutis ostendat prestante . . . Ff. 230rb–231rb.

306. C15. *Quis ascendet in montem* (Ps 23:3). Quia thema preponitur per modum interrogacionis . . .-. . . ? Ff. 231rb–233ra.

307. C15. *Quem eligero, germinabit virga illius* (Num 17:5). Sicud dicit beatus Augustinus 8 *Confessionum* capitulo 18, Diuerse voluntates descendunt cor hominis . . .-. . . vmbraculum valido robore. Ff. 233ra–234ra.

308. C15. *Eligite meliorem et eum qui vobis placuerit de filiis domini vestri unum et eum ponite super solium patris sui* (2 Kgs 10:3). Isti pictores et alii

prudenciores artifices quando vident quod opus bonum . . .-. . . Iesum Christum, gloriose Virginis filium dulcissimum, etc. Ff. 234ra–235rb. Thomas de Lisle, in Aberdeen 154, f. 344.

309. C19. *Fratres tui visitabis si recte agant, et quibus ordinati sint, disce* (1 Sam 17:18). Vnum verbum communiter dicitur, et est verum: Velit nolit vadit sacerdos ad synodum . . .-. . . ? Ff. 242ra–243vb. Thomas de Lisle, in Aberdeen 154, f. 329, and J/2-128.

310. C19. *Descendi in hortum meum, ut viderem poma convallium* (Cant 6:10). Fratres, scire debetis quod prelatus in Ecclesia Dei ponitur sicut ortolanus . . .-. . . ? Ff. 243vb–244vb. Thomas de Lisle, in Aberdeen 154, f. 335v.

311. C19*. *Descendi in hortum meum, ut viderem poma convallium et inspicerem, si floruissent vineae et germinassent mala punica* (Cant 6:10). Karissimi, isti diuites mundani sicud videmus ortos habent et virgulta sua . . .-. . . poma conuallium. Huius orti nos participes . . . F. 245ra–vb. Thomas de Lisle, in Aberdeen 154, f. 338v.

312. C19. *Vadam et videbo fratres meos* (1 Sam 20:29). Dicitur et multum bene, Quod oculus non videt, cordi non dolet . . .-. . . Rogemus Dominum Iesum Christum, gloriose Virginis Marie filium, etc. Ff. 245vb–246vb. Thomas de Lisle, in Aberdeen 154, f. 333.

313. C19 / C14. *Mundamini qui fertis vasa Domini* (Isa 52:11). Tali sancto talis offerenda, et tali domino talis familia . . .-. . . modo rogemus Dominum Iesum Christum, gloriose Marie Virginis filium, etc. Ff. 246vb–247va. Thomas de Lisle, in Aberdeen 154, f. 339.

314. C19. *Separavit vos Dominus ab omni populi, ut serviretis ei* (Num 16:9). Dicitur, et verum est, pactum vincit, hoc est dictu se ueniat venit hac condicione [?] . . .-. . . deducet eos ad vite fontis aquarum. Quod . . . Ff. 247va–248vb. Thomas de Lisle, in Aberdeen 154, f. 351v.

315. C19 / C14. *Resplenduit facies eius sicut sol et vestimentum eius sicut nix alba* (Matt 17:2). Dicitur: Quod oculus non videt, cor non dolet . . .-. . . fetus decursus a'm. Quod . . . Ff. 248vb–249va. Thomas de Lisle, in Aberdeen 154, f. 356.

316. C11. *Vere Dominus est in loco isto* (Gen 28:16). Res perdita inueniri non potest . . .-. . . modo rogemus Dominum, beate Marie Virginis filium, etc. Ff. 249va–250va. Thomas de Lisle, in Aberdeen 154, f. 340v.

317. C11. *Vere Deus est in loco isto* (Gen 28:16). Habentes in curia magnatorum aliqua negocia pertractare . . .-. . . et maxime in die pasche. Modo rogemus Dominum, etc. Ff. 250va–251rb. Thomas de Lisle, in Aberdeen 154, f. 342v.

318. C18. *Dilectus meus mihi et ego illi* (Cant 2:16). Gallice dicitur: Ky bien ayme, tard oblye. Hoc ad literam videmus . . .-. . . veni coronaberis. Modo rogemus . . . Ff. 251rb–252rb. Thomas de Lisle, see Schneyer 5: 670.

319. C18. *Relinquo mundum* (John 16:28). In natura sic est quod naturaliter vnumquemque quiescit in suo loco proprio et ibidem saluatur, extra vero locum suum nec quiescit . . .-. . . hic in excelsis habitabit. Vbi nos habitare . . . Ff. 252rb–253va.

320. S59. *Introduxit me rex in cellaria sua* (Cant 1:3). Munda [*or* viuida] res est amor quoniam vita est quedam duo compulans . . .-. . . replebuntur cellaria vniuersa substancia preciosa atque pulcherrima. Que cellaria . . . Ff. 254ra–vb.

321. S59. *Trahe me post te* (Cant 1:3). Qui indigerit aqua marina et transiret mare . . .-. . . nunquam fastidit fruentem eo. Igitur rogabimus . . . Ff. 254vb–255vb.

322. S59. *Quae est ista quae ascendit* (Cant 3:6). Clamant sancti et experiencia docet quod actus iste cui . . .-. . . inter sanctos est sors illorum. In qua sorte . . . Ff. 255vb–257vb.

323. S59*. *Una assumetur* (Matt 24:41). Celestis sponsus Christus Iesus domum maiestatis sue glorificare disponens . . .-. . . assumpsit in gloria die hodierna. Ipse nos per eius preces . . . Ff. 257vb–259rb.

324. S86*. *Venit in spiritu in templum* (Luke 2:27). Verba ista, dilectissimi, poterunt, vt michi videtur, ad predicatorem verbi Dei non incongrue referri . . .-. . . in templum claritatis eterne. Quod . . . Ff. 260ra–261va.

325. S86*. *Signum cui contradicetur* (Luke 2:34). Ecce reuelacio, signum; ecce rebellio, cui contradicetur . . .-. . . ?. Ff. 261va–263vb.

326. S86*. *Maria, invenisti gratiam* (Luke 1:30). Karissimi patres et domini, dicit Bernardus in sermone de Natiuitate Virginis gloriose quod si Maria pie fuerit inuocata . . .-. . . multiplicem graciam inuenisti etc. Ff. 264ra–265va.

327. S86*. *Tu* (Luke 1:28?). Si diligenter consideremus officium predicandi . . .-. . . nos regat et ducat ad gloriam regni celestis. Amen. Ff. 265va–268rb.

328. S86*. *Maria abiit in montana* (Luke 1:39). In quibus duo notantur: primum est amaritudo penitencie . . .-. . . ? F. 268rb–vb.

329. S86*. *Rorate, caeli, desuper* (Isa 45:8). Postquam terra cordis humani velud fenum exaruit . . .-. . . filius omnibus adoptiuus illustratur. Ff. 268vb–269rb.

330. S86. *Non est aliud nisi domus Dei et porta caeli* (Gen 28:17). Karissimi mei, licet gloriosa Virgo Maria secundum quod ait Alexander . . .-. . . est adhuc. Ff. 269rb–270ra.

331. S21. *Veniet ad templum* (Mal 3:1). Reuerendi mei, solent pauperes sedere ad portam . . .-. . . qui dedicauerunt templum sanctum suum. Ideo illud templum . . . Ff. 270va–271ra.

332. S86*. *Terra dedit fructum* (Ps 66:7). Reuerendi mei, tocius mundi machine eligans architectus . . .-. . . peruenire valeamus ad regnum celorum. Ad quod . . . Ff. 271ra–272ra. Repeats X-266.

333. S28. *Loquere* (Deut 19?). In principio Beatam Virginem [exoremus ut] nos medie[t] [mitiget] dirigat [et erigat] . . .-. . . ? F. 272rb–va.

334. S28. *Tu es* (Dan 5:13?). Beatus Ieronimus considerans gloriositatem Virginis Marie dixit ipsam esse . . .-. . . Dominus pars hereditatis etc. Quam hereditatem . . . F. 272va–b.

335. S28. *Ave, gratia plena, Dominus tecum, benedicta tu in mulieribus* (Luke 1:28). Aue inquiunt salutantes, de pleno [capiunt?] exorantes, domino assistunt famulantes . . .-. . . summe dote glorie. Ad quam . . . Ff. 272vb–273vb. Also V-40 and J/3-4.

336. S28. *Descendi in hortum meum* (Cant 6:10?). Spiritualiter quilibet predicator verbi Dei potest dici ortolanus pro quo quod ipse habet eradicare vicia et plantare virtutes . . .-. . . sed misericordiam volo et non iudicium. Ff. 274ra–277va.

Y – London, St. Paul's Cathedral Library, MS 8

Y/1

For the problems of recording these items see Part One, section 33, pp. 191–192.

1. ?. ?. Karissimi, quando aliquis per infirmitatem perdidit memoriam . . . , f. 1.

2. ?. Confessio. Reuerendi, secundum quod patet per beatum Gregorium . . . , f. 3.

3. ?. ?. Milicia est vita hominis super terram. Nam quamcito homo nascitur . . . , f. 4.

4. ?. Prepara. Karissimi, lego in libro Sapiencie quod in malivolam animam introibit sapiencia . . . , f. 5v.

5. ?. *Filius Dei es* (Matth 4:3). Reuerendi mei, tres sunt proprietates siue virtutes . . . , f. 8, inc.

6. ?. Tristicia. Karissimi, sicut scitis per, quod secundus [!] mors et tristicia intrauerunt in mundum . . . , f. 9v.

7. ?. ?. Legitur quod Scribe et Pharisey adduxerunt aliquam mulierem . . . , f. 12.

8. ?. ?. Karissimi, spiritualiter loquentes ramos de arboribus cedunt qui verba Dei predicant . . . , f. 13v.

9. T19*. *Caritate non ficta* (2 Cor 6:6). Reuerendi domini, secundum processum Apostoli in epistula hodierna . . . , f. 17. "Quod bannard in conuentu Wychie anno domini 1404 litera dominicalis d." (f. 20).

10. ?. Conuercio. Quatuor requiruntur ad hoc quod peccator conuertitur ad Dominum . . . , f. 21. Holcot, *Convertimini*, sermon 1.

11. ?. Castigacio. Triplici de causa fit castigacio . . . , f. 23.

12. ?. Caro. Caro concupiscit contra spiritum . . . , f. 24.

13. ?. Sanguis Christi. Refert Ouidius . . . , f. 24v.

14. ?. Habere. Sapiens Prouerbiorum 6 quecumque alloquitur dicens, Vade ad formicam, o piger . . . , f. 26.

15. ?. Vita. Karissimi, iuxta scripture sacre seriem, non nullorumque doctorum multiplex testimonium, triplex est vita . . . , f. 28v.

16. T28. Stare. Conualescentes de infirmitate corporali necesse habent stare in sanctitate. ., f. 31v.

17. T06. Signum. Gregorius 4 [*blank*], Signa sunt nobis necessaria, f. 33.

18. T06. Lux. Teste beato Augustino oculis egris odiosa lux . . . , f. 33v.

19. T06. De sole. Reuerendi patres et domini, Dei Filius duplici de causa soli assimilatur . . . , f. 35.

20. T06. Verbum Dei. In via lutosa et tenebrosa valde expedit homini . . . , f. 35v.

21. ?. Verbum Dei. Verbum Dei in sacra scriptura quatuor comparatur . . . , f. 37.

22. ?. Gracia Dei. Augustinus 1 *De ciuitate Dei* capitulo 2 dicit quod vates sacrorum carmen invenerunt . . . , f. 37v.

23. ?. Gracia Dei. Karissimi, sicut noueritis viri mendici . . . , f. 38v.

24. S20. ?. Reuerendi patres fratresque karissimi, secundum beatum Gregorium 24 *Moralium* capitulo 6 tres sunt conuersorum modi . . . , f. 39v.

25. S49. Dilexit. Karissimi, de sex mulieribus meminit scriptura. ., f. 40.

26. S52. Soluere. Karissimi, scitis quod in tenebris constituti . . . , f. 41.

27. ?. Iudicium. Precipites esse debeamus ne timere indiscussa . . . , f. 42v. "Istos duos sermones compilauit reuerendus Paulus Parden ordinis fratrum

Carmelitarum valarum. Qui si nimis prolixe videantur, possunt abbreuiari in quocumque membro sicut placet" (f. 43).

28. ?. Accipere et dare. Grammatici metrice dicunt quod hoc verbum das . . . , f. 44.

29. ?. ?. Karissimi, principium, finis, et medium tocius bonitatis presentis temporis . . . , f. 46.

30. ?. Pax. Dilectissimi, beatus Augustinus 19 *De ciuitate Dei* capitulo 13 commendans pacem dicit . . . , f. 46v.

31. ?. Iuste iudicare. Dicit Aristoteles 2 *Ethicorum* quod ad hoc quod homo sit iustus non sufficit . . . , f. 49v.

32. ?. *Idolorum servitus non habet hereditatem in regno Christi et Dei* (Eph 5:5). Karissimi, secundum beatum Augustinum . . . , f. 50x.

33. ?. *Requiescet pax* (Luke 10:6). Karissimi, Mathei 12 . . . , f. 54v. Also W-19.

34. ?. *Miserere mei* (Luke 18:38). Inter omnia que in mundo cernimus maxime deberet hominem delectare assidue cogitare . . . , f. 56v.

35. ?. *Videte quomodo caute ambuletis* (Eph 5:14). Inter multas questiones que ponuntur in sacra scriptura sub ista diccione quomodo . . . , f. 59.

36. ?. *Erudivit quasi pastor gregem suum* (Sir 18:13). Qualiter (?) dogmata pascencium et pastorum . . . , f. 61.

37. ?. *Diligite inimicos vestros* (Matt 5:44?). Karissimi, solempnitas huius martiris [Stephen?] celebranda est cum magna deuocione . . . , f. 62.

38. T10. *Venimus adorare eum*, etc. (Matt 2:2). Fratres karissimi, formam serui pro seruis accipiens . . . , f. 62v.

39. T01. *Veni, Domine* (Rev 22:20?). Karissimi, homo ex primorum parentum preuaricacione . . . , f. 64.

40. T01+. ?. Karissimi, secundum quod scribitur Prouerbiorum 17, Omni tempore. ., f. 65.

41. ?. ?. Karissimi, ante aduentum Domini in tanta caligine totum genus humanum . . . , f. 66.

42. ?. ?. Karissimi, secundum sentenciam beati Augustini in *Questionibus noui ac veteris* . . . , f. 67.

43. T06. ?. Karissimi, beatus Augustinus libro *De baptismo* . . . , f. 68.

44. ?. ?. Karissimi, Prouerbiorum [*blank*] scribitur, Si seruaueris doctrinam . . . , f. 69v–.

45. T06. ?. Karissimi, quando rex aliquis de longinquis partibus ad propria revertitur . . . , f. 71.

46. T01+. ?. Karisimi, sicut scitis prudens et discretus et curialiter educatus . . . , f. 72.

47. To1+. ?. Karissimi, secundum Philosophum cor [*canceled*?] hominis quadruplici affeccione mouetur . . . , f. 73v.

48. To1+. ?. Karissimi, quoniam ad misericordiam pertinet desolatos et afflictos consolare . . . , f. 74v.

49. To1+. ?. Karissimi, quantum magis desideratus appropinquat, eo amplius . . . , f. 75v.

50. To1+. ?. Karissimi, volentes primogenitum regis temporalis de nouo natum laudare . . . , f. 75v.

51. To6. *Operibus iustitiae quae fecimus nos*, etc. (Titus 3:5). Karissimi, iustus iudex, qui nec aduersario suo aliquod iniustum vult irrogare . . . , f. 77.

52. T29*. *Ostendit eis manus et latus* (John 20:20). Secundum magistrum in *Historia scolastica* . . . , f. 78.

53. ?. *Ascendit in montem ut oraret* (Luke 5:28). Karissimi, vt dicunt quidam naturales, est quoddam animal les [?] nomine, cuius natura . . . , f. 81.

54. ?. *Qui vicerit, non laedetur in morte secunda* (Rev 2:11). Refert Alexander Nequam quod Virgilius in ciuitate Romana . . . , f. 82v.

55. ?. *Caro mea requiescet in spe* (Ps 15:9). Propheta teste, karissimi, Iob capitulo 5, Si vt homo nasceretur . . . , f. 83v.

56. ?. *Memor esto iudicii mei sicut erat et tutum* (Sir 38:23). Sicud docet Augustinus 16 *Confessionum*, Omnis creatura loquitur . . . , f. 86. "Per iohannem turuey," f. 88.

57. ?. *Convertimini* (Joel 2:12). Karissimi, quatuor requiruntur ad hoc quod peccator conuertatur, scilicet gracie Dei infusio . . . , f. 88.

58. ?. *Maria, invenisti gratiam* (Luke 1:30). Videmus quod aliqui in hoc mundo graciam inveniunt coram rege . . . , f. 89, inc?

59. S59. ?. Karissimi, secundum consuetudinem humanam, mulieres in consorcium regum assumende . . . , f. 90.

60. To6. ?. Karissimi, sicut euidenter ostenditur vt in verbis istis sumitur, facta est lux, Genesis 1. Postquam Deus in principio celum et terram creauerat, tenebre erant super faciem abyssi . . . , f. 91.

61. S28. ?. Karissimi, sicut in conuiuiis mundanis dominus ostendit et assignat locum nobilioribus . . . , f. 94.

62. S28. ?. Karissimi, beata Virgo propter diuersas ipsius virtutes diuersis diuersemodo comparata . . . , f. 95.

63. Co9. ?. Karissimi, cum aliquis est in periculo indigens gracia . . . , f. 98.

64. S65. ?. Karissimi, vniuersum corporali aspectui variis floribus . . . , f. 99.

65. T28?. *Surrexit Dominus vere et apparuit Symoni* (Luke 24:34). Sunt que [?] Christi resurreccionem faciunt mirabilem. Primo resurgentis mira felicitas . . . , f. 108.

66. T28. *Probet autem seipsum homo* (1 Cor 11:28). Ceteri cibi sunt probandi et sic recipiendi; iste cibus non est probandus . . . , f. 109v.

67. ?. *Misit de summo et accepit me* (Ps 17:16). Karissimi, ante incarnacionem Filii Dei totum genus humanum . . . , f. 109v.

68. ?. *Adorate Dominum in atrio sancto eius* (Ps 28:2). Karissimi, Filius Dei venit ut nos in dupplici natura . . . , f. 110v.

69. ?. *Ecce nunc tempus acceptabile* (2 Cor 6:2). Karissimi, sicud legitur Luce 10, homo quidam descendebat ab Ierusalem . . . , f. 111v.

70. ?. *Paenitemini et convertimini ad Dominum, ut deleantur peccata vestra* (Acts 3:19). Karissimi, licet multiplex inueniatur penitencie effectus . . . , f. 112v.

71. C21*. *Redde quod debes* (Matt 18:28). Hec possunt esse verba Dei ad defuncti huius corpus . . . , f. 113.

72. ?. *Nunc scio* (John 11:22). Karissimi, in hac vita solum cognoscimus per fidem . . . , f. 115.

73. ?. *Iustum deduxit Dominus per vias rectas* (Wisd 10:10). In Psalmo scribitur, Iustus Dominus et iusticias dilexit, etc. Qui ergo vult . . . , f. 118v.

74. ?. *De morte transit ad vitam* (John 5:24). Karissimi mei, sicud dixit Philosophus 3 *Phisicarum*, omnis transitus siue motus est de contrario in contrarium . . . , f. 119v. "Per fratrem J. Turuay" (f. 121). Also E-11.

75. T26*. Occidere. Karissimi, hec verba prophete per multa annorum curicula ante Christi aduentum . . . , f. 122. Also W-98.

76. ?. Tenere. Karissimi, commune prouerbium est quod non est magnum amicum adquirere . . . , f. 125v. Also A-11 and X-126.

77. ?. Dies salutis. Secundum Aristotelem in *Secretis secretorum* 9 capitulo, quod salus siue sanitas corporalis homini est maxime . . . , f. 128.

78. ?. ?. Si quis in certamine positus ex vtraque parte et ita esset aduersariis circumspectus . . . , f. 129.

79. ?. ?. Sicut ex serie euangelii et in scriptura satis liquet, predicacionem Christi et apostolorum precessit quidam precursor, cui nomen Iohannes . . . , f. 132.

80. ?. Deieccio sompnus. Teste philosophia, contrariorum eadem est disciplina . . . , f. 133v, inc. Followed by four homilies from Bernard on *Super Missus est*, ff. 134–149v. "Turuey" (f. 149v).

81. S67. ?. Karissimi, secundum beatum Augustinum *De uera innocencia* . . . , f. 150.

82. C21. ?. Karissimi, secundum beatum Augustinum duplex est hominis malum . . . , f. 150v.

83. C21. ?. Karissimi, quilibet [!] irracionale et quilibet homo quando sentit aliquid sue nature delectabile . . . , f. 152.

84. C21. ?. Karissimi, si hec verba tractentur in exequiis alicuius magnatis . . . , f. 153.

85. T23. Mors. In sacre scripture lectis non paucis mortem assimilare reperimus . . . , f. 155.

86. ?. Dies. Aristoteles 4 *Phisicorum* . . . probat quod nichil habemus de tempore . . . , f. 156v.

87. T23. Mors. Videmus quod medicus scit prolongare vitam hominis . . . , f. 159v.

88. ?. Transire. Legitur in Vita beate Agnetis . . . , f. 161v–162.

Y/2

1. ?. *Eratis aliquando tenebrae, nunc lux in Domino* (Eph 5:8). Vt inteligatis modum loquendi Apostoli in his verbis est sciendum . . .-. . . ciuitas vbi nullus moritur, nullus infirmatur; ibi nullus perit amicus, ibi nullus accedet immutus [*read* inimicus?]. Quam. . . . Ff. 176–179v.

2. So1. *Discite a me, quia mitis sum* (Matt 11:29). Sunt nonnulli quos ad amorem celestis patrie plus exempla . . .-. . . ab hac vita ad eternam gloriam. Ad quam. . . . Ff. 179v–180v.

3. So1. *Christo confixus sum cruci* (Gal 2:19). Nauis in mari duobus indiget . . .- . . . sed habebit lumen vite. Ad quod, etc. Ff. 180v–181v. Also Jacobus de Losanna (Schneyer 3:89) and Michael de Furno (4:178).

4. So3. *Ponam super eum spiritum meum* (Matt 12:18). Sine spiritu uiuere nichil potest . . .-. . . sapienciam diuinam possit pertingere in gloria. Ad quam . . . Ff. 181v–182v.

5. So3. *Elegit eum ex omni carne* (Sir 45:4). Beatus Bernardus: Si maledictus est . . .-. . . de spiritu metet uitam eternam. Ad quam . . . Ff. 182v–183.

6. So5. *Benedixisti, Domine, terram tuam* (Ps 84:2). Res ordinata ad aliquod sacrum solet benedici sicut casulas . . .-. . . quia Deus que est nostra gloria. Ff. 183–184.

7. So5. *Statim sanctificata ab immundicia* (2 Sam 11:4). . . .-. . . Psalmo: Querite faciem eius semper. Ad quam . . . Ff. 184–185v.

8. So8. *Cum eum nec dimittam* (Cant 3:4). Duo sunt propter que res libenter et diligenter tenetur . . .-. . . Patris mei percipite regnum. Quod . . . Ff. 185v–186.

9. S08. *Oculus meus videt, idcirco me reprehendo* (Job 42:5–6). Duo sunt signa senectutis . . .-. . . Psalmo: Factus est michi in salutem. Ad quam . . . Ff. 186–187.

10. T06. *Sol egressus est super terram* (Gen 19:23). Motus solis super terram ex tribus cognoscitur . . .-. . . quando sol bene ascendit. Ff. 187r–v, inc.

The first seven sermons are lost but are listed in the table on f. 270v (medieval P. 170).

1. ?. *Recordare.*

2. ?. *Spe gaudentes.*

3. ?. *Relinquo mundum.*

4. ?. *Quodcumque dixerit vobis facite.*

5. ?. *Habitabit confidenter.*

6. ?. *Exaltavi te de medio populi.*

7. ?. *Exaltavit illum apud proximos suos.*

8. T36*. *Sedet a dextris Dei* (Mark 16:19). Rumores boni letificant cor . . .- . . . inquietum est cor nostrum, etc., donec requiescet. Quod . . . Ff. 199 (medieval page 25)-200. Also A-46.

9. ?. *Custodi virum istum* (1 Kgs 20:39). Karissimi, uulgariter dicitur, Aftyr þat þyng ys, hit ow to be nurryschyd and kepyd . . .-. . . quia Custos Domini sui gloriabitur, Prouerbiorum ultimo. Ff. 200–202.

10. ?. *Mortuus est rex* (Exod 2:23). Karissimi, in quolibet homine . . . Legitur in gestis Karoli . . .-. . . eo seculi in vitam eternam. Ad quid . . . Ff. 202– 205v.

11. ?. *Sequebatur eum* (John 6:2? [*ms* Luke 6]). Qui habet ire ire [!] ad mag- nam distanciam per vias duras . . .-. . . gloriam sequitur, quia Ecclesias- tici 23 dicitur, Gloria regine est sequere dominum. Quod . . . Ff. 205v– 207.

12. ?. *Sequebatur eum multitudo magna* (John 6:2). Reuerendi mei, tria sunt, propter que quilibet homo racionaliter mouetur . . .-. . . et finaliter ducet eum ad gaudium bonorum. Ad quod. . . . Ff. 207–210.

13. ?. *Refloruit caro mea* (Ps 27:7). Sicut dicit Albertus, odor vinee . . .-. . . et ego resuscitabo eum in nouissimo die. Ad istam . . . Ff. 217v–219.

14. ?. *Iam saturati estis, iam divites facti estis* (1 Cor 4:8). Testante beato Ambrosio omnes nos quamcito nascimur, quod iter ingredimur . . .-. . . sicud hodie spem sic . . . eternaliter saturare dignatur. Amen. Ff. 219–221v.

15. ?. *Stipendia peccati mors, ergo peccatum est rex* (Rom 6:23). Non [regnet?] peccatum sine vestro mortali corpore . . .-. . . mors depascet illos. Ff. 225v–226.

16. ?. *Remittuntur ei peccata, quoniam dilexit multum* (Luke 7:48). Tria notantur: crimina delinquentis . . .-. . . multi actus stulti. F. 226. Followed by distinctions, not listed in the table.

17. ?. *Sapientia aedificavit sibi domum* (Prov 9:11). Nota duplex est domus sapiencie . . .-. . . ? Ff. 228-?.

18. ?. *Quaerite* (Isa 21:12). Si queritis, querite. Tria sunt hic videnda: quare Deus querendus . . .-. . . qui est apud nos si nos velimus esse apud eum. F. 230v.

19. S70. *Angeli eorum semper vident faciem Patris mei* (Matt 18:10). In quibus tria: dignitas humane condicionis, ibi angelus . . .-. . . gloria eius stercus et vermis, hodie extollitur et cras non inuenietur. F. 231v.

20. S79. *Diligite Dominum, omnes sancti eius* (Ps 30:24). In quibus accio gloriosa et ideo delectabilis, ibi diligite . . .-. . . celestis premia exspectatis. Ff. 231v–232.

21. S80. *Opera illorum sequuntur illos* (Rev 14:13). Glossa: Opera, idest vices operum siue bonorum siue malorum . . .-. . . aut videre aut sentire aut cogitare quis potest? F. 232r–v.

22. S28. *Ave, gratia plena, Dominus tecum* (Luke 1:28). De Virgine tam gloriosa loquitur. Valde timendum est . . .-. . . quem totus non potest capere, etc. Ff. 232v–233.

23. C05. *Iustorum animae in manu Dei sunt* (Wisd 3:1). Anime iustorum sunt in manu Domini custodientis, ne rapiantur. Dyabolus enim ad modum milui circumuolat ad rapiendum . . .-. . . contra fraudulacionem suggestionum, etc. F. 233.

24. ?. *Date elemosynam, et omnia munda sunt vobis* (Luke 11:41). Duo notantur: primum est elemosinarum largicio . . .-. . . ? Ff. 233v–234.

25. ?. *Tempus revertendi nunc* (Heb 11:15). Karissimi, sanctus propheta Ysaias, sicud habetur Ysaie 55 capitulo, quando impletus erat spiritu sancto . . .- . . . reuertat ad Dominum et miserebitur ei. Quam misericordiam . . . Ff. 235–238.

26. ?. *Ramos de arboribus struebantur in via* (Matt 21:8). Augustinus super canonicam Johannis, tractatu 3 in fine, ostendit quod predicator sine gracia non fructificat . . .-. . . qui se humiliat exaltabitur. Quod nobis concedat Iesus. Amen. Ff. 238v–241v.

27. ?. *Voca operarios et redde illis mercedem* (Matt 20:8). Tullius 3 *De officiis* docet non solum homines . . .-. . . ideo nos peccatores vocauit ad gloriam suam. Ad quam. . . . Ff. 242–244v.

28. ?. *Nunc dies salutis* (2 Cor 6:2). Docet Aristoteles quod omne receptum est in recipiente . . .-. . . dies suos in bono et annos suos in gloria. Quam . . . Ff. 244v–245v.

29. ?. *Vindex est Dominus* (1 Thess 4:6). Karissimi, quandoque visum est si mulier habeat prolem . . .-. . . et irascitur demonibus suis frenus et tabescet etc. F. 246r–v.

30. ?. *Eicio daemonia* (Luke 11:19). Triplici de causa aliquis aliqua eicit . . .-. . . hec Augustinus. Quod gaudium . . . Ff. 247–248, 251r–v. Also P1-33.

31. ?. *Cum eiecisset daemonium, locutus est mutus* (Luke 11:14). Vbi nota quod egresso Spiritu Sancto de anima per peccatum ingreditur demonium . . .-. . . et honorabile nomen eorum coram illo. Quem honorem nobis concedat. Ff. 248v–250v.

32. ?. *Gentes ignorant Deum* (1 Thes 4:5). Sanctus Thomas 3 *Contra gentiles* capitulo 156, Deus inquit quantum in se est . . .-. . . in malignitate autem nostra consumpti sumus. Ff. 254–255v, 252–254. Also P1-30.

33. T21*. *Revertar* (Luke 11:24). Istud thema poterit tribus modis verificari. Primo modo, si quis incedit peruersam viam . . .-. . . reuertar ad eum qui me misit, idest principale bonum, etc. Ff. 255v–258. Also P2–32.

34. ?. *Benedictus fructus ventris tui* (Luke 1:42). Sicut docet Anselmus *De similitudinibus* capitulo 83, licet . . .-. . . mediante quo ducetur sursum ad celum. Ad quod. . . . Ff. 259–260v.

35. ?. *Quasi flos egreditur* (Job 14:2). Albertus 6 *De animalibus* dicit quod flores sunt vasa . . .-. . . fructiferam penitenciam ipsam contument [!], quod . . . Ff. 259v–261v.

35A. ?. *Terra dedit fructum* (Ps 66:7). Ad hoc quod terra fructum proferat tria necessaria requiruntur . . .-. . . remuneracio bonitatis. Dic ergo Terra dedit fructum. Ff. 261v–262. Not listed in the table.

36. ?. *Miserere mei Domine* (Matt 15:22). Karissimi, ista verba ad literam sunt verba mulieris Cananee . . .-. . . qui se suspendit laqueo, scilicet desperacionis. F. 262–262v.

37. ?. *Orate* (James 5:16). Karissimi, imploraturus graciam a principe siue rege . . .-. . . exspectamus misericordiam Domini nostri Iesu Christi in vita eterna. Ad quam . . . Ff. 263–264v.

38. ?. *Hic est Iesus rex* (Luke 23:38). Legimus in gestis Karoli imperatoris quod semel uoluit ciuitatem quandam lucrari . . .-. . . quid est Iesus nisi Saluator. Hec ille. F. 265r–v.

39. ?. *Hoc oro, ut caritas vestra magis ac magis abundet* (Phil 1:8). Videns Apostolus caritatem istis temporibus frigescentem . . .-. . . quam quis poterit ostendere proximo suo . . . Ff. 266r–v.

40. ?. *Vade* (John 4:16). Sicud enim videmus in istis corporalibus quod uadens situm mutat . . .-. . . Johannis 18: Vado ad eum qui me misit, scilicet Deum Patrem. Ad quem . . . (267). Ff. 266v–267.

41. ?. *Quomodo Christus resurrexit, ita et nos* (Rom 6:4). Karissimi, Augustinus sermone 64 distinguens de resurreccione . . .-. . . nam hec est terra viuencium. Ad quam nos perducat Iesus. Amen. Ff. 267–269.

42. ?. *Dum tempus habemus, operemur bonum* (Gal 6:10). Salomon dicit quod omnia tempus habent. Est enim tempus laborandi . . .-. . . voca operarios et redde illis mercedem, scilicet vitam eternam. Quam . . . F. 269r–v. Related to X-101.

43. ?. *Surge et ambula* (Matt 9:5?). Narrat Frontinus de quodam duas Affricorum . . .-. . . et corrigas te cum intencione non recidiuandi . . . Ff. 269v–270v.

Z – Arras, Bibliothèque de la ville, MS 184 (254)

1. T23 (Oxford, 1382). *Corruit in platea veritas* (acephalous; Isa 59:14). siue paciencia quod modo . . .-. . . peccati et culpe et hoc clauis. Amen. Ff. 1ra–4rb, acephalous and inc. Henry Chambron. Also V-37.

2. C21*. *Mortuus vivet* (John 11:25). Reuerendi, secundum sentenciam beati Anselmi in *De cura circa mortuos agenda*, inter omnia opera . . .-. . . in perpetuas eternitates, Danielis 12. Quam . . . Ff. 4rb–5va. Also E-38.

3. T19*. *Iesus* (Matt 4:1). Tria mouent me istud thema accipere: Dede, nede, and spede . . .-. . . et quem misisti, Iesum Christum, qui seipsum nobis donet . . . Ff. 5va–7vb. Also H-1 and CA/2-3.

4. T34*. *Petite et dabitur vobis* (Luke 11:9). Secundum Wallensem *De penitencia*, volens orari et aliquid a Deo petere . . .-. . . vbi tam corporis \et/ anime erit perfecta beatitudo. Ad quam etc. (f. 9rb). Similiter dicit Glossa: In hac vita est ieiunium . . . quid Christus docuit orare, quia Pater Noster. Ff. 7vb–9vb. Also J/5-24.

5. T28/2*. *Dicunt eum vivere* (Luke 24:23). Karissimi, ista verba dicebantur a quodam discipulo Christi nomine Cleophas. Nam prout dicitur in ewangelio hodierno, duo ex discipulis . . . .-. . . . reuertimini in regionem

vestram, scilicet in regionem gaudii et leticie sempiterne. Quod . . . Ff. 15rb–17rb.

6. Cii. *In domo tua oportet me manere* (Luke 19:5). Scribitur 2 Paralipomenon 6 de prima Ecclesia, templo scilicet Ierusalem . . .-. . . vitam et gloriam sempiternam tribuendo. Ad quas . . . Ff. 17rb–19rb. Also J/5-25.

7. T19+*. *Paenitentiam agite* (Matt 3:2). Karissimi, quod totum hoc sacrum tempus Quadragesime est specialiter dedicatum hominibus . . .-. . . agite, vbi prius. Sic igitur penitenciam veram agere . . . Ff. 22va–28rb.

8. ?. *Rex fecit grande convivium pueris suis* (Hester 1:3). Notandum quod opus mirabile, nobile, et subtile, cuius operarius eciam penitus [*read* et peritus?], solent queri tres questiones . . .-. . . ad terram promissionis attingere. Quam . . . Ff. 28rb–30ra.

9. ?. *Sanctus, sanctus, sanctus* (Rev 4:8). Nota secundum Ysidorum quod sanctus dicitur quasi sine terra . . .-. . . mercedem habemus, nonne puplicani hoc faciunt? Ideo diligenter fac finem si vis. F. 30ra–va.

10. ?. *Sequebatur eum multitudo magna* (John 6:2). Pro antethemate dicatur historia euangelii cum ista moralizacione: Mare Galilee signat mundum istum. . . .-. . . iudicantes duodecim tribus Israel habituri cum ipso gloriam eternam. Ad quam . . . Ff. 31rb–34va.

11. T31*. *Obsecro vos tamquam advenas et peregrinos abstinere vos a carnalibus desideriis* (1 Pet 2:11). Karissimi mei, cum vita cuiuslibet Christiani peregrinacio quedam versus Ierusalem sit . . .-. . . et debent frui sempiternis gaudiis. Qui . . . Ff. 34va–b, 36ra–vb.

12. ? (Oxford, 1395?). *Haec est autem vita eterna, ut cognoscant te solum verum Deum et quem misisti, Iesum Christum* (John 17:3). Cum diabolus qui est capitalis hominis inimicus laboret fortiter . . .-. . . et lumine claritatis consistit vita eterna. Ad quam vitam. Ff. 36vb–37vb, 35, 38ra–b. Robert Lychlade. Edited with translation in Wenzel, "Robert Lychlade's Oxford Sermon."

13. T28*. *Hoc facite in meam commemorationem* (Luke 22:19). Reuerendi domini, sicut patet ex processu sancti Ricardi *De sacramentis noui legis* . . .- . . . ut Christo ducente peruenias ad regnum celorum. Quod . . . Ff. 38rb–39vb, 42ra. Also G-28.

14. T28*. *Surge et comede* (1 Kings 19:5). Dicit Gregorius in *Morum* quod qui Deo loqui desiderat, de natura rerum confidere debet . . .-. . . accedite et commedite, ut cum Deo poteritis continue viuere. Quod . . . Ff. 42ra–vb, 40ra–41rb. Also H-7.

15. ?. *Inimici mei animam meam circumdederunt* (Ps 16:9). þe help of Crist, of wam is all wyt . . . Leue Cristen sovlus, experiens schewit and teches us al

day . . .-. . . of such mek men and humil in hert is þe kyndom of heuen. þe whych kyndam . . . Ff. 41ra–vb, 43ra–45ra.

16. ?. *Clausa est ianua.* (Matt 25:10). Sicut legitur in quadam historia quam ostendit nobis Virgilius. . . .-. . . ibi eritis coronati cum corona glorie sempiterne. Quod . . . Ff. 45ra–49rb.

17. ?. *Per triennium nocte et die non cessaui cum lacrimis monens vnumquemque vestrum, et nunc comendo vos Deo . . . sicut ipsi scitis.* (Acts 20:31–34). Amici, processus huius breuis collacionis . . .-. . . serui verum Dei in vitam eternam. Ad quam . . . Ff. 49rb–50vb.

18. ?. *Qui facit voluntatem Patris mei qui in celis est* (Matt 7:21). Karissimi, in hoc euangelio precipit nos Saluator cauere et vitare consilium falsorum prophetarum . . .-. . . intrabit ipse in regnum celorum. Quod regnum . . . Amen, Iesus Messias. Ff. 50vb–51rb.

19. T30*. *Christus passus est pro nobis, vobis reliquens exemplum ut sequamini.* (1 Pet 2:21). Anglice sic: Crist in hys passioun reliquit exemplum vobis quomodo ze schuld. Quamuis hec verba . . .-. . . quod interfecit patrem tuum. Quod . . . Ff. 51vb–61va. . Also S-1, H-25, W-6, and Christ Church 91. Edited from H-25 in Johnson, "Preaching the Passion," pp. 178–287.

20. T26*. *Quare rubrum est vestimentum tuum?* (Isa 63:2). Secundum sentenciam doctorum, he fuit questio angelorum in die ascensionis Domini . . .-. . . videlicet in premii accepcione. Quod premium . . . Ff. 61va–68va. Chambron. Also A-35, P2–71, S-19, and in CUL Ee.6.27, f. 73. Edited from S-19 in Johnson, "Preaching the Passion." pp. 288–322.

21. T06*. *Verbum caro factum est* (John 1:14). Primo queritur quando, cur, et vbi . . .-. . . secundo modo sapiencia inuenit dragmam perditam. Ff. 68va–69rb, inc?

22. ? (Council of Lyons, 1250). [No thema]. Dominus noster Iesus Christus, eternus eterni Dei Patris filius, de sacratissimo sinu Dei eterne [!] Patris descendit . . .-. . . plurimum est hodie et maxime in Anglia, etc. Ff. 69rb–72rb, inc. Grosseteste, sermon 14. Edited in *Fasciculus rerum* 2:250–257.

23. S49*. *Remittuntur tibi peccata tua* (Luce 7:48). In quibus verbis intelligitur primo illud quod causa est cuiuslibet doloris . . .-. . . iam noli amplius peccare, etc. Amen. Ff. 72rb–73ra.

24. S79. *Merces vestra copiosa est in celis* (Matthei 5:12). Sicut legitur in euangelio Matthei 4, Christus Iesus ante passionem suam circuibat. . . .-. . . quoniam merces vestra magna est in celis. Quam mercedem . . . Ff. 73rb–76ra. Also H-10.

25. T18. *Iesu, fili David, miserere mei* (Luke 18:38). Karissimi, legitur in primo libro Regum capitulo 11 quod viri Rabes. . . .-. . . mercedem scilicet vitam et gloriam sempiternam. Quam . . . Ff. 76rb–78rb.

26. T28. *Surrexit Dominus vere.* (Luke 24:34). Karissimi, sicut medicina corporalis, si fuerit conueniens complexioni. . . .-. . . de valle lacrimarum et miserie huius mundi ad patriam beatitudinis eterne. Quod . . . Ff. 78va–80vb. Also H-8 and E-2.

27. T23. *Qui est ex Deo, verba Dei audit* (John 8:47). Karissimi, sicut dicit Januensis, ista dominica vocatur Dominica in Passione. . . .-. . . in proximo sermone subsequente. Et fac finem sicut placet, etc. Ff. 80vb–82ra.

28. T24 / T26. *Hoc sentite in vobis, quod in Christo Iesu* (Phil 2:5). Karissimi, officium Ecclesie hodie reducit ad memoriam nostram diram Christi passionem. . . .-. . . vt possitis cum eo feliciter regnari. Quod . . . Ff. 82ra–84vb.

29. T39. *Ille vos docebit omnia* (John 14:26). Karissimi, legitur in primo libro Regum capitulo 11 quod viri Rabes . . .-. . . quorum primum est superbia, etc. Ff. 84vb–86rb.

30. T55. *Surge et vade, quia fides tua saluum te fecit* (Luke 17:19). Karissimi, sicut legitur in euangelio hodierno, factum est dum erat Iesus in Ierusalem. . . .-. . . a pena inferni et te perduxit ad vitam sempiternam. Quam . . . Ff. 86rb–87va.

31. T56. *Nemo potest duobus dominis servire* (Matt 6:24). Karissimi, in hoc euangelio monet nos Saluator noster specialiter de tria [!] . . .-. . . preparauit Deus diligentibus se. Quod . . . Ff. 87va–90vb.

32. T57. *Deus visitavit plebem suam* (Luke 7:17). Karissimi, sicut legitur in euangelio hodierno, Christus Iesus transiens in ciuitatem Naym. . . .-. . . ad liberandum nos a seruitute diaboli et ad restituendum ad gaudium regni celestis. Quod . . . Ff. 90vb–92vb. Also E-40.

33. T45. *Estote misericordes, sicut et Pater vester misericors est* (Luke 6:36). Karissimi, experimentum docet quod, si filius regis vel domini eiectus esset de terra. . . .-. . . et vitam eternam possidebitis. Quam . . . Ff. 92vb–94va.

34. T59. *Diliges Dominum Deum tuum* (Matt 22:37). Karissimi, sicut legitur in *Historia scolastica*, tres erant secte inter Iudeos. . . .-. . . decem Dei mandata. De quibus patet in sermone vnius virginis qui sic incipit: Clausa est ianua, etc. Ff. 94va–96ra.

35. T62. *Rogabat eum ut descenderet et sanaret filium eius* (John 4:47). Karissimi, siquis vellet in terra guerre pugnare contra iminicos. . . .-. . . angelicis canticis eternaliter confortati. Quod . . . Ff. 96ra–99rb.

36. ?. *Iohannes est nomen eius* (Luke 1:63). Karissimi, sicut videtis, quilibet homo componitur ex duobus, scilicet ex corpore et anima. . . .-. . . intrabit cum eo in gaudium sempiternum. Quod . . . Ff. 99rb–100va.

37. T19. *Ductus est Iesus in desertum a spiritu, ut temptaretur a diabolo* (Matt 4:1). Karissimi, duccio ista in desertum qua Iesus ducebatur a Spiritu Sancto . . .- . . . regnum a constitucione mundi. Quod . . . Ff. 100va–103va.

38. T20. *Miserere mei, fili David, filia mea a daemonio male vexatur* (Matt 15:22). Karissimi, sicut legitur in euangelio, Christus Iesus Saluator noster existens in terra Genasareth . . .-. . . et operis satisfaccio. De quibus patet in sermone precedenti, etc. F. 103va–b.

39. T21. *Locutus est mutus* (Luke 11:14). Karissimi, sicut experimentum docet, vox hominis muti per magnam distanciam faciliter non auditur. . . .-. . . cum magna melodia angelorum secum ducet ad celum in celesti gloria perpetuo regnaturos. Ad quam . . . Ff. 103vb–106vb.

40. T28 ("post prandium"). *Estote solliciti, ut custodiatis* (Josh 23:6). Karissimi, sicut legitur Exodi 16, quando Moyses eduxit filios per desertum versus terram promissionis . . .-. . . coronati corona glorie sempiterne. Quod . . . Ff. 106vb–109vb.

41. T01. *Abiciamus ergo opera tenebrarum et induamur arma lucis* (Rom 13:12). Karissimi, in aduentu magni regis uel principis, homines qui ipsum recipient locum . . .-. . . cum eo eternaliter in gaudio viuentes. Quod . . . Ff. 110ra–112vb.

42. ?. *Militia sive temptacio est vita hominis super terram* (Job 7:1). Duo genera sunt militum, scilicet spiritualium et corporalium . . .- . . . ad terram promissionis et terram viuencium. Quam etc. F. 113ra–va.

43. T26. *Hic est Iesus rex* (Matt 27:37). Scitis quoniam pauper et indigens qui haberet magnum negocium et viagium faciendum. . . .-. . . dederunt ei fel, etc., ad despectum. Ff. 120ra–126va, inc. Also J/5-23.

44. T19. *Hortamur vos, ne in vacuum gratiam Dei recipiatis* (2 Cor 6:1). Nota quod tripliciter in uacuum vas recipit aliquid . . .-. . . nisi abstuleris, crudelis esses. Sic, etc. Ff. 133rb–134va.

45. T21. *Omne regnum in seipsum divisum desolabitur* (Luke 11:17). Moraliter, quilibet suum corpus possidet quasi regnum. . . .-. . . [folio damaged]. Ff. 135rb–va?

46. T22. *Est puer unus hic qui habet quinque panes* (John 6:9). Puer iste potest dici Christus propter tria . . .-. . . gaudium vestrum nemo tollet a vobis. Illa gaudia . . . Ff. 136rb–137vb.

47. ?. *Vivus est sermo Dei et efficax,* etc. (Heb 4:12). Audistis, karissimi, quod frequenter incitaui vos ad libenter audiendum verbum Dei . . .-. . . libenter tam ceci quam alii. F. 138rb–vb.

48. T28/2. *Mane nobiscum, Domine* (Luke 24:29). Reuerendi, propter peccatum primi parentis expulsi fuimus a propria terra . . .-. . . rogemus, vt maneat nobiscum, hic per graciam et in fine per gloriam. Quod . . . Ff. 140ra–141ra.

49. T13. *Et ecce leprosus veniens adorabat eum dicens, Domine, si vis, potes me mundare.* (Matt 8:2). Karissimi, sicut videtis, quilibet homo componitur ex duobus, scilicet ex corpore et anima. . . .-. . . intrabit cum eo in gaudium sempiternum. Quod . . . Ff. 166va–168ra.

50. S21. *Nunc dimittis servum . . . pace* (Luke 2:29). Karissimi, sicut bene nostis, mos modernorum talis est quod mortuo aliquo nobili nobilior et eius sanguini propinquior faciet primo oblacionem. . . .-. . . in pace perfecta et leticia sempiterna. Ad quam . . . Ff. 168ra–169vb.

51. T60. *Surge, tolle lectum tuum, et vade in domum tuam* (Matth 9:6). Karissimi, postquam Iesus ostendisset plura miracula in terra Gerasenorum . . .- . . . patet in sermone vnius virginis, qui sic incipit: Clausa est ianua, etc. Ff. 169vb–170va.

52. ?. *Confitemini* (James 5:16). Nota quod est. . ab hominibus facta. . . .- . . . estote fortes in bello, etc. Quod regnum . . . Ff. 170vb–171va.

53. ?. *Facite vobis amicos de Mammona iniquitatis.* (Luke 16:9). Mammona Sira lingua diuicias sonat, et dicitur mammona iniquitatis quia. . . .-. . . nos ad eterna tabernacula dignetur perducere. Amen. Ff. 171va–172va.

54. ?. *Psallite Domino qui ascendit* (Ps 67:5). Dicit Boicius quod vir b[ene] [dispositus] et sanus audiens suauem melodiam . . .-. . . possitis ascendere et ibi eternaliter secum in gloria permanere. Amen. Ff. 172va–174vb.

55. ?. *Confitemini Domino quoniam bonus, quoniam in saeculum misericordia eius.* (Ps 105:1). Tria noscuntur precipue pertinere ad prelatum siue confessorem. . . .-. . . misericordie eius participes nos efficiat, qui . . . Ff. 175rb–176va.

56. ?. *Probet seipsum homo, et sic de pane illo edat.* (1 Cor 11:28). Karissimi, debetis in principio orare . . . Sicut scitis bene, ceteri cibi corporales sunt probandi. . . .-. . . pascet eum post hanc vitam in eterna gloria, que preparauit Dominus. Ad hanc . . . Ff. 176va–177vb. Also in Oxford, Magdalen College 112, f. 222va.

57. ?. *Sanguis Christi emundavit conscientias nostras.* (Heb 9:14). Christus pro sua magna passione, quam sustinuit pro toto genere humano . . .-. . . perducens nos ad vitam eternam. Sic ergo sanguis Christi emundet . . . Ff. 177vb–179ra.

Works cited

MANUSCRIPTS

For references to the collections with sigla (A, B/2, C, etc.), see the Index.

Aberdeen, University Library, MS 154: sermons by Thomas de Lisle, 140, 148, 223, 256, 257, 261, 262, 517, 651, 655

Arras, Bibliothèque de la Ville, MS 254: collection Z

Cambridge, Corpus Christi College, MS 392: collection K

MS 423: sermons, 316, 387

—, Gonville and Caius College, MS 52: priest's manual, including *Speculum iuniorum*, 218, 219, 221

MS 246: Jacobus de Voragine, sermons, 217

MS 334: works by Waldeby and collection CA; *see also* 41, 99, 172, 395, 413, 420

MS 356: collection C

—, Jesus College, MS 13: collection J

—, Pembroke College, MS 199: collection P1

MS 200: sermons, many shared with collection U, 8, 212–214, 598

MS 257: collection P2

—, Peterhouse, MS 210: Holcot, sermons, 127, 130, 565, 638, 640

—, St. John's College, MS 133: sermons and narrationes, some shared with Ross sermons, 173, 174

—, Sidney Sussex College, MS 74: English sermons, 465

—, Trinity College, MS B.1.45: miscellany, Latin and English, including sermons shared with Oxford, Merton College MS 112, 223

—, University Library, MS Ee.6.27: miscellany, containing Chambron's sermon *Quare rubrum*, 126, 183, 412, 565, 595, 668

MS Gg.6.16: Middle English sermons, 65

MS Gg.6.26: collection G

MS Ii.1.26: Pecham, *Collationes dominicales*, etc., 222

MS Ii.3.8: collection A

MS Ii.6.3: sermons by Michael of Hungary and others, 99

MS Kk.4.24: Bromyard's *Exhortaciones* and collection B/2

MS Additional 2943: Cistercian sermons, 284

MS Additional 3571: Woodford, commentary on Matthew, 114
MS Additional 5943: priest's notebook, 218
Charleville, Bibliothèque Municipale, MS 31: Cistercian sermons, 39
Dublin, Trinity College, MS 277: sermon *Amore langueo*, 87, 122, 416, 593, 598
Durham, Cathedral Library, MS Hunter 15: Peter Comestor and English works, 172
Gloucester, Cathedral Library, MS 22: sermons in English, including Felton, 57
Hereford, Cathedral Library, MS O.iii.5: collection E
    MS P.i.9: devotional works, 131
Lincoln, Cathedral Chapter Library, MS 10: collection RE, 357
    MS 68: materials for preachers including exempla, sermons, Robert Basevorn, etc., 249, 325
    MS 204: collection FE
London, BL, MS Additional 9066: *Gesta Romanorum* in English, 243
    MS Additional 37677: English sermons, including some by Alkerton and Wimbledon, 606
    MS Additional 38818: Basevorn, *Forma praedicandi* and sermons, 36, 149, 220, 466, 636, 637, 651
    MS Arundel 47: *De lingua*, etc., 55
    MS Arundel 200: *De lingua*, etc., 55
    MS Cotton Titus C.ix: monastic documents including a chapter sermon, 285
    MS Harley 52: Church legislation, including what to ask at visitation, 258
    MS Harley 206: Holcot, *Convertimini*, etc., 222
    MS Harley 331: collection H
    MS Harley 586: Simon de Hinton, *Summa iuniorum*, 221
    MS Harley 755: sermons by Jacobus de Voragine and others, 217
    MS Harley 1615: scattered Latin sermons, including some by a Wycliffite author, 4, 462, 528
    MS Harley 2247: Middle English sermons, 65
    MS Harley 2345: thirteenth-century sermons, including *Bis in anno*, 62, 63, 174, 222
    MS Harley 2346: priest's notebook, 218
    MS Harley 2385: Dominican notebook, 218, 453
    MS Harley 2388: collection I
    MS Harley 2977: Bury St. Edmunds, *Rituale*, 283
    MS Harley 3126: cycles of homilies, 358
    MS Harley 3130: theological dictionary, sermons, etc., 221
    MS Harley 3760: collection BR
    MS Harley 3838: John Bale's notes on Carmelite authors, 292
    MS Harley 4894: collection RY
    MS Harley 5275: *De lingua*, etc., 55
    MS Harley 5369: Holcot, *Convertimini*, etc., 223
    MS Harley 5396: Holcot, *Convertimini*, etc., 223
    MS Harley 5398: academic sermons, including *sermones examinatorii*, 153, 292, 299, 316
    MS Harley 7322: *exempla*, sermons, 219, 222
    MS Royal 5.C.iii: theological miscellany, 17

MS Royal 6.E.v: Grosseteste, *Dicta* and sermons, 19

MS Royal 7.A.viii: sermons by Richard Straddell, abbot of Dore, OCist. (+1346) and others, c. 1300, 284, 569

MS Royal 7.B.i: sermons by Bertrand de la Tour, 292

MS Royal 7.E.iv: Bromyard, *Summa predicancium*, 29, 261, 324

MS Royal 8.A.v: sermons by Richard Straddell, 284

MS Royal 8.C.ii: William of Pagula, *Oculus sacerdotis*, 233, 235, 238, 239, 352

MS Royal 10.C.x: Bromyard, *Tractatus iuris civilis*, 137

MS Royal 18.B.xxiii: Middle English sermons edited by Ross, Latin sermons, 25, 173, 214

MS Royal 18.B.xxv: Middle English sermons, 65

—, Lambeth Palace, MS 352: priest's notebook, including sermon *Dilexit nos*, 111, 222

—, St. Paul's Cathedral Library, MS 8: collection Y

—, University of London, MS 657: collection U

Longleat House, MS 4: English sermons, 358

Manchester, John Rylands Library, MS 367: collection M

Monte Cassino, MS 213: Franciscan sermons, 140, 506

Oxford, Balliol College, MS 149: collection S

MS 219: miscellany, containing *Confitemini*, 80, 144, 423, 521

—, Bodleian Library, MS Auct. D. 4.18: theological works, 38

MS Auct. F. infra 1.2: collection F

MS Auct. F. infra 1.3: sermons thought to be Carmelite, 292

MS Barlow 24: collection N

MS Bodley 4: thirteenth-century sermons, 39, 262, 476

MS Bodley 50: sermon notes and sermons by Gorran, 2, 223

MS Bodley 110: theological works including a Latin *Festial*, 62

MS Bodley 123: *Gesta Romanorum*, and sermons also found in Royal 173, 214

MS Bodley 144: collection FI

MS Bodley 440: handbook for priests, 62, 63

MS Bodley 448: *Floretum*, 259

MS Bodley 649: collection O

MS Bodley 677: John of Limoges, aid for making visitation sermons, 260

MS Bodley 687: *Fasciculus morum*, one sermon by Felton, Waldeby's *Novum opus dominicale*, 41, 57, 481

MS Bodley 692: notebook of John Lawerne, 280, 299, 301

MS Bodley 830: Grosseteste, sermons and *Dicta*, 386

MS Bodley 857: pastoral manual including sermons by Aquavilla, Grosseteste, *Confitemini*, 79, 83, 144, 218, 317, 353, 395, 423–424, 521, 555, 556, 559

MS Bodley 859: theological miscellany including Bromyard's *Distincciones* and other sermons, 128, 137–138, 294, 323, 395, 424–426, 570

MS e Musaeo 86: determinations by John Hornesby and others, 242, 292

MS Greaves 54: English sermons, 61

MS Hatton 101: Continental sermons, 499

MS Lat. th. d. 1: collection Q

MS Laud misc. 77: collection WA

MS Laud misc. 200: collection L

MS Laud misc. 511: Dominican sermons thirteenth century, 161

MS Laud misc. 635: Repingdon's sermons, 357

MS Laud misc. 706: collection R

MS Rawlinson A.362: *Speculum sacerdotale* in Latin, saints sermons, 62

—, Christ Church, MS 91: sermons, including Chambron's *Christus passus est*, 126, 129–130, 194, 395, 502, 593, 608, 668

—, Corpus Christi College, MS 54: collection RE

—, Lincoln College, MS 88: Jacobus de Voragine, *Sermones de sanctis et de festis*, 2

    MS 116: sermons by Radulfus Ardens, including prologue, 197

—, Magdalen College, MS 38: academic speeches, 301

    MS 57: Grosseteste, commentary on Galatians, 101

    MS 60: sermons by William Peraldus and moralized exempla, 100, 101, 102

    MS 61: homiliary, 101

    MS 67: *Ancrene Riwle* in Latin, 101

    MS 77: St. Bridget, *Revelations*, 101

    MS 79: collection DY

    MS 91: William Peraldus, sermons on the Sunday gospels, 101

    MS 93: collection T

    MS 96: collection CO

    MS 112: some scattered sermons, including *Amice ascende superius*, perhaps by Alkerton, 144, 161, 170, 183, 465, 523, 671

    MS 113: commentary on the Psalms, 101

    MS 141: treatises on the solitary life, 101

    MS 145: Nicholas de Byard, *Distinctiones*, 102

    MS 150: biblical exegesis, patristic, 101

    MS 154: Thomas Docking, biblical commentary, 101, 113

    MS 156: lectures on the gospels called homiliary, 31, 101, 112, 358

    MS 176: Januensis, sermons *de sanctis*, 101

    MS 177: Haymo of Halberstadt, biblical commentary, 101

    MS 182: astronomical works, 101

    MS 188: dictionary, 101

—, Merton College, MS 112: theological works and sermons, some shared with Cambridge, Trinity College, MS 223

    MS 216: sermons by Simon of Boraston, 2, 147, 631

    MS 217: William of Pagula, *Speculum prelatorum*, with sermons, 219, 238, 259

    MS 236: treatises and sermons by Francis of Meyronnes and others, 80, 215, 379, 540–545

    MS 248: sermons collected by John Sheppey, 26, 28, 87, 140, 177, 261, 517, 597

—, New College, MS 88: Dominican sermons, 299

    MS 92: collection SH

    MS 192: notebook of Robert Heete, 300

    MS 305: sermons by Januensis, Felton, and *Confitemini*, 80, 144, 217, 423, 521

—, Oriel College, MS 10: Felton's sermons, 479

    MS 15: academic sermons and quaestiones by FitzRalph and Holcot, 32, 484, 494

—, St. John's College, MS 77: theological miscellany, 101, 111

—, Trinity College, MS 7: pastoral manual, 353

MS 42: collection V

Padua, Biblioteca Antoniana, MS 515: sermons, including several by Holcot and by Chambron, 125, 126–128, 131, 299, 327, 363, 395, 425, 565, 572, 595, 630, 638

Paris, Bibliothèque Nationale, MS lat. 3804: material from Carolingian homiliaries, 173

MS lat. 18195: Franciscan sermons, 141, 147, 149, 633, 634, 637, 638

—, Bibliothèque de l'Université, MS 790: sermons by different authors including Rimington, 161, 462, 528

Philadelphia, University of Pennsylvania, MS Lat. 35: collection FE, 54, 481, 483

Siena, Biblioteca Comunale, MS F.ix.15: anonymous sermons, 211, 496, 497, 498

Toulouse, Bibliothèque Municipale, MS 340: anonymous sermons, France, 496, 497, 498

MS 342: collection D

Valencia, Biblioteca del Cabildo, MS 284: university sermons from Paris, 39, 475

Vatican, MS Borghese 166: Cistercian sermons, 39

MS Vat. lat. 11444: university sermons from Paris, 39

Winchester, Winchester College, MS 11: Odo of Cheriton, sermons, 217

Worcester, Cathedral Library, MS F.10: collection W

MS F.126: collection X

MS Q.46: thirteenth-century university sermons, 27, 38, 477–478

MS Q.56: lectures on Luke and collations, 152, 610, 620, 622

MS Q.63: thirteenth-century sermons, 147, 149, 631

PRINTED LITERATURE (INCLUDING DISSERTATIONS)

Acta capitulorum generalium Ordinis Praedicatorum. Benedictus Maria Reichert, OP, ed. 4 vols. Monumenta Ordinis Fratrum Praedicatorum 3, 4, 8, 9. Rome: In domo generalitia, 1898–1904.

Addleshaw, G. W. O. *Rectors, Vicars and Patrons in Twelfth and Early Thirteenth Century Canon Law.* St. Anthony's Hall Publications 8. York: St. Anthony's Press, 1956.

—. *The Development of the Parochial System from Charlemagne (768) to Urban II (1088–1099).* Second edn York: St. Anthony's Press, 1970.

—. *The Beginnings of the Parochial System.* Third edn. York: St. Anthony's Press, 1970.

Advent and Nativity Sermons from a Fifteenth-Century Revision of John Mirk's Festial. Susan Powell, ed. Middle English Texts 13. Heidelberg: Carl Winter, 1981.

Albertus Magnus. *Opera omnia.* A. Borgnet ed. 38 vols. Paris: Vivès, 1890–1899.

Alexander, J. J. G., and Elzbieta Temple. *Illuminated Manuscripts in Oxford College Libraries.* Oxford: Clarendon Press, 1985.

Amundesham, John. *Annales monasterii s. Albani.* H. T. Riley ed. *Chronica monasterii s. Albani,* part v, vol. 1. Rolls Series 28. London: Longmans, Green, 1870.

Archer, John R. "The Preaching of Philip Repingdon, Bishop of Lincoln (1405–1419): A Descriptive Analysis of His Latin Sermons." PhD dissertation. Graduate Theological Union, Berkeley, CA, 1984.

Aston, Margaret. "Corpus Christi and Corpus Regni: Heresy and the Peasants' Revolt." *Past and Present* 143 (1994), pp. 1–47.

—. "Lollards and Images." In Margaret Aston, ed., *Lollards and Reformers*. London: Hambledon Press, 1984. Pp. 135–192.

—. "Were the Lollards a Sect?" In Peter Biller and Barrie Dobson, eds., *The Medieval Church: Universities, Heresy, and the Religious Life. Essays in Honour of Gordon Leff*. Studies in Church History, Subsidia 11. Woodbridge, Suffolk: Boydell Press, 1999. Pp. 163–191.

Avril, Joseph. "A propos du 'proprius sacerdos': Quelques reflexions sur les pouvoirs du prêtre de paroisse." In *Proceedings of the Fifth International Congress of Medieval Canon Law. Salamanca, 21–25 Sept 1976*. Vatican City: Biblioteca Apostolica Vaticana, 1980. Pp. 471–486.

Baldwin, John W. *Masters, Princes, and Merchants: the Social View of Peter the Chanter and His Circle*. 2 vols. Princeton: Princeton University Press, 1970.

Ball, R. M. "The Opponents of Bishop Pecok." *Journal of Ecclesiastical History* 48 (1997), pp. 230–262.

Barlow, Frank. *Durham Jurisdictional Peculiars*. London: Oxford University Press, 1950.

—. *The English Church 1066–1154*. London: Longman, 1979.

Barré, Henri. *Les homéliaires carolingiens de l'école d'Auxerre: authenticité, inventaire, tableaux comparatifs, initia*. Studi e testi 225. Vatican City: Biblioteca Apostolica Vaticana, 1962.

Bataillon, Louis J. "Early Scholastic and Mendicant Preaching as Exegesis of Scripture." In Mark Jordan and Kent Emery, Jr., eds., *Ad litteram*. Notre Dame, IN: University of Notre Dame Press. Pp. 165–198.

—. "Les sermons attribués a saint Thomas: Questions d'authenticité." *Miscellanea mediaevalia* 19 (1988), pp. 325–341. Rpt. in Louis-Jacques Bataillon, *La Prédication au XIIIe siècle en France et Italie: Études et documents*. Collected Studies 402. Aldershot and Brookfield: Variorum, 1993, item XV.

Bell, David N. "A Cistercian at Oxford: Richard Dove of Buckfast and London BL, Sloane 513." *Studia monastica* 13 (1989), pp. 69–87.

Bennett, J. A. W. "The Date of the B-text of Piers Plowman." *Medium Aevum* 12 (1943), pp. 55–64.

Benrath, Gustav Adolf. *Wyclifs Bibelkommentar*. Berlin: Walter de Gruyter, 1966.

Bériou, Nicole. "Les sermons latins après 1200." In Beverly Mayne Kienzle, ed., *The Sermon*. Typologie des sources du moyen âge occidental 81–83. Turnhout: Brepols, 2000. Pp. 363–447.

—. Review article of Phillis B. Roberts, *Thomas Becket in the Medieval Latin Preaching Tradition* (Steenbrugge: Abbatia S. Petri, 1992), *Journal of Medieval Latin* 5 (1995), pp. 225–231.

Bernardino da Siena. *Prediche volgari sul Campo di Siena, 1427*, Carlo Delcorno, ed. 2 vols. Milan: Rusconi, 1989.

Bibliothèque Nationale, *Catalogue général des manuscrits latins*. 7 vols. Paris: Bibliothèque Nationale, 1939–1988.

Bihl, Michael, OFM. "Statuta generalia ordinis edita in capitulis generalibus celebratis Narbonae anno 1260, Assisii Anno 1279 atque Parisiis anno 1292." *AFH* 34 (1941), pp. 13–94, 284–358.

Binkley, Peter. "John Bromyard and the Hereford Dominicans." In Jan Willem Drijvers and A. A. MacDonald, eds., *Centres of Learning: Learning and Location in Pre-Modern Europe and the Near East*. Leiden: Brill, 1995. Pp. 255–264.

Blamires, Alcuin, and C. W. Marx. "Woman Not to Preach: A Disputation in British Library MS Harley 31." *Journal of Medieval Latin* 3 (1993), pp. 34–63.

Bloomfield, Morton W., with B.-G. Guyot, D. Howard, and T. Kabealo. *Incipits of Latin Works on the Virtues and Vices, 1100–1500 AD*, Cambridge, MA: Mediaeval Academy of America, 1979.

The Book of Margery Kempe. Sanford Brown Meech, ed., with a note by Hope Emily Allen. EETS 212. London: 1940; rpt. 1961.

Boyle, Leonard E., OP. "The Constitution *Cum ex eo* of Boniface VIII." *Medieval Studies* 24 (1962), pp. 263–302. Rpt. in Boyle, *Pastoral Care,* item VIII.

—. "The Date of the *Summa praedicantium* of John Bromyard." *Speculum* 48 (1973), pp. 533–537. Rpt. in Boyle, *Pastoral Care*, item X.

—. "Notes on the Education of the Fratres Communes in the Dominican Order in the Thirteenth Century." In *Xenia medii aevi historiam illustrantia oblata Thomae Kaeppeli*. Rome: Edizioni di storia e letteratura, 1978. Pp. 249–267. Rpt. Boyle, *Pastoral Care*, item VI.

—. "The *Oculus sacerdotis* and some other works of William of Pagula." *Transactions of the Royal Historical Society*, fifth series, 5 (1955), pp. 81–110. Rpt. in Boyle, *Pastoral Care*, item IV.

—. *Pastoral Care, Clerical Education and Canon Law, 1200–1400.* London: Variorum Reprints, 1981.

—. "Three English Pastoral Summae and a 'Magister Galienus'." In Ios. Forchielli and Alph. Stickler, eds., *Collectanea Stephan Kuttner. Studia Gratiana* 11 (1967), 1:133–144.

Brandt, William. "Church and Society in the Late Fourteenth Century: A Contemporary View." *Medievalia et Humanistica* 13 (1961), pp. 56–61.

Brecht, Martin. *Martin Luther.* Vol. 2: *Ordnung und Abgrenzung der Reformation 1521–1532.* Stuttgart: Calwer Verlag, 1981.

Briggs, Charles F. *Giles of Rome's "De regimine principum": Reading and Writing Politics at Court and University, c. 1275–c. 1525.* Cambridge: Cambridge University Press, 1999.

Brinton, Thomas. *The Sermons of Thomas Brinton, Bishop of Rochester (1373–1389).* Mary Aquinas Devlin, OP, ed. 2 vols. Camden Third Series 85–86. London: Royal Historical Society, 1954.

Briscoe, Marianne, and Barbara H. Jaye. *Artes praedicandi; artes orandi.* Typologie des sources du moyen âge occidental 61. Turnhout: Brepols, 1992.

Brooke, Rosalind B. *Early Franciscan Government: Elias to Bonaventure.* Cambridge: Cambridge University Press, 1959.

Burridge, A. W. "L'Immaculée Conception dans la théologie de l'Angleterre médiévale." *REH* 32 (1936), pp. 570–597.

A Calendar of Entries in the Papal Registers Relating to Great Britain and Ireland – Papal Letters (1198–1492). W. H. Bliss and J. A. Twemlow, eds. 18 vols. to date. London, 1893–.

A Calendar of the Register of Henry Wakefield, Bishop of Worcester 1375–1395. Warwick Paul Marett, ed. Worcestershire Historical Society, n. s. 7. Leeds: Worcestershire Historical Society, 1972.

A Calendar of the Register of Richard Scrope, Archbishop of York, 1398–1405. R. N. Swanson, ed. York: University of York, Borthwick Institute of Historical Research, 1981.

Works cited

Cannon, Joanna. "Panorama geografico, cronologico et statistico sulla distribuzione degli studia degli ordini mendicanti – Inghilterra." In *Le scuole degli ordini mendicanti (secoli XIII–XIV)*, Convegni del Centro di studi sulla spiritualità medievale 17. Todi: Accademia tudertina, 1978. Pp. 93–126.

The Canonization of St. Osmund, from the Manuscript Records in the Muniment Room of Salisbury Cathedral. A. R. Malden, ed. Wiltshire Record Society. Salisbury: Bennett Brothers, 1901.

Caplan, Harry. *Mediaeval "Artes praedicandi": A Hand-list.* Cornell Studies in Classical Philology 24. Ithaca, NY: Cornell University Press, 1934.

Carruthers, Leo. "'Know Thyself': Criticism, Reform and the Audience of Jacob's Well." In *Medieval Sermons and Society: Cloister, City, University*, Jacqueline Hamesse *et al.*, eds. Louvain-la-Neuve: Féderation Internationale des Instituts d'Etudes Médiévales, 1998. Pp. 219–240.

Casagrande, Carla, and Silvana Vecchio. *I peccati della lingua: disciplina ed etica della parola nella cultura medievale.* Roma: Enciclopedia Italiana, 1987.

A Catalogue of the Manuscripts Preserved in the Library of the University of Cambridge. 7 vols. in 6. Cambridge: Cambridge University Press, 1856–1867.

Catalogue of Romances in the Department of Manuscripts in the British Museum. 3 vols. London: British Museum, 1883–1910; rpt. 1961–62.

Catto, J. I. "Theology after Wycliffism." In Catto and Evans, eds., *Late Medieval Oxford.* Pp. 263–280.

— "Wyclif and Wycliffism at Oxford 1356–1430." In Catto and Evans, eds., *Late Medieval Oxford.* Pp. 175–261.

Catto, J. I., and Ralph Evans, eds. *Late Medieval Oxford.* Vol. 2 of *The History of the University of Oxford.* Oxford: Clarendon Press, 1992.

Chapters of the Augustinian Canons. H. E. Salter, ed. Canterbury and York Society 29. London: Canterbury and York Society, 1922.

Charland, Th.-M. *Artes praedicandi: Contribution à l'histoire de la rhétorique au moyen âge.* Paris: De Vrin, 1936.

Cheney, C. R. *Episcopal Visitation of Monasteries in the Thirteenth Century.* Second revised edn. Manchester: Manchester University Press, 1983.

The Chronicle of Adam Usk 1377–1421. C. Given-Wilson, ed. Oxford: Clarendon Press, 1997.

The Chronicle of Glastonbury Abbey: An Edition and Study of John of Glastonbury's "Cronica sive Antiquitates Glastoniensis Ecclesie." James P. Carley, ed., David Townsend, trans. Woodbridge, Suffolk: The Boydell Press, 1985.

Chronicon rerum gestarum monasterio sancti Albani. In *Annales Monasterii s. Albani*, part v. H. T. Riley ed. 2 vols. Rolls Series 28. London: Longmans, Green, 1870.

Clark, J. P. H. "A Defense of the Carmelite Order by John Hornby, O. Carm., AD 1374." *Carmelus* 32 (1985), pp. 74–106.

—. "Thomas Maldon, O. Carm., a Cambridge Theologian of the Fourteenth Century." *Carmelus* 29 (1982), pp. 193–235.

Clough, Cecil H., ed. *Profession, Vocation, and Culture in Later Medieval England: Essays Dedicated to the Memory of A. R. Myers.* Liverpool: Liverpool University Press, 1982.

Coleman, Janet. *English Literature in History 1350–1400.* Medieval Readers and Writers. London: Hutchinson, 1981.

Concilia Magnae Britanniae et Hiberniae, A.D. 446–1718. David Wilkins, ed. 4 vols. London: R. Gosling, F. Gyles, T. Woodward, C. Davis, 1737; rpt. Bruxelles: Culture et Civilisation, 1964.

Concilium basiliense: Studien und Quellen zur Geschichte des Concils von Basel. Johann von Haller, ed. 8 vols. Basel, 1896–1936; rpt. Nendeln/Liechtenstein: Kraus Reprint, 1971.

Congar, Yves M.-J. "Aspects ecclésiologiques de la querelle entre mendiants et séculiers dans la seconde moitié du xiiie siècle et le début du xive." *AHDMLA* 28 (1961), pp. 35–151.

Constable, Giles. "Monasteries, Rural Churches and the *cura animarum* in the Early Middle Ages." In *Cristianizzazione et organizzazione delle campagne nell' alto medioevo: espansione e resistenze. 10–16 aprile 1980,* Settimane di studio del Centro italiano di studi sull'alto medioevo 28. 2 vols. Spoleto: Centro italiano di studi sull'alto medioevo, 1982. 1:349–389.

Copsey, Richard, OCarm. "The Carmelites in England 1242–1540: Surviving Writings." *Carmelus* 43/1 (1996), pp. 175–224.

Corpus iuris canonici. Emil (Aemilius) Friedberg, ed. 2 vols. Leipzig, 1879; rpt. Graz: Akademische Druck- und Verlagsanstalt, 1959.

Coulet, Noel. *Les visites pastorales.* Typologie des sources du moyen âge occidental 23. Turnhout: Brepols, 1977.

Coulton, G. G. *Five Centuries of Religion (1000–1500).* 4 vols. Cambridge: Cambridge University Press, 1923–1950.

Councils and Synods, with Other Documents Relating to the English Church. F. M. Powicke and C. R. Cheney, eds. 2 vols. Oxford: Clarendon Press, 1964.

Courtenay, William J. *Schools and Scholars in Fourteenth-Century England.* Princeton: Princeton University Press, 1987.

Coxe, Henry O. *Catalogus codicum manuscriptorum qui in collegiis aulisque Oxoniensibus hodie adservantur.* 2 vols. Oxford: Oxford University Press, 1852; vol. 1 rpt. with introduction and annotations, 1972.

Crook, Eugene J. "A New Version of Ranulph Higden's *Speculum curatorum.*" *Manuscripta* 21 (1977), pp. 41–49.

Crook, Eugene J., and Margaret Jennings, "The Devil and Ranulph Higden." *Manuscripta* 22 (1978), pp. 131–140.

Cross, F. L., ed., *The Oxford Dictionary of the Christian Church.* 2nd edition. F. L. Cross and E. A. Livingstone, eds. Oxford: Oxford University Press, 1974.

Customary of the Benedictine Monasteries of Saint Augustine, Canterbury, and Saint Peter, Westminster. E. M. Thompson, ed. 2 vols. Henry Bradshaw Society 23. London: Harrison and Sons, 1902–1904.

d'Avray, D. L. "The Gospel of the Marriage Feast of Cana and Marriage Preaching in France." In Katharine Walsh and Diana Wood, eds., *The Bible in the Medieval World: Essays in Memory of Beryl Smalley.* Studies in Church History, Subsidia, 4. Oxford: Blackwell, 1985. Pp. 207–224.

—. *Medieval Marriage Sermons: Mass Communication in a Culture Without Print,* Oxford: Oxford University Press, 2001.

—. *The Preaching of the Friars: Sermons Diffused from Paris before 1300.* Oxford: Clarendon Press, 1985.

Davies, Richard G. "The Episcopate." In Cecil H. Clough, ed., *Profession, Vocation, and Culture in Later Medieval England: Essays Dedicated to the Memory of A. R. Myers*. Liverpool: Liverpool University Press, 1982. Pp. 51–89.

Deferrari, Roy J. "St. Augustine's Method of Composing and Delivering Sermons." *American Journal of Philology* 43 (1922), pp. 97–123, 193–219.

Delcorno, Carlo. "La diffrazione del testo omiletico: osservazioni sulle doppie reportationes delle prediche bernardiniane." *Lettere italiane* 38 (1986), pp. 457–477.

—. "Origini della predicazione francescana." In *Francesco d'Assisi e Francescanesimo dal 1216 al 1226*, Società Internazionale di Studi Francescani, Atti del IV Convegno Internazionale, Assisi 1976. Assisi: Società internazionale di studi francescani, 1977. Pp. 127–160.

—. "La predicazione agostiniana (sec. xiii–xv)." In *Gli agostiniani a Venezia e la Chiesa di S. Stefano*. Venice: Istituto Veneto di Scienze, Lettere ed Arti, 1997. Pp. 87–108.

Dictionary of Medieval Latin from British Sources, prepared by R. E. Latham. In progress. London: Oxford University Press, 1975–.

The Dictionary of National Biography. Leslie Stephen and Sidney Lee, eds. 21 vols. Oxford: Oxford University Press, 1917–.

Dictionnaire de Spiritualité ascétique et mystique. Marcel Viller, S. J., F. Cavallera, and J. de Guibert, SJ, eds. 17 vols. Paris: Beauchesne, 1937–1995.

Dobson, R. B. "The Religious Orders 1370–1540." In Catto and Evans, eds., *Late Medieval Oxford*. Pp. 539–579.

Documents Illustrating the Activities of the General and Provincial Chapters of the English Black Monks, 1215–1540. William A. Pantin, ed. 3 vols. Camden Third series 45, 47, 54. London: Royal Historical Society, 1931–37.

Documents Illustrating the History of S. Paul's Cathedral. W. Sparrow Simpson, ed. Camden Society, n.s. 26. Westminster: Camden Society, 1880.

Dohar, William J. *The Black Death and Pastoral Leadership: The Diocese of Hereford in the Fourteenth Century*. Philadelphia: University of Pennsylvania Press, 1995.

Doyle, A. I. "The European Circulation of Three Latin Spiritual Texts." In A. J. Minnis, ed., *Latin and Vernacular*. Cambridge: D. S. Brewer, 1990. Pp. 129–146.

Dunbabin, Jean. *A Hound of God: Pierre de la Palud and the Fourteenth-Century Church*. Oxford: Clarendon Press, 1991.

Durand, Guillaume. "Le pontifical de Guillaume Durand." In *Le pontifical romain au moyen âge*. Michel Andrieu, ed. 4 vols. Studi e testi 88. Vatican City: Biblioteca Apostolica Vaticana, 1940. 3:596–602.

Durantus, Guillelmus. *Rationale divinorum officiorum*. A. Davril and T. M. Thibodeau, eds. Corpus Christianorum, Continuatio Medievalis 140. Turnhout: Brepols, 1995.

Durrell, Lawrence. *Mountolive*. New York: E. P. Dutton, 1959.

The Early English Versions of the Gesta Romanorum. Sidney J. H. Herrtage, ed. EETS, e.s. 33. London: Kegan Paul, 1879.

"Ecclesiastica officia" Cisterciens du XII'ème siècle: texte latin selon les manuscrits édités de Trente 1711, Ljubljana 31 et Dijon 114, version française, annexe liturgique, notes, index et tables. Danièle Choisselet, OCSO, and Placide Verndt, OCSO, eds. Reiningue: La Documentation Cistercienne, 1989.

Edden, Valerie. "A Carmelite Sermon Cycle: British Library Royal 7.B.i." *Carmelus* 43 (1996), pp. 99–122.

—. "The Debate Between Richard Maidstone and the Lollard Ashwardby (ca. 1390)." *Carmelus* 34 (1987), pp. 113–134.

—. "Marian Devotion in a Carmelite Sermon Collection of the Late Middle Ages." *Medieval Studies* 57 (1995), pp. 101–129.

Edwards, K. *The English Secular Cathedrals in the Middle Ages.* Manchester: Manchester University Press, 1949.

Emden, A. B. *A Biographical Register of the University of Cambridge to 1500.* Cambridge: Cambridge University Press, 1963.

—. *A Biographical Register of the University of Oxford to A.D. 1500.* 3 vols. Oxford: Clarendon Press, 1957–1959.

English Works of John Fisher, Bishop of Rochester (1469–1535): Sermons and Other Writings, 1520–1535. Cecilia A. Hatt, ed. Oxford: Oxford University Press, 2002.

English Wycliffite Sermons. Anne Hudson and Pamela O. Gradon, eds. 5 vols. Oxford: Clarendon Press, 1983–1996.

The Episcopal Register of Robert Rede, Ordinis Praedicatorum, Lord Bishop of Chichester, 1397–1415. Cecil Deedes, ed. 2 vols. Sussex Record Society 8 and 11. London: Sussex Record Society, 1908–1910.

Erb, P. C. "Vernacular Material for Preaching in MS Cambridge University Library Ii.III.8." *Medieval Studies* 33 (1971), pp. 63–84.

Extracts from the Account Rolls of the Abbey of Durham, from the Original MSS. J. T. Fowler, ed. 3 vols. Surtees Society 99, 100, and 103. Durham: Surtees Society, 1898–1901.

Fasciculi zizaniorum Magistri Johannis Wyclif cum tritico, Ascribed to Thomas Netter of Walden. Walter Waddington Shirley, ed. Rolls Series 5. London, 1858.

Fasciculus morum: A Fourteenth-Century Preacher's Handbook. Siegfried Wenzel, ed. and trans. University Park and London: The Pennsylvania State University Press, 1989.

Fasciculus rerum expetendarum et fugiendarum. Edward Brown, ed. 2 vols. London: Richard Chiswell, 1690; rpt. Audax Press, Tucson, Arizona, 1967.

Feine, Hans Erich. *Kirchliche Rechtsgeschichte. Die katholische Kirche.* Fourth ed. Köln/Graz: Böhlau, 1964.

Fioravanti, Gianfranco. "Sermones in lode della filosofia e della logica a Bologna nella prima metà del xiv secolo." In Dino Buzzetti, Maurizio Ferriani, and Andrea Tabarroni, eds., *L'insegnamento della logica a Bologna nel xiv secolo.* Bologna, 1992. Pp. 165–185.

Fleming, John V. *An Introduction to the Franciscan Literature of the Middle Ages.* Chicago: Franciscan Herald Press, 1977.

Fletcher, Alan J. "The Authorship of the *Fasciculus morum*: A Review of the Evidence of Bodleian MS Barlow 24." *Note and Queries* 228 (1983), pp. 205–207.

—. "The Faith of a Simple Man: Carpenter John's Creed in the Miller's Tale." *Medium Aevum* 61 (1992), pp. 96–105. Rpt. in Fletcher, *Preaching*, pp. 239–248.

—. "'I sing of a maiden': A Fifteenth-century Sermon Reminiscence." *Notes and Queries* 223 (1978), pp. 107–108.

—. "John Mirk and the Lollards." *Medium Aevum* 56 (1987), pp. 217–224.

—. "'Magnus predicator et deuotus': A Profile of the Life, Work, and Influence of the Fifteenth-Century Oxford Preacher, John Felton." *Medieval Studies* 53 (1991), pp. 125–175. Rpt. in Fletcher, *Preaching*, pp. 58–118.

—. "The Manuscripts of John Mirk's *Manuale Sacerdotis*." *Leeds Studies in English* 19 (1988), pp. 105–139.

—. *Preaching, Politics and Poetry in Late-Medieval England*. Dublin: Four Courts Press, 1998.

—. "The Sermon Booklets of Friar Nicholas Philipp." *Medium Aevum* 55 (1986), pp. 188–202. Rpt. with minor revisions in Fletcher, *Preaching*, pp. 41–57.

—. "Unnoticed Sermons from John Mirk's *Festial*." *Speculum* 55 (1980), pp. 514–522.

Fletcher, Alan J., and Susan Powell. "The Origins of a Fifteenth-Century Sermon Collection: MSS Harley 2247 and Royal 18.B.XXV." *Leeds Studies in English*, n.s. 10 (1978), pp. 74–96.

Flood, Bruce P., Jr. "The Carmelite Friars in Medieval English Universities and Society, 1299–1430." *RTAM* 55 (1988), pp. 154–183.

Foley, Edward. "The Song of the Assembly in Medieval England." In Lizette Larson-Miller, ed., *Medieval Liturgy: A Book of Essays*. New York and London: Garland Press, 1997.

Forde, Simon. "New Sermon Evidence for the Spread of Wycliffism." In Thomas L. Amos, Eugene A. Green, and B. Kienzle, eds., *De Ore Domini: Preacher and Word in the Middle Ages*. Kalamazoo, MI: Medieval Institute Publications, 1989. Pp. 169–183.

—. "Nicholas Hereford's Ascension Day Sermon, 1382." *Medieval Studies* 51 (1989), pp. 205–241.

—. "Writings of a Reformer: A Look at Sermon Studies and Bible Studies through Repingdon's *Sermones super evangelia dominicalia*." PhD dissertation. 2 vols. University of Birmingham, 1985.

Formularies which Bear on the History of Oxford, c. 1204–1420. H. E. Salter, W. A Pantin, and H. G. Richardson, eds. 2 vols. Oxford Historical Society, n.s. 5. Oxford: Clarendon Press, 1942.

Forte, Stephen L., OP. "Simon of Boraston OP: Life and Writings." *AFP* 22 (1952), pp. 321–334.

Fowler, David C. *The Life and Times of John Trevisa, Medieval Scholar*. Seattle and London, University of Washington Press, 1995.

Franz, Adolph. *Der Magister Nikolaus Magni de Jawor: ein Beitrag zur Literatur- und Gelehrtengeschichte des 14. und 15. Jahrhunderts*. Freiburg im Breisgau: Herdersche Verlagsbuchhandlung, 1898.

The Friars' Libraries. K. W. Humphreys, ed. Corpus of British Medieval Library Catalogues. London: British Library, 1990.

Galloway, Andrew. "A Fifteenth-Century Confession Sermon on 'Unkyndeness' (CUL MS Gg.6.26) and its Literary Parallels and Parodies." *Traditio* 49 (1994), pp. 259–269.

Gascoigne, Thomas. *Loci e libro veritatum: Passages Selected from Gascoigne's Theological Dictionary Illustrating the Condition of Church and State 1403–1458*. James E. Thorold Rogers, ed. Oxford: Clarendon Press, 1881.

Gatch, Milton McC. *Preaching and Theology in Anglo-Saxon England: Aelfric and Wulfstan*. Toronto: University of Toronto Press, 1977.

Gerson, Jean. *Oeuvres complètes*. P. Glorieux, ed. 10 vols. Paris: Desclée & Cie., 1960–1973.

Works cited

Gesta Henrici Quinti: The Deeds of Henry the Fifth. Frank Taylor and John S. Roskell, trans. Oxford: Clarendon Press, 1975.

Gibbs, Marion, and Jane Lang. *Bishops and Reform 1215–1272, with Special Reference to the Lateran Council of 1215.* Oxford: Oxford University Press, 1934.

G[ibson], S[trickland]. "The Order of Disputations." *Bodleian Quarterly Review* 6 (1929–1931), pp. 107–112.

Gieben, Servus. "Robert Grossetete on Preaching, with the Edition of the Sermon *Ex rerum initiatarum* on Redemption." *Collectanea Franciscana* 37 (1967), pp. 100–141.

—. "*Rudimentum doctrinae* di Gilberto di Tournai, con l'edizione del suo *Registrum* o tavola della materia." In *Bonaventuriana. Miscellanea in onore di J.-G. Bougerol.* 2 vols. Rome: Edizioni Antonianum, 1988. 2:621–680.

—. "Thomas Gascoigne and Robert Grosseteste: Historical and Critical Notes." *Vivarium* 8 (1970), pp. 56–67.

Gillespie, Vincent. "Syon and the New Learning," in J. G. Clark, ed., *The Religious Orders in Pre-Reformation England.* Woodbridge: Boydell Press, 2002. Pp. 75–95.

Girsch, James Martin. "An Edition with Commentary of John Mirk's 'Manuale Sacerdotis'." PhD dissertation. University of Toronto, 1990.

Glorieux, P. "L'Enseignement au moyen âge: technique et méthodes en usage à la Faculté de Théologie de Paris, au XIIIe siècle." *Archives d'histoire doctrinale et littéraire du moyen âge* 35 (1968), pp. 65–186.

Godfrey, John. *The Church in Anglo-Saxon England.* Cambridge: Cambridge University Press, 1962.

Goering, Joseph, "The Summa 'Qui bene presunt' and Its Author," in Richard G. Newhauser and John A. Alford, eds., *Literature and Religion in the Later Middle Ages: Philological Studies in Honor of Siegfried Wenzel.* Binghamton, NY: Medieval and Renaissance Texts and Studies, 1995. Pp. 143–159.

—. *William de Montibus (c. 1140–1213): The Schools and the Literature of Pastoral Care.* Toronto: Pontifical Institute of Medieval Studies, 1992.

Goering, Joseph, and Daniel S. Taylor. "The Summulae of Bishops Walter de Cantilupe (1240) and Peter Quinel (1287)." *Speculum* 67 (1992), pp. 576–594.

Greatrex, Joan. "Benedictine Monk Scholars as Teachers and Preachers in the Later Middle Ages: Evidence from Worcester Cathedral Priory." In Joan Loades, ed., *Monastic Studies.* II. *The Continuity of Tradition.* Bangor: Headstart History, 1991. Pp. 213–225.

—. "Benedictine Sermons: Preparation and Practice in the English Monastic Cathedral Cloister." In Carolyn Muessig, ed., *Medieval Monastic Preaching.* Leiden, Boston, and Köln: Brill, 1998. Pp. 257–278.

—. *Biographical Register of the English Cathedral Priories of the Province of Canterbury c. 1066 to 1540.* Oxford: Clarendon Press, 1997.

Grégoire, Reginald. *Homéliaires liturgiques médiévaux: analyse de manuscrits.* Spoleto: Centro Italiano di Studi sull'Alto Medioevo, 1980.

Gribbin, Joseph A. *The Premonstratensian Order in Late Medieval England.* Studies in the History of Medieval Religion 16. Woodbridge, Suffolk, and Rochester, NY: Boydell and Brewer, 2001.

Gwynn, Aubrey, SJ. *The English Austin Friars in the Time of Wyclif.* Oxford and London: Oxford University Press, 1940.

—. "The Sermon-Diary of Richard FitzRalph, Archbishop of Armagh," *Proceedings of the Royal Irish Academy* 44 C (1937), pp. 1–57.

—. "Two Sermons of Primate Richard FitzRalph." *Archivum hibernicum* 14 (1949), pp. 50–65.

Haines, Roy M., "Church, Society and Politics in the Early Fifteenth Century as Viewed from an English Pulpit." In Derek Baker, ed., *Church, Society and Politics*. Studies in Church History 12. Oxford: Blackwell. Pp. 143–157.

—. *Ecclesia Anglicana: Studies in the English Church of the Later Middle Ages*. Toronto: University of Toronto Press, 1989.

—. "'Our Master Mariner, Our Sovereign Lord': A Contemporary Preacher's View of King Henry V." *Medieval Studies* 38 (1976), pp. 85–96.

—. "'Wilde wittes and wilfulnes': John Swetstock's Attack on Those 'poyswunmongeres,' the Lollards." In G. J. Cuming and Derek Baker, eds., *Popular Belief and Practice*. Studies in Church History 8. Cambridge: Cambridge University Press, 1972. Pp. 143–153.

Hamesse, Jacqueline. "*Reportatio* et transmission de textes." In Monika Asztalos, ed., *The Editing of Theological and Philosophical Texts from the Middle Ages*. Studia Latina Stockholmensia 30. Stockholm: Almqvist & Wiksell International, 1986. Pp. 11–34.

Hammerich, Louis L. "The Beginning of the Strife between Richard FitzRalph and the Mendicants, with an Edition of his Autobiographical Prayer and his Proposition 'Unusquisque'." *Det Kgl. Danske Videnskabernes Selskab. Historisk-filologiske Meddelelser*, 26.3 (1938), pp. 53–73.

Hanna, Ralph. *A Descriptive Catalogue of the Western Medieval Manuscripts of St. John's College, Oxford, Using Material Collected by the Late Jeremy Griffiths*. Oxford: Oxford University Press, 2002.

Hardy, Thomas Duffus. *Syllabus of the Documents relating to England and Other Kingdoms Contained in the Collection Known as Rymer's "Foedera"*. 3 vols. London: Longmans, Green, 1869–1885.

Haren, Michael J. "Bishop Gynwell of Lincoln, Two Avignonese Statutes and Archbishop FitzRalph of Armagh's Suit at the Roman Curia Against the Friars." *Archivum Historiae Pontificiae* 31 (1993), pp. 275–292.

—. "Friars as Confessors: The Canonist Background to the Fourteenth-Century Controversy." *Peritia* 3 (1984), pp. 503–516.

—. *Sin and Society in Fourteenth-Century England: A Study of the "Memoriale Presbiterum"*. Oxford: Clarendon Press, 2000.

Harvey, Barbara. "A Novice's Life at Westminster Abbey in the Century Before the Dissolution." In James G. Clark, ed., *The Religious Orders in Pre-Reformation England*. Woodbridge: Boydell Press, 2002. Pp. 51–73.

—. *Living and Dying in England, 1100–1540: The Monastic Experience*. The Ford Lectures delivered in the University of Oxford in Hilary Term 1989. Oxford: Clarendon Press, 1993.

Harvey, Margaret. *The English in Rome 1362–1420: Portrait of an Expatriate Community*. Cambridge: Cambridge University Press, 1999.

—. "Preaching in the Curia: Some Sermons by Thomas Brinton." *Archivum Historiae Pontificiae* 33 (1995), pp. 299–301.

Heffernan, Thomas J. "Sermon Literature." In A. S. G. Edwards, ed., *Middle English Prose: A Critical Guide to Major Authors and Genres*. New Brunswick, NJ: Rutgers University Press, 1984. Pp. 177–207.

Higden, Ranulf. *Polychronicon*. 9 vols. Vols. 1–2 ed. by Churchill Babbington, vols. 3–9 by Joseph R. Lumby. Rolls Series 41. London: Longmans & Co., 1865–1886.

Hinnebusch, W. A. *The Early English Friars Preachers*. Rome: Ad S. Sabinae, 1951.

The Historians of the Church of York and its Archbishops. James Raine, ed. 3 vols. Rolls Series 71. London: Longman, 1879–1894.

A History of the County of Cambridge and the Isle of Ely. Vol. 3: *The City and University of Cambridge*. J. P. C. Roach, ed. Victoria County History. London: Oxford University Press, 1959.

Hodnett, Dorothy K., and Winifred P. White. "The Manuscripts of the *Modus Tenendi Parliamentum*." *EHR* 34 (1919), pp. 209–225.

Holcot, Robert. *Super libros Sapientiae*. Hagenau, 1494; rpt. Frankfurt/Main: Minerva GmbH, 1974.

Holdsworth, Christopher. "Were the Sermons of St. Bernard on the Song of Songs Ever Preached?" In Carolyn Muessig, ed., *Medieval Monastic Preaching*. Leiden, Boston, and Köln: Brill, 1998. Pp. 295–318.

Horn, J. M., editor. *Chichester Diocese*. In John le Neve, *Fasti Ecclesiae Anglicanae 1300–1541*, vol. 4. London: Athlone Press, 1964.

Horner, Patrick J. "Benedictines and Preaching in Fifteenth-Century England: The Evidence of Two Bodleian Library Manuscripts." *Revue Bénédictine* 99 (1989), pp. 313–332.

—. "Benedictines and Preaching the *Pastoralia* in Late Medieval England: a Preliminary Inquiry." In Carolyn Muessig, ed., *Medieval Monastic Preaching*. Leiden, Boston, and Köln: Brill, 1998. Pp. 279–292.

—. "An Edition of Five Medieval Sermons from MS Laud misc. 706." PhD dissertation. State University of New York, Albany, 1975.

—. "John Paunteley's Sermon at the Funeral of Walter Froucester, Abbot of Gloucester (1412)." *American Benedictine Review* 28 (1977), pp. 147–166.

—. "Preachers at Paul's Cross: Religion, Society, and Politics in Late Medieval England." In Jacqueline Hamesse et al., eds, *Medieval Sermons and Society: Cloister, City, University*. Louvain-la-Neuve: Féderation Internationale des Instituts d'Etudes Médiévales, 1998. Pp. 261–282.

—. "A Sermon on the Anniversary of the Death of Thomas Beauchamp, Earl of Warwick." *Traditio* 34 (1978), pp. 381–401.

Horstmann, Carl, ed. *Altenglische Legenden, neue Folge*. Heilbronn: Gebrüder Henninger, 1881.

Hudson, Anne. "A Lollard Compilation and the Dissemination of Wycliffite Thought." *Journal of Theological Studies*, n.s. 23 (1972), pp. 65–81; rpt. in Hudson, *Lollards and Their Books*. London and Ronceverte: Hambledon Press, 1985. Pp. 13–29.

—. "'Poor Preachers, Poor Men': Views of Poverty in Wyclif and his Followers." In František Šmahel, ed., *Häresie und vorzeitige Reformation im Spätmittelalter*. Schriften des Historischen Kollegs, Kolloquien 39. Munich: Oldenbourg, 1998. Pp. 41–53.

—. *The Premature Reformation: Wycliffite Texts and Lollard History*. Oxford: Clarendon Press, 1988.

—. "'Springing cockel in our clene corn': Lollard Preaching in England around 1400." In Scott L. Waugh and Peter D. Diehl, eds., *Christendom and Its Discontents: Exclusion, Persecution, and Rebellion, 1000–1500.* Cambridge: Cambridge University Press, 1996. Pp. 132–147.

—. "A Wycliffite Scholar of the Early Fifteenth Century." In Katherine Walsh and Diana Wood, eds., *The Bible in the Medieval World: Essays in Memory of Beryl Smalley.* Oxford: Basil Blackwell, 1985. Pp. 301–315.

Jacobus a Voragine. *Legenda aurea.* Th. Graesse, ed. Third edn. 1890; rpt. Osnabrück: Otto Zeller Verlag, 1969.

James, M. R. *A Descriptive Catalogue of the Manuscripts in the Library of Corpus Christi College, Cambridge.* 2 vols. Cambridge: Cambridge University Press, 1912.

—. *A Descriptive Catalogue of the Manuscripts in the Library of Jesus College, Cambridge.* London and Cambridge: C. J. Clay and Sons, 1895.

—. *A Descriptive Catalogue of the Manuscripts in the Library of Gonville and Caius College Cambridge.* 2 vols. Cambridge: Cambridge University Press, 1907–1908.

—. *A Descriptive Catalogue of the Manuscripts in the Library of Pembroke College, Cambridge.* Cambridge: Cambridge University Press, 1905.

—. *On the Abbey of S. Edmund at Bury.* 2 vols. Cambridge Antiquarian Society, Octavo Publications 28. Cambridge: Cambridge Antiquarian Society, 1895.

—. *The Western Manuscripts in the Library of Trinity College, Cambridge: a Descriptive Catalogue.* 4 vols. Cambridge: Cambridge University Press, 1900–1904.

James, M. R., and Claude Jenkins. *A Descriptive Catalogue of the Manuscripts in the Library of Lambeth Palace.* Cambridge: Cambridge University Press, 1930–1932.

Jeffrey, David Lyle. *The Law of Love: English Spirituality in the Age of Wyclif.* Grand Rapids, MI: William B. Eerdmans Publishing Company, 1988.

John Damascene. *De fide orthodoxa: Versions of Burgundio and Cerbanus.* E. M. Buytaert, ed. St. Bonaventure, NY: Franciscan Institute, 1955.

John of Limoges. *Johannis Lemovicensis abbatis de Zirc Opera omnia.* Constantin (Konstatin) Horvath, OCist, ed. 3 vols. Veszprem, 1932.

Johnson, Holly. "Preaching the Passion: Good Friday Sermons in Late Medieval England." PhD dissertation. University of North Carolina at Chapel Hill, 2001.

Jolliffe, P. S. *A Check-List of Middle English Prose Writings of Spiritual Guidance.* Toronto: Pontifical Institute of Medieval Studies, 1974.

Kaeppeli, Thomas, OP. *Scriptores Ordinis Praedicatorum medii aevi.* 4 vols. Rome: Ad S. Sabinae, 1970–1993.

—. "Un sermonnaire anglais contenu dans le MS. Toulouse 342." *Archivum Fratrum Praedicatorum* 29 (1959), pp. 89–110.

Kedar, Benjamin V. "Canon Law and Local Practice: The Case of Mendicant Preaching in Late Medieval England." *Bulletin of Medieval Canon Law,* n.s. 2 (1972), pp. 17–32.

Kellogg, Alfred L., and Louis A. Haselmayer. "Chaucer's Satire of the Pardoner." In Alfred L. Kellogg, *Chaucer, Langland, Arthur: Essays in Middle English Literature.* New Brunswick, NJ: Rutgers University Press, 1972. Pp. 212–244. Originally published in *Publications of the Modern Language Association* 66 (1951), pp. 251–277.

Kellogg, Eleanor H. "Bishop Brunton and the Fable of the Rats." *Publications of the Modern Language Association* 50 (1935), pp. 57–67.

Works cited

Ker, N. R. *Medieval Manuscripts in British Libraries.* 5 vols. Oxford: Clarendon Press, 1969–2002.

Kienzle, Beverly Mayne, ed. *The Sermon,* Typologie des sources du moyen âge occidental 81–83. Turnhout: Brepols, 2000.

Kitchin, G. W. *Catalogus codicum mss. qui in Bibliotheca Aedis Christi apud Oxoniensis adservantur.* Oxford: Clarendon Press, 1867.

Knowles, David. *The Religious Orders in England.* 2 vols. Cambridge: Cambridge University Press, 1948–1955.

Langland, William. *Will's Vision of Piers Plowman, Do-well, Do-better and Do-best.* George Russell and George Kane, eds. London: The Athlone Press, 1997.

Lawrence, Veronica. "The Role of the Monasteries of Syon and Sheen in the Production, Ownership and Circulaton of Mystical Literature in the Late Middle Ages." *Analecta Cartusiana* 130: The Mystical Tradition and the Carthusians 10 (1996), pp. 101–115.

Le Neve, John. *Fasti Ecclesiae Anglicanae, 1300–1460.* Various editors. 12 vols. London: Institute of Historical Research, University of London, 1962–1967.

Leclercq, Henri. "Paroisses rurales." In *Dictionnaire d'archéologie chrétienne et de liturgie,* vol. XIII.2, cols. 2198–2235. Paris: Letouzey et Ané, 1938.

Lecoy de la Marche, Albert. *La chaire française au moyen âge, spécialement au XIIIe siècle d'après les manuscrits contemporains.* Second edn. Paris, 1886; reprinted Geneva: Slatkine Reprints, 1974.

Lekai, Louis J. *The Cistercians: Ideals and Reality.* Kent, OH: Kent State University Press, 1977.

—. *The White Monks: a History of the Cistercian Order.* Okauchee, WI: Cistercian Fathers, Our Lady of Spring Bank, 1953.

Lepine, David. *A Brotherhood of Canons Serving God: English Secular Cathedrals in the Later Middle Ages.* Woodbridge: Boydell Press, 1995.

Lesnick, Daniel R. *Preaching in Medieval Florence: The Social World of Franciscan and Dominican Spirituality.* Athens, GA: University of Georgia Press, 1989.

Lewis, R. E., N. F. Blake, and A. S. G. Edwards. *Index of Printed Middle English Prose.* New York: Garland Press, 1985.

Lewry, Osmund, OP. "Four Graduation Speeches from Oxford Manuscripts (c. 1270–1310)." *Medieval Studies* 44 (1982), pp. 138–180.

Little, A. G. "A Fifteenth-Century Sermon." In Little, *Franciscan Papers, Lists, and Documents,* pp. 244–256.

—. *Franciscan Papers, Lists, and Documents.* Manchester: Manchester University Press, 1943.

—. "The Franciscan School at Oxford in the Thirteenth Century." *Archivum Fratrum Historicum* 19 (1926), pp. 803–874.

—. *The Grey Friars in Oxford.* Oxford: Clarendon Press, 1892.

—. "Licence to Hear Confessions under the Bull *Super Cathedram.*" In Little, *Franciscan Papers, Lists, and Documents,* pp. 230–243.

—. *Studies in English Franciscan History.* Publications of the University of Manchester, Historical Series, 29. Manchester: University of Manchester, 1917.

Little, A. G., and F. Pelster. *Oxford Theology and Theologians c. AD 1282–1302.* Oxford Historical Society 96. Oxford: Clarendon Press, 1934.

Logan, F. Donald. "The Cambridge Canon Law Faculty: Sermons and Addresses." In M. J. Franklin and Christopher Harper-Bill, eds., *Medieval Ecclesiastical Studies in Honour of Dorothy M. Owen*. Woodbridge: Boydell Press, 1995. Pp. 151–164.

Lollard Sermons. Gloria Cigman, ed. EETS 294. Oxford: Oxford University Press, 1989.

Longère, Jean. *La Prédication médiévale*. Paris: Études Augustiniennes, 1983.

Lovatt, Roger. "John Blacman: Biographer of Henry VI." In R. H. C. Davis and J. M. Wallace-Hadrill, eds., with the assistance of J. I. Catto and M. H. Keen, *The Writing of History in the Middle Ages: Essays Presented to Richard William Southern*. Oxford: Clarendon Press, 1981. Pp. 415–444.

Maclure, Millar. *The Paul's Cross Sermons 1534–1642*. Toronto: University of Toronto Press, 1958.

Madan, Falconer, H. H. E. Craster, and N. Denholm-Young. *A Summary Catalogue of Western Manuscripts in the Bodleian Library at Oxford which have not hitherto been described in the Quarto Series, with references to the Oriental and other manuscripts*. 7 vols. Oxford: Clarendon Press, 1895–1953.

Maieru, Alfonso. *University Training in Medieval Europe*. D. N. Pryds, trans. and ed. Leiden, New York, Köln: E. J. Brill, 1994.

Mann, Jill. *Chaucer and Medieval Estates Satire*. Cambridge: Cambridge University Press, 1973.

Marshall, Peter. *The Catholic Priesthood and the English Reformation*. Oxford Historical Monographs. Oxford: Clarendon Press, 1994.

Marvin, Frank Clyde, Jr. "Diocesan Administration in the Late Fourteenth Century English Church: A Biographical Study." PhD dissertation. University of Michigan, 1976.

McNulty, Joseph. "William of Rymyngton, Prior of Salley Abbey, Chancellor of Oxford, 1372–3." *Yorkshire Archaeological Journal* 30 (1931), pp. 231–247.

McDonald, Peter. "The Papacy and Monastic Observance in Late Medieval England: The *Benedictina* in England." *Journal of Religious History* 14/2 (1986), pp. 117–132.

Meier, Ludgerus, OFM. "De schola franciscana Erfordiensi saeculi xv." *Antonianum* 5 (1930), pp. 57–94, 157–202, 333–362, 443–474.

Memorials of St. Edmunds Abbey. Thomas Arnold, ed. 3 vols. Rolls Series 96. London: H. M. Stationery Office, 1890–1896.

Mertens, Volker. "'Der implizierte Sünder.' Prediger, Hörer und Leser in Predigten des 14. Jahrhunderts. Mit einer Textpublikation aus den Berliner Predigten." In Walter Haug, Timothy R. Jackson, and Johannes Janota, eds., *Zur deutschen Literatur und Sprache des 14. Jahrhunderts: Dubliner Colloquium 1981*. Reihe Siegen, Germanistische Abteilung 45. Heidelberg: C. Winter, 1983. Pp. 76–116.

The Metropolitical Visitations of William Courtenay, Archbishop of Canterbury 1381–1396: Documents Transcribed from the Original Manuscripts of Courteney's Register, with an Introduction Describing the Archbishop's Investigations. Joseph Henry Dahmus, ed. Urbana, IL: University of Illinois Press, 1950.

Michaud-Quantin, Pierre. "Guy d'Evreux, OP, technicien du sermonnaire médiéval." *Archivum Fratrum Praedicatorum* 20 (1950), pp. 213–233.

Middle English Sermons Edited from British Museum MS Royal 18.B.xxiii. Woodburn O. Ross, ed. EETS 209. London: Oxford University Press, 1940; reprinted 1960.

The Middle English Translation of the Rosarium Theologie: a Selection Edited from Cambridge, Gonville and Caius College MS 354/581. Christina Von Nolcken, ed. Middle English Texts 10. Heidelberg: Winter, 1979.

Mifsud, G. "John Sheppey, Bishop of Rochester, as Preacher and Collector of Sermons." BLitt. thesis. Oxford, 1953.

Mirk, John. *The Advent and Nativity Sermons from a XV Revision of John Mirk.* Susan Powell, ed. Middle English Texts 13. Heidelberg: Winter, 1981.

—. *Instructions for Parish Priests by John Myrc: Edited from Cotton MS. Claudius A.II.* Edward Peacock, ed. EETS 31. London: Kegan Paul, Trench, Trübner, 1868; revised edition 1902.

—. *Instructions for Parish Priests, Edited from MS Cotton Claudius A.II and Six Other Manuscripts with Introduction, Notes and Glossary.* Gillis Kristensson, ed. Lund Studies in English 49. Lund: C. W. K. Gleerup, 1974.

—. *Mirk's Festial: A Collection of Homilies by Johannes Mirkus (John Mirk), Edited from Bodl. MS. Gough Eccl. Top. 4, With Variant Readings from Other MSS,* part 1. Theodore Erbe, ed. EETS, e.s., 96. London: Kegan Paul, Trench, Trübner, 1905.

Mollat, Guillaume. "Jean de Cardaillac, un prélat réformateur du clergé au XIVe siècle." *Revue d'Histoire Ecclésiastique* 48 (1953), pp. 74–121.

Monasticon anglicanum. William Dugdale, ed. 6 vols. London: Bohn, 1693.

Moorman, John R. H. *Church Life in England in the Thirteenth Century.* Cambridge: Cambridge University Press, 1946.

—. *A History of the Franciscan Order from its Origins to the Year 1517.* Oxford: Clarendon Press, 1968.

Morenzoni, Franco. "Aux origines des *Artes praedicandi*: Le *De artificioso modo predicandi* d'Alexandre d'Ashby." *Studi Medievali,* serie terza, 32.2 (1991), pp. 887–935.

Morrin, Margaret J. *John Waldeby, OSA, c. 1315–c. 1372: English Augustinian Preacher and Writer: With a Critical Edition of His Tract on the "Ave Maria".* Studia Augustiniana Historica 2. Rome: Analecta Augustiniana, 1972–1974.

Morrison, Stephen. "Lollardy in the Fifteenth Century: The Evidence From Some Orthodox Texts." *Cahiers Elisabéthains* 52.2 (1997), pp. 1–24.

Mulchahey, M. Michèle. *"First the Bow is Bent in Study." Dominican Education before 1350.* Toronto: Pontifical Institute of Medieval Studies, 1998.

Munimenta academica, or Documents Illustrative of Academical Life and Studies at Oxford. Henry Anstey, ed. 2 vols. Rolls Series 50. London: Longmans, Green, Reader, and Dyer, 1868.

Murphy, James J. *Rhetoric in the Middle Ages: A History of Rhetorical Theory from Saint Augustine to the Renaissance.* Berkeley, CA: University of California Press, 1974.

Mynors, R. A. B. *Catalogue of the Manuscripts of Balliol College, Oxford.* Oxford: Clarendon Press, 1963.

Mynors, R. A. B., and R. M. Thomson. *Catalogue of the Manuscripts of Hereford Cathedral Library.* Woodbridge: D. S. Brewer, 1993.

Neckam, Alexander. *De naturis rerum.* Thomas Wright, ed. Rolls Series 34. London: Longman, 1863.

Nicholson, Peter. "The Rypon Analogue of the *Friar's Tale*." *Chaucer Newsletter* 3 (1981), pp. 1–2.

Nighman, Chris L. "*Accipiant qui vocati sunt*: Richard Fleming's Reform Sermon at the Council of Constance." *Journal of Ecclesiastical History* 51 (2000), pp. 1–36.

Nold, Patrick. "British Library Royal 7.B.I Reconsidered: A Franciscan Sermon Cycle." *Carmelus* 45 (1998), pp. 155–162.

O'Brien, Robert. "Two Sermons at York Synod of William Rymyngton, 1372 and 1373." *Cîteaux: Commentarii Cistercienses* 19 (1968), pp. 40–67.

O'Carroll, Mary E., SND. *A Thirteenth-Century Preacher's Handbook: Studies in MS Laud Misc. 511*. Studies and Texts 128. Toronto: Pontifical Institute of Medieval Studies, 1997.

O'Carroll, Maura, SND. "The Lectionary for the Proper of the Year in the Dominican and Franciscan Rites of the Thirteenth Century." *Archivum Fratrum Praedicatorum* 49 (1979), 79–103.

O'Mara, V. M. *A Study and Edition of Selected Middle English Sermons: Richard Alkerton's Easter Week Sermon Preached at St. Mary Spital in 1406, a Sermon on Sunday Observance, and a Nunnery Sermon for the Feast of the Assumption*. Leeds Texts and Monographs, n.s. 13. Leeds: Leeds University Press, 1994.

Oberman, Heiko A., and James A. Weisheipl. "The *Sermo epinicius* Ascribed to Thomas Bradwardine (1346)." *Archives d'histoire doctrinale et littéraire du moyen âge* 25 (1958): pp. 295–329.

Observances in Use at the Augustinian Priory of St. Giles and St. Andrew at Barnwell, Cambridgeshire. John Willis Clark, ed. Cambridge: Macmillan and Bowes, 1897.

Offler, H. S. "Thomas Bradwardine's 'Victory Sermon' in 1346." In A. I. Doyle, ed., *Church and Crown in the Fourteenth Century: Studies in European History and Political Thought*. Aldershot: Ashgate, 2000. Pp. 1–40.

Owen, Nancy. "Thomas Wimbledon." *Medieval Studies* 24 (1962), pp. 377–381.

—. "Thomas Wimbledon's Sermon: 'Redde racionem villicacionis tue'." *Medieval Studies* 28 (1966): pp. 176–197.

Owst, G. R. "The 'Angel' and the 'Goliardeys' of Langland's Prologue." *Modern Language Review* 20 (1925), pp. 270–279.

—. *Literature and Pulpit in Medieval England: A Neglected Chapter in the History of English Letters and of the English People*. Cambridge: Cambridge University Press, 1933; second rev. edn Oxford: Basil Blackwell, 1961.

—. *Preaching in Medieval England: An Introduction to Sermon Manuscripts of the Period c. 1350–1450*. Cambridge: Cambridge University Press, 1926; rpt. New York: Russell & Russell, 1965.

Palmer, Nigel F. "'Antiquitus depingebatur.' The Roman Pictures of Death and Misfortune in the Ackermann of Böhmen." *Deutsche Vierteljahresschrift für Literaturwissenschaft und Geistesgeschichte* 57 (1983), pp. 121–239.

Pantin, W. A. *The English Church in the Fourteenth Century*. Cambridge: Cambridge University Press, 1955; Notre Dame, IN: University of Notre Dame Press, 1962.

—. "A Sermon for a General Chapter." *Downside Review* 51 (1933): pp. 291–308.

Parkes, M. B. *English Cursive Book Hands, 1250–1500*. Oxford: Clarendon Press, 1969.

Perroy, Édouard. *L'Angleterre et le grand schisme d'occident: étude sur la politique religieuse de l'Angleterre sous Richard II (1378–1399)*. Paris: Librairie J. Monnier, 1933.

Petrus Lombardus. *Sententiae*. Patres Collegii S. Bonaventurae, eds. 3rd edition. 2 vols. Grotta-ferrata: Collegio San Bonaventura, 1971–1982.

Pfaff, Richard W. *New Liturgical Feasts in Later Medieval England*. Oxford: Clarendon Press, 1970.

Pfander, Homer G. *The Popular Sermon of the Medieval Friar in England*. New York: New York University, 1937.

Les plus anciens textes de Cîteaux: sources, textes et notes historiques. Jean de la Croix Bouton and Jean Baptiste Van Damme, eds. Achel: Abbaye Cistercienne, 1974.

Political, Religious and Love Poems. J. F. Furnivall, ed. EETS 15, rev. edn. London: K. Paul, Trench, Trübner, 1903.

Poorter, A. de. "Un Manuel de prédication médiévale, le ms. 97 de Bruges." *Revue Neo-Scolastique de Philosophie* 25 (1923), pp. 192–205.

Pounds, N. J. G. *A History of the English Parish: The Culture of Religion from Augustine to Victoria*. Cambridge: Cambridge University Press, 2000.

Powell, Susan. "Connections between the *Fasciculus morum* and Bodleian MS Barlow 24." *Notes and Queries* 227 (1982), pp. 10–14.

—. "John Mirk's *Festial* and the Pastoral Programme." *Leeds Studies in English*, n.s. 22 (1991), pp. 85–102.

—. "A New Dating of John Mirk's *Festial*." *Notes and Queries* 227 (1982), pp. 487–489.

—. "Preaching at Syon Abbey." *Leeds Studies in English*, n. s. 31 (2000), pp. 229–267.

Powicke, F. M. *The Medieval Books of Merton College*. Oxford: Clarendon Press, 1931.

Quinto, Riccardo. "The Influence of Stephen Langton on the Idea of the Preacher in the 'De eruditione predicatorum' of Humbert of Romans and the 'Postille' on the Scriptures of Hugh of Saint-Cher." In Kent Emery, Jr., and Joseph Wawrykow, eds., *Christ among the Medieval Dominicans: Representations of Christ in the Texts and Images of the Order of Preachers*. Notre Dame, IN: University of Notre Dame Press, 1998. Pp. 49–91.

Rashdall, Hastings. *The Universities of Europe in the Middle Ages*. New edn, F. M. Powicke and A. B. Emden, eds. 3 vols. Oxford: Clarendon Press, 1936.

Raymo, Robert R. "Works of Religious and Philosophical Instruction." In Albert Hartung, ed., *A Manual of the Writings in Middle English, 1050–1500*, vol. 7. New Haven, CT: Connecticut Academy of Arts and Sciences, 1986. Pp. 2254–2378.

The Reception of the Church Fathers in the West: From the Carolingians to the Maurists. Irena Backus, ed. 2 vols. Leiden: Brill, 1997.

The Register of Bishop Philip Repingdon, 1405–1419. Margaret Archer, ed. 3 vols. Publications of the Lincoln Record Society 57, 58, and 74. Lincoln: Lincoln Record Society, 1963–1982.

The Register of Edmund Lacy, Bishop of Exeter, 1420–1455. G. R. Dunstan, ed. 5 vols. Canterbury and York Society 60–63 and 66. Torquay: Canterbury and York Society, 1963–1972.

The Register of Edmund Stafford (AD 1395–1419): An Index and Abstract of Contents. F. C. Hingeston-Randolph, ed. London: G. Bell & Sons, 1886.

The Register of Henry Chichele, Archbishop of Canterbury 1414–1443. E. F. Jacob, ed. 4 vols. Canterbury and York Society 42, 45–47. Oxford: Oxford University Press, 1937–1947.

The Register of John de Grandisson, Bishop of Exeter (AD 1327–1369). F. C. Hingeston-Randolph, ed. 3 vols. London: Bell & Sons, 1894–1899.

The Register of John Waltham, Bishop of Salisbury 1388–1398. T. C. B. Timmins, ed. Canterbury and York Society 80. Woodbridge, Suffolk: Boydell Press, 1994.

The Register of Thomas Langley, Bishop of Durham 1406–1437. R. L. Storey, ed. 5 vols. Surtees Society 164, 166, 169, 170, and 177. Durham: Surtees Society, 1956–1966.

The Register of William Edington, Bishop of Winchester, 1346–1366. S. F. Hockey, ed. 2 vols. Hampshire Record Society 7–8. Hampshire Record Office, 1986–1987.

Registrum abbatiae Johannis Whethamstede . . . iterum susceptae, in *Chronica monasterii s. Albani.* H. T. Riley, ed. Rolls Series 28, part vi, vol. 1. London: Longman, 1872.

Registrum Simonis Langham Cantuariensis archiepiscopi. A. C. Wood, ed. Canterbury and York Society 53. Oxford: Oxford University Press, 1956.

Reichl, Karl. *Religiöse Dichtung im englischen Hochmittelalter.* Munich: Fink Verlag, 1973.

Repertorium der lateinischen Sermones für die Zeit von 1350–1500. CD ROM edition, edited by L. Hödl and W. Knoch. Münster: Aschendorff, 2001.

Rishanger, William. *Chronica et annales regnantibus Henrico tertio et Edwardo primo.* Henry T. Riley, ed. Rolls Series 28, part 2. London: Longman, Green, Longman, Roberts, and Green, 1865.

Rites of Durham, Being a Description of All the Ancient Monuments, Rites, & Customs Belonging or Being within the Monastical Church of Durham before the Suppression Written 1593. J. T. Fowler, ed. Surtees Society 107. Durham: Andrews & Co., 1903.

Roberts, A. K. B. *St. George's Chapel Windsor Castle 1348–1416: A Study in Early Collegiate Administration.* Windsor: Dean and Canons of St. George's Chapel, by Oxley, 1947.

Roberts, Phyllis B. *Thomas Becket in the Medieval Latin Preaching Tradition: An Inventory of Sermons about St. Thomas Becket c. 1170–c. 1400.* Steenbrugge: Abbatia S. Petri, 1992.

Robertson, D. W., Jr. "Frequency of Preaching in Thirteenth Century England." *Speculum* 24 (1949), pp. 376–388; reissued in D. W. Robertson, Jr., *Essays in Medieval Culture.* Princeton: Princeton University Press, 1980. Pp. 114–128 and 351–355.

Robinson, P. R. *Catalogue of Dated and Datable Manuscripts, c. 737–1600, in Cambridge Libraries.* 2 vols. Cambridge: D. S. Brewer, 1988.

Robson, J. A. *Wyclif and the Oxford Schools: The Relation of the "Summa de ente" to Scholastic Debates at Oxford in the Later Fourteenth Century.* Cambridge: Cambridge University Press, 1961.

Roest, Bert. *A History of Franciscan Education (c. 1210–1517).* Education and Society in the Middle Ages and Renaissance 11. Leiden, Boston, and Cologne: Brill, 2000.

Roth, Francis, OSA. *The English Austin Friars, 1249–1538.* 2 vols. Cassiciacum 6–7. New York: Augustinian Institute, 1966 and 1961.

Rotuli parliamentorum. 6 vols. N.p., n.d.

Rouse, Richard H. "Cistercian Aids to Study in the Thirteenth Century." *Studies in Cistercian History* 2 (1976), pp. 123–134.

Rouse, Richard H., and Mary Rouse. *Preachers, Florilegia and Sermons: Studies on the "Manipulus florum" of Thomas of Ireland.* Toronto: Pontifical Institute of Medieval Studies, 1979.

Rubin, Miri. *Corpus Christi: The Eucharist in Late Medieval Culture.* Cambridge: Cambridge University Press, 1991.

Rusconi, Roberto. "Reportatio." *Medioevo e rinascimento* 3 (1989), pp. 7–36.

The Sarum Missal Edited from Three Early Manuscripts. J. Wickham Legg, ed. Oxford: Clarendon Press, 1916; rpt. 1969.

Schmitt, Jean-Claude. *La Raison des gestes dans l'occident médiéval.* Paris: Gallimard, 1990.

Schneyer, Johannes Baptist. *Geschichte der katholischen Predigt.* Freiburg im Breisgau: Seelsorgeverlag, 1969.

—. *Repertorium der lateinischen Sermones des Mittelalters, für die Zeit von 1150–1350.* 11 vols. Beiträge zur Geschichte der Philosophie und Theologie des Mittelalters 43. Münster: Aschendorff, 1969–1990.

—. *Die Unterweisung der Gemeinde über die Predigt bei scholastischen Predigern. Eine Homiletik aus scholastischen Prothemen.* Veröffentlichungen des Grabmann-Institutes, neue Folge 4. Munich: Schöningh, 1968.

Select Charters and Other Illustrations of English Constitutional History from the Earliest Times to the Reign of Edward the First. William Stubbs, ed. 8th edn. Oxford: Clarendon Press, 1905.

Sermons capitulaires de la Chartreuse de Mayence du début du XVe siècle: introduction, texte critique, traduction et notes. Philippe Dupont, ed. Analecta Cartusiana 46. Salzburg: Institut für Englische Sprache und Literatur, Universität Salzburg, 1978.

Sharpe, Richard. *A Handlist of the Latin Writers of Great Britain and Ireland before 1540.* Publications of the Journal of Medieval Latin 1. Turnhout: Brepols, 1997.

Shinners, John. "Parish Libraries in Medieval England." In Jacqueline Brown and William P. Stoneman, eds., *A Distinct Voice: Medieval Studies in Honor of Leonard E. Boyle, OP.* Notre Dame, IN: University of Notre Dame Press, 1997. Pp. 207–230.

Smalley, Beryl. *English Friars and Antiquity in the Early XIVth Century.* Oxford: Basil Blackwell, 1960.

—. Review of Thomas Brinton, *Sermons*, edited by Mary Aquinas Devlin. *Journal of Theological Studies* 6 (1955), p. 313.

Southern, R. W. *Robert Grosseteste: The Growth of an English Mind in Medieval Europe.* Second edn. Oxford: Clarendon Press, 1992.

Speculum sacerdotale. Edward H. Weatherly, ed. EETS 200. London: Oxford University Press, 1936.

Spencer, Helen. "English Vernacular Sunday Preaching in the Late Fourteenth and Fifteenth Century, with Illustrative Texts." DPhil. thesis. Oxford, 1982.

—. "A Fifteenth-Century Translation of a Late Twelfth-Century Sermon Collection." *RES*, n.s. 28 (1977), pp. 257–267.

Spencer, H. Leith. *English Preaching in the Late Middle Ages.* Oxford: Clarendon Press, 1993.

Stacpoole, Alberic. "Jean Sheppey." In *Dictionnaire de spiritualité ascétique et mystique*, 8:763–774.

Stainer, J. F. R., and C. Stainer. *Early Bodleian Music: Sacred and Secular Songs.* Sir John Stainer, ed. 2 vols. London: Novello, 1901; rpt. Farnborough, Hants.: Gregg, 1967.

Statuta antiqua universitatis Oxoniensis. Strickland Gibson, ed. Oxford: Clarendon Press, 1931.

Statuta capitulorum generalium Ordinis Cisterciensis, ab anno 1116 ad annum 1786. Josephus-Maria Canivez, ed. 8 vols. Louvain: Bureaux de la Revue, 1933–1941.

Statutes of Lincoln Cathedral. Henry Bradshaw and Christopher Wordsworth, eds. 2 parts in 3 vols. Cambridge: Cambridge University Press, 1892–1897.

Les Statuts synodaux français du XIII'e siècle précédés de l'histoire du synode diocésain depuis ses origines. Odette Pontal, ed. and trans. 2 vols. Paris: Bibliothèque Nationale, 1971 and 1983.

Steckman, Lillian Lois. "A Fifteenth Century Festival Book, edited from British Museum Harleian Manuscript 2247, with variant readings from British Museum Royal Manuscript 18.B.xxv." PhD dissertation. 2 vols. Yale University, 1934.

Stella clericorum, Edited from Wavreumont (Stavelot), Monastère St-Remacle, MS. s.n. Eric H. Reiter, ed. Toronto: Pontifical Institute of Medieval Studies, 1997.

Stemmler, Theo. "More English Texts from MS Cambridge UL Ii.III.8." *Anglia* 93 (1975), pp. 1–16.

Stone, John. *The Chronicle of John Stone, Monk of Christ Church 1415–1471.* William George Searle, ed. Cambridge Antiquarian Society, Octavo Publications 34. Cambridge: Cambridge Antiquarian Society, 1902.

Strohm, Paul. *England's Empty Throne: Usurpation and the Language of Legitimation, 1399–1422.* New Haven and London: Yale University Press, 1998.

Swanson, Jenny. *John of Wales: A Study of the Works and Ideas of a Thirteenth-Century Friar.* Cambridge: Cambridge University Press, 1989.

Swanson, R. N. *Church and Society in Late Medieval England.* Oxford: Blackwell, 1989.

—. "The 'Mendicant Problem' in the Later Middle Ages." In Peter Biller and Barrie Dobson, eds., *The Medieval Church: Universities, Heresy, and the Religious Life. Essays in Honour of Gordon Leff.* Studies in Church History, Subsidia, 11. Woodbridge: Boydell Press, 1999. Pp. 217–238.

Syon Abbey. Vincent Gillespie, ed. With "The Libraries of the Carthusians," ed. A. I. Doyle. Corpus of British Medieval Library Catalogues 9. London: The British Library, 2001.

Szittya, Penn R. *The Antifraternal Tradition in Medieval Literature.* Princeton: Princeton University Press, 1986.

Tachau, Katherine H. "Looking Gravely at Dominican Puns: The 'Sermons' of Robert Holcot and Ralph Friseby." *Traditio* 46 (1991), pp. 337–345.

Taylor, John. *The Universal Chronicle of Ranulf Higden.* Oxford: Clarendon Press, 1966.

Thompson, A. H. *The English Clergy and Their Organization in the Later Middle Ages.* Oxford: Clarendon Press, 1947.

Thompson, E. Margaret. *The Carthusian Order in England.* London: SPCK, 1930.

Thomson, R. M. *Catalogue of the Manuscripts of Lincoln Cathedral Chapter Library.* Woodbridge: D. S. Brewer, 1989.

—. *A Descriptive Catalogue of the Medieval Manuscripts in the Worcester Cathedral Library.* Cambridge: D. S. Brewer, 2001.

Thomson, S. Harrison. *The Writings of Robert Grosseteste, Bishop of Lincoln, 1235–1253.* Cambridge: Cambridge University Press, 1940.

Three Middle English Sermons from the Worcester Chapter MS F.10. D. M. Grisdale, ed. Leeds: University Press, 1939.

The Travels of Sir John Mandeville. C. W. R. D. Moseley, trans. Harmondsworth, Middlesex: Penguin Books, 1983.

Tubach, Frederic C. *Index Exemplorum.* Folklore Fellows Communications 204. Helsinki: Akademia scientiarum fennica, 1969.

Two Wycliffite Texts: The Sermon of William Thorpe 1406, The Testimony of William Thorpe 1407. Anne Hudson, ed. EETS 301. London: Oxford University Press, 1993.

Tyerman, Christopher. *England and the Crusades, 1095–1588.* Chicago: University of Chicago Press, 1988.

Works cited

Vincent of Beauvais. *Speculum quadruplex.* 4 vols. Douais: Baltazar Bellerus, 1624; rpt. Graz: Akademische Druck- und Verlagsanstalt, 1964–1965.

Visitations of Religious Houses in the Diocese of Lincoln. A. Hamilton Thompson, ed. 3 vols. Canterbury and York Society 17, 24, and 33. London: Canterbury and York Society, 1914–1929.

Von Nolcken, Christina. "An Unremarked Group of Wycliffite Sermons in Latin." *Modern Philology* 83 (1986), pp. 233–249.

Wabuda, Susan. *Preaching during the English Reformation.* Cambridge: Cambridge University Press, 2002.

Wakelin, M. F. "An Edition of John Mirk's *Festial* as it is Contained in the Brotherton Collection Manuscript." MA dissertation. Leeds University, 1960.

—. "The Manuscripts of John Mirk's *Festial.*" *Leeds Studies in English*, n.s. 1 (1967), pp. 93–118.

Walsh, Katherine. *A Fourteenth-Century Scholar and Primate, Richard FitzRalph in Oxford, Avignon, and Armagh.* Oxford: Oxford University Press, 1981.

—. "Preaching, Pastoral Care, and *sola scriptura* in Later Medieval Ireland: Richard FitzRalph and the Use of the Bible." In Katherine Walsh and Diana Wood, eds., *The Bible in the Medieval World: Essays in Memory of Beryl Smalley.* Studies in Church History, Subsidia 4. Oxford: Basil Blackwell, 1985. Pp. 251–268.

Walsingham, Thomas. *Gesta abbatum monasterii sancti Albani.* Henry Thomas Riley, ed. 3 vols. Rolls Series 28. London: Longmans, Green, 1867–1869.

—. *Historia anglicana.* In Henry Thomas Riley, ed., *Chronica monasterii s. Albani.* 2 vols. Rolls Series 28, part 1. London: Longmans, Green, 1863–1864.

Warner, Sir George F., and Julius P. Wilson. *British Museum. Catalogue of Western Manuscripts in the Old Royal and King's Collections.* 4 vols. London: British Museum, 1921.

Warner, Lawrence. "Jesus the Jouster: The Christ-Knight and Medieval Theories of Atonement in *Piers Plowman* and the 'Round Table' Sermons." *Yearbook of Langland Studies* 10 (1996), pp. 129–143.

Watson, Andrew G. *Catalogue of Dated and Dateable Manuscripts c. 435–1600 in Oxford Libraries.* 2 vols. Oxford: Clarendon Press, 1984.

Wenzel, Siegfried. "Academic Sermons at Oxford in the Early Fifteenth Century." *Speculum* 70 (1995), pp. 305–329.

—. "Chaucer's Pardoner and His Relics." *Studies in the Age of Chaucer* 11 (1989), pp. 37–41.

—. "The Classics in Late-Medieval Preaching." In Andries Welkenhuysen, Herman Braet, and Werner Verbeke, eds., *Mediaeval Antiquity.* Leuven: Leuven University Press, 1995. Pp. 127–143.

—. "The Continuing Life of Peraldus's *Summa vitiorum.*" In Mark D. Jordan and Kent Emery, Jr., eds., *Ad litteram: Authoritative Texts and their Medieval Readers.* Notre Dame Conferences in Medieval Studies 3. Notre Dame and London: University of Notre Dame Press, 1992. Pp. 135–163.

—. "A Dominican Preacher's Book from Oxford." *Archivum Fratrum Praedicatorum* 68 (1998), pp. 177–203.

—. "The Dominican Presence in Middle English Literature." In Kent Emery, Jr., and Joseph Wawrykow, eds., *Christ Among the Medieval Dominicans: Representations of Christ in the*

Works cited

Texts and Images of the Order of Preachers. Notre Dame, IN: University of Notre Dame Press, 1998. Pp. 315–331.

—. "Eli and His Sons." *The Yearbook of Langland Studies* 13 (1999), pp. 137–152.

—. "The Joyous Art of Preaching; or, the Preacher and the Fabliau." *Anglia* 97 (1979), pp. 304–325.

—. *Macaronic Sermons: Bilingualism and Preaching in Late Medieval England.* Recentiores: Later Latin Texts and Contexts. Ann Arbor, MI: University of Michigan Press, 1994.

—. *Monastic Preaching in the Age of Chaucer.* The Morton W. Bloomfield Lectures on Medieval English Literature 3. Kalamazoo, MI: Western Michigan University Press, 1993.

—. "The Moor Maiden: a Contemporary View." *Speculum* 49 (1974), pp. 69–74.

—. "A New Version of Wyclif's *Sermones quadraginta.*" *Journal of Theological Studies* 49 (1998), pp. 155–161.

—. "Notes on the Parson's Tale." *Chaucer Review* 16 (1982), pp. 237–256.

—. *Preachers, Poets, and the Early English Lyric.* Princeton, NJ: Princeton University Press, 1986.

—. "Preaching the Saints in Chaucer's England." In Susan J. Ridyard, ed., *Earthly Love, Spiritual Love, Love of the Saints.* Sewanee Medieval Studies 8. Sewanee: University of the South Press, 1999. Pp. 45–68.

—. "Preaching the Seven Deadly Sins." In Richard Newhauser, ed., *In the Garden of Evil: The Vices and Culture in the Middle Ages.* Toronto: Pontifical Institute of Medieval Studies. Forthcoming.

—. "Robert Grosseteste's Treatise on Confession, 'Deus est.'" *Franciscan Studies* 30 (1970): pp. 218–293.

—. "Robert Lychlade's Oxford Sermon of 1395." *Traditio* 53 (1998), pp. 203–230.

—. "Saints and the Language of Praise." In Susan J. Ridyard, ed., *Earthly Love, Spiritual Love, Love of the Saints.* Sewanee Medieval Studies 8. Sewanee: University of the South Press, 1999. Pp. 69–87.

—. "Sermon Collections and their Taxonomy." In Stephen Nichols and Siegfried Wenzel, eds., *The Whole Book: Cultural Perspectives on the Medieval Miscellany.* Recentiores: Later Latin Texts and Contexts. Ann Arbor, MI: University of Michigan Press, 1996.

—. "A Sermon in Praise of Philosophy." *Traditio* 50 (1995), pp. 249–259.

—. "A Sermon Repertory from Cambridge University." *History of Universities* 14 (1995/96), pp. 43–67.

—. *The Sin of Sloth: Acedia in Medieval Thought and Literature.* Chapel Hill, NC: The University of North Carolina Press, 1967.

—. *Verses in Sermons. "Fasciculus Morum" and its Middle English Poems.* Cambridge, MA: The Mediaeval Academy of America, 1978.

—. "Vices, Virtues, and Popular Preaching." In Dale B. J. Randall, ed., *Medieval and Renaissance Studies. Proceedings of the Southeastern Institute of Medieval and Renaissance Studies, Summer 1974.* Durham, NC: Duke University Press, 1976. Pp. 28–54.

—. "Why the Monk?" In Peter S. Baker and Nicholas Howe, eds., *Words and Works: Studies in Medieval English Language and Literature in Honour of Fred C. Robinson.* Toronto: Toronto University Press, 1998. Pp. 261–269.

Westminster Chronicle, 1381–1394. L. C. Hector and Barbara L. Harvey, eds. Oxford: Clarendon Press, 1982.

Works cited

Wimbledon's Sermon "Redde rationem villicationis tue": A Middle English Sermon of the Four-teenth Century. Ione Kemp Knight, ed. Pittsburgh, PA: Duquesne University Press, 1967.

Wolf, George. "La Préface perdue des sermons de Raoul Ardent, chapelain de Richard I." *Archives d'histoire doctrinale et littéraire du moyen âge* 46 (1979), pp. 35–39.

Workman, Herbert B. *John Wyclif: A Study of the English Mediaeval Church.* 2 vols. Oxford: Clarendon Press, 1926.

Wyclif, John. *Iohannis Wyclif Sermones.* Johann Loserth, ed. 4 vols. Wyclif's Latin Works 8, 9, 11, and 13. London: Wyclif Society, 1887–1890.

—. *Polemical Works in Latin.* Rudolf Buddensieg, ed. 2 vols. London: Wyclif Society, 1883.

Zerfass, Rolf. *Der Streit um die Laienpredigt.* Freiburg: Herder, 1974.

Index

Index

Athanasius, St., 113
Athboy, 241
Athelstan, 79
Augustine, St., 17, 27, 36, 37, 86, 88, 93, 110, 113, 124, 129, 157, 159, 245, 249, 250, 251, 315, 317, 318, 320, 322, 325, 329, 338, 340, 342, 368, 378, 381, 389, 418, 422, 425, 429, 433, 440, 441, 444, 446, 448, 452, 453, 462, 466, 469, 472, 475, 477, 480, 481, 483, 484, 493, 495, 513, 523, 524, 526, 527, 541, 544, 554, 555, 560, 571, 574, 577, 593, 594, 603, 606, 610, 613, 614, 618, 621, 622, 628, 629, 630, 631, 637, 642, 643, 648, 650, 651, 652, 654, 658–660, 661, 662, 664, 665, 666 passim, 667
Augustine of Canterbury, St., 37
    translation, 250
Augustinian Canons, 50, 58, 159, 220, 240, 241, 253, 266, 278, 284, 396
    general chapter, 281–282
aureate diction, 251, 287
Austin Friars, 40, 189, 190, 288, 289, 292, 293, 294, 310
authorities, 68, 76, 83, 93, 104, 113, 119–120, 137, 162, 175, 216, 219, 237, 245, 247, 249, 303, 314–332 passim, 382
    see also prooftexts; quotations
avarice, 187, 198, 273, 328, 339, 383
Ave Maria, 33, 41, 129, 348
Averey, Thomas, 215
Averroys, 113
Avicenna, 113, 246, 319, 414
Avignon, 31, 32, 45, 46, 142, 258, 305, 313, 314, 388

Bale, John, 292
Banard, John, 190, 658
baptism, 47, 52, 231, 233, 381
Barnabas, St., 86, 250
Bartholomaeus (de Sancto Concordio), 259
Bartholomaeus Turgelow, 213
Bartholomew the Englishman (Anglicus), 113, 319, 322, 552, 605
Basel, Council of, 119, 305, 317
Basevorn, Robert, 7, 39, 220, 238, 249, 294, 366
Basil, St., 113, 319, 466, 637
Bath, 253
Bath and Wells, 308
Beatific Vision, 32, 313
Beatitudes, 182, 186, 194, 275, 351
Beauchamp, Thomas, 89
Beaufort, Henry, 306
Bede, 36, 104, 113, 318, 322, 355, 356, 358, 441, 442, 574, 591, 621
Bedfordshire, 136, 241
Benedict, St., 86, 141, 250, 251, 603
Benedictines, 26, 29–30, 38, 40, 45, 66, 85, 86, 88, 89, 121, 141, 146, 149, 154, 245, 253, 255, 256,
257, 262, 278–281, 282, 283, 284, 286, 299, 301, 305, 323, 396
    general chapter, 47, 163, 166, 293–296, 299
Benedict XII, 29, 278
Bernardine of Siena, St., 17
Bernard of Clairvaux, St., 93, 104, 113, 189, 278, 280, 284, 302, 314, 317, 320, 322, 325, 329, 420, 427, 429, 433, 469, 472, 492, 493, 527, 528, 545, 563, 579, 581, 586, 593, 608, 611, 612, 636, 640, 649, 656, 661, 662
Berthold von Regensburg, 16
Bertrand de la Tour, 140, 292, 506
Bertrand of Tours, 113
Betson, Thomas, 283
Bible
    primacy of, 93, 338, 392
    sermons in praise of, 298, 299, 302; see also Introitus
    use in sermons, 2, 12, 39, 124, 213, 223, 245, 249, 287, 318–332 passim, 392
    vernacular translation, 330
    see also Gospel; Gospel events and parables; lection; Old Testament figures
Biblical commentary, 5, 101, 200, 318, 355–356
Birinus, St., 89, 250
bishops, 26, 45, 50–53
    cathedral preaching, 10, 253–255
    duty to preach, 229–230, 257, 397
    preaching, 31, 253–277
    see also visitation
Blackfriars Council, 45, 137
Black Monks: see Benedictines
Blackworth, Lady, 154
Blanche of Lancaster, 306
Boccaccio, 289
Boethius, 113, 119, 287, 320, 554, 561, 573, 624, 639, 671
Bohemia, 375
Bolew, William, 450
Bonaventure, St., 83, 113, 119, 127, 130, 149, 320, 321, 379, 522, 632
Boniface VIII, 231, 289, 297
Boniface IX, 156, 178
booklets, 23, 26–28, 36, 67, 74, 89, 96, 121, 128, 132, 140, 147, 151, 168, 173, 177, 189, 218, 219, 221
Boraston, Simon, 149, 222, 631
Bosworth, 113
boys, properties of, 326
Bradwardine, 52, 306, 318, 321
Brendan, St., 189
Bretone, Lawrence, 27
Bridget, St., 101, 119, 282, 317
Bridgettines, 282
Brinton, Thomas, xii, xv, 2, 3, 15, 18, 29, 45–49, 71, 123, 162, 177, 254, 255, 256, 258, 261, 266,

Huntingfield, Alice, 142, 143, 256
Hus, John, 208
Hussites, 208
Hynton, John, 285
Hynwood, 81, 435
hypocrisy, 374

Ilkalay, Peter de, 27
image worship, 11, 65, 72, 87, 90, 93, 119, 135, 145,
    158, 185, 187, 326, 332, 373, 381
Incarnation, 246, 316, 399
inception, 297, 301, 302
indices, 7, 27, 28, 66, 75, 95, 102, 132, 136, 138,
    140, 141, 146, 159, 175, 191, 198, 203, 212, 213,
    215, 217, 239, 325
Innocent III, 114, 129, 177, 229, 320, 322
introductio thematis, 11, 43, 55–56, 77, 361, 364, 367
Introitus, 32, 132, 133, 298, 299, 301, 303, 315, 484
Invention of the Cross, feast of, 203, 250, 255
invitation to pray, 37, 38, 55, 56, 60, 62, 71, 76, 82,
    97, 118, 162, 167, 196, 361
Invitatorium, 326
Isaac Stella, 278, 545
Isidore, St., 93, 114, 314, 319, 320, 322, 411, 416,
    445, 447, 473, 543, 544, 558, 577, 608, 617,
    667

Jacobus de Losanna, 127, 191, 213, 568, 569, 662
Jacobus de Voragine, 2, 52, 54, 55, 101, 110, 113,
    119, 129, 205, 211, 216, 217, 218, 316, 317, 318,
    319, 356, 362, 521, 535, 540, 545, 548, 574, 583,
    584, 585, 587, 669; *see also* Legenda aurea
Jacques de Vitry, 319
James, St., 101, 104, 105, 116, 212, 250
Januensis: *see* Jacobus de Voragine
Jean de Cardaillac, 132
Jeremiah, 314
Jerome, St., 86, 93, 104, 114, 152, 250, 317, 320,
    417, 478, 523, 527, 540, 542, 583, 626, 635,
    657
Jerome of Prague, 208
Jerusalem, 240
Jews, 46, 48, 118
Joachim of Flora, 171, 173, 178, 317
Johannes Andreae, 163
Johannes Balbi, 114, 353
Johannes de Rivo Forti, 119
Johannes de Scrata, 122, 292, 594
John the Baptist, St., 67, 91, 104, 116, 118, 150, 182,
    250, 251, 302, 314
    Decollation, 104, 250
John the Evangelist, St., 113, 137, 250, 251
John XXII, 128, 138
John, King, 256
John of Abbéville, 52, 114, 119, 211, 318, 499,
    583
John Beleth, 61, 114, 320

John Damascene, 114, 320, 382, 385
John de Erdesle, 127, 567
John of Limoges, 260
John of Salisbury, 319, 322, 653
John of Wales ('Wallensis'), 27, 29, 114, 119, 142,
    250, 294, 317, 319, 322, 523, 666
Jordan of Quedlinburg, 74
Jordan, William, 133, 134, 161, 446, 448–450
Josephus, 114, 319
Jude, St., 250

Kaeppeli, Thomas, 132, 133, 134
Katherine, St., 1, 32, 59, 251, 255
Kells, 241
Kempe, Margery, 16, 51, 240
Kenelm, St., 222
Ker, N. R., 189, 190, 212
key words, 117, 189, 190, 219, 239
Kilvington, Richard, 36, 37, 38, 315, 470
Kilwardby, Robert, 76, 133, 292, 321
King's Lynn, 94, 96, 97, 176, 240, 241
Knight, Ione Kemp, 172
Kyngton, Thomas, 265

Lactantius, 76, 541, 557
Lacy, Edmund, 266
ladder of perfection, 351
La Ferté, 285
Lambeth Constitutions: *see* Pecham, John
Lancham (Laueham), Philip, 27
Langdon, John, 265
Langham, Simon, 261
Langland, William, 49, 187, 289, 398
Langley, John, 133, 447–448
language: *see* macaronic; sermons, language of
Languebeyrky, John, 133, 447
Last Judgment, 169, 171, 177
Lateran IV, Council, 229–230, 233, 235, 253, 257,
    275, 289, 378, 387, 389
Lathbury, John, 119
Lawerne, John, 27, 280, 299, 301, 304
Lawrence, St., 104, 105, 182, 184, 250
Lawrence of Somercotes, 256
Lebreton, Thomas, 222
lechery, 273
lection, 11, 52, 67, 71, 82, 91, 102, 104, 112, 118, 185,
    199, 200, 205, 347
    moral-psychological interpretation of, 91–92
lectures, 146, 313, 324
    series, 112–115
Leeds, 242
Legat, Hugh, 153, 608
Legatine Council of, 257
Legenda aurea, 58, 59, 60, 61, 63, 110, 114, 205, 211,
    317, 319, 576
Leicester, 50, 281
Leighton Buzzard, 241

Lent, 2, 7, 34, 44, 55, 67, 68–71, 72, 84, 87, 88, 89,
98, 127, 129, 138, 139, 152, 161, 167, 175, 177,
178, 182, 184, 198, 200, 201, 211, 212, 213, 216,
217, 240, 241, 242, 244, 246, 248, 255, 298,
337, 344, 346, 354–357, 358, 362–366, 370,
382, 385, 387, 388, 389, 391, 392, 402
Leo I, St., 114
Liber de infancia Saluatoris, 114
Liber de perfeccione spiritualis vite, 114
Liber qui intitulatur Accenedon, 114
Lichfield, 31, 32, 96, 241, 253, 254, 255, 258, 348,
352
Lilleshall Abbey, 58, 65
Lincoln, 40, 50, 231, 254, 256, 257, 260,
305
Lincolniensis: *see* Grosseteste, Robert
literacy, 398
Little, A. G., 27, 38, 97
liturgical instruction, 60, 64
liturgical manuals, 236
liturgy, 62, 112, 256, 320
Llandaff, John of, 265
Lollards, xvi, 10, 11, 65, 71, 85, 90, 156, 158, 165,
185, 263, 286, 293, 309, 340, 370, 399
sympathy with, 109, 177, 179–180
Lollardy, 50–51, 173, 185, 335
London, 242, 307, 388
see also St. Paul's, London; St. Paul's Cross,
London
Louis, St., 335
Louis of Anjou, St., 46, 250
lovesickness, 87
Lugdunensis: *see* William Peraldus
Luke, St., 92, 250, 251
lust, 325
Luther, Martin, 16
Lychlade, Robert, 173, 181, 183, 186, 188, 275, 394,
395, 667
Lyme, 214
Lyndwood, William, 10, 265
Lyons, Council of, 183, 188

macaronic, 19, 85, 89, 97, 118, 123, 150, 164, 175,
222, 244, 277, 322, 361, 370, 380, 399
Maclure, Millar, 308
Macrobius, 319, 579
Malameyn, Nicholas, 28
Maldon, Thomas, 292
Malling, 28, 222
Mandeville, Sir John, 71, 317
Manipulus florum, 114, 317
manuscripts: *for manuscripts other than the
collections with sigla (see "collections" above),
see the section "Works Cited"*
Marcius, 114
Margaret, St., 104, 105, 250, 251
Margaret, Countess of Devon, 310

Mark, St., 250, 251, 368
marriage, 201, 233, 275
Marshall, William, 79, 218, 353
Martial, 114
Martin, St., 32, 103, 250, 251
Martin of Poland, 322
martyrdom, 105
Martyrs, 161, 203, 285
Mary, the Blessed Virgin, 32, 33, 41, 60, 129, 140,
141, 148, 157, 212, 250, 251, 255, 264, 326
Annunciation, 15, 103, 105, 167, 250
Assumption, 112, 142, 190, 240, 250, 254, 255,
280, 304, 401
Immaculate Conception, xiv, 32, 33, 36, 191,
250, 313–315
Nativity, 190, 250, 254, 285
Oblation, 251
Purification, 128, 138, 182, 250
virtues of, 105
Mary Magdalene, St., 67, 116, 190, 204, 250, 251,
369
Mass, 119, 221, 222, 233
preaching at, 236
see also eucharist
Matthew, St., 46, 190, 250, 355
Matthias, St., 46, 250
Mauleuerer, 27
Maundy Thursday, 28, 84, 147, 255, 283, 378
Maurice, St., 110, 250
Maximus, 114
May, John, 222
meditation, 106
Meldenham, Thomas, 157
Melton, 81, 96, 97, 98, 240, 435
mendicant preaching, 3, 29, 53, 142, 164, 278, 279,
288–296, 299, 387, 396
style, 293–296
Mercurius, 114
Michael, St., 250
Michael de Furno, 191, 662
Michael of Hungary, 44, 99, 440, 577
Mildred, St., 104, 110, 250
Minster-in-Thanet, 110
mirabilia, 379
miracles, 79, 104, 139, 199, 201, 205, 309, 338, 355,
372, 374, 383
Mirk, John, 24, 58–65, 139, 205, 219, 222, 250,
252, 284, 366, 395
model sermons, 3–4, 16, 18, 51, 52, 57, 87, 104, 216,
220–223, 244, 257, 260, 261, 291, 359, 395
monasticism, 14–16
education, 297
histories, 285, 286
perfection, 90
privileges, 237
virtues, 154
see also profession, monastic; individual orders

Index

prooftexts, 16, 93, 104, 163, 245, 261, 314, 315, 322, 325
  see also authorities
proprius sacerdos, 387–390
protheme, 11, 37, 39, 43, 47, 48, 55, 71, 76, 97, 117, 118, 122, 124, 141, 162, 167, 193, 198, 202, 247, 333, 359, 364, 377, 466–470
proverb, 19, 380
Pseudo-Boethius, 114
Pseudo-Chrysostom: *see* Chrysostom
Purgatory, prayer for souls in, 185, 326
Pynchebek, John, 120
Pythagoras, 114

quaestio, 52, 207, 301
question-and-answer structure, 52
Quinquagesima, 76, 359
quotations, 56, 119, 124, 130, 137, 171, 207, 211, 242, 244, 249, 269, 271, 287, 313–332 passim, 338, 351, 356, 364, 381; *see also* authorities

Rabanus Maurus, 114, 318, 322, 450, 547, 636
Raby Barathias, 114
Raby Moyses, 114
Raby Porcherius, 114
Raby Salomon, 114
Radulphus Ardens, 114, 197, 198, 533
Ralph Acton: *see* Radulphus Ardens
Ramsey Abbey, 282
Raymundus, 114
Raynaldus, 315
Reade, Robert, 254, 255, 260
Reading (monastery), 36, 38
reading text, 117
recidivism, 355
Reed, William, 26, 27, 38
Relics, 118, 158
Remigius, 102, 114, 318, 426, 448, 571, 622
Repingdon, Philip, xii, 8, 16, 50–53, 54, 60, 91, 103, 104, 118, 199–202, 203, 284, 308, 313, 316, 321, 327, 330, 342, 356, 357, 358, 359, 362, 364, 368, 381, 391, 394, 395, 396
  see also collections, RE
reportatio, 16–17, 127
rhetoric, 245–246, 256, 285, 294–296, 367–368, 400–402
  criticism of, 342–343
  warning against, 393
Richard II, 46, 78, 139, 156, 305, 308
Richard de Bury, 298
Richard of Chichester, St., 138, 667
Richard Middleton (of Mediavilla), 114, 321
Richard of St. Victor, 114, 249, 317, 497, 570
Richard Wethersette (Wethringset), 231
Richesdale, John, 122
Riddliton, John, 27

Ridevall, John, 293
Rigaud, Jean, 211
Rimington, William of, 4–5, 161–162, 208, 263, 266, 275, 284, 313, 395, 462, 528
Ringstead, Thomas, 318
Robert of Anjou, 213
Robert de Chamberleyn, 127
Robert de Gretham, 358
Robertson, D. W., Jr., 239
Rochester, 18, 26, 28, 29, 45, 255, 257, 261, 283
Rogation Days, 67, 78, 98, 103, 110, 142, 143, 203, 218, 254, 307
Roger Bacon, 113, 319, 322
Roger Meuland, 254
Roger Weseham, 353
Rolle, Richard, of Hampole, xi, 106, 111, 218, 222, 318
Rome, 45, 240
Ross, Woodburn O., xii, 173
Round Table, 316
Rouse, Mary, 236
Rouse, Richard, 236
Roxby, John, 265
Rubin, Miri, xiii
rubrics, 7, 9, 10, 18, 46, 68, 81, 82, 89, 93, 98, 101, 112, 116, 125, 126, 142, 153, 160, 169, 197, 207, 242, 261, 265, 280, 285, 309, 315
Rygge, Robert, 50, 298
Rypon, Robert, xii, xiv, 15, 17, 66–73, 238, 263, 266, 269, 279, 283, 313, 324, 327, 328, 329, 336, 337, 338, 348, 364, 382, 395, 396, 399, 402
  see also collections, RY

Sabellius, 372
sacraments, 33, 47, 160, 214, 218, 231, 233, 275, 351
  and unworthy priests, 52, 321, 381
  see also baptism; eucharist; marriage; penitence
saints sermons, 1, 9, 33, 41, 59, 60–61, 64, 67, 80, 84, 86, 89, 91, 94, 103, 104, 109, 132, 140, 149, 152, 182, 198, 216, 222, 250–252, 255
  generic, 1, 2, 37, 161, 203
Salisbury, 230, 252, 289, 305, 310
Salustius, 543
salvation, 368
Samson, St., 222
Sandes, John, 172
Sarum Use, 7, 8, 54, 363
Sawcemere (Sawremere), 27, 87
Sawles Warde, 198
Sawley (Sallay) Abbey, 161
Schneyer, Johannes Baptist, 173, 211, 213, 214, 395
scholasticism, 320
Scriptura sola: *see* Bible, primacy of
Scryn, 241
Secreta secretorum, 320

CAMBRIDGE STUDIES IN MEDIEVAL LITERATURE